America

The Essential Learning Edition

VOLUME ONE

DAVID EMORY SHI

Third Edition

W. W. Norton & Company, Inc.
New York • London

W. W. Norton & Company has been independent since its founding in 1923, when William Warder Norton and Mary D. Herter Norton first published lectures delivered at the People's Institute, the adult education division of New York City's Cooper Union. The firm soon expanded its program beyond the Institute, publishing books by celebrated academics from America and abroad. By midcentury, the two major pillars of Norton's publishing program—trade books and college texts—were firmly established. In the 1950s, the Norton family transferred control of the company to its employees, and today—with a staff of five hundred and hundreds of trade, college, and professional titles published each year—W. W. Norton & Company stands as the largest and oldest publishing house owned wholly by its employees.

Editor: Jon Durbin
Associate Managing Editor: Melissa Atkin
Assistant Editor: Lily Gellman
Editorial Assistant: Allen Chen
Managing Editor, College: Marian Johnson
Associate Director of Production: Benjamin Reynolds
Media Editor: Carson Russell
Associate Media Editor: Hillary Roegelein
Media Project Editor: Rachel Mayer
Media Editorial Assistant: Jennifer Jussel
Managing Editor, College Digital Media: Kim Yi
Ebook Production Manager: Kate Barnes
Marketing Manager, History: Sarah England Bartley
Design Director: Jillian Burr
Director of College Permissions: Megan Schindel
College Permissions Manager: Bethany Salminen
Text Permissions Specialist: Elizabeth Trammell
Photo Department Manager: Stacey Stambaugh
Photo Editor: Amla Sanghvi
Photo Researcher: Julie Tesser
Composition: Graphic World/Project Manager: Gary Clark
Cartography by Mapping Specialists
Manufacturing: Transcontinental—Beauceville, QC

ISBN: 978-0-393-54268-4
A catalogue record for the full edition is available from the Library of Congress.

This edition:
ISBN: 978-0-393-42299-3

W. W. Norton & Company, Inc., 500 Fifth Avenue, New York, NY 10110-0017
wwnorton.com
W. W. Norton & Company Ltd., 15 Carlisle Street, London W1D 3BS
1 2 3 4 5 6 7 8 9 0

For W. W. Norton & Company
A Group of Exceptional Professionals who Shape
the Future by Remembering the Past

About the Author

DAVID EMORY SHI is president emeritus at Furman University in Greenville, South Carolina. He is the author of several books focusing on American cultural history, including the award-winning *The Simple Life: Plain Living and High Thinking in American Culture* and *Facing Facts: Realism in American Thought and Culture, 1850–1920*. He remains highly engaged with students and instructors around the country with his many annual "author-in-residence" visits to campuses. Learn more about David Shi at usahistorian.com.

Contents in Brief

Contents

PART THREE | An Expanding Nation, 1815–1860 299

Maps

Thinking Like A Historian

What's It All About?
(In the Student Site)

These unique summary tables provide bullet point review summaries of major developments in each period.

Preface

With this Third Edition of *America: The Essential Learning* Edition, I have sought to improve on a textbook celebrated for its compelling narrative history of the American experience. In the late eighteenth century, the new republic of the United States of America emerged from a revolutionary war with Great Britain that was fought over hotly debated principles, especially the ideals of freedom and equality. To be sure, the integrity of those ideals was corrupted by the deeply rooted institution of slavery and equally entrenched notions of female inequality and racial and ethnic prejudice. Yet the founding principles, however unrealized in practice, remain the distinguishing element of American development. The United States has always been a work in progress, an experiment in building a republic based on the ideals of liberty and justice for all. Conflicts over how best to define and embody those ideals continue to be the shaping dynamic of the American experience. The nation is not perfect, but it remains committed to becoming less imperfect.

That commitment has generated much of the ambition, fortitude, and creativity that have distinguished the American experiment in representative democracy from the rest of the world. The ongoing struggle to create a beacon of freedom and equality to the world is what animates this textbook. I have sought to write an engaging account of the American experiment centered on political and economic developments animated by colorful characters informed by balanced analysis and social texture, and guided by the unfolding of transformational events. Those classic principles, combined with a range of affordably priced print and digital options, have helped make the *America: A Narrative History* family one of the most popular, enduring, and well-respected textbook families in the field.

This Third Edition of *America: The Essential Learning Edition* features important changes designed to make the text more teachable and classroom friendly. For the first time, *America: The Essential Learning Edition* shares the same narrative as the Brief Twelfth Edition of *America*. Readers will now experience the same famous narrative color and style that have long distinguished the original editions of *America: A Narrative History* with the added advantage of having a unique guided reading framework that highlights core learning objectives and major developments (more on that below).

The overarching theme of this Third Edition of *America: The Essential Learning Edition* is the importance of the Latino and Latina experience in American history (a phrase I will use to encompass the experiences of those variously called Hispanics, Chicano/Chicana, Latinx, and more specific national identities, for example, Cuban American, Mexican American and Puerto Rican American).

The story starts with the Spanish, who were the first Europeans to settle vast regions of what became the Union States. Their efforts to create a "New Spain" empire began a violent and often deadly process of colonial settlement. The frequent mixing of Spanish and Indigenous peoples and the resulting fusion of their cultures formed the social fabric of the southern borderlands and far western regions across several hundred years.

These regions would be acquired by the United States during the nineteenth century. After Mexico gained its independence from Spain in 1821 and Americans of European descent accelerated their expansion westward, more and more Spanish-speaking peoples would come to America to work and settle, joining those Spanish-speaking peoples already there. Many would face the ongoing challenges of poor working and living conditions and racial injustice.

Through all the challenges they faced, Mexican Americans and those of from other Latin American nations who have come to this country have persevered to exercise a profound influence on the development of American society and history. And they still do so today. American politics, prosperity, clothing, music, architecture, literature, language, food, and history have all been influenced by the growing presence of Latino and Latina people living throughout the entire country.

In 2003, Latinos (the term that displaced *Hispanics*, an earlier label used by the U.S. Census over several decades) passed African Americans as the nation's largest ethnic minority group. Today, immigrants from Spanish-speaking countries and their descendants occupy a more significant place in American cultural life than ever before, The Latino population in 2020 was more than 61 million, or nearly 20 percent of the total U.S. population.

While an introductory textbook must necessarily focus on major political, constitutional, diplomatic, economic, and social changes, it is also essential to highlight the diverse range of people who have contributed to the dynamic nature of the American experience. In addition to the focus on the Latino/Latina experience I just discussed, this edition includes ongoing enhanced coverage of diverse voices from women, African Americans, Native Americans, Asian Americans, immigrants, and LGBTQ Americans.

I also have enriched the political history that is the backbone of *America*'s narrative with an ongoing assessment of both the achievements and contradictions of well-known historical figures and fresh treatment of major historical events. This textbook also incorporates more social and cultural history by revealing how ordinary people managed everyday concerns—housing, jobs, food, recreation, religion, and entertainment. In doing so, they often overcame exceptional challenges to enhance the quality of American life in the face of depressions, wars, epidemics, and racial injustice.

Whether your interests are political, social, cultural, or economic, you'll find new material to consider in what remains the most well-balanced narrative history of America.

When asked what they most wanted in an introductory text, instructors said much the same as their students, but they also asked for a textbook that introduced students to the nature of historical research, analysis, and debate. Many professors also mentioned the growing importance to them and their institutions of *assessing* how well their students met the learning goals established by their department. Accordingly, I have aligned *The Essential Learning Edition* with specific learning outcomes for the introductory American history survey course approved by various state and national organizations, including the American Historical Association. These learning outcomes also inform the accompanying media package, enabling instructors to track students' progress toward mastery of these important learning goals.

These and other suggestions from students and professors have shaped the *Essential Learning Edition* and its unique guided reading framework. Each of the thirty chapters begins with a handful of **Core Objectives**, carefully designed to help students understand—and remember—the major developments and issues in each period. To make it easier for students to grasp the major developments, every chapter aligns the narrative with the learning objectives. Each chapter's Core Objective is highlighted at the beginning. Thereafter, **Core Objective flags** appear in the page margins to reinforce key topics in the narrative that are essential to understanding the broader Core Objectives. The Core Objective flags in the page margins also serve as a reference and review tool for students prior to quizzes and exams. **Key terms**, chosen to reinforce the major concepts, are bolded in the text and defined in the margin, helping reinforce their significance. At the end of each chapter, review features continue to reiterate the Core Objectives, including pithy chapter summaries, lists of key terms, and chapter chronologies.

This book continues to be distinctive for its creative efforts to make every component—text, maps, images, and graphs—a learning opportunity and teaching point. Map captions, for example, include lists of questions to help students interpret the data highlighted in them. Select image captions in each chapter also include questions designed to help students interpret a range of images from drawings, prints, photos, historic maps, and political cartoons.

Interactive maps are just one example of the innovative elements in this book designed to get students more *engaged* in the learning dynamic and thereby deepen their learning. Another unique new feature, called **Thinking Like a Historian**, helps students better understand—and apply—the research techniques and interpretive skills used by professional historians. Through carefully selected examples, the "Thinking Like a Historian" segments highlight the role of primary and secondary sources as the building blocks of historical research and illustrate the ways in which historians have differed in their interpretations of the past. Within the main text, there is one "Thinking Like a Historian" feature for each of the seven major periods of American history; each feature takes on a major interpretive issue in that era. In Part I of the activity, students first read excerpts from two original secondary sources that offer competing interpretive views framing that period. In Part II, students then read some of the original primary sources that those same historians used to develop their arguments. Finally, students must answer a series of questions that guide their reading and analysis of the sources.

To strengthen students' history skills, *America: The Essential Learning Edition* now offers a collection of new "Thinking Like a Historian" exercises for each chapter. Each online exercise highlights the foundational role of primary and secondary sources.

Among the new coverage in this Third Essential Learning Edition are the following:

Chapter 1: The Collision of Cultures in the Sixteenth Century

- New coverage on how gender status and the caste system based on ethnic hierarchy in Spanish America (Mestizos and Criollos) grew out of the impact of the ravages of smallpox.
- New discussions on how the crops native to the Americas crossed the Atlantic and improved the health of Europeans while spurring a dramatic population increase.

Chapter 2: England and Its American Colonies, 1607–1732

- New insights into how the population explosion in Europe in the seventeenth century led to the beginnings of mass migration to the New World.
- New coverage on the arrival of the first enslaved Africans brought to Jamestown in 1619 and how the growing European desire for new beverages—tea and coffee—dramatically increased the number and size of British sugar plantations in the Caribbean and the need for more enslaved Africans to work there.
- Discussion of how South Carolina became the wealthiest colony through its purposeful focus on developing coastal rice plantations using the forced labor of enslaved Africans and Native Americans.
- An expanded portrait of William Penn and how he developed strong relationships with Native Americans through the purchase of land titles from them.

Chapter 3: Colonial Ways of Life, 1607–1750

- New summaries comparing different types of slavery in different regions in colonial America.
- New segments explaining why the British first embraced enslaving Native Americans but then came to prefer enslaved Africans and what the slave system was like in New York City.
- A new vignette on a freedom seeker named Antonio, an enslaved West African man shipped to New Amsterdam and then to Maryland, who after his last escape attempt, in 1656, was tortured and killed by his owner, who was acquitted of murder by an all-White jury.

Chapter 4: From Colonies to States, 1607–1776

- New discussions on how French Jesuit missionaries integrated themselves into the Huron and Algonquin societies in French Canada.
- Updated discussions on how the American Revolution was often a civil war between colonists—Loyalists and Patriots—as demonstrated at the Battle of Moore's Creek Bridge, where the combatants were virtually all Americans.
- An updated and expanded biographical portrait of Thomas Paine and his writing of *Common Sense*.

Chapter 5: The American Revolution, 1775–1783

- New explanations of the British treatment of American prisoners of war during the Revolution and how the British policy to recruit enslaved men in the southern colonies to join the British army pushed many slave owners into the Patriots camp and motivated George Washington to allow free Blacks to fight with the Patriots.
- Expanded discussions of the American army's brutal winter encampment at Valley Forge, Pennsylvania.
- New coverage of the important Battle of King's Mountain, which was a decisive Patriot victory and another example of how the Revolution had turned into a violent civil war.
- A new segment on the Spanish-American alliance during the Revolutionary War that focuses on the Spanish general Bernardo de Gálvez, who organized a multicultural force of Spanish soldiers, Creole militiamen, Indians, free Blacks, and American volunteers and whose efforts helped compel the British to sign a peace treaty with the Americans guaranteeing their independence.

Chapter 6: Securing the Constitution and Union, 1783–1800

- New and expanded discussions on the Newburgh Conspiracy as a case study of the role of the military in a republic and how the Articles of Confederation laid the foundation for republicanism (representative democracy and majority rule).

Chapter 7: The Early Republic, 1800–1815

- Expanded biographical material about the achievements, contradictions, and legacy of Thomas Jefferson.
- New descriptions about the efforts of southerners to supply arms and ammunition to Haitian planters in hopes of quelling the uprisings of enslaved Haitians.
- Expanded discussions of the efforts of Tecumseh and his brother Tenskwatawa to forge an alliance of Native American nations to stop the influx of American settlers into their ancestral lands.

Chapter 8: The Emergence of a Market Economy, 1815–1850

- New and expanded discussions on innovations in travel and communications that grew out of the Industrial Revolution.
- New discussions describing the surge of Chinese immigrants to the West Coast during the California Gold Rush and the nativist attacks intended to deter the newcomers.

Chapter 9: Nationalism and Sectionalism, 1815–1828

- An expanded biography of President John Quincy Adams that discusses how his personality impacted his ability to govern.

Chapter 10: The Jacksonian Era, 1828–1840

- Expanded discussions of the origins of the Cherokee Nation and its first president, John Ross, and the story behind the signing of the Treaty of Echota and the Trail of Tears.

Chapter 11: The South and Slavery, 1800–1860

- New material about the centrality of slavery to the southern economy, the (mis)treatment of the enslaved on southern plantations, including the impact of separating and selling members of enslaved families, and the soaring profitability of new cotton plantations in the Gulf coast states of Alabama, Mississippi, Louisiana, and Texas.

Chapter 12: Religion, Romanticism, and Reform 1800–1860

- Fresh biographical portraits of Peter Cartwright, one of the most famous frontier revivalist ministers, Joseph Smith, the founder of the Mormon faith, and Abigail Kelley, an early abolitionist and a fiery advocate of female suffrage (voting rights).

Chapter 13: Western Expansion and Southern Secession, 1830–1861

- Fresh insights into life on the overland trails to the Far West, including more discussions on the role of women and the impact of the high death and divorce rates triggered by the hardships of pioneering.
- A new profile of Juan Seguín, the son of a prominent Tejano family from San Antonio, who fought with the Anglos in the Texas War of Independence and was made a captain in the Texian army before going on to serve as the mayor of San Antonio.
- A new segment on the Cart War in Texas, which resulted in seventy-five Mexican-born wagon (cart) drivers being murdered by White Texan drivers.
- New discussions on the mistreatment of Mexican Americans and Native Americans following the Mexican-American War and the signing of the Treaty of Guadalupe.
- New portraits of freedom-seeking enslaved people Anthony Burns and Margaret “Peggy” Garner.

Chapter 14: The War of the Union, 1861–1865

- Revelation of the critical role played by Tejanos and Mexicans in the Civil War, both as soldiers serving in the Confederate and Union armies and as cowboys driving Texas longhorn steers to feed Confederate armies in the East.

Chapter 15: The Era of Reconstruction, 1865–1877

- Exploration of the Memphis race riot of 1866 and the massacre of African Americans.
- New coverage on how western states before and after the Civil War passed laws to keep Chinese immigrants from gaining U.S. citizenship.
- A new profile of Henrietta Wood, a freed enslaved person living in Ohio, who sued the slave trader who had sold her originally for $20,000. The Ohio Court ruled in her favor, awarding her $2,500, and in doing so established a legal foundation for reparations for the formerly enslaved.

Chapter 16: Business and Labor in the Industrialized Era, 1860–1900

- A new vignette on Oliver Dalrymple, the "Wheat King of Minnesota," who created one of the first and largest bonanza farms worked by seasonal laborers from Mexico and Scandinavia.
- New discussions on how immigrant Chinese railroad laborers used work stoppages and strikes to demand better wages and treatment by their American bosses.
- A new segment focusing on the building of railroads in the Southwest and how developers set up recruiting centers in Mexico, leading to a 50 percent increase in the Mexican immigrant population in New Mexico from 1880 to 1900.

Chapter 17: The New South and the New West, 1865–1900

- New discussions on how the Duke family created the American Tobacco Company and other entrepreneurs joined the effort to industrialize the South after the Civil War.
- Expanded coverage of the Wilmington Insurrection.
- New discussions on how the Anglo cowboys learned how to ride horses and herd cattle from Mestizo Mexicans, called vaqueros, adopting their clothing, equipment, food, techniques, and terminology (*lasso, rodeo, rancho*).
- A new portrait of Callie Guy House, a former enslaved worker who launched a mass movement in the 1890s demanding pensions for former enslaved people.
- New discussions about the "Juan Crow" belt in south Texas where hundreds of Mexican Americans, many of them U.S. citizens, were lynched during the second half of the nineteenth century.

- New coverage of the Porvenir Massacre. Finally, Chapter 17 introduces to readers Las Gorras Blancas (the White Caps), who were Mexican American citizens in New Mexico who armed themselves to prevent Anglo settlers from seizing their land.

Chapter 18: Political Stalemate and Rural Revolt, 1865–1900

- Enhanced coverage of nativist efforts on the West Coast to discriminate against Asian immigrants by urging new laws such as the Page Act and the Chinese Exclusion Act.

Chapter 19: Seizing an American Empire, 1865–1913

- Expanded discussions on American imperial expansion, including the colonization of Cuba and the writing of the new Cuban Constitution and the Platt Amendment, which gave the United States the right to intervene militarily as needed in Cuban affairs.
- New discussions on how many of the American colonies were designated as "unincorporated" so that their residents would not be protected by the U.S. Constitution.
- New coverage of the Plan of San Diego, a rebellion against the United States by Mexican anarchists living in south Texas.

Chapter 20: The Progressive Era, 1890–1920

- New and revised details on how the women's suffrage movement achieved the vote, especially the key role played by western states such as Wyoming in spearheading the movement.
- New discussions on philosopher John Dewey's vision of a pragmatic and socially engaged education for young people.
- New coverage on how the tragic Triangle Factory Fire in New York City led to a myriad of improvements in workers' rights and the wages paid to child laborers.

Chapter 21: America and the Great War, 1914–1920

- New data on the diverse ethnic and racial composition of American soldiers in the Great War, including 400,000 African Americans and 100,000 Hispanic Americans.
- New discussions on the Jones Act, which granted U.S. citizenship to Puerto Ricans and allowed them to enlist in the U.S. Army (20,000 did during the Great War).

Chapter 22: A Clash of Cultures, 1920–1929

- A new profile of Alain Locke, the guiding force behind the Harlem Renaissance.
- Fresh treatment of the significance of Albert Einstein's scientific theories and their contribution to cultural modernism.
- New coverage of the Immigration Act of 1924 that introduced the term *illegal aliens* and required Mexican American migrant workers

to carry passports or visas before entering the United States to work.

Chapter 23: The Great Depression and the New Deal, 1933–1939

- New coverage of the "Cornbelt Rebellion" and how desperate farmers responded to the impact of the early stages of the Great Depression.
- A new segment about the massive deportation of Mexican workers and Mexican Americans in response to the soaring unemployment generated by the Great Depression.
- A refreshed biographical portrait of President Franklin D. Roosevelt.
- A new portrait of African American Mary McLeod Bethune, the first director of the National Youth Association.

Chapter 24: The Second World War, 1933–1945

- New insights into "Operation Barbarossa," the German invasion of the Soviet Union, including references to the Nazi "police" units that accompanied the invasion and murdered Russian Jews.
- A new vignette on A. Philip Randolph, the founder and head of the Brotherhood of Sleeping Car Porters, the largest African American labor union.
- A new profile of Harry T. Stewart, Jr., from Queens, New York, whose combat flights with the Tuskegee Airmen squadron earned him the Distinguished Flying Cross.
- Expanded treatment of the systematic prejudice against Jews working in the federal government during the war, and the role of the State Department in addressing the Holocaust in Europe.

Chapter 25: The Cold War and the Fair Deal, 1945–1952

- New segments showing how Harry Truman's views on racism evolved over time and led to his decision to integrate the federal government, including the military branches.
- A new section on "Operation Wetback," the deportation of Mexican Americans during the presidency of Dwight Eisenhower.

Chapter 26: Affluence and Anxiety in the Atomic Age, 1950–1959

- New discussions on the "Lavender Menace," the effort by federal agencies to identify and fire gay and lesbian people from working for the government.
- A new vignette on Frank Kameny, who protested the discriminatory government efforts and became one of the most prominent gay leaders.
- New discussion of *The Negro Motorist's Green Book,* a publication alerting African Americans to which motels and service stations served Blacks.
- New material on how women who were encouraged during the Second World War to work in defense plants were urged to resume their traditional roles as wives and mothers after the war.

Chapter 27: New Frontiers and a Great Society, 1960–1968

- A new segment on the Cold War and the race to the moon.
- Enhanced coverage of the Cuban Missile Crisis.
- Expanded discussions on the role of the Freedom Riders in propelling the civil rights movement into a national phenomenon.
- Expanded coverage of the civil rights march in Selma, Alabama, and how it prompted President Lyndon B. Johnson to insist that Congress pass the Voting Rights Act.
- Fresh coverage on Congressman John Lewis and his role in the civil rights movement.
- A new vignette on Fannie Lou Hamer and her role in the civil rights movement.

Chapter 28: Rebellion and Reaction, 1960s and 1970s

- A new segment about the Kerner Commission report on racism and urban violence.
- Expanded discussions of the feminist movement and the United Farm Workers movement with new biographical material on Cesar Chavez and Delores Huerta, its co-founders.
- New segments on Richard Nixon's Southern Strategy, his decision to expand the Vietnam War, the Kent State University shootings, and the controversy over the publication of the Pentagon Papers.

Chapter 29: Conservative Revival, 1977–2000

- A new biographical portrait of Mikhail Gorbachev, the leader of the Soviet Union.
- New treatment of the AIDS epidemic and the role of Larry Kramer in organizing the gay community to insist on more urgent government action to address the epidemic.
- New discussions of the impact of the Crime Bill of 1994 and the Illegal Immigration and Responsibility Act of 1996, which expanded the Border Patrol and the wall along the Mexican border.

Chapter 30: Twenty-First-Century America, 2000–Present

- A new framework for the Trump administration in the context of the ideological divide between supporters of economic nationalism and cooperative globalization and how this tension played out in the context of immigration policies, trade wars, and travel bans.
- New material on the COVID-19 pandemic, the Black Lives Matter movement, racial justice protests, the 2020 presidential election, the effort of pro-Trump rioters to storm the U.S. Capitol to prevent the certification of Joseph Biden as the new president, the second impeachment of Donald Trump, and the first 100 days of the Biden administration.

The new Third Edition of *America: The Essential Learning Edition* also makes history an *immersive* experience through its innovative pedagogy and digital resources. InQuizitive—W. W. Norton's adaptive learning program—helps students better grasp the textbook's key topics and enables instructors to assess learning progress at the individual and classroom levels. For the first time, instructors will have access to a library of guided primary sources plus a series of "Thinking Like a Historian" online exercises for every chapter, inviting students to work with both primary and secondary sources. Online activities such as the History Skills Tutorials and "Thinking Like a Historian" exercises support the discipline's efforts to develop students' critical thinking and analytical skills that are applicable to this course as well as a career in virtually any field. An array of valuable support materials ranging from author videos and online document collections to lecture slides and test banks are available for download or integration into a campus learning management system. See pages xxvii--xxxii for information about student and instructor resources.

Finally, a note on terminology. History is a dynamic discipline: as time passes, it benefits not only from the discovery of new evidence and refined interpretations but also from being in conversation with our contemporary culture. After much analysis and discussion, we have joined other publishers, magazines, and newspapers in capitalizing group identity terms such as *Black* and *White*. While respecting the various and at times conflicting opinions on this matter, we feel our new approach is consistent with the goals of making "a more perfect union" where all people are treated equally and with dignity, including the language choices many use to identify themselves. In this effort, we have also shifted from using the word *slave* in the narrative to *enslaved* and from *fugitive slave* to *freedom seeker*. After all, people did not choose to become slaves; they were instead forcibly *enslaved*. Once enslaved, they yearned to be free again and often risked their lives to liberate themselves. Where the words *slave* and *fugitive slave* are used in historical quotations, we have retained their original form.

No single term can precisely encompass social groups. In the new edition's references to people with Spanish-speaking ancestors, we use identifying terms that are the most historically accurate and relevant for a given context, region, time period, or group of people—Spanish, Hispanic, Tejano, Californio, Mexican American, Chicano and Chicana, Cuban American, Puerto Rican American, and Latino, Latina, and Latinx. Not only is this approach more historically accurate, but it also better demonstrates the dynamism of group identities in America.

This new edition follows a similar strategy for other significant groups such as African Americans, Native Americans, Asian Americans, immigrants, and LGBTQ Americans. We recognize that there are several ways to deal with these sensitive issues and that the issue of group terminology remains a subject of robust discussion within classrooms, homes, communities, and politics. Our efforts in this edition represent a continuing commitment to remain current in our treatment of such shifting preferences.

Media Resources for Instructors and Students

America's digital resources are designed to develop successful readers, guiding students through the narrative while simultaneously developing their critical thinking and history skills.

The comprehensive support package features an award-winning adaptive learning tool as well as new, innovative interactive resources, including the skill-building "Thinking Like a Historian" exercises, available for every chapter of the book, that encourage both primary and secondary source analysis. All of these resources are designed to help students master the Core Objectives in each chapter and continue to nurture their development as historians. W. W. Norton is unique in partnering to develop these resources exclusively with subject-matter experts who teach the course. As a result, instructors have all the course materials needed to manage their U.S. history survey class, whether they are teaching face-to-face, online, or in a hybrid setting.

New! Thinking Like a Historian Exercises

Chapter 19: Debating the Annexation of the Philippines wwnorton.com

Question 5 of 8

In the primary source excerpt below, click to identify the passage(s) that could be used to support Nell Irvin Painter's claim that, "The Philippine Islands—like Hawaii—represented the perfect stepping-stones to China, stops along the way where coal burning ships bound for Asia could refuel."

Click or tap on words, phrases, or items in the passage below to complete the question as instructed.

Henry Cabot Lodge, "The Retention of the Philippine Islands," Speech in the U.S. Senate (March 7, 1900)

I believe, we shall find arguments in favor of the retention of the Philippines as possessions of great value and a source of great profit to the people of the United States which cannot be overthrown. First, as to the islands themselves. They are over a hundred thousand square miles in extent, and are of the greatest richness and fertility. From these islands comes now the best hemp in the world, and there is no tropical product which cannot be raised there in abundance. Their forests are untouched, of great extent, and with a variety of hard woods of almost unexampled value… It is sufficient for me to indicate these few elements of natural wealth in the islands which only await development… A much more important point is to be found in the markets which they furnish. The total value of exports and imports for 1896 amounted in round numbers to $29,000,000, and this was below the average…

The Philippine Islands took from us imports to the value of only $94,000. There can be no doubt that the islands in our peaceful possession would take from us a very large proportion of their imports. Even as the islands are to-day there is opportunity for a large absorption of products of the United States, but it must not be forgotten that the islands are entirely

To strengthen students' history skills, *America* now offers a collection of new, assignable "Thinking Like a Historian" exercises for each chapter. Each online exercise highlights the foundational role of primary sources as the building blocks of history. A selection of exercises also includes secondary source document excerpts. Students examine a major historical debate or issue through the lens of primary source evidence and historians' differing interpretations of that evidence. A series of interactive questions with guiding feedback helps students dissect and compare the sources, building historical thinking skills throughout the semester. As a capstone assignment, follow-up short-answer writing prompts, delivered through the learning management system, encourage students to formulate their own interpretations about the historical debate in question.

INQUIZITIVE

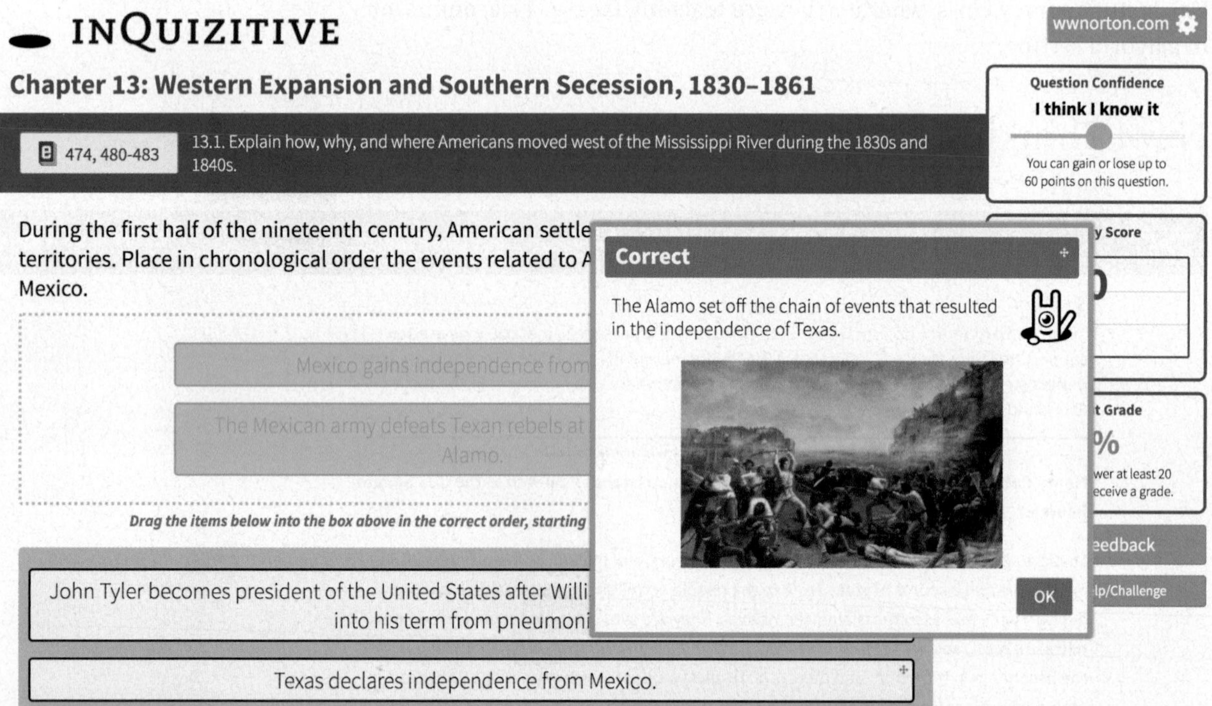

InQuizitive is W. W. Norton's award-winning, easy-to-use adaptive learning tool that personalizes the learning experience for students, helping them to grasp key concepts and achieve key learning objectives. Through a variety of question types, answer-specific feedback, and game-like elements such as the ability to wager points, students are motivated to keep working until they fully comprehend the concepts. As a result, students arrive better prepared for class, giving you more time for discussion and activities.

The InQuizitive course for *America* features over 1,500 engaging, interactive questions (approximately 20 percent of which are new or updated) tagged to each chapter's Core Objectives. Each activity ensures thorough coverage of the key concepts within the chapter reading, as well as questions that invite students to dig in and analyze maps, primary source excerpts, and other types of historical evidence such as artifacts, artworks, architecture, photographs, and more.

History Skills Tutorials

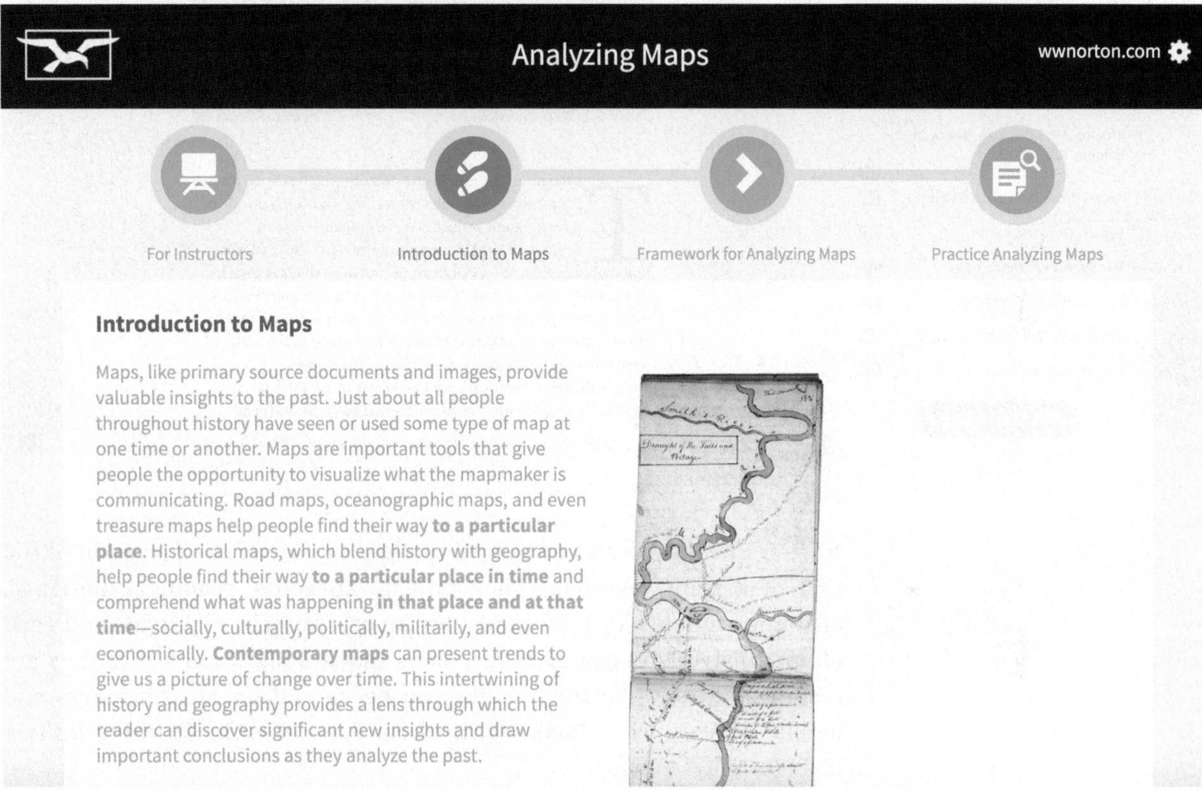

Analyzing Maps
wwnorton.com
For Instructors
Introduction to Maps
Framework for Analyzing Maps
Practice Analyzing Maps
Introduction to Maps
Maps, like primary source documents and images, provide valuable insights to the past. Just about all people throughout history have seen or used some type of map at one time or another. Maps are important tools that give people the opportunity to visualize what the mapmaker is communicating. Road maps, oceanographic maps, and even treasure maps help people find their way to a particular place. Historical maps, which blend history with geography, help people find their way to a particular place in time and comprehend what was happening in that place and at that time—socially, culturally, politically, militarily, and even economically. Contemporary maps can present trends to give us a picture of change over time. This intertwining of history and geography provides a lens through which the reader can discover significant new insights and draw important conclusions as they analyze the past.

The History Skills Tutorials are interactive, online modules that support student development of the key skills for the American history survey course. The tutorials for *America* focus on the following:

- Analyzing secondary source documents (new to this edition)
- Analyzing primary source documents
- Analyzing images
- Analyzing maps

With interactive practice assessments, helpful guiding feedback, and videos with author David Shi, these tutorials teach students the critical analysis skills that they will put to use in their academic and professional careers. These tutorials can be integrated directly into an existing learning management system, making for easy assignability and easy student access.

Norton Ebooks

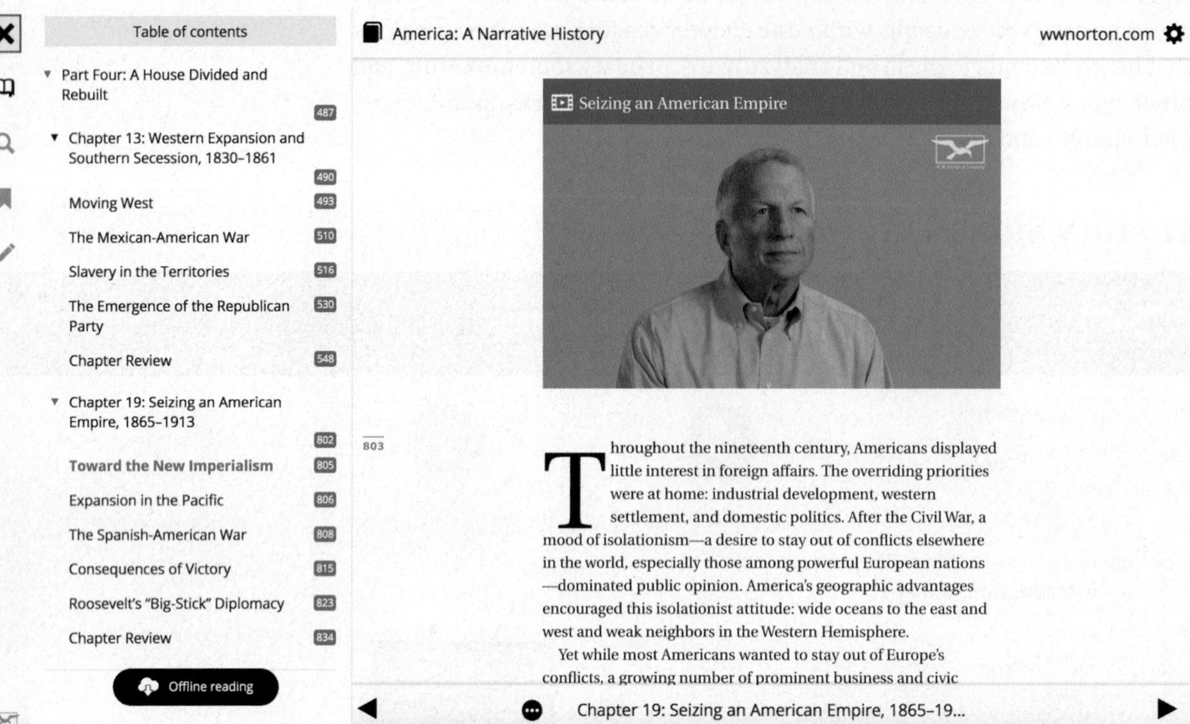

Norton Ebooks offer an enhanced reading experience at a fraction of the cost of a print textbook. They provide an active reading experience, enabling students to take notes, bookmark, search, highlight, and read offline. Instructors can even add notes that students can see as they are reading the text. Norton Ebooks can be viewed on all computers and mobile devices. The ebook for *America: The Essential Learning Edition* includes the following:

- Tool-tip key terms and definitions
- Clickable and zoomable maps and images
- Hundreds of embedded videos with author David Shi, including chapter overview videos that provide visual introductions to the key themes and historical developments students will encounter in each chapter

Student Site

A student website offers additional study and review materials for students to use outside of class. The resources include the following:

- An enhanced **Online Reader** featuring more than one hundred primary source documents and images, each with support materials such as brief headnotes and discussion prompts

- Hundreds of **Author Videos** featuring David Shi to help students understand the essential developments in the American History course
- **Flashcards** inviting students to review the key terms from the textbook
- **Chapter Outlines** giving students a detailed snapshot of the key topics of each chapter
- **iMaps** allowing students to view layers of information on various maps from the text
- **"What's It All About?" Infographics** employing the themes of continuity and change to frame visual overviews of important developments, such as the evolution of African Americans' legal status from the Civil War through Reconstruction

Test Bank

This test bank features more than 2,500 questions—including multiple-choice, true/false, and short-answer—aligned to each chapter of the book. Questions are classified according to level of difficulty and Bloom's Taxonomy, providing multiple avenues for comprehension and skill assessment and making it easy to construct tests that are meaningful and diagnostic.

Norton Testmaker brings W. W. Norton's high-quality testing materials online. Create assessments for your course from anywhere with an Internet connection, without downloading files or installing specialized software. Search and filter test bank questions by chapter, type, difficulty, learning objectives, and other criteria. You can also customize test bank questions to fit your course. Easily export your tests or W. W. Norton's ready-to-use quizzes to Microsoft Word or Common Cartridge files for your LMS.

Instructor's Manual

The instructor's manual for *America: The Essential Learning Edition*, Third Edition, is designed to help instructors prepare effective lectures. It contains chapter summaries, detailed chapter outlines, lecture ideas, in-class activities, discussion questions, and more.

Resources for Your LMS

High-quality Norton digital media can be easily added to online, hybrid, or lecture courses. Get started building your course with our easy-to-use integrated resources; all activities can be accessed right within your existing learning management system. Graded activities are configured to report to the LMS course grade book. The downloadable file includes integration links to the following resources, organized by chapter:

- Ebook
- InQuizitive
- History Skills Tutorials
- Thinking Like a Historian exercises

- Thinking Like a Historian writing prompts
- Chapter outlines
- Flashcards

Instructors can also add customizable multiple-choice, true/false, and short-answer questions to their learning management system using Norton Testmaker.

Classroom Presentation Tools

- **Lecture PowerPoint slides:** Available for download, these PowerPoints feature bullet points of key topics, art, and maps—all sequentially arranged to follow the book. The Lecture PowerPoints also include lecture notes in the Notes section of each slide, perfect for use in both in-person and online courses. These slides are customizable in order to meet the needs of both first-time and experienced teachers.
- **Image files:** All images and maps from the book are available separately in JPEG and PowerPoint format for instructor use. Alt-text is provided for each item.

Primary Source Readers to Accompany *America: A Narrative History*

- **NEW!** The Eighth Edition of **For the Record: A Documentary History of America,** by David E. Shi and Holly A. Mayer (Duquesne University), is the perfect companion reader for *America: The Essential Learning Edition.* It features over 250 primary source readings from diaries, journals, newspaper articles, speeches, government documents, and novels, including a noteworthy number of readings that highlight the role of the Latino and Latina Americans in this new edition of *America.* If you haven't perused *For the Record* in a while, now would be a good time to take a look. The reader is now available as an ebook for the first time!

Acknowledgments

This Third Edition of *America: The Essential Learning Edition* has been a team effort. Several professors who have become specialists in teaching the introductory survey course helped create the instructor resources and interactive media:

David Cameron, Lone Star College–University Park
Brian Cervantez, Tarrant County College–Northwest Campus
Manar Elkhaldi, University of Central Florida
Christina Gold, El Camino College
Maryellen Harman, North Central Missouri College

David Marsich, Germanna Community College
Brian D. McKnight, University of Virginia's College at Wise
Lise Namikas, Baton Rouge Community College
Matthew Zembo, Hudson Valley Community College

The quality and range of the professorial reviews on this project were truly exceptional. The book and its accompanying media components were greatly influenced by the suggestions provided by the following instructors for both current and previous editions:

Milan Andrejevich, Ivy Tech Community College
Carol A. Bielke, San Antonio Independent School District
April Birchfield, Asheville-Buncombe Technical Community College
Carl Boschert, Hinds Community College
Kevin Brady, Tidewater Community College
Matt Brent, Rappahannock Community College
Sharon J. Burnham, John Tyler Community College
Michael Collins, Texas State University
Scott Cook, Motlow State Community College
Carrie Coston, Blinn College
Nicholas P. Cox, Houston Community College
Tyler Craddock, J. Sargeant Reynolds Community College
Carl E. Creasman, Jr., Valencia College
Stephen K. Davis, Texas State University
Frank De La O, Midland College
Jim Dudlo, Brookhaven College
Jeffrey David Ewen, Ivy Tech Community College
Robert Glen Findley, Odessa College
Brandon Franke, Blinn College
Chad Garick, Jones County Junior College
Christopher Gerdes, Lone Star College–Kingwood and CyFair
Lanette Gonzalez, Ivy Tech Community College
Abbie Grubb, San Jacinto College–South Campus
Devethia Guillory, Lone Star College–North Harris
Jennifer Heth, Tarrant County College–South Campus
Justin Hoggard, Three Rivers College
Andrew G. Hollinger, Tarrant County College
David P. Hopkins, Jr., Midland College
Justin Horton, Thomas Nelson Community College
David Houpt, University of North Carolina, Wilmington
Bettye Hutchins, Vernon College
John Ivens, Glenville State College
Theresa R. Jach, Houston Community College
Robert Jason Kelly, Holmes Community College
Matthew Keyworth, Lone Star College
Deborah Kruger, Butler Community College
Jennifer Lang, Delgado Community College

David W. Marsich, Germanna Community College
Nina McCune, Baton Rouge Community College
Adam Meredith, University of Southern Indiana
Richard Randall Moore, Metropolitan Community College–Longview
Ken S. Mueller, Ivy Tech Community College
Lise Namikas, Colorado State University–Global
Brice E. Olivier, Temple College
Saul Panski, El Camino College
Candice Pulkowski, The Art Institutes
Shane Puryear, Lone Star College–Greenspoint and Victory Centers
Carey Roberts, Liberty University
John Schmitz, Northern Virginia Community College–Annandale
Nancy Schurr, Chattanooga State Community College
Donald Seals, Kilgore College
Greg Shealy, University of Wisconsin–Madison
Wendy Shuffett, Jefferson State Community College
Steve Siry, Baldwin Wallace University
Thomas Summerhill, Michigan State University
Kevin Sweeney, Wayland Baptist University
Christopher Thomas, J. Sargeant Reynolds Community College
Tracy S. Uebelhor, Ivy Tech Community College
Scott M. Williams, Weatherford College
Laura Matysek Wood, Tarrant County College–Northwest
Crystal R. M. Wright, North Central Texas College

As always, my colleagues at W. W. Norton shared with me their dedicated expertise and their poise amid tight deadlines, especially Jon Durbin, Melissa Atkin, David Bradley, Allen Chen, Lily Gellman, Carson Russell, Rachel Mayer, Alexander Lee, Hillary Roegelein, Jennifer Jussel, Benjamin Reynolds, Sarah England Bartley, Janise Turso, Julie Sindel, Carrie Polvino, Elizabeth Trammell, Amla Sanghvi, Debra Morton-Hoyt, Lissi Sigillo, Hope Goodell Miller, Lisa Buckley, Jen Montgomery, Jenna Barry, Alicia Jimenez, Rose Paulson, Anna Marie Anastasi, Harry Haskell, Ellen Lohman, Marne Evans, and Kelly Minot Rafey. In addition, Jim Stewart, a patient friend and consummate editor, helped winnow my wordiness.

Finally, I have dedicated this Third Essential Learning Edition of *America* to the incredible staff at W. W. Norton, a publisher whose dedicated employees are more interested in education than profit. I have been blessed to work with and learn from so many talented and dedicated professionals.

America

The Essential Learning Edition

I am very affectionately your Friend
Phillis Wheatley
Boston March 21. 1774.

PART

1

An Old "New" World

History is filled with surprises. Luck and accidents—the unexpected happenings of life—often shape events more than intentions do. Long before Christopher Columbus happened upon the Caribbean Sea in an effort to find a westward passage to the Indies (East Asia), the indigenous peoples he mislabeled "Indians" had transformed the lands of the Western Hemisphere for thousands of years. The "New World" was thus *new* only to the Europeans who began exploring, conquering, and exploiting the region at the end of the fifteenth century.

Over many centuries, ancient peoples in the Western Hemisphere (also called the Americas—North, Central, and South) had developed hundreds of strikingly different societies. Some were rooted in agriculture; others focused on trade or conquest. Many Native Americans (also called Amerindians) were healthier, were better fed, and lived longer than Europeans, but when the two civilizations—European and Native American—collided, Amerindians were often infected, enslaved, overworked, or exterminated. Yet the familiar story of invasion and conquest oversimplifies the process by which Indians, Europeans, and Africans interacted in the sixteenth and seventeenth centuries. Native Americans were also trading partners and military allies of the transatlantic newcomers. They became neighbors and advisers, religious converts and loving spouses. As such, they participated actively in the creation of America.

The Europeans who risked their lives to settle in the Western Hemisphere were a diverse lot. The explorers, conquerors, and colonists came from Spain, Portugal, France, the British Isles, the Netherlands (Holland), Scandinavia, Italy, and the German states. (Germany would not become a united nation until 1871.) What they shared was a presumption that Christianity was superior to all religions and that all other peoples were inferior to them and their culture.

A variety of motives inspired Europeans to undertake the dangerous transatlantic voyage. Some were fortune seekers lusting for glory and gold, silver, and spices. Others were Christian evangelists eager to create kingdoms of God in the New World. Still others were adventurers, convicts, debtors, servants, landless peasants, and political or religious exiles. Most were simply seeking a better way of life. As a Pennsylvania colonist noted, workers "here get three times the wages for their labor than they can in England."

Yet such wages never attracted enough workers to keep up with the rapidly expanding colonial economies, so Europeans eventually turned to Africa for their need for workers in the Americas. Beginning in 1503, European nations—especially Portugal and Spain—transported increasing numbers of captive Africans to the Western Hemisphere. Throughout the sixteenth century, enslaved Africans were taken to ports as far south as Chile and as far north as Canada. Thereafter, the English and Dutch joined the effort to sell enslaved Africans. Few Europeans acknowledged the contradiction between the promise of freedom in America for themselves and the expanding institution of race-based slavery.

The intermingling of these diverse peoples and cultures lent colonial American society its distinctive vitality and variety. The shared quest for a better life gave America much of its drama, conflict, and tragedy.

The Europeans unwittingly brought to the Americas infectious diseases that would prove disastrous for the indigenous peoples, who had no natural immunities. As many as 90 percent of Native Americans would eventually die from European-borne diseases. Proportionately, it would be the worst death toll in history.

At the same time, bitter rivalries among the Spanish, French, English, and Dutch triggered costly wars around the world. Amid such conflicts, the monarchs of Europe struggled to manage often-unruly colonies, which, as it turned out, played crucial roles in their frequent wars.

Many colonists displayed a feisty independence, which led them to resent government interference in their affairs. A British official in North Carolina reported that the colonists were "without any Law or Order. Impudence is so very high, as to be past bearing."

The colonists and their British rulers maintained an uneasy partnership throughout the seventeenth century. As royal authorities tightened their control during the mid–eighteenth century, they first met resistance, which in 1775 ignited into revolution.

HERNÁN CORTÉS AND EMPEROR MOCTEZUMA This seventeenth-century oil painting shows the first meeting of Spanish conquistador Hernán Cortés (*center right*) and Emperor Moctezuma of the Mexicas (*center left*) in 1519. Just behind Cortés stands Malinche, his mistress and interpreter. Moctezuma's people are not permitted to gaze upon his face, and a servant ensures his feet do not touch the ground.

CHAPTER 1

The Collision of Cultures

IN THE SIXTEENTH CENTURY

America was born in melting ice. Thousands of years ago, during a period known as the Ice Age, immense glaciers some two miles thick inched southward from the Arctic Circle at the top of the globe. The advancing ice crushed hills, rerouted rivers, gouged out lakebeds and waterways, and scraped bare all the land in its path.

The glacial ice sheets covered much of North America—Canada, Alaska, the Upper Midwest, New England, Montana, and Washington. Then, as the continent's climate began to warm, the ice slowly, century after century, melted, eventually opening pathways for the first immigrants to pass through. Over many centuries, curious people discovered a continent blessed with fertile soils, abundant game animals, and mighty rivers providing passageways throughout the interior.

North and South America were the last continents to be populated by *Homo sapiens*. Debate still rages about when and how humans first arrived in North America. Yet one thing is sure: the ancestors of every person living in the United States originally came from somewhere else. In this sense, America is a nation of immigrants, a diverse society of striving people attracted by a mythic new world promising new beginnings and a better life in a place of seemingly unlimited space—and freedoms. Geography may be destiny, as the saying goes, but without pioneering people of determination and imagination, geography would have destroyed rather than sustained the first Americans.

CORE OBJECTIVES INQUIZITIVE

1. Explain why there were so many diverse human societies in the Americas before Europeans arrived.
2. Summarize the significant developments in Europe that enabled the Age of Exploration.
3. Describe how the Spanish were able to conquer and colonize the Americas.
4. Assess the impact of the Columbian Exchange between the "Old" and "New" Worlds.
5. Analyze the legacy of the Spanish form of colonization on North American history.

THE FIRST MIGRATION

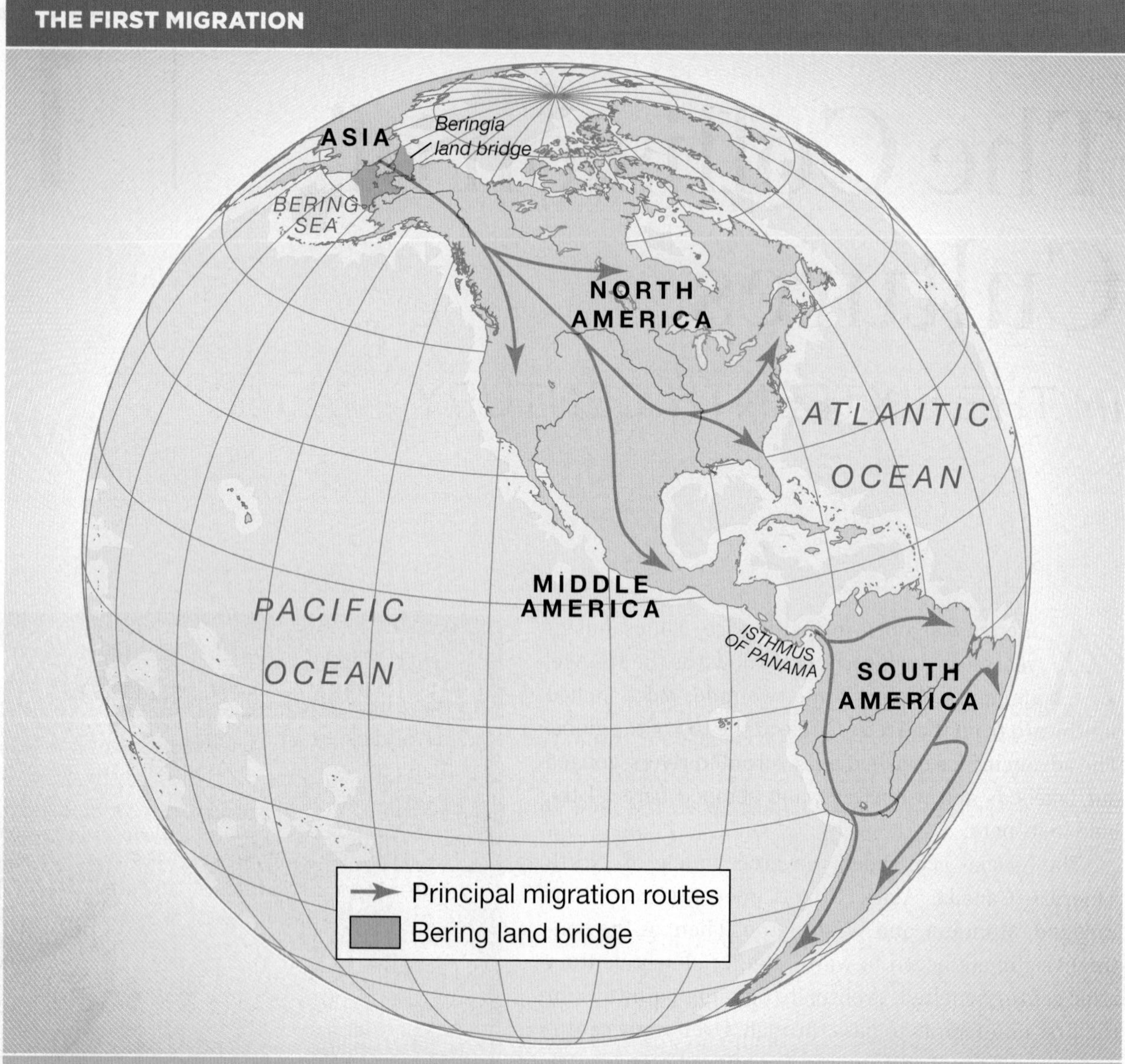

- When did people first cross the Bering Sea?
- What evidence have archaeologists and anthropologists found from the lives of the first people in America?
- Why did those people travel to North America?

Until recently, archaeologists had assumed that ancient peoples from northeast Asia were the first humans to arrive in the Western Hemisphere. Whether curious to explore new lands or attracted by herds of large game animals, they trekked across what is now the Bering Strait, a waterway that connects the Arctic and Pacific Oceans. During the Ice Age, however, the Bering Strait was dry—a treeless, frigid tundra known as Beringia that connected eastern Siberia with Alaska. Some Asians may have also ventured in boats to the coast of Alaska.

Over thousands of years, as the climate warmed and the glaciers and ice sheets melted, nomadic groups fanned out southward from Alaska and spread across the Western Hemisphere, forming primitive communities along the way. Archaeologists recently unearthed evidence of people in what is now Idaho dating back 16,500 years, a thousand years earlier than previously thought.

The Paleo Indians (also called Ancient Indians) lived in transportable huts with wooden frames covered by animal skins or grasses (thatch). They were skilled hunters and gatherers in search of game animals, whales, seals, fish, wild plants, berries, nuts, roots, and seeds. As they moved southward, they worked in groups to track and kill massive animals unlike any found today: mammoths, mastodons, giant sloths, camels, lions, saber-toothed tigers, cheetahs, and giant wolves, beavers, and bears.

Regardless of when, where, or how humans first set foot in North America, the continent eventually became a dynamic crossroads for adventurous peoples from around the world. They brought with them distinctive backgrounds, cultures, technologies, religions, and motivations that helped form the multicultural society known as America.

Early Cultures in the Americas

CORE **OBJECTIVE**

1. Explain why there were so many diverse human societies in the Americas before Europeans arrived.

Over many centuries, as the climate warmed, days grew so much hotter that many of the largest mammals—mammoths, mastodons, giant bison—became extinct. Hunters then began stalking smaller, yet more-abundant mammals: deer, antelope, elk, moose, and caribou. Over time, the Ancient Indians adapted to their varied environments—coastal forests, grassy plains, southwestern deserts, eastern woodlands. Some continued to hunt with spears and, later, bows and arrows; others fished or trapped small game. Some gathered wild plants and herbs and collected acorns and seeds, while others farmed. Most did some of each.

Global warming and climatic and environmental diversity

By about 7000 B.C.E. (before the Common Era), hunter-gatherer societies began transforming themselves into farming cultures, supplemented by seasonal hunting and gathering. Agriculture provided more nutritious food, which accelerated population growth and enabled once nomadic people to settle in villages. Indigenous peoples became expert at growing plants that would become the primary food crops of the hemisphere, chiefly **maize (corn)**, beans, and squash, but also chili peppers, avocados, and pumpkins.

Agricultural revolution

Maize-based societies viewed corn as the "gift of the gods" because it provided many essential needs. They made hominy by soaking dried kernels of corn in a mixture of water and ashes and then cooking it. They used corn cobs for fuel and the husks to fashion mats, masks, and dolls. They also ground the kernels into cornmeal, which could be mixed with beans to make protein-rich succotash.

maize (corn) The primary grain crop in Mesoamerica, yielding small kernels often ground into cornmeal. Easy to grow in a broad range of conditions, it enabled a global population explosion after being brought to Europe, Africa, and Asia.

The Maya, Incas, and Mexicas

In Middle America (*Mesoamerica*, what is now Mexico and Central America), agriculture supported the development of sophisticated communities complete with gigantic temple-topped pyramids, palaces, and bridges.

MAYA SOCIETY A fresco depicting a dressing ceremony of a high priest. He stands in the center garbed in a jaguar skin and an embroidered bell, surrounded by his less elaborately clad attendants. **What does this image reveal about the social hierarchy of Maya society?**

The Maya, who dominated Central America for more than 600 years, worshipped more than a hundred gods and developed a written language and elaborate works of art and architecture. They used mathematics and astronomy to create a yearly calendar more accurate than the one Europeans were using at the time of Columbus. Maya civilization featured sprawling cities, terraced farms, and spectacular pyramids.

In about 900 C.E., however, the Maya culture collapsed. Why it disappeared remains a mystery. Was its demise the result of civil wars or ecological catastrophe—drought, famine, disease, crop failure? The Maya destroyed much of the rain forest, upon whose fragile ecosystem they depended. As an archaeologist has explained, "Too many farmers grew too many crops on too much of the landscape." Deforestation led to hillside erosion and a catastrophic loss of nutrient-rich farmland.

Overpopulation added to the strain on Maya society, prompting civil wars. The Maya eventually succumbed to the Toltecs, who conquered most of the region in the tenth century. Around 1200 C.E., however, the Toltecs mysteriously withdrew after a series of droughts, fires, and invasions.

The Incas

Vast empires and monumental cities

Much farther south, many diverse people speaking at least twenty different languages made up the sprawling Inca Empire. By the fifteenth century, the Incas' vast realm stretched some 2,500 miles along the Andes Mountains in the western part of South America. It featured irrigated farms, stone buildings, and interconnected networks of roads paved with stones.

The Mexicas (Aztecs)

During the thirteenth century, the nomadic **Mexicas** (Me-SHEE-kas) began drifting southward from northwest Mexico. (They were not called Aztecs until 1821, when Mexico gained its independence from Spain.) Disciplined and imaginative, the Mexicas seized control of the central highlands, where they built the spectacular city of Tenochtitlán (place of the stone cactus) on an island in Lake Tetzcoco, at the site of present-day Mexico City.

Tenochtitlán would become one of the grandest cities in the world. It served as the capital of a sophisticated **Mexica Empire** ruled by a powerful emperor and divided into two social classes: nobles, warriors, and priests (about 5 percent of the population), and the free commoners—merchants, artisans, farmers, and enslaved people.

When the Spanish invaded Mexico in 1519, they found a vast Mexica Empire connected by a network of roads serving 371 city-states organized into 38 provinces. Towering stone temples, paved avenues, thriving marketplaces, and some 70,000 *adobe* (sunbaked mud) huts dominated Tenochtitlán.

Mexicas Otherwise known as Aztecs, a Mesoamerican people of northern Mexico who founded the vast Aztec Empire in the fourteenth century, later conquered by the Spanish under Hernán Cortés in 1521.

Mexica Empire The dominion established in the fourteenth century under the imperialistic Mexicas, or Aztecs, in the valley of Mexico.

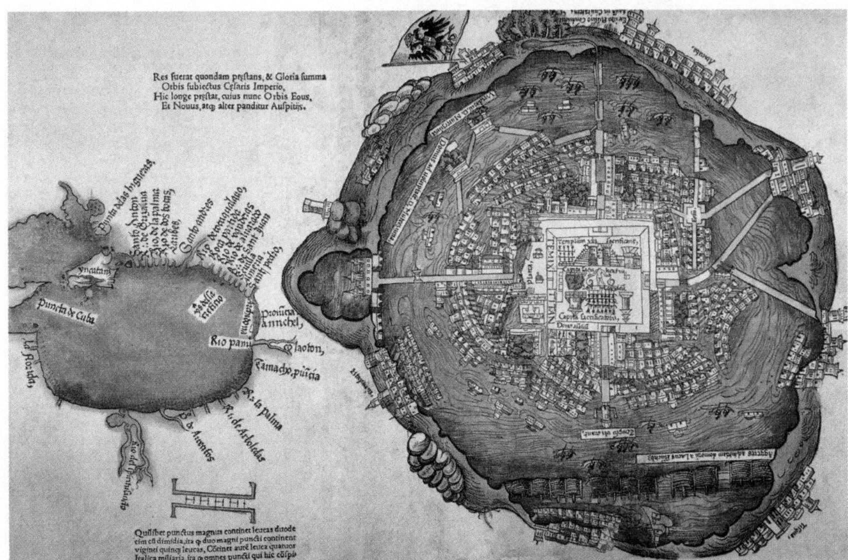

TENOCHTITLÁN This map of the Mexica capital (and the Gulf of Mexico) was published in a 1524 edition of the letters of Hernán Cortés. The capital bloomed in concentric circles, with the Great Temple and political buildings at the center, and the residences radiating outward. **What does the map of Tenochtitlán reveal about the people who lived there?**

As their empire expanded across central and southern Mexico, the Mexicas (Aztecs) developed elaborate societies supported by sophisticated legal and political systems. Their cities boasted lively markets and busy merchants and featured beautiful gardens and relaxing spas. The Mexicas practiced efficient new farming techniques, including terracing of fields, crop rotation, large-scale irrigation, and other engineering marvels. Their arts and architecture were magnificent.

Mexica rulers claimed godlike qualities, and nobles, priests, and warrior-heroes dominated the social system. The emperor's palace had 100 rooms and baths replete with statues, gardens, and a zoo; the aristocracy lived in large stone dwellings, practiced polygamy (multiple wives), and were exempt from manual labor.

Religion, war, tribute, and trade

Like most agricultural peoples, the Mexicas worshipped multiple gods. Their religious beliefs focused on the interconnection between nature and human life and the sacredness of natural elements—the sun, moon, stars, rain, mountains, rivers, and animals. They were obliged to feed the gods human hearts and blood. As a consequence, the Mexicas, like most Mesoamerican societies, regularly offered thousands of live human sacrifices to the gods. In elaborate weekly rituals, captured warriors or virgin girls would be daubed with paint, given a hallucinatory drug, and marched to the temple platform, where priests cut out their beating hearts and offered them to the sun god. The constant need for human sacrifices fed the Mexicas' relentless warfare against other indigenous groups. A Mexica song celebrated their warrior code: "Proud of itself is the city of Mexico-Tenochtitlán. Here no one fears to die in war. This is our glory." Warfare,

MEXICA SACRIFICES TO THE GODS Renowned for their military prowess, the Mexicas (Aztecs) preferred to capture and then sacrifice their enemies.

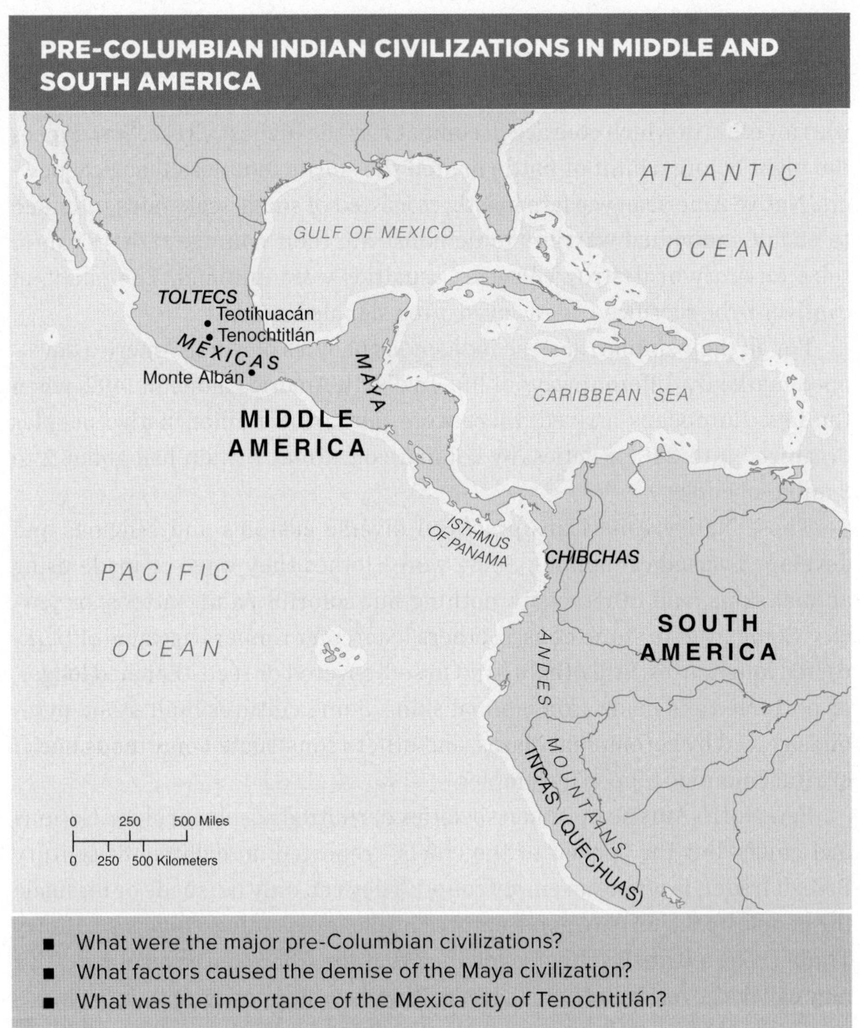

PRE-COLUMBIAN INDIAN CIVILIZATIONS IN MIDDLE AND SOUTH AMERICA

- What were the major pre-Columbian civilizations?
- What factors caused the demise of the Maya civilization?
- What was the importance of the Mexica city of Tenochtitlán?

therefore, was a sacred activity. Gradually, the Mexicas conquered many neighboring societies, forcing them to make payment of goods and labor as tribute to the empire.

North American Civilizations around 1500

Diverse regional societies

North of Mexico, in the present-day United States, many indigenous societies blossomed in the early 1500s. Over the centuries, small kinship groups (*clans*) had coalesced to form larger *bands* involving hundreds of people. The bands evolved into much larger regional groups, or *nations*, whose members spoke the same language. Although few indigenous societies had an alphabet or written language, they all developed rich oral traditions that passed spiritual myths and social beliefs from generation to generation.

Like the Mexicas, most indigenous peoples in the Americas believed in godlike "spirits." To the Sioux, God was Wakan Tanka, the Great Spirit. The Navajos believed in the Holy People: Sky, Earth, Moon, Sun, Thunders, and

Winds. Many Native Americans also believed in ghosts, who acted as their bodyguards in battle.

The importance of hunting to many Indian societies helped nurture a warrior ethic in which courage in combat was the highest virtue. War dances the night before a hunt or battle invited the spirits to unleash magical powers. Native American warfare mostly consisted of small-scale raids intended to enable individual warriors to demonstrate their courage rather than to seize territory or destroy villages. Casualties were minimal. The taking of captives to be sacrificed or enslaved often signaled victory.

For all their similarities, the indigenous peoples of North America developed markedly different ways of life. In North America alone in 1492, when the first Europeans arrived, there were perhaps 8 million native peoples organized into 240 societies. By comparison, Great Britain had about 2 to 3 million people.

These Native Americans practiced diverse customs and religions and developed varied economies. Some wore clothes they wove or made using animal skins, and others wore nothing but colorful paint, tattoos, or jewelry. Some lived in stone houses, others in circular timber wigwams or bark-roofed longhouses. Still others lived in sod-covered or reed-thatched lodges, or portable tipis made from animal skins. Some cultures built stone pyramids graced by ceremonial plazas, and others constructed enormous burial or ritual mounds topped by temples.

Few North American Indian societies permitted absolute rulers. Nations had chiefs, but the "power of the chiefs," reported an eighteenth-century British trader, is often "an empty sound. They can only persuade or dissuade the people by the force of good-nature and clear reasoning." Likewise, Henry Timberlake, a British soldier, explained that the Cherokee government, "if I may call it a government, which has neither laws nor power to support it, is a mixed aristocracy and democracy, the chiefs being chosen according to their merit in war."

Native Americans owned land in common rather than individually as private property. Men were hunters, warriors, and leaders. Women tended children; made clothes, blankets, jewelry, and pottery; cured and dried animal skins; wove baskets; built and packed tipis; and grew, harvested, and cooked food.

When the men were away hunting or fighting, women took charge of village life. Some Indian nations, like the Cherokee and the Five Nation League of the Iroquois (comprised of the Mohawk, Oneida, Onondaga, Cayuga, and Seneca Nations), gave women political power. The women "are much respected," a French priest reported on the Iroquois. "The Elders decide no important affair without their advice."

The Southwest

Southwest pueblo cultures

The often hot and dry Southwest (what is now Arizona, New Mexico, Nevada, and Utah) featured a landscape of high mesas, deep canyons, vast deserts, long rivers, and snow-covered mountains. The Hopis, Zunis, and others still live in the multistory adobe cliffside villages (called *pueblos* by the Spanish), which were erected by their ancient ancestors.

About 500 C.E. (Common Era), the Hohokam ("those who have vanished") people migrated from Mexico northward to southern and central Arizona, where they built extensive canals to irrigate crops. They also crafted decorative pottery and turquoise jewelry.

The most widespread of the Southwest pueblo cultures were the Anasazi (Ancestral Pueblos), or Basketmakers. Unlike the Mexicas and Incas, however, Ancestral Pueblo society did *not* have a rigid class structure. The Ancestral Pueblos engaged in warfare only as a means of self-defense, and the religious leaders and warriors worked much as the rest of the people did.

CLIFF DWELLINGS Ruins of Anasazi (Ancestral Pueblo) cliff dwellings in Mesa Verde National Park, Colorado. **Why might the Southwestern societies have built their villages deep into cliff faces?**

The Northwest

Along the narrow coastal strip running up the densely forested northwest Pacific coast, shellfish, salmon, seals, whales, deer, and edible wild plants were abundant. Here, there was little need to rely on farming. Many of the Pacific Northwest peoples, such as the Haida, Kwakiutl, and Nootka, needed to work only two days to provide enough food for a week.

The Pacific coast cultures developed intricate religious rituals and sophisticated woodworking skills. They carved towering totem poles featuring decorative figures of animals and other symbolic characters. For shelter, they built large, earthen-floored, cedar-plank houses up to 500 feet long, where groups of families lived together. They also created sturdy, oceangoing canoes made of hollowed-out tree trunks—some large enough to carry fifty people. Socially, they were divided into slaves, commoners, and chiefs.

The Great Plains

The many tribal nations living on the Great Plains, a vast, flat land west of the Mississippi River, included the Arapaho, Blackfeet, Cheyenne, Comanche, Crow, Apache, and Sioux. As nomadic hunter-gatherers, they tracked herds of bison (buffaloes) across a sea of grassland, collecting seeds, nuts, roots, and berries as they roamed.

Native Americans' religious beliefs

For all their differences, Native Americans developed a religious worldview distinctly different from the Christian perspective of Europeans. At the center of most hunter-gatherer religions is the idea that human beings are related to all living things, including natural objects: trees, rocks, rivers, mountains. As the Navajos sing, "All my surroundings are blessed as I found it." By contrast, the Bible portrays believers as separate from and superior to the natural world, encouraging them to exercise their "dominion" over the land and water.

GREAT SERPENT MOUND Over 1,300 feet in length and three feet high, this snake-shaped burial mound in Adams County, Ohio, is the largest of its kind in the world.

The Mississippians

Eastern "mound builders"

East of the Great Plains, in the vast woodlands reaching from the Mississippi River to the Atlantic Ocean, several "mound-building" cultures prospered. Between 700 B.C.E. and 200 C.E., the Adena and later the Hopewell societies developed communities in the Ohio valley. The Adena-Hopewell cultures grew corn, squash, beans, and sunflowers, as well as tobacco for smoking. They left behind enormous earthworks and elaborate **burial mounds** shaped like snakes, birds, and other animals.

Like the Adena, the Hopewell developed an extensive trading network with other Indian societies from the Gulf of Mexico to Canada, exchanging exquisite carvings, metalwork, pearls, seashells, copper ornaments, bear claws, and jewelry. By the sixth century, however, the Hopewell culture disappeared, giving way to a new phase of development east of the Mississippi River, the *Mississippian* culture.

burial mounds A funereal tradition, practiced in the Mississippi and Ohio Valleys by the Adena-Hopewell cultures, of erecting massive mounds of earth over graves, often shaped in the designs of serpents and other animals.

Cahokia The largest chiefdom of the Mississippian Indian culture located in present-day Illinois and the site of a sophisticated farming settlement that supported up to 15,000 inhabitants.

The Mississippians were corn-growing peoples who built substantial agricultural towns around central plazas and temples and developed a far-flung trading network that extended to the Rocky Mountains. Their ability to grow large amounts of corn in the fertile flood plains spurred rapid population growth around regional centers.

The largest of these advanced regional centers, called *chiefdoms*, was **Cahokia** (600–1300 C.E.), in southwest Illinois, near the confluence of the Mississippi and Missouri Rivers (across from what is now St. Louis). The

PRE-COLUMBIAN INDIAN CIVILIZATIONS IN NORTH AMERICA

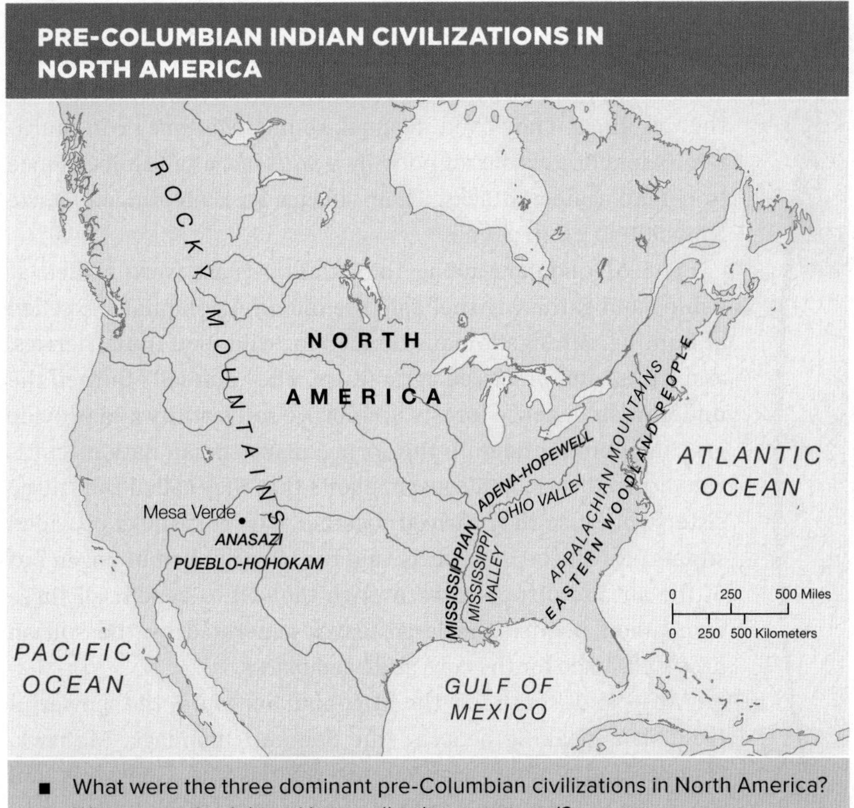

- What were the three dominant pre-Columbian civilizations in North America?
- Where was the Adena-Hopewell culture centered?
- How was the Mississippian civilization similar to that of the Maya or Mexicas?
- What made the Anasazi culture different from the other North American cultures?

Cahokians constructed an enormous farming settlement with monumental public buildings, spacious ceremonial plazas, and more than eighty flat-topped earthen mounds with thatch-roofed temples on top. At the height of its influence, Cahokia hosted 15,000 people on some 3,200 acres.

Cahokia, however, vanished around 1400. Its collapse remains a mystery, but the overcutting of trees to make fortress walls may have set in motion ecological changes that doomed the community when a massive earthquake struck. The loss of trees led to widespread flooding and the erosion of topsoil, which forced residents to seek better land across the Midwest and into what is now the American South.

Eastern Woodland Peoples and European Contact

After the collapse of Cahokia, the **Eastern Woodland peoples** spread along the Atlantic Seaboard from Maine to Florida and along the Gulf Coast to Louisiana. They included three groups distinguished by their different languages: the Algonquian, the Iroquoian, and the Muskogean. These were the indigenous societies that Europeans would first encounter when they arrived in North America.

Eastern Woodland peoples Various Native American societies, particularly the Algonquian, Iroquoian, and Muskogean regional groups, who once dominated the Atlantic seaboard from Maine to Louisiana.

The manner of their attire and
painting them selues when
they goe to their generall
huntings, or at theire
Solemne feasts.

ALGONQUIAN CHIEF IN WAR PAINT This sketch from the notebook of English settler John White depicts a Native American chief.

The Algonquian-speaking peoples stretched westward from the New England Seaboard to lands along the Great Lakes and into the Upper Midwest and south to New Jersey, Virginia, and the Carolinas. They lived in small, round *wigwams* or in multifamily longhouses surrounded by a *palisade*, a tall timber fence to defend against attacks. Their villages typically ranged in size from 500 to 2,000 people.

The Algonquians along the Atlantic coast were skilled at fishing and gathering shellfish; the inland Algonquians excelled at hunting. All Algonquians foraged for wild food (nuts, berries, and fruits) and practiced agriculture. They annually burned the underbrush in dense forests to improve soil fertility and provide grazing room for deer. In the spring, many Indian nations cultivated corn, beans, and squash, plants that they called the "three sisters" because they thrived together. The cornstalks provided support for the bean tendrils, and the beans pulled nitrogen out of the air and dispersed it through the soil to benefit all three companion plants. The large leaves generated by the squash provided shade for the corn and bean plants.

West and south of the Algonquians were the powerful Iroquoian-speaking peoples (the Seneca, Onondaga, Mohawk, Oneida, and Cayuga Nations, as well as the Cherokee and Tuscarora). Their lands spread from upstate New York southward through Pennsylvania and into the Carolinas and Georgia. The Iroquois were farmer/hunters who lived in extended family groups (clans), sharing bark-covered longhouses in towns of 3,000 or more people. The oldest woman in each longhouse served as the "clan mother."

Gender roles in Iroquoian culture

Unlike the Algonquian culture, in which men were dominant, women held the critical leadership roles in the Iroquoian culture. As an Iroquois elder explained, "In our society, women are the center of all things. Nature, we believe, has given women the ability to create; therefore, it is only natural that women be in positions of power to protect this function." Iroquois men and women operated in separate social domains. No woman could be a chief; no man could head a clan. Women selected the chiefs, controlled the distribution of property, supervised the enslaved, and planted and harvested the crops. They also arranged marriages. After a wedding ceremony, the man moved in with his wife's family. In part, the Iroquoian matriarchy reflected the frequent absence of Iroquois men, who as skilled hunters and traders traveled extensively for long periods.

The third major Native American group in the Eastern Woodlands included the peoples along the coast of the Gulf of Mexico who farmed and hunted and spoke the Muskogean language: the Creek, Choctaw, Chickasaw, Seminole, Natchez, Apalachee, and Timucua. Like the Iroquois, they were often matrilineal societies, meaning that ancestry flowed through the mother's line, but they had a more rigid class structure. The Muskogeans lived in towns arranged around a central plaza. Many of their thatch-roofed houses had no walls because of the mild winters and hot, humid summers.

Over thousands of years, the native North Americans had displayed remarkable resilience, adapting to the uncertainties of frequent warfare, changing climates, and varying environments. They would display similar resilience against the challenges created by the arrival of Europeans. In the process of adapting their heritage and ways of life to unwanted new realities, the Native Americans played a significant role in shaping America.

The Expansion of Europe

CORE **OBJECTIVE**

2. Summarize the significant developments in Europe that enabled the Age of Exploration.

The European exploration of the Western Hemisphere resulted from key developments during the fifteenth century. Dramatic scientific discoveries and technological improvements, along with sustained population growth, fueled European expansion abroad.

By the end of the fifteenth century, medieval feudalism's static agrarian social system, in which peasant serfs worked for nobles in exchange for living on and farming the land, began to disintegrate. People were no longer forced to remain in the same area and keep the same social status to which they were born. A "middle class" emerged committed to a more dynamic commercial economy fueled by innovations in banking, currency, accounting, and insurance.

Rise of a middle class

The growing trade-based economy in Europe freed kings from their dependence on feudal nobles. Monarchs unified the scattered cities ruled by princes (principalities) into large kingdoms with more-centralized governments. The rise of towns, cities, and a merchant class provided new tax revenues. Over time, the new class of monarchs, merchants, and bankers displaced the landed nobility as the ruling elite.

Powerful new nations

The Renaissance

The rediscovery of ancient Greek and Roman texts during the fourteenth and fifteenth centuries spurred the Renaissance (rebirth), an intellectual revolution that transformed the arts as well as traditional attitudes toward religion and science. The Renaissance began in Italy and spread across western Europe, bringing with it a more *secular* outlook that took greater interest in humanity than in religion. Rather than emphasizing God's omnipotence, Renaissance *humanism* highlighted the power of inventive people to exert command over nature.

The Renaissance was a crucial force in the transition from medievalism to early modernism. From the fifteenth century on, educated people throughout Europe began to challenge prevailing beliefs as well as the absolute authority of rulers and churchmen. They discussed controversial new ideas, engaged in scientific research, and unleashed their artistic creativity.

Innovations in shipbuilding, navigation, and weaponry led to global revolution in maritime trade

The Renaissance also sparked what came to be called the Age of Exploration. New knowledge and technologies made possible the construction of larger sailing ships capable of oceanic voyages. The development of more accurate navigational instruments helped sailors determine their ship's location at sea. The Renaissance also brought the invention of gunpowder, cannons, and firearms—and the printing press.

The Rise of Global Trade

By the sixteenth century, trade between western European nations and the Middle East, Africa, and Asia was booming. The Portuguese took the lead, bolstered by expert sailors and fast, three-masted ships called *caravels*. Portuguese ships traveled along the west coast of Africa collecting grains, gold, ivory, spices, and enslaved human cargo. Eventually, these ships continued around Africa to the Indian Ocean in search of the fabled *Indies* (India and Southeast Asia). They ventured on to China and Japan, where they acquired spices (cinnamon, cloves, ginger, nutmeg, black pepper) to enliven bland European food, sugar made from cane to sweeten food and drink, silk cloth, herbal medicines, and other exotic goods for burgeoning western markets.

Factors that facilitated global trade

Global trade flourished because of the emergence of four powerful nations: England, France, Portugal, and especially Spain. The arranged marriage of King Ferdinand II of Aragon and Queen Isabella I of Castile in 1469 unified their two kingdoms into one formidable new nation, Spain. The king and queen were eager to spread the Catholic faith. On January 1, 1492, after nearly eight centuries of warfare between Spanish Christians and Muslims, Ferdinand and Isabella declared victory for Catholicism at Granada. The monarchs then set about instituting a fifteenth-century version of ethnic cleansing. They gave Muslims and Jews in Spain one choice: convert to Catholicism or leave.

By ending the prolonged conflict over religious unity, the forced conversion of Muslims and Jews was one of many factors that enabled Europe's global explorations at the end of the fifteenth century. Other factors—urbanization, world trade, the rise of centralized nations, advances in knowledge, technology, and firepower—combined with natural human curiosity, greed, and religious zeal to spur efforts to find western sea routes to the Indies. More immediately, the decision of Chinese rulers to shut off land access to Asia in 1453 forced merchants to focus on seaborne options. For these reasons, Europeans set in motion the events that, as one historian has observed, would bind together "four continents, three races, and a great diversity of regional parts."

The Voyages of Columbus

These were the circumstances that prompted Christopher Columbus's efforts to find a faster route to Japan and China. Born in the Italian seaport of Genoa, in 1451, Columbus took to the sea at an early age, teaching himself geography, navigation, and Latin. By the 1480s, he was eager to spread Christianity across the globe and win glory and riches for himself.

Columbus spent a decade trying to convince European monarchs to finance a voyage across the Atlantic to Japan and China. England, France,

COLUMBUS'S VOYAGES

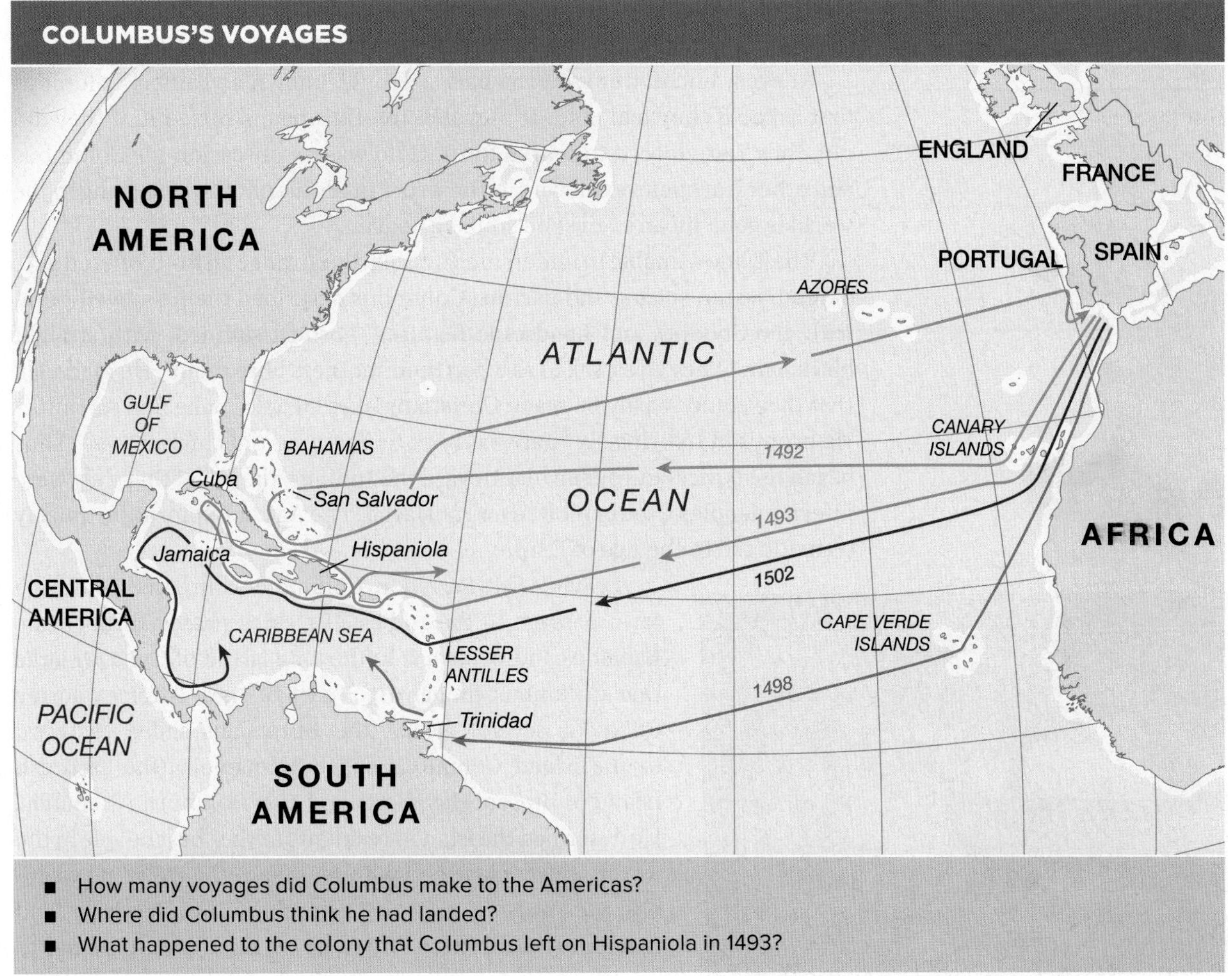

- How many voyages did Columbus make to the Americas?
- Where did Columbus think he had landed?
- What happened to the colony that Columbus left on Hispaniola in 1493?

Portugal, and Spain turned him down, but he eventually persuaded Ferdinand and Isabella to fund his voyage. They agreed to award him a one-tenth share of any riches he gathered; they would take the rest.

Columbus's First Voyage

On August 3, 1492, Columbus and a crew of ninety men and boys, mostly from Spain but from seven other nations as well, set sail on three tiny ships, the *Santa María*, the *Pinta*, and the *Niña*. They traveled first to Lisbon, Portugal, and then headed west to the Canary Islands, where they spent a month gathering supplies and making repairs. They then journeyed across the open sea. By early October, the worried sailors—none of whom had ever been away from land so long—rebelled at the "madness" of sailing blindly. They forced Columbus to agree to turn back if land were not sighted within three days.

As the ships sailed on, the crew's mood lightened as they saw evidence that land was nearby. Seagulls flew overhead, and the color of the ocean turned from dark blue to pale green. Then, at dawn on October 12, a sailor on watch yelled, *"Tierra! Tierra!"* ("Land! Land!"). He had spotted a small island in the Bahamas east of Florida that Columbus named San Salvador (Blessed Savior).

Columbus mistakenly assumed that they must be near the Indies, so he called the native people *Indios* and named the surrounding islands the West Indies.

Lust for gold

At every encounter with the native people, known as Tainos, Columbus first asked if they had gold. If they did, the Europeans seized it; if they did not, they were forced to search for it. Gold was an obsession for Columbus and other European explorers. As he wrote in his diary, "the best thing in the world is gold; it can even send souls to heaven."

The Tainos, unable to understand or repel the strange visitors, offered gifts of food, water, spears, and parrots. Columbus described them as "well-built, with good bodies, and handsome features"—brown-skinned, with straight black hair. "They go as naked as when their mothers bore them." He marveled that they could "easily be made Christians" and "would make fine servants." He promised to bring six "natives" back to Spain for "his highnesses." Thus began the typical European bias toward the Indians: the belief that they were inferior peoples to be exploited and enslaved. The Age of Exploration quickly transitioned to the Age of Empire.

Leaving San Salvador, Columbus continued to search for a passage to the Indies. His ships passed through the Bahamas and westward to the long island of Cuba, so large that Columbus thought it a part of Asia. After exploring Cuba for several weeks, the Europeans sailed eastward to the island Columbus called Hispaniola (the "Spanish Island"), present-day Haiti and the Dominican Republic. He described the island's residents as the "best people in the world," full "of love and without greed." They had no weapons, wore no clothes, and led a simple life. Columbus decided that the Indians were "fitted to be ruled and to be set to work" generating riches for Spain, "for there are great mines of gold and of other metals." He decreed that all Indians over age fourteen must bring him at least a thimbleful of gold dust every three months. The quota was often unattainable. Nevertheless, those who failed to supply enough gold had their hands cut off, causing many of them to bleed to death.

COLUMBUS IN THE "NEW WORLD" Christopher Columbus reached the island of San Salvador in 1492, though he was under the impression he had landed by the Indies. This woodcut, *Columbus's Landfall*, comes from a 1493 pamphlet describing this voyage—one of several trips he made back and forth across the Atlantic in the decade that followed.

Columbus's Return and the Treaty of Tordesillas

At the end of 1492, Columbus, still convinced he had reached an outer island of Japan, sailed back to Spain, where he received a hero's welcome, in part because everyone thought he had found the shortcut to Asia. "In thirty-three days," he reported, "I reached the *Indies*." He promised Ferdinand and Isabella that his discoveries would provide them "as much gold as they need . . . and as many slaves as they ask." Thanks to the newly invented printing press, news of Columbus's pathbreaking voyage spread rapidly across Europe and helped spur a desire to explore the world. The many voyages of discovery over the next two centuries would create a new outlook about knowledge. New plants, animals, peoples, cultures,

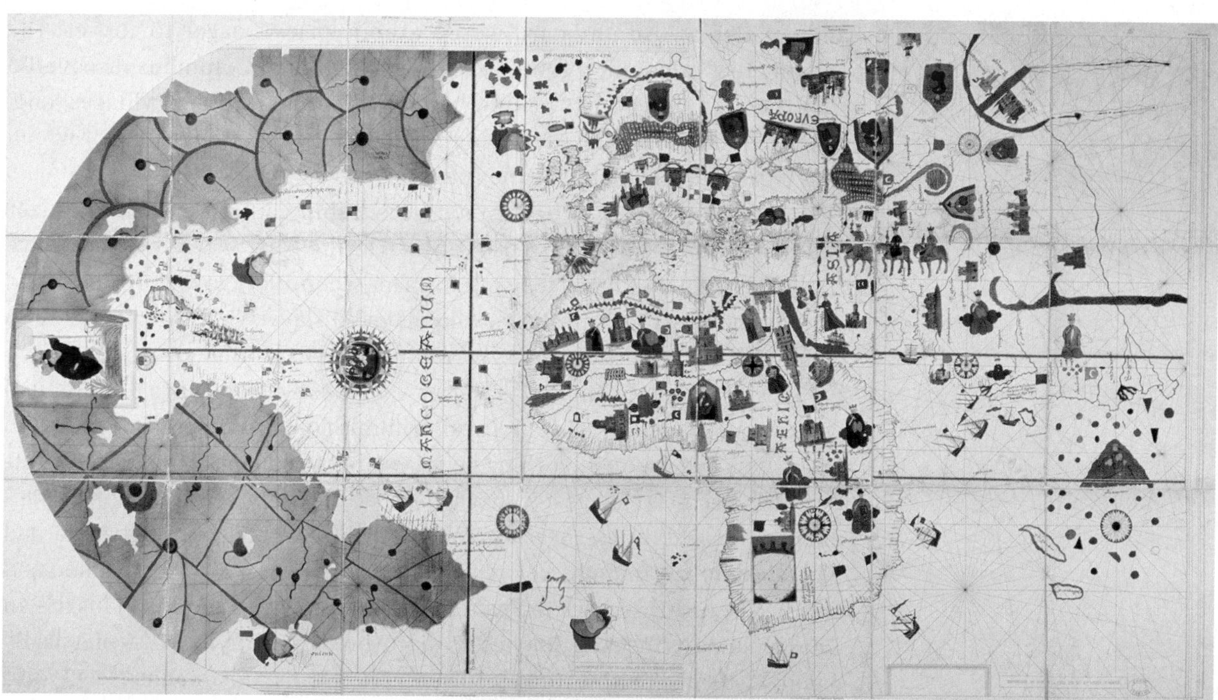

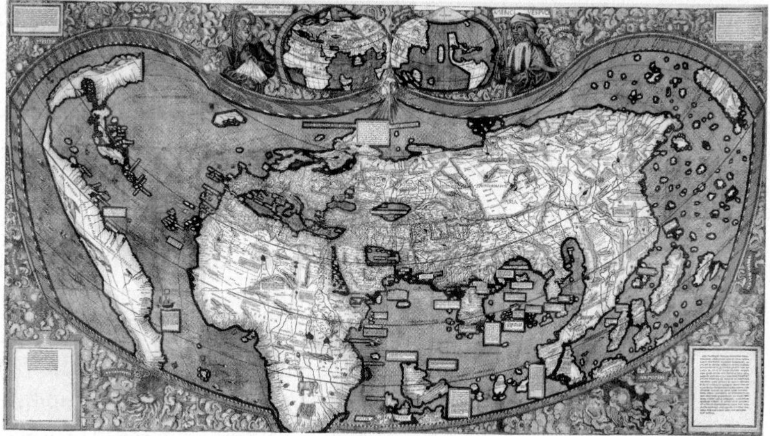

THE OLD AND NEW WORLDS (*Top*) The *mappa mundi*, or "map of the world," was drawn by Juan de la Cosa in 1500 and is the first known European map to include the "New World." (*Bottom*) Martin Waldseemüller's 1507 world map was the first to capture the full Western Hemisphere, and to use the name "America." **What do these maps represent and how might they have shaped European worldviews?**

and religions suddenly cast the traditional Christian worldview into doubt. The "New World" demanded new ways of thinking and new ways of scientific investigation.

The excited Spanish monarchs told Columbus to prepare for a second voyage, instructing him to "treat the Indians very well and lovingly and abstain from doing them any injury." Columbus and his men would repeatedly defy this order.

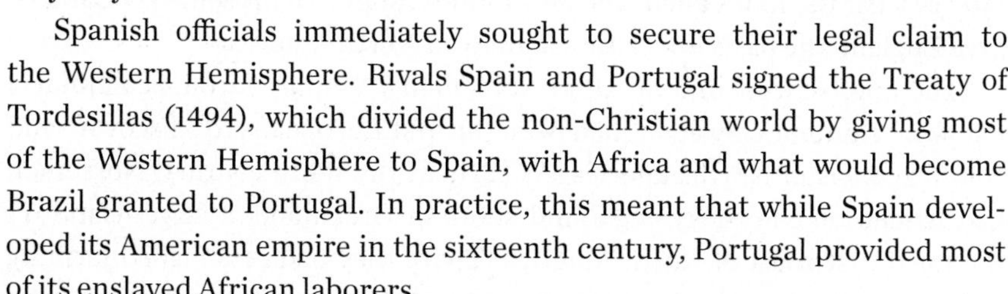

Spanish officials immediately sought to secure their legal claim to the Western Hemisphere. Rivals Spain and Portugal signed the Treaty of Tordesillas (1494), which divided the non-Christian world by giving most of the Western Hemisphere to Spain, with Africa and what would become Brazil granted to Portugal. In practice, this meant that while Spain developed its American empire in the sixteenth century, Portugal provided most of its enslaved African laborers.

Columbus's Troubled Second and Third Voyages

In 1493, Columbus returned to the New World with seventeen ships and 1,400 sailors, soldiers, and colonists—all men. They brought horses, pigs, cattle, chicken, sheep, goats, seeds, and plants. Unfortunately, the Spanish ships brought stowaway rats and infectious bacteria, measles, typhus, and smallpox. Also on board were Catholic priests eager to convert the Indians to Christianity. Upon reaching Hispaniola, Columbus discovered that the men he had left behind had raped women, robbed villages, and, as Columbus's son later added, committed "a thousand excesses for which they were mortally hated by the Indians."

Columbus proved to be a much better ship captain than a colonizer and governor. His first business venture in the New World was as a slave trader. When he returned to Spain from his second voyage with 400 enslaved Arawak Indians, Queen Isabella, who detested slavery, was horrified. "Who is this Columbus who dares to give out my vassals [Indians] as slaves?"

This incident prompted a series of investigations into Columbus's behavior. The queen sent a royal commissioner, Francis Bobadilla, to Hispaniola, where the first thing he saw were the corpses of six Spanish settlers who had been hanged. A shocked Bobadilla announced that he was supplanting Columbus as governor. When Columbus objected, Bobadilla had him jailed for two months before shipping the explorer, now nearly blind and crippled by arthritis, back to Spain in chains in 1500. To the end of his life, in 1506, Columbus insisted that he had discovered the outlying parts of Asia. By one of history's greatest ironies, this led Europeans to name the New World not for Columbus but another Italian sailor-explorer, Amerigo Vespucci.

Vespucci's New World continent

In 1499, with the support of Portugal's monarchy, Vespucci sailed across the Atlantic, landing first at Brazil and then exploring 3,000 miles of the South American coastline in search of a passage to Asia. In the end, Vespucci decided that South America was so extensive and so densely populated that it must be a *new* continent. In 1507, a German mapmaker paid tribute to Amerigo Vespucci's navigational skills by labeling the New World using the feminine Latin variant of the explorer's first name: America.

Professional Explorers

News of the voyages of Columbus and Vespucci stimulated many other expeditions. The first explorer to sight the North American continent was John Cabot, an Italian sponsored by King Henry VII of England. Cabot's landfall in 1497 at what the king called "the new founde lande," in present-day Canada, gave England the basis for a later claim to *all* North America.

The English were unaware that Norsemen ("Vikings") from Scandinavia (Norway, Denmark, Sweden) had been the first Europeans to "discover" and colonize areas of North America. As early as the tenth century, Norsemen had landed on the rocky, fogbound shore of Greenland, a large island off the northeast coast of North America. There they had established farming settlements lasting hundreds of years, until disappearing after prolonged cold weather forced them back to Scandinavia.

The Spanish were determined to keep other Europeans out of the New World. In 1505, a Spanish ship unloaded pigs and goats in Puerto Rico, intending them to grow and multiply in anticipation of settling a colony there. It would be the first European settlement on what would later become a territory of the United States of America.

Religious Conflict in Europe

While explorers were crossing the Atlantic, explosive religious conflicts were tearing Europe apart in ways that would shape developments in the Western Hemisphere. When Columbus sailed west in 1492, all of Europe acknowledged the supremacy of the Roman Catholic Church and its pope in Rome. The pope led a sprawling religious empire, and Catholics were eager to spread their faith around the world.

The brutal efforts of the Spanish to convert native peoples in the Western Hemisphere to **Roman Catholicism** illustrated the murderous intensity with which European Christians embraced religious life. People fervently believed in heaven and hell, demons and angels, magic and miracles—and were willing to kill and die for their religious beliefs.

Martin Luther

Protestant Reformation

The enforced unity of Catholic Europe began to crack on October 31, 1517, when an obscure, thirty-three-year-old German monk sent his ninety-five "theses" outlining the "corrupt" Catholic Church to church officials. Martin Luther (1483–1546) could not have known that his defiant stance and explosive charges would ignite history's fiercest spiritual drama, the **Protestant Reformation**.

Martin Luther fractured Christianity by undermining the authority of the Catholic Church. He called the pope "the greatest thief and robber that has appeared or can appear on earth," claiming the pope had subjected Christians to "satanic" abuse. Luther especially criticized the widespread sale of *indulgences,* whereby priests would "forgive" sins in exchange for money. The Catholic Church had forged a profitable business out of forgiving sins, using the revenue to raise massive armies and build lavish cathedrals. Luther insisted that God alone, through the grace and mercy of Christ, offered salvation; people could not purchase it from church officials or earn it through "good works." As he exclaimed, "By faith alone are you saved!" To Luther, the Bible was the sole source of Christian truth; believers did not need the "den of murderers"—Catholic priests, bishops, and popes.

Through this simple but revolutionary doctrine of "Protestantism," Luther sought to revitalize Christianity and rid it of priestly corruption. The common people, he declared, represented a "priesthood of all believers." Individuals could seek their salvation without the intervention of priests. "All Christians are priests," he said; they "have the power to test and judge what is correct or incorrect in matters of faith" by themselves in communion with the Bible. Luther went on to produce the first New Testament in a German translation so that everyone—male or female, rich or poor—could read it. No longer would worshippers need to rely on priests to translate Latin Bibles for them.

Luther's rebellion spread quickly across Europe thanks to the circulation of thousands of inexpensive hot-blooded pamphlets, which served as the social media of the time. "Every day it rains Luther's pamphlets," sighed

Roman Catholicism The Christian faith and religious practices of the Roman Catholic Church, which exerted great political, economic, and social influence on much of western Europe and, through the Spanish and Portuguese Empires, on the Americas.

Protestant Reformation Sixteenth-century religious movement initiated by Martin Luther, a German monk whose public criticism of corruption in the Roman Catholic Church and whose teaching that Christians can communicate directly with God gained a wide following.

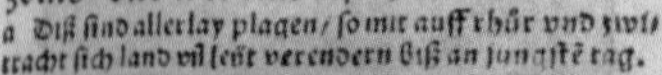

Sanct Johannes. CXLI

die Künig auff erden/vnd die öbersten/ vñ
die reychen/vnd die Hauptleütte/vnd die
gewaltigen/vnd alle knecht vnd alle frey
en/verborgen sich inn den klüfften vnnd
felsen an den bergen/vñ sprachen zů den
bergen vnd felsen/Fallet auff vns/vñ ver
berget vns vor dem angesicht deß/der auf
dem stůl sitzt/vnd vor dem zorn deß Lam-
mes/Dañ es ist komen der groß tag seines
zorns/vnd wer kan bestehn?

Von dem geschlecht Juda/zwelff tausent versigelt. Von dem geschlecht Rubē/
zwelff tausent versigelt. Von dem geschle
chte Gad/zwelff tausent versigelt. Von
dem geschlecht Aser/zwelff tausent versigelt. Von dem geschlecht Nephthali/
zwelff tausent versigelt. Von dē geschlecht
Manasse/zwelff tausent versigelt. Vō dē
geschlecht Simeon/zwelff tausent versigelt. Von dem geschlecht Leui/zwelff tau
sent versigelt. Vō dē geschlecht Isaschar/
zwelff tausent versigelt. Vō dē geschlecht

Das VII. Capitel.

MARTIN LUTHER'S BIBLE A page from Martin Luther's translation of the Bible, printed in 1535. A theologian and critic of the Catholic Church, Luther is best remembered for his ninety-five "theses," an incendiary document that served as a catalyst for the Protestant Reformation.

a Catholic official. Without the new printing presses publishing Luther's pamplets, there may not have been a Protestant Reformation.

Lutheranism began as a religious movement, but it soon developed profound social and political implications. By proclaiming that "all" are equal before God, Lutherans disrupted traditional notions of wealth, class, and monarchical supremacy. Their desire to practice a faith independent of papal or government interference contributed to the ideal of limited government.

What came to be called Lutheranism quickly found enthusiastic followers, especially in the German-speaking states. In Rome, however, Pope Leo X lashed out, calling Luther "a leper with a brain of brass and a nose of iron." Luther fought back, declaring that he was "born to war" against the "ignorant fools in Rome." He refused to abide by any papal decrees: "I will recant nothing!" The "die is cast, and I will have no reconciliation with the Pope for all eternity."

When the pope expelled Luther from the Catholic Church in 1521 and the Holy Roman emperor sentenced him to death, civil war erupted throughout the German principalities. Luther was now an outlaw, and he survived only because a powerful prince hid him in his castle.

Religious wars and upheavals

Luther's conflict with the pope plunged Europe into decades of religious warfare during which both sides sought to eliminate dissent by torturing and burning at the stake all "heretics." A settlement between Lutherans and Catholics did not come until 1555, when the Treaty of Augsburg allowed each German prince to determine the religion of his subjects. For a while, many people still deferred to the ruling princes. Most of the northern German states and Scandinavia became Lutheran. (Today there are 80 million Lutherans worldwide.) By undermining the authority of the Catholic Church, Luther opened the door for the creation of thousands of new churches representing dozens of new denominations.

John Calvin

If Martin Luther was the lightning that sparked the Reformation, John Calvin provided the thunder. Soon after Luther began his revolt against

Catholicism, Swiss Protestants also challenged papal authority. In Geneva, a city in the Swiss Alps, the rebellious movement looked to John Calvin (1509–1564), a brilliant French theologian and preacher. He had fled to Geneva at age twenty-seven and quickly brought it under the sway of his forceful personality and beliefs.

Calvin deepened and broadened the Reformation that Luther initiated by developing a strict way of life for Protestants to follow. His chief contribution was his emphasis upon humanity's inherent sinfulness and utter helplessness before an all-powerful God, a God that had predetermined who would be saved and who would suffer eternal damnation, regardless of their behavior. Calvin's followers believed that God had chosen them ("the elect") for salvation, and they would govern the world in peace.

Calvin ruled Geneva with uncompromising conviction. He summoned the citizenry to swear allegiance to a twenty-one-article confession of religious faith. No citizen could be outside the authority of the church, and Calvin viewed himself as God's appointed judge and jury. Dancing, card-playing, and theatergoing were outlawed, and informers were recruited to report wrongdoing. Visitors staying at inns had to say a prayer before dining. Everyone was required to attend church and to be in bed by nine o'clock. Even joking was outlawed.

Calvinism Spreads

For all its harshness, Calvinism spread like wildfire across France, Scotland, the Netherlands, and even into Lutheran Germany. Calvinism formed the basis for the German Reformed Church, the Dutch Reformed Church, the Presbyterians in Scotland, and the Huguenots in France, and it prepared the way for many forms of American Protestantism. Like Luther, Calvin argued that Christians did not need popes or kings, archbishops, and bishops to direct their search for salvation; each congregation should elect its own elders and ministers to guide their worship and nurture their faith.

Over time, John Calvin's ideas exerted a more significant effect upon religious belief and practice in the English colonies than did any other leader of the Reformation. His emphasis on humankind's essential depravity, his concept of predestination, his support for the primacy and autonomy of each congregation, and his belief in the necessity of theocratic government formed the ideological foundation for Puritan New England.

Catholic Counter-Reformation

The Catholic Church furiously resisted the emergence of new "Protestant" faiths by launching a "Counter-Reformation." In Spain, the monarchy established an "Inquisition" to root out Protestants and heretics. In 1534, a Spanish soldier, Ignatius de Loyola, organized the Society of Jesus, a militant monastic order created to revitalize Catholicism. Its members, the black-robed Jesuits, fanned out across Europe and the Americas as missionaries and teachers.

Throughout the sixteenth and seventeenth centuries, Catholics and Protestants persecuted, imprisoned, tortured, and killed each other. Every major international conflict in early modern Europe became, to some extent, a religious holy war.

The Reformation in England

In England, the Reformation followed a unique course. The Church of England (the Anglican Church) emerged through a gradual process of integrating Calvinism with English Catholicism. In early modern England, the Catholic Church and the national government were united and mutually supportive. The monarchy required people to attend religious services and to pay taxes to support the church.

The English Reformation originated because of purely political reasons. King Henry VIII, who ruled between 1509 and 1547, had won from the pope the title Defender of the Faith for initially refuting Martin Luther's revolutionary ideas. Henry, however, turned against the Catholic Church over the issue of divorce. His marriage to Catherine of Aragon, his elder brother's widow and the youngest daughter of the Spanish monarchs Ferdinand and Isabella, had produced a baby girl, Mary, but no boy. Henry's obsession for a male heir convinced him that he needed a new wife. First, however, he had to convince the pope to annul, or cancel, his twenty-four-year marriage to Catherine, who rebelled against her husband's plan. The pope refused to grant an annulment, and in 1533,

QUEEN ELIZABETH The *Armada Portrait*, painted in 1588 by George Gower, portrays Queen Elizabeth at the height of her reign. A scene in the background features England's victory over the attacking Spanish fleet, the Armada, while in the foreground Elizabeth's right hand rests on a globe, signifying the English expansion into the New World.

Henry VIII responded by severing England's nearly 900-year connection with the Catholic Church.

The pope then excommunicated Henry from the Catholic Church, after which Parliament passed an Act of Supremacy declaring that the king, not the pope, was head of the Church of England. Henry married Anne Boleyn, banned all Catholic "idols," required Bibles to be published in English rather than Latin, and seized the vast lands the Catholic Church owned across England.

In one of history's greatest ironies, Anne Boleyn gave birth not to a male heir but to a daughter named Elizabeth. The disappointed king accused Anne of adultery, had her beheaded, and declared the infant Elizabeth a bastard. (He would marry four more times.) Yet the unwanted Elizabeth grew up to be quick-witted, cunning, and courageous, a woman so tenacious, a ruler so skillful and charismatic, that she united a small, fragmented, and lowly island society into a nation of global ambition and reach. After the bloody reigns of her Protestant half-brother, Edward VI, and her Catholic half-sister, Mary I, Queen of Scots, Elizabeth ascended to the throne in 1558, at the age of twenty-five.

Queen Elizabeth, an unmarried Protestant in a Catholic- and male-dominated Europe, a monarch who escaped numerous assassination attempts and persecuted and executed Catholics, ruled confidently over England's golden age. She once told Parliament to remember her as "a Queen, having reigned, lived, and died a virgin." To the end, she was married only to England. Elizabeth proved to be one of the greatest rulers in history. Her forty-five-year reign witnessed political turmoil, religious strife, economic crises, menacing threats, and foreign wars. Yet she guided the nation with confidence and courage.

The Spanish Empire

CORE **OBJECTIVE**

3. Describe how the Spanish were able to conquer and colonize the Americas.

Between 1500 and 1650, some 450,000 Spaniards, most of them poor, single, unskilled men, made their way to the colonies in the Western Hemisphere. Once there, they used a mixture of courage, cruelty, piety, and greed to ship some 200 tons of gold and 16,000 tons of silver to Spain, which helped fuel the nation's "Golden Empire" and trigger the emergence of capitalism in Europe, enabling new avenues for trade, investment, and unimagined profits. By plundering, conquering, and colonizing the Americas and enslaving the inhabitants, the Spanish planted Christianity in the Western Hemisphere and gained the resources to rule the world.

A Clash of Cultures

Spanish foothold in the Caribbean

The Caribbean Sea was the gateway through which Spain entered the Americas. After establishing a trading post on Hispaniola, the Spanish proceeded to colonize Puerto Rico (1508), Jamaica (1509), and Cuba (1511–1514).

As its colonies multiplied to include Mexico, Peru, and what would become the American Southwest, the monarchy created an administrative bureaucracy to govern them and a name to encompass them: New Spain.

Many of the Europeans in the first wave of settlement in the New World died of malnutrition or disease. But the Native Americans suffered far more casualties, for they were ill-equipped to resist the European invaders. Civil disorder, rebellion, and tribal warfare abounded, leaving them vulnerable to division and foreign conquest. Attacks by well-armed soldiers and deadly germs from Europe overwhelmed entire indigenous societies.

Cortés's Conquest

Rivals collaborate against the Mexicas

The most dramatic European conquest of a formidable Indian civilization occurred in Mexico. On February 18, 1519, Spaniard Hernán Cortés set sail for Mexico, having grown weary of seeking a fortune in Cuba. He sold his Cuban lands to buy ships and supplies, then headed for Mexico on an unauthorized voyage of conquest. Cortés's eleven ships carried nearly 600 soldiers and sailors as well as 200 indigenous Cuban laborers, sixteen warhorses, greyhound fighting dogs, and cannon. They first stopped on the Yucatan Peninsula, where they defeated a group of Maya. To appease his European conqueror, the vanquished Maya chieftain gave Cortés twenty young women. The Spanish commander distributed them to his captains but kept one of the girls ("La Malinche") for himself and named her Doña Marina. She spoke Mayan as well as Nahuatl, the language of the Mexicas, with whom she had previously lived. She became Cortés's interpreter—and his mistress; she would later bear the married Cortés a son.

After leaving Yucatan, Cortés sailed west and landed at a place he named Veracruz (True Cross). There he convinced the local Totonacs to join his assault against the Mexicas, their hated rivals. To prevent his soldiers, called ***conquistadores*** (conquerors), from deserting, Cortés ordered the Spanish ships burned. He spared only one vessel to carry the expected riches back to Spain. With his small army and thousands of Indian allies, Cortés brashly set out to conquer the sprawling Mexica Empire. The 200-mile march through the mountains to the Mexica capital of Tenochtitlán took almost six months, during which Cortés recruited thousands of allies among the many indigenous societies the Mexicas had conquered.

Spanish Invaders

conquistadores Term from the Spanish word for "conquerors," applied to Spanish and Portuguese soldiers who conquered lands held by indigenous peoples in central and southern America as well as the current states of Texas, New Mexico, Arizona, and California.

As the Spanish army marched across Mexico, the conquistadores heard fabulous stories about Tenochtitlán, with its gleaming white buildings and beautiful temples. With some 200,000 inhabitants scattered among twenty neighborhoods, it was larger than London, Paris, and Seville, the capital of Spain. Laid out in a grid pattern on an island in a shallow lake, divided by long cobblestone avenues, crisscrossed by canals, connected to the mainland by wide causeways, and graced by formidable stone pyramids, the city

CORTÉS IN MEXICO A page from the *Lienzo de Tlaxcala*, a historical narrative from the sixteenth century. The scene, in which Cortés is shown seated on a throne, depicts the arrival of the Spanish in Tlaxcala.

seemed impregnable. The magnificent city, Cortés marveled, contained "all the things to be found under the heavens."

The Mexicas viewed themselves as having created the supreme civilization on the planet. "Are we not the masters of the world?" the emperor, Moctezuma II, said to his ruling council when he learned that the Europeans had landed on the coast. Through a combination of threats and deceptions, the Spanish entered Tenochtitlán peacefully. Moctezuma mistook Cortés for the exiled god of the wind and sky, Quetzalcoatl, come to reclaim his lands. The emperor stared at the newcomers with their long hair, sharp metal swords, gunpowder, and wheeled wagons. He gave the Spaniards a lavish welcome, housing them close to the palace and providing gifts of gold and women.

Within a week, however, Cortés executed a palace coup, taking Moctezuma hostage. The Spanish commander then ordered religious statues destroyed and coerced Moctezuma to end the ritual sacrifices of prisoners of war. Cortés explained why the invasion was necessary: "We Spaniards have a disease of the heart that only gold can cure."

For eight months, Cortés tried to convince the Mexicas to surrender, but they instead decided that Moctezuma was betraying them and resolved to resist the invaders. In the spring of 1520, the Spaniards attacked the Mexicas and killed many of the ruling elite. The Mexicas fought back, however, prompting Cortés to march Moctezuma to the edge of a balcony and forced him to order the warriors to lay down their weapons: "We must not fight them," the emperor shouted. "We are not their equals in battle. Put down your shields and arrows." The priests, however, denounced Moctezuma as a traitor and stoned him to death.

For the next seven days, Mexica warriors forced the Spaniards to retreat. The Spaniards lost about a third of their soldiers, but their 20,000 Indian allies remained loyal, and Cortés regrouped his forces. For months, sporadic fighting continued. In 1521, having been reinforced with more soldiers and horses from Cuba and thousands more indigenous warriors eager to defeat the despised Mexicas, Cortés surrounded the imperial city for eighty-five days, cut off the city's access to water and food, and watched as a smallpox epidemic devastated the inhabitants, killing 90 percent of them.

The ravages of smallpox and the support of 75,000 Indian allies help explain how such a small force of well-organized and highly disciplined Spaniards vanquished a proud imperial nation in August 1521. After 15,000 Mexicas were slaughtered, the others surrendered. A merciless Cortés ordered the leaders hanged and the priests devoured by dogs, but not before torturing them (literally putting their feet to the fire) in an effort to learn where more gold might be found. A conquistador remembered that the streets "were so filled with sick and dead people that our men walked over nothing but bodies." In two years, Cortés and his disciplined army had waged a genocidal war and seized an epic empire that had taken centuries to develop.

Cortés became the first governor-general of "New Spain" and quickly began replacing the Mexica leaders with Spanish bureaucrats and church officials. Mexico City became the imperial capital of New Spain, and Cortés ordered that a grand Catholic cathedral be built from the stones of Moctezuma's destroyed palace. Cortés's conquest of Mexico established the model for waves of plundering conquistadores to follow. Within fifty years, Spain had established a vast empire in Mexico and Central America, the Caribbean, and South America—calling it New Spain. The Spanish cemented their control through ruthless violence and enslavement of the indigenous peoples followed by oppressive rule over them—just as the Mexicas had done in forming their empire.

Cortés conquers the Mexicas, and Pizarro invades the Inca

In 1531, Francisco Pizarro led a band of 168 conquistadores and sixty-seven horses down the Pacific coast of South America. They brutally subdued the extensive Inca Empire and its 5 million people living in present-day Ecuador, Peru, Bolivia, Colombia, Chile, and Argentina. The Spanish killed thousands of Inca warriors, seized imperial palaces, took royal women as mistresses and wives, and looted the empire of its gold and silver.

From Peru, Spain extended its control southward through Chile and north to present-day Colombia. A government official in Spain reported in 1534 that the amount of gold and silver flowing into the treasury "was incredible." Soon, he predicted, Seville would be the "richest city in the world."

Spanish America

As the sixteenth century unfolded, the Spanish shifted from looting the indigenous peoples to enslaving them. To reward the conquistadores, the

Spanish government transferred to America a medieval socioeconomic system known as the ***encomienda.*** Favored soldiers or officials received large parcels of land—and control over the people who lived there. The conquistadores were told to Christianize the Indians and provide them with protection in exchange for "tribute"—a share of their goods and their forced labor.

New Spain thus became a society of extremes: wealthy *encomenderos* and powerful priests at one end, and Indians held in poverty at the other. The Spaniards used brute force to ensure that the Indians accepted their role. Nuño de Guzman, a governor of a Mexican province, loved to watch his massive fighting dog tear apart rebellious Indians. He was equally brutal with colonists. After a Spaniard talked back to him, he had the man nailed to a post by his tongue.

encomienda A land-grant system under which Spanish army officers (*conquistadores*) were awarded large parcels of land taken from Native Americans.

Columbian Exchange The transfer of biological and social elements, such as plants, animals, people, diseases, and cultural practices, among Europe, the Americas, and Africa in the wake of Christopher Columbus's voyages to the New World.

Imposing the Catholic Religion

Once in control of the Americas, the Spanish sought to convert the Indians into obedient Catholics. Hundreds of priests fanned out across New Spain, using force to convert the Indians. "Though they seem to be a simple people," a priest declared in 1562, "they are up to all sorts of mischief, and without compulsion, they will never speak the [religious] truth." By the end of the sixteenth century, there were more than 300 Catholic monasteries or missions in New Spain.

Some officials criticized the forced religious conversion of Indians and the harsh *encomienda* system. A Catholic priest, Bartolomé de Las Casas, was horrified by the treatment of Indians in Hispaniola and Cuba. The conquistadores behaved like "wild beasts," he reported, "killing, terrorizing, afflicting, torturing, and destroying the native peoples." Las Casas insisted that the role of Spaniards in the New World was to convert the Indians, "not to rob, to scandalize, to capture, or destroy them, or to lay waste their lands." He resolved in 1514 to devote himself to aiding the Indians, and he began urging Spanish officials to change their approach.

Las Casas spent the next fifty years advocating better treatment for indigenous people, earning the title Protector of the Indians. He eventually convinced the monarchy and the Catholic Church to issue new rules calling for better treatment of the Indians. Still, the use of "fire and the sword" continued, and angry Spanish colonists on Hispaniola banished Las Casas from the island.

The Columbian Exchange

CORE **OBJECTIVE**

4. Assess the impact of the Columbian Exchange between the "Old" and "New" Worlds.

Spain's seizure of the Americas produced unexpected consequences. The European ships that crossed the Atlantic carried more than human cargo. They also brought plants and animals that set in motion what came to be called the **Columbian Exchange**, a worldwide transfer of plants, animals, and diseases, which ultimately worked in favor of the Europeans at the expense of the indigenous peoples.

SMALLPOX The infectious diseases colonists carried with them to the New World decimated the Native American population. In this illustration, Mexica victims of the 1538 smallpox epidemic are covered in shrouds (*center*) as two others lie dying (*at right*).

The animals of the two worlds differed more than the peoples and their ways of life. Europeans had never encountered iguanas, buffaloes, cougars, armadillos, opossums, sloths, tapirs, anacondas, rattlesnakes, catfish, condors, or hummingbirds. Nor had Native Americans seen the horses, cattle, pigs, sheep, goats, and chickens that soon flooded the Americas. Sailing ships also brought stowaway creatures: earthworms, mosquitoes, and cockroaches, and honeybees, rats, and mice of every description. The European invasion of the Western Hemisphere thus generated an ecological transformation whose effects are still being felt. In this sense, the Europeans did not so much "discover" a new world as create one.

The exchange of plant life between the Western Hemisphere and Europe/Africa transformed the diets of both regions. Europeans brought plants never seen in the Americas: sugarcane (originally from New Guinea), wheat (from the Middle East), bananas, and coffee (both from Africa).

Before Columbus's voyage, Europeans did not know about foods such as maize (corn), potatoes (sweet and white), or many kinds of beans (snap, kidney, lima). Other Western Hemisphere food plants included peanuts, squash, peppers, tomatoes, pumpkins, pineapples, avocados, cacao (the source of chocolate), and chicle (for chewing gum).

The lowly white potato, for example, was transformational. Discovered in South America, it has more calories than an ear of corn, can yield more bushels per acre than wheat, can be stored through the winter, and is easy to cultivate. Explorers brought potatoes back to Europe, where they thrived. The "Irish potato" was eventually transported to North America by Scots-Irish immigrants during the early eighteenth century.

The new crops improved the health of Europeans and spurred a dramatic increase in the population. In turn, the surplus population provided the adventurous young people who would colonize the New World.

The most significant aspect of the Columbian Exchange was the transmission of **infectious diseases**. Europeans and enslaved Africans brought to the Western Hemisphere deadly diseases that Native Americans had never encountered: smallpox, typhus, malaria, mumps, chickenpox, and measles. The results were catastrophic. By 1568, just seventy-five years after Columbus's first voyage, infectious diseases had killed 80 to 90 percent of the Indian population in the Western Hemisphere—the most significant loss of life in history.

infectious diseases Also called contagious diseases, illnesses that can pass from one person to another by way of invasive biological organisms able to reproduce in the bodily tissues of their hosts. Europeans unwittingly brought many such diseases to the Americas, devastating the Native American peoples.

Smallpox was an especially ghastly killer; it came to be called the Great Dying. In central Mexico alone, some 8 million people, perhaps a third of the Indian population, died of smallpox within a decade of the arrival of the Spanish. Unable to explain or cure the hideous diseases, Native

American chieftains and religious leaders often lost their stature—and their lives—as they were usually the first to meet the Spanish and the first infected. The loss of their leaders made the indigenous peoples more vulnerable to invaders. Many Europeans, however, interpreted such epidemics as diseases sent by God to punish those who resisted conversion to Christianity.

The Spanish in North America

CORE **OBJECTIVE**

5. Analyze the legacy of the Spanish form of colonization on North American history.

Throughout the sixteenth century, no European nation other than Spain held more than a brief foothold in the Americas. While France and England were preoccupied with political disputes and religious conflict at home, Catholic Spain had forged a national and religious unity that enabled it to dominate Europe as well as the New World. Still, Spanish officials grew increasingly fearful that France and England would threaten their imperial monopoly in the Western Hemisphere.

Three centuries of Spanish domination and Hispanic influence

For most of the colonial period, Spain governed much of what is now the United States. Spanish culture etched a lasting imprint upon America's future. Hispanic place-names—San Francisco, Santa Barbara, Los Angeles, San Diego, Santa Fe, San Antonio, Pensacola, St. Augustine—survive to this day, as do Hispanic influences in art, architecture, literature, music, law, and food.

The Spanish Southeast

In 1513, Juan Ponce de León, the Spanish governor of Puerto Rico, made the earliest known European exploration of Florida. Other Spanish explorers sailed along the Gulf coast from Florida to Mexico, scouted the Atlantic coast to Canada, and established a short-lived colony on the Carolina coast.

In 1539, Hernando de Soto and 600 conquistadores landed on the western shore of La Florida (Land of Flowers) and soon set out on horseback to search for riches. Instead of gold, they found "great fields of corn, beans and squash . . . as far as the eye could see." De Soto led the expedition north as far as western North Carolina. The explorers then moved westward across Tennessee, Georgia, and Alabama before happening upon the Mississippi River near what today is Memphis.

After crossing the Mississippi, the conquistadores went up the Arkansas River, looting and destroying Indian villages along the way. In the spring of 1542, de Soto died near Natchez, Mississippi; the next year, the survivors among his party floated down the Mississippi River, and 311 of them made their way to Spanish Mexico.

In 1565, in response to French efforts to colonize north Florida, the Spanish king dispatched Pedro Menendez de Aviles with a ragtag group of 1,500 soldiers and colonists to create an outpost on the Atlantic coast of Florida. St. Augustine became the first permanent European settlement in the present-day United States.

- What were the Spanish conquistadores' goals for exploring the Americas?
- How did Cortés conquer the Mexicas?
- Why did the Spanish first explore North America, and why did they establish St. Augustine, the first European settlement in what would become the United States?

The Spanish positioned themselves in northern Florida to keep the French out. In the 1560s, French Protestant refugees (called Huguenots) established beachhead settlements on the coast of what became South Carolina and Florida. The settlements did not last long. At dawn on September 20, 1565, some 500 Spanish soldiers from St. Augustine assaulted the French Protestants at Fort Caroline in northeastern Florida. The Spanish hanged all the men over age fifteen; only women, girls, and young boys were spared. The Spanish commander notified his Catholic king that he had killed all the

French because "they were scattering the odious Lutheran doctrine in these Provinces." Later, when survivors from a shipwrecked French fleet washed ashore on Florida beaches, the Spanish commander told them they must abandon Protestantism and swear their allegiance to Catholicism. When they refused, his soldiers killed 245 of them.

The Spanish Southwest

The Spanish eventually established other permanent settlements in what are now New Mexico, Texas, and California. From the outset, however, the settlements were sparsely populated, inadequately supplied, and consistently neglected by Spanish colonial officials. The small number of Spanish colonists and the vast size of North America made it impossible for them to impose a European-style occupation. In the whole of Cuba, for example, there were only 322 Spanish households in 1550. Throughout the Western Hemisphere, there were only 25,000 Spanish households. By 1650, there were more enslaved Africans than there were Spaniards in the Western Hemisphere.

The Spanish were pitiless colonial rulers who exercised absolute power. In New Spain, people were expected to follow orders, no questions asked. There was no freedom of speech, religion, or movement; no local elections; no real self-government. The military officers, bureaucrats, wealthy landowners, and priests appointed by the king regulated every detail of colonial life. Settlers could not travel within the colonies without official permission.

New Mexico

The land that would later be called **New Mexico** was the first center of Catholic missionary activity in the American Southwest. In 1595, Juan de Oñate, the rich son of a Spanish family in Mexico, received a land grant for *El Norte,* the mostly desert territory north of Mexico above the Rio Grande—Texas, New Mexico, Arizona, California, and parts of Colorado. Over the next three years, he recruited colonists willing to move north with him. In 1598, the caravan of 250 colonists, including women, children, horses, goats, sheep, and 7,000 cattle, began moving north from the mountains above Mexico City. "O God! What a lonely land!" one traveler wrote to relatives. After walking more than 800 miles in seven months, they established the colony of New Mexico, the farthest outpost of New Spain. It took wagon trains eighteen months to travel to Mexico City and back. The Spanish labeled the local Indians Pueblos (a Spanish word meaning village) for the city-like aspect of their terraced, multistoried buildings, sometimes chiseled into the steep walls of cliffs.

New Mexico A region in the American Southwest, originally established by the Spanish, who settled there in the sixteenth century, founded Catholic missions, and exploited the region's indigenous peoples.

The goals of Spanish colonialism were to find gold, silver, and other valuable commodities while forcing the Native Americans to adopt the Spanish religion and way of life. Oñate, New Mexico's first Spanish governor, told the Pueblos that if they embraced Catholicism and followed his orders, they would receive

CULTURAL CONFLICT This Peruvian illustration, from a 1612–1615 manuscript by Felipe Guamán Poma de Ayala, shows a Dominican Catholic friar forcing an indigenous woman to weave. **What does this image show about the Spanish missionary's treatment of the indigenous peoples?**

"an eternal life of great bliss" instead of "cruel and everlasting torment." There was, however, little gold or silver in New Mexico. Nor were there enough corn and beans to feed the Spanish invaders, so Oñate forced the Indians to pay tributes (taxes) to the Spanish authorities in the form of a yard of cloth and a bushel of corn each year.

Once it became evident that New Mexico had little gold, the Spanish focused on religious conversion. Priests forced Indians to build and support Catholic missions and to work in the fields they had once owned. They also performed personal tasks for the priests and soldiers—cooking, cleaning, even sexual favors. Indians were herded to church services and whipped if they did not work hard enough. A French visitor reported that it "reminded us of a . . . West Indian [slave] colony." Some Indians welcomed the Spanish as "powerful witches" capable of easing their burdens. Others tried to use the European invaders as allies against rival Indian groups. Still others rebelled.

Before the end of New Mexico's first year of Spanish rule, in December 1598, the Acoma Pueblos revolted, killing eleven soldiers and two servants. Oñate's response was even more brutal. Over three days, Spanish soldiers destroyed the entire pueblo, killing 500 Pueblo men and 300 women and children. Survivors were found guilty of treason and enslaved. Children were separated from their parents and moved into a Catholic mission, where, Oñate remarked, "they may attain the knowledge of God and the salvation of their souls." He ordered that every male between the ages of twelve and twenty-five have a hand cut off, and that the left foot of every male over twenty-five be severed to ensure they never again would rebel.

The Mestizo Factor

Few Spanish women journeyed to New Spain in the sixteenth century. Those who did had to be married and accompanied by a husband. As a result, soldiers and settlers in North America were encouraged to marry Native American women. Intermarriage between Spaniards and indigenous peoples became common. Today, some three quarters of Mexicans are *Mestizo*—people of joint indigenous and Spanish or African genes. In downtown Mexico City, a plaque acknowledging the Spanish takeover in 1521 reads: "This was neither triumph nor defeat. It was the painful birth of the *mestizo* nation that is Mexico today."

By the eighteenth century, *Mestizos* were a majority in Mexico and New Mexico. Such widespread interbreeding and intermarriage led the Spanish to adopt a more inclusive social outlook toward the Indians than the English later did in their colonies along the Atlantic coast. Since most colonial officials were Mestizo themselves, they were less likely to belittle or abuse the Indians. At the same time, many Native Americans falsely claimed to be Mestizo to improve their legal status and avoid paying annual tribute. Over time, New Spain developed a caste system based on an ethnic hierarchy. At the top were the *Españoles* (Spaniards) followed by the *Criollos* (Spaniards born in the Americas). At the bottom were the *Indegenas* (Indians) and in between were enslaved Africans, Mulattoes (people of mixed Black and White ancestry), and Mestizos.

The Pueblo Revolt

Catholicism in New Spain and the Pueblo Revolt (1680)

In 1608, the Spanish government decided to turn New Mexico into a royal province and moved its capital to Santa Fe (Holy Faith in Spanish). It became the first permanent seat of government in the present-day United States. By 1630, there were fifty Catholic churches and monasteries in New Mexico as well as some 3,000 Spaniards. Roman Catholic missionaries in New Mexico claimed that 86,000 Pueblos had embraced Christianity during the seventeenth century.

However, resentment among the Indians increased as the Spanish stripped them of their ancestral ways of life. "The heathen," reported a Spanish soldier, "have conceived a mortal hatred for our holy faith and enmity [hatred] for the Spanish nation." In 1680, a charismatic Indian named Popé (meaning Ripe Plantings) organized a massive rebellion of warriors from nineteen villages. The Indians burned Catholic churches; tortured, mutilated, and executed twenty-one priests and 400 Spanish settlers; destroyed all relics of Christianity; and forced the 2,400 survivors to flee. The entire province of New Mexico was again in Indian hands.

The Pueblo Revolt was the most significant defeat Indians ever inflicted on European efforts to conquer the New World. It took twelve years and four military assaults for the Spanish to reestablish control over New Mexico.

Horses and the Great Plains

Horses and bison

Another major consequence of the Pueblo Revolt was the opportunity it gave Indian rebels to acquire Spanish **horses** (Spanish authorities had made it illegal for Indians to own horses). The Pueblos went on to establish a thriving horse trade with other Indian nations. By 1690, horses were in Texas, and soon they spread across the Great Plains, the vast, rolling grasslands extending from the Missouri valley in the east to the base of the Rocky Mountains in the west.

horses The animals that the Spanish introduced to the Americas, eventually transforming many Native American cultures.

Before the arrival of horses, Indians hunted on foot and used dogs as their beasts of burden. Dogs are carnivores, however, and it was difficult

PLAINS INDIANS The horse-stealing ride depicted in this hide painting demonstrates the essential role horses played in plains life.

to find enough meat to feed them. The vast grasslands of the Great Plains, however, were perfect for horses since the prairies offered plenty of forage. With horses, the Indians gained greater mobility and power. Horses could haul up to seven times as much weight as dogs, and their speed and endurance made the Indians more effective hunters and warriors.

Horses grew so valuable that they became a form of Indian currency and a sign of wealth and prestige. On the Great Plains, a warrior's status reflected the number of horses he owned. The more horses he had, the more wives he could support—and the more buffaloes he could kill and exchange the hides for more horses. By the late seventeenth century, horse-borne Indians were fighting the Spaniards on more equal terms. This helps explain why the Indians of the Southwest and Texas, unlike the Indians in Mexico, were able to sustain their cultures for the next 300 years.

Buffalo Hunting

The Arapaho, Cheyenne, Comanche, Kiowa, and Sioux reinvented themselves as horse-centered cultures. They left their traditional woodland villages and became nomadic buffalo hunters.

A bull buffalo could weigh more than a ton and stand five feet tall at the shoulder. Indians used virtually every part of the buffalo: meat for food; hides for clothing, shoes, bedding, and shelter; muscles and tendons for thread and bowstrings; intestines for containers; bones for tools; horns for eating utensils; hair for headdresses; and dung for fuel. One scholar has referred to the buffalo as the "tribal department store." Women and girls butchered and dried the buffalo meat and tanned the hides. As the value of the hides grew,

Indian hunters began practicing polygamy, because more wives could process more buffalo carcasses. The rising value of wives eventually led Plains Indians to raid other societies in search of brides.

While horses brought prosperity and mobility to the Plains Indians, they also triggered more conflicts. Over time, the Indians on horseback eventually killed more buffaloes than the herds could replace. Further, horses competed with the buffaloes for food, often depleting the prairie grass. As horse-centered culture enabled Indians to travel greater distances and encounter more people, infectious diseases spread. Yet horses overall brought a better quality of life.

French and Dutch Exploration of Americas

Spanish rivals for New World wealth

Catholic Spain's conquests in the Western Hemisphere spurred Portugal, France, England, and the Netherlands (Holland) to begin their explorations and exploitations of the New World. The French were the first to pose a serious threat. Spanish ships loaded with gold and silver taken from Mexico, Peru, and the Caribbean offered tempting targets for French pirates. At the same time, the French began explorations in North America. In 1524, the French king sent Italian Giovanni da Verrazano across the Atlantic. Upon sighting land (probably at Cape Fear, North Carolina), Verrazano ranged along the coast as far north as Maine. On a second voyage, in 1528, he was killed by Caribbean Indians.

Unlike the Verrazano voyages, those of Jacques Cartier led to the first French effort at colonization in North America. During three voyages, Cartier ventured up the St. Lawrence River, which today is the boundary between Canada and New York. Twice he got as far as present-day Montreal, and twice he wintered at Quebec, near which a short-lived French colony appeared in 1541–1542. France after midcentury, however, plunged into religious civil wars, and the colonization of Canada had to await the arrival of Samuel de Champlain, "the Father of New France," after 1600. Over thirty-seven years, Champlain would lead twenty-seven expeditions from France to Canada—and never lose a ship.

Greater threats to Spanish power in the New World arose from the Dutch and the English. In 1566, the Netherlands included seventeen provinces. The fragmented nation had passed by inheritance to the Spanish king in 1555, but the Dutch soon began a series of rebellions against Spanish Catholic rule.

A long, bloody struggle ensued in which the English under Queen Elizabeth aided the Dutch. The Dutch revolt, as much a civil war as a war for national independence, was a series of uprisings in different provinces at different times. Each province had its institutions, laws, and rights. Although seven provinces agreed to form the Dutch Republic, the Spanish did not officially recognize the independence of the entire Netherlands until 1648.

Almost from the beginning of the Protestant revolt in the Netherlands, the Dutch captured Spanish treasure ships in the Atlantic and conducted illegal trade with Spain's colonies. While England's Queen Elizabeth steered a tortuous course to avoid war with Spain, she desperately sought additional

ENGLISH, FRENCH, AND DUTCH EXPLORATIONS

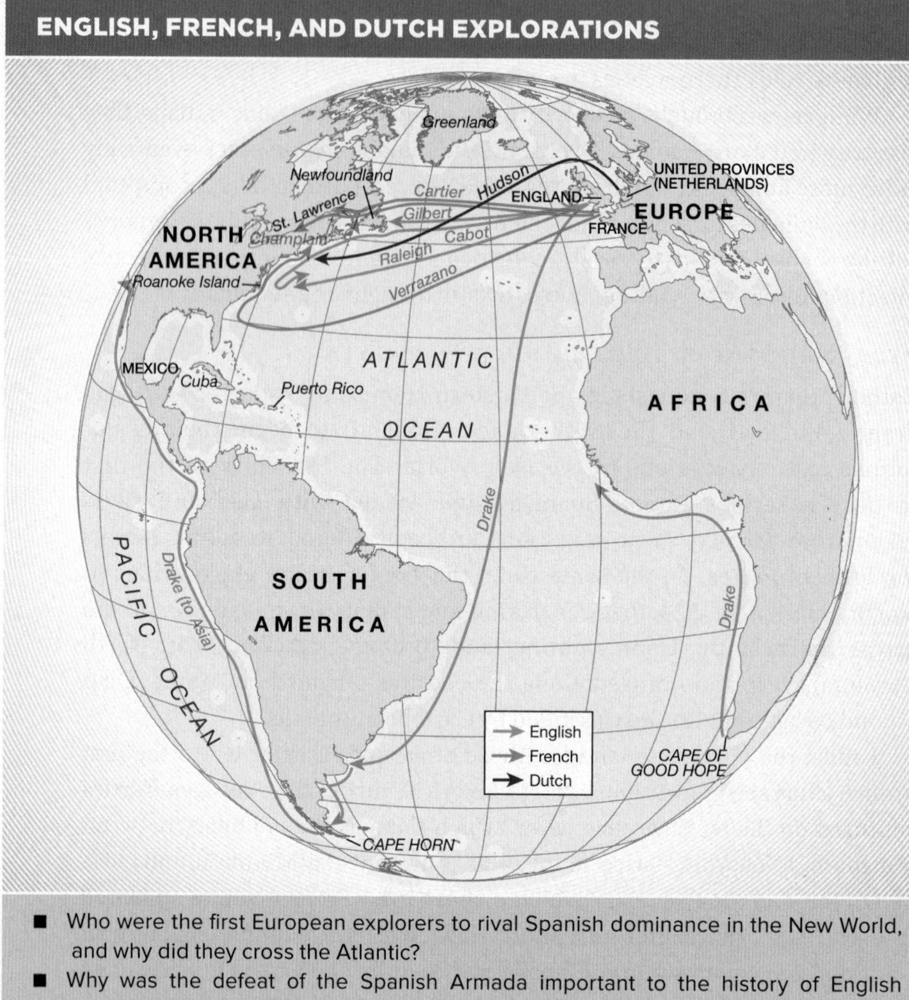

- Who were the first European explorers to rival Spanish dominance in the New World, and why did they cross the Atlantic?
- Why was the defeat of the Spanish Armada important to the history of English exploration?
- Why was the development of New France delayed after early exploration visits?

resources to defend her island nation. She encouraged dozens of English privateers to attack Spanish ships in the Americas, leading the Spanish to call her the "pirate queen."

The Defeat of the Spanish Armada

English raids on Spanish ships and settlements continued for some twenty years before war erupted between the two nations. Philip II, the king of Spain who was Elizabeth's brother-in-law and fiercest opponent, finally began plotting an invasion of England. To do so, he assembled the massive **Spanish Armada**: 132 warships, 7,000 sailors, and 17,000 soldiers. It was the greatest invasion fleet in history to that point.

Spanish Armada A massive Spanish fleet of 130 warships that was defeated at Plymouth in 1588 by the English navy during the reign of Queen Elizabeth I.

On May 28, 1588, the Armada set sail for the Netherlands to take on another 17,000 soldiers for the invasion of England. The English navy's ninety warships were waiting as the Spanish fleet moved through the English Channel. As the warships positioned themselves for battle, Queen Elizabeth donned a silver breastplate and told her forces, "I know I have the body of a weak and feeble woman, but I have the heart and stomach of a king, and a King of England too." As the nine-hour battle unfolded, the massive Spanish warships could not compete with the speed and agility of the English vessels. By the end of the day, the Spanish were forced to flee northward. For two weeks, the English fleet gave chase. Caught up in a mighty "Protestant wind," the Catholic invaders were swept into the North Sea, losing half their ships and a third of their sailors and soldiers.

By mid-August, the wounded Armada headed south toward home when ferocious storms in the North Atlantic sank more ships than had the English navy. In the end, only sixty of the original warships made it back to Spain, and some 15,000 sailors and soldiers had died.

The stunning victory marked the beginning of the steep decline of Spain's glorious empire, established Queen Elizabeth as an English hero, and cleared the way for colonizing America's "remote heathens and barbarous lands." By the end of the sixteenth century, Elizabethan England had begun an epic transformation from a poor, humiliated, and isolated nation into a mighty global empire.

The English defeat the Spanish Armada (1588).

English Exploration of America

English efforts to colonize America began a few years before the battle with the Spanish Armada. In 1584, Queen Elizabeth asked Sir Walter Raleigh to form a colony on the North American coast. His expedition happened upon the Outer Banks of North Carolina and landed at Roanoke Island. Raleigh named the area Virginia, in honor of Elizabeth, the "Virgin Queen."

After several false starts, Raleigh in 1587 sponsored another expedition of about 100 colonists, including twenty-six women and children, led by Governor John White. The governor spent a month helping launch the settlement on Roanoke Island and then returned to England for supplies. White left behind his daughter Elinor and his granddaughter Virginia Dare, the first English child born in the Americas.

White had to delay his journey back to Virginia because of the war with Spain. When he finally returned, in 1590, the Roanoke colony had been abandoned and pillaged. On a post at the entrance to the village, someone had carved the word *CROATOAN*. White concluded that the settlers had set out for the island of that name some fifty miles south, where friendly Indians lived.

The English never found the "lost colonists." Recent evidence indicates that the "Lost Colony" suffered from a horrible drought that prevented the settlers from growing enough food to survive. While some may have gone south, most went north, to the southern shores of the Chesapeake Bay, where they lived for years until Indians killed them.

The lost Roanoke colony

When Queen Elizabeth died in 1603, there were no English settlements in North America. This was about to change, however. Inspired by the success of the Spanish in exploiting the New World, the English—as well as

THE ENGLISH IN VIRGINIA This map depicts the arrival of English explorers on the Outer Banks. Roanoke Island and its colony are on the left.

the French and Dutch—would soon develop American colonial empires of their own.

New Spain in Decline

New Spain's legacy

During the one and a half centuries after 1492, the Spanish developed the most extensive empire the world had ever known. It spanned southern Europe and the Netherlands, much of the Western Hemisphere, and parts of Asia. Yet the Spanish rulers overreached with the combined costs of their involvement in the European religious wars of the sixteenth and seventeenth centuries and of administering of a large and complex empire overtaxing the government's resources.

During the sixteenth century, New Spain gradually developed into a settled society with the same rigid class structure as the home country. New Spain was essentially an extractive empire; its rulers were less interested in creating self-sustaining colonial communities than in removing gold, silver, and copper while enslaving the indigenous peoples and converting them to Christianity. Spain never encouraged vast numbers of settlers to populate New Spain.

Spain's colonial system was mostly disastrous for the peoples of Africa and the Americas. For three centuries after Columbus arrived in the New World, the Spanish explorers, conquistadores, and priests imposed Catholicism on the native peoples as well as a cruel system of economic exploitation and dependence. As Bartolomé de Las Casas concluded, "The Spaniards have shown not the slightest consideration for these people, treating them (and I speak from first-hand experience, having been there from the outset)... as piles of dung in the middle of the road. They have had as little concern for their souls as for their bodies." In the end, the lust for empire ("God, Glory, and Gold") brought decadence and decline to Spain and much of Europe.

Reviewing the
CORE OBJECTIVES | INQUIZITIVE

■ **Native American Societies** Asian hunter-gatherers came across the Bering Strait by foot and settled the length and breadth of the Americas, forming groups with diverse cultures, languages, and customs. Global warming enabled an agricultural revolution, particularly the growing of *maize,* that allowed former hunter-gatherer peoples like the *Mexicas* to settle and build empires in the *Mexica Empire.* Some North American, peoples, like the mississippians, developed an elaborate continental trading network and impressive cities like *Cahokia*; their burial mounds reveal a complex and stratified social organization. The *Eastern Woodland peoples* included both patriarchal and matriarchal societies as well as extensive language-based alliances. The Algonquian, Iroquoian, and Muskogean were among the major Indian nations. Warfare was an important cultural component, leading to shifting rivalries and alliances among indigenous communities and with European settlers.

■ **Age of Exploration** By the 1490s, Europeans were experiencing a renewed curiosity about the world. Warfare, plagues, and famine undermined the old agricultural feudal system in Europe, and in its place arose a middle class that monarchs could tax. Powerful new nations replaced the landed estates and cities ruled by princes. A revival of interest in antiquity led to the development of modern science and the creation of better maps and navigation techniques, as well as new weapons and ships. Navies became a critical component of global trade and world power. When the Spanish began to colonize the New World, the conversion of Indians to *Roman Catholicism* was important, but the search for gold and silver was primary. The national rivalries sparked by the *Protestant Reformation* in Europe shaped the course of conquest in the Americas.

■ **Conquering and Colonizing the Americas** Spanish *conquistadores* such as Hernán Cortés used their advantages in military technology, including steel, gunpowder, and domesticated animals such as *horses,* in order to conquer the powerful Mexica and Inca Empires. European diseases, first introduced by Columbus's voyages, did even more to ensure Spanish victories. The Spanish *encomienda* system demanded goods and labor from the indigenous peoples. As the Indian population declined, the Portuguese and Spanish began to import enslaved Africans into the Americas.

■ **Columbian Exchange** Contact between the Old World and the New resulted in a tremendous biological exchange, sometimes called the *Columbian Exchange.* Crops such as *maize,* beans, and potatoes became staples in the Old World. Native Americans incorporated into their culture Eurasian animals such as the *horse* and pig. But the invaders also carried *infectious diseases* that set off pandemics of smallpox, plague, and other illnesses to which Indians had no immunity. The Americas were depopulated and cultures destroyed.

■ **Spanish Legacy** Spain left a lasting legacy in the borderlands from California to Florida. Spanish horses eventually transformed Indian life on the plains. Catholic missionaries contributed to the destruction of the old ways of life by exterminating "heathen" beliefs in the Southwest, a practice that led to open rebellion in *New Mexico* in 1598 and 1680. Spain's rival European nation-states began competing for gold and glory in the New World. England's defeat of the *Spanish Armada* cleared the path for English dominance in North America.

KEY TERMS

maize (corn) *p. 9*

Mexicas *p. 11*

Mexica Empire *p. 11*

burial mounds *p. 16*

Cahokia *p. 16*

Eastern Woodland peoples *p. 17*

Roman Catholicism *p. 25*

Protestant Reformation *p. 25*

conquistadores *p. 30*

encomienda *p. 33*

Columbian Exchange *p. 33*

infectious diseases *p. 34*

New Mexico *p. 37*

horses *p. 39*

Spanish Armada *p. 42*

CHRONOLOGY

by 22,000 B.C.E.	Humans have migrated to the Americas
5000 B.C.E.	The agricultural revolution begins in Mexico
1050–1250 C.E.	The city of Cahokia flourishes in North America
1325	The Mexica (Aztec) Empire is established in Central Mexico
1492	Columbus leads first voyage of discovery in the Americas
1503	Spaniards bring the first enslaved Africans to the Americas
1517	Martin Luther launches the Protestant Reformation
1519	Cortés begins the Spanish conquest of Mexico
1531	Pizarro subdues the Inca Empire in South America for Spain
1565	Spaniards build settlement at St. Augustine, the first permanent European outpost in the present-day United States
1584–1587	Raleigh's Roanoke Island venture
1588	The English navy defeats the Spanish Armada
1680	Pueblo Revolt

INQUIZITIVE

Go to InQuizitive to see what you've learned—and learn what you've missed—with personalized feedback along the way.

OLD VIRGINIA As one of the earliest explorers and settlers of the Jamestown colony, John Smith put his intimate knowledge of the region to use by creating this seventeenth-century map of Virginia. In the upper right-hand corner is a Susquehannock, whom Smith called a "G[i]ant-like people."

CHAPTER 2

England and Its American Colonies

1607–1732

For tens of thousands of seekers and adventurers, America in the seventeenth century was a vast unknown land of new beginnings and new opportunities. They came seeking wealth, religious freedom, and new lives. The first European settlers found not a "virgin land" of uninhabited wilderness but Native American societies with established towns, fertile farms, networks of trading paths, a wide variety of governments, and many religions.

Indians dealt with Europeans in different ways. Many resisted, others retreated, and still others developed thriving trade relationships with the newcomers. In some areas, land-hungry colonists quickly decimated the Indians. In others, Indians found ways to live in cooperation with European settlers—if they were willing to adopt European ways of life.

After creating the Virginia, Maryland, and New England colonies, the English would go on to conquer the Dutch colony of New Netherland and much of the Spanish-controlled Caribbean, settle Carolina, and eventually establish the rest of the thirteen original colonies. The diverse colonies had one element in common: they all took part in the enslavement of other peoples, either Native Americans or Africans or both. Slavery, common throughout the world in the seventeenth and eighteenth centuries, enriched a few, corrupted many, and compromised the American promise of equal opportunity for all.

CORE OBJECTIVES INQUIZITIVE

1. Identify the economic, political, and religious motivations for the establishment of the diverse American colonies.
2. Describe the political, economic, social, and religious characteristics of English colonies in the Chesapeake region, New England, the Carolinas, and the middle colonies before 1700.
3. Analyze the ways by which English colonists and Native Americans adapted to each other's presence.
4. Evaluate the role of indentured servants and the development of slavery in colonial America.
5. Explain how the English colonies became the most populous, prosperous, and powerful region in North America by 1700.

CORE **OBJECTIVE**

1. Identify the economic, political, and religious motivations for the establishment of England's diverse American colonies.

The English Background

People and Profits

The English colonies differed in important ways from the Spanish colonies in North America. Spanish settlements were royal expeditions undertaken by the government; most of the wealth seized from Indians became the property of the monarchs who funded the conquistadores. In contrast, English colonization was led by two different groups: those seeking freedom from religious persecution—Protestants, Catholics, and Jews—and those seeking land and profits.

Joint-stock companies

English colonies were thus private business ventures or religious experiments—or both. The monarchy regulated rather than managed them. Because few people were wealthy enough to finance a colony, those interested in colonization banded together to share the financial risks. Investors purchased shares of stock in a colony to form **joint-stock companies**. That way, large amounts of money could be raised, and, if a colony failed, no investor would suffer the complete loss. If a colony succeeded, investors would share the profits.

The English settlements in America adjoined one another in concentrated geographical areas, and so were more compact than those in New Spain. The native peoples along the Atlantic coast were less numerous, more scattered, and less wealthy than the Mexicas and the Incas. Unlike the French and Spanish colonies, where fur traders and Spanish conquistadores often lived among the Indians and intermarried, most English settlers viewed the Indians as an impediment. The English settlers created family-based communities largely separate from Native American villages. By 1750, English colonists (male and female) outnumbered the French in North America (mostly male) nearly 20 to 1—1.3 million to 70,000—whereas in what became Texas, New Mexico, Arizona, Florida, and California, there were only 20,000 Spaniards.

Economic and social aims of colonization

The English government wanted colonies to provide raw materials such as timber for shipbuilding, tobacco for smoking, and fur pelts for hats and coats. It also wanted colonists to buy English-made goods. English monarchs viewed colonies as a safety valve to relieve social pressures at home. For decades, peasants had been pushed off the land by the *enclosure* movement, whereby landlords found it more profitable to raise sheep than host poor farmworkers, so they evicted many peasants. Doing so generated many beggars and vagrants and provided a compelling reason to send them to the colonies. In some cases, immigrants had no choice in their relocation. Some 50,000 British convicts were also shipped to America as servants for hire.

Massive displacement and immigration

The most powerful enticement for prospective colonists was to offer them land and the promise of a better life: what later came to be called the American dream. Land, plentiful and cheap, was America's prized treasure—once it was taken from the Native Americans.

joint-stock companies Businesses owned by investors, who purchase shares of stock and share the profits and losses.

Political Traditions

THE MAGNA CARTA English caricaturist John Leech's 1846 illustration of King John signing the Magna Carta in 1215 suggests the foundational document's lasting resonance.

European societies were tightly controlled hierarchies. From birth, people were not allowed to rise above the rank in the social order into which they were born. Commoners bowed to priests, priests bowed to bishops, peasants pledged their loyalty to landowners, and nobles knelt before monarchs, who claimed God had given them absolute ruling power to rule over their domain and its people.

Since the thirteenth century, however, English monarchs had *shared* power with the nobility and with a lesser aristocracy, the *gentry*. England's tradition of limited or constitutional monarchy began with the Magna Carta (Great Charter) of 1215, a statement of fundamental rights that rebellious nobles forced the king to approve. The Magna Carta established that England would be ruled by laws rather than tyrants. Everyone was equal before the law, and no one was above it, not even a king or queen—at least in theory.

Parliament, civil rights, and liberties

The people's representatives formed the national legislature known as **Parliament**, which comprised the hereditary and appointed members of the House of Lords and the elected members of the House of Commons. The crucial power allocated to Parliament was the authority to impose taxes on the people. By controlling tax revenue, the legislature exercised leverage over the monarchy, which needed tax revenues to sustain its power.

Religious Conflict and War

When Queen Elizabeth, who never married, died in 1603, her cousin, James VI of Scotland, became King James I of England. He called the combined kingdoms of Scotland and England *Great Britain*. While Elizabeth had ruled through constitutional authority, James claimed to govern by "divine right," which meant he answered only to God.

King James I confronted a divided Church of England, with the reform-minded **Puritans** in one camp and the Anglican archbishop and bishops in the other. The Puritans were theologically conservative dissenters who believed that the Church of England needed further "purifying." All "papist" (Roman Catholic) rituals must go. No use of holy water, candles, or incense. No "Devil's bagpipes" (pipe organs). No priestly vestments (robes). No lavish cathedrals, stained glass windows, or statues of Jesus. Puritans even sought to ban the use of the term *priest*.

Parliament Legislature of Great Britain, composed of the House of Commons, whose members are elected, and the House of Lords, whose members are either hereditary or appointed.

Puritans English religious dissenters who sought to "purify" the Church of England of its Catholic practices.

A divided Church of England and religious persecution

The Puritans wanted to simplify religion to its most basic elements: people worshipping God in plain, self-governing congregations without the formal trappings of Catholic and Anglican ceremonies and centered on the sufficiency of the Bible. They had hoped the new king would support their efforts. However, James I, who had been baptized in the Catholic faith, embraced the conservative Anglican Church to avoid a civil war and sought to imprison or banish the Puritans.

The most radical Puritans decided that the Church of England was too corrupt to be reformed. They therefore created congregations separate from the Anglican Church, thus earning the name *Separatists*. Such rebelliousness infuriated Anglican authorities, who required people to attend Anglican church services. The Separatists were violating church and civil laws. During the late sixteenth century, the Separatists (also called *Nonconformists*) were, said one of them, "hunted and persecuted on every side." Such persecution only deepened their spiritual convictions. Many Puritans left England, and some, who would be known as Pilgrims (people who travel to foreign lands), sailed to America.

EXECUTION OF CHARLES I
Flemish artist John Weesop witnessed the king's execution and painted this gruesome scene from memory. He was so disgusted by "a country where they cut off their King's head" that he refused to visit England again.

In 1625, King James's son, Charles I, succeeded his father and proved to be an even more stubborn defender of absolute royal power. He raised taxes without consulting Parliament, harassed the Puritans, and even disbanded Parliament from 1629 to 1640. The monarch went too far, however, when he forced Anglican forms of worship on Presbyterian Scotland. In 1638, the Scots rose in revolt, and in 1640, Charles, desperate to save his skin, revived Parliament, ordering its members to raise taxes for the defense of his kingdom. Parliament, led by militant Puritans, refused.

In 1642, when the king tried to arrest five members of Parliament, a civil war erupted between Royalists and Parliamentarians. In 1646, parliamentary forces led by Puritan Oliver Cromwell captured Charles and, in a public trial, convicted him of high treason and contempt of Parliament, labeling him a "tyrant, traitor, murderer, and public enemy." He was beheaded in 1649.

Oliver Cromwell ruled like a military dictator, outlawing Roman Catholics and Anglicans. Many Anglican Royalists, called *Cavaliers*, escaped by sailing to Virginia. After Cromwell's death in 1658, Parliament supported the Restoration of the monarchy under Charles II, eldest son of the executed king.

Unlike his father, King Charles II agreed to rule jointly with Parliament. His younger brother, the Duke of York (who became King James II in 1685), was more rigid. James embraced Catholicism, murdered or imprisoned political opponents, appointed Roman Catholics to crucial government posts, and defied Parliament.

The English tolerated James II's rule so long as they expected one of his Protestant daughters, Mary or Anne, to succeed him. In 1688, however, the birth of a royal son who would be raised Roman Catholic stirred a revolt. Political, religious, and military leaders urged the king's daughter Mary and her Protestant husband, William III of Orange (the ruling Dutch prince), to oust her father and assume the English throne as joint monarchs. A month after William and his powerful Dutch army landed in England, King James II fled to France.

Amid this dramatic transfer of power, which came to be called the Glorious Revolution, Parliament reasserted its right to counterbalance the authority of the monarchy. Kings and queens saw their authority limited; they could no longer suspend Parliament, create armies, or impose taxes without Parliament's consent. Kings and queens thereafter derived their power not from God ("divine right") but through elected representatives in Parliament.

Settling the American Colonies

CORE **OBJECTIVE**

2. Describe the political, economic, social, and religious characteristics of English colonies in the Chesapeake region, New England, the Carolinas, and the middle colonies before 1700.

During the seventeenth century, all but one of England's North American colonies—Georgia—were founded. The colonists were energetic, courageous, and often desperate and ruthless people people willing to risk their lives in hopes of improving them. Many of those who were jobless and landless in England would find their way to America, a place already viewed as a land of opportunity—and danger.

The Chesapeake Region

In 1606, King James I gave his blessing to a joint-stock enterprise called the Virginia Company. It was owned by merchant investors seeking to profit from the gold and silver they hoped to find. The king also ordered the Virginia Company to bring the "Christian religion" to the Indians, who "live in darkness and miserable ignorance of the true knowledge and worship of God." As was true of many colonial ventures, however, such missionary activities were quickly dropped in favor of making money.

Jamestown

A fragile Jamestown

In December 1606, the Virginia Company sent to America three ships carrying 104 colonists, all men and boys. In May 1607, after five storm-tossed months at sea, they reached Chesapeake Bay, which extends 200 miles along the coast of Virginia and Maryland. To avoid Spanish raiders, the colonists chose to settle about forty miles inland along a large river. They called it the

James, in honor of the king, and named their settlement James Fort, later renamed Jamestown.

On a marshy peninsula fed by salty water and swarming with mosquitos, the colonists built a fort, huts, and a church. They struggled to find enough to eat, for most of them were either townsmen unfamiliar with farming or "gentleman" adventurers who despised manual labor. Were it not for the food acquired or stolen from neighboring Indians, Jamestown would have collapsed.

The **Powhatan Confederacy** dominated the Indigenous peoples of the Chesapeake region. Chief Powhatan ruled several hundred villages (of about a hundred people each) organized into thirty chiefdoms in eastern Virginia. The Powhatans were farmers adept at growing corn. They lived in oval-shaped houses framed with bent saplings and covered with bark or mats.

Chief Powhatan lived in a massive lodge on the York River, not far from Jamestown. Forty bodyguards protected him, and a hundred wives bore him scores of children. Powhatan forced the rival peoples he had conquered to give him most of their corn. He also traded with the English colonists, exchanging corn and hides for hatchets, swords, and muskets. However, Powhatan realized too late that the newcomers planned to seize his lands and enslave his people.

NOVA BRITANNIA.
OFFERING MOST
Excellent fruites by Planting in
VIRGINIA.
Exciting all such as be well affected
to further the same.
LONDON
Printed for SAMVEL MACHAM, and are to be sold at
his Shop in Pauls Church-yard, at the
Signe of the Bul-head.
1609.

VIRGINIA COMPANY This pamphlet was printed in London in 1609 to promote immigration to Virginia. **What does this advertisement promise its potential settlers, and how does that promise conflict with the reality that greeted them?**

Pocahontas

One of the most remarkable Indians near Jamestown was Pocahontas, the favorite daughter of Chief Powhatan. In 1607, then only eleven years old, she figured in perhaps the best-known story of the settlement, her plea for the life of Captain John Smith. After Indians captured Smith and a group of Englishmen trespassing on their land, Chief Powhatan ordered his warriors to kill Smith. As they prepared to smash Smith's skull, young Pocahontas made a dramatic appeal for his life. She convinced her father to release him in exchange for muskets, hatchets, beads, and trinkets.

Schoolchildren still learn the story of Pocahontas and John Smith, but through the years the story's facts have become distorted or even falsified. Pocahontas and John Smith were friends, not lovers. Moreover, she saved Smith on more than one occasion, before she was kidnapped by English settlers eager to blackmail Powhatan.

Pocahontas, however, surprised her English captors by choosing to join them. She embraced Christianity, was baptized and renamed Rebecca, and fell in love with John Rolfe, a twenty-eight-year-old widower who introduced

Powhatan Confederacy An alliance of several powerful Algonquian societies under the leadership of Chief Powhatan, organized into thirty chiefdoms along much of the Atlantic coast in the late sixteenth and early seventeenth centuries.

CHIEF POWHATAN AND POCAHONTAS *(Left)* Chief Powhatan holds court in this 1624 line engraving from John Smith's "Generall Historie of Virginia." *(Right)* After being captured by English settlers, Pocahontas converted to Christianity and adopted the name "Lady Rebecca." She is shown here, in an illustration from 1616, in European dress.

tobacco to Jamestown. After their marriage, they moved in 1616 with their infant son, Thomas, to London. There the young princess drew excited attention from the royal family and curious Londoners. Just months after arriving, however, Lady Rebecca, only twenty years old, contracted a lung disease and died.

Hard Times

The Jamestown settlers had expected to find gold and silver, friendly Indians, and comfortable living in America. They instead found disease, drought, starvation, violence, and death. Virtually every colonist fell ill within a year. "Our men were destroyed with cruel diseases," a survivor wrote, "but for the most part they died of mere famine."

Fortunately for the Virginia colonists, they found a bold leader in Pocahontas's friend, Captain John Smith, a twenty-seven-year-old mercenary (soldier for hire). At five feet three inches, he was a sturdy runt of a man, full of tenacity, courage, and confidence. With the colonists on the verge of starvation, Smith imposed strict military discipline and forced all to work if they wanted to eat. Through Smith's often brutal efforts, Jamestown survived—but only barely.

During the winter of 1609–1610, the food supply again ran out, and most of the colonists died from "the sharp prick of hunger." Desperate settlers consumed their horses, cats, and dogs, then rats, mice, and snakes. A few "dug up dead corpses out of graves" and ate them. One hungry man killed, salted, and ate his pregnant wife. Horrified by such cannibalism, his fellow colonists executed him. Still, the cannibalism continued. "So great was our

EUROPEAN SETTLEMENTS AND INDIAN SOCIETIES IN EARLY AMERICA

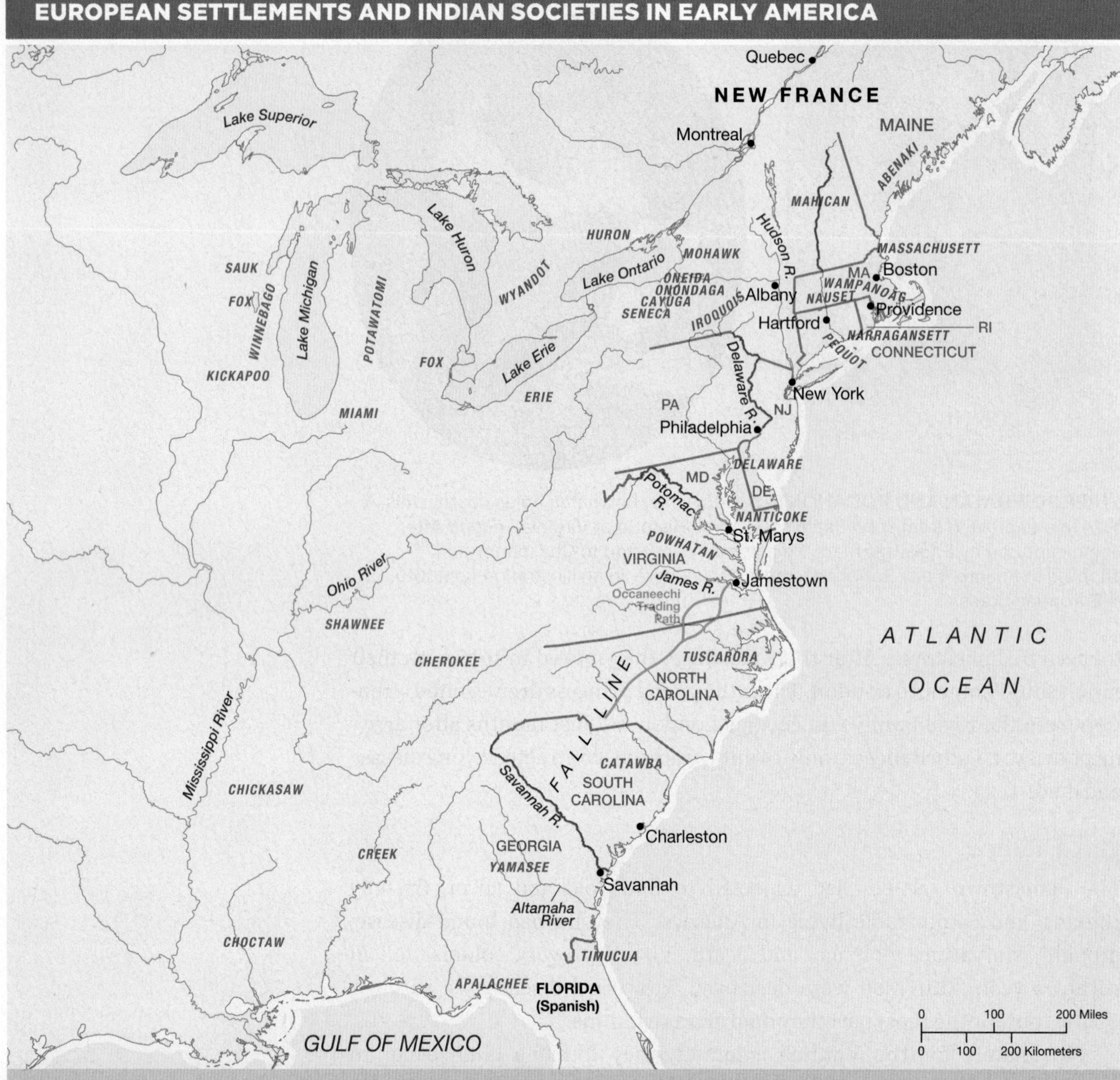

- Why did European settlement lead to the expansion of hostilities among the Indians?
- What were the consequences of the trade and commerce between the English settlers and the southern Indigenous peoples?
- How were the relationships between the settlers and the members of the Iroquois League different from those between settlers and Indians in other regions?

famine," Smith wrote, "that a savage we slew and buried, the poorer sort [of colonists] took him up again and ate him."

When the colonists discovered no gold or silver, the Virginia Company shifted its focus to the sale of land, which would rise in value as the colony grew in population. The company recruited more settlers, including a few courageous women, by promising that Virginia would "make them rich." In late May 1610, Sir Thomas Gates, a prominent English soldier and sea captain, brought some 150 new colonists to Jamestown. They found the settlement in shambles. The fort's walls and settlers' cabins had been used as firewood, and the church was in ruins. Of the original 104 Englishmen, only 38 had survived. They greeted the newcomers by shouting, "We are starved! We are starved!"

After nearly abandoning Jamestown to return to England, Gates led the rebuilding of the settlements and imposed a strict system of laws. The penalties for running away, for example, included shooting, hanging, or burning. Gates also ordered the colonists to attend church services on Thursdays and Sundays. Religious uniformity became a crucial instrument of public policy and civic duty in colonial Virginia.

Over the next several years, the Jamestown colony limped along until at last the settlers found a profitable crop: **tobacco**. Smoking had become a widespread habit in Europe, and tobacco plantations flourished on Caribbean islands. In 1612, settlers in Virginia began growing tobacco for export to England, using seeds brought from South America. By 1620, the colony was shipping 50,000 pounds of tobacco each year; by 1670, Virginia and Maryland were exporting 15 *million* pounds annually.

Despite its labor-intensive demands, the growing of tobacco became the most profitable enterprise in colonial Virginia and Maryland. Growing tobacco, however, quickly depleted the soil of nutrients, so large-scale tobacco farming required increasingly more land for planting and more laborers to work the fields. Much like sugar and rice, tobacco would be one of the primary crops that would drive the demand for indentured servants and enslaved Africans.

In 1618, Sir Edwin Sandys, a prominent member of Parliament, became head of the Virginia Company. He launched a new **headright** (land grant) policy: anyone who bought a share in the company and could pay for passage to Virginia could have fifty acres upon arrival and fifty more for each servant he brought along. The following year, the company promised that the settlers would have all the "rights of Englishmen." Those rights included a legislature elected by the people. This was a crucial development, for the English had long enjoyed the broadest civil liberties and the least intrusive government in Europe. Now the colonists in Virginia were to enjoy the same rights.

In 1619, the Virginia Company created the first elected legislature in the Western Hemisphere. The House of Burgesses, modeled after Parliament, would meet at least once a year to make laws and decide on taxes. It included the governor, his four councilors, and twenty-two burgesses elected by free White male property owners over the age of seventeen. The word *burgess* derived from the medieval *burgh*, meaning a town or community. The House of Burgesses represented the first experiment with representative government in the American colonies.

tobacco A "cash crop" grown in the Caribbean as well as the Virginia and Maryland colonies, made increasingly profitable by the rapidly growing popularity of smoking in Europe after the voyages of Columbus.

headright A land-grant policy that promised fifty acres to any colonist who could afford passage to Virginia and fifty more for each accompanying servant. The headright policy was eventually expanded to include any colonists—and was also adopted in other colonies.

LAND GRANTS TO THE VIRGINIA COMPANY

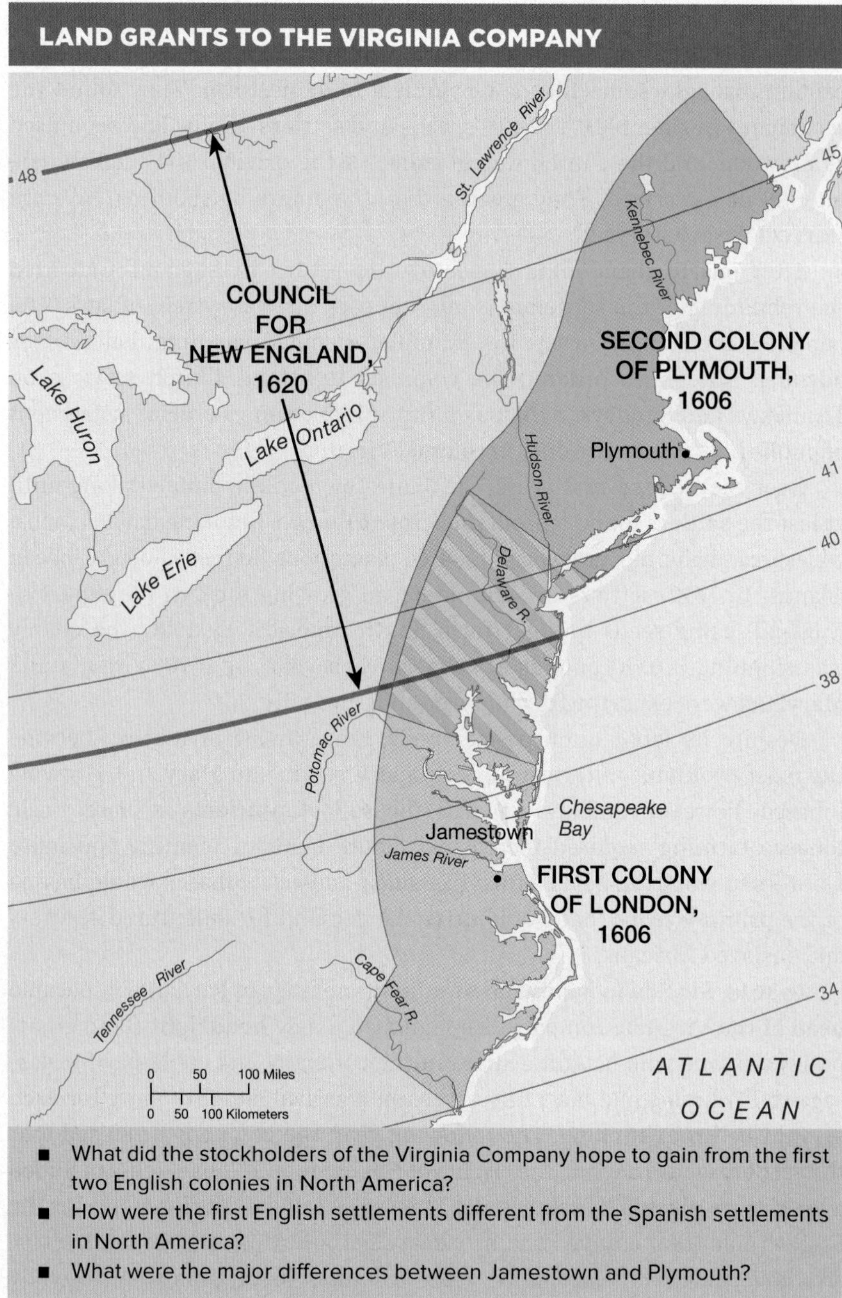

- What did the stockholders of the Virginia Company hope to gain from the first two English colonies in North America?
- How were the first English settlements different from the Spanish settlements in North America?
- What were the major differences between Jamestown and Plymouth?

The year 1619 was eventful in other respects. The settlement had outgrown James Fort and was formally renamed Jamestown. Also in that year, a ship arrived with ninety young women. Men rushed to claim them as wives by providing 125 pounds of tobacco to cover the cost of their trip.

Still another significant development occurred in 1619 when an English ship called the *White Lion* stopped at Point Comfort, Virginia, near Jamestown, and unloaded "20 and odd Negars," the first enslaved Africans known to have reached the British American mainland. Portuguese slave traders had captured them in Angola in West Africa. On their way to Mexico, the Africans were seized by the marauding *White Lion*, known to raid Portuguese and Spanish ships.

The first enslaved Africans

The arrival of Africans in Virginia marked the beginning of two and a half centuries of slavery in British North America. They were the first of some 450,000 Africans who would be seized and shipped to the mainland colonies. Overall, Europeans would transport 12.5 million enslaved Africans to the Western Hemisphere, 15 percent of whom died in transit. The majority were delived to Brazil and the Caribbean "sugar" islands—Barbados, Cuba, Jamaica, and others. There the heat, humidity, and awful working conditions brought an early death to enslaved workers. It is in this sense that institutionalized slavery is said to be the "original sin" committed by the English who settled the American colonies.

The year 1619 thus witnessed the terrible irony of the Virginia colony establishing the principle of representative government (the House of Burgesses) while enslaving Africans. From that point on, color-based slavery, America's original sin, would corrode the ideals of liberty and equality that would inspire the fight for independence .

By 1624, some 8,000 English men, women, and children had migrated to Jamestown, although only 1,132 had survived, and many of them were in "a sickly and desperate state." In 1622 alone, nearly 1,000 colonists died of disease or were victims of Indian attacks.

In 1624, the Virginia Company declared bankruptcy, and Virginia was converted from a joint-stock company to a royal colony controlled by the government. The settlers were now free to own property and start businesses. The king, however, would appoint their governors. Governor William Berkeley, who arrived in 1642, presided over the colony's rapid growth for most of the next thirty-five years. Tobacco prices surged, and wealthy planters began to dominate social and political life.

The Jamestown experience did not invent America, but the colonists' gritty will to survive, their mixture of greed and piety, and their exploitation of both Indians and Africans formed the model for many of the struggles, achievements, and hypocrisies that would come to define the American colonies and the American nation.

Maryland

Maryland: The first proprietary colony and a refuge for English Catholics

In 1634, ten years after Virginia became a royal colony, a neighboring settlement appeared on the northern shore of Chesapeake Bay. Named Maryland in honor of Henrietta Maria, the Catholic wife of King Charles I, its 12 million acres were granted to Sir George Calvert, Lord Baltimore. It thereby became the first *proprietary* colony—that is, an individual owned it—as opposed to a joint-stock company owned by investors.

Calvert, a Roman Catholic, asked the king to grant him an colony north of Virginia. Calvert, however, died before the king could act. So the charter went to Calvert's son Cecilius, the second Lord Baltimore, who founded the colony.

Cecilius Calvert envisioned Maryland as a refuge for English Catholics. Yet he also wanted the colony to be profitable and to avoid antagonizing Protestants. To that aim, he instructed his brother, Leonard, the colony's first governor, to ensure that Catholic colonists did not stir up trouble with Protestants. They must worship in private and remain "silent" about religious matters.

In 1634, the Calverts planted the first settlement in coastal Maryland at St. Mary's, near the mouth of the Potomac River, about eighty miles north of Jamestown. Cecilius sought to avoid the mistakes made at Jamestown. He recruited colonists made up of families intending to stay, rather than single men seeking quick profits. He and his brother also wanted to avoid the extremes of wealth and poverty that had developed in Virginia. To do so, they bought land from the Indians and provided 100 acres to each adult settler and 50 more for each child. The Calverts also promoted the "conversion and civilizing" of the "barbarous heathens." To avoid the frequent Indian wars

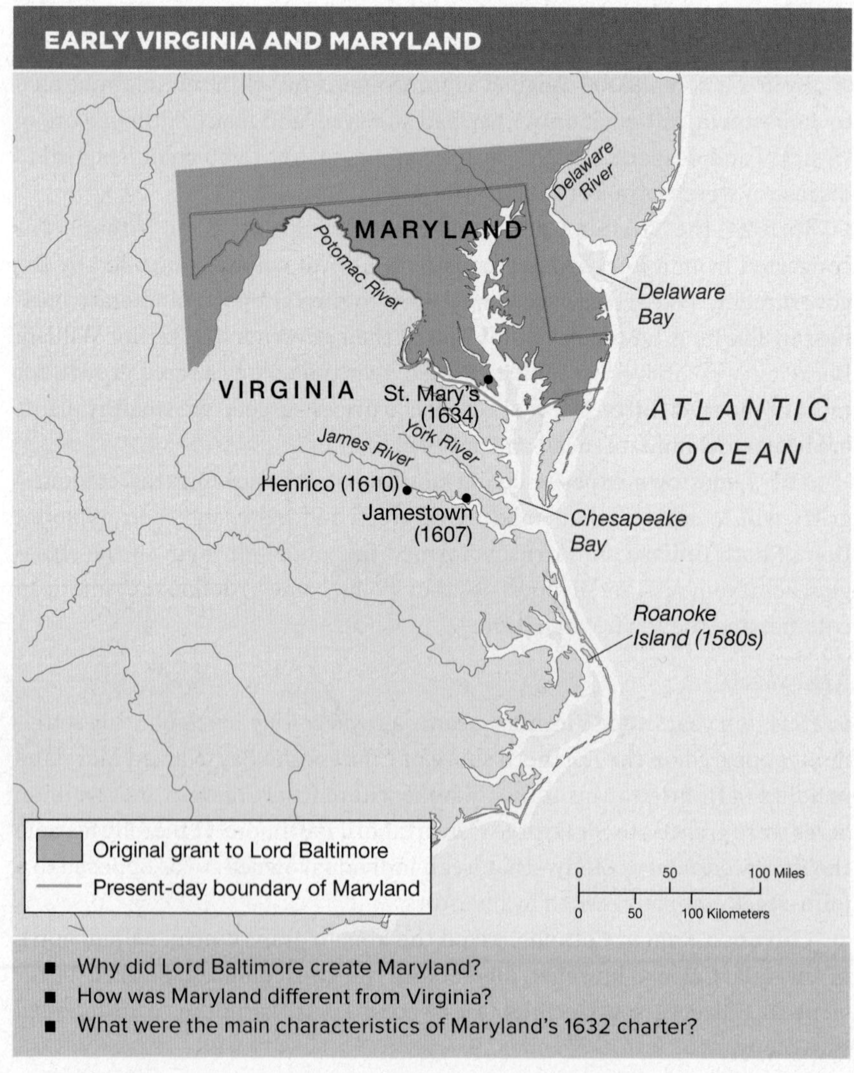

- Why did Lord Baltimore create Maryland?
- How was Maryland different from Virginia?
- What were the main characteristics of Maryland's 1632 charter?

suffered in Virginia, the Calverts pledged to purchase land from the Native Americans rather than take it by force.

Still, the early years in the Maryland colony were as difficult as in Virginia. Nearly half the colonists died before reaching age twenty-one. Some 34,000 colonists would arrive between 1634 and 1680, but in 1680 the colony's White population was only 20,000. The Calverts ruled with the consent of the *freemen* (all property holders). Yet they could not attract enough Roman Catholics to develop a self-sustaining economy. Most who came to the colony were Protestants. In the end, Maryland succeeded more quickly than Virginia because of its focus on growing tobacco from the start. Its long coastline along the Chesapeake Bay gave planters easy access to shipping.

Despite the Calverts' caution "concerning matters of religion," Catholics and Protestants feuded as violently as they had in England. When Oliver Cromwell and the Puritans took control in England and executed King Charles I in 1649, Cecilius Calvert feared he might lose his colony. To avoid such a catastrophe, he appointed Protestants to the colony's ruling council. He also wrote the Toleration Act (1649), a revolutionary document that welcomed all Christians, regardless of their denomination or beliefs. (It also promised to execute anyone who denied the divinity of Jesus.)

Toleration Act (1649)

Still, Calvert's efforts were not enough to prevent the new government in England from installing Puritans in positions of control in Maryland. They rescinded the Toleration Act in 1654, stripped Catholic colonists of voting rights, and denied them the right to worship. The once-persecuted Puritans had become persecutors themselves, at one point driving Calvert out of his own colony. Were it not for its success in growing tobacco, Maryland may well have disintegrated. In 1692, following the Glorious Revolution in England, officials banned Catholicism in Maryland. Only after the American Revolution would Marylanders again be guaranteed religious freedom.

New England

Quite different English settlements emerged north of the Chesapeake Bay colonies. Unlike Maryland and Virginia, the "New" England colonies were intended to be self-governing religious utopias. The New England settlers were not servants as in the Chesapeake colonies; they were mostly middle-class family groups that could pay their way across the Atlantic. Most male settlers were small farmers, merchants, seamen, or fishermen. Although its soil was not as fertile as that of the Chesapeake region and its growing season was much shorter, New England was a healthier place to live. Because of its colder climate, settlers avoided the infectious diseases like malaria that ravaged the southern colonies.

The Pilgrims and Puritans who arrived in Massachusetts were willing to sacrifice everything to create a model Christian society. These self-described

CROSSING THE ATLANTIC This sixteenth-century woodcut depicts sailors on an oceangoing vessel using the stars to chart their course, the same method English colonists used to navigate across the Atlantic.

"saints" remained subjects of the king, but they ruled themselves by following God's biblical commandments. They also resolved to "purify" their church of all Catholic and Anglican rituals. Such holy colonies, they hoped, would provide a living example of righteousness for a wicked England to imitate.

During the seventeenth century, only 21,000 colonists arrived in New England, compared with the 120,000 who went to the Chesapeake Bay colonies. By 1700, however, New England's thriving White population *exceeded* that of Maryland and Virginia.

Plymouth

The first permanent English settlement in New England was established by the Plymouth Company, a group of seventy British investors. Eager to make money by exporting the colony's abundant natural resources, the joint-stock company agreed to finance settlements in exchange for the furs, timber, and fish the colonists would ship back to England for sale. Among the first to accept the company's offer were Puritan separatists who had been forced to leave England because they refused to worship in Anglican churches. The separatist "saints" demanded that each congregation govern itself rather than be ruled by a corrupt bureaucracy of bishops and archbishops. The Separatists, mostly simple farm folk, initially left England for Holland, where, over time, they worried that their children were embracing urban ways of life in Dutch Amsterdam. Such concerns led them to leave Europe and create a holy community in America.

The Pilgrims at Plymouth and the Mayflower Compact (1620)

In September 1620, a group of 102 women, men, and children crammed aboard the tiny *Mayflower*, a leaky, three-masted vessel barely 100 feet long, and headed across the Atlantic, bound for the Virginia colony, where they had obtained permission to settle. Each colonist received one share in the enterprise in exchange for working seven years in America as servants. It was hurricane season, however, and violent storms blew the ship off course to Cape Cod, southeast of what became Boston, Massachusetts. Having exhausted most of their food and water after spending sixty-six days crossing 2,812 miles, they had no choice but to settle there in "a hideous and desolate wilderness full of wild beasts and wild men."

Once safely on land, William Bradford, who would become the colony's second governor, noted that the pious settlers, whom he called Pilgrims, "fell upon their knees and blessed the God of Heaven who had brought them over the vast and furious ocean." They called their hillside settlement Plymouth, after the English port city from which they had embarked.

The Mayflower Compact (1620)

Since the *Mayflower* colonists were outside the jurisdiction of any organized government, forty-one of them, all men, resolved to rule themselves. They signed the **Mayflower Compact**, a covenant (group contract) to form "a civil body politic" based on "just and civil laws" designed "for the general good." The Mayflower Compact was not democracy in action, however. The saints granted only themselves the rights to vote and hold office. Their "inferiors"—the "strangers" and servants who also had traveled on the *Mayflower*—would have to wait for their civil rights.

The colonists settled in a deserted Indian village that had been devastated by smallpox. Those who had qualms about squatting on Indian lands rationalized them away. One Pilgrim soothed his guilt by explaining that the Indians were "not industrious." They had neither "art, science, skill nor faculty to use either the land or the commodities of it." The Pilgrims experienced a "starving time" as had the early Jamestown colonists. During their first winter, almost half the colonists died, including fourteen of the nineteen women and six children. Only the theft of Indian corn enabled the English colony to survive.

Eventually, a local Indian named Squanto (Tisquantum) taught the colonists to grow corn, catch fish, gather nuts and berries, and negotiate with the Wampanoags. Still, when a shipload of colonists arrived in 1623, they "fell a-weeping" as they found the original Pilgrims in such a "low and poor condition." By the 1630s, Governor Bradford was lamenting the failure of Plymouth to become the thriving holy community he and others had envisioned.

Mayflower Compact (1620) A formal agreement signed by the Separatist colonists aboard the *Mayflower* to abide by laws made by leaders of their choosing.

Massachusetts Bay Colony English colony founded by Puritans in 1630 as a haven for persecuted Congregationalists.

Massachusetts Bay

The Plymouth colony's population never rose above 7,000, and after ten years it was overshadowed by its much larger neighbor, the **Massachusetts Bay Colony**. Like Plymouth, the new colony was also intended to be a holy commonwealth for Puritans, but the Massachusetts Bay Puritans were

EARLY NEW ENGLAND SETTLEMENTS

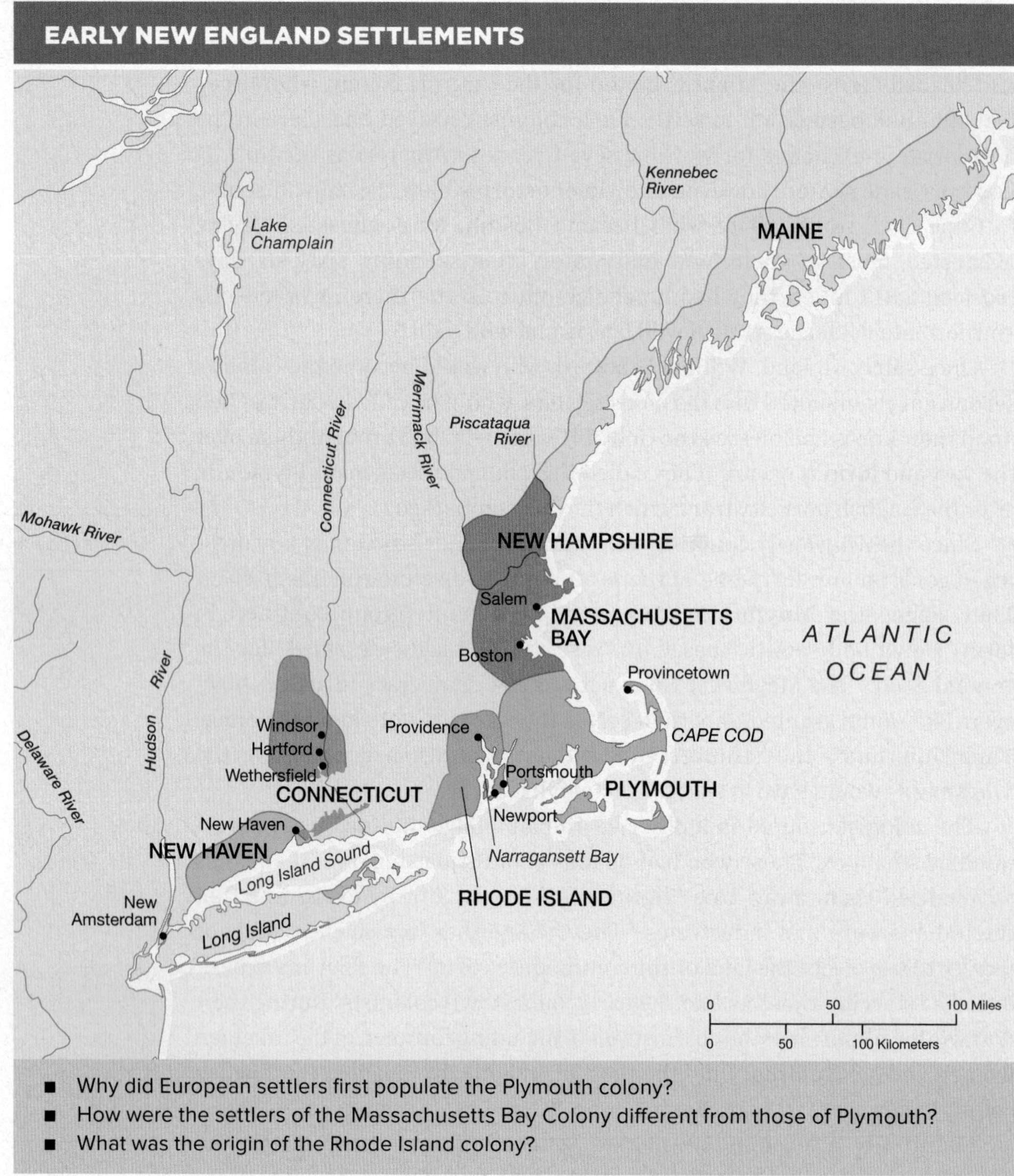

- Why did European settlers first populate the Plymouth colony?
- How were the settlers of the Massachusetts Bay Colony different from those of Plymouth?
- What was the origin of the Rhode Island colony?

different from the Pilgrims. They remained Anglicans—they wanted to purify the Church of England from within. They were called non-separating *Congregationalists* because their churches were governed by their independent congregations rather than by an Anglican bishop in England. The Puritans believed they were God's "chosen people." They limited church membership to "visible saints"—those who could demonstrate to the congregation that they had received the gift of God's grace.

In 1629, King Charles I gave a royal charter to the Massachusetts Bay Company, a group of Calvinist Puritans making up a joint-stock company. They were led by John Winthrop, a lawyer with intense religious convictions and mounting debts. Winthrop wanted the colony to be a haven for Puritans and a model Christian community where faith would flourish. They would create "a City upon a Hill," as he declared, borrowing the phrase from Jesus's Sermon on the Mount. "The eyes of all people are on us," Winthrop said, so the Puritans must live up to their sacred destiny.

JOHN WINTHROP The first governor of the Massachusetts Bay Colony, Winthrop envisioned a community that would be "a City upon a Hill."

In 1630, Winthrop, his wife, three of his sons, and eight servants joined some 700 Puritan settlers on eleven ships loaded with cows, horses, supplies, and tons of beer, which remained safely drinkable much longer than did water. Unlike the first colonists in Virginia, most of the Puritans in Massachusetts arrived as family groups; they landed near the mouth of the Charles River, where they built a village and called it Boston, after the English town of that name. Winthrop was delighted to discover that the local Indians had been "swept away by the smallpox . . . so God hath hereby cleared our title to this place." Disease knew no boundaries, however. Within eight months, some 200 Puritans had died of various illnesses, and many others had returned to England. Planting colonies was not for the faint-hearted. Anne Bradstreet, who became one of the first colonial poets, lamented the severe living conditions: "After I was convinced it was the way of God, I submitted to it." What eventually allowed the Massachusetts Bay Colony to thrive was a flood of additional colonists who brought money, skills, and needed supplies.

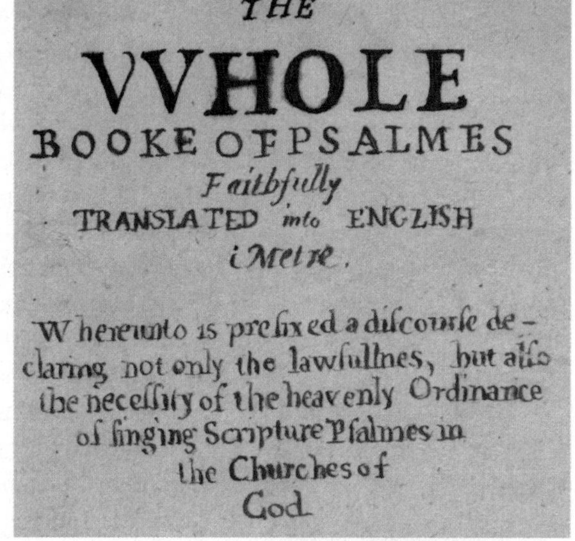

THE
VVHOLE
BOOKE OF PSALMES
Faithfully
TRANSLATED into ENGLISH
Metre.
Whereunto is prefixed a discourse declaring not only the lawfullnes, but also the necessity of the heavenly Ordinance of singing Scripture Psalmes in the Churches of God.

PURITAN WORSHIP The Whole Book of Psalmes Faithfully Translated into English Metre (Massachusetts, 1640) was the first book printed in the English mainland colonies. This copy was missing its title page, and so its owner wrote one out by hand, imitating the type and layout of the printed original.

John Winthrop had cleverly taken the royal charter for the colony with him to America, thereby transferring government authority from London to Massachusetts, where he and others hoped to govern their godly colony with little oversight by the monarchy. John Winthrop was determined to enforce religious devotion and ensure social stability. He and other Puritan leaders prized stability and hated the idea of democracy—the people ruling themselves. As the Reverend John Cotton explained, "If the people be governors, who shall be governed?" For his part, Winthrop claimed that a democracy was "the worst of all forms of government." Puritan leaders never embraced religious toleration, political freedom, social equality, or cultural diversity. They believed that the role of government should be to enforce religious beliefs and ensure social stability. Ironically, the same Puritans who had fled persecution in England did not hesitate to persecute people of other religious views in New England. Catholics, Anglicans, Quakers, and Baptists had no rights; they were punished, imprisoned, banished, tortured, or executed.

Unlike "Old" England, New England had no powerful lords or bishops, kings or queens. The Massachusetts General Court, wherein power rested under the royal charter, consisted of all the shareholders, called freemen.

At first, the freemen had no power except to choose "assistants," who in turn elected the governor and deputy governor. In 1634, however, the freemen turned themselves into the General Court, with two or three deputies to represent each town. A final stage in the democratization of the government came in 1644, when the General Court organized itself like the Parliament. Henceforth, all decisions had to be ratified by a majority in each house.

Rights and representation in New England

Thus, over fourteen years, the joint-stock Massachusetts Bay Company evolved into the governing body of a holy commonwealth in which freemen exercised increasing power. Puritans had fled not only religious persecution but also political repression, and they ensured that their liberties in New England were spelled out and protected. Over time, membership in a Puritan church replaced the purchase of stock as the means of becoming a freeman in Massachusetts Bay.

Rhode Island

Roger Williams challenges Puritan control

More by accident than design, the Massachusetts Bay Colony became the staging area for other New England colonies created by people dissatisfied with Puritan control. Young Roger Williams, who had arrived from England in 1631, was among the first to cause problems, precisely because he was the purest of Puritans—a Separatist. He criticized Puritans for not completely cutting their ties to the "whorish" Church of England. Where John Winthrop cherished strict governmental and clerical authority, Williams championed individual liberty and criticized the way colonists were mistreating Indians.

The combative Williams sought to be the holiest of the holy—at whatever cost. To that end, he posed a fundamental question: If one's salvation depends solely upon God's grace, why bother to have churches at all? Why not give individuals the right to worship God in their way? In Williams's view, true *puritanism* required complete separation of church and government and freedom from all coercion in matters of faith. "Forced worship," he declared, "stinks in God's nostrils." According to Williams, governments should be impartial regarding religions.

ROGER WILLIAMS An outspoken Separatist, Williams challenged John Winthrop's strict authority and brutal treatment of Native Americans.

Such radical views led the General Court to banish him to England. Before Williams could be deported, however, he escaped during a blizzard and found shelter among the Narragansett Indians. In 1636, he bought land from the Indians and established the town of Providence at the head of Narragansett Bay, the first permanent settlement in Rhode Island and the first in America to allow complete freedom of religion.

From the beginning, the Colony of Rhode Island and Providence Plantations was the most democratic of the colonies, governed by the heads of households rather than by church members. Newcomers could be admitted to full citizenship by a majority vote, and all who fled religious persecution were welcomed. For their part, the Massachusetts Puritans came to view Rhode Island as a refuge for rogues. A Dutch visitor reported that

Rhode Island was "the sewer of New England. All the cranks of New England retire there."

Roger Williams was only one of several prominent Puritans who clashed with Governor John Winthrop's stern, unyielding governance of the Bay Colony. Another, Anne Hutchinson, quarreled with Puritan leaders for different reasons. The strong-willed wife of a prominent merchant, Hutchinson raised thirteen children and hosted meetings in her Boston home to discuss sermons. Soon, however, the discussions turned into large gatherings (of both men and women) at which Hutchinson discussed religious matters. According to one participant, she "preaches better Gospel than any of your black coats [male ministers]." Blessed with extensive biblical knowledge and a quick wit, Hutchinson claimed to know which of her neighbors had gained salvation and which were damned, including ministers.

THE TRIAL OF ANNE HUTCHINSON In this nineteenth-century wood engraving, Anne Hutchinson stands her ground against charges of heresy from the all-male leaders of Puritan Boston.

A pregnant Hutchinson was hauled before the all-male General Court in 1637 for trying to "undermine the Kingdom of Christ." For two days she sparred on equal terms with the Puritan leaders steadfastly refusing to acknowledge any wrongdoing. Hutchinson's ability to cite chapter-and-verse biblical defenses of her actions led an exasperated Governor Winthrop to explode: "We are your judges, and not you ours. . . . We do not mean to discourse [debate] with those of your sex." As the trial continued, the Court lured Hutchinson into convicting herself when she claimed to have received direct revelations from God. This was blasphemy in the eyes of Puritans, for if God were speaking directly to her, there was no need for ministers or churches.

In 1638, the General Court excommunicated Hutchinson from the church and banished her for having behaved like a "leper" not fit for "our society." She initially settled with her family and followers on an island in Rhode Island's Narragansett Bay. The hard journey took its toll, however. Hutchinson grew sick, and her fourteenth baby was stillborn.

Hutchinson's spirits never recovered. After her husband's death, in 1642, she moved near New Amsterdam (New York City), which was then under Dutch control. The following year, Indians massacred Hutchinson and six of her children. Her fate, wrote a spiteful John Winthrop, was "a special manifestation of divine justice."

Connecticut, New Hampshire, and Maine

Connecticut had a more conventional beginning than did Rhode Island. In 1636, the Reverend Thomas Hooker led three congregations from Massachusetts Bay to the Connecticut Valley, where they organized the self-governing colony of Connecticut. Three years later, the Connecticut General Court adopted the Fundamental Orders, laws that provided for a "Christian Commonwealth" like that of Massachusetts, except that voting was not limited to church members.

New England expands

In 1622, the king gave a vast tract of land that would encompass the states of New Hampshire and Maine to Sir Ferdinando Gorges and Captain John Mason. In 1629, the two divided their territory. Mason took the southern part, which he named the Province of New Hampshire, and Gorges opted for the northern region, which became the Province of Maine. During the early 1640s, Massachusetts took over New Hampshire and in the 1650s extended its authority to the scattered settlements in Maine. The land grab led to lawsuits, and in 1678 English judges decided against Massachusetts. In 1679, New Hampshire became a royal colony, but Massachusetts continued to control Maine. A new Massachusetts charter in 1691 finally incorporated Maine into Massachusetts.

The Carolinas

Carolina, the southernmost mainland British American colony in the seventeenth century, began as two widely separated areas which, in 1712, officially became **North and South Carolina**. The northernmost part, long called Albemarle, had been settled in the 1650s by colonists who had drifted southward from Virginia. For a half-century, Albemarle remained a remote scattering of farms along the shores of Albemarle Sound.

North and South Carolina English proprietary colonies, originally formed as the Carolina colonies, officially separated into the colonies of North and South Carolina in 1712, whose semitropical climate made them profitable centers of rice, timber, and tar production.

The Barbados Connection

The eight prominent nobles, called lords proprietors, to whom the king had given Carolina neglected Albemarle and instead focused on more-promising sites to the south. They recruited established English planters from Barbados, the most easterly of the Caribbean "sugar islands" and Barbados was the oldest, most profitable, and most horrific colony in English America, a place notorious for its brutal treatment of enslaved workers, many of whom were literally worked to death.

To seventeenth-century Europeans, sugar was a new and much-treasured luxury item. The sugar trade fueled the wealth of European nations and enabled them to finance their colonies in the Americas. By the 1720s, half the ships traveling to and from New York City were carrying Caribbean sugar. In the 1640s, English planters transformed Barbados, into an agricultural engine dotted by fields of sugarcane. Like the bamboo it resembles, sugarcane thrives in hot, humid climates. Barbadian sugar, then called white gold, generated more money for the British than the rest of their American colonies combined.

The British had developed an insatiable appetite for Asian tea and West Indian coffee, both of which they sweetened with Caribbean sugar. As one planter noted, sugar was no longer "a luxury; but has become by constant use, a necessary of life."

Sugar was hard to produce. Enslaved Africans used machetes to harvest the canes, then hauled them to wind-powered grinding mills where they were crushed to extract the sap. The sap was boiled, and the hot "juice"—liquid sugar—was poured into troughs to granulate, before being shoveled into barrels, which were stored in a curing house to allow for the molasses to drain off. The resulting brown sugar, called *muscovado*, would be shipped to refiners to be prepared for sale. The molasses was distilled into rum, the most popular drink in the colonies. By the early seventeenth century, the British sugar colonies—Barbados, St. Kitts, Nevis, Antigua, and Jamaica—were sending tons of molasses and sugar to Europe and British America.

CARIBBEAN SUGAR Enslaved Africans plant sugarcane cuttings on a sugar plantation in Antigua in this 1823 engraving. The windmill (in the background) powers the grinding mill.

Barbados was dominated by a few wealthy planters who depended on hordes of enslaved Africans to do the work. An Englishman pointed out in 1666 that Barbados and the other "sugar colonies" thrived because of enslaved "Negroes" and "without constant supplies of them cannot subsist." So many of the enslaved in Barbados died from overwork, poor nutrition, and disease that the sugar planters required a steady stream of Africans to replace them. Because all available land on the island was under cultivation, the sons and grandsons of the planter elite were forced to look elsewhere to find plantations of their own. Many seized the chance to settle Carolina and bring with them the Barbadian plantation system. In this sense, Carolina became "the colony of a colony," an offspring of the sugar-and-slave culture in Barbados.

Charles Town

The first 145 English colonists in South Carolina arrived in 1669 at Charles Town (later Charleston), on the west bank of the Ashley River. They brought three enslaved Africans with them. Over the next twenty years, half the colonists came from Barbados and other island colonies in the Caribbean, such as Nevis, St. Kitts, and Jamaica. Six of South Carolina's royal governors between 1670 and 1730 were Barbadian English planters.

Slavery in the Carolinas

The Carolina coastal plain so impressed settlers with its flatness that they called it the low country. As one of them reported, "it is so level that it may be compared to a bowling alley." Planters from the Caribbean brought to Carolina enormous numbers of enslaved Africans to clear land, plant crops, herd cattle, and slaughter pigs and chickens. Carolina, a Swiss immigrant said, "looks more like a negro country than like a country settled by white people."

The government of Carolina grew out of a unique document, the Fundamental Constitutions of Carolina, drafted by one of the eight proprietors, Lord Anthony Ashley Cooper with the help of his secretary John Locke.

EARLY SETTLEMENTS IN THE SOUTH

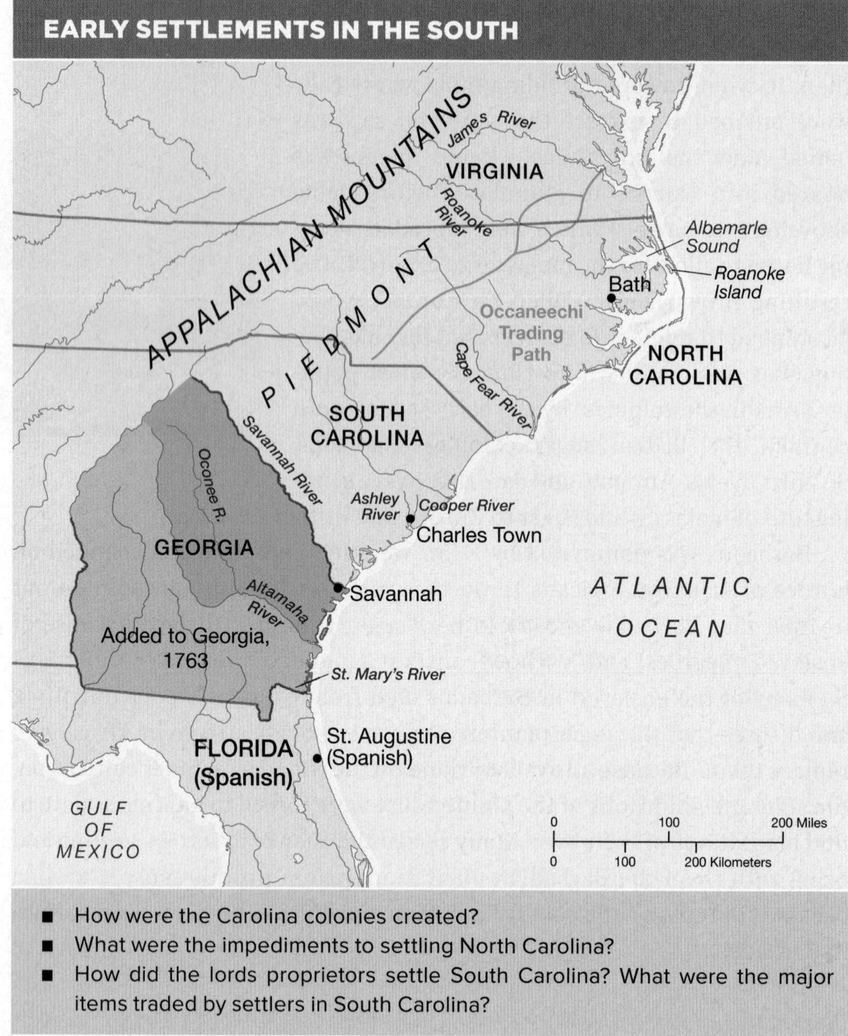

- How were the Carolina colonies created?
- What were the impediments to settling North Carolina?
- How did the lords proprietors settle South Carolina? What were the major items traded by settlers in South Carolina?

The constitution called for a royal governor, a council, and a Commons House of Assembly. In practice, however, what became South Carolina was dominated by prominent Englishmen who were awarded larger land grants. To generate an agricultural economy, the Carolina proprietors awarded land grants (headrights) to every male immigrant who could pay for passage across the Atlantic. The Fundamental Constitutions granted religious toleration, which gave Carolina a higher degree of religious freedom (extending to Jews and "heathens") than in England or any other colony except Rhode Island.

Religious tolerance

In 1685, the the Carolina colony received an unexpected surge of immigrants after French King Louis XIV revoked the Edict of Nantes, which had guaranteed the civil rights of the Huguenots, French Protestants. Hundreds of Huguenots settled in Carolina to avoid religious persecution at the hands of the Catholic monarchy.

The early settlers in Carolina experienced morale-busting hardships. "I have been here for six months," twenty-three-year-old Judith Manigault, a Huguenot refugee serving as a servant, wrote to her brother in Europe, reporting that she had been "working the ground like a slave," and had "suffered all sorts of evils." But "God surely gave us good grace to have been able to withstand all sorts of trials." Her son Gabriel benefited from her perseverance; he would become one of the richest men in the province.

In 1712, the proprietors divided the Carolina colony into North and South, and seven years later, South Carolina became a royal colony. North Carolina remained under the proprietors' rule until 1729, when it, too, became a royal colony.

The division of North and South Carolina

The two Carolinas proved to be wise investments. Both colonies had vast forests of pine trees that provided lumber and other materials for shipbuilding. The sticky pine resin could be boiled to make tar, which was used to waterproof the seams of wooden ships, which is why North Carolinians came to be called Tar Heels.

Rice rather than sugar became the dominant crop in South Carolina because it was perfectly suited to the hot, humid growing conditions. Rice, like sugarcane and tobacco, is a labor-intensive crop, and plantation owners preferred enslaved Africans to work their fields rather than employing indentured servants. This was largely because West Africans had been growing rice for generations. A British traveler noted that rice in the low country could only be profitable through "the labor of slaves."

By the start of the American Revolution in 1775, South Carolina would be the most profitable of the thirteen colonies, and some of its rice planters were among the wealthiest men in the world. It also hosted the most enslaved Blacks, over 100,000 of them compared with only 70,000 Whites. In 1737, the lieutenant governor warned, "Our negroes are very numerous and more dreadful to our safety than any Spanish invaders."

The Middle Colonies and Georgia

The area between New England and the Chesapeake—Maryland and Virginia—included the "middle colonies" of New York, New Jersey, Delaware, and Pennsylvania, which were initially controlled by the Dutch. The Dutch Republic, a coalition of seven provinces also called the Netherlands or Holland, comprised 2 million people who gained their independence from Spanish control in 1581. By 1670, the mostly Protestant Dutch had the largest fleet of merchant ships in the world and controlled northern European trade. They had become one of the most diverse and tolerant societies in Europe—and England's fiercest competitor in international commerce.

New Netherland Becomes New York

The Dutch in North America

The Dutch East India Company (organized in 1602) had hired English sea captain Henry Hudson to explore America in hopes of finding a northwest passage to the Indies. Sailing along the coast of North America in 1609, Hudson crossed Delaware Bay and then sailed ninety miles up the "wide and deep" river that eventually would be named for him. The Hudson River would become one of the most strategically important waterways in America. It was deep enough for oceangoing vessels to travel north into the interior, where the Dutch acquired thousands of beaver and otter pelts harvested by Indians. In exchange, the Indians received iron kettles, axes, knives, weapons, rum, cloth, and various trinkets.

The **New Netherland** colony emerged as a profit-making enterprise owned by a corporation, the Dutch West India Company. "Everyone here is a trader," explained one resident. Like the French, the Dutch were interested mainly in the fur trade, as the European demand for beaver hats created huge profits. In 1610, the Dutch established fur-trading posts on Manhattan Island and upriver at Fort Orange (later called Albany).

New Netherland Dutch colony conquered by the English in 1667, out of which four new colonies were created—New York, New Jersey, Pennsylvania, and Delaware.

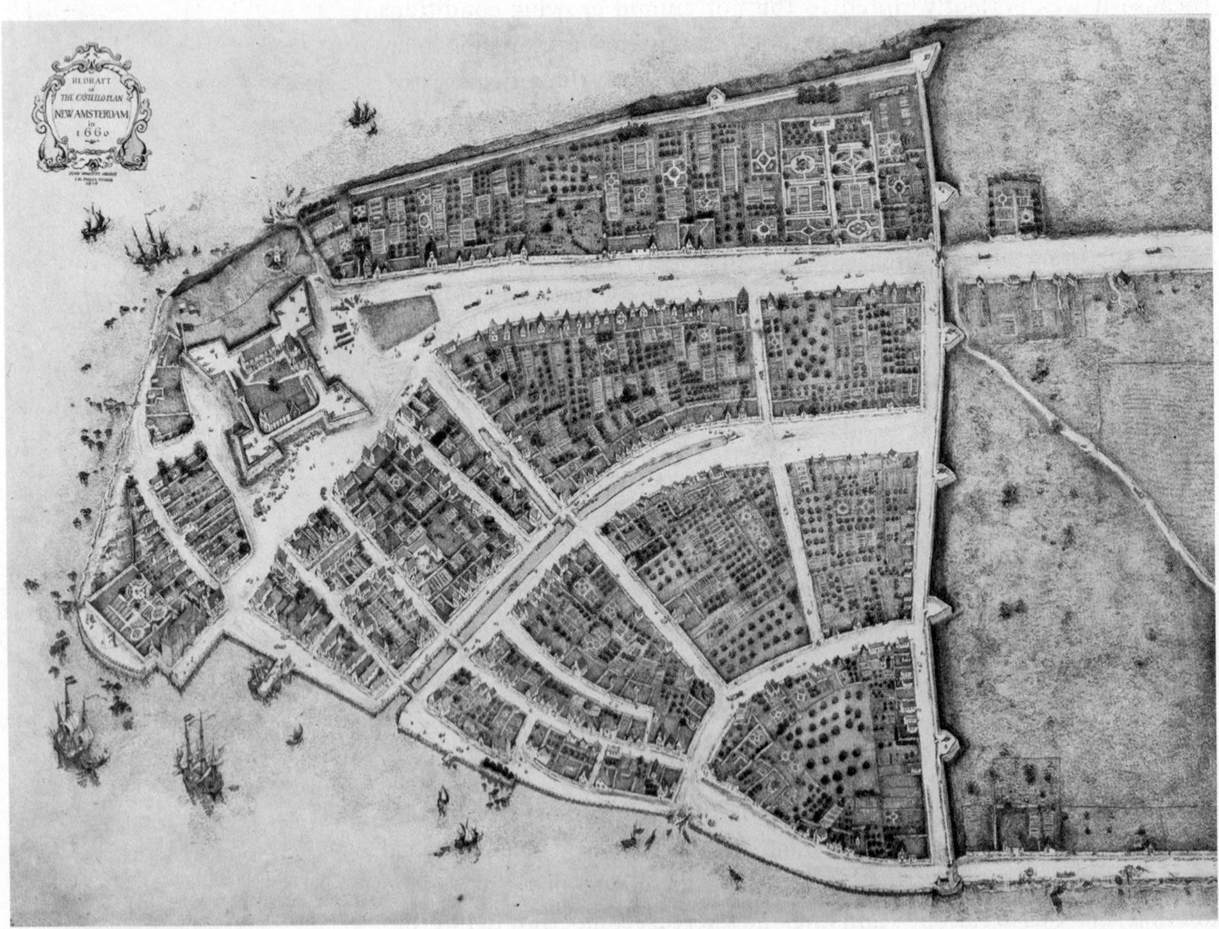

CASTELLO PLAN OF NEW AMSTERDAM A map of New Amsterdam in 1660, shortly before the English took the colony from the Dutch and christened it New York City.

In 1626, the Dutch governor purchased Manhattan (an Indian word meaning "island of many hills") from the Indians for 60 guilders, or about $1,000 in current value. The Dutch then built a fort and a fur-trading post at the lower end of the island. The village of New Amsterdam (eventually New York City), which grew up around the fort, became the capital of New Netherland. The Dutch West India Company controlled political life in New Netherland. It appointed the colony's governor and advisory council and prohibited any form of elected legislature. All commerce with the Netherlands had to be carried in the company's ships, and the company controlled the fur trade with the Indians.

JEWISH CEMETERY
A seventeenth-century Jewish cemetery in New York City shows the legacy of religious diversity in New Amsterdam, enduring even as the city developed around it.

In 1629, the Dutch West India Company, needing more settlers outside Manhattan to protect the colony from Indian attacks, awarded wealthy individuals large estates called *patroonships.* In exchange, the patroons had to host at least fifty settlers. Like a feudal lord, the *patroon* (from the Latin word for father) provided cattle, tools, and buildings. His tenants paid him rent, used his gristmill for grinding flour, and submitted to a court he established.

Unlike most English colonists, the Dutch embraced ethnic and religious diversity; their passion for profits outweighed their social prejudices. Barely half the residents in the Dutch colony were Dutch. New Netherland welcomed exiles from across Europe: Spanish and German Jews, French Protestants (Huguenots), English Puritans, and Catholics. There were even Muslims in New Amsterdam, where in the 1640s the 500 residents communicated in eighteen different languages.

The Dutch did not show the same tolerance for Native Americans, however. Soldiers regularly massacred neighboring Indians. At Pound Ridge, Anglo-Dutch soldiers surrounded an Indian village, set it ablaze, and killed all who tried to escape. Such horrific acts led the Indians to respond in kind.

The first Jewish settlers

Dutch tolerance had other limitations. In September 1654, a French ship arrived in New Amsterdam harbor carrying twenty-three *Sephardim,* Jews of Spanish-Portuguese descent. They had come seeking refuge from Portuguese-controlled Brazil and were the first Jewish settlers to arrive in North America. The colonial governor, Peter Stuyvesant, refused to accept them. He dismissed Jews as a "deceitful race" and "hateful enemies." Dutch officials overruled him, however, pointing out that it would be "unreasonable and unfair" to refuse to provide the Jews a haven. They wanted to "allow everyone to have his own belief, as long as he behaves quietly and legally, gives no offense to his neighbor, and does not oppose the government."

Not until the late seventeenth century could Jews worship in public, however. Such restrictions help explain why the American Jewish community grew so slowly. In 1773, more than 100 years after the first refugees arrived, Jews represented only one-tenth of 1 percent of the entire colonial population. Not until the nineteenth century would the Jewish community in the United States witness dramatic growth.

In 1626, the Dutch West India Company began importing enslaved Africans to meet its labor shortage. By the 1650s, New Amsterdam had one of the largest slave markets in America.

The extraordinary success of the Dutch economy also proved to be its downfall, however. Like imperial Spain, the Dutch Empire expanded too rapidly. The Dutch dominated the European trade with China, India, Africa, Brazil, and the Caribbean, but they could not control their far-flung possessions, and it did not take long for European rivals to exploit the sprawling empire's weak points. The Dutch in North American especially distrusted the English. A New Netherlander complained that the English were a people "of so proud a nature that they thought everything belonged to them."

England seizes New Netherland

In London, King Charles II decided to seize New Netherland. In 1664, the residents of New Amsterdam balked when Governor Stuyvesant called on them to defend the colony against an English invasion fleet. After the English surrounded New Amsterdam and threatened the "absolute ruin and destruction of fifteen hundred innocent souls," Stuyvesant surrendered the colony without firing a shot.

The Dutch negotiated an unusual surrender agreement that allowed New Netherlanders to retain their property, churches, language, and local officials. The English renamed the harbor city of New Amsterdam as New York, in honor of James Stuart, the Duke of York and the king's brother, who had led the successful invasion. As a reward, the king granted his sibling the entire Dutch region of New Netherland and named it for him: New York.

New Jersey

Shortly after the conquest of New Netherland, James Stuart, the Duke of York, granted the lands between the Hudson and Delaware Rivers to Sir George Carteret and Lord John Berkeley (brother of Virginia's governor) and named the territory for Carteret's native Jersey, an island in the English Channel. In 1676, by mutual agreement, New Jersey was divided into East and West Jersey, with Carteret taking the east, Berkeley the west.

New settlements arose in East Jersey. Disaffected Puritans from the New Haven colony in Connecticut founded Newark, Carteret's brother brought a group to found Elizabethtown, and a group of Scots founded Perth Amboy. In the west, a scattering of Swedes, Finns, and Dutch remained, but they were soon overwhelmed by swarms of English and Welsh Quakers, as well as German and Scots-Irish settlers.

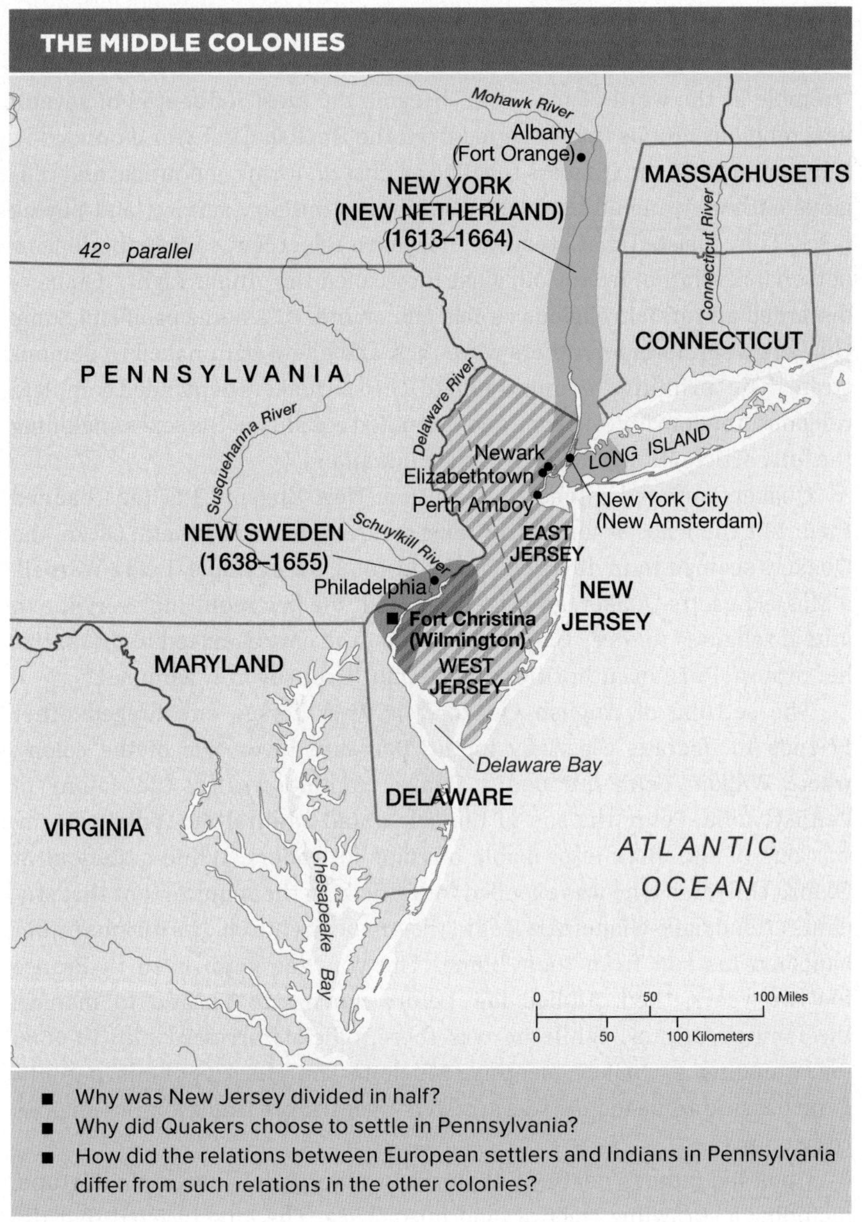

THE MIDDLE COLONIES

- Why was New Jersey divided in half?
- Why did Quakers choose to settle in Pennsylvania?
- How did the relations between European settlers and Indians in Pennsylvania differ from such relations in the other colonies?

The Scots-Irish were mostly Presbyterian Scots recruited by the English government during the first half of the seventeenth century to migrate to Ulster, in northern Ireland, and thereby dilute the appeal of Catholicism and anti-English rebellions. Many of them struggled to make a living in Ulster. One of them highlighted the benefits of life in America: "The price of land [here] is so low . . . forty or fifty pounds will purchase as much ground [in America] as one thousand pounds [would buy in Ireland]. In 1702, East and West Jersey were united as the single royal colony of New Jersey.

Pennsylvania

The Society of Friends, known as Quakers because they were supposed to "tremble at the word of the Lord," became the most influential of several new religious groups that emerged from the English Civil War. Founded in England in 1647, the Quakers rebelled against *all* forms of political and religious authority, including salaried ministers, military service, and paying taxes. They insisted that everyone, not just a select few, could experience a personal revelation from God, what they called the "Inner Light." Quakers discarded all formal religious rituals and embraced a fierce pacifism. Some Quakers went barefoot, others wore rags, and a few went naked to demonstrate their "primitive" commitment to Christ. Quakers demanded complete religious freedom for everyone and promoted equality of the sexes, including the full participation of women in religious affairs.

Persecution of Quakers

Quakers suffered intense persecution. New England Puritans banned them, slit their noses, lopped off their ears, and executed them. Often, the Quakers seemed to invite such abuse. In 1663, for example, Lydia Wardell, a Massachusetts Quaker, grew so upset with the law requiring everyone to attend religious services that she arrived at the church naked to dramatize her protest. Puritan authorities ordered her "to be severely whipped."

The settling of English Quakers in West Jersey encouraged other Friends to migrate, especially to the Delaware River side of the colony, where William Penn founded a Quaker commonwealth, the colony of Pennsylvania. Penn, the son of the celebrated admiral Sir William Penn, was one of the most improbable of colonial leaders. While a student at Oxford University, he was expelled for criticizing the requirement that students attend daily chapel services in the Anglican church. His furious father banished his son from their home. The younger Penn lived in France for two years, then studied law before moving to Ireland to manage the family's estates. While he was there, officials arrested him in 1666 for attending a Quaker meeting. Much to the chagrin of his parents, Penn became a Quaker and was arrested several more times for his religious convictions.

Quaker-controlled Pennsylvania

Upon his father's death, William Penn inherited a substantial fortune, including a sprawling tract of land in America. The king insisted that the land be named in honor of Penn's father—Pennsylvania (literally, Penn's Woods). Unlike John Winthrop in Massachusetts, Penn encouraged people of all faiths, nations, and social standing to live together in harmony. By the end of 1681, thousands of immigrants embracing different religions had settled in his new colony, and a town was emerging at the junction of the Schuylkill and Delaware Rivers. Penn called it Philadelphia (meaning City of Brotherly Love).

The relations between the Native Americans and the Pennsylvania Quakers were unusually good because of the Quakers' friendliness and Penn's policy of purchasing land titles from Native Americans. Penn told the Delaware Nation that he wanted to enjoy the land "with your love and consent, that way we may always live together as neighbors and friends." For some fifty years, the Pennsylvania colonists and Native Americans lived in peace.

The colony's government resembled that of other proprietary colonies except that the freemen (owners of at least fifty acres) elected the council members as well as the assembly. The governor had no veto, although Penn, as proprietor, did. Penn hoped to show that a colonial government could abide by Quaker principles. It could maintain peace and order, while demonstrating that religion could flourish without government support and with absolute freedom of conscience.

Over time, however, the Quakers struggled to forge a harmonious colony. In Pennsylvania's first ten years, it went through six governors. A disappointed Penn, who only visited his colony twice, wrote from London: "Pray [please] stop those scurvy quarrels that break out to the disgrace of the province." Even more ironic was that as Penn's colony began to flourish, he slid into poverty, eventually landing in debtor's prison.

Delaware

In 1682, the Duke of York granted William Penn the area known as Delaware. It was another part of the former Dutch territory (which had been New Sweden before being acquired by the Dutch in 1655). Delaware took its name from the Delaware River, which had been named to honor Thomas West, Baron De La Warr (1577–1618), Virginia's first colonial governor. Delaware became part of Pennsylvania, but after 1704 it was granted the right to choose its legislative assembly. From then until the American Revolution, Delaware had a separate assembly but shared Pennsylvania's governor.

Georgia

The last English colony to be founded, Georgia, emerged a half century after Pennsylvania. During the seventeenth century, settlers pushed southward into the borderlands between Carolina and Spanish Florida. They brought enslaved Africans and a desire to win the Indian trade from the Spanish. Each side used guns, gifts, and rum to court the Native Americans, and they, in turn, played the English against the Spanish.

Georgia established for the "worthy poor"

In 1732, King George II gave the land between the Savannah and Altamaha Rivers to twenty-one trustees appointed to govern the Province of Georgia, named in honor of the king. Georgia provided a military buffer against Spanish Florida. It also served as a social experiment by bringing together settlers from different countries and religions, many of them refugees, debtors, or members of the "worthy poor." General James E. Oglethorpe, a prominent member of Parliament, was appointed to head the colony.

In 1733, about 120 colonists established Savannah on the Atlantic coast near the Savannah River. Carefully laid out by Oglethorpe, the town, with its geometric pattern of crisscrossing roads graced by numerous parks, remains a splendid example of city planning. Protestant refugees from

SAVANNAH, GEORGIA The earliest known view of Savannah, Georgia (1734). The town's layout was carefully planned to incorporate parks and public spaces, and today constitutes one of the country's biggest National Historic Landmark Districts.

Austria began to arrive in 1734, followed by Germans and German-speaking Moravians and Swiss, who for a time made the colony more German than English. The addition of Welsh, Highland Scots, Sephardic Jews, and others gave the early colony a diverse ethnic character like that of Charleston, South Carolina.

As a buffer against Spanish Florida, the colony succeeded, but as a social experiment creating a "common man's utopia," Georgia failed. Initially, landholdings were limited to 500 acres to promote economic equality. Rum was banned, and the importation of the enslaved was forbidden. The idealistic rules soon collapsed, however, as the colony struggled to become self-sufficient. The regulations against rum and slavery were widely disregarded and finally abandoned. By 1759, all restrictions on landholding had been removed.

In 1752, Georgia became a royal colony. It developed slowly but boomed in population and wealth after 1763, when it came to resemble the plantation society in South Carolina. Georgians exported rice, lumber, beef, and pork, and they carried on a lively trade with the islands in the West Indies. Almost unintentionally, the colony had become an economic success and a slave-centered society.

Native Peoples and English Settlers

> CORE **OBJECTIVE**
> **3.** Analyze the ways by which English colonists and Native Americans adapted to each other's presence.

The process of creating English colonies in America did not occur in a vacuum: Native Americans played a crucial role in the development of British America. Most English colonists adopted a different strategy for dealing with the Indians than the French and the Dutch used. Merchants from France and the Netherlands focused on exploiting the profitable fur trade. The thriving commerce in animal skins—especially beaver, otter, and deer—helped spur exploration of the vast American continent. Yet it both enriched and devastated the lives of Indians. To acquire fur pelts from the Indians, the French and Dutch built trading outposts in upper New York and along the Great Lakes. There they established friendly relations with the Hurons, Algonquian, and other Indians, who greatly outnumbered them. The Hurons and Algonquians also sought French support in their ongoing wars with the mighty Iroquois Nations. In contrast, the English colonists were more interested in pursuing their "God-given" right to hunt and farm on Indian lands and to fish in Indian waters.

Food and Land

The English settled along the Atlantic Seabord, where Indian populations were much smaller than those in Mexico or on the islands in the Caribbean. Moreover, the Indigenous peoples of North America were fragmented, often fighting among themselves over disputed lands.

The Jamestown settlers had come to America expecting to find gold, friendly Indians, and easy living. Most did not know how to exploit the area's abundant game and fish. When some of the starving Jamestown residents tried to steal food from Indian villages, the Indians ambushed and killed them. One colonist was captured, skinned alive by Indian women using oyster shells, and then burned. Only the capable leadership of Captain John Smith and timely trade with the Indians, who taught the colonists to grow corn, enabled a remnant of the original colonists to survive.

> Battles over Indian lands

By 1616, the discovery that tobacco flourished in Virginia intensified the settlers' lust for more land. English tobacco planters coveted Indian fields because they had been cleared and were ready to be planted. In 1622, the Indians tried to repel the land-grabbing English. Captain Smith reported that the "wild, naked natives" attacked twenty-eight farms and plantations along the James River, "not sparing either age or sex, man, woman, or child," killing a fourth of the settlers. The English retaliated by decimating the Indians of Virginia. Smith said the colonists were determined to "force the Savages to leave their Country."

Bacon's Rebellion

> Intensified conflict with Indians

The relentless stream of settlers into Virginia produced growing tensions with the Indians. The wealthiest planters seized the most fertile land along the coast and rivers, compelling freed servants to become farmworkers

STRANGE NEWS
FROM
VIRGINIA;
Being a full and true
ACCOUNT
OF THE
LIFE and DEATH
OF
Nathanael Bacon Efquire,

Who was the only Caufe and Original of all the late Troubles in that COUNTRY.

With a full Relation of all the Accidents which have happened in the late War there between the Chriftians and Indians.

LONDON,
Printed for *William Harris*, next door to the Turn-Stile without *Moor-gate*. 1677.

NEWS OF THE REBELLION
A pamphlet printed in London provided details about Bacon's Rebellion to the British public, curious to hear the "strange news from Virginia."

or forcing them to move inland if they wanted farms of their own. In either case, the impoverished English settlers found themselves at a disadvantage. By 1676, one fourth of the free White men were landless. They were forced to roam the countryside, squatting on private property, working at odd jobs, poaching game, or committing other petty crimes to survive.

In the mid-1670s, simmering tensions caused by falling tobacco prices (stemming from overproduction), rising taxes, and crowds of landless freed servants sparked what came to be called **Bacon's Rebellion**. The discontent erupted when a squabble between a White planter and Indians on the Potomac River led to the murder of the planter's herdsman. Frontier vigilantes retaliated by killing some two dozen Indians. Enraged Indians took revenge by attacking frontier settlements.

Scattered attacks continued southward to the James River, where Indians killed Nathaniel Bacon's farm manager. In 1676, when Governor William Berkeley refused to attack the Indian raiders, Bacon organized a rebel group to terrorize the "protected and darling Indians." He pledged he would kill all the Indians in Virginia.

The rebellion became a battle of landless servants, small farmers, and even enslaved Africans against Virginia's wealthiest planters and political leaders. Bacon, however, was also the spoiled son of a wealthy family and had a talent for trouble. The vicious assaults by his followers against peaceful Indians and his greed for power and land sparked the conflict with the governing authorities and the planter elite.

Governor Berkeley declared Bacon a rebel, ordered him arrested, and challenged him to a duel with swords (Bacon declined). Thereafter, the colony plunged into civil war. Berkeley opposed Bacon's plan to destroy the Indians, not because he liked Native Americans but because he did not want to disrupt the deerskin trade. Bacon, whose ragtag "army" now numbered in the hundreds, issued a "Declaration of the People of Virginia" accusing Berkeley of corruption and attempted to take the governor into custody. Berkeley's forces resisted—feebly—and Bacon's men burned Jamestown in frustration. Bacon, however, fell ill from dysentery and died a month later, after which the rebellion disintegrated. Berkeley, disappointed that Bacon had died before he could be executed, satisfied his wrath by having twenty-three of Bacon's lieutenants hanged. For such severity, King Charles II denounced Berkeley and recalled him to England in 1677, where he died within a year.

Bacon's Rebellion (1676)
Unsuccessful revolt led by planter Nathaniel Bacon against Virginia governor William Berkeley's administration, which, Bacon charged, had failed to protect settlers from Indian raids.

Native Americans and Christianity

In the spring of 1621, the Pilgrims in Plymouth were struggling with hunger and disease, just as the Jamestown settlers had before them. And as was true in Virginia, the food and advice provided by Indians were crucial to their survival. Nevertheless, once they were established, the New England Puritans aggressively tried to convert Native Americans to Christianity and "civilized" living. They insisted that Indians abandon their religions and languages, their clothes, long hair, names, and villages, and forced them to move to what was called praying towns to separate them from their "heathen" brethren.

Religious conversion and land confiscation

One of the reasons that Roger Williams of Rhode Island was considered so dangerous by Puritan leaders was his insistence that all faiths, including those of Indians, should be treated equally.

The Pequot War

Most New England Puritans, like the colonists in Virginia, viewed Indians as demonic savages, "barbarous creatures," "merciless and cruel heathens." As one colonist asserted, Indians had no place in a "new England."

Bloody war between Puritans and Pequots

In 1636, settlers in Massachusetts accused a Pequot of murdering a colonist; they took revenge by setting fire to a Pequot village. As Indians fled the flames, the Puritans killed them—men, women, and children. William Bradford, the governor of Plymouth, acknowledged that it was "a fearful sight to see them thus frying in the fire," but "the victory seemed a sweet sacrifice" provided by God.

ALGONQUIAN CEREMONY As with most Native Americans, Algonquian religious beliefs were shaped by their dependence on nature for survival, as illustrated in this celebration of the harvest.

Sassacus, the Pequot chief, organized the survivors and counter-attacked. During the ensuing Pequot War of 1636–1637, the colonists and their Mohegan and Narragansett allies killed hundreds of Pequots, including unarmed women and children, in their village near West Mystic, in the Connecticut River Valley. Under the terms of the Treaty of Hartford (1638), the Pequot Nation was dissolved.

KING PHILIP'S WAR A 1772 engraving by Paul Revere depicts Metacom (King Philip), leader of the Wampanoags. **How does this representation of King Philip compare with John White's sketch of a Native American chief on p. 18?**

King Philip's War

After the Pequot War, relations between colonists and Indians improved, but the era of peaceful coexistence came to a bloody end during the last quarter of the seventeenth century. Native American leaders, especially the chief of the Wampanoags, Metacomet (known to the colonists as King Philip), resented the English efforts to convert Indians to Christianity. In the fall of 1674, John Sassamon, a Christian Indian who had graduated from Harvard College, warned the English that the Wampanoags were preparing for war. A few months later, Sassamon was found dead in a frozen pond. Colonial authorities convicted three Wampanoags of murder and hanged them. Enraged Wampanoag warriors then burned Puritan farms on June 20, 1675. Three days later, an Englishman shot a Wampanoag, and the Wampanoags retaliated by ambushing and beheading a group of Puritans. (One colonist had his stomach ripped open and a Bible stuffed inside.)

The gruesome violence soon spun out of control in what came to be called **King Philip's War (1675–1678)**, or Metacomet's War. The fighting killed more people in proportion to the population than any American conflict since. Vengeful bands of warriors destroyed fifty colonial towns while killing and mutilating hundreds of men, women, and children. Rival Indians fought on both sides.

Within a year, the colonists launched a surprise attack that killed 300 Narragansett warriors and 400 women and children. The Narragansetts retaliated by destroying Providence, Rhode Island. The situation grew so desperate that the colonies passed America's first conscription laws, drafting males into the militia.

King Philip's War (1675–1678) A war in New England resulting from the escalation of tensions between Native Americans and English settlers; the defeat of the Native Americans led to broadened freedoms for the settlers and their dispossessing the region's Native Americans of most of their land.

In the end, 5 percent of the colony's male English population died during the war. The Wampanoags and their allies suffered even higher casualty rates. Some surrendered, many succumbed to disease, and others fled westward. Those who remained were forced to move to villages supervised by English officials. Metacomet escaped, only to be hunted down and killed. The victorious colonists marched his severed head to Plymouth, where it sat atop a pole for twenty years—a grisly reminder of the English determination to ensure their dominance over Native Americans.

Enslaving Indians in Carolina

Unlike the New England experience, English colonists in Carolina developed a profitable trade with Indians. By 1690, traders from Charles Town

CHEROKEE CHIEFS A print depicting seven Cherokee chiefs who had been taken from Carolina to England in 1730.

had made their way up the Savannah River to arrange deals with the Cherokees, Creeks, and Chickasaws. Between 1699 and 1715, Carolina exported to England an average of 54,000 deerskins per year. The valuable hides were transformed into leather gloves, belts, hats, work aprons, and book bindings. The growing trade in deerskins entwined Indians in a dependent relationship with Europeans that would prove disastrous to their traditional way of life. Beyond seizing and enslaving Indians, English traders provided firearms and rum as payment for their capturing rivals to be sold into slavery.

Native American slave trade

The profitability of captive Indian workers, compared to enslaved Africans and servants, prompted a frenzy of slaving activity. As many as 50,000 Indians, most of them women and children, were sold into slavery in Charleston. Thousands more were sold to "slavers" who took them to Caribbean islands. The growing trade in enslaved Native Americans triggered bitter struggles between rival Indian nations, ignited unprecedented colonial warfare, and generated massive internal migrations across the southern colonies.

The Iroquois League

Iroquois relations with French and English

One of the most significant effects of European settlement in North America during the seventeenth century was the intensification of warfare among Indians. The same combination of forces that wiped out the Indian populations of New England and Carolina affected the Indigenous peoples around New York City and the Lower Hudson Valley. The inability of various Indian groups to unite against the Europeans, as well as their vulnerability to infectious diseases, doomed them to conquest and exploitation.

In the interior of New York, however, a different situation arose. There, sometime before 1600, the Iroquois Nations had forged an alliance so strong that the outnumbered Dutch and, later, English traders were forced to work with them to acquire beaver pelts. By the early seventeenth century, some fifty sachems (chiefs) governed the 12,000 members of the **Iroquois League**,

Iroquois League An alliance of the Iroquois Nations, originally formed sometime between 1450 and 1600, that used their combined strength to pressure Europeans to work with them in the fur trade and to wage war across what is today eastern North America.

known to its members as the *Haudenosaunee*. Its capital was Onondaga, a bustling town a few miles south of what later became Syracuse, New York.

The League was governed by a remarkable constitution, called the Great Law of Peace, which had three main principles: peace, equity, and justice. Each person was to be a shareholder in the tribe's wealth or poverty. The constitution established a Great Council of fifty male *royaneh* (religious-political leaders), each representing one of the female-led clans of the Iroquois Nations. The Great Law of Peace gave power to the people. It insisted that every time the *royaneh* dealt with "an especially important matter or a great emergency," they had to "submit the matter to the decision of their people," both men and women.

WAMPUM BELT Woven to certify treaties or record transactions, the white squares on this belt likely denote nations and alliances, while the purple likely conveys apprehension.

The search for furs and captives led Iroquois war parties to range widely across eastern North America. For more than twenty years, warfare raged across the Great Lakes region between the Iroquois (supported by Dutch and English fur traders) and the Algonquian and Hurons (and their French allies). In the 1690s, the French and their Indian allies destroyed Iroquois crops and villages, infected them with smallpox and other diseases, and reduced the male population by more than a third. Facing extermination, the Iroquois made peace with the French in 1701. During the first half of the eighteenth century, they played the English off against the French while creating a thriving fur trade for themselves.

CORE **OBJECTIVE**

4. Analyze the role of indentured servants and the development of slavery in colonial America.

Servitude and Slavery in the Colonies

Indentured Servitude

Indentured servitude solves the labor shortage

During the seventeenth century, the English colonies, especially Virginia and Maryland, grew so fast that they needed many more workers than there were settlers. The colonies needed what a planter called "lusty laboring men . . . capable of hard labor, and that can bear and undergo heat and cold."

indentured servants Settlers who signed on for a temporary period of servitude to a master in exchange for passage to the New World.

To solve the labor shortage, the planters first recruited **indentured servants** from England, Ireland, Scotland, and continental Europe. The term derived from the *indenture*, or contract, which enabled a person to pay for passage to America by promising to work for a fixed number of years (usually between three and seven). As tobacco production soared, indentured servants did most of the work. Of the 500,000 English immigrants to America from 1610 to 1775, some 350,000 came as indentured servants. Not all servants came voluntarily. Many homeless children in London were "kid-napped" and sold into servitude in America. Also, Parliament in 1717 declared that convicts could avoid prison or the hangman by relocating to the colonies.

Once in the colonies, servants were provided food and a bed, but life was harsh, and their rights were limited. As a Pennsylvania judge explained in 1793, indentured servants occupied "a middle rank between slaves and free men." They could own property but could not engage in trade. Marriage required the master's permission. Masters could whip servants and extend their length of service as punishment for bad behavior. Once the indenture ended, the servant could claim the "freedom dues" set by custom and law: a little money, a few tools, some clothing and food, and occasionally small tracts of land. Some former servants did very well. In 1629, seven members of the Virginia legislature were former indentured servants.

JUST ARRIVED,
THE SEARSDALE, Capt. REED,
with one hundred thirty-nine healthy
SERVANTS,
Men, women, and boys,
Among which are many tradeſmen, viz.
SMITHS, bricklayers, plaiſterers, ſhoemakers, houſe-carpenters and joiners, weavers, barbers and perukemakers, a clerk, a hatter, a rope-maker, a plumber, a glazier, a taylor, a printer, a bookbinder, a painter, a matuamaker, ſeveral ſempſtreſſes, and others; there are alſo farmers, waggoners, and other country labourers. The ſale will commence on *Wedneſday* the 10th of *October*, at *Leeds* town, on *Rappahannock*. A reaſonable credit will be allowed, giving bond with approved ſecurity, to
THOMAS HODGE.

INDENTURED SERVANTS An advertisement from the *Virginia Gazette*, October 4, 1779, publicizing the upcoming sale of indentured servants. **What does this advertisement indicate about the people who entered into indentured servitude?**
Earl Gregg Swem Library, Special Collections Research Center, William & Mary Libraries

African Slavery in North America

Growth of slavery in the colonies

In 1700, there were enslaved Africans in every colony, and they made up 11 percent of the total population (the enslaved would constitute more than 20 percent by 1770). Slavery in English North America differed significantly from region to region, however. Africans were a tiny minority in New England (about 2 percent). Because there were no large plantations there and less need for forced labor, "family slavery" prevailed, with both owners and the owned usually living under the same roof.

Slavery was much more common in the Chesapeake colonies and the Carolinas, where large plantations dominated. By 1730, the enslaved Black population in Virginia and Maryland had become the first in the Western Hemisphere to achieve a self-sustaining rate of population growth. By 1750, about 80 percent of the enslaved Blacks in the Chesapeake region had been born there.

African Roots

The transport of African captives, mostly young, across the Atlantic to the Americas was the most massive forced migration in world history. More than 10 million Africans eventually made the terrifying journey; the vast majority went to Brazil or the Caribbean sugar islands.

Enslaved Africans came from different places in Africa, spoke as many as fifty distinct languages, and worshipped diverse gods. Some had lived in large kingdoms and others in dispersed villages. In their homelands, warfare was

THE AFRICAN SLAVE TRADE, 1500–1800

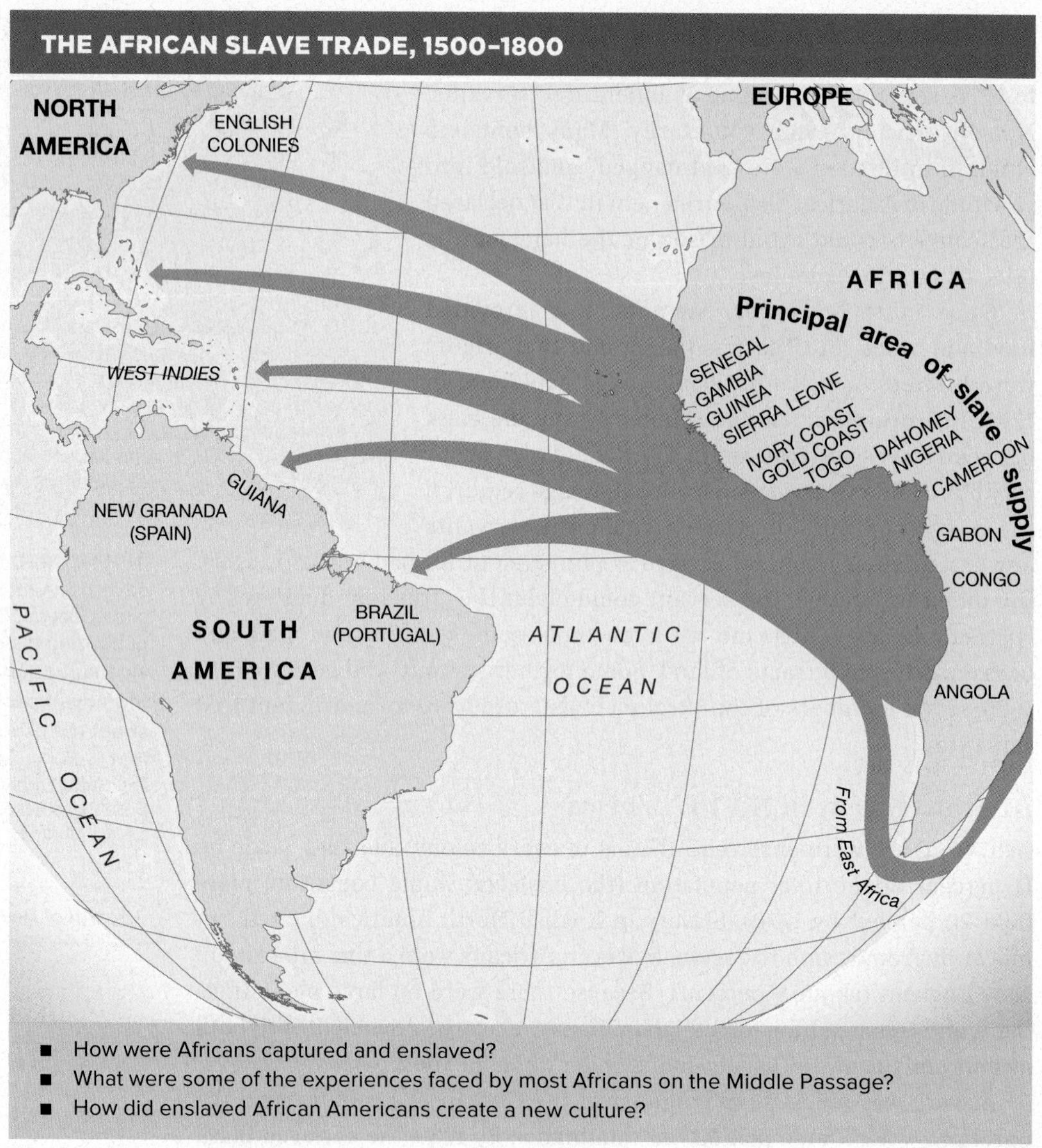

- How were Africans captured and enslaved?
- What were some of the experiences faced by most Africans on the Middle Passage?
- How did enslaved African Americans create a new culture?

as common as in Europe, as rival warriors conquered, kidnapped, enslaved, and sold one another.

During the seventeenth and eighteenth centuries, African slave traders brought captives to dozens of "slave forts" built along the West African coast, where they were sold to Europeans. Few of the captives had ever seen the ocean, a sailing ship, or a White person. Once purchased, the millions destined for slavery were branded with a company mark, chained, and crowded into slave ships. Forced to stay below deck, they were packed as tightly as livestock in the constant darkness. With no bedding, they slept in their own urine and excrement. Only twice a day were they allowed to go above deck for fresh air and exercise.

Middle Passage The hellish and often deadly middle leg of the transatlantic "triangular trade" in which European ships carried manufactured goods to Africa, then transported enslaved Africans to the Americas and the Caribbean, and finally conveyed American agricultural products back to Europe.

The transatlantic voyage of the slave ships was known as the **Middle Passage** because it served as the middle leg of the so-called triangular

SLAVE SHIP One in six Africans died from the brutal and cramped conditions while crossing the Atlantic in ships like this one, from an American diagram ca. 1808.

trade. On the first leg, European ships carried rum, clothing, household goods, and guns to Africa, which they exchanged for enslaved Africans. The captives then were taken on the second (or "middle") leg of the triangular trade to the Americas. Once the human cargo was unloaded, the ships were filled with timber, tobacco, rice, sugar, rum, and other products for the return voyage to English and European ports.

The Middle Passage was horrific. One in six African captives died along the way. Almost one in ten of these floating prisons experienced a slave revolt. Some captives committed suicide by jumping off the ships. Almost half the 12.5 million enslaved Africans went to Brazil. Jamaica received over a million, almost twice as many as were sent to America.

Those in the business of trading enslaved Africans justified their activities by embracing a widespread racism that viewed Africans as beasts of burden rather than human beings. Once in America, Africans were treated as property (chattel), herded in chains to public slave auctions, and sold to the highest bidder. Their owners required them to cook and clean; care for the owner's babies and children; dig ditches; drain swamps; clear, plant, and tend fields; and feed livestock.

AFRICAN HERITAGE IN THE SOUTH The survival of African culture among enslaved Americans is evident in this late-eighteenth-century painting of a South Carolina plantation. The musical instruments and pottery are of African (probably Yoruban) origin.

On large southern plantations that grew tobacco, sugarcane, or rice, the enslaved worked in gangs supervised by Black "drivers" and White overseers. The enslaved people were often housed in crude barracks, fed like livestock, and issued ill-fitting work clothes and shoes so uncomfortable that many enslaved people preferred to go barefoot. To ensure that they worked hard and did not cause trouble, they were whipped, branded, shackled, castrated, or sold away, often to the Caribbean islands, where few survived the harsh working conditions.

Slave Culture

Enslaved Africans, however, found ingenious ways to resist. Some rebelled by resisting work orders, sabotaging crops, stealing tools, faking illness or injury, or running away. If caught, the freedom seekers faced certain punishment—whipping, branding, and even the severing of an Achilles tendon. Runaways also faced uncertain freedom. Where would they run *to* in a society ruled by Whites and governed by racism?

African and American cultural exchange

In the process of being forced into lives of bondage in a new world, Africans from diverse homelands forged a new identity as African Americans. At the same time, they wove into American culture many strands of their African heritage, including new words that entered the language, such as *tabby, tote, goober, yam,* and *banana,* as well as the names of the Coosaw, Pee Dee, and Wando Rivers in South Carolina. More significant are African influences upon American music, folklore, and religious practices. The enslaved often used songs, stories, and religious preachings to circulate coded messages expressing their distaste for owners or overseers. The fundamental theme of Black religion, adapted from the Christianity they were forced to embrace, was deliverance. God, many of them believed, would eventually open the gates to heaven's promised land.

CORE **OBJECTIVE**

5. Explain how the English colonies became the most populous, prosperous, and powerful region in North America by 1700.

Thriving Colonies

By the early eighteenth century, England's colonies had outstripped those of both the French and the Spanish as tensions among the three major European powers grew. English America, both the mainland colonies and those in the Caribbean, had become the most populous, prosperous, and powerful of the European empires. American colonists were better fed, clothed, and housed than their counterparts in Europe, where a majority of the people lived in landless poverty. This higher standard of living for "white" colonists was in part built on the lands taken from Native Americans, the coerced labor of enslaved Africans and Native Americans, and the trading of goods in the Atlantic World.

The American colonists enjoyed crucial advantages over their European rivals. The tightly controlled colonial empires created by the monarchs of Spain and France stifled innovation. By contrast, the English and Dutch organized colonies as profit-making enterprises with a minimum of royal control. Where New Spain was dominated by wealthy men, many of whom intended to return to Spain, many English colonists ventured to America because, for them, life in England had grown intolerable. The leaders of the Dutch and non-Puritan English colonies, unlike the Spanish and French, welcomed people from many nationalities and religions who came in search of a new life. Perhaps most important, the English colonies enjoyed a greater degree of self-government, which made them more dynamic and innovative than their French and Spanish counterparts.

Organized for profit and self-governing, with widespread land ownership

Throughout the seventeenth century, geography reinforced England's emphasis on concentrated settlements in America. No single great river offered a highway to the interior. The farthest westward expansion of English settlement stopped at the eastern slopes of the Appalachian Mountains. To the east of the mainland colonies lay the Atlantic Ocean, which served as a highway for the transport of people, ideas, commerce, and ways of life from Europe to America. The Atlantic, however, also provided a barrier separating old ideas from new, allowing the English colonies to evolve in new ways in a "new world"—while developing new ideas about economic freedom and political liberties that would flower in the eighteenth century.

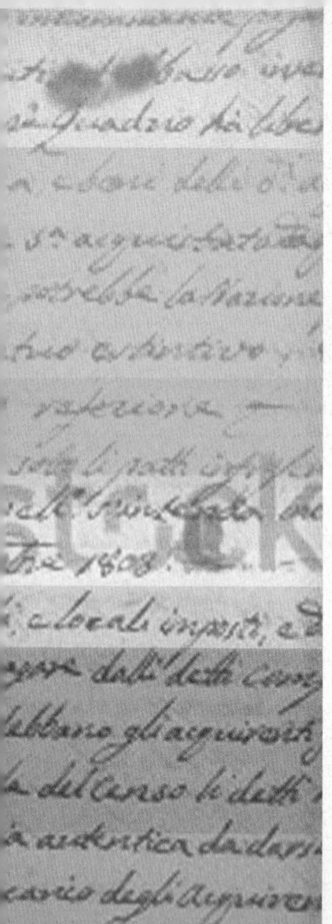

Reviewing the CORE OBJECTIVES | INQUIZITIVE

■ **English Background** England's colonization of North America differed from that of its European rivals. While chartered by the Crown, English colonization was funded by *joint-stock companies,* groups of proprietors eager for profits. Their colonial governments reflected the governmental model of a two-house *Parliament* and long-held English views on civil liberties and representative institutions. The colonization of the eastern seaboard of North America occurred at a time of religious and political turmoil in England, strongly affecting colonial culture and development.

■ **Settling the American Colonies** The early years of Jamestown and Plymouth were grim. The Virginia and Plymouth companies enticed colonists with headrights, or land grants. The *tobacco* economy flourished, but success also initiated a slave-based economy in the South. Sugar and rice plantations developed in the proprietary *Carolina colonies,* which operated with minimal royal intrusion. Family farms and a mixed economy characterized the middle and New England colonies. Religion was the primary motivation for the founding of several colonies. *Puritans* drafted the *Mayflower Compact* and founded *Massachusetts Bay Colony* as a Christian commonwealth. Rhode Island was established by Roger Williams, a religious dissenter from Massachusetts. Maryland was founded as a refuge for English Catholics. William Penn, a Quaker, founded *Pennsylvania* and invited Europe's persecuted religious sects to his colony. The Dutch, allowed members of all faiths to settle in *New Netherland* which was surrendered to the English in 1664.

■ **Indian Relations** Trade with the *Powhatan Confederacy* enabled Jamestown to survive its early years, but brutal armed conflicts such as *Bacon's Rebellion* occurred as settlers invaded Indian lands. Puritans retaliated in the Pequot War of 1636–1637 and *King Philip's War (1675-1678).* Among the chief colonial leaders, only Roger Williams and William Penn treated Indians as equals. The powerful *Iroquois League* played the European powers against each other to control territories.

■ **Indentured Servants and the Enslaved** The colonies increasingly relied on *indentured servants* for their labor supply. By the end of the seventeenth century, however, enslaved Africans had replaced indentured servants as the primary source of labor in the Chesapeake. The demand for coerced labor in the sugar plantations of the West Indies drove European slave traders to organize the transport of Africans via the dreaded *Middle Passage* across the Atlantic. Planters in the Carolinas also adopted African slavery as the preferred labor system. African cultures fused with others in the Americas to create a native-born African American culture.

■ **Thriving English Colonies** By 1700, English America was the most populous and prosperous region of North America. Minimal royal interference in the proprietary for-profit colonies, widespread landownership, and religious diversity attracted a variety of investors.

KEY TERMS

joint-stock companies, *p. 50*

Parliament, *p. 51*

Puritans, *p. 51*

Powhatan Confederacy *p. 54*

tobacco, *p. 57*

headright, *p. 57*

Mayflower Compact (1620), *p. 63*

Massachusetts Bay Colony, *p. 63*

North and South Carolina, *p. 68*

New Netherland, *p. 72*

Bacon's Rebellion (1676), *p. 80*

King Philip's War (1675–1678), *p. 82*

Iroquois League, *p. 83*

indentured servants, *p. 84*

Middle Passage, *p. 86*

CHRONOLOGY

1603 James I becomes king of England

1607 Jamestown established; the first permanent English colony

1612 John Rolfe begins growing tobacco for export

1619 The first enslaved Africans arrive in English America

1620 Plymouth Colony is founded by Pilgrims; Mayflower Compact

1622 War between Indians and colonists begins

1630 Massachusetts Bay Colony is founded

1634 The settlement of Maryland begins

1636–1637 Pequot War in New England

1642–1651 English Civil War (Puritans vs. Royalists)

1649 Toleration Act in Maryland

1660 Restoration of English monarchy

1669 Charles Town is founded in the Carolina colony

1675–1678 King Philip's War in New England

1676 Bacon's Rebellion erupts in Virginia

1681 Pennsylvania is established

1733 Georgia is founded

INQUIZITIVE

Go to InQuizitive to see what you've learned—and learn what you've missed—with personalized feedback along the way.

THE ARTISANS OF BOSTON (1766) While fishing, shipbuilding, and maritime trade dominated New England economies, many young men entered apprenticeships, learning a trade from a master craftsman in the hopes of becoming blacksmiths, carpenters, gunsmiths, printers, candlemakers, leather tanners, and more.

CHAPTER

3

Colonial Ways of Life

1607–1750

The process of carving a new civilization out of an abundant New World involved often-violent encounters among European, African, and Indian cultures. War, duplicity, conquest, displacement, and enslavement were the tragic results. On another level, however, the process of transforming the American continent was a story of blending and accommodation, of diverse peoples and resilient cultures engaged in the everyday tasks of building homes, planting crops, trading goods, raising families, enforcing laws, and worshipping their gods.

Those who colonized America during the seventeenth and eighteenth centuries were part of a massive social migration occurring throughout Europe and Africa. Everywhere, it seemed, people were in motion—moving from farms to villages, from villages to cities, and from homelands to colonies.

Most of the Europeans who migrated to America were responding to powerful social and economic forces. Rapid population growth and the rise of commercial agriculture squeezed poor farmworkers off the land and into cities, where they struggled to survive. That most Europeans in the seventeenth and eighteenth centuries were desperately poor helps explain why so many were willing to risk their lives by journeying to the American colonies. Others sought political security or religious freedom.

CORE OBJECTIVES INQUIZITIVE

1. Explain the major factors that contributed to the demographic changes in the English colonies during the eighteenth century.
2. Describe women's various roles in the English colonies.
3. Compare the societies and economies of the southern, New England, and middle colonies.
4. Describe the creation of race-based slavery during the seventeenth century and its impact on the social and economic development of colonial America.
5. Analyze the impact of the Enlightenment and Great Awakening on the colonies.

A tragic exception was the Africans, who were captured and transported to new lands against their will.

Those who initially settled in colonial America were mostly young (more than half were under twenty-five), male, and poor, and almost half were indentured servants or enslaved people. During the eighteenth century, England would transport some 50,000 convicts to the British colonies to relieve its own overcrowded jails and to address the constant demand for more workers in North America. Once in America, many of the newcomers kept moving in search of better lands or new business opportunities. This extraordinary mosaic of adventurous people created America's enduring institutions and values as well as its distinctive spirit and restless energy.

CORE **OBJECTIVE**

1. Explain the major factors that contributed to the demographic changes in the English colonies during the eighteenth century.

The Shape of Early America

Population Growth

Life in colonial America was hard. Many of the first colonists died of disease or starvation; others were killed by Native Americans. The average **death rate** was 50 percent. Once colonial life became more settled, however, the population grew rapidly. On average, it doubled every twenty-five years. By 1750, the number of colonists had passed 1 million; by 1775, it approached 2.5 million. By comparison, the combined population of England, Scotland, and Ireland in 1750 was 6.5 million. An English visitor reported in 1766 that America would surely become "the most prosperous empire the world had ever seen." But that would mean trouble for Britain: "How are we to rule them?"

Plentiful land, scarce labor, and better living conditions

Benjamin Franklin, a keen observer of life in British America, said that the colonial population grew so rapidly because land was plentiful and cheap, and laborers were scarce and expensive. In contrast, Europe suffered from overpopulation and expensive farmland. From this reversal of conditions flowed many of the changes that European culture underwent during the colonization of America—not the least being that land and good fortune lured enterprising immigrants and led the colonists to have large families, in part because farm children could help in the fields.

Birth and Death Rates

Rapid population growth

Colonists tended to marry and start families at an earlier age than was common in Europe. In England, the average age at marriage for women was twenty-five or twenty-six; in America, it was twenty. The **birth rate** rose accordingly, since women who married earlier had time for about two additional pregnancies during their childbearing years. On average, a married woman had a child every two to three years before menopause. Some women had as many as twenty pregnancies (Benjamin Franklin, for example, had sixteen siblings).

death rate Proportion of deaths per 1,000 of the total population; also called *mortality rate*.

birth rate Proportion of births per 1,000 of the total population.

Birthing children was also dangerous, however, since most babies were delivered at home in often unsanitary conditions. Miscarriages were common. Between 25 and 50 percent of women died during birthing or soon thereafter, and almost a quarter of all babies did not survive infancy, especially during the early stages of a colonial settlement.

Disease and epidemics were commonplace. Half the children born in Virginia and Maryland died before reaching age twenty. Boston minister Cotton Mather lost eight of fifteen children in their first year of life. Martha Custis, the Virginia widow who married George Washington, had four children during her first marriage. They all died young, at ages two, three, sixteen, and seventeen. Overall, however, mortality rates in the colonies were lower than in Europe.

COLONIAL FARM This plan of a newly cleared farm shows how trees were cut and the stumps left to rot.

Equally responsible for the fast-growing colonial population was a much lower death rate than that in Europe. By the middle of the seventeenth century, infants had a better chance of reaching maturity in New England than in England, and adults lived longer in the colonies. Lower mortality rates in the colonies resulted from several factors. Because fertile land was plentiful, famine seldom occurred after the early years of colonization, and although the winters were more severe than in England, firewood was abundant. Being younger—the average age in 1790 was sixteen—Americans were less susceptible to disease than were Europeans. That they were more scattered than in Europe also meant they were less exposed to infectious diseases. That fact of life began to change as colonial cities grew larger and more densely populated. By the mid-eighteenth century, the colonies experienced levels of disease much like that in Europe.

Nativism: Anti-immigrant Prejudice

Nativism emerged in the colonies as the population grew. Although Pennsylvania was founded as a haven for all people, by the mid-eighteenth century, concerns arose about the influx of Germans. Benjamin Franklin described Germans as "the most ignorant stupid sort of their own nation." They "herded together" in their own communities, and many refused to learn English. He feared that they would be a source of constant tension. Why, Franklin asked, "should Pennsylvania, founded by the English, become a Colony of Aliens?" He was "not against the admission of Germans in general, for they have their Virtues," but he urged that they be spread across the colonies.

As the number of desperately poor Irish immigrants soared, so too did the prejudice against them. In 1726, Franklin, then twenty years old, watched as a shipload of Irish immigrants disembarked in New York City. He wondered how the more affluent passengers could have put up with being "confined and stifled up with such a lousy, stinking rabble."

The Irish and Scots-Irish kept coming. An Irish immigrant in New York wrote home to his minister, urging him to "tell all the poor folk . . . that God has opened a door for their deliverance" in America. (*Scotch-Irish* is the more common but inaccurate name for the Scots-Irish, the mostly Presbyterian population that the British government transplanted from Scotland to the province of Ulster, in northern Ireland, to "protestantize" Catholic Ireland.)

CORE **OBJECTIVE**

2. Describe women's various roles in the English colonies.

Women in the Colonies

In contrast to New Spain and New France, British America had far more women. But more women did not mean greater equality. As a New England minister stressed, "The woman is a weak creature not endowed with [the] strength and constancy of mind [of men]."

Women, as had been true for centuries, were expected to focus on "housewifery," or the "domestic sphere." They were to obey and serve their husbands, nurture their children, and maintain their households. Governor John Winthrop insisted that a "true wife" would find contentment only "in subjection to her husband's authority." Not surprisingly, the lopsided gender relationship in colonial households at times generated tensions. One long-suffering wife commissioned the following inscription on her husband's tombstone: "Stranger, call this not a place of fear and gloom / To me it is a pleasant spot—It is my husband's tomb." Another woman focused on her own tombstone. It read: "She lived with her husband fifty years / And died in confident hope of a better life."

Women in most colonies could not vote, own property, hold office, attend schools or colleges, bring lawsuits, sign contracts, or become ministers. Divorces were allowed only for desertion or "cruel and barbarous treatment," and no matter who was named the "guilty party," the father received custody of the children. Virtually every member of a colonial household worked, and no one was expected to work harder than women. As John Cotton, a Boston minister, admitted in 1699, "Women are creatures without which there is no Comfortable living for a man." Women who failed to perform household work were punished as if they were servants or enslaved.

During the eighteenth century, **women's work** typically centered on activities in the house, garden, and fields. Yet the scarcity of workers in the colonies created new opportunities for women outside the home or farm. In towns, women commonly served as tavern hostesses and shopkeepers and occasionally also worked as doctors, printers, upholsterers, painters, and silversmiths. Other women operated laundries or bakeries. Technically, any money earned by a married woman was the property of her husband.

women's work Traditional term referring to routine tasks in the house, garden, and fields performed by women; eventually expanded in the colonies to include medicine, shopkeeping, upholstering, and the operation of inns and taverns.

Farm women usually rose by sunrise. They were responsible for building the fire, hauling water, and making meals. They fed and watered the

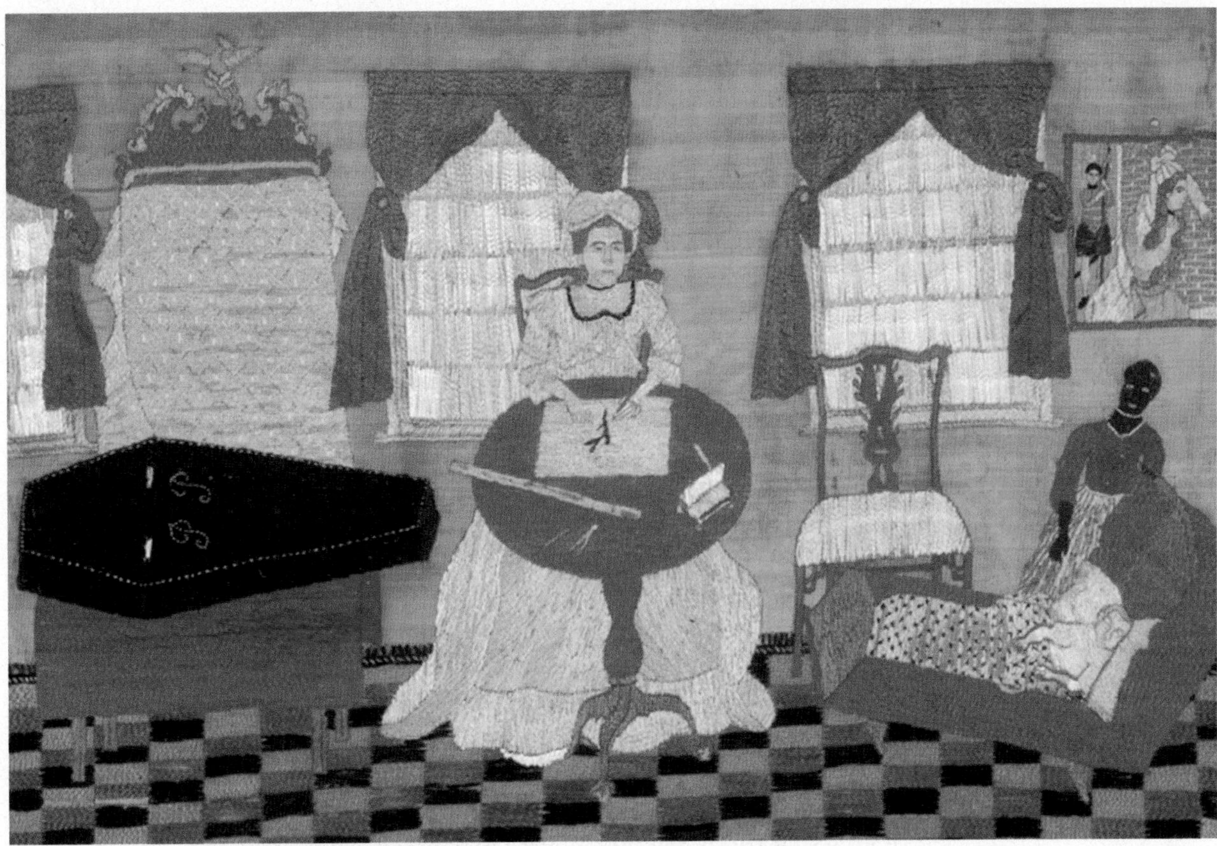

THE FIRST, SECOND, AND LAST SCENE OF MORTALITY Prudence Punderson's needlework (ca. 1776) shows the domestic path, from cradle to coffin, followed by most affluent colonial women.

livestock, cared for the children, tended the garden, prepared lunch (the main meal) and dinner, milked the cows, and cleaned the kitchen before retiring soon after dark. Women also spun wool for clothing; knitted linen and cotton, hemmed sheets, and pieced quilts; made candles and soap; chopped wood, mopped floors, and washed clothes. Female indentured servants in the southern colonies commonly worked as field hands.

Prostitution was one of the most lucrative trades among colonial women who could not find other work. Port cities had thriving brothels. They catered to sailors and soldiers, but men from all walks of life frequented what were called "bawdy houses," or, in Puritan Boston, "disorderly houses." Local authorities frowned on these "loose women." In Massachusetts, convicted prostitutes were stripped to the waist, tied to the back of a horse-drawn cart, and whipped as it moved through town. In South Carolina, several elected public officials were dismissed because they were caught "lying with wenches."

On occasion, circumstances forced women to exercise leadership outside the home. Such was the case with South Carolinian Elizabeth Lucas Pinckney (1722–1793). Born in the West Indies, raised on the island of Antigua, and educated in England, "Eliza" moved to Charleston, South Carolina, when her father, George Lucas, a British army officer, inherited three plantations.

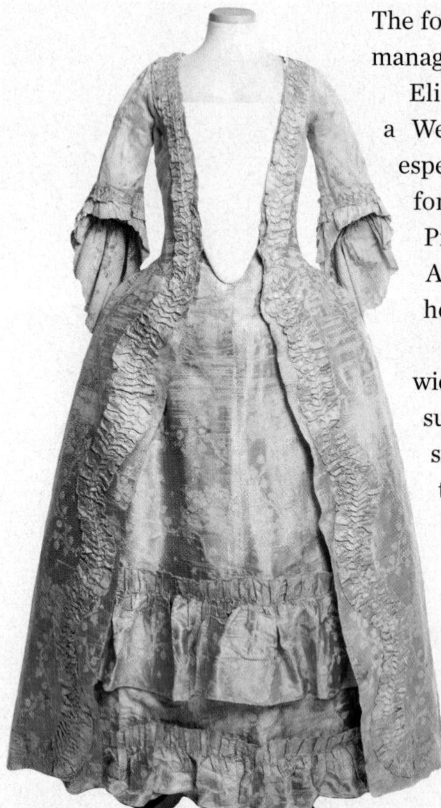

ELIZABETH LUCAS PINCKNEY'S DRESS This rare sack-back gown made of eighteenth-century silk has been restored and displayed at the Charleston Museum in South Carolina.
Courtesy of The Charleston Museum, Charleston, South Carolina, www.charlestonmuseum.org

The following year, however, he was called back to Antigua, leaving Eliza to manage three plantations worked by enslaved people.

Eliza loved the "vegetable world" and focused on growing *indigo*, a West Indian weed that produced a blue dye for coloring fabric, especially military uniforms. Indigo made Eliza's family a fortune, as it did for many other Carolina plantation owners. In 1744, she married Charles Pinckney, a wealthy widower, who was a leader of the South Carolina Assembly. She made him promise that she could continue to manage her plantations.

Fourteen years later, Charles died of malaria. Now a thirty-six-year-old widow, Eliza responded by adding her husband's plantations to her already substantial responsibilities. Self-confident and fearless, Eliza demonstrated the possibility of (White) women breaking out of the confining tradition of housewifery and subordination and assuming roles of social prominence and economic leadership.

Women and Religion

During the colonial era, no religious denomination allowed women to be ordained as ministers. Puritans cited biblical passages claiming that God required "virtuous" women to submit to male authority and remain silent in congregational matters. Women who challenged ministerial authority were usually prosecuted and punished. Yet by the eighteenth century, as is true today, most church members were women.

In colonial America, the religious roles of Black women were different from those of their White counterparts. In most West African societies, women served as priests and cult leaders. Although some enslaved Africans had been exposed to Christianity or Islam, most tried to sustain their African religions in the colonies.

The acute shortage of women in the early years of colonial settlement made them more highly valued in British America than in Europe; over time, women's status improved slightly. The Puritan emphasis on a well-ordered family life led to laws protecting wives from physical abuse and allowing for divorce. In addition, colonial laws gave wives greater control over the property that they brought into a marriage or that was left after a husband's death. However, the notion of female subordination and domesticity remained firmly entrenched.

CORE **OBJECTIVE**

3. Compare the societies and economies of the southern, New England, and middle colonies.

Society and Economy in the Colonies

In the early eighteenth century, England and Scotland merged, and in 1707 adopted a new name for the joint monarchies: Great Britain. The British American colonies were part of a complex North Atlantic commercial network. Companies, merchants, and farmers traded sugar, wheat, tobacco, rum, rice, and many other commodities, including enslaved Africans and Indians, with Great Britain and its highly profitable island colonies in the West Indies—Bermuda, Barbados, and Jamaica. In addition, American merchants also traded (smuggled) with Spain, France, Portugal, Holland, and their colonies, which were often at war with Britain and therefore officially off limits. Out of necessity, the colonists were dependent on Britain and Europe for manufactured goods and luxury items such as wine, glass, and jewelry.

Finding laborers for a rapidly expanding economy

The colonies were blessed with abundant natural resources, but they struggled to find enough laborers for the rapidly expanding economy. The primary solution to the shortage of workers was indentured servitude. This practice, whereby servants agreed to work three to seven years in exchange for their "master" paying for their travel to America, accounted for probably half the White settlers (mostly from England, Ireland, Scotland, or Germany). During the late seventeenth and eighteenth centuries, however, the southern colonies turned from using indentured servants to purchasing Indians or Africans as lifelong coerced laborers to satisfy the growing demand for workers on tobacco and rice plantations.

The Southern Colonies

Rising inequality and a slave-based economy in the South

As the southern colonies matured, inequalities of wealth became more visible, and social life grew more divided by marked differences in clothing, housing, wealth, and status. The use of enslaved Indians and Africans to grow tobacco, sugar cane, rice, and indigo generated enormous wealth for a few landowners. Socially, the planters and merchants became a class apart from the "common folk." They dominated the legislatures, bought luxury goods from London and Paris, and built brick mansions with formal gardens—all the while looking down upon their "inferiors," both White and Black.

Warm weather and plentiful rainfall helped the southern colonies grow the profitable **staple crops** (also called cash crops) valued by the mother country. Tobacco production soared. "In Virginia and Maryland," wrote a royal official in 1629, "tobacco . . . is our All, and indeed leaves no room for anything else." So much tobacco was grown in Virginia that the royal governor in 1616 passed "Dale's Laws" requiring every farmer to plant at least two acres of corn to ensure an adequate food supply.

Rice cultivation experienced a similarly phenomenal rate of growth. It was first grown in 1685 in low-country South Carolina and Georgia, a strip of wetlands and pine barrens paralleling the Atlantic Ocean and fed by tidal rivers. By 1700, South Carolina was exporting 400,000 pounds of rice each year; by 1768, some 66 *million* pounds of rice were shipped to Great Britain and northern Europe. Rice accounted for more than half of the colony's exports during the eighteenth century.

Planters adopted a system of rice cultivation that drew heavily on the labor patterns and technical knowledge of enslaved West Africans who had been growing rice for generations. Using only hand tools, male coerced

staple crops Profitable market crops, such as cotton, tobacco, and rice, that predominate in a region.

VIRGINIA PLANTATION WHARF Southern colonial plantations were often constructed along rivers, with easy access to oceangoing vessels, as shown on this 1730 tobacco label. **How does this illustration represent the rigid class system of the southern colonies?**

labor transformed the landscape, removing trees from wetlands infested with snakes, alligators, and malaria-carrying mosquitos, then digging miles of dikes, canals, levees, ditches, and culverts. Because "wet rice" is grown in standing water, it required an irrigation system to enable workers to drain or flood the fields using the daily tidal action of coastal rivers.

Over time, South Carolina rice planters became the wealthiest group in the British colonies. They situated their plantations along coastal rivers so they could use barges to transport rice to nearby ports for shipment to Europe. As rice plantations grew, the demand for enslaved laborers rose dramatically, for White colonists balked at working long hours in "mud and water." Almost 90 percent of the enslaved Africans transported to America went to the southern colonies. South Carolina had a majority Black population throughout the eighteenth century.

New England

New England townships

Environmental, social, and economic factors contributed to the remarkable diversity among the early American colonies. New England was quite different from the southern and middle Atlantic regions: it was more governed by religious concerns, less focused on commercial agriculture, more engaged in trade, more centered on village and town life, and much less reliant on slavery.

Close relationship between church and state

Religion Whenever New England towns were founded, the first public structure built was usually a church. The Puritans believed that God had created a *covenant* through which people formed a congregation for common worship. This led to the idea of people joining together to form governments, but the principles of democracy and equality were not part of Puritan political thought. Puritan leaders sought to do the will of God, and the ultimate source of authority was not majority rule but the Bible as interpreted by ministers and magistrates (political leaders). Over time, growing numbers of children and grandchildren of the original "visible saints" could not give the required testimony of spiritual conversion. Another blow to Puritan ideals came with the Massachusetts royal charter of 1691, which required the Puritan colony to "tolerate" religious dissenters (such as Quakers) and based the right to vote on property ownership rather than church membership. By law, every town had to collect taxes to support a church, and every resident—church member or not—was required to attend midweek and Sunday religious services. The average New Englander heard more than 7,000 sermons in a lifetime.

Although the Puritans sailed to America to create pious, prosperous communities, the traditional caricature of the dour, black-clothed Puritan is false. Yes, they banned card playing, dancing in taverns, swearing, and bowling. They even fined people for celebrating Christmas, for in their view only pagans marked the birth date of their rulers with merrymaking. Puritans also frowned on hurling insults, disobeying parents, and disrespecting civil and religious officials. In 1631, a servant named Phillip Ratcliffe had both of his ears cut off for making scandalous comments about the governor and the church in Salem.

HOUSING IN COLONIAL NEW ENGLAND This frame house, built in the 1670s, belonged to Rebecca Nurse, one of the women hanged as a witch in Salem Village in 1692.

Yet Puritans wore colorful clothing, enjoyed secular music, and imbibed prodigious quantities of beer and rum. "Drink is in itself a good creature of God," said the Reverend Increase Mather, "but the abuse of drink is from Satan." Drunks were arrested, and repeat offenders were forced to wear the letter *D* in public.

Moderation in all things was the Puritan guideline, and it applied to sexual life as well. Although sexual activity outside of marriage was strictly forbidden, New England courts overflowed with cases of adultery and illicit sex. A man found guilty of sleeping with an unwed woman could be jailed, whipped, fined, and forced to marry the woman. Female offenders were also jailed and whipped, and judges required adulterers to wear the letter *A* in public.

Over time, Puritan New England experienced a gradual erosion of religious commitment. More and more children and grandchildren of the original "visible saints" could not give the required testimony of spiritual conversion. Another blow to Puritan ideals came with the Massachusetts royal charter of 1691, which required toleration of religious dissenters (such as Quakers) and based the right to vote in public elections on property ownership rather than church membership.

Witches in Salem The strains generated by Massachusetts's transition from Puritan utopia to royal colony reached a climax in 1692–1693 amid the witchcraft hysteria at Salem Village (now called Danvers), a community on the northern edge of Salem Town, a flourishing port some fifteen miles north of Boston. Belief in witchcraft was widespread throughout Europe and the colonies in the seventeenth century. Prior to the dramatic episode in Salem, almost 300 New Englanders (mostly middle-aged women) had been accused of practicing witchcraft, and more than 30 had been hanged.

Salem witch trials

The Salem outbreak was unique, however. During the brutally cold winter of 1692, several preteen girls became fascinated with a fortune teller named Tituba, an enslaved woman from Barbados. Two of the girls, nine-year-old Betty Parris and eleven-year-old Abigail Williams, the daughter and niece of the village minister, Samuel Parris, began to behave oddly. They thrashed, shouted, barked, sobbed hysterically, and flapped their arms as if to fly. When asked who was tormenting them, they replied that three women—Tituba, Sarah Good, and Sarah Osborne—were Satan's servants.

Parris beat Tituba until she confessed to doing Satan's bidding. (Under the rules of the era, those who confessed were jailed; those who denied the charges were hanged.) Authorities arrested Tituba and the other accused women. Two of them were hanged, but not before they named other supposed witches and more young girls experienced convulsive fits. The mass hysteria extended to surrounding towns, and within a few months, the Salem Village jail was filled with more than 150 men, women, and children—and two dogs—all accused of practicing witchcraft.

As the allegations and executions multiplied and spread beyond Salem, leaders of the Massachusetts Bay Colony began to worry that the witch hunts were spinning out of control. The governor finally intervened when his wife was accused of serving the devil. He disbanded the special court in Salem and ordered the remaining suspects released. By then, nineteen people (fourteen women and five men, including a former minister) had been hanged. A year after it had begun, the witchcraft frenzy was finally over.

What explains Salem's mass hysteria? It may have represented nothing more than theatrical adolescents eager to enliven the dreary routine of everyday life. Others suggest community tensions may have led people to accuse neighbors, masters, relatives, or rivals as an act of spite or vengeance. Some historians have stressed that most of the accused witches were women, many of whom had in some way defied the traditional roles assigned to females.

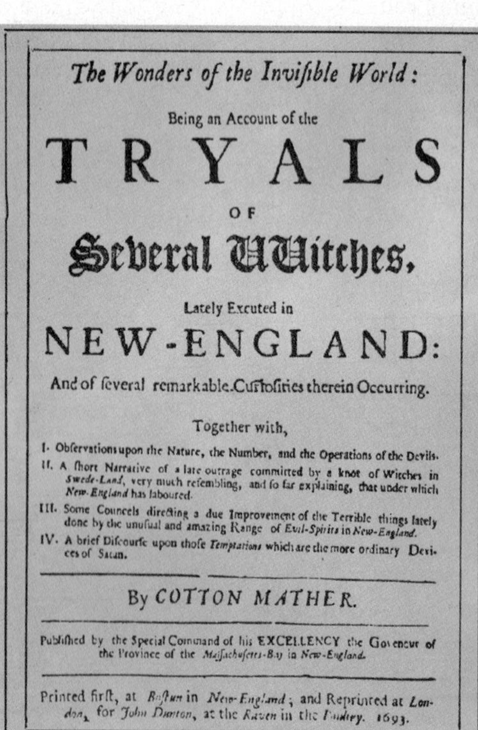

The Wonders of the Invisible World:

Being an Account of the

TRYALS

OF

Several Witches,

Lately Excuted in

NEW-ENGLAND:

And of several remarkable Curiosities therein Occurring.

Together with,

I. Observations upon the Nature, the Number, and the Operations of the Devils.

II. A short Narrative of a late outrage committed by a knot of Witches in *Swede-Land*, very much resembling, and so far explaining, that under which *New-England* has laboured.

III. Some Councels directing a due Improvement of the Terrible things lately done by the unusual and amazing Range of *Evil-Spirits* in *New-England*.

IV. A brief Discourse upon those *Temptations* which are the more ordinary Devices of Satan.

By *COTTON MATHER.*

Published by the Special Command of his EXCELLENCY the Govenour of the Province of the *Massachusetts-Bay* in *New-England*.

Printed first, at *Bostun* in *New-England*; and Reprinted at *London*, for *John Dunton*, at the *Raven* in the *Poultry*. 1693.

THE SALEM WITCHCRAFT TRIALS *(Left)* Title page of the 1693 London edition of Cotton Mather's account of the Salem witchcraft trials. Mather, a prominent Boston minister, warned his congregation that the devil's legions were assaulting New England. *(Right)* In *Examination of a Witch* (1853), artist Tompkins Harrison Matteson sought to render a dramatic scene from the trials.

Still another interpretation suggests that the accusations may have reflected the psychological strains caused by frequent Indian attacks just north of Salem. Some of the convulsing girls had seen their families killed or mutilated by Indians and suffered from what today is called post-traumatic stress disorder. Whatever its actual causes, the witchcraft controversy reflected the peculiar social tensions of Salem village. Nothing quite like it occurred anywhere else in the colonies.

Dwellings and Daily Life The first colonists in New England initially lived in caves, tents, or cabins, but they eventually built simple wood-frame houses with steeply pitched roofs to reduce the buildup of snow. Interior walls were often plastered and whitewashed, but it was not until the eighteenth century that the exteriors of most houses were painted, usually a deep "Indian" red, as the colonists called it. The interiors were dark and illuminated by candles or oil lamps, both of which were expensive; most people usually went to sleep soon after sunset. There were no bathrooms (privies). Most families relieved themselves outside, often beside the house. Family life revolved around the main room on the ground floor, called the hall, where meals were cooked in a fireplace and where the family lived most of the time. Hence, they came to be called *living* rooms.

Food was served at a table of rough-hewn planks, called the board, and the only eating utensils were spoons and fingers. The father was sometimes referred to as the "chair man" because he sat in the only chair (the origin of the term *chairman of the board*). The rest of the family usually stood or sat on stools or benches. A typical meal consisted of corn, boiled meat, and vegetables washed down with beer, cider, rum, or milk. Cornbread was a daily favorite, as was cornmeal mush, known as hasty pudding.

PROFITABLE FISHERIES
Fishing for, curing, and drying cod in Newfoundland in the early 1700s. The rich fishing grounds of the North Atlantic provided New Englanders with a prosperous industry for centuries. **Who provided the labor for northern fisheries?**

Economy As John Winthrop and the Puritans prepared to embark for New England in 1630, he stressed that God had made some people powerful and rich and others helpless and poor—so that the elite would show mercy and the masses would offer obedience. He reminded the Puritans that all were given a noble "calling" by God to work hard and ensure that material pursuits never diminished the importance of spiritual devotion.

Early New England farmers and their families led hard lives. The growing season was short, and the crops and livestock were those familiar to the English countryside: wheat, barley, oats, some cattle, pigs, and sheep.

Many New Englanders turned to the sea for their livelihood; the waters off the New England coast had the heaviest concentrations of cod in the world. Whales supplied ambergris, a waxy substance used in the manufacture of perfumes and lubrications, and which the colonists burned as lamp oil. New Englanders exported dried fish to Europe, with lesser grades going to the West Indies as food for enslaved laborers. The thriving fishing industry encouraged the development of shipbuilding and spurred transatlantic commerce. Rising incomes and a booming trade with Britain and Europe soon brought a taste for luxury goods that clashed with the Puritan ideal of plain living and high thinking.

Fishing and transatlantic trade

Trade in New England and the middle colonies differed from that in the South in two respects. The lack of agricultural staple crops to exchange for English goods was a relative disadvantage, but the success of shipping and commercial enterprises worked in their favor. After 1660, to protect its agriculture and fisheries, the English government placed prohibitive duties

ATLANTIC TRADE ROUTES

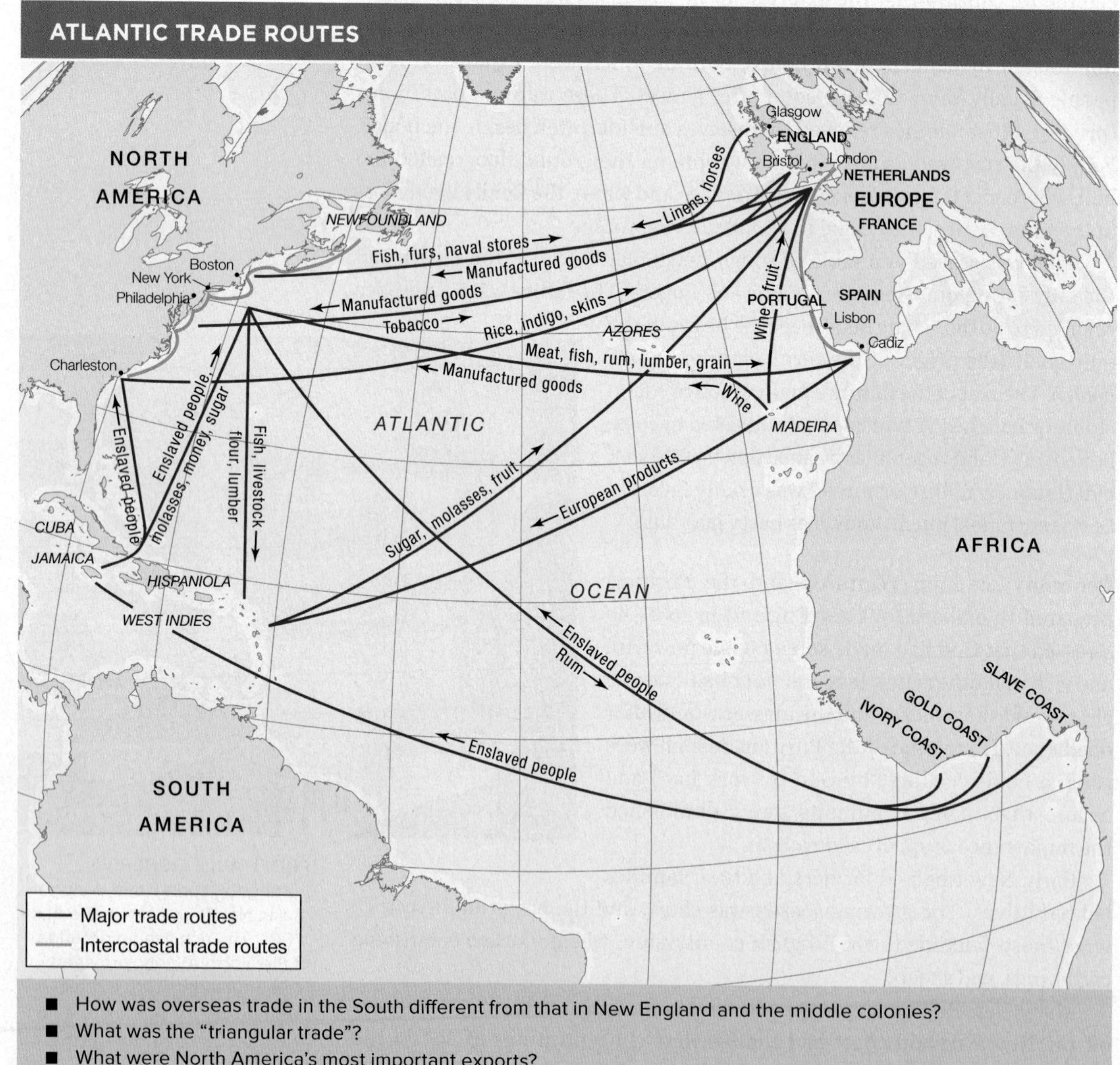

- How was overseas trade in the South different from that in New England and the middle colonies?
- What was the "triangular trade"?
- What were North America's most important exports?

(taxes) on fish, flour, wheat, and meat, while leaving the door open to high-demand products such as timber, furs, and whale oil. Between 1698 and 1717, New England and New York bought more from England than they exported to it, creating an unfavorable trade balance.

"Triangular" trade networks

These circumstances gave rise to the **triangular trade.** New England merchants shipped rum to the west coast of Africa, where it was exchanged for enslaved people. Ships then took the captive Africans to profitable Caribbean islands to sell. The ships returned home with various commodities, including molasses, from which New Englanders manufactured rum. In another version, shippers sent foodstuffs to the Caribbean, carried sugar and molasses to England, and returned with goods manufactured in Europe.

The Middle Colonies

Both geographically and culturally, the middle colonies (New York, New Jersey, Pennsylvania, Delaware, and Maryland) stood between New England and the South. As such, they more completely reflected the diversity of colonial life and more fully foreshadowed the pluralism of America.

They produced surpluses of foodstuffs for export to the slave-based plantations of the South and the West Indies: wheat, barley, oats and other grains, flour, and livestock. Three great rivers—the Hudson, Delaware, and Susquehanna—and their tributaries provided access to the backcountry of Pennsylvania and New York, and to a rich fur trade with Native Americans.

Land policies followed the *headright* system prevalent in the Chesapeake colonies. In New York, the early royal governors continued the Dutch practice of the patroonship, granting vast estates to influential men (called patroons). The patroons controlled large domains farmed by tenants (renters) who paid fees to use the landlords' mills, warehouses, smokehouses, and docks. With free land available elsewhere, however, New York's population languished, and new waves of immigrants sought the promised land of Pennsylvania.

Ethnic diversity in the middle colonies

In the makeup of their population, the middle colonies differed from New England's Puritan settlements and the biracial plantation colonies in the South. In New York and New Jersey, Dutch culture and language lingered. Along the Delaware River near Philadelphia, the first settlers—Swedes and Finns—were overwhelmed by an influx of Europeans. By the mid-eighteenth century, the middle colonies were the fastest-growing region in North America.

Germans came to America (primarily to Pennsylvania) mainly from the Rhineland region of Europe, where brutal religious wars had pitted Protestants against Catholics. William Penn's recruiting brochures circulated throughout central Europe, and his promise of religious freedom appealed to many persecuted sects, especially the Mennonites, German Baptists whose beliefs resembled those of the Quakers.

Throughout the eighteenth century, a quarter-million Scots-Irish immigrants moved still farther out into the Pennsylvania backcountry. Plentiful land in America was the great magnet for the cash-poor Scots-Irish, most

triangular trade A network of trade in which exports from one region were sold to a second region; the second sent its exports to a third region that exported its own goods back to the first country or colony.

WILLIAM PENN In this eighteenth-century engraving, William Penn welcomes a German immigrant to Philadelphia. **What factors in Europe brought so many Germans to Pennsylvania in the eighteenth century?**

of whom were farmworkers with the expectation "to have land for nothing" and were "unwilling to be disappointed." In most cases, the lands they "squatted on" were the ancestral acres claimed by Native Americans. In 1741, a group of Delaware Indians protested that the Scots-Irish were taking "our land" without giving "us anything for it." If the colonial government did not stop the flow of Whites, the Delawares threatened, they would "drive them off."

The Scots-Irish and Germans became the largest non-English ethnic groups in the colonies. Other ethnic minorities also enriched the population: Huguenots (French Protestants whose religious freedom had been revoked in 1685, forcing many to leave France), Irish, Welsh, Swiss, and Jews. New York had inherited from the Dutch a tradition of ethnic and religious tolerance, which had given the colony a diverse population: French-speaking Walloons (a Celtic people of southern Belgium), French, Germans, Danes, Portuguese, Spaniards, Italians, Bohemians, Poles, and others, including some New England Puritans.

In the eighteenth century, the population in British North America soared, and the colonies grew more diverse. In 1790, the White population was 61 percent English; 14 percent Scottish and Scots-Irish; 9 percent German; 5 percent Dutch, French, and Swedish; 4 percent Irish; and 7 percent "unidentifiable," a category that included people of mixed origins as well as "free Blacks." If one adds to the 3,172,444 Whites in the 1790 census the 756,770 non-Whites, without even considering the almost 100,000 Native Americans who went uncounted, only about half the nation's inhabitants, and perhaps fewer, could trace their origins to England.

Pennsylvania became the great distribution point for the ethnic groups of European origin, just as the Chesapeake Bay region and Charleston, South Carolina, became the distribution points for African peoples. During the eighteenth century, 40 percent of enslaved Africans brought to America arrived in Charleston. Many of the captives died while crossing the Atlantic. "There are few ships that come here from Africa but have had many of the cargoes [captives] thrown overboard," reported Alexander Garden, the port physician. "Some [have lost] one-fourth, some one-third, some lost half; and I have seen some that have lost two-thirds of their slaves."

Before the mid-eighteenth century, White settlers in the Pennsylvania backcountry had reached the Appalachian mountain range. A British official described the colonists as natural wanderers who "forever imagine the lands further off are still better than those upon which they are already settled." Rather than crossing the steep mountain ridges, the Scots-Irish and Germans filtered southward. Germans were the first White settlers in the

MAJOR IMMIGRANT GROUPS IN COLONIAL AMERICA

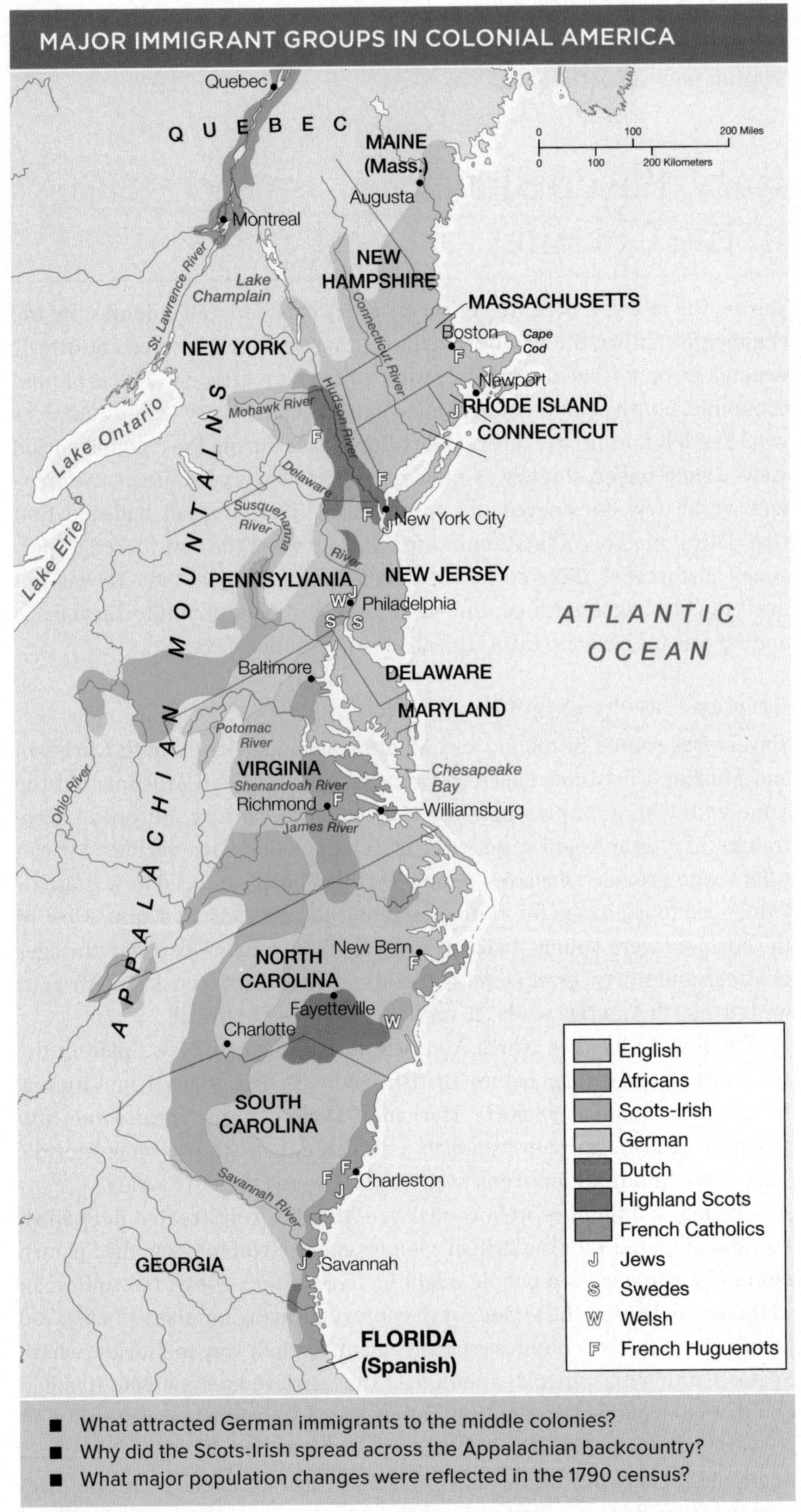

- What attracted German immigrants to the middle colonies?
- Why did the Scots-Irish spread across the Appalachian backcountry?
- What major population changes were reflected in the 1790 census?

Upper Shenandoah Valley in southern Pennsylvania, western Maryland, and northern Virginia, and the Scots-Irish filled the lower valley in western Virginia and North Carolina.

CORE **OBJECTIVE**

4. Describe the creation of race-based slavery during the seventeenth century and its impact on the social and economic development of colonial America.

Race-Based Slavery in the Colonies

During the late seventeenth century, slavery existed in all colonies. By the eighteenth century, the economy in the southern colonies had become utterly dependent on enslaved workers, either Indians or Africans. The profound economic, political, and cultural effects of African slavery in the Americas would be felt far into the future. Most Europeans during the colonial period viewed **race-based slavery** as a normal aspect of everyday life in an imperfect world; few considered it a moral issue. They instead believed that God determined one's "station in life." Slavery was thus considered a "personal misfortune" dictated by God rather than a social evil. It was not until the late eighteenth century that large numbers of White Europeans and Americans began to raise ethical questions about slavery.

African Slavery in North America

Slavery was rooted in the ancient Mediterranean societies, both Christian and Muslim. Christians enslaved captured Muslims, and Muslims did the same with Christian prisoners. By the sixteenth century, European slave traders had established a network of relationships with various African rulers, who provided enslaved people that had been captured in warfare or kidnapped in exchange for cloth, metal objects, muskets, and rum. Most of the enslaved were young—twice as many men as women—between the ages of fifteen and thirty. Over some 400 years, about 500,000 enslaved Africans went to North America while 3.5 million were taken to Brazil.

The first Africans in North America were brought to New Spain in the sixteenth century, long before British colonists first arrived in Virginia. In 1539, the Spanish explorer Hernando DeSoto transported some fifty enslaved Africans to help establish a settlement in what is now Florida. Thereafter, hundreds more enslaved Africans were taken to Florida.

Enslaved Africans in Spanish Florida versus the British colonies

The major difference in how enslaved Africans were treated in Spanish Florida compared with the British colonies centered on religion: the Spanish monarchy said enslaved people might be freed if they converted to Roman Catholicism. During the seventeenth century, growing numbers of enslaved people in the British colonies escaped and made their way to Florida, where Spanish authorities in 1623 announced that enslaved people who touched Spanish-controlled soil, requested refuge, agreed to serve in the militia, and converted to Catholicism could become free Spanish citizens. Creek and Seminole Indians in Florida also provided refuge for enslaved people who escaped from British colonies. In the eighteenth century, a British official

race-based slavery Institution that uses racial characteristics and myths to justify enslaving a people by force.

reported that for decades freedom seekers from Georgia and South Carolina had made their way to "Indian towns, from whence it proved very difficult to get them back."

In the Chesapeake colonies of Virginia and Maryland, Africans were initially treated much like indentured servants, with a limited term of service, after which they gained their freedom (but not equality). Gradually, however, *lifelong* slavery for Blacks became the custom—and the law of the land. During the 1660s, colonial legislatures formalized the institution of race-based slavery, with detailed **slave codes** regulating most aspects of enslaved people's lives. The South Carolina code, for example, defined all "Negroes, Mulattoes, and Indians" sold into bondage as having become enslaved *for life*, as were the children born of enslaved mothers.

SLAVERY IN NEW AMSTERDAM (1642) The significance of race-based slavery to the colonial economy is the focus of this engraving of the Dutch colony New Amsterdam, later known as New York City.

In 1667, the Virginia legislature declared that enslaved individuals could not serve on juries, travel without permission, or gather in groups of more than two or three. Some colonies even prohibited manumission, the practice whereby owners could free their enslaved people. The codes allowed owners to punish enslaved people by whipping them, slitting their noses, cutting their ankle cords, castrating men, or killing them. A 1669 Virginia law declared that accidentally killing an enslaved person who was being whipped or beaten was not a serious crime. In 1713, a South Carolina planter punished one of his enslaved people by closing him up in a coffin to die, only to have the trapped man's son slip in a knife so that he could kill himself rather than suffocate.

During the seventeenth and eighteenth centuries, the sugar-based economies of the French and British West Indies and Portuguese Brazil sparked greater demand for enslaved Africans. By 1675, the island colonies in the Caribbean had more than 100,000 enslaved peoples, while the American colonies had about 5,000.

As tobacco, rice, and indigo crops became more established in Maryland, Virginia, and the Carolinas, however, the number of enslaved Africans in those colonies grew substantially, while the flow of White indentured servants from Britain and Europe to America slowed. Until the eighteenth century, English immigrants made up 90 percent of American colonists. After 1700, the largest number of new arrivals were enslaved Africans, who totaled five times more than all European immigrants combined. While most enslaved people were in the southern colonies, all thirteen colonies allowed slavery.

slave codes Ordinances passed by a colony or state to regulate the behavior of enslaved people, often including severe punishments for infractions.

During the late seventeenth century, the profitability of African slavery led to the emergence of dozens of slave-trading companies, both in Europe and America, thus expanding the availability of enslaved Africans and lowering the price. Colonists favored enslaved people over servants because enslaved people were viewed as property with no civil rights, and as servants for life. The colonists preferred Africans over enslaved Indians because Africans could not escape easily in a land where they stood out because of their dark skin. In short, enslaved Africans offered a better investment.

Colonial Race Relations

Most enslaved workers were eventually used in virtually every activity within the expanding colonial economy. The vast majority of enslaved Africans worked on farms or plantations from dawn to dusk, in oppressive heat and humidity. As Jedidiah Morse, a prominent Charleston minister, admitted in the late eighteenth century, "No white man, to speak generally, ever thinks of settling a farm, and improving it for himself, without negroes." By 1750, there were almost 250,000 enslaved people in British America. The vast majority, about 150,000, resided in Virginia and Maryland, with 60,000 in South Carolina and Georgia.

As the number of enslaved people grew, so, too, did their talents and expertise. Over time, some became skilled workers: blacksmiths, carpenters, bricklayers, harbor pilots. Many enslaved women worked as household servants and midwives, helping to deliver babies. Despite the power and authority of slave owners, enslaved people found ways to resist and rebel—and escape. A Georgia slave owner, for example, asked newspaper readers to be on the lookout for "a negro fellow named Mingo, about 40 years old, and his wife Quante, a sensible wench about 20 with her child, a boy about 3 years old, all this country born."

Slavery in New York City In contrast to their experience in the southern colonies, most enslaved people in the northern colonies lived in towns or cities. Ethnically diverse New York City had more enslaved people than any other American city, and by 1740, it was second only to Charleston in the percentage of enslaved people in its population.

Acts of resistance to enslavement

As the number of enslaved people increased in the city, fears and tensions mounted—and occasionally exploded. In 1712, several dozen enslaved people revolted; they started fires, then killed Whites as they fought the blaze. Called out to suppress the "Negro plot," the militia captured twenty-seven enslaved people, six of whom committed suicide. The rest were executed. New York officials thereafter passed a citywide *black code* that strictly regulated the behavior of both free and enslaved Blacks.

The harsh regulations did not prevent other acts of resistance. In March 1741, city dwellers worried that enslaved people were setting a series of suspicious fires, including one at the governor's house. "The Negroes are rising!" shouted terrified Whites.

Mary Burton, a sixteen-year-old White indentured servant, told authorities that enslaved people and poor Whites were plotting to "burn the whole town" and kill the White men. The plotters were supposedly led by John Hughson, a White trafficker in stolen goods. His wife, two enslaved people, and a prostitute were charged as coconspirators. Despite their denials, all were convicted and hanged. Within weeks, more than half of the adult enslaved males in the city were in jail. What came to be called the Conspiracy of 1741 ended after seventeen enslaved people and four Whites were hanged. Thirteen more Blacks were burned at the stake, while many others were deported to the Caribbean colonies.

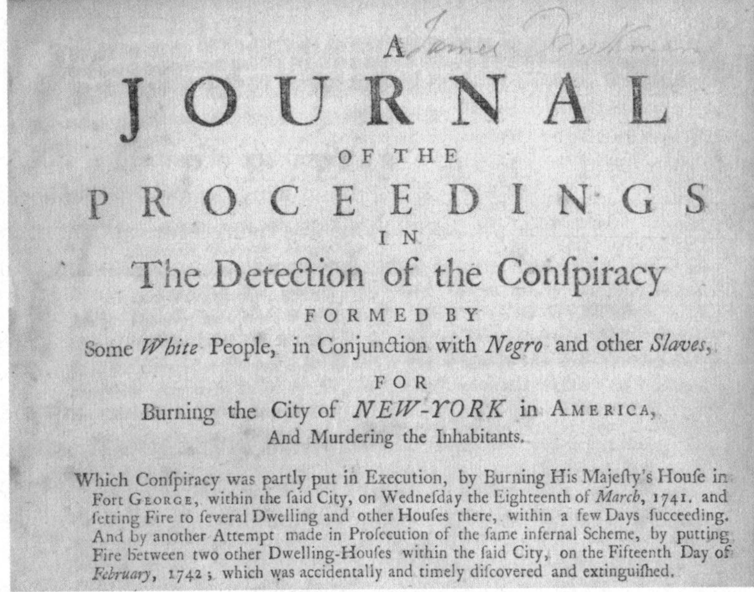

A
JOURNAL
OF THE
PROCEEDINGS
IN
The Detection of the Conſpiracy
FORMED BY
Some *White* People, in Conjunction with *Negro* and other *Slaves*,
FOR
Burning the City of *NEW-YORK* in AMERICA,
And Murdering the Inhabitants.

Which Conſpiracy was partly put in Execution, by Burning His Majeſty's Houſe in Fort GEORGE, within the ſaid City, on Wedneſday the Eighteenth of *March*, 1741. and ſetting Fire to ſeveral Dwelling and other Houſes there, within a few Days ſucceeding. And by another Attempt made in Proſecution of the ſame infernal Scheme, by putting Fire between two other Dwelling-Houſes within the ſaid City, on the Fifteenth Day of *February*, 1742; which was accidentally and timely diſcovered and extinguiſhed.

THE CONSPIRACY OF 1741 A detail of the title page of *A Journal of the Proceedings in the Detection of Conspiracy* (1741) summarizing the alleged plot by the enslaved and poor Whites to set a series of fires in New York City.

Freedom Seekers and Slave Rebellions Many enslaved people who ran away (freedom seekers) in colonial America faced ghastly punishments when caught. Antonio, a West African man shipped as an enslaved person to New Amsterdam and then to Maryland, tried to escape several times. After his last attempt, in 1656, his owner, a young Dutch planter named Syman Overzee, tortured and killed him. Authorities charged Overzee with murder—and an all-White jury acquitted him.

In a few cases, enslaved people organized rebellions in which they stole weapons, burned and looted plantations, and killed their captors. On Sunday morning, September 9, 1739, while White families were attending church, some twenty African-born enslaved people attacked a store in Stono, South Carolina, twenty miles southwest of Charles Town. Led by an enslaved person named Jemmy, the rebels seized weapons, killed and decapitated two shopkeepers, and fled south toward Spanish Florida. Along the way, they gathered more recruits. Within a few days, the enslaved people had burned six plantations and killed about two dozen Whites. They spared one innkeeper because he was "kind to his slaves." The rebels continued to free enslaved people as they moved southward. Then well-armed militiamen on horseback caught up with them. Most of the rebels were killed, and sixty of those captured were decapitated by enraged planters.

Stono Rebellion

The **Stono Rebellion,** the largest uprising of the colonial period, so frightened White planters that they convinced the South Carolina assembly to ban the importation of enslaved Africans for ten years and pass the Negro Act of 1740, which called for more oversight of enslaved people's activities and harsher punishments for rebellious behavior. Enslaved people could no longer grow their own food, gather in groups, learn to read or write, or earn money on the side. Those leaving their owner's supervision were required to have a pass documenting their whereabouts. The law also reduced the penalty for a White killing an enslaved person to a minor offense, and it banned enslaved people from testifying in courts.

Stono Rebellion A 1739 slave uprising in South Carolina that was brutally quashed, leading to executions as well as a severe tightening of the slave codes.

CORE **OBJECTIVE**

5. Analyze the impact of the Enlightenment and Great Awakening on the colonies.

First Stirrings of a Common Colonial Culture

By the middle of the eighteenth century, the thirteen colonies were growing and maturing. Schools and colleges were springing up, and the standard of living was rising. More and more colonists were able to read about the latest ideas circulating in London and Paris while purchasing the latest consumer goods from Europe.

Commerce and culture

The rage for luxury goods, especially jewelry, fine clothing, and beaver hats, heightened the recognition of social inequality, particularly in the cities. Many ministers complained that the wealthy were ignoring their commitment to Christian ideals. In 1714, a Bostonian regretted the "great extravagance that people are fallen into, far beyond their circumstances, in their purchases, buildings, families, expenses, apparel—generally in their whole way of living."

English merchants required Americans to buy their goods only with *specie* (gold or silver coins). This left little "hard money" in the colonies. Merchants tried various ways to get around the shortage of specie. Some engaged in *barter*, using commodities such as tobacco or rice as currency in exchange for manufactured goods and luxury items. The issue of money—what kind and how much—would become a major dispute between the colonies and Britain.

THE RAPALJE CHILDREN (1768) John Durand painted the children of a wealthy Brooklyn merchant wearing clothing typical of upper-crust urban society.

Colonial Cities

Throughout the seventeenth and eighteenth centuries, the colonies were mostly populated by farmers or farmworkers. However, a handful of cities blossomed into dynamic centers of political and social life. Economic opportunity drove most city dwellers. In New York City, for example, a visitor said the "art of getting money" dominated everything the residents did.

Colonial cities hugged the coastline or, like Philadelphia, sprang up on rivers large enough to handle oceangoing vessels. Never comprising more than 10 percent of the colonial population, the large coastal cities had a disproportionate influence on commerce, politics, society, and culture. By the end of the colonial period, Philadelphia, with some 30,000 people, was the largest city in the colonies, and New York City, with about 25,000, ranked second. Boston numbered 16,000; Charleston, South Carolina, 12,000; and Newport, Rhode Island, 11,000.

The Social and Political Order

The urban social elite was dominated by wealthy merchants and property owners served by a middle class of shop owners, innkeepers, and skilled craftsmen. Almost two thirds of urban male workers were artisans—carpenters and coopers (barrel makers), shoemakers and tailors, silversmiths and blacksmiths, sailmakers, stonemasons, weavers, and potters. At the bottom of the social order were sailors, manual laborers, servants, and enslaved laborers.

Urban problems and social support

Colonial cities were busy and crowded, and killer epidemics such as cholera, malaria, and yellow fever were common. Frequent fires led to the development of fire companies. Rising crime and violence required increased policing by sheriffs and local militias. Urban elites grew concerned about the poor and homeless. The number of Boston's poor receiving aid rose from 500 in 1700 to 4,000 in 1736; in New York City, it rose from 250 in 1698 to 5,000 in the 1770s. Those designated "helpless" were often provided money, food, clothing, and fuel. In some towns, "poorhouses" were built to house the homeless and provide them with jobs.

The Urban Web

The first American roads were Indian trails widened with frequent travel. "The roads all along this way are very bad," wrote Sarah Kemble Knight in 1704 after a harrowing five-day trip from Boston to New Haven, Connecticut. The route was "encumbered with rocks and mountainous passages, which were very disagreeable to my tired carcass."

Overland travel was initially by horse or foot. Eventually wagons and coaches were used. Inns and taverns (also called public houses, or pubs) were essential social institutions, since travel at night was treacherous—and Americans loved to drink. (It was said that when the Spanish settled an area, they would first build a church; the Dutch would first erect a fort; and the English would first construct a pub.)

Taverns and inns were places to eat, relax, read a newspaper, play cards, gossip and conduct business, and enjoy beer, hard cider, and rum. But

TAVERN CULTURE A tobacconist's business card from 1770 captures men talking in a Philadelphia tavern while they drink ale and smoke pipes.

ministers and magistrates began to worry that the pubs were promoting drunkenness and social rebelliousness. Not only were poor Whites drinking heavily but so too were Indians, which, one governor told the assembly, would have "fatal consequences to the Government." By the end of the seventeenth century, taverns had become the most important social institutions in the colonies—and the most democratic. They were places where rich and poor intermingled, and by the mid-eighteenth century, they would become gathering spots for people protesting British rule.

Travel and taverns: The circulation of new ideas

Long-distance communication was a more complicated matter. Postal service was almost nonexistent—people gave letters to travelers or sea captains in hopes that they would be delivered. Under a parliamentary law of 1710, the postmaster of London named a deputy in charge of the colonies. A postal system eventually emerged along the Atlantic Seaboard, providing the colonies with an effective means of communication that would prove crucial in the growing controversy with Great Britain. More reliable mail delivery also spurred the popularity of newspapers.

Citizenship in the Empire

The individual colonies needed settlers to generate economic growth and to conquer Native Americans. One way to entice immigrants was to give them the opportunity to acquire the same civil rights as those born in the colonies ("birthright citizenship"). To that end, the colonies developed "naturalization" policies outlining the path to citizenship. Each colony had slightly different rules, but for White men, the rights of naturalization typically included acquiring property, voting and holding office, and receiving royal grants of land.

From the start, therefore, British America was an immigrant-welcoming society. Why? Because, as South Carolina's law explained, "by their industry, diligence and trade, [immigrants] have very much enriched and advanced this colony and settlement thereof."

By contrast, England sought to restrict immigration to the home country, fearing that Presbyterians, Baptists, Quakers, and Methodists would undermine the authority of the Church of England. Others worried that naturalized immigrants, if given the right to vote and hold office, "might endanger our ancient polity and government, and by frequent intermarriages go a great way to blot out and extinguish the English race."

Naturalization Act (1740)

To sustain high levels of immigration to British America, Parliament in 1740 passed the Naturalization Act. It announced that immigrants living in America for seven years would become subjects in the British Empire after swearing a loyalty oath and providing proof that they were Protestants. While excluding "papists" (a disparaging term for Roman Catholics), the law did make exceptions for Jews.

Enlightenment A revolution in thought begun in Europe in the seventeenth century that emphasized reason and science over the authority and myths of traditional religion.

The Enlightenment

The most significant of the new European ideas circulating in eighteenth-century America grew out of a burst of intellectual activity known as the **Enlightenment**. The Enlightenment celebrated rational inquiry, scientific research, and individual freedom. Enlightened people were those who sought the truth wherever it might lead. Immanuel Kant, the eighteenth-century German philosopher, summed up the Enlightenment point of view: "Dare to know! Have the courage to use your own understanding." He and others applied the power of reason to analyze the workings of nature, and they employed new tools like microscopes and telescopes to engage in close observation, scientific experimentation, and precise mathematical calculation.

The Age of Reason in America

The scientific revolution

Often called the Age of Reason, the Enlightenment was triggered by a scientific revolution in the sixteenth century that transformed the way educated people observed and understood the world. Just as explorers alerted Europeans to the excitement of new geographical discoveries, early modern scientists began to realize that social "progress" could occur through a series of intellectual and technological discoveries enabled by the adaptation of mathematical techniques for observing the natural world.

The ancient Christian view that the God-created earth was at the center of the universe, with the sun revolving around it, was overthrown by the controversial solar system described by Nicolaus Copernicus, a Polish astronomer and Catholic priest. In 1533, Copernicus asserted that the earth and other planets orbit the sun. Catholic officials scorned his theory until it was later confirmed by other scientists using telescopes.

In 1687, Englishman Isaac Newton announced his transformational theory of the earth's gravitational pull. He challenged biblical notions of the world's workings by depicting a changing, dynamic universe moving in accordance with "natural laws" that could be grasped by human reason and explained by mathematics. He implied that natural laws (rather than God) govern all things, from the orbits of the planets to the effects of gravity to the science of human relations: politics, economics, and society.

Deism

Some enlightened people, called **Deists**, carried Newton's scientific outlook to its logical conclusion, claiming that God created the world and designed its natural laws, which governed the operation of the universe. In other words, God planned the universe and set it in motion, but no longer interacted directly with the earth and its people.

Evil, according to the Deists, resulted not from humanity's inherent *sinfulness* as outlined in the Bible but from human *ignorance* of the rational laws of nature. Therefore, the best way to improve society and human nature, according to Deists such as Thomas Jefferson and Benjamin Franklin, was by cultivating Reason, which was the highest Virtue. (Enlightenment thinkers often capitalized both words.)

Enlightened "freethinkers" refused to allow church and state to limit what they could study and investigate. In this sense, the Enlightenment was a disruptive and even dangerous force in European thought that spawned not just revolutionary ideas but revolutionary movements.

Faith in the possibility of human progress was one of the most important beliefs of the Enlightenment. Equally important was the notion of political

Deists Those who applied enlightenment thought to religion, emphasizing reason, morality, and natural law rather than scriptural authority or an ever-present god intervening in the daily life of humans.

BENJAMIN FRANKLIN A champion of rational thinking and commonsense behavior, Franklin was an inventor, philosopher, entrepreneur, and statesman. This depiction of him, by Benjamin West, emphasizes his scientific achievements, one of which was his demonstration of the electrical nature of lightning in 1752.

freedom. Both Thomas Jefferson and Benjamin Franklin were intrigued by English political philosopher John Locke, who maintained that "natural law" called for a government that rested on the consent of the governed and respected the "natural rights" of all. Those rights included the basic civic principles of the Enlightenment—human rights, political liberty, religious toleration—that would later influence colonial leaders' efforts to justify a revolution.

The American version of the Enlightenment was best exemplified by Benjamin Franklin. Born in Boston in 1706, he left home at the age of sixteen, bound for Philadelphia. Six years later, he bought a print shop and began editing and publishing the *Pennsylvania Gazette* newspaper. As his printing business prospered, his reputation grew.

Franklin celebrated the virtues and benefits of self-reliance, hard work, and public service. He taught himself to read in four languages. Before he retired from business at the age of forty-two, Franklin had founded a public library, started a fire company, helped create what became the University of Pennsylvania, and organized a debating club that grew into the American Philosophical Society.

Franklin was an inventive genius devoted to scientific investigation. His wide-ranging experiments extended to the fields of medicine, meteorology, geology, astronomy, and physics. He developed the Franklin stove, the lightning rod, bifocal spectacles, and a glass harmonica. The enlightened Franklin displayed an all-encompassing, lifelong curiosity that in turn nurtured the confidence and capacity to think critically.

The Great Awakening

Religious response to the Enlightenment

The growing popularity of Enlightenment rationalism posed a direct threat to traditional religious life. But in the early eighteenth century, the American colonies experienced a revival of spiritual zeal designed to restore the primacy of emotion in the religious realm. Between 1700 and 1750, when the controversial ideas of the Enlightenment were circulating among the best-educated colonists, hundreds of new Christian congregations were founded. Most Americans (85 percent) lived in colonies with an "established" church, meaning that a colony's government endorsed—and collected taxes to support—a single official denomination.

The Church of England was the established church in Virginia, Maryland, Delaware, and the Carolinas. Puritan Congregationalism was the official faith in most of New England. In New York, Anglicanism vied with the Dutch

Reformed Church for control. Pennsylvania had no state-supported church, but Quakers dominated the legislative assembly. New Jersey and Rhode Island had no official denomination and hosted numerous Christian splinter groups.

Most colonies organized religious life around local parishes. In colonies with official tax-supported religions, people of other faiths could not preach without the permission of the parish. In the 1730s and 1740s, the parish system was thrown into turmoil by the arrival of traveling evangelists, called *itinerants,* who claimed that most local parish ministers were incompetent. In their emotionally charged sermons, the itinerants, several of whom were White women and African Americans, insisted that Christians must be "reborn" in their convictions and behavior.

Traveling evangelists and intense revivals

During the early 1730s, worries about the erosion of religious fervor helped spark a series of revivals known as the **Great Awakening**. The revivals spread up and down the Atlantic coast. The highly emotional gatherings divided congregations, towns, and families, and fueled popular new denominations, especially the Baptists and Methodists. A skeptical Benjamin Franklin admitted that the Awakening was having a profound effect on social life: "Never did the people show so great a willingness to attend sermons. Religion is become the subject of most conversation."

The Awakening was the first popular movement before the American Revolution that affected all thirteen colonies, and as such, it helped create ties across the colonies that would later help coordinate revolutionary activities against the British government.

Jonathan Edwards In 1734–1735, a remarkable spiritual transformation occurred in the congregation of Jonathan Edwards, a prominent Congregationalist minister in the Massachusetts town of Northampton. A brilliant philosopher and theologian, Edwards had entered Yale College in 1716, at age thirteen, and graduated at the top of his class four years later.

JONATHAN EDWARDS One of the foremost preachers of the Great Awakening, Edwards dramatically described the torments that awaited sinners in the afterlife.

When Edwards arrived in Northampton in 1727, the town's lack of religious conviction shocked him. He claimed that the young people were preoccupied with sinful pleasures and indulged in "lewd practices" that "corrupted others." He warned that Christians had become obsessed with making and spending money, and that the controversial ideas associated with the Enlightenment were eroding the importance of religious life. The fiery, charismatic Edwards rushed to restore the emotional side of religion. His vivid descriptions of the torments of hell and the delights of heaven helped rekindle spiritual intensity among his congregants. By 1735, he reported that "the town seemed to be full of the presence of God; it never was so full of love, nor of joy."

In 1741, Edwards delivered his most famous sermon, "Sinners in the Hands of an Angry God," in which he reminded the congregation that hell is real and that God "holds you over the pit of hell, much as one holds a spider, or some loathsome insect, over the fire, abhors you, and is dreadfully provoked. . . . He looks upon you as worthy of nothing else, but to be cast into the fire." When he finished, he had to wait several minutes for the congregants to quiet down before he could lead them in a closing hymn.

Great Awakening Emotional religious revival movement that swept the thirteen colonies from the 1730s through the 1740s.

GEORGE WHITEFIELD PREACHING Another influential figure of the Great Awakening was George Whitefield, an Anglican preacher who made several trips to America to spread his religious sentiments. This painting by Englishman John Collet does not depict the massive crowds Whitefield was known to attract, but it does represent their diversity of age, sex, and class. **Why did the message of the Great Awakening appeal to such a wide range of people?**

George Whitefield The most celebrated promoter of the Great Awakening was a young, cross-eyed English minister, George Whitefield, who visited the colonies seven times between 1738 and 1748. Whitefield set out to restore the fires of religious intensity in America.

Starting in Georgia in 1738, the young evangelist began a fourteen-month tour of the colonies, preaching a fiery gospel of redemption to huge crowds gathered in barns, open fields, and cemeteries. He rejected the Calvinist assumption that people must prepare for salvation. In his view, the grace of God arrived suddenly and without warning, like the dawn. A Connecticut farmer who attended one of Whitefield's open-air sermons described the blond-haired evangelist, often dressed in sparkling white robes, as "almost angelical" in appearance. Another participant reported that Whitefield's theatrical performance entranced the crowd: "He exceedingly wept, stamped loudly and passionately and was frequently so overcome that, for a few seconds, you would suspect he would never recover."

Yet Whitefield's critics were as fervent as his admirers. Anglican ministers dismissed him as being preoccupied with converting commoners and "the ignorant." A disgusted Bostonian described a revival meeting's theatrics: "The meeting was carried on with . . . some screaming out in Distress and Anguish . . . some again jumping up and down . . . some lying along on the floor. . . . The whole with a very great Noise, to be heard at a Mile's Distance, and continued almost the whole night." Whitefield enthralled audiences with his golden voice, flamboyant style, and unparalleled eloquence. Even Benjamin Franklin, a confirmed rationalist who saw Whitefield preach in Philadelphia, was so excited by the sermon that he emptied his pockets into the collection plate.

Women and Revivals The Great Awakening's most controversial element was the emergence of women who defied convention by speaking at religious services. Among them was Sarah Haggar Osborne, a Rhode Island schoolteacher who organized prayer meetings that eventually included men and women, Black and White. When concerned ministers told her to stop, she refused to "shut my mouth and doors and creep into obscurity."

Similarly, in western Massachusetts, Bathsheba Kingsley spread the gospel because she had received "immediate revelations from heaven." When her husband tried to intervene, she pummeled him with "hard words and blows," praying loudly that he "go quick to hell." For all the turbulence created by the revivals, however, churches remained male bastions of political authority.

The Heart versus the Head

The Great Awakening subsided by 1750. Like the Enlightenment, it influenced the forces leading to the revolution against Great Britain and set in motion powerful currents that still flow in American life.

The Awakening implanted in American culture the evangelical impulse and the emotional appeal of revivalism, weakened the status of the old-fashioned clergy and state-supported churches, and encouraged believers to exercise their own individual judgment. By promoting the proliferation of denominations, it heightened the need for toleration of dissent.

In some respects, however, the Awakening and the Enlightenment led by different roads to similar ends, one stressing the urgings of the spirit and the other celebrating the cold logic of reason. Both movements spread across the mainland colonies and thereby helped bind the regions together. Both emphasized the power and right of individual decision-making, and both aroused hopes that America would become the promised land in which people might attain the perfection of piety or reason, if not both.

By urging believers to exercise their own spiritual judgment, revivals weakened the authority of the established churches and their ministers, just as resentment of British economic regulations would later weaken colonial loyalty to the king. As such, the Great Awakening and the Enlightenment helped nurture a growing commitment to individual freedom and resistance to authority that would play a key role in the rebellion against British "tyranny" in 1776.

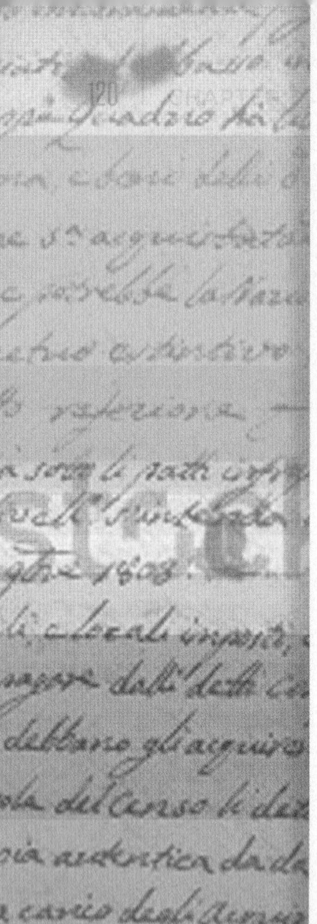

Reviewing the CORE OBJECTIVES | INQUIZITIVE

■ **Colonial Demographics** Cheap land lured poor immigrants to America. The initial shortage of women eventually gave way to a more equal gender ratio and a tendency to earlier marriage than in Europe, leading to higher *birth rates* and larger families. After the first years of settlement, *death rates* were lower in the colonies than in Europe, which led to rapid population growth.

■ **Women in the Colonies** English colonists brought their beliefs and prejudices with them to America, including convictions about the inferiority of women. Colonial women remained largely confined to *women's work* in the house, yard, and field. Over time, though, necessity created opportunities for women outside their traditional roles.

■ **Colonial Differences** A thriving colonial trading economy sent raw materials such as fish, timber, and furs to England in return for manufactured goods. The expanding economy created new wealth and a rise in the consumption of European goods, and it fostered the expansion of slavery. Tobacco was the *staple crop* in Virginia, rice in the Carolinas. Plantation agriculture based on slavery became entrenched in the South. New England's shipping industry created a profitable *triangular trade* among Africa, America, and England. By 1790, German, Scots-Irish, Welsh, and Irish immigrants, as well as other European ethnic groups, had settled in the middle colonies, along with Quakers, Jews, Huguenots, and Mennonites.

■ **Race-Based Slavery in the Colonies** Deep-rooted prejudice led to *race-based slavery*. Africans were considered "heathens" whose supposed inferiority entitled White Americans to enslave them. Africans brought diverse skills to help build America's economy. The use of enslaved Africans was concentrated in the South, where landowners used them to produce lucrative staple crops, such as tobacco, rice, and indigo. But enslaved people lived in cities, too, especially New York. As the enslaved population increased, race relations grew tense, and *slave codes* were created to regulate the movement of enslaved people. Sporadic slave uprisings, such as the *Stono Rebellion*, occurred in both the North and South.

■ **The Enlightenment and the Great Awakening** Printing presses, education, and city life generated a flow of new ideas that circulated via long-distance travel, tavern life, the postal service, and newspapers. The attitudes of the *Enlightenment* were transported along international trade routes. Sir Isaac Newton's scientific discoveries culminated in the belief that reason could improve society. Benjamin Franklin, who believed that people could shape their own destinies, became the face of the Enlightenment in America. *Deists* espoused the religious views of the Age of Reason. By the

1730s, a revival of faith, the *Great Awakening*, swept through the colonies. New congregations formed as evangelists insisted that Christians be "reborn." Individualism, not orthodoxy, was stressed in this first popular religious movement in America's history.

KEY TERMS

death rate *p. 94*

birth rate *p. 94*

women's work *p. 96*

staple crops *p. 99*

triangular trade *p. 105*

race-based slavery *p. 108*

slave codes *p. 109*

Stono Rebellion *p. 111*

Enlightenment *p. 114*

Deists *p. 115*

Great Awakening *p. 117*

CHRONOLOGY

1683 German Mennonites arrive in Pennsylvania

1687 Sir Isaac Newton publishes his theory of universal gravitation

1691 South Carolina passes first slave codes; other colonies follow

1692–1693 Salem witch trials

1712 Slave revolt in New York City; New York passes stricter laws governing the enslaved

1730s–1740s The Great Awakening

1738 Stono Rebellion

George Whitefield preaches his first sermon in America, in Georgia

1740 British Parliament passes the Naturalization Act

1741 Jonathan Edwards preaches "Sinners in the Hands of an Angry God"

The Conspiracy of 1741

1750 Colonial population passes 1 million

1775 Colonial population passes 2.5 million

INQUIZITIVE

Go to InQuizitive to see what you've learned—and learn what you've missed—with personalized feedback along the way.

BOSTON TEA PARTY In one of the most famous insurrections that contributed to the colonists' anti-British fervor, a swarm of Patriots disguised as Native Americans seized three British ships and dumped more than 300 chests of East India Company tea into the Boston harbor.

CHAPTER 4

From Colonies to States

1607–1776

Four great competing European powers—Spain, France, England, and the Netherlands (Holland)—created colonies in North America during the sixteenth and seventeenth centuries. Throughout the eighteenth century, wars raged across Europe, mostly pitting the Catholic nations of France and Spain against Protestant Great Britain and the Netherlands. The conflicts spread to North America, which became a primary battleground, involving both colonists and Native Americans allied with different European powers.

Spain's sparsely populated settlements in the borderlands north of Mexico were small and weak compared to those in the British colonies. Spain had failed to create substantial colonies with robust economies. Instead, it emphasized the conversion of native peoples to Catholicism, prohibited manufacturing within its colonies, strictly limited trade with Native Americans, and searched—mostly in vain—for gold.

The French and British colonies developed a thriving trade with Native Americans while the bitter rivalry between Great Britain and France gradually shifted the balance of power in Europe. By the end of the eighteenth century, Spain and the Netherlands were in decline, leaving France and Great Britain to fight for dominance. Their nearly constant warfare led Protestant Great Britain to tighten its control over the American colonies to raise the funds needed to combat

CORE OBJECTIVES INQUIZITIVE

1. Compare how the British and French Empires administered their colonies before 1763.
2. Analyze how the French and Indian War changed relations among the European powers in North America.
3. Describe how after the French and Indian War the British tightened their control over the colonies, and summarize the colonial responses.
4. Explain the underlying factors amid the events in the 1770s that led the colonies to declare their independence from Britain.

Catholic France and Spain. Tensions over these British efforts to preserve their empire at the expense of American freedoms would lead to rebellion and eventually to revolution.

CORE **OBJECTIVE**

1. Compare how the British and French Empires administered their colonies before 1763.

French and British Colonies

The French challenged the English presence in the Americas by establishing Catholic colonies in the Caribbean, Canada, and the Mississippi River Valley west of the Appalachian Mountains. Yet the French never invested enough people or resources in North America. By the mid-eighteenth century, the French residents of New France numbered less than 5 percent of the population in British America, and the relatively small French investment in Canada and Louisiana never turned a profit. In fact, New France became an enormous financial drain on the French economy, but imperial pride kept the monarchy from abandoning its North American colonies.

French fur-trading companies, forging alliances with indigenous peoples, religious restrictions, and limited immigration

New France

The actual settlement of New France began in 1605, when the intrepid soldier-explorer Samuel de Champlain founded Port-Royal in Acadia, along the Atlantic coast of Canada. Three years later, Champlain established Quebec, to the west, along the St. Lawrence River. Until his death in 1635, Champlain, "the Father of New France," governed Canada on behalf of trading companies eager to create a prosperous commercial colony tied to the robust fur trade with Indian nations and plentiful fishing opportunities off the Atlantic coast.

CHAMPLAIN IN NEW FRANCE Samuel de Champlain firing at a group of Iroquois, killing two chieftains (1609).

From the beginning, the French sought to work with the Indians. Champlain recruited Huron and Algonquian warriors to help conquer the feared Iroquois, their historic enemies. In his first confrontation with the Iroquois, the French commander fired his *arquebus* (forerunner to the rifle) at the Iroquois chiefs, killing two and wounding another. He then "pursued them and laid low still more of them." It was the Iroquois' first encounter with a firearm, and its explosive effects sent them caterwauling in fright. They dropped their weapons, abandoned their canoes and provisions, and fled.

In 1627, the French monarchy announced that only French Catholics could live in New France. This restriction stunted the settlement's growth—as did the harsh winter climate. As a consequence, the number of French colonists in Canada was *much* smaller than the number of British, Dutch, and Spanish in other North American colonies

Champlain knew that the French could survive only by befriending the native peoples. To that end, he dispatched trappers and traders to live with the indigenous nations, learn their languages and customs, and marry their women. Many of these hardy woodsmen pushed into the forested regions around the Great Lakes and developed a flourishing fur trade with the Indians.

The fur trade enticed the French to settle in Canada, but the activities of Catholic missionaries gave New France its dynamism. Like Spain, France aggressively sought to convert the Indians to Catholicism, in part because Christian Indians would become more reliable trading partners and military allies.

Jesuit missionaries led the way. The Society of Jesus (the Jesuits) had been founded in 1534, when Ignatius of Loyola, a Spanish soldier and nobleman, and six companions pledged to lead lives of poverty and chastity—and to defend the Roman Catholic Church. A year later, the pope officially recognized the Jesuits and urged them to convert the "pagan people" around the world.

The Jesuits became famous for their religious fervor, missionary zeal, and personal courage. They served as the "shock troops" of the Catholic Counter-Reformation, fighting the spread of Protestantism and traversing the globe as earnest missionaries. Some 3,500 Jesuits served in New Spain and New France.

French Jesuits in distinctive black robes fanned out from Quebec, traveling across the Great Lakes region and even down the Mississippi River.

JESUITS IN NEW FRANCE
Founded in 1539, the Jesuits sought to convert Indians to Catholicism, in part to make them more reliable trading and military partners.

The "Black Robes" carried with them smallpox and other infectious diseases that killed far more Indians than were converted to Christianity.

Unlike their Spanish counterparts, rarely were the Jesuits in French Canada accompanied by soldiers. Most of them lived among the Huron Nation in Canada. Jesuits and Indians borrowed from each other's practices and belief systems while never fully abandoning their own folkways. By befriending the Hurons and Algonquins, however, the French outraged other Indian nations. The tribes making up the Iroquois Confederacy (the Mohawk, Oneida, Onondaga, Cayuga, and Seneca) had long warred against the Hurons, and they loved nothing more than to destroy Catholic Huron villages and to capture Jesuit missionaries.

Royal control over New France

In 1663, French king Louis XIV converted New France into a royal colony led by a governor-general who modeled his rule after that of the absolute monarchy. New France was fully subject to the French king; colonists had no political rights or elected legislature. To solidify New France, Louis XIV dispatched soldiers and settlers, including shiploads of young women to become wives for the mostly male colonists. He also awarded large grants of land, called *seigneuries,* to lure aristocratic settlers. The poorest farmers usually rented land from the *seigneur*.

Yet none of these efforts transformed New France from being essentially a fur-trading outpost. Only about 40,000 French colonists came to the Western Hemisphere during the seventeenth and eighteenth centuries. By 1750, when the British in North America numbered about 1.5 million, the French population was only 70,000.

French geographical advantage over the British

New France, however, had one important advantage over the British: access to the great inland rivers that led to the heartland of the continent and thus to the pelts of fur-bearing animals such as beaver, otter, and mink.

From their Canadian outposts along the Great Lakes, French explorers in the early 1670s moved down the Mississippi River to the Gulf of Mexico. Louis Jolliet, a fur trader born in Quebec, teamed with Father Jacques Marquette, a Jesuit priest fluent in Indian languages, to explore the Wisconsin River south to the Mississippi. Traveling in canoes, they paddled to within 400 miles of the Gulf of Mexico, where they turned back for fear of encountering Spanish soldiers.

Other French explorers followed. In 1682, René-Robert Cavelier, sieur de La Salle, organized an expedition that started in Montreal, crossed the Great Lakes, and then went down the Mississippi to the Gulf of Mexico, the first European to do so. La Salle claimed for France the vast Ohio and Mississippi River Valleys—all the way to the Rocky Mountains. He named the region Louisiana, after King Louis XIV. Settlement of the Louisiana Territory finally began in 1699, when the French established a colony near Biloxi, Mississippi. The main settlement then moved to Mobile Bay and, in 1710, to what is now Mobile, Alabama.

For nearly fifty years, the driving force in Louisiana was Jean-Baptiste Le Moyne, sieur de Bienville. In 1718, he founded New Orleans, which soon

THE FRENCH IN NORTH AMERICA

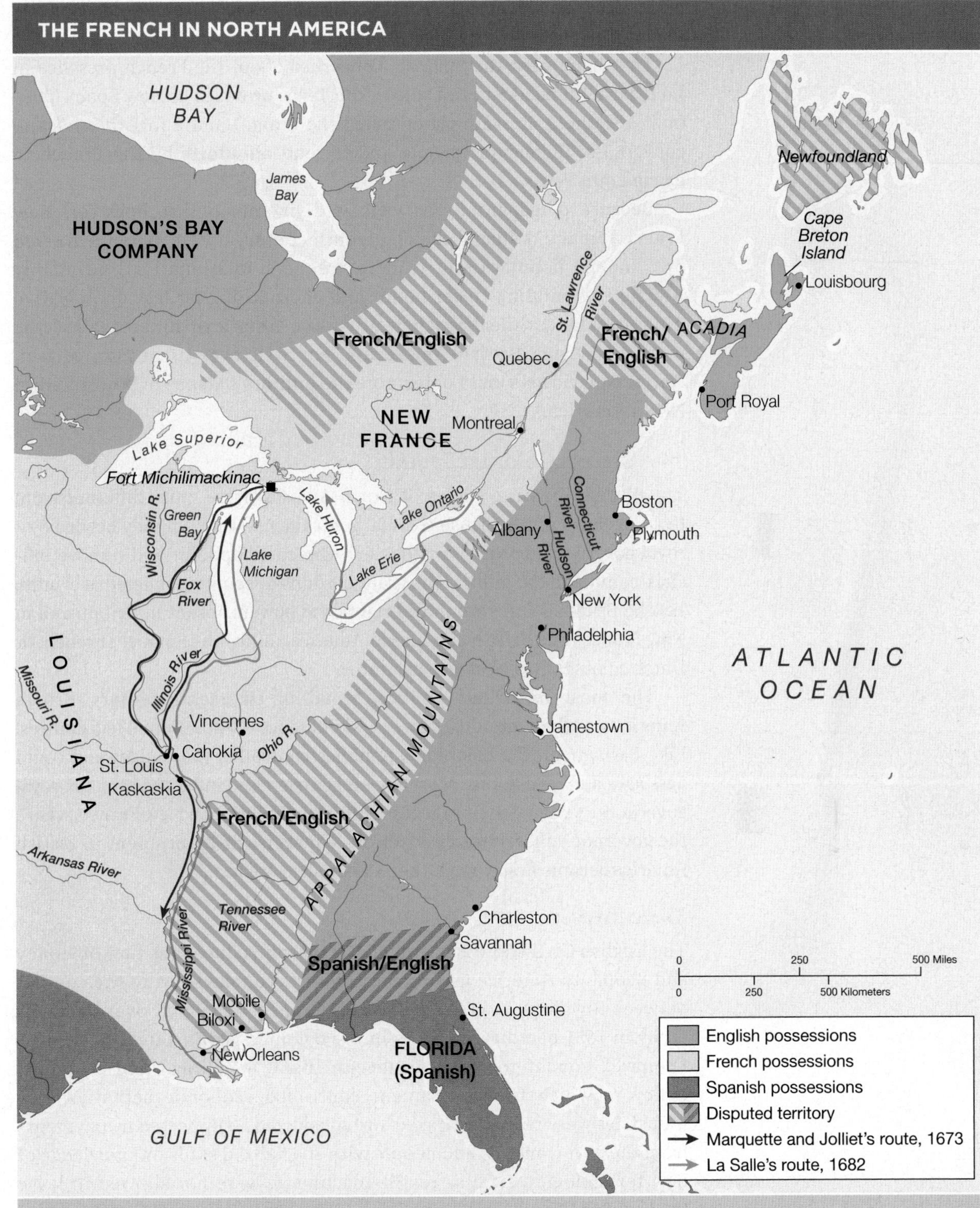

- Where were the largest French settlements in North America?
- How were they different from the Spanish and English colonies?
- Describe the French colonization of Louisiana.

became the capital of the sprawling Louisiana colony encompassing much of the interior of the North American continent.

That same year, the Spanish, concerned about the French presence in Louisiana, founded San Antonio in the Texas province of New Spain. They built a Catholic mission (later called the Alamo) and a fort (*presidio*) to convert the indigenous people and to fend off efforts by the French to expand into Texas.

Because of geography as well as deliberate policy, however, New France remained during the eighteenth century a vast region traversed by a mobile population of traders, trappers, missionaries, and mainly Indians. By building closer bonds and encroaching far less upon Native American lands, the French won Native American allies against the more numerous British Americans. For well over a century, in fact, Native Americans would determine the military balance of power within North America.

The British Colonial System

The diverse British colonies of North America were quite different from those of New France. British colonial governments were typically headed by a royal governor or proprietor (owner) who could appoint and remove officials, command the militia, and grant pardons to people convicted of crimes. Yet the British colonists enjoyed rights and powers absent in Britain and in New France. The British colonies in America, unlike the Spanish, French, or Dutch colonies, had *elected* legislatures.

The most important political trend in eighteenth-century British America was the expanding power and influence of the colonial legislatures. Like Parliament, the colonial assemblies controlled the budget and could pass laws and regulations. Most assemblies exercised influence over the royal governors by paying their salaries. Unlike the situation in New France, where the governor general exercised absolute power, self-government in British America became first a habit, then a cherished "right."

Mercantilism

The English Civil War during the 1640s sharply reduced the flow of money and people to America and forced colonists to take sides in the conflict between Royalists and Puritans. Oliver Cromwell's victory over the monarchy in 1651 had direct effects in the colonies. As England's new ruler, Cromwell sought to enforce **mercantilism**, a political and economic policy in which the government controlled economic activities. Key industries were regulated, taxed, or "subsidized" (supported by payments from the government), and people with specialized skills or knowledge of new technologies, such as textile machinery, were not allowed to leave the country.

mercantilism Policy of England and other imperial powers of regulating colonial economies to benefit the mother country.

Mercantilism also supported the creation of global empires. Colonies, it was assumed, enriched the mother country in several ways: (1) by providing silver, gold, and crucial raw materials such as furs, fish, and timber;

BOSTON FROM THE SOUTHEAST This view of eighteenth-century Boston shows the importance of shipping and its regulation in the colonies, especially in Massachusetts Bay.

(2) by creating a captive market of consumers who were forced to buy goods created in the home country; (3) by relieving social tensions and political unrest in the home country, because colonies could become a haven for the poor, unemployed, and imprisoned; and (4) by not producing goods that would compete with those produced in the home country.

Navigation Acts

Navigation Acts target the Dutch

Such mercantilist assumptions prompted Oliver Cromwell to adopt the first in a series of **Navigation Acts** intended to increase control over the colonial economies. The Navigation Act of 1651 required that all goods going to and from the colonies be transported *only* in English-owned ships. The law was intended to hurt the Dutch, who had developed a thriving shipping business between America and Europe. Dutch shipowners charged much less to transport goods than did the English, and they encouraged smuggling in the colonies as a means of defying the Navigation Acts. By 1652, England and the Netherlands were at war—the first of three naval conflicts between 1652 and 1674 involving the two Protestant rivals.

After the monarchy was restored to power in England in 1660, the Royalist Parliament passed the Navigation Act of 1660, which specified that certain colonial products (such as tobacco) were to be shipped *only* to England. The Navigation Act of 1663, called the Staples Act, required that *all* shipments from Europe to America first stop in Britain to be offloaded and taxed before being sent to the colonies.

Navigation Acts (1651–1775) Restrictions passed by Parliament to control colonial trade and bolster the mercantile system.

In 1664, English warships conquered New Netherland, ending Dutch colonial activity in North America. By 1700, the English had surpassed the Dutch as the world's leading maritime power, and most products sent to and from America via Europe and Africa were carried in English ships.

Resentment in the Colonies

Colonial merchants and shippers resented the Navigation Acts, but the English government refused to lift the restrictions. New England, which shipped 90 percent of all American exports, was particularly hard hit. In 1678, a defiant Massachusetts legislature declared that the Navigation Acts had no legal standing. In 1684, King Charles II responded by revoking the royal charter for Massachusetts. The following year, Charles died and his brother, King James II, succeeded him, becoming the first Catholic monarch in more than 100 years. The new king reorganized the New England colonies into a single supercolony called the Dominion of New England.

Dominion of New England

In 1686, a new royal governor of the Dominion of New England, the authoritarian Sir Edmund Andros, arrived in Boston. Andros stripped New Englanders of their civil rights, imposed new taxes, ignored town governments, strictly enforced the Navigation Acts, and punished smugglers.

The Glorious Revolution

In 1688, the Dominion of New England added the former Dutch provinces of New York, East Jersey, and West Jersey to its control, just a few months before the **Glorious Revolution** erupted in England. People called the revolution "glorious" because it took place with little bloodshed. Catholic king James II, fearing imprisonment, fled to France and was replaced by his daughter Mary and her husband William III, the ruling Dutch Prince (and the king's nephew). Both William and Mary were Protestants.

The English Bill of Rights

William III and Mary II would govern England as joint constitutional monarchs, their powers limited by Parliament. Both rulers signed the Declaration of Rights, which became known in England as the Bill of Rights. This document affirmed several constitutional principles, including the right for Parliament to meet regularly. It also mandated that elections be free from monarchical intervention and that freedom of speech in Parliament be protected. In addition, the Bill of Rights stipulated that no monarch could be a Roman Catholic. In May 1689, Parliament passed the Toleration Act, granting freedom of worship to many Protestant groups, but not Catholics.

After the Glorious Revolution, the monarchy in England would never again exercise absolute power. In addition, the long-standing geographical designation "Great Britain" for the united kingdoms of England, Scotland, and Wales was revived as the nation's official name.

Glorious Revolution (1688) Successful coup, instigated by a group of English aristocrats, that overthrew King James II and instated William of Orange and Mary, his English wife, to the English throne.

In 1689, Americans in Boston staged a revolt against the monarchy when a group of merchants, ministers, and militiamen (citizen-soldiers) arrested Governor Andros and his aides and removed Massachusetts Bay Colony from the new Dominion of New England. Within a few weeks, the other colonies that had been absorbed into the Dominion also restored their independence.

William and Mary, however, had no patience with American rebelliousness. They appointed new royal governors, who supported their reign, in Massachusetts, New York, and Maryland. In Massachusetts, the governor vetoed acts of the colonial assembly, and he removed the Puritans' religious qualification that only church members could vote in elections.

Amid the continuing tension between colonies and monarchy over governance issues, a powerful justification for revolution appeared in 1690 when English philosopher John Locke published *Two Treatises on Government*, which had an enormous impact on political thought in the colonies. Locke rejected the "divine" right of monarchs to govern with absolute power and insisted that people are endowed with **natural rights** to life, liberty, and property. When rulers failed to protect the property and lives of their subjects, Locke argued, the people had the right to overthrow the monarch and change the government.

JOHN LOCKE An English philosopher and strong believer in natural rights, Locke's writings rationalized revolutionary movements to overthrow unsatisfactory governments.

A New Emerging Colonial System

In early 1689 during the aftermath of the Glorious Revolution, New Yorkers sent a message to King William thanking him for delivering England from "tyranny, popery, and slavery." While the new monarchs also had rid the colonies of the much hated and more restrictive Dominion of New England, many colonists were disappointed, however, that earlier royal charters were restored and new royal governors appointed to run their colonies. Their disappointment further increased when the king took a series of steps to stop American smugglers from evading royal taxes. The Act to Prevent Frauds and Abuses of 1696 required royal governors to enforce the Navigation Acts, allowed customs officials in America to use "writs of assistance" (search warrants that did not have to specify the place to be searched), and ordered that accused smugglers be tried in royal admiralty courts (because juries in colonial courts rarely convicted their peers).

Soon, however, British efforts to enforce the Navigation Acts waned. King George I and George II, German princes who were descendants of James I, showed much less interest in enforcing colonial trade laws. Robert Walpole, the long-serving prime minister (1721–1742) and lord of the treasury, initiated a policy of **salutary neglect**, whereby the British government intentionally weakened the enforcement of the Navigation Acts. It did so in large part because rigid enforcement would have been too expensive. What Walpole did not realize was that his policy of salutary neglect would convince many colonists that they could avoid all royal regulations.

Decreased enforcement of colonial trade laws

The Habit of Self-Government

Government within the American colonies evolved during the eighteenth century as the colonial assemblies acquired powers, particularly with respect to government appointments, which Parliament had yet to exercise itself. By midcentury, the colonies had become largely self-governing.

The colonies benefited from elected legislative assemblies. Whether called the House of Burgesses (Virginia), Delegates (Maryland), Representatives

natural rights An individual's basic rights (life, liberty, and property) that should not be violated by any government or community.

salutary neglect Informal British policy during the first half of the eighteenth century that allowed the American colonies freedom to pursue their economic and political interests in exchange for colonial obedience.

Elected legislative assemblies

(Massachusetts), or simply the assembly, the "lower" houses were chosen by popular vote. Only male property owners could vote. Because property holding was much more widespread in America than in Europe, a greater proportion of the male population could vote and hold office. Members of the colonial assemblies tended to be wealthy, but there were exceptions. One unsympathetic colonist observed in 1744 that the New Jersey Assembly "was chiefly composed of mechanicks and ignorant wretches; obstinate to the last degree."

CORE **OBJECTIVE**

2. Analyze how the French and Indian War changed relations among the European powers in North America.

Warfare in the Colonies

The Glorious Revolution of 1688 transformed relations among the great powers of Europe. Protestant rulers William and Mary, passionate foes of Catholic France's Louis XIV, organized an alliance of European nations against the French in a transatlantic war known in the American colonies as King William's War (1689–1697). It would be the first of four major wars fought over the next seventy-four years pitting Britain and its European allies against France or Spain and their allies. By the end of the eighteenth century, the struggle between the British and French would shift the balance of power in Europe.

Wars have often been engines of change, sometimes in unexpected ways. The prolonged warfare between the British and French and their Indian allies had a devastating effect on New England, especially Massachusetts, which was closest to the battlefields of French Canada. It also reshaped the relationship between the colonies and Great Britain, which emerged from the wars as the most powerful nation in the world. Thereafter, international commerce became increasingly essential to the expanding British Empire, thus making the American colonies even more strategically significant.

The French and Indian War

The most important conflict between Britain and France (and its Catholic ally Spain) in North America was the **French and Indian War** (1756–1763), globally known as the **Seven Years' War**. Unlike the three previous wars between Britain, France, and their allies, it ended with a decisive British victory. The conflict started with frontier clashes in America in 1754, sparked by French and British competition for the ancestral Indian lands in the vast Ohio River Valley. The nation or colony (both Pennsylvania and Virginia claimed jurisdiction over it) that controlled the "Ohio Country" would control the entire continent because of the strategic importance of the Ohio and Mississippi Rivers.

French and Indian War (Seven Years' War) (1756–1763) The last and most important of four colonial wars between England and France for control of North America east of the Mississippi River.

To defend their interests, the French built forts in the Ohio Country. When Virginia's governor learned of the forts, he sent an ambitious twenty-two-year-old militia officer, Major George Washington, to warn the French to leave. But the French rudely rebuffed Washington.

A few months later, in the spring of 1754, Washington went back to the Ohio Country with 150 untrained volunteer soldiers and Indian allies.

MAJOR CAMPAIGNS OF THE FRENCH AND INDIAN WAR

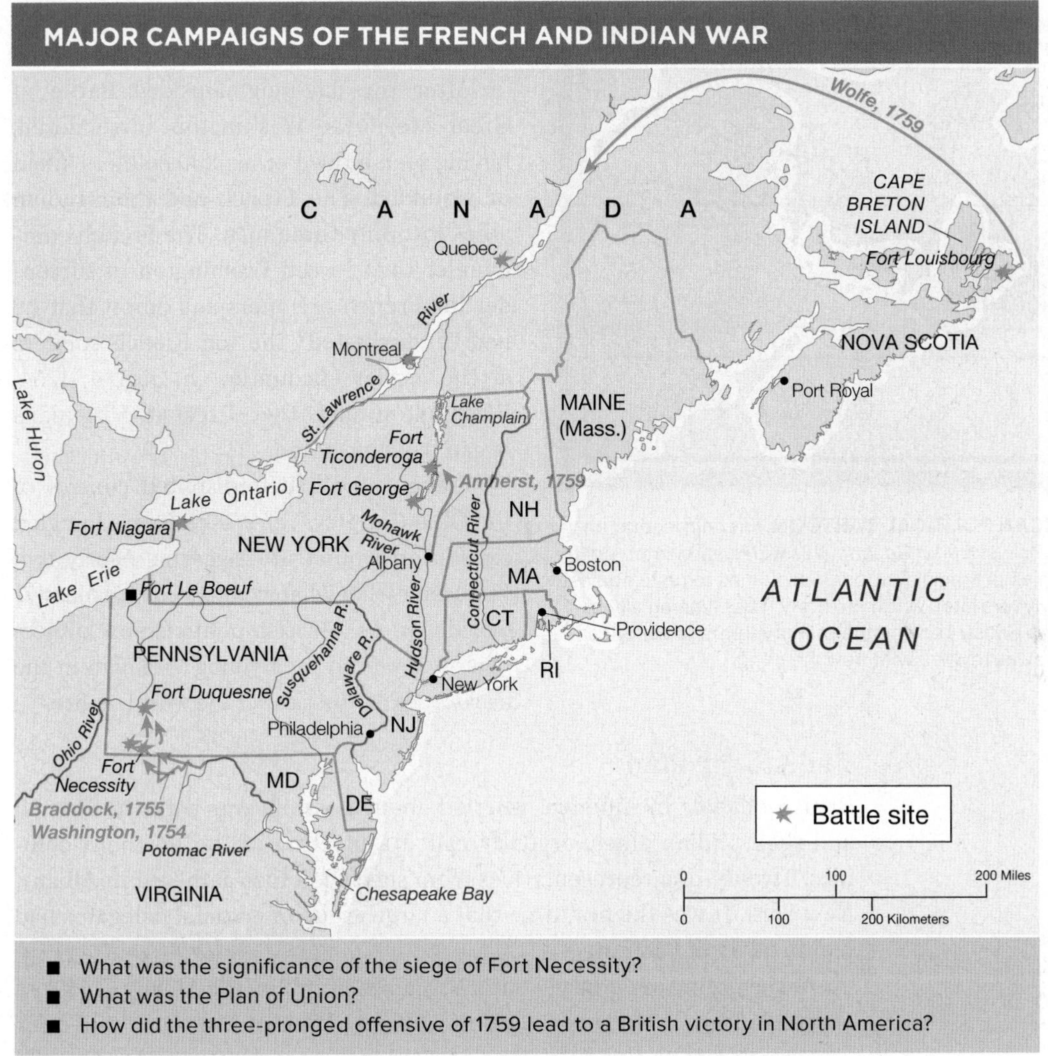

- What was the significance of the siege of Fort Necessity?
- What was the Plan of Union?
- How did the three-pronged offensive of 1759 lead to a British victory in North America?

They planned to build a fort where the Allegheny, Monongahela, and Ohio Rivers converged (where the city of Pittsburgh later developed). The so-called Forks of the Ohio was the key strategic gateway to the vast territory west of the Appalachian Mountains, and both sides were determined to control it.

After traveling for two months through dense forests and treacherous mountain passes, Washington learned that French soldiers had beaten him to the site and had built Fort Duquesne in western Pennsylvania. Washington decided to camp his men about forty miles away. The next day, the Virginians ambushed a French scouting party, killing ten—the first fatalities in what would become the French and Indian War.

Reinforced by more Virginians and British soldiers dispatched from South Carolina, Washington and his troops hastily constructed a tiny circular stockade, calling it Fort Necessity. Washington remarked that the valley provided "a charming field for an encounter," but there was nothing charming

THE FIRST AMERICAN POLITICAL CARTOON First appearing on May 9, 1754 in the *Pennsylvania Gazette*, this widely circulated political cartoon by Benjamin Franklin urged the colonies to unite against the French. Twenty years later, when the French became an ally of the colonies and the British became the primary threat to American liberty, this cartoon was revived with new meaning.

about the battle that erupted when a large French force attacked on July 3, 1754.

After the day-long, lopsided Battle of Great Meadows, Washington surrendered, having seen a third of his 300 soldiers killed or wounded. The French and their Indian allies lost only three men. The French commander then forced Washington to surrender his French prisoners and admit that he had "assassinated" the ten French soldiers at the earlier encounter. On July 4, 1754, Washington and the defeated Virginians began trudging home.

France now had undisputed control of the Ohio Country. Yet Washington's bungled expedition wound up triggering nearly two years later what what would become a massive world war. As a British politician exclaimed, "the volley fired by a young Virginian in the backwoods of America set the world on fire."

The Albany Plan

British officials in America, worried about possible war with the French and their Indian allies, urgently called a meeting of the northern colonies. Twenty-one representatives from seven colonies gathered in Albany, New York. It was the first time that a large group of colonial delegates had met to take joint action.

At the urging of Pennsylvania's Benjamin Franklin, the Albany Congress (June 19–July 11, 1754) approved the **Albany Plan of Union**. It called for eleven colonies to band together, headed by a president appointed by the king. Each colonial assembly would send two to seven delegates to a "grand council," which would have legislative powers. The Union would have jurisdiction over Indian affairs.

The Albany Plan of Union was too radical, however. British officials and the colonial legislatures, eager to maintain their individual powers, wanted simply a military alliance against Indian attacks, so they rejected the plan. Benjamin Franklin later maintained that the Plan of Union, had it been approved, might have postponed or eliminated the Revolutionary War. It would, however, become the model for the form of governance (Articles of Confederation) created by the new American nation in 1777.

Albany Plan of Union (1754) A failed proposal by the seven northern colonies in anticipation of the French and Indian War, urging the unification of the colonies under one Crown-appointed president.

War in North America

With the failure of the Albany Plan, the British decided to force a showdown with the "presumptuous" French. In June 1755, a British fleet captured the forts protecting French Acadia, along the Atlantic coast of Canada. The British then expelled 11,500 Acadians, the Catholic French residents. Hundreds of Acadians uprooted by the "Great Expulsion" eventually found their way to French Louisiana, where they became known as Cajuns.

In 1755, the British government sent 1,000 red-coated soldiers to dislodge the French from the Ohio Country. Their arrival on American soil would change the dynamics of British North America. Although the colonists endorsed the use of force against the French, they later would oppose the use of British soldiers to enforce colonial regulations.

FROM LA ROQUE'S *ENCYCLOPÉDIE DES VOYAGES* An Iroquois warrior in an eighteenth-century French engraving. **How does La Roque's representation of this Iroquois warrior differ from how Braddock viewed the Native Americans?**

Braddock's Defeat The British commander in chief in America, General Edward Braddock, was a stubborn, overconfident officer who, unlike the French, had no experience with frontier combat and little knowledge of American geography. He also failed to recruit large numbers of Indian allies. Braddock viewed Indians with contempt, telling the eight Indian scouts that he would not reward them with land as the French did, for "no savage should inherit the land." His dismissal of Indians and his ignorance of unconventional warfare would prove fatal.

With the addition of some American militiamen, including George Washington as a volunteer officer, Braddock's force left northern Virginia to confront the French, hacking a 125-mile-long road west through the Allegheny Mountains toward Fort Duquesne.

On July 9, 1755, as the British neared the fort, they were ambushed by French soldiers, Canadian militiamen, and Indians; they suffered shocking losses. Braddock was shot; he died three days later. Washington led a hasty retreat, despite having two horses shot dead under him and his coat and pants riddled by bullets. A British officer wrote that "the whole time," George Washington behaved "with the greatest courage."

What came to be called the Battle of Monongahela was one of the worst British defeats in history. The French and their Indian allies killed 63 of 86 British officers and 914 of 1,373 soldiers. A devastated Washington wrote his brother that the vaunted British redcoats had "been scandalously beaten by a trifling body of men" and had "broke & run as sheep pursued by hounds." The Virginians, he noted, "behaved like Men and died like Soldiers."

A World War

General Braddock's shocking defeat showed that the British army could be beaten. It also emboldened Indians allied with the French to attack English settlements throughout western Pennsylvania, Maryland, and

Virginia, killing, scalping, or capturing hundreds of men, women, and children. Desperate to respond, the Pennsylvania colonial government offered rewards for each Indian scalp.

The French and Indian War becomes the Seven Years' War

Indians and colonists fought mercilessly throughout 1755 and 1756. It was not until May 1756, however, that Protestant Britain and Catholic France formally declared war against one another in Europe. The first true "world war," the Seven Years' War in Europe (the battles in North America were called the French and Indian War) would eventually be fought on parts of five continents and three oceans. In the end, it would redraw the political map of North America. France, governed by the inept Louis XV, emerged from the war battered, humiliated, and bankrupt.

The onset of war brought into office a new British government, with William Pitt as prime minister. The fiery, self-confident Pitt provided expert leadership while declaring that he could "save this country and that no one else can." Pitt decided that defeating the French required a different military policy. Instead of forcing American colonists to help finance the war, he provided funds that convinced the legislatures to become full partners in the quest to oust the French from Canada.

Pitt's shrewd approach enabled his commanders to gather a force of 45,000 British troops and American militiamen. In August 1759, they captured French forts near the Canadian-American border at Ticonderoga, Crown Point, and Niagara.

In 1759, the French and Indian War reached its climax with a series of British triumphs. The most decisive victory was at Quebec, the hilltop fortress city and capital of French Canada. During the dark of night, some 4,500 British troops scaled the cliffs above the St. Lawrence River and at dawn surprised the French defenders in a battle that lasted only ten minutes. The French surrendered four days later.

GEORGE III In 1760 the young George III became King of Great Britain, and soon he governed the most powerful empire in the world.

The Battle of Quebec marked the turning point in the war. By 1761, France had lost Canada, its armies were bogged down in the killing fields of Germany, and its government was bankrupt. Thereafter, the conflict in North America ebbed, although sporadic combat continued until 1763.

A New British King

On October 25, 1760, the ailing British king George II arose at 6 A.M., drank his usual chocolate milk, and adjourned to his toilet closet. A few minutes later, a servant heard a strange noise, opened the door, and found the king dead, the result of a ruptured artery. His death brought an untested new king—his twenty-two-year-old grandson—to the throne. Although initially shy and insecure, King George III would become a strong-willed leader who would oversee the military defeat of France and Spain in the Seven Years' War.

The Treaty of Paris (1763)

The British gain most of North America; the Spanish gain the Louisiana Territory

The **Treaty of Paris**, signed in February 1763, gave Britain control of France's territories east of the Mississippi River. This encompassed all of Canada, what was then called Spanish Florida (including much of present-day Alabama and Mississippi), and several sugar-growing islands in the West Indies. As compensation, Spain received the vast Louisiana Territory, including the strategic port of New Orleans and all French land west of the Mississippi. France was left with no territory on the North American continent, while Great Britain emerged as the greatest empire in the world.

British Americans were delighted. The French menace had been removed from the Ohio River Valley, and British Americans could now enjoy the highest quality of life of any people in the Western Hemisphere. As a New England minister declared, Great Britain had reached the "summit of earthly grandeur and glory."

Yet Britain's military success created massive challenges. New territories had to be absorbed and funded. The staggering cost of maintaining the sprawling North American empire, including the permanent stationing of 10,000 British soldiers in the colonies, straned the government budget. In managing a vastly larger empire, the British would soon find themselves at war with their own colonies.

Managing a New Empire

No sooner was the Treaty of Paris signed than King George III and his cabinet, working through Parliament, began tightening control of the American colonies. With Britain no longer burdened by overpopulation, royal officials now rejected efforts by the colonies to encourage more immigrants by paying for their Atlantic crossing.

Colonists taxed to pay staggering British war debts

The king also ordered stiffer enforcement of economic regulations on the colonies to help reduce the crushing national debt caused by the war. In 1763, the average British citizen paid twenty-six times as much in annual taxes as did the average American colonist. British leaders thought it only fair that Americans should pay more of the expenses for administering and defending the colonies. Many Americans disagreed, however, arguing that the various Navigation Acts restricting their economic activity were already a form of taxation. "It is truly a miserable thing," said a Connecticut minister in December 1763, "that we no sooner leave fighting our neighbors, the French, but we must fall to quarreling among ourselves." The resulting tension set in motion a chain of events that would lead to revolution and independence.

Pontiac's Rebellion

After the war, colonists grew eager to take ownership of Indian lands west of the Appalachian Mountains that the French had ceded to the British in the Treaty of Paris. Native American leaders, none of whom

Treaty of Paris (1763) Settlement between Great Britain and France that ended the French and Indian War.

NORTH AMERICA, 1713

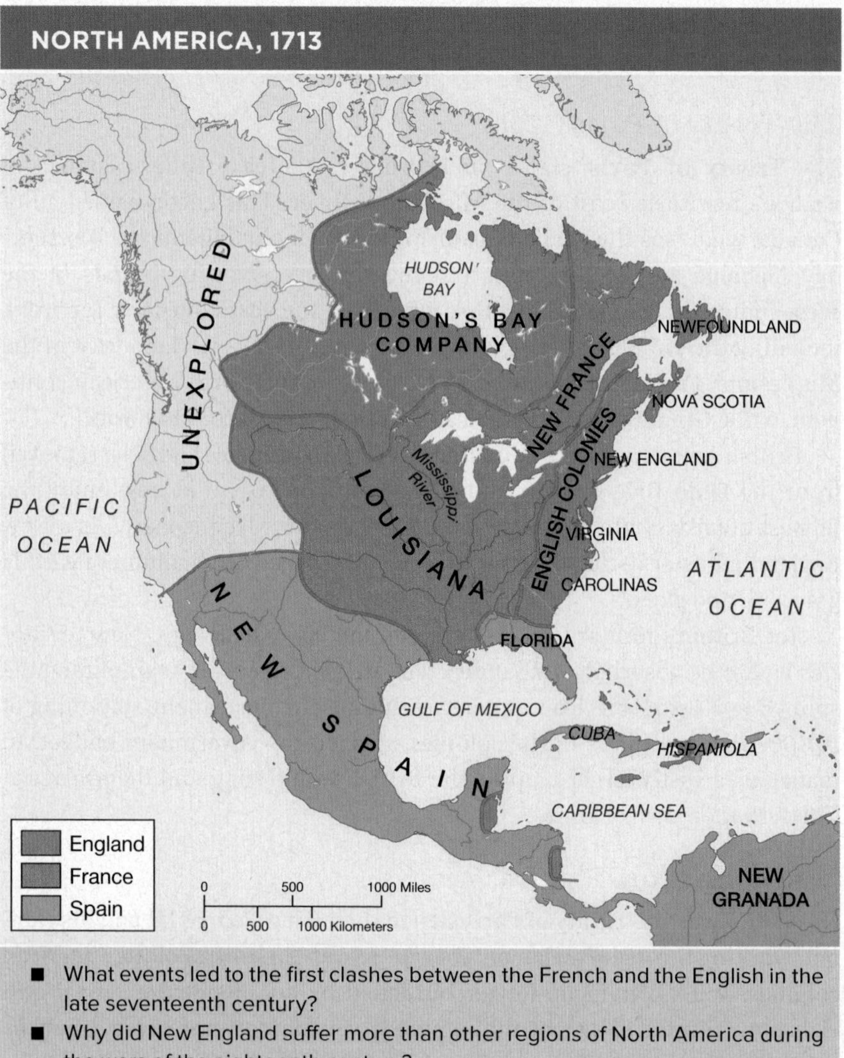

- What events led to the first clashes between the French and the English in the late seventeenth century?
- Why did New England suffer more than other regions of North America during the wars of the eighteenth century?
- What were the financial, military, and political consequences of the wars between France and Britain?

participated in the treaty negotiations, were shocked to learn that the French had "given" their ancestral lands to the British, who were intent upon imposing a harsh settlement on those Indians who had been allies of the French. The new British army commander in America, General Jeffrey Amherst, announced that the British would no longer provide "gifts" to the Indians, as the French had done. Ohio Indians complained to British army officers that "as soon as you conquered the French, you did not care how you treated us."

Frustrated Shawnees led by Chief Cornstalk fought back in the spring of 1763, capturing most of the British forts around the Great Lakes and in the Ohio River Valley. "Never was panic more general," reported the *Pennsylvania Gazette*, "than that of the Back[woods] Inhabitants, whose terrors at this time exceed that followed on the defeat of General Braddock." At Fort Pitt, formerly

NORTH AMERICA, 1763

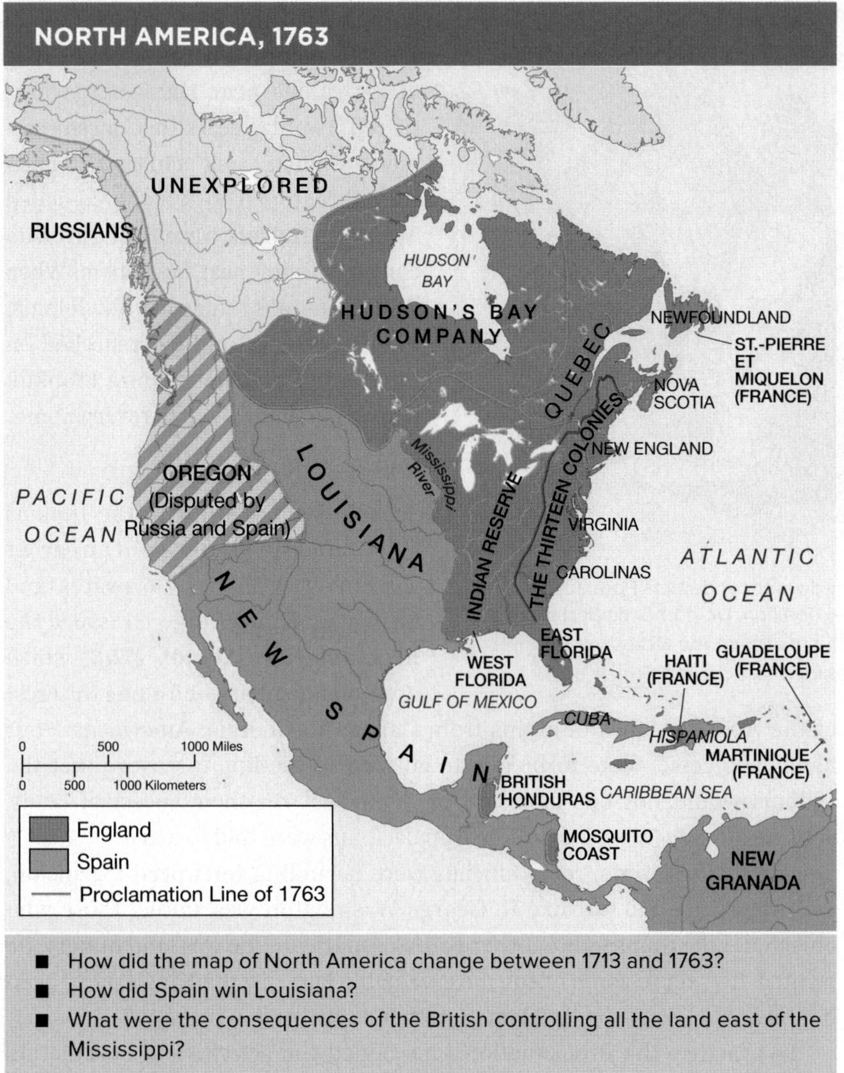

- How did the map of North America change between 1713 and 1763?
- How did Spain win Louisiana?
- What were the consequences of the British controlling all the land east of the Mississippi?

Fort Duquesne, a desperate General Amherst instituted an early form of biological warfare when he ordered that blankets infected with smallpox be circulated among the Indians. Native Americans raided colonial settlements in Pennsylvania, Maryland, and Virginia, destroying farms and killing hundreds.

The widespread Indian attacks came to be called **Pontiac's Rebellion** because of the prominent role played by the Ottawa chieftain in recruiting other tribes to help stop British expansion. Pontiac told a British official that the "French never conquered us, neither did they purchase a foot of our Country, nor have they a right to give it to you."

Pontiac's Rebellion (1763) A series of Native American attacks on British forts and settlements after France ceded to the British its territory east of the Mississippi River as part of the Treaty of Paris without consulting France's Native American allies.

British officials hoped to negotiate with Pontiac an arrangement whereby the two nations would trade generously with one another, but not fight each other. Colonists, however, had other goals, most notably revenge.

In December 1763, frontier ruffians in Pennsylvania took the law into their own hands. Outraged at the unwillingness of pacifist Quakers in the Pennsylvania assembly to protect White settlers from marauding Indians, a

PONTIAC'S REBELLION A hand-colored woodcut depicts Pontiac and allies meeting with British officials during the rebellion. No authentic portrait of Pontiac is known to exist. **What were the results of the Ottawa chieftain's resistance to British occupation of Native American land?**

group called the Paxton Boys, Scots-Irish farmers from Paxton, a cluster of log cabins near Harrisburg, massacred twenty peaceful Conestogas—men, women, and children. Then they threatened to kill the so-called Moravian Indians, a group of Christian converts living near Bethlehem. When the Indians took refuge in Philadelphia, some 1,500 Paxton Boys marched on the capital, where Benjamin Franklin helped persuade them to return home.

The Proclamation Line

To help keep peace with the Indians and to abide by the terms of an earlier agreement with the Delawares and Shawnees, King George III issued the **Proclamation Act of 1763**, which drew an imaginary line along the crest of the Appalachian Mountains from Canada to Georgia. Americans ("our loving subjects") were forbidden to go west of the line to ensure that the Indians would not be "molested or disturbed" on their ancestral lands. Settlers already living west of the Appalachians were told to leave.

For the first time, royal officials were curtailing territorial expansion, and Americans did not like it. George Washington was among those who objected. Like thousands of other British Americans, he was land hungry; he wanted "to secure some of the most valuable lands in the King's part" even if it meant defying "the Proclamation that restrains it at present."

In practice, the Proclamation Line ended the activities of speculators to buy huge tracts of Indian lands but did not keep settlers from pushing into the Indian lands in the Ohio River Valley. By 1767, an Indian chief was complaining that Whites were "making more encroachments on their Country than ever they had before."

Immigration Soars

One unexpected result of the war's end was a surge in European immigration to the American colonies. With the French no longer a threat, colonists were more comfortable in testing the American wilderness. Between 1763 and 1775, more than 30,000 English, 55,000 Protestant Irish, and 40,000 Scots arrived in the colonies, along with 12,000 German and Swiss settlers. At the same time, some 85,000 enslaved Africans were brought to the southern colonies. It was the greatest mass migration in history to that point, and it provided the impetus for much of America's development thereafter.

Proclamation Act of 1763 Proclamation drawing a boundary along the Appalachian Mountains from Canada to Georgia in order to minimize occurrences of settler–Native American violence; colonists were forbidden to go west of the line.

Most of the new arrivals were young males who had served as apprentices to learn a craft or trade. Many others were poor farm families who

"AN EAST PROSPECT OF THE CITY OF PHILADELPHIA" A detail of an engraving from 1771 showcases the religious diversity among European immigrants in the city of Philadelphia, as seen from across the Delaware River. An Anglican church, a Presbyterian church, a Dutch Calvinist church, and a Quaker meeting house—among others—punctuate the Philadelphia skyline.

emigrated as a group. Half of them could not afford to pay the cost of crossing the Atlantic and therefore arrived as indentured servants.

Tightening of Control Over The British Colonies

CORE **OBJECTIVE**

3. Describe how after the French and Indian War the British tightened their control over the colonies, and summarize the colonial responses.

As Britain tightened its hold over the colonies—and the Indians—after 1763, Americans reminded Parliament that their original charters guaranteed that they should have all the rights and liberties of English citizens. Why should they be governed by a distant legislature in which they had no elected representatives? Such arguments, however, fell on deaf ears in Parliament.

Grenville's Colonial Policy

British warships target American smugglers

Just as the Proclamation Act of 1763 was being drafted, a new British government, led by Prime Minister George Grenville, began to grapple with the huge debts accumulated during the Seven Years' War, along with the added expenses of maintaining troops in America. Grenville insisted that Americans pay for the British soldiers defending them. He also resented the large number of American smugglers who avoided British taxes on imported goods. Grenville ordered colonial officials to tighten enforcement of the Navigation Acts and sent warships to capture smugglers.

The Sugar Act (1764)

George Grenville's crackdowns posed a serious threat to New England's prosperity. Distilling rum out of molasses, a sweet syrup made from sugarcane, had become quite profitable, especially if the molasses could be smuggled in from Caribbean islands still controlled by the French.

New taxes and regulations

To raise more money from the colonies, Grenville put through the American Revenue Act of 1764, commonly known as the Sugar Act, which cut the tax on molasses in half. Doing so, he believed, would reduce the

THE GREAT FINANCIER A British cartoon from 1765 depicts the struggling British economy. Grenville stands in the center holding up a scale to measure British "Debts" and "Savings," the debts far outweighing the savings. On the left, a Native American woman wearing a yoke represents America, burdened by taxes without representation. **Why was Britain in such financial straits in the early 1760s and how did Grenville attempt to pay off Britain's debts?**

temptation to smuggle French molasses or to bribe royal customs officers. The Sugar Act, however, also added *duties* (taxes) on other goods (sugar, wines, coffee, spices) imported into America. The new tax revenues, Grenville believed, would help pay for "the necessary expenses of defending, protecting, and securing, the said colonies."

With the Sugar Act, Parliament sought to raise *revenues* from the colonies and not merely to *regulate* their trade with other nations, as had been the case up to that point. Colonists claimed that the Sugar Act taxed them without their consent, since they had no elected representatives in Parliament. British officials argued, however, that Parliament's power over the colonies was absolute and indivisible. If the Americans accepted parliamentary authority in *any* area, they had to accept it in *every* area including taxation.

The Currency Act (1764)

The colonies had long faced a chronic shortage of "hard" money (gold and silver coins, called *specie*), which kept flowing overseas to pay debts in England. To address the lack of specie, many colonies issued their own paper money, which could not be used in other colonies. British merchants feared being paid with a currency of such fluctuating value, so Grenville implemented the Currency Act of 1764. It prohibited the colonies from coining or printing money, while requiring that all payments for imported British goods be in gold or silver coins or in a commodity like tobacco. As a result, the value of existing paper money plummeted. As a Philadelphia newspaper complained, "The Times are Dreadful, Dismal, Doleful, Dolorous, and DOLLAR-LESS."

The Quartering Act (1765)

Then, in 1765, Grenville persuaded Parliament to pass the Quartering Act as part of his new system of colonial regulations. The Quartering Act required the colonies to feed and house many of the 10,000 British troops stationed in the colonies. Such a step seemed perfectly appropriate to Grenville, since he and many others in Britain believed that the Americans should contribute to the expense of defending the colonies. Many colonists, however, viewed the Quartering Act as yet another form of tax as well as another form of repression. Why, they asked, were so many British soldiers needed in colonial cities? If the British troops were there to defend against Indians, why were they based in cities rather than along the frontier? Some colonists decided that the Quartering Act was an effort to use British soldiers to bully Americans.

The TIMES are Dreadful, Dismal Doleful Dolorous, and DOLLAR-LESS.

of the STAMP
An Emblem of the Effects
O! the fatal Stamp

Thursday, October 31, 1765. THE NUMB. 1195.

PENNSYLVANIA JOURNAL;
AND
WEEKLY ADVERTISER.

EXPIRING: In Hopes of a Resurrection to LIFE again.

OPPOSITION TO THE STAMP ACT On October 31, 1765, the *Pennsylvania Journal* printed a skull and crossbones on its masthead in protest of the Stamp Act, which was to take effect the next day. **Why was the Stamp Act met with such opposition by the colonists?**

The Stamp Act (1765)

In February 1765, George Grenville pushed through an even more controversial measure. The **Stamp Act** required colonists to purchase paper from London embossed with a government revenue stamp. Only British currency could be used to purchase the stamped paper. It affected all colonists because it applied to paper for virtually every possible use: newspapers, pamphlets, bonds, leases, deeds, licenses, insurance policies, college diplomas, even playing cards. The requirement was to go into effect November 1.

The Stamp Act was the first effort by Parliament to place a tax directly on American goods and services rather than levying an "external" tax on imports and exports, and it offended just about everyone. Benjamin Franklin's daughter Sarah ("Sally") wrote to her father in London, where he was representing the colonies, reporting that the only subject of conversation in America was the Stamp Act, "and nothing else is talked of. . . . Everybody has something to say" about the hated tax, in part because, when combined with the Sugar and Currency Acts, it promised to bring American economic activity in the colonies to a halt.

The Stamp Act was even more hated, however, because it showed that Parliament was determined to deny Americans their rights to representation in Parliament. Boston lawyer John Adams, who would become the second president of the United States, led the opposition to the Stamp Act. In doing so, he unwittingly gave voice to the continuing contradiction among colonial rebels between their efforts to protect their civil liberties and their enslavement of hundreds of thousands of Africans and Indians. In a letter to a friend, Adams expressed his defiance of the Stamp Act by pledging, "We will not be their negroes." Another Boston agitator, James Otis, Jr., saw through the hypocrisy of Adams's statement. Yes, "the colonists are by the law of nature

Stamp Act (1765) Act of Parliament requiring that all printed materials in the American colonies use paper with an official tax stamp in order to pay for British military protection of the colonies.

free born," Otis acknowledged, but "indeed all men are, white or black." It was absurd, Otis argued, to claim that it was acceptable to "enslave a man [simply] because he is black."

The British controlled thirty colonies in the Western Hemisphere, but only the thirteen mainland colonies rose up against the new taxes. To Americans, however, the "engine" of British tyranny was a threat to their very existence.

The Whig Point of View

George Grenville's colonial policies ignited an intense debate about the proper relationship between Great Britain and her colonies. Americans who opposed British policies began to call themselves Patriots, or *Whigs*, a name earlier applied to British critics of royal power. In turn, Whigs labeled the king and his "corrupt" government ministers and Parliamentary supporters as *Tories*, a term of abuse meaning friends of the king.

In 1764 and 1765, colonial Whigs felt that Grenville was violating their rights in several ways. Although the French had been defeated and Canada was solidly under British control, thousands of British soldiers remained in America. Were the troops there to protect the colonists or scare them into obedience?

Virtual representation

Whigs also argued that although British citizens had the right to be taxed only by their elected representatives in Parliament, Americans had no such representatives. British leaders countered that the colonists enjoyed **virtual representation** in Parliament, but William Pitt, a staunch supporter of American rights in Parliament, dismissed virtual representation as "the most contemptible idea that ever entered into the head of a man." Many others, in both Britain and America, agreed. Sir Francis Bernard, the royal governor of Massachusetts, correctly predicted that the stamp tax "would cause a great Alarm & meet much Opposition."

Protests in the Colonies

Stamp Act Resolutions

The Stamp Act did arouse intense resentment and resistance. In a flood of pamphlets, speeches, resolutions, and street protests, critics repeated a slogan familiar to Americans: "No taxation without representation [in Parliament]." Rebels, calling themselves **Sons of Liberty**, emerged in every colony to organize protests, often meeting beneath "liberty trees"—in Boston a great elm, in Charleston a live oak. In Virginia, Patrick Henry convinced the assembly to pass the "Stamp Act Resolutions," which asserted that the colonists could not be taxed without being first consulted by the British government or being represented in Parliament by their own elected members.

virtual representation The idea that the American colonies, although they had no actual representative in Parliament, were "virtually" represented by all members of Parliament.

Sons of Liberty First organized by Samuel Adams in the 1770s, groups of colonists dedicated to militant resistance against British control of the colonies.

The Nonimportation Movement

Since the mid-seventeenth century, colonial consumers had become addicted to imported British manufactured goods—textiles, ceramics, glassware,

THE LIBERTY TREE At this mid-August meeting of the Sons of Liberty, the angry colonists hanged effigies of two tax collectors from the branches of a Liberty Tree.

and printed products. Now, however, patriots by the thousands signed nonimportation agreements pledging not to buy British goods.

Boycotts of British goods

The nonimportation movement united Whigs from different communities and different colonies. It also enabled women to play a key role in the resistance. Calling themselves **Daughters of Liberty**, Whig women stopped buying imported British clothes and quit drinking British tea to "save this abused Country from Ruin and Slavery." Using herbs and flowers, they made "Liberty Tea" instead. The Daughters of Liberty also participated in public "spinning bees," whereby they gathered in town squares to spin yarn and wool into fabric, known as "homespun." In 1769, the *Boston Evening Post* reported that the "industry and frugality of American ladies" were enabling "the political salvation of a whole continent."

Colonial Unity

Virginia Resolves and the Declaration of Rights and Grievances

The boycotts worked. Imports of British goods fell by 40 percent, and thousands of English workers lost their jobs as a result. At the same time, the Virginia House of Burgesses struck the first official blow against the Stamp Act with the Virginia Resolves, a series of resolutions inspired by Patrick Henry. Virginians, Henry asserted, could be taxed only by their elected legislature, not by Parliament.

Daughters of Liberty Colonial women who protested the British government's tax policies by boycotting British products, such as clothing, and who wove their own fabric, or "homespun."

In 1765, the Massachusetts House of Representatives invited the other colonial assemblies to send delegates to New York City to discuss opposition to the Stamp Act. Nine responded, and from October 7 to October 25, the twenty-seven men attending the Stamp Act Congress formulated a

REPEAL OF THE STAMP ACT This 1766 cartoon shows Grenville carrying the dead Stamp Act in its coffin. In the background, trade with America starts up again.

Declaration of the Rights and Grievances of the Colonies. The delegates insisted that they would accept no taxes being "imposed on them" without "their own consent, given personally, or by their representatives."

Repeal of the Stamp Act

George Grenville, having lost the confidence of King George III, was replaced by Lord Rockingham in July 1765. The growing rebellion in America convinced Rockingham that the Stamp Act was a mistake, and Parliament repealed it in February 1766. To save face, Parliament also passed the Declaratory Act, which asserted its power to govern the colonies "in all cases whatsoever." The repeal of the Stamp Act set off excited celebrations throughout the colonies. A British newspaper reported that the debate over the Stamp Tax had led some Americans to express a desire for "independence." The editor predicted that eventually the colonies would "shake off all subjection. If we yield to them . . . by repealing the Stamp Act, it is all over."

The Townshend Acts Fan the Flames

More taxes under Townshend

Townshend Acts (1767) Parliamentary measures to extract more revenue from the colonies; the Revenue Act of 1767, which taxed tea, paper, and other colonial imports, was one of the most notorious of these policies.

In July 1766, George III replaced Lord Rockingham with William Pitt, the former prime minister who had exercised heroic leadership during the Seven Years' War. For a time, the guiding force in the Pitt ministry was Charles Townshend, the treasury chief whose "abilities were superior to those of all men," said a colleague, "and his judgment [common sense] below that of any man."

In 1767, Townshend pushed through Parliament an ill-fated plan to generate more colonial revenue just a few months before he died, leaving a bitter legacy in British politics. The Revenue Act of 1767, which taxed colonial imports of glass, lead, paint, paper, and tea, posed an even more severe threat than George Grenville's taxes had, for Townshend planned to use the new tax revenues to pay the salaries of the royal governors in the colonies. Until that point, the colonial assemblies had paid the salaries, thus giving them leverage over the governors. John Adams observed that Townshend's plan would make the royal governor "independent of the people." Writing in the *Boston Gazette,* Adams insisted that such "an INDEPENDENT ruler, [is] a MONSTER in a free state."

Road to the American Revolution

CORE **OBJECTIVE**

4. Explain the underlying factors amid the events in the 1770s that led the colonies to declare their independence from Britain.

American Patriots

The **Townshend Acts** surprised and angered many colonists, including Samuel ("Sam") Adams of Boston, a failed beer brewer and tax collector who had become one of the most radical rebels and a driving force behind the Sons of Liberty. He decided that a small group of determined Whigs could generate a mass movement. "It does not take a majority to prevail," Adams insisted, "but rather an irate, tireless minority, keen on setting brushfires of freedom in the minds of men."

Early in 1768, Adams and James Otis, Jr., convinced the Massachusetts Assembly to circulate a letter that restated the illegality of taxation without representation. British officials ordered the Massachusetts Assembly to withdraw the letter. The delegates refused, and the king ordered the Massachusetts legislature dissolved.

SAMUEL ADAMS Adams was a fiery organizer of the Sons of Liberty.

In October 1768, in response to an appeal by the royal governor, 4,000 British troops arrived in Boston, the hotbed of colonial resistance. They disembarked with great ceremony, marching through the streets behind a brass band. **Loyalists**, as the Americans who supported the king and Parliament had begun to be called, welcomed the soldiers; **Patriots**, those rebelling against British authority, viewed the troops as an occupation force. Sam Adams growled that the king had "no right to send troops here . . . and I look upon them as foreign enemies." He then threatened violence: "We will destroy every soldier that dares put his foot on shore."

Meanwhile, in London, the king appointed still another new chief minister, Lord North, and told him to crack down on the rebellious colonists. "America must fear you—before she can love you," North told Parliament.

Loyalists Colonists who remained loyal to Britain before and during the Revolutionary War.

Patriots Colonists who rebelled against British authority before and during the Revolutionary War.

The Boston Massacre (1770)

In Boston, too, the presence of British soldiers had become a constant source of irritation. Crowds frequently heckled the soldiers, many of whom had earned the abuse by harassing Americans.

THE BLOODY MASSACRE Paul Revere created this engraving of the Boston Massacre about three weeks after the event, and it was one of the most effective pieces of political propaganda of the Revolutionary period. It inaccurately depicts an organized and merciless row of British soldiers shooting down an unarmed cluster of colonists, richly dressed and putting themselves in the line of fire as they carry their wounded compatriots to safety. **What would a more accurate representation of the Boston Massacre show?**

On the evening of March 5, 1770, two dozen "saucy" Boston rowdies—teens, Irishmen, and sailors—began throwing icicles and oyster shells at Hugh White, a young soldier guarding the Customs House. Someone rang the town fire bell, drawing a larger crowd to the scene, as the taunting continued: "Kill him, kill him, knock him down. Fire, damn you, fire, you dare not fire!"

A squad of soldiers arrived to help White, but the surly crowd surrounded them. When someone knocked a soldier down, he arose and fired his musket. Others joined in. After the smoke had cleared, five men lay dead or dying on the cobblestone street, and eight more were wounded. The first one killed was Crispus Attucks, a formerly enslaved man who worked at the docks. The *Boston Gazette* called it a "horrid massacre." More than 10,000 people attended the funerals of the murdered colonists.

Nine British soldiers were arrested and jailed. Never in Massachusetts had a trial generated such passion and excitement. Sam Adams and other firebrands demanded quick justice, but months passed before the trial convened. Finally, in late October, two of the British soldiers, convicted of manslaughter, were branded on the thumb with a hot iron.

Impact of the Boston Massacre

The so-called **Boston Massacre** sent shock waves throughout the colonies and all the way to London. Only the decision to postpone the trial for six months allowed tensions to ease. At the same time, the impact of the colonial boycott of British products persuaded Lord North to modify the Townshend Acts.

Late in April 1770, Parliament repealed all the Townshend duties except for the tea tax, which the king wanted to keep as a symbol of Parliament's authority. Colonial discontent subsided. The redcoats left Boston but remained in Canada, and the British navy continued to patrol the New England coast looking for smugglers.

The *Gaspée* Incident (1772)

The *Gaspée* incident

In June 1772, a naval incident further eroded the colonies' fragile relationship with the mother country. Near Warwick, Rhode Island, the *Gaspée*, a British warship, ran aground while chasing smugglers. Its hungry crew seized local sheep, hogs, and chickens. A crowd of enraged Americans then boarded the *Gaspée*, shot the captain, removed the crew, and looted and burned the ship.

In response to the *Gaspée* incident, Sam Adams organized in Boston the **Committee of Correspondence**, which issued a statement of American rights and grievances and invited other towns to do the same. Similar committees sprang up across the colonies, forming a unified network of resistance.

By 1772, Thomas Hutchinson, the royal governor of Massachusetts, could tell the colonial assembly that the choice facing Americans was stark: They must choose between obeying "the supreme authority of Parliament" and "total independence." Privately, Hutchinson grew convinced that colonial rebelliousness resulted from too much "democracy" in America. Where in England fewer than one in five men could vote, two-thirds of Americans voted. The sad result of such widespread participation, he complained, was constant disobedience.

The Boston Tea Party (1773)

The British prime minister, Lord North, soon provided the spark to transform American resentment into rebellion. In 1773, he tried to bail out the struggling East India Company, which had in its London warehouses some 17 million pounds of Asian tea that it desperately needed to sell before it rotted. Parliament passed the Tea Act of 1773 to allow the company to send its tea directly to America without paying taxes. British tea merchants could thereby undercut the prices charged by their American competitors, most of whom were smugglers who bought tea from the Dutch. At the same time, an obstinate King George III told Lord North to "compel obedience" in the colonies.

In Massachusetts, the Committees of Correspondence alerted colonists that the British government was trying to purchase colonial submission with

Boston Massacre (1770) Violent confrontation between British soldiers and a Boston mob on March 5, 1770, in which five colonists were killed.

Committee of Correspondence Group organized by Samuel Adams to address American grievances, assert American rights, and form a network of rebellion.

THE ABLE DOCTOR, OR AMERICA SWALLOWING THE BITTER DRAUGHT This 1774 engraving shows Lord North, the Boston Port Bill in his pocket, pouring tea down America's throat and America spitting it back.

cheap tea. ("Tea stands for Tyranny!") The reduction in the price of tea was a clever trick to make colonists accept taxation without consent. In Boston, furious citizens decided that their passion for liberty outweighed their love for tea.

Boston Tea Party

On December 16, 1773, scores of Patriots dressed as Mohawk Indians boarded three British cargo ships in Boston Harbor and dumped 342 chests filled with forty-six tons of East India Company tea into the icy water. The **Boston Tea Party** was, according to John Adams, "so bold, so daring" that it represented a turning point in relations with the monarchy.

The destruction of so much valuable tea convinced George III that a forceful response was required. "The die is now cast. The colonists must either submit or triumph. We must not retreat," he wrote to Lord North, who decided to make Boston an example to the rest of the colonies. In the end, the king's efforts to reassert royal control helped turn a rebellion into a revolution that would cost Britain far more than three shiploads of tea.

Boston Tea Party (1773) Demonstration against the Tea Act of 1773 in which the Sons of Liberty, dressed as Indians, dumped hundreds of chests of British-owned tea into Boston Harbor.

Coercive Acts (1774) Four parliamentary measures that required the colonies to pay for the Boston Tea Party's damages: closed the port of Boston, imposed a military government, disallowed colonial trials of British soldiers, and forced the quartering of troops in private homes.

The Coercive Acts

In 1774, Lord North convinced Parliament to punish Boston and the province of Massachusetts by passing a cluster of harsh laws, called the **Coercive Acts**. (Americans renamed them the "Intolerable" Acts.) The Port Act closed Boston Harbor until the city paid for the lost tea. (It never did.) The closing of the port cost many jobs, and the cost of consumer goods skyrocketed as trade ceased.

A new Quartering Act ordered colonists to provide lodging and supplies for British soldiers. The Impartial Administration of Justice Act said that any royal official accused of a major crime would be tried in London rather than in the colony.

Finally, the Massachusetts Government Act gave the royal governor the authority to appoint the colony's legislative council, which until then had been elected by the people, as well as local judges and sheriffs. It also banned town meetings. Collectively, these "Intolerable Acts" triggered a colonial uprising.

In May 1774, Lieutenant General Thomas Gage, commander in chief of British forces in North America, became military governor of Massachusetts. He believed that the British government had been too lenient with the colonists, and he resolved to clamp down on resisters. Gage assured the king that the colonists would not dare resist the latest British measures: "They will undoubtedly be very meek."

Meek they were not. The Intolerable Acts outraged colonists, deepened resentments, and transformed scattered resistance into widespread rebellion. By August 1774, Patriots across Massachusetts were taking control of local governments. They also began stockpiling weapons and gunpowder in anticipation of an eventual clash with British troops.

Elsewhere, colonists rallied to help Boston by boycotting, burning, or dumping British tea. In Virginia, George Washington found himself in a debate with Bryan Fairfax, an old friend and self-described Royalist. Fairfax blamed the Boston rebels for the tensions with London. Washington disagreed, defending the "quiet and steady conduct of the people of the Massachusetts Bay." It was time, he added, for Americans to stand up for their rights or submit to being treated like "abject slaves."

In Williamsburg, when the Virginia assembly (House of Burgesses) met in May, Thomas Jefferson suggested that June 1, the effective date of the Boston Port Act, become an official day of fasting and prayer throughout the colony.

The royal governor responded by dissolving the assembly, whose members then decided to form a Continental Congress to represent all the colonies in the growing dispute with the mother country. As Samuel Savage, a Connecticut colonist, wrote in May 1774, the conflict had come down to a single question: "Whether we shall or shall not be governed by a British Parliament."

The First Continental Congress (1774)

The First Continental Congress

On September 5, 1774, fifty-five delegates from twelve colonies (Georgia was absent) making up the First Continental Congress assembled in Philadelphia, the largest American city. The gathering was unprecedented. Never had representatives from all the colonies met to coordinate joint resistance to British policies. John Adams wrote his wife, Abigail, that every delegate "is a great man—an orator, a critic, a statesman," and they were beginning to imagine themselves as a nation rather than as individual colonies: "The distinctions between Virginians, Pennsylvanians, New Yorkers, and New Englanders are no more."

The Continental Congress endorsed the Suffolk Resolves, in which the colonists stressed their "allegiance and submission" to the king while pledging to resist British tyranny with force. The delegates then adopted a Declaration of American Rights, which proclaimed once again the rights of colonists as

British citizens and denied Parliament's authority to regulate internal colonial affairs. "We demand no new rights," said the Congress. "We ask only for peace, liberty, and security."

Finally, the Congress adopted the Continental Association of 1774, which recommended that every colony organize committees to enforce a complete boycott of all imported British goods, a dramatic step that would be followed by a refusal to export American goods to Britain. The county and city committees forming the Continental Association became the organizational network for the resistance movement. Seven thousand men across the colonies served on the local committees, and many more women helped put the boycotts into practice. The committees required colonists to sign an oath refusing to purchase British goods.

Public engagement: boycotts, volunteering, political action

Thousands of common people—men and women—participated in the boycott of British goods, volunteered in Patriot militia units, attended town meetings, and ousted royal officials. As the residents of Pittsfield, Massachusetts, affirmed in a petition, "We have always believed that the people are the fountain of power." Royal officials marveled at the colonists' ability to thwart British authority. "The ingenuity of these people," observed an army officer, "is singular in their modes of mischief." Loyalist Thomas Hutchinson, however, assured the king that Americans could not remain united because "the people were greatly divided among themselves in every colony." Hutchinson had no doubt "that all America would *submit*, and that they *must*, and moreover would, *soon*."

Hutchinson could not have been more wrong. The rebellion now extended well beyond simple grievances over taxation. Patriots decided that Parliament, the king, and his prime minister were engaged in a *conspiracy* against their liberties. By the end of 1774, more and more colonists were rejecting the authority of Parliament over their lives. Militant Patriots replaced royal governors with "committees of safety" that began secretly purchasing weapons and gunpowder from European nations. The colonies were mobilizing for war. In Boston, an increasingly nervous General Thomas Gage requested more troops to suppress the growing "flames of sedition." He reported that "civil government is near its end." Gage even tried to bribe Sam Adams to switch sides, but an insulted Adams refused.

Last-Minute Compromise

In London, King George fumed over his failure to control the colonies. He wrote Lord North that the Americans were displaying a "most daring spirit of resistance and disobedience" and "blows must decide" whether the colonists "are to be subject to this country or independent."

In early 1775, Parliament announced that Massachusetts was officially "in rebellion." London officials hired Samuel Johnson to write a pamphlet called *Taxation No Tyranny* (1775), expressing the government's perspective on the colonists and their slogan, "No taxation without representation." However much Americans might complain about taxes, they remained British subjects who should obey government actions. If the Americans wanted to participate in Parliament, Johnson suggested, they could move to England. Whatever the case, Johnson expressed confidence that the dispute between England and America would be resolved through "English superiority and American obedience."

PATRICK HENRY OF VIRGINIA Henry was a longtime advocate of colonial rights, fighting for the Stamp Tax Resolutions to be passed in Virginia in 1765. A decade later, in a speech to Virginia's Revolutionary Convention, he made the famous declaration, "Give me liberty, or give me death!"

Bold Talk of War

Patriots, however, were not in an obedient mood. Patrick Henry, soon to be governor of Virginia, announced that war with England had become unavoidable. The twenty-nine-year-old Henry, a farmer- and storekeeper-turned-self-taught-lawyer, claimed that the colonies had "done everything that could be done to avert the storm which is now coming on," but their protests had been met only by "violence and insult." Freedom, Henry shouted, could now be bought only with blood: "We must fight!" If forced to choose, he supposedly exclaimed, "Give me liberty"—he then paused dramatically, clenched his fist as if it held a dagger, and plunged it into his chest—"or give me death."

As Henry predicted, events quickly moved toward armed conflict. By mid-1775, the king and Parliament had lost control of the colonies; they could neither persuade nor force the Patriots to accept new regulations and taxes. In Boston, General Gage warned his superiors in London that armed conflict would unleash "civil war." But Lord Sandwich, head of the British navy, dismissed the rebels as "raw, undisciplined, cowardly men" without an army or navy. Joseph Warren, a fearless Boston physician, insisted that Americans were willing to die for their principles: "Our liberty must be preserved. It is far dearer than life." The assumption in London that the colonists would back down infuriated him. "These fellows say we won't fight. By heavens, I hope I shall die up to my knees in blood."

Fighting Begins: Lexington and Concord

On April 14, 1775, the British army received orders to stop the "open rebellion" in Massachusetts. General Gage decided to arrest rebel leaders such as Sam Adams and seize the militia's gunpowder stored at Concord, a village of 265 families sixteen miles northwest of Boston. Adams, however, had been alerted to the danger by none other than Gage's American-born wife, Margaret Kemble. The British governor-general was so humiliated by his wife's treason that he shipped her to his estate in England.

After dark on April 18, some 800 British soldiers converged near the Boston Common. Under a moonlit sky, the redcoats quietly boarded boats and crossed the Charles River to Cambridge, then set out on foot to Lexington, about eleven miles away. When Patriots got wind of the plan, Paul Revere and William Dawes mounted their horses for their famous "midnight ride" to warn rebel leaders that the British were coming. In Lexington, the church bell began to ring, and bonfires were lit across the countryside, alerting militiamen to grab their weapons and rush to the town square. Other riders fanned out to alert the militias in towns near Lexington.

Shots fired at Lexington and Concord

In the chilly gray dawn of April 19, an advance unit of 238 redcoats found American captain John Parker and seventy-six "Minutemen" (Patriot militia who could assemble at a "minute's" notice) lined up on the Lexington town green, while dozens of villagers watched. "Stand your ground," shouted Parker, a farmer with seven children who had fought in the French and Indian War. "Don't fire unless fired upon; but if they mean to have a war, let it begin here!"

Parker and his men intended only a silent protest, but British major John Pitcairn rode onto the Lexington Green, swinging his sword and yelling, "Disperse, you damned rebels! You dogs, run!"

The outnumbered militiamen were backing away when a shot rang out. Who fired first remains disputed, but after the first shot, the British unleashed a "continual roar of musketry" before charging the Minutemen with bayonets, leaving eight dead and nine wounded.

The sounds of gunfire "spread like electric fire," and militiamen in surrounding towns and villages spread the alarm. "Oh, what a glorious morning is this!" exulted Sam Adams, for he knew the Revolution had begun.

The British officers next led their men west to Concord, where they destroyed hidden military supplies, killed livestock, and burned Patriot houses. They shot or bayoneted those who resisted. More than a hundred bullet holes pockmarked a tavern where the owner, his wife, and two villagers

THE BATTLE OF LEXINGTON (1775) Amos Doolittle's impression of the Battle of Lexington as combat begins between the Royal Marines and the Minutemen.

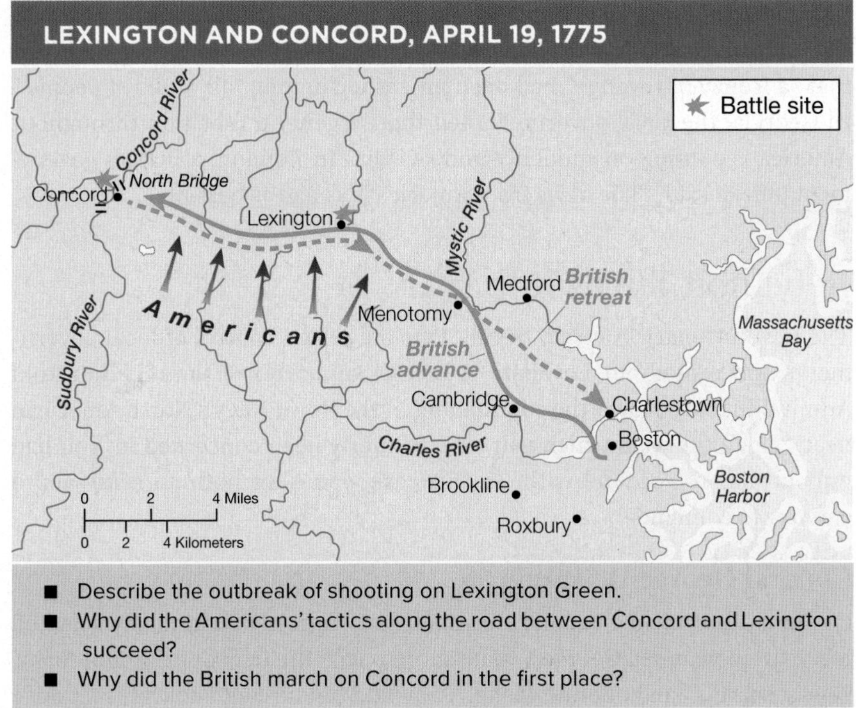

LEXINGTON AND CONCORD, APRIL 19, 1775

- Describe the outbreak of shooting on Lexington Green.
- Why did the Americans' tactics along the road between Concord and Lexington succeed?
- Why did the British march on Concord in the first place?

were found bayoneted, their skulls crushed. A young boy was so enraged at British atrocities that he used a hatchet to scalp a wounded redcoat and hack off his ears.

While marching out of Concord, the British encountered swarms of American riflemen. Shots were fired, and a dozen or so British soldiers were killed or wounded. More important, the short skirmish and ringing church bells alerted nearby rebel farmers, ministers, craftsmen, and merchants to grab their muskets. They were, as one of them said, determined to "be free or die."

By noon, the exhausted redcoats began a twenty-mile retreat that soon turned into a living hell. Less than a mile out of Concord, they suffered the first of many ambushes. The narrow road became a gauntlet of death as rebel marksmen fired from every direction, hidden behind stone walls, trees, barns, and houses. "It was a day full of horror," one of the soldiers recalled. The redcoats were no longer marching; they were fleeing. "We began to run rather than retreat," one of them said.

By nightfall, the redcoats were safely back in Boston, having marched some forty miles and suffered three times as many dead and wounded as the Americans. A British general reported that the colonists had earned his respect: "Whoever looks upon them as an irregular mob will find himself much mistaken." In Providence, Rhode Island, a rider appeared at the crowded wharf yelling, "War, war boys. There is war."

Until the Battles of Lexington and Concord, both sides had mistakenly assumed that the other would back down. Instead, the clash of redcoats and rebels in the two villages had turned a resistance movement into a war of rebellion. Thousands of New England militiamen, having heard that the redcoats had "engaged in butchering and destroying our brethren," began to converge on Boston, eager for revenge. In Virginia, Thomas Jefferson noted that "a frenzy of revenge" had been unleashed among "all ranks of people." In Georgia, the royal governor noted that "a general rebellion throughout America is coming on suddenly and swiftly." In London, a British government official said, "The news from America is as bad as possible."

Rebellion Turns into War

The Revolutionary War had begun. Patriots seized control of local governments and rooted out Loyalists. A British supporter of the rebellion told Admiral Richard Howe, the commander of the Royal Navy's North American fleet, "In all the wars which you have formerly been concerned in, you had only armies to contend with. In this case, you have both an army and a country to combat."

General George Washington

On June 15, 1775, the Second Continental Congress unanimously selected forty-three-year-old George Washington to lead the new Continental Army. It was, he said, "an honor he wished to avoid," but he could not refuse it once offered.

Washington had earned his new role. Having lost his father at an early age, he had hoped to serve in the British navy until his mother implored him to manage the family farm instead. His service in the French and Indian War had made him one of the few experienced American army officers. He was admired for his success as a planter, surveyor, and land speculator, as well as for his service in the Virginia legislature and the Continental Congress. Washington also married well; his wife, Martha Custis, had been the wealthiest widow in Virginia.

Perhaps most important to the Revolutionary cause, George Washington *looked* like a leader. Weighing 200 pounds and standing almost six feet four, he was an imposing figure, both powerful and graceful. His courage in battle, perseverance after defeat, and integrity in judgment would earn him the respect of his troops and the nation.

Washington refused to be paid for his service. Poet Mercy Otis Warren wrote a friend in London that Washington was "a man whose military abilities & public & private virtue place him in the first class of the Good & the Brave."

The Battle of Bunker Hill

The first major battle: Bunker Hill

On Saturday, June 17, the day that George Washington was named commander in chief, Patriot militiamen engaged British forces in their first major clash, the Battle of Bunker Hill (nearby Breed's Hill was the battle's actual location).

To strengthen their control over the area around Boston, some 2,400 British troops boarded twenty-eight barges and crossed over the Charles

River to the Charlestown Peninsula. With drums beating and bayonets glistening, they advanced up Breed's Hill in tight formation through waist-high grass, boosting themselves over fences and low stone walls as the American defenders watched from behind their earthworks. "Don't fire until you see the whites of their eyes," yelled Israel Putnam as he rode along the American lines. "Fire low because you are shooting downhill—and focus your fire on the officers." The militiamen, mostly farmers, waited until the redcoats ventured within thirty paces, then loosed a volley of lead that crumpled the first three rows of England's finest warriors and sent the attackers retreating in disarray. An American said the British fell like "grass when mowed."

The British regrouped and attacked again, but the Patriot riflemen forced them back a second time. General William Howe could not believe his eyes. All his aides had been killed or wounded, and his professional soldiers were being stymied by a "rabble" of untrained farmers. It was, he said, "a moment that I never felt before." During the third British assault, the colonists ran out of gunpowder and retreated, but the British were too tired to follow. In less than an hour, the British had suffered 1,054 casualties (killed or wounded), more than twice the American losses. A British officer reported to London that "we have lost a thousand of our best men and officers" because of "an absurd and destructive confidence, carelessness, or ignorance."

There followed a nine-month stalemate around Boston, with each side hoping for a negotiated settlement of the dispute. Thirty-eight days later, word of the Battle of Bunker Hill reached London. King George III and Lord North agreed that this meant all-out war. The king issued a Proclamation of Rebellion reminding his American subjects that they were "bound by law . . . to disclose all traitorous conspiracies . . . against us, our Crown and Dignity." If the American colonies were lost, he believed, Britain's other colonies would fall like dominoes.

Olive Branch Petition rejected

Three weeks after the Battle of Bunker Hill, in July 1775, the Continental Congress sent King George the Olive Branch Petition, urging him to negotiate. When the petition reached London, however, the king refused to read it. He instead denounced the "traitorous" Americans as "open and avowed enemies" trying to establish their own "independent empire."

Few Patriots were ready to call for independence, however. When the Second Continental Congress convened at Philadelphia on May 10, 1775, most delegates still wanted Parliament to restore their rights so that they could resume being loyal British colonists.

Independence

The Revolutionary War was well under way when Thomas Paine, a thirty-nine-year-old English tax collector who had lost his job, fallen deeply in debt, separated from his second wife (his first wife and child had died during birth), and immigrated to America in 1774, helped transform a rebellion into a revolution. He had arrived in America penniless and unknown but soon found work as a journalist writing for the *Pennsylvania Magazine* in Philadelphia.

THE COMING REVOLUTION The Continental Congress votes for independence, July 2, 1776.

In January 1776, Paine published a stirring fifty-page pamphlet titled ***Common Sense,*** in which he urged Americans to seize their independence. Nothing was more absurd, he maintained, than the notion that God had given kings the right to rule with absolute power or that an island nation (England) should exercise dominance over an entire continent (North America). Any colonist who favored reconciliation with Britain, he asserted, has "the heart of a coward."

Paine's *Common Sense* musters public support for independence

Until *Common Sense* appeared, most Patriots had directed their grievances at Parliament. Paine, however, directly attacked the king. The "common sense" of the matter, he stressed, was that George III, "the royal brute unfit to be the ruler of a free people," had caused the rebellion and had ordered the violation of American rights. Paine urged Americans to abandon the monarchy and proclaim their independence: "The blood of the slain, the weeping voice of nature cries, 'TIS TIME TO PART.'" It was time for those who "oppose not only the tyranny but the tyrant [King George] to stand forth! . . . Time hath found us!"

Paine's passionate pamphlet changed the course of history by convincing many anxious American rebels that independence was necessary and inevitable. "The cause of America is in great measure the cause of all mankind," he wrote, and the rest of the world would embrace an independent America; it would be the "glory of the earth." Paine concluded that the "sun had never shined on a cause of greater worth."

Common Sense (1776) Popular pamphlet written by Thomas Paine attacking British principles of hereditary rule and monarchical government and advocating a declaration of American independence.

Within three months of the pamphlet's appearance, more than 150,000 copies were circulating throughout the colonies and around the world.

"*Common Sense* is working a powerful change in the minds of men," George Washington observed. In Paris, John Adams reported that the French and other Europeans were enraptured by their reading of *Common Sense*. "Without the pen of the author of *Common Sense*," Adams later maintained, "the sword of Washington would have been raised in vain."

The Battle of Moore's Creek Bridge

Thomas Paine's words boosted Patriots' morale, but what they most needed was a true battlefield victory. It came near Wilmington, North Carolina, in late February 1776. The royal governor of North Carolina ordered the Tory (Loyalist) militia, mostly Scottish Highlanders who had served in the British army and were now promised 200 acres in exchange for their service, to don their kilts, sharpen their swords, sound their bagpipes, and head toward the coast to link up with British forces landing by sea. The governor, expecting a Loyalist victory, announced: "This is the moment when this country may be delivered from anarchy." The Patriots rushed to stop them.

On February 27, the two forces clashed at Moore's Creek Bridge, near the Cape Fear River. The battle was intense but brief, lasting three minutes. About fifty Tories were killed and twenty more wounded, while the victorious Patriots suffered only two casualties. Some 850 Loyalists were taken prisoner. The battle ended royal authority in North Carolina and revealed that the Revolution would be as much a civil war as a conflict between American and British forces, as only North Carolina Patriots and Loyalists fought at Moore's Creek Bridge. No British soldiers participated. Within two months of the American victory, on April 12, 1776, North Carolina became the first colony to vote in favor of independence from Britain.

Breaking the Bonds of Empire (1776)

During the spring and summer of 1776, some ninety local governments, towns, and colonial legislatures issued declarations of independence from Great Britain. In June 1776, one by one, the colonies authorized their delegates in the Continental Congress to take the final step. On June 7, Richard Henry Lee of Virginia moved "that these United Colonies are, and of right ought to be, free and independent states." At first, six colonies were not ready, but Lee's resolution finally passed on July 2, a date that John Adams predicted would "be the most memorable" in the history of America.

The more memorable date, however, became July 4, 1776, when fifty-six members of Congress formally adopted the **Declaration of Independence** creating the "United States of America." The stakes could not have been higher. The delegates knew that they were likely to be hanged if captured by British troops. "Well, Gentlemen," Benjamin Franklin told the Congress, "we must now hang together, or we shall most assuredly hang separately." Benjamin Harrison injected needed wit at that point, noting that when it was his turn to try on a British noose, his plentiful weight would bring him a mercifully swift death.

Declaration of Independence (1776) Formal statement, principally drafted by Thomas Jefferson and adopted by the Second Continental Congress on July 4, 1776, that officially announced the thirteen colonies' break with Great Britain.

Jefferson's Declaration

The risky decision to declare independence embodied a carefully reasoned political philosophy. A quest for freedom, for liberty from tyranny, animated the drama of American independence. Patriots wholeheartedly believed that the people should govern themselves and that they should enjoy both individual freedom and equal rights.

The formal rationale for independence was developed by thirty-three-year-old Thomas Jefferson, a brilliant Virginia planter and attorney serving in the Continental Congress. In Philadelphia, he drafted a justification for independence that John Adams and Benjamin Franklin then edited.

The Declaration of Independence was crucially important not simply because it marked the creation of a new nation (although the word *nation* was nowhere in the document) but because of the political ideals it expressed. Jefferson explained, "We hold these truths to be sacred and undeniable":

> That all men are created equal & independent, that from that creation they derive rights inherent & inalienable, among which are the preservation of life, liberty, & the pursuit of happiness; that to secure these ends, governments are instituted among men, deriving their just powers from the consent of the governed.

These were to be the new nation's founding principles. After reading Jefferson's draft, Benjamin Franklin saw fit to change the phrase "sacred & undeniable" to "self-evident" so as not to imply that the Declaration of Independence came from God.

Once Jefferson had established America's foundational principles, he listed the most acute grievances against British rule. Over the previous ten years, colonists had deplored acts of Parliament that impinged on their freedoms, especially efforts to impose "taxes on us without our consent." Now, Jefferson directed colonial resentment at King George III himself, arguing that the monarch should have reined in Parliament's efforts to "tyrannize" the colonies.

Jefferson, a slaveholder, then made the preposterous charge that the king had *imposed* slavery on Americans by stripping a "distant people who never offended him" (Africans) of their "most sacred right of life & liberty." In fact, however, as Jefferson knew full well, the British monarchy had not forced the system of race-based slavery on colonists; they had been eagerly lording over enslaved Africans since 1619, long before George III assumed the throne.

After listing the "repeated injuries and usurpations" committed against the thirteen colonies by the king and Parliament, Jefferson asserted that Americans had the fundamental right to create governments of their own choosing. The people, he explained, give governments their legitimacy, and are entitled to "alter or abolish" those governments when denied their rights. Because George III was trying to impose "an absolute tyranny over these states," the "Representatives of the United States of America" declared the thirteen "United Colonies" of British America to be "Free and Independent States." News of the Declaration of Independence so excited New Yorkers that they toppled a statue of King George and had it melted down to make 42,000 bullets for the war. General George Washington ordered the Declaration read to every unit in the Continental army.

The Contradictions of Freedom and Slavery

Once the Continental Congress chose independence, its members revised Jefferson's draft declaration before sending it to London. Southern representatives insisted on deleting Jefferson's passage criticizing George III for foisting slavery on the colonies. In doing so, they revealed the major paradox at work in the movement for independence. The rhetoric of freedom ("all men are created equal and independent") did not apply to the widespread system of slavery that fueled the colonial economy. Slavery was the absence of liberty, yet few Revolutionaries confronted the hypocrisy of their protests in defense of freedom—for Whites.

In 1764, a group of enslaved people in Charleston watching a demonstration against British tyranny by White Sons of Liberty got caught up in the moment and began chanting, "Freedom, freedom, freedom." But that was not what southern planters wanted for African Americans. In 1774, when a group of freedom seekers killed four Whites in a desperate attempt to gain their freedom, Georgia planters captured the rebels and burned them alive.

Harvard-educated attorney James Otis, Jr., was one of the few Patriots who demanded freedom for Blacks and women as well as the colonies. In 1764, he had argued that "the colonists, black and white, born here, are free British subjects, and entitled to all the essential civil rights of such." Otis went so far as to suggest that slavery itself should be ended, since "all men . . . White or black" were "by the law of nature freeborn."

Otis also asked, "Are not women born as free as men? Would it not be infamous to assert that the ladies are all slaves by nature?" His sister, Mercy Otis Warren, became a tireless advocate of American resistance to British "tyranny" through her poems, pamphlets, and plays. In a letter to a friend, she noted that British officials needed to realize that America's "daughters are politicians and patriots and will aid the good work [of resistance] with their female efforts."

Enslaved people insisted on independence too. In 1773, a group of four enslaved Bostonians addressed a public letter to the town government in which they referred to the hypocrisy of slaveholders who protested against British regulations and taxes. "We expect great things from men who have made such a noble stand against the designs of their fellow-men to enslave them," they noted. But freedom in 1776 was a celebration to which the enslaved were not invited.

George Washington acknowledged the contradictory aspects of the Revolutionary movement when he warned that the alternative to declaring

PHILLIS WHEATLEY A portrait of America's first celebrated African American poet.

independence was to become "tame and abject slaves, as the blacks we rule over with such arbitrary sway [absolute power]." Washington and other slaveholders at the head of the Revolutionary movement were in part so resistant to "British tyranny" because they witnessed every day what actual slavery was like.

Thomas Jefferson admitted the two-facedness of slave-owning Revolutionaries. "Southerners," he wrote to a French friend, are "jealous of their own liberties but trampling on those of others." Phillis Wheatley, the first African American writer to publish her poetry in America, highlighted the "absurdity" of White colonists claiming their freedom while continuing to exercise "oppressive power" over enslaved Africans.

"We Always Had Governed Ourselves"

Americans in 1775–1776 enjoyed a higher standard of living than most other societies. Their diet was better than that of Europeans, as was their average life span. In addition, the percentage of property owners in the thirteen colonies was higher than in Britain or Europe. At the same time, the taxes forced on Americans after 1763 were not as great as those imposed on the British people. And many colonists, perhaps as many as half, were indifferent, hesitant, or actively opposed to rebellion.

So why did so many Americans revolt? Historians have highlighted many factors: the clumsy British efforts to tighten their regulation of colonial trade, the restrictions on colonists eager to acquire western lands, the growing tax burden, the mounting debts to British merchants, the lack of American representation in Parliament, and the role of radicals such as Samuel Adams and Patrick Henry in arousing anti-British feelings.

Yet other reasons were not so selfless or noble. Many wealthy New Englanders and New Yorkers most critical of tighter British regulations, such as Boston merchant John Hancock, were smugglers; paying more British taxes would have cost them a fortune. Likewise, South Carolina's Henry Laurens and Virginia's Landon Carter, both prosperous planters, worried that the British might abolish slavery.

Overall, however, what Americans most resented were the British efforts to constrict colonists' civil liberties, thereby denying their rights as British citizens. As Hugh Williamson, a Pennsylvania physician, explained, the Revolution resulted not from "trifling or imaginary" injustices but from "gross and palpable" violations of American rights that had thrown "the miserable colonists" into the "pit of despotism."

Yet how did the diverse colonies develop such a unified resistance? Although most Patriots were of English heritage, many other peoples were represented: Scots, Irish, Scots-Irish, Welsh, Germans, Dutch, Swedes,

Finns, Swiss, French, and Jews, as well as growing numbers of Africans and diminishing numbers of Native Americans.

What most Americans—regardless of their backgrounds—had come to share by 1775 was a defiant attachment to the civil rights and legal processes guaranteed by the English constitutional tradition. This outlook, rooted in the defense of sacred constitutional principles, made the Revolution conceivable. Armed resistance made it possible, and independence, ultimately, made it achievable.

The Revolution would invent a new kind of nation: a large republic based on the shared political notion that all *citizens* were equal and independent, and that all governmental authority had to be based on long-standing constitutional principles and the consent of the governed. This "republican ideal" transformed a prolonged effort to preserve rights and liberties enjoyed by British citizens into a movement to create an independent nation. With their Declaration of Independence, the Revolutionaries—men and women, farmers, artisans, mechanics, sailors, merchants, tavern owners, and shopkeepers—had become determined to develop their own society. Americans wanted to trade freely with the world and to expand what Jefferson called their "empire of liberty" westward, across the Appalachian Mountains and into ancestral Indian lands.

The Revolutionaries knew the significance of what they were attempting. They were committing themselves, stressed John Adams, to "a Revolution, the most complete, unexpected, and remarkable of any in the history of nations."

Perhaps the last word on the reasons for the Revolution should belong to Levi Preston, a Minuteman from Danvers, Massachusetts, who was asked late in life about why he decided to fight for independence. "Young man," Preston explained, "what we meant in going for those redcoats was this: we always had governed ourselves, and we always meant to. They didn't mean we should."

Reviewing the

CORE OBJECTIVES | INQUIZITIVE

■ **British and French Colonies** France followed the model of absolute power in governing its far-flung trading outposts in Canada and the Louisiana Territory, but friendships with Native Americans and a profitable fur trade kept the balance of power in North America. The British government's decision to enforce more rigidly its policy of *mercantilism,* as seen in such measures as the *Navigation Acts* (1651–1775), became a means for Britain to enrich its global empire. The *Glorious Revolution* (1688) in Great Britain inspired new political philosophies that challenged the divine right of kings with the *natural rights* of free men.

■ **Warfare in the Colonies** The *Seven Years' War* (1756–1763), known as the *French and Indian War* in the American colonies, was the first world war, eventually won by the British. Worried colonies created the *Albany Plan of Union,* which was ultimately rejected but formed an early blueprint for an independent American government. In the *Treaty of Paris* in 1763, France lost all its North American possessions, Britain gained Canada and Florida, and Spain acquired the vast Louisiana Territory. With the war's end, Native Americans fought to regain control of their land in *Pontiac's Rebellion* (1763). Great Britain negotiated peace in the *Proclamation Act of 1763,* but land-hungry settlers ignored the Proclamation Line.

■ **British Colonial Policy** After the French and Indian War, the British government was saddled with an enormous national debt. To reduce that burden, George Grenville's colonial policy imposed various taxes to compel colonists to pay for their own defense. Colonists resisted, claiming that they could not be taxed by Parliament because they were not represented in Parliament. Colonial reaction to the *Stamp Act* of 1765 was the first sign of real trouble for British authorities. British officials tried to appease colonists with the argument that they were duly represented in Parliament through *virtual representation,* since parliamentarians were sworn to represent the entire nation as well as their particular district. Conflicts between Whigs and Tories intensified when the *Townshend Acts* (1767) imposed additional taxes. The *Sons of Liberty* and the *Daughters of Liberty* mobilized resistance with successful boycotts of British goods, helping convince Parliament to repeal the *Stamp Act* (1766).

■ **Road to the American Revolution** But the crisis worsened. Conflict between *Loyalists* and *Patriots* escalated. Spontaneous resistance led to the *Boston Massacre* (1770), and the First Continental Congress formed *Committees of Correspondence* to organize and spread resistance further. Organized protesters later staged the *Boston Tea Party* (1773). The British response, called the *Coercive Acts* (1774), sparked further violence. Thomas Paine's pamphlet *Common Sense* (1776) helped kindle Revolutionary fervor as well as plant the seed of independence, and conflicts over trade regulations, taxes, and expansion now erupted into war. In the heat of battle, compromise became less likely, and finally impossible, and the Continental Congress delivered its *Declaration of Independence* (1776).

KEY TERMS

mercantilism *p. 128*

Navigation Acts (1651–1775) *p. 129*

Glorious Revolution (1688) *p. 130*

natural rights *p. 131*

salutary neglect *p. 131*

French and Indian War (Seven Years' War) (1756–1763) *p. 132*

Albany Plan of Union (1754) *p. 134*

Treaty of Paris (1763) *p. 137*

Pontiac's Rebellion (1763) *p. 139*

Proclamation Act of 1763 *p. 140*

Stamp Act (1765) *p. 143*

virtual representation *p. 144*

Sons of Liberty *p. 144*

Daughters of Liberty *p. 145*

Townshend Acts (1767) *p. 147*

Loyalists *p. 147*

Patriots *p. 147*

Boston Massacre (1770) *p. 149*

Committee of Correspondence *p. 149*

Boston Tea Party (1773) *p. 150*

Coercive Acts (1774) *p. 150*

Common Sense (1776) *p. 158*

Declaration of Independence (1776) *p. 159*

CHRONOLOGY

1651	First Navigation Act passed by Parliament
1688–1689	Glorious Revolution
1754	Albany Plan of Union
1756–1763	Seven Years' War (French and Indian War); Treaty of Paris ends Seven Years' War; Pontiac's Rebellion begins; Proclamation Act
1764–1765	Sugar Act and Stamp Act; Stamp Act Congress
1766	Repeal of the Stamp Act
1767	Townshend Acts
1770	Boston Massacre
1773	Tea Act and Boston Tea Party
1774	Coercive Acts; First meeting of Continental Congress
1775	Military conflict at Lexington and Concord; The Continental Congress creates an army
1776	Thomas Paine publishes *Common Sense*; The Continental Congress declares independence

INQUIZITIVE

Go to InQuizitive to see what you've learned—and learn what you've missed—with personalized feedback along the way.

THINKING LIKE A HISTORIAN

DEBATING the Origins of the American Revolution

History is more than just the memorization of *what* happened. It also involves interpreting *why* the past unfolded as it did. In seeking to understand *why,* historians often find themselves disagreeing. This happens for many reasons. Historians themselves are influenced by their own outlook and the society they live in. Historians can revise their thinking in light of fresh information from newly discovered *primary sources.* They can also interpret previously examined sources in new ways by applying new methodologies and theories. The study of how interpretations of history have changed is called *historiography.* It is the history of the field of history! For Part 1, "An Old 'New' World," the case study of the origins of the American Revolution demonstrates how historians can disagree because they use different types of sources. Thus it is an excellent topic for sharpening your historiographical skills.

For this exercise you have two tasks:

PART 1: Compare the two secondary sources on the American Revolution.

PART 2: Using primary sources, evaluate the arguments of the two secondary sources.

PART I Comparing and Contrasting Secondary Sources

Below are excerpts from two prominent historians of the American Revolution who are at odds over its origins. The first piece comes from Bernard Bailyn of Harvard University, who has explored how *ideology* shaped the American Revolution—the system of ideas, ideals, and beliefs that undergird political and economic theory and practice. Bailyn focuses on the way that ideas from the English Whigs, who argued that the English constitution limited the power of the king (see page 144), influenced American Revolutionaries. The author of the second excerpt, Gary Nash of the University of California, Los Angeles, has studied the role that common people, as well as the economic forces that affected their lives, played in the American Revolution. Nash seeks to uncover not just the Whig ideology that is the focus of Bailyn's work but also the ideas and forces that motivated people to participate in this great struggle. While Bailyn and Nash agree on much, their work illustrates how different methodologies lead to different historical interpretations. On the one hand, Bailyn looks at the ideas and writings of the Revolutionary elite—their ideas and arguments—to explain what people actually did. On the other hand, Nash examines the actions and economic circumstances of Revolutionaries who produced no written records in order to understand their motivations. So while Bailyn seeks to understand the causes of the Revolution through the writing of the colonial elite, Nash looks at the actions of common people to understand why they participated in this struggle.

Compare the views of these two historians by answering the following questions. Be sure to find specific examples in the text to support your answers.

- What is the topic of each excerpt?
- Are there any similarities between these two excerpts?
- According to each author, what role did ideology play in the origins of the American Revolution?
- According to each author, what role did economics and material conditions play in the origins of the Revolution?
- What type of primary sources does each author mention?
- What might account for the differences (if any) in interpretation between the authors?

Secondary Source 1

Bernard Bailyn, *The Ideological Origins of the American Revolution* (1992)

Study of the pamphlets [thin booklets] confirmed my rather old-fashioned view that the American Revolution was above all else an ideological, constitutional, political struggle and not primarily a controversy between social groups undertaken to force changes in the organization of the society or the economy. It confirmed too my belief that intellectual developments in the decade before Independence led to a radical idealization and conceptualization of the previous century and a half of American experience, and that it was this intimate relationship between Revolutionary thought and the circumstances of life in eighteenth-century America that endowed the Revolution with its peculiar force and made it so profoundly a transforming event. But if the pamphlets confirmed this belief, they filled it with unexpected details and gave it new meaning.

. . . I began to see a new meaning in phrases that I, like most historians, had readily dismissed as mere rhetoric and propaganda: "slavery," "corruption," "conspiracy." These inflammatory words were used so forcefully by writers of so great a variety of social statuses, political positions, and religious persuasions; they fitted so logically into the pattern of radical and opposition thought; and they reflected so clearly the realities of life in an age in which monarchical autocracy flourished, in which the stability and freedom of England's "mixed" constitution was a recent and remarkable achievement, and in which the fear of conspiracy against constituted authority was built into the very structure of politics, that I began to suspect that they meant something very real to both the writers and their readers: that there were real fears, real anxieties, a sense of real danger behind these phrases, and not merely the desire to influence by rhetoric and propaganda the inert minds of an otherwise passive populace. The more I read, the less useful, it seemed to me, was the whole idea of propaganda in its modern meaning when applied to the writings of the American Revolution. . . . In the end I was convinced that the fear of a comprehensive conspiracy against liberty throughout the English speaking world—a conspiracy believed to have been nourished in corruption, and of which, it was felt, oppression in America was only the most immediately visible part—lay at the heart of the Revolutionary movement.

Source: Bailyn, Bernard. *The Ideological Origins of the American Revolution*. Cambridge, Mass.: Belknap Press of Harvard University Press, 1992. xx–xxiii.

Secondary Source 2

Gary Nash, "Social Change and the Growth of Prerevolutionary Urban Radicalism" (1976)

One of the purposes of this essay is to challenge these widely accepted notions that the "predicament of poverty" was unknown in colonial America, that the conditions of everyday life among "the inarticulate" had not changed in ways that led toward a revolutionary predisposition, and that "social discontent," "economic disturbances," and "social strains" can generally be ignored in searching for the roots of the Revolution. I do not suggest that we replace an ideological construction with a mechanistic economic interpretation, but argue that a popular ideology, affected by rapidly changing economic conditions in American cities, dynamically interacted with the more abstract Whig ideology borrowed from England. These two ideologies had their primary appeal within different parts of the social structure, were derived from different sensibilities concerning social equity, and thus had somewhat different goals. The Whig ideology, about which we know a great deal through recent studies, was drawn from English sources, had its main appeal within upper levels of colonial society, was limited to a defense of constitutional rights and political liberties, and had little to say about changing social and economic conditions in America or the need for change in the future. The popular ideology, about which we know very little, also had deep roots in English culture, but it resonated most strongly within the middle and lower strata of society and went far beyond constitutional rights to a discussion of the proper distribution of wealth and power in the social system. It was this popular ideology that undergirded the politicization of the artisan and laboring classes in the cities and justified the dynamic role they assumed in the urban political process in the closing decades of the colonial period.

To understand how this popular ideology swelled into revolutionary commitment within the middle and lower ranks of colonial society, we must first comprehend how the material conditions of life were changing for city dwellers during the colonial period and how people at different levels of society were affected by these alterations. We cannot fathom this process by consulting the writings of merchants, lawyers, and upper-class politicians, because their business and political correspondence and the tracts they wrote tell us almost nothing about those below them in the social hierarchy. But buried in more obscure documents are glimpses of the lives of both ordinary and important people—shoemakers and tailors as well as lawyers and merchants. The story of changing conditions and how life in New York, Philadelphia, and Boston was experienced can be discerned, not with perfect clarity but in general form, from tax, poor relief, and probate records.

The crescendo of urban protest and extralegal activity in the prerevolutionary decades cannot be separated from the condition of people's lives. . . . The willingness of broad segments of urban society to participate in attacks on narrowly concentrated wealth and power—both at the polls where the poor and propertyless were excluded, and in the streets where everyone, including women, apprentices, indentured servants, and slaves, could engage in action—should remind us that a rising tide of class antagonism and political consciousness, paralleling important economic changes, was a distinguishing feature of the cities at the end of the colonial period. It is this organic link between the circumstances of people's lives and their political thought and action that has been overlooked by historians who concentrate on Whig ideology, which had its strongest appeal among the educated and well-to-do.

Source: Nash, Gary. "Social Change and the Growth of Prerevolutionary Urban Radicalism." *The American Revolution: Explorations in the History of American Radicalism*, edited by Alfred F. Young, 6–7. DeKalb: Northern Illinois University Press, 1976.

PART II Using Primary Sources to Evaluate Secondary Sources

When historians are faced with competing interpretations of the past, they often look at *primary* source material as part of the process of evaluating the different arguments. Below is a selection of primary source materials relating to the origins of the American Revolution.

The first document is an excerpt from a series of letters by Pennsylvania Quaker John Dickinson that he published anonymously under the pen name "A Farmer." Dickinson wrote the first letter in 1767, following Parliament's suspension of the New York Assembly for failure to comply with the Quartering Act of 1765, which required the colonies to provide British troops with food and shelter.

The second document is an excerpt from a letter sent by Massachusetts Bay governor Francis Bernard to British officials in London following the Stamp Act Riots in Boston during August of 1765. The riots began on August 13 with an attack upon the house of Andrew Oliver, who was responsible for the collection of the tax. This act of destruction was widely celebrated by Samuel Adams and other Sons of Liberty. A few days later a mob ransacked and looted the house of the lieutenant-governor, Thomas Hutchinson. This mob acted without the support of Adams or other elite leaders.

Carefully read the primary sources and answer the following questions. Decide which of the primary source documents support or refute Bailyn's and Nash's arguments about this period. You may find that the documents do both but for different parts of each historian's interpretation. Be sure to identify which specific components of each historian's argument the documents support or refute.

- Which of the two historians' *arguments* is best supported by the *primary source* documents? If you find that both arguments are well supported by the evidence, why do you think the two historians had such different interpretations about the period?
- Based on your comparison of the two historians' arguments and your analysis of the primary sources, what have you learned about historiography and the ways historians interpret the past?

Primary Source 1

John Dickinson, "Letter from a Farmer in Pennsylvania" (1767)

My dear COUNTRYMEN,

I am a FARMER settled after a variety of fortunes, near the banks of the river *Delaware* in the province of *Pennsylvania*. . . . Being master of my time, I spend a good deal of it in a library. . . . I believe I have acquired a greater share of knowledge in history, and the laws and constitution of my country, than is generally attained by men of my class. . . . From my infancy I was taught to love humanity and liberty. Inquiry and experience have since confirmed my reverence for the lessons then given me, by convincing me more fully of their truth and excellence. . . . With a good deal of surprise I have observed, that little notice has been taken of an act of Parliament, as injurious in its principle to the liberties of these colonies, as the STAMP ACT was: I mean the act for suspending the legislation of New-York. . . . It [the Act] is a parliamentary assertion of the *supreme authority* of *the British legislature* over these colonies in *the part of taxation*; and is intended to COMPEL *New-York* into a submission to that authority. It seems therefore to me as much a violation of the liberty of the people of that province, and consequently of all these colonies, as if the parliament had sent a number of regiments to be quartered upon them till they should comply. For it is evident, that the suspension is meant as a compulsion; and the *method* of compelling is totally indifferent. It is indeed probable that the sight of red coats, and the beating of drums would have been most alarming, because people are generally more influenced by their eyes and ears than by their reason: But whoever seriously considers the matter, must perceive, that a dreadful stroke is aimed at the liberty of these colonies: For the cause of *one* is the cause of *all*. If the parliament may lawfully deprive *New-York* of any of its rights, it may deprive any, or all the other colonies of their rights; and nothing can possibly so much encourage such attempts, as a mutual inattention to the interests of each other. *To divide, and thus to destroy,* is the first political maxim in attacking those who are powerful by their union. He certainly is not a wise man, who folds his arms and reposes himself at home, viewing with unconcern the flames that have invaded his neighbour's house, without any endeavors to extinguish them.

Source: Dickinson, John. "Letters from a Farmer." *Letters from a Farmer in Pennsylvania, to the Inhabitants of the British Colonies*. Edited by R. T. H. Halsey, 6–12. New York: The Outlook Company, 1903.

Primary Source 2

Governor Francis Bernard, "Letter to the Lords of Trade" (1765)

The disorders of the town having been carried to much greater lengths than what I have informed your lordships of. After the demolition of Mr. Oliver's house was found so practicable and easy, and that the government was obliged to look on, without being able to take any one step to prevent it, and the principal people of the town publicly avowed and justified the act; the mob, both great and small, became highly elated, and all kinds of ill-humours were set on foot; everything that, for years past, had been the cause of any unpopular discontent, was revived; and private resentments against persons in office worked themselves in, and endeavoured to exert themselves under the mask of the public cause. . . . Towards evening, some boys began to light a bonfire before the town-house, which is an usual signal for a mob. Before it was quite dark, a great company of people gathered together, crying 'Liberty and Property;' which is their usual notice of their intention to plunder and pull down a house.

. . .

The lieutenant-governor [Thomas Hutchinson] . . . was at supper with his family when he received advice that the mob was coming to him. . . . As soon as the mob had got into the house, with a most irresistible fury, they immediately looked about for him, to murder him, and even made diligent enquiry whither he was gone. They went to work with a rage scarce to be exemplified by the most savage people. Every thing moveable was destroyed in the most minute manner, except such things of value as were worth carrying off. . . . It was now becoming a war of plunder, of general leveling, and taking away the distinction of rich and poor: so that those gentlemen, who had promoted and approved the cruel treatment of Mr. Oliver, became now as fearful for themselves as the most loyal person in the town could be. When first the town took this new turn, I was in hopes that they would have disavowed all the riotous proceedings; that of the first night, as well as the last. But it is no such thing; great pains are taken to separate the two riots: what was done against Mr. Oliver is still approved of, as a necessary declaration of their resolution not to submit to the Stamp Act.

Source: Bernard, Francis. "Extract from a Letter to the Lords of Trade, dated August 31, 1765." *The Parliamentary History of England, from the Earliest Period to the Year 1803. From which Last-Mentioned Epoch It Is Continued Downwards in the Work Entitled, "The Parliamentary Debates."* Vol. 16, A. D. 1765–1771. London: Printed by T. C. Hansard, Peterborough-Court, Fleet-Street: for Longman, Hurst, Rees, Orme, & Brown; J. Richardson; Black, Parry, & Co.; J. Hatchard; J. Ridgway; E. Jeffery; J. Booker; J. Rodwell; Cardock & Joy; R. H. Evans; E. Budd; J. Booth; and T. C. Hansard, 1813. 129–131.

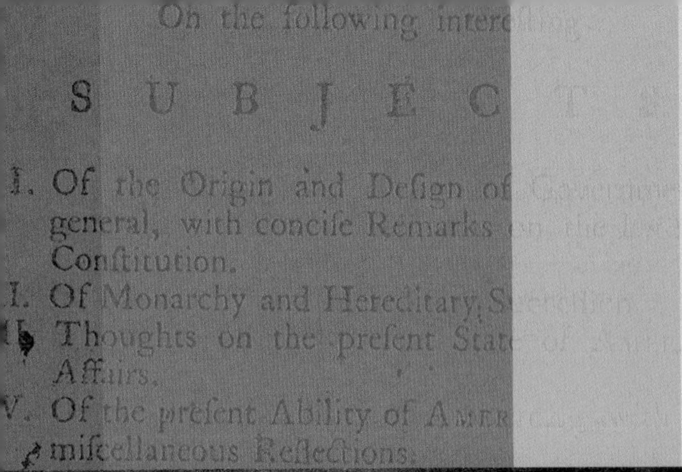

On the following interesting
SUBJECTS.
I. Of the Origin and Deſign of Governme
general, with conciſe Remarks on the Eng
Conſtitution.
II. Of Monarchy and Hereditary Succeſſion.
III. Thoughts on the preſent State of Amer
Affairs.
IV. Of the preſent Ability of Amer
miſcellaneous Reflections.

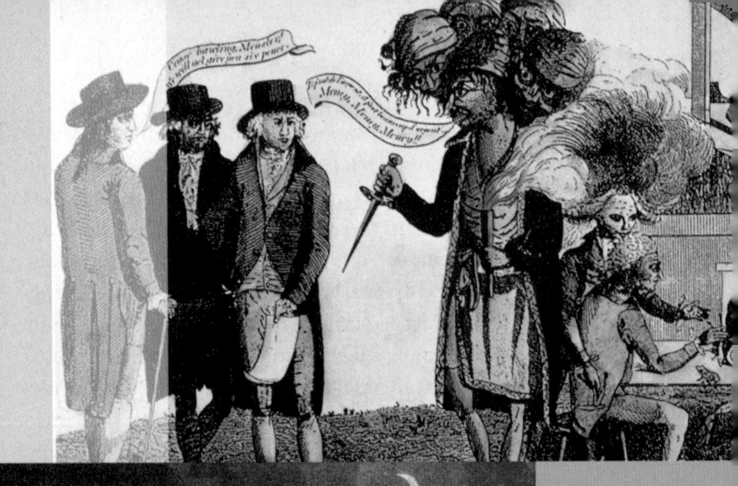

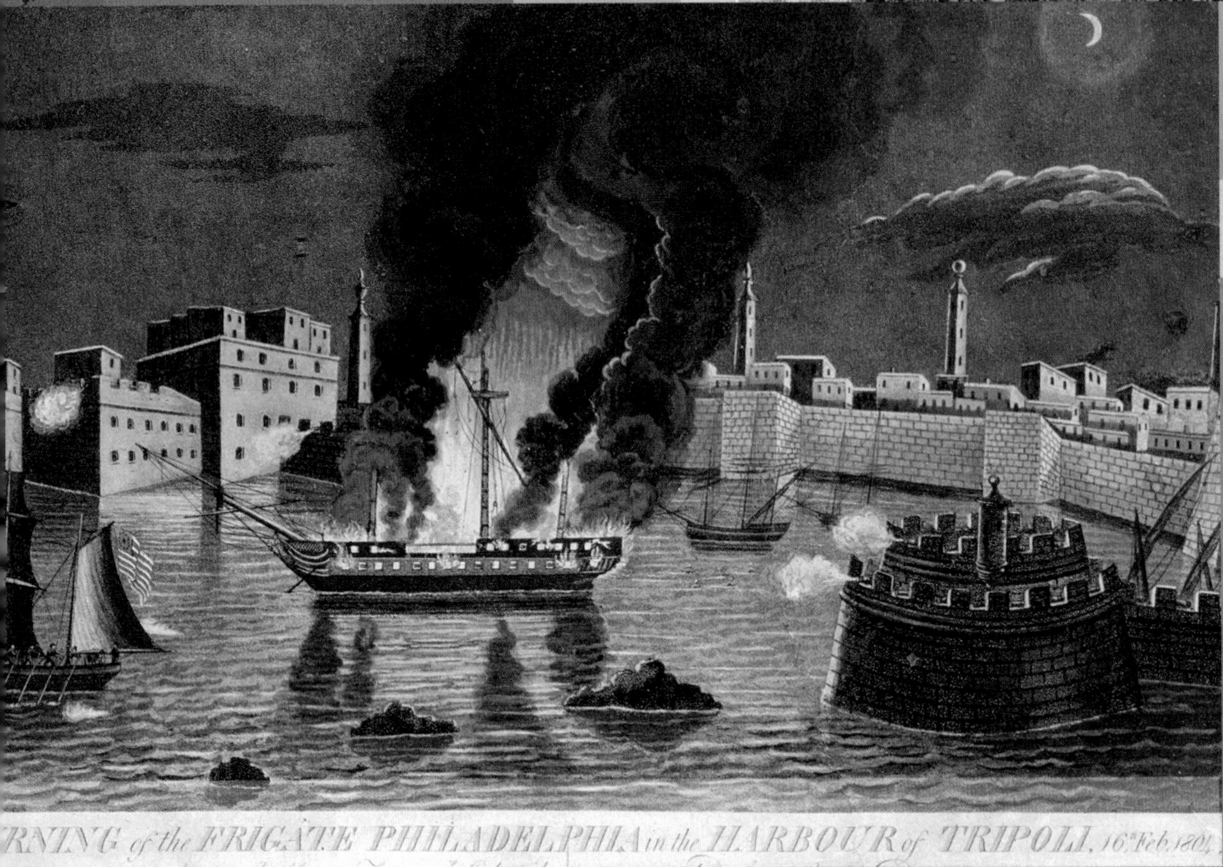

RNING of the FRIGATE PHILADELPHIA in the HARBOUR of TRIPOLI, 16th Feb. 1804.

INHABITANTS
OF
AMERICA,

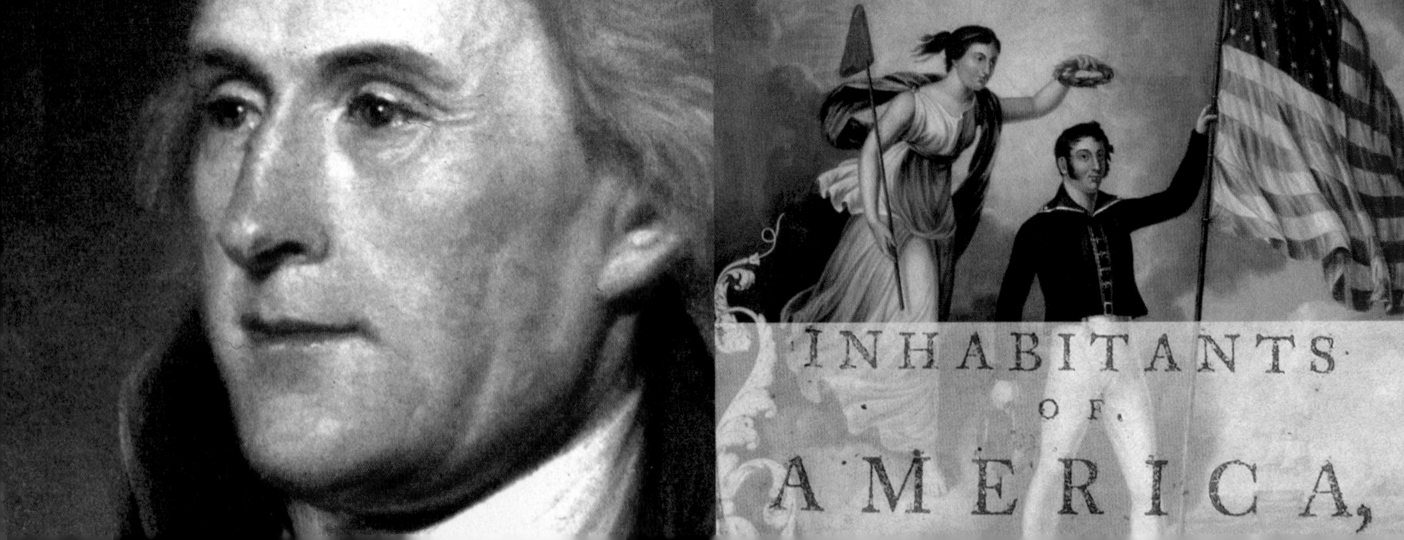

PART

2

Building a Nation

In August 1776, Benjamin Rush, a Philadelphia physician, recognized that the thirteen rebellious American colonies somehow had to behave like a united nation. Yet, it was one thing for Patriot leaders to declare independence and quite another to win it on the battlefield. The odds greatly favored Great Britain, the richest nation in Europe, with a population of some 11 million people. Fewer than half of the 2.5 million colonists were Patriots who *actively* supported the Revolution, and many others—the Loyalists, or Tories, as the Patriots mockingly called them—fought against it. Still others sought just to stay alive, often by changing sides.

Many Americans were suspicious of both sides and hesitant to embrace an uncertain cause. The thirteen independent states had new, untested governments; the Continental Congress struggled to serve as a national government with few powers; and General George Washington found himself in charge of an inexperienced and poorly equipped army facing the world's greatest military power.

Nevertheless, the Revolutionaries would persevere and prevail in almost miraculous fashion. As a military leader, Washington was no genius; he was more dogged than brilliant. Yet he was fearless and rarely lost his composure. His soldiers may have lacked the experience and equipment of their British counterparts, but they had extensive knowledge of the new nation's geography and used it to their advantage. Washington chose excellent advisers and officers, inspired loyalty, and quickly perceived that dealing with the Continental Congress was as crucial to victory as was gunpowder.

Equally important to the Revolutionary cause was the decision by the French (and later the Spanish and Dutch) to join the fight against Britain. The Franco-American alliance, negotiated in 1778, was the vital turning point in the war. In 1783, after eight years of sporadic fighting and heavy human and financial losses, the British gave up their American colonies.

While fighting the British, the Patriots also had to create new governments for themselves. Their deeply ingrained resentment of British imperial rule led Americans to give more power to the individual states than to the the *Confederation*—the new national government. As Thomas Jefferson declared, "Virginia is my country."

Such powerful local ties help explain why the Articles of Confederation, the original constitution organizing the league of thirteen independent, sovereign, and co-equal states, provided only minimal national authority. In fact, the Articles were not officially ratified by the states until 1781. And, even then, it remained unclear whether the American states would unite as a new nation or whether their ties would simply reflect a convenient alliance that might fragment at any moment. It often seemed that all they had in common was a desire for independence from British rule.

After the Revolutionary War, the flimsy political bonds authorized by the Articles of Confederation could not meet the needs of the new nation. This realization led to the calling of the Constitutional Convention in 1787. The process of drafting and approving the new constitution generated heated debate about the respective powers granted to the states and the national government, a debate that became the central theme of American political thought.

The Revolution also unleashed social forces that would help reshape American over time in terms of the role of women, African Americans, Hispanics, and Native Americans. Sectionalism between the different regions of the country, westward expansion into Native American ancestral lands, and foreign relations would also present major challenges.

These critical issues spawned the first national political parties. During the 1790s, the Federalist party, led by George Washington, John Adams, and Alexander Hamilton, and the Democratic-Republican party, led by Thomas Jefferson and James Madison, furiously debated the political and economic future of the republic.

With Jefferson's election as president in 1800, the Democratic-Republicans would remain dominant for the next quarter century. In the process, they presided over a maturing republic that expanded westward at the expense of Native Americans, embraced industrial development, engaged in a second war with Great Britain, and witnessed growing tensions between North and South over slavery.

THE DEATH OF GENERAL MERCER AT THE BATTLE OF PRINCETON (ca. 1789–1831) Soon after the American victory in Trenton, New Jersey, George Washington *(center, on horseback)* and his men had another unexpected win at the Battle of Princeton. One of the casualties, however, was Washington's close friend, General Hugh Mercer *(bottom)*, whose death became a rallying symbol for the Revolution.

CHAPTER 5

The American Revolution

1775–1783

Few Europeans thought the untested Americans could win against the world's most powerful empire. Although the British triumphed in most of the major battles, the Patriots outlasted them and eventually forced King George III to grant independence to the upstart United States of America. This stunning result reflected the tenacity of the Patriots as well as the difficulties the British faced in fighting a prolonged war 3,000 miles from home and in adjusting to the unorthodox American ways of warfare.

What began as a war for independence became both a *civil war* between Americans (Patriots/Whigs versus Loyalists/Tories), joined by their Indian allies, and a *world war* involving numerous "allied" European nations. The crucial development in the war was the ability of the United States to forge military alliances with France, Spain, and the Netherlands, all of which were eager to humble Great Britain. They provided the Revolutionaries with money, supplies, weapons, soldiers, and warships. The French and Spanish also sent warships to the English Channel, which forced much of the Royal Navy to remain at home and thus weakened the British effort to blockade American ports.

CORE OBJECTIVES INQUIZITIVE

1. Describe the ways in which the American Revolution was also a civil war.
2. Explain the challenges faced by both British and American military leaders in fighting the Revolutionary War.
3. Identify key turning points in the Revolutionary War, and explain how they changed the direction of the war.
4. Examine how the Revolutionary War was an "engine" for political and social change.
5. Compare the impact of the Revolutionary War on African Americans, women, and Native Americans.

Wars, of course, affect civilians as well as combatants. The Revolutionary War unleashed unexpected social and political changes, as it required "common people" to take a more active role in government at all levels—local, state, and national. In Virginia, voters in 1776 elected a new state legislature that, an observer noted, "was composed of men not quite so well dressed, nor so politely educated, nor so highly born" as had been the case in the past.

CORE **OBJECTIVE**

1. Describe the ways in which the American Revolution was also a civil war.

American Society at War

The Revolution was as much a barbaric civil war among bitterly opposed American factions (including the Native American peoples allied with both sides) as it was a prolonged struggle against Great Britain. It divided families and friends, towns and cities.

Benjamin Franklin's illegitimate son, William, for example, was the royal governor of New Jersey. An ardent Loyalist, he sided with Great Britain. His Patriot father removed him from his will and cut off all communication. Similarly, eighteen-year-old Bostonian Lucy Flucker defied her Loyalist father's wishes and married bookseller Henry Knox in 1774. (Knox would become a distinguished American general.) Lucy's estranged family fled with the British army when it left Boston in 1776, and she never saw them again. "I have lost my father, mother, brother, and sister, entirely lost them," she wrote.

Colonists divided

The colonists were similarly divided into three groups: (1) Patriots, who formed the Continental Army and fought in state militias; (2) Loyalists, or Tories, siding with Britain and the king; and (3) a middle group that sought to remain neutral but were eventually swayed by the better organized and more energetic Patriots. Loyalists may have represented 20 percent of the American population, but Patriots were the largest of the three groups.

***FOUR SOLDIERS* (CA. 1781)** This illustration by a French lieutenant captures the varied appearances of Patriot forces in the war *(left to right)*: a Black soldier (freed for joining the First Rhode Island Regiment), a New England militiaman, a frontiersman, and a French soldier. **What does this illustration show about the Patriot forces?**

Some Americans (like Benedict Arnold) switched sides during the war, some as many as four or five times. Both the Patriots and the British, once they took control of a city or community, would often require the residents to swear an oath of loyalty to their cause. In Pennsylvania, Patriots tied a rope around the neck of John Stevens, a Loyalist, and dragged him behind a canoe in the Susquehanna River because he refused to sign a loyalty oath to the American cause.

The Loyalists viewed the Revolution as an act of treason. The British Empire, they felt, was much more likely than an independent America to protect them from foreign foes and enable them to prosper. Loyalists were most numerous in the seaport cities and the Carolinas, and they came from all walks of life. Governors, judges, and other royal officials were almost all Loyalists; most Anglican ministers also preferred the mother country. Many small farmers who had largely been unaffected by the controversies over British efforts to tighten colonial regulations rallied to the British side. More New York men joined Loyalist regiments than enlisted in the Continental Army. In few places, however, were there enough Loyalists to assume control without the support of British troops.

The British were repeatedly frustrated by both the failure of Loyalists to materialize in strength and the collapse of Loyalist militia units once British troops departed. Because Patriot militias quickly returned whenever the British left an area, Loyalists faced a difficult choice: either accompany the British and leave behind their property, or stay and face the wrath of the Patriots. Even more disheartening was what one British officer called "the licentiousness of the [Loyalist] troops, who committed every species of rapine and plunder" and thereby converted potential friends to enemies.

The Patriots supported the war because they realized that the only way to protect their liberty was to separate themselves from British control. They also wanted to establish an American republic that would convert them from being *subjects* of a king to being *citizens* with the power to elect their own government and pursue their own economic interests.

Mobilizing for War

CORE **OBJECTIVE**

2. Explain the challenges faced by both British and American military leaders in fighting the Revolutionary War.

British Military Power

The British Empire sent some 35,000 soldiers and half of its huge navy to suppress the American rebellion. The British also hired foreign soldiers (mercenaries), as some 30,000 German soldiers served in the British armies. Most were from the German state of Hesse-Cassel. Americans called them ***Hessians***.

The British also recruited Loyalists, Native Americans, and African Americans, but never did as many enlist as they had hoped. Further, the British initially assumed that there would be enough food for their troops and forage for their horses in America. As the war ground on, however, most of their supplies had to come from Britain. The war's increasing costs—in human lives and war debt—demoralized the British.

American challenges: Massive British forces

Hessians German mercenary soldiers who were paid by the British royal government to fight alongside the British army.

GEORGE WASHINGTON AT PRINCETON Commissioned for Independence Hall in Philadelphia, this 1779 painting by Charles Willson Peale portrays Washington as the hero of the Battle of Princeton.

The British government under Lord North also lacked a consistent war strategy. At first, the British tried to use their naval superiority to blockade New England's seaports and strangle American commerce. When that failed, they sought to destroy George Washington's troops in New York. Despite early success, the British commanders failed to pursue the retreating American rebels. They next tried to drive a wedge between New England and New York, splitting the colonies in two. That too would fail, leading to the final British strategy: moving the main army into the southern colonies in hopes of rallying Loyalists in the region.

The Continental Army

While the Patriots had the advantage of fighting on their home ground, they also had to create an army and a navy from scratch. Before the war, **citizen-soldiers** (militiamen) were primarily civilians summoned from their farms and shops. During the Revolution, those called for military duty who had justifiable reasons could hire a substitute or simply pay a fine. Recruiting, supplying, equipping, training, and paying soldiers and sailors were monumental challenges for the new nation. At the start of the fighting, there were no uniforms, and American weapons were "as various as their costumes." Militiamen were at times unreliable and ungovernable. They were, reported General Washington, "nasty, dirty, and disobedient." They "come in, you cannot tell how, go, you cannot tell when, and act, you cannot tell where, consume your provisions, exhaust your stores [supplies], and leave you at last at a critical moment."

American challenges: Finance and supply for the military, citizen-soldiers

Washington knew that militiamen alone could not win the war. He therefore convinced the Continental Congress to create a **Continental Army** with full-time, well-trained soldiers. About half of the 200,000 Americans who served in the war were militiamen (Minutemen) and half were in the Continental Army. Most Continental Army recruits came from the margins of colonial society: poor farmers, unskilled laborers, indentured servants, or recently arrived immigrants. Most were young and single. Some 5,000 African Americans, virtually all formerly enslaved, also served.

citizen-soldiers Part-time non-professional soldiers, mostly poor farmers or recent immigrants who had been indentured servants, who played an important role in the Revolutionary War.

Continental Army Army authorized by Continental Congress, 1755–1784, to fight the British; commanded by George Washington.

What the Continental Army needed most at the start of the war were capable officers, intensive training, modern weapons, reliable supplies, and multiyear enlistment contracts. Its soldiers also needed strict discipline. As Washington and his officers began whipping the army into shape, those who violated the rules were jailed, flogged, sent packing, or even hanged as an example to others.

Many Patriots found army life unbearable and combat horrifying. As General Nathanael Greene, a Rhode Island Quaker who abandoned pacifism for the war effort and became Washington's ablest commander, pointed out, few Patriots had engaged in mortal combat, and they were hard-pressed to "stand the shocking scenes of war, to march over dead men, to hear without concern the groans of the wounded."

Desertions grew as the war dragged on. The Continental Army became an ever-shifting group, "part turnstile and part accordion." At times, General Washington could put only a few thousand men in the field. Eventually, Congress provided more generous enticements, such as land grants and cash bonuses, to encourage recruits to serve in the army for the duration of the war.

British maltreatment of prisoners of war

One of the unusual aspects of the Revolutionary war was that more Patriot soldiers and sailors died as British prisoners than as combatants. Some 18,000 Americans died in captivity, almost three times as many as those who died in combat. The British treated captured Patriot soldiers as traitors, which meant they could be as brutal to them as they wanted. Beatings and whippings were commonplace, as was the practice of denying food and water to prisoners deemed "rowdy."

As word seeped out about the horrific treatment of Patriot prisoners, outraged Americans deepened their resolve to gain independence. In 1777, Benjamin Franklin replied to a British friend who had asked if the Americans might abandon the war effort: "As to our submitting again to the government of Britain, 'tis vain to think of it. She has given us by her numberless barbarities, in the prosecution of the war and in the treatment of prisoners . . . that we can never again trust her in the management of our affairs."

Problems of Finance and Supply

Financing the Revolution was much harder for the Americans than it was for Great Britain. Lacking the power to impose taxes, Congress could only *ask* the states to provide funds for the national government. Yet the states rarely provided their expected share of the war's expenses, and Congress reluctantly had to allow Patriot armies to take supplies directly from farmers in return for written promises of future payment.

In a predominantly agricultural society like America, turning farmers into soldiers hurt the economy. William Hooper, a North Carolinian who signed the Declaration of Independence, grumbled that "a soldier made is a farmer lost." Many states found a source of revenue in the sale of abandoned Loyalist homes, farms, and plantations. Nevertheless, Congress and the states still fell short of funding the war's cost and were forced to print more and more paper money, which eroded its value.

Native Americans and the Revolution

American and British challenges: Recruiting Native Americans

Both the British and Americans recruited Indians to fight with them, but the British were far more successful at it, largely because they had long-standing relationships with chieftains and promised to protect Indian lands. The tribes making up the Iroquois League split their allegiances, with most Mohawk, Onondaga, Cayuga, and Seneca joining the British, and most Oneida and Tuscarora supporting the Patriots. In the Carolinas, the Cherokee joined the

British in hopes of driving out Americans who had taken their lands. Most Indians in New England tried to remain neutral or sided with the Patriots.

Disaster in Canada

In July 1775, the Continental Congress authorized a military expedition into British Canada to attack Quebec in the vain hope of convincing the French Canadians to become allies. The Americans, having spent six weeks struggling through dense forests, crossing roaring rapids, and wading through frost-covered marshes, arrived outside Quebec in September, tired, exhausted, freezing, and hungry. A silent killer then ambushed them: smallpox. As the virus raced through the American camp, General Richard Montgomery faced a brutal dilemma. Most of his soldiers had signed up for short tours of duty, and many were scheduled for discharge at the end of the year. Because of the impending departure of his men, Montgomery could not afford to wait until spring for the smallpox to subside. Seeing little choice but to fight, he ordered an attack on the British forces defending Quebec on December 31, 1775.

The assault was a disaster. More than 400 Americans were taken prisoner; the rest of the Patriot force retreated to their camp outside the walled city and appealed to the Continental Congress for reinforcements. The British, sensing weakness, attacked and sent the Patriots on a frantic retreat up the St. Lawrence River to the American-held city of Montreal and eventually back to New York and New England.

By the summer of 1776, the Patriots had come to realize that their quest for independence would be neither short nor easy. George Washington confessed to his brother that his efforts to form an effective army out of "the great mixture of troops" were filled with "difficulties and distresses."

Washington's Narrow Escape

New York City under threat

During the summer of 1776, the British decided to invade New York City, the new nation's leading commercial seaport. So many Loyalists lived there that it was called Tory Town. By the end of summer, two-thirds of the British army, veterans of many campaigns around the world, were camped on Staten Island, just a mile off the coast of Manhattan, preparing to invade the city.

The British commanders, General William Howe and his brother, Admiral Richard Howe, met with Patriot leaders to negotiate a settlement. After the negotiations failed, a British fleet of 427 ships began offloading 32,000 troops on Long Island near New York City. It was the largest seaborne military expedition in history.

Although George Washington's nearly 20,000 men were too few to protect New York, Congress insisted that the city be defended at all costs. As John Adams explained, New York was the "key to the whole continent."

In late August 1776, as the Americans entrenched on Long Island waited for the British attack, General Washington walked back and forth behind his greatly outnumbered men with two loaded pistols, warning them that he

LORD STIRLING AT THE BATTLE OF LONG ISLAND The Battle of Long Island was a devastating loss for George Washington, his troops, and American morale. In this dramatic painting by Alonzo Chappel, Patriot soldiers attack the British to enable the retreat of other units to Manhattan.

would shoot anyone who ran. He assured them that he would "fight as long as I have a leg or an arm."

Yet it would not be enough. As the Battle of Long Island and White Plains unfolded, the outgunned Americans were decimated. A Marylander reported that a British cannonball careened through the American lines. It "first took the head off a stout heavy man; then took off Chilson's arm, which was amputated. It then struck Sergeant Garret on the hip. What a sight that was to see men with legs and arms and packs all in a heap." It was impossible "for me to describe the confusion and horror," a soldier said of the panicked retreat across swampy marshes. As General Washington watched the disaster unfolding, he exclaimed, "Good God! What brave fellows I must lose this day!"

Over the course of six hours, the inexperienced American army suffered a humiliating defeat. The smoke and chaos of battle, the "confusion and horror," disoriented the undisciplined and untested Americans. They steadily gave ground, leading British commanders to assume that the Revolution was about to end. The lopsided British victory caused faith in General Washington to plummet. As John Adams lamented, "In general, our generals were outgeneraled."

American army retreats from New York

On August 29, General Washington realized the only hope for his battered army was to organize a hasty retreat to Manhattan that night. Thanks to a timely rainstorm and the heroic efforts of experienced New England boatmen, the 9,500 Americans and their horses and equipment were rowed across the East River throughout the night. A thick early-morning fog and a soaking mist cloaked the American retreat. General Washington was in the last boat to leave.

When the rain finally ceased and the fog lifted, British scouts reported startling news: the American army was gone. Admiral Howe's hopes for a quick end to the Revolution were dashed. Had the British army moved faster, it could have trapped Washington's entire force. But it did not happen. The British rested as the main American army made an astonishing escape from New York over the next several weeks. The Patriot troops crossed the Hudson River, retreated into New Jersey, and then crossed over the Delaware River into Pennsylvania.

Over the next two months, Washington was "wearied almost to death" as the remnants of his "broken and dispirited" army outraced their British pursuers. "In one thing only" did the British fail, reported an observer; "they could not run as fast as their Foe."

New York City became the headquarters of both the Royal Navy and the British army. Loyalists, or Tories, excitedly welcomed the British occupation. "Hundreds in this colony are against us," a New York City Patriot wrote to John Adams. "Tories openly express their sentiments in favor of the enemy."

Thomas Paine: "The Times That Try Men's Souls"

By December 1776, the Revolution was near collapse. "Our situation is truly distressing," George Washington admitted. A British officer reported that many "rebels" were "without shoes or stockings, and several were observed to have only linen drawers . . . without any proper shirt. They must suffer extremely" in the winter weather. Indeed, Washington had only 3,000 soldiers left. In a candid letter to his cousin, he confessed that his pitiful army was decimated by sickness and desertions. Unless he could organize "the speedy enlistment of a new army," the "game will be pretty well up."

Then, help emerged from an unexpected source: the English-born war correspondent Thomas Paine. Having opened 1776 with his inspiring pamphlet *Common Sense,* Paine now composed *The American Crisis*, in which he gave voice to the desperate struggle for independence:

> These are the times that try men's souls: The summer soldier and the sunshine patriot will, in this crisis, shrink from the service of his country; but he that stands it NOW deserves the love and thanks of man and woman. Tyranny, like Hell, is not easily conquered. Yet we

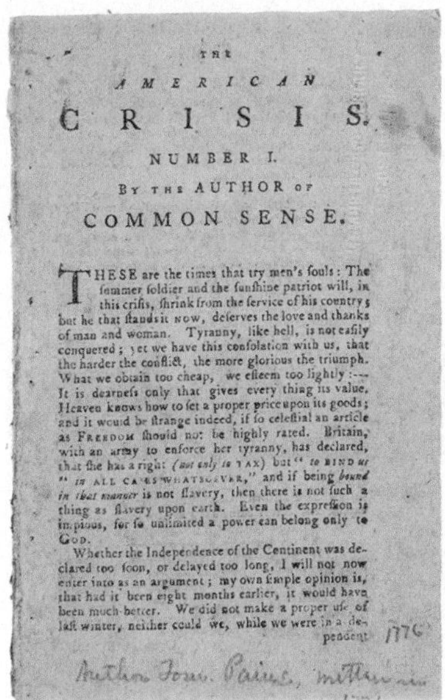

THE

AMERICAN

CRISIS.

NUMBER I.

By the AUTHOR of

COMMON SENSE.

THESE are the times that try men's souls: The summer soldier and the sunshine patriot will, in this crisis, shrink from the service of his country; but he that stands it NOW, deserves the love and thanks of man and woman. Tyranny, like hell, is not easily conquered; yet we have this consolation with us, that the harder the conflict, the more glorious the triumph. What we obtain too cheap, we esteem too lightly:— It is dearness only that gives every thing its value. Heaven knows how to set a proper price upon its goods; and it would be strange indeed, if so celestial an article as FREEDOM should not be highly rated. Britain, with an army to enforce her tyranny, has declared, that she has a right (*not only to* TAX) but "*to* BIND *us* "*in* ALL CASES WHATSOEVER," and if being *bound in that manner* is not slavery, then there is not such a thing as slavery upon earth. Even the expression is impious, for so unlimited a power can belong only to GOD.

Whether the Independence of the Continent was declared too soon, or delayed too long, I will not now enter into as an argument; my own simple opinion is, that had it been eight months earlier, it would have been much better. We did not make a proper use of last winter, neither could we, while we were in a de-

pendent

THOMAS PAINE'S *THE AMERICAN CRISIS* Thomas Paine's inspiring pamphlet was originally published anonymously "by the author of Common Sense," because the British viewed its content as evidence of treason. **What was the immediate impact of Paine's *The American Crisis*?**

have this consolation with us, that the harder the conflict, the more glorious the triumph.

Paine's rousing pamphlet boosted the Patriots' flagging spirits. "Who is the author of *Common Sense*?" asked a Rhode Island Patriot. "I can hardly refrain from admiring him." George Washington ordered that *The American Crisis* be read aloud to small groups of his dwindling army. Paine's stirring words also emboldened members of the Continental Congress, and on December 27, 1776, Congress gave Washington "large powers" to strengthen the war effort, including the ability to offer recruits cash, land, clothing, and blankets.

War Is a Stern Teacher

George Washington had learned some hard lessons. Dependence on state **militias**, he now realized, "would prove the downfall of our cause." The feisty frontier militiamen he had relied upon to bolster the Continental Army came and went as they pleased, in part because they resisted traditional forms of military discipline. Washington acknowledged that "a people unused to restraint must be led; they will not be driven." His strength as a commander was an ability to learn from his mistakes and to use resilience and flexibility as weapons.

With soldiers deserting every day, Washington modified his conventional top-down approach in favor of allowing soldiers to tell him their concerns and offer suggestions. What he heard led him to change his strategy. The Americans could not defeat veteran British soldiers in large battles. "On our side," Washington explained, "the war should be defensive." He would use the larger size and lumbering pace of the British forces against them. His focus would be on quickness and elusiveness, on launching hit-and-run campaigns to confuse and unsettle the British while preserving his struggling

militias Part-time "citizen-soldiers" called out to protect their towns from foreign invasion and ravages during the American Revolution.

army. Ultimately, the American commander planned to outlast his foes. The British fell into his trap.

In December 1776, General William Howe, commander of the British forces in North America, decided to wait out the winter in New York City. (Eighteenth-century armies rarely fought during the winter months.) By not pursuing the Americans into Pennsylvania, Howe had lost a great opportunity to end the Revolution.

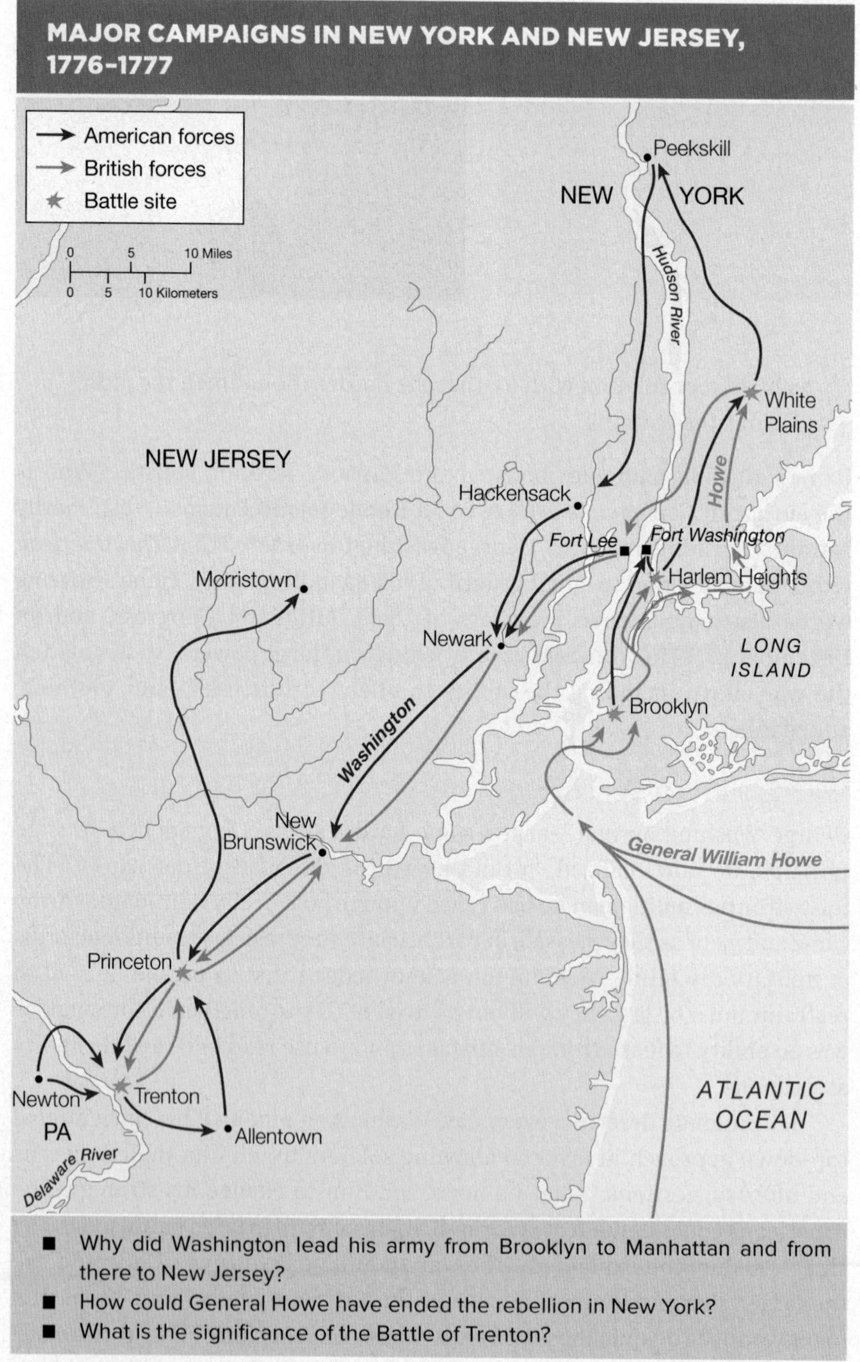

MAJOR CAMPAIGNS IN NEW YORK AND NEW JERSEY, 1776–1777

- Why did Washington lead his army from Brooklyn to Manhattan and from there to New Jersey?
- How could General Howe have ended the rebellion in New York?
- What is the significance of the Battle of Trenton?

A Desperate Gamble

George Washington, however, was not ready to hibernate. He decided that the Revolutionary cause desperately needed "some stroke" of good news. So he gambled on an audacious surprise attack. On a "fearfully cold and raw" Christmas night in 1776, Washington secretly led some 2,400 men, packed into forty-foot-long boats and maintaining a "profound silence," across the ice-clogged Delaware River into New Jersey. Near sunrise at Trenton, the Americans surprised 1,500 sleeping Hessians, many of them hungover from too much Christmas rum. The **Battle of Trenton** was a total rout. Just two of Washington's men were killed, and only four wounded. The Americans captured a thousand prisoners, forty horses, six cannon, a thousand muskets, and forty barrels of rum, much of which was consumed immediately.

After the battle, Washington hurried his men and their German captives back across the river, urging his troops to treat the prisoners "with humanity, and let them have no reason to complain of our copying the brutal example of the British army."

Four days later, the Americans again crossed the Delaware River, and attacked British forces around Princeton before taking shelter in winter quarters at Morristown, New Jersey. A British officer grumbled that the Americans had "become a formidable enemy."

The victories at Princeton and Trenton saved the cause of independence and shifted the war's momentum. A fresh wave of Patriots signed up to serve in the army, and Washington regained the confidence of his men. Although the "dark days" of late 1776 were over, unexpected challenges quickly chilled the Patriots' excitement.

Winter in Morristown

American challenges: Demoralized troops, disease

During the record-cold winter in early 1777, George Washington's ragged army was again much diminished, as six-month enlistment contracts expired and deserters fled the hardships caused by the brutal weather, inadequate food, and widespread disease. One soldier recalled that "we were absolutely, literally starved of. . . . I saw several of the men roast their old shoes and eat them."

Smallpox and other infectious diseases caused more casualties among the armies than did combat. By 1777, Washington had come to dread smallpox more than "the Sword of the Enemy." On any given day, a fourth of American troops were deemed unfit for duty. The threat was so great that Washington ordered a mass inoculation of the entire army, a risky undertaking that, in the end, paid off. The successful inoculation was one of Washington's greatest strategic accomplishments.

Only about 1,000 Patriots stayed through the brutal New Jersey winter. With the spring thaw, however, recruits began arriving to claim the bounty of $20 and 100 acres of land offered by Congress to those who would enlist for three years or for the duration of the conflict, if less. Having cobbled

Battle of Trenton (1776)
First decisive American victory that proved pivotal in reviving morale and demonstrating General Washington's abilities.

together some 9,000 regular troops, Washington began skirmishing with the British forces in northern New Jersey.

A Strategy of Evasion

British challenges: American evasion and selective confrontation; high supply costs

General William Howe had been making his own plans, however. He hoped to maneuver the Americans into fighting a single "decisive action" that the British would surely win—and thereby end the war.

Washington, however, refused to take the bait. The only way to win, he decided, was to evade the main British army, carefully select when and where to attack, and, in the end, wear down the enemy forces and their will to fight. He was willing to concede control of major cities to the British, for it was his army, "not defenseless towns, [that] they have to subdue." Britain, on the other hand, could win only by destroying the American will to resist.

CORE **OBJECTIVE**

3. Identify key turning points in the Revolutionary War, and explain how they changed the direction of the war.

Setbacks for the British (1777–1781)

In 1777, the British devised a fresh plan to defeat the "American rebellion." It centered on a three-pronged assault on the state of New York. The complicated plan called for an army, based in Canada and led by General John Burgoyne, to advance southward from Quebec via Lake Champlain to the Hudson River. At the same time, another British force would move eastward from Oswego, in western New York. General William Howe would lead a third army up the Hudson River from New York City. All three armies would eventually converge in central New York and strangle any remaining Patriot resistance. By gaining control of New York, the British would cut off New England from the rest of the colonies.

The British armies, however, failed in their execution—and in their communications with one another. At the last minute, Howe changed his mind and decided to move south from New York City to attack the Patriot capital, Philadelphia. General Washington withdrew most of his men from New Jersey to meet Howe's threat, while other American units banded together in upstate New York to deal with the British there.

Battles of Saratoga (1777)

On September 11, 1777, at Brandywine Creek, southwest of Philadelphia, the British overpowered Washington's army and occupied Philadelphia, then the largest and wealthiest American city. The members of the Continental Congress fled. Washington and his army withdrew to primitive winter quarters twenty miles away at the rural hamlet of Valley Forge, while Howe and his men remained in the comfortable confines of Philadelphia.

The Campaign of 1777

Meanwhile, an overconfident General Burgoyne (nicknamed "General Swagger") led his army southward from Canada, eventually reaching

Lake Champlain in June 1777. The British then pushed south through dense forests and rugged terrain toward the Hudson River. Eventually, they ran short of food and provisions, leaving them no choice but to make a desperate attempt to reach Albany. Growing numbers of Patriot soldiers slowed their advance, however.

GENERAL JOHN BURGOYNE After three weeks of fighting, Burgoyne, commander of Britain's northern forces, surrendered to the Americans at Saratoga on October 17, 1777.

The American army commander in New York was General Horatio Gates. Thirty-two years earlier, in 1745, he and Burgoyne had served as officers in the same British regiment. As Patriot militiamen converged from across central New York, Burgoyne pulled his forces back to the village of Saratoga (now called Schuylerville), where the reinforced American army surrounded the British. In the ensuing three-week-long **Battles of Saratoga**, the British, desperate for food and ammunition, twice tried—and failed—to break through the encircling Americans, losing a third of their men in the process. On October 17, 1777, Burgoyne surrendered. "The fortunes of war," he told Gates, "have made me your prisoner." Burgoyne also turned over 5,800 troops, 7,000 muskets, and 42 cannons.

The catastrophic British defeat unhinged King George. He fell "into agonies on hearing the account." The Saratoga campaign was the greatest loss that the British had ever suffered, and they would never recover. William Pitt, the former British prime minister, made a shocking prediction to Parliament after the defeat: "*You cannot conquer America.*"

The Crucial Alliance with France

The surprising victory at Saratoga was a strategic turning point for the new nation because it enabled an **alliance with France**, which was hungry for revenge after losing four wars to the British in the previous eighty years.

Under the Treaty of Alliance, signed on February 6, 1778, the parties agreed first, that when France entered the war, both countries would fight until American independence was won; second, that neither would conclude a "truce or peace" with Great Britain without "the formal consent of the other"; and, third, that each would guarantee the other's possessions in America "from the present time and forever against all other powers." France further agreed not to seek Canada or other British possessions on the mainland of North America. In the end, the French intervention determined the outcome of the war.

After the British defeat at Saratoga and the news of the French alliance with the United States, Parliament tried to end the war by granting all the demands the Americans had made before they had declared independence.

Battles of Saratoga (1777) Decisive defeat of almost 6,000 British troops under General John Burgoyne in several battles near Saratoga, New York, in October 1777; the American victory helped convince France to enter the war on the side of the Patriots.

alliance with France Critical diplomatic, military, and economic alliance between France and the newly independent United States, codified by the Treaty of Alliance (1778).

MAJOR CAMPAIGNS IN NEW YORK AND PENNSYLVANIA, 1777

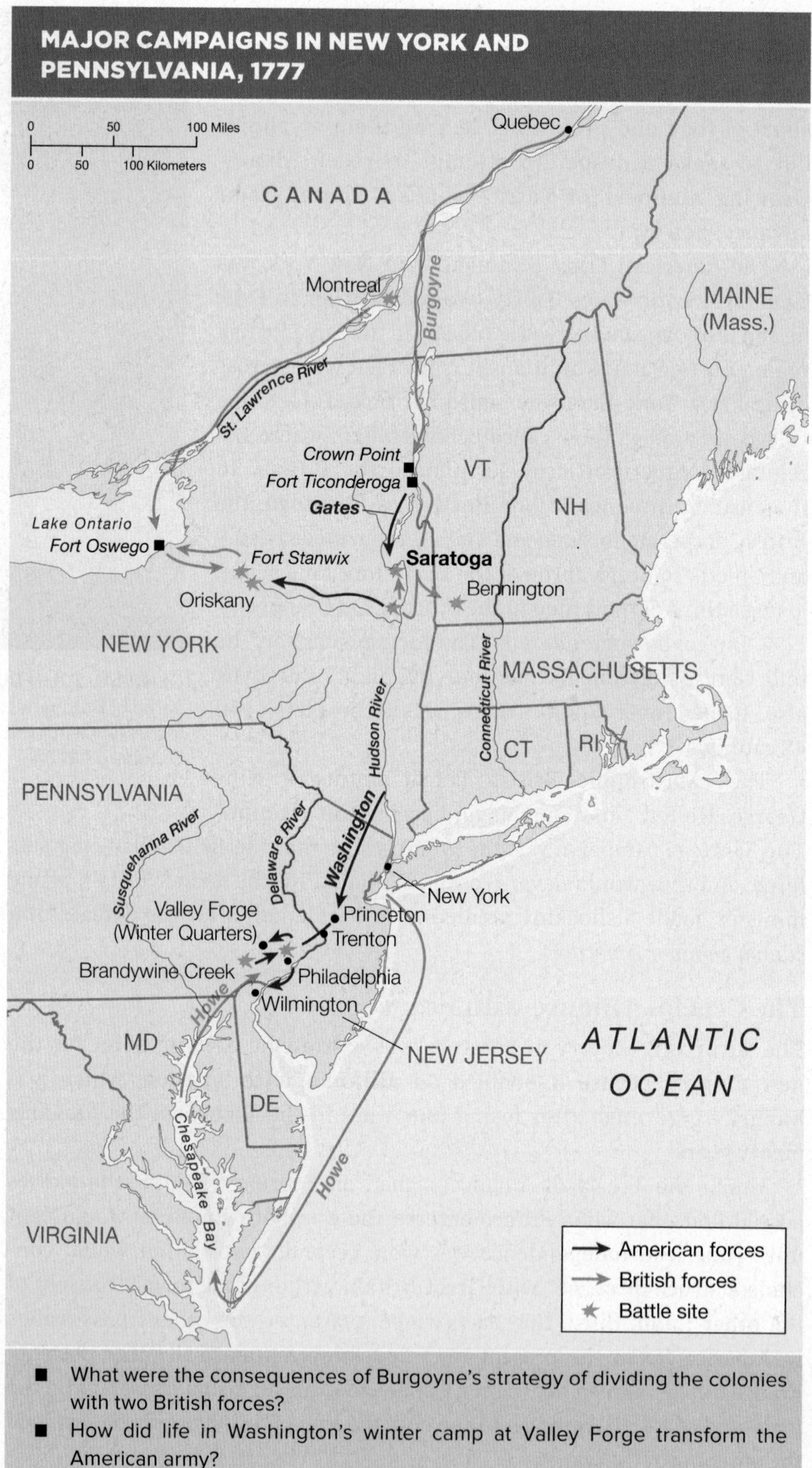

- What were the consequences of Burgoyne's strategy of dividing the colonies with two British forces?
- How did life in Washington's winter camp at Valley Forge transform the American army?
- Why was Saratoga a turning point in the American Revolution?

The Continental Congress, however, would not negotiate until Britain officially recognized American independence and withdrew its forces. King George III refused.

Valley Forge and Stalemate

For the American army at **Valley Forge**, near Philadelphia, the winter of 1777–1778 was a time of intense suffering. Keeping his ragtag army intact and preserving morale was George Washington's greatest leadership test. He wrote Henry Laurens, the president of Congress, that he could not find words to convey their predicament. It "must be seen to be believed."

BARON VON STEUBEN George Washington leads Baron von Steuben on a tour through Valley Forge, where Steuben would embark on a rigorous training program to ready the American soldiers for combat. **What conditions did Steuben find when he arrived at Valley Forge?**

The 11,000 Patriots, including some twelve-year-old soldiers accompanied by their mothers, lacked coats, shoes, and blankets. All were miserably hungry, and their 900 log-and-mud huts offered little protection from the icy winds. Bare feet froze, turned black, and were amputated.

By February 1778, some 7,000 troops were too ill for duty, and horses were dying from starvation. The first soldier to die at Valley Forge was known simply as Jethro, one of hundreds of free Blacks who served in the conflict. More than 2,500 soldiers died at Valley Forge; another 1,000 deserted, and several hundred officers resigned or left before winter's end. Washington warned Congress that if fresh food and supplies were not provided, the army would be forced "to starve, dissolve, or disperse."

Winter of 1777–1778 at Valley Forge

Fortunately for the Revolutionaries, General Howe again remained content to spend the winter amid the comforts of Philadelphia. Desperate to find relief for his long-suffering soldiers, Washington sent troops across New Jersey, Delaware, and the Eastern Shore of Maryland to confiscate horses, cattle, and hogs in exchange for "receipts" promising future payment.

In the early spring of 1778, Washington sought to boost morale by organizing a rigorous training program. To do so, he turned to an energetic, heavyset Prussian soldier of fortune, Friedrich Wilhelm, Baron von Steuben, who taught the Americans how to march, shoot, and attack in formation, and educated them on basic hygiene.

Steuben was one of several foreign volunteers who joined the American army at Valley Forge. Another was a nineteen-year-old, red-haired French orphan named Gilbert du Motier, the Marquis de Lafayette. A fabulously wealthy young idealist excited by the American cause, Lafayette offered to serve in the Continental Army for no pay in exchange for being named a major general. "It is not to teach but to learn that I have come hither," he explained. He gave $200,000 to the war effort, outfitted a ship, recruited other French volunteers, and left behind his pregnant wife and year-old daughter to join the "grand adventure."

Valley Forge (1777–1778) American military encampment near Philadelphia, where more than 3,500 soldiers deserted or died from cold and hunger in the winter.

George Washington was initially skeptical of the French aristocrat, barely twenty years old, but Lafayette soon became the commander in chief's most trusted aide. "I do not know a nobler, finer soul, and I love him as my own," Washington told a French diplomat, noting that Lafayette possessed "a large share of bravery and military ardor." The precocious French general also proved to be an able diplomat in helping to forge the crucial military alliance with France.

Patriot morale had risen when the Continental Congress promised extra pay and bonuses after the war, and again with the news of the military alliance with France. In the spring of 1778, British forces withdrew from Pennsylvania to New York City, with the American army in hot pursuit. From that time on, the combat in the north settled into a long stalemate.

War in the West

Terror tactics in Indian country

The one significant American military success of 1778 occurred in the West. The Revolution had created two wars. In addition to the main conflict in the east, a frontier guerrilla war pitted Indians and Loyalists against isolated Patriot settlers living along the northern and western frontiers. In the Ohio River Valley, as well as in western New York and Pennsylvania, the British urged Loyalists and their Indian allies to raid settlements and offered to pay bounties for American scalps.

To end the English-led attacks, early in 1778 George Rogers Clark took 175 Patriot frontiersmen down the Ohio River. On the evening of July 4, the Americans captured English-controlled Kaskaskia, in present-day

IROQUOIS AND LOYALISTS A nineteenth-century oil painting by Alonzo Chappel depicts Iroquois warriors joining Loyalists in a 1778 battle against Patriots during the Revolutionary War.

WESTERN CAMPAIGNS, 1776–1779

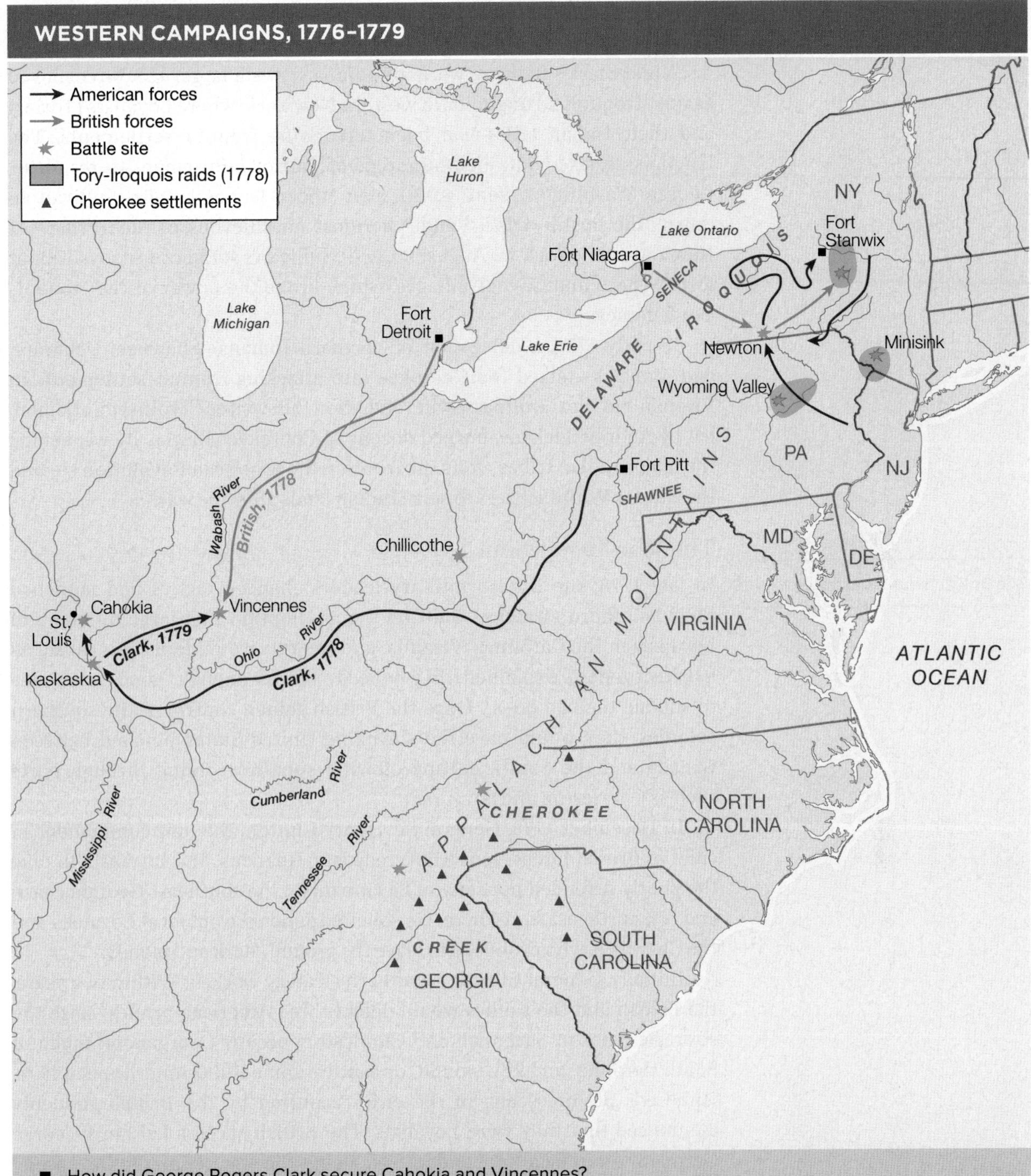

- How did George Rogers Clark secure Cahokia and Vincennes?
- Why did the American army destroy Iroquois villages in 1779?
- Why were the skirmishes between Indians and settlers on the western frontier significant for the future of the trans-Appalachian frontier?

Illinois. Then, without bloodshed, Clark took Cahokia (in Illinois across the Mississippi River from St. Louis) and Vincennes (in present-day Indiana).

While Clark's Rangers were in Indiana, a much larger U.S. force moved against Iroquois strongholds in western New York, where Loyalists (Tories) and their Indian allies had been terrorizing frontier settlements. The Iroquois attacks had killed hundreds of Patriot militiamen. In response, George Washington sent 4,000 men under General John Sullivan to crush "the hostile tribes" and "the most mischievous of the Tories." At Newtown, New York, on August 29, 1779, Sullivan's soldiers destroyed about forty Seneca and Cayuga villages, which broke the power of the Iroquois Confederacy.

In early 1776, a delegation of northern Indians—Shawnee, Delaware, and Mohawk—talked the Cherokee into attacking frontier settlements in Virginia and the Carolinas. Swift retaliation followed as Carolina militiamen, led by Andrew Pickens, burned dozens of Cherokee villages. By weakening the major Indian tribes along the frontier, the American Revolution cleared the way for White settlers to seize Indian lands after the war.

The War Moves South

The British "southern strategy"

In late 1778, the British military leaders changed tactics and launched their "southern strategy," built on the assumption that large numbers of Loyalists in the Carolinas, Virginia, and Georgia would join their cause. As a British general explained, they hoped to recruit enough "good Americans to subdue the bad ones." Once the British gained control of the southern colonies, they would have the shrinking United States pinched between Canada and the South, cutting off vital supplies coming through ports such as Charleston and Savannah.

In December 1778, General Sir Henry Clinton, the new commander in chief of British forces, sent 3,500 redcoats, Hessians, and Loyalists to take the poorly defended port city of Savannah, on the southeast Georgia coast, and roll northeast from there. He solicited support from local Loyalists and the Cherokee, who promised to leave the ground "dark and bloody."

Initially, General Clinton's southern strategy worked. Within two years, the British and their allies would defeat three American armies; seize the strategic cities of Savannah and Charleston; occupy Georgia and much of South Carolina; and kill, wound, or capture some 7,000 American soldiers. Hundreds of Americans in the cities captured by the British suddenly announced that they were Loyalists. The British success led Lord George Germain, the official in London overseeing the war, to predict a "speedy and happy termination of the American war."

Germain's optimistic prediction, however, fell victim to three developments: First, the Loyalist strength in the South was weaker than estimated; second, the British effort to unleash Indian attacks convinced many undecided backcountry settlers to join the Patriot side; and, third, some British and Loyalist soldiers behaved so harshly that they drove many Loyalists to switch sides.

Fighting in the Carolinas The Carolina campaign took a major turn when British forces, led by generals Henry Clinton and Charles Cornwallis, bottled up an entire American army on the Charleston Peninsula for six weeks.

Subsequently, on May 12, 1780, the American general surrendered Charleston and its 5,500 defenders. It was the greatest Patriot loss of the war, and one of the greatest disasters in the history of the U.S. Army.

More bad news followed in mid-August when General Cornwallis, now in charge of the British troops in the South, defeated a much larger American force led by General Horatio Gates at Camden, South Carolina. Some 700 Americans were killed or taken prisoner.

The British now had Georgia and most of South Carolina under their control. General Henry Clinton reported that he was now prepared "to conquer the southern provinces and perhaps much more." Most South Carolina men were "either our prisoners, or in arms with us."

The British and Loyalists alienate neutral frontiersmen

Then the British made a huge mistake by sending officers into the countryside to organize Loyalist fighters to assault Patriots, thereby transforming the conflict into a civil war. When Loyalists mercilessly burned homes and murdered surrendering rebels, they alienated many frontiersmen who had been neutral. Francis Kinlock, a Loyalist, warned a British official that "the lower sort of people, who were in many parts . . . originally attached to the British government, have suffered so severely and been so frequently deceived, that Great Britain now has a hundred enemies where it had one before."

In mid-1780, small bands of frontier Patriots based in the swamps and forests of backcountry South Carolina launched a series of savage hit-and-run raids. Led by colorful fighters such as Francis Marion, nicknamed "the Swamp Fox," and Thomas Sumter, "the Carolina Gamecock," the Patriot guerrillas gradually wore down British confidence and morale. By August 1780, the British commanders were forced to admit that the backcountry of South Carolina was "in an absolute state of rebellion."

In the backcountry of the Carolinas and Georgia, British commanders encouraged their Loyalist allies to wage a scorched-earth war of terror, arson, and intimidation. British general Charles Cornwallis urged his commanders to use the "most *vigorous* measures to *extinguish the rebellion*." Tory militiamen took civilian hostages, assaulted women and children, plundered and burned houses and churches, stole property, bayoneted wounded Patriots, and tortured and executed unarmed prisoners. Vengeful Patriots responded in kind.

The Battle of Kings Mountain (1780)

The Battle of Kings Mountain Cornwallis's most ruthless cavalry officers, Lieutenant Colonel Banastre Tarleton and Scotsman Major Patrick Ferguson, were in charge of training Loyalist militiamen. Yet eventually the cavalry officers overreached. Ferguson sealed his doom when he threatened to march over the Blue Ridge Mountains, hang the mostly Scots-Irish Presbyterian Patriot leaders ("backwater barbarians"), and destroy their farms. Instead,

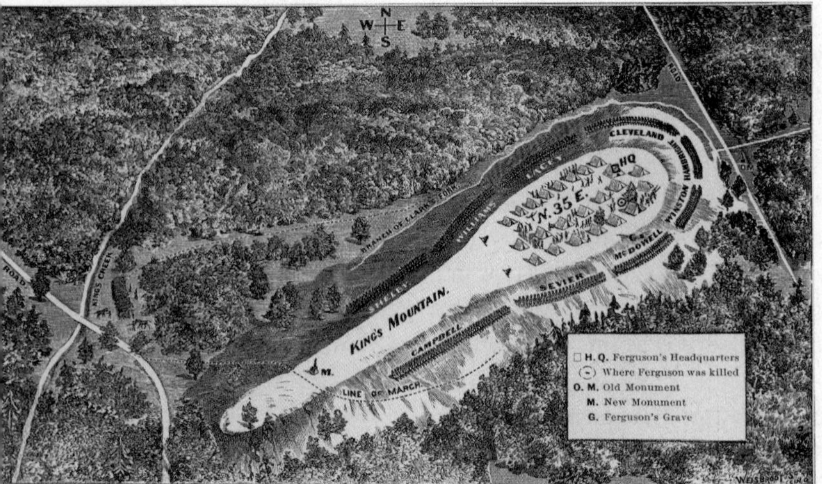

VICTORY AT KINGS MOUNTAIN A diagram of the Battle of Kings Mountain by historian Benson John Lossing shows how detachments of Patriots surrounded Major Ferguson and his encampment of Loyalists, taking them by surprise.

the feisty "over the mountain men" from southwestern Virginia and western North and South Carolina—all experienced hunters and riflemen who had often fought Cherokee—went hunting for Ferguson and his army of Loyalists in late September 1780.

After nearly two weeks in the saddle, the Patriots in early October 1780 found Major Ferguson and his Loyalist army camped near Kings Mountain along the border between North and South Carolina. The cocksure Major Ferguson had boasted beforehand that "all the rebels in hell could not push him off" Kings Mountain. He was dead wrong. By the end of the hour-long battle, his lifeless body was pocked with seven bullet holes, and both his arms were broken. Surrounding him were 157 dead Tories with 163 others too badly wounded to be moved. Seven hundred Loyalists were captured. Nine of them were hanged and many others brutalized during their long march to a North Carolina prison.

As with so many confrontations in the South, the Battle of Kings Mountain resembled an extended family feud. Seventy-four sets of brothers fought on opposite sides, as did twenty-nine sets of fathers and sons. Five brothers in the Goforth family from Rutherford County, North Carolina, fought at Kings Mountain; three were Loyalists, and two were Patriots. Only one of them survived. Two of the Goforth brothers, Preston and John Preston, fighting on opposite sides, recognized each other during the battle, took deadly aim as if in a duel, and fired simultaneously, killing each other.

The victory at Kings Mountain boosted American morale and undermined the British strategy in the South. Thomas Jefferson called the Patriot victory "the turn of the tide of success." General Cornwallis's forces retreated from Charlotte to South Carolina—and found it virtually impossible to recruit more Loyalists.

American victory at Cowpens

Patriots Gain Momentum in the South In late 1780, the Continental Congress chose a new commander for the American army in the South: General Nathanael Greene, "the fighting Quaker" of Rhode Island. Greene was bold and daring, and well suited to a drawn-out war. He arrived in Charlotte, North Carolina, to find that his troops lacked everything "necessary either for the Comfort or Convenience of Soldiers." Greene wrote Washington that the situation was "dismal, and truly distressing." Yet he also knew that if his army failed, the South would be "re-annexed" to Britain.

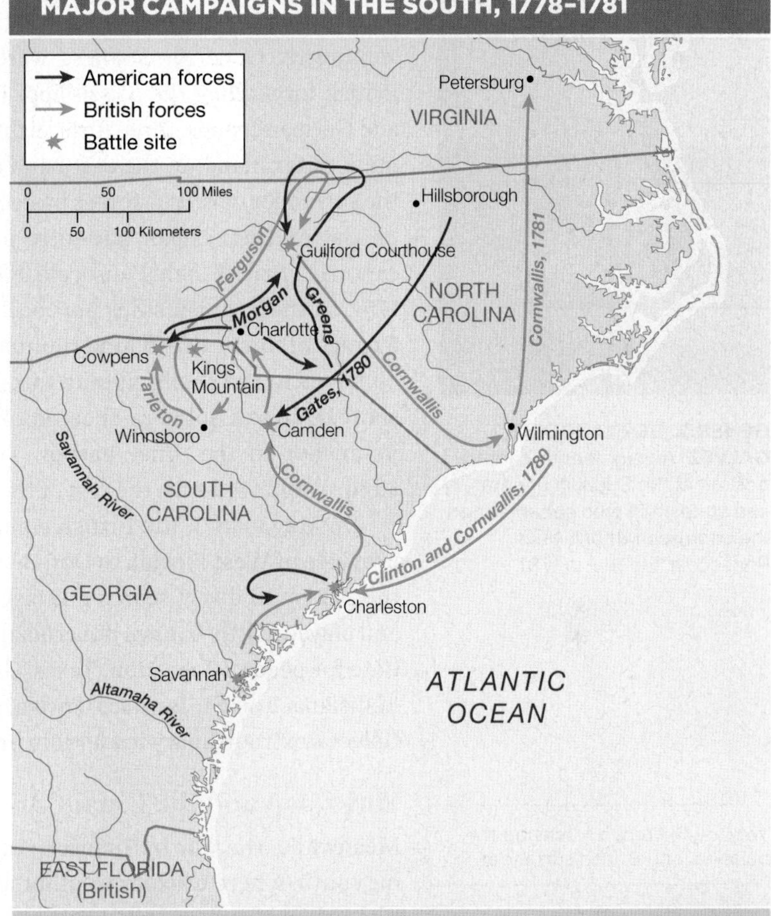

MAJOR CAMPAIGNS IN THE SOUTH, 1778–1781

- Why did the British suddenly shift their military campaign to the South in 1778?
- Why were the battles at Savannah and Charleston major victories for the British?
- How did Nathanael Greene undermine British control of the Carolinas?

Like General Washington, Greene adopted a hit-and-run strategy. From Charlotte, he moved his army eastward while sending General Daniel Morgan and about 700 riflemen on a sweep to the west of Cornwallis's headquarters at Winnsboro, South Carolina. Their assignment was to "annoy the enemy."

On a bitterly cold January 17, 1781, Morgan's force took up positions in a meadow called Cowpens in northern South Carolina. There Morgan lured Sir Banastre Tarleton's horsemen into an elaborate trap. Tarleton rushed his men forward, only to be ambushed by Morgan's cavalry. Tarleton escaped, but 110 British soldiers died and more than 700 were taken prisoner along with their horses and weapons.

Morgan's army then moved into North Carolina and joined Greene's troops. Greene lured the starving British army north, then attacked at Guilford Courthouse (near what became Greensboro, North Carolina) on March 15, 1781. In the end, the Americans lost the battle of Guilford Courthouse but inflicted such heavy losses that Cornwallis left behind his wounded and marched his weary men toward Wilmington, on the North Carolina coast, to lick their wounds and take on supplies from British ships. Cornwallis decided to abandon the Carolinas and move into Virginia, telling General Clinton in New York that he should march southward so that the two armies could merge and end the war in Virginia with a climactic victory that will "give us America."

The Spanish Alliance

In 1779, Spain, like France, forged an alliance with the United States. The Spanish had no great love for the Americans, but they were eager to deal a blow to Great Britain. Although the support provided by Spain was much less than the French effort, George Washington would later claim that the Spanish assistance was essential to the American victory.

Bernardo de Gálvez, a Spanish army general who was the new governor of the Spanish-controlled Louisiana Territory, provided weapons, ammunition,

GENERAL BERNARDO DE GÁLVEZ An eighteenth-century portrait of the Spanish general and statesman who spearheaded the capture of British-held Pensacola, Florida, in 1781.

and supplies to the American Revolutionaries. He then organized a multicultural force of Spanish soldiers, Creole militiamen, Indians, free Blacks, and American volunteers. Once his soldiers were equipped and trained, they attacked British forts along the Mississippi River, capturing over a thousand British and German troops, three forts, eight substantial ships, and thirteen hundred miles of farmland on the east bank of the river. In early 1780, Gálvez forced the surrender of British forces protecting the port city of Mobile, Alabama.

Gálvez then began patiently preparing for his most ambitious goal: capturing British-held Pensacola, Florida, on the Gulf of Mexico. In February 1781, as the Spanish ships approached the harbor, the British unleashed a barrage of thirty-two-pound cannonballs. Gálvez and his staff stood on deck, oblivious to the shells ripping through the canvas sails and rigging. On the shore, Gálvez's soldiers cheered and beat drums while his ship dropped its anchor in the inner harbor. The next day, the embarrassed Spanish admiral followed with the rest of the Spanish fleet.

On May 9, 1871, the British commander surrendered Pensacola and the province of West Florida to Don Bernardo de Gálvez. His success had forced the British to divert scarce military resources from fighting the Americans and played a little-known but crucial role in pressuring Great Britain to negotiate for peace. (Galveston, Texas, Galveston Bay, Galveston County, Galvez, Louisiana, and St. Bernard Parish, Louisiana, were all named in honor of Gálvez's extraordinary leadership in Spanish Louisiana.)

Yorktown and the Final Campaigns

Yorktown: French forces tip the balance, and British surrender

Meanwhile, the war in America ground on, with most of the fighting moving south, where warmer weather allowed combat to continue year-round. The Americans, however, knew they held the advantage in time, men, and supplies. Now they just needed to avoid a catastrophic defeat in any single battle. By September 1781, the Americans had narrowed British control in the South to Charleston and Savannah, although Patriots and Loyalists would continue to battle each other for more than a year in the backcountry.

Meanwhile, General Cornwallis had pushed his British army northward from Wilmington. Before the Carolinas could be subdued, he decided, Virginia must be eliminated as a source of American reinforcements and supplies.

Yorktown Cornwallis picked Yorktown, Virginia, a small tobacco port between the York and James Rivers on the Chesapeake Bay, as his base of operations. He was not worried about an American attack, since General Washington's main force remained in New York, and the British navy controlled American waters.

Washington, however, surprised the British. As Cornwallis's army moved into Virginia, Washington persuaded the commander of the French army in Rhode Island to join in an attack on the British army in New York. The two armies linked up in July, but before they could strike, word came that Admiral François Joseph Paul de Grasse was headed for the Chesapeake Bay with his large French fleet and some 3,000 soldiers.

The unexpected news led General Washington to change his strategy. He immediately began moving his army south toward Yorktown. At the same time, French ships slipped out of the British blockade at Newport, Rhode Island, and also headed south.

On August 30, Admiral de Grasse's fleet reached Yorktown, and French troops landed to join the Americans confronting Cornwallis's army. On September 6, the day after a British fleet appeared, de Grasse attacked and forced the British navy to abandon Cornwallis's army, leaving them with no way to get fresh food and supplies.

The climactic **Battle of Yorktown** began on September 28. The American and French troops closed off Cornwallis's last escape route and began bombarding the British with cannons. Cornwallis held out for three grim weeks, but on October 17, 1781—the anniversary of the American victory at Saratoga—he surrendered. Two days later, some 7,000 British soldiers laid down their weapons as the military band played "The World Turned Upside Down."

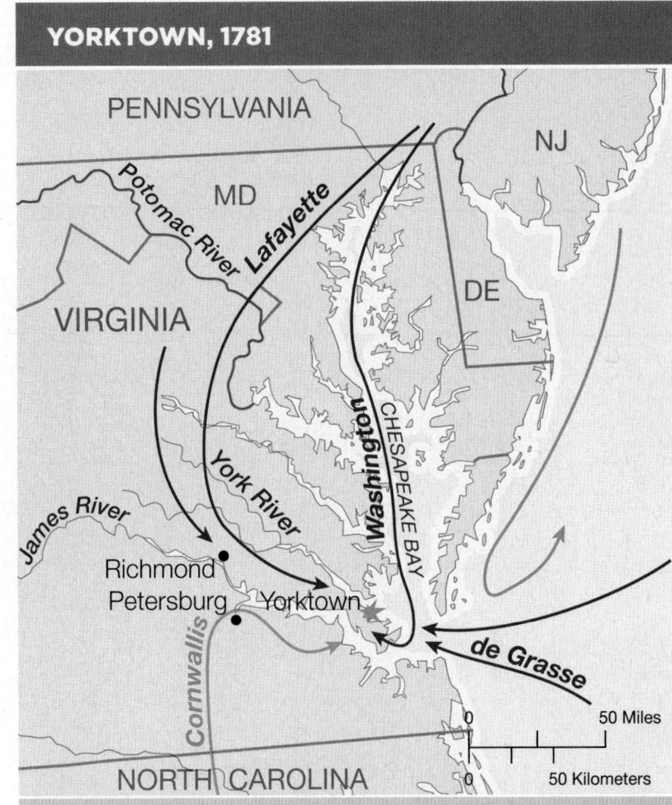

- Why did Washington and the French forces change their plans and head south to Yorktown?
- What made the Battle of Yorktown the final, decisive battle of the American Revolution?

Claiming to be ill but sick only with humiliation, a sullen General Cornwallis sent a painfully brief report to the British commander in chief in New York: "I have the mortification to inform your Excellency that I have been forced to surrender the troops under my command." A New Jersey Patriot noted that the British officers "behaved like boys who had been whipped at school. Some bit their lips, some pouted, others cried."

Interspersed among the surrendering British soldiers were hundreds of formerly enslaved people who had fled their southern masters and found refuge among the redcoats. Within days, American slave owners rushed to Yorktown in hopes of retrieving their freedom seekers. Among those eventually restored to captivity were seven freedom seekers from George Washington's Mount Vernon plantation and nine from Thomas Jefferson's Monticello.

Battle of Yorktown (1781) Last major battle of the Revolutionary War; General Cornwallis, along with over 7,000 British troops, surrendered to George Washington at Yorktown, Virginia, on October 17, 1781.

The Treaty of Paris (1783)

Although Cornwallis had surrendered his army, the war was not yet over; it would officially last for another fifteen months. The British still had more

NORTH AMERICA, 1783

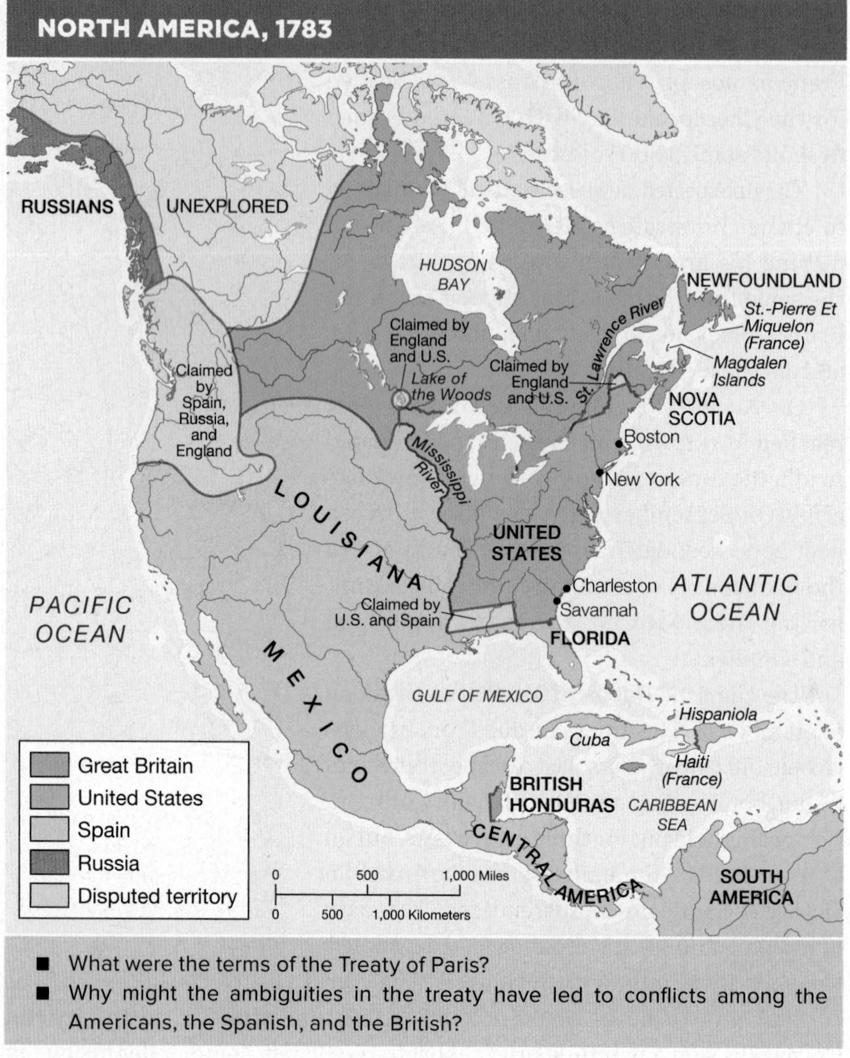

- What were the terms of the Treaty of Paris?
- Why might the ambiguities in the treaty have led to conflicts among the Americans, the Spanish, and the British?

than 20,000 redcoats in America. They controlled New York City, Charleston, and Savannah, and their warships still blockaded several American ports. Fighting continued, especially in the southern states, yet any lingering British hopes vanished at Yorktown. In London, Prime Minister Lord North exclaimed, "Oh God, it is all over."

In December 1781, King George decided against sending more troops to America. Early in 1782, British officials contacted Benjamin Franklin in Paris to ask if the Americans would be willing to sign a peace treaty without involving the French. Franklin replied that the United States had no intention of deserting its "noble" French ally to sign a treaty with "an unjust and cruel Enemy."

On February 27, 1782, Parliament voted to begin negotiations to end the war, and on March 20, Prime Minister North resigned. George III had earlier written out a letter to Parliament expressing his intention to give up the throne if the Americans won their independence.

In part, the British leaders chose peace in America so that they could concentrate on their continuing global war with France and Spain. At the same time, France let Franklin know that it was willing to let the United States negotiate its own treaty with Great Britain. Upon learning of the British decision to negotiate, Congress named a group of prominent Americans to go to Paris to discuss terms. They included John Adams, who was then representing the United States in the Netherlands; John Jay, minister (ambassador) to Spain; and Benjamin Franklin, already in France. On April 19, 1783, eight years to the day since the British had attacked American militiamen on Lexington Green, a permanent ceasefire began so that diplomats could agree to a peace treaty.

Those negotiations took almost six months. On September 3, 1783, the warring nations signed the **Treaty of Paris**. Its provisions were surprisingly favorable to the United States. Great Britain recognized the independence of the thirteen former colonies and agreed that the Mississippi River was America's western boundary, thereby more than doubling the territory of the new nation and making the new United States larger in size than any European nation. At a banquet celebrating the signing of the treaty, a French diplomat proposed a toast to "the growing greatness of America," now destined to become "the greatest empire in the world."

For now, however, the path to greatness was not so clear. A primary task in coming years would be to manage the new republic's ceaseless expansion westward without a national government capable of doing so. In addition, the peace treaty's vague references to America's northern and southern borders would be a source of dispute for years.

Native Americans had no role in the peace negotiations, and they were by far the biggest losers, as the English gave the Americans something that was not theirs to give; vast parcels of ancestral Indian lands. Florida, as it turned out, passed back to Spain. As for the prewar debts owed by Americans to British merchants, the U.S. negotiators promised that British merchants should "meet with no legal impediment" in seeking to collect money owed them.

However imperfect the peace treaty, the Americans had humbled the British Empire. "A great revolution has happened," acknowledged Edmund Burke, a prominent British politician. "A revolution made, not by chopping and changing of power in any one of the existing states, but by the appearance of a new state, of a new species, in a new part of the globe."

In winning the war, the Americans had earned their legitimate right to decide their own future. Whatever the failings and hypocrisies of the Revolution, it severed America's connection with monarchical rule and provided the catalyst for the creation of the world's only large representative democracy.

Treaty of Paris (1783) The treaty that ended the Revolutionary War recognized American independence from Britain, created the border between Canada and the United States, set the western border at the Mississippi, and ceded Florida to Spain.

The Greatest Man in the World

In late November 1783, the remaining British troops left New York City for home. As they departed, George Washington rode his gray horse into Manhattan, leading his soldiers down Broadway as thousands of New Yorkers cheered. At a noon luncheon on December 4, 1783, Washington, "with a heart full of love and gratitude," raised his wine glass and toasted his officers, several of whom were weeping: "To the memory of those heroes who have fallen for our freedom!" He then expressed the hope that his new nation would always provide shelter for immigrants and refugees: "May America be an asylum for the persecuted of the earth!"

Several days later, General Washington stunned the world when he appeared before Congress in Annapolis, Maryland, and surrendered his sword. With trembling hands and a rasping voice, he asked the members to accept his retirement so that he could return to managing his Mount Vernon plantation. "Having now finished the work assigned to me, I retire from the great theater of Action . . . and take my leave of all employments of public life."

CORE **OBJECTIVE**

4. Examine how the Revolutionary War was an "engine" for political and social change.

War as an Engine of Change

Like all major wars, the American war for independence had unexpected effects on political, economic, and social life. It upset traditional social relationships and affected the lives of people who had long been discriminated against—African Americans, women, and Indians. America had gained its liberty from British tyranny, but which Americans were to enjoy the blessings of freedom? In important ways, then, the Revolution was an engine for political experimentation and social change, and it ignited a prolonged debate about what new forms of government would best serve the new American republic.

The Loyalists Flee

The Loyalists suffered for their support of King George III and their refusal to pledge allegiance to the new United States. During and after the Revolution, their property was confiscated or destroyed, and many of them were assaulted, brutalized, and executed by Patriots (and vice versa).

After the American victory at Yorktown, tens of thousands of panicked Loyalists made their way to seaports to board British ships and flee the United States. Thousands of African Americans, mostly freedom seekers, also flocked to New York City, Charleston, and Savannah, with many of their owners in hot pursuit. Boston King, one of the freedom seekers, said he saw White slave owners grabbing their escaped enslaved prople "in the streets of New York, or even dragging them out of their beds." Of the 9,127 Loyalists who sailed from Charleston to various

British destinations, 5,327 were freedom seekers.

Some 80,000 desperate refugees—White Loyalists, free Blacks, freed enslaved people, and Native Americans who had allied with the British—dispersed throughout the British Empire. Among those who resettled in Canada were 3,500 formerly enslaved who had been freed in exchange for joining the British army. Some 2,000 freed Blacks chose to go to Sierra Leone, in Africa, where British abolitionists helped them create an experimental colony called Freetown.

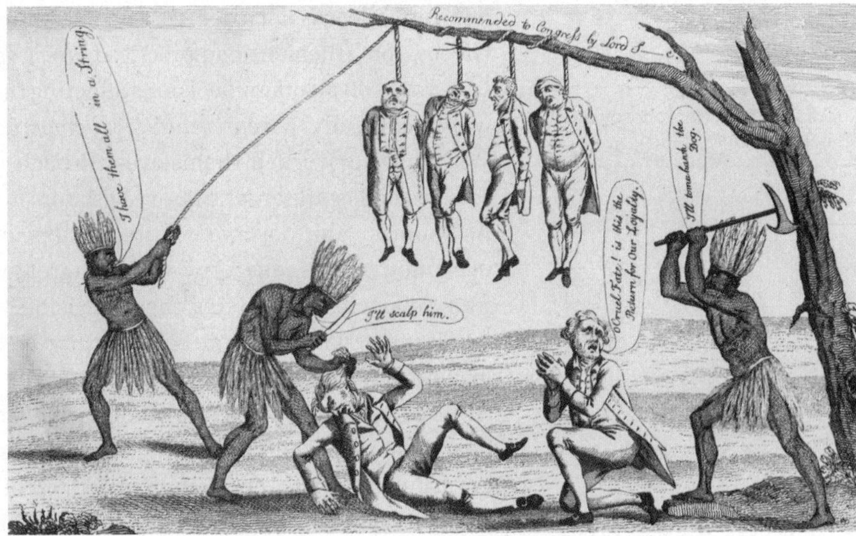

***THE FATE OF THE LOYALISTS* (1783)** After the Revolution, many Loyalists fled to British colonies in the Caribbean and Canada. This British cartoon shows Patriots, depicted as "savages let[ting] loose," mercilessly hanging and scalping Loyalists.

About 12,000 Georgia and South Carolina Loyalists, including thousands of their enslaved people (the British granted freedom only to the enslaved people of Patriots), went to British-controlled East Florida, only to see their new home handed over to Spain in 1783. Spanish authorities gave them a hard choice: swear allegiance to the Spanish king and convert to Catholicism or leave. Most of them left.

Some of the doubly displaced Loyalists sneaked back into the United States, but most went to British islands in the Caribbean. The departure of so many Loyalists was one of the most important social consequences of the Revolution. Their confiscated homes and lands and vacated jobs created new social, economic, and political opportunities for Patriots.

A Political Revolution

Debating the forms of government

The Americans had won their independence. Had they experienced a political revolution as well? Years later, retired President John Adams insisted that the Revolution had begun long before the shooting started. "The Revolution was in the minds and hearts of the people. . . . This radical change in the principles, opinions, sentiments, and affections of the people was the real American Revolution." Yet Adams's observation notwithstanding, the war itself ignited a prolonged debate about what political principles and forms of government would best serve the new American republic.

Republican Ideology

American Revolutionaries embraced a **republican ideology** instead of the aristocratic or monarchical outlook that had long dominated Europe. The

republican ideology Political belief in representative democracy in which citizens govern themselves by electing representatives, or legislators, to make key decisions on the citizens' behalf.

new republic was not a democracy in the purest sense of the word. In ancient Greece, the Athenians had practiced *direct democracy*, which meant that citizens voted on all major decisions affecting them. The United States, however, was technically a *representative democracy*, in which property-holding White men governed themselves through the concept of republicanism—they elected representatives, or legislators, to make decisions on their behalf. As Thomas Paine observed, representative democracy had many advantages over monarchies, one of which was greater transparency: "Whatever are its excellencies and defects, they are visible to all."

Representative democracy and individuals' rights

To preserve the delicate balance between liberty and power, Revolutionary leaders believed that they must protect the rights of individuals and states from being violated by the national government. The war for independence thus sparked the crafting of **state constitutions** to support the new governments that were being created, all of which were designed to reflect the principles of the republican ideology, limiting powers so as to protect the rights of the people.

State Governments

The first state constitutions created governments during the War of Independence much like the colonial governments, but with *elected* governors and senates instead of royally *appointed* governors and councils. Most of the constitutions also included a bill of rights that protected freedom of speech, trial by jury, and freedom from self-incrimination, while limiting the powers of governors and strengthening the powers of the legislatures.

The Articles of Confederation

Once the colonies had declared their independence in 1776, the new thirteen states needed to codify some form of collective or national government. Before March 1781, the Continental Congress had exercised emergency powers without any legal or official authority.

Plans for a permanent form of government emerged as early as July 1776, when a committee appointed by Congress had produced a draft constitution called the *Articles of Confederation and Perpetual Union*. But it took five years for the squabbling states to ratify the **Articles of Confederation** (March 1781), in part because there was a war to wage and in part because local and state concerns trumped national needs. The Articles essentially legalized how the government had been operating since independence had been declared, although the Continental Congress was renamed the Confederation Congress in 1781.

state constitutions Charters that define the relationship between the state government and local governments and individuals, while also protecting individual rights and freedoms.

Articles of Confederation The first form of government for the United States, ratified by the original thirteen states in 1781; weak in central authority, it was replaced by the U.S. Constitution drafted in 1787.

The Confederation revealed that developing a sense of *nationhood* would be as difficult for the thirteen states as achieving independence on the battlefields. The Articles reflected the long-standing fears of monarchy by not allowing for a president or chief executive. In the Confederation government, Congress had full power over foreign affairs and disputes between the states. Yet the Confederation had no national courts and no power to enforce its resolutions and ordinances. It could not levy taxes, and its budgetary needs depended on requisitions from the states, which state legislatures often ignored.

Limited government and states' rights

The states were in no mood to create a strong central government. The Confederation Congress, in fact, was granted less power than the colonists had once accepted in the British Parliament, since it could not regulate interstate and foreign commerce. For certain important acts, moreover, a "special majority" in the Confederation Congress was required. Nine of the thirteen states had to approve measures dealing with war, treaties, coinage, finances, and the military. Unanimous approval from the states was needed to impose tariffs (often called "duties," or taxes) on imports and to amend the Articles.

For all its weaknesses, however, the Confederation government represented the most practical structure for the new nation. After all, the Revolution had yet to be won, and an America besieged by British armies and warships could not risk divisive debates over the distribution of government power.

Expansion of Political Participation

The new political opportunities afforded by the creation of state governments enabled more citizens to participate in self-governance than ever before. Property qualifications for voting, which already allowed an overwhelming majority of White men to vote, were lowered after 1776. As a group of farmers explained, "No man can be free and independent" unless he possesses "a voice . . . in the most important offices in the legislature." In Pennsylvania, Delaware, North Carolina, and Georgia, any male taxpayer could vote, regardless of how much, if any, property he owned. A higher percentage of American males could vote in the late eighteenth and early nineteenth centuries than could their counterparts in Great Britain. Broader voting rights led to a more representative group of government officials. Farmers, tradesmen, and shopkeepers were elected to state legislatures.

A Social Revolution

The American Revolution was fought in the name of liberty, a virtuous ideal that proved elusive—even in victory. What did the Revolution's promise of liberty mean to the "poor and middling sort" who populated the Patriot army and navy—mechanics, artisans, apprentices, dock workers, servants, farmers, and those now free? Many hoped that American independence would remove the elite's traditional political and social advantages. Wealthy Patriots, on the other hand, would have been content to replace royal officials with the rich, the wellborn, and the well-educated.

In the end, the new republic's social fabric and political culture were visibly different after the war, and the energy created by the concepts of liberty, equality, and dignity for all changed the dynamics of social and political life. The Philadelphia doctor and scientist Benjamin Rush recognized

RELIGIOUS DEVELOPMENT The Congregational Church developed a national presence in the early nineteenth century. Lemuel Haynes, depicted here, was its first African American preacher. **What was the relationship between the American Revolution and religious freedom?**

that unexpected changes were on the way: "The American war is over: but this is far from being the case with the American Revolution. On the contrary, but the first act of the great drama is closed."

Freedom of Religion

The Revolution also tested traditional religious loyalties and triggered important changes in the relationship between churches and governments. Before the Revolution, Americans *tolerated* religious dissent; after the Revolution, they insisted on complete *freedom* of religion as embodied in the principle of separation of church and state.

The Anglican Church, established as the official religion in five colonies and parts of two others, was especially vulnerable to changes prompted by the war. Anglicans tended to be pro-British, and non-Anglicans, notably Baptists and Methodists, outnumbered Anglicans in all states except Virginia. All but Virginia eliminated tax support for the church before the fighting was over, and Virginia did so soon afterward. Although Anglicanism survived in the form of the new Episcopal Church, it never regained its pre-Revolutionary stature.

Religious freedom

In 1776, the Virginia Declaration of Rights had guaranteed the free exercise of religion. Ten years later, the **Virginia Statute of Religious Freedom** (written by Thomas Jefferson) declared that "no man shall be compelled to frequent or support any religious worship, place or ministry whatsoever" and "that all men shall be free to profess, and by argument to maintain, their opinions in matters of religion." These statutes, and the Revolutionary ideology that justified them, helped shape the course that religious life would take in the United States: diverse and voluntary rather than monolithic and enforced by the government.

CORE **OBJECTIVE**

5. Compare the impact of the Revolutionary War on African Americans, women, and Native Americans.

Equality and Its Limits

The Paradox of Slavery

The sharpest irony of the American Revolution was that Great Britain offered enslaved Blacks more opportunities for freedom than did the United States. In November 1775, the royal governor of Virginia, John Murray (Lord Dunmore), himself the owner of fifty-seven enslaved people, announced that all enslaved people and indentured servants would gain their freedom if they joined "Her Majesty's troops." Within a month, the British army had attracted more than 300 freedom seekers to what came to be called the Ethiopian Regiment. The number soon grew to almost 1,000 males and twice as many women and children.

The British recruitment of enslaved people outraged George Washington, Thomas Jefferson, and other White plantation owners in Virginia, where 40 percent of the population was Black. Washington knew all too well that the British offer would entice many enslaved people to escape. Dozens of his own enslaved people had fled his control since 1760. Jefferson expressed the same concerns after twenty-three enslaved people escaped from his plantation outside Charlottesville. He eventually reclaimed six of them, only to sell them for their "disloyalty."

AFRICAN AMERICANS AT WAR Peter Salem, a formerly enslaved person of a Massachusetts family, was freed so that he could join the American militia and is depicted here fighting in the Battle of Bunker Hill. **How did the British, the southerners, and the northerners differ in their approach to African Americans' involvement in the war?**

In 1775, authorities in Charleston, South Carolina, executed Thomas "Jerry" Jeremiah, a free man of color who was the wealthiest Black man in North America. A harbor pilot, Jeremiah owned enslaved people himself. His crime? He supposedly incited a rebellion by telling enslaved people that British troops were coming "to help the poor Negroes," and that he intended to side with the British.

At Jeremiah's "trial" in a "slave court," which had no judge, jury, or attorneys, Henry Laurens, a planter and former slave trader who would be elected president of the Continental Congress, charged that Jeremiah "was a forward fellow, puffed up by prosperity, ruined by Luxury & debauchery" and prone to "vanity & ambition." Laurens demanded that "nothing less than Death Should be the Sentence." On August 18, 1775, authorities hanged Jeremiah and burned his body to ashes.

British recruit and free enslaved people, while slavery is abolished in the North

Such brutalities led a British abolitionist to remark that America was "the land of the brave and the land of the slave." Many southern Revolutionaries were fighting less for independence from "British tyranny" than to retain their slave-labor system. That nearly 20 percent of American enslaved people risked death by joining British armies demonstrated how desperate they were to gain their freedom.

Southern Backlash

In the end, the British policy of recruiting enslaved people backfired. The "terrifying" prospect of enslaved people becoming British soldiers persuaded many fence-straddling southerners to join the Patriot cause. Edward Rutledge of South Carolina said that the British decision to arm enslaved people did more to create "an eternal separation between Great Britain and the colonies than any other expedient."

Virginia Statute of Religious Freedom (1786) A Virginia law, drafted by Thomas Jefferson in 1777 and enacted in 1786, that guarantees freedom of, and from, religion.

Racism and revolution

Racial prejudice thus helped fuel Revolutionary rebellion. What South Carolinians wanted from the Revolutionary War, explained Pierce Butler, "is that their slaves not be taken from them" by British armies.

In response to the British recruitment of enslaved African Americans, General Washington authorized the enlistment of free Blacks—but not enslaved people—into the American army. In February 1776, however, southern representatives convinced the Continental Congress to instruct Washington to enlist no more African Americans, free or enslaved. Two states, South Carolina and Georgia, refused to allow *any* Blacks to serve. As the American war effort struggled, however, Massachusetts organized two all-Black army units, and Rhode Island organized one, which also included Native Americans. About 5,000 African Americans fought on the Patriot side, most of them free Blacks from northern states.

While thousands of free Blacks and freedom seekers fought in the war, the vast majority of African Americans did not choose sides so much as they chose freedom. Several hundred thousand enslaved Blacks, mostly in the southern states, took advantage of the disruptions caused by the war to seize their freedom. In the North, which had far fewer enslaved people than the South, the ideals of liberty and freedom led most states to end slavery, either during the war or shortly afterward. But those same ideals had little impact in the southern states.

WOMEN AT WAR An 1856 Currier & Ives print celebrates "Molly Pitcher," the heroine of Monmouth, who loaded cannons in her husband's place after he fell in battle.

The Status of Women

The ideal of liberty spawned by the Revolution applied to the status of White women as much as to that of African Americans. The legal status of women was governed by British common law, which essentially limited their roles to child rearing and maintaining the household. Women could not vote or hold office, and few had access to formal education. Boys were taught to read and write; girls were taught to read and sew. Until married, women were subject to the dictates of their fathers.

However, once a woman married, she then became the possession of her husband, and all property she brought to the marriage became his. A married woman had no right to buy, sell, or manage property. Technically, any wages a wife earned belonged to the husband. Women could not sign contracts, file lawsuits, or testify in court. A husband could beat and even rape his wife without fearing legal action. Divorces were extremely difficult to obtain.

Yet the Revolution allowed women opportunities to broaden their social roles and to support the armies in various ways. They handled supplies, served as messengers or spies, and worked as "camp followers," cooking, washing, sewing, and nursing in exchange for daily rations. Some officers paid women to be their personal servants.

Women in war

Often women had no choice but to follow their husbands into war because they had no place to live or food to eat. Some tended cattle, sheep, or hogs, and guarded supplies. Others sold various items. A few of the single women were prostitutes. In 1777, George Washington ordered that commanders take measures to "prevent an inundation of bad women [prostitutes] from Philadelphia." He also urged that soldiers fraternize only with "clean" women to prevent the spread of venereal diseases.

Wives who were camp followers sometimes brought along their children. Washington was forced to accept them because he was afraid to lose "a number of men, who very probably would have followed their wives" home.

Women risked their lives in battle, tending the wounded or bringing water to the soldiers. On occasion, wives took the place of their soldier-husbands. In 1777, some 400 armed women mobilized to defend Pittsfield, Vermont. The men of the town had gone off to fight when a band of Loyalists and Indians approached the village. The women held off the attackers until help arrived.

Several women disguised themselves and fought as ordinary soldiers. Deborah Sampson joined a Massachusetts regiment as "Robert Shurtleff" and served from 1781 to 1783 thanks to the "artful concealment" of her gender. Ann Bailey did the same. In 1777, eager to get the enlistment bonus payment, she cut her hair, dressed like a man, and used a husky voice to join the Patriot army in New York as "Samuel Gay." Bailey performed so well that she was promoted to corporal, only to be discovered as a woman, dismissed, jailed, and fined.

Women Demand Liberty

America's war against Great Britain led some women to demand their own independence. Early in the struggle, Abigail Adams, one of the most learned and spirited women of the time, wrote to her husband John: "In the new Code of Laws which I suppose it will be necessary for you to make, I desire you would remember the Ladies. . . . Do not put such unlimited power into the hands of the Husbands." Since men were "Naturally Tyrannical," she wrote, "why then, not put it out of the power of the vicious and the Lawless to use us with cruelty and indignity with impunity." Otherwise, "if particular care and attention is not paid to the Ladies we are determined to foment a Rebellion, and will not hold ourselves bound by any Laws in which we have no voice, or Representation."

ABIGAIL ADAMS A 1766 portrait of Abigail Adams, the wife of John Adams. Though an ardent Patriot, she and other women like her saw few changes in women's rights emerging in the new United States.

John Adams laughed at his wife's radical proposals. He insisted on retaining the traditional privileges enjoyed by males: "Depend upon it, we know better than to repeal our Masculine systems." If women were to be granted equality, he warned, then "children and apprentices" and "Indians and Negroes" would also demand equal rights and freedoms.

In sum, America's Revolutionary leaders showed little interest in granting equal rights to women, empowering the poor, or freeing the enslaved. Liberty and equality "for all" would have to wait.

Native Americans Besieged

Most Native Americans sought to remain neutral in the war, but both British and American agents urged Indians to fight on their side. The result was chaos. Indians on both sides attacked villages, burned crops, and killed civilians. Americans, both frontiersmen and soldiers, exacted ruthless revenge.

Displacement and destruction of Native Americans

During and after the war, the new U.S. government assured its Indian allies that it would respect their lands and their rights. But many White Americans used the disruptions of war to destroy and displace Native Americans. Once the war ended and independence was secured, there was no peace for the Indians. By the end of the eighteenth century, land-hungry Americans were again pushing into Indian territories on the western frontier.

The Emergence of Nationalism

On July 2, 1776, when the Second Continental Congress resolved "that these United Colonies are, and of right ought to be, free and independent states," John Adams had written Abigail that future generations would remember that date as their "day of deliverance." Adams got everything right but the date. As luck would have it, July 4, the date the Declaration of Independence was approved, became Independence Day rather than July 2, when independence was formally declared.

The celebration of Independence Day quickly became the most important public ritual in the United States. People suspended their normal routines to devote a day to parades, patriotic speeches, and fireworks. In the process, the infant republic began to create its own myth of national identity.

From the democratic rhetoric of Thomas Jefferson to the pragmatism of George Washington to heady toasts bellowed in South Carolina taverns, patriots everywhere claimed a special role for America.

George Washington acknowledged that important work remained. While retiring from military service, he penned a letter to the thirteen states in which he told the American people it would be "their choice . . . and conduct" that would determine whether the United States would become "respectable and prosperous, or contemptible and miserable as a Nation." Yet he remained hopeful, for Americans had already done the impossible by winning their independence on the battlefield. In closing, he urged the citizenry to rejoice and be grateful as they set about demonstrating to a skeptical world that a large and unruly republic could survive and flourish—forever.

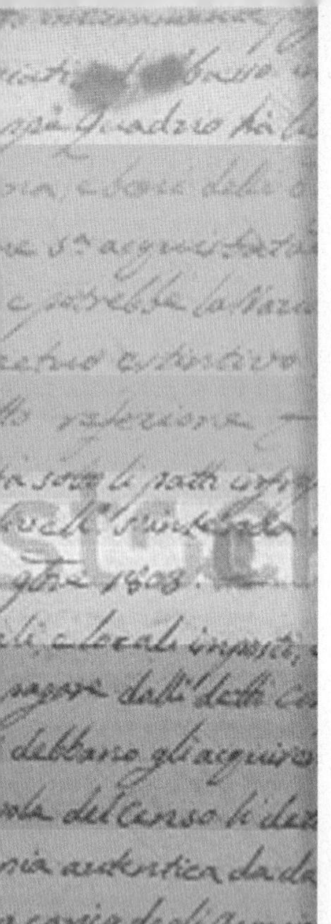

Reviewing the CORE OBJECTIVES | InQuizitive

■ **Civil War** The American Revolution was also a civil war, dividing families and communities. There were at least 100,000 Loyalists in the colonies. They included royal officials, Anglican ministers, wealthy southern planters, and the elite in large seaport cities; they also included many humble people, especially recent immigrants. After the hostilities ended, many Loyalists, including enslaved people who had fled their plantations to support the British cause, left for Canada, the West Indies, or Great Britain.

■ **Military Challenges** In 1776, the British had the mightiest army and navy in the world, and their ranks included thousands of *Hessians* (German mercenaries). The Americans had to create an army—the *Continental Army*—and sustain it. To defeat the British, George Washington realized that the Americans had to turn unreliable citizen-soldiers into a disciplined fighting force and draw on state *militias* for support. He decided to wage a long and costly hit-and-run war, wagering that since the British army was fighting thousands of miles from its home base, the king would eventually give up in order to cut the nation's mounting losses.

■ **Turning Points** The French were likely allies for the colonies from the beginning of the conflict because they resented their losses to Britain in the Seven Years' War. After the British defeat at the *Battles of Saratoga* (1777), the first major turning point, France agreed to fight with the colonies until independence was won. Washington was able to hold his ragged forces together despite daily desertions and two especially difficult winters in Morristown and *Valley Forge* (1777–1778), the second and third major turning points. The British lost support on the frontier and in their southern colonies when terrorist tactics backfired. The Battle of Kings Mountain (1780) drove southern Loyalists into retreat in the South, and the *alliance with France*, signed in 1778, meant that French supplies and the French fleet of warships would tip the balance of power and ensure the American victory at the *Battle of Yorktown* (1781), the final turning point that triggered negotiations leading to the *Treaty of Paris* (1783) ending the war and acknowledging America's independence.

■ **A Political and Social Revolution** The American Revolution disrupted and transformed traditional social relationships. American Revolutionaries embraced a *republican ideology* in contrast to a monarchy, and more White men gained the right to vote in the new nation as property requirements were lowered or removed entirely. But fears of a monarchy being reestablished led colonists to vest power in the states rather than a powerful national government under the *Articles of Confederation*. The states wrote new *state constitutions* that instituted more elected positions. The *Virginia Statute of Religious Freedom* (1786) led the way in guaranteeing the separation of church and state, and religious toleration was transformed into religious freedom for all, including Roman Catholics and Jews.

■ **African Americans, Women, and Native Americans** Northern states began to free the enslaved after the Revolutionary War, but southern states refused to do so. Although many women had undertaken nontraditional roles during the war, afterward they remained largely confined to the domestic sphere, with no changes broadening their legal or political status. The Revolution had catastrophic effects on Native Americans, regardless of which side they had supported during the war. During and after the Revolution, American settlers seized Native American land, often in violation of existing treaties.

KEY TERMS

Hessians *p. 177*

citizen-soldiers *p. 178*

Continental Army *p. 178*

militias *p. 183*

Battle of Trenton (1776) *p. 185*

Battles of Saratoga (1777) *p. 187*

alliance with France *p. 187*

Valley Forge (1777–1778) *p. 189*

Battle of Yorktown (1781) *p. 197*

Treaty of Paris (1783) *p. 199*

republican ideology *p. 201*

state constitutions *p. 202*

Articles of Confederation *p. 202*

Virginia Statute of Religious Freedom (1786) *p. 205*

CHRONOLOGY

1776 British forces seize New York City; General Washington's troops defeat British forces at the Battle of Trenton; States begin writing new constitutions

1777 American forces defeat the British in a series of battles at Saratoga, New York

1778 Americans and French form a crucial military alliance; George Rogers Clark's militia defeats British troops in the Mississippi River Valley; British seize Savannah and Charleston

1779 American forces defeat the Iroquois Confederacy at Newtown, New York

1780 Patriots defeat Loyalists at the Battle of Kings Mountain

1781 British invasion of southern colonies turned back at the Battles of Cowpens and Guilford Courthouse; American and French forces defeat British at Yorktown, Virginia

1783 Treaty of Paris is signed, formally ending Revolutionary War

1786 Virginia adopts the Statute of Religious Freedom

INQUIZITIVE

Go to InQuizitive to see what you've learned—and learn what you've missed—with personalized feedback along the way.

WASHINGTON AS STATESMAN AT THE CONSTITUTIONAL CONVENTION **(1856)** This painting by Junius Brutus Stearns is one of the earliest depictions of the drafting of the Constitution, capturing the moment after the convention members, including George Washington *(right)*, completed the final draft.

Securing the Constitution and Union

1783–1800

CHAPTER 6

During the 1780s, the United States of America was rapidly emerging as the lone large republic in an unstable world dominated by monarchies. The new nation was distinctive in that it was born out of a conflict over ideas, principles, and ideals rather than from centuries-old racial or ancestral bonds, as was the case in Europe and elsewhere.

America defined itself by certain self-evident political ideals—that people should govern themselves through their elected representatives, that everyone should have an equal opportunity to prosper ("the pursuit of happiness"), and that governments at all levels exist to protect liberty and promote the public good. Those ideals were captured in lasting phrases: All men are created equal. Liberty and justice for all. *E pluribus unum* ("Out of many, one"—the phrase on the official seal of the United States). How Americans understood, applied, and violated these ideals shaped the nation's development after 1783.

CORE OBJECTIVES INQUIZITIVE

1. Identify the strengths and weaknesses of the Articles of Confederation and explain how they prompted the creation of a new U.S. Constitution in 1787.
2. Describe the political innovations that the 1787 Constitutional Convention developed for the new nation.
3. Summarize the major debates surrounding the ratification of the Constitution and explain how they were resolved.
4. Compare the Federalists' vision for the United States with that of their Republican opponents during the 1790s.
5. Assess how attitudes toward Great Britain and France shaped American politics in the late eighteenth century.

CORE **OBJECTIVE**

1. Identify the strengths and weaknesses of the Articles of Confederation and explain how they prompted the creation of a new U.S. Constitution in 1787.

The Confederation Government

Americans had little time to celebrate victory in the Revolutionary War. As Alexander Hamilton, now an attorney in New York City, warned in 1783, the United States was facing a governance crisis: "We have now happily concluded the great work of independence, but much remains to be done to reach the fruits of it."

The transition from war to peace was neither simple nor easy. America was independent but not yet a self-sustaining nation. From the start, the new nation experienced political divisions, economic distress, and foreign troubles. Forging a new *nation* out of a *confederation* of thirteen colonies-turned-"free-and-independent"-states posed huge challenges, not the least of which was managing what George Washington called a "deranged" economy suffocating in war-related debts. The accumulated debt was $160 million, yet the Confederation Congress had no cash and could not impose taxes to raise it.

Three fundamental questions shaped political debate during the last quarter of the eighteenth century. Where would *sovereignty* (ultimate authority) reside in the new nation? What was the proper relationship of the states to each other and to the national government? And what was required for the republic to flourish as an independent nation? The efforts to answer those questions created powerful tensions that continue to complicate and enliven American life.

A Loose Alliance of States

A deliberately weak central government

The Articles of Confederation, formally approved in 1781, had created a loose alliance (confederation) of thirteen independent states that were united only in theory. In practice, each state government acted on its own.

The weak national government under the Articles had only one component, a one-house legislature. There was no president, no executive branch, no national judiciary (court system). State legislatures, not voters, appointed the members of the Confederation Congress, in which each state, regardless of size or population, had one vote. This meant that Rhode Island, with 68,000 people, had the same voting power as Virginia, with more than 747,000 inhabitants. George Washington called the Confederation "a half-starved, limping government." It could neither regulate trade nor create taxes to pay off the country's war debts. It could approve treaties but had no power to enforce their terms. It could call for raising an army but could not force men to serve.

The Congress, in short, could not enforce its own laws, and its budget relied on "voluntary" contributions from the states. In 1782, for example, the Confederation asked the states to provide $8 million for the national government; they sent $420,000. The lack of state support forced the Congress to print paper money, called Continentals, whose value plummeted to 2 cents on the dollar as more and more were printed. Virtually no gold and silver coins remained in circulation; they had all gone abroad to purchase war supplies.

It was hard to find people to serve in such a weak Congress, and many openly doubted the stability of the new republic. As John Adams wrote to Thomas Jefferson, "The Union is still to me an Object of as much Anxiety as ever independence was."

The Newburgh Conspiracy To garner support for their plan to finance the Confederation government, Superintendent of Finance Robert Morris and his nationalist friends in 1783 took a dangerous gamble. George Washington's army, encamped at Newburgh, New York, on the Hudson River, had grown restless after the Battle of Yorktown. The soldiers' pay was late, as usual, and the officers feared that the land grants promised them by the government might never be honored once their service was no longer needed.

Hamilton's *coup d'état*

A delegation of concerned officers traveled to Philadelphia, where they hatched a scheme to confront the states with the threat of a *coup d'état* unless the national government was given more power. New York congressman Alexander Hamilton sought to bring George Washington, his former commander, into the plan.

Washington sympathized with the basic purpose of Hamilton's scheme, but he was also convinced that a military coup would be both dishonorable and dangerous. In March 1783, he confronted the plotting officers and expressed his "horror and detestation" of any effort to assume dictatorial powers. A military revolt would open "the flood-gates of civil discord" and "deluge our rising empire in blood." When he finished speaking, his officers adopted resolutions denouncing the "infamous propositions," and the so-called Newburgh Conspiracy evaporated.

Support of republicanism

Yet in spite of its limitations, the Confederation Congress laid important foundations for the new national government. The Articles of Confederation were crucially important in supporting the political concept of *republicanism* (representative democracy and majority rule), which meant that America would be governed not by monarchs or aristocrats but "by the authority of the people," whose elected representatives would make decisions on their behalf. The Congress also created the national government's first executive departments and formulated the basic principles of land distribution and territorial government that would guide America's westward expansion.

Land Policy

In ending the Revolutionary War, the 1783 Treaty of Paris doubled the size of the United States, extending the nation's western boundary to the Mississippi River. Under the Articles of Confederation, land outside the boundaries of the thirteen original states became *public domain,* owned and administered by the national government.

In 1784, George Washington, now a civilian, left Mount Vernon, his Virginia plantation, and traveled west to lands he owned in the Ohio River Valley. Along the way, he saw pioneers streaming westward. "The spirit of emigration is great," he wrote to the president of the Confederation Congress. But chaos would ensue unless some orderly process for western settlement were devised. Settlers would not be stopped, but, he said, "It is yet in your power to mark the way."

Creation of land ordinances

Between 1784 and 1787, the Confederation Congress responded to such concerns by creating three major ordinances (policies) detailing how western lands would be surveyed, sold, and developed by the national government. These ordinances provided the framework for western settlement that would shape much of the nation's development during the nineteenth century.

Thomas Jefferson drafted the Land Ordinance Act of 1784, which urged states to divide the vast, unmapped area west of the Appalachian Mountains into as many as fourteen self-governing *territories* of equal size. In the new territories, all white males would be eligible to vote, hold office, and write constitutions for their territorial governments. When a territory's population equaled that of the smallest existing state (Rhode Island), it would be eligible for statehood. In other words, the western territories would not be treated as American colonies but as future states.

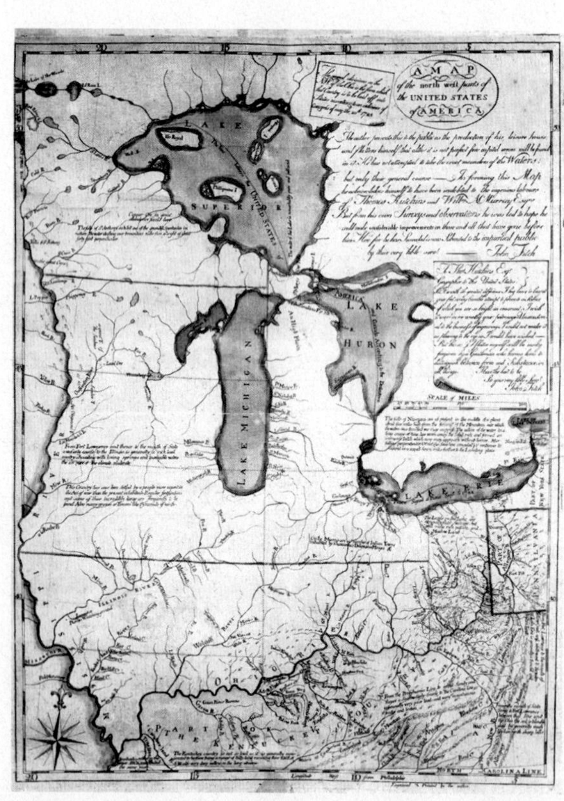

LAND ORDINANCE OF 1785 A map of the Northwest Territory of the United States as of 1785. The land was divided into a series of townships, which were split up into farms for auction.

Jefferson assumed that individual pioneers should be allowed to settle the western territories. George Washington and others, however, predicted chaos if migration were unregulated. Clashes with Indians would generate constant warfare, and disputes over land and boundaries would foster incessant bickering.

Before Jefferson's plan could take effect, the Confederation Congress created the Land Ordinance of 1785. It called for organizing the Northwest Territory (what would become the states of Ohio, Michigan, Indiana, Illinois, and Wisconsin) into townships of thirty-six square miles that would be surveyed, sold for less than a dollar an acre, and settled. Then the surveyors would keep moving westward, laying out more townships for settlement. Wherever Indian lands were purchased—or taken—they were surveyed and divided into six-mile-square townships laid out along a grid running east–west and north–south. Each township was in turn divided into thirty-six sections one mile square (640 acres), with each section divided into four farms. The 640-acre sections of "public lands" were to be sold at auctions, the proceeds of which would go to the national Treasury.

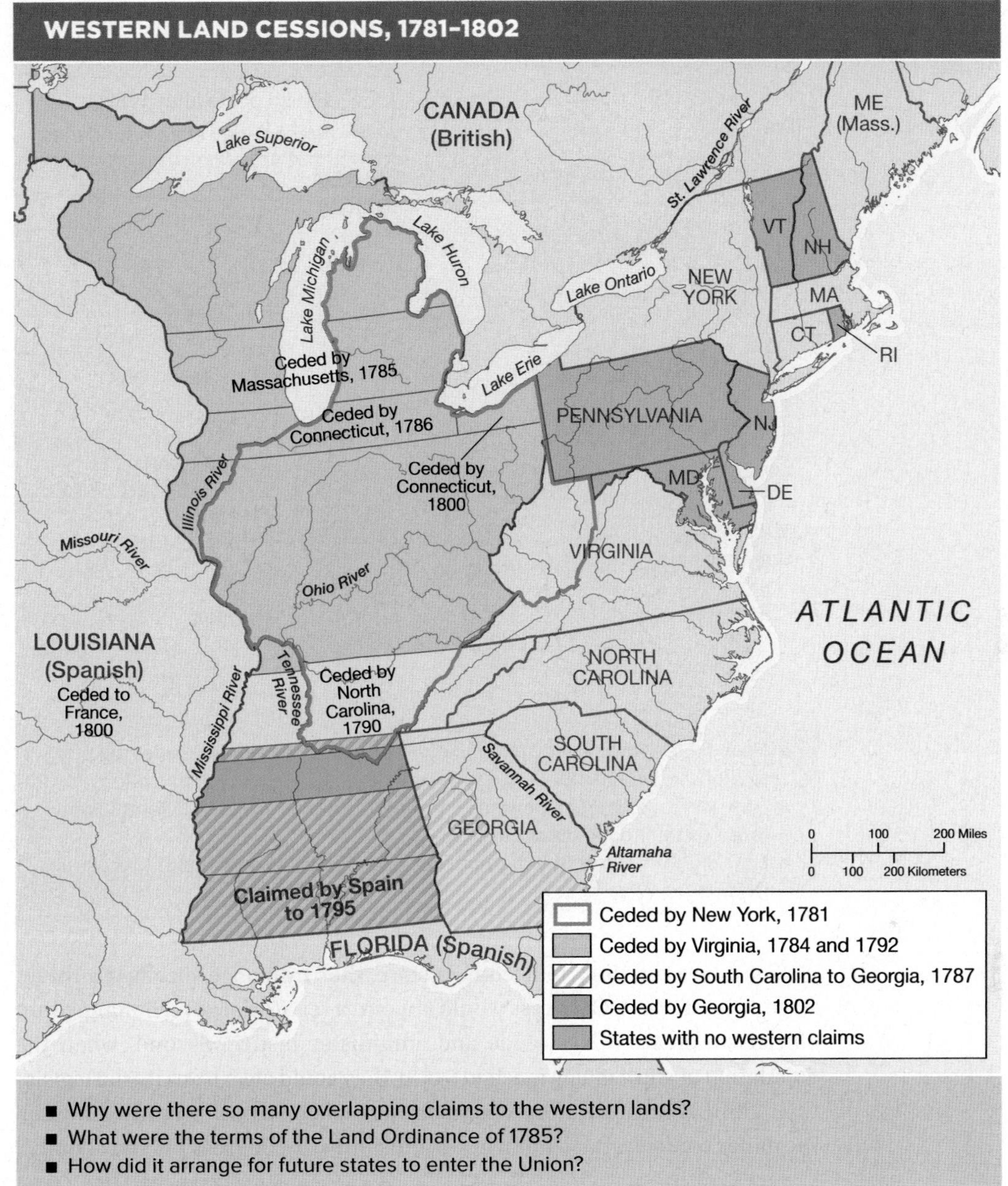

- Why were there so many overlapping claims to the western lands?
- What were the terms of the Land Ordinance of 1785?
- How did it arrange for future states to enter the Union?

The Northwest Ordinance

Two years after passage of the Land Ordinance of 1785, the Confederation Congress passed the third major land policy: the **Northwest Ordinance** of 1787. It set forth two key principles: the new territories would eventually become coequal states, as Jefferson had proposed, and slavery would be banned from the region north of the Ohio River. (Enslaved people already living there would remain in their state of bondage.) The Northwest Ordinance also included a promise, which would be repeatedly broken, that Indian lands "shall never be taken from them without their consent."

Northwest Ordinance (1787) Land policy for new western territories in the Ohio Valley that established the terms and conditions for self-government and statehood while also banning slavery from the region.

THE OLD NORTHWEST, 1785

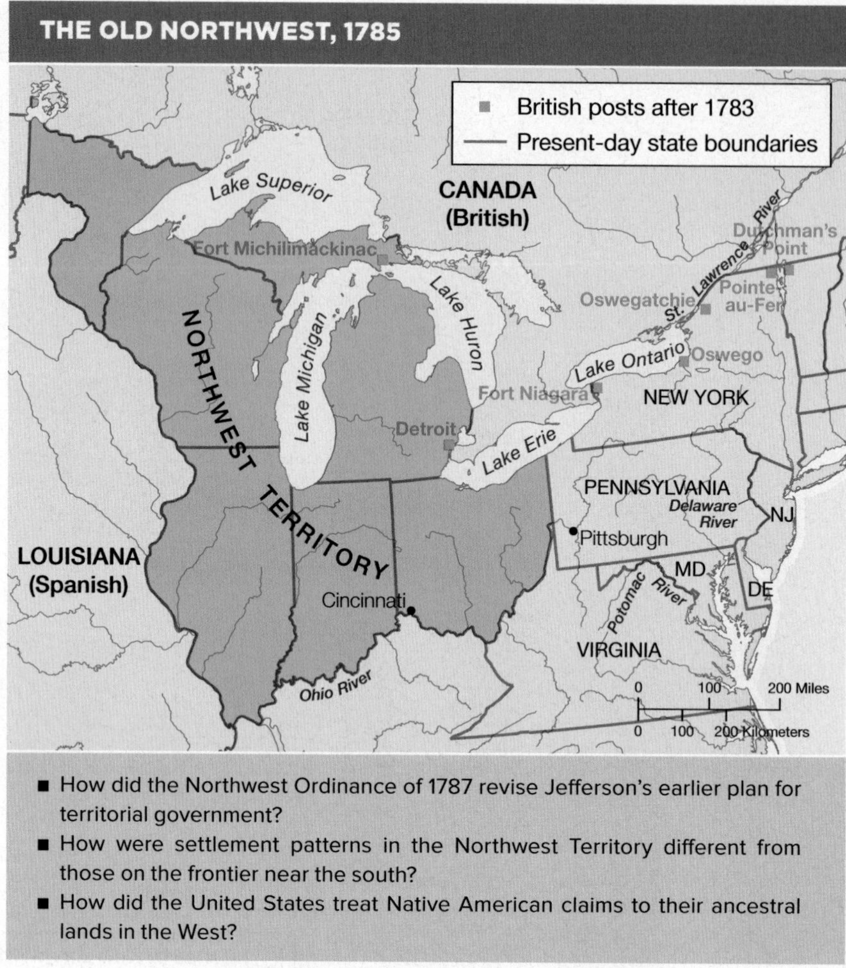

- How did the Northwest Ordinance of 1787 revise Jefferson's earlier plan for territorial government?
- How were settlement patterns in the Northwest Territory different from those on the frontier near the south?
- How did the United States treat Native American claims to their ancestral lands in the West?

For a new territory to become a state, the Ordinance specified a three-stage process. First, Congress would appoint a territorial governor and other officials to create a legal code and administer justice. Second, when the population of adult males reached 5,000, they could elect a territorial legislature. Third, when a territory's population reached 60,000 "free inhabitants," the males could draft a constitution and apply to Congress for statehood.

Foreign Tensions

After the Revolutionary War, relations with Great Britain and Spain remained tense because the two nations retained trading posts, forts, and soldiers on American soil, and both encouraged Indians to resist American efforts to settle on tribal lands. The British refused to remove their troops stationed south of the Canadian border in protest of the failure of Americans to pay their prewar debts. Another major irritant was the American seizure of Loyalist property during the war.

With Spain, the chief issues pertained to disputes about the location of the southern boundary of the United States and the right for Americans to send boats or barges down the Mississippi River.

After the Seven Years' War, in 1763 Spain had acquired the Louisiana Territory, which included the port of New Orleans, the Mississippi River, and all the area west to the Rocky Mountains. After the Revolution, Spain closed the Mississippi River to American use, infuriating settlers in Kentucky and Tennessee who used the river to send their crops and goods to New Orleans. Spain thought that closing the river to U.S. trade would deter American expansion to the west and the south.

Spain had also regained ownership of Florida, which then included southern Alabama. Thereafter, the Spanish governor in Florida provided firearms to Creek Indians, who resisted American encroachment on their native lands in southern Georgia.

Trade and the Economy

More troublesome than the behavior of the British and the Spanish was the fragile state of the economy. Seven years of warfare had nearly bankrupted the new nation. At the same time, many who had served in the army had never received their promised wages. Nor had civilians who had loaned money, supplies, crops, and livestock to the war effort been reimbursed.

After the war, the British treated the United States as an enemy nation, insisting that all Americans who had been born in England were still bound by allegiance to King George III. British warships began stopping and boarding American ships in the Atlantic, kidnapping English-born American sailors, and "impressing" them into service in the Royal Navy. The British also closed their Caribbean island colonies to American commerce. New England shipowners and southern planters were especially hard-hit, as exports of tobacco, rice, rum, and other commodities remained far below what they had been before the war. After 1783, American merchant ships were allowed to deliver American products to England and return to the United States with English goods. But U.S. vessels could not carry British goods anywhere else.

DOMESTIC INDUSTRY American craftsmen, such as these letterpress printers, favored tariffs on foreign goods that competed with their own products.

Failure to regulate interstate commerce and foreign relations

To punish Britain for banning U.S. trade with the British West Indies, many state governments imposed special taxes (called tonnage fees) on British vessels arriving in American ports and levied tariffs (taxes) on British goods brought to the United States. The British responded by sending their ships to ports in states whose tariff rates were lower. By charging different tariffs on the same products, the states waged commercial war with each other. The result was economic chaos. By 1787, it was evident that the national government needed to regulate interstate trade and foreign relations.

Money

High taxes and no national currency

Complex financial issues also hampered economic activity after the war. There were few gold and silver coins and no national paper currency. The nation had only three banks—in Philadelphia, New York City, and Boston—all of which had been chartered by state governments and were therefore limited to operating within a single state. Farmers found themselves squeezed by lower crop prices, mounting debts, and soaring state taxes. A Connecticut lawyer reported that high taxes were causing "civil discord in almost every state in the nation."

The widespread shortage of "hard money" (gold and silver coins) caused people to postpone paying their tax bills. By 1785, indebted citizens urged states to print new paper currency. Debtors believed that doing so would ease their plight by increasing the money supply (inflation). In 1785–1786, seven states began issuing paper money to help indebted farmers and to pay the cash bonuses promised to military veterans.

States grew reluctant to call out the militia to deal with tax protesters because militiamen were among those protesting loudest. Pennsylvania militiamen who refused to march argued that "the Poorer Sort of People were always Forced to Turn out" for militia duty while the "wealthy" used their "money" to exempt themselves from military service. In New Hampshire, in what was called the Exeter Riot, hard-pressed farmers surrounded the legislative building, demanding that the representatives print paper money to ease their plight. Similar appeals occurred in other states. The economic and political elites were horrified that the "new men" were endangering the real value of property by encouraging the printing of more money, for doing so would inflate the money supply and thereby reduce the purchasing power of currency.

Shays's Rebellion

Shays's Rebellion (1786–1787) Storming of the Massachusetts federal arsenal in 1787 by Daniel Shays and 1,200 armed farmers seeking debt relief from the state legislature through issuance of paper currency and lower taxes.

Fears of a taxpayer "revolt from below" became all too real in western Massachusetts, when struggling farmers demanded that the state issue more paper money and give them additional time to pay "unjust" state and local taxes. Farmers also resented the new state constitution because it *raised* the property qualifications for voting and holding elected office, thus stripping poorer men of political power.

When the merchant-dominated Massachusetts legislature refused to lower taxes or issue more paper money, three rural counties revolted in 1786. Armed groups of angry farmers, calling themselves Regulators, or "the voice of the people," banded together to force judges and sheriffs to stop seizing the cattle and farms of those "debtors" who could not pay their taxes. The insurgents were convinced that the state's political leaders were creating policies designed to make the wealthiest people even wealthier—at the expense of the poorest residents.

The situation worsened when a ragtag "army" of unruly farmers led by thirty-nine-year-old Daniel Shays, a distinguished war veteran, marched on the federal arsenal at Springfield in the winter of 1787. The state government responded by sending 4,400 militiamen, who scattered the debtor army with a single cannon blast that left four farmers dead and many wounded. Shays fled to Vermont. Several rebels were arrested, and two were hanged. The rebels nevertheless earned a victory of sorts, as the legislature agreed to eliminate some of the taxes and fees.

News of **Shays's Rebellion** sent shock waves across the nation. In Massachusetts, Abigail Adams dismissed the rebel farmers as "ignorant, restless desperadoes, without conscience or principles." George Washington was equally concerned. America, he said, needed a stronger national "government by which our lives, liberty, and properties will be secured."

SHAYS'S REBELLION In this hand-colored woodcut, a line of militiamen fire at Daniel Shays and his followers while the surviving rebels turn and flee. Shays demanded a more flexible monetary policy and the right to postpone paying taxes until the postwar agricultural depression lifted. **Why, given the rebels' defeat in combat, might the state legislature have decided to grant some of their demands?**

The Revolutionary elite resolved to create barriers to the unruly democracy spawned by the Revolution. Thomas Jefferson, however, urged state officials to be lenient with the rebels. He wrote James Madison that "a little rebellion now and then is a good thing" in a republic, where the people rule. Grassroots rebellions were "a medicine necessary for the sound health of government."

Creating the Constitution

CORE **OBJECTIVE**

2. Describe the political innovations that the 1787 Constitutional Convention developed for the new nation.

In the wake of Shays's Rebellion, what John Jay called "the better kind of people" sought to empower the national government to bring social order and provide economic stability. "Our present federal government," said Henry Knox, a Boston bookseller and Revolutionary War general, "is a name, a shadow, without power, or effect."

It was time, said James Madison, to create a federal constitution that would repair the "vices of the political system" and "decide forever the fate of republican government." Alexander Hamilton urged that a national gathering of delegates be given "full powers" to revise the Articles of Confederation so as to suppress "the amazing violence and turbulence of the democratic spirit" infecting the nation.

The Constitutional Convention

In 1787, the Confederation Congress responded to the unrest by calling for a special "federal" convention to gather in Philadelphia's State House (now known as Independence Hall) for the "purpose of revising the Articles of Confederation." Only Rhode Island refused to participate.

The delegates began work on May 25, 1787. Although the states appointed fifty-five delegates, there were never that many in attendance. Some quit in disgust; others were distracted by other priorities. Yet after fifteen weeks of deliberations, thirty-nine delegates signed the new federal Constitution on September 17.

The durability and defects of the Constitution reflect the individuals who created it. Their average age was forty-two, with the youngest being twenty-six. Most were members of the political and economic elite. Twenty-six were college graduates, two were college presidents, and thirty-four were lawyers. Others were planters, merchants, bankers, and clergymen. They were all White and male, and two dozen of them, including George Washington and James Madison, owned enslaved people.

SIGNING OF THE CONSTITUTION, SEPTEMBER 17, 1787 Thomas Pritchard Rossiter's painting shows George Washington presiding over what Thomas Jefferson called "an assembly of demi-gods" in Philadelphia.

The "Founding Fathers" were also practical men of experience. Twenty-two had fought in the Revolutionary War. Eight of the framers were immigrants, seven had been state governors, and eight had helped write their state constitutions. Most had been members of Congress, and eight had signed the Declaration of Independence.

JAMES MADISON This 1783 miniature shows Madison at thirty-two years old, just four years before he would assume a major role in drafting the Constitution.

Drafting the Constitution George Washington was unanimously elected as the presiding officer at the Federal Convention (later renamed the Constitutional Convention). He attended every session but participated little in the debates, for fear that people would take his opinions too seriously.

Most active was James Madison of Virginia, the ablest political theorist in the group. Madison was a thirty-six-year-old attorney who owned a huge tobacco plantation called Montpelier. Barely five feet tall and weighing only 130 pounds, Madison was too frail and sickly to serve in the Revolutionary army.

Madison is "a good and able man," remarked Fisher Ames of Massachusetts. But he "speaks low, his person [body] is little and ordinary," and he is "too timid in his politics." Although shy and soft-spoken, Madison had an agile mind and a commitment to public service. He had served in the Continental Congress, where he had become a full-blooded nationalist. Now he resolved to ensure the "supremacy of national authority." The logic of his arguments—and his willingness to compromise—proved decisive in shaping the new Constitution. "Every person seems to acknowledge his greatness," said a Georgia delegate.

Most delegates agreed with Madison that the republic needed a stronger national government, weaker state legislatures, and the power to restrain the "dangerous" democratic impulses unleashed by the Revolution. "The evils we experience," said Elbridge Gerry of Massachusetts, "flow from the excess of democracy."

Authority derived from "the people"

Two interrelated assumptions guided the Constitutional Convention: that the national government must have direct authority over the citizenry rather than governing through the state governments, and that it must derive its legitimacy from the "genius of the people" rather than from the state legislatures. Thus, the final draft of the Constitution begins: "We the people of the United States, in Order to form a more perfect Union, . . . do ordain and establish this Constitution for the United States of America."

The insistence that the voters were "the legitimate source of all authority," as James Wilson of Pennsylvania stressed, was the most important political innovation since the Declaration of Independence. No other nation in the world had endowed "the people" with such authority. By declaring the Constitution to be the voice of the people, the founders authorized the federal government to limit the powers of the states.

The delegates realized, too, that an effective national government needed authority to collect taxes, borrow and issue money, regulate commerce, fund an army and navy, and make laws. This meant that the states must be stripped of the power to print paper money, make treaties, wage war, and levy taxes and tariffs on imported goods. This concept of dividing authority between the national government and the states came to be called **federalism**.

The Virginia Plan

The Virginia and New Jersey Plans James Madison drafted the framework for the initial discussions at the Constitutional Convention. His proposals, called the Virginia Plan, started with a radical suggestion: that the delegates scrap their original instructions to *revise* the Articles of Confederation and instead create a *new* Constitution.

Madison's Virginia Plan called for a "*national* government [with] a *supreme* legislative, executive, and judiciary." It proposed a Congress divided into two houses (bicameral): a lower House of Representatives chosen by the "people of the several states" and an upper house of senators elected by the state legislatures. The more populous states would have more representatives in Congress than the smaller states. Madison also wanted to give Congress the power to veto state laws. The Virginia Plan sparked furious disagreements. When asked why the small states were so suspicious of the plan, Gunning Bedford of Delaware replied: "I do not, gentlemen, trust you."

The New Jersey Plan

On June 15, Bedford and other delegates submitted an alternative proposal called the New Jersey Plan, developed by William Paterson of New Jersey. It sought to keep the existing equal representation of the states in a unicameral (one-house) national legislature. It also gave Congress the power to collect taxes and regulate commerce and the authority to name a chief executive as well as a supreme court, but not the right to veto state laws.

The Structure of the Federal Government

The Great Compromise

The intense debate over congressional representation was resolved in mid-July by the so-called Great Compromise, which used elements of both plans. Roger Sherman of Connecticut suggested that one chamber of the proposed Congress have its seats allotted according to population, with the other preserving the principle of one vote for each state. And that is what happened. The more populous states won apportionment (the allocation of delegates to each state) by population in the proposed House of Representatives, while the delegates who sought to protect state power won equality of representation in the Senate, where each state would have two members elected by the legislatures.

The Legislature (Congress) The Great Compromise embedded the innovative concept of **separation of powers** into the new Congress. While James Madison believed that in "a republican government, the legislative authority necessarily predominates," he and others also sought to keep the Congress from becoming too powerful. To do so, they divided it into two houses, with the House of Representatives representing voters at large and the Senate representing state legislatures.

federalism Concept of dividing governmental authority between the national government and the states.

separation of powers Strict division of the powers of government among three separate branches (executive, legislative, and judicial), which in turn check and balance each other.

A bicameral Congress with a separation of powers

The members of the House of Representatives would be elected by voters every *two* years. (Under the Articles of Confederation, members of Congress had been chosen by state legislatures.) Madison argued that allowing individual citizens to elect the people's House was "essential to every plan of free government." Indeed, such representative democracy centered on majority rule was the essence of a republican form of government.

The framers viewed the upper house, or Senate, as a check on the excesses of democracy. John Adams, for example, argued that the Senate should be made up of "illustrious" and well-educated members elected for six-year terms so as to counterbalance those in the House of Representatives elected every two years by what he feared would be gullible and uninformed voters. The Senate could overrule the House or the president. Madison explained that the Senate would help "protect the minority of the opulent against the majority." Finally, the delegates decided that members of the House and Senate would be paid so that even those who were not wealthy could run for office.

The Executive (President) The Constitutional Convention also struggled over issues related to the executive branch. Some delegates wanted a powerful president who could veto acts of Congress. Others felt that the president should simply "execute" the laws as passed by Congress. Still others, like Benjamin Franklin, wanted a "plural executive" rather than a single man governing the nation. The eventual decision to have a single chief executive, a "natural born Citizen" at least thirty-five years old of any or no religion, worried many delegates. George Mason of Virginia feared that a single president might start behaving like a king.

Presidential powers

In the end, several compromises ensured that the president would be powerful enough to counterbalance the Congress. The president, to be elected for four-year terms, could veto acts of Congress, which would then be subject to being overridden by a two-thirds vote in each house. The president became the nation's chief diplomat and commander in chief of the armed forces and was responsible for implementing the laws made by Congress.

Checks on presidential power

Yet the president's powers were also limited. The chief executive could neither declare war nor make peace; only Congress could. Moreover, the president could be removed from office. The House of Representatives could impeach (bring to trial) the chief executive—and other civil officers—on charges of treason, bribery, or "other high crimes and misdemeanors." An impeached president must leave office if two-thirds of the Senate voted for conviction.

To preserve the separation of the three branches of government, the president would be elected every four years by a group of highly qualified "electors" chosen by "the people" in local elections. The number of each state's electors would equal the number of its congressional representatives and senators. This "Electoral College" was a compromise between those wanting the president elected by Congress and those preferring a direct vote of qualified citizens.

The Judiciary (Court System) The third proposed branch of government, the judiciary, sparked little debate. The Constitution called for a supreme national court headed by a chief justice. The court's role was not to make laws (a power reserved to Congress) or to execute and enforce the laws (reserved to the presidency), but to *interpret* the laws and to ensure that every citizen received *equal justice* under the law.

The U.S. Supreme Court had final authority in interpreting the Constitution and in settling constitutional disputes between states. Article VI of the Constitution declared that the federal Constitution, federal laws, and treaties were "the supreme Law of the Land."

The Limits of the Constitution

The men who drafted the new Constitution claimed to be representing all Americans. In fact, however, important groups were left out of the Constitution's protections. Native Americans, for example, could not be citizens unless they paid taxes, which few did. The Constitution declared that Native American "tribes" were not part of the United States but were separate "nations."

Addressing Slavery The enslaved were also denied political rights. Of all the issues that emerged during the Constitutional Convention of 1787, none was more explosive than slavery. As James Madison stressed, "the great division of interest" among the delegates "did not lie between the large & small states: it lay between the Northern & Southern," primarily from "their having or not having slaves." When the Patriots declared independence in 1776, slavery existed in every state. By 1787, however, Massachusetts, Pennsylvania, Connecticut, New Hampshire, and Rhode Island had ended the dreadful system.

***CHARLES CALVERT AND HIS SLAVE* (1761)** This image of Charles Calvert (direct descendant of Lord Baltimore) at age five dressed in full military attire towering over the kneeling enslaved boy, dressed as a military drummer, clearly establishes their roles and status within the Chesapeake colonial elite families.

How the framers handled slavery at the Constitutional Convention reflected the competing impulses driving the creation of the republic. Many delegates viewed slavery as an embarrassing contradiction to the principles of liberty and equality embodied in the Declaration of Independence ("all men are created equal") and the new Constitution. Luther Martin, Maryland's most brilliant attorney, pointed out that owning human beings was "inconsistent with the principles of the revolution and dishonorable to the American character."

Most southern delegates strongly disagreed. Many were planters who had grown dependent on enslaved African workers and who had been born and raised in a society where white supremacy and black inferiority were woven into the fabric of law and culture. These men did not hesitate to defend slavery. South

Carolinian Charles Pinckney stressed the practical reality in the southern states: "South Carolina and Georgia cannot do without slaves." Delegates owning enslaved people would have walked out of the negotiations had there been an attempt to abolish slavery. The framers therefore decided not to include in the Constitution any plan for limiting or ending slavery, nor did the document treat the enslaved as human beings with civil rights. The denial and evasion regarding slavery at the Constitutional Convention established the pattern adopted by elected officials thereafter.

Denying and evading the problem of slavery

If enslaved people were not to be freed or their rights to be acknowledged, however, how were the 700,000 of them to be counted? Since the size of state delegations in the proposed House of Representatives would be based on population, southerners argued that enslaved people should be counted to help determine how many representatives their state would have. Northerners maintained that it made no sense to count enslaved people for purposes of congressional representation when they were treated as property, not human beings.

The three-fifths compromise

The delegates finally agreed to a compromise in which three-fifths of "all other persons" (the enslaved) would be included in population counts as a basis for apportioning a state's congressional representatives. In a constitution intended to "secure the blessings of liberty to ourselves and our posterity," the three-fifths clause was a glaring example of compromise being divorced from principle. The corrupt bargain over slavery would bedevil the nation for the next seventy-five years, for the more enslaved people southern states imported from Africa, the more seats in Congress they gained.

In another concession to southerners, the original Constitution never mentions the word *slavery*. As slaveholder James Madison explained, it would be "wrong to admit in the Constitution the idea that there could be property in men." Instead, the document speaks of "free persons" and "all other persons" and of persons "held to service of labor." The word *slavery* would not appear in the Constitution until the Thirteenth Amendment abolished it in 1865.

The Absence of Women's Rights in the Constitution The delegates at the Constitutional Convention refused even to discuss political rights for women. In the new United States, women remained subservient to their husbands. They could not vote, hold elected office, or own property. Gaining a divorce remained extraordinarily difficult for women. "Every man, by the Constitution, is born with an equal right to be elected to the highest office," asserted Reverend John Ogden of Portsmouth, New Hampshire, in *The Female Guide* (1793). "And every woman is born with an equal right to be the wife of the most eminent man."

Advocates and arguments for gender equality

Yet not all women were willing to maintain their subordinate role. Just as the Revolutionary War enabled many African Americans to seize their freedom, it also inspired some brave women to demand political equality. Eliza Yonge Wilkinson, born in 1757 to a wealthy plantation family near

Charleston, South Carolina, lost her husband early in the war. In June 1780, after Wilkinson was assaulted and robbed by "inhuman" British soldiers, she became a fiery Patriot who "hated Tyranny in every shape." She assured a friend, "We may be *led*, but we never will be *driven*!"

Likewise, Wilkinson expected greater freedom for women after the war. "The men say we have no business [with politics]," she wrote to a friend. "I won't have it thought that because we are the weaker sex as to bodily strength, my dear, we are capable of nothing more than minding the dairy, visiting the poultry-house, and all such domestic concerns." Wilkinson demanded more. "They won't even allow us the liberty of thought, and that is all I want."

Judith Sargent Murray, a Massachusetts writer, argued that the rights and liberties fought for by Patriots belonged not just to men but to women, too. In her essay "On the Equality of the Sexes," published in 1790, she challenged the prevailing view that men had greater intellectual capacities than women. She insisted that any differences resulted from prejudice and discrimination that prevented women from having access to formal education and worldly experience.

The arguments for gender equality, however, fell mostly on deaf ears. Nowhere does the Constitution include the word *women*. Writing from Paris, Thomas Jefferson expressed the hope that American "ladies" would forget about political participation and be "contented to soothe and calm the minds of their husbands returning ruffled from political debate."

CORE **OBJECTIVE**

3. Summarize the major debates surrounding the ratification of the Constitution and explain how they were resolved.

The Fight for Ratification

On September 17, 1787, the Federal Convention reported that it had completed the new Constitution. George Washington was the first to sign. "Gentlemen," announced Benjamin Franklin, "you have a republic, if you can keep it." The Confederation Congress sent the final draft to thirteen special state conventions for official approval (ratification).

Over the next ten months, people from all walks of life debated the new Constitution's merits—on street corners and wharves, in taverns, at churches, in newspapers and pamphlets, in workplaces, and in the state conventions. Gilbert Livingston, a delegate to the New York ratifying convention, viewed his participation in the debate as the "greatest transaction of his life." At the Massachusetts ratifying convention, observers seated in the galleries refused to leave during meal breaks for fear of losing their seats. Richmond, the new state capital of Virginia, had trouble hosting the "prodigious number of People from all parts of the Country" who wanted to witness the debates.

Choosing Sides: Anti-Federalists versus Federalists

Advocates for the Constitution took the name Federalists; opponents were called **anti-Federalists**. The two sides formed the seeds for America's first two-party political system.

anti-Federalists Opponents of the Constitution as an infringement on individual and states' rights, whose criticism led to the addition of a Bill of Rights to the document. Many anti-Federalists later joined Thomas Jefferson's Democratic-Republican party.

The Federalists, led by James Madison and Alexander Hamilton, had several advantages. First, they had a concrete proposal, the draft Constitution itself; their opponents had nothing to offer but criticism. Second, their leaders were, on average, ten to twelve years younger and more energetic than the anti-Federalists; many Federalists had been members of the Constitutional Convention and were familiar with the disputed issues in the document. Third, they were more unified and better organized.

The anti-Federalist leaders—Virginians Patrick Henry, George Mason, Richard Henry Lee, and future president James Monroe; George Clinton of New York; Samuel Adams, Elbridge Gerry, and Mercy Otis Warren of Massachusetts; Luther Martin and Samuel Chase of Maryland—raised valid concerns. Some wanted to retain the Confederation. Others wanted to start over. Still others wanted to revise the proposed constitution.

Anti-Federalists feared that the new national government would eventually grow corrupt and tyrannical. A Philadelphia writer denounced those who drafted the Constitution as representing "the Aristocratic Party" intent upon creating a "monarchical" national government. George Mason of Virginia spoke for many in vowing that he would "sooner chop off my right hand" than approve the new Constitution. Mason and the other anti-Federalists especially criticized the absence of a "bill of rights" to protect individuals and states from the power of the national government. Other than the bill of rights, however, the anti-Federalists had no comprehensive alternative to the Constitution.

FEDERALISTS VERSUS ANTI-FEDERALISTS This satirical engraving by Amos Doolittle portrays the conflicts that arose over the ratification of the Constitution. In the center, stuck in the mud, is a wagon that represents Connecticut, laden with debt. On either side, the Federalists *(right)* and anti-Federalists *(left)* engage in a tug-of-war, pulling Connecticut in opposite directions. The three merchant ships at the bottom are carrying goods from Connecticut to New York, and the phrase below criticizes the tariffs that states imposed on such interstate imports. **Whom does Doolittle appear to agree with, the Federalists or the anti-Federalists?**

The Federalist Papers
Collection of eighty-five essays, published widely in newspapers in 1787 and 1788, written by Alexander Hamilton, James Madison, and John Jay in support of adopting the proposed U.S. Constitution.

The Federalist Papers

Among the supreme legacies of the debate over the Constitution is what came to be called ***The Federalist Papers***, a collection of eighty-five essays published in New York newspapers in 1787 and 1788. Written by James Madison, Alexander Hamilton, and John Jay, the essays were intended to convince New Yorkers to ratify the new Constitution.

The United States, according to *The Federalist Papers*, was to be a republic grounded in radically new notions: the people, not a king or queen, would be sovereign, and the rule of law would ensure that tyrants could never violate the civil rights protecting the citizenry.

In the most famous of the *Federalist* essays, No. 10, Madison turned the conventional wisdom about republics on its head. From ancient times, it had been assumed that republics ("representative democracies") survived only if they were small and homogeneous. Madison, however, argued that small republics usually fell victim to warring factions. In the United States, he explained, the size and diversity of the expanding nation would make it impossible for any single faction to form a majority that could corrupt the federal government—or society at large.

The genius of the Constitution was its creation of a legal and political system that protected minorities from majority despotism. Given a federal government in which power was shared among the three federal branches, a large republic, Madison argued, could work better than a small one to balance "clashing interests." "Extend the [geographic] sphere," Madison wrote, "and you take in a greater variety of parties and interests; you make it less probable that a majority of the whole will have a common motive to invade the rights of other citizens."

RATIFICATION OF THE CONSTITUTION

Order of Ratification	State	Date of Ratification
1	Delaware	December 7, 1787
2	Pennsylvania	December 12, 1787
3	New Jersey	December 18, 1787
4	Georgia	January 2, 1788
5	Connecticut	January 9, 1788
6	Massachusetts	February 6, 1788
7	Maryland	April 28, 1788
8	South Carolina	May 23, 1788
9	New Hampshire	June 21, 1788
10	Virginia	June 25, 1788
11	New York	July 26, 1788
12	North Carolina	November 21, 1789
13	Rhode Island	May 29, 1790

The States Decide

The heated debate over ratification of the Constitution at times boiled over into violence. Riots erupted in several cities. Newspapers took sides, leading one New Englander to remark that the papers were being "read more than the Bible."

Amid the intense discussions, ratification of the new Constitution gained momentum at the end of 1787. Delaware, New Jersey, and Georgia were among the first states to ratify the Constitution. Massachusetts, still sharply divided in the aftermath of Shays's Rebellion, was the first state in which the outcome was close, approving the Constitution by 187 to 168.

On June 21, 1788, New Hampshire became the ninth state to ratify the Constitution, thereby reaching the minimum number of states needed for approval. The Constitution, however, could hardly succeed without the approval of Virginia, the largest, wealthiest, and most populous state, or New York, which had the third-highest population and occupied a key position geographically. Both states included strong opposition groups that were eventually won over by an agreement to add a bill of rights.

Upon notification of New Hampshire's decision to ratify the Constitution, the Confederation Congress chose New York City as the national capital and called for the new government to assume power in 1789. The Constitution was adopted, but the resistance to it would help convince the new Congress to propose the first ten amendments to the Constitution, now known as the Bill of Rights.

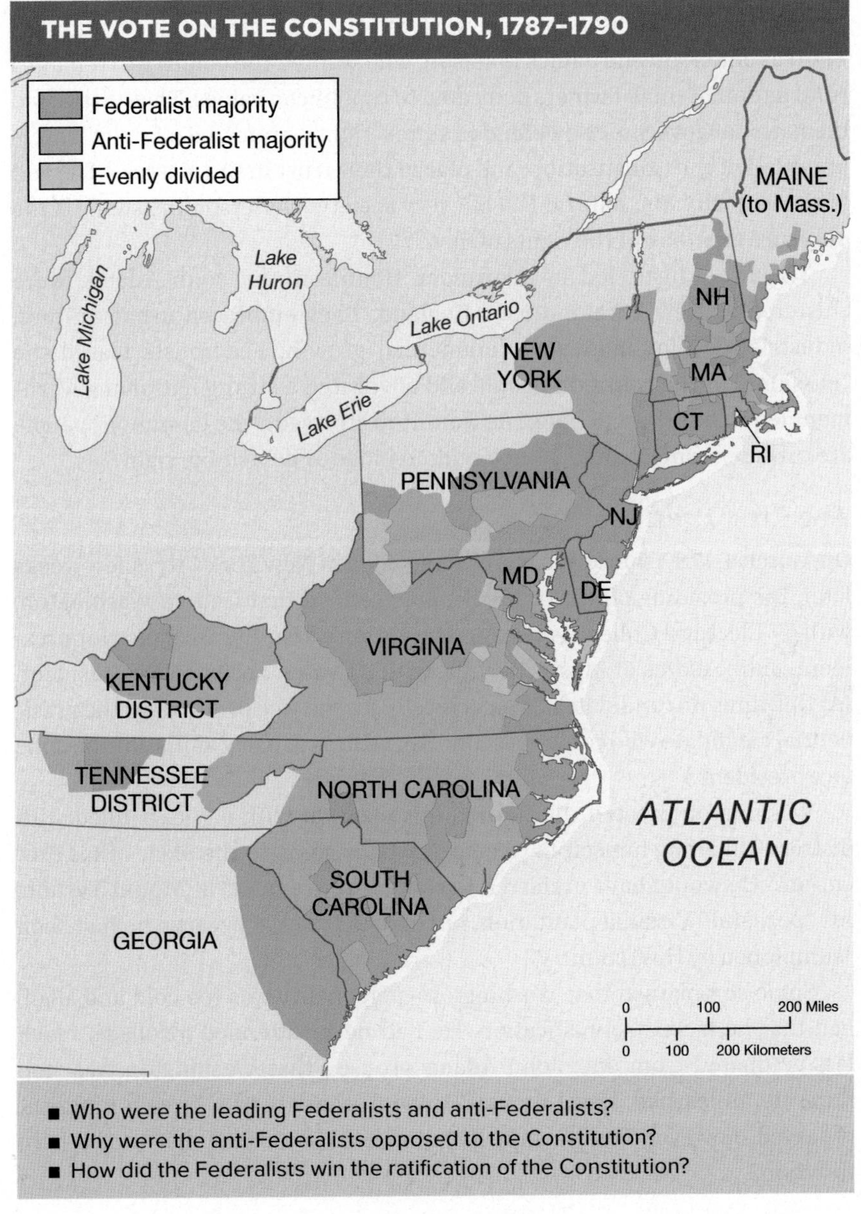

- Who were the leading Federalists and anti-Federalists?
- Why were the anti-Federalists opposed to the Constitution?
- How did the Federalists win the ratification of the Constitution?

CORE **OBJECTIVE**

4. Compare the Federalists' vision for the United States with that of their Republican opponents during the 1790s.

The Federalist Era

The Constitution promised to create a more powerful national government better capable of managing a rapidly growing republic. Yet it was one thing to ratify a new Constitution and quite another to make the new government run smoothly.

With each passing year, the United States debated how to interpret and apply the provisions of the new Constitution. During the 1790s, the federal government would confront rebellions, states threatening to secede, international tensions, and foreign wars, as well as the formation of competing political parties—Federalists and Democratic Republicans, more commonly known as **Jeffersonian Republicans**, or simply as Republicans.

The Democratic Republicans were mostly southerners, like Virginians Thomas Jefferson and James Madison, who wanted the country to remain a rural nation of small farmers dedicated to republican values. They distrusted the national government, defended states' rights, preferred a "strict" interpretation of the Constitution, and placed their trust in the masses. "The will of the majority, the natural law of every society," Jefferson insisted, "is the only sure guardian of the rights of men."

The Federalists, led by Alexander Hamilton and John Adams, were clustered in New York and New England. They embraced urban culture, industrial development, and commercial growth. Federalists feared the "passions" of the common people and advocated a strong national government led by "the best people." As Hamilton stressed, "the [common] people are turbulent and changing; they seldom judge or determine right."

The First President

On March 4, 1789, the new Congress convened in New York City. A few weeks later, the presiding officer of the Senate certified that George Washington, with 69 Electoral College votes, was the nation's unanimous choice for president. John Adams of Massachusetts, with 34 votes, became vice president. (At this time, no candidates ran specifically for the vice presidency; the presidential candidate who came in second, regardless of party affiliation, became vice president.)

Washington greeted the news of his election with a "heart filled with distress," likening himself to "a culprit who is going to the place of his execution." He would have preferred to stay in "retirement" at Mount Vernon, his "peaceful" Virginia plantation, but agreed to serve because he had been "summoned by [his] country."

Some complained that Washington's personality was too cold and aloof, and that he lacked sophistication. He had never attended a college, much less graduated from one. John Adams groused that Washington was "too illiterate, unlearned, [and] unread" to be president. As a French diplomat observed, however, Washington had "the soul, look, and figure of a hero in action."

Jeffersonian Republicans Political party founded by Thomas Jefferson in opposition to the Federalist party led by Alexander Hamilton and John Adams; also known as the Democratic-Republican party.

Born in Virginia in 1732, Washington was a largely self-educated former surveyor, land speculator, and soldier whose father had died when he was eleven. In 1759, he married Martha Dandridge Custis, a young widow with two small children and one of the largest fortunes in Virginia. In the years that followed, he became a prosperous tobacco planter, land speculator, and owner of enslaved people. A man of action rather than an intellectual, Washington loved riding horses, hunting foxes, playing cards or billiards, fishing, hosting oyster roasts, and drinking wine.

The fifty-seven-year-old Washington brought to the presidency both a detached reserve and a remarkable capacity for leadership. He had extraordinary stamina and patience, integrity and resolve, courage and resilience. Most of all, he was a fearless realist. He resolved to deal with "mankind as they are, since we cannot have them as we wish." Few doubted that he was the best person to lead the new nation. People were already calling him the "father of his country."

In his inaugural address, written by Alexander Hamilton, Washington appealed for unity, pleading with Congress to abandon "local prejudices" and "party animosities" to create the "national" outlook necessary for the fledgling

WASHINGTON'S INAUGURATION This portrayal of George Washington as he arrived at the Battery in New York for his 1789 inauguration was intended to enhance his legend as the founding father and to signify the importance that he was elected to become the first president of the United States. **Note the presence of the Native Americans in the lower right and the foreign flags in the distance—in what ways does this painting exaggerate Washington's support and in what ways is it an accurate representation of the sentiment at the time?**

republic to thrive. Within a few months, he would see his hopes dashed. Personal rivalries, sectional tensions, and partisan infighting would dominate political life in the 1790s.

Washington's Cabinet

President Washington faced massive challenges, and he knew that his every decision would have special significance because he was the first president. "The eyes of America—perhaps of the world—are turned to this Government," he said. He was entering "untrodden ground" and therefore must ensure that his actions were based on "true principles."

During the summer of 1789, Congress created executive departments corresponding to those formed under the Confederation. To head the Department of State, Washington named Thomas Jefferson. To lead the Department of the Treasury, he appointed Alexander Hamilton, who was widely read in matters of government finance. Henry Knox was secretary of war; and John Jay became the first chief justice of the Supreme Court.

Washington routinely called his chief staff members together to discuss matters of policy. This was the origin of the president's *cabinet*, an unofficial advisory body. The office of vice president, said its first occupant, John Adams, was the most "insignificant office . . . ever . . . contrived."

The Bill of Rights

Protecting individual rights vs. the power of the state

To address concerns raised by opponents of the new federal government, James Madison, now a congressman, presented to Congress a set of constitutional amendments intended to protect individual rights. After considerable debate, Congress approved twelve amendments in September 1789. By the end of 1791, the necessary three-fourths of the states had approved *ten* of the twelve proposed amendments, now known as the **Bill of Rights**.

The Bill of Rights provided safeguards for individual rights of speech, assembly, religion, and the press; the right to own firearms; the right to refuse to house soldiers; protection against unreasonable searches and seizures; the right to refuse to testify against oneself; the right to a speedy public trial, with an attorney present, before an impartial jury; and protection against "cruel and unusual" punishments. The Tenth Amendment addressed the widespread demand that powers not delegated to the national government "are reserved to the States respectively, or to the people."

The amendments were written in broad language that seemed to exclude no one. In fact, however, they technically applied only to property-owning white males. Native Americans were entirely outside the constitutional system, and, as such, an "alien people" in their own land. And, like the Constitution itself, the Bill of Rights gave no protections or civil rights to enslaved Americans. Similar restrictions applied to women, who could not vote in most state and national elections. Equally important, the Bill of Rights did not prevent *states* from violating the civil rights of citizens.

Bill of Rights (1791) First ten amendments to the U.S. Constitution, adopted in 1791 to guarantee individual rights and to help secure ratification of the Constitution by the states.

Still, the United States was the first nation to put such safeguards into its government charter. While the Constitution had designed a vigorous federal government binding together the thirteen states, the Bill of Rights provided something just as necessary: specifying the individual rights and freedoms that governments could not abuse or deny.

Religious Freedom

The debates over the Constitution and the Bill of Rights generated a religious revolution. Unlike the New England Puritans, whose colonial governments had rigidly enforced their religious beliefs, the Christian men who crafted the Constitution were determined to protect religious life from government interference and coercion. The Constitution, therefore, never mentions God. In contrast to the monarchies of Europe, the United States would keep the institutions of church and government separate and allow people to choose their own religions ("freedom of conscience"). To that end, the First Amendment declared that "Congress shall make no law respecting an establishment of [a single] religion or prohibiting the free exercise thereof." This statement has since become one of the most important—and controversial—principles of American government.

Separation of church and state

The First Amendment created a framework within which people of all religious persuasions could flourish and prohibited the federal government from endorsing or supporting any denomination or interfering with the religious choices that people make. As Thomas Jefferson later explained, the First Amendment erected a "wall of separation between church and State."

Immigration and Naturalization

The Constitution said little about immigration and naturalization (the process of gaining citizenship), and most of what it said was negative. In Article II, Section 1, it prohibits any immigrant from becoming president, limiting the office to a native-born "Citizen." On defining citizenship, the Constitution gives Congress the authority "to establish a uniform Rule of Naturalization" but offers no further guidance. As a result, naturalization policy has changed often over the years in response to fluctuating social attitudes and prejudices, economic needs, and political moods.

To ensure that America continued to share its "blessings of liberty" with immigrants, the Constitution called upon Congress to create policies to accommodate the continuing stream of immigrants from around the world.

The Naturalization Act

George Washington had strong feelings on the matter. He viewed America's open embrace of refugees and immigrants as one of the nation's most important values. The United States, he believed, should always serve as a refuge for the oppressed around the world. In his first address to Congress in 1790, President Washington urged legislators to craft a "liberal" naturalization law to attract immigrants.

Congress responded with the Naturalization Act of 1790, which specified that any "free white person" could gain citizenship ("naturalization") after living at least two years in the United States. (In 1795, Congress increased the residency requirement to five years.)

The Naturalization Act established an important principle: immigrants were free to renounce their original citizenship to become American citizens. The children of immigrants born in the United States, however, were immediately granted what came to be called birthright citizenship.

During the 1790s, some 100,000 European immigrants arrived in the United States, beginning a process that would grow with time. Because of its openness to immigrants and its liberal naturalization policy, the United States has admitted more people from more places than any other nation in the world.

Hamilton's Vision of a Prosperous America

In 1776, the same year that Americans were declaring their independence, Adam Smith, a Scottish philosopher, published a revolutionary book titled *An Inquiry into the Nature and Causes of the Wealth of Nations*. It provided the first full description of what would come to be called a *capitalist* economy. (The term *capitalism* would not appear until 1850.)

Adam Smith's *Wealth of Nations*

The Wealth of Nations was a declaration of independence from Great Britain's mercantilist system. Under *mercantilism*, national governments had exercised tight control over economic life. Smith argued that instead of controlling economic activity, governments should allow individuals and businesses to compete freely for profits in the marketplace. By liberating individual self-interest and entrepreneurial innovation from the constraints of government authority, he insisted, the public welfare would be enhanced. The poverty that had entrapped the masses of Europe for centuries would end to the extent that governments allowed for "free enterprise," by which individuals, through their hard work and ingenuity, could become prosperous. Smith also explained that the strongest national economies would be those in which *all* the major sectors were flourishing—agriculture, trade, banking, finance, and manufacturing.

ALEXANDER HAMILTON
A fervent Federalist and prolific contributor to *The Federalist Papers*, Hamilton served as George Washington's secretary of the Treasury from 1789 to 1795. Faced with the daunting challenge of repaying the national debt, Hamilton promoted an economic system that established federal taxes and a national bank.

Alexander Hamilton greatly admired *The Wealth of Nations*, and as secretary of the Treasury he took charge of the nation's financial affairs. Hamilton grasped the complex issues of government finance and envisioned what America would become: the world's most prosperous capitalist nation.

Hamilton was a self-made and self-educated aristocrat—and an immigrant. Born out of wedlock in the West Indies in 1755, he was deserted at age ten by his Scottish father and left an orphan at thirteen by the death of his mother. With the help of friends and relatives, he found his way to New Jersey in late 1772 before moving a year later to New York City. There he entered King's College (now Columbia University).

When the Revolutionary war with Britain erupted, Hamilton joined the Continental Army as a captain at age nineteen. He distinguished himself in battle and became one of General Washington's favorite aides. After the war, he established a thriving legal practice in New York City, married into a prominent family, and served as a member of the Confederation Congress.

Hamilton became the foremost advocate for an "energetic government" promoting vibrant economic development. The United States, he argued, was too dependent on agriculture. He therefore championed trade, banking, finance, investment, and manufacturing, as well as bustling commercial cities, as the most essential elements of America's future.

Paying Debts

Hamilton's economic reforms

The United States was born in debt. To fight the British, it had borrowed heavily from the Dutch and the French. After the war, the new nation had to find a way to pay off those debts. Yet there were no national bank and no national currency. In essence, the republic was bankrupt.

It fell to Alexander Hamilton to determine how the debts should be repaid and how the new government could balance its budget. Governments have four basic ways to pay their bills: (1) impose taxes or fees on individuals and businesses, (2) levy tariffs (taxes on imported goods), (3) borrow money by selling interest-paying government bonds to investors, and (4) print money.

Under Hamilton's leadership, the United States did all these things—and more. To raise funds, Congress enacted tariffs on a variety of imported items. By discriminating against imported goods, tariffs enabled American manufacturers to charge higher prices for their products sold in the United States. This penalized consumers, particularly those in the southern states that were most dependent upon imported goods.

In essence, tariffs benefited the nation's young manufacturing sector, most of which was in New England, at the expense of the agricultural sector, since farm produce was rarely imported. Tariff policy soon became an explosive political issue.

Raising Federal Revenue

The levying of tariffs marked but one element in Alexander Hamilton's plan to put the new republic on sound financial footing. In a series of reports submitted to Congress, he outlined a visionary program for the nation's economic development.

Nationalizing state's debts

The first report dealt with how the federal government should refinance the massive debt the states and the Confederation government had accumulated. Selling government bonds to pay the interest due on the war-related debts, Hamilton argued, would provide investors ("the monied interest") a direct stake in the success of the new government.

Hamilton also argued that the federal government should pay ("assume") the state debts from the Revolutionary War because they were a *national* responsibility; *all* Americans had benefited from the war for independence. A well-managed federal debt that absorbed the state debts, he claimed, would be a "national blessing," provide a "mechanism for national unity," and promote long-term prosperity by showing the world that America honored its obligations.

Settling Sectional Differences

Hamilton's farsighted proposals created a storm of controversy. James Madison, Hamilton's close ally in the fight for the new Constitution, broke with him over the federal government "assuming" the states' debts. Madison was troubled that northern states owed far more than southern states. Four states (Virginia, North Carolina, Georgia, and Maryland) had already paid off most of their war debts. The other states had not. Why should the southern states, Madison asked, subsidize the debts of the northern states?

Madison's opposition to Hamilton's debt-assumption plan ignited debate in Congress. In April 1790, the House of Representatives voted down the "assumption" plan, 32–29.

The Compromise of 1790

Hamilton did not give up, however. After failing to get members of Congress to switch their votes, he asked Thomas Jefferson to help break the impasse. In June 1790, Jefferson invited Hamilton and Madison to join him for dinner in New York City. By the end of the evening, they had reached a famous compromise. First, they agreed that the national capital should move from New York City to Philadelphia for the next ten years, and then move to a new city to be built in a ten-mile-square "federal district" astride the Potomac River, sandwiched between the slave states of Maryland and Virginia.

Hamilton agreed to find the votes in Congress to approve the move in exchange for Madison pledging to find the two votes needed to pass the debt-assumption plan.

The Compromise of 1790 went as planned. Congress voted as hoped, and the federal government moved in late 1790 to Philadelphia. Ten years later, the nation's capital moved again, this time to the new city of Washington, in the federal District of Columbia.

Once implemented, Hamilton's debt-funding scheme was successful. Investors purchased the bonds issued by the federal government in 1790, providing money to begin paying off the war debts. In addition, Hamilton obtained new loans from European governments.

To raise additional revenue, Hamilton convinced Congress to create *excise* taxes on particular products, such as carriages, sugar, and salt. Within a few years, the nation had a higher financial credit rating than all the nations of Europe. By making the new nation financially solvent, Hamilton set in motion the greatest economic success story in history.

A National Bank

Part of the opposition to Alexander Hamilton's debt-financing scheme grew out of opposition to Hamilton himself. Arrogant and headstrong, he viewed himself as President Washington's prime minister. That his Department of Treasury had *forty* staff members while Thomas Jefferson's State Department had *five* demonstrated the priority that George Washington gave to the nation's financial situation.

Hamilton's national bank

Hamilton promoted an urban-centered economy anchored in finance and manufacturing. After securing congressional approval of his debt-funding scheme, he called for a *national* bank modeled after the Bank of England. Such a bank, Hamilton believed, would foster greater "commerce among individuals" and provide a safe place for the federal government's revenues. A national bank, Hamilton explained, would increase the nation's money supply by issuing paper currency in amounts greater than the actual "reserve"—gold and silver coins and government bonds—in its vaults. By issuing loans and thereby increasing the amount of money in circulation, a national bank and its branches would serve as the engines of prosperity.

BANK OF THE UNITED STATES Proposed by Alexander Hamilton, the Bank of the United States opened in 1791 in Philadelphia, the nation's temporary capital.

Once again, James Madison and Thomas Jefferson led the opposition to Hamilton's banking scheme. They maintained that the Constitution said nothing about creating a national bank, so the government could not start one. Jefferson also believed that Hamilton's proposed bank would not help most Americans. Instead, an inner circle of self-serving financiers and investors would, over time, exercise corrupt control over the bank and Congress.

Hamilton, however, had the better of the argument. Representatives from the northern states voted 33–1 in favor of the national bank; southern congressmen opposed it 19–6. The lopsided vote illustrated the growing political division between the North and South.

Explicit vs. implied powers of the federal government

Before signing the bill, President Washington sought the advice of his cabinet, where he found an equal division of opinion. The result was the first great debate on constitutional interpretation. Were the powers of Congress only those *explicitly* stated in the Constitution, or were other powers *implied*? The argument turned chiefly on Article I, Section 8, which authorized Congress to "make all Laws which shall be necessary and proper for carrying into Execution the foregoing Powers."

Such language left lots of room for disagreement and led to a savage confrontation between Jefferson and Hamilton. The Treasury secretary had come to view Jefferson as a "contemptible hypocrite" guided by an "unsound & dangerous" agrarian economic philosophy. Jefferson hated commerce, speculators, factories, banks, and bankers—almost as much as he hated the "monarchist" Hamilton.

To thwart the proposed national bank, Jefferson argued that a bank might be convenient, but it was not *necessary*, as Article I, Section 8 specified. In a 16,000-word report to the president, Hamilton countered that the power to charter corporations was an "implied" power of any government. As he pointed out, the three banks already in existence had been chartered by states, none of whose constitutions specifically mentioned the authority to incorporate banks. Hamilton eventually convinced Washington to sign the bank bill.

The new **Bank of the United States** (B.U.S.) created in 1791, had three primary responsibilities: (1) to hold the government's revenues and pay its bills; (2) to provide loans to the federal government and to state-chartered banks to promote economic development; and (3) to manage the nation's money supply by regulating the power of state-chartered banks to issue paper currency or banknotes. The B.U.S. could issue national banknotes as needed to address the chronic shortage of gold and silver coins. Within a few years, the B.U.S. had added eight branches in major cities.

Encouraging Manufacturing

Hamilton's "Report on Manufactures"

In the last of his reports to Congress, the "Report on Manufactures," Alexander Hamilton set in place the capstone of his design for a modern capitalist economy: the active governmental promotion of new manufacturing and industrial enterprises (mills, mines, and factories).

Industrialization, Hamilton believed, would bring diversification to an economy dominated by agriculture and dependent on imported British goods; improve productivity through greater use of machinery; provide work for those not ordinarily employed outside the home, such as women and children; and encourage immigration of skilled industrial workers from other nations.

To foster industrial development, Hamilton recommended that the federal government increase tariffs on imports, most of which came from Britain, while providing financial incentives (called bounties) to key industries making crucial products such as wool, cotton cloth, and window glass. Such government support, he claimed, would enable new industries to compete "on equal terms" with long-standing British enterprises. Finally, Hamilton asked Congress to fund major transportation improvements, including the development of roads, canals, and harbors.

In the end, however, few of Hamilton's pro-industry ideas were enacted because of strong opposition from Thomas Jefferson, James Madison, and other southerners. Hamilton's proposals, however, provided arguments for future advocates of manufacturing and federally funded transportation projects (called "internal improvements").

Hamilton's Visionary Achievements

Alexander Hamilton's leadership was monumental. During the 1790s, as the Treasury department began to pay off the nation's war debts, foreigners invested heavily in the American economy, and European nations as well as China began a growing trade with the United States. Economic growth, so elusive in the 1780s, blossomed. A Bostonian reported that the nation had never "had a brighter sunshine of prosperity. . . . Our agricultural interest smiles, our commerce is blessed, our manufactures flourish."

All was not well, however. Hamilton had upset many people, especially in the agricultural South and along the western frontier.

Bank of the United States (1791) National bank responsible for holding and transferring federal government funds, making business loans, and issuing a national currency.

The Beginnings of Political Parties

Thomas Jefferson and James Madison were increasingly concerned that Hamilton's urban-industrial economic vision and his political deal-making threatened precious liberties. Jefferson's intensifying opposition to Hamilton's politics and policies fractured Washington's cabinet. Jefferson wrote that he and Hamilton "daily pitted in the cabinet like two cocks [roosters]." Washington urged them to rise above their toxic "dissensions," but it was too late. They had become mortal enemies, as well as the leaders of the first loosely organized political parties, the Federalists and the Democratic Republicans.

THOMAS JEFFERSON Jefferson, Alexander Hamilton's chief rival, fought against the New Yorker's emphasis on industrial development. Jefferson pushed for an agrarian America instead, inspired in part by his love of French culture.

The Federalists were centered in New York and New England and were also powerful among the planter elite in South Carolina. Generally, they feared the excesses of democracy, distrusted the "common people," and wanted a strong central government led by the wisest leaders who would be committed to economic growth, social stability, and national defense.

What most worried the Federalists, as Alexander Hamilton said, was the "poison" of "DEMOCRACY." The people, he stressed, were "turbulent and changing; they seldom judge or determine right [wisely]."

By contrast, the Democratic Republicans, led by Thomas Jefferson and James Madison, were most concerned about threats to individual freedoms and states' rights posed by a strong national government. They trusted the people. As Madison said, "public opinion sets bounds to every government and is the real sovereign in every free one."

Unexpected events in Europe influenced the two political parties. In July 1789, violence erupted in France when masses of the working poor, enraged over soaring prices for bread and in part inspired by the American Revolution, revolted against King Louis XVI.

The **French Revolution** captured the imagination of many Americans, especially Jefferson and the Democratic Republicans, as royal tyranny was displaced by a democratic republic that gave voting rights to all adult men regardless of how much property they owned. Americans formed forty-two Democratic-Republican clubs that hosted rallies on behalf of the French Revolution.

French Revolution Revolutionary movement beginning in 1789 that overthrew the monarchy and transformed France into an unstable republic before Napoléon Bonaparte assumed power in 1799.

Foreign and Domestic Crises

CORE **OBJECTIVE**

5. Assess how attitudes toward Great Britain and France shaped American politics in the late eighteenth century.

During the nation's fragile infancy, George Washington was the only leader able to rise above party differences. In 1792, he was unanimously reelected to a second presidential term—and quickly found himself embroiled in the cascading consequences of the French Revolution.

In 1791, the monarchies of Prussia and Austria had invaded France to stop the revolutionary movement from infecting their absolutist societies. The invaders, however, only inspired the French revolutionaries to greater efforts.

By early 1793, the most radical of the French revolutionaries, called *Jacobins*, had executed the king and queen, as well as hundreds of aristocrats and priests. The Jacobins not only promoted democracy, religious toleration, and human rights but social, racial, and sexual equality.

On February 1, 1793, the French revolutionary government declared war on Great Britain, Spain, and the Netherlands, thus beginning a European-wide conflict that would last twenty-two years.

As the French republic plunged into warfare, the French Revolution entered its vicious phase, the so-called Reign of Terror. In 1793–1794, Jacobins executed thousands of "counterrevolutionary" political prisoners and Catholic priests, along with many revolutionary leaders.

The French Revolution divides Federalists and Republicans

Secretary of State Thomas Jefferson, who loved French culture and democratic ideals, wholeheartedly endorsed the French Revolution, as did most Republicans. Jefferson even justified the Reign of Terror by asserting that the "tree of liberty must be refreshed from time to time with the blood of patriots and tyrants."

By contrast, Alexander Hamilton and John Adams saw the French Revolution as vicious and godless, and they sided with Great Britain and its allies. President Washington noted that Jefferson and the Republicans had become "the French Party," and their doing so had become "the curse of this country."

The European war tested the ability of the United States to remain neutral in world affairs. France and Britain sought to stop the other from trading with the United States, even if it meant attacking U.S. merchant ships.

CITIZEN GENÊT The French ambassador, known as Citizen Genêt, meets the disapproving George Washington after the French official had blatantly violated American neutrality laws.

As George Washington began his second presidential term in 1793, he faced an awkward decision. By the 1778 Treaty of Alliance, the United States was a *perpetual* ally of France. Americans, however, wanted no part of the war between France and Great Britain. Hamilton and Jefferson agreed that entering the conflict would be foolish. Where they differed was in how best to stay out. Hamilton wanted to declare the military alliance formed with the French during the American Revolution invalid because it had been made with a monarchy that no longer existed. Jefferson preferred to use the alliance with France as a bargaining point with the British.

In the end, Washington chose a wise middle course. On April 22, 1793, he issued a neutrality proclamation that declared the United States "friendly and impartial toward the belligerent powers" and warned U.S. citizens to remain neutral.

Instead of settling matters, however, the neutrality proclamation brought to a boil the ugly feud between Jefferson and Hamilton.

Citizen Genêt

At the same time that President Washington issued the neutrality proclamation, he accepted Thomas Jefferson's argument that the United States should officially recognize the French revolutionary government and welcome its ambassador to the United States, the cocky, twenty-nine-year-old Edmond-Charles Genêt.

In April 1793, Citizen Genêt, as he became known, landed at Charleston, South Carolina. He then openly violated U.S. neutrality by recruiting four American privateers (privately owned warships) to capture English and Spanish merchant vessels.

After five weeks in South Carolina, Genêt traveled to Philadelphia, where his efforts to draw America into the war on France's side embarrassed his friends in the Republican party. When Genêt threatened to go around President Washington and appeal directly to the American people, even Jefferson disavowed "the French monkey." In August 1793, President Washington, at Hamilton's urging, demanded that the French government replace Genêt.

The growing excesses of the radicals in France were quickly cooling U.S. support for the Revolution. Jefferson, however, was so disgusted by Hamilton and Washington's refusal to support the French that he resigned as secretary of state and returned to his Virginia home.

Vice President John Adams greeted Jefferson's departure by saying "good riddance." President Washington felt the same way. He never forgave Jefferson and Madison for organizing Democratic-Republican clubs to oppose his policies. After accepting Jefferson's resignation, Washington never spoke to him again.

Frontier Tensions

Meanwhile, new conflicts erupted in the Ohio River Valley between settlers and Native Americans. In the fall of 1793, General "Mad" Anthony Wayne led a military expedition into the Northwest Territory's "Indian Country" that sparked what became known as the Northwest Indian War, a conflict that arose after the British transferred the Ohio Country to the United States.

The Native Americans living in the region insisted that the British had no right to give away ancestral tribal lands. As pioneers moved into the Northwest Territory, the various Indian nations formed the Western Confederacy to resist American settlement.

In August 1794, the Western Confederacy of some 2,000 Shawnee,

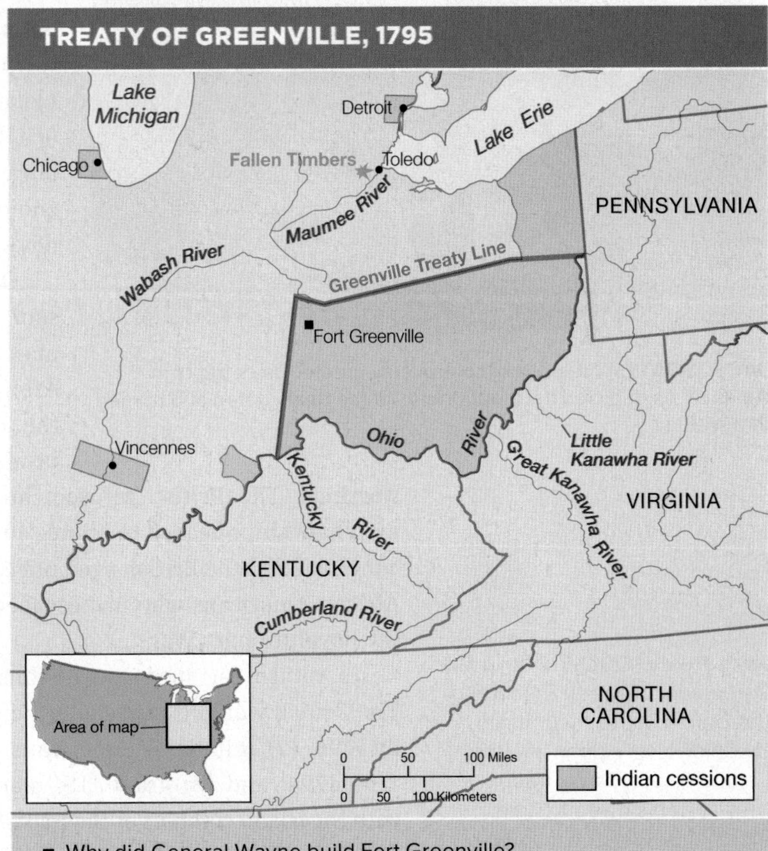

- Why did General Wayne build Fort Greenville?
- What happened at the Battle of Fallen Timbers?
- What were the terms of the Treaty of Greenville?

JAY'S TREATY A firestorm of controversy greeted Jay's treaty in America. As depicted here, opponents of the treaty rioted and burned Jay in effigy.

Ottawa, Chippewa, Delaware, and Potawatomi warriors, supported by the British, attacked General Wayne's troops and their Indian allies in the Battle of Fallen Timbers, along the Michigan-Ohio border.

The American soldiers defeated the Indians, destroyed their crops and villages, and built a line of forts in northern Ohio and Indiana. The Indians finally agreed to the Treaty of Greenville, signed in August 1795, by which the United States bought for $20,000 most of the territory that would form the state of Ohio and the cities of Detroit and Chicago.

Jay's Treaty

During 1794, the British efforts to incite Indian attacks on American settlements along the western frontier threatened to renew warfare between the old enemies. In addition, as England and France engaged in warfare on land and sea, British warships violated international law by seizing hundreds of U.S. merchant ships sailing for a French port. Their crews were given the terrible choice of being impressed into the British navy or being imprisoned.

On April 16, 1794, President Washington sent John Jay to London to settle the major issues between the two nations. After prolonged negotiations, Jay agreed to the British demand that America not sell products to France for the construction of warships. The British refused, however, to stop intercepting American merchant ships headed to France and "impressing" their sailors. Finally, Jay conceded that the British need not compensate U.S. citizens for the enslaved African Americans who had escaped to the safety of British armies during the Revolutionary War.

Jay's Treaty (1794) Controversial agreement between Britain and the United States, negotiated by Chief Justice John Jay, that settled disputes over trade, prewar debts owed to British merchants, British-occupied forts in American territory, and the seizure of American ships and cargo.

In return for such concessions, Jay won three important promises: The British would (1) evacuate their six forts along the northwest frontier by 1796, (2) reimburse Americans for the seizures of ships and cargo in 1793–1794, and (3) grant U.S. merchants a limited right to trade again with the island colonies of the British West Indies.

When the terms of **Jay's Treaty** were disclosed, many Americans, especially Republicans, were outraged. In Philadelphia, an angry crowd burned a copy of the treaty and an effigy of John Jay, shouting, "Kick this damned treaty to hell!" In New York City, Alexander Hamilton was pelted with rocks when he tried to defend the treaty. Even President Washington could not avoid abuse. "To follow Washington now is to be a Tory," wrote a newspaper editor, "and to deserve tar and feathers."

The sharp criticism stunned the president. "The cry against the treaty is like that against a mad dog," he wrote a supporter. Critics were "running it down" with "the most abominable mis-representations."

The wildly unpopular treaty created the most serious crisis of Washington's presidency. Some called for his impeachment. The president, however, decided that the proposed agreement was the only way to avoid another war with Britain, one that the United States was bound to lose.

WHISKEY REBELLION George Washington as commander in chief reviews the troops mobilized to quell the Whiskey Rebellion in 1794. Why did Washington's controversial action against the rebels lead to a surge in Republican support at the polls?

In 1795, with Washington's support, Jay's Treaty barely won the necessary two-thirds majority in the Senate. Some 80 percent of the votes *for* the treaty came from New England or the middle Atlantic states; 74 percent of those opposed were southerners, most of them Jeffersonian Republicans. While weary of partisan squabbles, George Washington had given the young nation a precious gift—peace. No other leader could have pushed the controversial treaty through Congress.

The Whiskey Rebellion

The Washington administration faced another challenge in the backcountry when frontier farmers launched the so-called **Whiskey Rebellion (1794)**. Alexander Hamilton's 1791 tax on "distilled spirits" had ignited resistance among cash-poor farmers throughout the western frontier. Liquor made from grain or fruit was the region's most valuable product; it even was used as a form of currency. Americans—men, women, and children—drank whiskey day and night. When efforts to repeal the tax failed, many turned to violence and intimidation. Beginning in September 1791, angry groups of farmers, militiamen, and laborers attacked federal tax collectors and marshals. In the summer of 1794, the discontent exploded into rebellion in western Pennsylvania, home to a fourth of the nation's whiskey stills. A mob of angry farmers threatened to assault nearby Pittsburgh, loot the homes of the rich, and set the town ablaze.

Whiskey Rebellion (1794) Violent protest by western Pennsylvania farmers against the federal excise tax on corn whiskey, put down by a federal army.

The Whiskey Rebellion was the first great domestic challenge to the federal government, and George Washington responded decisively. At Hamilton's urging, Washington ordered the whiskey rebels ("enemies of order") to disperse by September 1 or he would send in the militia.

When the rebels failed to respond, 13,000 militiamen began marching to western Pennsylvania. Washington donned his military uniform and rode on horseback to greet the soldiers.

The huge army, commanded by Virginia's governor, Henry "Lighthorse Harry" Lee, panicked the rebels, who vanished into the hills. Two were sentenced to hang, only to be pardoned by President Washington. The show of force led the rebels and their sympathizers to change their tactics. Rather than openly defying federal laws, they voted for Republicans, who won heavily in the next Pennsylvania elections.

Pinckney's Treaty

While events were unfolding in Pennsylvania, the Spanish began negotiations over control of the Mississippi River and the disputed northern boundary of their Florida colony. U.S. negotiator Thomas Pinckney pulled off a diplomatic triumph in 1795 when he convinced the Spanish to accept

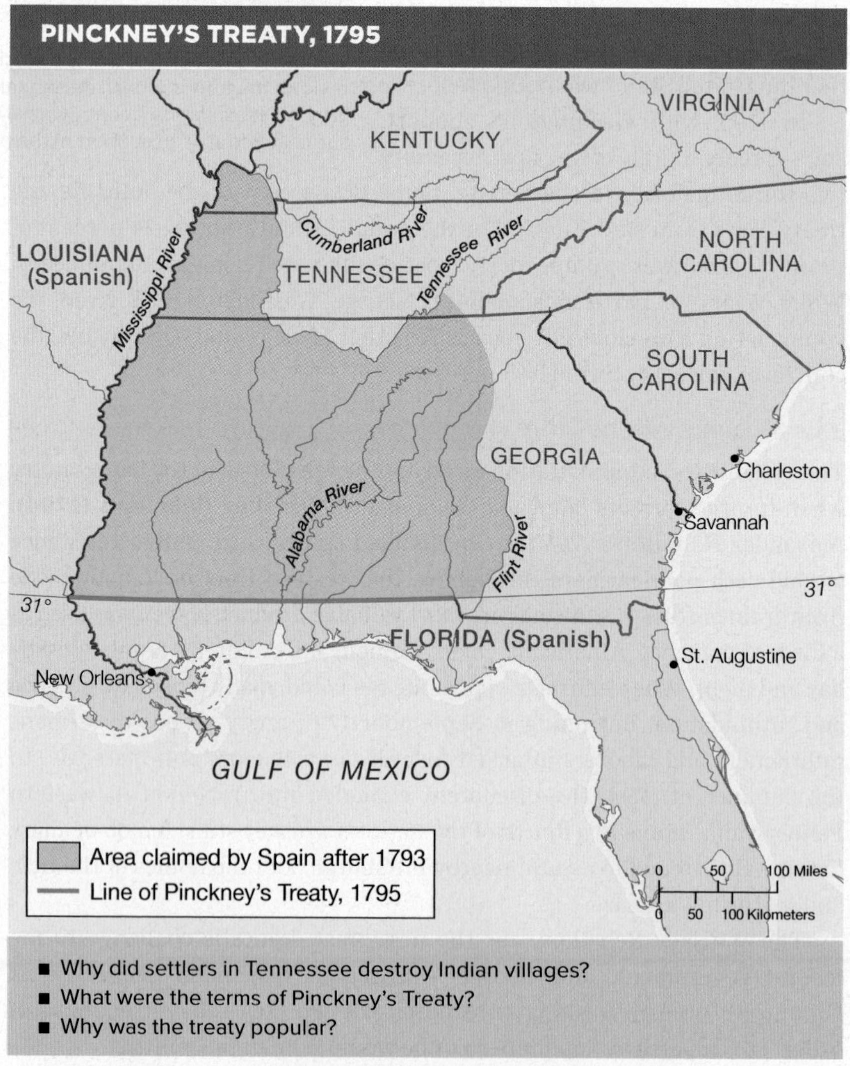

- Why did settlers in Tennessee destroy Indian villages?
- What were the terms of Pinckney's Treaty?
- Why was the treaty popular?

a southern American boundary in west Florida along the northern coast of the Gulf of Mexico (the current boundary between Florida and Georgia). The Spanish also agreed to allow Americans to ship goods, grains, and livestock down the Mississippi River to Spanish-controlled New Orleans. Senate ratification of Pinckney's Treaty (also called the Treaty of San Lorenzo) came quickly, for westerners were eager to transport their crops and livestock to New Orleans.

DANIEL BOONE ESCORTING SETTLERS THROUGH CUMBERLAND GAP
In this 1851 painting by George Caleb Bingham, a Missouri artist known for his mythologizing portraits of frontier life, Daniel Boone leads a group of settlers westward through the Appalachian Mountains. **How does Bingham's portrayal of the settlers reveal his vision of westward expansion and the spirit of those who made the difficult journey?**

Western Settlement and the Wilderness Road

The treaties signed by John Jay and Thomas Pinckney spurred a new wave of settlers into the western territories. Their lust for land aroused a raging debate in Congress over what the federal government should do with the vast areas it had acquired or taken from the British, the Spanish, and the Native Americans.

Federalists wanted the government to charge high prices for western lands to keep the East from losing both political influence and a labor force important to the growth of manufacture. They also preferred that government-owned lands be sold in large parcels to speculators, rather than in small plots to settlers. Thomas Jefferson and James Madison were reluctantly prepared to go along with these policies for the sake of reducing the national debt, but Jefferson preferred that government-owned land be sold to small farmers rather than speculators.

For the time being, the Federalists prevailed. With the Land Act of 1796, Congress doubled the price of federal land and required that much of it be sold in 640-acre sections, making the minimum cost well beyond the means of ordinary settlers.

Criticism of the policies led to the Land Act of 1800, which reduced the minimum parcel to 320 acres and spread payments over four years.

The lure of western lands led thousands of settlers to follow pathfinder Daniel Boone into the territory known as Kentucky, or Kaintuck, from the Cherokee KEN-TA-KE (Great Meadow). In the late eighteenth century, the Indian-held lands in Kentucky were a farmer's dream and a hunter's paradise, with their fertile soil, bluegrass meadows, abundant forests, and countless buffalo, deer, and wild turkeys.

Born of Quaker parents on a small farm in 1734 in central Pennsylvania, Boone became one of America's first folk heroes, a larger-than-life pioneer known as the "Columbus of the Woods."

After hearing numerous reports about the wonderful lands over the Appalachian Mountains, Boone set out from western North Carolina in 1769 to find a trail into Kentucky. He discovered what was called the Warriors' Path, a narrow footpath that buffalo, deer, and Native Americans had worn along the steep ridges of the Appalachian Mountains.

In 1773, Boone led a group of settlers into Kentucky, including his wife, Rebecca, and eight children. However, they were forced to abandon their migration after his eldest son was captured, tortured, and killed by Indians. Two years later, he and thirty woodsmen used axes to widen the 208-mile-long Warriors' Path into what became the Wilderness Road, a passageway through the Cumberland Gap that more than 300,000 settlers would use over the next twenty-five years.

Transfer of Power

In 1796, George Washington decided that two presidential terms in office were enough. He was eager to retire to Mount Vernon. He would leave behind a formidable record of achievement, including the organization of a new national government, a prosperous economy, the recovery of territory from Britain and Spain, a stable northwestern frontier, and the admission of three new states: Vermont (1791), Kentucky (1792), and Tennessee (1796). Of the nine presidents who were owners of enslaved people, he alone would free them upon his death.

Washington's farewell address warns against partisanship

On September 17, 1796, George Washington delivered a farewell address in which he criticized the rising spirit of political partisanship and the emergence of political parties. They endangered the republic, he felt, because they pursued the narrow interests of minorities rather than the good of the nation. In foreign relations, Washington advised, the United States should stay away from Europe's quarrels by avoiding "permanent alliances with any portion of the foreign world." His warning would serve as a fundamental principle in U.S. foreign policy until the early twentieth century.

The Election of 1796

With George Washington out of the race, the United States had its first contested election for president. The Federalist "caucus," a group of leading congressmen, chose Vice President John Adams as their candidate. The Republicans nominated Thomas Jefferson. Aaron Burr, a young New York attorney and senator, also ran as a Republican.

Adams elected president; Jefferson elected vice president (1796)

The campaign was nasty. The Federalists were attacked for unpopular taxes, excessive spending, and abuses of power. Republicans called the pudgy John Adams "His Rotundity" and labeled him a monarchist who despised "the people." (Adams wanted people to refer to the President as "His Highness.") Federalists countered that Jefferson was a French-loving atheist eager for another war with Great Britain. Adams won the election with seventy-one electoral votes, but in an odd twist, Jefferson, who received sixty-eight electoral votes, became vice president. The Federalists won control of both houses of Congress.

The Adams Administration

Vain and prickly, opinionated and stubborn, John Adams viewed everyone as less talented and less deserving than he believed himself to be—and he told them so. Popularity, he admitted, "had never been his mistress." An independent thinker with a combative spirit and volcanic temper, he fought as often with his fellow Federalists as with Republicans. Benjamin Franklin said Adams was "always an honest man, often a wise one, but sometimes . . . absolutely out of his senses."

JOHN ADAMS Political philosopher and politician, Adams won the election of 1796 by a thin margin, becoming the second president of the United States. He was the first president to take up residence in the White House, in early 1801.

The same could be said for Adams's talented wife, Abigail. She, too, was prone to letting her candor get ahead of her tact, as when she told her husband that Congress was full of cowardly imbeciles.

John Adams feared democracy and despised social equality. He once referred to ordinary Americans as the "common herd of mankind." He also felt that he was never properly appreciated—and he may have been right. Yet on the essential issue of his presidency, war and peace, he kept his head when others about him were losing theirs—probably at the cost of his reelection.

War with France

As America's second president, John Adams inherited a "Quasi War" with France, since it was undeclared, a by-product of French anger over Jay's Treaty between the United States and Great Britain. The navies of both warring nations were capturing U.S. ships headed for the other's ports. By the time of Adams's inauguration, in 1797, the French had plundered some 300 American vessels and broken diplomatic relations with the United States.

CONFLICT WITH FRANCE A cartoon indicating the anti-French sentiment generated by the XYZ Affair. In the background, a savage-looking figure bearing the French flag operates the guillotine, while on the left the three American negotiators reject the Paris Monster's demand for money.

Adams sought to ease tensions by sending three prominent Americans to Paris to negotiate. Upon their arrival, however, they were accosted by three French officials (labeled X, Y, and Z by Adams in his report to Congress) who announced that negotiations could begin only if the United States paid a bribe of $250,000 and loaned France $12 million.

The XYZ Affair

Such bribes were common in the eighteenth century, but the answer from the American side was "No, no, not a sixpence." When the so-called XYZ Affair became public, hostility toward France soared. Many Republicans—with the exception of Vice President Jefferson—joined with Federalists in calling for war. Federalists in Congress voted to construct warships and triple the size of the U.S. Army. By the end of 1798, French and American ships were engaged in an undeclared naval war in the Caribbean Sea.

War at Home

The conflict with France sparked an intense debate between Federalists eager for a declaration of war and Republicans sympathetic to France. For his part, President Adams had tried to take the high ground. Soon after his election, he had invited Vice President Jefferson to join him in creating a bipartisan administration. Jefferson refused, saying that he would not be a part of the cabinet and would only preside over the Senate as vice president, as the Constitution specified. Within a year, he and Adams were at each other's throats.

Jefferson and other Republicans were convinced that the real purpose of the French crisis was to give Federalists an excuse to quiet their American critics. Legislation of the **Alien and Sedition Acts of 1798** confirmed Republican suspicions. These partisan laws, passed amid a wave of patriotic war fervor, gave the president extraordinary powers to violate civil liberties protected by the Bill of Rights, all in a clumsy effort to stamp out criticism of the administration. They limited freedom of speech and of the press, as well as the liberty of "aliens" (immigrants who had not yet gained citizenship).

Adams's support of the Alien and Sedition Acts ("war measures") would prove to be the greatest mistake of his presidency. Timothy Pickering, his secretary of state, claimed that Adams agreed to the acts without consulting "any member of the government and for a reason truly remarkable—because he knew we should all be opposed to the measure."

Three of the four Alien and Sedition Acts reflected hostility toward French and Irish immigrants, many of whom had supported the French Revolution or the Irish Rebellion against British authority and had become militant Democratic Republicans in America.

The Naturalization Act lengthened from five to fourteen years the residency requirement for immigrants ("aliens") to gain U.S. citizenship. The Alien Friends Act empowered the president to jail and deport "dangerous" aliens, and the Alien Enemies Act authorized the president in wartime to expel or imprison aliens from enemy nations. Finally, the Sedition Act outlawed writing, publishing, or speaking anything of "a false, scandalous and malicious" nature against the government or any of its officers.

Alien and Sedition Acts of 1798 Four measures passed during the undeclared war with France that limited the freedoms of speech and press and restricted the liberty of immigrants.

CONGRESSIONAL PUGILISTS An infamous print of the fight between Roger Griswold and Matthew Lyon on the House Floor portrays the absurd degree of conflict between the Federalists and Republicans over the Sedition Acts. After a volley of verbal abuse, Lyon spat tobacco juice at Griswold, who retaliated by attacking Lyon with a wooden cane, who in turn took up a pair of fire tongs.

To counter the Alien and Sedition Acts, James Madison and Thomas Jefferson drafted the Kentucky and Virginia Resolutions, which were passed by the two state legislatures in late 1798. The resolutions were as troubling as the acts they denounced. While Jefferson appropriately described the Alien and Sedition Acts as "alarming infractions" of constitutional rights, he threatened disunion in claiming that state legislatures should "nullify" (reject and ignore) acts of Congress that violated the constitutional guarantee of free speech.

Meanwhile, President Adams was seeking peace. In 1799, he dispatched another team of diplomats to negotiate with a new French government under Napoléon Bonaparte, whose army had overthrown the republic. In a treaty called the Convention of 1800, the Americans dropped their demands to be repaid for the ships taken by the French, and the French agreed to end the military alliance with the United States dating to the Revolutionary War. The Senate quickly ratified the agreement.

Republican Victory in 1800

The furor over the Alien and Sedition Acts influenced the pivotal presidential election of 1800. The Federalists nominated John Adams, although Alexander Hamilton publicly questioned Adams's fitness to be president, citing his "disgusting egotism."

Thomas Jefferson and Aaron Burr, the Republican candidates, once again represented the alliance of the two most powerful states, Virginia and

THE ELECTION OF 1800

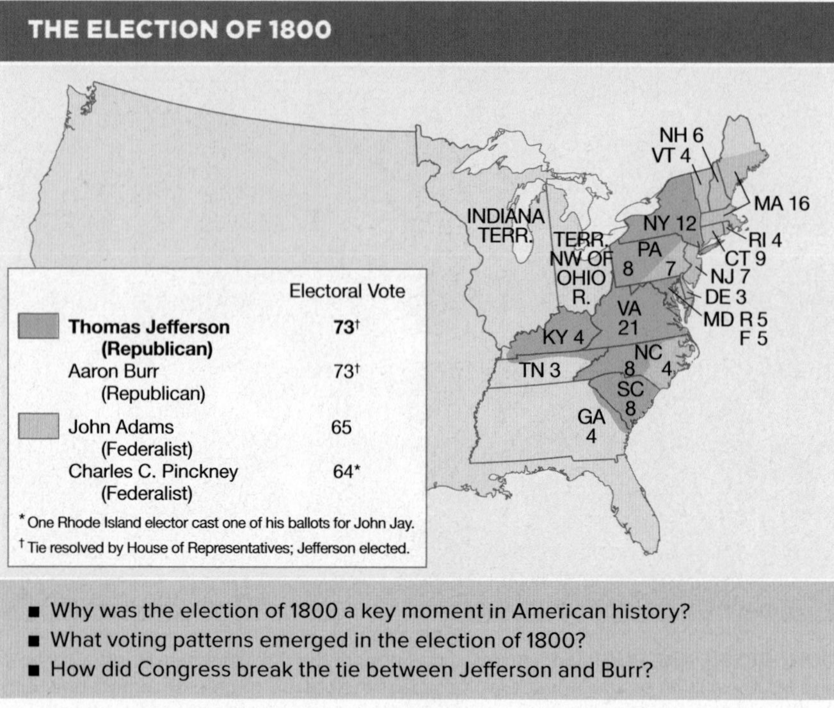

- Why was the election of 1800 a key moment in American history?
- What voting patterns emerged in the election of 1800?
- How did Congress break the tie between Jefferson and Burr?

New York. A Federalist newspaper predicted that if the "godless" Jefferson were elected, "murder, robbery, rape, adultery, and incest will be openly taught and practiced." Not to be outdone, a Republican newspaper dismissed Adams as a "blind, bald, crippled, toothless man who wants to start a war with France."

In the **election of 1800**, Jefferson and Burr emerged with seventy-three electoral votes each. Adams received sixty-five. When Burr refused to withdraw in favor of Jefferson, the tie vote in the Electoral College required a deciding vote in the House of Representatives.

After thirty-six ballots, a majority of House members chose Jefferson over Burr.

The Judiciary Act of 1801

Before the Federalists turned over power on March 4, 1801, President Adams and Congress passed the Judiciary Act of 1801, an effort to ensure Federalist control of the judicial system by creating sixteen federal circuit courts, with a new judge for each. It also reduced the number of Supreme Court justices from six to five in an effort to keep Jefferson from appointing a new member. Before he left office, Adams appointed Federalists to all the new positions. The Federalists, quipped Jefferson, had "retired into the judiciary as a stronghold." They never again would exercise significant political power.

election of 1800 Presidential election involving Thomas Jefferson and John Adams that resulted in the first Democratic-Republican victory after the Federalist administrations of George Washington and John Adams.

A New Era

The election of 1800 further divided the young republic into warring political factions and marked a major turning point in the nation's history. It was the first time one party had relinquished presidential power to the opposition, and it was the only election that pitted a sitting president (Adams) against his own vice president (Jefferson).

Jefferson's hard-fought victory signaled the emergence of a new, more democratic political culture dominated by bitterly divided parties and wider public participation. With the gradual elimination of the requirement that citizens must own property to vote, the electorate expanded enormously in the early nineteenth century.

Jefferson called his election the "Revolution of 1800," for it marked the triumph of the Republican party and the slaveholding South. Three Republican slaveholders from Virginia—Jefferson, James Madison, and James Monroe—would hold the presidency for the next twenty-four years.

John Adams was so upset by his defeat that he refused to participate in Jefferson's inauguration in the new federal capital in Washington, D.C. Instead, unnoticed and unappreciated, Adams boarded a stagecoach at 4 A.M. for the 500-mile trip to his home in Massachusetts. He and Jefferson would not communicate for the next twelve years. As Adams returned to work on his Massachusetts farm, he told his eldest son, John Quincy, who would become the nation's sixth president, that anyone governing the United States "has a hard, laborious, and unhappy life." Thomas Jefferson would soon feel the same way.

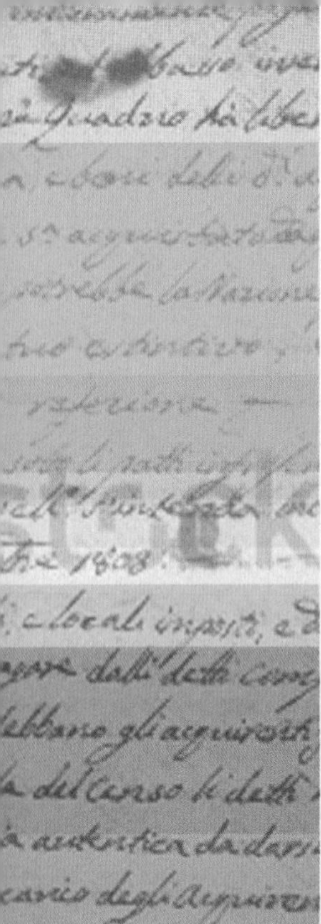

Reviewing the CORE OBJECTIVES | INQUIZITIVE

■ **Confederation Government** Despite the weak form of government organized under the Articles of Confederation, the Confederation government managed to construct important alliances during the Revolutionary War, help win the War of Independence, and negotiate the Treaty of Paris (1783). It created executive departments and established through the *Northwest Ordinance* the process by which new western territories would be organized and governments formed before they applied for statehood. The Articles of Confederation, however, did not allow the national government to raise taxes to fund its debts. *Shays's Rebellion* made many Americans fear that such uprisings would eventually destroy the new republic unless the United States formed a stronger national government.

■ **Constitutional Convention** When delegates gathered at the convention in Philadelphia in 1787 to revise the existing government, they decided to scrap the Articles of Confederation and start over. An entirely new document emerged, which created a system called *federalism* in which a strong national government with clear *separation of powers* among executive, legislative, and judicial branches functioned alongside state governments. Arguments about how best to ensure that the rights of individual states were protected and also that "the people" were represented in the new Congress were resolved by establishing a Senate, with equal representation for each state, and a House of Representatives, the number of whose delegates was determined by population counts.

■ **Ratification of the Constitution** Ratification of the Constitution was hotly contested. *Anti-Federalists* such as Virginia's Patrick Henry opposed the new structure of government because it lacked a bill of rights. To sway New York State toward ratification, Alexander Hamilton, James Madison, and John Jay wrote *The Federalist Papers*. Ratification became possible only when Federalists promised to add what came to be called the *Bill of Rights*.

■ **Federalists versus Republicans** Strengthening the economy was the highest priority of the Washington administration. Alexander Hamilton and the Federalists wanted to create a diverse economy in which agriculture was balanced by trade, finance, and manufacturing.

■ Thomas Jefferson and others, known as the *Jeffersonian Republicans*, worried that Hamilton's plans violated the Constitution and made the federal government too powerful. They envisioned a nation dominated by farmers and planters in which the rights of states would be protected against federal power. President Washington faced his first domestic crisis when rebellious farmers and moonshiners in Pennsylvania refused to pay the federal tax on whiskey. Washington organized a formidable force to suppress the *Whiskey Rebellion* (1794).

As part of Alexander Hamilton's economic reforms, he crafted a federal budget that funded the national debt through tax revenues and tariffs on imports, and he created a national bank, the first *Bank of the United States.*

▪ **Trouble Abroad** With the outbreak of war throughout much of Europe during the *French Revolution,* George Washington's policy of neutrality violated the terms of America's 1778 treaty with France. At the same time, Americans sharply criticized *Jay's Treaty* with the British for giving too much away. French warships began seizing British and American ships in an undeclared naval war. Federalists supported Washington's approach; Republicans were more supportive of France. During the presidency of John Adams, this undeclared naval war continued, which led to the controversial *Alien and Sedition Acts of 1798.* Criticism of the Adams administration spilled over into the hotly-contested presidential *election of 1800,* in which Thomas Jefferson defeated Adams.

KEY TERMS

Northwest Ordinance (1787) p. *217*

Shays's Rebellion (1787) *p. 221*

federalism *p. 224*

separation of powers *p. 224*

anti-Federalists *p. 228*

The Federalist Papers p. 230

Jeffersonian Republicans *p. 232*

Bill of Rights *p. 234*

Bank of the United States (1791) *p. 240*

French Revolution *p. 241*

Jay's Treaty (1794) *p. 244*

Whiskey Rebellion (1794) *p. 245*

Alien and Sedition Acts of 1798 *p. 250*

election of 1800 *p. 252*

CHRONOLOGY

1781	Articles of Confederation take effect
1783	Treaty of Paris ends the War of Independence
1784–1785	Land Ordinances
1786–1787	Shays's Rebellion
1787	Northwest Ordinance
	The Constitutional Convention is held in Philadelphia
1787–1788	*The Federalist Papers* are published
1789	President George Washington is inaugurated
1791	Bill of Rights is ratified
	Bank of the United States is created
1793	Washington issues a proclamation of neutrality
1794	Jay's Treaty is negotiated with England
	Whiskey Rebellion in Pennsylvania
	U.S. Army defeats Western Confederacy of Indian nations in the Battle of Fallen Timbers
1796	John Adams is elected president
1798–1800	Quasi-war with France
1798	Alien and Sedition Acts are passed
1800	Thomas Jefferson is elected president

INQUIZITIVE

Go to InQuizitive to see what you've learned—and learn what you've missed—with personalized feedback along the way.

***WE OWE ALLEGIANCE TO NO CROWN* (CA. 1814)** The War of 1812 generated a renewed spirit of nationalism, inspiring Philadelphia sign painter John Archibald Woodside to create this patriotic painting.

CHAPTER 7

The Early Republic

1800–1815

When President Thomas Jefferson took office in 1801, the United States and its western territories reached from the Atlantic Ocean to the Mississippi River. Nine of ten Americans lived on farms, and land-hungry easterners were rushing westward across the Appalachian Mountains to snatch up the ancestral hunting grounds of Native Americans in Tennessee and Kentucky. Everywhere people were on the make and on the move. Restless mobility and impatient striving soon came to define the American way of life.

Former president John Adams observed that "there is no people on earth so ambitious as the people of America . . . because the lowest can aspire as freely as the highest."

In 1800, people eager to own their own farms bought 67,000 acres of government-owned land; the next year, they bought 498,000 acres. Native Americans resisted the invasion of their ancestral lands but ultimately succumbed to a federal government (and an army) determined to relocate them. Most Whites, however, were more concerned with seizing their own economic opportunities than with the plight of Native Americans.

CORE OBJECTIVES INQUIZITIVE

1. Summarize the major domestic political developments that took place during Thomas Jefferson's administration.
2. Describe how foreign events affected the United States during the Jefferson and Madison administrations.
3. Explain the primary causes of the American decision to declare war on Great Britain in 1812.
4. Analyze the most significant outcomes of the War of 1812 on the United States.

CORE **OBJECTIVE**

1. Summarize the major domestic political developments that took place during Thomas Jefferson's administration.

Jeffersonian Republicanism

The "People's President"

The 1800 presidential campaign between Federalists and Jeffersonian Republicans had been so fiercely contested that some predicted civil war as the House of Representatives decided the outcome of the election. On March 4, 1801, however, fifty-seven-year-old Thomas Jefferson was inaugurated without incident. It was the first election in modern history that resulted in the orderly transfer of power from one political party to another.

Jefferson's inauguration marked the emerging dominance of the nation's political life by Republicans—and Virginians. The nation's most populous state, Virginia supplied a quarter of the Republican congressmen in the House of Representatives that convened in early 1801. Former secretary of state Timothy Pickering of Massachusetts acknowledged that the northeastern states, where Federalism dominated, could no longer "reconcile their habits, views, and interests with those of the South and West."

Jefferson was the first president inaugurated in the new national capital of Washington, District of Columbia. The unfinished city consisted of a few buildings clustered around two unfinished centers, Capitol Hill and the "Executive Mansion." (It would not be called the White House until 1901.) Cows grazed along the Mall while pigs and geese prowled the unpaved streets. Workers, many of them enslaved, had barely completed building the Capitol and the Executive Mansion before Jefferson was sworn in.

During his inauguration, Jefferson emphasized his connection to the "plain and simple" ways of the "common" people. Instead of wearing a ceremonial sword and riding in a horse-drawn carriage, as George Washington and John Adams had done, Jefferson walked to the Capitol Building, escorted by members of Congress. Jefferson's deliberate display of **republican simplicity** set the tone for his administration. He wanted Americans to notice the difference between the monarchical style of the Federalists and Republican simplicity.

In his eloquent inaugural address, Jefferson urged Americans to work together. "We are all Republicans—we are all Federalists," Jefferson stressed, noting that "every difference of opinion is not a difference of principle." But Jefferson's appeal for unity proved illusory. In a letter to a British friend, the Republican president said he feared that Federalists, a "herd of traitors," wanted to destroy "the liberties of the people" and convert the republic into a monarchy.

republican simplicity Deliberate attitude of humility and frugality, as opposed to monarchical pomp and ceremony, adopted by Thomas Jefferson in his presidency.

A More Democratic Society

Jefferson wanted common people to play a larger role in politics and social life. During and after the Revolutionary War, an increasing proportion of White males, especially small farmers, wage laborers, artisans, mechanics, and apprentices—long excluded from politics—gained the right to vote or hold office as states reduced or eliminated requirements that voters

THE CAPITOL BUILDING This 1806 watercolor of the Capitol Building was painted by Benjamin Henry Latrobe, its architect, and inscribed to Thomas Jefferson. A tall dome would be added later, after the building was damaged in the War of 1812.

Expanded political participation

and candidates own a specified amount of property. Thereafter, widespread public participation in the political process became a distinguishing feature of American life.

Many leaders in both political parties worried that men of humble origins, some of whom were uneducated and even illiterate, were replacing the social and political elite (referred to as the natural aristocracy) in the state legislatures. As the nineteenth century unfolded, voters were not content to be governed solely by "their betters"; they wanted to do the governing themselves. More than half the members of the Republican-controlled Congress elected in 1800 were first-time legislators. Federalist John Adams so detested the democratic forces transforming politics and social life that he despaired for the nation's future: "Oh my Country," he moaned, "how I mourn over" its "overweening admiration of fools and knaves! the never failing effects of *democracy!*"

A Contradictory Genius

Jefferson's hypocrisy

President Jefferson, who owned hundreds of enslaved people, was a unique bundle of contradictions. He was progressive and enlightened in some areas, self-serving and hypocritical in others. He loathed political maneuvering,

AT LEISURE AT MONTICELLO A scene of Jefferson's Monticello estate, showing his descendants playing in the garden. Designed by Jefferson himself after the sixteenth-century Italian architect Andrea Palladio, Monticello stands as a testament to Jefferson's classical tastes. **How did Jefferson's aristocratic lifestyle conflict with his persona as the "people's president"?**

yet excelled at it. He championed government frugality, yet nearly went bankrupt himself buying expensive wines, paintings, silverware, and furniture. Jefferson, who had written in the Declaration of Independence that "all men are created equal," also bought, bred, flogged, and sold enslaved people while calling slavery "an abominable crime" and a "hideous blot" on civilization.

Jefferson wrote about the evils of racial mixing because of what he claimed were the "inferior" attributes of African Americans. Yet after his wife, Martha, died, he used her half-sister, a beautiful enslaved mulatto woman named Sarah "Sally" Hemings, as his concubine; she gave birth to six of his children. For Jefferson, Hemings became what a friend called his "substitute for a wife" in a plantation world where a veil of silence cloaked the hypocrisy of slaveowning planters who celebrated the ideals of liberty and equality while benefiting from the coerced labor and sexuality of enslaved people.

At age fourteen, Sally Hemings accompanied Jefferson's daughter Maria to Paris, where Jefferson was serving as U.S. ambassador. Sally's descendants believe she began a sexual relationship with Jefferson in France. Before returning to Virginia in 1789, a pregnant Sally made a deal with Jefferson: Rather than remain in France, where she was legally free, Hemings would return to Monticello if Jefferson agreed to free any children they had. True to his word, Jefferson freed all six of Hemings's children, the only enslaved people he ever liberated.

Jefferson was an inventive genius of staggering learning and exceptional abilities. As a self-trained architect, he designed the state capitol in Richmond, Virginia, as well as his thirty-three-room mountaintop mansion near Charlottesville called *Monticello* (Little Mountain). He was an expert in constitutional law, civil liberties, and political philosophy; religion and ethics; classical history; progressive education; natural science, paleontology, and mathematics; music and linguistics; and farming, gardening, cooking, and wine.

Jefferson in Office

President as party leader

For all his shyness and admitted weakness as a public speaker, Thomas Jefferson was the first president to pursue the role of party leader, and he openly cultivated congressional support. In his cabinet, the leading figures were Secretary of State James Madison, his best friend and political ally, and Secretary of the Treasury Albert Gallatin, a Pennsylvania Republican whose financial skills had won him the respect of Federalists and Republicans alike.

In filling lesser offices, however, Jefferson often succumbed to pressure from Republicans to remove Federalists, only to discover that there were few qualified candidates to replace them. When Gallatin asked if he might appoint women to some posts, Jefferson revealed the limits of his liberalism: "The appointment of a woman to office is an innovation for which the public is not prepared, nor am I."

Marbury v. Madison (1803)

Marbury v. Madison (1803)

In one area—the federal judiciary—the new president decided to remove most of the offices altogether, in part because the court system was the only branch of the government still controlled by Federalists. In 1802, at Jefferson's urging, the Republican-controlled Congress repealed the Judiciary Act of 1801, which the Federalists had passed just before the transfer of power to the Jeffersonian Republicans. The Judiciary Act had ensured Federalist control of the judicial system by creating sixteen federal circuit courts and appointing—for life—a Federalist judge for each. The controversial effort to repeal the judgeships sparked the landmark case of the Supreme Court and ***Marbury v. Madison* (1803)**.

The case went to the Supreme Court, then presided over by Chief Justice John Marshall, an ardent Virginia Federalist. Marshall was largely self-educated, with no more than a year of formal schooling. He had joined the Continental Army during the Revolutionary War, served under George Washington, attended law school at the College of William and Mary, and become a respected attorney and an owner of enslaved people.

In 1788, Marshall helped James Madison convince Virginians to ratify the U.S. Constitution. He later served in Congress and became secretary of state under President John Adams, who appointed him chief justice of the Supreme Court early in 1801. Over the next three decades, Marshall almost single-handedly made the Court supreme, making it equal to the presidency and Congress in legitimacy and authority. Blessed with a keen intellect and an analytical mind, Marshall was a lifelong critic of Jefferson, whom he considered a war-shirking aristocrat who prized states' rights over the national government.

As the new president, Jefferson preferred a weak Supreme Court and feared centralized authority. John Marshall, however, sought to create a Supreme Court powerful enough to constrain the president and Congress. He worried that if Jefferson followed the desires of the radical democrats in the Republican party, "much calamity" would result. To avoid such a disaster, Marshall resolved to strengthen the young republic's judiciary system so as to ensure that the national government, rather than the states, remained supreme. He succeeded beyond everyone's expectations.

***Marbury v. Madison* (1803)** First Supreme Court decision to declare a federal law—the Judiciary Act of 1789—unconstitutional ("judicial review").

By the time Marshall completed thirty-four years on the Supreme Court (1801–1835), he had issued landmark decisions that made it the most powerful court in the world, distinctive for its emphasis on protecting individual rights while insisting upon the supremacy of the national government over the states. "Our Constitution is not a compact" of states, Marshall affirmed. "It is the act of [the] people of the United States." (Abraham Lincoln would make the same point in 1861 in denying the right of states to secede from the Union.)

The Marbury case involved the appointment of Maryland Federalist William Marbury as justice of the peace in the District of Columbia. Marbury's letter of appointment (called a commission), signed by President John Adams two days before he left office, was still undelivered when James Madison took office as secretary of state, and President Jefferson directed Madison to withhold it. Marbury then sued for a court order directing Madison to deliver his commission.

In the unanimous ruling, Marshall and the Court held that Marbury deserved his judgeship. Marshall, however, denied that the Court had jurisdiction in the case. The Federal Judiciary Act of 1789, which gave the Court authority in such proceedings, was unconstitutional, Marshall ruled, because the Constitution specified that the Court should have original jurisdiction only in cases involving foreign ambassadors or nations. The Court, therefore, could issue no order in the case.

With one bold stroke, Marshall had elevated the stature of the Court by reprimanding Jefferson while avoiding an awkward confrontation with an administration that might have defied his order. More important, the ruling subtly struck down a federal law, the Judiciary Act of 1789, because it violated provisions of the Constitution, the "fundamental and paramount law of the nation." Marshall stressed that the Supreme Court was "emphatically" empowered "to say what the law is," even if it meant overruling both Congress and the president.

Judicial review

The *Marbury* decision granted the Supreme Court a power not mentioned in the Constitution: the right of *judicial review,* whereby the Court determines whether acts of Congress (and the presidency) are constitutional. Marshall established that the Supreme Court was the final authority in all constitutional interpretations. Jefferson fumed over the ruling. Giving judges "the right to decide which laws are constitutional, and what not," he wrote Abigail Adams, "would make the judiciary a despotic branch."

Jefferson, however, would lose that argument. Although the Court did not declare another federal law unconstitutional for fifty-four years, it has since struck down more than 150 acts of Congress and more than 1,100 "unconstitutional" acts of state legislatures, all in an effort to protect individual liberties and civil rights. Marshall essentially created American constitutional law, making the unelected, life-tenured justices of the Supreme Court more-effective allies of a strong national government than even the framers had imagined.

Jefferson's Economic Policies

President Jefferson's first term included several triumphs. Surprisingly, he did not dismantle Alexander Hamilton's Federalist economic program, in part because he never could understand the logic of its elements. Instead, following the advice of Secretary of the Treasury Albert Gallatin, Jefferson learned to accept the national bank as essential to economic growth.

Jefferson, however, rejected Hamilton's argument that a federal debt was a national "blessing" because it gave bankers and investors who bought government bonds a financial stake in the success of the new republic. If the debt were not eliminated, Jefferson told Gallatin, "we shall be committed to the English career of debt, corruption, and rottenness, closing with revolution."

Limits on federal spending

To pay down the debt, Jefferson slashed the federal budget. He fired all federal tax collectors and cut the military budget in half, saying that state militias provided adequate protection against foreign enemies. Jefferson's was the first national government in history to *reduce* its own scope and power, leading a stunned Alexander Hamilton to snort, "What a poor starving system of administering a government!"

Jefferson and Gallatin also repealed the whiskey tax that Hamilton and George Washington had implemented in 1791, but the nation's prosperous economy helped the federal budget absorb the loss of the whiskey taxes. In addition, revenues from federal tariffs on imports rose with the growing European trade, and the sale of government-owned western lands soared as Americans streamed westward.

Western Expansion

Jefferson's focus on western expansion

Where Alexander Hamilton always faced east, looking to Great Britain for his model of national greatness, Thomas Jefferson looked to the west for his inspiration. Only by expanding westward, he believed, could America avoid the social turmoil and misery common in the cities of Europe—and remain a nation primarily of self-sufficient farmers. Ohio's admission to the Union in 1803 increased the number of states to seventeen. Government land sales west of the Appalachian Mountains skyrocketed as settlers shoved Indians aside and established homesteads. Jefferson, however, wanted even more western territory, and in 1803, a stroke of good fortune allowed him to double the new nation's size.

The Louisiana Purchase

In 1801, American diplomats in Europe heard rumors that Spain had been forced to transfer its huge Louisiana province back to France, now led by Napoléon Bonaparte. Short of stature but a giant on the battlefield, Napoléon was a military genius, the most feared ruler in the world, and conqueror of Egypt and Italy. After taking control of the French government in 1799, Napoléon set out to restore his country's North American empire (Canada and Louisiana) that had been lost to Great Britain in 1763. Napoléon left no doubt about his ultimate goal. He wanted, he boasted, "to rule the world. Who wouldn't in my place?"

THE CESSION OF NEW ORLEANS The United States purchased the Louisiana Territory from Napoléon in 1803, effectively doubling the nation's size. In this contemporary watercolor, the French flag is raised over the city of New Orleans one final time, soon to be replaced with the American flag. **Why was the city of New Orleans an important acquisition for the United States?**

The threat of Napoleonic France

President Jefferson labeled Napoléon a "scoundrel" who would become "a gigantic force" threatening the United States. Napoleonic France in control of the Mississippi River Valley would lead to "eternal friction" and eventually war. To prevent France from seizing the Mississippi River, Jefferson sent New Yorker Robert R. Livingston to Paris in 1801 as ambassador to France. Livingston's primary objective was to acquire from France the strategic port city of New Orleans, situated at the mouth of the Mississippi River. Jefferson told Livingston that "the day that France takes possession of New Orleans, . . . we must marry ourselves to the British fleet and nation" for protection.

Over the years, New Orleans had become a dynamic crossroads where some 50,000 people of different nationalities intermingled, garnering huge profits from the vast amount of goods floating down the Mississippi to the Gulf of Mexico. For years, Americans living in Tennessee and Kentucky had threatened to secede if the federal government did not ensure that they could send their crops and goods downriver to New Orleans.

In early 1803, Jefferson grew so concerned about the stalled negotiations in Paris that he sent Virginian James Monroe, his trusted friend, to assist the sixty-six-year-old Livingston. No sooner had Monroe arrived than Napoléon surprisingly offered to sell not just New Orleans but *all* of the immense, unmapped Louisiana Territory, from the Mississippi River west to the Rocky Mountains and from the Canadian border south to the Gulf of Mexico.

Touissaint L'Ouverture and his successful slave rebellion

The unpredictable Napoléon had reversed himself because his large army on the Caribbean island of Saint-Domingue (Haiti) had been decimated by epidemics of malaria and yellow fever. The colony also experienced a massive slave revolt in 1791 led by Toussaint L'Ouverture, a charismatic Black revolutionary who had proclaimed independence from France and the creation of the Republic of Haiti, the world's leading producer of sugar and coffee.

It was the first successful rebellion by enslaved people in history, and although it was in Haiti, the event panicked slaveholders in the southern states who feared that news of the revolt would spread to America. Between 1791 and 1793, southern planters sent arms, ammunition, and money to Haiti to help French forces put down the insurrection. Amid the turmoil, some 16,000 Black refugees from Haiti immigrated to the United States, and their arrival stoked fears of anti-slavery uprisings led by "French negroes" serving as "agents of rebellion." Such concerns explain why the U.S. government refused to allow Americans to do business in Haiti and did not even recognize Haiti's independence until 1862.

After losing more than 24,000 soldiers to disease and warfare, Napoléon decided to cut his losses by selling the entire Louisiana Territory to the United States and using the proceeds to finance his "inevitable" next war with Great Britain.

The Louisiana Purchase

On May 2, 1803, the United States agreed to pay $15 million (3¢ an acre) for the entire Louisiana Territory. A delighted Livingston said that "from this day the United States take their place among the powers of the first rank." He called the land transfer the "noblest work of our whole lives."

The arrival of the signed treaty in Washington, D.C., presented President Jefferson with a political dilemma. Nowhere did the Constitution mention the purchase of territory. Was such an action legal?

In the end, Jefferson's desire to double the size of the republic trumped his concerns about an unconstitutional exercise of executive power. Acquiring the Louisiana Territory, the president explained, would promote "the peace and security of the nation in general" by removing the French threat and creating a protective buffer separating the United States from the rest of the world. Jefferson also imagined that the distant region might be a place to relocate Indian nations or freed Blacks, since he feared the possibility of America becoming a multiracial society.

Opposition from the Federalists

New England Federalists strongly opposed the purchase. Fisher Ames of Massachusetts argued that the Louisiana Territory was a "wilderness unpeopled with any beings except wolves and wandering Indians." Ames and others feared that adding the vast territory would weaken New England and the Federalist party, since the new western states were likely to be settled by wage laborers from New England seeking cheap land and by southern slaveholders, all of whom were Jeffersonian Republicans. As a newspaper editorialized, "Will [Jefferson and the] Republicans, who glory in their sacred regard to the rights of human nature, purchase an *immense wilderness* for the purpose of cultivating it with the labor of slaves?"

In a reversal of traditional stances, Federalists found themselves arguing for strict construction of the Constitution in opposing the Louisiana

Louisiana Purchase (1803) President Thomas Jefferson's purchase of the Louisiana Territory from France for $15 million, doubling the size of U.S. territory.

Lewis and Clark expedition (1804–1806) Led by Meriwether Lewis and William Clark, a mission to the Pacific coast commissioned for the purposes of scientific and geographical exploration.

Purchase. "We are to give money of which we have too little for land of which we already have too much," argued a Bostonian in the *Columbian Centinel*.

Eager to close the deal, Jefferson called a special session of Congress on October 17, 1803, at which the Senate ratified the treaty by a vote of 26–6. On December 20, 1803, U.S. officials took formal possession of the Louisiana Territory. The purchase included 875,000 square miles of land (529,402,880 acres). Six states in their entirety, and most or part of nine more, would be carved out of the Louisiana Purchase, from Louisiana north to Minnesota and west to Montana.

The **Louisiana Purchase** was the most significant event of Jefferson's presidency and one of the most important developments in American history. It spurred western exploration and expansion, and it enticed cotton growers to settle in the Old Southwest—Alabama, Mississippi, and Louisiana.

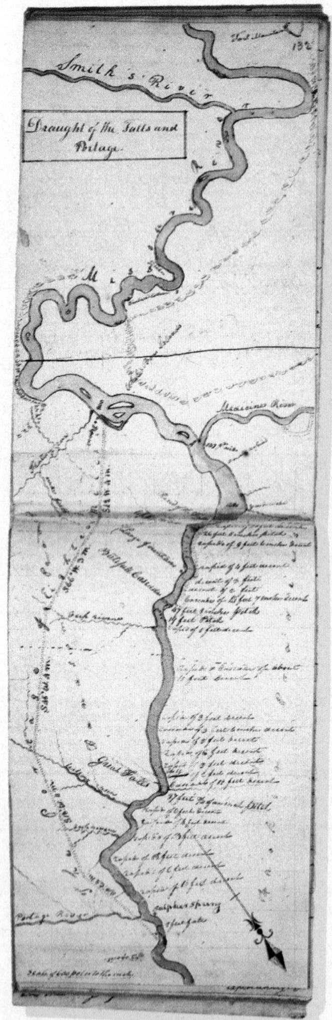

A MAP OF LEWIS AND CLARK'S JOURNEY In their journals, Lewis and Clark sketched detailed maps of previously unexplored regions, such as this one.

The Lewis and Clark Expedition (1804–1806)

To learn more about the Louisiana Territory and its prospects for trade and agriculture, Jefferson asked Congress to fund an expedition to find the most "practicable water communication across this continent." The president then appointed army captains Meriwether Lewis and William Clark to lead what came to be known as the **Lewis and Clark expedition**. The twenty-nine-year-old Lewis was Jefferson's private secretary. Jefferson admired his "boldness, enterprise, and discretion." The thirty-three-year-old Clark, from Louisville, Kentucky, was an accomplished frontiersman and "as brave as Caesar."

On a rainy May morning in 1804, Lewis and Clark's "Corps of Discovery," numbering about thirty "stout" men, set out from Wood River, a village near the former French town of St. Louis. They traveled in two large dugout canoes (called *pirogues*) and one large, flat-bottomed, single-masted keelboat filled with food, weapons, medicine, and gifts for the Indians. They traveled up the Mississippi to the Missouri River, the longest river in North America, where they added a dozen more men before proceeding. Unsure of where they were going and what or whom they might encounter, they were eager to discover if the Missouri made its way to the Pacific Ocean.

Six months later, near the Mandan Sioux villages in what would become Bismarck, North Dakota, the Corps of Discovery built Fort Mandan and wintered in relative comfort, sending downriver a barge loaded with maps and soil samples; the skins and skeletons of weasels, wolves, and antelope; and live specimens of prairie dogs and magpies, previously unknown in America.

In the spring of 1805, the Corps of Discovery added two guides: a French fur trader and his remarkable wife, a Shoshone woman named Sacagawea ("Bird Woman"), barely sixteen years old. In appreciation for Lewis and Clark's help in delivering her baby boy, Baptiste, Sacagawea provided crucial assistance as a guide, translator, and negotiator as they explored the Upper Missouri and encountered Native Americans, most of whom were "hospitable, honest, and sincere people."

From Fort Mandan, the adventurers crossed the Rocky Mountains and descended the Snake and Columbia Rivers to the Pacific Ocean, where they arrived in November. Near the future site of Astoria, Oregon, at the mouth of the Columbia River, they built Fort Clatsop, where they spent a cold, rainy winter.

In 1806 they headed back to St. Louis, having been forced to eat their dogs and horses. They had weathered blizzards, broiling sun, fierce rapids, pelting hail, grizzly bears, injuries, illnesses, and swarms of mosquitos. "I have been wet and as cold in every part as I ever was in my life," Clark noted. "Indeed I was at one time fearful my feet would freeze in the thin moccasins which I wore." Only one member of the group died, and that was because of a ruptured appendix.

The expedition, which lasted twenty-eight months and covered some 8,000 miles, returned with extensive journals that described their experiences and observations while detailing some 180 plants and 125 animals. Their splendid maps attracted traders and trappers to the region and led the United States to claim the Oregon Country (the entire Pacific Northwest) by right of discovery and exploration. Based on information from Lewis and Clark as well as other reports, Jefferson decided that the Native Americans living in the Louisiana Territory were as "incapable of self-government as children." Therefore, rather than follow the steps outlined in the Northwest Ordinance, Jefferson created a military government to rule the region until enough Americans had arrived to govern for themselves.

SACAGAWEA Sacagawea's services as a guide and translator were invaluable to Lewis and Clark's expedition. Of the many memorials devoted to Sacagawea, this statue by artist Alice Cooper was unveiled at the 1905 Lewis and Clark Centennial Exposition in the presence of several more pioneering women, including feminist Susan B. Anthony.

Political Schemes

The Lewis and Clark expedition and the Louisiana Purchase strengthened Thomas Jefferson's already solid support in the South and West. In New England, however, Federalists panicked because they assumed that new states carved out of the Louisiana Territory would be dominated by Jeffersonian Republicans.

To protect their interests, the Federalists hatched a scheme to link New York politically to New England by trying to elect Vice President Aaron Burr, Jefferson's ambitious Republican rival, as governor of New York. Burr chose to drop his Republican affiliation and run as an independent candidate.

EXPLORATIONS OF THE LOUISIANA PURCHASE, 1804–1807

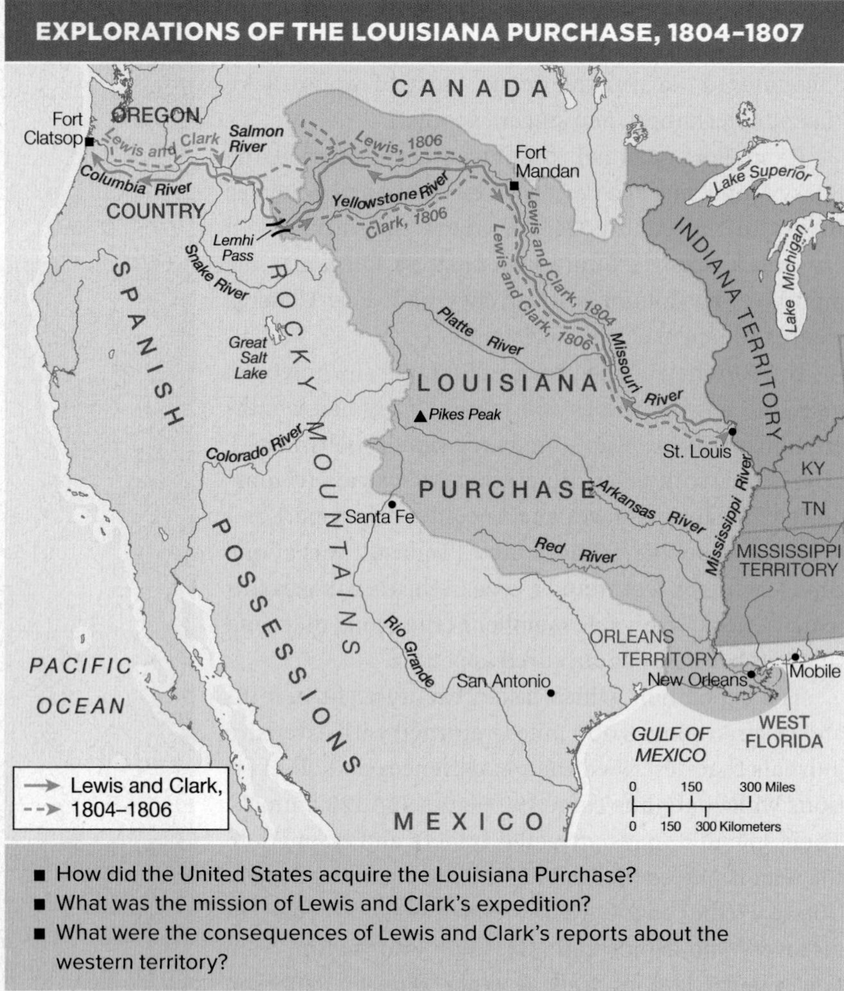

- How did the United States acquire the Louisiana Purchase?
- What was the mission of Lewis and Clark's expedition?
- What were the consequences of Lewis and Clark's reports about the western territory?

Several leading Federalists opposed the scheme, however. Alexander Hamilton urged Federalists not to vote for Burr, calling him a "dangerous" and "unprincipled" man "who ought not to be trusted with the reins of government."

The Burr-Hamilton duel

Burr ended up losing to the Republican candidate, who had been endorsed by Jefferson. A furious Burr blamed Hamilton for his defeat and challenged him to a duel. Burr had already been involved in three duels, while Hamilton had been to the brink of dueling ten times, but all those feuds had ended without combat. This time would prove different, however.

At dawn on July 11, 1804, the men met near Weehawken, New Jersey, on a ledge overlooking the Hudson River above New York City. Hamilton, whose oldest son, Philip, just nineteen, had been killed in a duel at the same location, fired first but intentionally missed ("threw away his shot") as a demonstration of his religious and moral principles.

Vice President Burr showed no such scruples. His shot struck Hamilton four inches above the hip; the bullet ripped through his ribs and liver before lodging in his spine. He died the next day, in his forty-seventh year. Charged with murder, Burr fled in disgrace to South Carolina, where his daughter lived, and later retreated to Europe.

Jefferson Reelected

In the meantime, the presidential campaign of 1804 began. A congressional caucus of Republicans renominated Jefferson and chose George Clinton of New York as the vice presidential candidate. To avoid the problems associated with parties running multiple candidates for the presidency, in 1803, Congress had ratified the Twelfth Amendment to the Constitution, stipulating that the members of the Electoral College must use separate ballots to vote for the president and vice president. Given Jefferson's first-term achievements, the Federalist candidate, South Carolinian Charles C. Pinckney, never had a chance. Jefferson had accomplished much: the Louisiana Purchase, a prosperous economy, and a reduction of both the federal government and the national debt. A Massachusetts Republican claimed that the United States was "never more respected abroad. The people were never more happy at home." Jefferson won 162 of 176 electoral votes.

The Burr Conspiracy

Meanwhile, Aaron Burr continued to connive and scheme. After the controversy over his duel with Alexander Hamilton subsided, he tried to carve out his own personal empire in the West. What came to be known as the Burr Conspiracy was hatched when Burr and General James Wilkinson, an old friend then serving as senior general of the U.S. Army and the self-serving, conniving governor of the Louisiana Territory, plotted to use a well-armed force of volunteers to separate part of lower Mississippi River Valley from the Union. They then planned to declare it an independent republic, with New Orleans as its capital and Burr as its ruler. Burr claimed that "the people of the western country were ready for revolt."

AARON BURR Burr graduated from what is now Princeton University at the age of sixteen, where he studied theology. After the United States gained its independence, Burr changed his focus to law, a profession he would return to after his failed conspiracy to take control of the Louisiana Territory ruined his hopes of government service.

In late 1806, Burr floated down the Ohio and Mississippi Rivers toward New Orleans with 100 volunteers, only to have Wilkinson turn on him and alert Jefferson to the scheme. The president ordered that Burr be arrested. Militiamen captured Burr in February 1807 and took him to Richmond, Virginia, where, in August, he was tried for treason before Supreme Court Chief Justice John Marshall.

Jefferson was hell-bent on seeing Burr hanged, claiming that he had tried to separate "the western states from us, of adding Mexico to them, and of placing himself at their head." In the end, however, Burr was acquitted because of a lack of evidence. Marshall had instructed the jury that a verdict of treason required an "act of war" against the United States confirmed by at least two witnesses.

Jefferson was disgusted. He charged that Marshall had bent the law "to twist Burr's neck out of the halter of treason." The president considered

SLAVERY'S ENDURANCE IN SOUTH CAROLINA Enslaved men, women, and children on a South Carolina plantation gathered for a photograph in 1862—a reminder of slavery's persistence in some parts of the United States decades after the bill outlawing the importation of enslaved people.

proposing a constitutional amendment to limit the power of the judiciary and even thought about asking Congress to impeach Marshall. In the end, however, he did nothing. With further charges pending, Burr skipped bail and took refuge first in England, then in France. He returned to America in 1812 and resumed practicing law in New York.

Ending the Transatlantic Slave Trade

In addition to shrinking the federal budget and reducing the national debt, Jefferson signed a landmark bill in 1808 that outlawed the importation of enslaved Africans into the United States. This came about in part because southerners had come to believe that captive African-born laborers were more prone to revolt. The new law took effect on January 1, 1808, the earliest date possible under the Constitution. At the time, South Carolina was the only state that still permitted the purchase of imported enslaved Africans. For years to come, however, illegal global trafficking in African people would continue.

CORE **OBJECTIVE**

2. Describe how foreign events affected the United States during the Jefferson and Madison administrations.

War in the Mediterranean and Europe

The Barbary Pirates

Upon assuming the presidency, Jefferson promised "peace, commerce, and honest friendship with all nations," but some countries preferred war. On the Barbary Coast of North Africa, the Islamic rulers of Morocco, Algiers,

Tunis, and Tripoli had for centuries preyed upon unarmed European and American merchant ships. The U.S. government made numerous blackmail payments to the **Barbary pirates** in exchange for captured American merchant ships and crews.

In 1801, however, the ruler of Tripoli upped his blackmail demands and declared war on the United States. Jefferson sent warships to blockade Tripoli, and a sporadic naval war dragged on until 1805, punctuated in 1804 by the notable exploits of Lieutenant Stephen Decatur, who slipped into Tripoli Harbor by night and set fire to the frigate *Philadelphia*, which had been captured after it ran aground.

BURNING OF THE FRIGATE *PHILADELPHIA* Lieutenant Stephen Decatur set fire to the captured *Philadelphia* during the United States' standoff with Tripoli over the enslavement of American sailors. **Why was the United States at war with Tripoli?**

A force of U.S. Marines marched 500 miles across the desert to assault Derna, Tripoli's second largest town, a feat highlighted in the Marine Corps hymn ("to the shores of Tripoli"). The Tripoli ruler finally agreed to a $60,000 ransom and released the *Philadelphia*'s crew. It was still blackmail (called "tribute" in the nineteenth century), but markedly less than the $300,000 the pirates had demanded and much less than the cost of an outright war.

Naval Harassment by Britain and France

In the spring of 1803, soon after completing the sale of Louisiana to America, Napoléon Bonaparte declared war on Great Britain. The conflict would last eleven years and eventually involve all of Europe. Most Americans wanted to remain neutral, but the British and French were determined to keep that from happening. During 1805, the European war reached a stalemate: the French army controlled most of Europe, and the British navy dominated the seas. Both nations were locked in a death struggle that led them to take extreme acts.

In May 1806, Britain issued a series of declarations called Orders in Council that imposed a naval blockade of the European coast to prevent merchant ships from other nations, including the United States, from making port in France. Although British leaders recognized America's independence in principle, they were eager to humble and humiliate the upstart republic by asserting their dominance over Atlantic trade.

Soon British warships began seizing American merchant ships bound for France. Congress responded by passing the Non-Importation Act, which banned the importation of British goods.

Barbary pirates North Africans who waged war (1801–1805) on the United States after Jefferson refused to pay tribute (a bribe) to protect American ships.

In early 1807, Napoléon announced that French warships would blockade the ports of Great Britain. The British responded that they would no longer allow foreign ships to trade with the French-controlled islands in the Caribbean. Soon thereafter, British warships appeared along the American coast and began searching U.S. merchant vessels as they headed for the Caribbean or Europe.

American merchant ships caught in the crossfire of French and British war

The tense situation posed a dilemma for American shippers. If they agreed to British demands to stop trading with the French, the French would retaliate by seizing U.S. vessels headed to and from Great Britain. If they agreed to French demands that they stop trading with the British, the British would seize American ships headed to and from France. Some American merchants decided to risk becoming victims of the Anglo-French war—and many paid a high price for their pursuit of overseas profits. During 1807, British and French warships captured hundreds of American ships.

Impressment

British impressment

For American sailors, the danger on the high seas was heightened by the practice of *impressment*, whereby British warships stopped U.S. vessels, boarded them, and kidnapped sailors they claimed were British citizens. American merchant ships attracted British deserters because they paid more than twice as much as did the Royal Navy. Fully half the sailors on American ships, about 9,000 men, had been born in Britain. The British often did not bother to determine the citizenship of those they "impressed" into service. Between 1803 and 1811, some 6,200 American sailors were "impressed" into the British navy.

The *Chesapeake* Incident (1807)

The crisis boiled over on June 22, 1807, when the British warship HMS *Leopard* stopped a smaller U.S. vessel, the *Chesapeake*, eight miles off the Virginia coast. After the *Chesapeake*'s captain refused to allow the British to search his ship for English deserters, the *Leopard* opened fire without warning, killing three Americans and wounding eighteen. A search party then boarded the *Chesapeake* and seized four men, one of whom, an English deserter, was hanged.

PREPARATION FOR WAR TO DEFEND COMMERCE
Shipbuilders, like those pictured here constructing the *Philadelphia*, played an important role in the war efforts against America's many rivals.

The attack was both an act of war and a national insult. Public anger was so great that President Jefferson could have declared war on the spot. "We have never, on any occasion, witnessed . . . such a thirst for revenge," the *Washington Federalist* reported. In early July, Jefferson banned all British warships from American waters. He also called on state governors to mobilize their militias. Like John Adams before him, however, Jefferson resisted war fever, in part because the undersized

U.S. Army and Navy were not prepared to fight. Jefferson's caution outraged his critics.

The Embargo Act (1807)

Unwilling to ignite a war, President Jefferson decided to use "peaceable coercion" to force Britain and France to stop violating American rights. Late in 1807, he convinced enough Republicans in Congress to cut off *all* American foreign trade. As Jefferson said, his choices were "war, embargo, or nothing."

OGRABME, OR, THE AMERICAN SNAPPING-TURTLE A merchant trying to trade with the British is held back by a so-called Ograbme (*embargo* spelled backward) in this political cartoon from 1807. **Why was Jefferson's Embargo Act so unpopular?**

The unprecedented **Embargo Act** (December 1807) stopped all American exports by prohibiting U.S. ships from sailing to foreign ports to "keep our ships and seamen out of harm's way." Jefferson and his secretary of state, James Madison, mistakenly assumed that the embargo would force the warring European nations to quit violating American rights. But neither the French nor the British were intimidated by the loss of trade with America.

What the embargo did achieve was the destruction of the U.S. economy. With each passing month, the loss of foreign markets devastated the economy while reviving the political appeal of the Federalists, especially in New England, where merchants howled because the embargo cut off their primary industry: oceangoing commerce. The value of U.S. exports plummeted from $48 million in 1807 to $9 million a year later, and federal revenue from tariffs plunged from $18 million to $8 million. Shipbuilding declined by two-thirds, and farmers and planters in the South and West saw prices for their exported crops cut in half.

The Embargo Act's toll on the U.S. economy

New England's once-thriving port cities became ghost towns; thousands of ships and sailors were out of work. Meanwhile, smuggling soared, especially along the border with British Canada. Americans raged at what critics called "Jefferson's embargo." One letter writer told the president that he had paid four friends "to shoot you if you don't take off the embargo," while another addressed the president as "you red-headed son of a bitch."

The embargo turned American politics upside down. To enforce it, Jefferson, once the leading advocate for *reducing* the power of the federal government, now found himself *expanding* federal power. In effect, the United States used its own warships to blockade its own ports. Jefferson even activated the New York state militia in an effort to stop smuggling across the Canadian border.

Congress finally voted 70–0 to end the embargo effective March 4, 1809, the day the "splendid misery" of Jefferson's second presidential term ended. A dejected Jefferson left the presidency feeling like a freed prisoner. No one, he said, could be more relieved "on shaking off the shackles of power."

Embargo Act (1807) A law promoted by President Thomas Jefferson prohibiting American ships from leaving for foreign ports, in order to safeguard them from British and French attacks. This ban on American exports proved disastrous to the U.S. economy.

Jefferson learned a hard lesson that many of his successors would also discover: a second presidential term is rarely as successful as the first. As

ANTI-JEFFERSON SENTIMENT This 1807 Federalist cartoon compares Washington *(left, flanked by a British lion and American eagle)* and Jefferson *(right, with a snake and a lizard)*. Below Jefferson are volumes of French philosophy, while Washington's volumes simply read: *Law*, *Order*, and *Religion*.

he admitted, "No man will ever carry out of that office the reputation which carried him into it."

In the election of 1808, the presidency passed to another prominent Virginian, Jefferson's secretary of state, James Madison. The Federalists, again backing Charles C. Pinckney of South Carolina and Rufus King of New York, won only 47 electoral votes to Madison's 122.

James Madison and the Drift to War

In his inaugural address, President Madison acknowledged that he inherited a situation "full of difficulties." He soon made things worse. Although Madison had been a talented legislator and the "Father of the Constitution," he proved to be a weak, indecisive chief executive. He was a persuader, not a commander.

Madison's sparkling wife, Dolley, was the only truly excellent member of the president's inner circle. Seventeen years younger than her husband, she was a superb First Lady who excelled at entertaining political leaders and foreign dignitaries. Journalists called her the "Queen of Washington City."

From the beginning, Madison's presidency was entangled in foreign affairs and crippled by his lack of executive experience. Madison and his advisers repeatedly overestimated the young republic's diplomatic leverage and military strength. The result was international humiliation.

Madison insisted on upholding the principle of freedom of the seas for the United States and other neutral nations, but he was unwilling to create a navy strong enough to enforce it. He continued the policy of "peaceable coercion" against the European nations, which was as ineffective for him as it had been for Jefferson.

In place of the disastrous embargo, Congress passed the Non-Intercourse Act (1809), which reopened trade with all countries *except* France and Great Britain and their colonies. It authorized the president to reopen trade with France or Great Britain if either should stop violating American rights on the high seas. In December 1810, France issued a vague promise to restore America's neutral rights, whereupon Madison gave Great Britain three months to do the same. The British refused, and the Royal Navy continued to seize American vessels, their cargoes, and crews.

The Non-Intercourse Act (1809)

A reluctant Madison asked Congress to declare war against the United Kingdom of Great Britain and Ireland on June 1, 1812. If the United States did not defend its maritime rights, he explained, then Americans were "not independent people, but colonists and vassals."

The congressional vote for war was the closest in American history. On June 5, the House of Representatives voted for war 79–49. Two weeks later, the Senate followed suit, 19–13. Every Federalist in Congress opposed "Mr. Madison's War," while 80 percent of Republicans supported it. The southern and western states wanted war; the New England states opposed it.

By declaring war, Madison and the Republicans hoped to unite the nation and discredit the Federalists. They also planned to end British-led Indian attacks along the Great Lakes and in the Ohio River Valley by invading British Canada. To generate popular support, Jefferson advised Madison that he needed, above all, "to stop Indian barbarities. The conquest of Canada will do this." Jefferson presumed that the French Canadians were eager to rise up against their British rulers. With their help, the Republicans predicted, American armies would conquer Britain's vast northern colony. It did not work out that way.

America declares war on Great Britain (1812)

The War of 1812

CORE **OBJECTIVE**

3. Explain the primary causes of the American decision to declare war on Great Britain in 1812.

The **War of 1812** marked the first time that Congress declared war. Great Britain was preoccupied with defeating Napoléon in Europe, and in fact, on June 16, 1812, it had promised to quit interfering with American shipping. President Madison and the Republicans, however, believed that only war would end the practice of impressment and stop British-inspired Indian attacks along the western frontier.

War of 1812 (1812–1815) Conflict fought in North America and at sea between Great Britain and the United States over American shipping rights and British-inspired Indian attacks on American settlements. Canadians and Native Americans also fought in the war on each side.

American Shipping Rights and National Honor

Why the United States chose to start the war is still debated by historians. Its main cause—the repeated British violations of American maritime rights and the practice of "impressing" sailors—dominated President Madison's war message. Most of the votes in Congress for war came from legislators representing rural regions where the economic interests

BRITISH IMPRESSMENT
Three American sailors are forced to abandon their ship and join the British forces in this contemporary print. This humiliating practice was common in the years before the War of 1812, and put merchant sailors at great risk. **How did Congress use impressment as one of its justifications for the war?**

of farmers and planters were being hurt by the raids on American merchant ships.

However, the representatives from the New England states, which bore the brunt of British attacks on U.S. shipping, voted 20–12 *against* the declaration of war. One explanation for this seeming inconsistency is that many Americans in the South and West, especially Tennessee, Kentucky, and South Carolina, voted for war because they believed America's national *honor* was at stake. Andrew Jackson, an anti-British Tennessean who was the state's first congressman, announced that he was eager to fight "for the re-establishment of our national character."

Native American Conflicts

Another factor leading to war was the growing number of British-inspired Indian attacks in the Ohio River Valley. The story took a new turn with the rise of two Shawnee leaders, Tecumseh and his half-brother, Tenskwatawa, who lived in a large village called Prophetstown on the Tippecanoe River in northern Indiana.

Born in 1768, Tecumseh ("Shooting Star") and his family had been forced to flee from invading armies five times between 1774 and 1782. By the 1790s, when Tecumseh became chief, his father and two brothers had been killed in battle and his nation was perennially threatened by starvation as the game animals in their ever-shrinking hunting grounds declined in number.

Tecumseh rallies the Native American nations against the Americans

Chief Tecumseh decided that the fate of the Indians depended on their diverse nations being unified. Tall and charismatic, Tecumseh hoped to create a single nation powerful enough, with British assistance, to fend off further American expansion.

His brother, Tenskwatawa (the "Open Door"), known as "the Prophet," gained a large following for his predictions that White Americans ("children of the devil") were on the verge of collapse. As a young man, Tenskwatawa had been a drunken ne'er-do-well, but he experienced a spiritual rebirth and became a charismatic spokesman for Indian resistance to the intrusion of American ways of life. Indians must, he stressed, abandon all things European: clothing, customs, Christianity, and especially liquor.

If they did so, the Great Spirit would reward them by turning the Whites' gunpowder to sand.

Inspired by his brother's spiritual message, Tecumseh traveled from Wisconsin to Alabama in an effort to form alliances with other Native American nations in 1811. In Alabama, he told a gathering of 5,000 Indians that they should "let the white race perish" because "they seize your land; they corrupt your women; they trample on the ashes of your dead!" The Whites "have driven us from the sea to the lakes," he noted. "We can go no further."

William Henry Harrison, governor of the Indiana Territory, met with Tecumseh twice and described him as "one of those uncommon geniuses who spring up occasionally to produce revolutions and overturn the established order of things." Yet in the fall of 1811, Harrison gathered 1,000 troops and advanced on Prophetstown.

What became the **Battle of Tippecanoe** was a disastrous defeat for the Native Americans, as Harrison's troops burned the village and destroyed its supplies. **Tecumseh's Indian Confederacy** went up in smoke, and he fled to Canada.

TECUMSEH A leader of the Shawnee, Tecumseh tried to unite Native American nations in opposition to European culture and in defense of their ancestral lands; he was later killed in 1813 at the Battle of the Thames.

The Lust for Canada and Florida

Some Americans demanded war with Great Britain because they wanted to seize British Canada. That there were nearly 8 million Americans and only 300,000 Canadians led many to believe that doing so would be quick and easy. Thomas Jefferson, for instance, wrote President Madison that the "acquisition of Canada" was simply a "matter of marching" north with a military force.

The British were also vulnerable far to the south. East Florida, which had returned to Spain's control in 1783, posed a threat because Spain was too weak, or too unwilling, to prevent Indian attacks across the border with Georgia. In the absence of a strong Spanish presence, British agents and traders remained in East Florida, smuggling goods and conspiring with Indians against Americans. Spanish Florida had also long been a haven for freedom-seeking enslaved people who had managed to flee enslavement in Georgia and South Carolina. Many Americans living along the Florida-Georgia border hoped that war would enable them to oust both the British and the Spanish from Florida.

Battle of Tippecanoe (1811) Battle in northern Indiana between U.S. troops and Native American warriors led by prophet Tenskwatawa, the half-brother of Tecumseh.

Tecumseh's Indian Confederacy A group of Native American nations under leadership of Shawnees Tecumseh and Tenskwatawa; its mission of fighting off American expansion was thwarted at the Battle of Tippecanoe (1811), when the Confederacy fell apart.

War Fever

In the Congress that assembled in late 1811, anti-British representatives from southern and western districts shouted for war to defend "national honor" and rid the Northwest of the "Indian problem" by invading Canada. Among the most vocal "war hawks" were Henry Clay of Kentucky and John C. Calhoun of South Carolina. Clay, the brash young Speaker of the House, was "for resistance by the *sword*." His bravado inspired others. "I don't like Henry Clay," Calhoun said. "He is a bad man, an imposter, a creator of wicked

The "war hawks" defend the war and America's national honor

schemes. I wouldn't speak to him, but, by God, I love him" for wanting war against Britain. When Calhoun learned that President Madison had finally decided on war, he threw his arms around Clay's neck and led his colleagues in a mock Indian war dance.

In New England and much of New York, however, there was little enthusiasm for war because military conflict would cripple the region's shipping industry. Both Massachusetts and Connecticut refused to send soldiers to fight, and merchants openly sold supplies to British troops in Canada.

War Preparations

Problems financing the war

One thing was certain: the United States was woefully unprepared for war, both financially and militarily, and James Madison lacked the leadership ability and physical stature to inspire public confidence and military resolve. The national economy was weak, too. In 1811, Republicans had let the charter of the Bank of the United States (B.U.S.) expire. Many Republican congressmen owned shares in state banks and wanted the B.U.S. dissolved because it both competed with and regulated the local banks. Once the B.U.S. shut down, however, the number of unregulated state banks mushroomed, all with their own forms of currency, creating commercial chaos.

Once war began, it did not go well. The British navy blockaded American ports, which caused federal tariff revenues to tumble. In March 1813, Treasury Secretary Albert Gallatin warned Madison that the United States had "hardly enough money to last till the end of the month." Furthermore, Republicans in Congress delayed approving tax increases needed to finance the war.

Problems with army recruitment

The military situation was almost as bad. In 1812, the British had 250,000 professional soldiers and the most powerful navy in the world. By contrast, the U.S. Army numbered only 3,287 ill-trained and poorly equipped men, led by mostly incompetent officers with little combat experience. In January 1812, Congress authorized an army of 35,000 men, but a year later, just 18,500 had been recruited—many of them Irish American immigrants who hated the English and were enticed to enlist by congressional promises of cash and land.

Madison, who refused to allow free Blacks or enslaved people to serve in the army, had to plead with state governors to provide militiamen, only to have the Federalist governors in anti-war New England decline. The British, on the other hand, had thousands of soldiers stationed in Canada and the West Indies, and they recruited more Native American allies than did the Americans.

The U.S. Navy was in better shape than the army, but it had only 16 warships compared with Britain's 600. The lopsided military strength of the British led Madison to mutter that the United States was in "an embarrassing situation."

A Continental War

For these reasons and more, the War of 1812 was one of the strangest conflicts in history. In fact, it was three wars fought on three fronts. One theater was the Chesapeake Bay along the coast of Maryland and Virginia, including

Washington, D.C. The second was in the South—Alabama, Mississippi, and West and East Florida—where American forces led by Andrew Jackson invaded lands owned by the Creeks and the Spanish. The third front might be more accurately called the Canadian-American War. It began in what is now northern Indiana and Ohio, southeastern Michigan, and the contested border regions around the Great Lakes. The fighting raged back and forth across the border as the United States repeatedly invaded British Canada, only to be repulsed.

U.S. NAVAL VICTORIES
In this cartoon, John Bull (the personification of England) is "stung to agony" by *Wasp* and *Hornet*, two American ships that clinched early victories in the War of 1812.

The War in the North

The War of 1812, often called America's second war for independence, was a civil war. Canadians, thousands of whom were former American Loyalists who had fled north after the Revolutionary War, remained loyal to the British Empire, while Americans and a few French Canadians and Irish Canadians sought to push Britain out of North America and annex Canada. In some cases, Americans fought former Americans, including families that were divided in their allegiances. Siblings even shot each other. Once, after killing an American militiaman, a Canadian soldier began taking the clothes off the corpse, only to realize that it was his brother. He grumbled that it served him right to have died for a bad cause.

Indians armed by the British dominated the wooded borderlands around the Great Lakes. Michigan's governor recognized that "the British cannot hold Upper Canada [Ontario] without the assistance of the Indians," but the "Indians cannot conduct a war without the assistance of a civilized nation [Great Britain]." So the American assault on Canada involved attacking Indians, Canadians, and British soldiers.

Invading Canada

President Madison approved a three-pronged plan for the invasion of British Canada. It called for one army to move north through upstate New York, along Lake Champlain, to take Montreal, while another was to advance into Upper Canada by crossing the Niagara River between Lakes Ontario and Erie. The third attack would come from the west, with an American force moving east into Upper Canada from Detroit, Michigan. The plan was to have all three attacks begin at the same time to force the British troops in Canada to split up.

Initial failures in the invasion of Canada

The plan, however, was a disaster. The underfunded and undermanned Americans could barely field one army, much less three, and communication was spotty at best. In July 1812, General William Hull, a Revolutionary War veteran and governor of the Michigan Territory, marched his ragtag army across the Detroit River into Canada. He told the Canadians that he had come to free them from British "tyranny and oppression."

The Canadians, however, did not want to be liberated, and the Americans were soon pushed back to Detroit by British troops, Canadian militiamen, and their Indian allies.

THE BATTLE OF QUEENSTON HEIGHTS The artist John David Kelly rendered the devastating American defeat at the Battle of Queenston Heights in this late nineteenth-century painting. The British can be seen in the foreground, fighting alongside Canadian militiamen and their Native American allies against the American forces. **What factors foiled Madison's plan to invade British Canada?**

Hull, tricked by the British commander's threats to unleash thousands of Indian warriors, did the unthinkable: he surrendered his entire force of 2,500 troops without firing a shot. His capitulation opened the western frontier to raids by British troops and their Canadian and Indian allies. President Madison felt humiliated. A Republican said General Hull must be a "traitor" or "nearly an idiot" or "part of both." Hull was eventually tried and sentenced to death. Although pardoned by Madison, he was dismissed from the army for his cowardice.

The second prong of the American plan, the assault on Montreal, never happened. The third prong began at dawn on October 13, 1812, when U.S. troops led by General Stephen Van Rensselaer rowed across the Niagara River from Lewiston, New York, to the Canadian village of Queenston, where they suffered a crushing defeat in the Battle of Queenston Heights. Almost a thousand U.S. soldiers were forced to surrender.

The losses in Canada led many Americans to lose hope. In early 1813, a Kentuckian warned that any more military disasters would result in "disunion" and that the "cause of Republicanism will be lost."

Then there was a glimmer of good news. In April 1813, Americans led by General Zebulon Pike attacked York (later renamed Toronto), the provincial capital of Upper Canada. The British and Canadian militiamen surrendered, and over the next several days, in part because Pike had been killed, the U.S. soldiers went on a rampage, plundering the city and burning government buildings.

After the torching of York, the Americans sought to gain naval control of the Great Lakes and other inland waterways along the Canadian border. If they could break the British naval supply line and secure Lake Erie, they could divide the British from their Indian allies.

Perry turns the tides in the north

In 1813, at Presque Isle, Pennsylvania, near Erie, twenty-eight-year-old Oliver Hazard Perry, the commander of U.S. forces, supervised the construction of warships from timber cut in nearby forests. By the end of the summer, Perry's new warships set out in search of the British, finally finding them at Lake Erie's Put-in-Bay on September 10. Two British warships pounded the *Lawrence*, Perry's flagship. After four hours, none of the *Lawrence*'s guns were working, and most crew members were dead or wounded. Perry refused to quit, however. He switched to another vessel, kept fighting, and, miraculously, ended up accepting the surrender of the entire British squadron. Hatless and bloodied, Perry famously reported, "We have met the enemy and they are ours."

The British were forced to evacuate Upper Canada. They gave up Detroit and were defeated at the Battle of the Thames in southern Canada on October 5, 1813. During the battle, the British fled, leaving the great chief Tecumseh and 500 warriors to face the wrath of the Americans. When Tecumseh was killed, the remaining Indians retreated. Perry's victory and the defeat

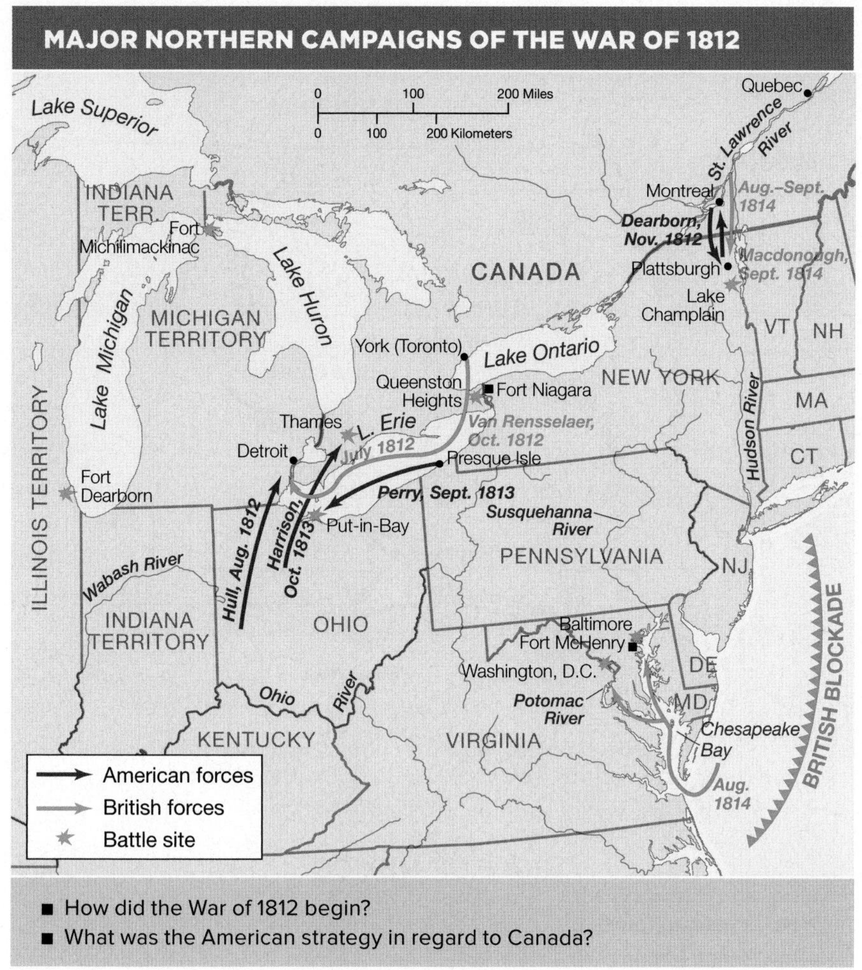

MAJOR NORTHERN CAMPAIGNS OF THE WAR OF 1812

- How did the War of 1812 begin?
- What was the American strategy in regard to Canada?

of Tecumseh enabled the Americans to recover control of most of Michigan and seize the Western District of Upper Canada. Thereafter, the war in the north lapsed into a military stalemate. (Tecumseh's legacy has lived on in the form of towns in five states named for him).

The Creek War

War also flared in the South in 1813. The Creek Nation consisted of several Indian groups that spoke different languages and had different customs. In the early nineteenth century, Creeks in western Georgia and Alabama had split into two factions: the Upper Creeks (called Red Sticks because of their bright-red war clubs), who opposed American expansion and sided with the British, and the Lower Creeks, who wanted to remain on good terms with the Americans. On August 30, Red Sticks attacked Fort Mims on the Alabama River and massacred hundreds of White and African American men, women, and children, as well as Lower Creeks.

Andrew Jackson's campaign in the south

Thirsting for revenge, Andrew Jackson, commanding general of the Army of West Tennessee, recruited about 2,500 volunteer militiamen and headed south. With him were David Crockett, a famous sharpshooter, and

MAJOR SOUTHERN CAMPAIGNS OF THE WAR OF 1812

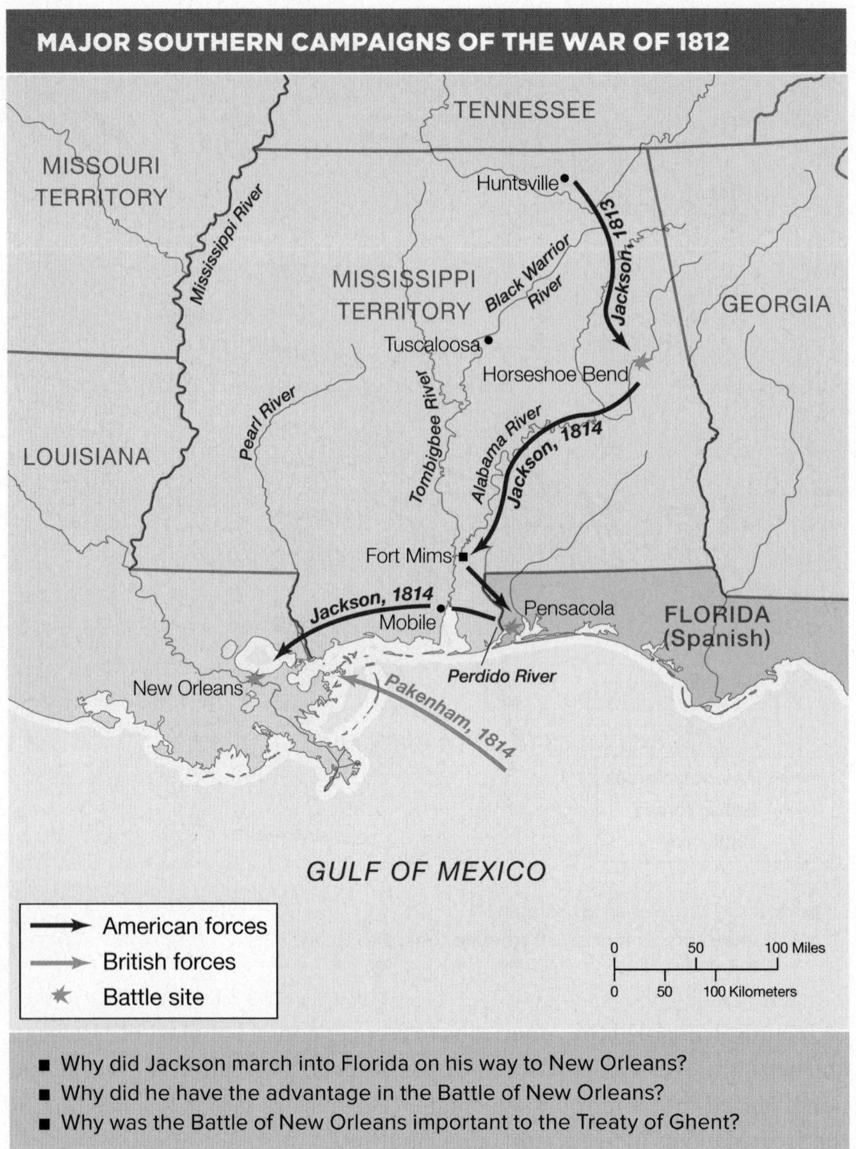

- Why did Jackson march into Florida on his way to New Orleans?
- Why did he have the advantage in the Battle of New Orleans?
- Why was the Battle of New Orleans important to the Treaty of Ghent?

Sam Houston, a nineteen-year-old Virginia frontiersman who would later lead the Texas War for Independence against Mexico.

Jackson was a natural warrior and gifted commander. His soldiers nicknamed him "Old Hickory" in recognition of his toughness. From a young age, he had gloried in violence and prospered by it. He told all "brave Tennesseans" that their "frontier [was] threatened with invasion by the savage foe" and that the Indians were advancing "with scalping knives unsheathed, to butcher your wives, your children, and your helpless babes. Time is not to be lost."

Jackson's expedition across Alabama was not easy. It was difficult to keep his men fed and supplied. Some of the men went home once their enlistment period ended. A few deserted or rebelled. When a seventeen-year-old soldier threatened an officer, he was tried and sentenced to death. Jackson had the young man shot in front of the rest of the army to demonstrate his steely determination to win the war. Jackson's grizzled volunteers crushed the Red Sticks in a series of bloodbaths.

The decisive battle in what came to be called the Creek War occurred on March 27, 1814, on a peninsula formed by the Horseshoe Bend on the Tallapoosa River. Jackson's soldiers, with crucial help from Cherokee and Creek allies, surrounded a Red Stick fort, set fire to it, and shot the Indians as they tried to escape. Nine hundred were killed, including 300 who drowned in a desperate effort to cross the river. Fewer than fifty of Jackson's soldiers were killed.

The Battle of Horseshoe Bend was the worst defeat ever inflicted upon Native Americans, and it effectively ended the Creeks' ability to wage war. With the Treaty of Fort Jackson, signed in August 1814, the Red Stick Creeks gave up two-thirds of their land—some 23 million acres—including southwest Georgia and much of Alabama. President Madison rewarded Jackson by naming him a major general in the regular U.S. Army.

Events in Europe soon took a dramatic turn when the British, Spanish, and Portuguese armies repelled French emperor Napoléon's attempt to conquer Spain and Portugal. Now free to focus on the American war, the British sent 16,000 soldiers to try yet again to invade America from Canada. The British navy also received reinforcement, enabling it to extend its blockade to New England ports and to bombard coastal towns from Delaware to Florida. The final piece of the British plan was to seize New Orleans and sever American access to the Mississippi River, the economic lifeline of the western states.

Fighting along the Chesapeake Bay

In February 1813, the British had more warships in the Chesapeake Bay than were in the entire U.S. Navy, and they frequently captured and burned U.S. merchant vessels. The British also launched numerous raids along the Virginia and Maryland shore.

The presence of British ships on the coast and inland rivers led many enslaved people to escape or revolt. As had happened during the Revolutionary War, British naval commanders promised freedom to fugitives from slavery who aided or fought with them. As many as 4,000 enslaved people in Maryland and Virginia escaped to the safety of British ships.

The British organize the Colonial Marines

In September 1813, the British organized some 400 former enslaved men into an all–African American military unit called the Colonial Marines. The recruits were provided uniforms, meals, $6 a month in wages, and the promise of a gift of land after their service. News of the Colonial Marines panicked Whites along the Chesapeake Bay; they feared that the freed men would "have no mercy on them."

The Burning of Washington, D.C.

During the late summer of 1814, U.S. forces suffered their most humiliating experience of the war when British troops captured and burned Washington, D.C. In August, 4,500 British soldiers, most of them veterans of the wars

THE BURNING OF THE CAPITOL In this illustration by Joseph Boggs Beale, residents of Washington, D.C., evacuate the city as the White House and the Capitol blaze with flames in the background.

against Napoléon, landed at Benedict, Maryland, routed the American militia at Bladensburg, and headed for the nation's capital just six miles away. President Madison called an emergency meeting of his cabinet. The secretary of war, John Armstrong, insisted that the British were not interested in the insignificant American capital. "They certainly will not come here," he told the president. "What the devil will they do here? No! No! Baltimore is the place, sir. That is of so much more consequence."

The British march on the capital

But the British were indeed headed for the American capital. Thousands of people panicked and fled the city. Madison frantically strapped two pistols onto his waist, called out the poorly led and untrained militia, then left Washington, D.C., to help rally the troops for the battle at Bladensburg. His efforts failed, however, as the American defense disintegrated. Many militiamen turned tail, some never slowing down until they reached home.

On August 24, British redcoats marched unopposed into the defenseless American capital. Madison and his wife, Dolley, fled just in time after first saving a portrait of George Washington and a copy of the Declaration of Independence.

The vengeful British, aware that American troops had burned York, the Canadian capital, torched the White House (then called the Executive

Mansion), the Capitol, the Library of Congress, and other government buildings before heading north to assault Baltimore. A tornado the next day compounded the damage, as did American scavengers who looted the White House of its silverware.

The destruction of Washington, D.C., shocked, embarrassed, and infuriated Americans. Even worse, people had lost confidence in the government and the military. David Campbell, a Virginia congressman, told his brother that America was "ruled by fools and the administration opposed by knaves." The secretary of war resigned; Madson, after escaping to Virginia, replaced him with James Monroe, who was also secretary of state. A desperate Monroe soon proposed enlisting free Blacks into the army. But many worried that such changes were too few and too late. A Virginia official noted that without a miracle, "*This union is inevitably dissolved*."

President Madison called an emergency session of Congress and appealed to Americans to "expel the invaders." A Baltimore newspaper reported that the "spirit of the nation is roused." That determination showed itself when fifty British warships sailed into Baltimore Harbor on September 13, while 4,200 British soldiers, including the all-Black Colonial Marines, assaulted the city by land. About 1,000 Americans held Fort McHenry, located on an island in the harbor.

Baltimore holds out against British warships

Throughout the night, the British bombarded Fort McHenry. Yet the Americans refused to surrender. At daybreak, the soldiers in the battered fort stood defiant, guns at the ready. The frustrated British sailed away.

Francis Scott Key, a slaveholding lawyer from a Maryland plantation family who later would become a district attorney for Washington, D.C., watched the assault from a British warship, having been sent to negotiate the release of a captured American. The sight of the massive U.S. flag still flying over Fort McHenry at dawn inspired Key to scribble the verses of what came to be called "The Star-Spangled Banner," which began, "Oh, say can you see, by the dawn's early light?"

Later revised and set to the tune of an English drinking song, it became America's national anthem in 1931. Less well known is that Key was a rabid White supremacist who declared that Africans in America were "a distinct and inferior race of people, which all experience proves to be the greatest evil that afflicts a community."

The lesser known third stanza of the "Star-Spangled Banner" refers to the slaughtering of enslaved men who had joined the British army in exchange for their freedom:

> No refuge could save the hireling and the slave
> From the terror of night or the gloom of the grave
> And the star-spangled banner in triumph doth wave
> O'er the land of the free and the home of the brave.

Key's celebration of America as being the "land of the free, [and] home of the oppressed" was for Whites only.

O say can you see ~~through~~ by the dawn's early light
What so proudly we hail'd at the twilight's last gleaming,
Whose broad stripes & bright stars through the perilous fight
O'er the ramparts we watch'd, were so gallantly streaming?
And the rocket's red glare, the bomb bursting in air,
Gave proof through the night that our flag was still there,
O say does that star-spangled banner yet wave
O'er the land of the free & the home of the brave?

On the shore dimly seen through the mists of the deep,
Where the foe's haughty host in dread silence reposes,
What is that which the breeze, o'er the towering steep,
As it fitfully blows, half conceals, half discloses?
Now it catches the gleam of the morning's first beam,
In full glory reflected now shines in the stream,
'Tis the star-spangled banner — O long may it wave
O'er the land of the free & the home of the brave!

And where is that band who so vauntingly swore,
That the havoc of war & the battle's confusion
A home & a Country should leave us no more?
— ~~[illegible]~~ Their blood has wash'd out their foul footstep's pollution.
No refuge could save the hireling & slave
From the terror of flight or the gloom of the grave,
And the star-spangled banner in triumph doth wave
O'er the land of the free & the home of the brave.

O thus be it ever when freemen shall stand
Between their lov'd home & the war's desolation!
Blest with vict'ry & peace may the heav'n rescued land
Praise the power that hath made & preserv'd us a nation!
Then conquer we must, when our cause it is just,
And this be our motto — "In God is our trust,"
And the star-spangled banner in triumph shall wave
O'er the land of the free & the home of the brave. —

A LESSER-KNOWN STANZA The third stanza of Francis Scott Key's "Star-Spangled Banner" celebrated the triumph of the "broad stripes and bright stars" over enslaved Africans who had aligned with the British in the course of seeking their freedom.

The Battle of Lake Champlain

The British failure to conquer Baltimore gave Americans a desperately needed morale boost. More good news arrived from upstate New York, where the outnumbered Americans at Plattsburgh, along Lake Champlain, were saved by the heroics of Commodore Thomas Macdonough, commander of the U.S. naval squadron.

On September 11, 1814, just days after the burning of Washington, D.C., British soldiers attacked at Plattsburgh while their navy engaged

Macdonough's warships in a battle that ended with the entire British fleet either destroyed or captured. The Battle of Lake Champlain (also called the Battle of Plattsburgh) forced the British to abandon the northern campaign and retreat into Canada.

Victories reinvigorate American morale

In November, an army led by Andrew Jackson in Florida seized Spanish-controlled Pensacola, on the Gulf coast, preventing another British army from landing and pushing northward into the southern states. The American victories in New York and Florida convinced Congress not to abandon Washington, D.C. Instead, the members voted to rebuild the Capitol and the Executive Mansion.

The Aftermath of the War

CORE **OBJECTIVE**

4. Analyze the most significant outcomes of the War of 1812 on the United States.

While the fighting raged, U.S. diplomats, including Henry Clay and John Quincy Adams, son of the former president, had begun meeting with British officials in Ghent, near Brussels in present-day Belgium, to discuss ending the war. Negotiations dragged on for weeks, but on Christmas Eve 1814, the diplomats finally reached an agreement.

The Treaty of Ghent (1814)

In the **Treaty of Ghent (1814)**, the two countries agreed to return each side's prisoners and restore the previous boundaries. This was a godsend for the Americans, since British forces at the time still controlled eastern Maine, northern Michigan, a portion of western New York, and several islands off the coast of Georgia. The British also pledged to stop supporting Indian attacks along the Great Lakes.

What had begun as an American effort to protect its honor, end British impressment, and conquer Canada had turned into a second war of independence. At the end of the negotiations, John Quincy Adams wrote to his wife that he had had the honor of "redeeming our union." Although the Americans lost the war for Canada and saw their national capital destroyed, they won the southern war, defeating the Indians and taking their lands. More important, the Treaty of Ghent saved the splintered republic from possible civil war and financial ruin.

The Battle of New Orleans (1815)

Because it took six weeks for news of the Treaty of Ghent to reach the United States, fighting continued at the end of 1814. On December 1, Andrew Jackson arrived in New Orleans to prepare for a British invasion. When Jackson learned of the British plan to seize New Orleans, he responded, "I will smash them, so help me God!" Jackson declared martial law and transformed New Orleans into an armed camp as he prepared its defense.

On December 12, a British fleet with sixty ships and thousands of soldiers took up positions on the coast of Louisiana, hoping to capture New Orleans

Treaty of Ghent (1814) Agreement between Great Britain and the United States that ended the War of 1812.

and thereby gain control of the Mississippi River, along which a third of American commerce flowed. But British general Sir Edward Pakenham's painfully careful preparation for an assault gave Jackson time to organize hundreds of enslaved people "loaned" by planters. They dug trenches, built ramparts bristling with cannons, stacked cotton bales and barrels of sugar, and dug a ten-foot-wide moat for protection.

The 4,500 Americans—including militiamen, Choctaws, African Americans, Tennessee and Kentucky sharpshooters, and Creole pirates—built an almost-invulnerable position at Chalmette Plantation seven miles south of New Orleans. On one side of their lines was a swamp and on the other was the Mississippi River.

Sporadic fighting occurred for more than three weeks before General Pakenham rashly ordered a frontal assault on the entrenched American defenders at dawn on Sunday, January 8, 1815. Andrew Jackson was having coffee at a home in New Orleans when a cannon ball passed through the room. The fearless American commander grabbed his sword and yelled to his staff: "Come on—we shall have a warm day."

The 5,300 British soldiers assaulted the Americans in two columns, each eighty men abreast. They soon encountered a murderous hail of artillery shells and rifle fire. Yet they kept coming, only to discover that an officer had forgotten to bring the ladders needed to scale the American ramparts. A brave but foolish British colonel was able to climb atop the American defenses, whereupon he ordered the "damned" Yankees to surrender, only to be shot and killed by an American rifleman.

When the smoke cleared, a Kentucky militiaman said that the battlefield looked first like "a sea of blood. It was not blood itself, but the red coats in which the British soldiers were dressed. The field was entirely covered in prostrate bodies."

In just 25 minutes, the British had lost some 2,100 men, including General Pakenham and his second in command. (The British stored Pakenham's corpse in a barrel of rum for burial in Britain).

Jackson and the Americans forced the remnants of the once proud British army to retreat and sail away empty-handed. The Americans suffered only seventy-one killed or wounded. Newspapers across America celebrated the unexpected victory. Said one editor: "Who would not be an American? Long live the Republic!'"

With New Orleans and the Mississippi River Valley liberated from British authority, the West was open for expansion, and Americans rushed to take advantage of western land sales made possible by Jackson's great victory.

Battle of New Orleans (1815) Final major battle in the War of 1812, in which the Americans under General Andrew Jackson unexpectedly and decisively countered the British attempt to seize the port of New Orleans, Louisiana.

Although the **Battle of New Orleans** occurred after the Treaty of Ghent had been signed, it was vitally important psychologically. Had the British won, they might have tried to revise the treaty in their favor. Jackson's victory ensured that both governments would act quickly to approve the treaty.

The surprising American triumph generated a wave of patriotism. The young nation had displayed the strength, fortitude, and courage to defend

JACKSON'S ARMY DEFENDS NEW ORLEANS Unaware that the war was over, in January 1815 Andrew Jackson led his troops and the enslaved people on loan from southern planters to a decisive victory over the British at New Orleans. **What was the diplomatic and symbolic importance of Jackson's victory?**

its freedom and prove to the world that it was becoming a great power. As a Washington, D.C., newspaper crowed, "ALMOST INCREDIBLE VICTORY!"

A diplomatic and symbolic victory

Such pride in the Battle of New Orleans would later help transform General Jackson into a dynamic presidential candidate. Jackson, wrote a southerner in April 1815, "is everywhere hailed as the savior of the country. . . . He has been feasted, caressed, & I may say idolized."

The Hartford Convention

On December 15, 1814, a few weeks before the Battle of New Orleans, New England Federalists, frustrated by the rising expense of "Mr. Madison's War," convened the **Hartford Convention** in Hartford, Connecticut.

Over the next three weeks, the Federalist delegates proposed seven constitutional amendments designed to limit Republican (and southern) political power. The amendments included abolishing the counting of enslaved people in determining a state's representation in Congress, requiring a two-thirds supermajority rather than a simple majority vote to declare war or admit new states, prohibiting trade embargoes lasting more than sixty days, excluding immigrants from holding federal office, limiting the president to one term, and barring successive presidents from the same state (a provision clearly directed at Virginia).

The delegates also discussed the possibility that some New England states might "secede" from the Union if their demands were dismissed. Yet the threat quickly evaporated. In February 1815, when messengers from the convention reached Washington, D.C., they found the capital celebrating the great American victory at New Orleans.

Hartford Convention (1814) A series of secret meetings in December 1814 and January 1815 at which New England Federalists protested American involvement in the War of 1812 and discussed several constitutional amendments, including limiting each president to one term, designed to weaken the dominant Republican party.

Ignored by Congress and the president, the Federalist delegates turned tail for home. The sorry episode proved fatal to the Federalist party, which never recovered from the shame of disloyalty stamped on it by the Hartford Convention. The victory at New Orleans and the arrival of the peace treaty from Europe transformed the national mood. Almost overnight, President Madison went from being denounced and possibly impeached to being hailed a national hero.

The War's Legacies

There was no clear military victor in the War of 1812, nor much clarification about the issues that had ignited the war. For all the clumsiness with which the war was managed, however, it generated an intense patriotism. The young republic was at last secure from British or European threats. As James Monroe said, "we have acquired a character and a rank among the other nations, which we did not enjoy before."

Economic independence

Most Americans viewed the war as a glorious triumph. Yet the conflict also revealed the limitations of relying on militiamen and the need for a larger professional army. The war also propelled the United States toward economic independence, as the interruption of trade with Europe forced America to expand its manufacturing sector and become more self-sufficient.

The British blockade of U.S. ports created a shortage of cotton cloth in the United States, leading to the creation of the nation's first cotton-manufacturing industry, in Waltham, Massachusetts. By the end of the war, there were more than 100 cotton mills in New England and 64 more in Pennsylvania. Even Thomas Jefferson admitted in 1815 that his beloved agricultural republic had been transformed: "We must now place the manufacturer by the agriculturalist." The new American republic was emerging as an agricultural, commercial, and industrial world power.

Reversal of political roles for Republicans and Federalists

Perhaps the strangest result of the War of 1812 was the reversal of attitudes among Republicans and Federalists.

The British invasion of Washington, D.C., convinced President Madison of the necessity of a stronger army and navy. In addition, the lack of a national bank had hurt the federal government's efforts to finance the war; state and local banks were so unstable that it was difficult to raise the funds needed to pay military expenses. In 1816, Madison created the Second Bank of the United States, where the national government deposited its revenue. The second B.U.S. also exercised a regulating influence over the many state banks that were issuing their own paper currency.

While business leaders appreciated the centralized control provided by the B.U.S., many wage workers, especially in the new western states, distrusted the national bank in Philadelphia. The rise of new industries prompted manufacturers to call for increased tariffs on imports to protect American companies from unfair foreign competition. Madison went along, despite his criticism of tariffs in the 1790s.

While Madison reversed himself by embracing nationalism and a broader interpretation of the Constitution, the Federalists reversed themselves and adopted Madison's and Jefferson's original emphasis on states' rights and strict construction of the Constitution to defend the special interests of their regional stronghold, New England. It was the first great reversal of partisan political roles in constitutional interpretation. It would not be the last.

Westward expansion and occupation of Native American lands

The War of 1812 proved devastating to the eastern Indian Nations, most of which had fought with the British. The war accelerated westward settlement, and Native American resistance was greatly diminished after the death of Tecumseh and his Indian Confederacy. The British essentially abandoned their Indian allies, and none of their former lands were returned to them.

Lakota chief Little Crow expressed the betrayal felt by Native Americans when he rejected the consolation gifts from the local British commander: "After we have fought for you, endured many hardships, lost some of our people, and awakened the vengeance of our powerful neighbors, you make peace for yourselves. . . . You no longer need our service; you offer us these goods to pay us for [your] having deserted us. But no, we will not take them; we hold them and yourselves in equal contempt."

As the Indians were pushed out, tens of thousands of Americans moved into the Great Lakes region and into Georgia, Alabama, and Mississippi, occupying more territory in a single generation than had been settled in the 150 years of colonial history. The federal government hastened western migration by giving war veterans 160 acres of land between the Illinois and Mississippi Rivers.

The trans-Appalachian population soared from 300,000 to 2 million between 1800 and 1820. By 1840, more than 40 percent of Americans lived west of the Appalachians in eight new states. The number of free Blacks tripled, from 59,000 in 1790 to more than 174,000 by 1810, while the number of enslaved people doubled to 1,191,364. At the same time, the growing dispute over slavery and its westward expansion into new territories set in motion an explosive debate that would once again test the grand experiment in republican government.

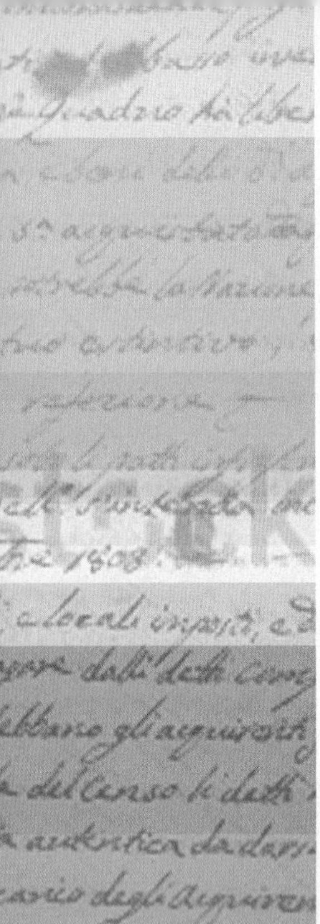

Reviewing the CORE OBJECTIVES | INQUIZITIVE

■ **Jeffersonian Republicanism** The Jeffersonian Republicans did not dismantle much of Hamilton's Federalist economic program, but they did repeal the whiskey tax, reduce government expenditures, and promote what was called *republican simplicity*—smaller government and plain living. In *Marbury v. Madison* (1803), the Federalist chief justice of the Supreme Court, John Marshall, declared a federal act unconstitutional for the first time. With that decision, the Court assumed the right of judicial review over acts of Congress and established the constitutional supremacy of the federal government over state governments.

While Republicans idealized the agricultural world that had existed prior to 1800, the first decades of the 1800s were a period of explosive economic and population growth in the United States, transforming the nation. Large-scale commercial agriculture and exports to Europe flourished; Americans moved west in huge numbers. The *Louisiana Purchase* (1803) dramatically expanded the boundaries of the United States. The *Lewis and Clark expedition* (1804–1806) explored the new region and published reports that excited interest in the Far West.

■ **War in the Mediterranean and Europe** Thomas Jefferson sent warships to subdue the *Barbary pirates* on the coast of North Africa and negotiated with the Spanish and French to ensure that the Mississippi River remained open to American commerce. Renewal of war between Britain and France in 1803 complicated matters for American commerce with Europe. Neither country wanted its enemy to purchase U.S. goods, so both blockaded each other's ports. In retaliation, Jefferson convinced Congress at the end of 1807 to pass the *Embargo Act*, which prohibited all foreign trade.

■ **The War of 1812** Renewal of the European war in 1803 created naval conflicts with Britain and France. President James Madison ultimately declared war against Great Britain over the issue of neutral shipping rights and the fear that the British were inciting Native Americans to attack frontier settlements. Indian nations took sides in the war. Tecumseh led the Confederacy against the Americans during the War of 1812. Earlier, at the *Battle of Tippecanoe* (1811), U.S. troops had defeated elements of *Tecumseh's Indian Confederacy*, an alliance of Indian nations determined to protect their ancestral lands. At the Battle of the Thames (1813), Tecumseh was killed and the Confederacy disintegrated soon thereafter.

■ **Aftermath of the War of 1812** The *Treaty of Ghent* (1814) ended the war by essentially declaring it a draw. A smashing American victory in January of 1815 at the *Battle of New Orleans* occurred before news of the peace treaty had reached the continent, but the lopsided American triumph helped ensure that the treaty would be ratified and enforced. One effect of the conflict was to establish the economic independence of the United States, as goods previously purchased from Great Britain were now manufactured at home. During and after the war, Federalists and Republicans seemed to exchange roles: delegates from the waning Federalist party met at the *Hartford Convention* (1814) to defend states' rights and threaten secession, while Republicans now promoted nationalism and a broad interpretation of the Constitution.

KEY TERMS

republican simplicity *p. 258*

Marbury v. Madison (1803) *p. 261*

Louisiana Purchase (1803) *p. 266*

Lewis and Clark expedition (1804–1806) *p. 266*

Barbary pirates *p. 271*

Embargo Act (1807) *p. 273*

War of 1812 (1812–1815) *p. 275*

Battle of Tippecanoe (1811) *p. 277*

Tecumseh's Indian Confederacy *p. 277*

Treaty of Ghent (1814) *p. 287*

Battle of New Orleans (1815) *p. 288*

Hartford Convention (1814) *p. 289*

CHRONOLOGY

1801	Thomas Jefferson inaugurated as president in Washington, D.C.
	Barbary pirates harass U.S. shipping and capture American sailors
	The pasha of Tripoli declares war on the United States
1803	Supreme Court issues *Marbury v. Madison* decision
	Louisiana Purchase
1804–1806	Lewis and Clark expedition
1804	Jefferson overwhelmingly reelected
1807	British interference with U.S. shipping increases, prompting President Jefferson to announce Embargo Act
1808	International slave trade ended in the United States
1811	Defeat of Tecumseh's Indian Confederacy at the Battle of Tippecanoe
1812	Congress declares war on Britain
	U.S. invasion of Canada
1813–1814	Creek War
1814	British capture and burn Washington, D.C.
	Hartford Convention
1815	Battle of New Orleans
	News of the Treaty of Ghent reaches the United States

INQUIZITIVE

Go to InQuizitive to see what you've learned—and learn what you've missed—with personalized feedback along the way.

THINKING LIKE A HISTORIAN

DEBATING Thomas Jefferson and Slavery

One of the more difficult tasks that historians face is assessing the actions of historical figures within an ethical framework. Should people in the past be assessed by the standards of their time or by those of today? Should we hold celebrated historical figures to a higher ethical standard? For Part 2, "*Building a Nation*," the complex relationship of Thomas Jefferson to slavery demonstrates how historians can disagree when they evaluate historic individuals from an ethical perspective.

This exercise involves two tasks:

PART 1: Compare the two secondary sources on Thomas Jefferson and slavery.
PART 2: Using primary sources, evaluate the arguments of the two secondary sources.

PART I Comparing and Contrasting Secondary Sources

Below are two secondary sources focused on the question of Jefferson and his relationship with slavery. The first is from Douglas L. Wilson, professor emeritus of English and codirector of the Lincoln Studies Center at Knox College; the second is written by Paul Finkelman, professor of law and public policy at the Albany Law School. In these selections, Wilson and Finkelman explore one of the great contradictions in early American history: that Thomas Jefferson, an outspoken critic of slavery, was himself a slave owner. Further complicating the matter was Jefferson's relationship with Sally Hemings, a slave with whom he had several children. Both passages grapple with the issue of *presentism*, the application of present-day ideas and beliefs onto the past.

Compare the views of these two scholars by answering the following questions. Be sure to find specific examples in the selections to support your answers.

- How does each author address the issue of presentism?
- What ethical standards do the authors use to evaluate Jefferson?
- What evidence do they offer when evaluating Jefferson?
- How does each author assess Jefferson's ethical standards?
- What ethical standard would you use?

Secondary Source 1

Douglas L. Wilson, "Thomas Jefferson and the Character Issue" (1992)

How could the man who wrote that "All men are created equal" own slaves? This, in essence, is the question most persistently asked of those who write about Thomas Jefferson, and by all indications it is the thing that contemporary Americans find most vexing about him.... The question carries a silent assumption that because he practiced slave holding, Jefferson must have somehow believed in it, and must therefore have been a hypocrite. My belief is that this way of asking the question . . . reflects the pervasive presentism of our time. Consider, for example, how different the question appears when inverted and framed in more historical terms: How did a man who was born into a slave holding society, whose family and admired friends owned slaves, who inherited a fortune that was dependent on slaves and slave labor, decide at an early age that slavery was morally wrong and forcefully declare that it ought to be abolished?

But when the question is explained in this way, another invariably follows: If Jefferson came to believe that holding slaves was wrong, why did he continue to hold them?... Obstacles to emancipation in Jefferson's Virginia were formidable, and the risk was demonstrably great that emancipated slaves would enjoy little, if any, real freedom and would, unless they could pass as white, be more likely to come to grief in a hostile environment. In short, the master whose concern extended beyond his own morality to the well-being of his slaves was caught on the horns of a dilemma. Thus the question of why Jefferson didn't free his slaves only serves to illustrate how presentism involves us in mistaken assumptions about historical conditions—in this case that an eighteenth-century slave holder wanting to get out from under the moral stigma of slavery and improve the lot of his slaves had only to set them free.

Although we may find Jefferson guilty of failing to make adequate allowance for the conditions in which blacks were forced to live, Jefferson did not take the next step of concluding that blacks were fit only for slavery. This rationalization of slavery was indeed the common coin of slave holders and other whites who condoned or tolerated the "peculiar" institution, but it formed no part of Jefferson's thinking. In fact, he took the opposite position: that having imposed the depredations of slavery on blacks, white Americans should not only emancipate them but also educate and train them to be self-sufficient, provide them with necessary materials, and establish a colony in which they could live as free and independent people.

Source: Wilson, Douglas L. "Thomas Jefferson and the Character Issue." *Atlantic Monthly* November 1992, pp. 57–74.

Secondary Source 2

Paul Finkelman, "Jefferson and Slavery" (1993)

An understanding of Jefferson's relationship to slavery requires analysis of his statements on and beliefs about the institution and an account of his actions as a public leader and a private individual. Scrutinizing the contradictions between Jefferson's professions and his actions does not impose twentieth-century values on an eighteenth-century man. Because he was the author of the Declaration of Independence and a leader of the American Enlightenment, the test of Jefferson's position on slavery is not whether he was better than the worst of his generation, but whether he was the leader of the best; not whether he responded as a southerner and a planter, but whether he was able to transcend his economic interests and his sectional background to implement the ideals he articulated. Jefferson fails the test. When Jefferson wrote the Declaration, he owned over 175 slaves. While many of his contemporaries freed their slaves during and after the Revolution, Jefferson did not.

In the fifty years from 1776 until his death in 1826, a period of extraordinary public service, he did little to end slavery or to dissociate himself from his role as the master of Monticello. To the contrary, as he accumulated more slaves he worked assiduously to increase the productivity and the property values of his labor force. Nor did he encourage his countrymen to liberate their slaves, even when they sought his blessing. Even at his death Jefferson failed to fulfill the promise of his rhetoric. In his will he emancipated only five bondsmen, condemning nearly two hundred others to the auction block. . . .

. . . He knew slavery was wrong. It could not have been otherwise for an eighteenth-century natural law theorist. Many of his closest European and American friends and colleagues were leaders of the new abolition societies. Jefferson was part of a cosmopolitan "republic of letters" that was overwhelmingly hostile to slavery. But, for the most part, he suppressed his doubts, while doing virtually nothing to challenge the institution. On this issue Jefferson's genius failed him. As David Brion Davis observes, "Jefferson had only a theoretical interest in promoting the cause of abolition."

Jefferson could not live without slaves. They built his house, cooked his meals, and tilled his fields. In contrast to George Washington, Jefferson carelessly managed his lands and finances and lived beyond his means. Washington refused to traffic in slaves. Chronically in debt, Jefferson overcame his professed "scruples about selling negroes but for delinquency or on their own request," selling scores of slaves in order to make ends meet. Jefferson could not maintain his extravagant life style without his slaves and, to judge from his lifelong behavior, his grand style was far more important than the natural rights of his slaves. . . .

Throughout his life, as he condemned slavery, Jefferson implied that, however bad it was for slaves, the institution was somehow worse for whites. His concerns about the institution had more to do with its effect on whites and white society than on its true victims. . . . Jefferson's concerns were solely with the "morals and manners" of the master class. He was concerned that slavery leads to despotism by the masters; but he never expressed regret for the mistreatment of the slave. Similarly, throughout his life Jefferson expressed his fears of miscegenation and a weakening of white society through contact with blacks. He favored some form of colonization that would put blacks "beyond the reach of mixture."

Source: Finkelman, Paul. "Jefferson and Slavery: 'Treason against the Hopes of the World.'" In *Jeffersonian Legacies*, edited by Peter S. Onuf, 181–221. Charlottesville: University Press of Virginia, 1993.

PART II Using Primary Sources to Evaluate Secondary Sources

When historians are faced with competing interpretations of the past, they often look at primary source material as part of the process of evaluating the different arguments. Below are primary source materials relating to Thomas Jefferson's relationship with slavery. The first document is an excerpt from a draft of the Declaration of Independence largely written by Thomas Jefferson. This excerpt was removed from the final version of the declaration. The second document is a selection from Jefferson's 1785 book on the state of Virginia, relating to slaves and slavery. The third document is a letter Jefferson wrote while serving in Paris as the U.S. minister (ambassador) to France in 1788, and the fourth is a letter from April 1820 expressing his feelings regarding the Missouri Compromise, which admitted Missouri as a slave state and created a northern boundary for slavery in the western territories.

Carefully read the primary sources and answer the following questions. Decide which of the primary source documents support or refute Wilson's and Finkelman's arguments about Jefferson. You may find that some documents do both but for different parts of each historian's interpretation. Be sure to identify which specific components of each historian's argument the documents support or refute.

- Which of the two historians' *arguments* is best supported by the *primary source* documents? If you find that both arguments are well supported by the evidence, why do you think the two historians had such different interpretations about Jefferson?
- Based on the ethical standard you choose in Part I and these documents, how would *you* assess Jefferson's relationship with slavery? You may consider how Jefferson's views change over time.
- What has using primary sources to evaluate the Wilson and Finkelman arguments taught you about making ethical assessments of historical figures?

Primary Source 1

Thomas Jefferson, a draft section omitted from the *Declaration of Independence* (1776)

He [King George III] has waged cruel war against human nature itself, violating its most sacred rights of life & liberty in the persons of a distant people [Africans] who never offended him, captivating & carrying them into slavery in another hemisphere, or to incur miserable death in their transportation thither. This piratical warfare, the opprobrium of infidel powers, is the warfare of the Christian king of Great Britain. Determined to keep open a market where men should be bought & sold, he has prostituted his negative for suppressing every legislative attempt to prohibit or to restrain this execrable [disgusting] commerce: and that this assemblage of horrors might want no fact of distinguished die, he is now exciting those very people to rise in arms among us, and to purchase that liberty of which he has deprived them, & murdering the people upon whom he also obtruded them; thus paying off former crimes committed against the liberties of one people, with crimes which he urges them to commit against the lives of another.

Source: Jefferson, Thomas. "Thomas Jefferson, June 1776, Rough Draft of the Declaration of Independence," 1776. *The Thomas Jefferson Papers Series 1. General Correspondence. 1651–1827.* American Memory, Library of Congress, Washington, D.C.

Primary Source 2

Thomas Jefferson, *Notes on the State of Virginia* (1787)

It will probably be asked, Why not retain and incorporate the Blacks into the State [after emancipation], and thus save the expense of supplying, by importation of white settlers, the vacancies they will leave? Deep-rooted prejudices entertained by the Whites; ten thousand recollections by the Blacks, of the injuries they have sustained; new provocations; the real distinctions which nature has made; and many other circumstances, will divide us into parties, and produce convulsions, which will probably never end but in the extermination of the one or the other race. To these objections, which are political, may be added others, which are physical and moral. . . . Comparing them by their faculties of memory, reason, and imagination, it appears to me, that in memory they are equal to the Whites; in reason much inferior, . . . and that in imagination they are dull, tasteless and anomalous. . . .

To our reproach it must be said, that though for a century and a half we have had under our eyes the races of Black and of Red men, they have never yet been viewed by us as subjects of natural history. I advance it therefore as a suspicion only, that the Blacks, whether originally a distinct race, or made distinct by time and circumstances, are inferior to the Whites in the endowments both of body and mind. It is not against experience to suppose, that different species of the same genus, or varieties of the same species, may possess different qualifications. Will not a lover of natural history then, one who views the gradations in all the races of animals with the eye of philosophy, excuse an effort to keep those in the department of man as distinct as nature has formed them? This unfortunate difference of colour, and perhaps of faculty, is a powerful obstacle to the emancipation of these people. Many of their advocates, while they wish to vindicate the liberty of human nature, are anxious also to preserve its dignity and beauty. Some of these, embarrassed by the question 'What further is to be done with them?' join themselves in opposition with those who are actuated by sordid avarice [greed] only. Among the Romans emancipation required but one effort. The slave, when made free, might mix with, without staining the blood of his master. But with us a second is necessary, unknown to history. When freed, he is to be removed beyond the reach of mixture. . . . There must, doubtless, be an unhappy influence on the manners of our people, produced by the existence of slavery among us. The whole commerce between master and slave is a perpetual exercise of the most boisterous passions, the most unremitting despotism on the one part, and degrading. . . . For if a slave can have a country in this world, it must be any other in preference to that in which he is born to live and labor for another.

Source: Jefferson, Thomas. "Laws, Query XIV." *Notes on the State of Virginia*. London: Printed for John Stockdale, Opposite Burlington-House, Piccadilly, 1787. 229–271.

Primary Source 3

Thomas Jefferson, Letter to M. Warville [a Frenchman] (February 11, 1788)

Sir,

I am very sensible of the honor you propose to me, of becoming a member of the society for the abolition of the slave-trade. You know that nobody wishes more ardently, to see an abolition, not only of the trade, but of the condition of slavery: and certainly nobody will be more willing to encounter every sacrifice for that object. But the influence and information of the friends to this proposition in France will be far above the need of my association. I am here as a public servant, and those whom I serve, having never yet been able to give their oice against the practice, it is decent for me to avoid too public a demonstration of my wishes to see it abolished. Without serving the cause here, it might render me less able to serve it beyond the water. I trust you will be sensible of the prudence of those motives, therefore, which govern my conduct on this occasion, and be assured of my wishes for the success of your undertaking, and the sentiments of esteem and respect, with which I have the honor to be, Sir, your most obedient, humble servant,

Th: Jefferson.

Source: Jefferson, Thomas. "Jean Plumard Brissot de Warville to Thomas Jefferson, February 11, 1788," 1788. *The Thomas Jefferson Papers*. Series 1: General Correspondence, 1651–1827. American Memory, Library of Congress, Washington, D.C.

Primary Source 4

Thomas Jefferson, Letter to John Holmes (April 22, 1820)

I thank you, dear Sir, for the copy you have been so kind as to send me of the letter to your constituents on the Missouri question [the admission of Missouri as slave state]. . . . The cession of that kind of property [slaves] (for so it is misnamed) . . . would not cost me a second thought, if, in that way, a general emancipation and expatriation could be effected: and, gradually, and with due sacrifices, I think it might be. But as it is, we have the wolf by the ears, and we can neither hold him, nor safely let him go. Justice is in one scale, and self-preservation in the other. Of one thing I am certain, that as the passage of slaves from one State to another, would not make a slave of a single human being who would not be so without it, so their diffusion over a greater surface would make them individually happier, and proportionally facilitate the accomplishment of their emancipation. . . .

Th: Jefferson.

Source: Jefferson, Thomas. "Thomas Jefferson to John Holmes, April 22, 1820," 1820. *The Thomas Jefferson Papers,* Series 1: General Correspondence, 1651–1827. American Memory, Library of Congress, Washington, D.C.

A CARD.

BLOUNT & DAWSON,

NERAL BROKERS

the Purchase and Sale of NEGROES and OTHER PROPERTY.

VANNAH, GEORGIA.

ken the Office and New Jail completed by Wm. Wright, Esq., we are
rd secure and good accommodations for all negroes left with us for Sale
ping, would respectfully solicit a share of public patronage.

Two Doors East of J. Bryan & Co., opposite the State Bank.

OUNT. W. C. DAWSON.

g leased the above gentlemen my office and jail, would take pleasure in
ling them to my patrons and the public generally.

WM. WRIGHT.

PART 3

An Expanding Nation, 1815–1860

During the nineteenth century, the United States experienced wrenching changes. With each passing decade, its predominantly agrarian society developed a more diverse economy, with factories and cities emerging alongside farms and towns. The pace of life quickened, and ambitions soared. A visiting Frenchman noted in 1831 that he knew "of no country where wealth has taken a stronger hold on the affections of men" than in America.

Between 1790 and 1820, the nation's boundaries expanded and its rate of population growth—both White and Black—was greater than anything known in Europe. By the early 1820s, the total number of enslaved Americans was more than two and a half times greater than in 1790, and the number of free Blacks had doubled. The White population increased just as rapidly.

Other nations marveled and grew worried about America's growing power. Spain's governor in New Orleans warned officials in Spain that the greatest threat to their possessions in North America was "not military but demographic." The rapid rate of population growth in the United States would eventually drive the Spanish out of the continent.

Accompanying the industrialization of the economy was relentless westward expansion. The West provided the key to the nation's nineteenth-century development, as millions migrated across the Allegheny and Appalachian Mountains into the Middle West, then crossed the Mississippi River and spread out across the Great Plains. By the 1840s, Americans had reached the Pacific Ocean, transported there by horses, wagons, canals, flatboats, steamboats, and, eventually, railroads and ocean-going steamships.

While the feverish expansion brought more conflict with Native Americans, Mexicans, the British, and the Spanish, most Americans believed it was their God-given destiny to spread across the continent—at whatever cost and at whosever's expense. In 1845, an editorial in the *United States Journal* claimed that "we, the American people, are the most independent, intelligent, moral, and happy people on the face of the earth." The constitutional republic governed by "natural aristocrats" such as Thomas Jefferson, James Madison, James Monroe, and John Quincy Adams gave way to the frontier democracy promoted by frontiersman Andrew Jackson. Americans began to demand government of, by, and for the people.

Two very different societies—North and South—developed. The North, the more dynamic and faster-growing region, embraced the Industrial Revolution, large cities, foreign immigrants, and the ideal of "free laborers" rather than enslaved workers. The South remained rural, agricultural, and increasingly committed to enslaved labor as the backbone of its cotton-centered economy. Two great underlying fears worried southerners: the threat of slave uprisings and the growing possibility that a northern-controlled Congress might abolish slavery. The planter elite's aggressive efforts to preserve and expand slavery stifled reform impulses in the South and ignited a prolonged political controversy with the North that would eventually lead to civil war.

The so-called Jacksonian era during the first half of the nineteenth century celebrated individual freedom and self-expression. Religious life experienced another wave of revival centered on the power of individuals

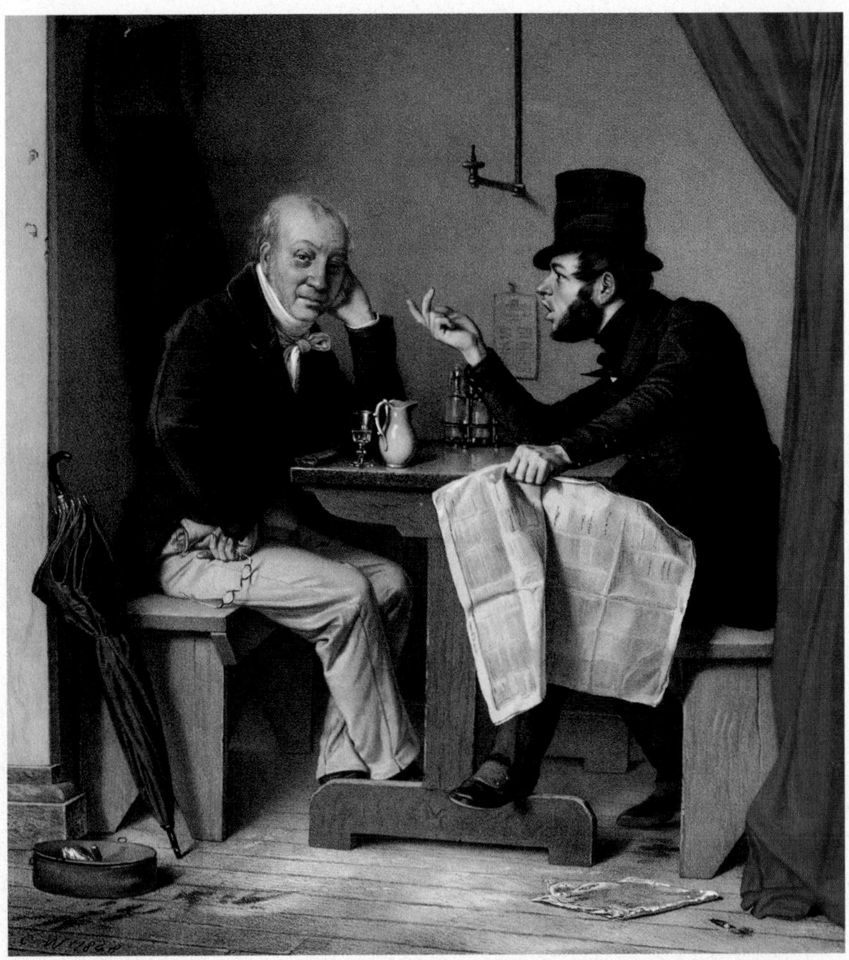

to embrace Christ and attain salvation on their own. Such an emphasis on individualism and freedom of expression shaped cultural life in general.

The Romantic movement applied democratic ideals to virtually every field: philosophy, religion, literature, and the fine arts. In New England, Ralph Waldo Emerson and Henry David Thoreau joined other "transcendentalists" in promoting a radical individualism. At the same time, activists fanned out to reform and even perfect society by creating public schools accessible to all children; working to abolish slavery; combating the consumption of alcohol; and striving to improve living conditions for the disabled, the insane, the poor, and the imprisoned.

During the first half of the nineteenth century, these and other developments combined to shape the America we live in today. Social reform, religious fervor, soaring immigration and nativist prejudices, unpopular wars triggered by presidential actions, and violent swings in the business cycle resemble many of the pressing issues garnering today's headlines.

***LACKAWANNA VALLEY* (1855)** Often hailed as the father of American landscape painting, George Inness was commissioned by a railroad company to capture its trains coursing through the lush Lackawanna Valley in northeastern Pennsylvania. New inventions and rapid industrial growth would continue to change the American landscape.

The Emergence of a Market Economy

1815–1850

CHAPTER 8

Amid the postwar celebrations in 1815, Americans set about transforming their victorious young nation. Soon after the war's end, prosperity returned as British and European markets again welcomed American ships and commerce. During the war, the loss of trade with Britain and Europe had forced the United States to develop more factories and mills, spurring the development of the more diverse economy that Alexander Hamilton had championed in the 1790s.

Between 1815 and 1850, the United States became a transcontinental power, expanding to the Pacific coast. Swarms of land-hungry people streamed westward. Between 1815 and 1821, six new states joined the Union (Alabama, Illinois, Indiana, Mississippi, Missouri, and Maine).

Nineteenth-century Americans were a restless, ambitious people, and the country's energy and mobility were dizzying. A Boston newspaper commented that the entire American "population is in motion." Everywhere, it seemed, people were moving to the next town, the next farm, the next opportunity. In many cities, half the population moved every ten years. In 1826, the newspaper editor in Rochester, New York, reported that 120 people left the city every day while 130 moved in.

The lure of cheap land and plentiful jobs, as well as the promise of political and religious freedom, attracted millions of immigrants. This great wave of humanity was not always welcomed, however. Ethnic prejudices, anti-Catholicism, and language barriers made it difficult for many

CORE OBJECTIVES INQUIZITIVE

1. Describe how changes in transportation and communications altered the economic landscape during the first half of the nineteenth century.
2. Explain the impact of the Industrial Revolution on the way people worked and lived.
3. Analyze how immigration altered the nation's population and shaped its politics.
4. Evaluate the impact of the expanding capitalist "market economy" on workers, professionals, and women.

immigrants, mostly from Ireland, Germany, and China, to adapt to American culture.

In the Midwest, large-scale commercial agriculture emerged as big farms grew corn and wheat and raised pigs and cattle to be sold in distant markets. In the South, cotton became so profitable that it increasingly dominated the region's economy, luring farmers and planters (wealthy farmers with hundreds or even thousands of acres worked by large numbers of enslaved people) into the new states of Alabama, Mississippi, Louisiana, and Arkansas. As the cotton culture expanded into the Gulf coast states, it required growing numbers of enslaved workers, many of whom were sold and relocated from Virginia and the Carolinas.

Meanwhile, the Northeast experienced a surge of industrial development. Labor-saving machines and water- and steam-powered industries reshaped the region's economic and social life. Mills and factories transformed the way people labored, dressed, ate, and lived. With the rise of the factory system, more and more economic activity occurred outside the home and off the farm. An urban middle class began to emerge as Americans, including young women, moved to towns and cities, lured by jobs in new mills, factories, stores, and banks.

By 1850, the United States boasted the world's fastest-growing economy. Dramatic technological innovations in communication and transportation transformed the economy into an interconnected national marketplace. The railroad, the steamboat, the telegraph, the clipper ship, and the photograph combined to shrink time and distance. Newly elected president Andrew Jackson, for example, arrived in Washington, D.C., in 1829 riding in a horse-drawn carriage. Eight years later, he left the presidency and returned to Tennessee in a railroad car.

Amid such dramatic changes, the nation began to divide into three powerful regional political blocs—North, South, and West—whose shifting alliances would shape political life until the Civil War.

CORE **OBJECTIVE**

1. Describe how changes in transportation and communications altered the economic landscape during the first half of the nineteenth century.

The Market Revolution

In the eighteenth century, most Americans were farm folk who operated within a "household economy." That is, they produced enough food, livestock, and clothing for their own family's needs and perhaps a little more to barter (exchange) with their neighbors. During the nineteenth century, however, farm families began producing surplus crops and livestock to sell, for cash, in regional and even international markets.

In 1851, the president of the New York Agricultural Society noted that until the nineteenth century, "'production for consumption' was the leading purpose" of the farm economy. Now, however, "no farmer could find it profitable to do everything for himself. He now sells for money." With the cash they earned, farm families were able to buy more land, better equipment, and the latest manufactured household goods.

Such large-scale commercial agriculture, the first stage of a **market economy**, produced boom-and-bust cycles, and was often built upon the backs of enslaved laborers, immigrant workers, and displaced Mexicans. Overall, however, the standard of living rose, and Americans enjoyed unprecedented opportunities for economic gain and geographic mobility. What the market economy most needed were "internal improvements"—deeper harbors, lighthouses, and a national network of canals, bridges, roads, and railroads—to improve the flow of goods across states. In 1817, for example, South Carolina congressman John C. Calhoun expressed his desire to "bind the Republic together with a perfect system of roads and canals." As the world's largest republic, the United States desperately needed a national transportation system. "Let us conquer space," he told the House of Representatives.

Economic gain and geographic mobility

Calhoun's idea sparked a fierce debate over how to fund such infrastructure improvements: Should it be the responsibility of the federal government, the individual states, or private corporations? Since the Constitution said nothing about the federal government's role in funding transportation improvements, many argued that such projects must be initiated by state and local governments. Others insisted that the Constitution gave the federal government broad powers to promote the "general welfare," which included enhancing transportation and communication. The debate over the funding of internal improvements would continue throughout the nineteenth century.

Transportation

New means of transportation

Until the nineteenth century, travel had been slow, uncomfortable, and expensive. For example, it took a stagecoach four days to get from New York City to Boston. Because of long travel times, many farm products could be sold only locally before they spoiled.

That soon changed, as an array of transportation innovations—larger horse-drawn wagons, called *Conestogas*; new roads; canals; steamboats; and the first railroads—knit together the expanding national market for goods and services and greatly accelerated the pace of life. Stagecoaches increased their speed as the quality of roads improved. In addition, coach lines began using continual relays, or "stages," of fresh horses made available every forty or so miles. These "stagecoaches" quickened travel, while making it less expensive and more accessible.

New Roads

As settlers moved west, people demanded better roads. In 1803, when Ohio became a state, Congress ordered that 5 percent of the money from the sale of federally owned land in the state should go toward building a National Road from the Atlantic coast across Ohio and westward. Construction finally began in 1811. Originally called the Cumberland Road, it was the first interstate roadway financed by the federal government. By 1818, the road was open from Cumberland, Maryland, to Wheeling, Virginia (now West Virginia),

market economy Large-scale manufacturing and commercial agriculture that emerged in America during the first half of the nineteenth century, displacing much of the premarket subsistence and barter-based economy and producing boom-and-bust cycles while raising the American standard of living.

where it crossed the Ohio River. By 1838, the National Road extended 600 miles farther westward to Vandalia, Illinois.

Road transportation: Building turnpikes

The National Road quickened the settlement of the West and the emergence of a truly national market economy by reducing transportation costs, creating new markets, and stimulating the growth of towns. To the northeast, a movement for paved roads gathered momentum after the Philadelphia-Lancaster Turnpike opened in 1794. (The term *turnpike* derived from a pole, or pike, at the tollgate, which was turned to admit the traffic in exchange for a small fee, or toll.) By 1821, some 4,000 miles of turnpikes had been built, and companies emerged to move more people and cargo at lower rates.

Water Transportation

By the early 1820s, the turnpike boom was giving way to advances in water transportation. Steamboats, flatboats (barges driven by men using long poles), and canal barges carried people and goods far more cheaply than did horse-drawn wagons. Hundreds of flatboats floated goods, farm produce, livestock, and people from Tennessee, Kentucky, Indiana, Ohio, western Pennsylvania, and other states down the Ohio and Mississippi Rivers. Flatboats, however, went only downstream. Once unloaded in Natchez, Mississippi, or New Orleans, Louisiana, they were sold and dismantled to provide lumber for construction.

Water transportation: Steamboats

The difficulties of getting back upriver were solved when Robert Fulton and Robert R. Livingston sent the *Clermont*, the first commercial steamboat, up the Hudson River from New York City to Albany in 1807. The 150-mile trip took 30 hours; a sailing vessel took four days. Thereafter, the use of wood-fired **steamboats** spread rapidly.

By bringing two-way travel to the rivers in the Mississippi River Valley, steamboats created a transcontinental market and a commercial agricultural empire that produced much of the nation's cotton, timber, wheat, corn, cattle, and hogs. By 1836, 750 steamboats operated on American rivers. As steamboat use increased, the price for shipping goods plunged, thus increasing profits and stimulating demand.

The use of steamboats transformed St. Louis, Missouri, into a booming river port. New Orleans developed even faster. By 1840, it was perhaps the wealthiest American city, having developed a thriving trade with the Caribbean islands and the new Latin American republics that had overthrown Spanish rule. The annual amount of trade shipped through the river city doubled that of New York City by 1843, in large part because of the explosion in cotton production.

Wood-burning steamboats were a risky form of transportation, however. Accidents, explosions, and fires were common, and sanitation was poor. Passengers crowded on board along with pigs and cattle. There were no toilets on steamboats until the 1850s; passengers shared the same two washbasins and towels. Despite the inconveniences, however, steamboats were the fastest and most convenient form of transportation in the first half of the nineteenth century.

steamboats Ships and boats powered by wood-fired steam engines that made two-way traffic possible in eastern river systems, creating a transcontinental market and an agricultural empire.

TRAVELING THE WESTERN WATERS Three steamboats are docked at the levee at St. Paul, Minnesota, in 1859.

Water transportation: Canal systems

Canals also sped the market revolution. The **Erie Canal** (finished in 1825) in central New York connected the Great Lakes and the Midwest to the Hudson River and New York City. New York governor DeWitt Clinton took the lead in promoting the risky project, boasting that New York had the opportunity to "create a new era in history, and to erect a work more stupendous, more magnificent, and more beneficial, than has hitherto been achieved by the human race."

It was not an idle boast. A "river of gold" flowed along the Erie Canal after it opened in 1825. It drew eastward much of the midwestern trade (furs, lumber, textiles) that earlier had been forced to go to Canada or make the long journey down the Ohio and Mississippi Rivers to New Orleans and the Gulf of Mexico. Thanks to the Erie Canal, the backwoods village of Chicago developed into a bustling city because of its commercial connection via the Great Lakes to New York City, and eventually to Europe.

The Erie Canal was an engineering triumph. Forty feet wide and four feet deep, it was the longest canal in the world, extending 363 miles across New York from Albany in the east to Buffalo and Lake Erie in the west, and rising some 675 feet in elevation. It crossed rivers and valleys, marshes and forests.

Erie Canal (1825) Most important and profitable of the many barge canals built in the early nineteenth century, connecting the Great Lakes to the Hudson River and conveying so much cargo that it made New York City the nation's largest port.

Thousands of laborers built the canal. They were mostly German and Irish immigrants who were paid less than a dollar a day to drain swamps, clear forests, build stone bridges and aqueducts, and blast through solid rock.

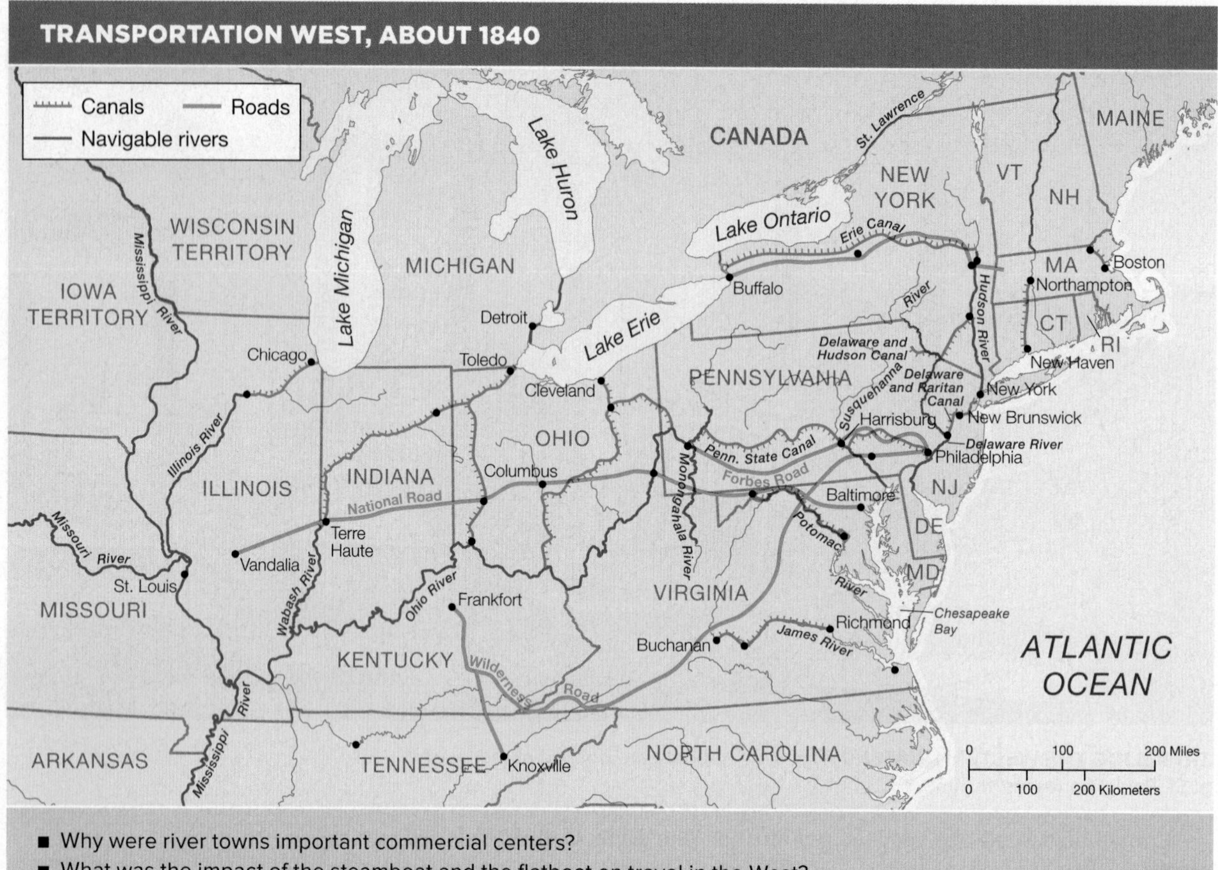

- Why were river towns important commercial centers?
- What was the impact of the steamboat and the flatboat on travel in the West?
- How did the Erie Canal transform the economies of New York and the Great Lakes region?

Canal boats brought lumber, grain, flour, and other goods, and they unlocked the floodgates of western settlement. Transporting goods from Buffalo to New York City previously took three weeks; now it took only eight days. The canal was so profitable that it paid off its construction costs in just seven years.

The Erie Canal also had enormous economic and political consequences, as it tied together the regional economies of the Midwest and the East while further isolating the Deep South. The Genesee Valley in western New York became one of the most productive grain-growing regions in the world; Rochester became a boom town, processing wheat and corn into flour and meal. Syracuse, Albany, and Buffalo experienced similarly dramatic growth.

The success of the Erie Canal and the entire New York canal system inspired other states to build some 3,000 miles of waterways by 1837. Canals spurred the economy by enabling speedier and less expensive transport of goods and people. They also boosted real estate prices for the lands bordering them and transformed sleepy villages into booming cities.

THE GROWTH OF RAILROADS, 1850 AND 1860

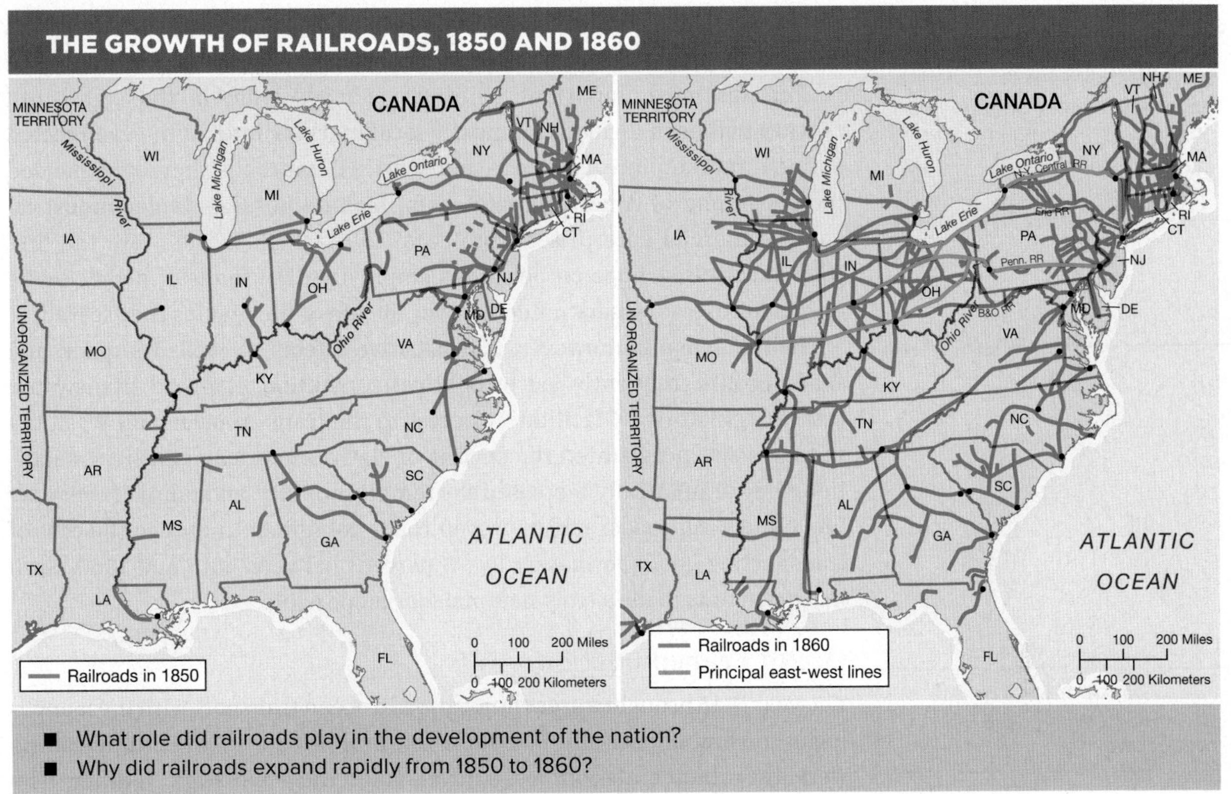

- What role did railroads play in the development of the nation?
- Why did railroads expand rapidly from 1850 to 1860?

Railroads

The canal era was short-lived, however. During the second quarter of the nineteenth century, a more versatile and powerful form of transportation emerged: the **railroad**. In 1825, the year the Erie Canal was completed, the world's first steam-powered railway began operating in England. Soon thereafter, a railroad-building craze struck the United States. In 1830, the nation had only 23 miles of railroad track. Over the next twenty years, railroad coverage grew to 30,626 miles.

Railroads connect the continent

The railroad surpassed other forms of transportation because trains could carry more people and freight faster, farther, and cheaper. The early railroads averaged ten miles per hour, more than twice the speed of stagecoaches and four times that of boats and barges. Railroads could also operate year-round, which gave them a huge advantage over canals that froze over in winter and dirt roads that became rivers of mud during rainstorms.

Railroads also encouraged western settlement and the expansion of commercial agriculture. A westerner reported that the opening of a new rail line resulted in the emergence of three new villages along the line. The depot or rail station became the central building in every town, a public place where people from all walks of life converged.

Building railroads stimulated the national economy not only by improving transportation but also by creating a huge demand for iron, wooden

railroads Steam-powered vehicles that improved passenger transportation, quickened western settlement, and enabled commercial agriculture in the nineteenth century.

clipper ships Tall, slender ships favored over older merchant ships for their speed; ultimately gave way to steamships because clipper ships lacked cargo space.

crossties, bridges, locomotives, freight cars, and other equipment. Railroads also became the nation's largest corporations and employers.

Perhaps most important, railroads changed what in the eighteenth century had been a cluster of mostly local markets into an interconnected national marketplace for goods and services. Railroads thereby expanded the geography of American capitalism, making possible larger industrial and commercial enterprises from coast to coast. Railroads were the first "big" businesses, huge corporations employing thousands of people while exercising extraordinary influence over the life of the regions they served.

Railroad mania, however, had negative effects as well. Its quick and shady profits frequently led to political corruption. Railroad titans often bribed legislators. By facilitating access to the trans-Appalachian West, the railroads also accelerated the decline of Native American culture. In addition, they dramatically increased the tempo, mobility, and noise of everyday life. Canals, railroads, and improved roads combined to reduce the cost of transporting goods to market by 95 percent between 1815 and 1860. Such improvements made a truly national market possible.

Ocean Transportation

Ocean transportation: Clipper ships enable high-speed ocean travel

The year 1845 brought a great innovation in ocean transport with the launching of the first clipper ship, the *Rainbow*. Built for speed, the **clipper ships** were the nineteenth-century equivalent of the supersonic jetliner. The three-masted schooners were twice as fast as the older merchant ships. Long and lean, with sleek hulls, flat bottoms, taller masts, and more sails, they cut

BUILDING A CLIPPER SHIP This 1833 oil painting captures the Messrs. Smith & Co. Ship Yard in Manhattan, where shipbuilders are busy shaping timbers to construct a clipper ship.

dashing figures during their brief but colorful career, which lasted less than two decades.

The American thirst for Chinese tea prompted the clipper boom. Asian tea leaves had to reach the market quickly after harvest, and the clipper ships made this possible. In addition, smugglers needed fast ships to get opium from India to China and then to America. A clipper ship loaded with opium was worth tens of millions of dollars at today's rates.

Even more important, the discovery of gold in California in 1848 lured thousands of prospectors and entrepreneurs from the Atlantic seaboard. The clipper ships were needed to make the run from Boston or New York to San Francisco, which required going around South America's dangerous Cape Horn. A clipper ship could make the trip in 123 days, some 80 days faster than a conventional ship.

The massive wave of would-be miners also generated an urgent demand for goods on the West Coast, and the clippers met it. But clippers, while fast, lacked space for cargo or passengers, and their tall masts often broke during storms. After the Civil War, the clipper ship would give way to the steamship and the transcontinental railroad.

Communications

Innovations in transportation also helped spark improvements in communications, which knit the nation even closer together. At the beginning of the nineteenth century, it took days—often weeks—for news to travel along the Atlantic seaboard. For example, after George Washington died in 1799 in Virginia, the news did not appear in New York City newspapers until a week later. By 1829, however, relay horse riders delivered President Andrew Jackson's inaugural address from Washington, D.C., to New York City in fewer than twenty hours.

Growth of newspapers

The number of newspapers also soared along with the creation of new towns and the rapid growth of cities. In 1790, there were 92 weekly newspapers; by 1810, there were 371, and many newspapers had become dailies. America had more newspaper readers than any nation. When a British traveler asked a milkman in Cincinnati why Americans spent so much time reading newspapers, he quickly replied: "How should freemen spend their time, but looking after their government, and watching that them fellers as we give offices to, does their duty?"

Development of the postal service

Mail deliveries also improved. The number of U.S. post offices soared from 75 in 1790 to 28,498 in 1860. In addition, new steam-powered printing presses reduced the cost of newspapers from 6¢ to a penny each, enabling virtually everyone to benefit from the news contained in the "penny press." In the new western states and territories, however, postal service was scarce and slow. To address the problem, two entrepreneurs, Henry Wells and William G. Fargo, formed an express delivery service called Wells Fargo & Company in 1852. Within a few years, Wells Fargo stagecoaches pulled by six horses were delivering passengers, mail, and "strongboxes" filled with gold

PONY EXPRESS Founded in 1860, the Pony Express Company pledged speedy delivery of mail from Missouri to as far west as California, relying on a relay team of 400 horses instead of the stagecoach of Wells Fargo & Company. In this hand-colored woodcut based on Frederic Remington's oil painting, Pony Express riders are shown changing horses.

across California and eventually from coast to coast. In 1857, Wells Fargo formed the Overland Mail Company, establishing regular twice-a-week mail service between St. Louis and San Francisco. Prior to that innovation, mail service was twice a month by steamship.

The Pony Express

Still, people sought even faster delivery. In 1860, Alexander Majors, William Russell, and William B. Waddell founded the Pony Express Company to deliver mail cross country between St. Joseph, Missouri, and Sacramento, California. By then, California had almost 400,000 people, and they needed faster connections to the rest of the nation. Majors, Russell, and Waddell decided to deliver mail by using horses instead of wagons. To do so, they acquired 400 fast horses and established 184 relay stations from Missouri west to California, enabling their 120 riders to change horses every ten to fifteen miles. The Pony Express riders set their fastest time delivering Abraham Lincoln's presidential inaugural address in 1861, which arrived in California in eight days. Riding day and night alone across western prairies, deserts, and snow-covered mountains was a dangerous enterprise. Indians attacked many of the relay stations, stealing the horses, killing the station keepers, and burning the buildings. The likelihood of Indian raids was a factor in the selection of horses for the express riders. Their ponies, fed with grain rather than grass, could outrun most Indian ponies.

telegraph system System of electronic communication invented by Samuel F. B. Morse that could transmit messages instantaneously across great distances.

The Pony Express Company, however, lasted only eighteen months. It was driven out of business by the most important advance in communications: the development of a national electromagnetic **telegraph system**.

Samuel F. B. Morse, a portrait-painter-turned-inventor, developed the telegraph. In May 1844, he sent the first intercity telegraph message from Washington, D.C., to Baltimore, Maryland. It read: "What hath God wrought?" By the end of the 1840s, most major cities benefited from telegraph lines. By enabling people to communicate faster and more easily across long distances, the telegraph system triggered many changes, not the least of which was helping railroad operators schedule trains more precisely and thus avoid collisions. A New Orleans newspaper claimed that with the invention of the telegraph "scarcely anything now will appear to be impossible."

Invention of the telegraph

The Role of Government

Government financing for internal improvements

Steamboats, canals, and railroads connected the western areas of the country with the East, boosted trade, helped open the Far West for settlement, and spurred dramatic growth in cities. Between 1800 and 1860, an undeveloped nation of scattered farms, primitive roads, and modest local markets became an engine of capitalist expansion, urban energy, and global reach.

The transportation improvements were financed by both state governments and private investors. The national government bought stock in turnpike and canal companies and, after the success of the Erie Canal, awarded land grants to several western states to support canal and railroad projects. In 1850, Stephen A. Douglas, a powerful Democratic senator from Illinois, convinced Congress to provide a major land grant to support a north–south rail line connecting Chicago and Mobile, Alabama. The 1850 congressional land grant set a precedent for other bounties that totaled about 20 million acres by 1860. However, this would prove to be a small amount when compared with the land grants that Congress would award transcontinental railroads during the 1860s and after.

Industrial Development

CORE **OBJECTIVE**

2. Explain the impact of the Industrial Revolution on the way people worked and lived.

The concentration of huge numbers of people in cities, coupled with the transportation and communication revolutions, greatly increased the number of potential customers for a given product. This in turn gave rise to *mass production*, whereby companies used new technologies (machine tools) to produce greater quantities of products, which could thereby be sold at lower prices while generating higher profits. The application of water-powered mills and coal-powered steam engines sparked an industrial revolution in Europe and America from the mid-eighteenth century to the late nineteenth century.

The **Industrial Revolution**, centered on the invention of the steam engine, was the most important development in human history since the advent of agriculture. Prior to 1800, most products were made by hand by skilled artisans. That changed quickly with the development of textile machinery, soon followed by a dazzling array of machinery invented to manufacture almost everything.

Factories, mills, mines, and industrial plants emerged to replace many artisans and craftsmen making clothing, shoes, clocks and watches, furniture, firearms, and an array of other items. "It is an extraordinary era in which we live," reported Daniel Webster in 1847. "It is altogether new. The world has seen nothing like it before."

American Technology

"Practical" inventiveness

During the nineteenth century, Americans became known for their "practical" inventiveness. Between 1790 and 1811, the U.S. Patent Office approved an annual average of seventy-seven patents certifying new inventions; by the 1850s, the Patent Office was approving more than 28,000 new inventions each year.

Many inventions generated dramatic changes. In 1844, for example, Charles Goodyear patented a process for "vulcanizing" rubber, which made the product stronger, more elastic, waterproof, and winter-proof. Vulcanized rubber was used for a variety of products, from shoes and boots to seals, gaskets, hoses, and eventually tires.

In 1846, Elias Howe patented his design of the sewing machine. It was soon improved by Isaac Merritt Singer, who founded the Singer Sewing Machine Company, which first produced industrial sewing machines for use in textile mills but eventually offered machines for home use. Sewing machines helped revolutionize "women's work." They dramatically reduced the time for making clothes at home, thus freeing up more leisure time for many women.

Technological advances improved living conditions because houses could be larger, better heated, and better illuminated. The first sewer systems helped clean up cities by ridding streets of human and animal waste. Machine-made clothes using standardized forms fit better and were cheaper than those sewn by hand; machine-made newspapers and magazines were more abundant and affordable, as were clocks, watches, guns, and plows.

The Cotton Gin

One invention launched an economic revolution. In 1792, Eli Whitney, a recent Yale graduate from New England, spent several months at Mulberry Grove Plantation on the Georgia coast, where he "heard much said of the difficulty of ginning cotton"—that is, separating the fibers from the seeds. Cotton had been used for clothing and bedding from ancient times, but cotton cloth was rare and expensive because it took so long to remove the seeds. One person working all day could separate barely one pound by hand.

Industrial Revolution Major shift in the nineteenth century from handmade manufacturing to mass production in mills and factories using water-, coal-, and steam-powered machinery.

At Mulberry Grove, Whitney learned that the person who could invent a "machine" to gin cotton would become wealthy overnight. That was incentive enough for him. Within just ten days, Whitney had devised "an absurdly simple contrivance," using nails attached to a roller, to remove the seeds from cotton bolls.

Completed in 1793, Whitney's **cotton gin** (short for *engine*) proved to be fifty times more productive than a hand laborer. Almost overnight, it transformed cotton from simply a local crop to a global industry led by the American South, whose climate from Virginia southward offered the 200 frost-free days required to grow the fibrous plant. In becoming America's most profitable crop, cotton transformed southern agriculture, northern industry, race-based slavery, national politics, and international trade.

COTTON GIN Before Eli Whitney's cotton gin, it would have taken the four people in this engraving days to pick through the avalanche of cotton depicted here and separate the cotton seeds from the fibers. **How did the cotton gin affect the economy of the South and the nation more broadly?**

King Cotton

During the first half of the nineteenth century, southern-grown **cotton** became the dominant force driving both the national economy and the controversial efforts to expand slavery into the western territories. People called it "white gold"; it brought enormous wealth to southern planters and merchants as well as New England textile mill owners and New York shipowners and cotton traders.

Slavery expanded accordingly. The number of enslaved people increased from 700,000 in 1787 to over 4 million on the eve of the American Civil War; approximately 70 percent were involved in some way with cotton production. So closely tied were cotton and slavery that the price of an enslaved person directly correlated to the price of cotton (except during years of excessive speculation). The commercial growing of cotton spread plantation slavery across the South, especially the Carolinas, Georgia, Tennessee, Alabama, Mississippi, Louisiana, Arkansas, and Texas.

By 1812, cotton gins had reduced the cost of producing cotton yarn by 90 percent. Suddenly, cotton clothing was affordable to everyone. By the mid-nineteenth century, people worldwide were wearing more-comfortable and easier-to-clean cotton clothing. When British textile manufacturers chose the less brittle American cotton over the varieties grown in the Caribbean, Brazil, and India, the demand for southern cotton skyrocketed, as did its price. Cotton became America's largest export. By 1860, British textile mills were processing a billion pounds of cotton a year, 92 percent of which

cotton gin Hand-operated machine invented by Eli Whitney that quickly removed seeds from cotton bolls, enabling the mass production of cotton in nineteenth-century America.

cotton White fibers harvested from plants that made comfortable, easy-to-clean products, especially clothing; the most valuable cash crop driving the economy in nineteenth-century United States and Great Britain.

came from the southern states. On the eve of the Civil War, cotton represented 60 percent of America's exports.

American cotton becomes an international commodity

The southern cotton boom also spurred the development of textile mills in New England; expanded the shipping fleets of New York City; and made the ports of New Orleans, Mobile, Savannah, and Charleston sources of enormous profits for the regional and national economies. The South harvested raw cotton, and northern buyers and shipowners carried it to New England, Great Britain, and France, where textile mills spun the fiber into thread and fabric. Bankers in New York City and London financed the growth of global cotton capitalism.

The Expansion of Slavery

Because cotton was a labor-intensive crop, growers were convinced that only enslaved Blacks could make their farms and plantations profitable. Many Virginia and Maryland planters sold their surplus enslaved people to work in the new cotton-growing areas in Georgia, Alabama, Mississippi, and Louisiana. In 1790, planters in Virginia and Maryland had owned 56 percent of all the enslaved people in the United States; by 1860, they owned only 15 percent, as some 835,000 enslaved people were "sold south."

In the search for higher profits, the price of enslaved workers soared as did the abuses they suffered—whippings, sexual assaults, children separated from mothers, and being overworked to death. Cotton created boom times in Alabama, Mississippi, and Louisiana, where land was cheap. "The ALABAMA FEVER rages here," a North Carolina planter lamented . . . and has *carried off* vast numbers of our citizens." A cotton farmer in Mississippi urged a friend in Kentucky to sell his farm and join him: "If you could reconcile it to yourself to bring your negroes to the Mississippi Territory, they would certainly make you a handsome fortune in ten years by the cultivation of Cotton." Enslaved people became so valuable that stealing them became a common problem.

Farming the Midwest

By 1860, more than half of Americans lived west of the Appalachian Mountains. The fertile farmlands in the Midwest—Ohio, Michigan, Indiana, Illinois, and Iowa—drew farmers from the rocky hillsides of New England and the exhausted soils of Virginia. People traveled on foot, on horseback, and in wagons, eager to make a fresh start on their *own* land made available by the government.

Squatters' claims on western farmland

A national land law of 1820 reduced the price of federal land. Even that was not enough for westerners, however. They demanded "preemption," the right of squatters (people who simply built a cabin and started farming without actually purchasing government land) to buy land at the minimum price, and "graduation," the progressive reduction of the price of land that did not sell immediately. Congress eventually responded with two bills. Under the Preemption Act of 1830, squatters could get 160 acres at the minimum price of $1.25 per acre. Under the Graduation Act of 1854, prices of unsold lands were to be lowered in stages over thirty years.

Growth of commercial agriculture: Steel plows (1837) and mechanical reapers (1831)

Technology also enabled greater agricultural productivity. The development of durable iron plows (rather than wooden plows) eased the backbreaking job of tilling the soil. In 1819, Jethro Wood of New York introduced an iron plow with separate parts that were easy to replace. Further improvements would follow, including Vermonter John Deere's steel plow (1837), whose sharp edges could cut through the tough prairie grass in the Midwest and the Great Plains. By 1845, Massachusetts alone had seventy-three plants making more than 60,000 plows per year. Most were sold to western farmers, illustrating the emergence of a national marketplace for goods and services made possible by the transportation revolution.

Other technological improvements quickened the growth of large-scale commercial agriculture. By the 1840s, new mechanical seeders had replaced the process of sowing seed by hand. In 1831, twenty-two-year-old Virginian Cyrus Hall McCormick invented a mechanical reaper pulled by horses to harvest wheat, a development as significant to the agricultural economy of the Midwest, Old Northwest, and Great Plains as the cotton gin was to the South.

In 1847, the **McCormick reaper** began selling so fast that its inventor moved to Chicago and built a manufacturing plant. Within a few years, McCormick had sold thousands of the giant machines, transforming the scale of commercial agriculture. Using a handheld sickle, a farmer could harvest a half-acre of wheat a day; with a McCormick reaper, two people could work twelve acres a day.

McCormick reaper Mechanical reaper invented by Cyrus Hall McCormick in 1831 that dramatically increased the production of wheat.

McCORMICK'S REAPING MACHINE This illustration appeared in the catalog of the Great Exhibition, held at the Crystal Palace in London in 1851. The plow eased the transformation of rough plains into fertile farmland, and the reaping machine accelerated the harvesting of hay, wheat, and other grains.

Early Textile Manufacturers

While technological breakthroughs such as the cotton gin, mechanical harvester, and railroads accelerated agricultural development and enabled a national economy, other technologies altered the economic landscape even more profoundly.

Industrial capitalists who financed and built the first factories were the revolutionaries of the nineteenth century, for they transformed the nature of work and the dynamics of workers' communities. People had never labored for twelve-hour shifts in large windowless buildings filled with deafening machines and scores or even hundreds of sweating workers. The informal routine of farmwork was replaced by the close supervision of managers and the regimentation signaled by the factory whistle and the time clock. As the German economic theorist Karl Marx pointed out in *Capital,* traditionally, "the workman makes use of a tool, [whereas] the machine makes use of him."

Rise of the factory system: Steam-powered mills

Mills and factories were initially powered by water wheels and then by coal-fired steam engines. The shift from river water to coal sped the growth rate of the textile industry (and industries of all types), and initiated an industrial revolution destined to end Great Britain's domination of the world economy.

In 1800, the output of America's mills and factories amounted to only one sixth of Britain's production. The growth of textile production was slow until Thomas Jefferson's embargo in 1807 stimulated the domestic production of cloth. By 1815, hundreds of textile mills in New England, New York, and Pennsylvania were producing thread, cloth, and clothing. By 1860, the output of America's mills and factories would be a third and by 1880 two thirds that of the British.

After the War of 1812, British textile companies had flooded American markets with cheap cotton cloth. Such "dumping" nearly killed the infant American textile industry by lowering the prices of thread and cloth. A delegation of New England mill owners traveled to Washington, D.C., to demand a federal tariff on imported cloth to deter the British from selling their cloth in the United States for less than the prices charged by American manufacturers. The efforts of the mill owners created a culture of industrial lobbying for congressional tariff protection that continues to this day.

Import tariffs to promote American-made textiles

The mill owners neglected to admit that tariffs hurt consumers by forcing them to pay higher prices for imported goods. Over time, as Scotsman Adam Smith explained in his pathbreaking book on capitalism, *The Wealth of Nations* (1776), consumers not only pay higher prices for imported goods as a result of tariffs but also pay higher prices for domestic goods, since businesses invariably take advantage of opportunities to raise the prices charged for their products.

Tariffs helped "protect" American industries from foreign competition, but competition is the engine of innovation and efficiency in a capitalist economy. New England shipping companies opposed higher tariffs because they would reduce the amount of goods sent from Britain and Europe.

Many southerners opposed tariffs because of fears that Britain and France would retaliate with tariffs on American cotton and tobacco shipped to their ports.

In the end, Congress passed the Tariff of 1816, which placed a tax on imported cloth. Such tariffs were a major factor in spurring industrialization. By impeding foreign competition, they enabled American manufacturers to dominate the national marketplace.

MILL GIRLS Massachusetts mill workers of the mid-nineteenth century, photographed holding shuttles. Thread was spun around the inner bobbin. **What sort of working conditions would Lowell girls like these have experienced?**

The Lowell System

The factory system emerged first at Waltham, Massachusetts, in 1813, when a group known as the Boston Associates constructed the first textile mill in which the mechanized processes of spinning yarn and weaving cloth (copied from English mills) were brought together under one roof. In 1822, the Boston Associates, led by Francis Cabot Lowell, developed another cotton mill at a village along the Merrimack River twenty-eight miles north of Boston, which they renamed Lowell. It soon became the model for mill towns throughout New England, often referred to as the **Lowell system**.

The founders of the Lowell system sought to develop ideal industrial communities. To avoid the wretched conditions of the overcrowded English textile-mill villages, they located their four- and five-story brick-built mills along rivers in the countryside and lined the streets with trees and tidy flower beds.

Women—mostly young women from farm families—were the first factory workers in the nation. Mill owners preferred women because of their dexterity in operating machines and their willingness to endure the mind-numbing boredom of operating spinning machines and looms for wages lower than those paid to men (even though their wages, $2.50 per week, were the highest in the world for women).

Moreover, by the 1820s New England had a surplus of women because so many men had migrated westward. Many, perhaps most, of the young women viewed their work in mills as temporary. "There are few who look upon factory labor as a pursuit for life," one of them reported. "It is but a temporary vocation; and most of the girls resolve to quit the Mill. . . . Money is their object."

Whatever their motives, in the early 1820s, a steady stream of lively girls and single women began flocking toward Lowell. To reassure worried parents, the mill owners promised to provide the "Lowell girls" with tolerable work, competitive wages, prepared meals, comfortable boardinghouses (four girls to a room), moral discipline, and educational and cultural opportunities. Work in the mill village would provide a righteous escape from the isolation and boredom of farm life.

Lowell system Model New England factory communities that provided employees, mostly young women, with meals, a boardinghouse, moral discipline, and educational opportunities.

Initially the "Lowell idea" worked. Visitors commented on the well-designed mills, with their lecture halls and libraries. The "Lowell girls" were "neatly dressed" and appeared "healthy and happy." They lived in dormitories

THE GROWTH OF INDUSTRY IN THE 1840S

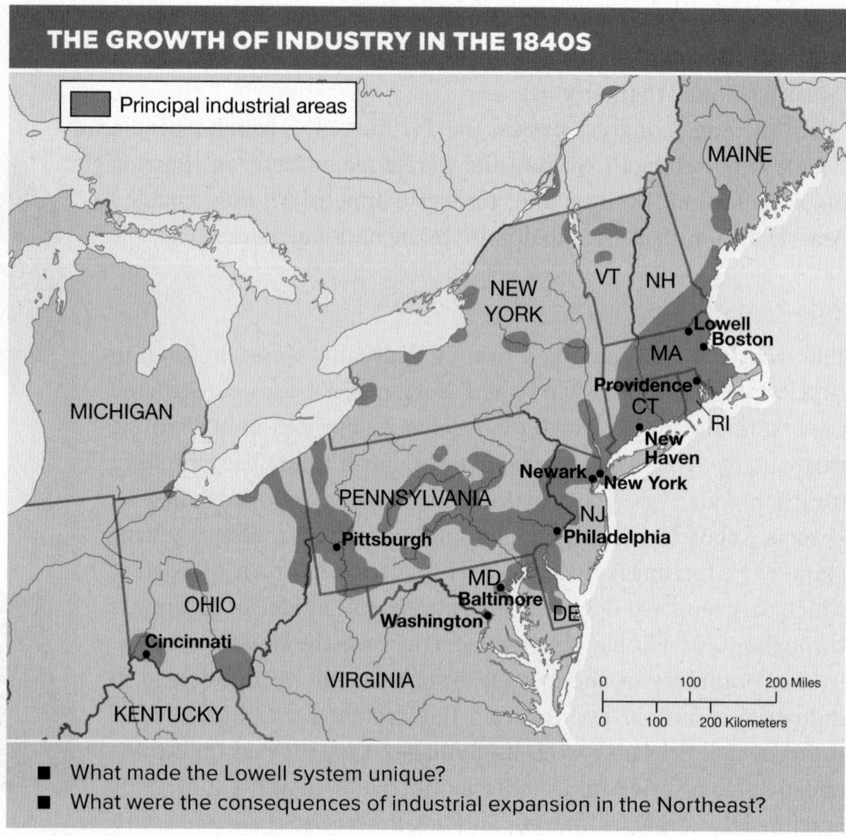

- What made the Lowell system unique?
- What were the consequences of industrial expansion in the Northeast?

staffed by "virtuous" matrons who enforced strict rules regarding contact with men, evening curfews, and mandatory church attendance. Despite thirteen-hour workdays and five-and-a-half-day workweeks (longer hours than those imposed upon prison inmates), some women still found the time and energy to form study groups, write poetry, publish a literary magazine, and attend lectures.

Declining conditions and labor strikes

Lowell, however, lost its innocence as it grew—and as the owners accumulated "unbelievable profits." By 1832, some 500 cotton mills were operating in New England. Eight years later, Lowell had come to house 8,000 textile workers. The once clean and tidy rural village had become a grimy industrial city, and the repetitive routine of tending a spinning machine or a loom all day led to boredom and fatigue. Greed led mill owners to produce too much cloth, which depressed prices. The owners slashed wages and quickened the pace of work. One worker described the situation as constituting "factory tyranny."

In 1834, the Lowell women went on strike to protest wage cuts and deteriorating working and living conditions. The angry mill owners labeled the hundreds of striking women "ungrateful" and "unfeminine"—and tried to get rid of the strike's leaders. One mill manager reported that "we have paid off several of these Amazons & presume that they will leave town on Monday."

The workers lost the strike. Labor activist Seth Luther denounced the mill system in New England for degrading the "bodies and minds of the producing classes, destroying the energies of both, and for no other object than to enable the 'rich' to 'take care of themselves,' while the poor 'must work or starve.'"

Two years later, the Lowell workers again walked out to protest rent increases in company-owned boarding houses. This time the owners backed down. Over time, however, the owners began hiring Irish immigrants who were so desperate for jobs that they rarely complained about the working conditions. By 1850, some 40 percent of the mill workers were Irish, and the mill owners also started hiring boys for jobs once reserved for girls only.

Industrialization, Cities, and the Environment

Urban growth

The rapid growth of commerce and industry spurred the growth of cities and mill villages. Lowell's population in 1820 was 200. By 1830, it was 6,500, and ten years later it had soared to 21,000. Other factory centers sprouted up across New England, displacing forests, farms, and villages while filling the air with smoke, noise, and stench. Between 1820 and 1840, the number of Americans engaged in manufacturing increased 800 percent, and the number of city dwellers more than doubled.

The United States was rapidly becoming a global industrial power, producing its own clothing and shoes, iron and engines. The Atlantic seaports of New York City, Philadelphia, Baltimore, and Boston remained the largest cities. New Orleans became the nation's fifth largest because of its role in shipping goods down the Mississippi River to the East Coast and to Europe. New York outpaced all its competitors in growth. By 1860, it was the first city whose population surpassed more than 1 million, largely because of its superior harbor and its access to the commerce floating down the Hudson River from the Erie Canal.

Popular Culture

During the colonial era, working-class Americans had little time for amusement. Most adults worked from dawn to dusk six days a week. In rural areas, free time was often spent in communal activities, such as barn raisings, shooting matches, and footraces, while coastal residents sailed and fished. In cities, people attended dances, went on sleigh rides and picnics, and played "parlor games" such as billiards, cards, and chess.

By the early nineteenth century, however, an increasingly urban society enjoyed more diverse forms of recreation. A distinctive urban culture emerged, and laborers and shopkeepers sought new forms of leisure and entertainment.

Urban Recreation Social drinking was pervasive during the first half of the nineteenth century. In 1829, the secretary of war estimated that three quarters of the nation's laborers drank at least four ounces of "hard liquor" daily. Taverns and social or sporting clubs served as centers of recreation and leisure.

THE GROWTH OF CITIES, 1820 AND 1860

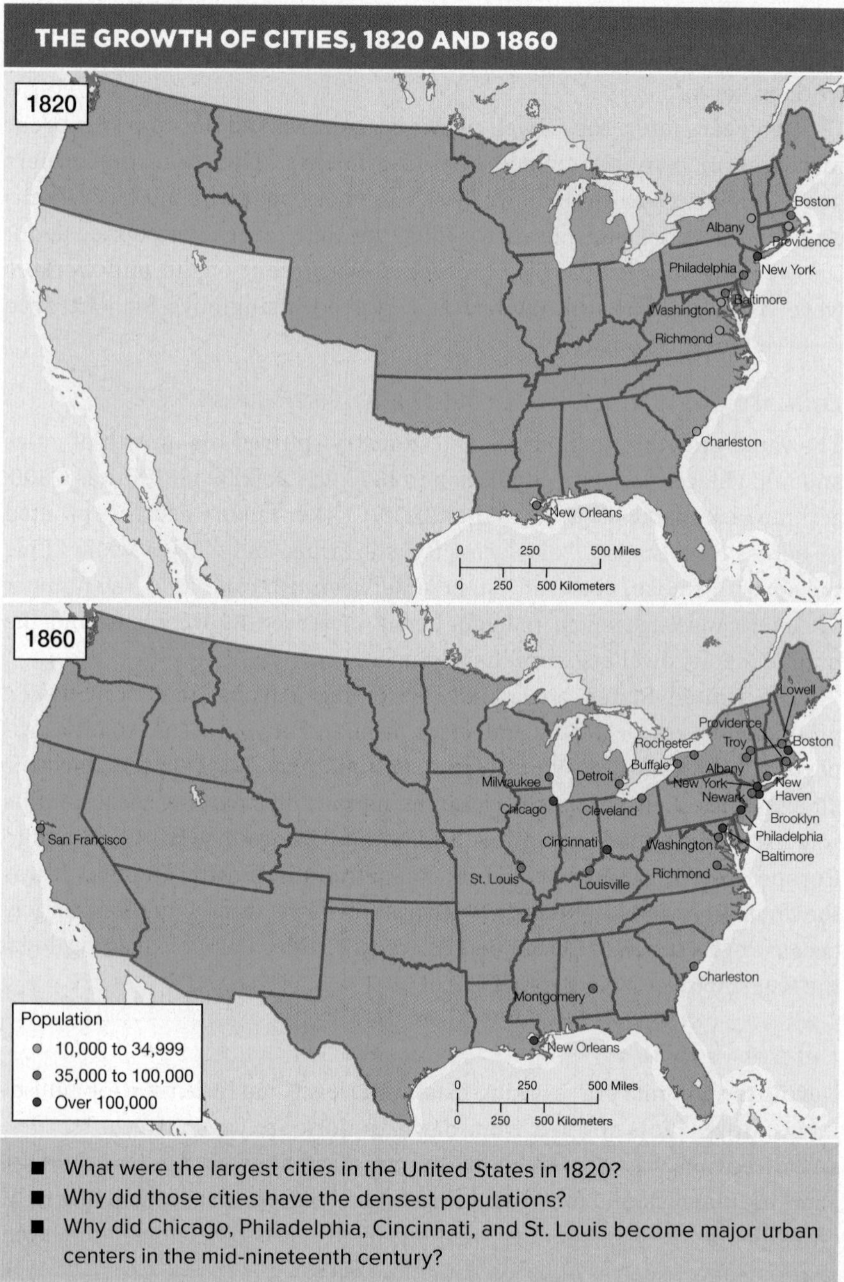

- What were the largest cities in the United States in 1820?
- Why did those cities have the densest populations?
- Why did Chicago, Philadelphia, Cincinnati, and St. Louis become major urban centers in the mid-nineteenth century?

Recreation: Blood sports

So-called blood sports were also popular, especially among the working poor. Cockfighting and dogfighting attracted frenzied betting, but prizefighting (boxing) eventually displaced the animal contests and proved popular with all social classes. The early contestants tended to be Irish or English immigrants who fought with bare knuckles, and the results were brutal. A match ended only when a contestant could not continue. One bout in 1842 lasted 119 rounds and ended when a fighter died in his corner. Such deaths prompted several cities to outlaw boxing, only to see it reappear as an underground activity.

BARE KNUCKLE BOXING Blood sports such as "bare-knuckle boxing," portrayed here in a contemporary painting George A. Hayes, emerged as popular urban entertainment for men of all social classes, but especially among the working poor.

The Popular Arts Theaters became the most popular form of indoor entertainment. People from all walks of life flocked to opera houses, playhouses, and music halls to watch a wide spectrum of performances: Shakespeare's tragedies, "blood and thunder" melodramas, comedies, minstrel shows, operas, and local pageants. Audiences were predominantly men. "Respectable" women rarely attended, as the prevailing "cult of domesticity" kept them at home.

White recreation: Minstrel shows

The 1830s brought the first uniquely American form of mass entertainment: "blackface" minstrel shows, featuring White performers made up as Blacks. "Minstrelsy," which drew upon African American folklore and reinforced racial stereotypes, featured banjo and fiddle music, "shuffle" dances, and lowbrow humor. Between the 1830s and the 1870s, minstrel shows were immensely popular, especially among northern working-class ethnic groups and southern Whites.

The most popular minstrel songs were written by a White composer named Stephen Foster. In 1846, he composed "Oh! Susanna," which immediately became a national favorite. Its popularity catapulted Foster into the limelight, and he responded with equally well-received tunes such as "Old Folks at Home" (popularly known as "Way Down upon the Sewanee River"), "Massa's in de Cold, Cold Ground," "My Old Kentucky Home," and "Old Black Joe," all of which perpetuated the sentimental myth of contented enslavement.

Immigration

CORE **OBJECTIVE**

3. Analyze how immigration altered the nation's population and shaped its politics.

During the forty years from the outbreak of the Revolution to the end of the War of 1812, immigration to America had slowed to a trickle. The French Revolution and the Napoleonic Wars restricted travel to and from Europe until 1815. Thereafter, however, the number of immigrants rose steadily. Ships overflowing with adventurous and desperate people arrived from across the world. They were eager to experience the American Dream—the seductive promise that in the United States everyone had a chance to improve their life.

After 1837, a worldwide financial panic and economic slump accelerated the pace of immigration. Employers aggressively recruited foreigners, in large part because they would work for lower wages than native-born Americans. The *Chicago Daily Tribune* observed that a German laborer was willing "to live as cheaply and work infinitely more intelligently than the negro."

POPULATION DENSITY, 1820 AND 1860

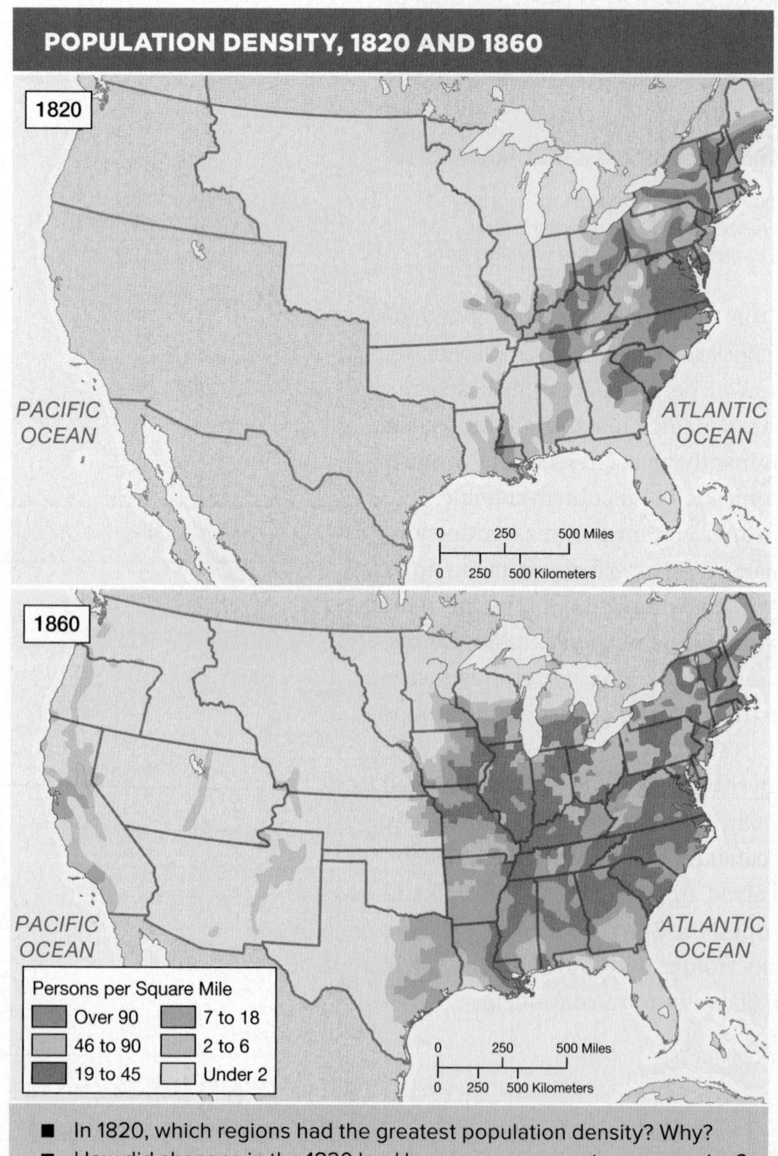

- In 1820, which regions had the greatest population density? Why?
- How did changes in the 1820 land law encourage western expansion?
- In 1860, which regions had the greatest population density? Why?
- How did new technologies allow farmers to grow more crops on larger pieces of land?

The years from 1845 to 1854 witnessed the greatest proportional influx of immigrants in U.S. history, 2.4 million, or about 14.5 percent of the total population in 1845. In 1860, more than one of every eight Americans was foreign born. British immigrants continued to arrive in large numbers. By the 1850s, the rapid development of California lured Chinese immigrants in significant numbers, while Scandinavians settled mostly in Wisconsin and Minnesota, where the climate and woodlands reminded them of home. By far, however, the largest number of immigrants between 1840 and 1860 came from Ireland and Germany.

The Irish

No nation proportionately sent more of its people to America than Ireland. They first arrived in British America in significant numbers during the 1720s. By 1790, they represented a sixth of the national population. During the mid-nineteenth century, however, their numbers soared. A prolonged agricultural crisis that brought immense social hardships caused many Irish to flee their homeland.

Irish farmers primarily grew potatoes; the average Irishman ate five pounds of potatoes a day. In 1845, a fungus destroyed the potato crop and triggered the potato famine. More than a million people died, and almost 2 million more left Ireland, whose total population was only 8 million.

Irish immigration: Unskilled labor

Most Irish immigrants, almost all of them Roman Catholics, traveled to Canada and the United States. In just one year, Boston's Irish population jumped from 30,000 to 100,000. As one group of immigrants explained, "All we want to do is get out of Ireland; we must be better anywhere but here." America, they knew, had paying jobs and "plenty to eat."

By the 1850s, the Irish made up more than half the population of Boston and New York City and were almost as dominant in Philadelphia. Most were desperately poor and crowded into filthy tenement houses. Irish neighborhoods became known for crime, deadly diseases, prostitution, and alcoholism. Almost 80 percent of infants born to Irish immigrants died.

Irish immigrants confronted humiliating stereotypes and intense anti-Catholic prejudice. Many employers posted signs reading "No Irish Need Apply." A Chicago newspaper reported that the "Irish fill our prisons, our poor houses. . . . Scratch a convict or a pauper, and the chances are that you tickle the skin of an Irish Catholic. Putting them on a boat and sending them home would end crime in this country."

Irish Americans, however, could be equally mean-spirited toward other groups, such as free African Americans, who competed with them for low-wage jobs. In 1850, the *New York Tribune* expressed concern that the Irish, having escaped from "a galling, degrading bondage" in their homeland, voted against proposals for equal rights for Blacks and frequently arrived at the polls shouting, "Down with the Colored people! Let them go back to Africa, where they belong."

Many African Americans viewed the Irish with equal contempt. In 1850, an enslaved person expressed a common sentiment: "My Master is a great tyrant, he treats me badly as if I were a common Irishman."

Irish immigrants in large cities often took jobs as waiters, dock workers, and deliverymen that had long been held by African Americans. A free Black person voiced a criticism of immigrants threatening to take over their low-skilled jobs that is still being made in the twenty-first century. The Irish, he said, were "crowding themselves into every place of business and labor and driving the poor colored American citizen out."

THE IGNORANT VOTE—HONORS ARE EASY Thomas Nast's racist caricature of an Irishman and African American southerner evenly balanced on a scale appeared on the cover of *Harper's Weekly* in December 1876. **How does Nast, a German-born immigrant, represent the race relations between the Irish and African Americans?**

Enterprising Irish immigrants forged remarkable careers, however. Twenty years after arriving in New York, Alexander T. Stewart became the owner of the nation's largest department store and accumulated vast real estate holdings. Michael Cudahy, who began working at age fourteen in a Milwaukee meatpacking business, became head of the Cudahy Packing Company and developed a process for the curing of meats under refrigeration.

Dublin-born Victor Herbert emerged as one of America's most revered composers, and Irish dancers and playwrights came to dominate the stage.

The growth of Roman Catholicism

By the start of the Civil War, the Irish had energized trade unions, become the most important ethnic group supporting the Democratic party, and made the Roman Catholic Church the nation's largest religious denomination. Years of persecution had instilled in Irish Catholics a fierce loyalty to the church as "the supreme authority over all the affairs of the world." Such passion for Catholicism generated unity among Irish Americans and fear among American Protestants. Picked on and discriminated against, the Irish were understandably clannish. Most of them settled in all-Irish neighborhoods in the nation's largest cities. They also formed powerful Democratic political organizations such as Tammany Hall in New York City that would dominate political life during the second half of the nineteenth century.

The Germans

German immigration: Skilled and diverse workers

German immigrants were almost as numerous as the Irish. Unlike the Irish, however, the German arrivals included a large number of skilled craftsmen and well-educated professional people—doctors, lawyers, teachers, engineers—some of whom were refugees from the failed German revolution of 1848.

In addition to an array of political opinions, Germans brought with them a variety of religious preferences. Most were Protestants (usually Lutherans), a third were Roman Catholics, and a significant number were Jews.

Among the German immigrants who prospered were Heinrich Steinweg, a piano maker who in America changed his name to Steinway and became famous for the quality of his instruments, and Levi Strauss, a Jewish tailor who followed the gold rush to California and began making work pants, later dubbed Levi's.

Germans settled more often in rural areas. Many were independent farmers, skilled workers, and shopkeepers. More so than the Irish, they migrated in families and groups. This clannish quality helped them better sustain elements of their language and culture in the New World. More of them also tended to return to their native country. About 14 percent of the Germans eventually went back to their homeland, compared with just 9 percent of the Irish.

Nativism

The nativists and widespread xenophobia

The flood of immigrants created a backlash among a growing number of "nativists," people born in the United States who resented the newcomers. The flood of Irish and German Catholics especially aroused hostility among Protestant nativists. A Boston minister described Catholicism as "the ally of tyranny, the opponent of material prosperity, the foe of thrift, the enemy of the railroad, the caucus, and the school."

Roving gangs of **nativists** terrorized and even murdered Catholic immigrants to keep them from voting. The Order of the Star-Spangled Banner, founded in New York City in 1849, grew into a powerful political group known officially as the American party. Members pledged never to vote for any foreign-born or Catholic candidates. When asked about the secretive

nativists Native-born Americans who viewed immigrants as a threat to their job opportunities and way of life.

organization, they were told to say, "I know nothing," a phrase that gave rise to the informal name for the American party: the **Know-Nothings**.

For a while, the Know-Nothings appeared on the brink of major-party status, especially during the 1850s, when the number of immigrants was five times as large as it had been during the 1840s. In the state and local campaigns of 1854, they swept the Massachusetts legislature, winning all but two seats in the lower house, and that fall they elected more than forty congressmen. Forty percent of the Pennsylvania state legislators were Know-Nothings.

KNOW-NOTHINGS This political cartoon (ca. 1850) visualizes the Know-Nothings' common complaints: that in contrast to hardworking Americans, the Irish and German immigrants were drunkards who were stealing American elections and disrupting the political status quo.

The Know-Nothings demanded that immigrants and Roman Catholics be excluded from public office and that the waiting period for naturalization (earning citizenship) be extended from five to twenty-one years. Their shouted battle cry was "America for Americans," and many of them engaged in riotous violence, assaulting Catholic neighborhoods, killing Catholic immigrants, and burning churches, convents, and homes.

Then, as now, nativists generated intense opposition. Abraham Lincoln expressed his revulsion at the anti-immigrant party in a letter to a friend in 1855:

> I am not a Know-Nothing—that is certain. How could I be? How can anyone who abhors the oppression of negroes, be in favor of degrading classes of white people just because of their religion or their place of origin? As a nation, we began by declaring that "all men are created equal." We now practically read it "all men are created equal, except negroes." When the Know-Nothings get control, it will read "all men are created equals, except negroes and foreigners and Catholics."

For a while, the Know-Nothings threatened to control New England, New York, and Maryland, but the anti-Catholic movement subsided when slavery became the focal issue of the 1850s, and after 1856 members opted for either the Republican or the Democratic party. By 1860, the nativist American party was dead.

Know-Nothings Nativist, anti-Catholic third party organized in 1854 in reaction to large-scale German and Irish immigration.

Organized Labor and New Professions

CORE **OBJECTIVE**

4. Evaluate the impact of the expanding capitalist "market economy" on workers, professionals, and women.

While most Americans continued to work as farmers during the nineteenth century, a growing number found employment in new or expanding enterprises: textile mills, shoe factories, banks, railroads, publishing, retail stores, teaching, preaching, medicine, law, construction, and engineering. Technological innovations (steam power, power tools, and new modes of

THE SHOE FACTORY When Philadelphia shoemakers went on strike in 1806, a court found them guilty of a "conspiracy to raise wages." Here shoemakers work in the bottoming room at a Massachusetts shoe factory.

transportation) and their social applications (mass communication, turnpikes, the postal service, banks, and corporations) transformed the nature of work for many Americans, both men and women.

Still, during the first half of the nineteenth century, most Americans continued to live on isolated farms, their lives revolving around the changing seasons and the hours of daylight. Most grew their own food and made their own clothes. Information from the outside world was scarce and usually stale by the time it appeared in rural areas. By the end of the century, however, all that had changed thanks to technological innovations.

Early Unions

Proud apprentices, journeymen, and master craftsmen, who controlled their labor and invested their work with an emphasis on quality rather than quantity, resented the spread of mills and factories populated by masses of "half-trained" workers dependent upon an hourly wage and subject to the sharp fluctuations of the larger economy. Skilled workers were called artisans, craftsmen, or mechanics. They made or repaired shoes, hats, saddles, silverware, jewelry, glass, ropes, furniture, and a broad array of other products. During the 1820s and 1830s, artisans struggled to compete with the low prices made possible by the new factories and mass-production workshops.

Trade associations of skilled craftspeople

In the early nineteenth century, a growing fear that they were losing status led artisans in the major cities to become involved in politics and unions. At first, they organized themselves into interest groups representing their individual skills or trades. Such "trade associations" were the first type of labor unions. They pressured politicians for tariffs to protect their industries from foreign imports, provided insurance benefits, and drafted regulations to improve working conditions. In addition, they sought to control the number of tradesmen in their profession so as to maintain wage levels.

Early labor unions were prosecuted as unlawful conspiracies. In 1806, for instance, Philadelphia shoemakers were found guilty of conspiring "to raise their wages." The court's decision broke the union. In 1842, though, the Massachusetts Supreme Court issued a landmark ruling in *Commonwealth v. Hunt* declaring that forming a trade union was not in itself illegal, nor was a demand that employers hire only members of the union. The court also said that union workers could strike if an employer hired laborers who refused to join the union.

Until the 1820s, labor organizations took the form of local trade unions, each confined to one city and one craft or skill. From 1827 to 1837, however, organization on a larger scale began to take hold. In 1834, the **National Trades' Union** was formed to organize the citywide trade unions into a stronger national association. At the same time, shoemakers, printers, carpenters, and weavers established national craft unions. But all the national groups and most of the local ones vanished during the economic depression in the late 1830s.

Women also formed trade unions. Sarah Monroe, who helped organize the New York Tailoresses' Society, explained that it was intended to defend "our rights." If it was "unfashionable for men to bear [workplace] oppression in silence," she wondered, "why should it not also become unfashionable with the women?" In 1831, the women tailors went out on strike demanding a "just price for labor."

The Rise of the Professions

The dramatic social changes of the first half of the nineteenth century opened up an array of new **professions**. Bustling new towns required new services—retail stores, printing shops, post offices, newspapers, schools, banks, law firms, medical practices, and others—that created more high status professions than had existed before.

Teaching Teaching became one of the fastest-growing vocations. Horace Mann of Massachusetts was instrumental in demanding free public education for all children as the best way to transform youths into citizens. Many states, especially in the North, agreed, and the number of schools exploded during the second quarter of the nineteenth century.

New schools required teachers, and Mann helped create "normal schools" to train teachers. Public schools initially preferred men as teachers, usually hiring them at age seventeen or eighteen. The pay was so low that few stayed in the profession their entire career, but for many young adults, teaching offered independence and social status, as well as an alternative to the

National Trades' Union Organization formed in 1834 to organize all local trade unions into a stronger national association; dissolved amid the economic depression in the late 1830s.

professions Occupations requiring specialized knowledge of a particular field; the Industrial Revolution and its new organization of labor created an array of professions in the nineteenth century.

THE COUNTRY SCHOOL A one-room schoolhouse in rural New England, as depicted by Winslow Homer in 1871. The young teacher presides over her class, which, as was custom, is arranged with boys on one side of the room and girls on the other (the youngest boy and girl, on the right, are likely siblings who have been allowed to sit next to each other). **What changes in American education took place in the mid-eighteenth century?**
Winslow Homer, American, 1836–1910; The Country School, 1871; oil on canvas; 21 1/4 x 38 1/4 inches; Saint Louis Art Museum, Museum Purchase 123:1946

rural isolation of farming. Church groups and civic leaders started private academies, or seminaries, for girls.

New professions for men: Lawyers, doctors, engineers

Law, Medicine, and Engineering Teaching was a common stepping-stone for men who became lawyers. In the decades after the Revolution, young men would teach for a year or two before joining an experienced attorney as an apprentice (what today would be called an *intern*). They would learn the practice of law in exchange for their labors.

Like attorneys, physicians in the early nineteenth century often had little formal academic training. Healers of every stripe assumed the title of *doctor* and established medical practices without regulation. Most were self-taught or had assisted a physician for several years, occasionally supplementing their internships with a few classes at the handful of medical schools. By 1860, there were 60,000 self-styled physicians, many of whom were "quacks" or frauds.

Industrial expansion also spurred the profession of engineering, a field that, by the outbreak of the Civil War, would become the largest professional occupation for men. Specialized expertise was required for the design and construction of canals and railroads, the development of machine tools and steam engines, and the building of roads, bridges, and factories.

Women in the Professional Workforce

New professions for women: Teachers and nurses

During the first half of the nineteenth century, most women still worked primarily in the home or on a farm. The only professions readily available to them were nursing (often midwifery, the delivery of babies) and teaching. Many middle-class women spent their time outside the home doing religious and social-service work. Then as now, women were the backbone of most churches and service organizations.

A few women, however, courageously pursued careers in male-dominated professions. Elizabeth Blackwell of Ohio gained admission to Geneva Medical College (now Hobart and William Smith College) in western New York despite the disapproval of the faculty. When she arrived at her first class, a hush fell upon the students "as if each member had been struck with paralysis."

Blackwell, however, had the last laugh when she finished first in her class in 1849, but thereafter the medical school refused to admit any more women. The first woman to earn a medical degree, Blackwell went on to start the New York Infirmary for Women and Children and later was a professor of gynecology at the London School of Medicine for Women.

Equal Opportunities

The dynamic market economy helped spread the idea that individuals should have an equal opportunity to better themselves through their abilities and hard work. Equality of opportunity, however, did not assume equal outcomes. Americans wanted an equal chance to earn unequal amounts of wealth.

The same ideals that prompted so many White immigrants to risk everything to come to the United States, however, were equally appealing to those groups denied equal opportunities to pursue their American dream: African Americans and women. By the 1830s, they, too, began to demand their right to "life, liberty, and the pursuit of happiness."

The desire of "common people" to pursue economic opportunities would quickly spill over into the political arena. The great theme of political life in the first half of the nineteenth century would be the continuing democratization of opportunities for White men, regardless of income or background, to vote and hold office.

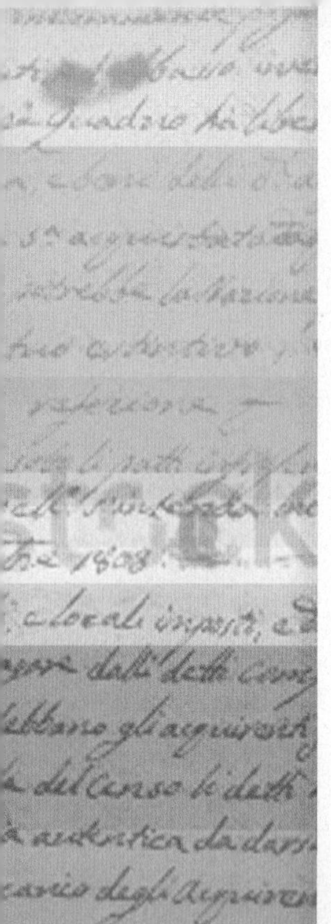

Reviewing the
CORE OBJECTIVES | INQUIZITIVE

■ **Transportation and Communication Revolutions** Canals and other improvements in transportation such as the *steamboat,* which could be used on the nation's rivers and lakes, allowed goods to reach markets more quickly and cheaply, helping to create a national *market economy* in which people bought and sold goods at longer distances. *Clipper ships* shortened the amount of time to transport goods across the oceans. The *railroads* (which expanded rapidly during the 1850s) and the *telegraph system* diminished the isolation of the West and united the country economically and socially. The *Erie Canal* (1825) contributed to New York City's emerging status as the nation's economic center even as it spurred the growth of Chicago and other midwestern cities. Improvements in transportation and communication linked rural communities to a worldwide marketplace.

■ **The Industrial Revolution** Inventions in machine tools and technology spurred an *Industrial Revolution* during the nineteenth century. The *cotton gin* dramatically increased cotton production, and a rapidly spreading *cotton* culture boomed in the South, with a resultant increase in slavery. Other inventions, such as John Deere's steel plow and the mechanized *McCormick reaper,* helped Americans, especially westerners, farm their land more efficiently and more profitably. In the North, mills and factories, at first water-powered and eventually powered by coal-fired steam engines, spread rapidly. They initially produced textiles for clothing and bedding from southern cotton, as well as iron, shoes, and other products. The federal government's tariff policy encouraged the growth of domestic manufacturing, especially cotton textiles, by reducing imports of British cloth. Between 1820 and 1840, the number of Americans engaged in manufacturing increased 800 percent. Many mill workers, such as the women employed in the *Lowell system* of New England textile factory communities, worked long hours for low wages in unhealthy conditions. Industrialization, along with increased commerce, helped spur the growth of cities.

■ **Immigration** The promise of cheap land and good wages drew millions of immigrants to America. By 1844, about 14.5 percent of the population was foreign born. Many of those who arrived in the 1840s came not just from the Protestant regions of Northern Europe that had supplied most of America's previous immigrants. The devastating potato famine led to an influx of poor Irish Catholic families. By the 1850s, they represented a significant portion of the urban population in the United States, constituting a majority in New York and Boston. German migrants, many of them Catholics and Jews, came to the country at the same time. Not all native-born Americans welcomed the immigrants. *Nativists* became a powerful political force in the 1850s, with the *Know-Nothings* nearly achieving major-party status with their message of excluding immigrants and Catholics from the nation's political community.

■ **Workers, Professionals, and Women** Skilled workers (artisans) in American cities had long formed trade associations to protect their members and to lobby for their interests. As the *Industrial Revolution* spread, some workers expanded these organizations nationally, forming the *National Trades' Union*. The growth of the *market economy* also expanded opportunities for those with formal education to serve in new or expanding *professions*. The number of physicians, teachers, engineers, and lawyers grew rapidly. By the mid-nineteenth century, women, African Americans, and immigrants began to agitate for equal social, economic, and political opportunities.

KEY TERMS

market economy *p. 305*
steamboats *p. 306*
Erie Canal (1825) *p. 307*
railroads *p. 309*
clipper ships *p. 310*
telegraph system *p. 312*
Industrial Revolution *p. 314*
cotton gin *p. 315*
cotton *p. 315*
McCormick reaper *p. 317*
Lowell system *p. 319*
nativists *p. 326*
Know-Nothings *p. 327*
National Trades' Union *p. 329*
professions *p. 329*

CHRONOLOGY

1793 Eli Whitney invents the cotton gin
1794 Philadelphia-Lancaster Turnpike is completed
1807 Robert Fulton and Robert Livingston launch steamship transportation on the Hudson River in New York
1825 Erie Canal opens in upstate New York
1831 Cyrus McCormick invents a mechanical reaper
1834 National Trades' Union is organized
1837 John Deere invents the steel plow
1842 Massachusetts Supreme Judicial Court issues *Commonwealth v. Hunt* decision
1845 The *Rainbow*, the first clipper ship, is launched
Irish potato famine
1846 Elias Howe invents the sewing machine
1848 California gold rush begins
1854 Know-Nothings (American party) formed

INQUIZITIVE

Go to InQuizitive to see what you've learned—and learn what you've missed—with personalized feedback along the way.

PROCESSION OF THE VICTUALLERS OF PHILADELPHIA On a beautiful day in March 1821, Philadelphia butcher William White organized a parade celebrating America's high-quality meats. This colored aquatint by Joseph Yeager, after John Lewis Krimmel, captures the new, vibrant nationalism that emerged in America after the War of 1812.

CHAPTER

9

Nationalism and Sectionalism

1815–1828

After the War of 1812, the British stopped interfering with American shipping. The United States could now develop new industries and exploit new markets around the globe.

It was not simply Alexander Hamilton's financial initiatives and the capitalistic energies of wealthy investors and entrepreneurs that sparked the nation's dramatic economic growth. Prosperity was also powered by the efforts of ordinary men and women who were willing to take risks, uproot families, use unstable paper money issued by unregulated local banks, and tinker with new machines and inventions. By 1828, the young agrarian republic was poised to become a sprawling commercial nation connected by networks of roads and canals as well as regional economic relationships—all energized by a restless spirit of enterprise, experimentation, and expansion.

Yet for all the energy and optimism exhibited by Americans after the war, the fundamental tension between *nationalism* and *sectionalism* (or *regionalism*) remained: how to balance the different economic, political, and social needs of the nation's three diverse regions—Northeast, South, and West—with the national interest.

CORE OBJECTIVES INQUIZITIVE

1. Analyze how the spirit of nationalism that emerged after the War of 1812 affected economic policies and judicial decisions.
2. Summarize the issues and ideas that promoted sectional conflict during this era.
3. Explain the emergence of the "Era of Good Feelings" and the factors that led to its demise.
4. Identify the federal government's diplomatic accomplishments during this era, and analyze their impact.
5. Evaluate the influence of Andrew Jackson on national politics in the 1820s and the developments that enabled him to become president.

Some sectionalists focused on promoting their region's priorities: shipping and manufacturing in the Northeast, slavery-based agriculture in the South, low land prices and transportation improvements in the West. Nationalists, on the other hand, promoted the interests of the nation as a whole. This required each region to recognize that no single section could get all it wanted without threatening the survival of the nation. Among the issues dividing the young republic, the passions aroused by the expansion of slavery proved to be the most difficult to resolve.

CORE **OBJECTIVE**

1. Analyze how the spirit of nationalism that emerged after the War of 1812 affected economic policies and judicial decisions.

A New Nationalism

After the War of 1812, Americans experienced a wave of patriotic excitement. They had won their independence from Britain for a second time, and a postwar surge of prosperity fed a widespread sense of optimism. In a message to Congress in 1815, President James Madison revealed how the challenges of the war, especially the weaknesses of the armed forces and federal finances, had changed his attitudes toward the role of the federal government.

Now, Madison and other leading southern Republicans, such as South Carolina's John C. Calhoun, acted like nationalists rather than states' rights sectionalists. They abandoned many of Thomas Jefferson's presidential policies (reducing the armed forces and opposing a national bank, for example) in favor of the *economic* nationalism promoted earlier by Federalists Alexander Hamilton and George Washington.

Madison now supported a larger army and navy, a new national bank, and tariffs to protect American manufacturers from foreign competitors. "The Republicans have out-Federalized Federalism," one New Englander commented after Madison's speech.

The Bank of the United States

Economic nationalism: New national bank and currency

After President Madison and congressional Republicans allowed the charter for the First Bank of the United States to expire, in 1811, the nation's finances fell into a muddle. States began chartering local banks with little or no regulation, and their banknotes (paper money) flooded the economy with different currencies of uncertain value. Imagine trying to do business on a national basis when each state-chartered bank had its own currency, which often was not accepted by other banks or in other states.

Second Bank of the United States Established in 1816 after the first national bank's charter expired; it stabilized the economy by creating a sound national currency; by making loans to farmers, small manufacturers, and entrepreneurs; and by regulating the ability of state banks to issue their own paper currency.

In response, President Madison in 1816 urged Congress to establish a **Second Bank of the United States** (B.U.S.). The B.U.S. was intended primarily to support a stable national currency that would promote economic growth. With the help of powerful legislators Henry Clay and John C. Calhoun, Congress created the new B.U.S., which, like its predecessor, was based in Philadelphia and was chartered for twenty years.

In return for issuing national currency and opening branches in every state, the B.U.S. was required to handle all the federal government's funds without charge, lend the government up to $5 million upon demand, and pay the government $1.5 million. The bitter debate over the B.U.S. helped set the pattern of regional alignment for most other economic issues. Generally speaking, westerners opposed the national bank because it catered to eastern customers.

A Protective Tariff

The long controversy with Great Britain over shipping rights convinced most Americans of the need to end their dependence on imported British goods. Efforts to develop iron and textile industries, begun in New York and New England during the embargo of 1807, had accelerated during the War of 1812, when America lost access to European goods.

After the war ended, however, British companies flooded U.S. markets with their less-expensive products. In response, northern manufacturers lobbied Congress for tariffs to protect their infant industries from "unfair" British competition.

Economic nationalism: Tariff of 1816 and federal financing for "internal improvements"

Congress responded by passing the **Tariff of 1816**, which placed a 20–25 percent tax on a long list of imported goods. Tariffs benefited some regions (the Northeast) more than others (the South), thus aggravating sectional tensions and grievances. Debates over federal tariffs would continue, in part because they provided much of the annual federal revenue and in part because they benefited manufacturers rather than consumers.

Internal Improvements

The third major element of economic nationalism in the first half of the nineteenth century involved federal financing of **internal improvements**, specifically the construction of roads, bridges, canals, and harbors. Most American rivers flowed from north to south, so the nation needed a network of roads running east to west.

In 1817, John C. Calhoun urged the House to fund internal improvements. He believed that a federally funded network of roads and canals in the West would help his native South by opening up trading relationships between the two regions. Support for his idea came largely from the West, which badly needed transportation infrastructure. Opposition was centered in New England, which expected to gain the least from projects intended to spur western development.

Using federal money to finance internal improvements remained controversial. Critics concerned about the expansion of federal power argued that the U.S. Constitution did not allow for such activities; only the local and state governments, or private investors, should fund road, canal, and harbor projects.

Tariff of 1816 Taxes on various imported items to protect America's emerging iron and textile industries from British competition.

internal improvements Construction of roads, canals, and other projects intended to facilitate the flow of goods and people.

Postwar Nationalism and the Supreme Court

The postwar emphasis on economic nationalism also flourished in the Supreme Court, where Chief Justice John Marshall strengthened the

THE NATIONAL ROAD, 1811–1838

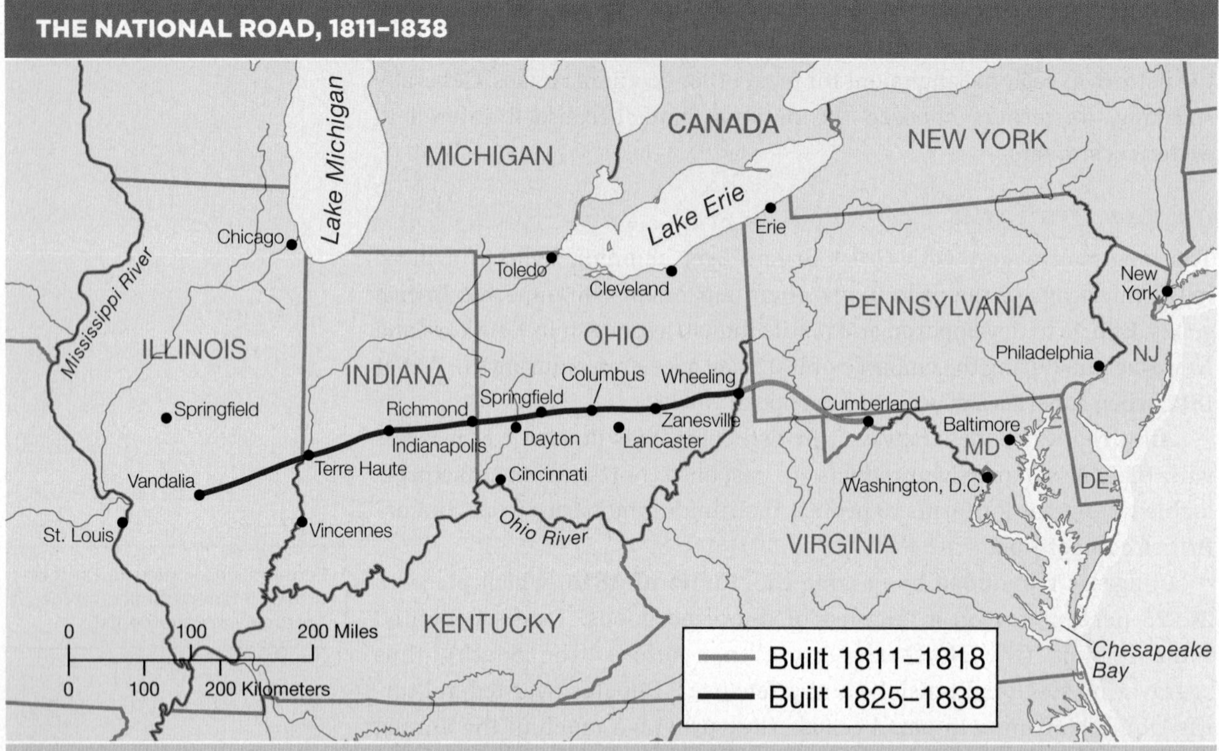

- Why were internal improvements so important in the early nineteenth century?
- How did the National Road affect agriculture and trade?
- What were the constitutional issues that limited the federal government's ability to enact internal improvements?

JOHN MARSHALL A pillar of judicial nationalism, Marshall became chief justice of the U.S. Supreme Court at the young age of forty-six, ruling on *Marbury v. Madison* just two years later.

constitutional powers of the federal government at the expense of states' rights. Marshall was a consistent nationalist. He viewed his cousin Thomas Jefferson and his Republican followers as a danger to the nation because they preferred states' rights over federal authority.

During Marshall's early years as chief justice (he served thirty-four years altogether), his judicial nationalism affirmed that the Supreme Court had the authority (and responsibility) to judge the constitutionality of state and federal legislative actions (oversight called *judicial review*). In the pathbreaking case of *Marbury v. Madison* (1803), the Court had, for the first time, declared a federal law unconstitutional. In the cases of *Martin v. Hunter's Lessee* (1816) and *Cohens v. Virginia* (1821), the Court ruled that the Constitution, as well as the nation's laws and treaties, could remain the supreme law of the land only if the Court could review and at times overturn the decisions of state courts.

Protecting Contract Rights

The Supreme Court made two more decisions in 1819 that strengthened the power of the federal government at the expense of the states. One,

Dartmouth College v. Woodward (1819), involved the New Hampshire legislature's effort to change Dartmouth College's charter to stop the college's trustees from electing their own successors. In 1816, the legislature created a new board of trustees for the college. The original group of trustees sued to block the move. They lost in the state courts but won on appeal to the Supreme Court. The college's original charter, wrote John Marshall in drafting the Court's opinion, was a valid contract that the state legislature had violated, an act forbidden by the Constitution.

Judicial nationalism: *Dartmouth College v. Woodward* (1819)

This decision implied an enlarged definition of *contract* that seemed to put corporations beyond the reach of the states that had chartered them. Thereafter, states commonly wrote into the charters incorporating businesses and other organizations provisions that made charters subject to modification. Such provisions were then part of the "contract."

Protecting a National Currency

Judicial nationalism: *McCulloch v. Maryland* (1819)

The second major Supreme Court case of 1819 was Chief Justice Marshall's most significant interpretation of the constitutional system: ***McCulloch v. Maryland*** (1819). James McCulloch, a B.U.S. clerk in Baltimore, had refused to pay state taxes on B.U.S. currency, as required by a Maryland law. The state indicted McCulloch. Acting on behalf of the national bank, he appealed to the Supreme Court, which ruled unanimously that Congress had the authority to charter the B.U.S. and that states had no right to tax the national bank.

Speaking for the Court, Chief Justice Marshall ruled that Congress had the right (that is, one of its "implied powers") to take any action not forbidden by the Constitution as long as the purpose of such laws was within the "scope of the Constitution." One great principle that "entirely pervades the Constitution," Marshall wrote, is "that the Constitution and the laws made in pursuance thereof are supreme: . . . They control the Constitution and laws of the respective states, and cannot be controlled by them." The effort by a state to tax a federal bank therefore was unconstitutional, for the "power to tax involves the power to destroy."

Regulating Interstate Commerce

John Marshall's last great decision, ***Gibbons v. Ogden*** (1824), affirmed the federal government's supremacy in regulating interstate commerce. In 1808, the New York legislature granted Robert Fulton and Robert R. Livingston the exclusive right to operate steamboats on the state's rivers and lakes. Fulton and Livingston then gave Aaron Ogden, a former New Jersey governor, the exclusive right to ferry people and goods up the Hudson River between New York and New Jersey. Georgia planter Thomas Gibbons, however, operated ships under a federal license that competed with Ogden.

On behalf of a unanimous Court, Marshall ruled in *Gibbons v. Ogden* (1824) that the monopoly granted by the state to Ogden conflicted with the

***Dartmouth College v. Woodward* (1819)** Supreme Court ruling that enlarged the definition of *contract* to put corporations beyond the reach of the states that chartered them.

***McCulloch v. Maryland* (1819)** Supreme Court ruling that prohibited states from taxing the Bank of the United States.

***Gibbons v. Ogden* (1824)** Supreme Court case that gave the federal government the power to regulate interstate commerce.

***STEAMBOAT TRAVEL ON THE HUDSON RIVER* (1811)** This watercolor of an early steamboat was painted by a Russian diplomat, Pavel Petrovich Svinin, who was fascinated by early technological innovations and the unique entrepreneurial culture of America.

Judicial nationalism: *Gibbons v. Ogden* (1824)

federal license issued to Gibbons. Marshall added that Congress could regulate commerce not only between states but also activities within a state "connected with" interstate commerce. He said that Congress could exercise power "to its utmost extent" in such circumstances.

Thomas Jefferson detested Marshall's judicial nationalism. To Jefferson, the Court's ruling in the *Gibbons* case revealed how "the Federal branch of our Government is advancing towards the usurpation of all the rights reserved to the States, and the consolidation in itself of all powers, foreign and domestic."

CORE **OBJECTIVE**

2. Summarize the issues and ideas that promoted sectional conflict during this era.

Debates over the American System

The major economic initiatives debated by Congress after the War of 1812—the national bank, federal tariffs, and federally financed roads, bridges, and canals—were interrelated pieces of a comprehensive economic plan called the **American System**. The term was coined by Henry Clay, the powerful Kentucky congressman. Clay wanted to free America's economy from its dependence on Great Britain while tying together the diverse regions of the nation politically. "I know of no South, no North, no East, no West to which I owe my allegiance," he asserted. "The Union is my country."

HENRY CLAY A committed nationalist, Clay was the chief architect of the American System. Here Clay is pictured on a $50 bill issued in the 1860s, long after his death.

In promoting the American System, Clay sought to deliver to each region of the country its top economic priority. He argued that high tariffs on imports were needed to block the sale of British products in the United States in order to protect new industries in New York and New England from unfair foreign competition. To convince western states to support the tariffs wanted by New England manufacturers, Clay first called for the federal government to use tariff revenues to build much-needed infrastructure—roads, bridges, canals, and other internal improvements—in the frontier West to enable speedier travel and faster shipment of goods to markets. Second, Clay's American System would raise prices for the purchase of federal lands and "distribute" the additional revenue to the states to help finance more roads, bridges, and canals. Third, Clay endorsed a strong national bank to create a single national currency and to regulate the unstable state and local banks.

Clay was the era's supreme political deal maker and economic nationalist. In many respects, he assumed responsibility for sustaining Alexander Hamilton's vision of a strong federal government nurturing a diversified national economy that combined agriculture, industry, and commerce. Clay ridiculed the Old Republicans for opposing factories and mills and encouraged an industrial revolution to help diversify the nation's economy and reduce its dependence on imports from Great Britain.

Regional controversies over the American System

Clay's program depended on the willingness of each region to compromise. For a while, it worked. Critics, however, argued that higher prices for federal lands would discourage western migration and that tariffs benefited the northern manufacturing sector at the expense of southern and western farmers and the "common" people, who had to pay higher prices for the goods produced by tariff-protected industries.

Many westerners and southerners also feared that the Philadelphia-based Second B.U.S. would become so powerful and corrupt that it could dictate the nation's economic future at the expense of states' rights and the needs of particular regions. Missouri senator Thomas Hart Benton feared that the West would be "devoured" by the East. Westerners, Benton worried, "are in the jaws of the monster! A lump of butter in the mouth of a dog! One gulp, one swallow, and all is gone!"

The bitter debate over the B.U.S. helped set the pattern of deepening sectional disputes over economic issues associated with Clay's proposed American System. Support for federal spending on internal improvements came largely from the West, while many New Englanders and southerners argued that the states should fund such projects.

American System Economic plan championed by Henry Clay of Kentucky that called for federal tariffs on imports, a strong national bank, and federally financed internal improvements—roads, bridges, canals—all intended to strengthen the national economy and end American economic dependence on Great Britain.

On his last day in office, in 1817, President Madison vetoed a bill that would have funded more internal improvements because he could not find a provision in the Constitution authorizing such federal expenditures.

Nor was he willing to claim that such funding was an "implied power" within the Constitution. As a result, internal improvements remained, with few exceptions, the responsibility of the states for another hundred years. The federal government did not enter the field again on a large scale until passage of the Federal Highways Act of 1916.

Conflict over extending slavery into the western states

In championing his American System, Henry Clay was forced to resolve explosive sectional conflicts over slavery in the western territories and states. Many Americans pouring across the Appalachian Mountains were southerners who took with them a commitment to cotton production and the slavery system that supported it. The possibility of new western states becoming "slave states" created the greatest political controversy of the nineteenth century. Thomas Jefferson admitted that the issue scared him "like a firebell in the night." It "awakened and filled me with terror. I considered it at once as the knell of the Union."

An aging Jefferson realized that the United States was increasingly at risk of disintegrating over the future of slavery, and like Jefferson, Clay lived with the contradiction of being a slave owner who denounced the evils of slavery and opposed its expansion into western territories. "I consider slavery as a curse—a curse to the master, a wrong, a grievous wrong to the slave," he explained. Nonetheless, he insisted that slavery was allowed by the Constitution and had become essential to the southern way of life.

CORE **OBJECTIVE**

3. Explain the emergence of the "Era of Good Feelings" and the factors that led to its demise.

"An Era of Good Feelings"

In the 1816 presidential election, Virginian James Monroe overwhelmed his Federalist opponent, Rufus King of New York, by a 183–34 margin in the Electoral College. The "Virginia dynasty" of presidents continued, although Monroe would be the last president to wear knee breeches, buckled shoes, and a tricornered hat.

The nation that Monroe would preside over was remarkably changed from the new republic led by George Washington. By 1817, the Union had nineteen states; five more would be added under Monroe. Perhaps the most remarkable evidence of the fast-growing nation was the number of post offices. There had been seventy-five in 1789, when George Washington was inaugurated as president. In 1817, there were 3,459. Soon after his inauguration, President Monroe embarked on a goodwill tour of New England, the stronghold of the Federalist party. In Boston, a Federalist newspaper complimented the Republican president for striving to "harmonize feelings, annihilate dissentions, and make us one people."

James Monroe

Like George Washington, Thomas Jefferson, and James Madison, James Monroe was a slaveholding Virginia planter who claimed that he hated slavery. He had joined the army at the age of sixteen, served under Washington during the Revolution, and later studied law with Jefferson.

***INDEPENDENCE DAY CELEBRATION,* 1819** Monroe's election and his presidential tour that followed became associated with an "Era of Good Feelings," here envisioned in watercolor by John Lewis Krimmel. In reality, Monroe's presidency was tainted by the Panic of 1819 and the controversial Missouri Compromise.

James Monroe was eminently qualified to be president. He had served as a representative in the Virginia Assembly; as governor of the state; as a representative in the Confederation Congress; as a U.S. senator; and as U.S. minister (ambassador) to Paris, London, and Madrid. Under President Madison, he had served as secretary of state and doubled as secretary of war. John C. Calhoun, who would serve as Monroe's secretary of war, said that the new president was "among the wisest and most cautious men I have ever known." Jefferson was even more lavish with his praise, noting that Monroe was "a man whose soul might be turned wrong side outwards without discovering a blemish to the world."

Monroe's administration began with the nation at peace and its economy flourishing. A Boston newspaper said the new president's arrival in office coincided with what a Boston editor called an "Era of Good Feelings," and the label became a popular catchphrase for the strong economy and political goodwill during Monroe's administration.

The nationalist priorities during the so-called Era of Good Feelings did not last long, however, for sectional loyalties continued to battle with national perspectives. Two crucial events signaled the end of the Era of Good Feelings and warned of stormy times ahead: the financial Panic of 1819 and the political conflict over statehood for Missouri.

The Panic of 1819

The **Panic of 1819** resulted from the sudden collapse of cotton prices after British textile mills quit buying high-priced American cotton—the nation's leading export—in favor of cheaper cotton from other parts of the world, especially the British colonies of Egypt and India.

Panic of 1819 A financial panic that began a three-year economic crisis triggered by reduced demand in Europe for American cotton, declining land values, and reckless practices by local and state banks.

Collapse of cotton prices

The collapse of cotton prices devastated southern planters, but it also reduced the world demand for other American goods. New factory owners struggled to find markets for their goods and to fend off more-powerful foreign competitors. The financial panic thus renewed sectional tensions between northern and southern economic interests.

Other factors caused the financial panic to become a depression. Business owners, farmers, and land speculators had recklessly borrowed money to expand their business ventures or purchase more land. With the collapse of crop prices and the decline of land values during and after 1819, both land speculators and settlers saw their income plummet.

Unregulated banks exacerbate the financial crisis

The reckless lending practices of the numerous unregulated new state banks compounded the economic confusion. Between 1815 and 1818, the number of banks grew some 30 percent. To generate more loans, the wobbly new banks issued more paper money. Even the B.U.S., which was supposed to provide financial stability, succumbed to the easy-credit mania.

The economic depression lasted about three years, and people blamed the B.U.S. After the panic subsided, many Americans, especially in the South and the West, remained critical of the national bank.

The Missouri Compromise

As the financial panic deepened, another cloud appeared on the horizon: the onset of a fierce sectional controversy between North and South over extending slavery into the new western territories. Ever since the drafting of the U.S. Constitution, most Americans had sought to bury the toxic issue of slavery in the misbegotten hope that it would simply die away. Instead, the importance of slavery grew enormously, year after year.

By 1819, the United States had an equal number of slave and free states—eleven of each. The Northwest Ordinance (1787) had *banned* slavery north of the Ohio River, and the Southwest Ordinance (1790) had *authorized* slavery south of the Ohio. In the vast region west of the Mississippi River, however, no move had been made to extend the dividing line across the vast Louisiana Territory, where slavery had existed since France and Spain first colonized the area. At the time, the Missouri Territory encompassed all the Louisiana Purchase except the state of Louisiana and the Arkansas Territory.

In 1819, residents in the Missouri Territory asked the House of Representatives to let them draft a constitution and apply for statehood, for its population had passed the required minimum of 60,000 White settlers. It would be the first state west of the Mississippi River, and a majority of its residents wanted to allow slavery.

At that point, Representative James Tallmadge, Jr., an obscure New York Republican, stunned Congress by proposing a resolution to ban any more enslaved people in Missouri.

The Tallmadge Amendment

Tallmadge's resolution infuriated southern slave owners, many of whom had developed a profitable trade selling enslaved people to be taken into the western territories. Any effort to restrict slavery, they believed, could lead to "disunion" and civil war. In addition, southerners worried

THE MISSOURI COMPROMISE, 1820

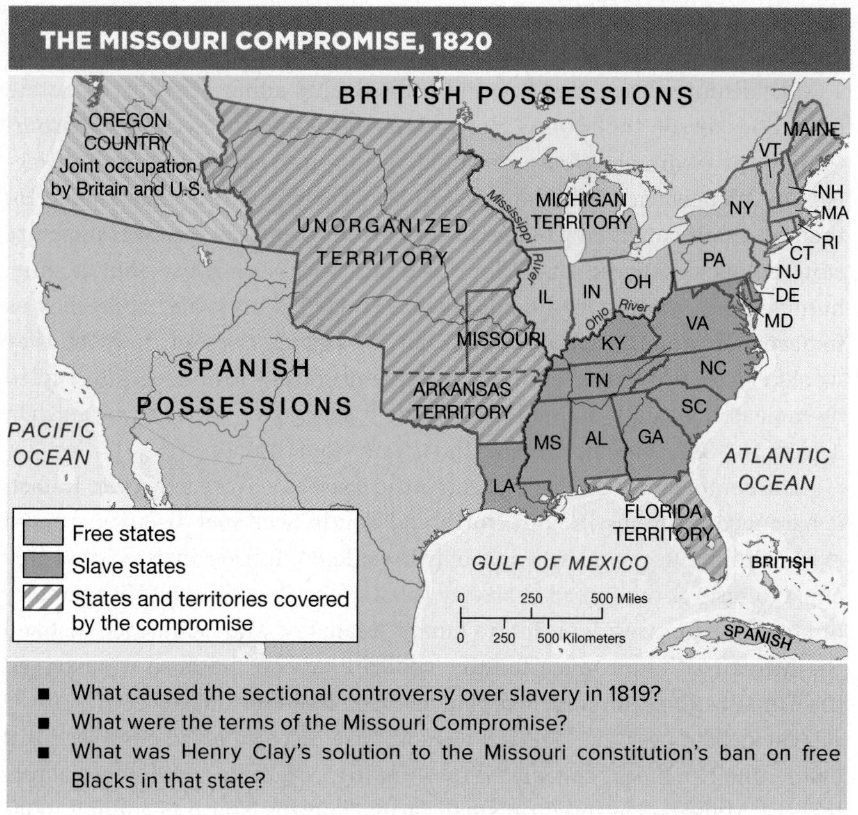

- What caused the sectional controversy over slavery in 1819?
- What were the terms of the Missouri Compromise?
- What was Henry Clay's solution to the Missouri constitution's ban on free Blacks in that state?

that the addition of Missouri as a free state would tip the balance of power in the Senate against the slave states. Their fears were heightened when congressman Timothy Fuller, an anti-slavery Republican from Massachusetts, declared that it was both "the right and duty of Congress" to stop the spread "of the intolerable evil and the crying enormity of slavery." After fiery debates, the House, with its northern majority, passed the Tallmadge Amendment on an almost strictly sectional vote. The Senate, however, rejected it—also along sectional lines.

At about the same time, Maine, which had been part of Massachusetts, applied for statehood. The Senate decided to link Maine's request for statehood with Missouri's, voting to admit Maine as a free state and Missouri as a slave state, thus maintaining the political balance between free and slave states.

The Missouri Compromise

Illinois senator Jesse Thomas revised the so-called **Missouri Compromise** by introducing an amendment to exclude slavery in the rest of the Louisiana Purchase territory north of latitude 36°30′, Missouri's southern border. Slavery thus would continue in the Arkansas Territory and in Missouri but would be excluded from the remainder of the area west of the Mississippi River. By a narrow margin, the Thomas Amendment passed on March 2, 1820.

Missouri Compromise (1820) Legislative decision to admit Missouri as a slave state while prohibiting slavery in the area west of the Mississippi River and north of the parallel 36°30′.

Then another issue arose. The pro-slavery faction in Missouri's constitutional convention inserted in the proposed state constitution a provision banning free Blacks and Mulattoes (mixed-race people). This violated the U.S. Constitution. Free Blacks were already citizens of many states.

The dispute threatened to unravel the deal to admit Missouri as a state until Speaker of the House Henry Clay fashioned a "second" Missouri Compromise whereby Missouri would be admitted as a state only if its legislature pledged never to deny free Blacks their constitutional rights. He then set about convincing others to support his proposal. A New Hampshire congressman observed that Clay "uses no threats or abuse—but is mild, humble, and persuasive—he begs, he instructs, adjures, and beseeches us to have mercy on the people of Missouri." If anyone resisted, however, they would experience Clay's wrath as "continuous peals of thunder, interrupted by repeated flashes of lightning." Clay's aggressive tactics worked. On August 10, 1821, Missouri became the twenty-fourth state.

The compromise did little to settle the issue of slavery, however. In fact, it hardened positions in both North and South. Sectional disputes erupted even within the president's cabinet. President Monroe insisted that any effort to restrict the spread of slavery violated the Constitution. His secretary of state, future president John Quincy Adams of Massachusetts, disliked the Missouri Compromise for the opposite reason: because it sustained the Constitution's immoral "bargain between freedom and slavery."

The debate over the Missouri Compromise revealed a widening sectional divide: the Northeast dominated by shipping, commerce, and manufacturing, the Midwest centered on small farms, and the South becoming more and more dependent on cotton and slavery.

CORE **OBJECTIVE**

4. Identify the federal government's diplomatic accomplishments during this era, and analyze their impact.

Nationalist Diplomacy

Henry Clay's *economic* nationalism and John Marshall's *judicial* nationalism were reinforced by efforts to practice *diplomatic* nationalism. Secretary of State John Quincy Adams aggressively exercised America's growing power to clarify and expand the nation's boundaries. He also wanted Europeans to recognize America's dominance in the Western Hemisphere.

Relations with Britain

The Treaty of Ghent had ended the War of 1812, but it left unsettled several disputes between the United States and Great Britain. American statesmen wanted to resolve those disputes in ways that would reinforce economic nationalism. During James Monroe's presidency, John Quincy Adams oversaw the negotiations of two important treaties, the Rush-Bagot Agreement of 1817 (named after the diplomats who arranged it) and the Convention of 1818, both of which eased tensions with Great Britain.

The Rush-Bagot Agreement of 1817 and the Convention of 1818

In the Rush-Bagot Agreement, the two nations limited the number of warships on the Great Lakes. The Convention of 1818 settled the disputed northern boundary of the Louisiana Purchase by extending it along the 49th parallel westward from what would become Minnesota to the Rocky

Mountains. West of the Rockies, the Oregon Country would be jointly occupied by the British and the Americans.

Florida

Still another disputed boundary involved western Florida. Spanish control over Florida during the early nineteenth century was more a technicality than an actuality. Spain was now a declining power, unable to enforce its obligations under Pinckney's Treaty of 1795 to keep Indians in the region from launching raids into southern Georgia.

In 1816, U.S. soldiers clashed with freedom seekers who had taken refuge in a British fort in West Florida, in the present-day Florida Panhandle. At the same time, Seminole warriors fought White settlers in the area. In 1817, Americans burned a Seminole village on the border, killing five Indians.

The First Seminole War

At that point, Secretary of War John C. Calhoun ordered General Andrew Jackson to lead an army from Tennessee into Florida, igniting what became known as the First Seminole War. Jackson was told to pursue marauding Indians into Spanish Florida but not to attack any Spanish forts.

When it came to Spaniards or Indians, few White Tennesseans—and certainly not Andrew Jackson, the hero of the Battle of New Orleans—bothered with legal technicalities. In early 1818, without presidential approval, General Jackson's force of 2,000 federal soldiers, volunteer Tennessee militiamen, and Indian allies crossed into Spanish Florida from southern Georgia.

BOUNDARY TREATIES, 1818–1819

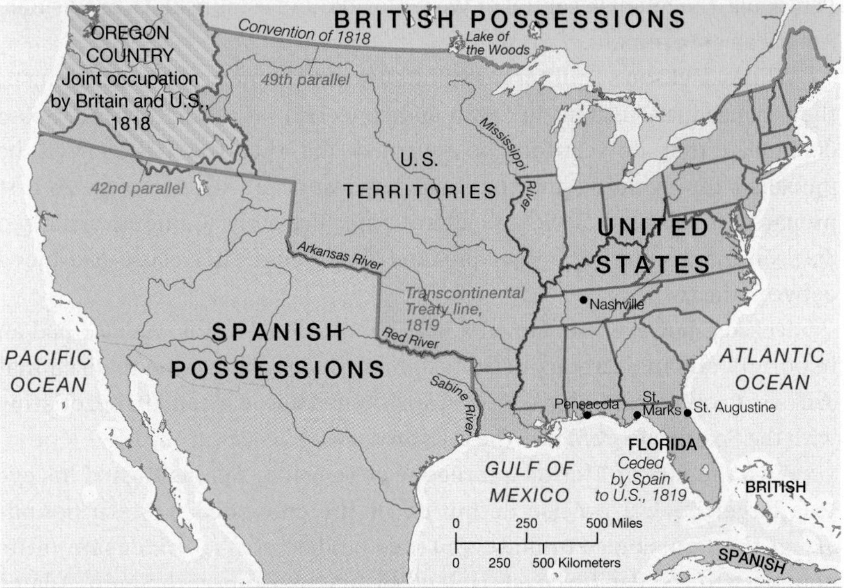

- What territorial disputes did the Convention of 1818 settle?
- How did Andrew Jackson's actions in Florida help Secretary of State John Quincy Adams claim the territory from Spain?
- What were the terms of the treaty with Spain?

***MASSACRE OF THE WHITES BY INDIANS AND BLACKS IN FLORIDA* (1836)** Published in a southerner's account of the Seminole War, this is one of the earliest known depictions of African Americans and Native Americans fighting as allies. **What motivated Americans to attack Native Americans to the west?**

The Americans assaulted a Spanish fort at St. Marks and destroyed several Seminole villages along the Suwannee River. They also captured and court-martialed British traders accused of provoking Indian attacks. When told that a military trial of the British citizens was illegal, Jackson gruffly replied that the laws of war did not "apply to conflicts with savages." Jackson ordered the immediate execution of the British troublemakers, an illegal action that angered the British government and alarmed President Monroe's cabinet. But the impulsive general kept moving. In May, he captured Pensacola, the Spanish capital of West Florida, and established a provisional American government.

While Jackson's military exploits excited American expansionists, they aroused resentment in Spain and concern in Washington, D.C. Spain demanded that its territory be returned and that the U.S. general be punished for violating international law. Monroe's cabinet was at first prepared to disavow Jackson's illegal acts. Privately, Calhoun criticized Jackson for disobeying orders—a stand that would later cause bad blood between the two.

Jackson, however, remained a hero to most Americans. He also had an important ally in Secretary of State John Quincy Adams, who realized that Jackson's conquest of Florida had strengthened his own hand in negotiating with the Spanish to purchase the territory.

With the fate of Florida a foregone conclusion, Adams turned his eye to a larger goal: a precise definition of the contested western boundary of the Louisiana Purchase and—his boldest stroke—extension of its boundary to the Pacific coast. In lengthy negotiations with Spain, Adams gradually gave ground on American claims to Texas, then a province of New Spain. In the final version of the deal, however, he stuck to his demand that the boundary of the Louisiana Purchase extend to the Pacific Ocean.

In 1819, Adams convinced the Spanish to sign the **Transcontinental Treaty** (also called the Adams-Onís Treaty), which gave all of Florida to the United States for $5 million. Florida thus became a U.S. territory; in 1845, it would become a state. The treaty also clarified the western boundary separating the Louisiana Territory from New Spain, explaining that it would run from the Gulf of Mexico north to the 42nd parallel and then west to the Pacific coast. The United States now spanned the continent.

Transcontinental Treaty makes Florida a U.S. territory

The Monroe Doctrine

The most important diplomatic policy crafted by President Monroe and Secretary of State Adams involved a determined effort to prevent future European colonialism in the Western Hemisphere. One consequence of the Napoleonic Wars raging across Europe and the French occupation of Spain and Portugal was a series of independence movements among the Spanish colonies. Between 1809 and 1830, Spain lost almost its entire empire in the Americas: La Plata (later Argentina), Bolivia, Chile, Ecuador, Peru, Colombia, Mexico, Paraguay, Uruguay, and Venezuela had all proclaimed their independence, as had Portuguese Brazil, and the United States was the first nation to recognize them. The only areas still under Spanish control were the islands of Cuba and Puerto Rico and the colony of Santo Domingo on the island of Hispaniola.

In 1823, rumors reached America that the monarchs of Europe were planning to help Spain recover its lost Latin American colonies. The British foreign minister, George Canning, told the United States that the two countries should jointly oppose any new incursions by European nations in the Western Hemisphere. Monroe initially agreed—if the British government would recognize the independence of the new nations of Latin America. The British refused.

Secretary of State Adams urged President Monroe to go it alone in prohibiting European involvement in the hemisphere. He stressed that "it would be more candid as well as more dignified" for America to ban further European intervention than to tag along with a British statement.

Monroe declares opposition to recolonization of the Americas

Monroe agreed. He incorporated the substance of Adams's views into his annual message to Congress in December 1823. The **Monroe Doctrine**, as it was named a generation later, contained four major points: (1) that "the American continents . . . are henceforth not to be considered as subjects for future colonization by any European powers"; (2) that the United States would oppose any attempt by European nations to impose their political system anywhere in the hemisphere; (3) that the United States would not interfere with the remaining European-controlled colonies; and (4) that the United States would keep out of the internal affairs of European nations and their wars.

Although the Monroe Doctrine became one of the cherished principles of American foreign policy, it had no standing in international law; it was merely a bold statement sent by an American president to Congress. No European nation recognized the legitimacy of the Monroe Doctrine. And,

Transcontinental Treaty (1819) Treaty between Spain and the United States that clarified the boundaries of the Louisiana Purchase and arranged for the transfer of Florida to the United States in exchange for cash.

Monroe Doctrine (1823) U.S. foreign policy that barred further colonization in the Western Hemisphere by European powers and pledged that there would be no American interference with any existing European colonies.

to this day, it has no official standing in international law. Symbolically, however, it has been an important statement of American intentions to prevent European involvement in the Western Hemisphere. Since the Monroe Doctrine was announced, not a single Latin American nation has lost its independence to an outside invader.

CORE **OBJECTIVE**

5. Evaluate the influence of Andrew Jackson on national politics in the 1820s and the developments that enabled him to become president.

The Rise of Andrew Jackson

America had become a one-party political system after the War of 1812. The refusal of the Federalists to support the conflict against Great Britain had virtually killed the party. In 1820, President Monroe was reelected without opposition.

While the Democratic Republican party was dominant for the moment, however, it was about to follow the Federalists into oblivion. If Monroe's first term was the Era of Good Feelings, his second term became the Era of Bad Feelings, as sectional controversies erupted into disputes so violent that they gave birth to a new political party: the Democrats, led by Andrew Jackson.

Andrew Jackson

Born in 1767 along the border between the Carolinas, Jackson grew up in a struggling single-parent household. His father was killed in a farm accident three weeks before Andrew was born, forcing his widowed mother, Elizabeth, to scratch out a living as a housekeeper while raising three sons.

During the Revolution, the Jackson boys fought against the British. One of them, sixteen-year-old Hugh, died of heat exhaustion during a battle; another, Robert, died while trudging home from a prisoner-of-war camp in Camden, South Carolina, some forty-five miles. In 1781, fourteen-year-old Andrew Jackson was captured. When a British officer demanded that the boy shine his boots, Andrew refused, explaining that he was a prisoner of war and expected "to be treated as such." The angry officer slashed him with his sword, leaving ugly scars on Andrew's head and hand. Soon after young Andrew was released, his mother died of cholera. "She was gentle as a dove," he remembered, "and as brave as a lioness."

ANDREW JACKSON The controversial general was painted by Anna Claypoole Peale in 1819, the year of his military exploits in Florida.

After the Revolution, Jackson went to Charleston, South Carolina, where he learned to love racehorses, card games, gambling, carousing, and fine clothes. He returned home and tried saddle-making and teaching before moving to Salisbury, North Carolina, where he earned a license to practice law. He also enjoyed life. A friend recalled that Jackson was "the most roaring, rollicking, game-cocking, card-playing, mischievous fellow that ever lived in Salisbury."

In 1788, at age twenty-one, Jackson moved to Nashville, Tennessee, and became an attorney. Eight years later, when Tennessee became a state, voters elected him to the U.S. House and later to the Senate, but he served only a year before returning home and becoming a judge. Jackson also made a lot of money, first as an attorney, then as a buyer and seller of horses, land, and enslaved people. He eventually owned 100 enslaved laborers on his cotton plantation, called the Hermitage, some twelve miles outside Nashville.

Many American political leaders cringed at the thought of the combative, short-tempered Jackson, who had run roughshod over international law when fighting the British and Seminoles in Florida, presiding over the nation. "His passions are terrible," said Thomas Jefferson. "He is a dangerous man." John Quincy Adams scorned Jackson "as a barbarian and savage who could scarcely spell his name." Jackson dismissed such criticism as an example of the "Eastern elite" trying to maintain control of American politics. He responded to Adams's criticism by commenting that he never trusted a man who could think of only one way to spell a word.

One-Party Politics

No sooner had James Monroe started his second presidential term, in 1821, than leading Republicans began positioning themselves to be the next president, including three members of the cabinet: Secretary of War John C. Calhoun, Secretary of the Treasury William H. Crawford, and Secretary of State John Quincy Adams. The powerful Speaker of the House, wily Henry Clay, also hungered for the presidency. And there was Andrew Jackson, who was elected to the Senate in 1823. The emergence of so many viable candidates revealed how fractured the Republican party had become.

Presidential Nominations

In 1822, the Tennessee legislature named Andrew Jackson as its choice to succeed President Monroe. Two years later, a mass meeting of Pennsylvanians endorsed Jackson for president and John C. Calhoun for vice president. Meanwhile, the Kentucky legislature had nominated its favorite son, Henry Clay, in 1822. The Massachusetts legislature nominated John Quincy Adams in 1824. That same year, a group of Republican congressmen nominated William Crawford of Georgia.

Crawford's friends emphasized his devotion to states' rights and strict construction (interpretation) of the Constitution. For his part, Clay continued to champion his American System. Adams shared Clay's belief that the national government should finance internal improvements to stimulate economic development, but he was less strongly committed to tariffs.

Jackson's appeal as "the common man"

As a self-made military hero, Jackson was an attractive candidate, especially to voters of Irish and Scots-Irish backgrounds. In Jackson, the Irish immigrants found a hero. The son of poor Scots-Irish colonists, he was beloved for having defeated the hated English in the Battle of New Orleans. In addition, the Irish immigrants' distaste for aristocracy, which they associated with centuries of English rule, attracted them to a politician who claimed to represent "the common man."

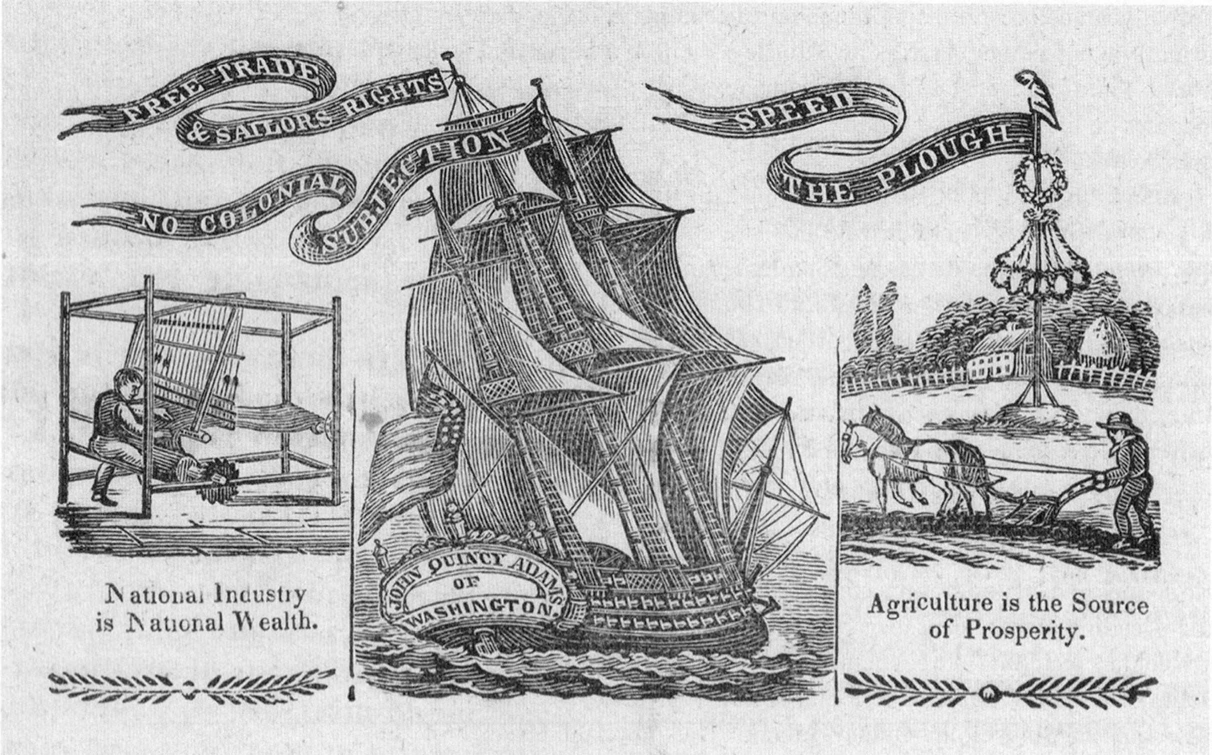

ELECTION CAMPAIGN OF 1824 In this illustration from an 1824 political broadside, John Quincy Adams advertises his allegiance to Henry Clay's American System. His presidential platform is portrayed as a ship, sailing under the banners of "No Colonial Subjugation" and "Free Trade." **How did Adams's platform differ from Jackson's?**

The "Corrupt Bargain"

A deadlocked election

The results of the 1824 election were inconclusive. In the Electoral College, Jackson had 99 votes; Adams, 84; Crawford, 41; and Clay, 37. Jackson, however, did not have a majority of the votes. In such a circumstance, as in the 1800 election, the Constitution specified that the House of Representatives would make the final decision from among the top three candidates. By the time the House could convene, however, Crawford had suffered a stroke and dropped out.

Whatever else might have been said about the outcome between Jackson and Adams, one thing seemed apparent—the election revealed how deeply divided the nation had become. Sectionalism had defeated nationalism as the Republicans split into warring regional factions.

The election was particularly humiliating for Henry Clay and his American System; voters in New England and New York opposed his call for federal funding of internal improvements, and the South rejected his promotion of the protective tariff.

Once the deadlocked election had been thrown into the House of Representatives, however, Clay's influence, as Speaker of the House, would prove decisive. While Adams and Jackson courted Clay's support, he claimed they provided only a "choice of evils." But he regarded Jackson as a "military chieftain," a frontier Napoleon unfit for the presidency. Jackson's election, Clay predicted, would "be the greatest misfortune that could befall the country."

Although Clay and Adams disliked each other, the nationalist Adams supported most of what Clay wanted policy-wise, particularly high tariffs, transportation improvements, and a strong national bank. Clay also expected Adams to name him secretary of state, the office that usually led to the White House. A deal between Clay and Adams broke the deadlock. Clay endorsed Adams, and the House of Representatives elected Adams with 13 state delegation votes to Jackson's 7 and Crawford's 4.

The backlash of the "corrupt bargain"

The controversial victory proved costly for Adams, however, as it united his foes and crippled his administration before it began. Jackson dismissed Clay as a "scoundrel," the "Judas of the West," who had entered into a self-serving "**corrupt bargain**" with Adams. Their "corruptions and intrigues," he charged, had "defeated the will of the People." American politics had now entered an Era of Bad Feelings.

Almost immediately, Jackson's supporters launched a campaign to undermine the Adams administration and elect their hero president in 1828. Crawford's supporters soon moved into the Jackson camp, as did the new vice president, John C. Calhoun of South Carolina, who quickly found himself at odds with the president.

John Quincy Adams

Adams was one of the ablest men, hardest workers, and finest intellects ever to enter the White House. Groomed for greatness by his parents, John and Abigail, the nation's second president and his accomplished wife, John Quincy began keeping a diary at age twelve and made daily entries until his death, eventually filling some 14,000 pages of text. In his diary, Adams often reflected on the stain of slavery. The Constitution that his father had helped enact was, he decided, "morally and politically vicious, inconsistent with the principles upon which alone our Revolution can be justified; cruel and oppressive."

Adams's political experience was unmatched. He had been ambassador to four European nations, during which he became fluent in three languages: German, Dutch, and French. After graduating from Harvard, he served as a U.S. senator, a Harvard professor, and an outstanding secretary of state, perhaps the greatest ever. He had helped negotiate the treaty ending the War of 1812 and had drafted the Monroe Doctrine (1823). And he promoted American isolation from global wars and causes. In 1821, he had explained that America "goes not abroad in search of monsters to destroy. She is the well-wisher to the freedom and independence of all. She is the champion and vindicator only of her own."

corrupt bargain Scandal in which presidential candidate and Speaker of the House Henry Clay secured John Quincy Adams's victory over Andrew Jackson in the 1824 election, supposedly in exchange for naming Clay secretary of state.

JOHN QUINCY ADAMS A brilliant man but an ineffective leader, he appears here in his study in 1843. He was the first U.S. president to be photographed.

Adams was also an unbending moralist obsessed with public service and self-improvement. After becoming president, he awoke every morning at 4 A.M. to swim naked in Tiber Creek, which fed into the Potomac River. Then he walked six miles before having breakfast.

Yet for all his accomplishments, John Quincy Adams proved to be an ineffective president, undercut from the start by the controversy surrounding his deal with Henry Clay. In his inaugural address, Adams promised to govern with "talents and virtue" but admitted to voters that he was "less possessed of your confidence . . . than any of my predecessors."

Self-righteous to a fault and "cold as an iceberg," Adams lacked the common touch and the politician's gift for compromise. "I am," he confessed, "a man of reserved, cold, austere, and forbidding manners." The stiff and stern Adams was unable to "reform" himself. His sour personality was shaped in part by family tragedies: he saw two brothers and two sons die from alcoholism. Adams himself suffered from chronic bouts of depression that reinforced his grim outlook and tendency toward self-pity, qualities that did not endear him to fellow politicians or the public.

Adams also detested the democratic politicking that Andrew Jackson represented. He worried, as had his father, that republicanism was rapidly turning into democracy, and that government *of* the people was degenerating into government *by* the people, many of whom, in his view, were uneducated and incompetent. He wanted politics to be a "sacred" arena for the "best men," a profession limited to the "most able and worthy" leaders motivated by a sense of civic duty rather than a selfish quest for power and stature.

An Active Government

Public opposition to Adams's active government

John Quincy Adams was determined to create an activist federal government with expansive goals. His first State of the Union message, in December 1825, included a grand blueprint for national development, but it was set forth so bluntly that it became a political disaster.

The federal government, Adams stressed, should finance vast internal improvements (new roads, canals, harbors, and bridges), create a national university, support scientific explorations of the Far West, build astronomical observatories, and establish a department of the interior to manage government-owned lands. To refrain from using such broad federal powers, Adams insisted, "would be treachery to the most sacred of trusts." He challenged Congress to approve his proposals and not be paralyzed "by the will of our constituents."

The reaction was overwhelmingly negative. Newspapers charged that Adams was behaving like an aristocratic tyrant, and Congress approved none of his proposals. The disastrous start shattered Adams's confidence. He wrote in his diary that he was in a "protracted agony of character and reputation."

A partisan split between the Democrats and Republicans

Adams's effort to expand the powers of the federal government was so divisive that the Democratic-Republican party split. Those who agreed with the economic nationalism of Adams and Clay began calling themselves National Republicans. Those Democratic Republicans supporting Andrew Jackson and states' rights would eventually drop the name Republican and become simply Democrats.

President Adams proved to be a great statesman at the wrong time, an arrogant and stubborn visionary unable to excite voters by his ideas. America was not ready for a dominant federal government. But it was ready for a charismatic and domineering president.

The Election of Andrew Jackson

The defiant congressional opposition to the Adams presidency launched the savage **campaign of 1828** between the National Republicans and the Jacksonian Democrats. Both sides engaged in vicious personal attacks. As a Jackson supporter observed, "The floodgates of falsehood, slander, and abuse have been hoisted" by the Adams campaign, "and the most nauseating filth is [being] poured" on Jackson's head.

Adams's supporters denounced Jackson as a hot-tempered, ignorant barbarian and slave trader who had participated in numerous duels and frontier brawls, a man whose fame rested upon his reputation as a killer.

Such charges were not inaccurate. The iron-willed Jackson had always displayed an explosive temper. He loved a good fight. In 1806, he challenged attorney and rival racehorse breeder Charles Dickinson to a duel, claiming that the arrogant young attorney had not paid off a racing bet and had insulted his wife, Rachel.

The two proud men and their supporters agreed to meet across the border in Kentucky, where dueling was not yet illegal.

Although Dickinson was considered the best shot in Tennessee and was said to have already killed twenty-six men in duels, Jackson let him fire first from twenty-four feet away. For his gallantry, Jackson received a bullet in his chest that fractured ribs and lodged so close to his heart it could not be removed. "My God! Have I missed him?" Dickinson asked, not knowing that his bullet had indeed wounded Jackson.

The dueling code of honor had been satisfied, since Jackson had stood his ground. At that point, he could have generously spared his opponent, but the wounded Jackson clenched his teeth from the pain, straightened himself, patiently took aim, and coolly killed his foe. The doctor at the scene told Jackson, "I don't see how you stayed on your feet after that

campaign of 1828 Bitter presidential contest between Democrat Andrew Jackson and National Republican John Quincy Adams (running for reelection), resulting in Jackson's victory.

JACKSON AND DICKINSON DUEL The future president Andrew Jackson demonstrated both his fiery temper and the pertinacity that his supporters found so admirable in his duel with Charles Dickinson. Dickinson shot Jackson square in the chest, but Jackson stood his ground, fired, and fatally shot his opponent.

wound." Jackson replied, "I should have hit him if he had shot me through the brain."

Defamatory attacks on Jackson

The most scurrilous political attack on Jackson was that he had lived in adultery with his wife, Rachel, a deeply pious woman. In fact, they had lived together for two years in the mistaken belief that her divorce from her abusive first husband was final. As soon as the divorce became official, Andrew and Rachel had remarried. Jackson blamed Henry Clay for the slurs against his wife, calling the Kentuckian "the basest, meanest scoundrel that ever disgraced the image of his god." Thereafter, the two proud men developed a consuming hatred for each other and a bitter political rivalry.

In the 1828 campaign, the Jacksonians condemned John Quincy Adams as an aristocrat and monarchist, dismissing him as a professional politician who had never had a "real" job. Newspapers claimed that the president had been corrupted by foreigners in the courts of Europe. The most outlandish charge was that Adams had delivered up an American girl to Czar Alexander I while serving as ambassador to Russia. Adams was left to gripe about the many "forgeries now swarming in the newspapers against me."

Jackson held most of the advantages in the campaign. As a fabled Indian fighter, he was beloved in the western and southern states, and as a plantation owner, lawyer, and slaveholder, he had the trust of the southern elite. Jackson promoted small federal government, individual liberty, an expanded military, and White supremacy. Above all, he was a nationalist committed to preserving the Union in the face of rising sectional tensions.

Candidate Jackson benefited from a growing spirit of democracy in which many voters viewed John Quincy Adams as an elitist. When Adams's supporters began referring to the rough-hewn Jackson as a "jackass," the Tennessean embraced the name, using the animal as a symbol for his "tough" campaign. The jackass eventually became the enduring symbol of the Democratic party.

The "Common Man" in Politics

Democratization of voting

Jackson's campaign explicitly appealed to the "common" voters, many of whom were able to vote in a presidential election for the first time. After the Revolution, and especially after 1800, more and more White men had gained the right to vote. Only Virginia and the Carolinas, still dominated by the planter elite, continued to resist the democratizing trend. This "democratization" of politics also affected many free Black males in northern states, half of which allowed African American men to vote.

The extension of voting rights to people with little or no wealth led to the election of politicians sprung from the people rather than the social elite. Jackson, a frontiersman of humble origin who had made a fortune and scrambled up the political ladder by will and tenacity, fit this more democratic ideal. "Adams can write," went one of the campaign slogans, "but Jackson can fight."

Labor Politics

Political participation by labor unions and reformers

With the widespread removal of property qualifications for voting, the working poor became an important political force in the form of the Workingmen's parties, first organized in Philadelphia in 1828. The Workingmen's parties were reformist groups in the nation's largest cities devoted to promoting the interests of laborers, including shorter working hours and allowing all males to vote regardless of the amount of property owned.

The Workingmen's parties faded quickly, however. The inexperience of labor politicians left them prey to manipulation by political professionals. In addition, major national parties, especially the Democrats, co-opted some of their issues.

Yet the working-class parties succeeded in drawing attention to their demands, many of which attracted the support of middle-class reformers. They promoted free public education for all children and sought to end the practice of imprisoning people for indebtedness, causes that won widespread popular support. In large part because of his background as a "common man," union members loved Andrew Jackson.

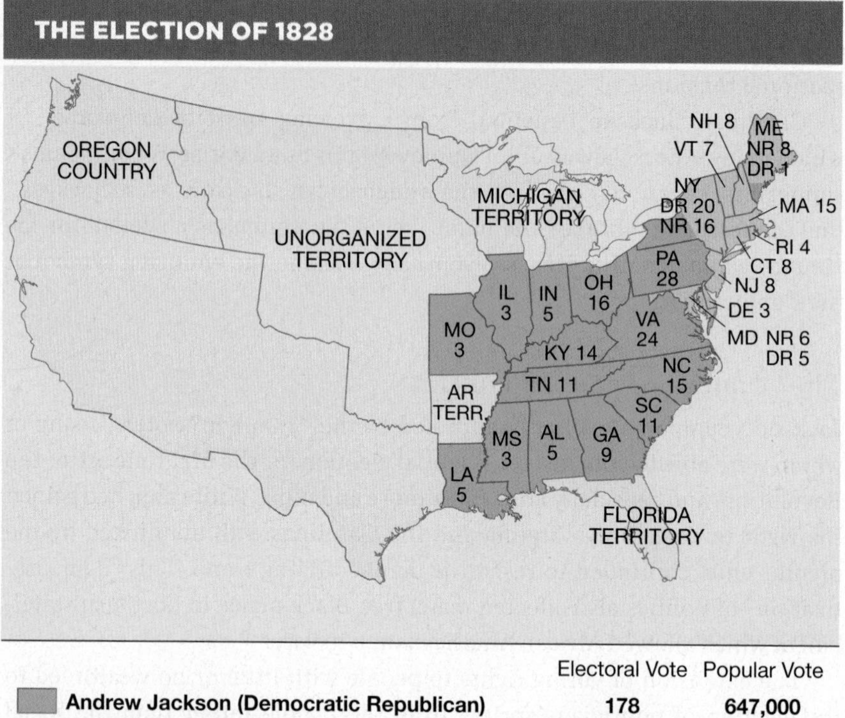

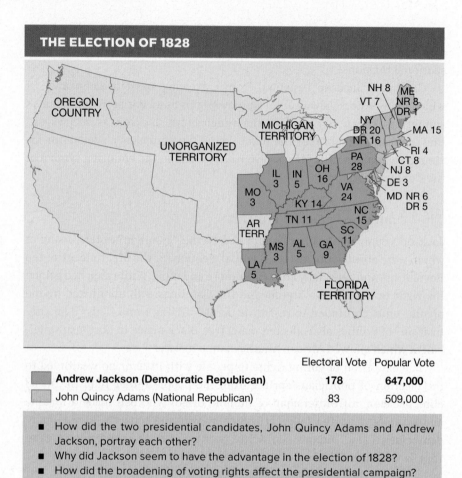

- How did the two presidential candidates, John Quincy Adams and Andrew Jackson, portray each other?
- Why did Jackson seem to have the advantage in the election of 1828?
- How did the broadening of voting rights affect the presidential campaign?

President Jackson

Record-breaking voter turnout for Jackson

When the 1828 election returns came in, Andrew Jackson had won handily, taking every state west and south of Pennsylvania. Equally important was the surge in voter turnout that brought more than twice as many men to vote as in the 1824 election.

Adams was stunned by his defeat. He was only the second president to be denied a second term (his father was the first), and his loss dragged him into "the deepest gloom." But he was elated to leave the White House. "The four most miserable years of my life," he later noted, "were my four years in the presidency."

Jackson, the first president from a western state, entered office still seething with resentment at the way his opponents had smeared his wife, who had died a few days after learning of the political attacks on her and her "tarnished" marriage.

Now the president-elect relished the chance to take revenge on those whose "vile falsehoods" had caused Rachel's heart attack and death in December 1828, just weeks before his inauguration. "My heart is nearly broke," he confessed to a friend. At the funeral, Jackson declared that those "vile wretches who have slandered her must look to God for mercy," for he would offer none.

Jackson was determined to launch a new "democratic" era that would silence his critics, restore government to "the people," and take power away from the "Eastern elite." In doing so, he would transform the nation's political landscape—for good and for ill, as it turned out.

Reviewing the

CORE OBJECTIVES | INQUIZITIVE

▪ **Nationalism** After the War of 1812, the federal government pursued many policies to strengthen the national economy. The *Tariff of 1816* protected American manufacturers from foreign competition, and the *Second Bank of the United States* provided a stronger national currency. Madison, Monroe, and Adams all promoted an active role for the federal government in promoting economic growth. Led by John Marshall, the Supreme Court limited the powers of states and strengthened the power of the federal government in *Dartmouth College v. Woodward* (1819) and *McCulloch v. Maryland* (1819). The Marshall court interpreted the Constitution as giving Congress the right to take any action not forbidden by the Constitution as long as the purpose of such laws was within the "scope of the Constitution." In *Gibbons v. Ogden* (1824), the Marshall court established the federal government's authority over interstate commerce.

▪ **Sectionalism** Henry Clay's *American System* supported economic nationalism by endorsing a national bank, a protective tariff, and federally funded *internal improvements*, such as roads and canals. Many Americans, however, remained more tied to the needs of their particular sections of the country. People in the different regions—North, South, and West—disagreed about which economic policies best served their interests. As settlers streamed west, the extension of slavery into the new territories became the predominant political concern, eventually requiring both sides to compromise repeatedly to avoid civil war.

▪ **Era of Good Feelings** James Monroe's term in office was initially labeled the Era of Good Feelings because it began with peace and prosperity. Two major events spelled the end of the Era of Good Feelings: the financial *Panic of 1819* and the controversial *Missouri Compromise* (1820). The explosive growth of the cotton culture transformed life in the South, in part by encouraging the expansion of slavery, which moved west with migrating southern planters. In 1819, however, the sudden collapse of world cotton prices devastated the southern economy. The *Missouri Compromise,* a short-term solution to the issue of allowing slavery in the western territories, exposed the emotions and turmoil that the tragic system generated.

▪ **National Diplomacy** The main diplomatic achievements of the period after the War of 1812 extended America's contested boundaries and enabled the resumption of trade with Great Britain. To the north, U.S. diplomatic achievements established northern borders with Canada. To the south, the *Transcontinental Treaty* (1819) with Spain extended the boundaries of the United States. The *Monroe Doctrine* (1823) declared that the Americas were no longer open to European colonization.

▪ **The Election of 1828** The demise of the Federalists ended the first party system in America, leaving the Republicans as the only national party. The seeming unity of the Republicans was shattered by the election of 1824, which Andrew Jackson lost as a result of what he believed was a *corrupt bargain* between John Quincy Adams and Henry Clay. Jackson won the presidency with the *campaign of 1828* by rallying southern and western voters with his promise to serve the interests of common people. His election opened a new era in national politics that reflected the democratization of voting in most states (at least for White men).

KEY TERMS

Second Bank of the United States *p. 336*

Tariff of 1816 *p. 337*

internal improvements *p. 337*

Dartmouth College v. Woodward (1819) *p. 339*

McCulloch v. Maryland (1819) *p. 339*

Gibbons v. Ogden (1824) *p. 339*

American System *p. 341*

Panic of 1819 *p. 343*

Missouri Compromise (1820) *p. 345*

Transcontinental Treaty (1819) *p. 349*

Monroe Doctrine (1823) *p. 349*

corrupt bargain *p. 353*

campaign of 1828 *p. 355*

CHRONOLOGY

1811 Construction of the National Road begins

1816 Second Bank of the United States is established

First protective tariff goes into effect

1817 Rush-Bagot Agreement between the United States and Great Britain creates an unfortified border between the United States and Canada

1818 The Convention of 1818 establishes the northern border of the Louisiana Purchase at the 49th parallel and the joint occupation of Oregon by the United States and Great Britain

1819 Supreme Court issues *McCulloch v. Maryland* decision

United States and Spain agree to the Transcontinental Treaty

Tallmadge Amendment

1820 Congress accepts the Missouri Compromise

1823 President Monroe enunciates the principles of the Monroe Doctrine

1824 Supreme Court issues *Gibbons v. Ogden* decision

John Quincy Adams wins the presidential election by what some critics claim is a corrupt bargain with Henry Clay

1828 Andrew Jackson wins presidential contest

INQUIZITIVE

Go to InQuizitive to see what you've learned—and learn what you've missed—with personalized feedback along the way.

HARD TIMES IN THE JACKSONIAN ERA Although Andrew Jackson championed the "poor and humble," his economic policies contributed to the Panic of 1837, a financial crisis that hit the working class the hardest. This cartoon illustrates New York City during the seven-year depression: a frantic mob storms a bank, while in the foreground, a widow begs on the street with her child, surrounded by a banker or landlord and a barefoot sailor. At left, there is a drunken member of the Bowery Toughs gang and a down-on-his-luck militiaman. The cartoonist places the blame on Jackson, whose hat, glasses, and pipe overlook the scene. The white flag at left wryly states: "July 4th, 1827, 61st Anniversary of Our Independence." The banners demanding "specie," or payments in gold rather than paper money, illustrate the controversy over banks and bankers during the Jacksonian era.

CHAPTER 10

The Jacksonian Era

1828–1840

President Andrew Jackson was a unique personality and a transformational leader. He was the first president from a western state (Tennessee), the first to have been born in a log cabin, the first *not* from a prominent colonial family, the first to be censured by the Senate, the first to experience an attempted assassination, and the first to carry two bullets in his body from a duel and a barroom brawl. Most important, Jackson was the polarizing emblem of a new democratic era.

Jackson had a gaunt, chiseled face topped by a shock of unruly white hair. A self-made man, he was well-mannered but short-tempered and proud. Jackson believed in simple pleasures; he read three chapters of the Bible each day. He smoked a corncob pipe and chewed—and spit—tobacco. (As president, he had a servant place twenty gold spittoons throughout the White House.) He stood ramrod straight and was tall and lean. Although Jackson weighed only 140 pounds, he cut an intimidating figure with penetrating blue eyes, long nose, jutting chin, and weather-beaten face. Jackson was dubbed "Old Hickory" because of his grit and toughness, yet despite appearances, he was not in good health when he assumed the presidency. He suffered from blinding headaches, a constant cough, and other ailments that led rival Henry Clay to describe him as "feeble in body and mind."

CORE OBJECTIVES INQUIZITIVE

1. Describe Andrew Jackson's major beliefs regarding democracy, the presidency, and the proper role of government in the nation's economy.
2. Evaluate Jackson's response to the nullification crisis.
3. Analyze Jackson's legacy regarding the status of Indians in American society.
4. Explain the causes of the economic depression of the late 1830s and the emergence of the Whig party.
5. Assess the strengths and weaknesses of Jackson's transformational presidency.

Despite his physical challenges, Jackson remained sharply focused and keenly sure of himself. He relished the rough-and-tumble combat of the raucous new democratic political culture. "I was born for a storm," he once boasted.

Jackson took the nation by storm. No political figure was so widely loved or more deeply despised. As a soldier, lawyer, slave-owning planter, and politician, he helped create and shape the Democratic party, and he ushered new elements of presidential campaigning into the electoral process. Jackson championed the emergence of the "common man" in politics (by which he meant White men only) and resolved to "*preserve the union of these states, although it may cost me my life.*" In the end, he stamped his name and, more important, his ideas, personality, and values on an entire era of American history.

CORE **OBJECTIVE**

1. Describe Andrew Jackson's major beliefs regarding democracy, the presidency, and the proper role of government in the nation's economy.

Jacksonian Democracy

Andrew Jackson's election marked the culmination of thirty years of democratic innovations in politics. During the 1820s and 1830s, political life was transformed as more and more landless White men were allowed to vote and to hold office. "The principle of universal suffrage," announced the *U.S. Magazine and Democratic Review*, "meant that white males of age constituted the political nation." Jackson promised to protect "the poor and humble" from the "tyranny of wealth and power." His populist goal was to elevate the "laboring classes" of White men who "love liberty and desire nothing but equal rights and equal laws." Such democratization was unique in the world, for it gave previously excluded White men equal status as citizens regardless of their wealth or background. No longer was politics the arena for only the most prominent and wealthiest Americans.

Promoting the "common man"

Campaigning was also democratized. Politics became the most popular form of mass entertainment, as people from all walks of life passionately engaged in political campaigns and were remarkably well-informed about public policy issues. Politics was "the only pleasure an American knows," observed visiting Frenchman Alexis de Tocqueville. "Even the women frequently attend public meetings and listen to political harangues as a recreation from their household labors."

An openly partisan president

Jackson was the most openly partisan and politically involved president to that point. Unlike previous presidents, who viewed political campaigning as unseemly, he actively sought votes among the people, lobbied congressmen, and formed "Hickory Clubs" across the nation to campaign for him.

Jackson also benefited from a powerful Democratic party "machine" run by his trusted secretary of state (later his vice president) Martin Van Buren, a New York lawyer with a shrewd political sense. Unlike the founders who drafted the Constitution, Van Buren did not worry over the rise of political parties. He saw them as necessary elements of a republic. And to him goes much of the credit for nurturing the development of Jackson's Democratic party.

Democracy, of course, is a slippery and elastic concept, and Jacksonians rarely defined what they meant by the "rule of the people." Noah Webster, the Connecticut Federalist who produced the nation's first dictionary of homegrown American English, complained that "the men who have preached these doctrines [of democracy] have never defined what they mean by the *people*, or what they mean by *democracy*, nor how the *people* are to govern themselves."

Jacksonian Democrats also showed little concern for the *undemocratic* constraints on African Americans, Native Americans, and women, all of whom were denied political and civil rights. Many southern slaveholders worried that the surge of democratic activism would eventually threaten the slave system. Virginian Muscoe Garnett, a planter and attorney, declared that "democracy is indeed incompatible with slavery, and the whole system of Southern society." His fellow Virginian, George Fitzhugh, was more explicit in his disdain for democratic ideals. In every society, he asserted, "some were born with saddles on their backs, and others booted and spurred to ride them."

Expanded presidential authority

As the first president to view himself as a representative of "the people," Jackson resolved to exercise expanded executive powers at the expense of the legislative and judicial branches. The ruling political and economic elite must be removed, he said, for "the people" are "the government, the sovereign power" in the United States, and they had elected him president.

Jackson's inauguration ceremony set the tone for his controversial presidency. The self-described people's president stepped out of the U.S. Capitol at noon on March 4, 1829. Waiting for him in the cold were 15,000 people who collectively roared and waved their hats when they saw Jackson emerge. "I've never seen anything like it before," marveled Daniel Webster, the great senator from Massachusetts.

Concerns about Jackson's fitness for the presidency were heightened by riotous scenes at the White House after his inauguration ceremony in March 1829. In a symbolic effort to reach out to the "common" people, Jackson opened the party to anyone. To his surprise, the huge crowd of jubilant Democrats turned into a drunken mob smashing dishes and glasses and breaking furniture. "The reign of KING MOB seemed triumphant," said Supreme Court Justice Joseph Story, who witnessed the destruction.

ALL CREATION GOING TO THE WHITE HOUSE In this depiction of Jackson's inauguration party, satirist Robert Cruikshank draws a visual parallel to Noah's Ark, suggesting that people of all walks of life were now welcome to what would be called the White House. **What demographics are *not* featured in Cruikshank's illustration?**

Upon taking office, the nation's seventh president wanted to reduce federal spending, pay off the federal debt (a "national curse"), destroy the Second Bank of the United States (B.U.S.), and relocate the "ill-fated race" of Indians from the East to the West so that Whites could exploit their ancestral lands. In pursuing these ambitious goals, he exercised presidential authority more boldly than any of his predecessors.

The Spoils System and Presidential Conventions

Spoils system

To dislodge the eastern political elite, Jackson launched a policy he called "rotation in office," whereby he replaced many federal officials with his supporters. Government jobs, he argued, belonged to the people, not to career bureaucrats. During Jackson's two presidential terms, he replaced about a fifth of the federal officeholders with his friends and supporters, not all of whom were qualified for their new positions. Such partisan behavior came to be called "the spoils system," since, as a prominent Democrat declared, "to the victor goes the spoils."

Birth of presidential nominating conventions

Jackson also sought to "democratize" the way that presidential candidates were selected. Since the presidency of George Washington, most nominees had been chosen by party "caucuses" of prominent congressmen and senators. Jackson hated the idea of legislators nominating presidents. In 1832, he would convince the Democrats to stage their first presidential nominating convention as a means of involving more people in the process of selecting a candidate. The innovation of presidential nominating conventions reinforced Jackson's image as a man of the people fighting against entrenched party leaders.

The Eaton Affair

Yet Jackson soon found himself preoccupied with squabbles within his own cabinet. From the outset, his administration was divided between supporters of Secretary of State Martin Van Buren, a New Yorker, and the allies of Vice President John C. Calhoun of South Carolina. Both men wanted to succeed Jackson as president. Jackson turned mostly to Van Buren for advice because he did not trust Calhoun, a Yale graduate of towering intellect and fiery determination. Although earlier a Republican nationalist, Calhoun now was focused on defending southern interests, especially the preservation of the slave-based cotton economy that had made him a rich planter.

The Peggy Eaton affair

In his rivalry with Calhoun, Van Buren took full advantage of a juicy social scandal known as the Peggy Eaton affair. Widower John Eaton, a former U.S. senator from Tennessee and one of Jackson's closest friends, had long been associated with Margaret "Peggy" O'Neale Timberlake, an outspoken Washington woman married to John Timberlake, a naval officer frequently at sea. While her husband was away, she was involved with several "gentlemen," including Senator John Eaton. In April 1828, John Timberlake died at sea. Although the official cause of death was pulmonary failure, rumors swirled that he had committed suicide after learning of his wife's affair with Eaton.

Soon after the 1828 presidential election, Eaton had written President-elect Jackson about the spiteful gossip aimed at himself and Peggy Timberlake. Jackson responded: "Marry her and you will be in a position to defend her." Eaton did so on January 1, 1829. Eaton's enemies quickly criticized the "unseemly haste" of the marriage and continued to demean Peggy Eaton. The mean-spirited gossip about Peggy Eaton reminded Jackson of the efforts of his political opponents to defame his wife, Rachel. Intensely loyal to John Eaton, the president defended Peggy. His cabinet members, however, were unable to cure their wives of what Martin Van Buren dubbed "the Eaton Malaria." The rumoring and sniping became a time-consuming distraction for the president.

PEGGY O'NEAL This 1870 cigar box label illustrates the dramatic life of Peggy O'Neal, the wife of Andrew Jackson's secretary of war. To the left, President Jackson gives her a bouquet after she is shunned by the wives of his cabinet. To the right, her husband kills an adversary in a duel for insulting her honor.

Martin Van Buren used the affair to curry favor with Jackson. As a widower, he was able to serve as Peggy Eaton's escort at social events. He also accompanied Jackson on horse rides around the capital. In the process, he displaced Vice President Calhoun as the nation's second most powerful political figure; he would become president himself in 1837.

Jackson blamed the Eaton scandal, also known as the "Petticoat Affair," on Henry Clay and John C. Calhoun. The president assumed that Calhoun and his wife had targeted John Eaton because Eaton did not support Calhoun's desire to be president. One of Calhoun's friends wrote in April 1829 that the United States was "governed by the President—the President by the Secretary of War—and the latter by his Wife." Jackson concluded that Calhoun "would sacrifice his friend, his country, and forsake his god, for selfish personal ambition." For his part, Calhoun dismissed Jackson as a "self-infatuated man . . . blinded by ambition [and] intoxicated by flattery and vanity!"

Internal Improvements

Concerns that Jackson was not in control of things quickly disappeared, however, for he decisively used his executive authority to limit the role of the federal government—while at the same time delivering additional blows to John C. Calhoun and to Henry Clay, the man Jackson blamed for having "stolen" the 1824 election from him.

Jackson vetoes the Maysville Road Bill

In 1830, Congress passed a bill pushed by Calhoun and Clay that authorized the use of federal funds to build a sixty-mile-long road from Maysville, Kentucky, to Lexington, Kentucky, Clay's hometown. Urged on by New Yorker Martin Van

Buren, who wanted to preserve the Erie Canal's monopoly over western trade, Jackson vetoed the bill. The president claimed that the proposed road was a "purely local matter," because the proposed Maysville road would run solely through the state of Kentucky. That single-state boundary therefore placed the project outside the domain of Congress, which had authority only over interstate commerce. Federal funding for such local projects would thus require a constitutional amendment. The veto left Clay stunned. "We are all shocked and mortified by the rejection of the Maysville road," he wrote a friend. But he had no luck convincing Congress to override the presidential veto. Jackson ruled the day.

The Bank War

Andrew Jackson showed the same principled stubbornness in dealing with the national bank. The charter for the First Bank of the United States had expired in 1811 but was renewed in 1816 as the Second Bank of the United States, and it soon became the largest corporation in the nation. The Second B.U.S. held all federal funds, mostly the proceeds from land sales and tariff revenues. It also issued paper money (backed by gold and silver) as the national currency. Headquartered in Philadelphia and supported by twenty-nine branches around the nation, the B.U.S. had helped accelerate business expansion by making loans to individuals, businesses, and state banks. It had also supplied a stable currency by forcing the 464 state banks to keep enough gold coins in their vaults to back their own paper currency, which they loaned to people and businesses. With federal revenues soaring from land sales during the early 1830s, the B.U.S., led by the brilliant but arrogant Nicholas Biddle, had accumulated massive amounts of money—and economic power.

KING ANDREW THE FIRST
Opponents considered Jackson's veto of the Maysville Road Bill an abuse of power. This cartoon shows "King Andrew" trampling on the Constitution, internal improvements, and the Bank of the United States.

Even though the B.U.S. benefited the national economy, it had been controversial from the start. Local banks and state governments, especially those in the South and West, feared its growing "monopolistic" power. Southerners and westerners claimed that Biddle and the massive B.U.S. were restricting lending by state banks and impeding businesses from borrowing as much as they wanted.

Throughout his life Andrew Jackson, like many westerners, had hated banks and bankers, whom he called "vipers and thieves." He admitted that he had "always been afraid of banks"—especially the national bank—because they exercised too much power over the economy and the people. Jackson wanted only gold and silver coins to be used for economic transactions. He distrusted paper money because banks printed too much of it, causing prices to rise (inflation). "I think it right to be perfectly frank with you," Jackson told Nicholas Biddle in 1829. "I do not dislike your Bank any more than [I dislike] all banks."

Early on, the president resolved to destroy the B.U.S., pledging "to put his foot upon the head of the monster and crush him to the dust." The national

RECHARTERING THE BANK Jackson's effort to defeat the recharter of the B.U.S. is likened to fighting a hydra, a many-headed serpent from Greek mythology. Just as the hydra would sprout two heads when one was severed, for every B.U.S. supporter that Jackson subdued, even more B.U.S. supporters would emerge to take his place.

bank may have become too powerful, but the **Bank War** between Jackson and Biddle revealed that the president never understood the bank's role or policies. The national bank had provided a stable currency for the expanding economy, as well as a mechanism for controlling the pace of economic growth by regulating the ability of branch banks and state banks to issue paper currency.

The Recharter Effort

Although the Second Bank's charter would run through 1836, Nicholas Biddle could not afford to wait until then for its renewal. Leaders of the newly named National Republican party, especially Henry Clay and Daniel Webster (who was legal counsel to the B.U.S. as well as a senator), told Biddle that he needed to get the charter renewed before the 1836 presidential election. They assured Biddle that the Congress would renew the charter. Biddle himself grew overconfident about his bank's future. "This worthy President," Biddle claimed, "thinks because he has scalped Indians . . . he is to have his way with the Bank." Biddle thought otherwise. "I have been for years in the daily exercise of more personal authority than any President habitually enjoys." He was certain that the B.U.S. "will destroy" Jackson.

Biddle and his political allies, however, failed to grasp both Jackson's tenacity and the depth of public resentment toward the national bank. Jackson's disgust for the B.U.S. reflected the concerns of many voters. In the end, Biddle, Clay, and the National Republican party, also called the Anti-Jackson party, unintentionally handed Jackson a powerful issue on the eve of the 1832 election.

Bank War Political struggle in the early 1830s between President Jackson and financier Nicholas Biddle over the renewing of the Second Bank's charter.

Jackson vetoes renewal of B.U.S. charter

Early in the summer of 1832, both houses of Congress passed the Bank Recharter Bill. On July 10, 1832, however, Jackson vetoed the bill, sending it back to Congress with a blistering criticism of the bank. Jackson claimed that the B.U.S. was both unconstitutional (although the Supreme Court disagreed) and "dangerous to our liberties." The B.U.S. made "the rich richer and the potent more powerful" while discriminating against "the humble members of society—the farmers, mechanics, and laborers."

Daniel Webster accused Jackson of using the bank issue "to stir up the poor against the rich." To Henry Clay, Jackson's veto represented another example of the president's desire to concentrate "all power in the hands of one man." Jackson responded by dismissing Clay as "reckless as a drunken man in a brothel." In the end, Clay and Webster could not convince the Senate to override the veto, thus setting the stage for a nationwide debate and a dramatic presidential campaign.

CORE **OBJECTIVE**

2. Evaluate Jackson's response to the nullification crisis.

Nullification

The vetoes of the Maysville Road Bill and the B.U.S. recharter illustrated Jackson's forceful personality. He eventually would veto twelve congressional bills, more than all the previous presidents combined. Critics claimed that his behavior was "monarchical" in its frequent defiance of the will of Congress. Jackson, however, remained determined to strengthen the executive branch in order to strengthen the Union. His commitment to nationalism over sectionalism was nowhere more evident than in his handling of the nullification crisis in South Carolina.

Calhoun and the Tariff

Vice President John C. Calhoun became President Jackson's fiercest critic because of changing conditions in his home state of South Carolina. The financial Panic of 1819 had sparked a nationwide depression, and throughout the 1820s, South Carolina had suffered from a collapse in cotton prices. The state lost almost 70,000 residents who had moved west during the 1820s in search of cheaper and more fertile land for growing cotton; twice as many would leave during the 1830s.

Most South Carolinians blamed their economic woes on the Tariff of 1828, which they labeled the "**Tariff of Abominations**." By taxing British textiles coming into U.S. markets, the 1828 tariff on imported cloth hurt southern cotton growers by reducing British demand for raw cotton from America. It also hurt southerners by raising the prices they had to pay for imports.

Tariff of Abominations (1828) Tax on imported goods, including British cloth and clothing, that strengthened New England textile companies but hurt southern consumers, who experienced a decrease in British demand for raw cotton grown in the South.

But the tariff was not the only factor explaining South Carolina's problems. Thousands of acres of farmland across the state were nutritionally exhausted from constant overplanting. In addition, South Carolina cotton planters now faced competition from the new cotton-growing states in the Old Southwest: Alabama, Mississippi, Louisiana, and Arkansas.

In a lengthy pamphlet called the *South Carolina Exposition and Protest* (1828), written in secret by John C. Calhoun, the South Carolinian claimed that the Tariff of 1828 favored the interests of New England textile manufacturing over southern agriculture. Under such circumstances, he argued, a state could "nullify," or veto, a federal law it deemed unconstitutional.

Nullification was the ultimate weapon for those determined to protect states' rights against federal authority. As President Jackson and others pointed out, however, allowing states to pick and choose which federal laws they would follow would create chaos.

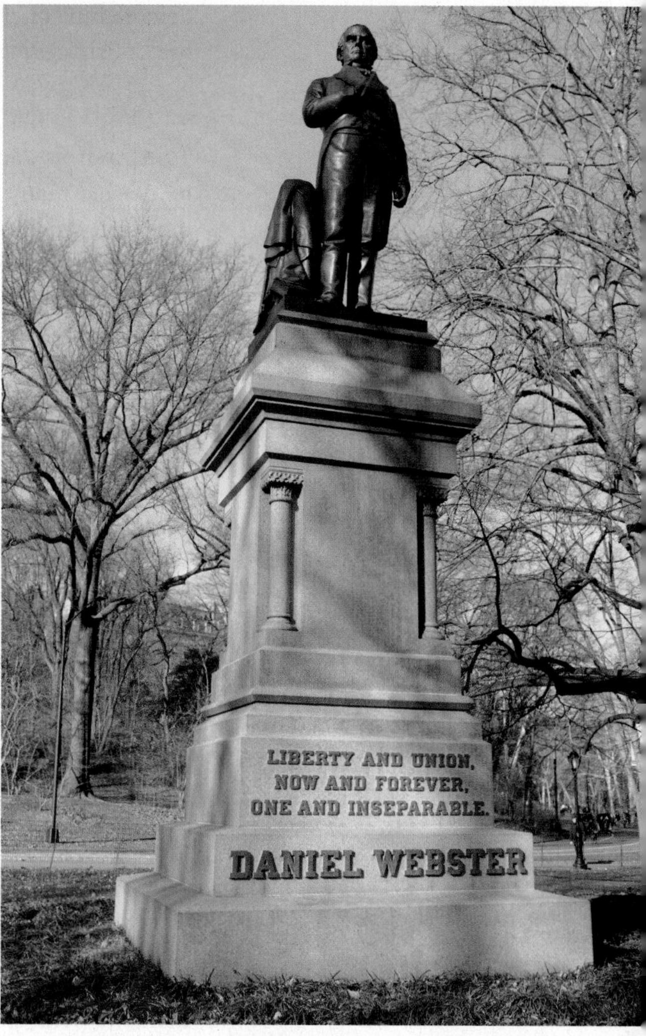

WEBSTER'S REPLY TO SENATOR HAYNE Shortly before his death, a sculpture was made of the eloquent Massachusetts senator Daniel Webster by Thomas Ball, commemorating his denunciation of nullification in the Webster-Hayne debate. A cast of this statue was placed in New York's Central Park in 1876, with a pedestal quoting Webster's final line: "Liberty and union, now and forever, one and inseparable."

The Webster-Hayne Debate

The controversy over the Tariff of 1828 simmered until 1830, when the great Webster-Hayne debate in Congress ignited the tension between states' rights and national authority. In a fiery speech, Senator Robert Y. Hayne of South Carolina argued that anti-slavery Yankees were invading the South, "making war upon her citizens, and endeavoring to overthrow her principles and institutions." In Hayne's view, the Union was created by the states, and the states therefore had the right to nullify, or ignore, federal laws they did not like. The independence of the states was to him more important than the preservation of the Union.

Massachusetts senator Daniel Webster then rose to defend the North—and the Union. Blessed with a thunderous voice and a theatrical flair, Webster was an unapologetic Unionist determined "to strengthen the ties that hold us together." He pointed out that the U.S. Constitution was created not by the states but by the people. If states were allowed to nullify a federal law, the Union would be nothing but a "rope of sand." South Carolina's defiance of federal authority, he charged, "is nothing more than resistance by *force*—it is disunion by *force*—it is secession by *force*—it is civil war."

Webster's powerful closing statement appeared in virtually every newspaper in the nation: "Liberty and Union, now and forever, one and inseparable." Abraham Lincoln later called it "the very best speech ever delivered." Even Hayne was awestruck. He told Webster that "a man who can make such speeches as that ought never to die."

Webster-Hayne debate: States' rights vs. national unity

In the end, Webster had the better argument. Most political leaders agreed that the states could not act separately from the national government. President Jackson did not attend the debate, but he kept in touch with it from the White House. When he asked an aide how Webster was doing, the answer was what he wanted: "He is delivering a most powerful speech . . .

nullification Right claimed by some states to veto a federal law deemed unconstitutional.

demolishing our friend Hayne." The president was pleased. As Jackson said, the Constitution and its laws were "supreme."

Jackson versus Calhoun

That Andrew Jackson, like John C. Calhoun, was a cotton-planting slaveholder led many southerners to assume that the president would support their resistance to the federal tariff. Jackson was sympathetic—until Calhoun and others in South Carolina threatened to "nullify" federal laws they did not like. He then turned on them with the same fury he had directed toward the advancing British army at New Orleans in 1815.

Jackson's toast to the preservation of the Union

On April 13, 1830, the Democratic party hosted members of Congress at the first annual Jefferson Day dinner to honor the birthday of the former president. When it was Jackson's turn to propose a toast to Jefferson's memory, he rose to his feet, raised his glass, glared at Calhoun, and announced: "Our Union—it must be preserved!"

People gasped, knowing that the vice president must reply to Jackson's threat to nullification. Calhoun, trembling with emotion, countered with a defiant toast to "the Union, next to our liberty the most dear!" In that dramatic exchange, Jackson and Calhoun laid bare the fundamental tension between federal authority and states' rights that has remained an animating theme of the American republic.

A New Cabinet

Soon thereafter, another incident deepened the animosity between the two men. On May 12, 1830, the president saw for the first time a letter from 1818 in which Calhoun, then secretary of war under President James Monroe, had wanted to discipline General Jackson for his unauthorized invasion of Spanish-held Florida. After exchanging heated letters about the incident with Calhoun, Jackson told a friend that he was finally through with the "double dealing of J.C.C."

The rift prompted Jackson to take a dramatic step suggested by Secretary of State Martin Van Buren. During one of their frequent horseback rides together, Van Buren offered himself up as a political sacrifice as a way to remove all Calhoun supporters from the cabinet and also end the ongoing Eaton affair that had fractured the administration.

As the first step in the cabinet coup, Van Buren convinced John Eaton to resign as secretary of war on April 4, 1831. Four days later, Van Buren resigned as secretary of state. "The long agony is over," crowed Samuel Ingham, the secretary of the Treasury, in a letter to Attorney General John Berrien. "Mr. V. B. and Major Eaton have resigned." What Ingham and Berrien did not realize was that a few days later, Jackson would force them—both Calhoun supporters—to resign as well. Jackson now had a clean slate on which to create another cabinet.

Critics saw through the secretary of state's scheme: "Mr. Van Buren may be called the 'Great Magician,'" wrote the *New York Courier*, "for he *raises his wand, and the whole Cabinet disappears*." Others claimed that the cabinet

JACKSON'S KITCHEN CABINET Faced with a cabinet already divided by the Eaton affair, Jackson and his closest adviser Martin Van Buren emptied the cabinet of Calhoun supporters and filled it instead with Jackson loyalists. **What did Jackson's new "kitchen cabinet" advise him to do?**

purge showed that Jackson did not have the political skill to lead the nation. One newspaper announced that the ship of state "is sinking and the rats are flying! The hull is too leaky to mend, and the hero of two wars and a half has not the skill to keep it afloat."

Jackson's "kitchen cabinet"

By the end of August 1831, President Jackson had appointed a new cabinet. At the same time, he increasingly relied upon the advice of Martin Van Buren and others making up his so-called kitchen cabinet, an informal group of close friends and supporters, many of them Democratic newspaper editors. The kitchen cabinet soon convinced Jackson to drop his pledge to serve only one term. They explained that it would be hard for Van Buren, the president's chosen successor, to win the 1832 Democratic nomination because Calhoun would do everything in his power to stop him—and might win the nomination himself.

The South Carolina Nullification Ordinance

In the fall of 1831, President Jackson tried to defuse the confrontation with South Carolina by calling on Congress to reduce the tariff. Congress responded with the Tariff of 1832, which lowered taxes on many imported items.

The new tariff, however, was not enough to satisfy Calhoun and others in his home state. South Carolina seethed with resentment toward Jackson and the federal government. One hotheaded South Carolina congressman called the Union a "foul monster." He and other White South Carolinians, living in the only state where enslaved Africans were a majority of the population, feared that if the northern representatives in Congress were powerful enough to create such discriminatory tariffs, they might eventually vote to end slavery.

South Carolina threatens to secede from the Union

In November 1832, just weeks after Andrew Jackson was elected for a second term, a South Carolina state convention overwhelmingly adopted a Nullification Ordinance that repudiated the "unconstitutional" federal tariff acts of 1828 and 1832 (declaring them "null, void, and no law"). If federal authorities tried to use force to collect the tariffs, South Carolina would secede from the Union, they vowed. The state legislature then chose Senator Robert Hayne as governor and elected Calhoun to succeed him as U.S. senator. Calhoun resigned as Jackson's vice president so that he could defend the nullification policy in the Senate.

Jackson's Firm Response

In the nullification crisis, South Carolina, "feisty as a gamecock," found itself standing alone. Other southern states expressed sympathy, but none endorsed nullification. President Jackson's public response was measured yet forthright. He promised to use "firmness and forbearance" with South Carolina but stressed that nullification "means insurrection and war; and the other states have a right to put it down."

In private, however, Jackson was furious. He threatened to hang Calhoun, Hayne, and other "nullifiers" if there were any bloodshed. "Surely the president is exaggerating," Governor Hayne of South Carolina remarked to Senator Thomas Hart Benton of Missouri. Benton, who years before had been in a fistfight with Jackson, replied: "I have known General Jackson a great many years, and when he speaks of hanging [people] it is time to look for a rope."

In his annual message to the nation, delivered December 4, 1832, Jackson appealed to the people of South Carolina not to follow false leaders such as Calhoun: "The laws of the United States must be executed. . . . Those who told you that you might peaceably prevent their execution, deceived you. . . . Their object is disunion. . . . Disunion by armed force is treason."

Clay's Compromise

Jackson asks Congress to issue a Force Bill

President Jackson then sent federal soldiers and a warship to Charleston, the South Carolina port city. Governor Hayne responded by mobilizing the state militia, and the two sides verged on civil war. In early 1833, the president requested from Congress a "**Force Bill**" authorizing him to use the U.S. Army to "force" compliance with federal law in South Carolina. Calhoun exploded on the Senate floor, exclaiming that he and others defending his state's constitutional rights were being threatened "to have our throats cut, and those of our wives and children." The greatest threat facing the nation, he argued, was not nullification but presidential despotism. Calhoun and the nullifiers, however, soon backed down, and the South Carolina legislature postponed implementation of the nullification ordinances in hopes that Congress would pass a more palatable tariff bill.

Force Bill (1833) Legislation, sparked by the nullification crisis in South Carolina, that authorized the president's use of the army to compel states to comply with federal law.

Passage of the compromise bill in Congress, however, depended upon the support of Senator Henry Clay, himself a slaveholding planter. A senator told Clay that these "South Carolinians are good fellows, and it would be a pity to see Jackson hang them." Clay agreed. On February 12, 1833, he circulated a plan to reduce the federal tariff gradually. It was less than South Carolina preferred, but it got the nullifiers out of the dilemma they had created. Calhoun supported the compromise: "He who loves the Union must desire to see this agitating question [the tariff] brought to a termination."

On March 1, 1833, Congress passed the compromise tariff and the Force Bill, and the next day Jackson signed both. Calhoun rushed home to convince the rebels in his state to back down. The South Carolina convention then met and rescinded its nullification of the tariff acts. In a face-saving gesture, the delegates nullified the Force Bill, which Jackson no longer needed.

Both sides claimed victory. Jackson had upheld the supremacy of the Union, and South Carolina had secured a reduction of the federal tariff. But there remained the fundamental issue of southern slaveholders feeling increasingly threatened by growing anti-slavery sentiment in the North. "The struggle, so far from being over," a defiant Calhoun wrote, "is not more than fairly commenced."

Jackson's Indian Policy

CORE **OBJECTIVE**

3. Analyze Jackson's legacy regarding the status of Indians in American society.

If President Jackson's firm stance against nullification constituted his finest hour, his forcible removal of Indians from their ancestral lands was his lowest moment. Like most White frontiersmen, Jackson believed that Indians and land-hungry White settlers could never live in harmony, so the Indians had to be relocated if they were to survive.

After his election in 1828, Jackson recommended that the remaining eastern Indians (those east of the Mississippi River) be moved west of the Mississippi River, in what became Oklahoma. State laws in Alabama, Georgia, and Mississippi had already abolished tribal units and stripped them of their powers, rejected ancestral Indian land claims, and denied Indians the right to vote or testify in court. Jackson claimed that relocating the eastern Indians was an act of mercy, a "wise and humane policy" that would save the Indians from "utter annihilation" if they tried to hold on to their lands.

Indian Removal

In response to a request from Jackson, Congress in 1830 debated the **Indian Removal Act**, which authorized the president to ignore previous treaty commitments and force the 74,000 Indians remaining in the East and South to move to federal lands west of the Mississippi River. Opponents of the policy flooded Congress with petitions warning that Jackson's efforts would bring "enduring shame" on the nation. But Jackson won the battle. In late

Indian Removal Act (1830) Law permitting the forced relocation of Indians to federal lands west of the Mississippi River in exchange for the land they occupied in the East and South.

INDIAN REMOVAL, 1820–1840

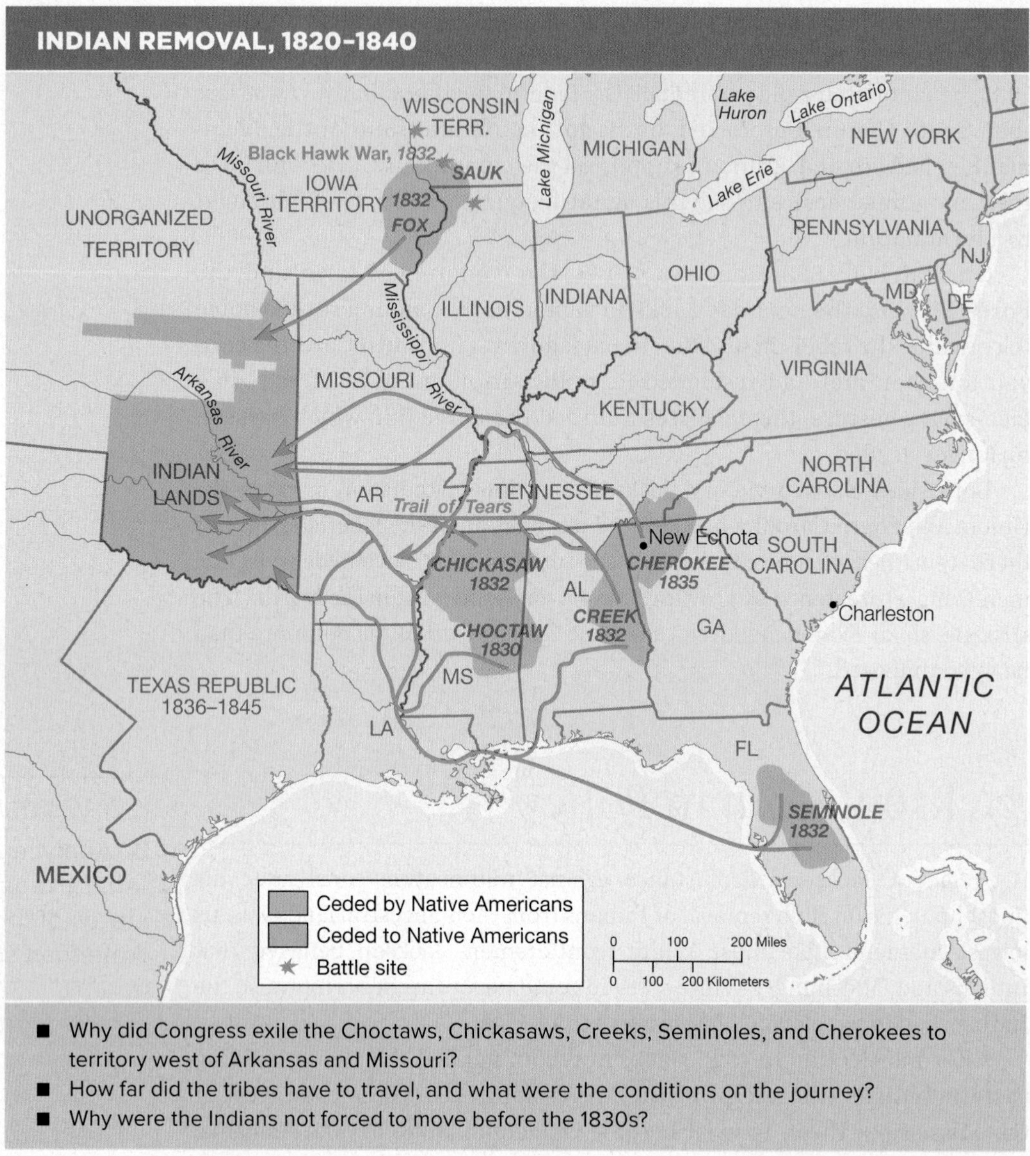

- Why did Congress exile the Choctaws, Chickasaws, Creeks, Seminoles, and Cherokees to territory west of Arkansas and Missouri?
- How far did the tribes have to travel, and what were the conditions on the journey?
- Why were the Indians not forced to move before the 1830s?

May 1830, the Senate passed the Indian Removal Act by a single vote. The Cherokees responded by announcing, "We see nothing but ruin before us."

Indians Resist Resettlement

By 1836, some 46,000 Indians, including most in the North, had been relocated across the Mississippi River. In Illinois and the Wisconsin Territory, however, Sauk and Fox Indians fought to regain their ancestral lands.

The Black Hawk War erupted in April 1832, when Chief Black Hawk led 1,000 Sauks—men, women, and children who had been relocated to the Iowa Territory—back across the Mississippi River to their homeland in Illinois, land shared with the Fox Nation. After several skirmishes, Indiana and Illinois militiamen chased the Sauk and Fox into the Wisconsin Territory and caught them on the eastern bank of the Mississippi, a few

HIDING IN A MANGROVE SWAMP An armed group of Seminoles crouch under a mangrove in the Florida Everglades during the Second Seminole War, out of sight of the American sailors passing by. It was not until 1934 that the few surviving Seminoles in Florida became the last Native American tribe to end their war with the United States.

miles downstream from the mouth of the Bad Axe River. The soldiers misinterpreted the Indians' effort to surrender and fighting erupted. In what became known as the Bad Axe Massacre, the militiamen murdered hundreds of women and children as they tried to escape. The soldiers then scalped the dead Indians and cut long strips of flesh from several of them for use as strops to sharpen razors. Six weeks later, Black Hawk was captured and imprisoned.

In Florida, the Seminoles, led by Osceola, son of an English trader and a Muskogee mother who herself was of mixed parentage, ferociously resisted the federal removal policy. For eight years, the Seminoles would fight a guerrilla war in the swamps of the Everglades—the longest, most costly, and deadliest war ever fought by Native Americans. Some 1,500 were killed on both sides. At times, Seminole women killed their children rather than see them captured.

Seminole resistance waned after 1837, however, when Osceola was captured under a white flag of truce, imprisoned, and left to die of malaria at

Fort Moultrie near Charleston, South Carolina. After 1842, only a few hundred Seminoles remained. It was not until 1934 that the surviving Seminoles in Florida became the last Native American tribe to end its war with the United States.

The Cherokees

Members of the Cherokee Nation also defied the federal removal policy, but its leaders chose to use the courts as their battleground. Cherokees had long occupied northwest Georgia and the mountainous areas of northern Alabama, northwest South Carolina, eastern Tennessee, and western North Carolina. In 1827, relying upon their established treaty rights, they adopted a constitution as an independent nation in which they declared that they were not subject to the laws or control of any state or federal government. Georgia officials had other ideas.

In 1828, shortly after Andrew Jackson's election, the Georgia government announced that after June 1, 1830, the authority of state law would extend to the Cherokees. The "barbarous and savage tribes" must give way to the march of White civilization. Under the new state laws, the Cherokees would not be allowed to vote, own property, or testify against Whites in court. The continuing profitability of cotton and the discovery of gold in north Georgia in 1829 had increased Whites' lust for Cherokee land and led to the new law, which prohibited the Cherokees from digging for gold on their own lands. The Cherokees sought relief in the Supreme Court, arguing, "We wish to remain on the land of our fathers. We have a perfect and original right to remain without interruption or molestation."

Cherokee Nation v. Georgia (1831)

In *Cherokee Nation v. Georgia* (1831), Chief Justice John Marshall ruled that the Cherokees had "an unquestionable right" to maintain control of their ancestral lands, but the Court could not render a verdict because of a technicality: the Cherokees had filed suit as a "foreign nation," but in Marshall's view they were "domestic dependent nations." If it was true that "wrongs have been inflicted," Marshall explained, "this is not the tribunal which can redress the past or prevent the future."

Worcester v. Georgia (1832)

The following year, the Supreme Court *did* rule in favor of the Cherokees in *Worcester v. Georgia* (1832). The case arose when Georgia officials arrested a group of White Christian missionaries living among the Cherokees in violation of a state law forbidding such interaction. Two of the missionaries, Samuel Worcester and Elihu Butler, were sentenced to four years at hard labor. They appealed to the Supreme Court.

In the *Worcester* case, Marshall said the missionaries must be released. The anti-Cherokee laws passed by the Georgia legislature, he declared, had violated "the Constitution, laws, and treaties of the United States." He added that the Cherokee Nation was "a distinct political community" within which Georgia law had no force. Jackson, however, refused to enforce the Court's "wicked" decisions, claiming that he had no constitutional authority to intervene in Georgia. A New York newspaper editor reported that Jackson said, "John Marshall has made his decision, now let him enforce it."

Thereafter, Jackson gave the Cherokees and other Indian nations a terrible choice: either abide by discriminatory new state laws or relocate to federal lands west of the Mississippi River, which would be theirs "forever." Jackson told the Creeks that they and his "white children" could not live "in harmony and peace" if the Creeks remained on their ancestral lands; their only option, he concluded, was "a speedy removal" to the West, where "your father [Jackson] has provided a country large enough for all of you."

CHEROKEES DIVIDED While many Cherokee elite fought against Jackson's policies, Elias Boudinot, editor of the first Native American newspaper, *Cherokee Phoenix*, signed the Treaty of New Echota in 1835. He was subsequently murdered by a rival faction of Cherokees.

The irony of the new Georgia policy was that of all the southern nations, the Cherokees had come closest to adopting the customs of White America. They had abandoned traditional hunting practices to develop farms, build roads, schools, and churches, and create trading posts and newspapers. Many Cherokees had married Whites, adopted their clothing and food, and converted to Christianity. And the Cherokees owned some 2,000 enslaved African Americans.

The Cherokees also had their own constitution modeled after the U.S. Constitution. They elected as their first president John Ross, a wealthy, mixed-race Christian who had served with General Andrew Jackson's forces against the Creeks. The Cherokees, Ross told the U.S. Senate, were "like the white man in manners, morals, and religion." He added that they were not "savages" but "civilized" members of the American republic. Should not their property rights and treaty rights be respected?

His plea fell on mostly deaf ears, however. President Jackson declared that he would not allow a separate Indian nation to exist amid American communities. The Cherokees, he concluded, must either submit to Georgia's authority or move west. In essence, the Indians would be treated as colonists, not as equals. Former president John Quincy Adams lamented that Jackson's plan "was not republican at all." It was instead something an empire would mandate, an act of "despotism."

The Trail of Tears

The federal officials responsible for implementing the Indian Removal Act developed a strategy of divide and conquer with the Cherokees. In 1835, for example, a minority faction among the Cherokees led by Major Ridge (He Who Walks on Mountaintops) signed the fraudulent Treaty of New Echota, which called for the relocation of the Cherokee Nation to Oklahoma. Cherokee president John Ross was outraged. Since the Europeans had arrived, he asserted, "we have been made to drink the bitter cup of humiliation; treated like dogs; our lives, our liberties, the sport of the white men; our country and the graves of our fathers torn from us." Ridge, however, urged submission to President Jackson's orders: "They are strong, and we are weak. We are few, they are many."

Although 90 percent of the Cherokee people had rejected the New Echota treaty, the U.S. Senate readily accepted it, and the U.S. Army set about enforcing its provisions. Former president John Quincy Adams called the treaty "an eternal disgrace upon the country." Major Ridge knew that his decision

TRAIL OF TEARS Thousands of Cherokees died on a nightmarish forced march from Georgia to Oklahoma after being evicted from their native lands.

to abide by the federal decree outraged most Cherokees. "I have signed my death warrant," he muttered. Indeed, he had. In 1839, rival Cherokees executed Ridge and his son, John.

In 1838, when Martin Van Buren was president, 17,000 Cherokees were evicted and moved west under military guard on the **Trail of Tears**, an 800-mile forced journey. Some 4,000 of the refugees, including John Ross's wife, died along the way from exposure, disease, or starvation. Van Buren told Congress in December 1838 that he took "sincere pleasure" in reporting that the Cherokees had been relocated. "You can expel us by force, we grant," Chief John Ross wrote to Van Buren in 1838, "but you cannot make us call it fairness."

The Trail of Tears was, according to a White Georgian, "the cruelest work I ever knew." A few Cherokees held out in the mountains of North Carolina; they became known as the "Eastern Band" of Cherokees. The Creeks and Chickasaws followed the Trail of Tears a few years later, after Alabama and Mississippi used the same techniques as the Georgia government to take control of their tribal lands.

Trail of Tears (1838–1839) The Cherokees' 800-mile journey from the southern Appalachians to Indian Territory.

President Van Buren predicted that the controversies dogging his administration would disappear over time, but the forced removal of the Indians would "endure . . . as long as the government itself." In 2009, Congress passed and President Barack Obama signed an official document apologizing for the Trail of Tears.

Political Battles

CORE **OBJECTIVE**

4. Explain the causes of the economic depression of the late 1830s and the emergence of the Whig party.

Andrew Jackson's controversial policies regarding the Indians, nullification, and the B.U.S. aroused intense opposition. Some congressional opponents talked of impeaching him. Jackson received so many death threats that he decided his political opponents were trying to kill him.

In January 1835, the threat became real. After attending the funeral service for a member of Congress, Jackson was leaving the Capitol when an unemployed English-born housepainter named Richard Lawrence emerged from the shadows and pointed a pistol at the president's heart. When he pulled the trigger, however, the gun misfired. Jackson lifted his walking stick and charged at Lawrence, who pulled out another pistol, but it, too, miraculously misfired. Jackson claimed that his political foes, including John C. Calhoun, had planned the attack. A jury, however, decided that Lawrence, the first person to try to kill a U.S. president, was insane and ordered him confined in an asylum.

A Third Party

In 1832, for the first time in a presidential election, a third party entered the field. The grassroots movement known as the Anti-Masonic party grew out of popular hostility toward the Masonic fraternal order, a large all-male social organization that originated in Great Britain early in the eighteenth century. By 1830, there were some 2,000 Masonic "lodges" scattered across the United States with about 100,000 members, including Andrew Jackson and Henry Clay.

The Anti-Masonic party

Suspicions of the Masonic order as a secret elite organization intent on undermining democracy gave rise to the movement. More than a hundred Anti-Masonic newspapers emerged across the nation. Their common purpose was to stamp out an organization that was contaminating the "heart of the republic." Former president John Quincy Adams said that disbanding the "Masonic institution" was the most important issue facing "us and our posterity."

Opposition to a fraternal organization was hardly the foundation upon which to build a lasting political party. The Anti-Masonic party, however, had three important firsts to its credit: in addition to being the first third party, it was the first party to hold a national convention to nominate a presidential candidate and the first to announce a "platform" of specific policy goals.

The 1832 Election

In preparing for the 1832 election, the Democrats and the National Republicans followed the example of the Anti-Masonic party by holding presidential nominating conventions of their own for the first time. In December 1831, the National Republicans gathered to nominate Henry Clay.

Eager to demonstrate popular support for his own party's candidates, Jackson endorsed the idea of a nominating convention for the Democratic party as well. The Democratic convention named New Yorker Martin Van Buren as Jackson's running mate. The Democrats, unlike the other two parties, adopted no formal platform and relied upon the popularity of the president to carry their cause.

Jackson and Van Buren win the 1832 election

The outcome was an overwhelming endorsement of Jackson in the Electoral College, with 219 votes to 49 for Clay, and a solid victory in the popular vote, 688,000 to 530,000. William Wirt, the Anti-Masonic candidate, carried only Vermont, winning seven electoral votes. Wayward South Carolina, unable to stomach either Jackson or Clay, delivered its 11 votes to Governor John Floyd of Virginia. Dazzled by the president's strong showing, Wirt observed that Jackson could "be President for life if he chooses."

The Removal of Government Deposits

Andrew Jackson interpreted his lopsided reelection as a "decision of the people against the bank." Having vetoed the charter renewal of the B.U.S., he ordered the Treasury Department to transfer federal monies from the national bank to twenty-three state banks—called "pet banks" by Jackson's critics because many were in the western states and were run by Jackson's friends and allies. When the Treasury secretary balked, a furious Jackson fired him.

Transferring the government's money from the B.U.S. to the pet banks was probably illegal, and the Senate, led by Henry Clay, voted on March 28, 1834, to *censure* (a formal statement of disapproval) Jackson for it, the only time an American president has been reprimanded in this way as opposed to actual impeachment. Jackson was so angry after being censured that he wanted to challenge Clay to a duel to "bring the rascal to a dear account."

Biddle's Response

Nicholas Biddle responded to Jackson's actions by ordering the B.U.S. to quit making loans and demanded that state banks exchange their paper currency for gold or silver coins as quickly as possible. Through such deflationary policies that reduced the amount of money circulating in the economy, the desperate Biddle was trying to create an economic depression to reveal the importance of maintaining the national bank. An enraged Jackson said the B.U.S. under Biddle was "trying to kill me, but I will kill it!"

Jackson's "pet banks" create financial chaos

Jackson prevailed in the Bank War; the B.U.S. would shut down by 1841. With the restraining effects of Biddle's national bank removed, hundreds of new state banks sprouted like mushrooms, each printing its own paper currency to lend to land speculators and new businesses. Sales of federal or state-owned lands rose from 4 million acres in 1834 to 20 million in 1836. At the same time, the states plunged themselves heavily into debt to finance the building of roads and canals. By 1837, total state indebtedness had soared.

The irony of Jackson's war on the national bank was that it sparked the dangerous misbehavior among small state banks that he most feared. As

Senator Thomas Hart Benton, one of Jackson's most loyal supporters, said in 1837, those who helped kill the B.U.S. did not intend to create a "wilderness of local banks. I did not join in putting down the paper currency of a national bank to put up a national paper currency of a thousand local banks."

But that is what happened. During the "free banking era" after 1837, anyone who could raise a certain minimum amount of money (capital) could open a bank. And many did. With no central bank to regulate and oversee the operations of "wildcat" banks, many of them went bankrupt after only a few months or years, leaving their depositors empty-handed. Jackson's war against Biddle had ended the central bank only to unleash banking chaos.

The Money Question

During the 1830s, the federal government acquired huge amounts of money from the sale of government-owned lands. Initially, the Treasury department used the annual surpluses from land sales to pay down the accumulated federal debt, which it eliminated in 1835, the first time that any nation had done so. By 1836, the federal budget was generating an annual budget surplus, which led to intense discussions about what to do with the increasingly worthless paper money flowing into the Treasury's vaults.

The Distribution Act (1836)

The surge of unstable paper money issued by state banks peaked in 1836, when events combined suddenly to destroy the value of the bank notes. Two key developments, the passage of the **Distribution Act** and the Specie Circular, would play havoc with the economy and devastate the nation's financial system.

In June 1836, Congress approved a Distribution Act that required the federal government to "distribute" surplus revenue from land sales to the states by "depositing" the funds into eighty-one state banks in proportion to each state's representation in Congress. The state governments would then draw upon those deposits to fund roads, bridges, and other internal improvements, including the construction of new public schools.

Specie Circular (1836)

A month later, President Jackson issued the Specie Circular (1836), which announced that the federal government would accept only specie (gold or silver coins) in payment for land purchased by speculators (farmers could still pay with paper money). Westerners opposed the Specie Circular because most of the government land sales were occurring in the western states. They helped convince Congress to pass an act overturning Jackson's policy. The president, however, vetoed it.

Once enacted, the Distribution Act and the Specie Circular put added strains on the nation's already-tight supplies of gold and silver. Eastern banks had to transfer much of their gold and silver reserves to western banks. As banks reduced their reserves of gold and silver coins, they had to reduce their lending. Soon, the once-bustling economy began to slow into a recession as the money supply contracted. Nervous depositors rushed to their local banks to get their money out, only to learn that there was not enough specie in their vaults to redeem their deposits.

Distribution Act (1836) Law requiring distribution of the federal budget surplus to the states, creating chaos among unregulated state banks dependent on such federal funds.

THE DOCTORS PUZZLED, OR THE DESPERATE CASE OF MOTHER U.S. BANK In this satire of Jackson's Distribution Act and Specie Circular, the B.U.S. is portrayed as an oversized patient vomiting gold and silver coins into pans representing local banks. Clay, Webster, and Calhoun discuss various prescriptions while Jackson leans on the windowsill, insisting he knows the best cure.

Censoring the Mail

While concerns about the strength of the economy grew, slavery emerged again as a flashpoint issue. In 1835, northern abolitionist organizations began mailing anti-slavery pamphlets and newspapers to prominent White southerners, hoping to convince them to end the "peculiar institution."

Francis Pickens of South Carolina urged southerners to stop abolitionists from spreading their "lies." Angry pro-slavery South Carolinians in Charleston broke into the federal post office, stole bags of abolitionist mailings, and ceremoniously burned them. Southern state legislatures passed laws banning such "dangerous" publications. Jackson asked Congress to pass a federal censorship law that would prohibit "incendiary" materials intended to incite "the slaves to insurrection."

Controversy over the censorship of abolitionist literature

Congress took action in 1836, but instead of banning abolitionist materials, a bipartisan group reaffirmed the sanctity of the federal mail. As a practical matter, however, southern post offices began censoring the mail anyway, arguing that federal authority ended when the mail arrived at the post office door. Jackson decided not to enforce the congressional action. His failure of leadership created what would become a growing split in the Democratic party over the future of slavery. Some northern Democrats decided that Jackson, for all of his celebrations of democracy and equality, was no different from John C. Calhoun and other southern White racists.

The controversy over the mails proved to be a victory for the growing abolitionist movement. One anti-slavery publisher said that instead of stifling their efforts, Jackson and the southern radicals "put us and our principles up before the world—just where we wanted to be." Abolitionist groups now started mailing their pamphlets and petitions to members of Congress.

James Hammond, a pro-slavery South Carolinian, called for Congress to ban such anti-slavery petitions. When that failed, Congress in 1836 adopted an informal solution suggested by Martin Van Buren: whenever a petition calling for the end of slavery appeared, someone would immediately move that it be tabled rather than discussed. The plan, Van Buren claimed, would preserve the "harmony of our happy Union."

Van Buren's "gag rule" stifles abolitionists

The supporters of this "gag rule" soon encountered a formidable obstacle in John Quincy Adams, the former president who now was a congressman from Massachusetts. An ardent opponent of slavery, he devised several procedures to get around the gag rule. Henry Wise, a Virginia opponent, called Adams "the acutest, the astutest, the archest enemy of southern slavery that ever existed." In the 1838–1839 session of Congress, thanks to Adams, some 1,500 anti-slavery petitions were filed with 163,845 signatures. Andrew Jackson dismissed Adams, his longtime rival, as "the most reckless and depraved man living."

The Whig Coalition

Whigs vs. "King Andrew I"

Jackson had removed the Indians from the eastern United States and had slain the dual monsters of nullification in South Carolina and the national bank in Philadelphia, and many loved him for it. But in 1834, a new anti-Jackson coalition emerged, united chiefly by their hostility to the president's authoritarian style. They claimed that he was ruling like a domineering monarch, dubbing him "King Andrew I," and labeled his Democratic followers *Tories*. The new anti-Jackson coalition called itself the **Whig party**, a name that had been used by the Patriots of the American Revolution (as well as the parliamentary opponents of the Tories in Britain).

The Whig party grew directly out of the National Republican party led by John Quincy Adams, Henry Clay, and Daniel Webster. The Whigs also found support among Anti-Masons and even some Democrats who resented President Jackson's war on the national bank. Of the forty-one Democrats in Congress who had voted against Jackson on rechartering the national bank, twenty-eight had joined the Whigs by 1836. For the next twenty years, the Whigs and the Democrats would be the two major political parties, and for a second time a **two-party system** emerged.

The Whigs supported Henry Clay and his "American System" of economic nationalism. They favored federal support for internal improvements to foster economic growth. They also supported a national bank and high tariffs. In the South, the Whigs tended to be bankers and merchants. In the West, they were mostly farmers who valued government-funded infrastructure improvements: more roads, canals, and railroads. Unlike the Democrats, who attracted Catholic voters from Germany and Ireland, northern Whigs tended to be native-born Protestants—Congregationalists, Presbyterians, Methodists, and Baptists—who advocated the abolition of slavery and efforts to restrict alcoholic beverages. For the next twenty years, the Whigs and the Democrats would be the two major political parties.

Whig party Political party founded in 1834 in opposition to the Jacksonian Democrats; supported federal funding for internal improvements, a national bank, and high tariffs on imports.

two-party system Domination of national politics by two major political parties, such as the Whigs and Democrats during the 1830s and 1840s.

The Election of 1836

In 1835, eighteen months before the presidential election, the Democrats nominated Jackson's handpicked successor, Vice President Martin Van Buren. The Whig coalition, united chiefly in its opposition to Jackson, adopted a strategy of nominating multiple candidates, hoping to throw the election into the House of Representatives.

Martin Van Buren wins the election of 1836

The Whigs put up three regional candidates: New Englander Daniel Webster, Hugh Lawson White of Tennessee, and William Henry Harrison of Indiana. But the multi-candidate strategy failed. In the popular vote of 1836, Van Buren defeated the entire Whig field, winning 170 electoral votes while the others collected only 113 combined.

The Eighth President

MARTIN VAN BUREN Van Buren earned the nickname the "Little Magician" for not only his short stature but also his "magical" ability to exploit his political and social connections.

Born into a family of Dutch-speaking New York farmers, Martin Van Buren remains the only president for whom English was a second language. Like Andrew Jackson, Van Buren was an outsider and took great pride in his successful efforts to strip the political "old guard" of their powers.

Martin Van Buren was largely responsible for the formation of the Democratic party. Elected governor of New York in 1828, he had resigned to become Andrew Jackson's secretary of state, then became vice president in 1833.

Van Buren had been Jackson's closest political adviser and ally, but many thought he was too self-centered. John Quincy Adams wrote in his diary that Van Buren was "by far the ablest" of the Jacksonians, but he had wasted "most of his ability upon mere personal intrigues. His principles are all subordinate to his ambition." Van Buren's rival John C. Calhoun was even more cutting. "He is not of the race of the lion or the tiger." Rather, he "belongs to a lower order—the fox."

At his inauguration, Van Buren promised to follow "in the footsteps of President Jackson." Before he could do so, however, the nation's financial sector began collapsing. On May 10, 1837, several large state banks in New York, running out of gold and silver, suddenly refused to convert customers' paper money into coins. Other banks across the nation quickly did the same. This financial crisis, the worst yet faced by the young nation, would become known as the **Panic of 1837**. It would soon mushroom into the republic's worst depression, lasting some seven years.

The Panic of 1837

Reasons for the Panic: European economy

The causes of the financial crisis went back to the Jackson administration, but Van Buren got the blame. The problem actually started in Europe. During the mid-1830s, Great Britain, America's largest trading partner, experienced an acute financial crisis when the Bank of England, worried about a run on the gold and silver in its vaults, curtailed its loans. This forced most British companies to reduce their trade with America. As British demand for American cotton plummeted, so did the price paid for cotton. On top of everything else, in 1836 there had been a disastrous wheat crop in the United States.

Panic of 1837 A financial calamity in the United States brought on by a dramatic slowdown in the British economy and falling cotton prices, failed crops, high inflation, and reckless state banks.

As creditors hastened to foreclose on struggling businesses and farms, the inflationary spiral went into reverse. Government spending plunged. Many canals under construction were shut down. In many cases, state governments could not repay their debts. In the crunch, 40 percent of the hundreds of recently created state banks failed. In April 1837, some 250 businesses failed in New York City alone. By early fall, 90 percent of the nation's factories had closed. Those who still had jobs saw their wages plummet, sometimes in half. Hundreds of thousands of people across the nation were not only jobless but homeless as well.

Reasons for the Panic: Jackson's policies

The nation's worst economic crisis was frightening. As a newspaper editorial complained in December 1836, the economy "has been put into confusion and dismay by a well-meant, but *extremely mistaken*" decisions by Congress and President Jackson: the destruction of the B.U.S. and the Specie Circular.

The first mistake was the Specie Circular. Its requirement that all federal land purchases be transacted in gold or silver coins greatly reduced government land sales, thus pinching the federal budget. Struggling American banks had to borrow gold from European banks, but they could not get enough to prevent a financial panic and a deepening depression.

Jackson's second mistake was his decision to eliminate rather than reform the B.U.S. It could have acted as a stabilizing force amid the financial panic. Instead, unregulated state banks around the country flooded the economy with worthless paper money without adequate backing in gold or silver.

In April 1836, *Niles' Weekly Register*, the nation's leading business journal, reported that the economy was "approaching a momentous crisis." The federal government was lucky to sell land for $3 an acre that had been going for $10 an acre. State governments canceled plans to build roads, bridges, railroads, canals, and ports. More and more people were caught short by the crisis and could not pay their debts: farmers, merchants, bankers. Many desperate people fled their debts altogether by moving to Texas, then a province of Mexico. Forty percent of the state banks shut their doors. Even the federal government itself, having put most of its gold and silver in state banks, was verging on bankruptcy. The *National Intelligencer* newspaper reported in May that the federal treasury "has not a dollar of gold or silver in the world!"

JACKSONIAN TREASURY NOTE A parody of the often-worthless fractional notes issued by local banks and businesses in lieu of coins. These notes proliferated during the panic of 1837, with the emergency suspension of gold and silver payments. In the main scene, Martin Van Buren, a monster on a wagon driven by John C. Calhoun, is about to pass through an arch labeled "Wall Street" and "Safety Fund Banks."

The poor, as always, were particularly hard hit. By the fall of 1837, a third of workers were jobless, and those still fortunate enough to have jobs had their wages slashed. At the same time, prices for food and clothing soared. As the winter of 1837 approached, a

New York City journalist reported that 200,000 people were "in utter and hopeless distress with no means of surviving the winter but those provided by charity." The nation had a "poverty-struck feeling."

Politics amid Depression

The unprecedented economic calamity sent shock waves through the political system. Critics called the president "Martin Van Ruin" because he did not believe that the government had any responsibility to rescue hard-pressed farmers, bankers, or businessmen or to provide relief for the jobless and homeless. He did call a special session of Congress in 1837, which canceled the distribution of the federal surplus to the states because there was no longer any surplus to distribute.

How best to deal with the unprecedented depression divided Democrats from Whigs. Unlike Van Buren, Whig Henry Clay insisted that suffering people were "entitled to the protecting care of a parental Government." To him, an enlarged role for the federal government was the price of a maturing, expanding republic in which elected officials had an obligation to promote public "safety, convenience, and prosperity." Van Buren and the Democrats believed that the government had no such obligations. Henry Clay, among others, savaged the president for his "cold and heartless" attitude.

An Independent Treasury

Van Buren believed that the federal government should stop risking its deposits in shaky state banks. Instead, he wanted to establish an independent Treasury system whereby the government would keep its funds in its own bank vaults and do business entirely in gold or silver, not paper currency. Van Buren wanted the federal government to regulate the nation's supply of gold and silver and let the marketplace regulate the supply of paper currency printed by state banks.

Independent Treasury Act (1840)

It took Van Buren more than three years to convince Congress to pass the **Independent Treasury Act** on July 4, 1840. Although it lasted little more than a year (the Whigs repealed it in 1841), it would be restored in 1846. Not surprisingly, the state banks that lost control of the federal funds howled in protest.

The "Log Cabin and Hard Cider" Campaign

By 1840, an election year, the Van Buren administration and the Democrats were in deep trouble. The depression continued to worsen and the suffering spread, leading the Whigs to grow confident they could win the presidency. At their nominating convention, they passed over Henry Clay, the Kentucky legislator who had been Jackson's consistent foe, in favor of William Henry Harrison, whose credentials were impressive: victor at the Battle of Tippecanoe against Tecumseh's Shawnees in 1811, former governor of the Indiana Territory, and former congressman and senator from Ohio. To balance the ticket geographically, the Whigs nominated John Tyler of Virginia as their vice president. Henry Clay, who yearned to be president, was bitterly

Independent Treasury Act (1840) System created by Van Buren that moved federal funds from favored state banks to the U.S. Treasury, whose financial transactions could only be in gold or silver.

UNCLE SAM'S PET PUPS! A woodcut showing William Henry Harrison luring "Mother Bank," Andrew Jackson, and Martin Van Buren into a barrel of hard (alcoholic) cider. While Jackson and Van Buren sought to destroy the B.U.S., Harrison promised to reestablish it, hence his providing "Mother Bank" a refuge in this scene.

disappointed, grousing, "My friends are not worth the powder and shot it would take to kill them. I am the most unfortunate man in the history of parties."

The Whigs refused to take a stand on major issues. They did, however, seize upon a catchy campaign slogan: "Tippecanoe and Tyler Too." When a Democratic newspaper declared that General Harrison was the kind of man who would spend his retirement "in a log cabin [sipping apple cider] on the banks of the Ohio [River]," the Whigs chose the cider and log cabin symbols to depict Harrison as a simple man sprung from the people, in contrast to Van Buren's wealthy, aristocratic lifestyle. (Harrison was actually from one of Virginia's wealthiest families).

Harrison wins the 1840 election with record-breaking voter turnout

Harrison defeated Van Buren easily, winning 234 electoral votes to 60. The Whigs had promised a return to prosperity without explaining how it would happen. It was simply time for a change. The most remarkable aspect of the election of 1840 was the turnout. More than 80 percent of White American men voted, many for the first time—the highest turnout before or since, as almost every state had dropped property qualifications for voting.

Jackson's Legacy

CORE **OBJECTIVE**

5. Assess the strengths and weaknesses of Jackson's transformational presidency.

The nation that new president William Henry Harrison governed was vastly different from that led by George Washington in the 1790s. In 1828, when Andrew Jackson took office, the United States boasted twenty-four states and nearly 13 million people, many of them recent arrivals from Germany and Ireland. The national population was growing at a phenomenal rate, doubling every twenty-three years.

During the so-called Jacksonian era, the nation witnessed continuing industrialization, rapidly growing cities, rising tensions between the North and South over slavery, accelerating westward expansion, and the emergence of the second two-party system, featuring Democrats and Whigs.

A surge in foreign demand for southern cotton and other American goods, along with substantial British investment in an array of new American enterprises, helped generate an economic boom and a transportation revolution. That President-elect Jackson rode to his inauguration in a horse-drawn carriage and left Washington, D.C., eight years later on a train symbolized the dramatic changes occurring in American life.

A New Political Landscape

A transformational figure in a transformational era, Andrew Jackson helped reshape the political landscape. Even his ferocious opponent, Henry Clay, acknowledged that Jackson had "swept over the Government . . . like a tropical tornado."

Like all great presidents, however, Jackson left a messy, even contradictory, legacy. Jackson championed opportunities for the "common man" to play a greater role in the political arena at the same time that working men were forming labor unions to increase their economic power and political clout. He helped establish the modern Democratic party and attracted to it the working poor and immigrants from eastern cities, as well as farmers from the South and East. Through a nimble combination of force and compromise, he saved the Union by suppressing the nullification crisis.

In Jackson's 1837 farewell address, he stressed that he had worked on behalf of "the farmer, the mechanic, and the laboring classes of society—the bone and sinew of the country—men who love liberty and desire nothing but equal rights and equal laws."

And, with great fanfare on January 1, 1835, Jackson announced that the government had paid off the national debt accumulated since the Revolutionary War, which he called a "national curse." The *Washington Globe* noted that the elimination of the debt coincided with the twentieth anniversary of the Battle of New Orleans, writing, "New Orleans and the National Debt—the first of which paid off our scores to *our enemies*, whilst the latter paid off the last cent to *our friends*."

Jackson's concept of "the people," however, was limited to a "white men's democracy," as it had been for all previous presidents. The phenomenon of Andrew Jackson, the heroic symbol of the common man and the democratic ideal, continues to spark historical debate, as it did during his lifetime.

Jackson was so convinced of the rightness and righteousness of his ideals that he was willing to defy constitutional limits on his authority when it suited his interests and satisfied his rage. He did not embrace the rule of law unless he was the one making the laws. In this sense, he was both the instrument of democracy and its enemy, protecting "the humble people" and the Union by expanding presidential authority in ways that the founders had never envisioned, including removing federal money from the national bank, replacing government officials with party loyalists, censoring the mails, and ending nullification in South Carolina. In doing so, he both symbolized and aggravated the perennial tension in the American republic between a commitment to democratic ideals and the exercise of presidential power, states' rights, and federal actions.

Reviewing the CORE OBJECTIVES | INQUIZITIVE

■ **Jackson's Views and Policies** The Jacksonians sought to democratize the political process and expand economic opportunity for the "common man" (that is, "poor and humble" White men). As the representative of "the people," he expanded the role of the president in economic matters, reducing federal government spending and eliminating the powerful Second Bank of the United States. His *Bank War* painted the national bank as full of "vipers and thieves" and was hugely popular, but Jackson did not understand its long-term economic consequences. In addition, his views on limited government were not always reflected in his policies. He left the high taxes on imports from the *Tariff of Abominations* (1828) in place until opposition in the South created a national crisis.

■ **Nullification Controversy** The concept of *nullification*, developed by South Carolina's John C. Calhoun, enabled a state to disavow a federal law. When a South Carolina convention nullified the Tariffs of 1828 and 1832, Jackson requested that Congress pass a *Force Bill* (1833) authorizing the U.S. Army to compel compliance with the tariffs. After South Carolina, under the threat of federal military force, accepted a compromise tariff put forth by Henry Clay, the state convention nullified the *Force Bill*. The crisis was over, with both sides claiming victory.

■ **Indian Removal Act of 1830** The *Indian Removal Act* authorized the relocation of eastern Indians to federal lands west of the Mississippi River. The Cherokees used the federal court system in *Cherokee Nation v. Georgia* and *Worcester v. Georgia* to try to block this relocation. Despite the Supreme Court's decisions in their favor, President Jackson forced them to move; the event and the route they took came to be called the *Trail of Tears* (1838–1839). By 1840, only a few Seminoles and Cherokees remained in remote areas of the Southeast.

■ **Democrats and Whigs** Jackson's arrogant behavior, especially his use of the veto, led many to regard him as "King Andrew I." Groups who opposed him organized a new political party, known as the *Whig party*, thus producing the country's second *two-party system*. Two acts—the *Distribution Act* (1836) and the Specie Circular—ultimately destabilized the nation's economy. Andrew Jackson's ally and vice president, Martin Van Buren, succeeded Jackson as president, but Jacksonian bank policies led to the financial *Panic of 1837* and an economic depression. Van Buren responded by establishing the *Independent Treasury Act* (1840) to safeguard the nation's economy but offered no help for individuals in distress. The economic calamity ensured a Whig victory in the election of 1840.

■ **The Jackson Years** Andrew Jackson's America was very different from the America of 1776. Most White men had gained the vote when states removed property qualifications for voting, but political equality did not mean economic equality. Democrats wanted every American to have an equal chance to compete in the marketplace and in the political arena, but they never promoted equality of results. Inequality between rich and poor widened during the Jacksonian era.

KEY TERMS

Bank War *p. 369*

Tariff of Abominations (1828) *p. 370*

nullification *p. 371*

Force Bill (1833) *p. 374*

Indian Removal Act (1830) *p. 375*

Trail of Tears (1838–1839) *p. 380*

Distribution Act (1836) *p. 383*

Whig party *p. 385*

two-party system *p. 385*

Panic of 1837 *p. 386*

Independent Treasury Act (1840) *p. 388*

CHRONOLOGY

1828 Andrew Jackson wins presidential election

Tariff of Abominations goes into effect

1830 Congress passes the Indian Removal Act

Andrew Jackson vetoes the Maysville Road Bill

The Eaton affair divides Andrew Jackson's warring cabinet

1831 Supreme Court issues *Cherokee Nation v. Georgia* decision

1832 Supreme Court issues *Worcester v. Georgia* decision

Andrew Jackson vetoes the Bank Recharter Bill

South Carolina passes Nullification Ordinance

1833 Congress passes the Force Bill, authorizing military force in South Carolina

Congress passes Henry Clay's compromise tariff with Jackson's support

1836 Democratic candidate Martin Van Buren is elected president

1837 Financial panic deflates the economy

1838–1839 Eastern Indians forced west on Trail of Tears

1840 Independent Treasury Act established

1840 Whig candidate William Henry Harrison is elected president

INQUIZITIVE

Go to InQuizitive to see what you've learned—and learn what you've missed—with personalized feedback along the way.

THE OLD SOUTH One of the enduring myths of the South before the Civil War is captured in this late nineteenth-century painting of a plantation on the Mississippi River, depicting strong, well-dressed enslaved people tending the lush cotton fields while the planter and his family presumably are relaxing in the coolness of their white-columned mansion. Novels and films like *Gone with the Wind* (1939) would perpetuate the notion of the Old South as a stable, paternalistic agrarian society worked by "happy" enslaved people and led by White planters who claimed they were the "natural" aristocracy of virtue and talent governing their communities.

CHAPTER

11

The South and Slavery

1800–1860

Of all the nation's regions during the first half of the nineteenth century, the South was the most distinctive. What had once been a narrow band of settlements along the Atlantic coast dramatically expanded westward and southward to form a subcontinental empire rooted in cotton—and slavery.

The southern states remained rural and agricultural long after the rest of the nation had embraced cities, hired immigrants, and built factories, but the Old South was also instrumental in enabling the nation's industrial development. After the War of 1812, southern-grown cotton fed the bustling textile mills of Great Britain and New England. The price of raw cotton doubled in the first year after the war, and the fibrous "white gold" quickly displaced sugar as the most profitable crop produced by enslaved labor. Its stunning profitability soon entwined the economies of the North and much of the world. Investors in Boston, New York City, and Philadelphia provided loans to southerners to buy more land and more enslaved workers. Northerners also provided the cotton industry with other essential needs: insurance, financing, and shipping. In this sense, the South coerced enslaved people to create a cotton empire, and northern financiers, shippers, and merchants manipulated the South to create an industrial and financial empire.

CORE OBJECTIVES INQUIZITIVE

1. Explain the various factors that made the South distinct from the rest of the United States during the early nineteenth century.
2. Discuss the role that cotton production and slavery played in the South's economic and social development.
3. Distinguish among the major groups within southern White society and explain why each group supported the expansion of slavery.
4. Describe the impact of slavery on African Americans, both free and enslaved, throughout the South.
5. Analyze how enslaved peoples responded to the inhumanity of their situation.

Slavery was more than a moral disgrace; it was a profit-making *system* built upon forced labor exploitation, a vicious form of racial capitalism that created vast inequalities in income, wealth, power, and status. A group of Virginia enslaved people recognized their essential role in the surging national economy when they asked, "Didn't we clear the land, and raise the crops of corn, of tobacco, rice, of sugar, of everything? And then didn't the large cities in the North grow up on the cotton and the sugars and the rice that we made?"

CORE **OBJECTIVE**

1. Explain the various factors that made the South distinct from the rest of the United States during the early nineteenth century.

The Distinctiveness of the Old South

People have long debated what set the Old South apart from the rest of the nation. Most arguments focus on the region's climate and geography in shaping its culture and economy. The warm, humid climate was ideal for cultivating commercial crops such as tobacco, cotton, rice, indigo, and sugarcane, which led to the plantation system of large commercial agriculture and its dependence upon enslaved laborers working from dawn to dusk, six days a week.

Unlike the North, the South had few large cities, few banks, few railroads, few factories, and few schools. Most of the commerce in the South dealt with the storage, distribution, and sale of agricultural products, especially cotton. With the cotton economy booming, there was little reason to create a robust industrial sector. "We want no manufactures; we desire no trading, no mechanical, or manufacturing classes," an Alabama politician told an English visitor. Profitable farming built on the backs of enslaved African Americans thus remained the South's ideal pursuit of happiness.

A Multiracial Region

What made the Old South most distinctive was not its climate or soil but its expanding system of race-based slavery to support its agricultural economy. Most southern Whites did not own enslaved people, but everyone was affected by the social norms and economic imperatives of what southern leaders euphemistically referred to as the South's "**peculiar institution**" of enslaved labor.

Racial hierarchies in the Old South

Most southerners viewed those held in bondage not as human beings but as investment property. A South Carolina planter asserted that the enslaved "are yet the best stock a man can own.... The truth is there is no investment so safe & so profitable as land & negroes." The profitability and convenience of owning laborers created a sense of social unity among Whites that bridged class differences. Poor Whites who owned no enslaved people and resented the planters (referred to as cotton snobs) could still claim racial superiority over enslaved Blacks. Because of race-based slavery, explained Georgia attorney Thomas Reade Cobb, every White "feels that he belongs to an elevated class. It matters not that he is no slaveholder; he is not of the inferior race; he is a free-born citizen."

The Old South also differed from other sections of the country in its high proportion of native-born Americans. The region attracted few European immigrants after the Revolution, in part because of geography. The main

peculiar institution Phrase used by Whites in the antebellum South to refer to slavery without using the word *slavery*.

shipping routes from Britain and Europe took immigrants to northern port cities such as Boston, New York, and Philadelphia, and most immigrants could not afford to travel to the South. Moreover, southern planters preferred enslaved Africans over European immigrants as their primary source of labor.

Low immigration rates to the South

Conflicting Myths

Southerners, a North Carolina editor wrote, are "a mythological people . . . who live in a still-legendary land." Myths are beliefs made up partly of truths and partly of lies. During the nineteenth century, a powerful myth emerged among White southerners—that the southern way of life was both different from *and* better than that in the North. Even today, many southerners tenaciously cultivate a defiant pride and identity separate from the rest of the nation.

Southerners' myth of the Old South: Agrarian "aristocracy"

In defending the South and slavery from northern critics, southerners claimed that their region was morally superior. Kind planters, according to the prevailing myth, provided happy enslaved people with food, clothing, shelter, and security—in contrast to a North populated with greedy bankers and heartless factory owners who treated their White wage laborers worse than enslaved workers. South Carolina's John C. Calhoun insisted that in the northern states the quality of life for free people of color had "become worse" because slavery there had been banned while in the South, the standard of living among enslaved African Americans had "improved greatly in every respect."

In this mythic version of the Old South, slavery supposedly benefited enslaved people as much as owners. In *Aunt Phillis's Cabin; or, Southern Life as It Is* (1852), Virginia novelist Mary Henderson Eastman stressed "the necessity of the existence of slavery at present in our Southern States," and claimed "that, as a general thing, the slaves are comfortable and contented, and their owners humane and kind."

NEGRO VILLAGE ON A SOUTHERN PLANTATION The opening engraving of Mary Henderson Eastman's novel *Aunt Phillis's Cabin* depicts a jovial scene of enslaved people at leisure, dancing or relaxing in the shade. **How does this portrayal fit into the myth of the Old South?**

The southern passion for guns, horsemanship, hunting, and the military filled in the self-gratifying image of the Old South as a region governed by aristocratic gentlemen, young belles, and beautiful ladies who led leisurely lives of well-mannered graciousness, honor, and courage, all the while sipping mint juleps in a carefree romanticized world of white-columned mansions.

Northerners' myth of the Old South: Immoral exploiters

The contrasting myth of the Old South was much darker. Northern abolitionists pictured the region as being rooted in an immoral economic system dependent on the exploitation of Blacks and the displacement of Native Americans. In this version of the southern myth, White planters were ambitious self-made men who had seized opportunities to become rich by planting and selling cotton—and trading in enslaved people.

Abolitionists such as Harriet Beecher Stowe portrayed southern planters as cunning capitalists who raped enslaved women, brutalized enslaved people, and lorded over their communities with arrogant disdain. They treated enslaved people like cattle, treated enslaved women like prostitutes, broke up enslaved families, and sold enslaved people "down the river" to toil in the gruesome sugar mills and rice plantations in South Carolina, Georgia, and Louisiana. An English woman traveling in the South in 1830 noted that what enslaved people in Virginia and Maryland feared most was being "sent to *the south* and sold. . . . The sugar plantations [in Louisiana] and, more than all, the rice grounds of Georgia and the Carolinas, are the terror of the American negroes."

Several Souths

The Old South included three regional subsections with distinct patterns of economic development and diverging degrees of commitment to slavery. Throughout the first half of the nineteenth century, the seven states of the Lower South (South Carolina, Georgia, Florida, Alabama, Mississippi, Louisiana, and parts of Texas) grew increasingly reliant on cotton production, which was dependent upon slave labor. By 1860, enslaved people represented nearly half the population of the Lower South, largely because they were the most efficient producers of cotton in the world and the most profitable form of capital investment.

The states of the Upper South (Virginia, North Carolina, Tennessee, and Arkansas) had more varied agricultural economies—a mixture of large commercial plantations and small family farms, where crops were grown mostly for household use. Many states also had large areas without slavery, especially in the mountains of Virginia, the western Carolinas, eastern Tennessee, and northern Georgia, where the soil and climate were not suited to growing cotton or tobacco.

In the Border South (Delaware, Maryland, Kentucky, and Missouri), slavery was slowly disappearing because cotton could not thrive there. By 1860, 90 percent of Delaware's Black population and half of Maryland's were already free. Slave owners in the Lower South, however, had a much larger investment in slavery. They also believed that only constant supervision, intimidation, and punishment would keep enslaved workers under control, in part because working and living conditions for the enslaved were so brutal. "I'd rather be dead," said a White overseer in Louisiana, "than a [colored person] in one of those big [sugarcane] plantations."

The Cotton Kingdom

CORE **OBJECTIVE**

2. Discuss the role that cotton production and slavery played in the South's economic and social development.

Tobacco, Rice, Sugar, and Livestock

After the Revolution, as the tobacco fields in Virginia and Maryland lost their fertility, tobacco farming spread into Kentucky and as far west as Missouri. Rice continued to be grown in the coastal areas (low country) of the Carolinas and Georgia, where fields could easily be flooded and drained by tidal rivers flowing into the ocean. Sugarcane, like rice, was also expensive to produce, requiring machinery to grind the cane to release the sugar syrup. During the early nineteenth century, only southern Louisiana focused on sugar production.

In addition to such cash crops, the South led the nation in the production of livestock: hogs, horses, mules, and cattle. For southerners, both Black and White, pork was "king of the table." John S. Wilson, a Georgia doctor, called the region the "Republic of Porkdom." Southerners ate pork or bacon "morning, noon, and night." Corn was on southern plates as often as pork. During the early summer, corn was boiled on-the-cob. By late summer, it was ground into meal or flour. Cornbread and hominy, a "mush" or porridge made of whole-grain corn mixed with milk, were almost daily fare.

"King Cotton"

During the first half of the nineteenth century, cotton surpassed rice as the most profitable cash crop in the South. Southern cotton drove much of the national economy and the industrial revolution, feeding the textile mills in New England and Great Britain.

Cotton became one of the transforming forces in nineteenth-century history. It shaped the lives of the enslaved who cultivated it, the planters who grew rich by it, the ship owners who transported it, the mill girls who turned it into fabric and thread, the merchants who sold it, the people who wore it, and the politicians who warred over it. "Cotton is King," exclaimed the *Southern Cultivator* in 1859, "and wields an astonishing influence over the world's commerce." In 1832, over eighty of America's largest companies were New England textile mills.

Technological innovations: British textile mills and the cotton gin

The Cotton Kingdom resulted largely from two crucial developments. Until the late eighteenth century, cotton fabric was a rarity produced by women in India using hand looms. Then British inventors developed

ATOP THE COTTON KINGDOM This photograph offers a glimpse of the staggering rates of cotton production. These cotton bales fill this Mississippi steamboat to capacity and are so densely packed and plentiful that men are able to walk on top of them.

machinery to convert raw cotton into thread and cloth. The mechanical production of cotton thread, cloth, and clothing made Great Britain the world's first industrial nation, and British textile mills grew so fast that they could not get enough cotton fiber to meet their needs (cotton could not be grown in the British climate). Cotton remained a tough crop to process because the sticky seeds had to be removed by hand. American Eli Whitney solved the problem in the 1790s by constructing the first cotton gin.

Taken together, these two mechanical breakthroughs helped create the world's largest industry—and transformed the South. By 1815, just months after General Andrew Jackson's victory over British troops at New Orleans, some thirty British ships tied up at the city's wharves because, as an American merchant reported, "Europe must, and will have, cotton for her manufacturers." During that year alone, more than 65,000 bales of cotton were shipped down the Mississippi River to New Orleans. By 1860, southern states were providing 77 percent of the cotton used in British textile mills and 90 percent of the fiber used in France's mills.

The Lower South (the Old Southwest)

Because of its warm climate and plentiful rainfall, the Lower South became the global leader in cotton production. The region's cheap, fertile land and the profits provided by cotton and the sale of enslaved people generated a frenzied mobility as people eager to better themselves searched for more opportunities and better land. Henry Watson, a New Englander who moved to Alabama, complained in 1836 that "nobody seems to consider himself settled [here]; they remain one, two, three or four years & must move on to some other spot."

Massive migration to Lower South / Old Southwest

The cotton belt moved south and west during the first half of the nineteenth century. As Virginia and the Carolinas experienced soil exhaustion from the overplanting of tobacco and cotton, restless farmers and many sons of planters moved to the **Old Southwest**—western Georgia, Alabama, Mississippi, Louisiana, Arkansas, and, eventually, Texas. They found cheap land and fertile soil—a promised land made possible by the worldwide demand for cotton clothing.

Old Southwest Region covering western Georgia, Alabama, Mississippi, Louisiana, Arkansas, and Texas, where low land prices and fertile soil attracted droves of settlers after the American Revolution.

Many southern women were not excited about leaving the coastal states for the southwestern frontier. As Mary Ann Taylor prepared to leave South Carolina for Alabama, she confessed to a friend, "You *cannot* imagine the state of despair I am in." Her despair deepened when she reached Alabama in 1834. There she was "surrounded by strangers with whom I have not a single congenial feeling."

In 1820, Virginia, the Carolinas, and Georgia had produced two-thirds of the nation's cotton. By 1830, the states in the Old Southwest were producing two-thirds of all cotton. An acre of land in South Carolina produced about 300 pounds of cotton, while an acre in Alabama or in the Mississippi delta, a 200-mile-wide strip of fertile soil between the Yazoo and Mississippi Rivers, could generate 800 pounds. It was the most profitable farmland in the world. As a British visitor noted, people in the Old Southwest "buy cotton, sell cotton, think cotton, eat cotton, drink cotton, and dream cotton. They marry cotton wives, and unto them are born cotton children. . . . It is the great staple—the sum and substance of Alabama."

Such profits, however, required backbreaking labor, most of it performed by enslaved Blacks, whose working environment was one of danger, disease, and deprivation. A White Virginian noted that "there is a great aversion amongst our Negroes to be carried to distant parts, and particularly to our new countries [in the Old Southwest]."

Hot-tempered Samuel Townes was typical of planters in the Old Southwest who worked enslaved people to the limit. After graduating from the University of Virginia, he trained as an attorney in upstate South Carolina while yearning to be a wealthy planter. The South Carolina soil, however, was worn out, so in 1833 he took his new bride and three enslaved people to Marion, Alabama.

As the months passed, however, Townes grew frustrated with two enslaved women, Marcelena and Phillis, because they were picking only 40 pounds of cotton a day when the other women were picking 70 pounds. Townes screamed at his overseer to "make those bitches go to at least 100 [pounds a day] or whip them like the devil." Townes even took pride in his young son for abusing enslaved girls, describing him as "the terror of the back yard little negroes."

Cotton boom expands slavery

The formula for growing rich in the Lower South was simple: cheap land, improved cotton seed, and enslaved people forced to work at a brutal pace. A planter who moved to the Mississippi Territory urged a friend back in Kentucky to join him: "If you could . . . bring your negroes to the Miss. Terr., they would certainly make you a handsome fortune in ten years by the cultivation of Cotton."

Between 1810 and 1840, the combined population of Georgia, Alabama, and Mississippi increased from about 300,000 (252,000 of whom were in Georgia) to 1,657,799. As Virginian Richard Ambler made his way to Alabama, he marveled that "the number of emigrants surpasses all calculations. . . . For six or eight miles at a time you see an uninterrupted line of walkers, wagons, and carriages." By 1860, annual cotton production in the United States had grown to 4 *million* (a bundle of cotton weighing between 400 and 500 pounds).

The Spreading Cotton Kingdom

By 1860, the center of the "**cotton kingdom**" stretched from eastern North Carolina, South Carolina, and Georgia through the Alabama-Mississippi

cotton kingdom Cotton-producing region, relying predominantly on slave labor, that spanned from North Carolina west to Louisiana and reached as far north as southern Illinois.

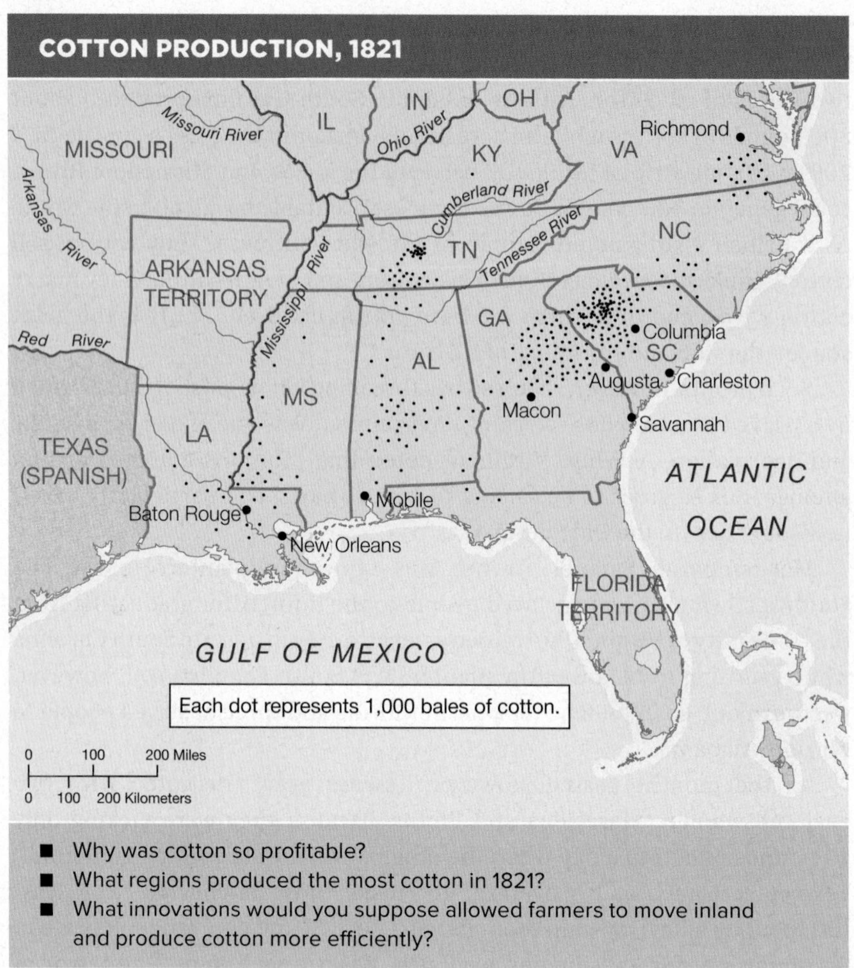

- Why was cotton so profitable?
- What regions produced the most cotton in 1821?
- What innovations would you suppose allowed farmers to move inland and produce cotton more efficiently?

"black belt" (so called for the color of the fertile soil), through Louisiana, on to Texas, and up the Mississippi River Valley as far as southern Illinois.

Steamboats transport cotton along the Mississippi River

With the emergence of steamboats, the Mississippi River became the cotton highway, transporting millions of bales downriver from Kentucky, Tennessee, Arkansas, Mississippi, and Louisiana to New Orleans, where ships took the cotton to New York City, New England, Great Britain, and France. King Cotton accounted for more than half of all U.S. exports. By 1860, Alabama, Mississippi, and Louisiana were the top-producing cotton states, and two-thirds of the richest Americans lived in the South.

The spreading system of slavery was, as John Quincy Adams wrote in his diary, "the great and foul stain" upon the nation's commitment to liberty and equality. It expanded because it was such a powerful engine of economic development—and the most visible sign of economic success. Enterprising young White men judged wealth and status by the number of human beings they owned. By 1860, the dollar value of enslaved Blacks outstripped the value of *all* American banks, railroads, and factories combined.

POPULATION GROWTH AND COTTON PRODUCTION, 1821–1859

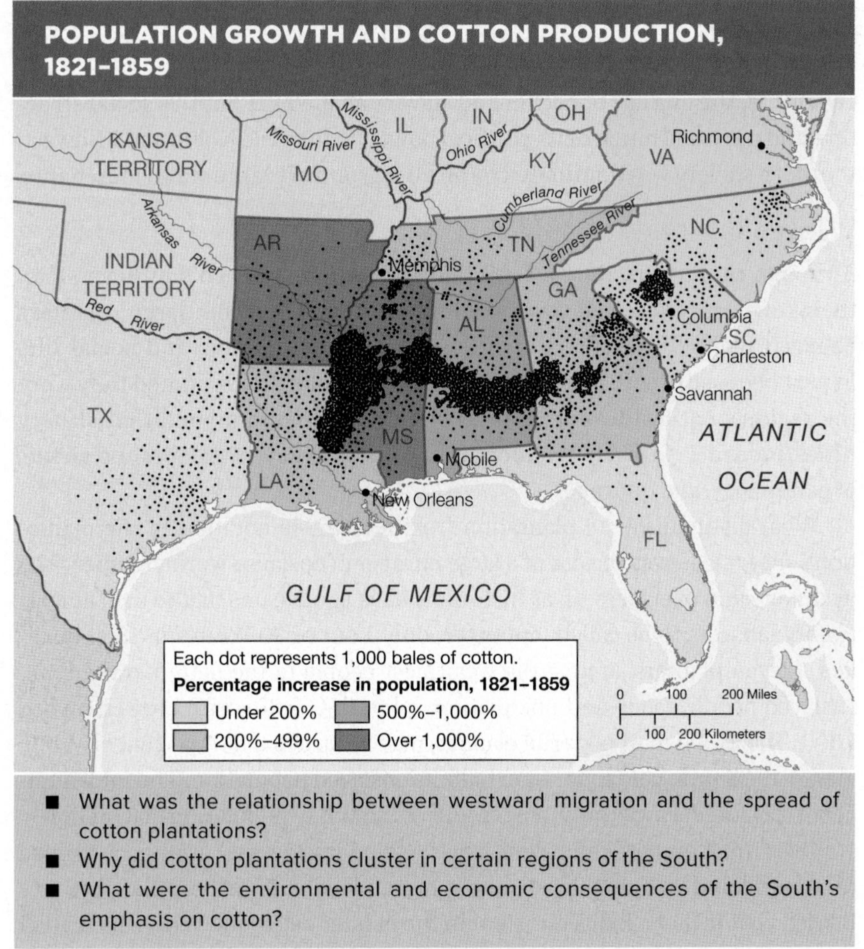

- What was the relationship between westward migration and the spread of cotton plantations?
- Why did cotton plantations cluster in certain regions of the South?
- What were the environmental and economic consequences of the South's emphasis on cotton?

The soaring profitability of cotton fostered a false sense of economic security. In 1860, a Mississippi newspaper boasted that the South, "safely entrenched behind her cotton bags . . . can defy the world—for the civilized world depends on the cotton of the South." Cotton bred cockiness. In a speech to the U.S. Senate in 1858, South Carolina's former governor James Henry Hammond, who owned a huge cotton plantation worked by more than 300 enslaved laborers, warned critics: "You dare not make war on cotton. No power on earth dares make war upon it. Cotton is King."

Unsustainable southern dependence on Britain purchasing cotton

What Hammond failed to acknowledge was that the southern economy had grown dangerously dependent on European demand for raw cotton. By 1860, Great Britain was importing more than 80 percent of its cotton from the South. Southern leaders did not anticipate what they could least afford: a collapse in world demand for southern cotton. In 1860, the expansion of the British textile industry peaked, and the price paid for southern cotton began a steady decline. By then, however, it was too late to change; the Lower South was committed to large-scale cotton production for generations to come.

CORE **OBJECTIVE**

3. Distinguish among the major groups within southern White society and explain why each group supported the expansion of slavery.

Whites in the Old South

Over time, the culture of cotton and slavery shaped the South's social structure and provided much of its political power. Unlike the North and Midwest, southern society was dominated by an elite group of planters and merchants.

White Planters

Although there were only a few giant plantations in each southern state, their owners exercised overwhelming influence. The large planters behaved like aristocrats, controlling political, economic, and social life, in part because of self-interest and in part because they assumed they were the region's natural leaders. James Henry Hammond argued that slavery "does indeed create an aristocracy—an aristocracy of talents, of virtue, of generosity, and courage."

The planter elite

What distinguished a plantation from a farm—in addition to the plantation's sheer size—was the use of a large number of enslaved workers supervised by drivers and overseers. If, as historians have agreed, one had to own at least twenty laborers to be called a **planter**, only 1 out of 30 Whites in 1860 qualified. Eleven planters, among the wealthiest people in the nation, owned 500 enslaved people each—and one planter, a South Carolina rice grower, owned 1,000. The 10,000 most powerful planters, making up less than 3 percent of White men in the South, held more than half the enslaved population. The total number of slaveholders was only 383,637 out of the White population of 8 million.

Over time, planters and their wives (called mistresses) grew accustomed to being waited on by enslaved people, day and night. A Virginia planter told a British visitor that a Black girl slept in the master bedroom. When his British guest asked why, he replied: "Good heaven! If I wanted a glass of water during the night, what would become of me?"

When not working, planters enjoyed hunting, horse racing, and card games. As an enslaved plantation worker recalled, his master on Sundays liked to "gamble, run horses, or fight game-cocks [roosters], discuss politics, and drink whisky, and brandy and water all day long."

Honor and violence: Dueling

Most southern White men, but especially the planter and political elite, embraced an unwritten social code centered on a prickly sense of personal honor in which they felt compelled to defend their reputation—with words, fists, or guns. Duels to the death (called affairs of honor) were the ultimate expressions of manly virtue.

Although not confined to the South, dueling was much more common there than in the rest of the nation. Many prominent southern leaders—congressmen, senators, governors, editors, and planters—engaged in duels, although dueling was technically illegal in many states.

The Plantation Mistress

planters Owners of large farms in the South that were worked by twenty or more enslaved people and supervised by overseers.

The South, like the North, was a male-dominated society, only more so because of the slavery system. South Carolinian Christopher Memminger explained that slavery heightened the need for a hierarchical social and family structure. White wives and children, he stressed, needed to be as subservient and compliant

A SOUTHERN PLANTATION An 1859 engraving of a rice planter's mansion. Behind the mansion can be seen a set of humble cabins that housed the plantation's enslaved workers.

MARY BOYKIN CHESNUT Chesnut's diary describing southern life and the Civil War was published posthumously and won the Pulitzer Prize in 1981.

as enslaved Blacks were required to be. "Each planter," he declared, "is in fact a Patriarch" who requires "obedience and subordination."

The **plantation mistress** may have been expected to be meekly submissive, but few were the frail, helpless creatures that many husbands demanded. Although wives had enslaved people to attend to their needs, they supervised the domestic household in the same way that planters took care of the cotton business. Wives oversaw the supply and preparation of food and linens, the housecleaning and care of the sick, the birthing of babies, and the operations of the dairy.

An enslaved plantation worker remembered that her mistress "was with all the slave women every time a baby was born. Or, when a plague of misery hit the folks, she knew what to do and what kind of medicine to chase off the aches and pains." At the same time, however, southern women often treated enslaved workers harshly. South Carolinian Martha Burt, the niece of John C. Calhoun, was notorious for "always scolding and whipping" her enslaved people.

Some White women complained that they too were enslaved. Mary Boykin Chesnut, a plantation mistress in South Carolina, complained that "there is no slave, after all, like a wife." She admitted that she had few rights, since her husband was the "master of the house." George Fitzhugh, a Virginia attorney and writer, spoke for most southern men when he said that a "man loves his children because they are weak, helpless, and dependent. He loves his wife for similar reasons."

White women living in a slaveholding culture confronted a double standard in terms of moral and sexual behavior. They were expected to be exemplars of Christian morality and sexual purity and to "obey" their fathers and husbands, even as their husbands, brothers, and sons followed an unwritten rule of self-indulgent hedonism and adultery—often forcing themselves on their enslaved workers. "The enjoyment of a Negro or Mulatto [people of mixed parentage] woman is spoken of as quite a common thing," a guest of

plantation mistress Matriarch of a planter's household, responsible for supervising the domestic aspects of the estate.

southern planters noted in 1764. "No reluctance, delicacy, or shame is made about the matter." White owners assaulting enslaved women was common because the crime of rape did not apply. A slave owner could treat his human property as he wished.

The practice of forced sexual relations between enslaved person and master created perverse family relations. "Under slavery," Mary Chesnut wrote in her famous diary, "we live surrounded by prostitutes." Yet she did not blame enslaved women for playing that role. White planters forced them to do so. In fact, many planters justified their behavior by highlighting the additional money they were creating by impregnating enslaved women.

"God forgive us," Chesnut added, "but ours is a monstrous system. Like the patriarchs of old, our men live all in one house with their wives and their [enslaved] concubines [lovers]; and the [people of mixed races] one sees in every family partly resemble the white children. Any lady is ready to tell you who is the father of all the mulatto children in everybody's household but her own. Those, she seems to think, drop from the clouds."

Yet for all their private complaints and daily burdens, plantation mistresses largely accepted the domestic role assigned them by men such as George Howe, a South Carolina religion professor. In 1850, he complimented southern women for understanding their subordinate status. "Born to lean upon others, rather than to stand independently by herself, and to confide in an arm stronger than hers," the southern woman had no desire for "power" outside the home, he said. The few women who were demanding equality, he claimed, were "unsexing" themselves and were "despised and detested" by their families and communities.

Most plantation mistresses agreed. With but a few exceptions, observed Julia Gardiner Tyler, the northern-born wife of President John Tyler, a Virginia slaveholder, women should limit themselves to the roles that "God designed for them"—"as wife, mother, mistress." Another prominent southern woman, Mary Howard Schoolcraft, described herself and other plantation wives in South Carolina as "old fogies" who refused to believe that "slavery is a sin." She could not imagine doing without the comforts and conveniences "afforded by slaves."

Overseers and Drivers

The Whites who worked on large plantations were usually *overseers* who managed the enslaved people. They were also responsible for maintaining the buildings, fences, and grounds. They usually were farmers or skilled workers, or sons of planters, or simply poor Whites eager to rise in stature. Some were themselves slaveholders.

The overseers moved often in search of better wages and cheaper land. A Mississippi planter described White overseers as "a worthless set of vagabonds." Frederick Douglass, who escaped from slavery in Maryland, said his overseer was "a miserable drunkard, a profane swearer, and a savage monster" armed with a blood-stained bullwhip and a club that he used so cruelly that he even "enraged" the plantation owner.

OVERSEEING ENSLAVED WORKERS A well-dressed overseer supervises a line of enslaved people harvesting sugarcane. On the left, playing in the shade, are two White boys, about the same age as the African American children laboring in the field.

Usually, the highest managerial position an enslaved person could hope for was that of *driver,* a favored man whose job was to oversee a small group ("gang") of enslaved people, getting them up and organized each morning by sunrise, and then directing their work (and punishing them) until dark. There were numerous examples of enslaved people murdering drivers for being too cruel.

"Plain White Folk"

The most numerous White southerners were small farmers—the "**plain white folk**," usually uneducated and often illiterate, eking out hardscrabble lives of bare self-sufficiency. These small farmers ("yeomen") lived with their families in two-room cabins, raised a few hogs and chickens, grew some corn and cotton, and traded with neighbors more than they bought from stores.

Women on these farms worked in the fields during harvest time but spent most of their days doing household chores while raising lots of children. Some of these "middling" farmers owned a handful of enslaved people, but most had none. Farm children grew up fast. By age four they could carry a water bucket from the well to the house and collect eggs from the henhouse.

Southern farmers tended to be fiercely independent and suspicious of government authority, and they overwhelmingly identified with the Democratic party of Andrew Jackson and the spiritual energies of the evangelical Protestant denominations such as Baptists and Methodists. Although only a minority of the small farm owners held enslaved people, most supported the slave system for economic and racial reasons. They feared that the enslaved people, if freed, would compete with them for land and jobs, and they enjoyed the privileged status that race-based slavery afforded them. As a White farmer told a northern traveler, "Now suppose they [enslaved people] was free. You see they'd all think themselves as good as we."

plain white folk Yeoman farmers who lived and worked on their own small farms, growing food and cash crops to trade for necessities.

"Poor Whites"

Visitors to the Old South often had trouble telling small farmers apart from the "poor whites," desperately poor people relegated to the least desirable land and living on the fringes of polite society. The poor Whites, often derided as "crackers," or "hillbillies," or "rednecks," were day laborers or squatters who owned neither land nor enslaved people. Some 40 percent of White southerners were landless "tenants," renting land from others, or working as farm laborers, toiling for others. They were often forced to take refuge in the pine barrens, the mountain hollows, and the swamps after having been pushed aside by the more enterprising and the more successful in southern society. They usually lived in log cabins, barely managing to keep their families clothed, warm, dry, and fed.

CORE **OBJECTIVE**

4. Describe the impact of slavery on African Americans, both free and enslaved, throughout the South.

White over Black: Unequal Society in the South

However immoral and degrading, slavery was the fastest-growing element of southern life during the first half of the nineteenth century. Owning, working, and selling enslaved workers was the quickest way to wealth and social status. In 1790, the United States had fewer than 700,000 Black enslaved people. By 1830, it had more than 2 million, and by 1860, 4 million. As the enslaved population grew, slave owners felt the need to develop a complex system of rules, regulations, and restrictions governing the behavior of their enslaved workers.

Most southern Whites viewed enslaved people as property rather than people. "We believe the negro to belong to an inferior race," one planter asserted. Thomas Reade Cobb proclaimed that African Americans were better off "in a state of bondage."

Slave codes

Black babies became enslaved at birth; enslaved people could be moved, sold, rented out, whipped, or raped, as their master or mistress saw fit. Formal **slave codes** in each state governed the treatment of enslaved people. They could not leave their owner's land or household without permission or stay out after dark (curfew) without an identification pass.

Some codes made it a crime for enslaved people to learn to read and write, for fear that they might use notes to plan a revolt. A former enslaved man from Kentucky, John W. Fields, remembered that the White slaveholders "were very harsh if we were caught trying to learn or write. . . . Our ignorance was the greatest hold the South had on us." Enslaved people in most states could not testify in court, legally marry, own firearms, or hit a White man, even in self-defense. Yet despite such restrictions and brutalities, the enslaved managed to create their own community and culture within the confines of the slave system.

slave codes Regulations governing the treatment of enslaved people in each state in order to deter freedom seekers and rebellions.

Whites believed that effective slave management required teaching enslaved people to understand that they were supposed to be treated like animals. As Henry Garner, a freedom seeker, explained, the aim of slaveholders was "to make you as much like brutes as possible." Others justified slavery as a form of benevolent paternalism. George Fitzhugh said that the enslaved Black was "but a grown-up child and must be governed as a child."

Such self-serving paternalism had one purpose: profits. Planters, explained a southerner, "care for nothing but to buy Negroes to raise cotton & raise cotton to buy Negroes." Many viewed enslaved people as a form of *human capital*, commodities to be bought and sold.

In 1829, the North Carolina Supreme Court declared that slavery existed to increase "the profit of the Master." The role of the enslaved person was "to toil while another [the owners] reap the fruits."

Those in the business of buying and selling enslaved people grew wealthy. One of them reported in the 1850s that "a [colored person] that wouldn't bring over $300, seven years ago, will fetch $1000, cash, quick, this year." Thomas Clemson of South Carolina, the son-in-law of John C. Calhoun, candidly explained, "My object is to get the most I can for the property [enslaved people]. . . . I care but little to whom and how they are sold, whether together [as families] or separated."

Few slave owners balked at splitting up enslaved families. Charles Ball was an enslaved four-year-old in Maryland when his owner died. The owner's family then sold Ball, his mother, and his siblings to different buyers. "My poor mother, when she saw me leaving her for the last time, ran after me, took me down from the horse, clasped me in her arms, and wept loudly and bitterly over me," Ball recalled. "My master . . . endeavored to soothe her distress by telling her that he would be a good master to me." Still, his mother would not let go. She begged the slave owner to buy her and the rest of her children.

At that point the man who had bought Ball's mother "came running in pursuit of her with a raw hide [whip] in his hand. When he overtook us, he told her . . . to give that little Negro to its owner and come back with him. My mother . . . cried, 'Oh, master, do not take me from my child!' Without making any reply, he gave her two or three heavy blows on the shoulders with his raw hide, snatched me from her arms, handed me to my [new] master, and seizing her by one arm, dragged her back towards the place of sale."

Ball was then locked in chains, dragged across the Patuxent River, and marched some 500 miles across Virginia and North Carolina before finally reaching his new home on the South Carolina coast. Years later, after he had escaped to freedom, the memory of his family being sold and separated remained an open wound: "Young as I was, the horrors of that day sank deeply into my heart, and even at this time, though half a century has elapsed, the terrors of the scene return with painful vividness upon my memory."

"Free Persons of Color"

African Americans who were not enslaved were called free persons of color. In fact, however, they were anything but free; they occupied an uncertain social status between slavery and freedom. In South Carolina, for example,

YARROW MAMOUT As an enslaved African Muslim, Mamout purchased his freedom, acquired property, and settled in present-day Washington, D.C. Charles Willson Peale executed this portrait in 1819 when Mamout was over 100 years old.

free Blacks had to pay an annual tax and were not allowed to leave the state. After 1823, they were required to have a White "guardian" and an identity card.

Blacks came to be "free" in a number of ways. Some enslaved people were able to purchase their freedom, and others were freed (manumitted) by their owners. By 1860, approximately 250,000 free people of color lived in the slave states, most of them in coastal cities such as Baltimore, Charleston, Mobile, and New Orleans. Some were tailors or shoemakers or carpenters; others were painters, bricklayers, butchers, blacksmiths, or barbers. Still others worked on the docks or on ships. Free Black women usually worked as seamstresses, laundresses, or house servants.

Among the free Black population were **Mulattoes**, people of mixed ancestry. The 1860 census reported 412,000 Mulattoes in the United States, or about 10 percent of the Black population—probably a drastic undercount. In cities such as Charleston, and especially New Orleans, Mulattoes occupied a status somewhere between that of Blacks and that of Whites.

Although most free people of color were poor, some Mulattoes built substantial fortunes and even became slaveholders themselves. In Natchez, Mississippi, William Johnson, son of a White father and a Mulatto mother, operated three barbershops, owned 1,500 acres, and held several enslaved people. Black or Mulatto slaveholders were few in number, however. The 1830 census reported that 3,775 free Blacks, about 2 percent of the total free Black population, owned 12,760 enslaved people.

The Slave Trade

The rapid rise in the nation's enslaved population during the early nineteenth century mainly occurred through the births of enslaved people already living in the United States. This was especially the case after Congress and President Thomas Jefferson outlawed the purchase and importation of enslaved people from Africa in 1808. By 1820, more than 80 percent of captive people had been born in America. But banning the trafficking of enslaved people from Africa increased the cash value of slaves within the United States. This in turn convinced some owners to treat their enslaved workers better. As one planter remarked in 1849, "The time has been that the farmer would kill up and wear out one Negro to buy another, but it is not so now."

The surge in the dollar value of enslaved workers prompted better treatment for many. "Massa was purty good," one formerly enslaved person recalled. "He treated us jus' 'bout like you would a good mule." Another said his owner "fed us reg'lar on good, 'stantial food, jus' like you'd tend to you hoss [horse], if you had a real good one." An enslaved person born in 1850 had a life expectancy of thirty-six years; the life expectancy of Whites was forty years. Some slaveholders hired White wage laborers, often Irish

Mulattoes Mixed-race people who constituted most of the South's free Black population.

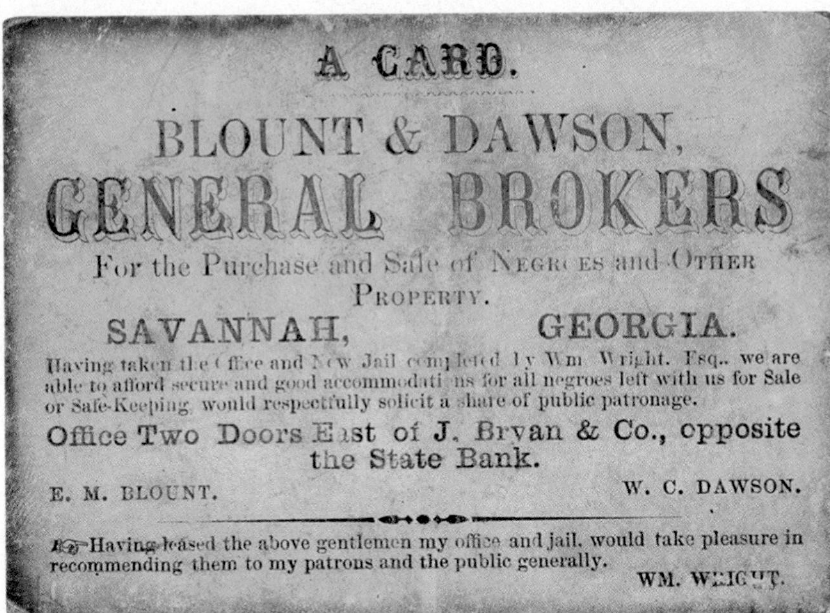

THE BUSINESS OF SLAVERY
This advertisement for the Blount & Dawson slave traders guarantees its clients "secure and good accommodations for all negroes left with us for Sale or Safe-Keeping" in its newly acquired jail, opposite the state bank.

immigrants, for dangerous work rather than risk the lives of the more valuable enslaved people.

Domestic slave trade

Once the African slave trade was outlawed, the slave-trading network *within* the United States became much more important—and profitable. Between 1800 and 1860, the average price of enslaved people *quadrupled*, as breeding and selling enslaved people became a big business. Over a twenty-year period, a Virginia plantation owned by John Tayloe III recorded 252 enslaved births and 142 deaths of enslaved people, thus providing him with 110 extra enslaved workers to be deployed on the plantation, given to his sons, or sold to traders.

To manage the growing slave trade, markets and auction houses sprang up in every southern city. New Orleans alone had twenty slave-trading businesses. Each year, thousands of enslaved people circulated through the city's "slave pens," forced to become products with prices. They were bathed and groomed, "fattened up" with bacon, milk, and butter, like cattle; assigned categories such as Prime, No. 1, No. 2, and Second Rate; and packaged for sale in identical blue suits or dresses. On auction day, they were paraded into the sale room. The tallest, strongest, and "blackest" brought the highest prices. As a slave trader stressed, "I must have if possible the *jet black* Negroes, for they stand the [hot, humid] climate best."

Buyers physically inspected each enslaved person on the "auction block." They squeezed their muscles, felt their joints, worked their fingers back and forth, and pried open their mouths to examine their teeth and gums. They forced enslaved people to undress and inspected their naked bodies, looking for signs of disease or deformities. As formerly enslaved Solomon Northup noted, "scars on a slave's back were considered evidence of a rebellious or unruly spirit and hurt [the enslaved person's

ESTATE SALE AND AUCTION OF THE ENSLAVED This engraving from 1842 depicts an estate sale in New Orleans, where enslaved people are auctioned off beside art and other valuable items. An enslaved man, woman, and child stand on the auction block. **How were enslaved people treated and evaluated in auctions like this?**

chances for] sale." Once the inspections ended, buyers bid on the enslaved people, purchased them, and transported them to their new homes.

Almost a million captive African Americans, many of them children, were "sold South" or "down river" and taken to the Old Southwest during the first half of the nineteenth century. "It is better to buy *none in families*," said a Mississippi buyer, "but to select *only choice, first rate, young hands from 16 to 25 years of age* [buying no children or aged negroes]."

The worst aspect of the slave trade was the separation of children from parents and husbands from wives. In Missouri, one enslaved woman saw six of her seven children, ages one to eleven, sold to six different owners. Only Louisiana and Alabama prohibited separating a child younger than ten from his or her mother, and no state prevented the separation of an enslaved husband from his wife.

Slave markets in New Orleans engaged in what was called the "fancy trade," which meant selling women as forced sexual partners. "I sold your fancy girl Alice for $800," a New Orleans slave trader wrote to a partner in Richmond. "There is great demand for fancy maids."

A reporter watching a slave sale in New Orleans spied on the auction block "one of the most beautiful women [he] had ever saw. She was about sixteen, dressed in a cheap striped woolen gown, and bareheaded." Her name was Hermina, and she was "sold for $1250 [$35,000 today] to one of the most lecherous brutes I ever set eyes on." The same reporter noted that "a noble-looking woman with a bright-eyed seven-year-old" son were offered for sale as a pair. When no one bid on them, the auctioneer offered them separately. A man from Mississippi bought the boy, while the mother went to a Texan. As her son was dragged away, the woman "burst forth into the most frantic wails that ever despair gave utterance to."

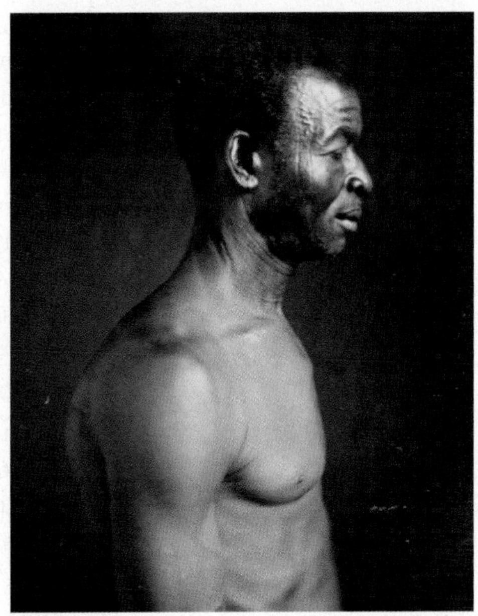

JACK (1850) Daguerreotype of an enslaved man identified only as Jack, on the plantation of B. F. Taylor in Columbia, South Carolina.

Slavery as a Way of Life

The lives of enslaved people differed greatly from place to place, depending in part on the personality of their owner, in part on whether they were focused on growing rice, sugar, tobacco, or cotton, and in part on whether they were on farms or in cities. Although many enslaved people were artisans or craftsmen (carpenters, blacksmiths, furniture makers, butchers, ship pilots, house servants, cooks, nurses, maids, weavers, basketmakers, etc.), the vast majority were **field hands** who were often organized into work gangs supervised by a Black driver or White overseer. Some enslaved people were "hired out" to other planters or to merchants, churches, or businesses. Others worked on Sundays or holidays to earn cash of their own.

Plantation field hands

Enslaved plantation workers were usually housed in one- or two-room cabins with dirt floors. The wealthiest planters built them cabins out of brick. Beds were a luxury, even though they were little more than boards covered with straw. Most enslaved people slept on the floor with only a coarse blanket for warmth. They received a set of cheap linen or cotton clothes twice a year, but shoes were generally provided only in winter; enslaved people went barefoot most of the year. About half of enslaved babies died in their first year, a death rate more than twice that of Whites. The food given enslaved people was cheap and monotonous: cornmeal, pork, molasses, and chicken.

Field hands worked from sunrise to sunset, six days a week. At times they were worked at night as well, ginning cotton, milling sugarcane, grinding corn, or doing other indoor tasks. Women, remembered an enslaved person, "had to work all day in de fields an' den come home an' do the housework at night." Sundays were precious days off. Enslaved people used them to hunt, fish, dance to banjo and fiddle music, tell stories, or tend their own small gardens.

field hands Enslaved people who toiled in the cotton or cane fields in organized work gangs.

Beginning in August and lasting several months, the focus was on picking cotton. Gangs of enslaved men and women would sweep across a field, pull the bolls from the thorny pods, and stuff them in large sacks or baskets. All the while, they were watched and prodded by an overseer, bullwhip in hand. Solomon Northup remembered picking cotton until it was "too dark to see, and when the moon is full, they oftentimes labor till the middle of the night." Each evening, the overseer or planter weighed the baskets and recorded the number of pounds on a slate board by each picker's name. Those who fell short of the daily goal were whipped.

The Violence of Slavery

Although some owners and enslaved people developed close and even affectionate relationships, slavery remained a system rooted in brutal force. The difference between a good owner and a bad one, according to one enslaved man, was the difference between one "who did not whip you too much" and one who "whipped you till he'd bloodied you and blistered you."

Allen Sidney, an enslaved person, recalled an incident on a Mississippi plantation. An enslaved worker who fell behind while picking cotton resisted when a Black driver started to "whip him up." Upon seeing the fracas, the White overseer, mounted on horseback, galloped over and shot the resisting enslaved man, killing him. "None of the other slaves," Sidney noted, "said a word or turned their heads." They were so fearful of being shot themselves that they "kept on hoeing as if nothing had happened."

Brutal violence against the rural enslaved population

At times, Whites turned the punishment of enslaved people into theatrical spectacles to strike fear into anyone considering rebellion or escape. In Louisiana, whippings often followed a horrific procedure, as a visitor reported: "Three stakes is drove into the ground in a triangular manner, about six feet apart. The culprit [enslaved person] is told to lie down . . . flat on his belly. The arms is extended out, sideways, and each hand tied to a stake hard and fast. The feet is both tied to the third stake, all stretched tight." The overseer would then step back "seven, eight or ten feet and with a rawhide whip about 7 feet long . . . lays on with great force and address across the Buttocks," cutting strips of flesh "7 or 8 inches long at every stroke."

Urban Slavery

Enslaved people living in southern cities such as Richmond, Memphis, Atlanta, New Orleans, or Charleston had a much different experience from those on isolated farms and plantations. "A city slave is almost a freeman," claimed an enslaved person living in Maryland.

Greater mobility for enslaved people in the cities

Enslaved people in urban households tended to be better fed and clothed and had more privileges. They interacted not only with their White owners but with the extended interracial community—shopkeepers and police, neighbors and strangers. Some were hired out to others and allowed to keep a portion of their wages. In general, enslaved people in cities enjoyed greater mobility and freedom than their counterparts in rural areas.

Enslaved Women

Although enslaved men and women often performed similar chores, they did not experience slavery in the same way. "Slavery is terrible for men," the former enslaved North Carolinian Harriet Jacobs stressed in her autobiography, *Incidents in the Life of a Slave Girl*, "but it is far more terrible for women."

Enslaved women and reproduction

Once slaveholders realized how profitable a fertile enslaved woman could be by giving birth to babies that could later be sold, they "encouraged" enslaved women to have as many children as possible. Some owners rewarded pregnant enslaved women by giving them less work and more food and gifted new mothers with dresses and silver dollars.

But if motherhood provided enslaved women with greater stature and benefits, it also was exhausting. Within days after childbirth, the mothers were put to work spinning, weaving, or sewing. A few weeks thereafter, they were sent back to the fields; breast-feeding mothers were often forced to take their babies with them, strapped to their backs. Enslaved women were expected to do "man's work": cut trees, haul logs, spread fertilizer, plow fields, dig ditches, slaughter animals, hoe corn, and pick cotton.

Enslaved women and sexual abuse

Enslaved girls, women, and some men were often sexually abused by their owners, both men and women. Hundreds of thousands of Mulattoes provided physical proof of interracial sexual assault.

James Henry Hammond, the prominent South Carolina planter and politician, confessed that he sexually assaulted one of his enslaved women, Sally Johnson, who bore several of his children—all of whom he kept in slavery as "their happiest earthly condition." He also abused one of her daughters, twelve-year-old Louisa.

Sometimes a White master or overseer would rape a woman in the fields or cabins. Sometimes a woman would be locked in a cabin with an enslaved

***VIRGINIAN LUXURIES*, ca. 1825**
This painting alludes to two privileges of the slave owner: to sexually abuse enslaved women and to physically abuse all enslaved people.

man whose task was to impregnate her. Enslaved women responded in different ways. Some seduced their owner away from his wife. Others fiercely resisted the advances—and were usually whipped or even killed for their disobedience. Some women aborted or killed their babies rather than see them grow up in slavery.

Celia

Enslaved people often could improve their circumstances only by making horrible choices that offered no guarantee of success. The tragic story of a girl named Celia reveals the moral complexity of slavery for African American women and the limited legal options available to them.

In 1850, fourteen-year-old Celia was purchased by Robert Newsom, a prosperous Missouri farmer who told his daughters that he had bought the girl to be their servant. In fact, however, the recently widowed Newsom wanted a sex slave. After purchasing Celia, he raped her, and for the next five years treated her as his mistress, even building her a brick cabin fifty yards from his house. During that time, she gave birth to two of his children.

Eventually, Celia reached her breaking point. She warned Newsom that the rapes must stop. He paid no attention. On June 23, 1855, the sixty-five-year-old Newsom entered Celia's cabin, ignored her frantic appeals, and kept assaulting her until she struck and killed him with a large stick and then burned his body in the fireplace.

Celia was not allowed to testify at her murder trial because she was an enslaved person. The judge and jury, all White men, pronounced her guilty, and on December 21, 1855, she was taken to the Calloway Courthouse in Fulton, Missouri, and "hanged until she died."

Celia's grim story illustrates the lopsided power structure in southern society at the time. She bore a double burden, being both an enslaved person and a woman living in a male-dominated society rife with racism and sexism.

CORE **OBJECTIVE**

5. Analyze how enslaved peoples responded to the inhumanity of their situation.

Forging an Enslaved Community

Enslaved African Americans were victims of terrible injustice and abuse, but such an obvious truth neglects important evidence of their endurance, resilience, and achievement. The Africans who were brought to America represented a variety of ethnic, linguistic, and tribal origins. Wherever they could, they forged their own sense of community, asserted their individuality, and devised ingenious ways of resisting their confinement. They invented stories of resistance such as "Brer [Brother] Rabbit," where the smart little rabbit eludes the animals stalking it by hiding in a patch of prickly briars. Many **spirituals** (sacred folk songs) expressed a longing to be free. Although most enslaved people were prohibited from marrying, the law did not prevent them from choosing partners and forging a family life within the rigid constraints of slavery.

spirituals Songs with religious messages sung by enslaved people to help ease the strain of field labor and to voice their suffering at the hands of their masters and overseers.

ENSLAVED FAMILY IN A GEORGIA COTTON FIELD An enslaved family toils in a cotton field together, the young children working alongside the men and women. **What factors extended enslaved African Americans' concept of family?**

The Enslaved Family

Marriages between enslaved people had no legal status, but many slaveholders accepted unofficial marriages as a stabilizing influence on the plantation. Sometimes they performed the marriage ceremonies themselves or had a minister officiate. Whatever the formalities, the norm for the slave community, as for the White, was the nuclear family, with the father regarded as the head of the household. Most enslaved children were socialized by means of the nuclear family, which afforded some degree of independence from White influence.

Childhood was short for enslaved people. At five or six years of age, children were put to work; they collected trash and firewood, picked cotton, scared away crows from planted fields, weeded gardens and fields, and ran errands. By age ten they were full-time field hands.

The frequent buying and selling of enslaved people meant that children were often separated from their parents and sold to new masters. Given the fragility of the family, enslaved African Americans often extended the fellowship of family to those who worked together, with older enslaved women being addressed as "granny," or coworkers as "sis" or "brother."

African American Religion

Among the most important elements of African American culture was its dynamic religion, a unique mixture of African, Caribbean, and Christian elements often practiced in secret and at night because many slaveholders feared enslaved workers might use group religious services to organize rebellions.

***PLANTATION BURIAL* (1860)** The enslaved people of Mississippi governor Tilghman Tucker gather together in the woods to bury and mourn for one of their own. The painter of this scene, Englishman John Antrobus, would serve in the Confederate army during the Civil War.

Enslaved people found in religion both relief for the soul and release for their emotions. "We used to slip off into the woods," a former enslaved person recalled, "... to sing and pray to our own liking. We prayed for freedom."

African American religion and spirituals

Most Africans brought with them to the Americas belief in a Creator, or Supreme God, whom they could recognize in the Christian God, and whom they might identify with Christ, the Holy Ghost, and the saints. But they also maintained beliefs in spirits, magic, and conjuring. Most slave owners tried to erase African religion and spirituality from the experience of slavery.

By 1860, about 20 percent of enslaved adults had joined Christian denominations. Many others displayed aspects of the Christian faith in their forms of worship. As a White minister observed, "some slaves had heard of Jesus Christ, but who he is and what he has done for a ruined world, they cannot tell."

Enslaved people found the Bible inspiring in its support for the poor and oppressed, and they embraced its promise of salvation through the sacrifice of Jesus. Likewise, the lyrics of religious songs (called spirituals) offered enslaved people the promise of deliverance from their worldly woes. One popular spiritual, "Go Down, Moses," derived from the plight of the ancient Israelites held captive in Egypt, says: "We need not always weep and moan, / Let my people go. / And wear these slavery chains forlorn, / Let my people go."

Enslaved Rebellions

Southern Whites feared slave uprisings more than anything. As a prominent Virginian explained, a slave revolt would "deluge the southern country with blood." Any sign of resistance or rebellion therefore risked a brutal response.

Gabriel's Rebellion The overwhelming authority and firepower of southern Whites made organized slave resistance difficult and risky. The nineteenth-century South witnessed only four major slave insurrections. On August 30, 1800, a twenty-four-year-old enslaved man named Gabriel, who worked as a blacksmith near Richmond, Virginia, launched a revolt. His plan was to kill his owner and then gather perhaps a thousand other enslaved people, free Blacks, working-class Whites, abolitionists, and Quakers. His rebel army would then seize key points in the city, capture the governor (future president James Monroe), and terrorize the White elite.

Gabriel's foiled rebellion

Yet the rebellion never occurred because two enslaved workers on a neighboring plantation alerted Whites to the scheme. Gabriel, his two older brothers, and twenty-four of his fellow "soldiers" were captured, tried, and hanged. Before his execution, Gabriel explained that he was only imitating George Washington: "I have ventured my life in endeavoring to obtain the liberty of my countrymen."

German Coast Uprising In early 1811, the largest slave revolt in American history occurred just upriver from New Orleans on a ribbon of land known as the German Coast. There, wealthy sugarcane planters had acquired one of the largest populations of enslaved people in North America, five times as many as the Whites who owned them. Many of those enslaved people were ripe for revolt. Sugarcane was known as a "killer crop" because the working conditions were so harsh.

Deslondes's rebellion

Late on January 8, a group of enslaved people broke into their owner's plantation house along the Mississippi River. The planter escaped, but his son was hacked to death. The leader of the assault was Charles Deslondes, a trusted slave overseer who was the light-skinned son of a planter. Deslondes and his fellow rebels seized weapons, horses, and militia uniforms from the plantation. Reinforced by more enslaved people and emboldened by liquor, they headed toward New Orleans, burning houses and killing Whites along the way. Over the next two days, the ranks of the rebels swelled to over 200.

Their success was short-lived, however. Angry Whites—as well as several free Blacks who were later praised for their "tireless zeal and dauntless courage"—suppressed the insurrection. U.S. Army units and local militiamen joined the effort. Dozens of enslaved people were killed or wounded; most who fled were eventually captured.

Deslondes had his hands severed and thighs broken before he was shot and his body roasted. As many as 100 enslaved people were tortured, killed, and beheaded. Their heads were placed on poles along the Mississippi River to strike fear into enslaved workers. A month after the rebellion was put down, a White resident noted that "all the negro difficulties have subsided and gentle peace prevails."

Denmark Vesey Revolt The Denmark Vesey plot in Charleston, South Carolina, discovered in 1822, involved a similar effort to assault the White population. Vesey, born in 1767 on the Caribbean island of St. Thomas, was bought by a slave trader based in Charleston. In 1799, Vesey purchased a lottery ticket and won $1,500, which he used to buy his freedom. He thereafter opened a carpentry shop and organized a Bible study class in the African Methodist Episcopal Church. His several wives and children, however, remained enslaved, and he could visit them only with the permission of their masters.

The Vesey plot

In 1822, Vesey and several others plotted a massive slave revolt. They would first capture the city's arsenal and distribute its hundreds of rifles to free and enslaved Blacks, who outnumbered Whites in the city. All the Whites would then be killed, along with any Blacks who refused to join the rebellion. Vesey's plan then would have them burn the city, seize ships in the harbor, and head for the Black republic of Haiti, where enslaved people in the former French sugar colony, then called Saint-Domingue, had staged a successful revolt in 1791.

The Vesey plot never got off the ground, however. As Vesey and others secretly tried to recruit enslaved people, one of them told his master what was going on. Soon Vesey and a hundred other supposed rebels were captured and tried. The court found Vesey guilty of plotting a slave uprising intended to "trample on all laws, human and divine; to riot in blood, outrage, rapine . . . and conflagration, and to introduce anarchy and confusion in their most horrid forms." Vesey and thirty-four others were executed; three dozen more were transported to Spanish Cuba and sold. When told that he would be hanged, Vesey replied that "the work of insurrection will go on."

Denmark Vesey's planned rebellion led officials in South Carolina to place even more restrictions on the mobility of free Blacks and Black religious gatherings. It also influenced John C. Calhoun to abandon the nationalism of his early political career and become the South's most forceful spokesman for states' rights.

Whites' indiscriminate murder of enslaved people in reaction to rebellion

Nat Turner Rebellion The Nat Turner rebellion of August 1831, in Southampton County, Virginia, again panicked Whites throughout the South. Turner, a trusted Black overseer, was also a preacher who believed God had instructed him to lead a slave rebellion. The revolt began when a small group of enslaved people joined Turner in killing his owner's family. Arming themselves with axes and swords, farm tools and muskets, they then repeated the process at other farmhouses, where other enslaved people joined in. Before the revolt ended, fifty-seven Whites had been killed, most of them women and children. Turner later explained that he had also killed the "man who was to me a kind master."

Federal troops, Virginia militiamen, and volunteers killed nearly 200 enslaved people in the process of putting down the rebels. Seventeen enslaved people were hanged; several were decapitated, and their heads placed on poles along the highway. Turner, called the "blood-stained monster," avoided capture for six weeks. He then was tried and found guilty. While waiting to be hanged, he was asked if the revolt was worth it. "Was not Christ crucified?" he replied. His dead body was dismembered, with body parts given to the victims' families.

More than any other slave uprising, **Nat Turner's Rebellion** terrified Whites across the South. The Virginia legislature debated whether slavery should be abolished. That proposal was defeated, and instead the delegates restricted the ability of enslaved people to learn to read and write and gather for religious meetings. "We were no more than dogs," an enslaved woman recalled. "If they caught us with a piece of paper in our pockets, they'd whip us. They was afraid we'd learn to read and write, but I never got the chance."

After Nat Turner's Rebellion, southern states created vigilante groups of Whites to patrol their communities looking for freedom seekers. A former enslaved person highlighted the "thousand obstacles thrown in the way of the flying slave. Every White man's hand is raised against him—the patrollers are watching for him—the hounds are ready to follow on his track, and the nature of the country is such as renders it impossible to pass through it with any safety."

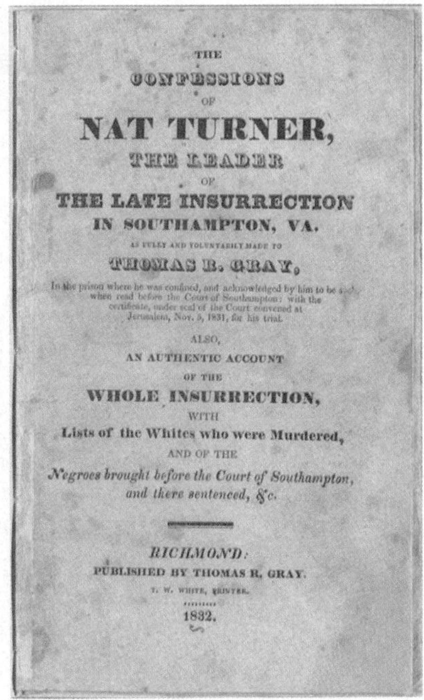
THE
CONFESSIONS
OF
NAT TURNER,
THE LEADER
OF
THE LATE INSURRECTION
IN SOUTHAMPTON, VA.
AS FULLY AND VOLUNTARILY MADE TO
THOMAS R. GRAY,
In the prison where he was confined, and acknowledged by him to be such when read before the Court of Southampton; with the certificate, under seal of the Court convened at Jerusalem, Nov. 5, 1831, for his trial.
ALSO,
AN AUTHENTIC ACCOUNT
OF THE
WHOLE INSURRECTION,
WITH
Lists of the Whites who were Murdered,
AND OF THE
Negroes brought before the Court of Southampton, and there sentenced, &c.

RICHMOND:
PUBLISHED BY THOMAS R. GRAY.
T. W. WHITE, PRINTER.
1832.

THE CONFESSIONS OF NAT TURNER Following Nat Turner's trial and conviction, his lawyer, Thomas R. Gray, published an account of Turner's life and rebellion in which he explained that Turner believed that God had called upon him to murder slave owners. **What sentiments did Turner's rebellion, and accounts such as this, provoke among White southerners?**

The Dream of Freedom

Yet thousands of enslaved people kept running away each year—a powerful example of the enduring dream of freedom and the extraordinary courage of those who yearn for it. Frederick Douglass decided that risking death was better than staying in bondage: "I had as well be killed running as die standing." In 1834, Douglass and two other enslaved people on the Maryland coast stole a canoe and paddled toward the Chesapeake Bay and freedom. They were caught, however, and jailed. His owner threatened to sell him to a friend in Alabama, but in the end, Douglass was kept and taught a skill: caulking the seams in ships.

Freedom seekers: the "Underground Railroad"

As Douglass experienced, the odds were stacked against escape, in part because most enslaved people could not read, had no maps, and could not use public transportation such as stagecoaches, steamboats, and railroads. Blacks, whether free or enslaved, had to have an identity pass or official emancipation papers to go anywhere on their own. Most freedom seekers were tracked down by bloodhounds or bounty hunters. Even in the 1850s, the height of efforts by many northerners to help freedom seekers through the "Underground Railroad," only 1,000 to 1,500 enslaved people each year made it to safety.

Nat Turner's Rebellion (1831) Insurrection in rural Virginia led by Black overseer Nat Turner, who murdered slave owners and their families; in turn, federal troops indiscriminately killed hundreds of enslaved people in the process of putting down Turner and his rebels.

THE ENSLAVED POPULATION, 1820 AND 1860

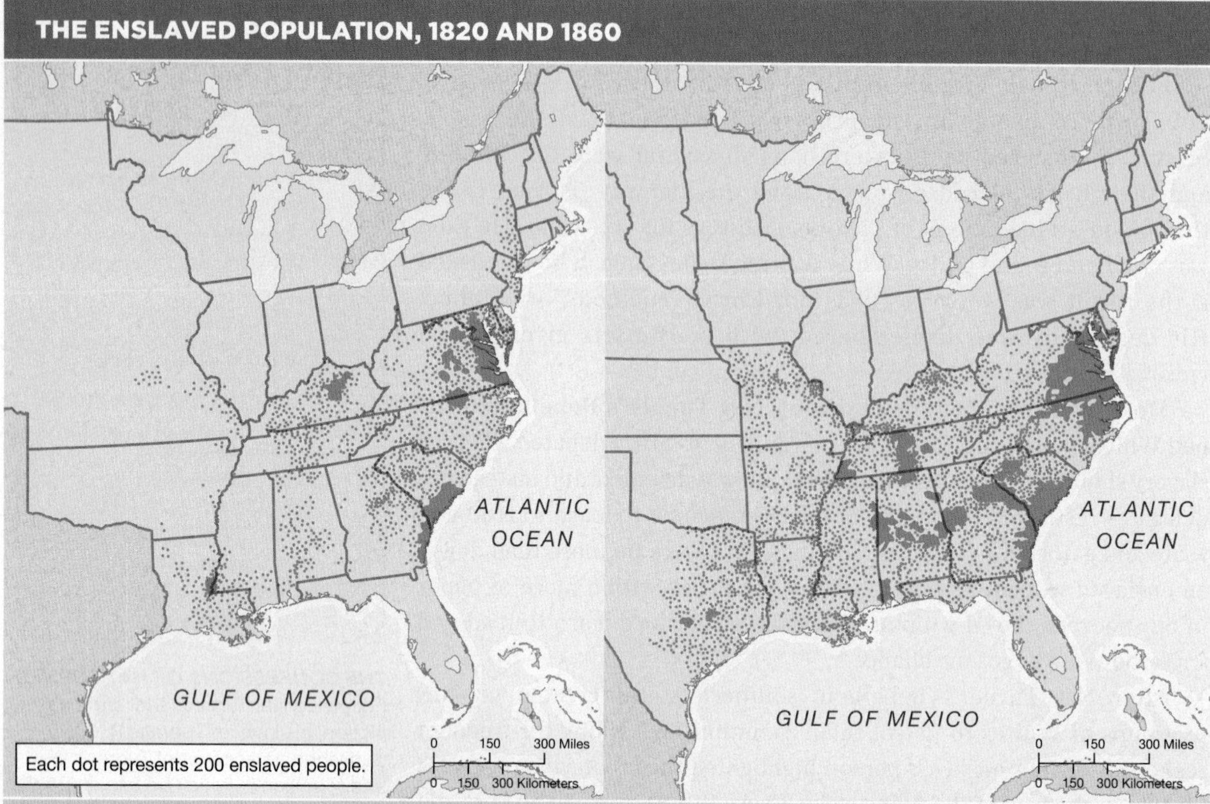

- Consider where the largest populations of enslaved people were clustered in the South in 1820. Why were most enslaved people in these regions and not in others?
- Compare these maps with the maps of cotton production on pages 402–403. What patterns do you see?
- Why did slavery spread west? Why did many enslaved people resist migrating west?

Everyday forms of resistance

Enslaved people who did not escape resisted in other ways. They often faked illness, engaged in sabotage, stole or broke tools, or destroyed crops or livestock. Yet there were constraints on such behavior, for laborers would likely eat better on a prosperous plantation than on a struggling one. And the shrewdest slaveholders knew that offering rewards was more profitable than inflicting pain.

The South—a Region Apart

The recurring theme of southern politics and culture from the 1830s to the outbreak of the Civil War in 1861 was the region's determination to remain a society dominated by Whites who debased people of color. Slavery increasingly became the paramount issue controlling all else. A South Carolinian explained that "slavery with us is no abstraction—but a great and vital fact. Without it, our every comfort would be taken from us."

Protecting their right to own, transport, and sell enslaved people in the new western territories became the overriding focus of southern political leaders. Throughout the 1830s, southern state legislatures were "one and indivisible" in their efforts to preserve and expand slavery. Virginia's General

Assembly, for example, declared that only the southern states had the right to control slavery and that such control must be "maintained at all hazards." The Georgia legislature agreed, announcing that "upon this point there can be no discussion—no compromise—no doubt." The increasingly militant efforts of northerners to restrict or abolish slavery helped reinforce the sense of southern unity while provoking an emotional defensiveness that would result in secession and war—and the unexpected end of slavery.

Reviewing the CORE OBJECTIVES | INQUIZITIVE

■ **Southern Distinctiveness** The South remained rural and agricultural in the first half of the nineteenth century as the rest of the nation embraced urban industrial development. The region's climate favored the growth of cash crops such as tobacco, rice, indigo, and, increasingly, cotton. These crops led to the spread of the plantation system of large commercial agriculture dependent upon enslaved labor. The Southern planter elite sought not only to preserve slavery in the nineteenth century but also to expand it, despite growing criticism of this *peculiar institution* outside the region.

■ **A Cotton Economy** Throughout the pre–Civil War era the South became increasingly committed to a cotton economy dependent upon slave labor. Despite efforts to diversify the economy, the wealth and status associated with cotton, as well as soil exhaustion and falling prices from Virginia to Georgia, prompted the westward expansion of the plantation culture to the *Old Southwest.* Moreover, sons of southern planters wanted to take advantage of cheap land on the frontier in order to make their own fortunes. By 1860, the *Cotton Kingdom* stretched from the Carolinas and Georgia through eastern Texas and up the Mississippi River to Illinois. More than half of all enslaved people worked on cotton plantations.

■ **Southern White Culture** White society was divided between the planter elite, or those who owned at least twenty enslaved people or more, and all the rest. *Planters* made up around 4 percent of the White population and exercised a disproportionately powerful political and social influence. Other Whites owned a few enslaved people, but most owned none. A majority of Whites were *plain white folk*—simple farmers who raised corn, cotton, hogs, and chickens. Southern White women spent most of their time on household chores. The *plantation mistress* supervised her enslaved people in the home and household. Most Whites were fiercely loyal to the institution of slavery. Even those who owned no enslaved people feared the competition they believed they would face if enslaved people were freed, and they enjoyed the privileged status that race-based slavery gave them.

■ **Southern Black Culture** As the southern economy became more dependent on slave labor, the enslaved faced more regulations and restrictions on their behavior. The vast majority of southern Blacks were enslaved people who served as *field hands.* They had few rights and could be bought and sold and moved at any time. Their own movements were severely limited, and they had no ability to defend themselves. Any violation of these restrictions could result in severe punishments. Most southern Blacks were enslaved, but a small percentage were free. Many of the free Blacks were *Mulattoes,* having mixed-race parentage. Free Blacks often worked for wages in towns and cities.

■ **African American Resistance and Resilience** Originally, enslaved people were treated more as indentured servants, eligible for freedom after a specified number of years, but during the eighteenth-century *slave codes* codified practices of treating enslaved people as property rather than as people. The enslaved responded to their oppression in a variety of ways. Although many enslaved people attempted to run away, only a few openly rebelled because the consequences were so harsh. Organized revolts such as *Nat Turner's Rebellion* (1831) in Virginia were rare. Most enslaved people survived their hardships by relying on their own communities, family ties, and Christian faith, and by developing their own culture, such as the singing of *spirituals* to express frustration, sorrow, and hope for their eventual deliverance.

KEY TERMS

peculiar institution *p. 396*

Old Southwest *p. 400*

cotton kingdom *p. 401*

planters *p. 404*

plantation mistress *p. 405*

plain white folk *p. 407*

slave codes *p. 408*

Mulattoes *p. 410*

field hands *p. 413*

spirituals *p. 416*

Nat Turner's Rebellion (1831) *p. 421*

CHRONOLOGY

1790	Enslaved population of the United States reaches nearly 700,000
1791	Slave revolt in Saint-Domingue (Haiti)
1800	Gabriel conspiracy in Richmond, Virginia
1808	U.S. participation in the international slave trade is outlawed
1811	Charles Deslondes revolt in Louisiana
1815	Annual cotton production in the United States is 150,000 bales
1822	Denmark Vesey conspiracy is discovered in Charleston, South Carolina
1830	Enslaved population exceeds 2 million in the United States
1831	Nat Turner leads slave insurrection in Virginia
1840	Population in the Old Southwest tops 1.5 million
1860	Annual cotton production in the United States reaches 4 million bales
	Enslaved population in the United States reaches 4 million

INQUIZITIVE

Go to InQuizitive to see what you've learned—and learn what you've missed—with personalized feedback along the way.

***THE INDIAN'S VESPERS* (1847)** In the wake of the Enlightenment, the Romantic ideals of personal spirituality and honor for the uncorrupted natural world swept America. This work, by the artist and transcendentalist Asher B. Durand, depicts a Native American saluting the sun. It celebrates the reverence for nature that kindled religion, activism, education, and reform in the first half of the nineteenth century.

Religion, Romanticism, and Reform

CHAPTER 12

1800–1860

During the first half of the nineteenth century, the United States was overflowing with restless energy, expansive optimism, and confidence in the future. "America is the country of the Future," Massachusetts philosopher-poet Ralph Waldo Emerson observed. "It is a country of beginnings, of projects, of designs, and expectations."

However, the dynamic young republic was also experiencing growing pains as the market revolution widened the gap between rich and poor. At the same time, sectional tensions over economic policies and increasingly heated debates over the morality and future of slavery created a combative political environment whose conflicts overflowed into social and cultural life.

After the Revolution, American Christians also became as interested in religious salvation as they were in exercising political rights. A theological revolution led most people to reject Calvinist determinism. Salvation, they argued, was open to everyone, not just the "elect." By this logic, sin was voluntary rather than innate. People were not helplessly depraved; they could choose salvation and improve themselves and society.

CORE OBJECTIVES INQUIZITIVE

1. Describe the major changes in the practice of religion in America in the early nineteenth century and assess their influence.
2. Examine the emergence of transcendentalism in American culture in the early nineteenth century.
3. Explain the origins of the major social reform movements in the early nineteenth century and analyze their influence on society and politics.
4. Evaluate the impact of the anti-slavery movement on society and politics.

Such notions democratized Christianity by giving everyone the path to salvation. So-called free-will ministers promised that everyone could *choose* to be saved simply by embracing Jesus's promise of salvation.

Evangelicals believed that America had a God-given mission to provide a shining example of representative government, much as Puritan New England had once stood as an example of an ideal Christian community. The concept of a Godly *mission* to create an ideal society (often called manifest destiny) still carried strong spiritual overtones.

It also contained an aspiration toward perfectionism: People could become more and more perfect by reforming themselves and society. Throughout the first half of the nineteenth century, reformers fanned out across the United States to root out injustice or suffering. The combination of religious energy and intense social activism brought major advances in human rights. It also triggered cynicism and disillusionment.

CORE **OBJECTIVE**

1. Describe the major changes in the practice of religion in America in the early nineteenth century and assess their influence.

A More Democratic Religion

The energies of the rational Enlightenment and the spiritual Great Awakening flowed from the colonial period into the nineteenth century. In different ways, these two powerful modes of thought, one scientific and rational and the other religious and optimistic, led many Christians to embrace the more democratic religious outlook that offered salvation to everyone. Just as Enlightenment rationalism stressed humanity's natural goodness and encouraged belief in progress through democratic reforms and individual improvement, a growing number of Protestant churches stressed that all people were capable of perfection through the guiding light of Christ and their own activism.

Rational Religion

Enlightenment ideas, including the religious concept of *Deism,* inspired prominent leaders such as Thomas Jefferson and Benjamin Franklin. Deists believed in a rational God—the creator of the rational universe—and that all people were equals in the eyes of God. Deists prized science and reason over traditional religion and unquestioning faith.

The rise of *Deism*

Interest in Deism increased after the American Revolution. By using reason and scientific research, Deists believed, people might grasp the natural laws governing the universe. Deists did not believe that every statement in the Bible was literally true, and they questioned the divinity of Jesus. They defended free speech and opposed religious coercion.

Unitarianism and Universalism

The ideals of Enlightenment rationalism that excited Deists soon began to make inroads into Protestantism. The churches in and around Boston proved especially vulnerable to the appeal of anti-Puritan (anti-Calvinist) religious liberalism. By the end of the eighteenth century, well-educated New Englanders, most of them Congregationalists, were embracing Unitarianism, a "liberal" faith that emphasized the compassion of a loving God, the natural goodness of humankind, the superiority of calm reason over emotional forms of worship, the rejection of the Calvinist belief in predestination (that God had only chosen a select few for salvation), and a general rather than literal reading of the Bible.

Unitarians abandoned the concept of the Trinity (God the Father, the Son, and the Holy Ghost) that had long been central to the Christian faith, believing instead that God and Jesus were separate. Jesus was a saintly man (but not divine) who set a shining example. Unitarians also stressed that people were not inherently sinful. By following the teachings of Jesus and trusting their own consciences, *all* people were eligible for salvation. Boston became the center of the Unitarian movement. "Liberal" churches adopted the name *Unitarian*, a spiritual outlook especially popular with the educated elite in major cities.

CHURCH OF THE FIRST PARISH MEETING HOUSE HILL Located in Dorchester, Massachusetts, it was one of the first Puritan churches in the New World before it became a Unitarian Universalist congregation in the early nineteenth century.

A parallel anti-Calvinist movement, Universalism, attracted a different—and much larger—social group: the working poor. In 1779, John Murray, a British clergyman, founded the first Universalist church, in Gloucester, Massachusetts. Like the Unitarians, **Universalists** proclaimed the dignity and worth of all people. They stressed that believers must liberate themselves from the rule of priests and ministers and use their own God-given reasoning to explore the mysteries of existence.

To Universalists and Unitarians, hell was a myth; it did not exist. Salvation was "universal," available to everyone through the sacrifice of Jesus. In essence, Universalists thought God was too caring to damn people to hell, while Unitarians thought themselves too good to be damned. (The two denominations would combine in 1961, becoming the Unitarian Universalist faith.)

The Second Great Awakening

The rise of Universalism and Unitarianism did not mean that traditional religious beliefs were disappearing. Fire and brimstone evangelism remained widespread. During the first Great Awakening in the early 1700s, traveling revivalists had promoted a more intense and personal relationship with God. In addition, Anglicanism suffered from being aligned with the Church of England; it lost its status as the official religion in most states after the American Revolution. To help erase their pro-British image, Virginia Anglicans renamed themselves *Episcopalians*.

Yet the new name did not prevent the Episcopal Church from losing its leadership position in the South. Newer denominations, especially Baptists and Methodists, 20 percent of whom were African American, attracted excited followers by promoting more-democratic principles and allowing individual congregations to exercise more power than did the Anglican Church.

Around 1800, the United States experienced a massive wave of religious revivals called the **Second Great Awakening**. While all denominations grew as a result of the Second Great Awakening, the evangelical sects—Baptists,

Unitarians Members of the liberal New England Congregationalist offshoot, who profess the oneness of God and the goodness of rational worshippers, often well-educated and wealthy.

Universalists Generally working-class members of a New England religious movement, who believed in a merciful God and universal salvation.

Second Great Awakening Religious revival movement that arose in reaction to the growth of secularism and rationalist religion; spurred the growth of the Baptist and Methodist denominations.

Methodists, and Presbyterians—experienced explosive popularity. In 1780, the nation had only 50 Methodist churches; by 1860, there were 20,000, far more than any other denomination. The percentage of Americans who joined Protestant churches increased sixfold between 1800 and 1860.

The Second Great Awakening involved two centers of activity. One developed among New England colleges that were founded as religious centers of learning, then spread across western New York into Pennsylvania and Ohio, Indiana, and Illinois. The other emerged in the backwoods of Tennessee and Kentucky and spread across rural America. Both shared a simple message: Salvation is available to *anyone* who repents and embraces Christ.

Frontier Revivals

In its frontier phase, the Second Great Awakening generated tremendous excitement and emotional excesses. It gave birth to two religious phenomena—the traveling backwoods evangelist and the frontier camp meeting.

People found the supernatural inside as well as outside of churches; they readily believed in magic, dreams, visions, miraculous healings, and speaking in tongues (a spontaneous babbling precipitated by the workings of the Holy Spirit). Evangelists and "exhorters" (spiritual speakers who were not formal ministers) with colorful nicknames such as Jumpin' Jesus, Crazy

RELIGIOUS REVIVALISM Frontier revivals and prayer meetings ignited religious fervor within both minister and participant. In this 1830s camp meeting, the women are so intensely moved by the sermon that they shed their bonnets and fall to their knees.

Dow, and Mad Isaac found ready audiences among lonely frontier folk hungry for spiritual intensity and a more authentic sense of community.

Mass revivals along the western frontier were family-oriented, community-building events that bridged social, economic, political, and even racial divisions. Women, especially, flocked to the revivals and served as the backbone of religious life on the frontier.

At the end of the eighteenth century, ministers visiting the western territories reported that there were few frontier churches and few people attending them. To remedy the situation, traveling evangelists organized "camp meetings."

New religious phenomenon: camp meetings

The first large camp meeting occurred in 1801 on a Kentucky hillside called Cane Ridge, east of Lexington. A Scots-Irish Presbyterian minister named James McGready invited Protestants to attend, and as many as 20,000 camped in tents for nine days at what came to be called the Great Revival. McGready sought to help people see heaven's "glories and long to be there" while reminding them of "hell and its horrors." To him, the purpose of Christianity was simple: to convince sinners to convert themselves to saints assured of eternal bliss. His sermons left his listeners "powerless, groaning, praying, and crying for mercy."

The frontier revivals generated intense emotions. As news of the unscrubbed energy of the Cane Ridge gathering spread, Protestant evangelists, especially Methodists, organized similar revivals in other states. "Hell is trembling, and Satan's kingdom falling," reported a South Carolinian in 1802. "The sacred flame" of religious revival is "extending far and wide." In 1776, about one in six Americans belonged to a church; by 1850, it was one in three.

Denominational Growth

Frontier revivals included many Presbyterians, but Baptists and Methodists predominated. Of the established denominations, Presbyterianism was entrenched among those with Scots-Irish backgrounds, from Pennsylvania to Georgia. Since the Presbyterians and the Congregationalists agreed on theology, they were able to form unified congregations and "call" (recruit) a minister from either denomination. The result through much of the Old Northwest (Ohio, Michigan, Indiana, and Illinois) was that New Englanders became Presbyterians by way of the "Presbygational" churches.

Mechanisms of religious dissemination: unified congregations and circuit riders

Baptist theology was grounded in biblical fundamentalism—a certainty that every word and story in the Bible were divinely inspired and literally true. Unlike the Puritans, however, Baptists believed that *everyone* could gain salvation by choosing (via "free will") to receive God's grace and being baptized as adults. Baptists also stressed the social equality of everyone before God.

Methodists, who also believed in free will, developed the most effective evangelical method: the "circuit rider," a traveling evangelist ("itinerant") on horseback who sought converts in remote frontier settlements. The itinerant system began with Francis Asbury, a British-born revivalist who traveled across fifteen states and preached thousands of sermons.

frontier revivals Religious revival movement within the Second Great Awakening, which took place in frontier churches in western territories and states in the early nineteenth century.

PETER CARTWRIGHT AND HIS WIFE FRANCINE GAINES Cartwright experienced a religious epiphany at a frontier revival meeting, and henceforth became a traveling evangelist, the first to integrate evangelical preaching into politics.

After Asbury, Peter Cartwright emerged as the most successful circuit rider. He grew up in a violent, lawless region of Kentucky. His brother was hanged as a murderer, and his sister was said to be a prostitute. Cartwright himself had been a hellion until, at age fifteen, he attended a frontier revival meeting: "Divine light flashed all around me, unspeakable joy sprung up in my soul. I rose to my feet, opened my eyes, and it really seemed as if I was in heaven. . . . My mother raised the shout, my Christian friends crowded around me and joined me in praising God; and though I have been since then, in many instances, unfaithful, yet I have never for one moment, doubted that the Lord did, then and there, forgive my sins and give me religion."

The following year, Cartwright became a religious exhorter, preaching the faith even though he was not yet an ordained minister. At age eighteen, he began working as a circuit rider. For more than twenty years, he preached a sermon a day, three hours at a time.

Revivalism and African Americans

Revivals broke down social barriers. Free African Americans were especially attracted to the emotional energies of the Methodist and Baptist churches, in part because many White circuit riders opposed slavery. They also infused their churches with exuberant energy and emotional songs called *spirituals*. Richard Allen, a formerly enslaved person in Philadelphia, claimed in 1787 that "there was no religious sect or denomination that would suit the capacity of the colored people as well as the Methodist." He decided that the "plain and simple gospel suits best for any people; for the unlearned can understand [it]." Even more important, the Methodists actively recruited Blacks.

***BLACK METHODISTS HOLDING A PRAYER MEETING* (1811)** This caricature of an African American Methodist meeting in Philadelphia shows a preacher in the church doorway, while his congregation engages in exuberant worship. **How does this illustration compare with the frontier prayer meeting depicted on page 430?**

Yet racial tensions increased as the mostly White Methodist congregations required Blacks to sit in designated pews. Such discrimination led Allen and others to organize the Bethel African Methodist Episcopal Church in 1793. In 1816, as racial discrimination continued, Allen helped found a new denomination: the African Methodist Episcopal (AME) Church.

The rise of the African Methodist Episcopal Church

The denomination grew quickly. By 1846, it boasted 296 churches, almost 200 ministers, and 17,375 members. During the nineteenth century, AME extended its outreach, initiating the first civil rights movement and promoting economic and educational opportunities for people of color. (Allen University in South Carolina is named in honor of Richard Allen.)

Camp Meetings and Women

Religious leadership for women

Baptist, Methodist, and Presbyterian ministers often worked as a team at revivals, and crowds frequently numbered in the thousands. Infusions of the spirit sparked strange behavior. Some people went into trances; others contracted the "jerks," a spasmodic twitching. Still others babbled in unknown tongues or got down on all fours and barked like dogs to "tree the devil."

The camp meetings also offered a social outlet to isolated rural folk, especially women. Evangelical ministers repeatedly applauded the spiritual energies of women and affirmed their right to give public witness to their faith and to play a leading role in efforts at social reform.

At a time when women were banned from preaching, Jarena Lee, a free Black who lived near Philadelphia, was the first African American woman to become a minister in the AME. As she wrote, "If the man may preach, because the Saviour died for him, why not the woman? Seeing [as] he died for her also." Lee became a tireless revivalist; according to her records, she "traveled 2,325 miles and preached 178 sermons."

Women found public roles within evangelical denominations because of their emphasis on individual religious experiences rather than conventional, male-dominated church structures. Phoebe Worrall Palmer, who traveled the country as a camp-meeting exhorter, claimed her right to preach by citing the biblical emphasis on obeying God rather than man. "It is always right to obey the Holy Spirit's command," she stressed, "and if that is laid upon a woman to preach the Gospel, then it is right for her to do so; it is a duty she cannot neglect without falling into condemnation." Such religious enthusiasm often inspired women to pursue social reforms for their benefit, including greater educational opportunities and the right to vote.

JARENA LEE A pathbreaking revivalist, Lee traveled thousands of miles on foot to preach to diverse crowds across America. Lee also published a detailed autobiography about her religious experiences, spreading her message through print, as well.

Religion and Reform

Regions roiled by revival fever were compared to forests devastated by fire. Western New York experienced so much evangelical activity that people labeled it the *burned-over district*. One reason the area was such a hotbed was the Erie Canal, which opened in 1825. Both the construction of and traffic on the canal turned many towns into rollicking scenes of lawlessness: gambling, prostitution, public drunkenness, and crime. Such widespread sinfulness made the region ripe for revivalism.

Charles G. Finney

The most successful evangelist in the burned-over district was a former-attorney-turned-Presbyterian-minister named Charles Grandison Finney. In the winter of 1830–1831, he preached for six months in Rochester, a canal boomtown in upstate New York. In the process, he became the most celebrated minister in the country.

Finney and the religious revival in New York

While rural camp-meeting revivals attracted farm families and other working-class groups, Finney's Northeast audiences attracted more-prosperous seekers. "The Lord," Finney declared, "was aiming at the conversion of the highest classes of society." In 1836, he built a huge church in New York City to accommodate his rapidly growing congregation.

Finney focused on one question: What role can the individual play in earning salvation? He and other free-will evangelists insisted that everyone, rich or poor, Black or White, could *choose* to be "saved."

By choosing Christ, a convert could thereafter be free of sin, but Christians also had an obligation to improve society by perfecting themselves. Christians should "aim to be holy and not rest satisfied until they are as perfect as God."

The revivals provided much of the energy behind the reform impulse that swept across America during Andrew Jackson's presidency. By the time the waves of reform crested at midcentury, the fabric of society had been transformed. Catharine Beecher, a leading advocate for evangelical religion and social reform, stressed that the success of democracy "depends upon the intellectual and moral character of the mass of people. If they are intelligent and virtuous, democracy is a blessing; but if they are ignorant and wicked, it is only a curse."

The Mormons

The Second Great Awakening also spawned new religious groups. The burned-over district in New York gave rise to several movements, the most important of which was Mormonism. Its founder, Joseph Smith Jr., the child of an intensely religious Vermont farm couple who settled in the western New York village of Palmyra, was born and raised amid the excitement of revivalism.

Joseph Smith founds Mormonism

In 1823, eighteen-year-old Smith reported that an angel named Moroni had appeared by his bedside and announced that God needed Smith's help. The angel then led him to a hillside near his father's farm, where he had unearthed a box containing golden plates on which was etched, in an ancient language, a lost "gospel" explaining the history of ancient America. It described a group of Israelites ("Nephites") who crossed the Atlantic and settled America 2,100 years before Columbus. After his death and resurrection, Jesus Christ appeared before the "Nephites" in the New World.

Smith set about laboriously translating the inscriptions on the plates, which no one else ever saw. Much of the language he transcribed was in fact drawn from the Bible. In 1830, he convinced a friend to pay for the publication of the first 5,000 copies of the 500-page text he called *The Book of Mormon: An Account Written by the Hand of Mormon upon Plates Taken from the Plates of Nephi*.

NAUVOO The magnificent scale and stately architecture of Joseph Smith's original temple in Nauvoo is captured in this 1890 print. **How did Joseph Smith organize the new community of Nauvoo?**

With this book as his gospel, young Smith became Jesus's prophet, and he began telling the story of his "marvilous [*sic*] experience" and gathering thousands of converts (he referred to as saints) who shared his desire to live together in accordance with the teachings of Jesus. Eventually, Smith formed what he called the Church of Jesus Christ of Latter-day Saints, often informally known as the **Mormon Church**. In keeping with the teachings of Jesus and the democratic spirit of the times, Smith maintained that God, angels, and people were all members of the same flesh-and-blood species. God "is a man like one of you," Smith told his followers.

In his self-appointed role as the Mormon Prophet, Smith dismissed as frauds all Christian denominations (Protestant and Catholic); criticized the sins of the rich; preached universal salvation; denied that there was a hell; urged his followers to avoid liquor, tobacco, and caffeine; and asserted that the Second Coming of Christ was near. He promised followers "a nation, a new Israel, a people bound as much by heritage and identity as by belief." Within a few years, he had gathered thousands of converts ("saints"), most of them poor farmers.

Years of Persecution From the outset, Mormons tested the social and democratic boundaries of the era with their secret rituals, their refusal to abide by local laws and conventions, and their separateness. In their search for a "promised land" freed from persecution, the Mormons moved from western New York to Ohio, then to Missouri, where the governor called for them to be "exterminated or driven from the state."

Forced out of Missouri, Smith and the Mormons moved in 1839 to the half-built town of Commerce, Illinois on mosquito-infested wetlands along the Mississippi River. They renamed the town Nauvoo, a rough translation of a Hebrew word meaning "beautiful land."

Within five years, Nauvoo had become the second largest city in the state, and Joseph Smith, the Prophet, and his saints referred to it as the Kingdom of God. The community established a new form of theocratic government with its own constitution. As "the Prophet," Smith had substantial control over the community. He owned the hotel and general store; published the newspaper; and served as mayor, chief justice, and commander

Mormon Church The Church of Jesus Christ of Latter-day Saints, founded by Joseph Smith, emphasizing universal salvation and a modest lifestyle; often persecuted for separateness and practice of polygamy.

MORMON TREK, 1830–1851

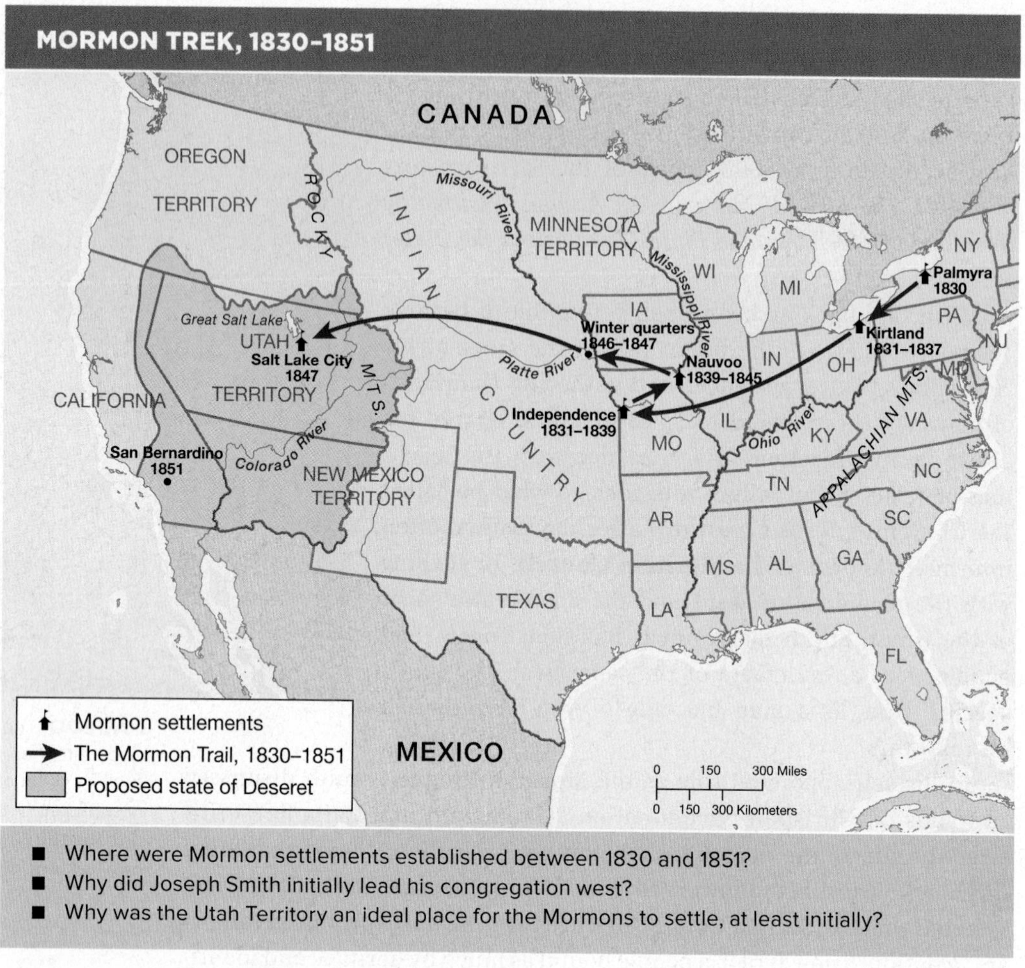

- Where were Mormon settlements established between 1830 and 1851?
- Why did Joseph Smith initially lead his congregation west?
- Why was the Utah Territory an ideal place for the Mormons to settle, at least initially?

of the city's army. With his strong belief in priestly authority, however, Smith began excommunicating dissidents.

Dissent over issue of polygamy

Smith pushed conventional social and marital boundaries too, when he announced that God wanted men to have multiple wives—"plural marriage" (polygamy). Over time, Smith took more than two dozen wives, many of them already married to others. In 1844, Mormon dissenters, including Smith's first wife, Emma, denounced his polygamy. The result was not only a split in the church but also an attack on Nauvoo by non-Mormons. (The Mormon Church would ban polygamy in 1889.)

When an opposition newspaper was destroyed, Smith and his brother Hyrum were arrested and charged with treason. While awaiting trial, a mob from surrounding communities stormed the jail and killed the Smith brothers.

Brigham Young The Mormons quickly found a new leader in the charismatic Brigham Young. Because Nauvoo continued to arouse the suspicions of non-Mormons, Young began to look for another home. It turned out to be 1,300 miles away, near the Great Salt Lake in Utah, a vast, sparsely populated area that was then part of Mexico. After leading over 2,000 followers across the Great Plains and Rocky Mountains, Young found in 1847 "a broad and barren plain hemmed in by the mountains, blistering in the burning rays of the mid-summer sun. No waving fields, no swaying forests, no verdant meadows." Young, however, declared that "this is the place" to settle.

By the end of 1848, the Mormons had developed an irrigation system for their farms, and over the next decade they brought about a spectacular greening of the Utah desert. They called their settlement Deseret (meaning Land of the Honeybee) and elected Young governor.

But their independence was short-lived. In 1848, Mexico signed the Treaty of Guadalupe Hidalgo, transferring to the United States what are now California, Nevada, Utah, Texas, and parts of Arizona, New Mexico, Colorado, and Wyoming. Two years later, Congress incorporated the Utah Territory into the United States. Nevertheless, when Young was named the territorial governor, the new arrangement gave the Mormons virtual independence.

BRIGHAM YOUNG Taking over from Joseph Smith after his death, Young served as president of the Mormons for thirty years and led them on their exodus to Utah.

For more than twenty years, Young ruled Utah with an iron hand. But the growing desire for statehood finally led the Mormons to disavow polygamy, thereby enabling Utah to be admitted as a state. Out of its traumatic and violent early struggles, the tremendous work ethic of its people, and the strong religious faith of its members and their commitment to spreading that faith worldwide through their missionary work, Mormonism today is the fourth largest religious denomination in the world.

Romanticism in America

CORE **OBJECTIVE**

2. Examine the emergence of transcendentalism in American culture in the early nineteenth century.

The revival of religious life during the early 1800s was one of many efforts to unleash the stirrings of the spirit throughout the United States and Europe. Another great cultural shift was the Romantic movement in thought, literature, and the arts. The Romantic movement began in Europe as a rebellion against the well-ordered rational world promoted by scientific objectivity. Were there not, after all, more things in the world than reason, science, and logic could categorize and explain: spontaneous moods, impressions, and feelings; mysterious, unknown, and half-seen things?

In areas in which science could neither prove nor disprove concepts, the Romantics insisted that people were justified in believing what they felt. They preferred the stirrings of the heart over the calculations of the head, nonconformity over traditional behavior, and the mystical over the rational. Americans especially embraced Romanticism's emphasis on individualism and the virtues of common people and civic democracy.

THE OXBOW This 1836 landscape by the American artist Thomas Cole is an iconic work of Romanticism, capturing the view from Mount Holyoke, Massachusetts, after a thunderstorm. **What might Cole be symbolizing by his juxtaposition of untamed wilderness to the left and domesticated farmland to the right?**

Transcendentalism

The rise of transcendentalism in New England

The most intense American advocates of Romantic ideals were the transcendentalists of New England. Transcendentalism promoted a radical individualism and personal spirituality separate from organized religion. The word **transcendentalism** came from an emphasis on thoughts and behaviors that *transcend* (or rise above) the limits of reason and logic. To transcendentalists, the inner life of the spirit took priority over the hard facts of science and the rigidities of organized religion. Transcendentalism, said one of its champions, meant an interest in areas "a little beyond" the scope of reason.

Transcendentalism rejected both religious orthodoxy and the "corpse-cold" rationalism of Unitarianism. Reality was not simply what could be touched and seen and analyzed; it included the innate stirrings of the mind and the unscientific urgings of the spiritual world. Above all, transcendentalists believed in "self-reliance" over group conformity and embraced a pure form of personal spirituality uncorrupted by theological dogma and denominational creeds. They wanted individuals to look *within* themselves for spiritual insights and to nurture a romantic spirituality in harmony

transcendentalism Philosophy of New England writers and thinkers who advocated personal spirituality, self-reliance, social reform, and harmony with nature.

with nature. They believed that all people had the capacity to tap the divine "spark" present throughout God's creations. Ralph Waldo Emerson, the movement's leader, viewed nature as the "symbol of spirit."

In short, transcendentalists wanted everyone to think their *own* thoughts and develop their *own* beliefs. Self-discovery was essential. By the 1830s, New England transcendentalism had become the most influential force in American culture.

Ralph Waldo Emerson

More than anyone, Ralph Waldo Emerson embodied the transcendentalist gospel. To Emerson, self-knowledge opened the doors to self-improvement and self-realization.

Emerson became the nation's most popular speaker during the 1840s. "We have listened too long to the courtly muses of Europe," he said. "We will walk on our own feet; we will work with our own hands; we will speak with our own minds." He exhorted the young republic to shed its cultural inferiority complex and create its own distinctive literature, art, and thought.

The son of the minister of Boston's First Unitarian Church and the descendant of eight generations of clergymen, Emerson graduated from Harvard College in 1821 and became a Unitarian parson in 1829. But three years later, following the death of his wife after only eighteen months of marriage, he turned away from organized religion. He sought instead to cultivate a personal spirituality in communion with nature. As he explained, "I am more of a Quaker than anything else. I believe in the 'still, small voice,' and that voice is Christ within us."

After traveling in Europe, where he met England's greatest Romantic writers, Emerson settled in Concord, Massachusetts, and became an essayist, poet, and lecturer ("preacher to the world"). He celebrated self-reliance and the individual's unlimited potential—if people would only learn to think for themselves and defy traditional assumptions and beliefs.

RALPH WALDO EMERSON Emerson is most remembered for leading the transcendentalist movement, and his message of self-reliance affirmed the integrity of the individual and inspired generations of thinkers.

In 1836, Emerson published the pathbreaking book *Nature*, which helped launch the transcendental movement. In it, he stressed that people could "transcend" the limitations of the material world and rational thinking and discover the "spirit" animating the universe. Every human being, said Emerson, should enjoy an "original relation to the universe."

Emerson's lectures and writings provided the energetic core of the transcendentalist outlook. His essay "Self-Reliance" (1841) expressed the transcendentalist ideal of intellectual independence: "Whoso would be a man," he declared, "must be a nonconformist. . . . Nothing is at last sacred but the integrity of your own mind. . . . It is easy in the world to live after the world's opinion; it is easy in solitude to live after our own; but the great man is he who in the midst of a crowd keeps with perfect sweetness the independence of solitude."

MARGARET FULLER Margaret Fuller (May 23, 1810–July 19, 1850) was an illustrious American journalist, editor, and critic. In 1839 she began a conversation group among Boston's women that led to the classic treatise *Woman in the Nineteenth Century.* Drowned in a shipwreck with her husband and baby boy, Margaret Fuller is the tragic heroine of the transcendentalist movement.

The Transcendental Club

In 1836, a diverse, informal discussion group that came to be called the Transcendental Club began to meet in Boston and nearby Concord to discuss philosophy, literature, and religion. In describing life in Concord, writer Nathaniel Hawthorne said there "never was a poor, little country village infested with such a variety of queer, strangely dressed, oddly behaved mortals."

The club included cultural rebels; social critics; liberal clergymen; utopian reformers; militant abolitionists; innovative writers; and brilliant women such as Elizabeth Peabody, her sister Sophia (who married Hawthorne), and Margaret Fuller, the author of *Woman in the Nineteenth Century* (1845). A dazzling conversationalist, Fuller organized a transcendentalist discussion group that met in Peabody's Boston bookstore. Their "Conversations" were designed to embolden women to think and act for themselves. Fuller helped launch and edit the *Dial* (1840–1844), an experimental transcendentalist magazine that introduced Romanticism to readers. "A much greater range of occupations," Fuller asserted, must be made available to women to enable them to express their full potential.

Henry David Thoreau

Ralph Waldo Emerson's younger friend, Henry David Thoreau, practiced the thoughtful self-reliance and pursuit of perfection that Emerson preached. "I like people who can do things," Emerson said, and Thoreau could do many things: carpentry, masonry, painting, surveying, sailing, gardening, lecturing. Thoreau was America's original wild child. Armed with a headstrong sense of uncompromising integrity, prickly individuality, and proud rebelliousness, he loved to unearth forbidden questions and lay bare everyday hypocrisies. He celebrated his feisty individuality. "If a man does not keep pace with his companions," he wrote, "perhaps it is because he hears a different drummer."

Thoreau described himself as "a mystic, a transcendentalist, and a natural philosopher" who questioned tradition and challenged authority. Emerson delighted in Thoreau, whom he called "stubborn and implacable; always manly and wise, but rarely sweet." A neighbor was more blunt. "I love Henry," said Elizabeth Hoar, "but I do not like him."

Born in Concord in 1817, Thoreau graduated from Harvard, worked as a teacher, and then helped his father, a celebrated pencil maker. Like Emerson, however, Thoreau frequently escaped to the woods. He viewed "the indescribable innocence" of nature as a living bible; the earth to him was a form of poetry, full of hidden meanings. Christianity, he believed, was a dying institution. His priorities were inward.

Thoreau showed little interest in social life and no interest in wealth. "The mass of men," he wrote, "lead lives of quiet desperation" because they were preoccupied with making money and exploiting nature. Money was not Thoreau's goal. He yearned to escape the constraints of stuffy traditions, unjust laws, and the opinions of his elders. He committed himself to what Emerson called a simple life centered on "plain living and high thinking." Thoreau rented a room at the Emerson home, where he tended the garden, worked as a handyman, and took long walks with his host.

HENRY DAVID THOREAU A model transcendentalist, Thoreau celebrated the right and willingness of individuals to think and act for themselves, influencing activists throughout the twentieth century and since.

In 1844, when Emerson bought fourteen acres along Walden Pond, Thoreau decided to embark upon an unusual experiment in self-reliance. On July 4, 1845, just shy of his twenty-eighth birthday, he took to the woods to live in a tiny, one-room cabin he had built at Walden Pond, a mile outside of Concord. His hut featured three chairs: "one for solitude, two for friendship, and three for society."

Living at Walden Pond was Thoreau's personal declaration of independence. His goal was to discover what nature "had to teach" about those things that money can't buy. "I went to the woods because I wished to live deliberately," he wrote in *Walden, or Life in the Woods* (1854), ". . . and not, when I came to die, discover that I had not lived." Thoreau ate only one meal a day and disdained coffee, alcohol, jam, tobacco, and salt. He regarded sex with disgust and suspicion. His minimalist ethic led Emerson to observe that he "was never affectionate, but superior, didactic," forever scorning his neighbors and claiming that he was "more favored by the gods."

Walden contains some of the most evocative nature writing in American literature. A first-rate naturalist, Thoreau was blessed with superhuman powers of observation. He urged readers to open their eyes and hearts to the infinite spontaneity of everyday sensory experiences. "We can never have enough of nature," he wrote. "We need to witness our own limits transgressed, and some life pasturing freely where we never wander."

To Thoreau, there was something sacred and liberating about nature's beauty and sensuality. His ecstatic descriptions of the natural world have made him the patron saint of the environmental movement. (Nearly a million people visit his cabin site at Walden Pond each year.) "In wildness is the preservation of the world," he wrote, and his scriptural statement later became the motto of the Sierra Club.

During Thoreau's two years, two months, and two days at Walden Pond, his conscience was pricked by the abolitionist movement. He harbored a freedom seeker and considered President James K. Polk's declaration of war against Mexico an unjust action pushed by southern cotton planters eager to add more slave territory. His disgust for the war led him to refuse to pay taxes, for which he was put in jail (for only one night; an aunt paid his overdue tax bill).

This incident inspired Thoreau to write "Civil Disobedience" (1849), a classic essay that would influence Martin Luther King, Jr., in shaping the civil rights movement 100 years later. "If the law is of such a nature that it requires you to be an agent of injustice to another," Thoreau wrote, "then, I say, break the law."

Until his death in 1862, Thoreau kept a journal of "close observations" and philosophical reflections. He also attacked slavery and applauded those who worked to undermine it. The continuing influence of his creed of individual action against injustice shows the impact that a thoughtful person can have on an imperfect world.

An American Literature

Impact of transcendentalism on American literature

Henry David Thoreau and Ralph Waldo Emerson portrayed the transcendentalist movement as an expression of moral idealism; critics dismissed it as outrageous self-centeredness. Although the transcendentalists attracted only a small following in their time, they inspired a generation of writers that produced the first great age of American literature.

The 1840s and 1850s brought an outpouring of extraordinary writing. Among the works produced were *Representative Men* by Emerson; *Walden, or Life in the Woods* by Thoreau; *The Scarlet Letter* and *The House of the Seven Gables* by Nathaniel Hawthorne; *Moby-Dick* by Herman Melville; *Leaves of Grass* by Walt Whitman; and hundreds of unpublished poems by Emily Dickinson.

Nathaniel Hawthorne

Nathaniel Hawthorne, the supreme writer of the New England group, never shared the sunny optimism of his neighbors or their perfectionist belief in reform. A native of Salem, Massachusetts, he was haunted by the knowledge of evil bequeathed to him by his Puritan forebears, one of whom (John Hathorne) had been a judge at the Salem witchcraft trials. After college, Hawthorne worked in obscurity in Salem before earning a degree of fame with *Twice-Told Tales* (1837). The central theme of his stories and novels was sin and its consequences: pride and selfishness, secret guilt, and the impossibility of rooting sin out of the human soul.

EMILY DICKINSON Although her works were rarely published during her lifetime, Dickinson offered the literary world of New England a fresh female voice.

Emily Dickinson

Emily Dickinson, the most strikingly original of the New England poets, lived with her parents and sister in Amherst, Massachusetts. There in a spartan corner bedroom on the second floor of the family house, the slim, red-haired Dickinson found independence and self-expression in poetry, ever grateful that "one is one's self & not somebody else." Only 10 or so of her almost 1,800 poems appeared in print (anonymously) before her death in 1886 at fifty-five. As she once prophetically wrote, "Success is counted sweetest/By those who ne'er succeed."

Once, when Emily's niece Matty visited, Dickinson locked the bedroom door and excitedly announced, "Matty: here's freedom," for in her room her soul had "moments of Escape." Dickinson lived what her niece called a life of "exquisite self-containment," in part because her patriarchal and often tyrannical father prohibited her from exploring the world of ideas outside the home. Enlivened by "the light of insight and the fire of emotion," Dickinson wrote verse remarkable for its simplicity, brevity, and depth.

Whether her seclusion and intensity resulted from severe eye trouble, aching despair generated by her love for a married minister, or fear of her possessive father, Dickinson's isolation and lifelong religious doubts led her to probe the "white heat" of heartbreak and disappointment in ways unusual for the time. Her often-abstract themes were elemental: life, death, fear, loneliness, nature, and above all, the withdrawal of God, "a distant, stately lover" who no longer could be found.

Edgar Allan Poe

Edgar Allan Poe was fascinated by the menace of death. Born in Boston in 1809 and orphaned as a child, he was raised by foster parents in Richmond, Virginia. After attending the University of Virginia, he moved to Philadelphia in 1837, where he edited magazines and wrote scathing reviews and terrifying mystery stories. As the creator of the detective story, his influence on literature has been enormous.

The poem "The Raven," about a man who lost his lover, made Poe a household name. In 1847, however, his young wife died of tuberculosis. Thereafter, he was seduced as much by alcohol and drug abuse as by writing. He died at age forty of mysterious causes. Poe left behind an extraordinary collection of "unworldly" tales and haunting poems. He used horror to explore the darkest corners of human psychology and satisfy his lifelong obsession with death. To him, fear was the most powerful emotion, so he focused on making the grotesque and supernatural seem disturbingly real. Anyone who has read "The Tell-Tale Heart" or "The Pit and the Pendulum" can testify to his success.

Herman Melville

Herman Melville was a New Yorker who went to sea as a youth. In 1851, the thirty-two-year-old Melville published *Moby-Dick*, one of the world's greatest novels. It is the story of Captain Ahab's obsessive quest for an "accursed" white whale that had devoured his leg. On one level, the book is a ripping good yarn of adventure on the high seas. On another level, it explores the unfathomable depths and darkness of human complexity, as Ahab's crazed obsession with finding and killing the white whale turns him into a monster who sacrifices his ship and crew.

Walt Whitman

The most controversial writer during the nineteenth century was Walt Whitman, a New York journalist and poet. He was a self-promoting, robust personality. Whitman wrote excitedly about industrial development, urban life, working men, sailors, and "simple humanity."

By the time he met Ralph Waldo Emerson, Whitman had been "simmering, simmering." Emerson "brought him to a boil" with his emphasis on defying tradition and celebrating the commonplaces of life, including sexuality

***POLITICS IN AN OYSTER HOUSE* (1848)** Commissioned by social activist John H. B. Latrobe, this painting captures the public conversations that were fueled by newspapers and other print periodicals. **What issues were being tackled by activists in the mid-1800s?**

and the body. These themes found their way into Whitman's controversial first book of unconventional, free-verse poems, *Leaves of Grass* (1855). In its first year, it sold ten copies. One reviewer called it "an intensely vulgar, nay, absolutely *beastly* book." *Leaves of Grass*, however, became more influential with each passing year.

Whitman's poems, remarkable for their energy, exuberance, and intimacy, were seasoned with frank sexuality and homoerotic overtones. Although *Leaves of Grass* was banned in Boston because of its explicit sexuality, Emerson found it "the most extraordinary piece of wit and wisdom that America has yet contributed." More conventional literary critics, however, shuddered at the shocking "grossness" of Whitman's homosexual references ("manly love"; "the love of comrades"; "for the friend I love lay sleeping by my side"). Yet Whitman could never be truly honest about his sexuality (he identified as gay or bisexual in today's terms), for even discussing such perspectives was a felony in the nineteenth century.

Newspapers

The flowering of American literature coincided with a massive expansion in newspaper readership sparked by rapid improvements in printing technology. The availability of newspapers costing only a penny transformed daily reading into a form of popular entertainment.

By 1850, the United States had more newspapers than any nation, and they forged a network of communications across the republic. As readership soared, the content of the papers expanded beyond political news and commentary to include society gossip, sports, and reports of sensational crimes and accidents. The proliferation of newspapers was largely a northern and western phenomenon, as literacy rates in the South lagged behind those of the rest of the country.

CORE **OBJECTIVE**

3. Explain the origins of the major social reform movements in the early nineteenth century and analyze their influence on society and politics.

The Reform Impulse

In 1842, the United States was awash in reform movements led by dreamers and activists eager to fight social injustice or immorality. Lyman Beecher, a prominent preacher and champion of evangelical Christian revivalism (and the father of writer Harriet Beecher Stowe), stressed that the Second Great Awakening was not focused simply on promoting individual conversions; it was also intended to "reform human society."

While an impulse to "perfect" people and society helped excite the reform movements, social and economic changes, including the Panic of 1837 and the ensuing depression, invigorated many reformers, most of whom were women. The rise of an urban middle class enabled growing numbers of women to hire cooks and maids, thus freeing them to devote more time to societal concerns. Many joined churches and charitable organizations, most of which were led by men.

Both women and men belonging to evangelical societies fanned out across America to organize Sunday schools, spread the gospel, and distribute Bibles to the children of the working poor. Other reformers tackled issues such as living/working conditions in prisons and workplaces, care of the disabled, temperance (reducing the consumption of alcoholic beverages), women's rights, and the abolition of slavery. Transcendentalists sought to improve the lot of the poor, the disenfranchised, and the enslaved.

That these reformers often met resistance, persecution, violence, and even death testified to the sincerity of their convictions and the power of their example. As Ralph Waldo Emerson said, "Never mind the ridicule, never mind the defeat, up again, old heart!" For there is "victory yet for all justice."

Temperance

The **temperance** crusade was among the most widespread of the reform movements. Many people argued that the worst social problems were rooted in alcohol abuse. William Cobbett, an English reformer who traveled in the United States, noted in 1819 that virtually every time he visited an American home his hosts asked him "to drink wine or spirits, even *in the morning*."

In 1826, a group of ministers in Boston organized the American Society for the Promotion of Temperance, which sponsored lectures, press campaigns, and the formation of local and state societies. A favorite tactic was to ask everyone who pledged to quit drinking to put by their signature a letter *T* for "total abstinence." With that, a new word entered the English language: *teetotaler*.

Like nearly every reform movement of the day, the temperance movement had a wing of absolutists. Those absolutists formed the American Temperance Union in 1833, and three years later it passed a resolution that liquor ought to be prohibited by law. Three years later, the Temperance Union called for abstinence from all alcoholic beverages—which caused moderates to abstain from the temperance movement.

Social reform can be a conservative force. Those who feared the rise of Jacksonian democracy and worried about the surge of poor immigrants from Ireland and Germany, or who dreaded change itself, viewed reform as a means of restoring social control. They were afraid of anything that upset the social status quo.

For example, fears that Americans were turning away from the Protestant faith led Lyman Beecher and other evangelicals to found societies such as the American Bible Society, the American Sunday School Union, and the American Tract Society—all designed to shore up the centrality of religion and churches in community life. Evangelical reformers sought to restrict freedom: no more Sunday mail service or Sunday recreation, no more families without Bibles, no communities without ministers, no more liquor.

temperance A widespread reform movement led by militant Christians that focused on reducing the use of alcoholic beverages.

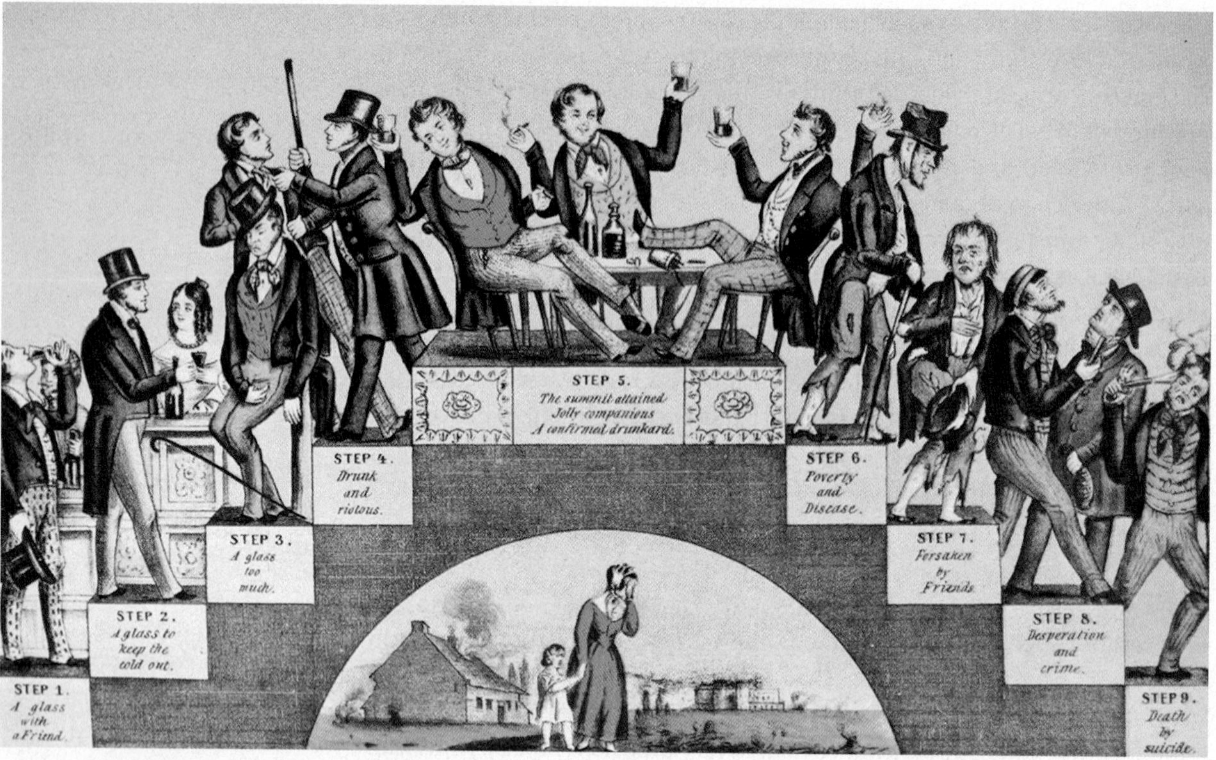

THE DRUNKARD'S PROGRESS This 1846 pro-temperance print outlines a nine-step process of alcoholism, beginning with "a glass with a friend" and ending with "death by suicide." Below the arc are a weeping wife and her child.

Prisons and Asylums

Romantics believed that people are innately good and capable of perfection. Such an optimistic view brought about major changes in the treatment of prisoners, the disabled, and orphans. Public institutions (often called asylums) emerged for the treatment of social ills. If removed from society, the theory went, the needy and deviant could be made whole again. Unhappily, however, the underfunded and understaffed asylums often became breeding grounds for brutality and neglect.

Romanticism and rehabilitative justice

The idea of the penitentiary—a place where the guilty paid for their crimes but also underwent rehabilitation—developed as a new approach to reforming criminals. An early model of the system was the Auburn Penitentiary, which opened in New York in 1816.

The prisoners at Auburn had separate cells and gathered only for meals and group labor. Discipline was severe. The men marched in lockstep and were never put face-to-face or allowed to talk. The system, its advocates argued, had a beneficial effect on the prisoners and saved money, since the facility's workshops supplied prison needs and produced goods for sale at a profit. By 1840, the nation had twelve Auburn-type penitentiaries.

The Romantic reform impulse also found an outlet in the care of the insane. Before 1800, the insane were usually confined at home, with hired keepers, or in jails or almshouses, where homeless debtors were housed. After 1815, however, asylums that separated the disturbed from the criminal began to appear.

Dorothea Dix's activism for the mentally ill

The most important figure in boosting awareness of the plight of the mentally ill was Dorothea Lynde Dix. A pious Boston schoolteacher, she was asked to instruct a Sunday-school class at a prison in 1841. There she found a roomful of insane people who had been completely neglected. The scene so disturbed her that she began a two-year investigation of jails and almshouses in Massachusetts. In a report to the state legislature in 1843, Dix revealed that insane people were confined "in *cages, closets, cellars, stalls, pens! Chained, naked, beaten with rods,* and *lashed* into obedience." Her crusading efforts on behalf of "the miserable, the desolate, and the outcast" spread throughout the country and abroad. In the process, she helped to transform social attitudes toward mental illness.

Women's Rights

While countless middle-class women devoted themselves to improving the quality of life in America, some argued that women should focus on enhancing home life. In 1842, Catharine Beecher published *A Treatise on Domestic Economy,* which promoted the **cult of domesticity**, a powerful ideology that called upon women to accept and celebrate their role as manager of the household and nurturer of the children, separate from the man's sphere of work outside the home. Beecher argued that young women should be trained not for careers outside the home but for a life centered in the household. As a result, the prospects for women remained relatively unchanged. They were barred from the ministry and most other professions. They could not vote or serve on juries. College was rarely an option. A wife often had no control over her property or her children. She could not make a will, sign a contract, or bring suit in court without her husband's permission.

Julia Ward Howe and the women's suffrage movement

Julia Ward Howe, known mostly as the poet who would provide the lyrics to the "Battle Hymn of the Republic," the anthem of the Union army during the Civil War, was living testimony to the deadening aspects of the cult of domesticity. Like most nineteenth-century women, she spent her time at home with her children. Yet she was anything but happy. "My books are all that keeps me alive," she sighed in private frustration. After her husband's death in 1876, Howe would become a leader of the women's suffrage movement. A few years before her death in 1910, she wrote in her journal: "I do not desire ecstatic, disembodied sainthood. . . . I would be human, and American, and a woman."

Gradually, women began to protest their subordinate status, and some men began to listen. In 1848, two prominent women's rights advocates, abolitionists Lucretia Mott, a Philadelphia Quaker, and Elizabeth Cady Stanton of New York, called a convention of men and women to gather in Stanton's hometown of Seneca Falls, in western New York, to discuss "the social, civil, and religious condition and rights of women."

cult of domesticity Pervasive nineteenth-century ideology urging women to celebrate their role as manager of the household and nurturer of the children.

ELIZABETH CADY STANTON AND SUSAN B. ANTHONY Stanton *(left, in 1856)* was a young mother who called the Seneca Falls Convention, while Anthony *(right, in 1848)* started as an anti-slavery and temperance activist in her twenties. The two would meet in 1851 and form a lifelong partnership in the fight for women's suffrage.

On July 19, 1848, when the **Seneca Falls Convention** convened, revolution was in the air. In Europe, militant nationalists, including many women, rebelled against monarchies and promoted unification. In France, the Society for the Emancipation for Women demanded that women receive equal political rights. In April, the French government abolished slavery in its Caribbean colonies, and in June, European feminists called for "the complete, radical abolition of all the privileges of sex, of birth, of race, of rank, and of fortune."

Seneca Falls Convention (1848) Convention organized by feminists Lucretia Mott and Elizabeth Cady Stanton to promote women's rights and issue the pathbreaking Declaration of Rights and Sentiments.

Declaration of Rights and Sentiments (1848) Document based on the Declaration of Independence that called for gender equality, written primarily by Elizabeth Cady Stanton and signed by Seneca Falls Convention delegates.

The activists at Seneca Falls did not go that far, but they did issue a clever paraphrase of the Declaration of Independence. The **Declaration of Rights and Sentiments** proclaimed that "all men and women are created equal." All laws that placed women "in a position inferior to that of men, are contrary to the great precept of nature, and therefore of no force or authority." The convention's most controversial demand was the right to vote.

Such ambitious goals were too radical for most of the 300 delegates, and only about a third of them signed the Declaration of Rights and Sentiments. The editors of the *Philadelphia Public Ledger* asked why women would want to climb down from their domestic pedestal and get involved with politics: "A woman is nothing. A wife is everything. A pretty girl is equal to ten thousand men, and a mother is, next to God, all powerful." Despite such opposition, the Seneca Falls gathering represented an important first step in the campaign for women's rights.

From 1850 until the outbreak of the Civil War in 1861, women's rights advocates held conventions, delivered lectures, and circulated petitions. While the movement struggled in the face of meager funds and widespread opposition, it eventually succeeded because of a few undaunted women.

Susan B. Anthony, already active in temperance and anti-slavery groups, joined the women's crusade in the 1850s. Unlike Elizabeth Cady Stanton and Lucretia Mott, she was unmarried and therefore able to devote most of her attention to the movement. As one observer put it, Stanton "forged the thunderbolts and Miss Anthony hurled them." Both lived into the twentieth century, focusing after the Civil War on women's suffrage (the right to vote).

Women nationwide did not gain the vote in the nineteenth century, but they did make legal gains. In 1839, Mississippi became the first state to grant married women control over their property; by the 1860s, eleven more states had done so. Still, the only jobs open to educated women in any number were nursing and teaching, both of which brought relatively lower status and pay than "men's work."

Early Public Schools

Early America, like most rural societies, offered few educational opportunities. That changed in the first half of the nineteenth century as reformers lobbied for **public schools** to serve all children. The working poor wanted free schools to give their children an equal chance to pursue the American dream. Education, advocates argued, would improve manners while reducing crime and poverty.

A well-informed, well-trained citizenry was considered one of the basic premises of a republic. Because political power resided with the people, as the Constitution asserted, the citizenry needed to be well educated. By 1830, however, no state had a public school system.

Horace Mann, a Massachusetts state legislator and attorney, led the early drive for statewide, tax-supported public schools. Schools, he insisted, should be free to all children regardless of class, race, or ethnicity—including immigrant children. Universal access to education, Mann argued, "was the great equalizer of the conditions of men—the balance-wheel of the social machinery."

Mann saw public schools as the only way to ensure that everyone had a basic level of knowledge and skills. Schooling would also reinforce values such as hard work and clean living. "If we do not prepare children to become good citizens, if we do not enrich their minds with knowledge," Mann warned, "then our republic must go down to destruction."

By the 1840s, most states in the North and Midwest had joined the public school movement. Still, funds for buildings, books, and equipment were limited; teachers were poorly paid and often poorly prepared. Most students going beyond the elementary grades attended private academies,

public schools Elementary and secondary schools funded by the state and free of tuition.

THE GEORGE BARRELL EMERSON SCHOOL, BOSTON (ca. 1850) Although higher education for women initially met with some resistance, seminaries, like this one, started in the 1820s and 1830s, and taught women mathematics, physics, and history as well as music, art, and social graces.

often organized by churches. In 1821, Boston English High School opened as the nation's first free public *secondary* school. Beginning in 1827, Massachusetts required every town of 500 or more residents to have a high school.

Regional inequalities in access to education

Other states were not as progressive, however. Public high schools flourished only after the Civil War. Yet by 1850, half the nation's White children between ages five and nineteen were enrolled in primary schools. Few were southerners, however. With only a few exceptions, southern states did not establish public schools until after the Civil War. In most states, enslaved children were prohibited from learning to read and write or to attend school. The South had some 500,000 illiterate Whites, more than half the total in the country. In the South, North Carolina led the way in state-supported education, enrolling more than two thirds of its White school-age population by 1860. But the school year was only four months long because of the state's need for children to do farmwork.

The prolonged disparities between North and South in educational opportunities helped explain the growing economic and cultural differences between the two regions. Then, as now, undereducated people were more likely to remain poor, less healthy, and less engaged in political life.

Utopian Communities

Amid the climate of reform, the quest for everyday utopias—ideal communities with innovative social and economic relationships—flourished. Plans for creating heaven on earth had long been an American passion, at least since the Puritans set out to build a holy colony in New England.

utopian communities Ideal communities that offered innovative social and economic relationships to those who were interested in achieving salvation—now.

In the nineteenth century, more than 100 **utopian communities** were established. Religious motives animated many of them, while others reflected faith in the Enlightenment ideal that every social problem had a solution discoverable by scientific study.

Some utopias were *communitarian* experiments emphasizing the welfare of the entire community rather than individual freedom and private profits. Others experimented with "free love," socialism, and special diets. What they shared was a conviction that mainstream society was fundamentally flawed and irredeemable.

The Shakers Communities founded by the Shakers (the United Society of Believers in Christ's Second Appearing) proved to be long lasting. Ann Lee (known as Mother Ann Lee) arrived in New York from England with eight followers in 1774. The illiterate daughter of a blacksmith and the wife of an abusive husband, she came to believe in the "depravity of human nature and the odiousness of sin." No sooner did she marry than she was constantly pregnant, bearing four children, none of whom lived beyond six years of age. The trauma of childbirth and the loss of her children convinced Ann Lee that sexual activity was "indecent" and sinful. She eventually took shelter among a group of renegade Shaking Quakers who nurtured in her the dream of a celibate, spotlessly clean utopia devoted to the Second Coming of Christ in which she would play the role of Jesus's female counterpart. She also believed that God and Jesus spoke directly to her (direct revelation).

As Ann Lee recounted her visions of Christ, listeners decided that "the candle of the Lord was in her hand." She was both a prophet and a seer who equated cleanliness, hard work, and chastity with saintliness. Under her leadership, the Shakers publicly attacked the Anglican Church, adopted lives of strict celibacy, and developed eccentric forms of worship featuring loud singing, "inspired" dancing, shrieking, stamping feet, speaking in unknown tongues, and "shaking," hence their name.

Ann Lee founds New Lebanon Shaker Society

After immigrating to America, Ann Lee and her followers settled on 200 acres in upstate New York that they named New Lebanon (in the biblical Old Testament Lebanon is a community in the Promised Land). They first built a log cabin that housed men on the first floor and women on the second, and then they pursued their goal of Christian perfection. Six years later, they began recruiting others to their austere paradise.

Mother Ann died in 1784, but new leaders spread the Shaker movement from New York into New England, Ohio, and Kentucky. By 1830, an estimated 4,000 Shakers lived in about twenty settlements. In these earnest communities, there were no pets, no rugs (favorite hiding places of the devil, they believed), no mixing of garden plants, no more than one rocking chair in a room. All property was held in common. Life and labor were communal, and men and women were equal. People of color were welcome. Shaker farms became leading sources of garden seed and medicinal herbs, and many Shaker products, especially handcrafted furniture, came to be prized for their clean lines and simple beauty.

The Shakers took great pride in their ability to create stable colonies outside the mainstream of American life. They displayed their utopian faith in the perfectibility of life on earth. What they did not perfect was an ability to convince the orphaned children under their care to follow their example.

Of the nearly 200 orphans raised at New Lebanon, only one decided to become a Shaker.

Oneida John Humphrey Noyes, founder of the Oneida Community in upstate New York, developed a much different utopian community. The son of a Vermont congressman, Noyes attended Dartmouth College and Yale Divinity School. But in 1834 he was expelled from Yale and his license to preach was revoked after he announced that he was "perfect" and free of all sin, and that God had singled him out to shepherd people to perfection. In 1836, Noyes gathered a group of "Perfectionists" in Putney, Vermont.

Ten years later, Noyes announced a new doctrine, "complex marriage," which meant that every man in the community was married to every woman, and vice versa. "In a holy community," he claimed, "there is no more reason why sexual intercourse should be restrained by law than why eating and drinking should be." Local authorities disagreed, and they charged Noyes with adultery for practicing his theology of "free love."

John Humphrey Noyes founds the Oneida Community

Noyes fled to New York and in 1848 established the Oneida Community, which became famous for producing fine silverware. Oneida would survive by promoting free sex. Adults had multiple sexual partners and access to surprisingly effective birth control methods. Noyes separated couples that grew too fond of each other ("sticky love") and conveniently announced that it was his duty as "first husband" to initiate virgin women into sexual activity. Equally repellent were his experiments in scientific breeding, where he paired couples based on their positive genetic attributes. Over ten years, Oneida produced sixty-two children from these pairings, ten of them fathered by Noyes. It was Noyes that Emerson had in mind when he wrote that many reformers "have their high origin in an ideal justice, but they do not retain the purity of an idea." Like the Shakers, the Oneida Community banned private property. Everyone labored for the common good; selfishness would be eliminated on the road to perfection.

ONEIDA COMMUNITY Known for its practice of "complex marriage," Oneida was a utopian community that disavowed private property and emphasized "free love." In this photo from 1870, members of the Oneida Community relax on the front lawn of the Oneida Mansion.

What none of the utopian experiments resolved was the fundamental tension inherent in all perfectionist schemes: how to maintain solidarity when residents with different personalities and convictions display conflicting notions of paradise and perfection. Although only a few utopian communities survived, they provided inspiration and hope for seekers who had given up on life as it was. In the end, utopianism also provided a dose of everyday reality sufficient to send them back to mainstream society. Idealists desperate enough to build a heaven on earth are usually destined for an unexpected hell of their own making.

The Anti-Slavery Movement

CORE **OBJECTIVE**

4. Evaluate the impact of the anti-slavery movement on society and politics.

The collapse of perfectionist utopias created a vacuum in the reform movement that the anti-slavery crusade quickly filled. Many of those who participated in communitarian experiments ended up playing key roles in the abolitionist movement. Transcendentalist reformer Theodore Parker declared that slavery was "the blight of this nation, the curse of the North and the curse of the South."

Early Opposition to Slavery

The first organized emancipation movement appeared in 1816 with the formation of the **American Colonization Society (ACS)** in Washington, D.C., whose mission was to raise funds to transport free Blacks back to Africa. Its supporters included James Madison, James Monroe, Andrew Jackson, Henry Clay, John Marshall, and Daniel Webster.

Some supported the colonization movement because they opposed slavery; others saw it as a way to get rid of free Blacks. "We must save the Negro," one missionary explained, "or the Negro will ruin us." White supremacy remained a powerful assumption, even among abolitionists.

Leaders of the free Black community denounced the colonization idea. The United States, they stressed, was their native land, and they had as valid a claim on U.S. citizenship as anyone else. "America is more our country than it is the whites," argued David Walker, an African American living in Boston. "We have enriched it with our blood and tears."

American Colonization Society sends free Blacks to West Africa

Nevertheless, the ACS acquired land on the Ivory Coast of West Africa, and on February 6, 1820, the *Elizabeth* sailed from New York with eighty-eight Black emigrants who formed the nucleus of a new nation, the Republic of Liberia. Thereafter, however, the African colonization movement waned, and in the end only about 15,000 African Americans resettled in Africa.

From Gradualism to Abolitionism

The fight against slavery started in Great Britain in the late eighteenth century, and the movement's success in ending British involvement in the African slave trade helped spur the anti-slavery cause in America. British abolitionists lectured across the northern United States and often bought freedom for the enslaved. Most of the leading American abolitionists visited Great Britain and came away inspired by the breadth and depth of anti-slavery organizations there.

The British example helped convince leaders of the cause in America to adopt an aggressive new strategy in the early 1830s. Equally important

American Colonization Society (ACS) Established in 1816, an organization whose mission was to return formerly enslaved people to Africa.

was the realization that slavery in the cotton-growing southern states was not dying out; it was rapidly growing.

This harsh reality led to a change in tactics among anti-slavery organizations, many of which were energized by evangelical religions and the emerging social activism of transcendentalism. Their initial efforts to promote a *gradual* end to slavery by prohibiting it in the western territories and using moral persuasion to convince owners to free their enslaved people steadily gave way to demands for *immediate* **abolitionism** everywhere.

Religious revivalism strengthens the abolitionist movement

The reason for the shift was largely religious: to a new generation of reformers who came of age during the Second Great Awakening, slavery was a sin, and Christians had an obligation to purge all sins, personal and societal. The abolitionists found in the goal of immediate emancipation a perfectionist formula for casting off the guilt of slavery. Theirs would be a moral crusade rather than a political movement. As the preamble to the American Anti-Slavery Society promised: "We shall send forth agents to lift up the voice of remonstrance, of warning, of entreaty, and of rebuke" to slaveholders everywhere.

By the 1820s, every northern state had abolished slavery. As the anti-slavery movement grew, it came to encompass a wide spectrum of attitudes. Some, like Abraham Lincoln, were gradualists who focused on preventing the extension of slavery into the new western territories in the hope that slavery would eventually die out in the South. Others, known as immediatists, called for the immediate abolition of slavery.

William Lloyd Garrison

A zealous White activist named William Lloyd Garrison drove the abolitionist movement. Born in 1805 in Newburyport, Massachusetts, Garrison learned the printing trade and moved to Boston. There he embraced the reform spirit of the era, writing anonymous letters and essays decrying alcohol abuse, Sabbath-breaking, and war.

But it was slavery that most excited his indignation. In 1831, free Blacks helped convince Garrison to launch an anti-slavery newspaper, *The Liberator,* which became the voice of the nation's first civil rights movement. Of the first 500 subscribers, 450 were free Blacks, leading Garrison to explain that *The Liberator* did not belong to Whites but to people of color: "It is their organ."

In the first issue, Garrison condemned "the popular but pernicious doctrine of gradual emancipation." He dreamed of immediate equality in all spheres of American life, including the status of women, and vowed to be "as harsh as truth, and as uncompromising as justice. . . . I am in earnest—I will not equivocate—I will not excuse—I will *not retreat a* single inch—and I WILL BE HEARD."

Garrison's courage in denouncing slavery outraged slaveholders in the South, as well as some Whites in the North. In 1835, a mob of angry Whites dragged him through the streets of Boston. The South Carolina and Georgia legislatures promised a $5,000 reward to anyone who kidnapped Garrison and brought him south for trial. The intensity of the southern reaction

abolitionism Movement that called for an immediate end to slavery throughout the United States.

MASTHEAD OF *THE LIBERATOR* Masthead of abolitionist newspaper, *The Liberator*, dated Friday, April 21, 1861. William Lloyd Garrison's weekly newspaper appealed to the morality of its readers to abolish African American slavery. In the center is an image of Jesus Christ and the text, "I come to break the bonds of the oppressor."

wrecked the assumption of "Garrisonians" that moral righteousness would trump evil and that their fellow Americans would listen to reason.

Founding of the American Anti-Slavery Society

Garrison's unflagging efforts helped make the impossible—abolition—seem possible. Two wealthy New York City merchants, Arthur and Lewis Tappan, provided financial support, and in 1833, they joined with Garrison and a group of Quaker reformers, free Blacks, and evangelicals to organize the American Anti-Slavery Society (AASS).

That same year, Parliament freed some 800,000 enslaved colonial peoples throughout the British Empire by passing the Emancipation Act, which paid slaveholders to give up their "human property." In 1835, the Tappans hired revivalist Charles G. Finney to head the anti-slavery faculty at Oberlin, a new college in northern Ohio that would be the first to admit Black students.

In 1835, the AASS began flooding the South with anti-slavery pamphlets and newspapers. The materials enraged southern slaveholders. A Louisiana community offered a $50,000 reward for the capture of the "notorious abolitionist, Arthur Tappan, of New York," and post offices throughout the South began destroying "anti-slavery propaganda."

By 1840, some 160,000 people belonged to the American Anti-Slavery Society, which stressed that "slaveholding is a heinous crime in the sight of God, and that the duty, safety, and best interests of all concerned, require its *immediate abandonment*." Even more radically, the AASS argued that Blacks should have full social and civil rights.

David Walker

The most radical figure among the Garrisonians was David Walker, a free Black who owned a used clothing store in Boston serving mostly seamen. In 1829, he published his *Appeal to the Colored Citizens of the World*, a pamphlet that denounced the hypocrisy of White Christians in the South for defending slavery, calling them "an unjust, jealous, unmerciful, avaricious, and bloodthirsty" people. He urged enslaved people to revolt. "The whites want slaves, and want us for their slaves," Walker warned, "but some of them will curse the day they ever saw us." Walker challenged African Americans, enslaved and free, to use the "crushing arm of power" to gain their freedom. "Woe, woe will be to you," he threatened Whites, "if we have to obtain our freedom by fighting."

Walker's *Appeal* compels Mississippi to censor incendiary texts

Copies of Walker's *Appeal* were secretly carried to the South by Black sailors who had frequented his shop, but Whites in major cities seized the "vile" pamphlet. In 1830, the state of Mississippi outlawed efforts to "print, write, circulate, or put forth . . . any book, paper, magazine, pamphlet, handbill or circular" intended to arouse the "colored population" by "exciting riots and rebellion." By then, however, David Walker had been discovered dead near the doorway of his Boston shop. His murderer was never found.

A Split in the Movement

As the abolitionist movement spread, debates over tactics intensified. The Garrisonians, who felt that slavery had corrupted all aspects of life, embraced every important reform movement of the day: abolition, temperance, pacifism, vegetarianism, and women's rights. William Lloyd Garrison's unconventional religious ideas and social ideals led him to break with the established Protestant churches, which, to his mind, were in league with slavery, as was the federal government. The U.S. Constitution, he charged, was "a covenant with death and an agreement with hell."

Other reformers saw American society as fundamentally sound and concentrated on purging it of slavery. Garrison struck them as an unrealistic fanatic whose radicalism hurt the cause. The Tappan brothers eventually broke with Garrison over religion. They argued that the anti-slavery movement should be led only by men of "evangelical piety" and declared that the Unitarians and Universalists in New England failed to meet that standard.

The Grimké Sisters

A showdown between the rival anti-slavery camps erupted in 1840 over the issue of women's rights, with the scandalous activities of the Grimké sisters serving as the catalyst. Sarah and Angelina Grimké, born to a wealthy South Carolina family, grew up being served by enslaved people. In 1821, shortly after her father's death, Sarah moved from Charleston to Philadelphia, joined the Society of Friends (Quakers), and renounced slavery. Angelina soon followed her, and in 1835, the sisters joined the abolitionist movement. After they appealed to southern Christian women to end slavery, the mayor of Charleston told their mother that they would be jailed if they returned home.

THE GRIMKÉ SISTERS After moving away from their slaveholding family, Sarah *(left)* and Angelina *(right)* Grimké devoted themselves to abolitionism and feminism.

The Grimké sisters traveled widely throughout the North, speaking first to audiences of women and eventually to groups of both sexes. Their unconventional (promiscuous) behavior in speaking to mixed-gender audiences prompted sharp criticism from ministers in the anti-slavery movement. Catharine Beecher reminded the sisters that women occupied "a subordinate relation in society to the other sex" and that they should limit their activities to the "domestic and social circle."

Uniting abolition of slavery with women's rights

Angelina Grimké firmly rejected such arguments: "The investigation of the rights of the slave has led me to a better understanding of my own [rights]." For centuries, she noted, women had been raised to view themselves as "inferior creatures." Now, she insisted, "It is a woman's right to have a voice in all laws and regulations by which she is to be governed, whether in church or in state." Soon, Angelina and her sister began linking their efforts to free the enslaved with their desire to free women from male domination. "Men and women are CREATED EQUAL!" Sarah Grimké said. "Whatever is right for man to do is right for woman." Sarah asked "no favors for my sex. All I ask . . . [of men] is that they will take their feet off our necks and permit us to stand upright."

The Role of Women

The debate over the role of women in the anti-slavery movement exploded at the American Anti-Slavery Society's meeting in 1840, where the Garrisonians convinced delegates that women should participate equally in the organization. The Tappans and their supporters walked out and formed the American and Foreign Anti-Slavery Society.

A third faction of the American Anti-Slavery Society had grown skeptical that the nonviolent "moral suasion" promoted by Garrison would

Formation of the Liberty Party (1840)

ever lead to abolition. They decided that political action was the most effective way to pursue their goal. In 1840, activists formed the Liberty party to elect an American president who would restrict the spread of slavery. The party's presidential nominee, James Gillespie Birney, was a former Alabama slaveholder turned anti-slavery activist. His slogan was "Vote as you pray and pray as you vote." The platform called not for immediate abolition but for banning slavery in the western territories and the District of Columbia.

In the 1840 election, Birney polled only 7,000 votes. In 1844, however, he would win 60,000. Thereafter, an anti-slavery third-party candidate contested every national election until the Thirteenth Amendment officially ended slavery in 1865.

Black Anti-Slavery Activity

Although many Whites worked to end slavery, most of them, unlike William Lloyd Garrison, still insisted that Blacks were socially inferior, and many expected free Blacks to take a backseat in the abolitionist movement.

Yet free African Americans were crucial in transforming the struggle against slavery into a more ambitious fight against racial discrimination, which remained widespread. Even free Blacks were barred from public places—churches, schools, hotels, railroad stations, and cemeteries. As Garrison reported from Boston, "Hardly any doors but those of our state prisons were open to our colored brethren."

William Wells Brown Much of the energy and appeal of the abolitionist movement derived from the compelling testimonies provided by formerly enslaved people, such as William Wells Brown, a freedom seeker from Kentucky; Frederick Douglass, who had escaped from Maryland; and Sojourner Truth, a freedom seeker from New York. They became the most effective critics of the South's "peculiar institution."

Brown was just twenty years old when he escaped from his owner, a steamboat pilot on the Ohio River. An Ohio Quaker named Wells Brown provided shelter to the freedom seeker, and Brown adopted the man's name while forging a new identity as a free man. He settled in Cleveland, Ohio, where he was a dockworker. He married, had three children, and helped freedom seekers cross the border into Canada. By 1842, Brown had learned to read and write, begun to publish columns in abolitionist newspapers, and was in great demand as a speaker at anti-slavery meetings. In 1847, he moved to Boston, where the Massachusetts Anti-Slavery Society hired him as a traveling lecturer.

Narrative of William W. Brown (1847)

That same year, the organization published Brown's autobiography, *Narrative of William W. Brown, A Fugitive Slave, Written by Himself*, which became a best seller. Brown gave thousands of speeches calling for an end to slavery and equality for both Blacks and women. He stressed that African Americans were "endowed with those intellectual and amiable qualities which adorn and dignify human nature."

FREDERICK DOUGLASS AND SOJOURNER TRUTH Douglass *(left)* escaped slavery and came to Massachusetts, where he began his career as a traveling speaker and advocate for abolitionism, eventually earning enough money to purchase his freedom and found the *North Star,* an abolitionist newspaper. Sojourner Truth *(right)* was also a captivating speaker and toured the North advocating for abolitionism and women's rights.

Frederick Douglass Frederick Douglass was an even more effective spokesman for abolitionism. Born into slavery in Maryland to a mother he rarely saw, Douglass suspected that his White owner was also his father. At age eight he was sent to Baltimore to be a house servant. There he taught himself to read. When Douglass was about fifteen years old, his owner relocated him again, this time to a plantation to strip him of his "rebelliousness," but the experience only hardened Douglass's resolve to escape.

Back in Baltimore, Douglass was rented out yet again, this time to a shipyard. There, he plotted his escape. After disguising himself as a sailor and forging documents certifying that he was a free Black, he escaped from Maryland and made his way to Massachusetts, where he began speaking at anti-slavery meetings in Black churches. The Massachusetts Anti-Slavery Society recruited him as a traveling speaker, sending him across New England and west to Ohio and Indiana. At numerous abolitionist gatherings, he recounted his painful encounters with "the whip, the chain, the gag, the thumbscrew, the bloodhound, the stocks, and all the other bloody paraphernalia of the slave system." Through his writings and presentations, Douglass became the best-known man of color in America and the courageous voice of the abolitionist movement. "I appear before the immense assembly this evening as a thief and a robber," he told a Massachusetts group in 1842. "I stole this head, these limbs, this body from my master, and ran off with them."

Narrative of the Life of Frederick Douglass (1845)

After publishing his *Narrative of the Life of Frederick Douglass, An American Slave* (1845), Douglass left for an extended lecture tour of the British Isles. He returned two years later with enough money to purchase his freedom. He then started an abolitionist newspaper for Blacks, the *North Star*, in Rochester, New York. He named the newspaper after the star that freedom seekers used to guide them toward freedom.

Sojourner Truth African American women were immensely influential in the abolitionist movement. Sojourner Truth was born to enslaved parents in upstate New York in 1797. She was given the name Isabella "Bell" Hardenbergh but renamed herself in 1843 after experiencing a conversation with God, who told her "to travel up and down the land" preaching "the truth" against slavery.

Enslaved until freed in 1827, Truth spoke with conviction about the evils of the "peculiar institution" as well as the inequality of women. She traveled throughout the North during the 1840s and 1850s. As she told the Ohio Women's Rights Convention in 1851, "I have plowed, and planted, and gathered into barns, and no man could head me—and ar'n't I a woman? I have borne thirteen children, and seen 'em mos' all sold off into slavery, and when I cried out with a mother's grief, none but Jesus heard—and ar'n't I a woman?"

Through such compelling testimony, Sojourner Truth tapped the distinctive energies that women brought to reformist causes. "If the first woman God ever made was strong enough to turn the world upside down all alone," she concluded in her address to the Ohio gathering, "these women together ought to be able to turn it back, and get it right side up again!"

The Underground Railroad

Between 1810 and 1850, tens of thousands of enslaved people in the South fled north. Freedom seekers would make their way, usually at night, from one "station," or safe house, to the next. The organizations and the systems of safe houses and shelters in the border states such as Maryland and Kentucky (and farther north) were referred to as the **Underground Railroad**. The "conductors" helping the freedom seekers included freeborn Blacks, White abolitionists, formerly enslaved people, and Native Americans. Unitarians, Quakers, Presbyterians, Methodists, and Baptists also participated.

In Philadelphia, William Still, a free Black who was a clerk at the Pennsylvania Society for the Abolition of Slavery, sheltered freedom seekers as they made their way to Canada. In the fourteen years he worked as a conductor for the Underground Railroad, he helped almost 800 freedom seekers. He later published an account of his efforts, explaining, "It was my good fortune to lend a helping hand to the weary travelers flying from the land of bondage."

Underground Railroad A secret system of routes, safe houses, and abolitionists that helped freedom seekers reach freedom in the North.

A few courageous people of color returned to the South to organize more escapes. Harriet Tubman, the most celebrated member of the Underground Railroad, was born an enslaved person on Maryland's Eastern Shore in 1820 but escaped to Philadelphia in 1849, traveling some 90 miles on foot across Delaware. "I was free," she recalled, "but there was no one to welcome me to the land of freedom. I was a stranger in a strange land." Dressed like a man, she would return to the South nineteen times to help some 300 freedom seekers, including her parents and brothers, and "never lost a passenger." She carried a pistol, and when a freedom seeker would panic and have second thoughts about escaping, she would pull out her gun, point it at the ambivalent runaway, and say, "You'll be free or die a slave."

During the Civil War, Tubman worked as a nurse, a Northern spy and a scout, leading Union gunboats in the Carolinas to liberate some 750 enslaved Confederates. By then, slave owners in Maryland were demanding her arrest, dead or alive, and placed a $40,000 bounty on her head. The fearless Tubman explained, "There was two things I had a right to, liberty or death: if I could not have one, I would have the other."

Reactions to Abolitionism

Elijah P. Lovejoy Despite the growing efforts of anti-slavery organizations, racism remained widespread in the North. Abolitionist speakers confronted hostile White crowds who disliked Blacks or found anti-slavery agitation bad for business. In 1837, a mob in Illinois killed Elijah P. Lovejoy, editor of an anti-slavery newspaper, giving the movement a martyr to the causes of both abolition and freedom of the press.

Lovejoy had begun his career as a Presbyterian minister in New England. After receiving a "sign by God" to focus on the "destruction of slavery," he moved to St. Louis, in slaveholding Missouri, where his newspaper denounced alcohol, Catholicism, and slavery. When a pro-slavery mob destroyed his printing office, he moved across the Mississippi River to a warehouse in Alton, Illinois, where he tried to start an anti-slavery society. White mobs, however, twice more destroyed his printing press. When a new press arrived, Lovejoy and several supporters armed themselves and took up defensive positions.

Mob violence against abolitionists

On November 7, 1837, White racists began hurling stones and firing shots into the building. One of Lovejoy's allies fired back, killing a rioter. The mob then set fire to the warehouse. A shotgun blast killed Lovejoy, and his murder aroused a frenzy of indignation. John Quincy Adams said the murder "sent a shock as of any earthquake throughout this continent." In Illinois, young Abraham Lincoln noted that Lovejoy's murder was an "ill omen," for the "mob violence" threatened America's core values: "liberty and equal rights."

Abigail Kelley The powerful appeal of abolitionism and the broader reform impulse is illustrated in the colorful life of Abigail "Abby" Kelley.

A teacher born in Pelham, Massachusetts, in 1811, she initially became a Grahamite, giving up coffee, alcohol, meat, and tea in favor of vegetables and Graham crackers. Soon thereafter, she attended a lecture by William Lloyd Garrison and embraced abolitionism, joining the Female Anti-Slavery Society. In 1837, she wrote her sister that she was supporting a variety of "moral enterprises—Grahamism, Abolition, and Peace."

Abigail Kelley becomes an officer for the American Anti-Slavery Society

In 1840, Kelley became the first woman elected an officer in the American Anti-Slavery Society. Many male abolitionists were furious. One of them described Kelley as one of those "women of masculine minds and aggressive tendencies . . . who cannot be satisfied in domestic life." The prejudice she experienced among male officers revealed to her that she and other women "were manacled [chained] *ourselves*."

During the 1850s, Kelley, while still a passionate abolitionist, began to champion women's rights and temperance. She spoke at the fourth national woman's rights convention in Cleveland. Lucy Stone, one of the women's rights leaders, called Kelley a heroine who "stood in the thick of the fight for the slaves, and at the same time, she hewed out that path over which women are now walking toward their equal political rights."

The Defense of Slavery

Attempts to justify slavery with the Bible

The growing strength and visibility of the abolitionist movement, coupled with the profitability of cotton, prompted southerners to launch an aggressive defense of slavery. During the 1830s and after, pro-slavery leaders worked out an elaborate rationale for what they considered the benefits of slavery. The Bible was their favorite weapon. Had not the patriarchs of the Hebrew Bible held people in bondage? Had not Saint Paul advised servants to obey their masters and told a runaway servant to return to his master? And had not Jesus remained silent on slavery?

Soon, bolder arguments emerged. In February 1837, South Carolina's John C. Calhoun told the Senate that slavery was "good—a great good," rooted in the Bible. He asserted that the "savage" Africans brought to America "had never existed in so comfortable, so respectable, or so civilized a condition, as that which is now enjoyed in the Southern states." If slavery were abolished, Calhoun warned, the principle of White racial supremacy would be compromised.

One of Calhoun's friends, James Henry Hammond, was the South's loudest defender of slavery. Like Calhoun, a South Carolina planter, Hammond proclaimed that the people he enslaved were "happy, content . . . and utterly incapable, from intellectual weakness, ever to give us any trouble by their aspirations." He repudiated the "ridiculously absurd . . . dogma of Mr. Jefferson, that 'all men are born equal.'"

Hammond, Calhoun, and others also claimed that Blacks were naturally shiftless, and if freed, they would be a danger to themselves and to others. White workers, on the other hand, feared the competition for jobs if enslaved people were freed.

The increasingly heated debate over slavery drove a deep wedge between North and South. In 1831, William Lloyd Garrison predicted that an eventual "separation between the free and slave States" was "unavoidable." By mid-century, many Americans had decided that southern slavery was an abomination that should not be allowed into the western territories. The militant reformers who were determined to prevent slavery from expanding outside the South came to be called Free Soilers. Their crusade would reach a fiery climax in the Civil War.

Reviewing the CORE OBJECTIVES | INQUIZITIVE

■ **Religious Developments** Starting in the late eighteenth century, *Unitarians* and *Universalists* in New England challenged the notion of predestination by arguing that all people could receive salvation, not just a select few. The evangelical preachers of the *Second Great Awakening* generated fiery *frontier revivals*. The more democratic sects, such as Baptists and Methodists, which promoted the idea of free-will salvation, gained huge numbers of converts, including women and African Americans. Religion went hand in hand with reform in the burned-over district in western New York, which was also the birthplace of several religious movements, including the Church of Jesus Christ of Latter-day Saints (often called the *Mormon Church*).

■ **Transcendentalists** Transcendentalists were poets, writers, artists, ministers, and philosophers who embraced a moral and spiritual idealism (Romanticism) in reaction to scientific rationalism and Christian orthodoxy. They sought to "transcend" reason and the material world and encourage more independent thought and reflection. At the same time, *transcendentalism* influenced the works of novelists, essayists, and poets, who created a uniquely American literature. A cultural nationalism emerged with political ideals for a more moral American society.

■ **Social Reform Movements** The most widespread reform movement was for *temperance*, the elimination of excessive drinking. At the same time, the dominant *cult of domesticity* celebrated a "woman's sphere" in the home and argued that young women should be trained not for the workplace but in the domestic arts—managing a kitchen, running a household, and nurturing the children. However, the rise of an urban middle class offered growing numbers of women more time to devote to societal concerns. Social reformers—many of them women—left their homes to eradicate social evils. Many were also active in reforming prisons and asylums. At the *Seneca Falls Convention* (1848), social reformers launched the women's rights movement with the *Declaration of Rights and Sentiments* (1848). In many parts of the country, social reformers called for greater access to education through free *public schools* for the nation's young. One educational reformer, Horace Mann, said that public school teaching was a way for women to become "mothers away from home" for the students. Amid the pervasive climate of reform during the early nineteenth century, more than 100 *utopian communities* were established, including the Shakers and the Oneida Community.

■ **Anti-Slavery Movement** Northern opponents of slavery promoted several solutions, including the *American Colonization Society*'s call for gradual emancipation and the deportation of free African Americans to colonies in Africa. *Abolitionism* emerged in the 1830s, demanding an immediate and complete end of slavery. Some abolitionists went even further, calling for full social and political equality among the races, although they disagreed over tactics.

Abolitionist efforts in the North provoked a strong reaction among southern Whites, stirring fears for their safety and resentment of interference. Yet many northerners shared the belief in the racial inferiority of Africans and were hostile to the tactics and message of the abolitionists. African Americans in the North joined with abolitionists to create an *Underground Railroad*, a network of safe havens and courageous abolitionists, both White and Black, which helped freedom seekers escape their bondage in the South.

KEY TERMS

Unitarians *p. 429*

Universalists *p. 429*

Second Great Awakening *p. 429*

frontier revivals *p. 431*

Mormon Church *p. 435*

transcendentalism *p. 438*

temperance *p. 445*

cult of domesticity *p. 447*

Seneca Falls Convention (1848) *p. 448*

Declaration of Rights and Sentiments (1848) *p. 448*

public schools *p. 449*

utopian communities *p. 450*

American Colonization Society (ACS) *p. 453*

abolitionism *p. 454*

Underground Railroad *p. 460*

CHRONOLOGY

1779	Universalist Church founded in Massachusetts
1816	Auburn Penitentiary opens in New York
1826	Ministers organize the American Society for the Promotion of Temperance
1830	Percentage of American churchgoers has doubled since 1800
	Joseph Smith reveals the Book of Mormon
1830–1831	Charles G. Finney leads revivals in upstate New York
1831	William Lloyd Garrison begins publishing *The Liberator*
1833	American Anti-Slavery Society is founded
1836	Transcendental Club holds its first meeting
1837	Abolitionist editor Elijah P. Lovejoy is murdered
1840	Abolitionists form the Liberty party
1845	*Narrative of the Life of Frederick Douglass* is published
1846	Mormons, led by Brigham Young, make the difficult trek to Utah
1848	At the Seneca Falls Convention, feminists issue the Declaration of Rights and Sentiments
	John Humphrey Noyes establishes the Oneida Community
1851	Sojourner Truth delivers her famous speech "Ar'n't I a Woman?"
1854	Henry David Thoreau's *Walden, or Life in the Woods* is published

INQUIZITIVE

Go to InQuizitive to see what you've learned—and learn what you've missed—with personalized feedback along the way.

THINKING LIKE A HISTORIAN

DEBATING Separate Spheres

Politics and present-day events often influence *historiography,* the study of how historians develop contrasting interpretations over time. In the 1960s, *social* history gained popularity as scholars sought to tell the story of previously unrepresented groups—the poor, women, minorities. Three concepts of great importance to social historians are *race, class,* and *gender.* Part 3, *"An Expansive Nation,"* shows how historians use these concepts to debate the importance of the "separate spheres" ideology. In the first half of the nineteenth century, before the Civil War, the separate spheres ideology promoted separate and distinct roles for women and men. The female sphere was "domestic," within the home, while the male sphere was centered on economic and political life.

This exercise has two tasks:

PART 1: Compare the two secondary sources on women and separate spheres.
PART 2: Using primary sources, evaluate the arguments of the two secondary sources.

PART I Comparing Secondary Sources

Below are secondary sources from two social historians. The first is from Catherine Clinton of Queens University in Belfast, Northern Ireland; the second, from Nancy Hewitt of Rutgers, the State University of New Jersey. Both Clinton and Hewitt use race, class, and gender analysis to assess how the dominant tradition of separate spheres impacted women and how women responded.

In comparing the views of these two scholars, answer the following questions. Use specific examples in the selections to support your answers.

- What is the subject of each article?
- What classes of women does each author highlight?
- According to each author, how did the ideology of separate spheres impact women?
- In what ways does each author use race, class, and gender to construct her argument?

Secondary Source 1

Catherine Clinton, "The Ties That Bind" (1984)

The nineteenth century ushered in a social as well as an economic revolution for American women. The refinement of middle-class ideology profoundly affected females during the antebellum [pre–Civil War] era. . . . The creation of the cult of domesticity, the redefinition of the home as women's domain, was a delicate process designed to channel women's contributions into a proper course. . . .

[I]nstead of liberty and equality, subordination and restriction were drummed into women, a refrain inherited from the colonial era. Women's only reward was lavish exaltation of their vital and unmatchable contributions to the civic state as mothers. This rejuvenated ethic was accompanied by a confinement to the domestic sphere.

Once segregated from men by the confines of a new ideological order, women set about turning their liabilities into assets. Forbidden traditional pathways to success, post-Revolutionary women pursued other means of achieving esteem and influence within their society. These alternatives were pioneered by women who were in search of new influence but who refrained from invading the male domain—not for the sake of modesty, but rather as a strategy. . . .

Woman's domain was, despite confinement, expansive. She was charged with the moral, spiritual, and physical well-being of her entire family. . . . She was supervisor of the education of her children, tender of the heath, and the symbol of the home. These indispensable functions, although primarily carried out within the home, were not restricted to it. Women perceived that they might extend female jurisdiction into the public and hitherto exclusively male realm by using their "domestic" role as a lever—wedging themselves into positions of power, however limited, through exploitation of their domesticity. In the early decades of the century, creative women took their rather circumscribed nooks and crannies, within the culture, and turned them into springboards. Women's talents and contributions were soon apparent within the larger social arena.

Source: Clinton, Catherine. "The Ties That Bind." Chap. 3 in *The Other Civil War: American Women in the Nineteenth Century*. New York: Hill & Wang, 1984. 40–42.

Secondary Source 2

Nancy A. Hewitt, "Beyond the Search for Sisterhood: American Women's History in the 1980s" (1985)

The bonds that encircled past generations of women were initially perceived as restrictive, arising from female victimization at the hands of patriarchs in such institutions as medicine, education, the church, the state, and the family. Historians soon concluded, however, that oppression was a double-edged sword; the counterpart of subordination in or exclusion from male-dominated domains was inclusion in an all-female enclave. The concept of womanhood, it soon appeared, "bound women together even as it bound them down."

The formative works in American women's history have focused on the formation of these separate sexual spheres, particularly among the emerging urban bourgeoisie in the first half of the nineteenth century. Reified in prescriptive literature, realized in daily life, and ritualized in female collectivities, this 'woman's sphere' came to be seen as the foundation of women's culture and community in antebellum [pre–Civil War] America. . . . The community that has become the cornerstone of North American women's history was discovered within the Victorian middle class. . . . Yet evidence from the lives of slaves, mill operatives, miners' wives, immigrants, and southern industrial workers as well as from "true women" indicates that there was no single woman's culture or sphere. There was a culturally dominant definition of sexual spheres promulgated by an economically, politically, and socially dominant group.

That definition was firmly grounded in the sexual division of labor appropriate to that class, just as other definitions developed based on the sexual division of labor in other class and racial groups. All these divisions were characterized by sufficient sex-stereotyping to assure the formation of distinct female circles of labor and distinct rituals and values rooted in that laboring experience.

To date historians have focused on the parallels in the establishment of women's spheres across classes, races, and ethnic groups and have asserted certain commonalities among them, assuming their common origin in the modernization of society during the nineteenth century.

A closer examination now reveals that no such universal sisterhood existed, and in fact that the development of a sense of community among various classes of women served as a barrier to an all-embracing bond of womanhood. Finally, it is now clear that privileged women were willing to wield their sex-specific influence in ways that, intentionally or unintentionally, exploited other women in the name of "true-womanhood."

Source: Hewitt, Nancy A. "Beyond the Search for Sisterhood: American Women's History in the 1980s." *Social History* 10 (1985): 299–321.

PART II Using Primary Sources to Evaluate Secondary Sources

When historians are faced with conflicting interpretations of the past, they often look at primary source material as part of the process of evaluating the different arguments. Below are three excerpts from political statements by three remarkable but very different women. The first is from Lucretia Mott, a middle-class and highly educated woman who became a prominent Quaker speaker, leading abolitionist, and co-organizer of the first women's rights convention, the Seneca Falls Convention. The second excerpt is from Sojourner Truth, a formerly enslaved woman and leading abolitionist. The final excerpt is from Harriett Robinson, who at the age of ten began work in the textile mills of Lowell, Massachusetts. Robinson went on to write her autobiography and was involved in the women's suffrage movement.

While not all these documents directly address the term *separate spheres*, each addresses women's place in American society.

Carefully read each of the primary sources and answer the following questions. Decide which of the primary source documents support or refute Clinton's and Hewitt's arguments about women's separate sphere. Be sure to identify which specific components of each historian's argument the documents support or refute.

- How did the ideology of separate spheres impact the lives of these three women?
- Which of the primary sources do you think Clinton and Hewitt would find most useful, and how might the authors use them to support their arguments?
- Which of the secondary sources do you think is best supported by the primary source evidence?
- What have these primary sources taught you about using race, class, and gender in historical analysis?

Primary Source 1

Lucretia Mott, *Discourse on Women* (1849)

This age is notable for its works of mercy and benevolence—for the efforts that are made to reform the inebriate and the degraded, to relieve the oppressed and the suffering. Women as well as men are interested in these works of justice and mercy. They are efficient co-workers, their talents are called into profitable exercise, their labors are effective in each department of reform. The blessing to the merciful, to the peacemaker is equal to man and to woman. It is greatly to be deplored, now that she is increasingly qualified for usefulness, that any view should be presented, calculated to retard her labors of love.

Why should not woman seek to be a reformer? . . . [I]f she is to fear to exercise her reason, and her noblest powers, lest she should be thought to "attempt to act the man," and not "acknowledge his supremacy"; if she is to be satisfied with the narrow sphere assigned her by man, nor aspire to a higher, lest she should transcend the bounds of female delicacy; truly it is a mournful prospect for woman. We would admit all the difference, that our great and beneficent Creator has made, in the relation of man and woman, nor would we seek to disturb this relation; but we deny that the present position of woman, is her true sphere of usefulness: nor will she attain to this sphere, until the disabilities and disadvantages, religious, civil, and social, which impede her progress, are removed out of her way. These restrictions have enervated her mind and paralyzed her powers. . . .

So far from her "ambition leading her to attempt to act the man," she needs all the encouragement she can receive, by the removal of obstacles from her path, in order that she may become a "true woman." As it is desirable that man should act a manly and generous part, not "mannish," so let woman be urged to exercise a dignified and womanly bearing, not womanish. Let her cultivate all the graces and proper accomplishments of her sex, but let not these degenerate into a kind of effeminacy, in which she is satisfied to be the mere plaything or toy of society, content with her outward adornings, and with the tone of flattery and fulsome adulation too often addressed to her. True, nature has made a difference in her configuration, her physical strength, her voice, etc.—and we ask no change, we are satisfied with nature. But how has neglect and mismanagement increased this difference! It is our duty to develop these natural powers, by suitable exercise, so that they may be strengthened "by reason of use."

Source: Mott, Lucretia. *Discourse on Women*. Philadelphia, Penn.: T. B. Peterson, 1850.

Primary Source 2

Sojourner Truth, "And Ar'n't I a Woman?" (1851)

And ar'n't I a woman? Look at me! Look at my arm! (*And she bared her right arm to the shoulder, showing her tremendous muscular power.*) I have plowed, and planted, and gathered into barns, and no man could head [surpass] me—and ar'n't I a woman? I could work as much and eat as much as a man when I could get it and bear de lash as well—and ar'n't I a woman? I have borne thirteen children, and seen 'em mos' all sold off to slavery, and when I cried out with my mother's grief, none but Jesus heard me—and ar'n't I a woman? . . . If my cup won't hold but a pint, and your'n holds a quart, wouldn't ye be mean not to let me have my little half-measure full? . . . He say women can't have as much rights as men, 'cause Christ wan't a woman! Whar did your Christ come from? . . . From God and a woman! Man had nothin' to do with Him.

Source: Truth, Sojourner. "And Ar'n't I a Woman?" (Speech at the Ohio Women's Rights Convention, 1851, Akron, Ohio). *History of Woman Suffrage*. Vol. 1, *1848–1861*. Edited by Elizabeth Cady Stanton, Susan B. Anthony, and Matilda Joslyn Gage. Rochester, NY: Susan B. Anthony, 1887.

Primary Source 3

Harriett H. Robinson, *Loom and Spindle or Life among the Early Mill Girls* (1898)

One of the first strikes of cotton-factory operatives that ever took place in this country was that in Lowell, in October,

1836. When it was announced that the wages were to be cut down, great indignation was felt, and it was decided to strike, en masse. This was done. The mills were shut down, and the girls went in procession from their several corporations to the "grove" on Chapel Hill, and listened to "incendiary" speeches from early labor reformers. One of the girls stood on a pump, and gave vent to the feelings of her companions in a neat speech, declaring that it was their duty to resist all attempts at cutting down the wages. This was the first time a woman had spoken in public in Lowell, and the event caused surprise and consternation among her audience. . . . It was estimated that as many as twelve or fifteen hundred girls turned out, and walked in procession through the streets. They had neither flags nor music, but sang songs, a favorite (but rather inappropriate) one being a parody on "I won't be a nun."

Oh ! isn't it a pity, such a pretty girl as I—

Should be sent to the factory to pine away and die?

Oh ! I cannot be a slave,

I will not be a slave,

For I'm so fond of liberty

That I cannot be a slave.

Source: Robinson, Harriett H. *Loom and Spindle or Life among the Early Mill Girls*. New York: Thomas Y. Crowell & Company, 1898.

unanimously at 1.15 o'clock, P. M., Dec
20th, 1860.
AN ORDINANCE
olve the Union between the State of South Caroli
States united with her under the compact entitle
titution of the United States of America."
ple of the State of South Carolina, in Convention assembled, do declare and
reby declared and ordained,
e Ordinance adopted by us in Convention, on the twenty-third day of
Lord one thousand seven hundred and eighty-eight, whereby the Constitu
tes of America was ratified, and also, all Acts and parts of Acts of t
FOR SALE HERE
AN EDITION FOR THE MILLION, COMPLETE IN 1 Vol., PRICE 37 1-2 CENT
" " IN GERMAN, IN 1 Vol., PRICE 50 CENTS.
" " IN 2 Vols., CLOTH, 6 PLATES, PRICE $1.50.
SUPERB ILLUSTRATED EDITION, IN 1 Vol., WITH 153 ENGRAVINGS,
PRICES FROM $2.50 TO $5.00.
ON DEMAND, THE
UNITED STATES
Promise to pay to the Bearer

A House Divided and Rebuilt

PART 4

During the first half of the nineteenth century, America's population and its boundaries continued to expand. In 1800, there were slightly more than 5 million residents; by 1850, that number had soared to 23 million. Adventurous people continued to move westward, where vast lands lured farmers, ranchers, and miners. Alexis de Tocqueville, a French visitor who was a keen observer of American life, noted that "western migration is an extraordinary phenomenon, in which Americans band together in search of fortune." He added that this massive migration westward benefited the nation "because it prevents the population from being concentrated in only a few places."

By the end of the 1840s, the United States had expanded its territory from Texas to California and the Pacific Northwest. Neither Mexican Americans, nor Native Americans, nor Chinese immigrants could withstand the assault on their lands and civil rights. In the process of displacing Mexicans, abusing Chinese, and exterminating Native Americans, Americans amassed a continental empire from the Atlantic to the Pacific.

This surge of territorial expansion was a mixed blessing, however. Managing the western territories became the nation's flashpoint issue. The economic and political differences among the nation's three distinctive regions—North, South, and West—grew even more explosive.

During the first half of the nineteenth century, a series of political compromises had glossed over the fundamental issue of slavery's future, but growing numbers of activists opposed efforts to extend slavery into the western territories acquired from Mexico. Moreover, the 1850s witnessed the emergence of a new generation of national politicians who were less willing to compromise over the volatile issue.

The continuing debate over allowing slavery into new western territories eventually led people to decide that the nation, as Abraham Lincoln maintained in 1858, could not survive half enslaved and half free.

It was Lincoln's election in 1860 that prompted southern states to secede from the Union and form the Confederate States of America. Their "peculiar institution" of slavery had to be preserved at all costs. When Confederate cannons fired on Fort Sumter in Charleston Harbor and forced its surrender, northerners, led by President Lincoln, mobilized for a civil war to restore the Union. The war would take the lives of more than 700,000 people in four years of fighting and transform the nation in the process.

The Northern victory in 1865 restored the Union and helped accelerate America's transformation into a modern urban-industrial superpower. A national consciousness began to replace the sectional divisions of the prewar era, and a Republican-led Congress passed legislation to promote industrial and commercial development and western expansion. In the process, the United States began to leave behind the Jeffersonian dream of remaining a decentralized agrarian republic.

The Civil War ended slavery, but the status of the freed African Americans remained uncertain. Although legally free, few formerly enslaved people had money, property, homes, education, or training. While the Fourteenth Amendment (1868) guaranteed the civil rights of African Americans and the Fifteenth Amendment (1870) declared that Black men could vote, southerners often ignored the new federal laws. At the same time, African Americans continued to suffer social abuse and physical harm at the hands of White supremacists.

Although former Confederate leaders lost the right to vote and hold office, they continued to exercise considerable authority in political and economic matters. In 1877, when the last federal troops withdrew from the South, former Confederates declared themselves “redeemed” from the stain of Northern military occupation. By the end of the nineteenth century, most states of the former Confederacy had developed a system of legal discrimination against Blacks that re-created many aspects of slavery.

EMIGRANTS CROSSING THE PLAINS, OR THE OREGON TRAIL **(1869)** German American painter Albert Bierstadt captures the majestic sights of the frontier, though the transcontinental trek was also grueling and bleak for many pioneers.

CHAPTER 13

Western Expansion and Southern Secession

1830–1861

During the 1840s and after, waves of enterprising Americans moved westward. By 1860, some 4.3 million people had crossed the mile-wide Mississippi River and spread out across the Great Plains, over the Rocky Mountains, and along the Pacific coast.

Westward expansion was especially crucial to southerners, many of whom wanted access to inexpensive new lands on which they could grow cotton using enslaved workers. Southerners had long enjoyed disproportionate political power because the U.S. Constitution included enslaved people as part of the population in determining the number of congressional seats for each state. Nine of the first twelve presidents were from the South, and southerners held most congressional leadership positions.

Southern political influence, however, began to wane as the population in the industrializing Midwest and Northeast grew more rapidly than population in the South. Southerners wanted new western states to boost pro-southern representation in Congress and thus ensure that northerners could never abolish slavery. Such motives made the addition of new western

CORE OBJECTIVES INQUIZITIVE

1. Explain how, why, and where Americans moved west of the Mississippi River during the 1830s and 1840s.
2. Examine the impact of the Mexican-American War on national politics.
3. Describe how the federal government tried to resolve the issue of slavery in the western territories during the 1850s.
4. Analyze the appeal of the Republican party to northern voters and how it led to Abraham Lincoln's victory in the 1860 presidential contest.
5. Explain why seven southern states seceded from the Union shortly after Lincoln's election in 1860.

territories a flashpoint of sectional debate. Would they be slave states or free?

People migrated west mainly for economic reasons, usually fueled by gold fever or land lust. Trappers, farmers, miners, ministers, merchants, hunters, ranchers, teachers, servants, and prostitutes, among others, headed west. Others—such as the Mormons and Christian missionary organizations—sought religious freedom and the chance to win converts to their faith.

The Indians and Hispanics who had long inhabited the region were swept aside by the onslaught of Americans, an onslaught enabled by presidents and members of Congress eager to complete the nation's expansion to the Pacific coast.

CORE **OBJECTIVE**

1. Explain how, why, and where Americans moved west of the Mississippi River during the 1830s and 1840s.

Moving West

In 1845, a New York newspaper editor named John L. O'Sullivan gave a catchy name to America's aggressive spirit of westward expansion. "Our manifest destiny," he wrote, "is to overspread the continent allotted by Providence for the free development of our yearly multiplying millions."

The idea of a "**manifest destiny**" implied that the United States had a God-given mission to extend its Christian republic and capitalist economy from the Atlantic to the Pacific—and beyond. It flattered American vanity and offered a powerful, if self-serving, religious justification for expansion at the expense of Native Americans and Hispanics, Spaniards and the British.

The Western Frontier

Western migration

Most western pioneers were American-born Whites from the Upper South and the Midwest. Only a few free Blacks joined in the migration. What spurred the massive migration westward was the continuing population explosion in the United States and the widespread desire for *land*. Americans viewed owning land as the essential condition of liberty. After all, voting rights initially were tied to land ownership, and farming or ranching provided the best opportunity for self-sufficiency.

Although some people traveled 13,000 miles by sea from New York City or Boston to California, most took the overland route across the Mississippi River, the Great Plains, and the Rocky Mountains. Between 1841 and 1867, some 400,000 men, women, and children made the trek to California or Oregon, while many others settled in areas such as Colorado, Texas, and Arkansas. As many as 70,000 Mormons emigrated to the Far West, making them one of the leading forces in western settlement.

Most of the pioneers on the **Overland Trails** traveled in family groups. A wagon train was a "moving village," explained Narcissa Whitman, a Christian missionary from New York who settled with her family in the Pacific Northwest. To her and others, the Great Migration was a community-building enterprise. "Our manner of living is far preferable to any in the States," Whitman reported. "I never was so contented and happy before."

manifest destiny The widespread belief that America was "destined" by God to expand westward across the continent into lands claimed by Native Americans as well as European nations and Mexico.

Overland Trails Trail routes followed by wagon trains bearing settlers and trade goods from Missouri to the Oregon Country, California, and New Mexico, beginning in the 1840s.

WAGON TRAILS WEST

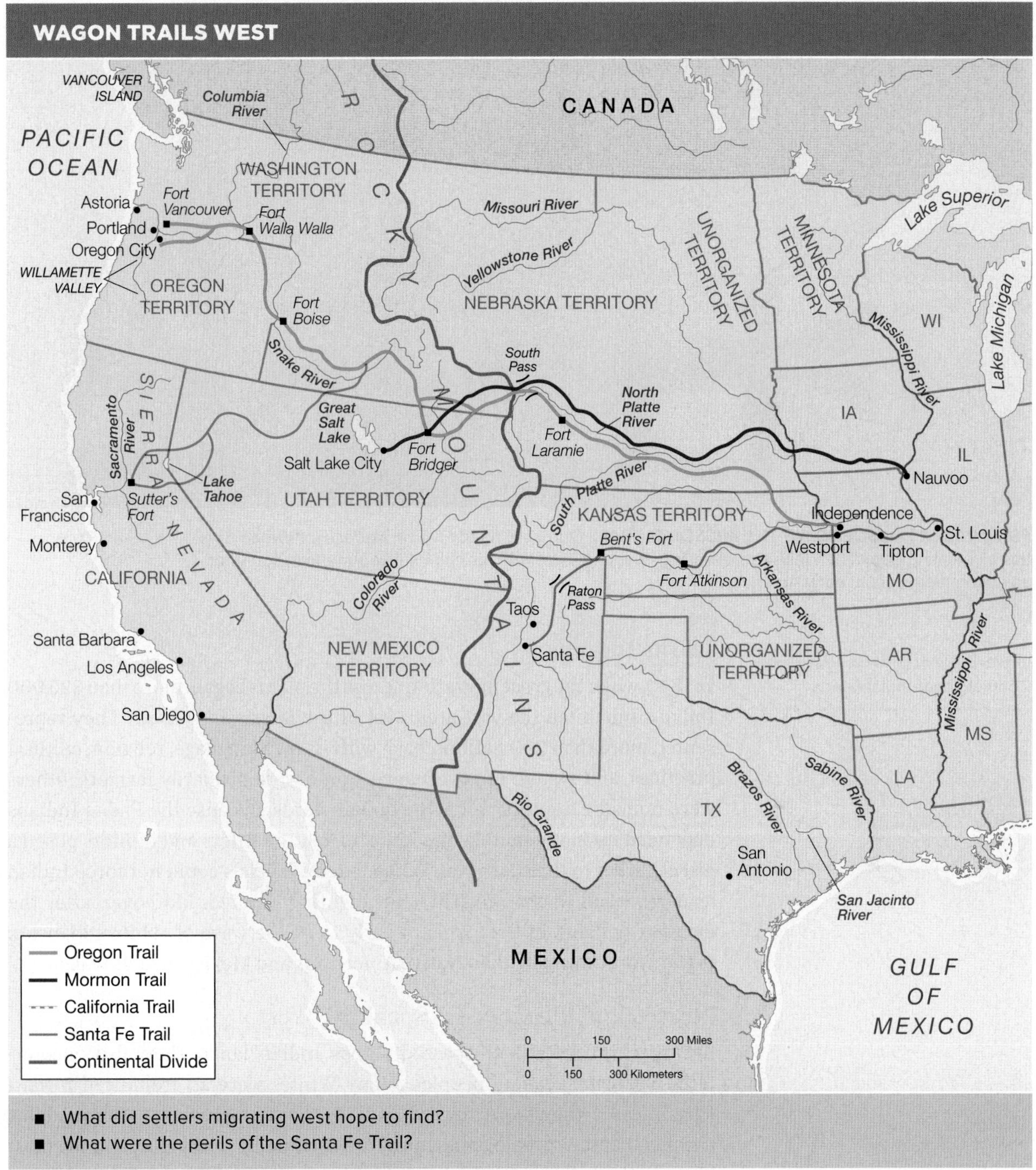

- What did settlers migrating west hope to find?
- What were the perils of the Santa Fe Trail?

Still, it was not easy to pull up stakes and become a pioneer in unknown lands. Lucy Cooke's family left their Iowa farm headed for Oregon, only to endure terrible hardships. After the first day on the trail, her mother exclaimed, "I wish we never had started." Another woman felt the same way. "What had possessed my husband," she wailed, "that he should have thought of bringing us way out through this God forsaken country?" Thousands died along the trail from hunger, disease, accidents, or violence.

***FUR TRADERS DESCENDING THE MISSOURI* (1845)** Originally titled *French-Trader, Half-Breed Son,* this oil painting depicts a White settler sailing down the river with his half–Native American son—not an uncommon sight in early America.

Plains Indians

Conflicts over Indian lands

In 1840, when the great migration across the plains began, more than 325,000 Indians inhabited the vast area west of the Mississippi River. They represented more than 200 nations, each with its own language, religion, cultural practices, and system of governance. Some were primarily farmers; others were nomadic hunters, following buffalo herds. Because the Plains Indians depended upon the buffalo, the influx of White settlers and hunters posed a direct threat to their survival. When federal officials could not force Indian leaders to sell their ancestral lands, fighting erupted. Moreover, after the discovery of gold in California in early 1848, the wave of White expansion to the West Coast engulfed Native Americans and Mexicans in its wake.

Mexico and the Spanish-Speaking West

As American settlers trespassed across Indian lands, they also encountered Spanish-speaking peoples. Many Whites were as prejudiced toward Hispanics as they were toward Indians. Former president John Adams insisted that the "people of [Spanish] America are the most ignorant, the most bigoted, the most superstitious of all the Roman Catholics in Christendom." Senator Lewis Cass from Michigan expressed the expansionist view when he declared: "We do not want the people of Mexico, either as citizens or as subjects. All we want is their . . . territory."

The Santa Fe Trail to New Mexico

In 1821, Mexico had gained its independence from Spain, but the new nation's leaders failed to manage or protect their vast territory that stretched westward to California and north to Wyoming. Americans were eager to take advantage of Mexico's instability. Fur traders streamed into New Mexico and Arizona, developing a profitable trade in beaver pelts. A Mexican official called for restrictions on American immigration: "Where others send invading armies," he explained, Americans "send their colonists."

During the 1830s and 1840s, thousands of Americans traversed the Santa Fe Trail from Missouri to New Mexico. The trek was not for the fainthearted. In 1847 alone, marauding Indians killed forty-seven Americans, destroyed 330 wagons, and stole 6,500 horses, cattle, mules, and oxen along the trail.

PIONEERS ON THE SANTA FE TRAIL In this engraving from the 1850s, a line of covered wagons make their way along the Santa Fe Trail to New Mexico.

The Rocky Mountains and Oregon Country

During the early nineteenth century, the Far Northwest consisted of the Nebraska, Washington, and Oregon Territories. The Oregon Country included what became the states of Oregon, Idaho, and Washington, as well as parts of Montana, Wyoming, and the Canadian province of British Columbia. It was an unsettled region claimed by both Great Britain and the United States. By the Convention of 1818, the two nations had agreed to "joint occupation" of the Oregon Country.

Word of Oregon's fertile soil, plentiful rainfall, mild climate, and magnificent forests spread eastward. By the late 1830s, farmers, missionaries, fur traders, and shopkeepers were traveling along the Oregon Trail, a 2,100-mile pathway that became the most strategic land route in North America. It spanned the waist of the continent, passing over windswept plains, flood-swollen rivers, scorching deserts, and treacherous mountain passes to the Pacific coast.

The Oregon Trail to British-American Oregon Country

Soon, **Oregon Fever** swept the nation, "raging like any other contagion," as a journalist wrote in 1843. In 1841 and 1842, the first sizable wagon trains made the trip, and in 1843 the movement became the largest voluntary overland migration in history.

For many, then and since, the migration across the punishing terrain came to symbolize the mythic American Dream, whereby a determined people risked everything to gain their own land and ultimately enjoy unparalleled prosperity and independence. "Eastward I go only by force," said poet Henry David Thoreau. "But westward I go free." George Law Curry, a Missouri newspaper editor, crossed the Oregon Trail in 1846 and eventually became Oregon's governor. While traveling through what became the state of Kansas, he wrote a friend: "Life on the plains far surpasses my expectation; there is a freedom and a nobleness about it that tend to bring forth the full manhood."

Oregon Fever The lure of fertile land and economic opportunities in the Oregon Country that drew hundreds of thousands of settlers westward, beginning in the late 1830s.

Those who settled Oregon found it in a "primitive state" requiring back-breaking work to create self-sustaining homesteads. Women labored as hard as men. "I am a very old woman," reported twenty-nine-year-old Sarah Everett. "My face is thin, sunken, and wrinkled, my hands bony, withered, and hard." One Oregon pioneer warned that a "woman that cannot endure almost as much as a horse has no business here." By 1845, there were about 5,000 settlers in Oregon's fertile Willamette Valley.

The long journey west, usually five to six months long, was full of hardship amid climatic extremes: broiling summers, fierce thunderstorms and tornadoes, and bitterly cold winters. Wagons broke down, mules and oxen died, and diseases took their toll.

Cholera

Cholera claimed many lives. Tainted water and contaminated food spread the poisonous bacteria, which multiply rapidly in the small intestine. Those infected experienced acute diarrhea followed by convulsions and vomiting; most died within hours of contracting the disease. Illinois emigrant John Nevin King found it awful to see "an acquaintance at noon well and in the enjoyment of health and learn in the evening that he is a corpse." On average, one grave appeared every eighty yards along the overland trails.

Decimation of Native American lands

As the number of migrants traveling along the Oregon Trail grew, they tore through Native American lands. Buffalo disappeared, and nations like the Cheyenne and the Arapaho were forced to split into northern and southern branches. As the federal government negotiated new treaties with Native Americans, it insisted that they move onto reservations far from the Oregon Trail.

The Settlement of California

California was as powerful a magnet for new settlers and adventurers as was the Oregon Territory. By the nineteenth century, Spanish Catholic missionaries, aided by Spanish soldiers, controlled most of the coastal Indians. The

THE JOURNEY WEST A photo from the nineteenth century shows a westward-bound man and woman beside their covered wagon. Life on the Overland Trails was rough and tiring, and even in these moments of apparent rest the pioneers had to cook their meals, tend to their horses or oxen, and maintain their wagon. **What challenges did the westward-bound face on their journey?**

friars (priests) lured Indians into "missions" by offering gifts or impressing them with their "magical" religious rituals.

Once inside the missions, the Indians were baptized as Catholics, taught Spanish, and stripped of their native heritage. Soldiers living in the missions enforced the will of the friars; rebellious Indians were whipped or imprisoned. Mission Indians died at an alarming rate, mostly as the result of infectious diseases.

The Spanish and then the Mexicans wanted to preserve Indians as mission inmates or as cheap farm laborers. Nevertheless, the Native American population along the California coast declined from 72,000 in 1769 to 18,000 by 1821. Saving souls cost many lives.

For all its natural resources, California remained thinly populated well into the nineteenth century, with Native Americans still outnumbering Hispanics (called *Californios*) and Americans. The residents took comfort that Mexico City, the Mexican capital, was too far away to exercise effective control over them.

Ranchos dominate Mexican-owned California

The shift from Spanish to Mexican rule did produce one dramatic change in California. In 1824, Mexico passed a colonization act that granted hundreds of enormous *ranchos* (estates) to prominent Mexicans. Yet the *rancheros* (largest landowners) wanted more, especially the vast estates controlled by the Catholic missions along the coast.

In 1833–1834, the *rancheros* persuaded the Mexican government to pass the "secularization act," which had a disastrous effect on the Native Americans. It allowed the government to take the missions, release the Indians from church control, and transfer the missions' farmlands to *rancheros*. Within a few years, the government issued some 700 new *rancho* grants of 4,500 to 50,000 acres along the California coast. These sprawling ranches resembled southern plantations—but the death rate among Indian workers was twice as high as that among enslaved Blacks in the Lower South.

Mission Santa Clara de Asis, California, 1777

SPANISH MISSIONS The Spanish Mission, Santa Clara de Asis, California in 1777 was one of a series of religious outposts founded by Spanish Catholics to spread the Christian doctrine to the Native Americans. Once part of the missions, Native Americans were stripped of their heritage and forced to work on mission lands.

John Sutter Among the most ambitious White pioneers in California was forty-four-year-old John Augustus Sutter, a German-Swiss entrepreneur who left behind his wife, four children, crushing debts, and a warrant for his arrest to make his fortune in America. At the junction of the Sacramento and American Rivers (later the site of the city of Sacramento), Sutter built a bustling trading outpost called Sutter's Fort. Completed in 1843, it stood at the end of the California Trail.

Sutter's Fort and the development of the Sacramento Valley

Sutter set about creating a wilderness empire in the Sacramento Valley after convincing the Mexican government to grant him 230 square *miles* of land. In addition to trading furs, Indians made wool blankets and hats; cultivated vast acres of wheat and corn; and raised huge herds of cattle, sheep, hogs, and horses. Sutter paid his Indian workers, but he also whipped, jailed, and even executed Indians who disobeyed his orders. In the process, Sutter helped spur the American settlement of Hispanic California.

By 1845, there were perhaps 800 Americans in California, along with approximately 10,000 *Californios* and 150,000 Native Americans. Some 3,000 Americans arrived the next year. California's Mexican governor, Pio Pico, warned in 1845, "We find ourselves threatened by hordes of Yankee emigrants, who have already begun to flock into our country, and whose progress we cannot arrest."

The Donner Party The most tragic story of pioneers traveling to California involved the group headed by George Donner, a sixty-two-year-old farmer from Illinois. In mid-April 1846, Donner led his family and seventy-four other settlers from Springfield, Illinois, to the Oregon Trail. But tragedy interrupted their journey.

The group started too late in the spring, overloaded their wagons, and took a shortcut that turned into a disaster. They had brought too little food, water, and clothing, and their inexperience would prove to be fatal. In the Utah Territory's Wasatch Mountains, the party got lost, wasting three

SUTTER'S FORT Marking the end of the California Trail, Sutter's Fort was a prominent trading hub that depended on the labor and craftsmanship of the Native Americans who worked for Sutter. **How were the Native Americans at Sutter's Fort treated?**

precious weeks. Then, crossing the desert before the Great Salt Lake, they suffered in the heat. Over 100 oxen were lost, forcing them to abandon several wagons with precious supplies.

The Donner Party and cannibalism

Reaching Truckee Pass in eastern California, the Donner Party confronted a two-week blizzard. Facing twenty feet of snow and rationing a dwindling supply of food, they separated into two camps. As their food ran out, they were forced to eat cowhides, with one family cooking and eating their dog. When a group of seventeen, calling themselves the "Forlorn Hope," attempted to push on, they were met by more snow. Eight would die. Billy Graves urged his two daughters to eat his corpse—and they did. Soon, two other members died and were eaten.

Back at the main camps, the survivors had slaughtered and eaten the last of the livestock, then killed two Indian guides and ate them. By the time a rescue party reached the camps two months later, thirteen people had died, and cannibalism had become commonplace. The rescuers were appalled to find around the fire the bones, skulls, and half-eaten limbs of those who had died. As the survivors were led over the pass, George Donner, too weak and distressed to walk, stayed behind to die. His wife, Tanzene, chose to die with him.

American Settlements in Texas

The American passion for western land focused on the northern Mexican province of Texas, a vast land sweeping westward from Louisiana to the Rocky Mountains in the north and the Rio Grande in the south (*Rio Grande* is a Spanish phrase meaning "Big River"). During the 1820s, the United States had twice offered to buy Texas, but the Mexican government refused to sell.

"Texians" settle lands in northern Mexico

By 1823, some 3,000 Americans (or Texians, also called Anglos because they spoke English), were living in Texas in violation of Mexican law. The unstable Mexican government could not stop the illegal immigrants from America trespassing into Texas. Between 1824 and 1858, Mexico had fifty pitiful presidents who turned the government into a comic opera.

The leading promoter of American settlement in Mexican-controlled Texas was Stephen Fuller Austin, a visionary land developer (*empresario*). His father, Moses Austin, had convinced the Mexican government that American settlers could provide a buffer zone between Comanches to the north and Mexicans in the south.

Moses Austin died before he could enact his plan, but his son Stephen set it in motion in 1822. Thousands of hardy souls settled in Austin's Anglo-Texas "colony" on the lower Brazos and Colorado Rivers. Stephen Austin intended his colony to be a thriving community of cooperating families. He believed that Anglo-Americans would "redeem Texas from the wilderness" and "*Americanize* Texas."

By 1830, far more Americans lived in coastal Texas than Mexicans—about 20,000 Anglo-Texans and 1,000 enslaved Blacks. In 1828, José María Sánchez, a Mexican official, visited Austin's settlement. Afterward, he reported that the effort by Americans to take Texas from Mexico "will start from this colony" because the Mexican government was not taking "vigorous measures to prevent it." For their part, the settlers displayed a racist contempt for the brown-skinned Mexican people, who could not sustain an effective government.

The Texas War for Independence

Mexican officials grew so worried about the intentions of the Americans living in Texas that in April 1830 they abruptly outlawed immigration from the United States. They also banned any additional enslaved people and built forts housing Mexican soldiers to enforce the new law.

Such efforts were too little too late, however. Americans kept coming. By 1835, the Texians and their enslaved Blacks outnumbered the *Tejanos* (Texans born in Spain or Mexico) ten to one.

Texas Revolution against Santa Anna (1835–1836)

Changing political circumstances in Mexico aggravated the growing tensions. General Antonio López de Santa Anna served as the Mexican president eleven times between 1833 and 1854. Texians feared that the Mexican president planned to free "our slaves and to make slaves of us." When the Mexican president eliminated exemptions for slaveholders and imprisoned Stephen Austin in 1834 for inciting rebelliousness, Texians began transforming themselves into revolutionaries.

In the fall of 1835, Texians rebelled against the "despotism" of the Mexican government. A furious Santa Anna ordered all Americans expelled from Texas, and all rebels arrested and executed. As sporadic fighting erupted, hundreds of armed volunteers from southern states rushed to assist the 30,000 Texians in the **Texas Revolution** against a Mexican nation of 7 million people. "The sword is drawn!" Stephen Austin proclaimed, promising 800 acres of land to anyone who joined the rebellion.

The Alamo and Goliad At San Antonio, in southern Texas, Santa Anna's 1,800-man army assaulted a small group of fewer than 200 Texians, Tejanos, and recently arrived American volunteers holed up in an abandoned Catholic mission called the Alamo. Leading the outmanned rebels was William B. Travis, a hot-tempered, pro-slavery, twenty-six-year-old Alabama lawyer and teacher. He ignored orders to retreat, insisting that "death was preferable to disgrace."

Among the Americans at the Alamo, the most celebrated was David Crockett, the Tennessee frontiersman, bear hunter, and sharpshooter who had fought Indians under Andrew Jackson and served as an anti-Jackson Whig congressman. Having lost his reelection bid, he encouraged those Tennesseans who voted against him "to go to hell," while "I go to Texas." Upon his arrival in San Antonio, Crockett told the Alamo defenders that he had come "to aid you all that I can in your noble cause."

Texas Revolution (1835–1836) Conflict between Texas colonists and the Mexican government that resulted in the creation of the separate Republic of Texas in 1836.

Also among those in the Alamo was Juan Seguín, the son of a prominent Tejano family in San Antonio. At age eighteen, he had become the mayor (*alcalde*) of San Antonio. Like many other Mexicans living in Texas, he resented Santa Anna's tyranny so much that he joined the Texas independence movement and was made a captain in the Texian army.

Battle of the Alamo (1836)

In February 1836, Santa Anna demanded that the Americans in the Alamo surrender. Travis answered with cannon fire and a letter, promising that he was determined to "die like a soldier. *I shall never surrender or retreat. . . .* VICTORY OR DEATH!" Santa Anna's forces then launched a series of assaults. During the fighting, Travis sent Seguín to gather reinforcements and to deliver a message to Sam Houston, the commander of the Texian army: the Texans at the Alamo would "never surrender or retreat."

For eleven days, the Mexicans suffered heavy losses. Then, before dawn on March 6, the Alamo defenders awakened to the sound of Mexican bugles playing the dreaded "Degüello" ("Take No Prisoners"). Wave after wave of Santa Anna's men attacked. They were twice forced back, but on the third try, they broke through the battered north wall. As Travis was directing his men, a bullet smashed into his forehead, killing him instantly. The rebels ran out of bullets but fought on with tomahawks, knives, and rifle butts. In the end, however, virtually all were killed. A few days later, Juan Seguín returned with more troops, only to discover that they were too late.

Victory at the Alamo was costly for the Mexicans, however, as they lost more than 600 soldiers and also alienated many Texians. While Santa Anna

THE ALAMO David Crockett, pictured fighting with his rifle over his head after running out of bullets, joined the legendary battle to defend the Alamo against the Mexican army. **What were the consequences of the Battle of the Alamo?**

SAM HOUSTON Having led the Texans to a sweeping victory over the Mexicans in the Battle of San Jacinto, Houston went on to serve as the first president of the Republic of Texas.

proclaimed a "glorious victory," his aide wrote in his diary, "One more such 'glorious victory' and we are finished."

The furious fighting at the Alamo turned the rebellion into a war for Texas independence. On March 2, 1836, delegates from all fifty-nine Texas towns met at Washington-on-the-Brazos, 150 miles northeast of San Antonio. There they signed a declaration of independence from Mexican control. Over the next seventeen days, they drafted a constitution establishing the Republic of Texas.

Two weeks later, at the Battle of Coleto, a Mexican force again defeated a smaller Texian army. The Mexicans marched 465 captured Texians to a fort in the nearby town of Goliad. Despite pleas from his men to show mercy, Santa Anna ordered the captives killed as "pirates and outlaws." On Palm Sunday, March 27, 1836, 303 Texians were marched out of Goliad and murdered.

The Battle of San Jacinto

The commander in chief of the still-forming Texian army was Sam Houston, a fearless, hard-drinking frontiersman born in Virginia and raised in eastern Tennessee. As a young teen, he had left his widowed mother and eight siblings to live among the Cherokees for a time, learning their language and customs. He also developed a lifelong weakness for alcohol.

Like David Crockett, Sam Houston had served under General Andrew Jackson during the War of 1812. At the Battle of Horseshoe Bend in Alabama in 1814, he was seriously wounded but insisted on rejoining his unit, only to be shot twice in the right arm and shoulder. Jackson marveled at his tenacity and became a lifelong friend and mentor.

After the war, Sam Houston became an attorney, a U.S. congressman, and, in 1827, governor of Tennessee. In 1829, despondent and often drunk, Houston resigned the governorship and went "home" to the Cherokees in Arkansas Territory. There he married a Cherokee woman and was formally "adopted" by the Cherokee Nation. In December 1832, he moved to Texas, became a Mexican citizen, and started a law practice.

When the Americans in Texas declared their independence from Mexico on March 4, 1836 Houston became "Commander in Chief of the Armies of the Republic of Texas." Houston was fearless, a quality sorely needed against the much larger Mexican army.

Santa Anna is defeated

After learning of the massacre at the Alamo, Houston's troops retreated, hoping that Santa Anna's pursuing army would make a mistake. On April 21, 1836, the cocky Mexican general walked into a trap. Houston's ragtag army surprised the Mexican encampment near the San Jacinto River, about twenty-five miles southeast of the modern city of Houston. At 4:30 in the afternoon, the Texians charged the Mexican lines screaming "Remember the Alamo! Remember Goliad!" The Texians and Tejanos overwhelmed the Mexicans, most of whom had been caught napping during the afternoon *siesta*.

The Battle of San Jacinto lasted only eighteen minutes, but Houston's vengeful troops spent two more hours slaughtering fleeing Mexican soldiers.

It was, said a Texian, a "frightful sight to behold." Some 650 Mexicans were killed and 300 captured. The Texians lost only eleven men.

General Santa Anna, who had been enjoying an opium-induced nap when the battle erupted, escaped in his underwear only to be captured the next day. Brought before Sam Houston, the Mexican leader begged the American leader to be "generous to the vanquished." Houston replied, "You should have remembered that at the Alamo." In the end, Santa Anna bought his freedom by signing a treaty recognizing the independence of the Republic of Texas. The Texas Revolution had succeeded in just seven weeks.

The Lone Star Republic

In 1836, the Lone Star Republic, as Texians called their new nation, drafted a constitution that legalized slavery and banned free Blacks. Voters elected Sam Houston president and voted overwhelmingly for annexation by the United States.

Delayed recognition of the Republic of Texas

The American president at the time was Andrew Jackson, who eagerly wanted Texas to join the Union. Jackson, however, decided it was better to wait, for adding Texas as a slave state would ignite a quarrel between North and South that would fracture his own Democratic party. Worse, any effort to add Texas to the Union would likely mean a war with Mexico, which refused to recognize Texan independence. So Jackson delayed official recognition of the Republic of Texas until his last day in office, early in 1837. New Yorker Martin Van Buren, Jackson's successor, did as predicted: he avoided all talk of Texas annexation during his single term as president.

The Tyler Presidency and Texas

When William Henry Harrison became president in 1841, he was the oldest man (sixty-eight) and the first Whig to win the office. The Whigs had emerged in opposition to Andrew Jackson, promoting federal government support for industrial development and economic growth through high tariffs to deter imports and federal funding for internal improvements. Harrison, however, was elected primarily on the strength of his military record, a singular victory at the Battle of Tippecanoe thirty years before. In the end, it mattered little, for Harrison served the shortest term of any president.

Death of Willian Henry Harrison

On April 4, 1841, exactly one month after his inauguration, Harrison died of pneumonia, the first president to die in office. Vice President John Tyler of Virginia assumed the presidency, only to discover that the powerful anti-Jackson Whig, Senator Henry Clay, intended to dominate the new president.

Tyler, however, was not easily dominated. At fifty-one, the tall, thin, slave-owning Virginian was the youngest president to date, but he had lots of political experience, having served as a state legislator, governor, congressman, and senator. Initially a Democrat, Tyler had broken with the party over President Andrew Jackson's "condemnation" of South Carolina's attempt to nullify federal laws. Tyler believed that South Carolina had a constitutional right to secede from the nation.

Now, as president, Tyler began working to make Texas the twenty-eighth state. At the same time, however, he opposed Clay's "American System," the program of economic nationalism that called for the federal government to promote industrial development.

Conflicts between Clay and Tyler

When Congress met in a special session in 1841, Clay introduced a series of controversial resolutions. He demanded the repeal of the Independent Treasury Act and the creation of another Bank of the United States. He also pledged to revive the "distribution" program whereby the money raised from federal land sales went to the states, and he urged that tariffs be raised on imported goods.

Clay then used threats and intimidation to push his program through Congress. Legislators began calling Clay "the Dictator." With more tact, Clay might have avoided a series of nasty disputes with Tyler over financial issues. For once, however, driven by his lust to be president, Clay, the Great Compromiser, lost his instinct for compromise and bullied legislators to follow his lead.

Tyler vetoes national bank bill

Although Tyler agreed to the repeal of the Independent Treasury Act and signed a higher tariff bill, he vetoed Clay's pet project: a new national bank. Clay responded by calling the president a traitor to his party. He then convinced Tyler's entire cabinet to resign, except for Secretary of State Daniel Webster. Tyler replaced the defectors with anti-Jackson Democrats who, like him, had become Whigs.

The Whigs then took the unprecedented step of expelling Tyler from the party, dismissing him as "His Accidency" and the "Executive Ass." By 1842, Tyler had become a president without a party, shunned by both Whigs and Democrats but loved by those promoting territorial expansion.

A festering economic depression coincided with the political turmoil. Bank failures mounted, and unemployment soared. Riots erupted in Philadelphia, and an armed rebellion flared up in Rhode Island when non-landowners were denied the right to vote. Tyler, however, remained determined to annex Texas.

Efforts to Annex Texas

Texas annexation treaty defeated

In April 1843, South Carolinian John C. Calhoun, then secretary of state, sent to the Senate for ratification a treaty annexing Texas. There it died by a vote of 35–16. Northern senators, many of whom were abolitionists, refused to add another slave state. Others feared that annexing Texas would trigger a war with Mexico.

Texan leaders were frustrated that independence had not led to annexation. Sam Houston threatened to expand the Republic of Texas to the Pacific. But with little money in the treasury, rising government debt, and continuing tensions with Mexico, which insisted that it remained at war with Texas, the new republic was in no position to spread its borders.

The Lone Star Republic had no infrastructure—no banks, no schools, and no industries. It remained a frontier community of scattered log cabins and few cities. Houston decided that Texas had two choices: annexation to the United States or closer economic ties to Great Britain, which had begun to buy cotton from Texas planters. Meanwhile, thousands more Americans poured into Texas. The population more than tripled between 1836 and 1845, from 40,000 to 150,000, and the enslaved Black population grew even faster than the White population.

ELECTION OF 1844 A political cartoon depicts the decline of the Whig party—represented by a raccoon—from 1810 to 1844. What used to be a plump, well-fed raccoon was now an emaciated animal with a fraction of the strength. **Based on the 1844 election, how accurate was this illustration's representation of the Whigs?**

The Election of 1844

Both political parties hoped to keep the divisive Texas issue out of the 1844 presidential campaign. Whig Henry Clay and Democrat Martin Van Buren, the leading candidates for each party's nomination, agreed that adding Texas to the Union would be a mistake. Van Buren's stance cost him the support of southerners.

At the Democratic Convention, annexationists, including Andrew Jackson, nominated James Knox Polk, former Speaker of the House and former governor of Tennessee. Like Tyler, Polk was an aggressive expansionist with a dull personality. On the ninth ballot, he became the first "dark horse" (unexpected) candidate to win a major-party nomination. At Polk's insistence, the Democrats' platform called for the annexation of both the Oregon Country and Texas.

The 1844 election proved to be one of the most significant in American history. By promoting southern and western expansionism, the Democrats offered a winning strategy that forced Whig candidate Henry Clay to alter his position on Texas at the last minute. He dropped his "objection to the annexation" if it could be achieved "without dishonor, without war, with the common consent of the Union, and upon just and fair terms."

James K. Polk elected president (1844)

Clay's change of heart shifted more anti-slavery votes to the new Liberty party (the anti-slavery party formed in 1840), which increased its count in the presidential election from about 7,000 in 1840 to more than 62,000 in 1844. In the western counties of New York, the Liberty party drew enough votes from Clay and the Whigs to give the state to Polk and the Democrats. Had he carried New York, Clay would have won by seven electoral votes. Instead, Polk won a narrow national plurality of 38,000 popular votes (the first president since John Quincy Adams to win without a majority) but a clear majority of the Electoral College, 170–105. Clay had lost his third and last attempt to win the presidency.

James K. Polk

Born near Charlotte, North Carolina, Polk had graduated first in his class at the University of North Carolina, then moved to Tennessee, where he became a successful lawyer, planter, and political figure. He served fourteen years in Congress (four as Speaker of the House) and two years as governor.

At age forty-nine, Polk was the youngest president up to that time. Yet he worked so hard during his four years in the White House that his health failed, and he died in 1849, at fifty-three, just three months after leaving office.

Polk owed his election to two people: Andrew Jackson, his hero and mentor, and Sarah Childress Polk, his charming wife who served as his unofficial chief of staff. She managed his correspondence and used her considerable social skills to practice what was called parlor politics, hosting numerous dinner gatherings as a means of gaining political intelligence her husband could use in pursuing his priorities. For the Polks, politics was a family enterprise.

The State of Texas

Texas joined the Union just *before* James K. Polk became president. In his final months as president, John Tyler convinced Congress to annex Texas. On March 1, 1845, in his final presidential action, Tyler signed the resolution admitting Texas to the Union as the fifteenth slave state. By 1850, the population—both White and Black—had soared by almost 50 percent. (The census did not include Native Americans.)

Expulsion of the Tejanos

After gaining their independence from Mexico, White Texans had turned on the Tejanos (Mexican-born Texans) who had supported the revolution. "White folks and Mexicans were never made to live together," an American woman explained to a visiting journalist. "The Mexicans had no business [living] here." By then, Tejanos were being uprooted and expelled.

In 1857, White Texan wagon drivers (teamsters) killed seventy-five Mexican-born competitors in what was called the Cart War. Juan Seguín, who had led a cavalry unit against Mexican forces at San Jacinto and had served as mayor of San Antonio, lamented that he "had become a foreigner in my native land."

Polk's Goals

Polk's goals: territorial expansion, reducing import tariffs, reestablishing the Independent Treasury

Perhaps because he pledged to serve only one term, Polk was a president in a hurry. His top priority was territorial expansion. He wanted to add Oregon, California, and New Mexico to the Union. In keeping with long-standing Democratic beliefs, Polk wanted lower tariffs to allow more foreign goods to compete in the American marketplace and thereby help drive consumer prices down. Congress agreed by approving the Walker Tariff of 1846, named after Robert J. Walker, the Treasury secretary.

In the same year, Polk persuaded Congress to restore the Independent Treasury Act, which established independent treasury deposit offices separate from private or state banks to receive all federal government funds. The system was intended to replace the Second Bank of the United States, which Jackson had "killed." This would offset the rapid growth of unregulated state banks, whose reckless lending practices had helped cause the depression of the late 1830s.

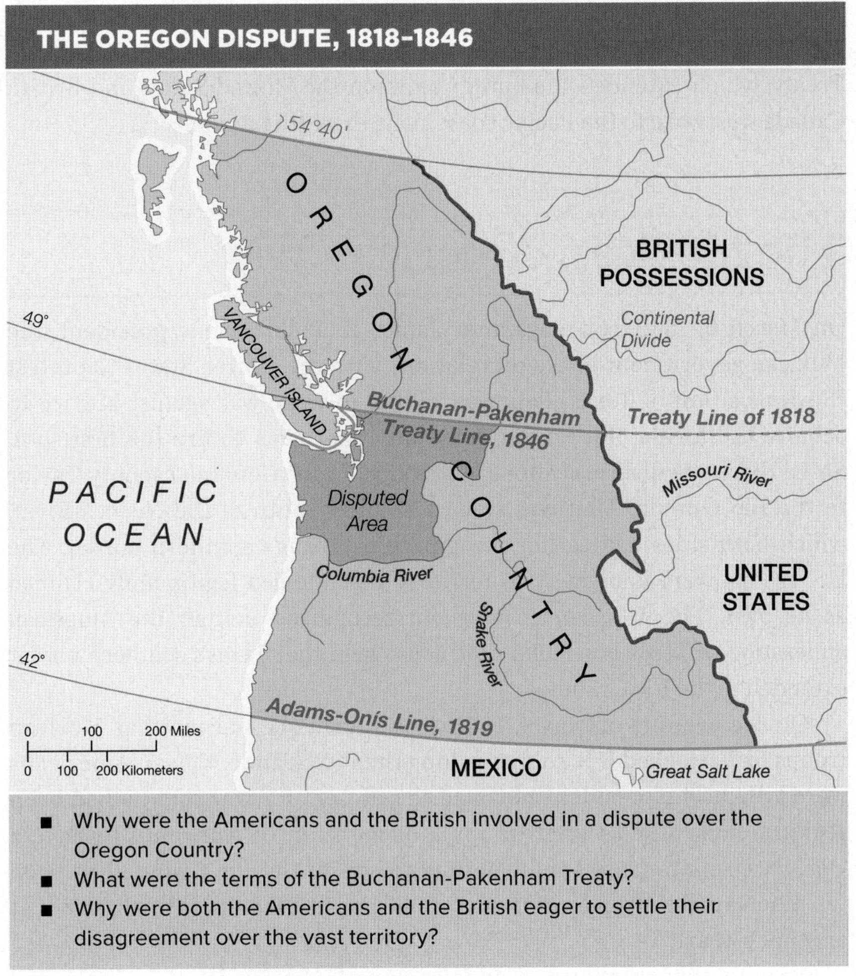

THE OREGON DISPUTE, 1818–1846

- Why were the Americans and the British involved in a dispute over the Oregon Country?
- What were the terms of the Buchanan-Pakenham Treaty?
- Why were both the Americans and the British eager to settle their disagreement over the vast territory?

The Independent Treasury entrusted the federal government, rather than favored state banks, with the exclusive management of government funds and required that all disbursements be in gold or silver, or paper currency backed by gold or silver.

Polk also twice vetoed Whig-passed bills for federally funded infrastructure projects. His efforts to reverse Whig economic policies satisfied the slaveholding South but angered northerners, who wanted higher tariffs to protect their industries from British competition, and westerners, who wanted federally financed roads and harbors.

Oregon

Meanwhile, the dispute with Great Britain over the Oregon Country boundary heated up as expansionists insisted that Polk take the whole region rather than split it with the British. Polk was willing to go to the brink of war to do so. "If we do have war," the president blustered, "it will not be our fault."

Buchanan-Pakenham Treaty (1846): Oregon becomes American territory

Fortunately, the British were not willing to risk war. On June 15, 1846, James Buchanan, Polk's secretary of state, signed the Buchanan-Pakenham Treaty, which extended the border between the United States and British Canada westward to the Pacific coast along the 49th parallel.

CORE **OBJECTIVE**

2. Examine the impact of the Mexican-American War on national politics.

The Mexican-American War

On March 6, 1845, two days after James K. Polk became president, the Mexican government broke off relations with the United States to protest the annexation of Texas. Polk was willing to wage war against Mexico to acquire California, but he did not want Americans to fire the first shot. So he dispatched several thousand troops under General Zachary Taylor to the Rio Grande. That was some 150 miles south of the Nueces River, which both sides had earlier recognized as Texas's southern border. The U.S. troops were knowingly in territory that Mexico legitimately claimed as its own. The Mexican government recognized neither the American annexation of Texas nor Polk's ridiculous claim that Texas's southern border extended to the Rio Grande.

Polk and Congress declare war

On the evening of May 9, 1845, President Polk learned that Mexican troops had attacked U.S. soldiers along the Rio Grande. Eleven Americans were killed. The president now had the pretext for war that he had been seeking. Polk asked Congress for a declaration of war, only to have a Delaware senator insist that sending troops to the Rio Grande had been "as much an act of aggression on our part as is a man pointing a pistol at another's heart."

Despite such concerns, Congress complied with Polk's request and authorized the recruitment of 50,000 soldiers. The outbreak of fighting thrilled many Americans. In the South, where expansion fever ran high, the war was immensely popular. So many men rushed to volunteer that thousands had to be turned back. Eventually, 112,000 Whites served in the war (Blacks were banned).

The United States had formidable advantages in the war. America's population was 20 million compared with Mexico's 7 million. The Mexican economy was essentially bankrupt, while America prospered. The U.S. forces had better weapons, training, resources, and leadership. The main Mexican advantage was fighting on its own territory.

Opposition to the War

In New England, however, there was much less enthusiasm for "Mr. Polk's War." Congressman John Quincy Adams, the former president, called it "a most unrighteous war." He intended to extend slavery into new territories taken from Mexico. The fiery Boston abolitionist William Lloyd Garrison charged that the war was one of American "aggression, of invasion, of conquest."

Most Whigs across the North, including a young Illinois congressman named Abraham Lincoln, also opposed the war, stressing that President Polk had maneuvered the Mexicans to attack. The United States, they argued, had no reason for placing its army in the disputed border region between Texas and Mexico.

Preparing for Battle

Regardless of the conflict's legitimacy, the United States was again ill-prepared for a major war. At the outset, the regular army numbered barely 7,000, in contrast to the Mexican force of 32,000. Before the war ended, the U.S. military had grown to almost 79,000 troops, including frontier toughs who lacked uniforms, equipment, and discipline.

Many U.S. soldiers abused and slaughtered Mexicans wherever they found them—men, women, and children. George Gordon Meade, who would become a celebrated Union general during the Civil War, noted that the undisciplined Americans murdered Mexicans simply "for their amusement." General Winfield Scott also admitted that his troops had committed numerous atrocities, including "murder, robbery, and rape of [Mexican] mothers and daughters."

The Mexican-American War, from March 1846 to April 1848, was fought on four fronts: southern Texas, central Mexico, New Mexico, and California. Early in the fighting, General Zachary Taylor's army scored two victories north of the Rio Grande, at Palo Alto (May 8) and Resaca de la Palma (May 9).

On May 18, Taylor's army crossed the Rio Grande and occupied Matamoros. These quick victories brought Taylor, a Whig, instant popularity, and Polk grudgingly agreed to public demands that Taylor be named the overall commander.

Zachery Taylor becomes commander

The Annexation of California

Of all the Mexican territories President Polk coveted, California was the grand prize, for he saw it as the commercial gateway to the riches of Asia. Accordingly, Polk fashioned an elaborate scheme to seize Mexico's westernmost province.

Polk's plan centered on using John C. Frémont, a self-promoting army officer famous for having helped map the Oregon Trail. Near the end of 1845, Frémont recruited sixty-two frontiersmen, scientists, soldiers, marksmen, and hunters for a secret mission. After equipping his men with the finest weapons and supplies, Frémont led them into California's Sacramento Valley. His official purpose was to find the best route for immigrants; his actual goal was to conquer Mexican California.

Frémont was a free-spirited adventurer who disobeyed orders, violated promises, and never acknowledged mistakes. Once in California, he and his troops abandoned their exploration and research mission and focused on organizing a rebellion against the Mexican officials. The Mexican governor quickly ordered Frémont and his "band of robbers" to leave.

They grudgingly did so, traveling north to Oregon, only to return after receiving secret messages from President Polk. The messages revealed

CALIFORNIA BEAR FLAG REVOLT OF 1846 General Frémont's soldiers joined other Americans and proclaimed the Republic of California on June 14, 1846, and hoisted a flag featuring a grizzly bear and star, a version of which would later become the state flag.

that the United States would soon be at war with Mexico and that Frémont should seize control of California. Frémont's men then joined other Americans in capturing Sonoma, the largest settlement in northern California, on June 14, 1846. They proclaimed the Republic of California and hoisted a flag featuring a grizzly bear and star, a version of which would later become the state flag.

California becomes an American territory (1846)

The Bear Flag Republic lasted only a month, however. In July, the commander of the U.S. Pacific Fleet, having heard of the outbreak of hostilities with Mexico, sent troops ashore at Monterey to raise the American flag and claim California as part of the United States.

Before the end of July, another navy officer, Robert F. Stockton, led the American occupation of Santa Barbara and Los Angeles, on the southern California coast. By mid-August 1846, Mexican resistance in California had evaporated. On August 17, Stockton declared himself governor, with Frémont as military governor in the north.

U.S. Army takes New Mexico (1846)

At the same time, another U.S. military expedition headed for New Mexico. On August 18, General Stephen Kearny and a small army entered Santa Fe. Kearny then led 300 men westward toward southern California, where they joined Stockton's forces at San Diego. They took control of Los Angeles on January 10, 1847, and the remaining Mexican forces surrendered.

War in Northern Mexico

Both California and New Mexico had been taken from Mexican control before General Zachary Taylor fought his first major battle in northern Mexico. In September 1846, Taylor's army assaulted the fortified city of Monterrey, which surrendered after a five-day siege. The dictator General Antonio López de Santa Anna, forced out of power in 1845, got word to Polk from his exile in Cuba that he would end the war if allowed to return.

Santa Anna returns to Mexico

In August 1846, on Polk's orders, Santa Anna was permitted to return to Mexico on the condition that he stay out of politics and the military. The treacherous Mexican leader had lied, however. Soon he was again president of Mexico and in command of the Mexican army. In October 1846, he prepared to attack. When the Mexican general invited the outnumbered Americans to surrender, Zachary Taylor responded, "Tell him to go to hell."

The Battle of Buena Vista (1847)

That launched the hard-fought Battle of Buena Vista (February 22–23, 1847). Both sides claimed victory, but the Mexicans suffered five times as many casualties as the Americans. One of the U.S. soldiers killed was Henry Clay, Jr., whose famous father had lost to Polk in the 1844 presidential campaign. The elder Clay, devastated by his son's death, condemned Polk's "unnecessary" war of "offensive aggression" and opposed any effort to use the war as a means of acquiring Mexican territory "for the purpose of introducing slavery into it."

In August, General Winfield Scott's outnumbered invasion force marched from Veracruz on the eastern coast toward heavily defended Mexico City, the national capital some 200 miles away. After four battles in which they overwhelmed the Mexican defenders and needlessly killed hundreds of civilians, U.S. forces arrived at the gates of Mexico City in early September 1847.

The Saint Patrick's Battalion

General Winfield Scott's triumphant assault on Mexico City was not without problems. Since the start of the war, some 7,000 American soldiers had deserted. Several hundred of them, mostly poor Catholic Irish and German immigrants, changed sides and formed the Saint Patrick's Battalion in the Mexican army.

The American soldiers, called *San Patricios* in Spanish, switched sides because they resented the abuse they received from Protestant officers and

ST. PATRICK'S "PATRICIOS" BATALLION In this painting, Samuel E. Chamberlain depicts some of the seventy-two Catholic Americans charged with joining the Mexican army, which promised greater respect and opportunity. On September 13, 1847, they were lined up outside the Chapultepec fortress and forced to watch it fall before being hanged, themselves.

the atrocities they saw committed against Catholic Mexicans. An Ohio volunteer, for example, yearned to destroy Catholic churches and "put the greasy priests, monks, friars, and other officials at work on the public highways."

The Mexican army circulated leaflets to American soldiers, offering higher pay, land grants, and citizenship, and urging the foreign born to switch sides and fight for their shared "sacred imperiled religion. If you are Catholic, the same as we, if you follow the doctrines of Our Savior, why are you murdering your brethren? Why are you antagonistic to those who defend their country and your own God?"

Whatever their motives, the *San Patricios* fought tenaciously. During one of the battles for Mexico City, the Americans captured seventy-two of the Catholic defectors, most of whom were sentenced to death.

At dawn on September 13, 1847, the *San Patricios,* their hands and feet bound, were made to stand in the hot sun in sight of Chapultepec, the last Mexican fortress protecting Mexico City. They were forced to watch the battle unfold. When the American troops scaled the walls of the fortress and raised the U.S. flag, the *San Patricios* were all hanged simultaneously.

The Treaty of Guadalupe Hidalgo (1848)

After the fall of Mexico City, Mexican leader Santa Anna resigned and fled the country. Peace talks began on January 2, 1848. News of the victory thrilled American expansionists. The editor John O'Sullivan, who had coined the phrase "manifest destiny," shouted, "More, More, More! Why not take all of Mexico?"

By the **Treaty of Guadalupe Hidalgo**, signed on February 2, a humiliated Mexico gave up half its entire territory: all of Texas north of the Rio Grande, the territories that would become the states of California, Arizona, New Mexico, and significant parts of Colorado, Utah, Wyoming, and Nevada.

The treaty guaranteed the 150,000 Native Americans and the 80,000 Mexicans living in the ceded territories that they could keep their property, receive U.S. citizenship, and retain their Catholic religion. About 90 percent of them chose to stay in the new American territories.

Americans' treatment of the Mexicans and Native Americans

Over time, however, as Americans streamed in, the ruthless among them—and there were many—scorned, cheated, and killed Mexican-born residents and Native Americans. Mexican Americans were forced to accept the lowest-paying jobs under the worst working conditions. Most of them were manual laborers, vaqueros (cowboys), miners, railroad workers, or cartmen, transporting food and supplies.

Americans also found ways to cheat Mexicans out of their lands. By the Land Act of 1851, Congress required that all landowners whose property was granted earlier by Spanish or Mexican authorities had to have documented titles. Those who did not have such land titles had their property confiscated.

Treaty of Guadalupe Hidalgo (1848) Treaty between United States and Mexico that ended the Mexican-American War.

Except for a small addition made by the Gadsden Purchase of 1853, the annexations of Mexican territory rounded out the continental United States and nearly doubled its size. In return for what President Polk called "an immense empire," the United States paid Mexico $15 million. The disgraced Mexican leader Santa Anna spoke for most Mexicans when he said the treaty would always be a source of "eternal shame and bitter regret for every Mexican."

The War's Legacies

The Mexican-American War marked the first time that U.S. military forces had defeated and occupied another country. More than 13,000 Americans died in the conflict, 11,550 of them from disease. The war remains the deadliest in American history in terms of the percentage of soldiers killed. Of every 1,000 U.S. soldiers in Mexico, some 110 died.

The U.S. victory helped end the prolonged economic depression. As the years passed, however, critics charged that the conflict was a shameful war of conquest and imperialistic plunder directed by a president to grab more territory for slavery. Ulysses S. Grant, who fought in the war, later called it "one of the most unjust wars ever waged by a stronger against a weaker nation."

The revolutionary republic of 1776 devoted to liberty from colonial rule had become a continental empire built upon the conquest and exploitation of native peoples. (There are no grand statues in Washington, D.C., celebrating the Mexican-American War.)

The annexation of so much Mexican territory worried some prominent Americans determined to defend their notions of racial superiority. "More than half the Mexicans are Indians," South Carolina's John C. Calhoun harrumphed, "and the other half is composed chiefly of mixed tribes. I protest against such a union as that! Ours, sir, is the government of a white race."

Slavery in the Territories

CORE **OBJECTIVE**

3. Describe how the federal government tried to resolve the issue of slavery in the western territories during the 1850s.

At midcentury, political storm clouds were forming over the fate of slavery. The United States was a powerful nation, but, as Henry Clay said, it was an "unhappy country" torn by the "uproar, confusion, and menace" caused by the deepening agony over slavery. The United States had developed two different societies, one in the North and the other in the South, and the two sections increasingly disagreed over the nation's future. In 1833, Andrew Jackson had predicted that southerners "intend to blow up a storm on the slave question." He added that pro-slavery firebrands like John C. Calhoun "would do any act to destroy this union and form a southern confederacy bounded, north, by the Potomac River." By 1848, Jackson's prediction seemed close to reality.

The Wilmot Proviso

President Polk had naively assumed that the expansion of American territory to the Pacific would strengthen "the bonds of Union." Instead, the fate of slavery in the new western territories ignited a violent political debate that would lead to secession and civil war.

THE WILMOT PROVISO Taylor would refuse to veto the proviso as president, even though he was a slave owner. This political cartoon, "Old Zack at Home," points out his seeming hypocrisy.

The Mexican-American War was less than three months old when it sparked a new political conflict over slavery. On August 8, 1846, an obscure Democratic congressman from Pennsylvania, David Wilmot, delivered a speech to the House of Representatives in which he proposed that if any Mexican territory should be acquired, slavery would be banned there.

The proposed **Wilmot Proviso** reignited the debate over the westward expansion of slavery that had been lurking since the Missouri controversy of 1819–1821. The Missouri Compromise had provided a temporary solution by protecting slavery in states where it already existed but not allowing it in newly acquired territories north of the 36°30′ latitude. Now, with the territories taken from Mexico, the political dispute over slavery would explode.

Congressional controversy over the Wilmot Proviso

The House of Representatives approved the Wilmot Proviso, but the Senate balked. President Polk dismissed the proviso as "mischievous and foolish" but privately worried that "the slavery question is assuming a fearful... aspect" that might "ultimately threaten the Union itself." If slavery were banned from the western territories, all new states would be free states, thus putting at risk the future of slavery everywhere and shifting the political balance in Congress against the slave states.

Wilmot Proviso (1846) Proposal by Congressman David Wilmot, a Pennsylvania Democrat, to prohibit slavery in any lands acquired in the Mexican-American War.

Polk convinced Wilmot to withhold his amendment from any bill dealing with the annexation of Mexican territory. By then, however, others were ready to take up the cause. In one form or another, Wilmot's proposal would frame the furious debate in Congress over the expansion of slavery. Abraham Lincoln recalled that during his one term as a congressman, in 1847–1849, he voted for restricting slavery in the new territories forty times.

Senator John C. Calhoun, meanwhile, countered Wilmot's proviso with a pro-slavery plan, which he introduced on February 19, 1847. Calhoun insisted that Wilmot's effort to exclude enslaved people from territories would violate the Fifth Amendment, which forbids Congress to deprive any person of life, liberty, or property without due process of law. Enslaved people, he argued, were *property*.

By this clever stroke of logic, Calhoun turned the Bill of Rights into a guarantee of slavery. Senator Thomas Hart Benton of Missouri, a slaveholder but also a nationalist eager to calm sectional tensions, found in Calhoun's stance a set of dangerous abstractions "leading to no result." Wilmot and Calhoun between them, he said, had fashioned a pair of scissors. Neither blade alone would cut very well, but joined together they could sever the nation in two.

Popular Sovereignty

Thomas Hart Benton and others tried to deflect the brewing conflict over slavery by suggesting that Congress simply extend the Missouri Compromise line, dividing free and slave territory at the latitude of 36°30′, all the way to the Pacific Ocean. Senator Lewis Cass of Michigan suggested a different solution: that the citizens of each territory "regulate their own internal concerns in their own way," like the citizens of a state. Such an approach would take the issue of slavery in new territories out of Congress and put it in the hands of those directly affected. "**Popular sovereignty**," as Cass called his idea, appealed to many eager to protect states' rights.

President Polk had promised to serve only one term, and, having accomplished his goals, he refused to run again in 1848. Cass won the Democratic presidential nomination, but the party refused to endorse his "popular sovereignty" plan. Instead, their platform denied the power of Congress to interfere with slavery in the states and criticized all efforts by anti-slavery activists to bring the question before Congress.

The Whigs, as they had in 1840, passed over their party leader, Henry Clay, in favor of General Zachary Taylor, the hero of the Mexican-American War. Taylor owned a Louisiana plantation with more than 100 enslaved people. Yet he vigorously opposed the extension of slavery into new western territories.

The Free-Soil Coalition

As it had done in the 1840 election, the Whig party in 1848 offered no platform to avoid the divisive issue of slavery. The anti-slavery crusade, however, was not easily silenced. Americans who worried about slavery but could not endorse outright abolition could support banning slavery from the western territories. As a result, "Free Soil" in the western territories became the rallying cry for a new political party: the Free-Soil coalition, which focused on preventing the spread of slavery.

The **Free-Soil party** attracted northern Democrats, anti-slavery northern Whigs, and members of the abolitionist Liberty party, created in 1840.

popular sovereignty Legal concept by which the White male settlers in a U.S. territory would vote to decide whether to permit slavery.

Free-Soil party A political coalition created in 1848 that opposed the expansion of slavery into the new western territories.

In 1848, Free-Soilers nominated former Democratic president Martin Van Buren as their candidate. The party's platform stressed that slavery would not be allowed in the western territories.

The Free-Soilers split the Democratic vote enough to throw New York to the Whig Zachary Taylor, and they split the Whig vote enough to give Ohio to the Democrat Lewis Cass. However, Van Buren's approximately 291,000 third-party votes lagged well behind the 1,361,000 for Taylor and 1,222,000 for Cass.

The California Gold Rush

Meanwhile, a new development emerged in the Mexican province of Alta California. On January 24, 1848, on part of John Sutter's land along the south fork of the American River, a group of Mormon and Indian workers building a sawmill in eastern California discovered gold. Just nine days later, California would be labeled the "great prize" transferred to the United States through the treaty ending the Mexican-American War.

Word of the gold strike spread rapidly after President Polk confirmed the news in a speech to Congress. In 1849, nearly 100,000 Americans, mostly young men infected with gold fever, quit jobs, left farms, deserted from the army, abandoned wives and children, and sold businesses to set off for California. Within a matter of weeks after the news, three-quarters of the men living in San Francisco had rushed to the gold fields. By 1854, the number would top 300,000, vastly outnumbering the disinherited Mexican population. Thousands more came from across the world—Mexico, Central and South America, Canada, Australia, New Zealand, Asia, and Europe.

A U.S. army officer reported that the "vast deposits of gold" had "entirely changed the character of Upper California." Within two years, San Francisco was transformed from a sleepy coastal village of 800 residents to a bustling city of 20,000.

"We are on the brink of an Age of Gold," gushed Horace Greeley, editor of the *New York Tribune*. "Go West, young man, go west!" So many New England

SAN FRANCISCO A view of San Francisco during 1849 shows the city in the midst of rapid growth. The Bay is crowded with ships, and a blend of tents and newly constructed buildings dot the coastline.

men left for the California gold fields that it would take years to restore the region's gender balance, leading some women to form ambiguous same-sex partnerships in what novelist Henry James called "Boston marriages."

Gold seekers, called forty-niners, found the long trip to California grueling beyond description. The favorite route to California was by sea around Cape Horn, the southern tip of South America, and then up the Pacific to San Francisco. The 13,000-mile journey took an average of six months, twice as long as the trek overland.

Mass migration to California

For all its hardships, however, the **California Gold Rush** became the greatest mass migration in American history. Between 1851 and 1855, the "diggings" throughout California produced almost half the world's output of gold, and the nation's supply of gold coinage increased twentyfold.

Decimating Native Americans and Mexican Americans

For Native Americans in California, however, the Gold Rush was a disaster. In 1848, there were 150,000 Indians in California, ten times as many Whites; by 1870, there were only 30,000 left (80% decrease). Starvation, disease, and a declining birth rate took a heavy toll. But many, perhaps 40 percent, were murdered by gold miners, soldiers, "Indian killers," and others.

In 1851, Peter W. Burnett, the California territorial governor, pledged to continue "a war of extermination . . . between the two races until the Indian race becomes extinct." His commitment to exterminating the Indians contradicted the Treaty of Guadalupe Hidalgo, which granted U.S. citizenship to the indigenous peoples in California.

With the governor's approval and the added enticement of bounties paid for Indian scalps or ears, bands of White Indian-killers roamed the state massacring indigenous peoples. Sally Bell, a Sinkyone survivor of one of the raids, reported that "some white men came. They killed my grandfather and my mother and my father. . . . Then they killed my baby sister and cut her heart out and threw it in the brush where I ran and hid." A California senator applauded the mass murders of Indians because "the interest of the white man demands their extinction."

The infusion of California gold into the U.S. economy triggered a surge of prolonged prosperity. The Gold Rush also shifted the nation's focus westward, spurred the construction of transcontinental railroads and telegraph lines, and prompted dreams of an American commercial empire linking the Pacific coast to Asia's teeming markets.

Senator Stephen Douglas, a Democratic senator from Illinois, urged the federal government to build a transcontinental railroad from California through Indian Country to Chicago. Another senator, William Seward of New York, pointed out that there were eighteen Indian nations living along the proposed route. "Where will they go?" Seward asked. "Back across the Mississippi? . . . To the Himalayas?"

Cherokees were aghast. "No matter how little is left the red man," warned an editorial in the *Cherokee Advocate*, the federal government would not "rest until the Indians are made landless and homeless."

California Gold Rush (1849) A massive migration of gold hunters, mostly young men, who transformed the national economy after massive amounts of gold were discovered in northern California.

Actions against Mexican *Californios*

While native peoples were being targeted for removal, the influx of miners into California proved deadly for Mexican *Californios*. "Mexicans have no business in this country," a miner wrote in a letter to the *Stockton Times*. "I don't believe in them. The men were made to be shot at, and the women were made for *our* purposes. I'm a white man—I am. A Mexican is pretty near black. I hate all Mexicans." In 1850, White miners convinced the new state legislature to pass a Foreign Miners' Tax that drove most Mexicans from the diggings.

White miners treated Indians as roughly as Mexicans. In 1850, the California state legislature allowed Whites to force "unemployed" Indians to work for them in exchange for food and clothing. Some miners went further, forcing them out of the diggings and killing those who resisted.

Mining Life

Women in California

The few women who dared to live in the mining camps could demand a premium for their work as cooks, laundresses, entertainers, and prostitutes. One placed a candid ad for a husband in a local newspaper: "Her age is none of your business. She is neither handsome nor a fright, yet an *old* man need *not* apply, nor any who have not a little more education than she has, and a great deal more gold, for there must be $20,000 settled on her [paid] before she will" marry.

Sacramento, closer to the diggings, became the staging area for the northern mines. Many of the wealthiest Californians were providing goods and services to the miners. New business enterprises—saloons, taverns, gambling halls, restaurants, laundries, general stores—emerged to serve the miners. One of the new businesses made sturdy denim work pants, their pockets reinforced by copper rivets. The blue jeans, known to this day as Levi's, were developed in San Francisco by the German-Jewish immigrant Levi Strauss.

The flannel-shirted forty-niners included people from every social class and every state and territory, as well as local Indians and enslaved people brought by their owners. Louis Manigault, the son of a South Carolina rice planter, reported that California was "filled with castoffs and exiles from almost every nation, the true and perfect scum of the Earth." Life in the mining camps, he noted, "was not safe, and almost every [news]paper informed us of some dreadful murder, or horrible crime—everyone was armed."

Chinese immigrants in California

The miners were mostly unmarried men of varied ethnic and cultural backgrounds, including some 20,000 Chinese immigrants. A Chinese shipowner recruited immigrants by portraying California as utopia: "Americans are very rich people. They want the Chinese to come and will make him welcome. There will be big pay, large houses, and food and clothing of the finest description. . . . It is a nice country, without mandarins [aristocrats] or soldiers. All alike: big man no larger than little man. . . . Never fear, and you will be lucky."

Few Chinese immigrants were interested in staying in California; they wanted to strike it rich and return home, in part because of the prejudice against them. "The manners and habits of the Chinese are very repugnant to Americans in California," reported a San Francisco newspaper. "Of different language, blood, religion, and character, and inferior in most mental and bodily qualities, the Chinaman is looked upon . . . as only a little superior to the Negro."

GOLD MINERS Chinese immigrants and White settlers mine for gold in the Auburn Ravine of California in 1856. **What were living and working conditions like in the mining camps?**

Most forty-niners did not strike it rich. Mining camps sprang up like mushrooms and disappeared almost as rapidly. As soon as rumors of a new strike made the rounds, prospectors abandoned one site for another; when no more gold could be found, they picked up and moved on again.

The mining camps and shantytowns may have had colorful names—Whiskey Flat, Murderers' Bar, Sucker Flat, Lousy Ravine, Petticoat Slide, Piety Hill—but they were raw, dirty, lawless, disease-ridden, and dangerous places. "In the short space of twenty-four days," one miner reported, "we have had murders, fearful accidents, bloody deaths, a mob, whippings, a hanging, an attempt at suicide, and a fatal duel."

Within six months of arriving in California in 1849, one gold seeker in every five was dead. The gold fields and mining towns were so dangerous that insurance companies refused to provide coverage. Suicides were common, as were deadly illnesses triggered by contaminated water—cholera, malaria, dysentery, and typhoid.

Twenty-seven-year-old prospector Olney Thayer of Massachusetts recognized the larger significance of the Gold Rush in 1852 when he predicted in a letter home that "California is destined to exert a powerful influence, not only upon the destiny of this nation, but upon the whole civilized globe." He died nine months later of typhoid fever.

California Statehood

New president Zachary Taylor decided in 1849 to use California's request for statehood to end the congressional stalemate over slavery. Why not make California and New Mexico free states immediately, he argued, and thereby bypass the volatile issue of slavery?

California and New Mexico establish free-state governments

Californians, however, were ahead of him. By December 1849, without consulting Congress, they had put a free-state (no-slavery) government into operation. New Mexico responded more slowly, but by 1850 it had also adopted a free-state constitution.

Yet while banning African American slavery, the new western states preserved *peonage* (involuntary servitude) of Native Americans. In California, the Indian Act (1850) allowed some 25,000 "unemployed" Indians ("vagrants"), including thousands of children, to be auctioned off to White settlers as forced laborers. Five years later, the state legislature passed the Anti-Vagrancy Act, also known as the Greaser Act. The act's supporters claimed it was created

Compromise of 1850 A package of five bills presented to the Congress by Henry Clay intended to avoid secession or civil war by reducing tensions between North and South over the status of slavery.

"to protect honest people from the excesses of vagabonds." In fact, however, it was directed at those of "Spanish and Indian blood," commonly "known as greasers." The Anti-Vagrancy Act allowed police to arrest any person suspected of being a vagabond and force them to work, usually on ranches or in mines.

The Compromise of 1850

On December 4, 1849, President Zachary Taylor endorsed the immediate admission of California for statehood and urged Congress to avoid injecting slavery into the issue. The new Congress, however, was in no mood for simple solutions.

Angry southerners threatened to leave the Union if Taylor brought California and New Mexico in as free states. Doing so, they feared, would upset the political balance of fifteen slave states and fifteen free states.

The spotlight then fell on the Senate, where an all-star cast—Henry Clay, John C. Calhoun, and Daniel Webster (all of whom would die within two years), with William H. Seward, Stephen A. Douglas, and Jefferson Davis in supporting roles—staged one of the great dramas of American politics: the **Compromise of 1850**.

Saving the Union

With southern extremists threatening secession, congressional leaders again turned to Henry Clay, now seventy-two, who, as Abraham Lincoln said, was "regarded by all, as *the* man for the crisis."

On January 29, 1850, having gained Daniel Webster's support, Henry Clay presented to Congress several resolutions meant to settle the "controversy between the free and slave states, growing out of the subject of slavery."

CLAY'S COMPROMISE (1850) Warning against an impending sectional conflict, Henry Clay outlines his plan for "compromise and harmony" on the Senate floor.

THE COMPROMISE OF 1850

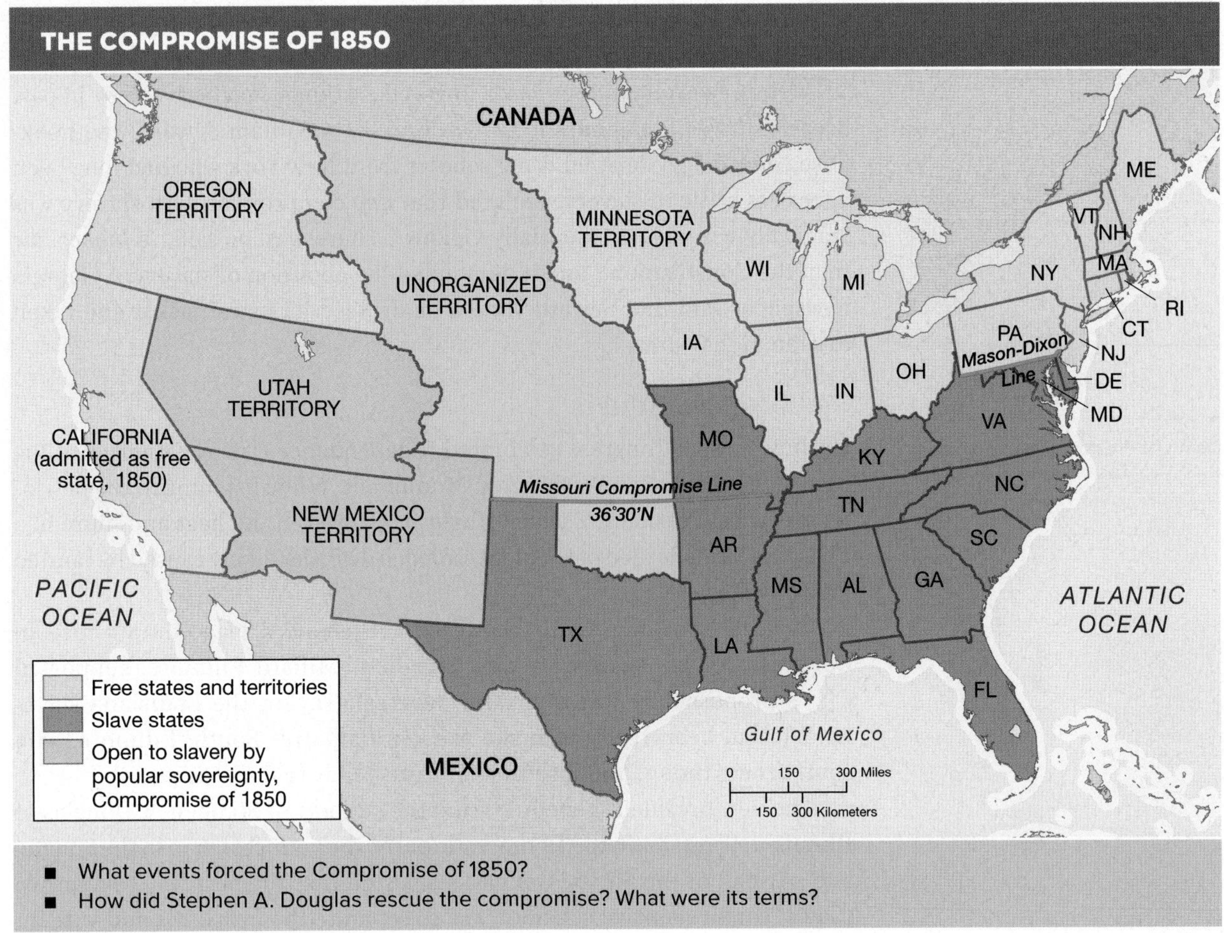

- What events forced the Compromise of 1850?
- How did Stephen A. Douglas rescue the compromise? What were its terms?

Clay proposed to (1) admit California as a free state; (2) organize the territories of New Mexico and Utah without restrictions on slavery, allowing the residents to decide the issue for themselves; (3) deny Texas its claim to much of New Mexico; (4) compensate Texas by having the federal government pay the pre-annexation Texas debts; (5) retain slavery in the District of Columbia but abolish the *sale* of enslaved people in the nation's capital; (6) adopt a more stringent federal fugitive slave law; and (7) deny congressional authority to interfere with the interstate slave trade.

His complex proposals became in substance the Compromise of 1850, but only after months of negotiations punctuated by the most celebrated debates in congressional history. On March 4, a grim John C. Calhoun, the unbending defender of slavery, left his sickbed, draped himself in a black cloak, and sat in the Senate chamber, where he listened to a colleague read his defiant rejection of Clay's proposal.

Three days later, John C. Calhoun, who would die in just three weeks, returned to the Senate to hear the "golden-throated" Daniel Webster. "I wish to speak today," Webster began, "not as a Massachusetts man, not as a Northern man, but as an American. . . . I speak today for the preservation of the Union." He criticized extremists on both sides for their "violent" actions and suggested that some new territories should become slave states and others free states.

Webster's evenhanded speech angered extremists on both sides—in part because it was four hours long. On March 11, William Seward, the hook-nosed and shaggy-browed Whig senator from New York who had long been a fearless critic of slavery, declared that *any* compromise with slavery was "radically wrong and essentially vicious." There was, he said, "a *higher law* than the Constitution," and it demanded the abolition of slavery. A Georgia newspaper said that Seward should be dressed in a straitjacket and taken to a lunatic asylum.

Compromise Efforts

Death of President Zachary Taylor

On July 4, 1850, Congress celebrated Independence Day by gathering at the base of the unfinished Washington Monument. While listening to the patriotic speeches, President Zachary Taylor collapsed in the heat and humidity. Five days later, he died of a violent stomach disorder, likely caused by tainted food or water.

Taylor's shocking death bolstered the chances of a compromise in Congress, for his successor, Vice President Millard Fillmore, supported Clay's proposals. It was a striking reversal: Taylor, the Louisiana slaveholder, had been ready to make war on his native South; Fillmore, who southerners thought opposed slavery, was ready to make peace.

The new president benefited from the support of Stephen A. Douglas of Illinois, a rising star in the Democratic party, the youngest man in the Senate, and a friend of the South. Douglas suggested that the best way to approve Clay's "comprehensive scheme" was to separate the proposals and vote on each of them, one at a time. The plan worked. By September 20, President Fillmore had signed the last of the measures into law.

The Compromise of 1850 passes

In its final version, the Compromise of 1850 included the following elements: (1) California entered the Union as a free state, ending forever the balance of free and slave states; (2) the Texas–New Mexico Act made New Mexico a separate territory and set the Texas state boundary at its present location (in return for giving up its claims to much of New Mexico, Texas received $10 million to erase the state's debt); (3) the Utah Act set up the Utah Territory and gave the territorial legislature authority over "all rightful subjects of legislation," including slavery; (4) a Fugitive Slave Act required the federal government and northern states to help capture and return freedom seekers to the South; and (5) as a gesture to antislavery groups, the public sale of enslaved people, but not slavery itself, was abolished in the District of Columbia.

The Fugitive Slave Act

Fugitive Slave Act (1850) A part of the Compromise of 1850 that authorized federal officials to help capture and then return freedom seekers to their owners without trials.

The **Fugitive Slave Act** was the most controversial element of the Compromise of 1850. It did more than strengthen the hand of slave catchers; it sought to recover freedom-seekers who had already escaped. The law also unwittingly enabled slave traders to kidnap free Blacks in northern "free" states, claiming that they were freedom seekers, and it required citizens to help locate and capture freedom seekers. The act assigned federal officers to assist in slave-catching. Finally, the act denied freedom seekers the right to a jury trial and increased the penalty for interfering with slave catchers to $1,000 and six months in jail.

Abolitionists fumed. Ralph Waldo urged people to break the new law. In New York, Reverend Jermain Loguen, himself a freedom seeker, shouted: "I don't respect this law—I don't fear it—I won't obey it! It outlaws me, and I outlaw it."

In late October 1850, two slave catchers from Georgia arrived in Boston, determined to use the Fugitive Slave Act to recapture William and Ellen Craft, husband-and-wife cabinetmakers. Abolitionists mobilized to prevent the Crafts from being seized by the "man stealers." After five days, the slave catchers gave up and returned to Georgia.

THE

BOSTON SLAVE RIOT,

AND

TRIAL

OF

Anthony Burns,

CONTAINING THE

REPORT OF THE FANEUIL HALL MEETING; THE MURDER OF BACHELDER; THEODORE PARKER'S LESSON FOR THE DAY; SPEECHES OF COUNSEL ON BOTH SIDES, CORRECTED BY THEMSELVES; VERBATIM REPORT OF JUDGE LORING'S DECISION; AND, A DETAILED ACCOUNT OF THE EMBARKATION.

BOSTON:
FETRIDGE AND COMPANY.
1854.

TRIAL OF ANTHONY BURNS
Title page from the pamphlet, *The Boston Slave Riot, and Trial of Anthony Burns*, which captured the detailed judicial proceedings of one of the most transformative events in the abolitionist movement.

Anthony Burns had a much different experience, however. In 1853, he had escaped from slavery in Virginia and settled in Boston. The following year, his former owner captured him on his way home from work. Although Burns, as a freedom seeker, had no legal rights, his antislavery attorneys found ingenious ways to postpone the court date when he would be released to his former master.

Then something extraordinary occurred. Some 7,000 Black and White abolitionists stormed the courthouse in an effort to free Burns. During the fracas, a U.S. Marshal was killed and a dozen more people were wounded. Some 1,500 federal troops were sent to restore order and ensure that Burns's hearing proceeded on schedule. The judge ruled that Burns must be returned to Virginia and his enslaved existence.

Amos Lawrence, one of the wealthiest men in Boston, was transformed by the government's effort to return Burns to a life of forced servitude. He wrote his uncle that "we went to bed one night old-fashioned, conservative, Compromise Union Whigs and waked up stark mad Abolitionists." Lawrence and other abolitionists began to endorse the use of violence to end slavery.

In Springfield, Massachusetts, fiery abolitionist John Brown formed an armed band of African Americans to attack slave catchers. Such efforts led Horace Greeley, the prominent New York newspaper editor, to write that the Fugitive Slave Act was "a very bad investment for slaveholders" because it was creating such a backlash against slavery throughout the northern states.

Several northern states countered the Fugitive Slave Act by passing what were called personal liberty laws. Some allowed jury trials for freedom seekers who had been captured and others prohibited state authorities from cooperating with slave catchers. Still others imposed stiff penalties on anyone who falsely accused African Americans of being freedom seekers.

MARGARET "PEGGY" GARNER This image depicts Peggy Garner, the determined freedom seeker who escaped from Kentucky to Ohio with four of her children, one of whom she killed when discovered by slave catchers. She said she did not want her children raised in slavery.

Slavery: A Fate Worse than Death

The divisive Fugitive Slave Act polarized the debate over the future of slavery. It also generated tragic consequences, the most poignant example of which occurred along the Kentucky-Ohio border. On January 28, 1856, a twenty-two-year-old enslaved woman, Margaret "Peggy" Garner, escaped from Maplewood, a northern Kentucky plantation. With her was Robert, her enslaved "husband," four children, and several other enslaved families. They stole horses and a sleigh and made their way sixteen miles to the frozen Ohio River. At dawn, the seventeen escapees walked across the iced-over waterway and made their way to Cincinnati, where they split up. At long last, they were free—or so they thought.

Within hours, slave catchers, federal marshals, and Archibald Gaines, the owner of Maplewood, found Garner and others barricaded in what they thought was a safe house. The posse, armed with warrants, stormed the house. Frantic with fright, Margaret killed her two-year-old daughter Mary with a butcher knife rather than see her returned to slavery. She was about to kill her other children and then herself when marshals arrested her.

Accounts of the incident spread quickly across the nation and the world. Both the Ohio governor and President Franklin Pierce took keen interest in the case, and more than a thousand people lined the streets each day to observe the trial.

On the trial's final day, Garner called slavery a fate "more cruel than death," especially for young women subject to daily sexual assaults. It was better for her children "to go home to God than back to slavery."

In the end, the Ohio judge ruled that Garner was "property" to be returned to slave-state Kentucky. Yet no sooner was she back in Kentucky than abolitionists in Ohio got the state to issue warrants to have her returned to be tried for murder. (They assumed the governor would pardon her if convicted.) These efforts prompted Archibald Gaines to sell Margaret and her children to his brother in Arkansas. She died of typhoid fever in 1858.

Uncle Tom's Cabin

During the 1850s, anti-slavery advocates gained a powerful new weapon in the form of Harriet Beecher Stowe's best-selling novel, *Uncle Tom's Cabin; or Life among the Lowly* (1852). Stowe epitomized the powerful moral and religious underpinnings of the abolitionist movement. The sister and daughter of prominent ministers and the wife of a theology professor, she could not help but absorb the deep religiosity and moral activism prevalent among her extended family members. While raising six children in Cincinnati, Ohio, during the 1830s and 1840s, she helped freedom seekers who had crossed the Ohio River from Kentucky.

Stowe detested the Fugitive Slave Act. In the spring of 1850, having moved to Maine, she began writing *Uncle Tom's Cabin.* "The time has come," she wrote, "when even a woman or a child who can speak a word for freedom and humanity is bound to speak." The novel ended with Stowe predicting that Almighty God's wrath would destroy America if slavery were not abolished.

Uncle Tom's Cabin is a bestseller

Uncle Tom's Cabin was a smashing success. Within two days, the first printing had sold out, and by the end of its first year, it had sold 300,000 copies in the United States and more than a million in Great Britain. By 1855, it was "the most popular novel of our day."

Uncle Tom's Cabin depicts improbable saints and sinners, crude stereotypes, impossibly virtuous Black victims, and sensational incidents. The novel tells the story of Eliza, a desperate freedom seeker who, clutching her baby, barely escapes her pursuers by taking a dangerous "flying leap" over the water onto "rafts of ice" in the Ohio River, frantically jumping from one ice "cake" to another until "she saw the Ohio side, and a man helping her up the bank" to freedom.

In the process of describing this young woman's liberation, Stowe revealed how the brutal realities of slavery harmed everyone associated with it. The book incensed slaveholders, who called Stowe that "wretch in petticoats." One of them mailed her a parcel containing the severed ear of a disobedient enslaved man.

The Election of 1852

In 1852, the Democrats chose Franklin Pierce of New Hampshire as their presidential candidate; their platform endorsed the Compromise of 1850. For their part, the Whigs repudiated Millard Fillmore, who had faithfully supported the Compromise of 1850, and chose General Winfield Scott, another hero of the Mexican-American War.

Scott, an inept campaigner, carried only Tennessee, Kentucky, Massachusetts, and Vermont. Pierce overwhelmed him in the Electoral

College, 254–42, although the popular vote was close: 1.6 million–1.4 million. The third-party Free-Soilers mustered only 156,000 votes for John P. Hale.

Franklin Pierce elected president (1852)

The forty-eight-year-old Pierce had fought in the Mexican-American War and was, like James Polk, touted as another Andrew Jackson despite his undistinguished record as a congressman and senator. He promoted western expansion, even if it meant adding more slave states to the Union. Yet he also acknowledged that the nation had recently survived a "perilous crisis," and he urged both North and South to avoid aggravating the other.

By the end of his first year in office, Democratic leaders had decided he was a failure. By trying to be all things to all people, Pierce was labeled a "doughface": a "Northern man with Southern principles."

The Kansas-Nebraska Crisis

During the mid–nineteenth century, American merchants discovered the vast markets of Asia. As commerce with China and Japan grew, demand grew for a transcontinental railroad line connecting the eastern seaboard with the Pacific coast to facilitate both the flow of commerce with Asia and the settlement of the western territories. Those promoting the railroad did not realize that the issue would also reignite the debate over the westward extension of slavery.

Democrats pass Kansas-Nebraska Act

In 1852 and 1853, Congress debated several proposals for a transcontinental rail line. Secretary of War Jefferson Davis of Mississippi favored a southern route across the territories acquired from Mexico. Senator Stephen Douglas of Illinois insisted that Chicago be the transcontinental railroad's Midwest hub. To promote that idea, he urged Congress to pass the **Kansas-Nebraska Act** so that the vast territory west of Missouri and Iowa could be settled—by Whites.

To win the support of southern legislators, Douglas championed the principle of "popular sovereignty," whereby voters in each new western territory would decide whether to allow slavery. It was a clever way to get around the 1820 Missouri Compromise, which excluded slavery north of the 36th parallel, where Kansas and Nebraska were located.

Southerners demanded more, however, and Douglas complied, in part because he would make a fortune if a railroad were built through the territory. He supported the formal repeal of the Missouri Compromise and the creation of *two* new territorial governments: Kansas, west of Missouri, and Nebraska, which then included the Dakotas. In 1854, Douglas and the Democrats pushed through the Kansas-Nebraska Act by a vote of 37–14 in the Senate and 113–100 in the House.

Kansas-Nebraska Act (1854) Controversial legislation that created two new territories taken from Native Americans, Kansas and Nebraska, where resident males would decide whether slavery would be allowed (popular sovereignty).

The anti-slavery faction in Congress, mostly Whigs, had been crushed, and the national Whig party died with them. Out of its ashes would emerge a new party, the Republicans.

The Emergence of the Republican Party

CORE **OBJECTIVE**

4. Analyze the appeal of the Republican party to northern voters and how it led to Abraham Lincoln's victory in the 1860 presidential contest.

The dispute over the Kansas-Nebraska Act led northern Whigs to align with one of two new parties. One was the nativist American party, which had emerged in opposition to the surge of mostly Catholic immigrants from Ireland and Germany during the 1840s, when the number of newcomers soared. The anti-Catholic "Know-Nothings" proposed that newcomers be denied citizenship and the right to run for public offices. In the early 1850s, Know-Nothings won several local elections in Massachusetts and New York.

The other new party, the Republicans, attracted even more northern Whigs. The party coalesced in 1854 when the anti-slavery "conscience Whigs" split from the southern pro-slavery "cotton Whigs." They then joined with independent Democrats and Free-Soilers to form the new party dedicated to excluding slavery from the western territories.

A young Kentucky-born Illinois congressman named Abraham Lincoln, the son of an illiterate farmer and a mother who died when he was nine, made the transition from Whig to Republican. He said that the passage of Douglas's Kansas-Nebraska Act angered him "as he had never been before" and transformed his views on slavery. Unless the North mobilized to stop the efforts of pro-slavery southerners, Lincoln believed, the future of the Union was imperiled. He was determined to reverse the Kansas-Nebraska Act, for it had been "conceived in violence, passed in violence, is maintained in violence, and is being executed in violence."

"Bleeding Kansas"

The passage of the Kansas-Nebraska Act soon placed Kansas at the center of the increasingly violent debate over slavery. While Nebraska would become a free state, Kansas was up for grabs. According to the Kansas-Nebraska Act, the residents of the Kansas Territory, not Congress, would decide whether to allow slavery. The law, however, said nothing about *when* Kansans would decide about slavery, so each side tried to gain political control of the vast territory and worked to recruit emigrants to the Kansas territory.

Anti-abolitionist voting fraud in Kansas

When Kansas's first federal governor arrived in 1854, he scheduled an election for a territorial legislature in 1855. On Election Day, 5,000 "border ruffians" from Missouri crossed into Kansas. They seized polling places, illegally elected pro-slavery legislators (casting four times as many votes as there were residents), and vowed to kill every "God-damned abolitionist in the Territory." The governor denounced the fraudulent vote but did nothing to alter the results for fear of being killed himself. The territorial legislature expelled its few anti-slavery members and declared the territory open to slavery.

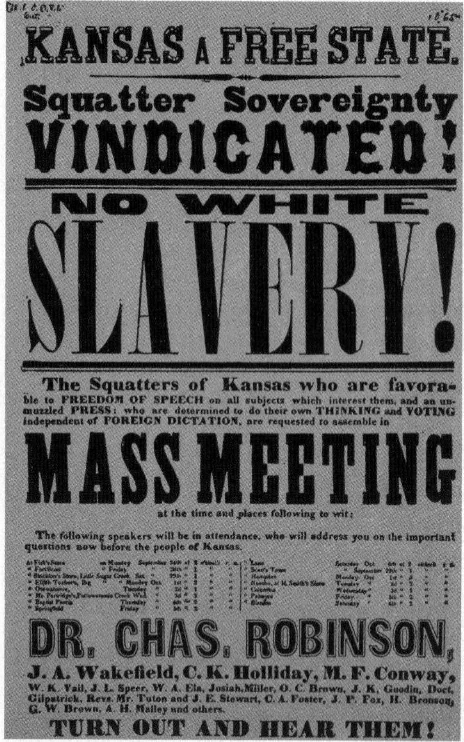

KANSAS A FREE STATE This broadside advertises a series of mass meetings in Kansas in support of the free-state cause, based on the principle of "squatter" or popular sovereignty.

Outraged free-state advocates in Kansas spurned this "bogus" legislature and elected their own delegates to a "free state" constitutional convention that met in Topeka in 1855. The convention drafted a new state constitution excluding slavery and applied for statehood. By 1856, a free-state "governor" and "legislature" were operating in Topeka; thus, there were two illegal governments in the Kansas Territory. Soon the political conflict mushroomed into a civil war, which journalists called "**Bleeding Kansas**."

In May 1856, a pro-slavery force of 500 Missourians, Alabamans, and South Carolinians invaded the free-state town of Lawrence, near the Missouri border. Democrat David Atchison, a former U.S. senator from Missouri, urged the pro-slavery raiders not to stop fighting "until every spark of free-state, free-speech, free-[colored people], or free in any shape is quenched out of Kansas." As they prepared to use "the bayonet and blood" to teach the "damned abolitionists a southern lesson," Atchison yelled: "Boys, this is the happiest day of my life!"

The aroused mob rampaged through the town, destroying the newspaper offices, burning the governor's house, and demolishing the Free-State Hotel.

The "Sack of Lawrence" ignited the passions of abolitionist John Brown. He believed that Christians must "break the jaws of the wicked," and that the wickedest Americans were those who owned and traded enslaved people. Upon meeting Brown, many declared him crazy; those who supported his efforts thought he was a saint. He was some of both.

By the mid-1850s, the fifty-five-year-old Brown, the father of twenty children, had left his home in Springfield, Massachusetts, to become a merciless holy warrior against slavery. In his view, Blacks deserved both liberty and full social equality.

The Pottawatomie Massacre

Two days after the attack on Lawrence, Brown led four of his sons to Pottawatomie, Kansas, a pro-slavery settlement near the Missouri border. There they dragged five men from their houses and hacked them to death with swords. "God is my judge," Brown told one of his sons afterward. "We were justified under the circumstances."

The Pottawatomie Massacre (May 24–25, 1856) ignited a guerrilla war in the Kansas Territory. On August 30, pro-slavery Missourians raided a free-state settlement at Osawatomie, Kansas. They looted and burned houses and shot Frederick Brown, John's son, through the heart. By the end of 1856, about 200 settlers had been killed in "Bleeding Kansas."

Violence in the Senate

Bleeding Kansas (1856) A series of violent conflicts in the Kansas Territory between anti-slavery and pro-slavery factions over the status of slavery.

The violence in Kansas spilled over into Congress. On May 22, 1856, the day after the burning of Lawrence and two days before the Pottawatomie Massacre, an ugly incident in the Senate shocked the nation. Two days before, Republican senator Charles Sumner of Massachusetts had delivered

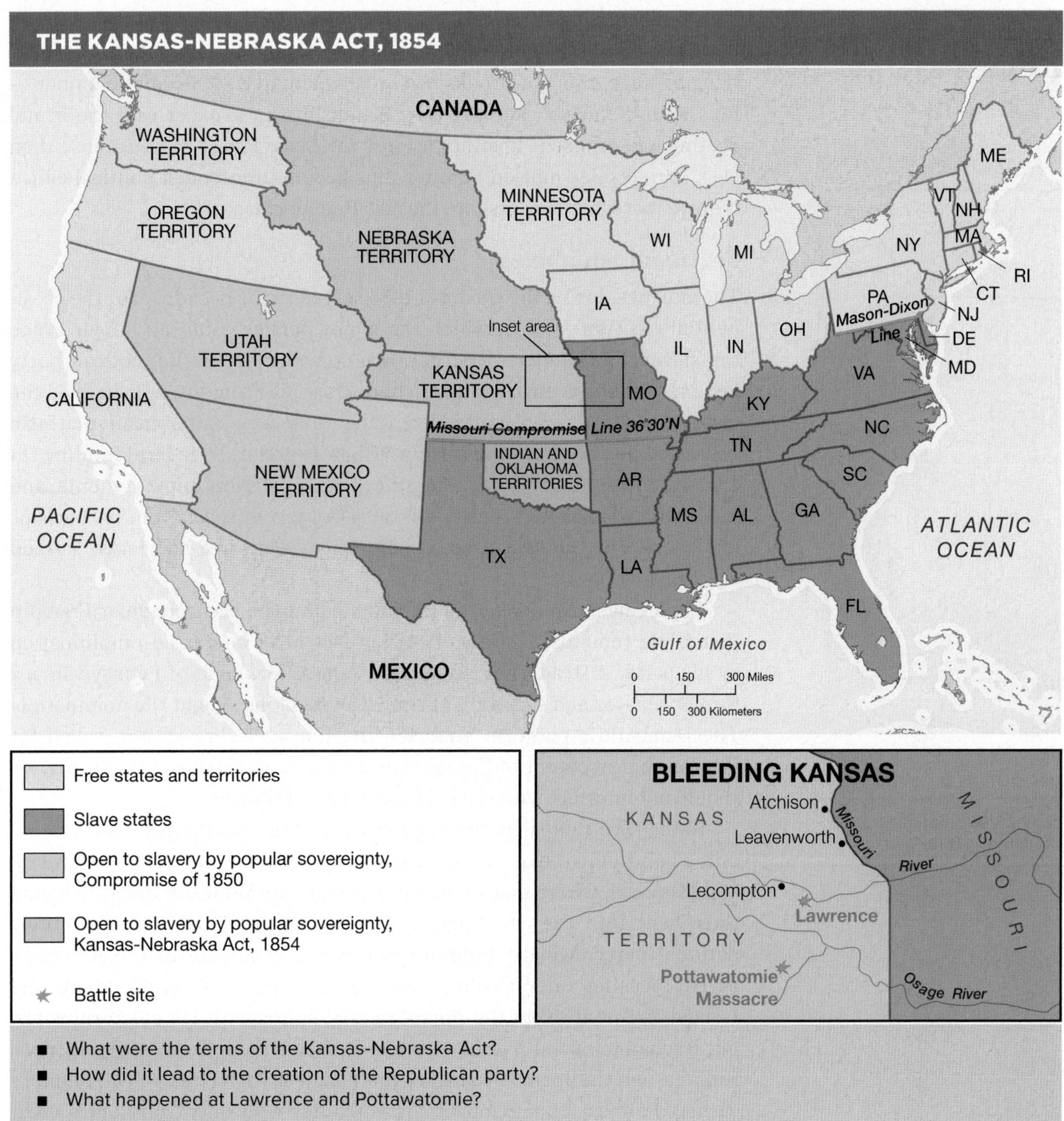

- What were the terms of the Kansas-Nebraska Act?
- How did it lead to the creation of the Republican party?
- What happened at Lawrence and Pottawatomie?

a fiery speech that insulted slave owners, including Andrew Pickens Butler, an elderly senator from South Carolina.

Sumner's speech enraged Butler's young cousin, Preston S. Brooks, a hotheaded South Carolina congressman. On May 22, Brooks resolved to defend the honor of his family, state, and region. He strode into the Senate, confronted Sumner, and began beating him about the head and shoulders with a gold-knobbed cane. Sumner nearly died; he would not return to the Senate for almost four years.

"Bleeding Sumner": A Republican martyr

Southerners celebrated Brooks as a hero; dozens of supporters sent him new canes, one of which carried the inscription: "Hit Him Again." In satisfying his rage, though, Brooks had created a martyr—"Bleeding Sumner"—for the anti-slavery cause. A New Hampshire newspaper said the brutal beating had aroused "hostility against the Slave Power more intense than ever." Brooks's assault on Sumner thus had an unintended political effect: it drove more northerners into the new Republican party.

Sectional Squabbles

The violence during the spring of 1856 served as the backdrop for the presidential election—one in which the major parties could no longer evade the slavery issue. At its first national convention, the Republican party fastened on an eccentric military hero, John C. Frémont, who had led the conquest of Mexican-controlled California. The Republican platform borrowed heavily from the former Whigs. It endorsed federal funding for a transcontinental railroad and other transportation improvements, and it denounced the repeal of the Missouri Compromise and the "barbarism" of slavery. For the first time, a major-party platform had taken a stand against slavery.

In picking a candidate, the Democrats dumped the unpopular Franklin Pierce. He remains the only elected president to be denied renomination by his party. Instead, they nominated James Buchanan of Pennsylvania, a former senator and secretary of state who had long sought the nomination. The Democratic platform endorsed the Kansas-Nebraska Act, called for vigorous enforcement of the fugitive slave law, and stressed that Congress should not interfere with slavery in states or territories.

James Buchanan elected president (1856)

In the 1856 campaign, the Republicans had few southern supporters and only a handful in the border slave states of Delaware, Maryland, Kentucky, and Missouri, where fear of disunion held many Whigs in line. Buchanan thus went into the campaign as the candidate of the only remaining national party. Millard Fillmore ran as the candidate of the American party, focusing on opposing Catholic immigrants from Germany and Ireland. Frémont swept the northernmost states with 114 electoral votes, but Buchanan added five free states—Pennsylvania, New Jersey, Illinois, Indiana, and California—to his southern majority for a total of 174. Fillmore garnered almost 22 percent of the votes but won only Maryland's eight electoral votes.

President James Buchanan

James Buchanan had built his career on his commitment to states' rights and his aggressive promotion of territorial expansion. Saving the Union, he believed, depended upon making concessions to the South. Republicans charged that he lacked the backbone to stand up to the southern slaveholders who dominated the Democratic majorities in Congress.

The sixty-five-year-old Buchanan was—and remains—America's only president who was a lifelong bachelor. (His niece, Harriet Lane, handled the duties of First Lady during his term in office.) He was also rumored to be the first gay president.

To be gay or lesbian or bisexual in the mid-nineteenth century (the term "homosexual" had yet to appear) was to risk arrest or social censure—or both. Most states enforced "anti-sodomy" laws prohibiting "unnatural acts," forcing same-sex relationships underground. For that reason, historians struggle to know with certainty the sexual orientation of people determined to camouflage their behavior.

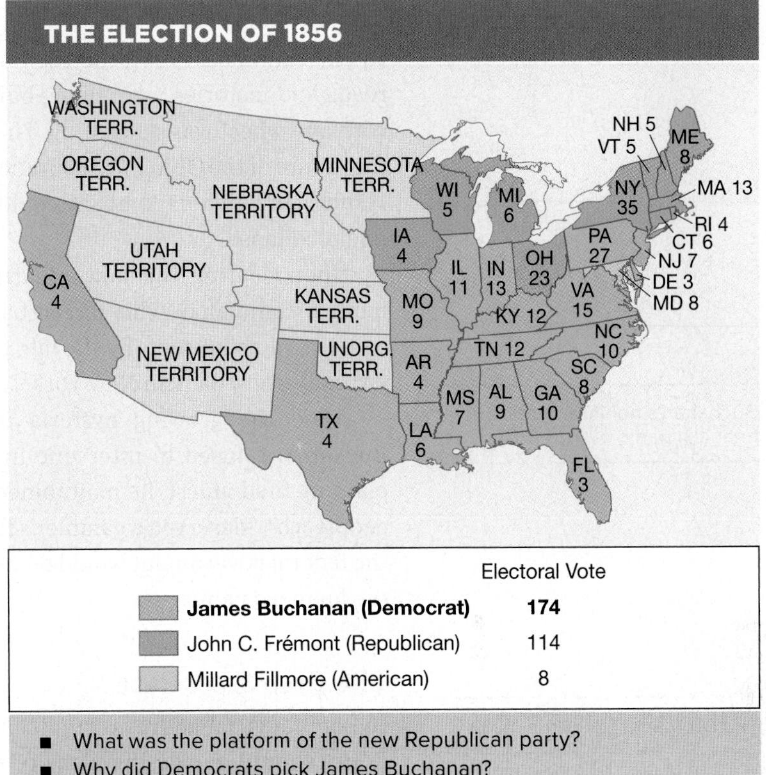

That is the case with James Buchanan. Before becoming president, he had lived for sixteen years with Democrat William Rufus King, a former U.S. senator from Alabama who had also served as ambassador to France. King and Buchanan attended many official functions and social events together. And they shared a bed. To be sure, it was not uncommon in the nineteenth century for single men to room together or even sleep together, whether they knew each other or not. In the case of Buchanan and King, however, there seemed to be more at stake than simple expediency. Friends referred to King as Buchanan's "better half," and one congressman nicknamed him "Mrs. B." When King left for Paris, Buchanan confessed that he was "now 'solitary and alone,' having no companion in the house with me. I have gone a wooing to several gentlemen but have not succeeded with any one of them."

King preferred that Buchanan not find another companion while they were separated. As he wrote from France, "I am selfish enough to hope you will not be able to procure an associate who will cause you to feel no regret at our separation." That King and Buchanan had family members destroy their correspondence after their deaths has added to the speculation about their relationship.

Whatever Buchanan's sexual orientation, there is no doubt that he was a "doughface," a northerner with southern sympathies. No sooner was he elected president than he chose mostly slave-state men for his cabinet.

Although Buchanan had vast political experience, he had limited leadership ability—and bad luck. During his first six months in office in 1857, three main events brought about his undoing: (1) a sharp downturn in the economy; (2) the controversial Supreme Court decision in the *Dred Scott* case; and (3) new troubles in the strife-torn Kansas Territory.

The Panic of 1857

By the summer of 1857, the economy was growing too fast. Too many railroads and factories were being built, and European demand for American corn and wheat was slackening. The result was a financial panic triggered by the failure of the Ohio Life Insurance and Trust Company on August 24, 1857. If such a prestigious company could fail, people worried, the entire economy might collapse.

Upon hearing the news, fearful customers began withdrawing their money from banks. This forced banks to call in loans, causing many businesses to go bankrupt. By the fall, tens of thousands had lost their jobs, and virtually every bank in New York City had closed its doors.

Buchanan's nonintervention in financial panic

Amid the growing hysteria over the economic collapse, President Buchanan refused to intervene in the Panic of 1857. Most of those complaining the loudest, he maintained, were speculators in land and enslaved people who "deserved a gambler's fate." While he was president, he pledged, the federal government would do nothing to address the suffering caused by the financial panic.

The *Dred Scott* Case

The *Dred Scott* decision (1857)

In his inaugural address, President Buchanan asserted that the Supreme Court should decide the issue of slavery in the western territories. Two days later, on March 6, 1857, the Court delivered a momentous decision in the long-awaited case of ***Dred Scott v. Sandford***, which had taken eleven years to work its way through the state and federal courts. The *New York Times* declared it "the most important decision ever made by the Supreme Court."

Scott, born into slavery in Virginia, had been taken to Missouri in 1830, where slavery was legal. There he was sold to an army surgeon, who took him to Illinois, then to the Wisconsin Territory (later Minnesota), and finally back to St. Louis in 1842. While in the Wisconsin Territory, Scott had married Harriet Robinson, and they had two daughters.

In 1846, Scott filed suit in Missouri, claiming that his residence in Illinois and the Wisconsin Territory had made him free because slavery was outlawed there. A Missouri jury decided in his favor, but the state supreme court ruled against him. When the case finally arose on appeal to the U.S. Supreme Court, the nation anxiously awaited its ruling.

Seven of the nine justices were Democrats, and five of the seven were southern slaveholders. Buchanan violated the separation of powers between the judicial and executive branches by browbeating a justice to go along with the southerners. The final vote was 7–2 against Scott.

Chief Justice Roger B. Taney of Maryland, a devoted supporter of the South and of slavery, wrote the majority opinion. He ruled that Scott lacked legal standing because, like all enslaved people, he was property, not a human being. As such, he was not a U.S. citizen and could never become one, nor was he eligible to file suit in a court.

***Dred Scott v. Sandford* (1857)** U.S. Supreme Court ruling that enslaved people were not U.S. citizens and that Congress could not prohibit slavery in territories.

Taney said much more, however. He claimed that slaveholding was a fundamental constitutional right that neither Congress nor territorial legislatures could restrict. Taney argued that the compromises of 1820 and 1850 had deprived citizens of property by prohibiting slavery in selected territories and states, an action "not warranted by the Constitution."

The *Dred Scott* case thus directly challenged the concept of "popular sovereignty." If Congress could not exclude slavery from a territory, as Taney argued, then neither could a territorial government created by an act of Congress. Suddenly, all the West—and the North—was open to slavery.

Pro-slavery advocates loved the Court's decision, as did President Buchanan. A Georgia newspaper said the decision "covers every question regarding slavery and settles it in favor of the South." Republicans and abolitionists, on the other hand, protested the *Dred Scott* decision because it nullified the very basis of the anti-slavery movement—that the enslaved were people, not property.

DRED SCOTT Scott's lawsuit over his family's freedom fanned the flames of the nation's debate on slavery.

The Lecompton Constitution (1857)

Meanwhile, in the Kansas Territory, the fight over slavery intensified. Just before James Buchanan's inauguration, in early 1857, the pro-slavery territorial legislature scheduled a constitutional convention. The governor vetoed the measure, but the legislature overrode his veto. The governor resigned in protest, and Buchanan replaced him with Robert J. Walker.

With Buchanan's approval, Walker pledged to free-state Kansans (the overwhelming majority of residents) that the new constitution would receive a fair vote. But the delegates at Lecompton did not represent the majority, and they drafted a constitution that allowed slavery to be continued in Kansas. Opponents reacted by boycotting the referendum, thus allowing it to be approved and sent to Congress for endorsement. At that point, Buchanan urged Congress to approve the pro-slavery Lecompton Constitution. A new wave of outrage swept across the northern states. Stephen A. Douglas, the most prominent midwestern Democrat, sided with anti-slavery Republicans because Buchanan's action would deny Kansas voters their right to decide the issue in a general election.

Kansans twice reject the Lecompton Constitution

Meanwhile, in Kansas, a new acting governor had convened the anti-slavery legislature. It called for another election to vote the Lecompton Constitution up or down. Most pro-slavery settlers boycotted this election. The result, on January 4, 1858, was decisive: 10,226 voted against the constitution, while only 138 voted for it. In April 1858, the U.S. Congress ordered that Kansans vote again. They did so, rejecting the Lecompton Constitution, 11,300–1,788. With that vote, Kansas cleared the way for its eventual admission as a free state.

LINCOLN AND DOUGLAS A tall, rawboned small-town lawyer, Lincoln *(left)* was motivated by the Kansas-Nebraska Act to vie for an Illinois Senate seat, running against the current Democratic senator and author of the act, Stephen Douglas *(right)*.

Douglas versus Lincoln (1858)

The controversy over slavery in Kansas fractured the Democratic party. Stephen A. Douglas, one of the few remaining Democrats with support in both the North and the South, struggled to keep the party from fragmenting. First, however, he had to secure his home base in Illinois, where in 1858 he faced a demanding Senate reelection campaign.

To challenge Douglas, Illinois Republicans selected a respected lawyer from Springfield, Abraham Lincoln. Lincoln was the son of a frontier farmer/carpenter so poor that he rented out his hardworking son to neighbors.

When Abraham was seven, the family moved from Kentucky across the Ohio River to Indiana. Two years later, Lincoln's "angel mother" Nancy died, and his father remarried. In March 1830, the Lincolns moved to Illinois. In Springfield, Lincoln worked as a farmer, rail-splitter, and surveyor. He later became an attorney and married Mary Todd, from a wealthy, slave-owning family in Lexington, Kentucky.

In 1834, Lincoln was elected to the Illinois legislature, and he served four successive terms as a Whig. He was a true believer in Henry Clay's leadership and Clay's promotion of the American System. "My politics are short and sweet," Lincoln said. "I am in favor of a national bank. I am in favor of the internal improvement system and a high protective tariff." And he was opposed to the expansion of slavery into the western territories.

In 1846, Lincoln won a seat in the U.S. Congress while pledging to serve only one term. After his single unremarkable term, he returned to lawyering in Springfield. In 1854, however, Lincoln's disgust at Douglas's Kansas-Nebraska Act drew him back into the political arena.

Lincoln hated slavery but was not yet an abolitionist. He did not believe that the nation should force the South to end "the monstrous injustice" of slavery, but he did insist that slavery be banned in the new western territories.

In 1856, Lincoln joined the Republican party, and two years later he emerged as the obvious choice to oppose Douglas in the Illinois senatorial race. Lincoln sought to raise his profile by challenging Douglas to a series of debates. The seven **Lincoln-Douglas debates** took place from August 21 to October 15, 1858. They attracted thousands of spectators and transformed the statewide race into a battle for the future of the entire republic.

The two men differed as much physically as they did politically. The brash and brilliant Douglas was short and stocky, barely five feet tall, but had an enormous head that inspired the nickname "the Little Giant." He wore custom-tailored suits and traveled to the debates in a private railroad car.

By contrast, Lincoln was homely—tall (six feet four inches) and thin, with a long neck, big ears, enormous hands and feet, shaggy eyebrows, and deep-set, brooding eyes. Poet Walt Whitman said that Lincoln's face was "so awful ugly it becomes beautiful." His coarse black hair never looked the same from day to day, and his ill-fitting suits made him so unkempt a Bostonian considered Lincoln "the ugliest man" he had ever seen.

Lincoln, however, dazzled people with the rawboned genius of his speeches, which were highlighted by folksy humor, entertaining stories, and biblical eloquence. His opponent, Stephen Douglas, acknowledged that Lincoln was "the strong man of the [Republican] party—full of wit, facts, dates, and the best stump speaker . . . in the West."

Lincoln-Douglas debates over the issue of slavery in the West

The basic dispute between the two rivals, Lincoln insisted, lay in Douglas's indifference to the immorality of slavery. Douglas, he said, did not care whether slavery in the territories was "voted up, or voted down." Instead, he was preoccupied only with process ("popular sovereignty"); Lincoln claimed to be focused on principle. "I have always hated slavery as much as any abolitionist," he stressed. The American government, he predicted, could not "endure, permanently half *slave* and half *free*. . . . It will become *all* one thing or *all* the other."

Douglas responded that the United States was founded on the principle of White supremacy. "It was made by the white man, for the benefit of the white man, to be administered by the white man." Blacks and Indians, he added, were members of an "inferior race."

If Lincoln had the better of the argument, Douglas had the better of a close election. But Lincoln's energetic campaign had made him a national figure.

An Outnumbered South

Continued violence in Congress

In May 1858, the free state of Minnesota entered the Union; in February 1859, another non-slave territory, Oregon, gained statehood. The slave states were quickly becoming a besieged minority, and their political insecurity deepened.

As tensions over the future of slavery rose, decorum in Congress plummeted. Legislators threatened each other with clenched fists. A few of them killed opponents in duels. In 1858, members of Congress engaged in the largest brawl ever staged on the floor of the House of Representatives.

Harsh words about slavery incited the free-for-all. According to a reporter, the House floor "was a sea of writhing bodies, a dozen Southerners

Lincoln-Douglas debates (1858) In the Illinois race between Republican Abraham Lincoln and Democrat Stephen A. Douglas for a seat in the U.S. Senate, a series of seven dramatic debates focusing on the issue of slavery in the territories.

pummeling—or being pummeled by—a dozen Northerners. The Speaker shouted and rapped for order, and the sergeant at arms, thinking he could make a difference, rushed among the combatants showing the House mace. One representative picked up a heavy stoneware spittoon and rushed into the fray. Several Quakers urged calm and peace."

The fracas ended when John "Bowie Knife" Potter of Wisconsin yanked off the hairpiece of a Mississippi congressman and shouted, "I've scalped him."

Like the fighting members of Congress, more and more Americans decided that compromise over the extension of slavery was impossible. The editor of a pro-slavery Kansas newspaper confessed he wanted to kill abolitionists: "If I can't kill a man, I'll kill a woman; and if I can't kill a woman, I'll kill a child."

Some southerners were already talking of secession again. In 1858, former Alabama congressman William L. Yancey, a member of a group of hot-tempered southerners called fire-eaters, boasted that it would be easy "to precipitate the Cotton States into a revolution."

John Brown's Raid (1859)

Raid on Harpers Ferry (1859)

Such violent threats drove John Brown into a desperate act. On the cool, rainy night of October 16, 1859, Brown launched his supreme effort to end slavery. From a Maryland farm, he crossed the Potomac River with about twenty young men, including three of his sons and five African Americans. They walked five miles to the federal rifle arsenal in Harpers Ferry, Virginia (now West Virginia). There they took the sleeping residents by surprise, cut the telegraph lines, and occupied the arsenal with its 100,000 rifles.

Brown then sent several men to kidnap prominent slave owners and arm thousands of enslaved people in the area, in the hope of triggering mass uprisings. "I want to free all the negroes in this state," Brown said. "If the citizens interfere with me, I must burn the town and have blood."

Only a few enslaved people heeded the call, however, and by dawn, enraged townsmen had surrounded the raiders. Brown and a dozen of his men, along with eleven White hostages and two of their enslaved workers, holed up in the firehouse.

In response, hundreds of armed men poured into Harpers Ferry, Among them was Lieutenant Colonel Robert E. Lee, who arrived with a force of U.S. Marines. On the morning of October 18, the marines broke down the firehouse's barricaded doors and rushed in. The siege was over. Brown's men had killed four townspeople and wounded another dozen. Of their own group, ten were killed (including two of Brown's sons), and five were captured; another five escaped.

JOHN BROWN On his way to the gallows, Brown predicted that slavery would end only "after much bloodshed."

A jury quickly convicted John Brown and his accomplices of treason, murder, and "conspiring with Negroes to produce insurrection." A wounded Brown, appearing more rational than crazed, delivered a stirring speech: "Now, if it is deemed necessary that I should forfeit my life for the furtherance of the ends of justice, and mingle my blood further with the blood of my children and with the blood of millions in this slave country whose rights are disregarded by wicked, cruel, and unjust enactments, I say, let it be done."

On December 2, 1859, Brown, wearing a black coat and black pants stained with blood, climbed into a wagon, sat on his empty black walnut coffin, and rode to the gallows, which was surrounded by 1,500 soldiers. (Among the onlookers was a popular actor named John Wilkes Booth, who would later assassinate Abraham Lincoln.)

Brown's raid ignites fears of abolitionists and insurrections

If Brown had failed to ignite a massive slave rebellion, he had become a martyr for the anti-slavery cause. In the North, church bells tolled in his honor, and cannons fired salutes. In the South, he had stirred the region's worst nightmare: that armed enslaved people would revolt. John Brown, wrote the African American abolitionist Frederick Douglass, "began the war that ended American slavery."

Throughout the fall and winter of 1859–1860, rumors of abolitionist conspiracies and slave insurrections swept through the southern states. Some 300 abolitionists were murdered or forced out of the region. "We regard every man in our midst an enemy to the institutions of the South," said the *Atlanta Confederacy*, "who does not boldly declare that he believes African slavery to be a social, moral, and political blessing."

The Democrats Divide (1860)

Amid such hysteria, the nation mobilized for another presidential election, destined to be the most fateful in its history. In April 1860, Democrats gathered for what would become a disastrous nominating convention in Charleston, South Carolina.

President Buchanan decided not to seek a second term, leaving Stephen A. Douglas as the front-runner. His northern supporters tried to straddle the issue of slavery by promising to defend the institution in the South while assuring northerners that it would not spread to new states. Southern militants, however, used the *Dred Scott* ruling to demand federal protection for slavery in the territories as well as the states.

When the pro-slavery advocates lost, delegates from eight southern states walked out, and the convention disintegrated. Before departing, William Preston, a plantation owner, left no doubt about the reason for the split: "Slavery is our King; Slavery is our truth; Slavery is our divine right." Douglas's supporters reassembled in Baltimore on June 18 and nominated him for president.

Southern Democrats met first in Richmond and then in Baltimore, where they adopted the pro-slavery platform that had been defeated in Charleston. They named John C. Breckinridge, vice president under Buchanan, as their candidate because he promised to protect the right of emigrants to take their enslaved workers to the western territories. Thus another cord binding the nation together had snapped: the fracturing of the Democratic party made a Republican victory in 1860 almost certain.

THE ELECTION OF 1860

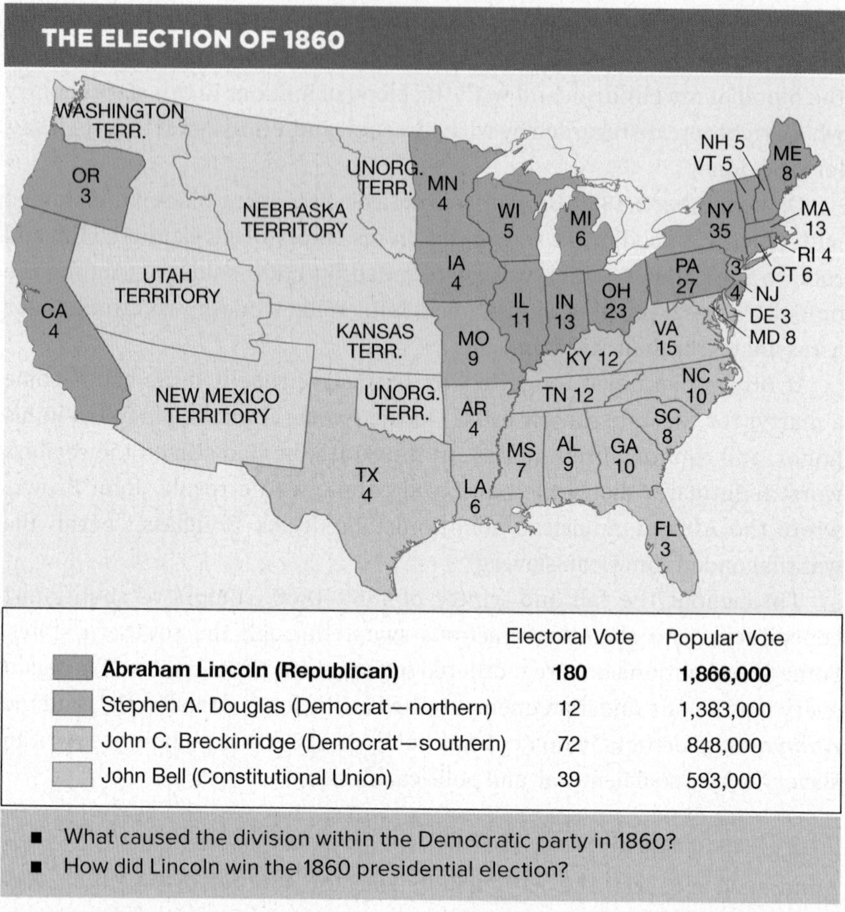

	Electoral Vote	Popular Vote
Abraham Lincoln (Republican)	**180**	**1,866,000**
Stephen A. Douglas (Democrat—northern)	12	1,383,000
John C. Breckinridge (Democrat—southern)	72	848,000
John Bell (Constitutional Union)	39	593,000

- What caused the division within the Democratic party in 1860?
- How did Lincoln win the 1860 presidential election?

That President Buchanan refused to endorse candidate Douglas revealed how splintered the Democrats had become.

Lincoln's Election (1860)

The Republicans gathered in Chicago, where everything came together for Abraham Lincoln. Inside the convention building, the "wildest excitement and enthusiasm" swelled to a "perfect roar" as Lincoln was nominated. The convention reaffirmed the party's opposition to the extension of slavery and endorsed a series of traditional Whig policies promoting a higher protective tariff, free farms ("homesteads") on federal lands out west, and federally financed internal improvements, including a transcontinental railroad.

The rival conventions revealed that opinions about the future of slavery tended to be more extreme in the Northeast and the Lower South. Attitude followed latitude. In the border states of Maryland, Delaware, Kentucky, and Missouri, former Whigs made one more try at sectional reconciliation. Meeting in Baltimore a week before the Republicans met in Chicago, they reorganized as the Constitutional Union party and nominated John Bell of Tennessee for president. Their platform promoted "the

Constitution of the Country, the Union of the States, and the Enforcement of the Laws."

The bitterly contested presidential campaign became a choice between Abraham Lincoln and Steven A. Douglas in the North (Lincoln was not even on the ballot in the South), and between Breckinridge and Bell in the South. Douglas, the only candidate to mount a nationwide campaign, promised that he would "make war boldly against" extremists in both regions. His heroic effort did little good, however.

Abraham Lincoln elected president (1860)

At midnight on November 6, Lincoln won with 39 percent of the popular vote, the smallest plurality ever, but he captured a clear majority (180 votes) in the Electoral College. He carried *all* eighteen free states but *none* of the slave states. Douglas came in second and had worn himself out in doing so. He would die just seven months later at age forty-eight.

Lincoln's political experience was meager, his learning limited, and his popular support shallow. "Never did a President enter upon office with less means at his command," the poet James Russell Lowell remarked. Yet the unassuming lawyer from Springfield, Illinois, would become, as Walt Whitman wrote, "the grandest figure yet, on all the crowded canvas of the Nineteenth Century."

The Southern Response

CORE **OBJECTIVE**

5. Explain why seven southern states seceded from the Union shortly after Lincoln's election in 1860.

Between November 8, 1860, when Abraham Lincoln was elected, and March 4, 1861, when he was inaugurated, the United States of America disintegrated. Lincoln's election panicked southerners who believed that the Republican party, as a Richmond newspaper asserted, was founded for one reason: "hatred of African slavery."

After Lincoln's victory, South Carolina's entire congressional delegation resigned. The state's legislature then appointed a convention to decide whether the state should secede from the Union. Nearly all the delegates owned enslaved people. Delegate Thomas Jefferson Withers declared that the "true question for us all is how shall we sustain African slavery in South Carolina from a series of annoying attacks."

South Carolina secedes

Meeting in Charleston on December 20, 1860, the special convention unanimously approved an Ordinance of Secession, explaining that Lincoln was a man "whose opinions and purposes are hostile to slavery." Secession was a revolutionary act, the most radical step a state could take. James L. Petigru, one of the few Unionists in Charleston, claimed that those who voted for secession were lunatics. South Carolina, he quipped, "is too small to be a Republic and too large to be an insane asylum."

As the news spread across the state, church bells rang and shops closed. "THE UNION IS DISSOLVED!" screamed the headline of the *Charleston Mercury*. One Unionist kept a copy of the newspaper, scribbling on the bottom of it: "You'll regret the day you ever done this. I preserve this to see how it ends."

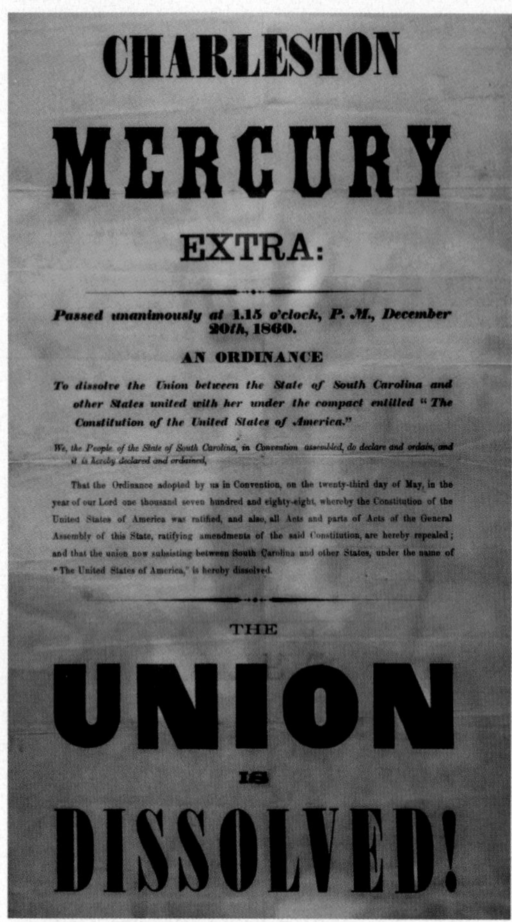

CHARLESTON

MERCURY

EXTRA:

Passed unanimously at 1.15 o'clock, P. M., December 20th, 1860.

AN ORDINANCE

To dissolve the Union between the State of South Carolina and other States united with her under the compact entitled "The Constitution of the United States of America."

We, the People of the State of South Carolina, in Convention assembled, do declare and ordain, and it is hereby declared and ordained,

That the Ordinance adopted by us in Convention, on the twenty-third day of May, in the year of our Lord one thousand seven hundred and eighty-eight, whereby the Constitution of the United States of America was ratified, and also, all Acts and parts of Acts of the General Assembly of this State, ratifying amendments of the said Constitution, are hereby repealed; and that the union now subsisting between South Carolina and other States, under the name of "The United States of America," is hereby dissolved.

THE

UNION

IS

DISSOLVED!

"THE UNION IS DISSOLVED!" A newspaper headline announcing South Carolina's secession from the Union.

President Buchanan's Waiting Game

Other southern states soon followed South Carolina's lead in descending into disunion. The imploding nation desperately needed a bold, decisive president to intervene. Instead it suffered under James Buchanan, who blamed the crisis on fanatical abolitionists. He declared secession illegal, then claimed that he lacked the constitutional authority to stop it. "I can do nothing," he sighed. In the face of the president's clueless inaction, armed southern firebrands surrounded federal forts in the seceded states.

Among the federal forts under siege was Fort Sumter, nestled on a tiny island at the mouth of Charleston Harbor. When South Carolina secessionists demanded that Major Robert Anderson, a Kentucky Unionist, surrender the fort, he refused.

On January 5, 1861, President Buchanan sent an unarmed commercial steamship, the *Star of the West*, to resupply Fort Sumter. As the ship approached Charleston Harbor after midnight on January 9, Confederate cannons operated by cadets from The Citadel, the state's military college, opened fire and drove it away. It was an act of war, but Buchanan chose to ignore the attack, hoping that a compromise might avert civil war. Southern leaders, however, were not in a compromising mood. "We spit on every plan to compromise," sneered a secessionist. The issue was no longer slavery in the territories; it was the survival of the nation. That same day, Mississippi left the Union, followed by Alabama three days later.

Secession of the Lower South (1861)

By February 1, 1861, the other states of the Lower South—Florida, Georgia, Louisiana, and Texas—had also seceded. Although their secession ordinances mentioned various grievances, they made clear that the primary reason for leaving the Union was the preservation of slavery.

The formation of the Confederacy

On February 4, 1861, fifty representatives of the seceding states, all but one of them slave owners, met in Montgomery, Alabama, where they adopted a constitution for the Confederate States of America (CSA) modeled closely after the federal constitution. Unlike the 1787 constitution, which made no mention of God, the Rebel founders proclaimed that the CSA honored "Almighty God." The Confederate constitution also outlawed tariffs and federal funding for internal improvements, and it enabled the president to veto specific items within the annual federal budget. The president could serve only one six-year term and could not remove federal officials without Senate approval.

The CSA was to have only an agricultural economy. As one of its framers, the South Carolina–born Texan Louis Wigfall, insisted, "We want no manufactures: we desire no trading, no mechanical or manufacturing classes" of workers.

Perhaps most important, the constitution mandated that "the institution of negro slavery, as it now exists in the Confederate States, shall be recognized and protected" by the new government.

Jefferson Davis elected Confederate president

The delegates unanimously elected as president Mississippi's Jefferson Finis Davis (his middle name chosen because he was the last of ten children). Davis, a West Point graduate who had been a much-decorated officer in the Mexican-American War, became a U.S. senator and then served as secretary of war under President Franklin Pierce. It took him five days by train to reach Montgomery. Along the way, he delivered twenty-five speeches. In Jackson, Mississippi, he claimed that if "only the North would recognize our independence, all would be well." Still, at every stop, he told his cheering listeners to prepare for "a long and bloody conflict."

Georgia's Alexander H. Stephens, Davis's vice president, told supporters that the Confederacy was founded to sustain the slave system upon which the southern economy depended. The new nation, he said, embodied "the great truth that the negro is not equal to the white man; that slavery, subordination to the superior [White] race, is his natural and normal condition."

Compromise Effort Fails

President-elect Lincoln still assumed that the southerners were bluffing. Members of Congress, meanwhile, sought to avert civil war. On December 18, 1860, slave owner John J. Crittenden of Kentucky, the oldest member of the Senate, had suggested that slavery be allowed in the western territories *south* of the 1820 Missouri Compromise line (36°30′ parallel) and be guaranteed to continue where it already existed. Lincoln, however, opposed any plan that would expand slavery westward, and the Senate defeated the Crittenden Compromise, 25–23.

Lincoln's Inauguration

In mid-February 1861, Abraham Lincoln boarded a train in Springfield, Illinois, headed to Washington, D.C., for his inauguration. Alerted to a plot to assassinate him when he changed trains in Baltimore, federal officials had Lincoln wear a disguise and board a secret train in Pennsylvania. The train carrying Lincoln slipped through Baltimore unnoticed.

In his inaugural address on March 4, the most highly anticipated speech in U.S. history, the fifty-two-year-old Lincoln repeated his pledge not "to interfere with the institution of slavery in the states where it exists" because he had no authority to do so. The immediate question, however, had shifted to secession. Lincoln insisted that "the Union of these States is perpetual," and therefore the notion of a Confederate nation was a fiction. No state, he stressed, "can lawfully get out of the Union." He pledged to defend "federal forts in the South," such as Fort Sumter, but beyond that "there [would] be no invasion, no using of force against or among the people anywhere."

In closing, Lincoln appealed for regional harmony:

> We are not enemies, but friends. We must not be enemies. Though passion may have strained, it must not break our bonds of affection. The mystic chords of memory, stretching from every battlefield and patriot grave to every living heart and hearthstone all over this broad land, will yet swell the chorus of the Union, when again touched, as surely they will be, by the better angels of our nature.

Southerners were not impressed. A North Carolina newspaper warned that Lincoln's speech made civil war "inevitable." The editor of the *Richmond Enquirer* dismissed the new president as a "fanatic" eager to bring on the "horrors of civil war." A New Orleans newspaper blamed northern voters, for by electing Lincoln, they had "perpetuated a deliberate, cold-blooded insult and outrage on the people of the slaveholding states."

Both sides assumed that if fighting erupted, it would be over quickly and that their daily lives would go on as usual. That perception would soon be proven terribly wrong.

The End of the Waiting Game

On March 5, 1861, his first day in office, President Lincoln found a letter on his desk from Major Robert Anderson, the army commander at Fort Sumter. Anderson reported that his men had enough food for only a few weeks and that the Confederates were encircling the fort with a "ring of fire."

Civil War begins (April 12, 1861)

On April 4, Lincoln ordered unarmed ships to resupply the sixty-nine soldiers at Fort Sumter. His Confederate counterpart, Jefferson Davis, resolved to stop any such effort. On April 11, Confederate general Pierre G. T. Beauregard, who had studied under Major Anderson at West Point, demanded that his former professor surrender Fort Sumter. Anderson refused. At four-thirty in the morning darkness of April 12, Confederates began firing on Fort Sumter. After some thirty-four hours, his ammunition exhausted, Anderson lowered the "Stars and Stripes."

The Confederate attack on Fort Sumter changed everything. It "has made the North a unit," New York Democratic congressman Daniel Sickles wrote. "We are at war with a foreign power." On April 15, the *Charleston Mercury* newspaper ran a simple headline: "Lincoln Declares War." A civil war of unimagined horrors had begun. "War begins where reason ends," said the African American abolitionist Frederick Douglass, and the South's outsized fears confirmed the logic of his statement.

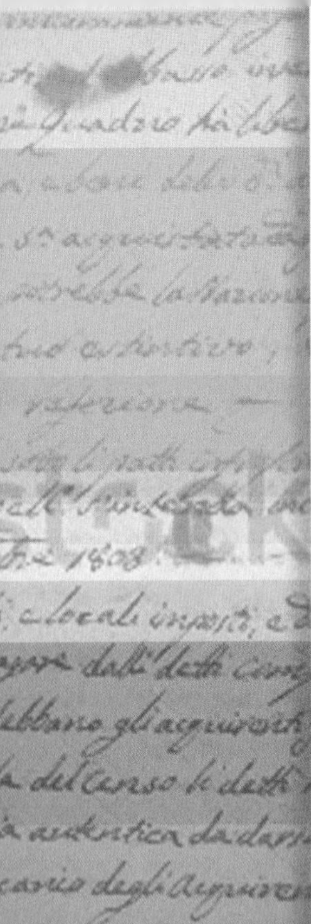

Reviewing the CORE OBJECTIVES | INQUIZITIVE

■ **Westward Migration** In the 1830s, Americans came to believe in *manifest destiny*—that the U.S. expansion to the Pacific coast was divinely ordained. A population explosion and the lure of cheap, fertile land prompted large numbers of Americans to endure the hardships of the *Overland Trails* to settle in Oregon (*Oregon Fever*) and California. At the same time, many southerners ("Texians") moved to the Mexican province of Texas with their enslaved people. The Mexican government outlawed slavery, however, and in 1830 forbade further immigration. Texians rebelled, winning their independence from Mexico in the *Texas Revolution (1835–1836)*. Texas, however, would not become a state for another decade because the United States was determined to avoid both war with Mexico and the divisive issue of adding another slave state to the Union.

■ **Mexican-American War** When the United States finally annexed Texas in 1845, the Mexican government refused to recognize the loss of its northern province. President Polk sought to acquire California, New Mexico, and Texas, but negotiations failed. When Mexican troops crossed the Rio Grande and fired on U.S. soldiers, Polk urged Congress to declare war, which U.S. forces won. By the terms of the *Treaty of Guadalupe Hidalgo (1848)*, Mexico ceded California and New Mexico to the United States and gave up claims to disputed land north of the Rio Grande.

■ **Slavery in the Territories** The *Wilmot Proviso (1846)* never became law, but by seeking to ban slavery in the newly acquired Mexican territories, it outraged pro-slavery legislators. The controversy helped create a new *Free-Soil party* that demanded that slavery be banned in the new territories. In 1849, the *California Gold Rush* further escalated sectional tensions. Most Californians wanted their territory to become a free state. Southerners feared losing federal protection of slavery if free states outnumbered slave states. Some political leaders urged the voters in each territory to decide the issue (*popular sovereignty*). The much celebrated *Compromise of 1850* allowed California to enter the Union as a free state, established the territories of Texas, New Mexico, and Utah without direct reference to slavery, banned the slave trade in Washington, D.C., and strengthened the *Fugitive Slave Act (1850)*. Tensions turned violent with the passage of the *Kansas-Nebraska Act (1854)*, which overturned the Missouri Compromise by allowing slavery in the territories where it had been banned in 1820.

■ **The Republican Party's Appeal** Northerners were outraged by violent pro-slavery mobs as the territory of Kansas prepared to enter the Union. Yet anti-slavery zealots were equally violent, such as John Brown in *Bleeding Kansas (1856)*. The Supreme Court's pro-slavery *Dred Scott v. Sandford (1857)* decision further fueled sectional conflict. The *Lincoln-*

Douglas debates (1858) in Illinois centered on the controversy over extending slavery into the territories. Northern voters increasingly gravitated toward the anti-slavery Republican party. Republicans also advocated for protective tariffs and the development of national infrastructure, which appealed to northern manufacturers and commercial farmers. In the 1860 presidential election, Abraham Lincoln carried every free state and won a clear Electoral College victory.

- **The Secession of the Lower South** South Carolina seceded from the Union a month after Lincoln's presidential victory. Before Lincoln was inaugurated, six other states joined South Carolina to form the Confederate States of America. South Carolinians bombarded Fort Sumter in Charleston Harbor, and so the Civil War began.

KEY TERMS

manifest destiny *p. 476*

Overland Trails *p. 476*

Oregon Fever *p. 479*

Texas Revolution (1835–1836) *p. 484*

Treaty of Guadalupe Hidalgo (1848) *p. 496*

Wilmot Proviso (1846) *p. 498*

popular sovereignty *p. 499*

Free-Soil party *p. 499*

California Gold Rush (1849) *p. 501*

Compromise of 1850 *p. 504*

Fugitive Slave Act (1850) *p. 506*

Kansas-Nebraska Act (1854) *p. 510*

Bleeding Kansas (1856) *p. 512*

Dred Scott v. Sandford (1857) *p. 516*

Lincoln-Douglas debates (1858) *p. 519*

CHRONOLOGY

1821	Mexico gains independence from Spain
1836	American "Texians" are defeated at the Alamo
1845	United States annexes Texas
1846	Mexican-American War begins
1848	Treaty of Guadalupe Hidalgo ends Mexican-American War
1849	California Gold Rush begins
1854	Congress passes Kansas-Nebraska Act
	The Republican party founded
1856	Bleeding Kansas and Bloody Sumner
1857	*Dred Scott v. Sandford* and Lecompton Constitution
1858	Lincoln-Douglas debates
1859	John Brown's raid at Harpers Ferry, Virginia
1860–1861	Seven southern states secede from the Union
March 4, 1861	Abraham Lincoln is inaugurated president
April 1861	Fort Sumter falls to Confederate forces

INQUIZITIVE

Go to InQuizitive to see what you've learned—and learn what you've missed—with personalized feedback along the way.

***LINCOLN'S DRIVE THROUGH RICHMOND* (1866)** Shortly after the Confederate capital of Richmond, Virginia, fell to Union forces in April 1865, President Abraham Lincoln visited the war-torn city. Formerly enslaved people and White Unionists swarmed his carriage.

CHAPTER 14

The War of the Union

1861–1865

The fall of Fort Sumter started the Civil War and triggered a wave of patriotic bluster on both sides. A southern woman prayed that God would "give us strength to conquer the Yankees, to exterminate *them*, to lay waste every Northern city, town and village, to destroy them utterly." Northern sentiment was similarly bloodthirsty. Writer Nathaniel Hawthorne reported from Massachusetts that his transcendentalist friend Ralph Waldo Emerson was "breathing slaughter" as the Union army prepared for its first battle. Emerson, a pacifist, now said that "sometimes gunpowder smells good."

Many Southerners, then and since, argued that the Civil War was not about slavery but about the South's effort to defend states' rights against the federal government. Confederate president Jefferson Davis claimed that the Confederates fought for the South's right to secede from the Union and its need to defend itself against a "tyrannical majority"—meaning those who had elected President Abraham Lincoln, the anti-slavery Republican.

For his part, Lincoln stressed that the "paramount object in this struggle *is* to save the Union, and is *not* either to save or to destroy slavery. If I could save the Union without freeing *any* slave I would do it, and if I could save it by freeing *all* the slaves I would do it; and if I could save it by freeing some and leaving others alone I would also do that." If the southern states returned to the Union, he promised, they could retain their enslaved people. None of the Confederate states accepted

CORE OBJECTIVES INQUIZITIVE

1. Identify the respective advantages of the North and South in the war, and explain how they affected the military strategies of the Union and the Confederacy.
2. Evaluate Lincoln's decision to issue the Emancipation Proclamation and its impact on the war.
3. Analyze how the war affected social and economic life in the North and South.
4. Describe the military turning points in 1863 and 1864 that ultimately led to the Confederacy's defeat.
5. Explain how the Civil War changed the nation.

JEFFERSON DAVIS President of the Confederacy.

Lincoln's offer, in large part because most White Southerners were convinced that he was lying. They believed the "Black Republican," as they called the president, was determined to end slavery.

Southerners claimed their *right* to secede, but protecting slavery was the *reason* Confederate leaders used to justify secession and war. The South Carolina Declaration on the Immediate Causes of Secession, for example, explained that the state left the Union because of the "increasing hostility on the part of the non-slaveholding states to the institution of slavery." Mississippi mentioned one reason: preserving slavery. Georgian Alexander Stephens, vice president of the Confederate States of America, said that slavery was the "immediate cause" of secession and war and that White supremacy was the "cornerstone" of the Confederacy. The "great truth" on which the Confederate government was founded, he stressed, is "that the negro is not equal to the White man; that slavery—subordination to the superior race—is his natural and normal condition."

CORE **OBJECTIVE**

1. Identify the respective advantages of the North and South in the war, and explain how they affected the military strategies of the Union and the Confederacy.

Mobilizing Forces in the North and South

On April 15, three days after the Confederate attack on Fort Sumter, Lincoln directed the "loyal" states to supply 75,000 militiamen for ninety days to suppress the rebellion. The Civil War would force everyone—men and women, White and Black, immigrants, Hispanic-Americans, and Native Americans, free and enslaved—to choose sides. Neither the Union nor the Confederacy enjoyed unanimous support. Some 100,000 Southerners fought for the Union; thousands of Northerners fought for the Confederacy. Thousands more European volunteers fought on each side.

Choosing Sides

The first seven states that seceded were all from the Lower South—South Carolina, Mississippi, Florida, Alabama, Georgia, Louisiana, and Texas—where the cotton economy was strongest and where most enslaved people lived. All the states in the Upper South, especially Tennessee and Virginia, had areas (mainly in the mountains) where Whites were poor, enslaved people were scarce, and Union support remained strong. Nevertheless, the outbreak of fighting led four more southern slave states to join the Confederacy: Virginia, Arkansas, Tennessee, and North Carolina.

Of the slaveholding states along the border between North and South, Delaware remained in the Union, but Maryland, Kentucky, and Missouri went through bitter struggles to decide which side to support. "I think to lose Kentucky is nearly the same as to lose the whole game," Lincoln told a friend. If Kentucky were to join the Confederacy, "we cannot hold Missouri, nor, as I think, Maryland." Lincoln was so determined to keep slaveholding Kentucky on the Union side that he muffled all talk of abolition.

SECESSION, 1860–1861

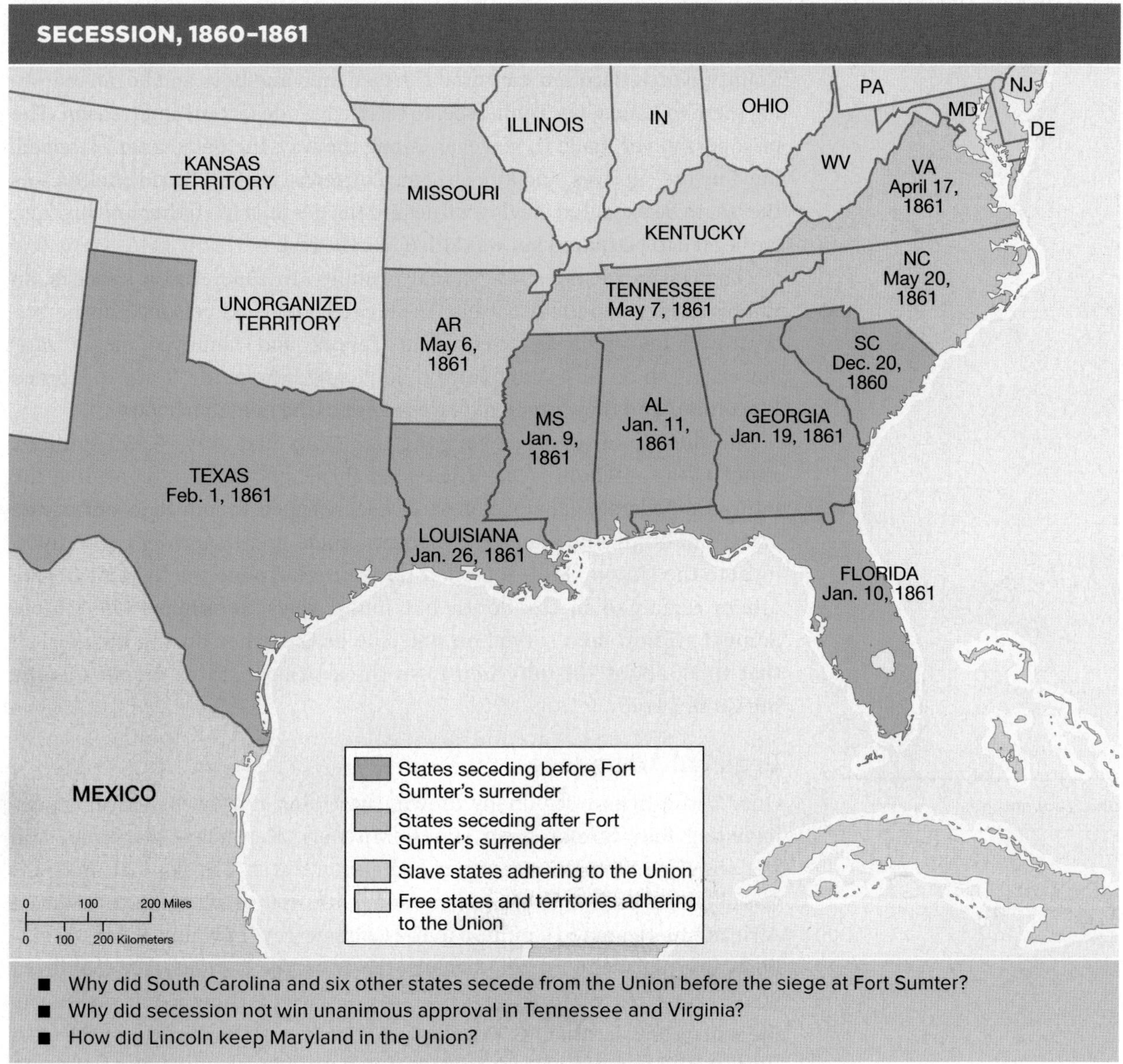

- Why did South Carolina and six other states secede from the Union before the siege at Fort Sumter?
- Why did secession not win unanimous approval in Tennessee and Virginia?
- How did Lincoln keep Maryland in the Union?

If Maryland had seceded, Confederates would have surrounded Washington, D.C. To keep Maryland in the Union, Lincoln had pro-Confederate leaders there arrested. The fragile neutrality of Kentucky lasted until September 3, when Confederate and Union armies moved into the divided state. Kentucky voters elected a secessionist governor and a Unionist majority in the state legislature, as did Missouri, a state with many European immigrants, most of whom were German.

In eastern Tennessee, however, the mountain counties would supply more volunteers to the Union army than to the Confederate cause. Thirty-nine counties in mountainous western Virginia were so loyal to the Union that they split off and formed the new state of West Virginia in October 1861.

In areas of the South where Union sentiment remained strong, the Civil War was brutally uncivil. In January 1863, Confederate soldiers in Madison County, North Carolina, captured thirteen men and boys and began marching them to Knoxville, Tennessee, to be tried for desertion and treason. The prisoners never made it, however. Along the way, the detachment stopped, lined up the captives, and killed them. Thirteen-year-old David Shelton was the last to be executed, having witnessed the death of his father and brother. He begged to be spared but was killed like the rest.

The Northern states saw similar brutality. In 1863, Anson Babcock, an Illinois farmer, reported that his "rebel neighbors" had poisoned his horses, destroyed his orchards, wrecked his fences, and "annoyed me in various ways," all because "'my politics don't suit'" them, for "I am 'a damned Lincolnite,' and they intend to drive me out of the neighborhood."

On the eve of the Civil War, the U.S. Army had only 16,400 soldiers, about 1,000 of whom were officers. Of these, about 25 percent, like the future Confederate general Robert E. Lee, resigned to join the Confederate army. But similarly, many Southerners made great sacrifices to remain loyal to the Union. Some left their native region once the fighting began; others remained in the South but found ways to support the Union. Some 3 million men served on one side or the other during the war. Of that total, about 100,000 men from the southern states fought *against* the Confederacy.

Regional Advantages

Union advantage: Population

Once battle lines were finally drawn, the Union had twenty-three states, including four border slave states—Missouri, Kentucky, Maryland, and Delaware—while the Confederacy had eleven states. The population count was about 22 million in the Union (some 400,000 of whom were enslaved African Americans) to 9 million in the Confederacy (of whom about 3.5 million were enslaved). To help balance the odds, the Confederacy mobilized 80 percent of its military-age White men, a third of whom would die during the four-year war. About 2.75 million soldiers and sailors fought in the Civil War—2 million for the North and 750,000 for the South. As many as 400,000 boys under age fifteen served on both sides.

Union advantage: Industrial development

An even greater asset for the North was its superior industrial development. The Southern states produced just 7 percent of the nation's manufactured goods. The Union states generated 97 percent of the firearms and 96 percent of the railroad equipment.

The North also had a huge advantage in transportation, particularly ships. At the start of the war, the Union had ninety warships; the South had none. Federal gunboats and transports played a direct role in securing the Union's control of the Mississippi River and its larger tributaries, which provided easy invasion routes into the center of the Confederacy. Early on, the Union navy's blockade of major Southern ports sharply reduced the amount of cotton that could be exported to Britain and France as well as the flow of goods (including military weapons) imported from Europe. In addition, the Union had more wagons and horses and an impressive edge in railroad locomotives.

Confederate advantage: Defending its own territory

The Confederates, however, had major geographic and emotional advantages: they could fight on their own territory in defense of their homeland. In warfare, it is usually easier to defend than to attack, since defending troops have the opportunity to dig protective trenches and fortifications. In the Civil War, armies that assaulted well-defended positions were mauled 90 percent of the time. Many Confederate leaders thought that if they could hold out long enough, disgruntled Northern voters might convince Lincoln and Congress to end the war.

A Conflict of Goals

The Confederacy's top priority was to convince the Union and the world to recognize its newly declared independence. The United States, on the other hand, fought to restore the Union, as Abraham Lincoln repeatedly said.

Early expectations for the war

After the fall of Fort Sumter, newspaper editors and politicians on both sides pressured the generals to strike quickly. "Forward to Richmond!" screamed a New York newspaper headline. Most people thought the war would be, in President Lincoln's words, "a short and decisive one." They were sorely wrong.

In the summer of 1861, Jefferson Davis told General Pierre G. T. Beauregard to rush the main Confederate army to Manassas Junction, a railroad crossing in northern Virginia, about twenty-five miles west of Washington. Lincoln hoped that the Union army (often called *Federals*) would overrun the outnumbered Confederates and quickly push on to Richmond, only 107 miles to the south.

First Bull Run

When word reached Washington, D.C., that the armies were converging for battle, hundreds of civilians packed picnic lunches and rode out to watch, assuming that the first clash of arms would be short, glorious, and bloodless.

It was a hot, dry day on July 21, 1861, when 37,000 untested Union recruits marched to battle, some of them breaking ranks to eat blackberries or drink water from streams along the way. Many of them died with the berry juice still on their lips as they engaged the Confederates dug in behind a tree-choked branch of the Potomac River called Bull Run.

For most soldiers, the battle provided their first taste of the chaos and confusion of combat. Many were disoriented by the smoke from gunpowder and saltpeter, the roar of cannon fire, the screaming of fallen comrades, and the sound of bullets whizzing past. Because neither side yet wore standard-colored uniforms, the soldiers had trouble deciding friend from foe.

The Union troops almost won the battle early in the afternoon. "We fired a volley," wrote a Massachusetts private, "and saw the Rebels running. . . . The

BULL RUN Moments before battle, a spectator in a top hat chats with Union soldiers *(bottom right)*, while an artist sketches the passing troops heading to combat *(at left)*. **What was the outcome of the First Battle of Bull Run?**

boys were saying constantly, in great glee, 'We've whipped them.' 'We'll hang Jeff Davis from a sour apple tree.' 'They're running.' 'The war is over.'"

But Confederate reinforcements poured in. A South Carolina officer rallied his troops by pointing to the courageous example of Thomas Jackson: "Look! There is General Jackson with his Virginians, standing like a stone wall!" Jackson, an eccentric, god-fearing professor at the Virginia Military Institute who had graduated from West Point, ordered his men to charge, urging them to "yell like furies!" From that day forward, "Stonewall" became Jackson's nickname, and he would be the most celebrated—and feared—Confederate field commander.

Confederate advantage: Victory at First Battle of Bull Run (1861)

The Union army panicked, and fleeing soldiers and terrified civilians clogged the road to Washington, D.C. The victorious Confederates, however, were so disorganized and exhausted that they failed to give chase.

THOMAS "STONEWALL" JACKSON The aggressive commander of a Confederate brigade at Bull Run, Jackson would later die of friendly fire in the Battle of Chancellorsville.

The news of the Confederate victory at Bull Run shocked Northerners. Senator Benjamin Wade, an Ohio Republican, reported from Washington, D.C., that "all is gloomy & despairing here." The surprising Yankee defeat triggered sharp criticism of President Lincoln. Michigan senator Zachariah Chandler, a Republican, dismissed the president as "timid, vacillating & inefficient." An Ohio Republican was even more critical, denouncing Lincoln as "an admitted failure" who "has no will, no courage, no executive capacity."

The hallmark of Lincoln's presidency, however, was his ability to acknowledge mistakes, to learn from them, and to move forward. The self-educated president with limited political and executive experience surrounded himself with capable cabinet members and advisers, both Republicans and Democrats, conservatives and radicals. All were independent thinkers and prickly personalities with their own agendas, yet Lincoln found a way to forge them into an effective team. With each passing year, Lincoln would grow surer of himself. He grew into greatness as the war grew in scope and unspeakable horrors.

The Union's "Anaconda" Plan

The Battle of Bull Run demonstrated that the war would not be decided with one sudden stroke, as many had assumed. General Winfield Scott, the seventy-five-year-old commander of the Union effort, devised a three-pronged strategy. First, the Army of the Potomac, the main Union army, would defend Washington, D.C., and exert constant pressure on the Confederate capital at Richmond.

Union strategy: Naval blockade and control of rivers

Second, the Federal navy's blockade of southern ports would cut off the Confederacy's access to foreign goods and weapons. The third component called for other Union armies to divide the Confederacy by pushing south along the crucial inland water routes: the Mississippi, Tennessee, and Cumberland Rivers. This so-called **Anaconda Plan** was intended to slowly trap and crush the southern resistance, like an anaconda snake strangling its prey.

Confederate Strategy

Confederate strategy: Prolonged war to erode Northern support

The Confederate plan was simpler. If the Union forces could be stalemated and the war prolonged, as Jefferson Davis and others hoped, then the British or French, desperate for Southern cotton, might be persuaded to join the cause. Or perhaps a long war would change public sentiment in the North and force President Lincoln to seek a negotiated settlement. So, while armies were forming in the South, Confederate diplomats were seeking military and financial assistance in London and Paris, and Confederate sympathizers in the North were urging an end to the Union's war effort.

Confederate strategy: Cotton diplomacy in Europe

The Confederate representatives in Paris won a promise from France to recognize the Confederacy as a new nation *if* Great Britain would do the same. But the British refused, partly in response to pressure from Lincoln and partly out of their desire to maintain trade with the United States.

Confederate leaders had assumed that Britain would support the South in order to get its cotton. As it turned out, however, the British were able to import enough cotton from India to maintain production. In the end, Confederate diplomacy in Europe was more successful in purchasing military supplies than in gaining official recognition as an independent nation.

Forming Armies

Diverse Union army

Once fighting began, President Lincoln called for 500,000 more men, a staggering number that the Confederacy struggled to match. Although the average age of soldiers in the Civil War was twenty-six, the Union army included more than 100,000 soldiers younger than fifteen. Almost a fifth of Union soldiers and sailors were immigrants—French, Germans, Poles, Italians, and other Europeans—and many could not speak English. The Union army also included 50,000 Canadians and an equal number of Englishmen. Some 210,000 Irish-born men served in the war, 170,000 of them on the Union side. At the outset of the war, some 3,500 Hispanics, mostly Mexican Americans, Puerto Ricans, and Cubans living in the United States, joined the war, with most fighting for the Confederacy. By the end of the war, the number of Hispanic soldiers had risen to 10,000.

Anaconda Plan Union's primary war strategy calling for a naval blockade of major Southern seaports and then dividing the Confederacy by gaining control of the Tennessee, Cumberland, and Mississippi Rivers.

UNION SOLDIERS Smoking their pipes, these soldiers share a moment of rest and a bottle of whiskey. **Which ethnic groups participated in the Union and Confederate armies? Which did not?**

Immigrants fought for many reasons: a strong belief in the Union cause, cash bonuses, extra food, regular pay, the need for a steady job. Whatever the reason, the high proportion of immigrants in the Union army gave it an ethnic diversity absent in the Confederate ranks.

The Confederacy's smaller male population forced Jefferson Davis to enact a conscription law (mandatory military draft). On April 16, 1862, all White males between eighteen and thirty-five were required to serve in the army for three years. "From this time until the end of the war," a Tennessee soldier wrote, "a soldier was simply a machine, a conscript. . . . All our pride and valor had gone, and we were sick of war and cursed the Southern Confederacy."

The conscription law included controversial loopholes. A draftee might avoid service either by paying a "substitute" who was not of draft age or by paying $500 to the government. Elected officials and key civilian workers, as well as planters with twenty or more enslaved people, were exempted from military service.

Drafted Confederate army, with loopholes

The Union waited nearly a year before forcing men into service. In 1863, with the war going badly, the U.S. government began to draft men. As in the South, Northerners found ways to avoid military service. A draftee might pay $300 to avoid service, and exemptions were granted to selected federal and state officeholders and to others on medical or compassionate grounds. Such exemptions led to bitter complaints on both sides about the conflict being "a rich man's war and a poor man's fight."

Why They Fought

Most of those who fought were volunteers. Why did they risk their lives? Many felt compelled by duty, honor, and patriotism. As an Alabama planter who joined the Confederate army explained to his wife, "My honor, my duty, your reputation & that of my darling little boy" forced him to don a uniform "when our bleeding country needs the services of every man." Likewise, an Illinois officer felt that Union soldiers were guided by "a high and noble sentiment, but after all a sentiment [preserving the Union and ending slavery]. They [Confederates] are fighting for independence and are animated by passion and hatred against invaders [Yankees]."

PRIVATE WAKEMAN Sarah Rosetta Wakeman, alias Lyons Wakeman, served in the Union army.

A New York Private Nineteen-year-old Lyons Wakeman, the eldest of nine children in an upstate New York farm family, enlisted in the Union army in 1862. In exchange for a $152 cash bonus, the five-foot-tall, blue-eyed Wakeman signed up for three years. The pay was $13 a month. Initially, at least, army life was tolerable, and the prospect of death did not faze Wakeman: "I don't fear the rebel bullets, nor do I fear the cannon. If it is God's will for me to be killed here, it is my will to die." In letters home, first from Virginia and later from Louisiana, Private Wakeman asked about the family farm, how many hogs were slaughtered, what the new barn looked like, and how much it might cost to buy a farm on the Wisconsin prairie.

Yet Wakeman never became a farmer. In a fierce battle, the New Yorker faced "enemy bullets with my regiment. I was under fire about four hours and lay on the field of battle all night." Wakeman did not die from wounds but did succumb a few weeks later to dysentery (chronic diarrhea), after drinking from a stream contaminated with the carcasses of dead horses. Wakeman was buried in a New Orleans cemetery, under a headstone that simply read: "Lyons Wakeman—N.Y."

What might have been added was that Lyons Wakeman was a woman. Born Sarah Rosetta Wakeman, she, like hundreds of women on both sides, had disguised her gender to serve in the war. Why? Was it simply patriotism? Or did it also involve seizing the opportunity afforded by the war to explore alternative modes of gender identity?

What Was at Stake Many Confederates were convinced that defeat would enslave Southern Whites. "If we was to lose," a Mississippi private wrote his wife in 1862, "we would be slaves to the Yanks and our children would have a yoke of bondage thrown around their necks."

Most Confederates could not imagine life without Black slavery. "This country without slave labor would be completely worthless," wrote a Mississippi lieutenant. "We can only live & exist by that species of labor: hence I am willing to fight to the last."

Many Union soldiers were fighting to preserve the Union rather than free men, women, and children in bondage, but a substantial number of Yankee soldiers insisted that winning the war meant ending slavery. A private from Minnesota felt that the war "will never end until we end slavery."

Despite the patriotic fervor, people remained ambivalent about their loyalties. In Virginia, for example, Confederate Joseph Waddill admitted in his diary in 1863 that he actually regretted secession. "I never ceased to deplore the disruption [of the Union], and never could have loved my country and government as I loved the old United States."

Divided Families The Civil War divided families. President Lincoln's wife, Mary Todd of Kentucky, for example, saw her youngest brother join the Confederate army, as did three of her half-brothers and a brother-in-law. At the same time, Varina Davis, the Confederate First Lady, had divided loyalties; she was privately pro-Union. Ulysses Grant, who would become the foremost Union general, struggled with his father-in-law, Colonel Frederick Dent, who was a fiery Missouri Confederate. Dent swore that if his "worthless son-in-law" ever came on his land he would "shoot him as if he were a rabbit."

The Life of a Soldier

The average Civil War soldier stood five feet eight inches tall and weighed 143 pounds. A third of the Southern soldiers could neither read nor write. Half of the Union soldiers and two-thirds of the Confederates were farmers.

Because most of the fighting occurred in the spring and summer, soldiers spent far more time preparing for war than fighting. A Pennsylvania private wrote home that "the first thing in the morning is drill. Then drill, then drill again. Then drill, drill, a little more drill, then drill, lastly drill."

When not training, soldiers relaxed outdoors in makeshift shelters or small tents—talking, reading, playing cards or checkers, singing songs, smoking pipes, washing and mending clothes, and fighting lice, ticks, chiggers, and mosquitoes. Their diet was dull: baked bread crackers (called hardtack), salted meat (pork or beef), and coffee.

Some soldiers on both sides were so overwhelmed by the rigors of combat and camp life or so concerned about their families and farms that they deserted, even though they risked execution if caught. Desertions soared with each passing year, as did incidents of drunkenness, thievery, and insubordination.

Punishments varied. Some deserters were shot or hanged. Others were tied to a ball and chain, forced to bury dead horses or tend to animals, or

DAILY LIFE These souvenir cards show various parts of life in Civil War camps, from enduring illnesses and a bland diet of hardtack to getting stuck in the mud and hiding from enemy fire.

drummed out of the service. Most soldiers on both sides, however, came to view their military experience as beneficial.

Prisoner-of-war camps

One of every four Civil War soldiers, more than 670,000 men, surrendered at some point in the war. More than 400,000 soldiers on both sides were sent to prisoner-of-war camps, where conditions were so miserable that some 30,000 Union prisoners and nearly 26,000 Confederates died in captivity. The worst of the prisons was Camp Sumter, in southwest Georgia near Andersonville. Built to house 10,000 prisoners, it overflowed with 45,000 Union soldiers. Nearly a third of them died in captivity.

Becoming Warriors

Only a few of those who fought in the Civil War had any combat experience. Sullivan Ballou, a thirty-two-year-old Rhode Island lawyer and legislator who enlisted in the Union army, wrote his wife in July 1861 that he would have loved nothing more than to have stayed home and seen their sons grow to "honorable manhood," but his ultimate priority was serving his country. A week later, Ballou was killed in the first Battle of Bull Run. In his last letter to his wife, he had expressed a premonition of death: "Do not mourn me dead. . . . Wait for me, for we shall meet again."

Southerners felt the same sense of patriotism and manly honor. As the months passed, however, enthusiasm faded. Charles Biddlecom, a farmer from upstate New York, volunteered in May 1861 for the Union army, eager to whip the "Southern whelps." By 1863, however, Biddlecom had had enough. Sick with dysentery, overrun with lice, and miserably lonesome, he and three comrades were forced to live in a "little dog kennel" just four feet high. Although Biddlecom hated slaveholders, he now felt it might have been "better in the end to have let the South go out peaceably and tried her hand at making a nation."

Like those of many, Biddlecom's moods and motives fluctuated depending upon the course of the war. In 1864, he confessed that the Union army was "worn out, discouraged, [and] demoralized." He stuck it out, but "as for men fighting from pure love of country, I think them as few as White blackbirds." He declared that he was neither a "Union saver" nor a "freedom shrieker." At war's end, however, Biddlecom celebrated the defeat of the Confederacy, since it affirmed that "freedom shall extend over the whole nation."

Blacks in the South

As had happened during the Revolutionary War and the War of 1812, enslaved African Americans took advantage of the confusion created by the war to run away, engage in sabotage, join the fighting, or pursue their own interests.

Enslaved people support the Union

Perhaps the most dramatic instance of enslaved people's rebelliousness occurred in Charleston Harbor. On May 13, 1862, twenty-three-year-old Robert Smalls, an enslaved harbor pilot aboard the C.S.S. *Planter,* stole the gunboat and headed out to sea in a desperate quest for freedom. Sneaking past Confederate forts and cannons, he guided the *Planter* up the Cooper River and

ROBERT SMALLS Robert Smalls, a twenty-three-year-old enslaved harbor pilot, stole a Confederate gunboat, the C.S.S. *Planter*. Smalls steered it to the Union side and was lauded a hero in the North.

docked at a wharf where his wife, two children, and the families of his enslaved crew were waiting.

Once the seventeen Black passengers (nine men, five women, and three children) boarded the *Planter*, the warship crept out of the harbor. As the sun rose, Smalls had a crew member hoist a white bed sheet to signal their intention to surrender as he steered the gunboat toward the Union fleet then blockading Charleston Harbor. A warship summoned Smalls onboard, whereupon he announced: "I am delivering this war material, including these cannons, and I think Uncle Abraham Lincoln can put them to good use."

Smalls was hailed as a hero in the North. He met with President Lincoln at the White House, toured Northern cities urging that Blacks be allowed to serve in the Union army and navy, and became a ship pilot for the Union navy. After the war, he would buy his former owner's house and become a South Carolina legislator and U.S. congressman.

Fighting in the West

Fighting spilled across the Mississippi River into the Great Plains and all the way to California. In 1862, a small Confederate army based in Texas tried to conquer the New Mexico Territory to gain control of the western region, including the gold fields of Colorado and the ports of California. But the attack was repelled by Union forces led by the "New Mexico Volunteer Infantry," which boasted 157 Hispanic officers.

Amid the sporadic fighting, western settlement slowed but did not stop. New discoveries of gold and silver in eastern California and in Montana and Colorado lured more prospectors. Dakota, Colorado, and Nevada gained territorial status in 1861, Idaho and Arizona in 1863. Both Montana and silver-rich Nevada gained statehood in 1864.

Kansas and Indian Nations

The most intense fighting west of the Mississippi occurred along the Kansas-Missouri border, where the disputes that had developed between pro-slavery and anti-slavery settlers in the 1850s turned into brutal guerrilla warfare.

William Quantrill versus the Jayhawkers in Kansas

The most prominent pro-Confederate leader was William Quantrill. He and his troops, mostly teenagers, fought under a black flag, meaning that they would kill anyone who surrendered. In destroying Lawrence, Kansas, in 1863, Quantrill ordered his men to "kill every male and burn every house." By the end of the day, they had massacred 182 men and boys. Their opponents, the Jayhawkers (originally slang for thieves), responded by torturing and hanging pro-Confederate prisoners, burning houses, and destroying livestock.

Native Americans pick sides

Many Indian nations were caught up in the war. Some 20,000 Native Americans allied with one side or the other. Several Indian tribes owned enslaved African Americans and felt a bond with Southern Whites. Stand Watie, an Oklahoma Cherokee leader, chose the Confederacy in 1861 and raised a volunteer regiment called the Cherokee Mounted Rifles. By the end of the war, he had been promoted to brigadier general and was the principal chief of the Confederate Cherokees.

Oklahoma's proximity to Texas influenced the Choctaws and Chickasaws to support the Confederacy. The Cherokees, Creeks, and Seminoles were more divided in their loyalties. The Cherokees, for example, split in two, some supporting the Union and others the Confederacy. Caught in the crossfire of battle, one-third of Cherokee women ended up widows.

STAND WATIE Stand Watie commanded the Confederate Indian cavalry of the Army of the Trans-Mississippi after the Cherokee Nation allied with the Confederacy during the Civil War.

Texans in the War

Although Texas would never be a primary battleground, it did have an outsized influence on the Civil War, sending east vast numbers of soldiers in diverse uniforms, cowboy hats, and Mexican sombreros. No sooner was war declared than 25,000 Texans volunteered. Eventually more than half of the military-aged men in Texas fought in the war. One of them explained that he was willing to go to war because "we want more slaves—we need them."

Several Texans emerged as prominent Confederate generals, and Texas units were the most ethnically diverse of all the states. The 4,400-strong Texas Brigade led by John Bell Hood included Mexicans, Native Americans, and Europeans of all sorts—English, Welsh, Irish, Scots, Germans, and French. They became one of the most celebrated units in the war, in part because they were willing to absorb the highest rate of casualties. Only 600 were still serving at war's end. Texan and *Tejano* cowboys also drove vast herds of longhorn steers hundreds of miles east across Louisiana and the Mississippi River to feed Confederate armies.

Not all Texans chose the Confederate cause, however. Among the Union soldiers from Texas were many *Tejanos* and Mexican nationals. Their motives were varied, but many sought revenge against White Texans who had taken their lands. Others were attracted by the enlistment bonuses and military pay. If captured by Confederates, Texas Unionists often paid with their lives. Several dozen were executed as traitors.

Kentucky and Tennessee

Little happened of military significance east of the Appalachian Mountains before May 1862. On the other hand, important battles occurred in the West (from the Appalachians to the Mississippi River).

Early in 1862, General Ulysses S. Grant made the first Union thrust against the Confederate army that was defending Kentucky and Tennessee. To combat his weakness for liquor, he looked to his chief of staff, John A. Rawlins, a teetotaler, to keep him sober. When Grant was sober, he had only one equal as a military commander: Robert E. Lee.

Union victories at Fort Henry, Fort Donelson, and Nashville

Moving on boats out of Cairo, Illinois, and Paducah, Kentucky, the Union army captured two hastily built Confederate strongholds twelve miles apart: Fort Henry on the east bank of the Tennessee River, and nearby Fort Donelson, perched on a hill overlooking the Cumberland River. On February 16, some

12,000 Confederates met the demands of General Grant and surrendered immediately and unconditionally. Eight days later, Union forces took control of Nashville, then serving as Tennessee's capital.

Early victories ensure Kentucky's loyalty to the Union

These first major victories ignited wild celebrations throughout the North. They helped ensure that Kentucky would stay within the Union and gave the North access to the Cumberland and Tennessee Rivers. At the same time, the victory at Fort Donelson gave Grant a catchy nickname: "Unconditional Surrender" Grant.

President Lincoln's delight with the Union army's success, however, was tempered by the death of his eleven-year-old son, Willie, of typhoid fever. The tragedy "overwhelmed" the president. A White House staff member said she had never seen "a man so bowed down in grief."

Shiloh

After the defeats in Kentucky and Tennessee, the Confederate forces fled southward before regrouping under General Albert Sydney Johnston at Corinth, in northern Mississippi, near the Tennessee border. Their goal was to protect the Memphis and Charleston Railroad linking the lower Mississippi River Valley and the Atlantic coast.

While planning his attack on Corinth, General Grant exposed his 42,000 troops on a rolling plateau between Lick and Snake Creeks flowing into the Tennessee River. He also failed to have his men dig defensive trenches. Johnston recognized Grant's blunder, and at dawn on Sunday, April 6, he launched a surprise attack.

The Confederates, screaming the blood-curling "Rebel yell," struck the unsuspecting Union lines near Shiloh, a tiny Methodist church in the center of the Union camp in southwestern Tennessee. Many of Grant's troops, half of whom had yet to see combat, were still sleeping or eating breakfast; some died in their tents.

After a day of confused fighting and terrible losses on both sides—including Confederate general Johnston—the fleeing Union soldiers were pinned against the river as heavy rain began to fall. General William Tecumseh Sherman found Grant and said, "we've had the devil's own day, haven't we?" Grant puffed on his cigar and replied, "Yes, but we will lick 'em tomorrow though."

The new Confederate commander, Pierre G. T. Beauregard, telegraphed President Jefferson Davis that his army had scored "a complete victory, driving the enemy from every position." His celebration was premature, however.

The next morning, reinforced by 25,000 fresh troops, Grant's army took the offensive, and the Confederates glumly withdrew twenty miles to Corinth. The Union troops were too battered and weary to pursue. Confederate private Sam Watkins observed that "those Yankees were whipped, fairly whipped, and according to all the rules of war they ought to have retreated. But they didn't."

Shiloh, a Hebrew word meaning "Place of Peace," had become a place of anguish. The battle's first day was the bloodiest in American history to that point. Viewing the scene afterward, said General Sherman, "would have

CAMPAIGNS IN THE WEST, FEBRUARY–APRIL 1862

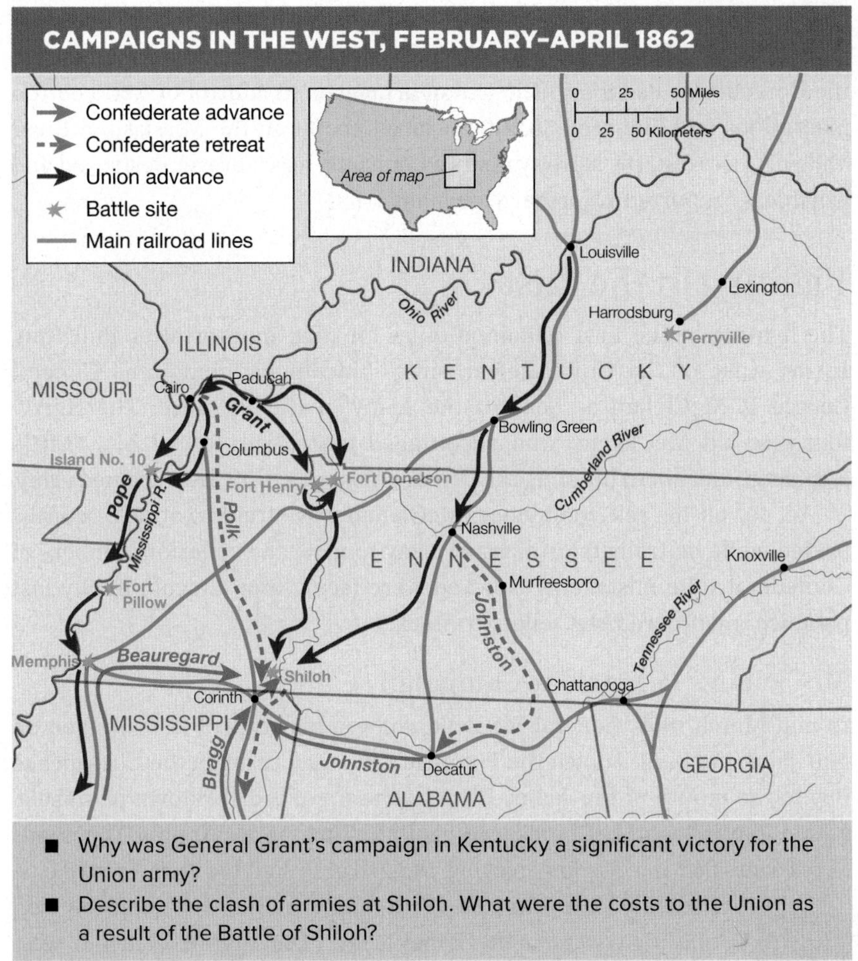

- Why was General Grant's campaign in Kentucky a significant victory for the Union army?
- Describe the clash of armies at Shiloh. What were the costs to the Union as a result of the Battle of Shiloh?

cured anybody of war." Sherman himself had three horses shot and killed under him, and he suffered a buckshot wound in the hand and a bruised shoulder from a spent bullet.

Devastating casualties at the Battle of Shiloh

Of the 100,000 men who participated, a quarter were killed or wounded, seven times the casualties at the Battle of Bull Run. And like Bull Run earlier and so many battles to come, Shiloh was less a story of brilliant strategy than it was missed opportunities and lucky accidents. Throughout the war, winning armies would fail to pursue their retreating foes, allowing the wounded opponent to slip away, recover, and fight again.

After Shiloh, Union general Henry Halleck, a military bureaucrat jealous of Grant's success, spread a false rumor that Grant had been drinking during the battle. Grant stressed in a letter to his wife that he had been "sober as a deacon." Some urged Abraham Lincoln to fire the "unmilitary" Grant, but the president refused: "I can't spare this man; he fights."

New Orleans

Union seizes New Orleans

Just three weeks after the Battle of Shiloh, the Union won a great naval victory at New Orleans, as Admiral David G. Farragut's warships blasted their way past Confederate forts to take control of the largest city in the Confederacy and its principal port. The loss of New Orleans was a devastating blow to the Confederate economy. The Union army gained control of 1,500 cotton plantations and liberated 50,000 enslaved people in the Mississippi River Valley. As a result, the slave system in Louisiana was "forever destroyed and worthless," reported a Northern journalist.

Fighting in the East

George B. McClellan heads the Army of the Potomac

The fighting in the East remained quiet for nine months after Bull Run. In the wake of the Union defeat there, Lincoln had appointed General George B. McClellan as head of the Army of the Potomac. The thirty-four-year-old McClellan, who encouraged journalists to call him "Little Napoleon," set about building the Union's most powerful, best-trained army.

Yet for all his self-confidence, McClellan was afraid to attack. Months passed while he trained his massive army to meet the superior numbers of Confederates he mistakenly believed were facing him. Lincoln finally lost patience and ordered McClellan to attack.

McClellan's Peninsular Campaign

Robert E. Lee heads Army of Northern Virginia

In mid-March 1862, General McClellan moved his army of 122,000 men on 400 ships and barges down the Potomac River and through the Chesapeake Bay to the mouth of the James River at the tip of the Yorktown peninsula, within sixty miles of the Confederate capital of Richmond, Virginia. Thousands of residents fled the city in panic, but McClellan waited too long to strike. A frustrated Lincoln told McClellan that the war could be won only by *engaging* the Rebel army. "Once more," Lincoln telegraphed, "it is indispensable that you strike a blow."

ROBERT E. LEE The Confederacy's greatest general, Lee served as military adviser to President Jefferson Davis and as commander of the Army of Northern Virginia.

On May 31, 1862, Confederate general Joseph E. Johnston struck at McClellan's army along the Chickahominy River, six miles east of Richmond. In the Battle of Seven Pines (Fair Oaks), only the arrival of Federal reinforcements prevented a disastrous Union defeat. Both sides took heavy casualties.

At this point, Robert E. Lee assumed command of the main Confederate army, the Army of Northern Virginia, a development that changed the course of the war. Lee, a slave-owning planter who believed slavery was "a moral and political evil," had graduated second in his class at West Point. During the Mexican-American War, he had impressed General Winfield Scott as the "very best soldier I ever saw in the field." Lee would prove to be a daring strategist who was as aggressive as McClellan was timid. "He is silent, inscrutable, strong, like a God," said a Confederate officer. Lee also looked the part. "He was a model of manly beauty," said another officer, "large, well-made, and graceful." The mere sight of him, added a soldier, "was awe-inspiring."

On July 9, when Lincoln visited McClellan's headquarters on the coast of Virginia, the general complained that the administration had

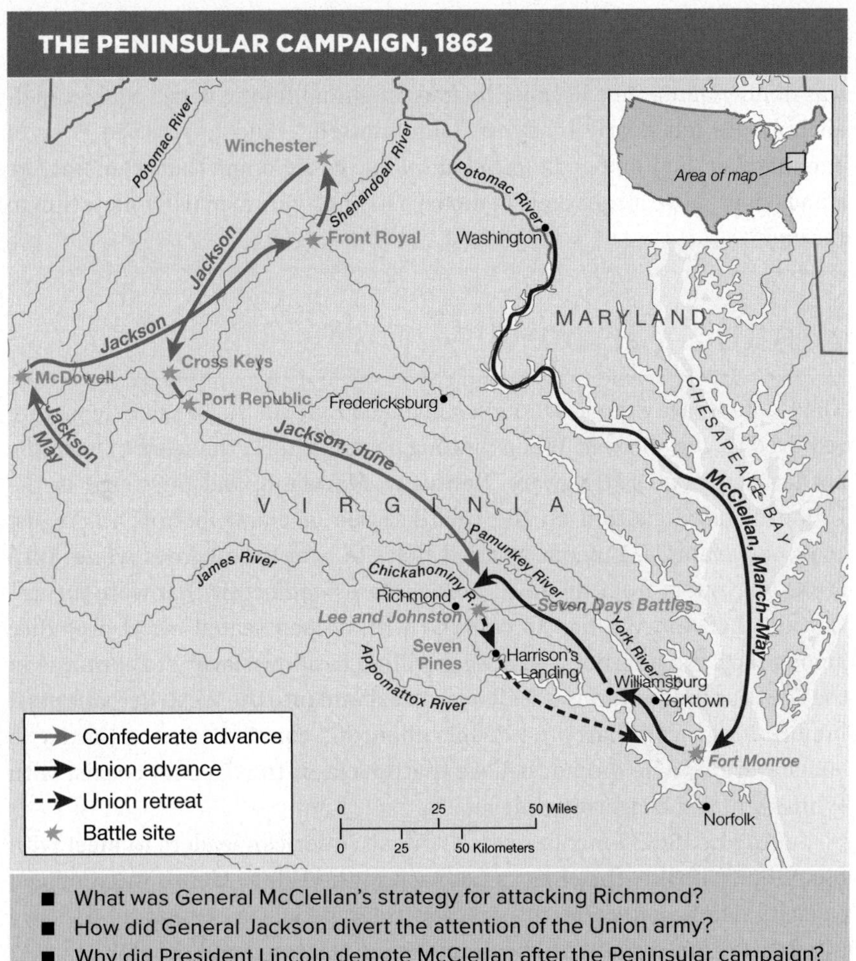

- What was General McClellan's strategy for attacking Richmond?
- How did General Jackson divert the attention of the Union army?
- Why did President Lincoln demote McClellan after the Peninsular campaign?

failed to support him and lectured the president on military strategy. Such insubordination was ample reason to relieve McClellan of his overall command. After returning to Washington, Lincoln named Henry Halleck general in chief of all Union forces.

Second Bull Run

General McClellan was ordered to move his Army of the Potomac back to Washington, D.C., and join General John Pope, commander of the Union Army of Virginia, in a new assault on Richmond. Robert E. Lee realized that his only chance was to drive a wedge between the two larger Union armies so that he could deal with them one at a time. He moved northward to strike Pope's army before McClellan's troops could arrive. At the Second Battle of Bull Run (or Manassas), fought on almost the same site as the earlier battle, August 30, 1862, Lee boldly divided his forces, sending Stonewall Jackson's troops around the flank to attack from the rear. A confused Pope assumed that he faced only Jackson, but Lee's main army by that time had joined in.

Confederate victory at the Second Battle of Bull Run (1862)

The crushing Confederate attack drove the larger Union army from the field, giving the Confederates a sensational victory and leading a disheartened

Union officer to confess, "General Pope had been outwitted. . . . Our generals have defeated us." The news of another defeat left Lincoln depressed, which was doubly dangerous because he had fought a lifelong battle against melancholy. He felt nearly ready to "hang himself." Lincoln relieved Pope of command on September 12. A Rebel soldier wrote home that "General Lee stands now above all generals in modern history. Our men will follow him to the end."

CORE **OBJECTIVE**

2. Evaluate Lincoln's decision to issue the Emancipation Proclamation and its impact on the war.

Emancipation

The Confederate victories in 1862 convinced Lincoln that bolder steps were required to win the war. When fighting began in 1861, the need to keep the border slave states (Delaware, Kentucky, Maryland, and Missouri) in the Union dictated caution on the volatile issue of emancipation. In August 1862, for example, Lincoln worried that "to arm the negroes would turn 50,000 bayonets from the loyal Border states *against* us that were *for* us." Beyond that, Lincoln had to contend with a deep-seated racial prejudice among most Northerners, who were willing to allow slavery to continue in the South as long as it was not allowed to expand into the West. Perhaps most important, Lincoln harbored doubts about his constitutional authority to end slavery, and he did not believe that Blacks, if freed, could coexist with Whites without triggering violence.

In August 1862, Lincoln invited African American leaders to meet with him—the first time that Blacks had visited the White House in an official capacity. He urged them to persuade their people to emigrate, to leave America for Africa, the Caribbean, and other places around the globe.

Enslaved People in the War

"Contrabands of war"

The expanding war forced the issue of the status of slavery. As Federal forces pushed into the Confederacy, freedom seekers began arriving in Union army camps needing food and shelter. Initially, commanders did not know what to do with them—or what to call them. Were they "freedmen" or "vagrants" or something else? One general designated them as "contraband of war," a military phrase referring to captured military equipment. Thereafter, the eventual half million enslaved people who arrived at Union army camps seeking protection and freedom were known as **contrabands**, but the more accurate term for them was *refugees*.

Most Union officers put the freedom seekers to work digging trenches, building fortifications, tending livestock, washing clothes, assisting in hospitals, burying the dead, and serving as guides or spies; some were provided land to grow cotton or vegetables. Still others were simply set free.

contrabands Freedom seekers who sought refuge in Union military camps or who lived in areas of the Confederacy under Union control.

As time passed and the number of refugees soared, Union armies erected some 500 camps to house them in secondhand tents or slapdash cabins. The camps were intended to help the enslaved make the transition to freedom,

CONTRABANDS Formerly enslaved people freed by the war's chaos on a farm in Cumberland Landing, Virginia, 1862. **How were freedom seekers treated by the Union forces?**

but they were often disease-ridden and dangerous places that were soon overwhelmed by the growing number of refugees.

Still, the former enslaved-turned-refugees much preferred to live in Union army camps than with their former Southern overlords. "They will endure every privation for the sake of freedom," noted a Union officer in 1862. "And they seem too happy in their escape from slavery to feel very keenly any present and temporary suffering."

"What Shall We Do with the Negro?"

However much Lincoln and others asserted that the conflict was about saving the Union rather than ending slavery, the prolonged war changed outlooks. In 1862, the editors of the *New York Times* asked, "What Shall We Do with the Negro?" Lincoln's answer was to edge toward ending slavery as a way to help win the war. On April 16, 1862, he signed an act that abolished slavery in the District of Columbia; on June 19, he signed another bill that excluded slavery from the western territories. Still, he insisted that the war was about restoring the Union and ending secession, not freeing the enslaved.

Circumstances, however, transformed Lincoln's outlook. In March 1862, he urged representatives of the four border slave states to begin to free their enslaved people. The next month, the Republican-controlled Congress passed the Second Confiscation Act, which declared that contrabands who had made it to Union army camps were "forever free."

Emancipation as a military necessity

That summer, Lincoln decided that as commander in chief he could eliminate slavery in the Confederate states as a necessary step to win the war and save the Union. In July 1862, he confided to his cabinet that emancipation had become "a military necessity, absolutely necessary to the preservation of the Union. We must free the slaves or be ourselves subdued." Secretary of State William H. Seward agreed but advised Lincoln to delay the announcement until after a Union battlefield victory, to avoid being viewed as desperate.

Antietam: A Turning Point

Robert E. Lee made his own momentous decision in the summer of 1862: He would invade Maryland and force the "much weakened and demoralized" Army of the Potomac and its "timid" commander George McClellan to leave northern Virginia, thereby relieving the pressure on Richmond, the Confederate capital. "The idea of waiting for blows, instead of inflicting them, is altogether unsuited to the genius of our people," explained the *Richmond Examiner*.

Lee hoped an invasion would influence the upcoming elections in the North. He also wanted to gain British and French recognition of the Confederacy, which would bring his troops desperately needed supplies. In addition, Lee and Jefferson Davis planned to capture Maryland (with its many Confederate supporters), separate it from the Union, and gain control of its farms, crops, and livestock.

In September 1862, Lee and his 40,000 troops pushed north across the Potomac River into western Maryland amid sweltering heat and humidity. "I have never seen such a mass of filthy, strong-smelling men," said a Marylander. "They are the roughest looking set of creatures I ever saw, their features, hair, and clothing matted with dirt and filth."

The Battle of Antietam (1862)

On September 17, Union and Confederate armies clashed in the furious **Battle of Antietam** (Sharpsburg). Had Union soldiers not discovered Lee's battle plans wrapped around three cigars that a Rebel courier had carelessly dropped on the ground, the Confederates might have won.

And had McClellan acted preemptively and moved his men more quickly, he could have destroyed Lee's Army of Northern Virginia while it was scattered and still on the march, since McClellan's army was twice as large as Lee's. As always, however, McClellan mobilized slowly, enabling Lee and his troops to regroup at Sharpsburg, Maryland, between Antietam Creek and the Potomac River.

There, over the course of fourteen hours, the poorly coordinated Union army launched repeated attacks. The fighting was savage; a Union officer counted "hundreds of dead bodies lying in rows and in piles." The scene after "five hours of continuous slaughter" was "sickening, harrowing, horrible. O what a terrible sight!" With nearly 23,000 killed and wounded on both sides, it was the bloodiest single day of the war and the bloodiest day in American history.

Battle of Antietam (1862) Turning-point battle near Sharpsburg, Maryland, leaving almost 25,000 soldiers dead or wounded, in which Union forces halted a Confederate invasion of the North.

The next day, Lee braced for another Union attack that never came. That night, cloaked by fog and drizzling rain, the battered Confederates slipped back across the Potomac River to the safety of Virginia. "The 'barefoot boys' have done some terrible fighting," a Georgian wrote his parents. "We are a dirty, ragged set [of soldiers], mother, but courage & heroism find many a true disciple among us."

Although the battle was technically a draw, Lee's northern invasion had failed. McClellan, never known for his modesty, told his wife that he "had fought the battle splendidly" against great odds. To him, the Battle of Antietam was "the most terrible battle of the age." Some 6,400 soldiers on both sides were killed, twice as many as at Shiloh, and another 17,000 were wounded or listed as missing.

President Lincoln was pleased that Lee's army had been forced to retreat, but he was disgusted by McClellan's failure to pursue the Confederates and win the war. The president sent a sarcastic message to the general: "I have just read your dispatch about sore-tongued and fatigued horses. Will you pardon me for asking what the horses of your army have done . . . that fatigues anything?" Failing to receive a satisfactory answer, Lincoln sacked McClellan as commander of the Army of the Potomac. Never again would McClellan command troops, but he would challenge Lincoln for the presidency in 1864.

CASUALTIES AT THE BATTLE OF ANTIETAM A photograph taken on September 19, 1862, captures a wagon road known as "Bloody Lane." Used as a rifle pit by Confederate troops, it served as their gravesite after the deadliest day in American history.

The Battle of Antietam revived sagging Northern morale and dashed the Confederacy's hopes of forging military alliances with Great Britain and France. It also convinced Lincoln to transform the war from an effort to restore the Union to a crusade to end slavery.

Emancipation Proclamation

On September 22, 1862, five days after the Battle of Antietam, President Lincoln issued the preliminary **Emancipation Proclamation**, which changed the course of history. It warned Confederate leaders that if they did not stop fighting and return to the Union, all enslaved people still under their control would be made "forever free" in exactly 100 days, on January 1, 1863.

Civil War becomes war to end slavery

The Emancipation Proclamation was not based on ideas of racial equality or abstract ideals of human dignity. It was, according to Lincoln, a "military necessity" and therefore a legitimate use of presidential "war powers." His concept of military-necessitated emancipation would free only those enslaved in areas still controlled by the Confederacy; it had no bearing on those enslaved in the four border states because they remained in the Union, and Lincoln had no constitutional authority to free them.

When Lincoln signed the actual Emancipation Proclamation in January, however, he amended his original message, adding that the proclamation was "an act of justice" as well as a military necessity. He said, "I never, in my life, felt more certain that I was doing the right thing than I do in signing this paper." Simply restoring the Union was no longer the purpose of the war; the transformation of the South and the slave system was now the goal.

Emancipation Proclamation (1863) Military order issued by President Abraham Lincoln that freed enslaved people in areas still controlled by the Confederacy.

UNION VIEW OF THE EMANCIPATION PROCLAMATION A thoughtful Lincoln composes the proclamation with the Constitution and the Holy Bible in his lap. The Scales of Justice hang on the wall behind him.

Reactions to Emancipation

Abraham Lincoln's threat to free enslaved people under Confederate control triggered emotional reactions. The *New York Times* proclaimed that "there has been no more far reaching document ever issued since the founding of this government." The *Illinois State Register* disagreed. It savaged the president for violating the Constitution and causing "the permanent disruption of the republic." Democrats called his decision dictatorial, unconstitutional, and catastrophic. "We Won't Fight to Free the [colored person]," proclaimed one popular banner.

Many others felt likewise. In the months following the proclamation, thousands of Union troops deserted, explaining that they did not enlist to free enslaved people, much less to provide racial equality. In the November elections, Democrats, scolding Republicans as "[colored person] Worshippers," took twenty-eight Republican seats.

Lincoln responded forcefully. "You say you will not fight to free negroes," he wrote. "Some of them seem willing to fight for you; but, no matter. Fight you, then, exclusively to save the Union. I issued the [emancipation] proclamation on purpose to aid you in saving the Union."

Although Lincoln's proclamation technically would free only the enslaved people where Confederates remained in control, many enslaved people in the Northern border states and the South claimed their freedom anyway. As Lincoln had hoped, word spread rapidly among enslaved communities in the Confederacy, creating general confusion in the cities and encouraging hundreds of thousands to escape.

George Washington Albright, an enslaved teen in Mississippi, recalled that although White planters tried to prevent enslaved people from learning

CONFEDERATE VIEW OF THE EMANCIPATION PROCLAMATION Surrounded by demonic faces hidden in his furnishings, Lincoln pens the proclamation with a foot trampling on a bound copy of the Constitution. The devil holds the inkwell before him.

about the emancipation proclamation, word slipped through the "grapevine." His father was inspired to escape and join the Union army, and the younger Albright served as a "runner" for the 4Ls ("Lincoln's Legal Loyal League"), a secret group created to spread the news to enslaved people throughout the region.

Lincoln's proclamation incensed Confederate leaders, who predicted it would ignite a race war. By contrast, Frederick Douglass, the African American abolitionist leader, loved the "righteous decree"; he knew it would inspire abolitionists in the North and set in motion the eventual end of slavery everywhere.

Union effort boosted by freed African Americans and European sympathy

As Lincoln had hoped, the Emancipation Proclamation boosted the Union war effort. It enabled African Americans to enlist in the Union army and navy, and it undermined support for the Confederacy in Europe. The conversion of the Civil War from a conflict to restore the Union into a crusade to end slavery gave the Federal war effort moral legitimacy in the eyes of Europeans.

As Union armies advanced deeper into the Southern states, they became forces of liberation. At Camp Saxton, a former plantation on the coast of South Carolina, the First South Carolina Volunteers, a Union regiment made up of formerly enslaved men, gathered on January 1, 1863, to celebrate Lincoln's signing of the Emancipation Proclamation.

After the proclamation was read aloud, it was "cheered to the skies." As Colonel Thomas W. Higginson, the unit's commander, unfurled an American flag, the Black troops spontaneously began singing "My Country 'Tis of Thee / Sweet land of liberty / Of thee I sing!" "I never saw anything so electric," Higginson reported; "it made all other words cheap; it seemed the choked voice of a race at last unloosed."

Fredericksburg

Meanwhile, the war was growing in scope and destruction. In Richmond, Mary Chesnut reported that everyone she encountered seemed shell-shocked by Confederate losses: "They press your hand, tears stand in their eyes or roll down their cheeks.... They have brothers, fathers, or sons—as the case may be—in the battle. And this thing now never seems to stop."

Ambrose E. Burnside made general

In his search for an effective commanding general, Lincoln turned in the fall of 1862 to Ambrose E. Burnside, whose greatest attribute was that he looked like a general: tall and imposing, with massive facial hair that gave rise to the term *sideburns*. Twice before, Burnside had turned down the job, saying he was unfit for such responsibility. Now he accepted, although he remained wracked by self-doubts.

Burnside decided to try again to capture Richmond, the Confederate capital. In mid-November 1862, he positioned most of the 122,000 men in the Army of the Potomac east of the icy Rappahannock River overlooking the town of Fredericksburg, Virginia. Robert E. Lee rushed his Army of Northern Virginia to defend the town.

As the days passed, Lee's outnumbered forces established impregnable positions along a line of ridges and behind a stone wall at the base of Marye's Heights, west of Fredericksburg. The Confederates positioned so many cannons atop the ridge that an officer boasted: "A chicken could not live on that field when we open up on it." A Union soldier predicted what was to happen: "It looks to me as if we are going over there to get murdered."

On December 13, the Union soldiers began to assault Lee's entrenched positions. Confederate cannons and muskets chewed up the Federals as they advanced uphill across a half mile of open land. The series of six futile assaults was, a Union general regretted, "a great slaughter-pen." The awful scene of dead and dying Federals, some stacked three deep on the battlefield, led General Lee to remark: "It is well that war is so terrible—we should grow too fond of it."

Union defeated at Battle of Fredericksburg (1862)

After 12,600 Federals were killed or wounded, compared with fewer than 5,300 Confederates, a weeping General Burnside told his shattered army to withdraw across the river as darkness fell. When Burnside rode past his retreating men, his aide called for three cheers for their commander. All he got was sullen silence. It was the worst Union defeat of the war.

The year 1862 ended with a stalemate in the East and with the Union thrust in the West mired down. Northern morale plummeted. Many Democrats were calling for a negotiated peace, and Republicans—even Lincoln's own cabinet members—grew increasingly critical of the president's leadership. "If there is a worse place than hell," Lincoln sighed, "I am in it."

New York City Draft Riots

Lincoln's proclamation freeing enslaved people in the Confederacy created anxiety and anger among many Northern laborers who feared that formerly enslaved people would eventually migrate north and take their jobs. In New York City, such fears erupted into violence. In July 1863, a group of 500

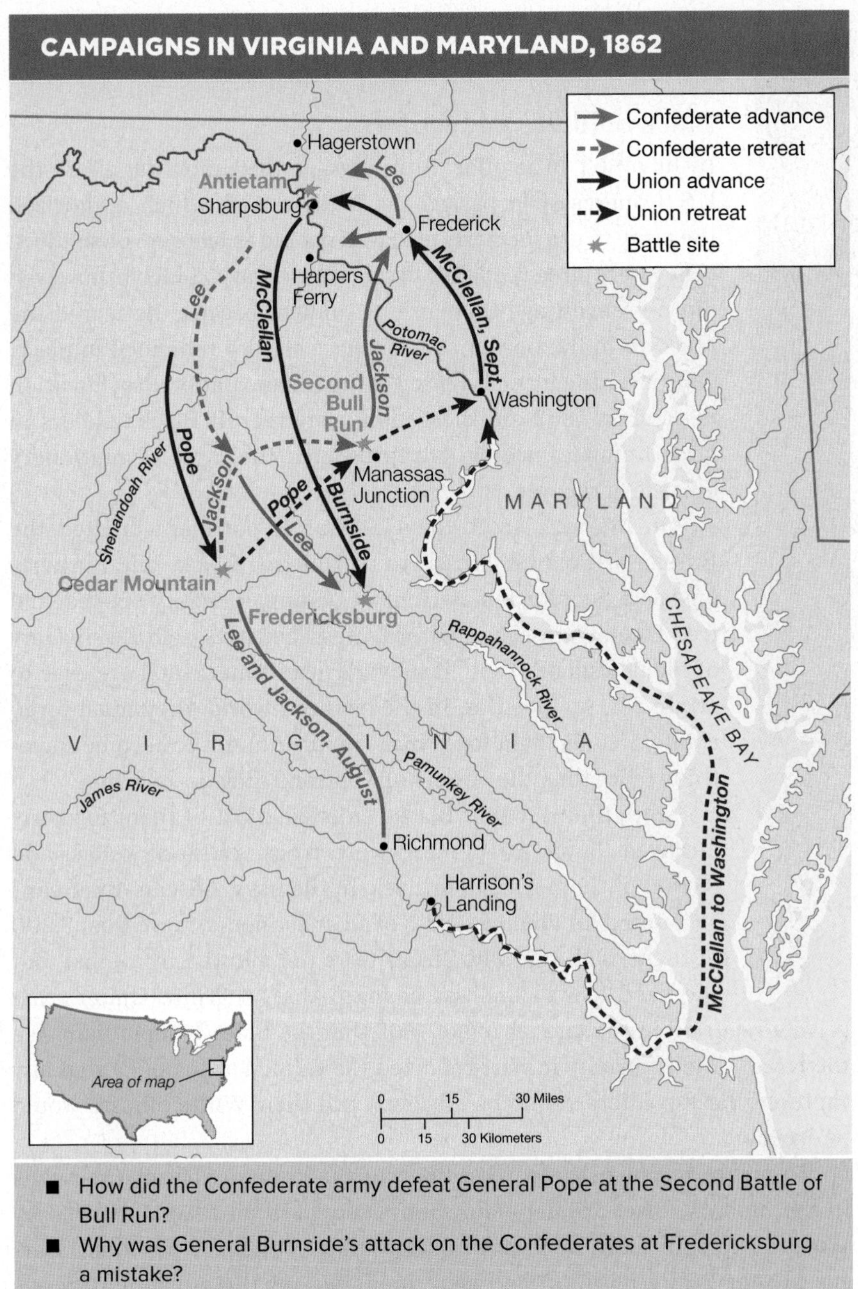

- How did the Confederate army defeat General Pope at the Second Battle of Bull Run?
- Why was General Burnside's attack on the Confederates at Fredericksburg a mistake?

Whites, led by volunteer firemen, assaulted the army draft office, shattered its windows, and burned it down.

Northern resistance to the war effort

Swollen by thousands of working-class Whites, mostly Irish, the rioters then ruthlessly began taking out their frustrations on Blacks. For four days and nights, mobs rampaged through the streets of Manhattan, tearing up rail lines, cutting telegraph wires, toppling streetcars, and randomly attacking African Americans. The protesters also burned down more than fifty buildings, including the mayor's home, police stations, two Protestant churches, and the Colored Orphan Asylum, forcing 233 children to flee.

BLACK UNION ARMY SERGEANT Wearing the uniform and sword of the North, this Black Union sergeant poses with a copy of J. T. Headley's *The Great Rebellion* in his hand.

The violence killed 120 people and injured thousands. Only the arrival of Union soldiers ended it.

Black Soldiers and Sailors

In July 1862, in an effort to strengthen the Union war effort, the U.S. Congress had passed the **Militia Act**, which authorized the army to use formerly enslaved people as laborers or soldiers. (They were already eligible to serve in the navy.) Lincoln, however, did not encourage their use as soldiers because he feared the reaction in the border states, where slavery remained in place. Only after the formal signing of the Emancipation Proclamation in January 1863 did the Union army recruit Black soldiers in large numbers. Doing so represented the most revolutionary episode of the war.

On May 22, 1863, the U.S. War Department created the Bureau of Colored Troops to recruit free Blacks and formerly enslaved people. James Henry Gooding, a twenty-six-year-old free Black from New Bedford, Massachusetts, told the readers of his newspaper that "if they [African Americans] are ever to attain . . . any position in the civilized world, they must forgo comfort . . . and fight for it; make up their minds to become something more than the hewers of wood and drawers of water."

More than 180,000 Blacks enlisted, most of them formerly enslaved. Some 80 percent were from Southern states, and 38,000 of them gave their lives. In the navy, African Americans accounted for about a fourth of all enlistments; more than 2,800 of them died. Initially, Blacks were not allowed in combat, but the need to win the war changed that. A White Union army private reported in the late spring of 1863 that the Black troops "fight like the Devil." Their tenacity in part reflected the Confederate policy that any captured Black soldiers would be enslaved and their White officers would be executed.

Inequalities in the Union army

To be sure, racism in the North influenced the status of African Americans in the military. Black soldiers and sailors served in all-Black units led by White officers. Initially, they were paid less than Whites ($7 per month versus $16 for White recruits) and were ineligible for the enlistment bonus paid to Whites. Still, as Frederick Douglass declared, "this is no time for hesitation. . . . This is our chance, and woe betide us if we fail to embrace it."

Service in the Union army or navy provided formerly enslaved people a unique opportunity to grow in confidence, awareness, and maturity. A Northern social worker in the South Carolina Sea Islands was "astonished" at the positive effects of "soldiering" on the formerly enslaved: "Some who left here a month ago to join [the army were] cringing, dumpish, slow," but now they "are ready to look you in the eye—are wide awake and active." President Lincoln reported that "some of our commanders . . . believe that . . . the use of colored troops constitutes the heaviest blow yet dealt to the

Militia Act (1862) Congressional measure that permitted formerly enslaved people to serve as laborers or soldiers in the U.S. Army.

rebels." One African American soldier who recognized his former owner among a group of Confederate prisoners called out: "Hello master. Bottom rail on top this time!"

The War behind the Lines

> CORE **OBJECTIVE**
> **3.** Analyze how the war affected social and economic life in the North and South.

Feeding, clothing, supplying, and nursing the vast armies required tremendous sacrifices. Farms and villages were transformed into battlefields, churches became makeshift hospitals, civilian life was disrupted, and families grieved for those who would not be coming home.

Civil War Medicine

Medical knowledge lagged the development of military weapons during the war. Antibiotics had yet to be developed, and pain-killing medicines were in short supply. Amputation was the common treatment for gunshot wounds to the arm or leg, and stomach wounds were usually fatal because resulting infection (peritonitis) could not be prevented. Of those killed by combat, some 60 percent died in battle, and 40 percent succumbed later.

Women and the War

The Civil War also loosened traditional restraints on female activity. "No conflict in history," a journalist wrote, "was such a woman's war as the Civil War."

Women played prominent roles on both sides. They worked in mills and factories, sewed uniforms, raised money and supplies, and volunteered as nurses. In Greenville, South Carolina, when T. G. Gower went off to fight, his wife, Elizabeth, took over the family business, converting production in their carriage factory to military wagons and ambulances. Three thousand Northern women worked as nurses with the U.S. Sanitary Commission, which provided medical relief and other services for soldiers. Countless women, Black and White, supported the freedmen's aid movement to feed, clothe, shelter, and educate formerly enslaved people.

In the North, thousands of women served as untrained nurses and health-related volunteers. The most famous were Clara Barton and Dorothea Lynde Dix. Barton explained that her place was "anywhere between the bullet and the battlefield." For her part, Dix, who was appointed superintendent of Union nurses in 1861, issued an appeal for "plain looking" women between the ages of thirty-five and fifty who wore no jewelry and could "bear the presence of suffering and exercise entire self-control."

It was not easy for the women who volunteered as nurses to interact with the surgeons, most of whom were male. Georgie Woolsey, who volunteered along with her sister, reported that none of the surgeons treated them with "even common courtesy." Yet to her and others it was worth the effort to help the wounded and the dying, comforting "them in their weary and dark hours."

WOMEN IN THE WAR EFFORT Claiming that her place was "anywhere between the bullet and the battlefield," Clara Barton *(left)* oversaw the distribution of medicines to Union troops and later helped found the American Red Cross. Susie King Taylor *(right)* served as a nurse in Union-occupied Georgia and later operated a school for freedpeople.

Barton, who later founded the American Red Cross, decided to go to the battlefields on her own, delivering medical supplies and food. At Fredericksburg, she nursed some 1,200 wounded in a single building. "I wrung the blood from the bottom of my clothing before I could step," she reported, "for the weight about my feet" kept her from moving.

In many Southern towns and counties, the home front became a world of White women and children and enslaved African Americans. A resident of Lexington, Virginia, reported that there were "no men left" in town by mid-1862. Women suddenly found themselves full-time farmers or plantation managers, clerks, and schoolteachers.

Other women traveled with the armies, cooking meals, writing letters, and assisting with amputations. Several dozen served as spies. New Yorker Mary Edwards Walker, a Union battlefield surgeon, was captured and imprisoned by the Confederates for spying, but later released in a prisoner exchange. She was the only woman in the war (and since) to be awarded the Congressional Medal of Honor, the nation's highest military award, which Lincoln had authorized in 1861.

Wartime Government

While freeing the enslaved people in the Confederacy was a transformational development, a political revolution resulted from the shift in congressional power from the South to the North after secession.

In 1862, the Republican-dominated Congress sought to promote the "prosperity and happiness of the whole people" by passing a more comprehensive tariff bill (called the Morrill Tariff in honor of its sponsor, Vermont Republican congressman Justin Smith Morrill) to raise government revenue and "protect" America's manufacturing, agricultural, mining, and fishing industries from foreign competition.

Republicans expand national economy and federal government

Republicans in Congress, with Lincoln's support, enacted legislation reflecting their belief that the federal government should actively promote economic development. To that end, Congress approved the **Pacific Railway Act (1862)**, which provided funding and grants of land for construction of a 1,900-mile-long transcontinental railroad line from Omaha, Nebraska, to Sacramento, California. In addition, a **Homestead Act (1862)** granted 160 acres of public land to each settler who agreed to work the land for five years. To help farmers become more productive, Congress created a new federal agency, the Department of Agriculture.

Two other key pieces of legislation were the **Morrill Land-Grant College Act (1862)**, which provided states with 30,000 acres of federal land to finance the establishment of public universities that would teach "agriculture and mechanic arts," and the **National Banking Act (1863)**, which created national banks that could issue paper money that would be accepted across the country. These wartime measures had long-term significance for the growth of the national economy—and the expansion of the federal government.

Union Finances

In December 1860, the federal Treasury was virtually empty. To meet the war's huge expenses, Congress needed money fast—and lots of it. It focused on three options: raising taxes, printing paper money, and selling government bonds to investors. The taxes came chiefly in the form of the Morrill Tariff on imports and a 3 percent tax on manufactures and most professions.

In 1862, Congress created the Internal Revenue Service to collect the first income tax on citizens and corporations. Yet only 250,000 people out of a population of 39 million had income high enough to pay taxes.

In the end, the tax revenues met only 21 percent of wartime expenditures. To fill the gap, Congress approved the printing of paper money to help finance the war. With the Legal Tender Act of 1862, the Treasury issued $450 million in new paper currency, called *greenbacks* because of the green ink used to print the bills.

The federal government also relied upon the sale of bonds. A Philadelphia banker named Jay Cooke (the "Financier of the Civil War") mobilized a nationwide campaign to sell $2 billion in government bonds to private investors.

Confederate Finances

In comparison to the Union, Confederate efforts to finance the war were a disaster. Jefferson Davis had to create a Treasury department and a revenue-collecting system from scratch. Moreover, the South's agrarian economy

Pacific Railway Act (1862) Congress provided funding for a transcontinental railroad from Nebraska west to California.

Homestead Act (1862) Legislation granting "home-steads" of 160 acres of government-owned land to settlers who agreed to work the land for at least five years.

Morrill Land-Grant College Act (1862) Federal statute that granted federal lands to states to help fund the creation of land-grant colleges and universities, which were founded to provide technical education in agriculture, mining, and industry.

National Banking Act (1863) The U.S. Congress created a national banking system to finance the enormous expense of the Civil War. It enabled loans to the government and established a single national currency, including the issuance of paper money ("greenbacks").

STATE CURRENCY Both the Union and the Confederacy issued paper money to stimulate the economy. Generally, the better the art on the note, the more it was trusted.

was land-rich but cash-poor. While the Confederacy owned 30 percent of America's assets (businesses, land, enslaved people) in 1861, its currency in circulation was only 12 percent of that in the North.

Financing the war: Tax-evasion and inflation

In its first year, the Confederacy created a property tax, which should have yielded a hefty amount of revenue. Collecting taxes was left to the states, however, and the result was chaos. In 1863, the desperate Confederate Congress began taxing nearly everything, but enforcement was poor and evasion easy. Altogether, taxes covered no more than 5 percent of Confederate war costs, and bond issues accounted for less than 33 percent. Treasury notes (paper money) accounted for more than 60 percent.

During the war, the Confederacy issued more than $1 billion in paper money, which, along with a shortage of consumer goods, caused prices to soar. By 1864, a turkey sold in the Richmond market for $100, and bacon was $10 a pound. Such steep price increases caused great distress, and frustrations over the burdens of war erupted into rioting, looting, and mass protests.

By 1865, some 100,000 Confederate soldiers, hungry, weary, and frustrated by delayed pay, were deserting and heading home. As one said, he and his comrades were "tired of fighting for this negro-owning aristockracy [*sic*]."

Union Politics

The North also had its share of dissension and factionalism, but President Lincoln proved to be a remarkable conflict manager. He loved the jockeying of backroom politics, and he excelled at fending off uprisings and attempts to subvert his leadership.

Led by Thaddeus Stevens in the House and Charles Sumner in the Senate, the so-called Radical Republicans wanted more than the Confederacy's defeat; they wanted to "reconstruct" the rebellious region by having Union armies seize Southern plantations and give the land to the former enslaved workers. Most Republicans, however, continued to back Lincoln's more cautious approach.

The Democratic party was devastated by the loss of its long-dominant southern wing and the death of its nationalist spokesman, Stephen A. Douglas. Peace Democrats favored restoring the Union "as it was [before 1860] and the Constitution as it is." They reluctantly supported Lincoln's war policies but opposed Republican economic legislation. Those referred to as the War Democrats, such as Tennessee senator Andrew Johnson and Secretary of War Edwin M. Stanton, backed Lincoln.

Civil Liberties

Lincoln suspends *habeas corpus*

The growing support in the North for the enemy led President Lincoln to crack down hard. His challenge was to balance the urgent needs of winning a war with the protection of civil liberties. Using his authority as commander in chief, Lincoln exercised emergency powers, including suspending the writ of *habeas corpus*, which guarantees arrested citizens a speedy hearing before a judge. The Constitution states that the government may suspend habeas corpus only in cases of foreign invasion, but Supreme Court justice Roger Taney and several congressional leaders argued that Congress alone had the authority to take such action.

By the Habeas Corpus Act of 1863, Congress allowed the president to have people arrested on the "suspicion" of treason. Thereafter, Union soldiers and local sheriffs arrested thousands of Confederate sympathizers in the Northern states without using a writ of habeas corpus. Union general Henry Halleck jailed a Missourian for saying, "[I] wouldn't wipe my ass with the stars and stripes."

Confederate Politics and States' Rights

As the war dragged on, discontented Confederates directed much of their frustration toward their leaders. A Richmond newspaper reported in 1862 that the Confederacy had "reached a very dark hour" because of Jefferson Davis's faulty leadership. It described the Rebel leader as "cold, haughty, peevish, narrow-minded, pig-headed, [and] malignant."

Poor White Southerners resented the planter elite while food grew scarce and prices skyrocketed. In August 1862, planter/politician J. F. H. Claiborne wrote a letter to the Mississippi governor in which he acknowledged, "We are proving our loyalty by starvation." The military's demands for food and supplies pitted the needs of civilians against soldiers.

Riots in the South

A food riot erupted in Richmond on April 2, 1863, when an angry mob, mostly women armed with pistols or knives, marched to the governor's mansion to demand that bread in Confederate military warehouses be shared with civilians. When the governor announced that nothing could be done, the protesters shouted, "Bread or blood!" They broke into markets and stores, stealing shoes and clothing as well as food. The riot ended only when President Davis arrived and threatened to shoot the protesters. Over several days, police arrested forty-four women and twenty-nine men. "We had forgotten Yankees and were fighting each other," Mary Chesnut confessed.

Davis's greatest challenge came from Southern politicians who criticized the "tyrannical" powers of the Confederate government. Critics asserted states' rights against the Confederate government, just as they had against the Union. Georgia governor Joseph Brown explained that he had joined the Confederacy to "sustain the rights of the states and prevent the consolidation of the Government, and I am still a *rebel* . . . *no* matter who may be in power."

While Lincoln was a shrewd pragmatist, Davis was a brittle ideologue with a waspish temper. Once he'd made a decision, nothing could change his mind, and he could never admit his mistake. South Carolina's James Henry Hammond charged that Davis displayed "the most perverse & mulish obstinacy, spleen, spite & illimitable conceit & vanity."

Such a dogmatic personality was ill-suited to the chief executive of a new—and quarrelsome—nation. Cabinet members resigned almost as soon as they were appointed. During its four years, the Confederacy had three secretaries of state and six secretaries of war.

CORE **OBJECTIVE**

4. Describe the military turning points in 1863 and 1864 that ultimately led to the Confederacy's defeat.

The Faltering Confederacy

Amid the political infighting, the war ground on. The Confederate strategy of fighting mostly a defensive war was working well, and President Lincoln was still searching for a general in chief comparable to Robert E. Lee.

Chancellorsville

Joseph Hooker heads the Army of the Potomac

After the Union disaster at Fredericksburg at the end of 1862, President Lincoln fired Ambrose Burnside and appointed General Joseph "Fighting Joe" Hooker to lead the Army of the Potomac. With a force of 130,000 men, the largest Union army yet gathered, an overconfident Hooker attacked the Confederates at Chancellorsville, in eastern Virginia, during the first week of May 1863. "My plans are perfect," Hooker boasted. "May God have mercy on General Lee, for I will have none."

Hooker spoke too soon. Lee, with perhaps half as many troops, split his army in thirds and gave Hooker a painful lesson in the art of elusive mobility when Stonewall Jackson's 28,000 Confederates surprised the Union army by smashing into its exposed right flank. Jackson's stunning attack resulted in a devastating defeat for the Union. "My God, my God," moaned Lincoln when he heard the news. "What will the country say?"

Death of Stonewall Jackson

The Confederate victory was costly, however. As night fell during the second day of battle, General Jackson and several aides rode out beyond the Rebel lines to locate Union forces. Shooting erupted in the darkness, and nervous Confederates mistakenly opened fire on Jackson's group. Three bullets struck the celebrated commander, shattering his left arm and right hand.

The next day, a surgeon amputated his arm. The indispensable Jackson seemed to be recovering, but he then contracted pneumonia and died. "I have lost my right arm," Lee lamented, and "I do not know how to replace him."

ULYSSES S. GRANT Lincoln finally found a general to rival Lee in Grant, pictured here at his headquarters in City Point (now Hopewell), Virginia.

Vicksburg

While General Lee frustrated the Federals in the East, General Grant had been inching his army down the Mississippi River toward the Confederate stronghold of Vicksburg, Mississippi, a busy commercial town situated on high bluffs overlooking a bend in the river. Capturing the most important Rebel outpost in the western theater, Grant stressed, "was of the first importance," because Vicksburg was the only rail and river junction between Memphis, Tennessee, and New Orleans. By gaining control of the lower Mississippi River, the Union could cut off and isolate Texas, Arkansas, and most of Louisiana from the rest of the Confederacy.

While Union warships sneaked past the Confederate cannons overlooking the river, Grant moved his army eastward across Mississippi, living off the land on a campaign that President Lincoln later called "one of the most brilliant in the world." In three weeks, Grant's men marched 180 miles, won five battles, and captured some 6,000 prisoners before pinning the main Rebel army inside Vicksburg so tightly that "not a cat could have crept out . . . without being discovered."

In late May and early June 1863, Federal troops dug twelve miles of interconnected trenches around the besieged city and positioned 220 cannons to make life miserable for the Vicksburg defenders. Yet taking the river city would not be easy. One of Grant's generals declared that "no place on earth is favored by nature with natural defense such as Vicksburg."

Ulysses S. Grant holds Vicksburg under siege

In the **Battle of Vicksburg**, Grant decided to use constant bombardment from gunboats and cannons to starve and gradually wear down the trapped Confederate soldiers, 10 percent of whom would be killed or wounded. Many civilians were forced to live in cellars or caves dug as protection from the unending shelling. A woman trapped by the siege stressed that "we are utterly cutoff from the world, surrounded by a circle of fire. The fiery shower of [Union] shells goes on day and night." All the "dogs and cats must be killed or starved. I don't see any more pitiful animals prowling around."

The Rebel soldiers and the city's residents could neither escape nor be reinforced nor resupplied with food and ammunition. As the weeks passed, they ate their horses and mules, then dogs and cats, and, finally, rats, which sold for a dollar each. A young lady noted in her diary how the "hollow-eyed, ragged, footsore, [and] bloody" soldiers "limped along" in "aimless confusion." Attempts at rescue failed, and the living conditions for both military personnel and civilians deteriorated rapidly.

Battle of Vicksburg (1863) A protracted battle in northern Mississippi in which Union forces under Ulysses S. Grant besieged the last major Confederate fortress on the Mississippi River, forcing the inhabitants into starvation and then submission on July 4, 1863.

General John C. Pemberton, the Confederate commander at Vicksburg, wrote Jefferson Davis that the situation was "hopeless." A group of ragged soldiers pleaded with their commander: "If you can't feed us, you had better surrender us, horrible as that idea is." Yet Pemberton, a Pennsylvanian whose Virginia-born wife convinced him to fight for the Confederacy, was determined to outlast Grant's troops.

Gettysburg

General Lee leads Confederate troops north

Vicksburg's dilemma led Jefferson Davis to ask General Lee to send troops from Virginia to Mississippi to break the Union siege. Lee, however, thought he had a better plan. He would make another daring strike into the North in hopes of forcing the Union army surrounding Vicksburg to rush home to defend the Northern heartland. He also wagered that a bold northern offensive would persuade peace-seeking Democrats to try again to end the war on terms favorable to the Confederacy. The stakes were high. A Confederate general said the invasion across Maryland and into Pennsylvania would "either destroy the Yankees or bring them to terms." Or be a disaster for Lee.

In June 1863, the fabled Army of Northern Virginia, which Lee said was made up of "invincible troops" who would "go anywhere and do anything if properly led," moved northward, taking thousands of animals and wagons as well as throngs of enslaved people for support.

One reason Lee moved into the North was to find food for his men and horses. The Union armies had spent so much time in northern Virginia that there were not enough rations to go around. So as Lee's army moved north, his soldiers and enslaved people confiscated thousands of horses, cattle, and hogs, as well as tons of wheat and corn. They also captured free Blacks in Maryland and Pennsylvania, returning them to slavery in Virginia.

Once the Union commander General George Meade realized that the Confederates were again moving north, he gave chase, knowing that the next battle would "decide the fate of our country and our cause." As Lee's army moved into Pennsylvania, he lost track of the Federals following him because of the unexplained absence of General J. E. B. Stuart's 5,000 horse soldiers, who were Lee's "eyes and ears." Stuart, it turned out, had decided on his own to threaten an attack on Washington, D.C. On June 28, an exasperated Lee exploded: "I cannot think what has become of Stuart. I ought to have heard from him long before now."

Battle of Gettysburg (1863)

Neither side expected Gettysburg, a hilly farming town in southeastern Pennsylvania, to be the site of the largest battle ever fought in North America. Unsuspecting Confederate troops entered the town at dawn on June 30 and collided with Union cavalry units that had been tracking their movements.

Battle of Gettysburg (1863) A monumental three-day battle in southern Pennsylvania, widely considered a turning point in the war, in which Union forces defeated Lee's Confederate army and forced it back into Virginia.

The main forces of both sides—65,000 Confederates and 85,000 Federals—then raced to the scene, and on July 1, the armies clashed in what came to be called the **Battle of Gettysburg**, the most dramatic contest of the war.

Initially, the Confederates forced the Federals to retreat, but the Union troops regrouped to stronger positions on high ridges overlooking the town.

PICKETT'S CHARGE In a courageous and doomed effort, the Confederate soldiers *(in the foreground)* led by General Pickett prepare to advance on a line of well-armed Union troops.

General Meade rushed in reinforcements. That night he wrote his wife that both armies had been "shattered" by the first day's combat.

On July 2, wave after wave of screaming Confederates assaulted Meade's army, pushing the Federals back but never breaking through. A wounded Confederate officer scrawled a note before he died: "Tell my father I died with my face to the enemy." Some 16,000 were killed or wounded on both sides during the second day. Worse was to come.

The next day, against the objections of his senior general, Georgian James Longstreet, Robert E. Lee risked all on a gallant but doomed assault against the well-defended Union lines along Cemetery Ridge. For two hours, both sides bombarded the other, leading a Union soldier to write that it felt "as if the heavens and earth were crashing together."

Then, at two o'clock on the broiling summer afternoon, the cannons stopped. Three infantry divisions—about 12,500 men—rose together and emerged from the woods into the brilliant sunlight. General George Pickett, commander of the lead division, told his men, "Charge the enemy and remember Old Virginia!"

Picket's "grand charge"

A gray wave of sweating Rebels began a mile-long dash up a grassy slope of newly mown hay crisscrossed with split-rail fences. Awaiting them behind a low stone wall at the top of Cemetery Ridge were 120 Union cannons and thousands of riflemen.

When the Federals opened fire, the attacking Rebels were "enveloped in a dense cloud of dust. Arms, heads, blankets, guns, and knapsacks were tossed into the clear air." Half of the Confederates were killed or wounded. Only a few made it to the top, where they grappled with Federals in hand-to-hand combat. The Union line held, and the Confederates fell back.

With stunning suddenness, the carnage was over. The surviving Confederates retreated to the sheltering woods, and the once roaring

A HARVEST OF DEATH Timothy H. O'Sullivan's grim photograph of the dead at Gettysburg.

battlefield was left covered with the corpses of men and horses, a scene made ghastlier by the "moanings and groanings" of thousands of wounded. Each corpse told a poignant story. Scattered beside a dead Federal officer were papers granting him leave to go home and be married, and a letter from his soon-to-be bride expressing her "happiness at the approaching event."

What General Lee had called the "grand charge" was a grand failure. As he watched the survivors straggle back, he muttered, "All this has been my fault. It is I who have lost this fight." He ordered General Pickett to prepare his battered division for another attack, only to have Pickett reply: "General Lee, I have no division now." Half his men lay dead or wounded.

Lee sought to console Pickett by assuring him that he and his troops "have covered yourselves with glory." Pickett would have none of it. "Not all the glory in the world, General Lee, can atone for the widows and orphans this day has made."

Some 42,000 were dead, wounded, or missing after three days at Gettysburg. Thousands of horses were also killed and left to rot. A Union soldier wrote home: "Great God! When will this horrid war stop?"

Others asked the same question. John Futch, a Confederate private from North Carolina, had seen his brother shot in the head. He wrote his wife that the slaughter had left him "half crazy." A few weeks after the battle, he quit his post and headed home, only to be captured, tried as a deserter, and executed.

Union soldiers were ecstatic after the climactic battle. Never had they soundly beaten Lee's army. Now their resounding victory boosted morale and confidence. "The great battle of the war has been fought," a Rhode Islander wrote to his family, "and thanks be to God the Army of the Potomac has been victorious at last."

Lee's Retreat

Again, as after Antietam, Robert E. Lee's mangled army retreated to Virginia—and again, the Federals were slow to give chase. Had General Meade quickly pursued Lee's battered army, he might have ended the war. President Lincoln was outraged: "We had them within our grasp! Your golden opportunity is gone, and I am distressed immeasurably because of it."

The war would grind on for another twenty-one months. Still, Rebel morale plummeted. A Georgia soldier wrote his mother that "the Army is broken hearted" and "don't care which way the war closes, for we have suffered very much."

CAMPAIGNS IN THE EAST, 1863

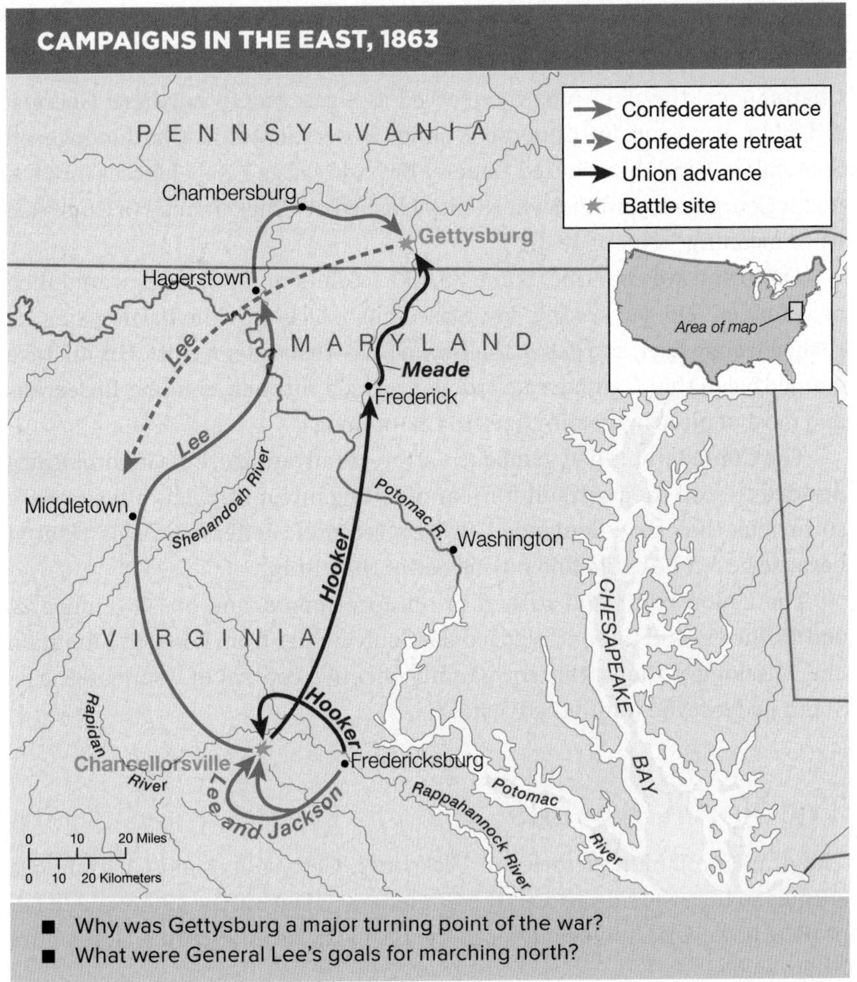

- Why was Gettysburg a major turning point of the war?
- What were General Lee's goals for marching north?

Lee's desperate gamble had failed in every way, not the least being its inability to relieve the pressure on the Confederate army trapped in Vicksburg, Mississippi. On July 4, General John Pemberton, the Confederate commander at Vicksburg, surrendered, ending the forty-seven-day siege. Union vessels now controlled the Mississippi River, and the Confederacy was effectively split in two.

The Gettysburg Address

After the Battle of Gettysburg, a group of Northern states funded a military cemetery in commemoration of the thousands killed in the battle. On November 19, 1863, President Lincoln spoke to 15,000 people gathered to dedicate the new national cemetery. In his brief remarks (only nine sentences), known now as the Gettysburg Address, he expressed the pain and sorrow of the uncivil war. The prolonged conflict was testing whether a nation "dedicated to the proposition that all men are created equal . . . can long endure." In stirring words, Lincoln predicted that "this nation, under God, shall have a new birth of freedom—and that government of the people, by the people, and for the people, shall not perish from the earth."

Chattanooga

The third Union triumph of 1863 occurred in southern Tennessee around Chattanooga, the river port that served as a gateway to northern Georgia. A Union army led by General William Rosecrans took Chattanooga on September 9 and then chased General Braxton Bragg's Rebel forces into the north Georgia mountains, where they clashed at Chickamauga (a Cherokee word meaning "river of death").

The result was horrific. Some 35,000 soldiers on both sides were killed or wounded. On the second day, Rosecrans nearly lost the battle when he rushed troops to close a gap in the Union line—that did not exist. His mistake opened a gap that Confederate troops stormed through, sending Rosecrans and most of his army reeling back to Chattanooga.

The Confederates had gained the strategic advantage, but General Bragg decided to stop their pursuit for fear of falling into a trap. His officers were so furious that they demanded Bragg's removal. Jefferson Davis refused because he felt he could find no one better than Bragg.

The Battle of Chattanooga secures Union victory in the West

The Union command rushed in reinforcements, and on November 24 and 25, the Federal troops dislodged the Confederates from Lookout Mountain and Missionary Ridge, thereby gaining effective control of Tennessee. The South had lost the war in the West.

The North Prevails

The dramatic Union victories at Vicksburg, Gettysburg, and Chattanooga seemed to turn the tide against the Confederacy. During the summer and fall of 1863, however, Union generals in the East lost the momentum Gettysburg had provided.

By 1864, Robert E. Lee, whose offer to resign after Gettysburg was refused by Jefferson Davis, was ready to renew the war. His men were "in fine spirits and anxious for a fight." Still, the tone had changed. Confederate leaders had long assumed they could win the war. Now, they began to worry about defeat. A Confederate officer in Richmond noted in his diary after the defeat at Gettysburg that "today absolute ruin seems to be our fortune. The Confederacy totters to its destruction."

A Wartime Election

War or no war, 1864 was a presidential election year, and by autumn the contest would become a referendum on the war itself. No president since Andrew Jackson had won reelection, and Abraham Lincoln became convinced that he would lose without a dramatic change in the course of the war. "This war is eating my life out," Lincoln confessed to an Illinois friend in 1864. "I have a strong impression I shall not live to see the end."

Radical Republicans, frustrated that the war had not been won, tried to prevent Lincoln's nomination for a second term, but he consistently outmaneuvered them. Once Lincoln was assured of the nomination, he selected

Andrew Johnson, a War Democrat from Tennessee, as his running mate on the "National Union" ticket. Johnson was the only U.S. senator from the southern states to remain in Congress and not join the Confederacy in 1861. By choosing Johnson as his running mate, Lincoln sought to make a bipartisan appeal to Union voters, both Republicans and Democrats.

The War Democrats had indiscreetly asked General Grant to be their candidate. He firmly declined, explaining, "I am not a politician, never was, and hope never to be." Becoming president, he said, "is the last thing in the world I desire."

Spurned by Grant, the Democrats nominated General George B. McClellan, the former Union commander who had clashed with Lincoln. McClellan pledged to stop the war and, if the Rebels refused to return to the Union, to allow the Confederacy to "go in peace."

Lincoln was convinced he would lose the election unless Union armies won a major battlefield victory. To save the Union—and his presidency—Lincoln had brought Grant, his best commander, to Washington, D.C., in March 1864; promoted him to general in chief; and given him overall command of the war effort, promising all the troops and supplies he needed.

A New York newspaper reported that Lincoln's presidency was now "in the hands of General Grant, and the failure of the General will be the overthrow of the president." When a delegation visited the White House to complain about Grant's reputation as a heavy drinker, Lincoln told the visitors that if he could find the brand of whiskey Grant used, he would distribute it to the rest of his generals.

Grant's Strategy

General Grant was a hard-nosed warrior with unflagging energy and persistence. One soldier said that Grant always looked like he was "determined to drive his head through a brick wall and was about to do it." Yet the Union commander hated war. "I never went into battle willingly or with enthusiasm," he admitted. Nevertheless, he was a brilliant military strategist driven by a simple concept: "Find out where your enemy is, get to him as soon as you can, and strike him as hard as you can, and keep moving on."

Grant's predecessors had focused on trying to capture Richmond; his purpose was to defeat Confederate armies. He would wage a relentless war of attrition, one in which victory would favor the side that could absorb the most punishment and keep fighting. Grant, as Abraham Lincoln noted, understood that winning the war was a matter of "awful arithmetic." The Union had the greater numbers, so victory was "only a matter of time."

Grant's strategy of total war

To that end, Grant ordered the three largest Union armies, one in Virginia, one in Tennessee, and one in Louisiana, to launch offensives in the spring of 1864. No more short battles followed by long pauses. They would force the outnumbered Confederates to keep fighting, day after day, week after week, until they were worn out.

Grant assigned his trusted friend, General William Tecumseh Sherman, a rail-thin, red-haired Ohioan, to lead the Union army in Tennessee southward and apply a strategy of "complete conquest." Sherman and Grant would now

FORT PILLOW MASSACRE The Confederate general Nathan Bedford Forrest oversaw the brutal execution of roughly 300 surrendered Union soldiers, most of them Black, at Fort Pillow in 1864.

wage total war, destroying any property that might have military value. It was a ruthless and costly plan, but in the end, it would prove effective in shortening the war.

Fort Pillow Massacre

As the war ground on, the fighting grew more brutal. The worst war crime occurred at Fort Pillow on the western edge of Tennessee. Built in 1861 by Confederates, Fort Pillow was perched on a bluff overlooking a bend in the Mississippi River some forty miles north of Memphis, Tennessee. In 1862, as Union forces took control of the Mississippi, Confederates abandoned the fort and Union troops had moved in.

On April 12, 1864, Confederate troops under General Nathan Bedford Forrest, a former slave trader and planter, assaulted Fort Pillow and murdered some 300 surrendering Union soldiers. Most of them were African Americans. A Confederate sergeant reported that "the slaughter was awful. Words cannot describe the scene. The poor, deluded negroes would run up to our men, fall upon their knees, and with uplifted hand scream for mercy, but were ordered to their feet and then shot down. . . . I with several others tried to stop the butchery . . . but Gen. Forrest ordered them shot down like dogs, and the carnage continued. Finally, our men became sick of blood, and the firing ceased."

Word of the Fort Pillow Massacre raced across the nation. Violence begat violence. A few weeks later, a Union soldier from Wisconsin fighting in north Georgia wrote to his future wife about a recent battle: "Twenty-three of the Rebs surrendered but our boys asked if they remembered Fort Pillow and killed all of them. Where there is no officer with us, we take no prisoners. . . . We want revenge for our brother soldiers and will have it."

Chasing Lee

Battle of the Wilderness (1864)

In May 1864, General Grant's massive Army of the Potomac, numbering about 115,000 (nearly twice the size of General Lee's Army of Northern Virginia), moved south across the Rappahannock and Rapidan Rivers in eastern Virginia. In the nightmarish Battle of the Wilderness (May 5–6), halfway between Washington, D.C., and Richmond, the armies clashed in an impenetrable tangle of scrub oaks, stunted pines, and thorny thickets interspersed with ravines, streams, and swamps. Exploding shells set off brushfires that burned many wounded soldiers to death.

At one point, the Union forces threatened to overrun Lee's headquarters. Lee himself helped organize a counterattack, lining up soldiers from Texas to lead the effort. He then turned to lead the charge himself, but was stopped by one of his soldiers. Lee's mood brightened as the Confederates swept the Federals from the field.

Grant's men suffered more casualties than the Confederates, but the Rebels struggled to find replacements. Always before, when bloodied by Lee's troops, Union armies had quit fighting to rest and nurse their wounds, but now Grant refused to halt. His army continued to push southward, forcing the Rebels to keep fighting.

Lee knew what he was up against. As he told aides, the "great thing about Grant is his perfect coolness and persistency of purpose . . . he is not easily excited . . . and he has the grit of a bull-dog! Once let him get his 'teeth' in, and nothing can shake him off." When General John B. Gordon boasted after the Battle of the Wilderness that Grant was retreating, Lee corrected him: "You are mistaken, quite mistaken. Grant is not retreating; he is not a *retreating* man."

Lee predicted that Grant's army would head for Spotsylvania, which it did. There, it engaged Lee's men near Spotsylvania Court House, eleven miles southwest of Fredericksburg, on the road to Richmond. For twelve brutally hot days in May, the opposing armies were locked in some of the fiercest combat of the war. The result was inconclusive, with both sides declaring victory.

Grant suffers terrible defeat at Cold Harbor

In the first days of June, just as Republican leaders were gathering to renominate Abraham Lincoln as their presidential candidate, Grant approved a poorly coordinated frontal assault on Lee's entrenched Rebels ten miles east of Richmond, at Cold Harbor (the name derived from a tavern that offered overnight rooms but no hot meals).

In twenty minutes, amid pitiless heat and choking dust, almost 7,000 Federals, caught in a blistering crossfire, were killed or wounded; the Rebel count was only 1,500. It was, according to a Union general, "one of the most disastrous days the Army of the Potomac has ever seen." A Confederate commander reported that "it was not war; it was murder."

The frightful losses nearly unhinged Grant, who later admitted that the botched attack was his greatest mistake as a commander. Critics called Grant "a butcher" who was "not fit to be at the head of an army." In just two months, Grant's massive offensive across Virginia, labeled the Overland Campaign, had cost some 65,000 killed, wounded, or missing Union soldiers while the Confederate losses were only half that number.

Northern outcry against Grant

Criticism of Grant's campaign skyrocketed. Even Horace Greeley, the powerful Unionist publisher of the *New York Tribune*, urged Lincoln to negotiate with Confederate leaders to save the "bleeding, bankrupt, almost dying country." The Union war effort came close to ending.

Yet Grant, for all his mistakes, knew that his army could replace its dead and wounded; the Rebels could not. A Union victory, he insisted, "was only a question of time." And, Grant reminded Lincoln, he was slowly pushing Lee's army toward Richmond, backing the Confederates into a corner from which they could not escape.

In June 1864, Grant brilliantly maneuvered his battered forces around Lee's army, crossed the James River, and headed for Petersburg, a major supply center and railroad hub twenty-five miles south of Richmond. As the opposing armies dug in above and below Petersburg, Grant began a long siege

GRANT IN VIRGINIA, 1864–1865

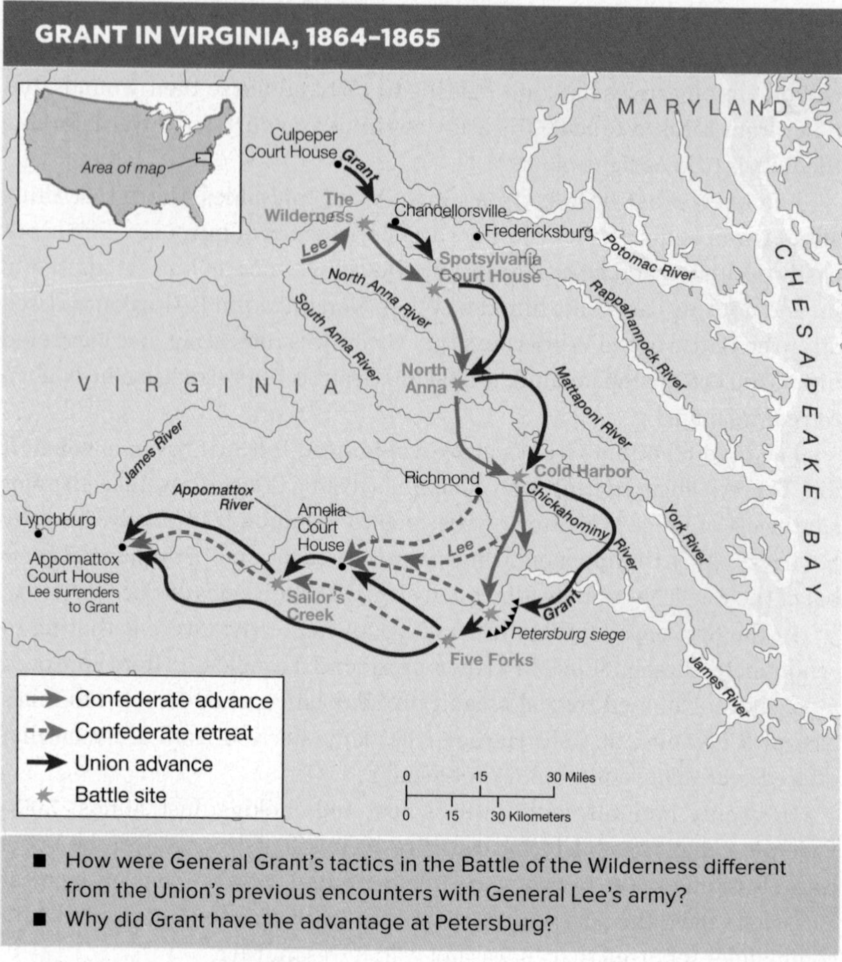

- How were General Grant's tactics in the Battle of the Wilderness different from the Union's previous encounters with General Lee's army?
- Why did Grant have the advantage at Petersburg?

of the trapped Confederate army, tightening the noose as he had done at Vicksburg.

At the end of August, Robert E. Lee reported to Jefferson Davis that Grant was "reducing us by starvation." For nine months, the two sides held each other in check around Petersburg. Grant's troops were generously supplied by Union vessels moving up the James River, while the Confederates wasted away. The number of deserters grew so large that Lee asked permission to shoot them when caught.

Petersburg had become Lee's prison while disasters piled up for the Confederacy elsewhere. He admitted that it was "a mere question of time" before he would have to retreat or surrender. A Rebel soldier noted in his diary that "our affairs do look gloomy."

Sherman Pushes South

Meanwhile, General Grant ordered William T. Sherman to drive through the heart of Dixie and inflict "all the damage you can." As Sherman moved his army south from Chattanooga toward the crucial railroad hub of Atlanta, he sent a warning to the city's residents: "Prepare for my coming."

By the middle of July, Sherman's troops had reached the outskirts of heavily fortified Atlanta, trapping 40,000 Confederate soldiers there. General John Bell Hood, the Confederate commander from Texas, was a fearless fighter. A Confederate senator's wife said that "a braver man, a purer patriot, a more gallant soldier never breathed than General Hood." General Grant's opinion of him was more mixed. He viewed Hood as "a gallant brave fellow" but believed he would likely "dash out and fight every time you raised a [Union] flag before him." And that is just what Grant and Sherman wanted him to do.

Hood's arm had been shattered at Gettysburg, and he had lost a leg in Tennessee. Strapped to his saddle, he refused simply to "defend" Atlanta; instead, he attacked. Three times in eight days, the Confederates lashed out at the Union lines encircling the city. Each time they were repulsed, suffering *seven* times as many casualties as the Federals. "All lion," Robert E. Lee said of Hood, "none of the fox."

Sherman seizes and burns Atlanta

Finally, on September 1, the Confederates evacuated the city. Sherman then moved in, gleefully telegraphing Lincoln in September 1864, "Atlanta is ours and fairly won." Confederates were crestfallen at the news. A distraught Mary Chesnut decided "the end has come. . . . We are going to be wiped off the face of the earth. . . . No hope."

In the North, the news from Atlanta generated the opposite reaction. Joseph Medill, a Chicago newspaper publisher and leading Republican, worried no more about his friend Lincoln's upcoming reelection bid. "The dark days are over," he crowed. "Thanks be to God. The Republic is safe."

Sherman's soldiers stayed in Atlanta until November, resting and resupplying themselves. The 20,000 residents were told to leave before he destroyed much of the city. When they protested, the Union commander replied: "War is cruelty." His men then set fire to the city's railroad station, iron foundries, shops, mills, hotels, and businesses. After Grant congratulated Sherman, he ordered him to commence another campaign, for "we want to keep the enemy constantly pressed to the end of the war."

Lincoln Reelected

William Tecumseh Sherman's conquest of Atlanta enabled Abraham Lincoln to win a second term in the **election of 1864**. Up to that point, the president was convinced that he would lose. "I am a beaten man, unless we have some great victory," he predicted at the end of August. Now, the tide had turned in Lincoln's favor. As a Republican senator said, the Union victory in Georgia "created the most extraordinary change in public opinion here [in the North] that ever was known." A Union newspaper editor reported that the fall of Atlanta "has secured a sudden unanimity for Mr. Lincoln."

In the 1864 election, the Democratic candidate, George McClellan, carried only New Jersey, Delaware, and Kentucky, winning just 21 Electoral College votes to Lincoln's 212 and 1.8 million popular votes (45 percent) to Lincoln's 2.2 million (55 percent). Union soldiers and sailors voted in large numbers, and almost 80 percent voted for Lincoln, who became the first president since Andrew Jackson to win a second term. The president's

election of 1864 Abraham Lincoln's successful reelection campaign, capitalizing on Union military successes in Georgia, to defeat his Democratic opponent, former general George B. McClellan, who ran on a peace platform.

victory sealed the fate of the Confederacy, for it ensured that Union armies would keep the pressure on the Rebels. There would be no negotiated peace—only surrender. In a telegram to the president, General Grant said his reelection was "worth more to the country than a battle won."

Sherman's "March to the Sea"

In November 1864, General Sherman led 60,000 soldiers out of Atlanta on their fabled 300-mile "March to the Sea" southeastward to the coastal city of Savannah. Sherman planned to wage a modern war against all the Confederates—soldiers and civilians—and their economy. He intended to "whip the rebels, to humble their pride, to follow them into their inmost recesses, and make them fear and dread us." Showing Rebel sympathizers the "hard hand of war," he believed, would shatter civilian morale and trigger a wave of military desertions, thereby shortening the war. Sherman telegraphed Grant that he planned to abandon Atlanta and then "ruin Georgia" as a source of Confederate supplies. President Lincoln agreed that the power of terror and psychological warfare could break the will of the Confederacy.

John Bell Hood's Confederate Army of Tennessee, meanwhile, tried a desperate gamble by heading in the opposite direction, pushing northward into Alabama and then Tennessee. Hood hoped to trick Sherman into chasing him, but Sherman refused to take the bait. He was determined to keep his main army moving southward to the Georgia coast and then into South Carolina, the seedbed of secession.

Sherman, however, did send General George Thomas and 30,000 soldiers to shadow Hood's Confederates. The two forces clashed in the Battle of Franklin (November 30, 1864), near Nashville, where Hood's 18,000 soldiers launched a suicidal frontal assault against entrenched Union troops backed by cannons.

Hood's Confederate Army of Tennessee defeated

In just five hours, Hood lost six generals and saw 6,252 of his men killed or wounded, a casualty figure higher than "Pickett's Charge" at Gettysburg and three times that of the Union troops at Franklin. The following morning, a Tennessee private noted that the battlefield resembled "a grand holocaust of death. . . . The dead were piled the one on the other all over the ground."

Many of the surviving Confederates blamed their reckless commander. A captain wrote that the "wails and cries of the widows and orphans made at Franklin, Tennessee, will heat up the fires of the bottomless pit to burn the soul of General J. B. Hood for murdering their husbands and fathers." Two weeks later, in the Battle of Nashville, the Federals scattered what was left of Hood's bloodied army.

On November 15, 1864, Sherman's army also began its 300-mile March to the Sea, racing southeastward across Georgia from Atlanta to coastal Savannah, living off the land while destroying plantations, barns, crops, warehouses, mills, bridges, and rail lines. An Ohio sergeant told his men, "Every house, barn, fence, and cotton gin gets an application of the torch. That prospect is revolting, but war is an uncivil game, and can't be civilized."

DESTROYING SOUTHERN RAILROADS Sherman's troops cut a swath of destruction across Georgia in his "March to the Sea." Here, Union troops rip up railroad tracks in Atlanta. **Why did Sherman adopt a strategy that included the destruction of railroads, homes, barns, and cities?**

Sherman's "March to the Sea" became infamous among Southerners as a supposed example of Union ruthlessness. After the war, however, a Confederate officer acknowledged that the campaign was well-conceived and well-managed. "I don't think there was ever an army in the world that would have behaved better, in a similar expedition, in an enemy country. Our army certainly wouldn't have."

On December 24, 1864, General Sherman sent a whimsical telegram to President Lincoln offering him the coastal city of Savannah as a Christmas present. By the time Union troops arrived in Savannah, they had freed more than 40,000 enslaved people, burned scores of plantations, and destroyed the railroads. "God bless you, Yanks!" shouted a formerly enslaved man. "Come at last! God knows how long I been waitin'. "

South Carolina

On February 1, 1865, Sherman's army headed north across the Savannah River into South Carolina, the "hell-hole of secession." Sherman reported that his "whole army is burning with an insatiable desire to wreak vengeance upon South Carolina. I almost tremble at her fate, but feel she deserves all that seems in store for her."

Sherman's "March to the Sea" (1864) The Union army's devastating march through Georgia from Atlanta to Savannah led by General William T. Sherman, intended to demoralize civilians and destroy the resources the Confederate army needed to fight.

South Carolina paid a high price for having led the southern states out of the Union. Sherman's men burned more than a dozen towns, including Barnwell, which they called "Burnwell." On February 17, 1865, they captured the state capital of Columbia. Soon thereafter, Charleston surrendered after Confederate soldiers torched buildings containing material that would be valuable to the Yankees.

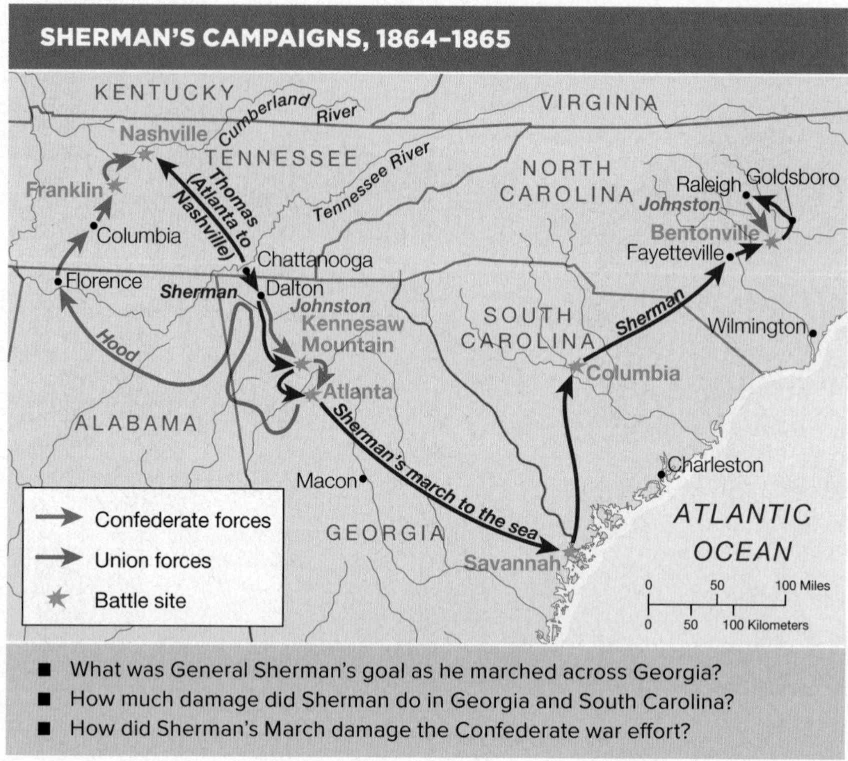

- What was General Sherman's goal as he marched across Georgia?
- How much damage did Sherman do in Georgia and South Carolina?
- How did Sherman's March damage the Confederate war effort?

It was no accident that Sherman ordered two all-Black regiments to lead the Union troops into the city. On April 14, the Union commander gave Major Robert Anderson the honor of raising the U.S. flag once again over Fort Sumter.

Jefferson Davis refuses to surrender

During late 1864 and early 1865, the Confederacy found itself besieged on all sides. Some Rebel leaders wanted to negotiate a peace settlement, but Jefferson Davis stubbornly rejected any talk of surrender. If his armies should be defeated, he wanted soldiers to scatter and fight an unending guerrilla war. "The war came and now it must go on," he insisted, "till the last man of this generation falls in his tracks, and his children seize his musket and fight our battle."

A Second Term

While Confederate forces made their last stands, Abraham Lincoln prepared for his second term as president. The weary commander in chief had weathered constant criticism during his first term, but he now garnered deserved praise. The *Chicago Tribune* observed that Lincoln "has slowly and steadily risen in the respect, confidence, and admiration of the people."

On March 4, 1865, amid rumors of a Confederate attempt to abduct or assassinate the president, some 30,000 people, half of them African Americans, defied frigid weather to attend Lincoln's second inauguration. Dressed in a black suit and stovepipe hat, Lincoln delivered his address on the east portico of the Capitol. Sharpshooters lined the roofs to protect the president—and with good reason. Looking down from the Capitol porch, not 100 feet away, was twenty-six-year-old stage actor John Wilkes Booth, who five weeks later would kill the president in a desperate attempt to do something "heroic" for his beloved South.

Lincoln's second inaugural address (1865)

Lincoln's five-minute second inaugural address (703 words) was more a powerful sermon than a predictable political speech. He chose not to celebrate Union victories, nor did he denounce Confederates. Instead, Lincoln revealed what he had learned during four years of killing and suffering and untold stories of heartbreak and mourning in homes across both nations. He insisted that everyone bore some guilt for the shame of racial injustice and the tragic but just war to end it.

Lincoln longed for peace. "Fondly do we hope—fervently do we pray—that this mighty scourge of war may speedily pass away." As Lincoln looked ahead to a "just and lasting peace," he stressed that the destructive spirit of vengeance must be trumped by humility and forgiveness. Reconciliation must be pursued "with malice toward none; with charity for all." Those eight words captured his hopes for a restored Union. Redemption and reunion were his goals, not reprisals. Afterward, Lincoln asked abolitionist and formerly enslaved Frederick Douglass what he thought of the speech. "Mr. Lincoln," he replied, "that was a sacred effort."

Appomattox

During the spring of 1865, General Grant's army kept pounding the encircled Rebels defending Petersburg, Virginia. Robert E. Lee had no way to replace the men he was losing, and his dwindling army couldn't kill enough Yankees to make Grant quit. On April 2, 1865, after General Philip Sheridan's horse soldiers cut off the last railroad serving the Confederate army in Petersburg, a desperate Lee made a desperate decision: the badly outnumbered Confederates abandoned Petersburg and headed west, with the Union army in hot pursuit.

At the same time, the Confederate government fled Richmond, but not before burning anything of value. While the fires raged, Union troops, led by the all-Black Fifth Massachusetts Cavalry, entered the capital of the dying Confederacy. African Americans clogged the streets to welcome the soldiers. They shouted, danced, prayed, and sang songs of liberation. The next day, April 4, Abraham Lincoln toured the fallen Rebel capital. "The colored population," wrote a Black reporter for a Philadelphia newspaper, "went wild with excitement."

Lee prepares to surrender at Appomattox Court House

The Confederacy was in chaos. "Women were weeping, children crying," noted a reporter in Richmond. "Men stood speechless, haggard, woebegone." Five days later, on April 7, General Grant sent a note urging General Lee to surrender. With the remnants of his army virtually surrounded and no food, Lee recognized that "there is nothing left for me to do but go and see General Grant, and I would rather die a thousand deaths."

On April 9 (Palm Sunday), four years to the day since the Confederate attack on Fort Sumter, the tall, dignified Lee, stiff and formal in his impeccable dress uniform, ceremonial sword, and shiny boots, met the short, mud-spattered Grant in a small brick house in the village of **Appomattox Court House**. Grant apologized for his "rough" appearance, explaining that

Appomattox Court House Virginia village where Confederate general Robert E. Lee surrendered to Union general Ulysses S. Grant on April 9, 1865.

THE END OF THE WAR General Lee *(right)* surrenders to General Grant *(left)* at Appomattox Court House on April 9, 1865.

he had left behind his dress uniform. Lee, in turn, stressed that he was in a new uniform because it was the only one he had left, and he fully expected to be arrested after surrendering.

After some awkward exchanges about their service as junior officers in the Mexican-American War, Lee asked Grant about the terms of surrender. In keeping with Lincoln's desire for a gracious peace with "malice toward none," a cigar-chewing Grant let the Confederates keep their pistols, horses, and mules, and he promised that none of them would be tried for treason. Lee replied that "this would have a most happy effect" upon his men and accepted the terms as "more than he expected." He then confessed that his men were starving, and Grant ordered that they be provided food.

After signing the surrender documents, Lee mounted his horse. Grant and his men saluted him, raising their hats, and Lee responded in kind before returning to his defeated army. Grant ordered that there be no cheering or gloating. "The war is over," he said, adding that "the rebels are our countrymen again, and the best sign of rejoicing after the victory will be to abstain from all demonstrations in the field."

The next day, as the gaunt Confederates formed ranks for the last time, Joshua Chamberlain, the Union general in charge of the surrender ceremony, told his men to salute the Rebel soldiers as they paraded past to give up their muskets. His Confederate counterpart signaled his men to do likewise. Chamberlain remembered that there was not a sound, simply an "awed stillness . . . as if it were the passing of the dead."

The remaining Confederate forces in Texas and North Carolina surrendered in May. Jefferson Davis, who had fled Richmond ahead of the advancing Federal troops, was captured in Georgia on May 10. He was eventually imprisoned in Virginia for two years.

Some Confederates never surrendered. They fled to the Caribbean or to Central or South America or to Europe. In June 1865, General Joseph Shelby of Missouri and almost a thousand Rebel troops crossed the Rio Grande and entered Mexico. Once they reached Mexico City, the government gave them land to form a refugee colony, but most of the expatriates returned to the United States within a few years.

Other unrepentant Confederates vowed revenge. John Wilkes Booth wrote in his diary that "something *decisive* and great must be done." He began plotting with others to kill President Lincoln and members of his cabinet.

Two days after Lee surrendered, Lincoln gave a speech on the White House lawn in which he said he looked forward to "reconstructing" the Confederate states. He also hoped that literate freed Blacks and those who had served in the Union military would gain voting rights. Booth, who was in the audience, noted that Lincoln's pledge "meant [colored person] citizenship. Now, by God, I'll put him through [kill him]. That is the last speech he will ever make."

A Transformational War

CORE **OBJECTIVE**

5. Explain how the Civil War changed the nation.

The Civil War was the most traumatic event in American history. "We have shared the incommunicable experience of war," reflected Oliver Wendell Holmes, Jr., a twice-wounded Union officer who would become chief justice of the Supreme Court. "We have felt, we still feel, the passion of life to its top. . . . In our youth, our hearts were touched by fire."

Throughout the South, however, a vengeful gloom covered Dixie like the dew. In Virginia, Edmund Ruffin, the fervent secessionist who had fired the first shot at Fort Sumter in 1861, was utterly devastated by the Confederate surrender. In the final entry to his diary, he wrote: "I hereby declare my unmitigated hatred to Yankee rule—to all political, social and business connections with the Yankees and to the Yankee race." He then put a shotgun barrel in his mouth and blew off the top of his head.

The war had transformed the nation. A *New York Times* editorial reflected that the war had left "nothing as it found it. . . . It leaves us a different people in everything." The war destroyed the South's economy, many of its railroads and factories, much of its livestock, and several of its cities. In 1860, the northern and southern economies had been essentially equal in size. By 1865, the southern economy's productivity had been halved, while the Union established the United States as a modern industrial nation.

The Union Preserved

The war restored a Union destined for global leadership; ended what Lincoln called the "monstrous injustice" of slavery; shifted the political balance of power in Congress, the U.S. Supreme Court, and the presidency from South to North; strengthened the Republican party; and boosted the northern economy's industrial development, commercial agriculture, and western settlement.

Impacts of war: Expansion of federal government

The Homestead Act (1862) made more than a billion acres in the West available to the landless. The power and scope of the federal government were expanded at the expense of states' rights. In 1860, the annual federal budget was $63 million; by 1865, it was more than $1 billion. In winning the war, the federal government had become the nation's largest employer.

Impacts of war: New industries

By the end of the war, the Union was spending $2.5 million per day on the military effort, and whole new industries had been established to meet its needs for weapons, uniforms, food, equipment, and supplies. The massive amounts of preserved food required by the Union armies, for example, helped create the canning industry and transformed Chicago into the meatpacking capital of the world.

Federal contracts also provided money needed to accelerate the growth of new industries, such as the production of iron, steel, and petroleum, thus laying the groundwork for a postwar economic boom. Ohio senator John Sherman, in a letter to his brother, General William T. Sherman, said the war had dramatically expanded the vision "of leading capitalists" who now talked of earning "millions as confidently as formerly of thousands."

Impacts of war: New cotton exporters

The war also influenced world events. Southern cotton had fed national prosperity during the first half of the nineteenth century, but the onset of war in 1861 changed that. In 1860, the South had sent nearly 4 million bales of cotton to Europe. By 1862, hardly any arrived in Europe. By cutting off the supply of southern cotton to Great Britain and Europe, the war fueled global colonialism, as European nations looked for other sources of cotton in India, Egypt, and West Africa.

The First "Modern" War

In many respects, the Civil War was one of the first modern wars. Its scope and scale were unprecedented, as it was fought across the entire continent. For the first time, armies used railroads and steamboats to move around and photographers used cameras to record the carnage.

Devastating human losses

One of every twelve men served in the war, and few families were unaffected. More than 750,000 soldiers and sailors (37,000 of whom were African Americans fighting for the Union) died, 50 percent more than would die in World War II. The number killed exceeds that in *all* other American wars combined. Of the surviving combatants, 50,000 returned home with one or more limbs amputated. Disease, however, was the greatest threat to soldiers, killing twice as many as were lost in battle. Some 50,000 civilians died as well, and virtually every community had uncounted widows and orphans.

Changing attitudes to firearms

The Civil War also accelerated the American love affair with guns. Hundreds of thousands of men who had never owned or used a pistol or rifle now believed that the "right to own and use weapons" was an essential constitutional principle.

Unlike previous conflicts, much of the fighting had been distant and impersonal, in part because of improvements in the effectiveness of muskets, rifles, and cannons. Men were killed at long distance, without knowing who had fired the shots that felled them. Among the array of new weapons and instruments were cannons with "rifled," or grooved, barrels for greater accuracy; repeating rifles; ironclad ships; railroad artillery; the first military telegraph; observation balloons; and wire entanglements. Civilians could also follow the war by reading the newspapers that sent reporters to the front lines, or by visiting exhibitions of photographs taken at the battlefields and camps.

Social Changes Wrought by the War

The war also generated significant social changes. Women's roles were transformed. "No conflict in history," a journalist wrote at the time, "was such a woman's war as the Civil War." The requirements of war enabled women to become nurses, farm or business managers, and executives of new organizations. So many ministers left their congregations to become military chaplains that laypeople, especially women, assumed even greater responsibility for religious services in churches and synagogues. The war's awful carnage took a terrible personal toll on women. Hundreds of thousands of wives were widowed by the war or saw their lives permanently transformed by the return of husbands with missing limbs or ghastly wounds.

Thirteenth Amendment

The most important result of the war was the liberation of almost 4 million enslaved people. The Emancipation Proclamation had technically freed only those enslaved in areas still controlled by the Confederacy. It had no bearing on those enslaved in the four border states that remained in the Union—Maryland, Delaware, Kentucky, and Missouri. As the war entered its final months, however, freedom for all enslaved people emerged as a legal reality, as President Lincoln moved from viewing emancipation as a military weapon to seeing it as the mainspring of the conflict itself. At last, Lincoln had become an abolitionist.

Thirteenth Amendment: Banning of slavery

Three major steps occurred in January 1865. Missouri and then Tennessee abolished slavery, and, at Lincoln's insistence, the U.S. House of Representatives passed an amendment to the Constitution that banned slavery everywhere. Every Republican voted in favor. As the final tally was announced, the House erupted in "an outburst of enthusiasm." Men threw their hats and some "wept like children."

Upon ratification by three-fourths of the reunited states, the **Thirteenth Amendment** became law eight months after the war ended, on December 18, 1865. That date, said the *New York Times*, "will be forever memorable in the annals of the republic." The amendment removed any lingering doubts about the legality of emancipation.

The Debate Continues

Historians continue to debate the reasons for the Union victory. Some have focused on the weaknesses of the Confederacy: the lack of industry and railroads in the South, the tensions between the states and the central government in Richmond, poor political leadership, faulty coordination and communication, the expense of preventing enslaved people from escaping, and the advantages in population and resources enjoyed by the North. Still others have highlighted the erosion of Confederate morale in the face of terrible food shortages and unimaginable human losses.

The debate about why the North won and the South lost will never end, but Robert E. Lee's explanation remains accurate: "The Army of Northern Virginia has been compelled to yield to overwhelming numbers and resources."

An indissoluble Union

Whatever the reasons, the North's victory resolved a key issue: no state could divorce itself from the Union. The Union, as Lincoln had always maintained, was indissoluble. At the same time, the war led to the Constitution being permanently amended to eliminate slavery. The terrible war thus served to clarify the meaning of the ideals ("All men are created equal") on which the United States had been established. The largest slaveholding nation in the world had at last chosen liberty—for all.

In his first message to Congress in December 1861, Lincoln had recognized early on what was at stake: "The struggle of today is not altogether for today; it is for a vast future also." So it was. The "fiery trial" of a war both "fundamental and astounding" produced, as Lincoln said, not just a preserved Union but "a new birth of freedom."

Thirteenth Amendment (1865) Amendment to the U.S. Constitution that ended slavery and freed all enslaved people in the United States.

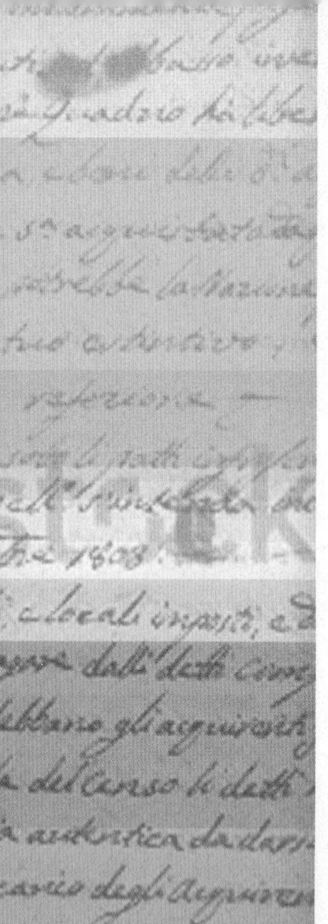

Reviewing the CORE OBJECTIVES | INQUIZITIVE

▪ **Civil War Strategies** The Confederacy had a geographic advantage of fighting a defensive war on its own territory. The Union, however, had a larger population and greater industrial capability, particularly in the production of weapons, ships, and railroad equipment. The Union quickly launched a military campaign to seize the Confederate capital, Richmond, Virginia. Initial hopes for a rapid victory died at the First Battle of Bull Run. The Union then adopted the *Anaconda Plan,* which involved imposing a naval blockade on Southern ports and slowly crushing resistance on all fronts.

▪ **Emancipation Proclamation** Gradually, President Lincoln came to see that winning the war required ending slavery. He justified the *Emancipation Proclamation* (1863) as a military necessity because it would deprive the South of its captive labor force. After the *Battle of Antietam* in September 1862, he announced his plans to free the enslaved people living in areas under Confederate control. Many enslaved people freed themselves by escaping to Union army camps. In July 1862, with the *Militia Act,* Congress had declared that formerly enslaved people (*contrabands*) could join the Union army. During 1863, Blacks, both free and freed, joined the Union army in large numbers, giving the Union military a further advantage over the Confederacy.

▪ **Wartime Home Fronts** Some Northerners were sympathetic to the Confederates and urged Lincoln and the Republicans to negotiate an end to the fighting. The Union government proved much more capable with finances than did its Confederate counterparts. Through tariffs, income taxes, government bond issues, and the printing of paper money, the Union was better able to absorb the war's soaring costs. The Confederate finances, on the other hand, were pitiful in the cash-poor South. The Confederate Treasury Department had to print so much money that it created spiraling inflation of consumer prices and civil unrest. Also, most of the warfare took place in the South; thus, although the North had more casualties, the physical destruction in the South was much greater.

▪ **The Winning Union Strategy** The Union victories at the *Battle of Vicksburg* and the *Battle of Gettysburg* in July 1863 were a major turning point of the war. With the capture of Vicksburg, Union forces cut the Confederacy in two, depriving armies in the east of western supplies and manpower. General Robert E. Lee and the Army of Northern Virginia lost a third of its troops after the defeat at Gettysburg, forcing the Confederates to adopt a defensive strategy. In 1864, Lincoln placed General Ulysses S. Grant in charge of the Union's war efforts, and thereafter Grant's forces constantly attacked Lee's in Virginia while, farther south, General William T. *Sherman's March to the Sea* (1864) resulted in the conquest of Georgia and South Carolina. Sherman's successes helped propel Lincoln to victory in the *election of 1864.* After that, Southern resistance wilted, forcing Lee to surrender his army to General Grant at *Appomattox Court House* in April 1865.

■ **The Significance of the Civil War** The Civil War involved the largest number of casualties of any American war, and the Union's victory changed the course of the nation's development. Most important, the war ended slavery, embodied in the adoption of the *Thirteenth Amendment* to the U.S. Constitution in late 1865. Not only did the power of the federal government increase, but the center of political and economic power shifted away from the South and the planter class.

KEY TERMS

Anaconda Plan *p. 537*

contrabands *p. 548*

Battle of Antietam (1862) *p. 550*

Emancipation Proclamation (1863) *p. 551*

Militia Act (1862) *p. 556*

Pacific Railway Act (1862) *p. 559*

Homestead Act (1862) *p. 559*

Morrill Land-Grant College Act (1862) *p. 559*

National Banking Act (1863) *p. 559*

Battle of Vicksburg (1863) *p. 563*

Battle of Gettysburg (1863) *p. 564*

election of 1864 *p. 573*

Sherman's "March to the Sea" (1864) *p. 575*

Appomattox Court House *p. 577*

Thirteenth Amendment (1865) *p. 581*

CHRONOLOGY

April 1861	Virginia, North Carolina, Tennessee, and Arkansas join Confederacy; West Virginia splits from Virginia to stay with Union
July 1861	First Battle of Bull Run (Manassas)
March–July 1862	Peninsular campaign
April–August 1862	Battles of Shiloh, Second Bull Run, and Antietam; New Orleans seized by Union forces
July 1862	Congress passes the Militia Act
September 1862	Lincoln issues Emancipation Proclamation
May–July 1863	New York City draft riots; Battles of Vicksburg and Gettysburg
November 1863	Battle of Chattanooga
March 1864	General Grant takes charge of Union military operations
September 1864	General Sherman seizes and burns Atlanta
November 1864	Lincoln is reelected
	Sherman's "March to the Sea"
April 9, 1865	General Lee surrenders at Appomattox Court House
1865	Thirteenth Amendment is ratified

INQUIZITIVE

Go to InQuizitive to see what you've learned—and learn what you've missed—with personalized feedback along the way.

THOMAS NAST'S *EMANCIPATION* (1865) This wood engraving based on Thomas Nast's *Emancipation* represents his vision of an optimistic future for Blacks in the United States after emancipation, which would not outlast Reconstruction. The central scene of a joyous family contrasts with the background depicting enslavement and subordination prior to emancipation.

CHAPTER

15

The Era of Reconstruction

1865–1877

CORE OBJECTIVES INQUIZITIVE

1. Identify the federal government's major challenges in reconstructing the South after the Civil War.
2. Describe how and why Reconstruction policies changed over time.
3. Assess the attitudes of White and Black Southerners toward Reconstruction.
4. Analyze the political and economic factors that helped end Reconstruction in 1877.
5. Explain the significance of Reconstruction to the nation's future.

In the spring of 1865, the terrible conflict finally ended. The United States was a "new nation," said an Illinois congressman, because it was now "wholly free." At a cost of some 750,000 lives and the destruction of the southern economy, the Union had won the war, and almost 4 million enslaved Americans had seized their freedom.

Most civil wars, however, never end completely. Peace did not bring everyday equality or civil rights to people of color, nor did it end racism, in the South or the North. Many White Southerners opposed the decision of Confederate generals to surrender their armies and bitterly resented the freeing of the enslaved. In the North, racism persisted too. The *New York Times* declared that African Americans, even if freed from slavery, had no more business voting than did women or Indians, and that it was "little short of insane" to think otherwise. The *Times* was also relieved to learn that most Blacks would stay in the South and would not "swarm to the North."

The defeated Confederates had seen their world turned upside down. The abolition of slavery, the disruptions to the southern economy, and the horrifying human losses and physical devastation had shattered the plantation system and upended racial relations in the South. "Change, change, indelibly stamped upon everything I meet, even upon the faces of the people!" sighed Alexander Stephens, vice president of the former Confederacy. His native region now had to adjust to a new order as the

U.S. government set about "reconstructing" the South and using federal troops to police defiant ex-Confederates.

Formerly enslaved people felt just the opposite. Yankees were their liberators. No longer would enslaved workers be sold and separated from their families or prevented from learning to read and write or attending church. "I felt like a bird out of a cage," said formerly enslaved Houston Holloway of Georgia, who had been sold to three different owners during his first twenty years. "Amen. Amen. Amen. I could hardly ask to feel any better than I did that day."

Many previously enslaved people rushed to change their names. Some only had a first name under slavery; others had used the same last name as their owners. Now, they could rename themselves as freed people. In Alabama, a formerly enslaved person who had served in the Union army explained that after returning home after the war, "I was wearing the name of Lewis Smith, but I found that the negroes after freedom, were taking the names of their father like the white folks often did. So I asked my mother and she told me my father was John Barnett, a white man, and I took up the name of Barnett."

Many slaveowners refused to free enslaved people until forced to by the arrival of Union soldiers. In South Carolina, violence against freed people was widespread. Federal troops found "the bodies of murdered Negroes" strewn in a forest. When a South Carolina White man caught an enslaved mother and her children running toward freedom, he "drew his bowie-knife and cut her throat; also the throat of her boy, nine years old; also the throat of her girl, seven years of age; threw their bodies into the river, and the live baby after them."

Such brutal incidents testified to the extraordinary challenges the nation faced in "reconstructing" a ravaged and resentful South while helping to transform formerly enslaved people into free workers and citizens. It would not be easy. The Rebels had been conquered, but they were far from being loyal Unionists, and few of them supported the federal effort to create a multiracial democracy in the former Confederacy.

The Reconstruction era, from 1865 to 1877, witnessed a complex debate about the role of the federal government in ensuring civil rights. Some Northerners wanted the former Confederate states returned to the Union with little or no changes. Others wanted Confederate leaders imprisoned or executed and the South rebuilt in the image of the rest of the nation. Still others cared little about reconstructing the South; they wanted the federal government to focus on promoting northern economic growth and westward expansion.

Although the Reconstruction era lasted only twelve years, it was one of the most challenging and significant periods in U.S. history. At the center of the debate over how to restore the Union were profound questions: Who is deserving of citizenship, and what does it entail? What rights should all Americans enjoy? What role should the federal government play in ensuring freedom and equality? Those questions are still shaping American life nearly 150 years later.

The War's Aftermath in the South

CORE **OBJECTIVE**

1. Identify the federal government's major challenges in reconstructing the South after the Civil War.

In the spring of 1865, Southerners were emotionally exhausted; fully a fifth of southern White males had died in the war, and many others had been maimed for life. In 1866, Mississippi spent 20 percent of the state's budget on artificial limbs for Confederate veterans. The economy was also ravaged. Property values had collapsed. In the year after the war ended, eighty-one Mississippi plantations sold for a tenth of what they had been valued in 1860. Confederate money was worthless; personal savings had vanished; tens of thousands of horses and mules had been killed; and countless farm buildings and agricultural tools had been destroyed.

Many of the largest southern cities—Richmond, Atlanta, Columbia—were devastated. Most railroads and many bridges were damaged or destroyed, and Southerners, White and Black, were homeless and hungry. Along the path that General William T. Sherman's Union army had blazed across Georgia and the Carolinas, the countryside "looked for many miles like a broad black streak of ruin and desolation." Burned-out Columbia, South Carolina, said another witness, was "a wilderness of ruins"; Charleston, the birthplace of secession, had become a place of "vacant houses, of widowed women, of rotting wharves, of deserted warehouses, of weed-wild gardens, of miles of grass-grown streets, of acres of pitiful and voiceless barrenness."

Economic disparities between the North and South

Between 1860 and 1870, northern wealth grew by 50 percent while southern wealth dropped 60 percent. Emancipation wiped out almost $3 billion invested in the slave labor system, which had enabled the explosive growth

RICHMOND AFTER THE CIVIL WAR Before evacuating the capital of the Confederacy, Richmond, Virginia, residents set fire to warehouses and factories to prevent their falling into Union hands. Pictured here is one of Richmond's burnt districts in April 1865. Women in mourning attire walk among the shambles.

of the cotton culture. Not until 1879 would the cotton crop again equal the record harvest of 1860. Tobacco production did not regain its prewar level until 1880, the sugar crop of Louisiana did not recover until 1893, and the rice economy along the coasts of South Carolina and Georgia never regained its prewar levels of production or profit.

In 1860, just before the Civil War, the South had generated 30 percent of the nation's wealth; in 1870, it produced but 12 percent. Amanda Worthington, a planter's wife from Mississippi, could not believe "that we are no longer wealthy—yet thanks to the Yankees, the cause of all unhappiness, such is the case."

Resentment boiled over. Union soldiers were cursed and spat upon. A Virginia woman expressed a common spirited defiance: "Every day, every hour, that I live increases my hatred and detestation, and loathing of that race. They [Yankees] disgrace our common humanity. As a people I consider them vastly inferior to the better classes of our slaves." Fervent southern nationalists implanted in their children a similar hatred of Yankees and a defiance of northern rule.

Legal and social controversies over Reconstruction

The issues related to "reconstructing" the former Confederacy were complicated and controversial. For example, the process of forming new state governments required first determining the official status of the states that had seceded: were they now conquered territories? If so, then the Constitution assigned Congress authority to re-create their state governments. But what if, as Abraham Lincoln argued, the Confederate states had never officially left the Union because the act of secession was itself illegal? In that circumstance, the president, not Congress, would be responsible for re-forming state governments.

Whichever branch of government—Congress or the presidency—directed the reconstruction of the South, it would have to address the most difficult issue: what would be the political, social, and economic status of the freedpeople? They were free but by no means independent. Were they citizens? If not, what was their status?

What formerly enslaved people most wanted was to become self-reliant, to be paid for their labor, to reunite with their family members, to gain education for their children, to enjoy full participation in political life, and to create their own community organizations and social life. Most southern Whites were determined to prevent that from happening.

CORE **OBJECTIVE**

2. Describe how and why Reconstruction policies changed over time.

Battles over Political Reconstruction

Reconstruction of the former Confederate states began during the war and went through several phases, the first of which was called Presidential Reconstruction. In 1862, President Lincoln had named army generals to serve as temporary military governors for conquered Confederate areas.

By the end of 1863, he had formulated a plan to reestablish governments in states liberated from Confederate rule.

Lincoln's Wartime Reconstruction Plan

Presidential Reconstruction: Lincoln's Proclamation of Amnesty and Reconstruction

In late 1863, President Lincoln issued a Proclamation of Amnesty and Reconstruction, under which former Confederate states could re-create a Union government once a number equal to 10 percent of those who had voted in 1860 swore allegiance to the Constitution. They also received a presidential pardon acquitting them of treason. Certain groups, however, were denied pardons: Confederate government officials; senior officers of the Confederate army and navy; judges, congressmen, and military officers of the United States who had left their posts to join the rebellion; and those who had abused captured African American soldiers.

Congressional Wartime Reconstruction Plans

A few conservative and most moderate Republicans supported President Lincoln's "10 percent" program that immediately restored pro-Union southern governments. Radical Republicans, however, argued that Congress, not the president, should supervise Reconstruction. **Radical Republicans** favored a drastic transformation of southern society that would immediately grant formerly enslaved people full citizenship. Many Radicals believed that all people, regardless of race, were equal in God's eyes. They wanted no compromise with the "sin" of racism. They also hoped to replace the White, Democratic planter elite with a new generation of small farmers. "The middling classes who own the soil, and work it with their own hands," explained Radical leader Thaddeus Stevens, "are the main support of every free government."

In 1864, with war still raging, the Radicals tried to take charge of Reconstruction by passing the Wade-Davis Bill, named for two leading Republicans. In contrast to Lincoln's 10 percent Reconstruction plan, the Wade-Davis Bill required that a *majority* declare their allegiance to the Union before a formerly Confederate state could be readmitted.

Lincoln vetoes Wade-Davis Bill

The bill never became law, however, because Lincoln vetoed it. In retaliation, Radicals issued the Wade-Davis Manifesto, which accused Lincoln of exceeding his constitutional authority. Unfazed by the criticism, Lincoln continued his efforts to restore the Confederate states to the Union. He also rushed assistance to the freedpeople in the South.

The Freedmen's Bureau

In early 1865, Congress approved the Thirteenth Amendment to the Constitution, officially abolishing slavery in the United States. It became law in December. Yet what did freedom mean for the formerly enslaved, most of whom had no land, no home, no food, no job, and no education? The debate over what freedom should entail became the central issue of Reconstruction. "Liberty has been won," Senator Charles Sumner noted. "The battle for Equality is still pending."

Radical Republicans Congressmen who identified with the abolitionist cause and sought swift emancipation of the enslaved, punishment of the Rebels, and tight controls over former Confederate states.

FREEDMEN'S SCHOOL IN VIRGINIA As part of its effort to support formerly enslaved people in their transition to freedom, the Freedmen's Bureau established schools for the freedpeople across the southern states. **The freedmen schools were not only meant for children—who is being taught in this illustration from 1866?**

Establishment of the Freedmen's Bureau (1865)

To address the complex issues raised by emancipation, Congress on March 3, 1865, created within the War Department the Bureau of Refugees, Freedmen, and Abandoned Lands (known as the **Freedmen's Bureau**) to assist "freedmen and their wives and children." It was the first federal effort to provide help directly to people rather than to states. And its task was daunting. When General William T. Sherman learned that his friend, General Oliver O. Howard, had been appointed to lead the Freedmen's Bureau, he warned: "It is not . . . in your power to fulfill one-tenth of the expectations of those who framed the Bureau."

Undeterred by such concerns, Howard declared that emancipated people "must be free to choose their own employers and be paid for their labor." He assigned army officers to negotiate labor contracts between freedpeople and White landowners, many of whom resisted. The Bureau also provided the now free African Americans with medical care, clothing, shelter, and food. By 1868, the Bureau had distributed more than 20 million meals. It also assisted formerly enslaved people in seeking justice in courts, managed abandoned lands, and helped formalize marriages and find relatives.

The Bureau also helped establish schools and colleges. A Mississippi freedman explained that education was his essential priority, for it "was the next best thing to liberty." By 1870, the Freedmen's Bureau was supervising more than 4,000 new schools serving almost 250,000 students in the former Confederate states. The Bureau recruited thousands of teachers from the northern states. Charlotte Forten, an African American teacher, ventured south from Philadelphia after the war to be a volunteer teacher at a school for formerly enslaved people. She marveled at the passion for learning displayed by the students: "I never before saw children so eager to learn."

Freedmen's Bureau Federal Reconstruction agency established to protect the legal rights of formerly enslaved people and to assist with their education, jobs, health care, and land ownership.

Yet the Freedmen's Bureau had significant limitations. It never had more than 900 agents across thirteen states to deal with 3.5 million formerly enslaved people spread across a million square miles, not nearly enough to implement the Bureau's broad goals. The number of federal troops supporting the Freedmen's Bureau was also inadequate. As a Texas officer stressed, the Bureau agents were helpless "unless in the vicinity of our troops." Perhaps the most glaring weakness of the Bureau was its failure to redistribute land to formerly enslaved people.

The Assassination of Lincoln

The possibility of a lenient federal Reconstruction of the Confederacy would die with Abraham Lincoln. The president who had yearned for a peace "with malice toward none, with charity for all" offered his last view of Reconstruction in the final speech of his life. On April 11, 1865, Lincoln rejected calls for a vengeful peace. He wanted "no persecution, no bloody work," no hangings of Confederate leaders, and no extreme efforts to restructure southern social and economic life.

Lincoln assassinated (April 14, 1865)

Three days later, on April 14, Lincoln and his wife attended a play at Ford's Theatre in Washington, D.C. With his trusted bodyguard called away to Richmond, Lincoln was defenseless as twenty-six-year-old John Wilkes Booth, a celebrated actor and rabid Confederate, slipped into the presidential box and shot the president behind the left ear. As Lincoln slumped forward, Booth pulled out a knife, stabbed the president's military aide, and jumped from the box to the stage, breaking his leg in the process. He then mounted a waiting horse and fled the city. Lincoln died nine hours later, the first president to be killed in office.

LINCOLN'S FUNERAL PROCESSION After Lincoln's assassination, his body was taken on a two-week-long funeral procession through five different states, allowing millions of people the chance to see his casket. This photograph was taken on April 25, when the procession passed through New York City.

As Booth was shooting the president, other Confederate assassins were hunting Vice President Andrew Johnson and Secretary of State William H. Seward. Johnson escaped injury because his would-be assassin got drunk in the bar of the vice president's hotel. Seward and four others, including his son, however, suffered severe knife wounds when attacked at home.

The government was suddenly leaderless, and the nation was overwhelmed with shock, horror, and anguish. African American leader Frederick Douglass described Lincoln's murder as "an unspeakable calamity." In his view, Lincoln was "the black man's President: the first to show any respect for their rights as men" by rising "above the prejudice of his times." Confederates had a different view. A seventeen-year-old South Carolina girl celebrated the news of Lincoln's murder. As she wrote in her diary, "Old Abe Lincoln has been assassinated!"

Vice President Andrew Johnson became the new president shortly after Lincoln was declared dead. Eleven days later, Union troops found John Wilkes Booth hiding in a Virginia tobacco barn. In his diary the night before, he had vowed never to be taken alive: "I have too great a soul to die like a criminal!" The soldiers set the barn on fire, and, a few minutes later, one of them shot and killed Booth. As he lay dying, the assassin whispered, "Tell my mother I died for my country."

Three of Booth's collaborators were convicted by a military court and hanged, as was Mary Surratt, a middle-aged widow who owned the Washington boardinghouse where the assassination had been planned. Surratt and her extended family were ardent supporters of the Confederacy.

The outpouring of grief after Lincoln's death transformed the fallen president into a sacred symbol. Lincoln's body lay in state for several days in Washington, D.C., before being transported 1,600 miles by train for burial in Springfield, Illinois. In Philadelphia, 300,000 mourners paid their last respects; in New York City, 500,000 people viewed the president's body. On May 4, Lincoln was laid to rest.

ANDREW JOHNSON
A Jacksonian Democrat from Tennessee, Johnson stepped into the role of president after Lincoln's assassination. He introduced a Restoration Plan that required southern states to ratify the Thirteenth Amendment and limited the political power of rich ex-Confederates.

Johnson's Reconstruction Plan

The new president, Andrew Johnson of Tennessee, was a pro-Union Democrat who had been added to Lincoln's National Union ticket in 1864 to help the president win reelection. Humorless, insecure, combative, and self-righteous, Johnson hated both the White southern elite and the idea of racial equality. He also had a weakness for liquor.

Like Lincoln, Johnson was a self-made man, but he displayed none of Lincoln's dignity or eloquence. Born in 1808 in a log cabin near Raleigh, North Carolina, he lost his father when he was three and never attended school. His illiterate mother apprenticed him to a tailor to learn a trade. He ran away from home at thirteen and eventually landed in Greeneville, in the mountains of East Tennessee. There he taught himself to read, and his sixteen-year-old wife showed him how to write and do basic arithmetic.

Over time, Johnson prospered and acquired five enslaved people, which he sold in 1863. A natural leader, he served as mayor, state legislator, governor, congressional representative, and U.S. senator. A friend described the trajectory of Johnson's life as "one intense, unceasing, desperate upward struggle" during which he identified with poor farmers and came to hate the "pampered, bloated, corrupted aristocracy" of wealthy planters.

During the Civil War, Johnson supported "putting down the [Confederate] rebellion, because it is a war [of wealthy plantation owners] against democracy." Yet Johnson was also a venomous racist. "Damn the negroes," he exclaimed during the war. "This is a country for white men," he exclaimed, "and by God, as long as I am president, it shall be a government for white men."

Johnson adapts Lincoln's plan for reconstruction

Early in his presidency, Johnson stressed that he would continue Lincoln's policies in restoring the former Confederate states to the Union. **Johnson's Restoration Plan** included a few twists, however. In May 1865, Johnson issued a new Proclamation of Amnesty that excluded not only those ex-Confederates whom Lincoln had barred from a presidential pardon but also anyone with property worth more than $20,000. Johnson was determined to keep the wealthiest Southerners from regaining political power.

Surprisingly, however, by 1866 President Johnson had pardoned some 7,000 former Confederates, and he eventually pardoned most of the White "aristocrats" he claimed to despise. What brought about this change of heart? Johnson had decided that he could buy the political support of prominent Southerners by pardoning them, improving his chances of reelection.

Johnson appointed a Unionist as provisional governor in each southern state. Each governor called a convention of men elected by "loyal" (not Confederate) voters. Johnson's plan required that each state convention ratify the Thirteenth Amendment. Except for Mississippi, each former Confederate state held a convention that met Johnson's requirements.

Freedmen's Conventions

Neither Abraham Lincoln nor Andrew Johnson saw fit to ask freedpeople in the South what they most needed. The formerly enslaved people therefore took matters into their own hands. They met and marched, demanding not just freedom but citizenship and full civil rights, land of their own, and voting rights. Especially in large cities such as New Orleans, Mobile, Norfolk, Wilmington, Nashville, Memphis, and Charleston, they organized regular meetings, chose leaders, protested mistreatment, learned the workings of the federal bureaucracy, and sought economic opportunities.

African Americans mobilize at freedmen's conventions

During the summer and fall of 1865, emancipated Southerners and free Blacks from the North ("missionaries") and South organized freedmen's conventions (sometimes called Equal Rights Associations). The conventions met in state capitals "to impress upon the white men," as the Reverend James D. Lynch told the Tennessee freedmen's convention, "that we are part and parcel of the American republic." As such, the freedmen were eager to counter the Whites-only state conventions organized under President Johnson's Reconstruction plan.

Johnson's Restoration Plan Plan to require southern states to ratify the Thirteenth Amendment, disqualify wealthy ex-Confederates from voting, and appoint a Unionist governor.

FREEDMEN'S CONVENTION In this 1868 woodcut, a group of southern freedpeople meet to discuss their political and social resolutions. **Who is participating in this freedmen's convention, and how might the demographic diversity have contributed to the freedmen's initiatives?**

The North Carolina freedmen's convention elected as its president James Walker Hood, a free Black from Connecticut. In his acceptance speech, he said: "We and the white people have to live here together. Some people talk of emigration for the Black race, some of expatriation, and some of colonization. I regard this as all nonsense. We have been living together for a hundred years and more, and we have got to live together still; and the best way is to harmonize our feelings as much as possible, and to treat all men respectfully." Hood then demanded three constitutional rights for African Americans: the right to testify in courts, the right to serve on juries, and "the right to carry [a] ballot to the ballot box."

In sum, the freedmen's conventions demanded that their voices be heard. As the Virginia convention asserted, "Any attempt to reconstruct the states . . . without giving to American citizens of African descent all the rights and immunities accorded to white citizens . . . is an act of gross injustice."

The Radical Republicans

President Johnson's initial assault on the southern planter elite pleased Radical Republicans, but not for long. The most extreme Radical Republicans, led by Thaddeus Stevens of Pennsylvania and Charles Sumner of Massachusetts, wanted Reconstruction to provide social and political equality for Blacks.

Stevens and other Radicals resented Johnson's efforts to bring the South back into the Union as quickly as possible. They viewed the Confederate states as "conquered provinces" to be readmitted to the Union by the U.S. Congress, not the president.

Little change among southern representatives

Johnson, however, balked at such an expansion of federal authority. He was committed to letting the states control their affairs. When the U.S. Congress met in December 1865 for the first time since the end of the war, the new southern state governments looked remarkably like the former Confederate governments. Southerners had refused to extend voting rights to the formerly enslaved population.

White voters in southern states elected former Confederate leaders as their new U.S. senators and congressmen. Across the South, four Confederate generals, eight colonels, six Confederate cabinet members, and several Confederate legislators were elected as new U.S. senators and congressmen. Outraged Republicans denied seats to all such "Rebel" officials and appointed a Joint Committee on Reconstruction to develop a plan to bring the former Confederate states back into the Union.

The joint committee discovered that White violence against Blacks in the South was widespread. A formerly enslaved man from Shreveport, Louisiana, testified that Whites still bullwhipped Blacks as if they were enslaved. He estimated that 2,000 freedpeople had been killed in Shreveport in 1865.

Race riots

In 1866, White mobs murdered African Americans in Memphis and New Orleans. In Memphis, a clash between African American military

RACE RIOTS IN MEMPHIS, TENNESSEE In 1866, African Americans were murdered by White mobs in Memphis, Tennessee. Black neighborhoods, schools, and churches were destroyed. Forty-six African Americans were killed.

veterans and city police triggered a race riot in which rampaging Whites raped and murdered Blacks before setting fire to their neighborhoods. Over two days, Black schools and churches were destroyed. Forty-six African Americans and two Whites were killed. Only the arrival of federal troops quelled the violence.

The racial massacres, Radical Republicans argued, resulted from Andrew Johnson's lenient policy toward White supremacists. Senator Charles Sumner asked, "Who can doubt that the President is the author of these tragedies?" The race riots helped spur the Republican-controlled Congress to pass the Fourteenth Amendment (1868), extending federal civil rights protections to African Americans.

Black Codes

Southern states issue Black codes

The new all-White southern state legislatures quickly passed laws discriminating against formerly enslaved people. These "**Black codes**," as a White Southerner explained, would ensure "the ex-slave was not a free man; he was a free Negro." A Northerner visiting the South observed that the Black codes would guarantee that "the blacks at large belong to the whites at large."

Black codes varied from state to state. In South Carolina, African Americans were required to remain on their former plantations, forced to labor from dawn to dusk. Mississippi prohibited Blacks from hunting or fishing, making them even more dependent on their White employers.

Some Black codes recognized Black marriages but prohibited interracial marriage. Mississippi stipulated that "no white person could intermarry with a freedman, free negro, or mulatto." Violators faced life in prison.

The codes also barred African Americans from voting, serving on juries, or testifying against Whites. In Mississippi, every Black male over eighteen had to be apprenticed to a White, preferably a former slave owner. Any Blacks not apprenticed or employed by January 1866 would be jailed as "vagrants." If they could not pay the vagrancy fine—and most could not—they were jailed and forced to work for Whites as convict laborers in "chain gangs."

Exploitative labor practices under "convict leasing"

In part, states employed this "convict lease" system as a means of increasing government revenue and cutting the expenses of housing prisoners. Many southern prisons were destroyed during the war, and states lacked the funds to rebuild them. Since most prisoners were Black (only in Texas were White prisoners a majority), the popular solution was to rent them out to White farmers and businesses.

At its worst, convict leasing turned out to be one of the most exploitative labor systems in history, as people convicted of crimes, often African Americans who were falsely accused, were hired out by county and state governments to work for individuals and businesses—coal mines, lumber camps, brickyards, railroads, quarries, mills, and plantations. Convict leasing, in other words, was a thinly disguised form of slavery and often more brutal. More than 10 percent of Black convicts died on the job. A southern planter explained that before the Civil War "we owned the negroes. If a man had a

Black codes Laws passed in southern states to restrict the rights of formerly enslaved people.

good negro he could afford to keep him. . . . But these convicts, we don't own 'em. [If] one dies, [we] get another."

The Black codes infuriated Republicans. "We [Republicans] must see to it," Senator William Stewart of Nevada resolved, "that the man made free by the Constitution of the United States is a freeman indeed."

"SLAVERY IS DEAD (?)" Thomas Nast's 1867 cartoon argues that Blacks were still being treated as if they were enslaved despite the passage of the Fourteenth Amendment. This detail illustrates a case in Raleigh, North Carolina: a Black man was whipped for a crime despite federal orders specifically prohibiting such forms of punishment.

Johnson's Battle with Congress

Early in 1866, the Radical Republicans openly challenged Andrew Johnson over Reconstruction policies after he vetoed a bill renewing funding for the Freedmen's Bureau. The Republicans could not overturn the veto. Then, on February 22, 1866, Johnson criticized Radical Republicans for promoting Black civil rights. Moderate Republicans thereafter deserted the president and supported the Radicals. Johnson had become "an alien enemy of a foreign state," Thaddeus Stevens declared.

In mid-March 1866, the Radical-led Congress passed the pathbreaking Civil Rights Act, the first federal law to define citizenship. It declared that "all persons born in the United States," including the children of immigrants, but excluding Native Americans, were citizens entitled to "full and equal benefit of all laws."

Congress passes the Civil Rights Act

The Civil Rights Act infuriated President Johnson. Congress, he fumed, could not grant citizenship to Blacks, who did not deserve it. Claiming that the proposed legislation trespassed on states' rights, Johnson vetoed it. This time, however, Republicans overrode the veto. The government, said Senator Richard Yates of Illinois, never intended "to set 4 million slaves free . . . and at the same time leave them without the civil and political rights which attach to a free citizen." It was the first time that Congress had overturned a presidential veto of a major bill. From that point on, Johnson steadily lost both public and political support.

Fourteenth Amendment

Republicans unilaterally pass the Fourteenth Amendment (1866)

To remove all doubt about the legality of the new Civil Rights Act, Congress passed the **Fourteenth Amendment** to the Constitution in 1866. (It gained ratification in 1868.) It guaranteed citizenship not just to freedpeople but also to immigrant children born in the United States (known as birthright citizenship).

Fourteenth Amendment (1866) Amendment to the U.S. Constitution guaranteeing equal protection under the law to all U.S. citizens, including formerly enslaved people.

The Fourteenth Amendment overturned the Black codes by prohibiting any efforts to violate the civil rights of "citizens," Black or White or Yellow; to deprive any person "of life, liberty, or property, without due process of law"; or to "deny any person . . . the equal protection of the laws."

The Fourteenth Amendment gave the federal government responsibility for protecting (and enforcing) civil rights. Not a single Democrat in the House or Senate voted for it. All states in the former Confederacy were required to ratify the amendment before they could be readmitted to the Union and to Congress. President Johnson urged the southern states to refuse to ratify the amendment. He predicted that the Democrats would win the congressional elections in November and then nix the amendment.

Johnson versus the Radical Republicans

To win votes for Democratic candidates in the 1866 congressional elections, Andrew Johnson went on a nineteen-day speaking tour during which he gave more than 100 speeches promoting his plan for reconstructing the South. He drew large crowds in Baltimore, Philadelphia, and New York City, during which he denounced Radical Republicans as traitors who should be hanged. His partisan speeches backfired, however.

In Cleveland, Ohio, Johnson savaged Radical Republicans as "factious, domineering, tyrannical" men. When a heckler shouted that Johnson should hang Jefferson Davis as a war criminal, the thin-skinned president retorted, "Why not hang Thad Stevens?" Then a crowd member yelled, "Is this dignified?" Johnson shouted: "I care not for dignity."

The backlash was intense. One newspaper denounced Johnson's remarks as "the most disgraceful speech ever delivered" by a president. Even the pro-Johnson *New York Times* concluded that the president's boorish behavior was "compromising his official character."

Republicans win two-thirds majority in Congress

Voters agreed. The 1866 congressional elections brought a devastating defeat for Johnson and the Democrats; in each house, Radical Republican candidates won more than a two-thirds majority, the margin required to override presidential vetoes. Congressional Republicans would now take over the process of reconstructing the former Confederacy.

Congress Takes Charge of Reconstruction

On March 2, 1867, Congress passed, over President Johnson's vetoes, the First Reconstruction Act, which included three laws creating what came to be called **Congressional Reconstruction**: the Military Reconstruction Act, the Command of the Army Act, and the Tenure of Office Act.

Military Reconstruction Act (1867)

The Military Reconstruction Act abolished the new governments "in the Rebel States" established under Andrew Johnson's lenient Reconstruction policies. In their place, Congress established military control over ten of the eleven former Confederate states. (Tennessee was exempted because it had already ratified the Fourteenth Amendment.) The other ten states were divided into five military districts, each commanded by an army general who acted as governor.

Congressional Reconstruction Phase of Reconstruction directed by Radical Republicans through the passage of three laws: the Military Reconstruction Act, the Command of the Army Act, and the Tenure of Office Act.

Yet only 10,000 federal troops, mostly African Americans, were dispatched to police the sprawling "military districts." Between 1865 and 1871, the federal army shrank from more than a million men to 30,000, most of them stationed in the West to suppress Indian uprisings. The entire state of Mississippi, for instance, had fewer than 400 U.S. soldiers assigned to ensure compliance with Reconstruction.

The Military Reconstruction Act required each former Confederate state to create a constitution that guaranteed all adult males the right to vote—Black or White, rich or poor, landless or property owners. Women—Black or White—were still not included.

The act also stipulated that the new state constitutions were to be drafted by conventions elected by male citizens "of whatever race, color, or previous condition." Once a majority of voters ratified the new constitutions, the state legislatures had to ratify the Fourteenth Amendment; once the amendment became part of the Constitution, the former Confederate states would be entitled to send representatives to Congress. Several hundred African American delegates participated in the constitutional conventions.

Command of the Army Act (1867)

The Command of the Army Act required that the president issue all army orders through general in chief Ulysses S. Grant. (The Radicals feared that President Johnson would appoint anti-Black generals to head the military districts who would be too lenient toward defiant Whites.)

Tenure of Office Act (1867)

The Tenure of Office Act stipulated that the Senate must approve any presidential effort to remove federal officials whose appointments the Senate had confirmed. Radicals intended this act to prevent Johnson from firing Secretary of War Edwin Stanton, the president's most outspoken critic in the cabinet.

Congressional Reconstruction embodied the most sweeping peacetime legislation in history to that point. It sought to ensure that formerly enslaved people could participate in the creation of new state governments in the former Confederacy. As Thaddeus Stevens explained, the Congressional Reconstruction plan would create a "perfect republic" based on the principle of *equal rights* for all citizens. "This is the promise of America," he insisted. "No More. No Less."

Impeaching the President

The first two years of Congressional Reconstruction produced dramatic changes in the South, as new state legislatures rewrote their constitutions and ratified the Fourteenth Amendment. Radical Republicans were in control of Reconstruction, but one person still stood in their way—Andrew Johnson. During 1867 and early 1868, more and more Radicals decided that the president must be removed from office.

Johnson himself opened the door to impeachment (the formal process by which Congress charges the president with "high crimes and misdemeanors") when, in violation of the Tenure of Office Act, he suspended Secretary of War Edwin Stanton, who had refused to resign despite his harsh criticism of the president's Reconstruction policy.

Johnson, who considered the Tenure of Office Act an illegal restriction of presidential power, fired Stanton and replaced him with Ulysses S. Grant. The Radicals now saw their chance to impeach the president. By removing

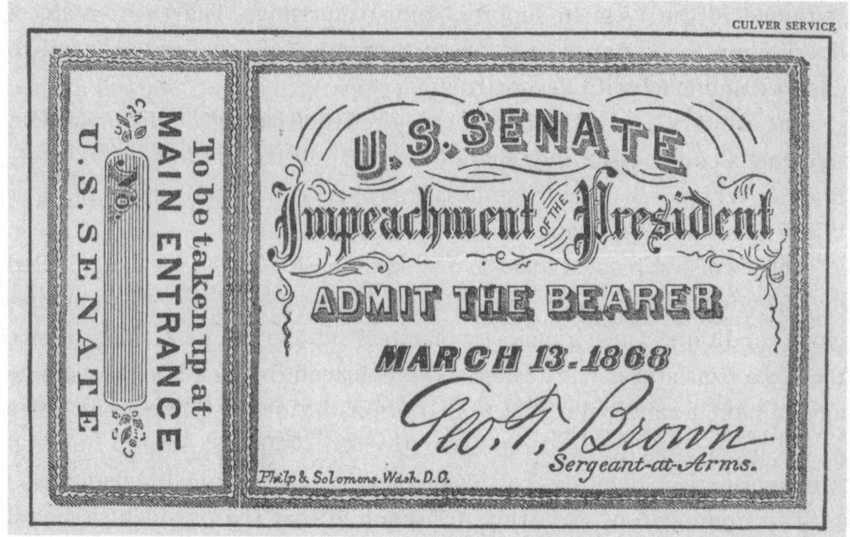

TICKET TO THE U.S. SENATE IMPEACHMENT TRIAL OF ANDREW JOHNSON President Andrew Johnson's impeachment trial was the first in American history. To follow the trial's progress, spectators needed a ticket to gain admission into the U.S. Senate chambers.

Stanton without congressional approval, Andrew Johnson had violated the law.

Impeachment of President Johnson

On February 24, 1868, the Republican-dominated House passed eleven articles of impeachment (that is, specific charges against the president), most of which dealt with Stanton's firing—and all of which were flimsy. In reality, the essential grievance against the president was that he had opposed the policies of the Radical Republicans and in doing so had brought "disgrace, ridicule, hatred, contempt, and reproach" onto the Congress. According to Secretary of the Navy Gideon Welles, Radicals were so angry at Johnson that they "would have tried to remove him had he been accused of stepping on a dog's tail."

The first Senate trial of a sitting president began on March 5, 1868. The Republicans held a majority, but not the two-thirds required to convict. It was a dramatic spectacle before a packed gallery of journalists, foreign dignitaries, and political officials. As the trial began, Stevens warned the president: "Unfortunate, unhappy man, behold your doom!"

Johnson acquitted

The five-week trial came to a stunning end when the Senate voted 35–19 for conviction, only *one* vote short of the two-thirds needed for removal. Senator Edmund G. Ross, a young Republican from Kansas, cast the deciding vote in favor of acquittal. He later explained that despite tremendous pressure from his fellow Republicans, he decided that the evidence against Johnson was both insufficient for conviction and overtly partisan. More recent research, however, suggests that Ross secretly sold his vote for acquittal. After the impeachment trial ended, Ross asked the embattled president to get friends appointed to federal jobs, and Johnson agreed to every request. The president may also have given Ross cash from a $150,000 slush fund raised by Johnson's supporters.

In the end, the effort to remove Johnson weakened public support for Congressional Reconstruction. The *Richmond Daily Dispatch* stressed that Johnson's acquittal was "a terrible rebuke on the Radical party and diminished its physical force (it never had any other)." Nevertheless, the Radical cause did gain Johnson's private agreement to stop obstructing Congressional Reconstruction. (He would later break his pledge by turning a deaf ear to pleas for federal support in suppressing Ku Klux Klan violence.)

Republican Rule in the South

Congress passes the Fifteenth Amendment

In June 1868, congressional Republicans announced that eight southern states could again send delegates to Congress. The remaining former Confederate states—Virginia, Mississippi, and Texas—were readmitted in 1870, with the added requirement that they ratify the **Fifteenth Amendment**, which gave voting rights to African American men. As the formerly enslaved Frederick Douglass had declared in 1865, "slavery is not abolished until the black man has the ballot."

The Fifteenth Amendment prohibited states from denying a citizen's right to vote on grounds of "race, color, or previous condition of servitude." Prior to its ratification, the individual states determined voting eligibility. But Susan B. Anthony and Elizabeth Cady Stanton, the leaders of the movement to secure voting rights for women, insisted that the amendment should have included women. As Anthony stressed, the U.S. Constitution refers to "We, the people; not we, the white male citizens; nor yet we, the male citizens; but we, the whole people, who formed the Union—women as well as men."

Prejudice against Chinese Americans

Still another group ignored by the Fifteenth Amendment was Chinese Americans. In California, Nevada, and Oregon, state laws prevented them from voting. *People v. Hall*, an 1857 California supreme court case, described the Chinese as "a race of people whom nature has marked as inferior, and who are incapable of progress."

During Reconstruction, elected officials from the western states insisted that citizenship and voting rights were appropriate for Blacks but not Asians. The Chinese, asserted Senator Henry W. Corbett of Oregon, were "a different race entirely" and should not be allowed to vote. A Nevada congressman added that there were not "ten American citizens" in the Far West "who favor Chinese suffrage."

Voting rights remain restricted

In the end, California and Oregon refused to ratify the Fifteenth Amendment because of the Chinese issue. Federal policies continued to bar Chinese Americans from citizenship and voting until 1943. In 1952, Asian Americans were made eligible for citizenship and voting.

Native Americans were precluded from citizenship until 1924, and many states continued to deny them voting rights until 1947. Most men also remained opposed to voting rights for women. Radical Republicans tried to deflect the issue by declaring that it was the "Negro's hour." Anyway, argued Senator Richard Yates, allowing a woman to vote would be "destructive of her womanly qualities." Another Radical Republican, John M. Broomall, added that

Fifteenth Amendment (1870) Amendment to the U.S. Constitution forbidding states to deny any male citizen the right to vote on grounds of "race, color or previous condition of servitude."

"the head of the family does the voting for the family." Women seeking voting rights would have to wait—another fifty years, as it turned out.

CORE **OBJECTIVE**

3. Assess the attitudes of White and Black Southerners toward Reconstruction.

Black Society under Reconstruction

When a federal official asked Garrison Frazier, a freedman from Georgia, if he and others wanted to live among Whites, Frazier said that they preferred "to live by ourselves, for there is a prejudice against us in the South that will take years to get over." In forging new lives, Frazier and many other formerly enslaved people set about creating their own social institutions.

Freed but not Equal

African Americans were active in affecting the course of Reconstruction. It was not an easy process, however, because Whites, both northern and southern, still embraced racism. Once the excitement of freedom wore off, most southern Blacks realized that their best chance to make a living was by working for pay for their former owners. In fact, the Freedmen's Bureau and federal soldiers urged and even ordered them to sign labor contracts with Whites. Many planters, however, conspired to control the amount of wages paid to freedmen. "It seems humiliating to be compelled to bargain and haggle with our own servants about wages," complained a White planter's daughter.

After emancipation, Union soldiers and northern observers often expressed surprise that formerly enslaved people did not leave the South. But why would they leave what they knew so well? As a group of African Americans explained, they did not want to abandon "land they had laid their fathers' bones upon." A Union officer noted that southern Blacks seemed "more attached to familiar places" than any other group in the nation.

Black Churches and Schools

African American religious life in the South was transformed during and after the war. Many formerly enslaved people identified with the biblical Hebrews, who were led out of slavery into the "promised land." Emancipation demonstrated that God was on *their* side. Before the war, enslaved people who attended White churches were forced to sit in the back. After the war, with the help of many northern Christian missionaries, both Black and White, formerly enslaved people established their own churches that became the crossroads for Black community life.

African American churches

Ministers emerged as social and political leaders. Many African Americans became Baptists or Methodists, in part because these were already the largest denominations in the South and in part because they reached out to the working poor. In 1866 alone, the African Methodist Episcopal (AME) Church gained 50,000 members. By 1890, more than 1.3 million African Americans in

THE FIRST AFRICAN CHURCH In June 1874, *Harper's Weekly* featured this illustration of the First African Church of Richmond, Virginia, on the eve of its move to a new building. **What accounted for the rise of religious membership among African Americans?**

the South had become Baptists, nearly three times as many as had joined any other denomination.

African American schools

African American communities also rushed to establish schools. Starting schools, said a formerly enslaved person, was the "first proof" of freedom. Before the Civil War, most plantation owners had denied an education to their enslaved people to keep them from reading abolitionist literature and organizing uprisings. After the war, the White elite worried that education would distract poor Whites and Blacks from their work in the fields or encourage them to leave the South in search of better social and economic opportunities.

The Union League

The Fifteenth Amendment had enormous political consequences. No sooner was it ratified than northern Republicans, Black and White, sought to convince freedmen to join the party of Lincoln. To do so, they organized Union Leagues throughout the former Confederacy. Republicans had founded the Union League (also called the Loyal League) in 1862 to rally voters behind Lincoln, the war, and the party. By late 1863, the league claimed over 700,000 members in 4,554 councils across the nation.

Union Leagues mobilize Black voters

In the postwar South, these Union League chapters were organized like fraternities, with formal initiations and rituals and secret meetings to protect the freedpeople from being persecuted by angry White Democrats. The leagues met in churches, schools, homes, and fields, often listening to northern speakers who traveled the South extolling the Republican party and encouraging Blacks to register and vote. By the early 1870s, the Union League in the South had become one of the largest Black social movements in history.

Through the help of the Union Leagues, some 90 percent of southern freedmen registered to vote, almost all of them as Republicans, and

Risks of voting

they voted in record numbers (often 80–90 percent). Their doing so often required great courage, for most White Southerners were Democrats eager to deny freedmen the vote. "All the blacks who vote against my ticket shall walk the plank," threatened Howell Cobb, a Georgia Democrat who had been a Confederate general and former governor. Throughout the postwar South, angry Whites persecuted, evicted, or fired African American workers who "exercised their political rights," as a Union officer reported from Virginia.

Black Republicans were at times equally coercive. "The Negroes are as intolerant of opposition as the whites," a White South Carolina Democrat observed. They shunned, expelled, and even killed any "of their own" who "would turn democrats." He added that freedwomen were as partisan as the men—and as intolerant of opposition: "[The] women are worse than the men, refusing to talk to or marry a renegade [Black Democrat], and aiding [men] in mobbing him."

Yet the net result of the Union Leagues was a remarkable mobilization of Blacks whose votes enabled men of color to gain elected offices for the first time in the states of the former Confederacy. Francis Cardozo, a Black minister who served as president of the South Carolina Council of Union Leagues, declared in 1870 that South Carolina had "prospered in every respect" as a result of the enfranchisement of Black voters enabled by the Union Leagues. "The fierce and determined opposition to us," he maintained, illustrated how powerful a force for equality the leagues had become.

Politics and African Americans

Black military veterans formed the core of the African American political leaders in the postwar South. Participation in the Union army or navy had given many freedmen training in leadership. Military service also gave many formerly enslaved people their first opportunities to learn to read and write and alerted them to new possibilities for economic advancement, social respectability, and civic leadership.

African American men elected to office

With many ex-Confederates denied voting rights, new African American voters helped elect some 600 Blacks—most of them formerly enslaved people—as state legislators. In Louisiana, Pinckney Pinchback, a northern free Black and former Union soldier, was elected lieutenant governor. Several other African Americans were elected to high state offices. There were two Black senators in Congress, Hiram Revels and Blanche K. Bruce, both Mississippi natives who had been educated in the North, while fourteen Blacks served in the U.S. House of Representatives.

The election of Black politicians appalled southern Whites. Democrats claimed that Radicals were trying to "organize a hell in the South" by putting "the Caucasian race" under the rule of "their own negroes." Southern Whites complained that emancipated Blacks were illiterate and had no civic experience or appreciation of political issues and processes. In this regard, however, Blacks were no different from millions of poor or immigrant White males who had been voting and serving in office for years. While Black political representation and influence did increase significantly, major obstacles

AFRICAN AMERICAN POLITICAL FIGURES OF RECONSTRUCTION As Blacks gained the right to vote, many ex-Confederate Whites were stripped of that right. As a consequence, several formerly enslaved men were elected to positions in government, such as Blanche K. Bruce *(left)* and Hiram Revels *(right)*, who served in the U.S. Senate. Between them is Frederick Douglass, who was a major figure in the abolitionist movement.

remained within state legislatures. Only South Carolina's Republican state convention had a Black majority. Louisiana's was evenly divided racially, and in only two other state conventions were more than 20 percent of the members Black: Florida and Virginia.

Land, Labor, and Disappointment

Land granted to former slaves revoked by President Johnson

Many formerly enslaved people argued that what they needed most was land. In several southern states, Blacks had been given land by Union armies after they had taken control of Confederate areas during the war. But Andrew Johnson reversed such transfers of White-owned property to formerly enslaved workers.

In South Carolina, the Union general responsible for evicting formerly enslaved people urged them to "lay aside their bitter feelings, and become reconciled to their old masters." The assembled freedmen instead shouted, "No, never!" and "Can't do it!"

Ownership of land was the foundation of freedom in the postwar South. They may have had no deeds or titles for the land they now worked, but it had been "earned by the sweat of *our* brows," said a group of Alabama freedmen. "Our wives, our children, our husbands, has been sold over and over again to purchase the lands we now locate on," a Virginia freedman noted. "Didn't we clear the land and raise de crops? We have a right to [that] land."

Thousands of formerly enslaved workers were forced to return their farms to White owners. In addition, it was virtually impossible for Blacks to get loans to buy farmland because few banks were willing to lend to them. A formerly enslaved man in Mississippi said that he and others were left with nothing: "no *land*, no *house*, not so much as a place to lay our head."

SHARECROPPERS This 1899 photograph by Frances Benjamin Johnston, one of the earliest female photojournalists, shows a sharecropping family outside their Virginia cabin. **How did the living conditions of sharecroppers compare to the life of enslaved people in the antebellum South?**

Sharecropping replaces slavery

As freedpeople were stripped of their land, they had little choice but to participate in a new labor system: **sharecropping**. It worked like this: White landowners would provide land, seed, and tools in exchange for a *share* of the crop. This essentially reenslaved workers because, as a federal army officer said, no matter "how much they are abused, they cannot leave without permission of the owner." If they left, they would forfeit their portion of the crop. Workers who violated the terms of the contract could be evicted, leaving them jobless and homeless—and subject to arrest as "vagrants."

The rapid growth of sharecropping revealed that most White plantation owners and small farmers were determined to control African Americans as if they were still enslaved. And if bad weather or insects or disease stunted the harvest, it pushed the sharecropper deeper in debt.

Many freed Blacks preferred sharecropping over working for wages, since it freed them from day-to-day supervision by White landowners. Over time, however, most sharecroppers, Black and White, found themselves deeply in debt to the landowner, with little choice but to remain tied to the same discouraging system of dependence that felt much like slavery. As a formerly enslaved person acknowledged, he and others had discovered that "freedom could make folks proud, but it didn't make 'em rich."

Tensions among Southern Blacks

African Americans in the postwar South were by no means a uniform community. They had their own differences and disputes, especially between the few who owned property and the many who did not. Affluent northern Blacks and the southern free Black elite, most of whom were city dwellers and Mulattoes (people of mixed-racial parentage), often opposed efforts to redistribute land to the freedmen, and many insisted that political equality did not mean social equality. As an African American leader in Alabama stressed, "We do not ask that the ignorant and degraded shall be

sharecropping A farming system developed after the Civil War by which landless workers farmed land in exchange with the landowner for farm supplies and a share of the crop.

put on a social equality with the refined and intelligent." In general, however, unity prevailed within the Black community, and African Americans focused on common concerns. "All we ask," said a Black member of the state constitutional convention in Mississippi, "is justice, and to be treated like human beings."

"Carpetbaggers" and "Scalawags"

White Southerners who resisted reconstruction called Whites who served in the new Republican state governments carpetbaggers or scalawags. Carpetbaggers, critics argued, were the 30,000 scheming Northerners who rushed south with their belongings in cheap suitcases made of carpeting ("carpetbags") to grab political power or buy plantations.

Some Northerners who migrated south were corrupt opportunists. However, most were Union military veterans drawn to the South by the desire to rebuild the region's wrecked economy. Many other so-called carpetbaggers were teachers, social workers, attorneys, physicians, editors, and ministers motivated by a genuine desire to help free Blacks and poor Whites.

Northerners who moved south

For example, Union general Adelbert Ames, who won the Congressional Medal of Honor, stayed in the South after the war because he felt a "sense of Mission with a large M" to help formerly enslaved people develop healthy communities. He served as the military governor of Mississippi before being elected a Republican U.S. senator in 1870. Southern Democrats especially hated the scalawags, or southern White Republicans, calling them traitors to their region. A Nashville newspaper editor described them as the "merest trash." They were prominent in the mountain counties of Georgia and Alabama and especially in the hills of eastern Tennessee. What the scalawags had in common was a willingness to work with Republicans to rebuild the southern economy.

Southern Resistance

With each passing year during Reconstruction, African Americans suffered increasing exploitation and abuse. The Black codes created by White state governments in 1865 and 1866 were the first of many efforts to deny equality. As a formerly enslaved person protested to President Johnson, the new state codes were "returning us to slavery again." Whites also used terror, intimidation, and violence to disrupt Black Republican meetings, target Black and White Republican leaders for beatings or killings, and prevent Blacks from exercising their political rights. Hundreds were killed and many more injured in systematic efforts to "keep blacks in their place."

In Texas, a White farmer, D. B. Whitesides, told a former enslaved man named Charles Brown that his newfound freedom would do him "damned little good . . . as I intend to shoot you"—which he did, shooting Brown in the chest as he tried to flee. Whitesides then rode his horse beside Brown and asked, "I got you, did I Brown?" "Yes," a bleeding Brown replied. "You got me good." Whitesides yelled that the wound would teach "[Negroes like you] to put on airs because you are free."

A VISIT FROM THE KU KLUX KLAN African Americans in the South lived in constant fear of racial violence, as this 1872 engraving from *Harper's Weekly*, published to elicit northern sympathy, illustrates.

Rise of White supremacy groups

Such ugly incidents revealed a harsh truth: the death of slavery did not mean the birth of true freedom for African Americans. A growing number of southern Whites used violence to resist Radical Reconstruction. Secretive terrorist groups, including the Ku Klux Klan, the Knights of the White Camelia, the White Line, and the White League, emerged to harass, intimidate, torture, and kill African Americans.

The **Ku Klux Klan** (KKK) was formed in 1866 in Pulaski, Tennessee. The name *Ku Klux* derived from the Greek word *kuklos*, meaning "circle" or "band"; *Klan* came from the English word *clan*, or family. The Klan, and other groups like it, began as a social club, with spooky costumes and secret rituals. But its members, most of them former Confederate soldiers, soon began harassing Blacks and White Republicans.

General Philip Sheridan, who supervised the military district that included Louisiana and Texas, reported that Klansmen were "terrorists" intent on suppressing Black political participation. Klansmen marauded at night on horseback, spreading rumors, issuing threats, and burning schools and churches. "We are going to kill all the Negroes," a White supremacist declared during one massacre.

The Legacy of Congressional Reconstruction

Ku Klux Klan A secret terrorist organization founded in Pulaski, Tennessee, in 1866 targeting formerly enslaved people who voted and held political offices, as well as people the KKK labeled as carpetbaggers and scalawags.

The widespread use of racial violence helped overturn Republican state governments. Yet they left behind an important accomplishment: the new constitutions they created remained in effect for years, and later constitutions incorporated many of their most progressive features.

Some of the significant innovations instituted by the Republican state governments protected Black voting rights and restructured legislatures. More state offices were changed from appointed to elective positions to weaken

Radical Republican achievements

the "good old boy" tradition of rewarding political supporters with state government jobs. In South Carolina, former Confederate leaders opposed the Republican state legislature not simply because of its Black members but because poor Whites were also enjoying political clout for the first time, thereby threatening the dominance of wealthy White plantation owners and merchants.

Given the hostile circumstances under which Republican state governments operated in the South, their achievements were remarkable. They provided free public schools for the first time in most southern counties and allowed women to keep their private property rather than transfer it to their husbands, rebuilt an extensive railroad network, and established public school systems open to all children, although the buildings were segregated by race. Some 600,000 Black pupils had enrolled in southern schools by 1877.

Southern Republicans also gave more attention to the poor and to orphanages, asylums, and institutions for the deaf and blind of both races.

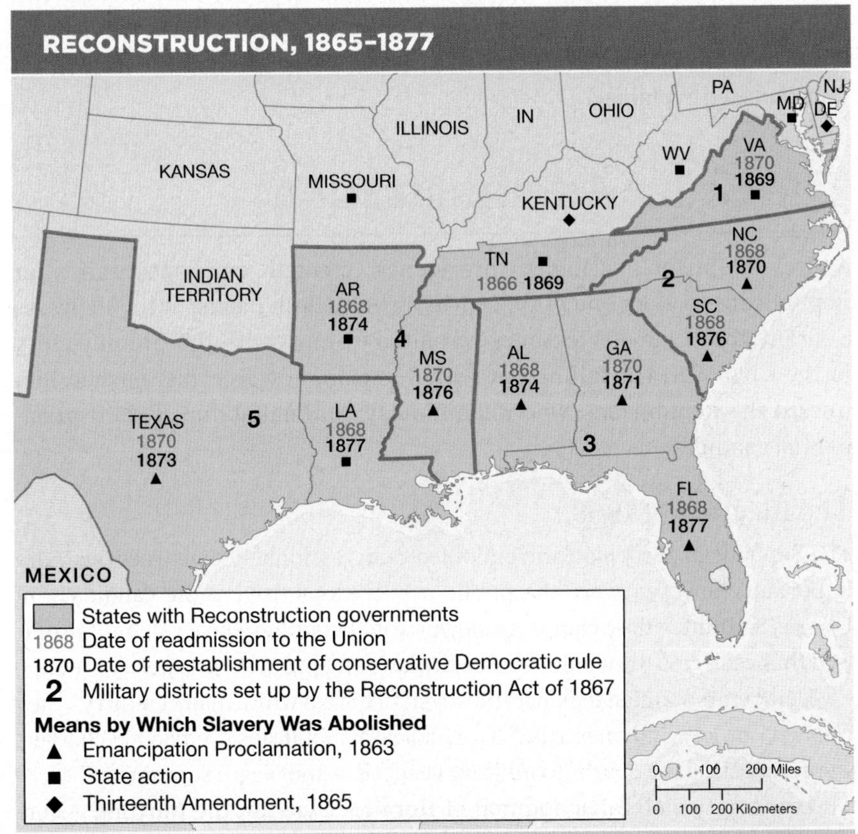

- How did the Military Reconstruction Act reorganize governments in the South in the late 1860s and 1870s?
- What did the former Confederate states have to do to be readmitted to the Union?
- Why did "conservative" parties gradually regain control of the South from the Republicans in the 1870s?

Much-needed infrastructure—roads, bridges, and buildings—was repaired or rebuilt. African Americans achieved rights and opportunities that would repeatedly be violated but would never completely be taken away, at least in principle, such as equality before the law and the rights to own property, attend schools, learn to read and write, enter professions, and carry on business.

Continued corruption in government

Yet government officials also engaged in corrupt practices. Bribes and kickbacks, whereby companies received government contracts in return for giving government officials cash or stock, were commonplace. In Louisiana, twenty-six-year-old Henry Clay Warmoth somehow turned an annual salary of $8,000 into a million-dollar fortune during his four years as governor. "I don't pretend to be honest," he admitted. "I only pretend to be as honest as anybody in politics." Warmoth would eventually be impeached and removed from office.

As was true in the North and the Midwest, southern state governments awarded money to corporations, notably railroads, under conditions that invited shady dealings and outright corruption. Some railroad corporations received state funds but never built railroads, and bribery was rampant. But the Radical Republican regimes did not invent such corruption, nor did it die with them. Warmoth recognized as much: "Corruption is the fashion" in Louisiana, he explained.

CORE **OBJECTIVE**

4. Analyze the political and economic factors that helped end Reconstruction in 1877.

The Grant Administration

Andrew Johnson's crippled presidency created an opportunity for Republicans to elect one of their own in 1868. Both parties wooed Ulysses S. Grant, the "Lion of Vicksburg" credited by most with the Union victory in the Civil War. His falling-out with Johnson, however, had pushed him toward the Republicans, who unanimously nominated him as their presidential candidate.

The Election of 1868

The Republican party platform endorsed Congressional Reconstruction. More important, however, were the public expectations driving the candidacy of Ulysses S. Grant, whose campaign slogan was "Let us have peace." Grant promised that, if elected, he would enforce the laws and promote prosperity for all.

Democrats shouted defiance, however. "This is a white man's country," they claimed, so "let white men rule." The Radical Republicans, Democrats charged, were subjecting the South "to military despotism and Negro supremacy."

Black votes help to elect President Grant (1868)

Democratic delegates nominated Horatio Seymour, the wartime governor of New York and a passionate critic of Congressional Reconstruction, who dismissed the Emancipation Proclamation as "a proposal for the butchery of women and children." His running mate, Francis P. Blair, Jr., a former Union general from Missouri who had served in Congress, was an avowed racist who wanted to "declare the reconstruction acts null and void" and withdraw all federal troops from the South. He attacked Grant for exercising military tyranny "over the eight millions of white people in the South, fixed to the earth with his bayonets." A Democrat later said that Blair's "stupid and indefensible" remarks cost Seymour a close election. Grant won all but eight states and swept the Electoral College, 214–80, but his popular majority was only 307,000 out of almost 6 million votes.

More than 500,000 African American voters, mostly in the South, accounted for Grant's margin of victory. Although Klan violence soared during the campaign, and hundreds of African Americans paid with their lives, the efforts of Radical Republicans to ensure voting rights for southern Blacks had paid off.

Grant, the youngest president (forty-six years old when inaugurated), had said during the Civil War that he was not "a politician, never was and never hope to be." Now he was the politician in chief. Although a courageous defender of Congressional Reconstruction and civil rights for Blacks, Grant was not a great president. He later admitted that he thought "I could run the government of the United States as I did the staff of my army. It was my mistake, and it led me into other mistakes."

"LET US HAVE PEACE" In the midst of the social and political turbulence of Reconstruction, Ulysses S. Grant's slogan, "Let us have peace"—as stamped on campaign coins like this one—struck a chord with voters.

Grant passively followed the lead of Congress and was often blind to the political forces and self-serving influence peddlers around him. He showed poor judgment in his selection of cabinet members, often favoring friendship, family, loyalty, and military service over integrity and ability.

During Grant's two presidential terms, his seven cabinet positions changed twenty-four times. His close friend, General William T. Sherman, said he felt sorry for Grant because so many supposedly loyal Republicans used the president for selfish gains.

Yet Grant excelled at bringing diversity to the federal government. During his two presidential terms, he appointed more African Americans, Native Americans, Jews, and women than any of his predecessors, and he fulfilled his campaign pledge to bring the nation "peace and prosperity."

The Battle to Enforce the Fifteenth Amendment

President Grant viewed Reconstruction as the nation's top priority, and he insisted that African Americans be allowed to exercise their civil rights without fear of violence. On March 30, 1870, Grant delivered a speech to Congress in which he celebrated the ratification of the Fifteenth Amendment, giving voting rights to African American men nationwide. "It was," he declared, "... the most important event that has occurred since the nation came into life ... the realization of the Declaration of Independence."

To African American leader Frederick Douglass, the Thirteenth, Fourteenth, and Fifteenth Amendments seemed to ensure that Blacks would at last gain true equality. "Never was revolution more complete," Douglass announced in 1870. To President Grant, "more than any other man, the Negro owes his enfranchisement."

Backlash against the Fifteenth Amendment

But Douglass and others were soon bitterly disappointed. The "revolution" turned out to be incomplete as the Fifteenth Amendment ignited a violent backlash in the South. In Georgia, White officials devised new ways to restrict Black voting, such as poll taxes and onerous registration procedures. Other states followed suit. "What is the use of talking about equality before the law," a freedman wrote as ex-Confederates took control of southern society. "There is none."

Four months after the Fifteenth Amendment became the law of the land, Congress passed the Naturalization Act of 1870. For the first time, it extended the process whereby immigrants had gained citizenship to include *"aliens of African nativity and to persons of African descent."* Efforts to include Asians and Native Americans in the naturalization law were defeated, however.

Indian Policy

President Grant was almost as progressive in his outlook toward Native Americans as he was toward African Americans. In 1869, he appointed General Ely Parker, a Seneca chief trained as an attorney and engineer, as the new commissioner of Indian Affairs, the first Native American to hold the position. Parker had served as Grant's military secretary during the war. Now, as commissioner, Parker faced formidable challenges in creating policies for the 300,000 Indians across the nation, many of whom continued to be pressured by White settlers, miners, railroads, and telegraph companies to give up their ancestral lands.

Grant's "Peace Policy"

Working with Parker, Grant created a "Peace Policy" toward Native Americans. "The Indians," he observed, "require as much protection from the whites as the white does from the Indians." He did not want the army "shooting these poor savages; I want to conciliate them and make them peaceful citizens." His experiences had shown that the "Indian problem" was in fact the result of "bad whites."

Grant believed that lasting peace could only result from Indians abandoning their nomadic tradition and relocating to government reservations, where federal troops would provide them "absolute protection." Even Lieutenant General William T. Sherman, no friend of the Indians, acknowledged the injustice of the situation. "The poor Indians are starving," he reported to his wife in 1868. "We kill them if they attempt to hunt," yet if they stay "within the reservation, they starve."

Grant also promised to end the chronic corruption whereby congressmen appointed cronies as licensed government traders with access to Indian reservations. Many traders used their positions to swindle Native Americans out of the federally supplied food, clothing, and other provisions intended solely for the reservations. One of the accused traders was the president's brother.

To clean up the so-called Indian Ring, Grant moved the Bureau of Indian Affairs out of the control of Congress and into the War Department. He also created a ten-man Board of Indian Commissioners, a civilian agency whose mission was to oversee the operations of the Bureau of

Indian Affairs. Grant then appointed Quakers as reservation traders, assuming that their honesty, humility, and pacifism would improve the distribution of government resources. "If you can make Quakers out of the Indians," Grant told them, "it will take the fight out of them. Let us have peace." Yet Quakers proved no more able to manage Indian policy than government bureaucrats could.

Like other presidents, Grant discovered that there was often a gap between the policies he created and their implementation. Many of the officers and soldiers sent to "pacify" Indian peoples in the Great Plains displayed an attitude toward Native Americans quite different from Grant's. For example, General Philip Sheridan coined the infamous statement, "The only good Indians I know are dead." He also dismissed Indians as "the enemies of our race and of our civilization." General William T. Sherman agreed. He stressed to Sheridan that "the more [Indians] we kill this year, the less we would have to kill next year." Several members of Congress openly called for the "extermination" of the Indians.

Such attitudes led the abolitionist Wendell Phillips to ask why Indians were one of the only groups still denied citizenship. "The great poison of the age is race hatred" directed at both African Americans and Native Americans, Phillips charged. Most White Americans, however, did not care. "Wendell Phillips' new [Negro]," the editors of the *New York Herald* observed with disdain, "is the 'noble red man.'" Phillips responded, "We shall never be able to be just to other races . . . until we 'unlearn' contempt" for others different from us.

Scandals

President Grant's naive trust in people, especially rich people, led his administration into a cesspool of scandal. Perhaps because of his disastrous efforts as a storekeeper and farmer before the Civil War, Grant was awestruck by men of wealth. As they lavished gifts and attention on him, he was lured into their webs of self-serving deception. In the summer of 1869, two unprincipled financial schemers, Jay Gould and James Fisk, Jr., plotted with Abel Corbin, the president's brother-in-law, to "corner" (manipulate) the nation's gold market. They intended to create a public craze for gold by purchasing massive quantities of the precious metal to drive up its value.

Gould-Fisk scheme to corner the gold market

The only threat to the scheme lay in the possibility that the federal Treasury would burst the bubble by selling large amounts of its gold, which would deflate its market value. When Grant was seen in public with Gould and Fisk, people assumed that he supported their scheme. As the false rumor spread in New York City's financial district that the president endorsed the run-up in gold, its value soared.

On September 24, 1869—soon to be remembered as Black Friday—the Gould-Fisk scheme worked, at least for a while. Starting at $150 an ounce, the price of gold rose, first to $160, then $165, leading more and more investors to join the stampede.

Then, around noon, Grant and his Treasury secretary realized what was happening and began selling government gold. Within fifteen minutes,

CORNERING THE GOLD MARKET In this political cartoon of the "Black Friday" gold scheme, Jay Gould attempts to manipulate the gold market, represented by caged and enraged bulls and bears. In the background, President Grant dashes from the U.S. Treasury to the scene, frantically trying to bring down the soaring price of gold.

the price plummeted to $138. Schemers lost fortunes amid the chaotic trading. Soon the turmoil spread to the entire stock market, claiming thousands of victims. As Fisk noted, each man was left to "drag out his own corpse."

For weeks after the gold bubble collapsed, financial markets were paralyzed and business confidence was shaken. Congressman James Garfield wrote privately to a friend that Grant had compromised his office by his "indiscreet acceptance" of gifts from Fisk and Gould and that any investigation of Black Friday would lead "into the parlor of the President." One critic announced that U. S. Grant's initials actually stood for "uniquely stupid."

The plot to corner the gold market was the first of several scandals that rocked the Grant administration. The secretary of war's wife, it turned out, had accepted bribes from merchants who traded with Indians at army posts in the West. And in St. Louis, whiskey distillers bribed federal Treasury agents in an effort to avoid paying excise taxes on alcohol. Grant's personal secretary participated in the scheme, taking secret payments in exchange for confidential information. Grant urged Congress to investigate. "Let no guilty man escape," he stressed.

Liberal Republicans

Disputes over political corruption and the fate of Reconstruction helped divide Republicans into two factions: Liberals (or Conscience Republicans) and Stalwarts (or Grant Republicans).

Liberal Republicans, led by Senator Carl Schurz, a Union war hero from Missouri, embraced free enterprise capitalism and opposed government regulation of business and industry while championing gold coins as the only reliable currency. They wanted to oust Grant from the presidency and end what Schurz called "Negro supremacy" in the South. The "horror" of Reconstruction, Schurz insisted, must be stopped and federal troops withdrawn.

As the *Nation* magazine stressed, "Everybody is heartily tired of discussing [the Negro's] rights."

Schurz and other Liberal Republicans also sought to lower the tariffs lining the pockets of big corporations and promote "civil service reforms" to end the "partisan tyranny" of the "patronage system," whereby new presidents rewarded the "selfish greed" of political supporters with federal government jobs.

The 1872 Election

In 1872, the Liberal Republicans, many of whom were elitist newspaper editors suspicious of the "working classes," held their own national convention in Cincinnati, during which they accused the Grant administration of corruption, incompetence, and "despotism." They then committed political suicide by nominating Horace Greeley, the eccentric editor of the *New York Tribune* and a longtime champion of causes ranging from abolitionism to socialism, vegetarianism, and spiritualism (communicating with the dead).

Most Northerners were appalled by Greeley's selection. E. L. Godkin, editor of the *Nation* and a Liberal Republican sympathizer, dismissed Greeley as "a conceited, ignorant, half-cracked, obstinate old creature."

Southern Democrats, however, liked Greeley's criticism of Reconstruction. His newspaper charged that Radical Republicans had given the vote to "ignorant" formerly enslaved people whose "[Negro] Government" exercised "absolute political supremacy" in several states and was transferring wealth from the "most intelligent" and "influential" southern Whites to themselves.

President Grant reelected (1872)

In the 1872 balloting, Greeley carried only six southern states and none in the North. Grant won thirty-one states and a large popular majority, gaining 56 percent of the votes. An exhausted Greeley confessed that he was "the worst beaten man who ever ran for high office." Greeley died three weeks later.

Grant was delighted that the "soreheads and thieves who had deserted the Republican party" were defeated, and he promised to avoid the "mistakes" he had made in his first term.

The Money Supply

Greenbacks vs. gold coins

Complex financial issues—especially monetary policy—dominated Ulysses S. Grant's second term. Prior to the Civil War, the economy operated on a gold standard; state banks issued paper money that could be exchanged for an equal value of gold coins. So, both gold coins and state bank notes circulated as currency. **Greenbacks** (so called because of the dye used on the printed dollars) were issued by the federal Treasury during the Civil War to help pay for the war.

When a nation's supply of money grows faster than the economy itself, prices for goods and services increase (inflation). This happened when the greenbacks were issued. After the war, the U.S. Treasury assumed that the greenbacks would be recalled from circulation so that consumer prices

greenbacks Paper money issued during the Civil War, which sparked currency debates after the war.

would decline and the nation could return to a "hard-money" currency—gold, silver, and copper coins—which had always been viewed as more reliable in value than paper currency.

Public Credit Act (1869)

The most vocal supporters of a return to hard money were eastern creditors (mostly bankers and merchants) who did not want their debtors to pay them in paper currency. Critics tended to be farmers and other debtors. These so-called soft-money advocates opposed taking greenbacks out of circulation because shrinking the supply of money would bring lower prices (deflation) for their crops and livestock. In 1868, congressional supporters of such a soft-money policy—mostly Democrats—forced the Treasury to stop withdrawing greenbacks.

President Grant sided with the hard-money camp. On March 18, 1869, he signed the Public Credit Act, which said that investors who purchased government bonds to help finance the war effort must be paid back in gold. The act led to a decline in consumer prices that hurt debtors and helped creditors. It also ignited a ferocious debate over the merits of hard and soft money that would last throughout the nineteenth century—and beyond.

Financial Panic

President Grant's effort to withdraw greenbacks from circulation triggered a major economic collapse. During 1873, two dozen railroads stopped paying their bills, forcing Jay Cooke and Company, the nation's leading business lender, to go bankrupt and close its doors on September 18, 1873.

The shocking news created a snowball effect, as other hard-pressed banks and investment companies began shutting down. A Republican senator sent Grant an urgent telegram from New York City: "Results of today indicate imminent danger of general national bank panic."

The resulting **Panic of 1873** caused a deep depression. Tens of thousands of businesses closed, 3 million workers lost jobs, and those with jobs saw their wages slashed. In major cities, the unemployed and homeless roamed the streets and formed long lines at soup kitchens. A quarter of New Yorkers were jobless.

The depression signaled that the maturing industrial economy was entering a long phase of instability punctuated by periods of soaring prosperity followed by desperate panics, bankruptcies, unemployment, recessions, and even prolonged depressions.

Republicans lose congressional majority

The Panic of 1873 led the U.S. Treasury to reverse course and begin printing more greenbacks to increase the nation's money supply. For a time, the supporters of paper money celebrated, but in 1874, Grant vetoed a bill to issue even more greenbacks. His decision pleased the financial community but ignited a barrage of criticism. A Tennessee Republican congressman called the veto "cold-blooded murder," and a group of merchants in Indiana charged that Grant had sold his soul to those "whose god is the dollar."

Panic of 1873 Financial collapse triggered by President Grant's efforts to withdraw greenbacks from circulation and transition the economy back to hard currency.

In the end, Grant's decision only prolonged what was then the worst depression in the nation's history. It also brought about a catastrophe for Republicans in the 1874 congressional elections. In the House, Republicans

PANIC OF 1873 The depression in 1873 left millions unemployed and destitute. In this contemporary woodcut, a line of somber men hugs the wall of a New York City hospice, where they hope to get a hot meal.

went from a 70 percent majority to a 37 percent minority. As a result, the Republican effort to reconstruct the South ground to a halt.

Domestic Terrorism

President Grant initially fought to enforce federal efforts to reconstruct the postwar South, but southern resistance increased and turned brutally violent. In Grayson County, Texas, a White man and two friends murdered three formerly enslaved people because they wanted to "thin the [Negroes] out and drive them to their holes."

Anti-Black terrorism escalates

Klansmen focused on intimidating prominent Republicans, Black and White—elected officials, teachers in Black schools, state militias. In Mississippi, they killed a Black Republican leader in front of his family. Three White Republicans were murdered in Georgia in 1870, and that same year an armed mob of Whites attacked a Republican political rally in Alabama, killing four Blacks and wounding fifty-four. An Alabama Republican pleaded with Grant to intervene. "Give us poor people some guarantee of our lives," G. T. F. Boulding wrote. "We are hunted and shot down as if we were wild beasts."

In South Carolina, White supremacists were especially violent. In 1871, some 500 masked men laid siege to the Union County jail and eventually lynched eight Black prisoners. In March 1871, Klansmen killed thirty African Americans in Meridian, Mississippi.

Enforcement Acts (1870–1871)

At Grant's urging, Republicans in Congress responded with three Enforcement Acts (1870–1871). The first imposed penalties on anyone who interfered with a citizen's right to vote. The second dispatched federal supervisors to monitor elections in southern districts where political terrorism flourished. The third, called the Ku Klux Klan Act (1871), outlawed the main activities of the KKK—forming conspiracies, wearing disguises, resisting officers, and intimidating officials. It also allowed the president to send federal troops to any community where voting rights were being violated.

Once the legislation was approved, Grant sent Attorney General Amos Akerman, a Georgian, to recruit prosecutors and marshals to enforce it. In South Carolina alone, Akerman and federal troops and prosecutors convinced local juries to convict 1,143 Klansmen. By 1872, Grant's tough actions had effectively killed the Klan. In general, however, the Enforcement Acts were not consistently enforced. As a result, the violent efforts of southern Whites to thwart Reconstruction escalated.

Colfax Massacre

On Easter Sunday 1873 in the small Black township of Colfax, Louisiana, some 140 White vigilantes, most of them well-armed ex-Confederate soldiers led by Klansmen, used a cannon, rifles, and pistols to force a group of Black Republicans holed up in the courthouse to surrender. The Whites then called out the names of the African Americans, told them to step forward, and either shot them, or slit their throats, or hanged them, slaughtering a total of eighty-one people.

When federal troops arrived, an officer reported that they found heaps of Black bodies being picked over by dogs and buzzards. Many of the dead "were shot in the back of the head and neck." Most had "three to a dozen wounds."

President Grant told the Senate that the Colfax Massacre was unprecedented in its "barbarity." He declared parts of Louisiana to be in a state of insurrection and imposed military rule. Federal prosecutors used the Enforcement Acts to indict seventy Whites, but only nine were put on trial and just three were convicted—but of "conspiracy," not murder, and none were sent to prison.

Southern "Redeemers"

The Klan's impact on southern politics varied from state to state. In the Upper South, it played a modest role in helping Democrats win local elections. In the Lower South, however, Klan violence had more serious effects. In overwhelmingly Black Yazoo County, Mississippi, vengeful Whites used terrorism to reverse the political balance of power.

In the 1873 elections, Republicans cast 2,449 votes and Democrats 638; two years later, Democrats polled 4,049 votes, Republicans 7. Once Democrats regained power, they ousted Black legislators, closed public schools for Black children, and instituted poll taxes to restrict Black voting.

The activities of White supremacists disheartened Black and White Republicans alike. "We are helpless and unable to organize," wrote a Mississippi Republican. "[We] dare not attempt to canvass [campaign for candidates] or make public speeches." At the same time, Northerners displayed a growing weariness with using federal troops to reconstruct the South. "The plain truth is," noted the *New York Herald,* "the North has got tired of the Negro."

Civil Rights Act of 1875

President Grant, however, desperately wanted to use more federal force to preserve peace. He asked Congress to pass new legislation that would "leave my duties perfectly clear." Congress responded with the Civil Rights Act of 1875, which said that people of all races must be granted equal access to hotels and restaurants, railroads and stagecoaches, theaters, and other "places of public amusement."

Unfortunately for Grant, the new anti-segregation law provided little enforcement authority. Those who felt their rights were being violated had to file suit in court, and the penalties for violators were modest.

Civil Rights Cases (1883) allow for more racial segregation measures

In 1883, the U.S. Supreme Court struck down the Civil Rights Act on the grounds that the Fourteenth Amendment focused only on the actions of state governments; it did not have authority over the policies of private businesses or individuals. Chief Justice Joseph Bradley added that it was time for Blacks to assume "the rank of a mere citizen" and stop being the "special favorite of the laws." As a result, the *Civil Rights Cases* (1883) opened the door for a wave of racial segregation that washed over the South during the late nineteenth century.

Republican political control in the South and public interest in protecting civil rights gradually loosened during the 1870s as all-White "conservative" parties mobilized the anti-Reconstruction vote. They called themselves conservatives to distinguish themselves from northern Democrats. Conservatives—the so-called **redeemers** who supposedly "saved" the South from Republican control and "black rule"—used the race issue to excite the White electorate and threaten Black voters. Where persuasion failed to work, conservatives used trickery to rig the voting. As one conservative boasted, "The white and black Republicans may outvote us, but we can outcount them."

Republican political control ended in Virginia and Tennessee as early as 1869 and collapsed a year later in Georgia and North Carolina, although North Carolina had a Republican governor until 1876. Reconstruction lasted longest in the Lower South, where Whites abandoned Klan robes for barefaced intimidation in paramilitary groups such as the Mississippi Rifle Club and the South Carolina Red Shirts. The last Radical Republican regimes ended, however, after the elections of 1876, and the return of the old White political elite further undermined the country's commitment to Congressional Reconstruction.

The Supreme Court

Key rulings by the U.S. Supreme Court further eroded Congressional Reconstruction. The *Slaughterhouse Cases* (1873) limited the "privileges or immunities" of U.S. citizenship as outlined in the Fourteenth Amendment.

In 1869, the Louisiana legislature had granted the New Orleans livestock slaughtering business to a single company as a means of protecting public health. Competing butchers sued the state, arguing that the monopoly violated their "privileges" as U.S. citizens under the Fourteenth Amendment and deprived them of property without due process of law.

In a 5–4 decision, the Court ruled that the monopoly did not violate the Fourteenth Amendment because its "privileges and immunities" clause applied only to U.S. citizenship, not state citizenship. States, in other words, retained legal jurisdiction over their citizens, and federal protection of civil rights did not extend to the property rights of businesses.

redeemers Postwar White Democratic leaders in the South who supposedly saved the region from political, economic, and social domination by Northerners and Blacks.

Dissenting Justice Stephen J. Field argued that the Court's ruling rendered the Fourteenth Amendment a "vain and idle enactment" with little scope or authority. By designating the rights of state citizens as being beyond the jurisdiction of federal law, the *Slaughterhouse Cases* unwittingly opened the door for states to discriminate against African Americans.

Supreme Court limits federal enforcement of Reconstruction measures

Three years later, in *United States v. Cruikshank* (1876), the Supreme Court further eroded the protections of individuals by overturning the convictions of William Cruikshank and two other White men who had led the Colfax Massacre. In doing so, the Court argued that the equal protection and due process clauses in the Fourteenth Amendment governed only state actions, not the behavior of individuals. Furthermore, the prosecution's failure to prove racial intent placed the convictions outside the reach of the equal protection clause of the Fourteenth Amendment.

Chief Justice Morrison Waite and the other justices struck down the Enforcement Acts, ruling that the states, not the federal government, were responsible for protecting citizens from attack by other private citizens.

Taken together, the *Slaughterhouse* and *Cruikshank* cases so gutted the Fourteenth Amendment that freedpeople were left even more vulnerable to violence and discrimination. The federal government was effectively abandoning its role in enforcing Reconstruction as Northerners shifted their attention to corruption in Washington, D.C.

Seeking Restitution

After the Civil War, a few resolute formerly enslaved people fought to be compensated for their years of forced labor. Henrietta Wood had grown up enslaved on a northern Kentucky plantation before being separated from her mother and sold several times. In 1848, the woman who owned Wood moved across the Ohio River to Cincinnati, where she freed Henrietta. Wood then worked at a boarding house cleaning rooms until one day in 1853 the owner, Rebecca Boyd, took her on a carriage ride to Kentucky. "I have some friends to see, and we can get back in time for supper," she assured Henrietta. Yet as they left the ferry on the Kentucky side of the river, Wood's employer handed her over to a slave trader who sold her to a Mississippi planter.

Eventually, Wood ended up enslaved on a Texas plantation so isolated that she did not learn of the Union victory in the Civil War until months after Robert E. Lee's surrender. Once freed, Wood returned in 1869 to Cincinnati with her young son, Arthur, who was likely the result of her having been raped by her Texas owner.

In 1870, a resilient, determined Henrietta Wood took slave trader Zebulon Ward to federal court in Cincinnati, arguing that she should be reimbursed $20,000 for the wages she had earned but never received after he reenslaved and sold her. Ward had grown wealthy in Arkansas after the war by leasing imprisoned Blacks to area farmers. After numerous delays, a jury of twelve White men ruled in favor of Wood in 1878. The judge, a former slaveowner himself, awarded her $2,500. It was the largest settlement of its kind, enabling her to buy a house and later send her son to college and law school.

Wood's victory in court was the exception, but in part it would plant the idea to formerly enslaved people and their descendants to seek restitution for all their unpaid work when in bondage.

The Contested Election of 1876

President Grant wanted to run for an unprecedented third term in 1876, but many Republicans had lost confidence in his leadership. In the summer of 1875, he acknowledged the inevitable and announced that he would retire, confessing that he "never wanted to get out of a place as much as I did to get out of the Presidency."

James Gillespie Blaine of Maine, former Speaker of the House, initially seemed the likeliest Republican to succeed Grant, but his candidacy crumbled when newspapers revealed that he had secretly promised political favors to railroad executives in exchange for shares of stock in the company.

The scandal led the Republican convention to select Ohio's favorite son, Rutherford B. Hayes. Orphaned at birth and raised by a single mother, he graduated first in his class at Kenyon College, then received a law degree from Harvard before becoming an anti-slavery attorney in Cincinnati. When the Civil War erupted, he joined the Union army and eventually became a major general; he was wounded four times. After the war, Hayes served three terms as governor of Ohio. He was a civil service reformer eager to reduce the number of federal jobs subject to political appointment. But his chief virtue was that, as a journalist put it, he was "obnoxious to no one."

The Democratic convention was uncharacteristically harmonious. On the second ballot, the nomination went to Samuel J. Tilden, a wealthy corporate lawyer and reform governor of New York.

The 1876 campaign avoided controversial issues. In the absence of strong ideological differences, Democrats highlighted the Republican scandals. Republicans responded by repeatedly waving "the bloody shirt," linking the Democrats to secession, civil war, and the violence committed against Republicans in the South. As Robert G. Ingersoll, the most celebrated

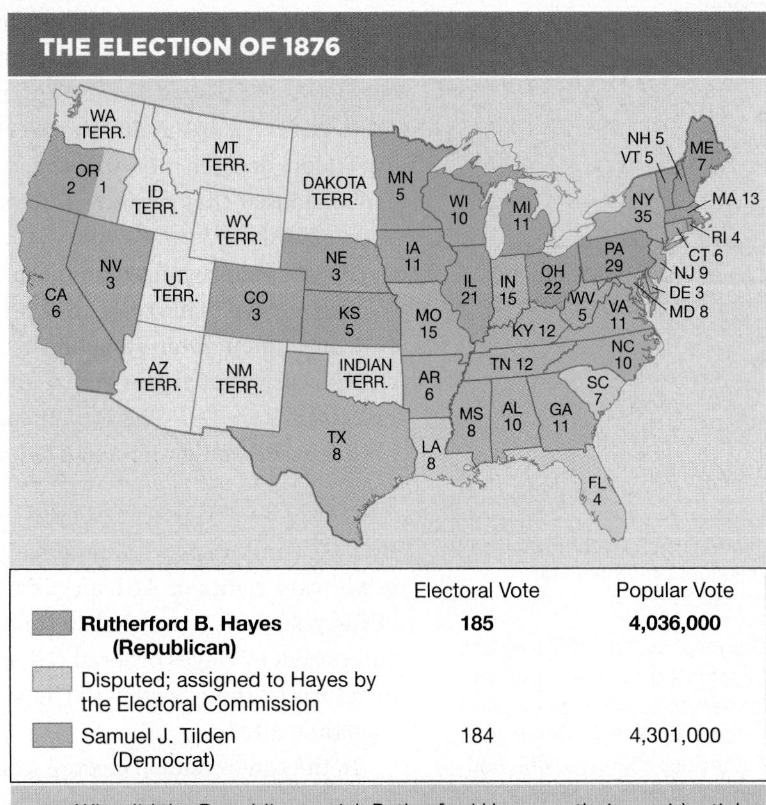

	Electoral Vote	Popular Vote
Rutherford B. Hayes (Republican)	**185**	**4,036,000**
Disputed; assigned to Hayes by the Electoral Commission		
Samuel J. Tilden (Democrat)	184	4,301,000

- Why did the Republicans pick Rutherford Hayes as their presidential candidate?
- Why were the electoral votes of several states disputed?
- What was the Compromise of 1877?

COMPROMISE OF 1877 This illustration represents the compromise between Republicans and southern Democrats that ended Radical Reconstruction.

Republican public speaker of the time, insisted: "The man that assassinated Abraham Lincoln was a Democrat. . . . Soldiers, every scar you have on your heroic bodies was given you by a Democrat!"

Early returns pointed to a victory for Tilden. Nationwide, he outpolled Hayes by almost 300,000 votes, and by midnight following Election Day, Tilden had won 184 electoral votes, just 1 short of the total needed for victory. Republican activists realized that the election hinged on 19 disputed electoral votes from Florida, Louisiana, and South Carolina.

The Democrats needed only one of the challenged votes to claim victory; the Republicans needed all nineteen. Republicans in the three states had engaged in election fraud, while Democrats had used violence to keep Black voters at home. All three states, however, were governed by Republicans who appointed the election boards, each of which reported narrow victories for Hayes. The Democrats challenged the results.

Congress chooses Hayes; Tilden concedes

In all three states, rival election boards submitted conflicting vote counts. Weeks passed with no solution. On January 29, 1877, Congress appointed an electoral commission to settle the dispute. On March 1, the commission voted 8–7 in favor of Hayes. The next day, the House of Representatives declared Hayes president by an electoral vote of 185–184.

Tilden decided not to protest the decision. His campaign manager explained that they preferred "four years of Hayes's administration to four years of civil war."

Compromise of 1877

Hayes's victory hinged on the defection of key southern Democrats, who, it turned out, had made secret deals with the Republicans. On February 26, 1877, prominent Ohio Republicans and powerful southern Democrats had struck a private bargain—the **Compromise of 1877**—at Wormley's Hotel in Washington, D.C. The Republicans promised that if Hayes were named president, he would remove all federal troops from the South.

The End of Reconstruction

Federal troops withdrawn from civil rights enforcement

By 1877, Americans were no longer willing to pay the price to protect the newly won rights of African Americans. The Democrat-controlled House of Representatives refused to fund federal troops in the South after July, and President Hayes ordered U.S. soldiers in the South Carolina statehouse to return to their barracks. The state's Republican government collapsed soon thereafter.

Compromise of 1877 Secret deal forged by congressional leaders to resolve the disputed election of 1876; Republican Rutherford B. Hayes, who had lost the popular vote, was declared the winner in exchange for his pledge to remove federal troops from the South, marking the end of Reconstruction.

In the congressional elections of 1878, Hayes admitted that the balloting in southern states was corrupted by "violence of the most atrocious character," but he would not send federal troops again. The Democrats controlling the House went a step further and banned the use of federal troops to enforce civil rights in the former Confederacy. The news led a South Carolina African

American to dread his future. "I am an unprotected freedman. O God save the Colored People."

Without the sustained presence of federal troops, African Americans could not retain their newly won civil rights. New White Democratic state governments rewrote their constitutions, ousted the "carpetbaggers, scalawags, and blacks," and cut spending. As the years passed, White supremacists found various ways to prevent Blacks from voting or holding office or even sharing the same railcar. State colleges and universities that had admitted Blacks now reversed themselves. In short, the North had won the Civil War but lost the peace. "The Yankees helped free us, so they say," a formerly enslaved North Carolinian named Thomas Hall remembered, "but [in 1877] they let us be put back in slavery again."

In an 1876 speech to the Republican National Convention, Frederick Douglass recognized that the party had won the Civil War, freed the enslaved, and passed amendments protecting their civil and voting rights, yet "what does it all amount to if the black man, after having been made free by the letter of your law, is unable to exercise that freedom . . . and is [again] to be subject to the slaveholder's shotgun?"

Reconstruction's Significance

CORE **OBJECTIVE**

5. Explain the significance of Reconstruction to the nation's future.

Yet for all its unfulfilled promises, Congressional Reconstruction did leave an enduring legacy—the Thirteenth, Fourteenth, and Fifteenth Amendments. Taken together, they represented a profound effort to extend the principle of personal and political equality to African Americans. As Frederick Douglass proclaimed in 1870 after the passage of the Fifteenth Amendment, "We have all [that] we asked, and more than we expected."

If Reconstruction's experiment in interracial democracy failed to provide true social equality or substantial economic opportunities for African Americans, it did create the essential constitutional foundation for future advances in the quest for equality and civil rights—and not just for African Americans, but for women and other minority groups.

Until the pivotal Reconstruction era, the states were responsible for protecting citizens' rights. Thereafter, thanks to the Fourteenth and Fifteenth Amendments, Blacks had gained equal rights (in theory), and the federal government had assumed responsibility for ensuring that states treated Blacks equally. A hundred years later, the cause of civil rights would finally be embraced again by the federal government. "With malice toward none, with charity for all, with firmness in the right," as Abraham Lincoln urged in his second inaugural address, "let us strive to finish the work we are in, to bind up a nation's wounds, to . . . cherish a just and lasting peace." His vision for a reconstructed America retains its relevance and urgency today.

Reviewing the

CORE OBJECTIVES | INQUIZITIVE

■ **Reconstruction Challenges** With the defeat of the Confederacy and the passage of the Thirteenth Amendment, the federal government had to develop policies and procedures to address a number of difficult questions: What was the status of the defeated states, and how would they be reintegrated into the nation's political life? What would be the political status of the formerly enslaved people, and what would the federal government do to integrate them into the nation's social and economic fabric?

■ **Reconstruction over Time** Abraham Lincoln and his successor, Southerner Andrew Johnson, preferred a more lenient and faster *Restoration Plan* for the southern states. The *Freedmen's Bureau* attempted to educate and aid formerly enslaved people, negotiate labor contracts, and reunite families. Lincoln's assassination led many Northerners to favor the *Radical Republicans,* who wanted a more transformative plan designed to end the grasp of the old plantation elite on the South's society and economy. Southern Whites resisted and established *Black codes* to restrict the lives of formerly enslaved people. *Congressional Reconstruction* responded by stipulating that to reenter the Union, former Confederate states had to ratify the *Fourteenth Amendment* (1868) and *Fifteenth Amendment* (1870) to the U.S. Constitution to expand and protect the rights of African Americans.

■ **Views of Reconstruction** Many formerly enslaved people found comfort in their families and the independent churches they established, but land ownership reverted to the old White elite, reducing newly freed Black farmers to *sharecropping.* African Americans enthusiastically participated in politics, with many serving as elected officials. Along with White southern Republicans (scalawags) and northern carpetbaggers, they worked to rebuild the southern economy. Many White Southerners, however, blamed their poverty on formerly enslaved people and Republicans, and they supported the *Ku Klux Klan*'s violent intimidation of the supporters of these Reconstruction efforts and the goal of "redemption," or White Democratic control of southern state governments.

■ **Political and Economic Developments and the End of Reconstruction** Scandals during the Grant administration involved an attempt to corner the gold market and the "whiskey ring's" plan to steal millions of dollars in tax revenue. In the face of these troubles and the economic downturn caused by both the *Panic of 1873* over railroad defaults and disagreement over whether to continue the use of *greenbacks* or return to the gold standard, northern support for Reconstruction eroded. Southern White *redeemers* were elected in 1874, successfully reversing the political progress of Republicans and Blacks. In the *Compromise of 1877,* Democrats agreed to the election of Republican Rutherford B. Hayes, who put an end to the Radical Republican administrations in the southern states.

■ **The Significance of Reconstruction** Southern state governments quickly renewed long-standing patterns of discrimination against African Americans, but the *Fourteenth* and *Fifteenth Amendments* remained enshrined in the Constitution, creating the essential constitutional foundation for future advances in civil rights. These amendments give the federal government responsibility for ensuring equal treatment and political equality within the states, a role it would increasingly assume in the twentieth century.

KEY TERMS

Radical Republicans *p. 589*

Freedmen's Bureau *p. 590*

Johnson's Restoration Plan *p. 593*

Black codes *p. 596*

Fourteenth Amendment (1866) *p. 597*

Congressional Reconstruction *p. 598*

Fifteenth Amendment (1870) *p. 601*

sharecropping *p. 606*

Ku Klux Klan *p. 608*

greenbacks *p. 615*

Panic of 1873 *p. 616*

redeemers *p. 619*

Compromise of 1877 *p. 622*

CHRONOLOGY

1865	Congress sets up the Freedmen's Bureau
	Lincoln assassinated on April 14, 1865
	Johnson issues Proclamation of Amnesty
1865–1866	Southern state legislatures pass Black codes
1866	Ku Klux Klan organized
	Congress passes Civil Rights Act
1867	Congress passes Military Reconstruction Act
	Freedmen begin participating in elections
1868	Fourteenth Amendment is ratified
	The U.S. House of Representatives impeaches President Andrew Johnson; the Senate fails to convict him
	Grant elected president
	Six former Confederate states readmitted to the Union
1869	Reestablishment of White Democratic rule ("redeemers") in former Confederate states
1870	Fifteenth Amendment ratified
	First Enforcement Acts passed
1872	Grant wins reelection
1873	Panic of 1873 triggers depression
1877	Compromise of 1877 ends Reconstruction

INQUIZITIVE

Go to InQuizitive to see what you've learned—and learn what you've missed—with personalized feedback along the way.

THINKING LIKE A HISTORIAN

DEBATING Reconstruction

Historians' interpretations of the past change over time. This happens for many reasons. Historians can revise their thinking in light of information from newly discovered *primary sources*. They can also interpret previously examined sources in new ways by applying new methodologies and theories. Finally, historians themselves are influenced by the values of their own society and times. Present-day events or particular personal interests can influence how historians think about the past. The study of how interpretations of history have changed is called *historiography*. It is the history of the field of history. For Part 4, *"A House Divided,"* the case study of debating Reconstruction demonstrates how the views of historians have changed dramatically over time.

For this exercise you have two tasks:

PART 1: Compare the two secondary sources on Reconstruction.

PART 2: Using primary sources, evaluate the arguments of the two secondary sources.

PART I Comparing and Contrasting Secondary Sources

Two *secondary sources*, the work of prominent historians from different eras, are included below for you to review. The first selection comes from William Dunning's (1857–1922) *Reconstruction, Political and Economic, 1865–1877*, written in 1907. Dunning was born on the eve of the Civil War to a well-to-do New Jersey family and enrolled at Columbia University soon after the end of Reconstruction. He lived during a time when racial segregation and White supremacy were the unchallenged law of the land, and he wrote some of the first books about Reconstruction.

Dunning was such a compelling force in the first half of the twentieth century that the many historians trained and influenced by him are referred to as the "Dunning School." He was particularly hostile to political idealists, a group that, in his mind, included abolitionists and Radical Republicans. Like many historians of his day, Dunning never questioned his own objectivity. However, later historians and activists have noted that his writings reflect the political beliefs and prejudices of his generation.

Interpretations of Reconstruction have undergone many changes since Dunning's time. The second excerpt, written ninety-one years later, is from Eric Foner's *The Story of American Freedom*. Born in 1943, Foner is the son of civil rights activists (one of them a historian) deeply concerned with the plight of African Americans. Foner completed his Ph.D. in 1969 during the height of the civil rights movement. Widely regarded as the leading interpretation of Reconstruction, Foner's writing on the period brings together much of the scholarship that has revised "Dunning School" interpretations of Reconstruction, particularly as they described the role of African Americans in American society.

Before reading these excerpts, review Chapter 15 on the transition from President Andrew Johnson's Restoration Plan to Congressional Reconstruction.

Compare the work of these two historians by answering the following questions. Be sure to support your answers with specific examples drawn from the selections by Dunning and Foner.

- What is the *topic* of each excerpt? What period of Reconstruction is the author writing about? What groups are examined?
- Generally, how does each author portray the Reconstruction process? What in each author's writing reveals the author's attitude about Reconstruction? How do those feelings—whether positive or negative—affect each author's point of view?
- What are the similarities in these two excerpts?
- What are the major differences in interpretation between the excerpts?

- What is the main *argument* each historian makes?
- How do these interpretations compare to that presented in Chapter 15?
- These two excerpts were written ninety-one years apart. How might this have influenced the development of their arguments?

Secondary Source 1

William Dunning, *Reconstruction, Political and Economic, 1865–1877*

It was, indeed, no novelty for the people of the South to be subject to government by the United States army. . . . The reasoning by which the policy of Congress was justified in the North was regarded in the South as founded on falsehood and malice. So far as the "Black codes" were concerned, it was pointed out that they could not be alleged as evidences of a tendency to restore slavery or introduce peonage [dependence], since the offensive acts had in many of the states been repealed by the legislatures themselves, and in all had been duly superseded by the civil rights act. The much-exploited outrages on freedmen and Unionists were declared to be exaggerated or distorted reports of incidents which any time of social tension must produce among the criminal classes. The rejection of the Fourteenth Amendment was considered as merely a dignified refusal by honorable men to be the instruments of their own humiliation and shame.

Under all these circumstances the southerners felt that the policy of Congress had no real cause save the purpose of radical politicians to prolong and extend their party power by means of negro suffrage [voting rights]. This and this alone was the purpose for which major-generals had been empowered to remodel the state governments at their will, to exercise through general orders the functions of executive, legislature, and courts, and to compel the white people to recognize the blacks as their equals wherever the stern word of military command could reach. It was as inconceivable to the southerners that rational men of the North should seriously approve of negro suffrage per se as it had been in 1860 to the northerners that rational men of the South should approve of secession per se. Hence, in the one case as in the other, a craving for political power was assumed to be the only explanation of an otherwise unintelligible proceeding.

Source: Dunning, William. *Reconstruction, Political and Economic, 1865–1877.* New York: Harper & Bros., 1907. 109–112.

Secondary Source 2

Eric Foner, *The Story of American Freedom*

Rejecting the idea that emancipation implied civil or political equality or opportunities to acquire property or advance economically, rights northerners deemed essential to a free society, most white southerners insisted that blacks must remain a dependent plantation workforce in a laboring situation not very different from slavery. During Presidential Reconstruction—the period from 1865 to 1867 when Lincoln's successor, Andrew Johnson, gave the white South a free hand in determining the contours of Reconstruction—southern state governments enforced this view of black freedom by enacting the notorious Black Codes, which denied blacks equality before the law and political rights and imposed on them mandatory year-long labor contracts, coercive apprenticeship regulations, and criminal penalties for breach of contract. Through these laws, the South's white leadership sought to ensure that plantation agriculture survived emancipation.

Thus, the death of slavery did not automatically mean the birth of freedom. But the Black Codes so flagrantly violated free labor principles that they invoked the wrath of the Republican North. Southern reluctance to accept the reality of emancipation resulted in a monumental struggle between President Andrew Johnson and the Republican Congress over the legacy of the Civil War. The result was the enactment of laws and constitutional amendments that redrew the boundaries of citizenship and expanded the definition of freedom for all Americans. . . .

Much of the ensuing conflict over Reconstruction revolved around the problem, as Senator Lyman Trumbull of Illinois put it, of defining "what slavery is and what liberty is." . . . By 1866, a consensus had emerged within the Republican Party that civil equality was an essential attribute of freedom. The Civil War had elevated "equality" to a status in the vocabulary of freedom it had not enjoyed since the Revolution. . . . In a remarkable, if temporary, reversal of political traditions, the newly empowered national state now sought to identify and protect the rights of all Americans.

Source: Foner, Eric. *The Story of American Freedom*. New York: W. W. Norton & Company, 1998. 103–105.

PART I I Using Primary Sources to Evaluate Secondary Sources

When historians are faced with competing interpretations of the past, they often look at primary source material as part of the process of evaluating the different arguments. In the following selections, you'll find *primary sources* relating to the period of Reconstruction.

Carefully read the primary sources and answer the following questions. Decide how the primary source documents support or refute Dunning's and Foner's arguments about this period. You may find that some documents do both but for different parts of each historian's interpretation. Be sure to identify which specific components of each historian's argument the documents support or refute.

- Which of the two historians' arguments is best supported by the primary source documents? If you find that both arguments are well supported by the evidence, why do you think the two historians produced such different interpretations?
- Based on your comparison of the two arguments and your analysis of the primary sources, how has the interpretation of Reconstruction by historians shifted over time? What can you conclude about historiography from the work of these two historians?

Primary Source 1

Union army general Carl Schurz, *Report on the Condition of the South*

A belief, conviction, or prejudice, or whatever you may call it, so widely spread and apparently so deeply rooted as this, that the negro will not work without physical compulsion, is certainly calculated to have a very serious influence upon the conduct of the people entertaining it. It naturally produced a desire to preserve slavery in its original form as much and as long as possible—and you may, perhaps, remember the admission made by one of the provisional governors, over two months after the close of the war, that the people of his State still indulged in a lingering hope slavery might yet be preserved—or to introduce into the new system that element of physical compulsion which would make the negro work. Efforts were, indeed, made to hold the negro in his old state of subjection, especially in such localities where our military forces had not yet penetrated, or where the country was not garrisoned in detail. Here and there planters succeeded for a limited period to keep their former slaves in ignorance, or at least doubt, about their new rights; but the main agency employed for that purpose was force and intimidation. In many instances negroes who walked away from the plantations, or were found upon the roads, were shot or otherwise severely punished, which was calculated to produce the impression among those remaining with their masters that an attempt to escape from slavery would result in certain destruction. A large proportion of the many acts of violence committed is undoubtedly attributable to this motive.

Source: Schurz, Carl. *Report on the Condition of the South.* 39th Cong., 1st sess., Senate Executive Document 2, 1865. 19.

Primary Source 2

Mississippi Vagrant Law, 1865

All freedmen, free negroes and mulattoes in this State, over the age of eighteen years, found on the second Monday in January, 1866, or thereafter, with no lawful employment or business, or found unlawfully assembling themselves together, either in the day or night time, and all white persons so assembling themselves with freedmen, free negroes or mulattoes, or usually associating with freedmen, free negroes or mulattoes, on terms of equality, or living in adultery or fornication with a freed woman, free negro or mulatto, shall be deemed vagrants, and on conviction thereof shall be fined in a sum not exceeding, in the case of a freedman, free negro, or mulatto, fifty dollars, and a white man two hundred dollars, and imprisoned at the discretion of the court, the free negro not exceeding ten days, and the white man not exceeding six months. . . . All fines and forfeitures collected under the provisions of this act shall be paid into the county treasury for general county purposes, and in case any freedman, free negro or mulatto shall fail for five days after the imposition of any fine or forfeiture upon him or her for violation of any of the provisions of this act to pay the same, that it shall be, and is hereby, made the duty of the sheriff of the proper county to hire out said freedman, free negro or mulatto, to any person who will, for the shortest period of service, pay said fine and forfeiture and all costs. . . .

Source: Mississippi Vagrant Law, *Laws of Mississippi, 1865*, 90. In *Documentary History of Reconstruction: Political, Military, Social, Religious, Educational & Industrial, 1865 to the Present Time.* Edited by Walter Lynwood Fleming, 1:283–286. Cleveland, Ohio: The Arthur H. Clark Company, 1906.

Primary Source 3

Civil Rights Act of 1866

Be it enacted, . . . That all persons born in the United States and not subject to any foreign power, excluding Indians not taxed, are hereby declared to be citizens of the United States; and such citizens, of every race and color, without regard to any previous condition of slavery or involuntary servitude, except as a punishment for crime whereof the party shall have been duly convicted, shall have the same right, in every State and Territory in the United States, to make and enforce contracts, to sue, be parties, and give evidence, to inherit, purchase, lease, sell, hold, and convey real and personal property, and to full and equal benefit of all laws and proceedings for the security of person and property, as is enjoyed by white citizens, and shall be subject to like punishment, pains and penalties, and to none other, any law, statute, ordinance, regulation, or custom, to the contrary notwithstanding.

Source: Civil Rights Act of 1866, 14 Stat. 27 (April 9, 1866).

Primary Source 4

Radical Republican Thaddeus Stevens, "The Advantages of Negro Suffrage"

Unless the rebel States, before admission, should be made republican in spirit, and placed under the guardianship of loyal men, all our blood and treasure will have been spent in vain. . . . There is more reason why colored voters should be admitted in the rebel States than in the Territories. In the States they form the great mass of the loyal men. Possibly with their aid loyal governments may be established in most of those States. Without it all are sure to be ruled by traitors; and loyal men, black and white, will be oppressed, exiled, or murdered. . . . Have not loyal blacks quite as good a right to choose rulers and make laws as rebel whites? In the second place, it is a necessity in order to protect the loyal white men in the seceded States. The white Union men are in a great minority in each of those States. With them the blacks would act in a body; and it is believed that in each of said States, except one, the two united would form a majority, control the States, and protect themselves. Now they are the victims of daily murder. They must suffer constant persecution or be exiled. . . . Another good reason is, it would insure the ascendency of the Union party. . . . I believe . . . that on the continued ascendency of that party depends the safety of this great nation. If impartial suffrage is excluded in the rebel States, then every one of them is sure to send a solid rebel representative delegation to Congress, and cast a solid rebel electoral vote. . . . I am for negro suffrage in every rebel State. If it be just, it should not be denied; if it be necessary, it should be adopted; if it be a punishment to traitors, they deserve it.

Source: Stevens, Thaddeus. *Congressional Globe*, January 3, 1867, 252. In *Documentary History of Reconstruction: Political, Military, Social, Religious, Educational & Industrial, 1865 to the Present Time.* Edited by Walter Lynwood Fleming, 1:149–150. Cleveland, Ohio: The Arthur H. Clark Company, 1906.

Glossary

abolitionism Movement that called for an immediate end to slavery throughout the United States.

affirmative action Programs designed to give preferential treatment to women and people of color as compensation for past injustices and to counterbalance systematic inequalities.

Affordable Care Act (ACA) (2010) Vast health-care-reform initiative championed by President Obama and widely criticized by Republicans that aimed to make health insurance more affordable and make health care accessible to everyone, regardless of income or prior medical conditions.

Agricultural Adjustment Act (1933) Legislation that paid farmers to produce less in order to raise crop prices for all; the AAA was later declared unconstitutional by the U.S. Supreme Court in the case of *United States v. Butler* (1936).

Albany Plan of Union (1754) A failed proposal by the seven northern colonies in anticipation of the French and Indian War, urging the unification of the colonies under one Crown-appointed president.

Alien and Sedition Acts of 1798 Four measures passed during the undeclared war with France that limited the freedoms of speech and press and restricted the liberty of immigrants.

alliance with France Critical diplomatic, military, and economic alliance between France and the newly independent United States, codified by the Treaty of Alliance (1778).

American Anti-Imperialist League Coalition of anti-imperialist groups united in 1899 to protest American territorial expansion, especially in the Philippine Islands; its membership included prominent politicians, industrialists, labor leaders, and social reformers.

American Colonization Society (ACS) Established in 1816, an organization whose mission was to return freed, formerly enslaved people to Africa.

American Federation of Labor Founded in 1886 as a national federation of trade unions made up of skilled workers.

American System Economic plan championed by Henry Clay of Kentucky that called for federal tariffs on imports, a strong national bank, and federally financed internal improvements—roads, bridges, canals—all intended to strengthen the national economy and end American economic dependence on Great Britain.

American Tobacco Company Business founded in 1890 by North Carolina's James Buchanan Duke, who combined the major tobacco manufacturers of the time, controlling 90 percent of the country's booming cigarette production.

Anaconda Plan Union's primary war strategy calling for a naval blockade of major Southern seaports and then dividing the Confederacy by gaining control of the Tennessee, Cumberland, and Mississippi Rivers.

anti-Federalists Opponents of the Constitution as an infringement on individual and states' rights, whose criticism led to the addition of a Bill of Rights to the document. Many anti-Federalists later joined Thomas Jefferson's Democratic-Republican party.

Appomattox Court House Virginia village where Confederate general Robert E. Lee surrendered to Union general Ulysses S. Grant on April 9, 1865.

Articles of Confederation The first form of government for the United States, ratified by the original thirteen states in 1781; weak in central authority, it was replaced by the U.S. Constitution drafted in 1787.

Atlanta Compromise (1895) Speech by Booker T. Washington that called for the Black community to strive for economic prosperity before demanding political and social equality.

Atlantic Charter (1941) Joint statement crafted by Franklin D. Roosevelt and British prime minister Winston Churchill that listed the war goals of the Allied Powers.

"Axis" alliance Military alliance formed in 1937 by the three major fascist powers: Germany, Italy, and Japan.

baby boom Markedly high birth rate in the years following World War II, leading to the biggest demographic "bubble" in U.S. history.

Bacon's Rebellion (1676) Unsuccessful revolt led by planter Nathaniel Bacon against Virginia governor William Berkeley's administration, which, Bacon charged, had failed to protect settlers from Indian raids.

Bank of the United States (1791) National bank responsible for holding and transferring federal government funds, making business loans, and issuing a national currency.

Bank War Political struggle in the early 1830s between President Jackson and financier Nicholas Biddle over the renewing of the Second Bank's charter.

Barbary pirates North Africans who waged war (1801–1805) on the United States after Jefferson refused to pay tribute (a bribe) to protect American ships.

Battle of Antietam (1862) Turning-point battle near Sharpsburg, Maryland, leaving almost 25,000 soldiers dead or wounded, in which Union forces halted a Confederate invasion of the North.

Battle of Gettysburg (1863) A monumental three-day battle in southern Pennsylvania, widely considered a turning point in the war, in which Union forces defeated Lee's Confederate army and forced it back into Virginia.

Battle of Midway A 1942 battle that proved to be the turning point in the Pacific front during World War II; it was the Japanese navy's first major defeat in 350 years.

Battle of New Orleans (1815) Final major battle in the War of 1812, in which the Americans under General Andrew Jackson unexpectedly and decisively countered the British attempt to seize the port of New Orleans, Louisiana.

Battle of Tippecanoe (1811) Battle in northern Indiana between U.S. troops and Native American warriors led by prophet Tenskwatawa, the half-brother of Tecumseh.

Battle of Trenton (1776) First decisive American victory that proved pivotal in reviving morale and demonstrating General Washington's abilities.

Battle of Vicksburg (1863) A protracted battle in northern Mississippi in which Union forces under Ulysses S. Grant besieged the last major Confederate fortress on the Mississippi River, forcing the inhabitants into starvation and then submission on July 4, 1863.

Battle of Yorktown (1781) Last major battle of the Revolutionary War; General Cornwallis, along with over 7,000 British troops, surrendered to George Washington at Yorktown, Virginia, on October 17, 1781.

Battles of Saratoga (1777) Decisive defeat of almost 6,000 British troops under General John Burgoyne in several battles near Saratoga, New York, in October 1777; the American victory helped convince France to enter the war on the side of the Patriots.

Bay of Pigs (1961) Failed CIA operation that deployed Cuban rebels to overthrow Fidel Castro's Communist regime.

Beats Group of bohemian writers, artists, and musicians who flouted convention in favor of liberated forms of self-expression.

Berlin airlift (1948–1949) Effort by the United States and Great Britain to fly massive amounts of food and supplies into West Berlin in response to the Soviet land blockade of the city.

Berlin Wall Twenty-seven-mile-long concrete wall constructed in 1961 by East German authorities to stop the flow of East Germans fleeing to West Berlin.

Bill of Rights (1791) First ten amendments to the U.S. Constitution, adopted in 1791 to guarantee individual rights and to help secure ratification of the Constitution by the states.

birth rate Proportion of births per 1,000 of the total population.

Black codes Laws passed in southern states to restrict the rights of formerly enslaved people.

Black Lives Matter (BLM) Sociopolitical movement in protest of police brutality toward Black people, with origins in Missouri and a growing global presence.

Black Power movement Militant form of civil rights protest focused on urban communities in the North that emerged as a response to impatience with the nonviolent tactics of Martin Luther King, Jr.

Bleeding Kansas (1856) A series of violent conflicts in the Kansas Territory between anti-slavery and pro-slavery factions over the status of slavery.

blitzkrieg (1940) The German "lightning war" strategy characterized by swift, well-organized attacks using infantry, tanks, and warplanes.

Bonus Expeditionary Force (1932) Protest march on Washington, D.C., by thousands of military veterans and their families, calling for immediate payment of their service bonus certificates; violence ensued when President Herbert Hoover ordered their tent villages cleared.

Boston Massacre (1770) Violent confrontation between British soldiers and a Boston mob on March 5, 1770, in which five colonists were killed.

Boston Tea Party (1773) Demonstration against the Tea Act of 1773 in which the Sons of Liberty, dressed as Indians, dumped hundreds of chests of British-owned tea into Boston Harbor.

bracero program (1942) System that permitted seasonal farmworkers from Mexico to work in the United States on yearlong contracts.

Brown v. Board of Education **(1954)** Landmark Supreme Court case that struck down racial segregation in public schools and declared "separate but equal" unconstitutional.

burial mounds A funereal tradition, practiced in the Mississippi and Ohio Valleys by the Adena-Hopewell cultures, of erecting massive mounds of earth over graves, often shaped in the designs of serpents and other animals.

Bush Doctrine National security policy launched in 2002 by which the Bush administration claimed the right to launch preemptive military attacks against perceived enemies, particularly outlaw nations or terrorist organizations believed to possess WMD.

Cahokia The largest chiefdom of the Mississippian Indian culture located in present-day Illinois and the site of a sophisticated farming settlement that supported up to 15,000 inhabitants.

California Gold Rush (1849) A massive migration of gold hunters, mostly young men, who transformed the national economy after massive amounts of gold were discovered in northern California.

campaign of 1828 Bitter presidential contest between Democrat Andrew Jackson and National Republican John Quincy Adams (running for reelection), resulting in Jackson's victory.

Camp David Accords (1978) Peace agreement facilitated by President Carter between Prime Minister Menachem Begin of Israel and President Anwar el-Sadat of Egypt, the first Arab head of state to officially recognize the state of Israel.

Carnegie Steel Company Corporation under the leadership of Andrew Carnegie that came to dominate the American steel industry.

Central Intelligence Agency (CIA) Intelligence-gathering government agency founded in 1947; under President Eisenhower's orders, it secretly undermined elected governments deemed susceptible to communism.

Chicago Democratic National Convention Convention in 1968 where the social unrest over the Vietnam War and civil rights movement came to a violent head between student protesters and the Chicago police. Hubert H. Humphrey was ultimately nominated as the presidential candidate for the Democratic Party.

Chinese Exclusion Act (1882) Federal law that barred Chinese laborers from immigrating to America.

Christian Right Christian conservatives with a faith-based political agenda that includes prohibition of abortion and allowing prayer in public schools.

citizen-soldiers Part-time non-professional soldiers, mostly poor farmers or recent immigrants who had been indentured servants, who played an important role in the Revolutionary War.

Civil Rights Act of 1964 Legislation that outlawed discrimination in public accommodations and employment, passed at the urging of President Lyndon B. Johnson.

civil service reform An extended effort led by political reformers to end the patronage system; led to the Pendleton Act (1883), which called for government jobs to be awarded based on merit rather than party loyalty.

Clayton Anti-Trust Act (1914) Legislation that served to enhance the Sherman Anti-Trust Act (1890) by clarifying what constituted "monopolistic" activities and declaring that labor unions were not to be viewed as "monopolies in restraint of trade."

clipper ships Tall, slender ships favored over older merchant ships for their speed; ultimately gave way to steamships because clipper ships lacked cargo space.

Coercive Acts (1774) Four parliamentary measures that required the colonies to pay for the Boston Tea Party's damages: closed the port of Boston, imposed a military government, disallowed colonial trials of British soldiers, and forced the quartering of troops in private homes.

Columbian Exchange The transfer of biological and social elements, such as plants, animals, people, diseases, and cultural practices, among Europe, the Americas, and Africa in the wake of Christopher Columbus's voyages to the New World.

Committee of Correspondence Group organized by Samuel Adams to address American grievances, assert American rights, and form a network of rebellion.

***Common Sense* (1776)** Popular pamphlet written by Thomas Paine attacking British principles of hereditary rule and monarchical government and advocating a declaration of American independence.

Compromise of 1850 A package of five bills presented to the Congress by Henry Clay intended to avoid secession or civil war by reducing tensions between North and South over the status of slavery.

Compromise of 1877 Secret deal forged by congressional leaders to resolve the disputed election of 1876; Republican Rutherford B. Hayes, who had lost the popular vote, was declared the winner in exchange for his pledge to remove federal troops from the South, marking the end of Reconstruction.

Comstock Lode A mine in eastern Nevada acquired by Canadian fur trapper Henry Comstock that between 1860 and 1880 yielded almost $1 billion worth of gold and silver.

Congressional Reconstruction Phase of Reconstruction directed by Radical Republicans through the passage of three laws: the Military Reconstruction Act, the Command of the Army Act, and the Tenure of Office Act.

conquistadores Term from the Spanish word for "conquerors," applied to Spanish and Portuguese soldiers who conquered lands held by indigenous peoples in central and southern America as well as the current states of Texas, New Mexico, Arizona, and California.

consumer culture A society in which mass production and consumption of nationally advertised products comes to dictate much of social life and status.

containment U.S. cold war strategy to exert political, economic, and, if necessary, military pressure on global Soviet expansion as a means of combating the spread of communism.

Continental Army Army authorized by Continental Congress, 1755–1784, to fight the British; commanded by George Washington.

contrabands Freedom seekers who sought refuge in Union military camps or who lived in areas of the Confederacy under Union control.

Contract with America (1994) List of conservative promises in response to the supposed liberalism of the Clinton administration; drafted by Speaker of the House Newt Gingrich and other congressional Republicans as a campaign tactic for the 1994 midterm elections.

corrupt bargain Scandal in which presidential candidate and Speaker of the House Henry Clay secured John Quincy Adams's victory over Andrew Jackson in the 1824 election, supposedly in exchange for naming Clay secretary of state.

cotton White fibers harvested from plants that made comfortable, easy-to-clean products, especially clothing; the most valuable cash crop driving the economy in nineteenth-century United States and Great Britain.

cotton gin Hand-operated machine invented by Eli Whitney that quickly removed seeds from cotton bolls, enabling the mass production of cotton in nineteenth-century America.

cotton kingdom Cotton-producing region, relying predominantly on slave labor, that spanned from North Carolina west to Louisiana and reached as far north as southern Illinois.

counterculture Unorganized youth rebellion against mainstream institutions, values, and behavior that more often focused on cultural radicalism rather than political activism.

COVID-19 pandemic Global pandemic resulting from the airborne and contagious coronavirus disease which took millions of lives, debilitated governments and institutions, and necessitated new cultural norms of distancing and face masking.

crop-lien system Credit system used by sharecroppers and share tenants who pledged a portion ("share") of their future crop to local merchants or landowners in exchange for farming supplies, food, and clothing.

Cuban missile crisis (1962) Thirteen-day U.S.-Soviet standoff sparked by the discovery of Soviet missile sites in Cuba; closest the world has come to nuclear war since 1945.

cult of domesticity Pervasive nineteenth-century ideology urging women to celebrate their role as manager of the household and nurturer of the children.

***Dartmouth College v. Woodward* (1819)** Supreme Court ruling that enlarged the definition of *contract* to put corporations beyond the reach of the states that chartered them.

Daughters of Liberty Colonial women who protested the British government's tax policies by boycotting British products, such as clothing, and who wove their own fabric, or "homespun."

Dawes Severalty Act of 1887 Federal legislation that divided ancestral Native American lands among the heads of each Indian family in an attempt to "Americanize" Indians by forcing them to become farmers working individual plots of land.

death rate Proportion of deaths per 1,000 of the total population; also called *mortality rate.*

Declaration of Independence (1776) Formal statement, principally drafted by Thomas Jefferson and adopted by the Second Continental Congress on July 4, 1776, that officially announced the thirteen colonies' break with Great Britain.

Declaration of Rights and Sentiments (1848) Document based on the Declaration of Independence that called for gender equality, written primarily by Elizabeth Cady Stanton and signed by Seneca Falls Convention delegates.

détente Period of improving relations between the United States and Communist nations, particularly China and the Soviet Union, during the Nixon administration.

Deists Those who applied Enlightenment thought to religion, emphasizing reason, morality, and natural law rather than scriptural authority or an ever-present god intervening in the daily life of humans.

de Lôme letter (1898) Private correspondence written by the Spanish ambassador to the United States, Depuy de Lôme, that described President McKinley as "weak"; the letter was stolen by Cuban revolutionaries and published in the *New York Journal* in 1898, deepening American resentment of Spain and moving the two countries closer to war in Cuba.

Dien Bien Phu Cluster of Vietnamese villages and site of a major Vietnamese victory over the French in the First Indochina War.

Distribution Act (1836) Law requiring distribution of the federal budget surplus to the states, creating chaos among unregulated state banks dependent on such federal funds.

Dixiecrats Breakaway faction of White southern Democrats who defected from the national Democratic party in 1948 to protest the party's increased support for Black civil rights and to nominate their own segregationist candidates for elective office.

dollar diplomacy Practice advocated by President Theodore Roosevelt in which the U.S. government fostered American investments in less developed nations and then used U.S. military force to protect those investments.

***Dred Scott v. Sandford* (1857)** U.S. Supreme Court ruling that enslaved people were not U.S. citizens and that Congress could not prohibit slavery in territories.

Dust Bowl Vast area of the Midwest where windstorms blew away millions of tons of topsoil from parched farmland after a long drought in the 1930s, causing great social distress and a massive migration of farm families.

Eastern Woodland peoples Various Native American societies, particularly the Algonquian, Iroquoian, and Muskogean regional groups, who once dominated the Atlantic seaboard from Maine to Louisiana.

Economic Opportunity Act of 1964 Key legislation in President Johnson's "War on Poverty" that created the Office of Economic Opportunity and programs like Head Start and the work-study financial-aid program for low-income college students.

election of 1800 Presidential election involving Thomas Jefferson and John Adams that resulted in the first Democratic-Republican victory after the Federalist administrations of George Washington and John Adams.

election of 1864 Abraham Lincoln's successful reelection campaign, capitalizing on Union military successes in Georgia, to defeat his Democratic opponent, former general George B. McClellan, who ran on a peace platform.

Emancipation Proclamation (1863) Military order issued by President Abraham Lincoln that freed enslaved people in areas still controlled by the Confederacy.

Embargo Act (1807) A law promoted by President Thomas Jefferson prohibiting American ships from leaving for foreign ports, in order to safeguard them from British and French attacks. This ban on American exports proved disastrous to the U.S. economy.

encomienda A land-grant system under which Spanish army officers (*conquistadores*) were awarded large parcels of land taken from Native Americans.

Enlightenment A revolution in thought begun in Europe in the seventeenth century that emphasized reason and science over the authority and myths of traditional religion.

Environmental Protection Agency (EPA) Federal environmental agency created by Nixon to appease the demands of congressional Democrats for a federal environmental watchdog agency.

Erie Canal (1825) Most important and profitable of the many barge canals built in the early nineteenth century, connecting the Great Lakes to the Hudson River and conveying so much cargo that it made New York City the nation's largest port.

ethnic cleansing Systematic removal of an ethnic group from a territory through violence or intimidation in order to create a homogeneous society; the term was popularized by the Yugoslav policy brutally targeting Albanian Muslims in Kosovo.

Exodusters African Americans who migrated west from the South in search of a haven from racism and poverty after the collapse of Radical Republican rule.

Fair Deal (1949) President Truman's proposals to build upon the New Deal with national health insurance, the repeal of the Taft-Hartley Act, new civil rights legislation, and other initiatives; most were rejected by the Republican-controlled Congress.

"falling-domino" theory This theory that if one country fell to communism, its neighboring countries would necessarily follow suit.

Farmers' Alliances Like the Granger movement, these organizations sought to address the issues of small farming communities; however, Alliances emphasized more political action and called for the creation of a third party to advocate their concerns.

fascism A radical form of totalitarian government that emerged in 1920s Italy and Germany in which a dictator uses propaganda and brute force to seize control of all aspects of national life.

Federal Deposit Insurance Corporation (FDIC) (1933) Independent government agency, established to prevent bank panics, that guarantees the safety of deposits in citizens' savings accounts.

Federal Reserve Act (1913) Legislation passed by Congress to create a new national banking system in order to regulate the nation's currency supply and ensure the stability and integrity of member banks that made up the Federal Reserve System across the nation.

Federal Trade Commission (1914) Independent agency created by the Wilson administration that replaced the Bureau of Corporations as an even more powerful tool to combat unfair trade practices and monopolies.

Federal-Aid Highway Act (1956) Largest federal project in U.S. history, which created a national network of interstate highways.

federalism Concept of dividing governmental authority between the national government and the states.

The Federalist Papers Collection of eighty-five essays, published widely in newspapers in 1787 and 1788, written by Alexander Hamilton, James Madison, and John Jay in support of adopting the proposed U.S. Constitution.

field hands Enslaved people who toiled in the cotton or cane fields in organized work gangs.

Fifteenth Amendment (1870) Amendment to the U.S. Constitution forbidding states to deny any male citizen the right to vote on grounds of "race, color or previous condition of servitude."

First New Deal (1933–1935) Franklin D. Roosevelt's ambitious first-term cluster of economic and social programs designed to combat the Great Depression.

First Red Scare (1919–1920) Outbreak of anti-Communist hysteria that included the arrest without warrants of thousands of suspected radicals, most of whom (especially Russian immigrants) were deported.

flappers Young women of the 1920s whose rebellion against prewar standards of femininity included wearing shorter dresses, bobbing their hair, dancing to jazz music, driving cars, smoking cigarettes, and indulging in illegal drinking and gambling.

Force Bill (1833) Legislation, sparked by the nullification crisis in South Carolina, that authorized the president's use of the army to compel states to comply with federal law.

Fourteen Points President Woodrow Wilson's proposed plan for the peace agreement after the Great War, which included the creation of a "league" of nations intended to keep the peace.

Fourteenth Amendment (1866) Amendment to the U.S. Constitution guaranteeing equal protection under the law to all U.S. citizens, including formerly enslaved people.

Freedmen's Bureau Federal Reconstruction agency established to protect the legal rights of formerly enslaved people and to assist with their education, jobs, health care, and land ownership.

Freedom Riders Activists who, beginning in 1961, traveled by bus through the South to test federal court rulings that banned segregation on buses and trains.

Free-Soil party A political coalition created in 1848 that opposed the expansion of slavery into the new western territories.

French and Indian War (Seven Years' War) (1756–1763) The last and most important of four colonial wars between England and France for control of North America east of the Mississippi River.

French Revolution Revolutionary movement beginning in 1789 that overthrew the monarchy and transformed France into an unstable republic before Napoléon Bonaparte assumed power in 1799.

frontier revivals Religious revival movement within the Second Great Awakening, which took place in frontier churches in western territories and states in the early nineteenth century.

Fugitive Slave Act (1850) A part of the Compromise of 1850 that authorized federal officials to help capture and then return freedom seekers to their owners without trials.

Ghost Dance movement A spiritual and political movement among Native Americans whose followers performed a ceremonial "ghost dance" intended to connect the living with the dead and make the Native Americans bulletproof in battles intended to restore their homelands.

***Gibbons v. Ogden* (1824)** Supreme Court case that gave the federal government the power to regulate interstate commerce.

GI Bill of Rights (1944) Provided unemployment, education, and financial benefits for World War II veterans to ease their transition back to the civilian world.

Gilded Age (1860–1896) An era of dramatic industrial and urban growth characterized by widespread political corruption and loose government oversight of corporations.

glasnost Russian term for "openness"; applied to the loosening of censorship in the Soviet Union under Mikhail Gorbachev.

globalization An important and controversial transformation of the world economy led by the growing number of multinational companies and the internet, whereby an international marketplace for goods and services was created.

Glorious Revolution (1688) Successful coup, instigated by a group of English aristocrats, that overthrew King James II and instated William of Orange and Mary, his English wife, to the English throne.

Granger movement Began by offering social and educational activities for isolated farmers and their families and later started to promote "cooperatives" where farmers could join together to buy, store, and sell their crops to avoid the high fees charged by brokers and other middlemen.

Great Awakening Emotional religious revival movement that swept the thirteen colonies from the 1730s through the 1740s.

Great Depression (1929–1941) Worst economic downturn in American history; it was spurred by the stock market crash in the fall of 1929 and lasted until the Second World War.

Great Migration Mass exodus of African Americans from the rural South to the Northeast and Midwest during and after the Great War.

Great Recession (2007–2009) Massive, prolonged economic downturn sparked by the collapse of the housing market and the financial institutions holding unpaid mortgages; resulted in 9 million Americans losing their jobs.

Great Sioux War Conflict between Sioux and Cheyenne Indians and federal troops over lands in the Dakotas in the mid-1870s.

Great Society Term coined by President Lyndon B. Johnson in his 1965 State of the Union address, in which he proposed legislation to address problems of voting rights, poverty, diseases, education, immigration, and the environment.

greenbacks Paper money issued during the Civil War, which sparked currency debates after the war.

Harlem Renaissance The nation's first self-conscious Black literary and artistic movement; centered in New York City's Harlem district, which had a largely Black population in the wake of the Great Migration from the South.

Hartford Convention (1814) A series of secret meetings in December 1814 and January 1815 at which New England Federalists protested American involvement in the War of 1812 and discussed several constitutional amendments, including limiting each president to one term, designed to weaken the dominant Republican party.

Haymarket Riot (1886) Violent uprising in Haymarket Square, Chicago, where police clashed with labor demonstrators in the aftermath of a bombing.

headright A land-grant policy that promised fifty acres to any colonist who could afford passage to Virginia and fifty more for each accompanying servant. The headright policy was eventually expanded to include any colonists—and was also adopted in other colonies.

Hessians German mercenary soldiers who were paid by the British royal government to fight alongside the British army.

Hiroshima (1945) Japanese port city that was the first target of the newly developed atomic bomb on August 6, 1945. Most of the city was destroyed.

HIV/AIDS Human immunodeficiency virus (HIV) transmitted via the bodily fluids of infected persons to cause acquired immunodeficiency syndrome (AIDS), an often-fatal disease of the immune system when it appeared in the 1980s.

holding company Corporation established to own and manage other companies' stock rather than to produce goods and services itself.

Holocaust Systematic efforts by the Nazis to exterminate the Jews of Europe, resulting in the murder of over 6 million Jews and more than a million other "undesirables."

Homestead Act (1862) Legislation granting "home-steads" of 160 acres of government-owned land to settlers who agreed to work the land for at least five years.

Homestead Steel Strike (1892) Labor conflict at the Homestead steel mill near Pittsburgh, Pennsylvania, culminating in a battle between strikers and private security agents hired by the factory's management.

horses The animals that the Spanish introduced to the Americas, eventually transforming many Native American cultures.

House Committee on Un-American Activities (HUAC) Committee of the U.S. House of Representatives formed in 1938; originally tasked with investigating Nazi subversion during the Second World War and later focused on rooting out Communists in the government and the motion-picture industry.

Immigration Act of 1924 Federal legislation intended to favor northern and western European immigrants over those from southern and eastern Europe by restricting the number of immigrants from any one European country to 2 percent of the total number of immigrants per year, with an overall limit of slightly over 150,000 new arrivals per year.

Immigration and Nationality Services Act of 1965 Legislation that abolished discriminatory quotas based upon immigrants' national origin and treated all nationalities and races equally.

imperialism The use of diplomatic or military force to extend a nation's power and enhance its economic interests, often by acquiring territory or colonies and justifying such behavior with assumptions of racial superiority.

indentured servants Settlers who signed on for a temporary period of servitude to a master in exchange for passage to the New World.

Independent Treasury Act (1840) System created by Van Buren that moved federal funds from favored state banks to the U.S. Treasury, whose financial transactions could only be in gold or silver.

Indian Removal Act (1830) Law permitting the forced relocation of Indians to federal lands west of the Mississippi River in exchange for the land they occupied in the East and South.

Indian wars Bloody conflicts between U.S. soldiers and Native Americans that raged in the West from the early 1860s to the late 1870s, sparked by American settlers moving into ancestral Indian lands.

Industrial Revolution Major shift in the nineteenth century from handmade manufacturing to mass production in mills and factories using water-, coal-, and steam-powered machinery.

infectious diseases Also called contagious diseases, illnesses that can pass from one person to another by way of invasive biological organisms able to reproduce in the bodily tissues of their hosts. Europeans unwittingly brought many such diseases to the Americas, devastating the Native American peoples.

***The Influence of Sea Power upon History,* 1660–1783** Historical work in which Rear Admiral Alfred Thayer Mahan argued that a nation's greatness and prosperity come from the power of its navy; the book helped bolster imperialist sentiment in the United States in the late nineteenth century.

Intermediate-Range Nuclear Forces (INF) Treaty (1987) Agreement signed by U.S. president Ronald Reagan and Soviet premier Mikhail Gorbachev to eliminate the deployment of intermediate-range missiles with nuclear warheads.

internal improvements Construction of roads, canals, and other projects intended to facilitate the flow of goods and people.

Interstate Commerce Commission (ICC) (1887) An independent federal agency established in 1887 to oversee businesses engaged in interstate trade, especially railroads, but whose regulatory power was limited when tested in the courts.

Iran-Contra affair (1987) Reagan administration scandal over the secret, unlawful U.S. sale of arms to Iran in partial exchange for the release of hostages in Lebanon; the arms money in turn was used illegally to aid Nicaraguan right-wing insurgents, the Contras.

Iranian hostage crisis (1979) Storming of the U.S. embassy in Tehran by Iranian revolutionaries, who held fifty-two Americans hostage for 444 days, despite President Carter's appeals for their release and a botched rescue attempt.

iron curtain Term coined by Winston Churchill to describe the cold war divide between Western Europe and the Soviet Union's Eastern European satellite nations.

Iroquois League An alliance of the Iroquois Nations, originally formed sometime between 1450 and 1600, that used their combined strength to pressure Europeans to work with them in the fur trade and to wage war across what is today eastern North America.

J. Pierpont Morgan and Company An investment bank under the leadership of J. Pierpont Morgan that bought or merged unrelated American companies, often using capital acquired from European investors.

Jay's Treaty (1794) Controversial agreement between Britain and the United States, negotiated by Chief Justice John Jay, that settled disputes over trade, prewar debts owed to British merchants, British-occupied forts in American territory, and the seizure of American ships and cargo.

Jazz Age Term coined by writer F. Scott Fitzgerald to characterize the spirit of rebellion and spontaneity among young Americans in the 1920s, a spirit epitomized by the hugely popular jazz music of the era.

Jeffersonian Republicans Political party founded by Thomas Jefferson in opposition to the Federalist party led by Alexander Hamilton and John Adams; also known as the Democratic-Republican party.

Johnson's Restoration Plan A plan to require southern states to ratify the Thirteenth Amendment, disqualify wealthy ex-Confederates from voting, and appoint a Unionist governor.

joint-stock companies Businesses owned by investors, who purchase shares of stock and share the profits and losses.

Kansas-Nebraska Act (1854) Controversial legislation that created two new territories taken from Native Americans, Kansas and Nebraska, where resident males would decide whether slavery would be allowed (popular sovereignty).

King Philip's War (1675–1678) A war in New England resulting from the escalation of tensions between Native Americans and English settlers; the defeat of the Native Americans led to broadened freedoms for the settlers and their dispossessing the region's Native Americans of most of their land.

Knights of Labor A national labor organization with a broad reform platform; reached peak membership in the 1880s.

Know-Nothings Nativist, anti-Catholic third party organized in 1854 in reaction to large-scale German and Irish immigration.

Ku Klux Klan A secret terrorist organization founded in Pulaski, Tennessee, in 1866 targeting formerly enslaved people who voted and held political offices, as well as people the KKK labeled as carpetbaggers and scalawags.

laissez-faire An economic doctrine holding that businesses and individuals should be able to pursue their economic interests without government interference.

League of Nations Organization of nations formed in the aftermath of the Great War to mediate disputes and maintain international peace; despite President Wilson's intense lobbying for the League of Nations, Congress did not ratify the Versailles Treaty, and the United States failed to join.

Lend-Lease Act (1941) Legislation that allowed the president to lend or lease military equipment to any country whose own defense was deemed vital to the defense of the United States.

Lewis and Clark expedition (1804–1806) Led by Meriwether Lewis and William Clark, a mission to the Pacific coast commissioned for the purposes of scientific and geographical exploration.

Lincoln-Douglas debates (1858) In the Illinois race between Republican Abraham Lincoln and Democrat Stephen A. Douglas for a seat in the U.S. Senate, a series of seven dramatic debates focusing on the issue of slavery in the territories.

Louisiana Purchase (1803) President Thomas Jefferson's purchase of the Louisiana Territory from France for $15 million, doubling the size of U.S. territory.

Lowell system Model New England factory communities that provided employees, mostly young women, with meals, a boardinghouse, moral discipline, and educational opportunities.

Loyalists Colonists who remained loyal to Britain before and during the Revolutionary War.

Lusitania British ocean liner torpedoed and sunk by a German U-boat; the deaths of nearly 1,200 of its civilian passengers, including many Americans, caused international outrage.

maize (corn) The primary grain crop in Mesoamerica, yielding small kernels often ground into cornmeal. Easy to grow in a broad range of conditions, it enabled a global population explosion after being brought to Europe, Africa, and Asia.

manifest destiny The widespread belief that America was "destined" by God to expand westward across the continent into lands claimed by Native Americans as well as European nations.

***Marbury v. Madison* (1803)** First Supreme Court decision to declare a federal law—the Judiciary Act of 1789—unconstitutional ("judicial review").

March on Washington (1963) Civil rights demonstration on the National Mall, where Martin Luther King, Jr. gave his famous "I Have a Dream" speech.

market economy Large-scale manufacturing and commercial agriculture that emerged in America during the first half of the nineteenth century, displacing much of the premarket subsistence and barter-based economy and producing boom-and-bust cycles while raising the American standard of living.

marriage equality Legal right for gay and lesbian couples to marry; the most divisive issue in the culture wars of the early 2010s as increasing numbers of court rulings affirmed this right across the United States.

Marshall Plan (1948) Secretary of State George C. Marshall's post–World War II program providing massive U.S. financial and technical assistance to war-torn European countries.

Massachusetts Bay Colony English colony founded by Puritans in 1630 as a haven for persecuted Congregationalists.

massive resistance White rallying cry for disrupting federal efforts to enforce racial integration in the South.

massive retaliation Strategy that used the threat of nuclear warfare as a means of combating the global spread of communism.

Mayflower Compact (1620) A formal agreement signed by the Separatist colonists aboard the *Mayflower* to abide by laws made by leaders of their choosing.

McCarthyism Anti-Communist hysteria led by Senator Joseph McCarthy's witch hunts attacking the loyalty of politicians, federal employees, and public figures, despite a lack of evidence.

McCormick reaper Mechanical reaper invented by Cyrus Hall McCormick in 1831 that dramatically increased the production of wheat.

***McCulloch v. Maryland* (1819)** Supreme Court ruling that prohibited states from taxing the Bank of the United States.

Medicare and Medicaid Health-care programs designed to aid the elderly and disadvantaged, respectively, as part of President Johnson's Great Society initiative.

mercantilism Policy of England and other imperial powers of regulating colonial economies to benefit the mother country.

Mexica Empire The dominion established in the fourteenth century under the imperialistic Mexicas, or Aztecs, in the valley of Mexico.

Mexicas Otherwise known as Aztecs, a Mesoamerican people of northern Mexico who founded the vast Aztec Empire in the fourteenth century, later conquered by the Spanish under Hernán Cortés in 1521.

microprocessor An electronic circuit printed on a tiny silicon chip; a major technological breakthrough in 1971, it paved the way for the development of the personal computer.

Middle Passage The hellish and often deadly middle leg of the transatlantic "triangular trade" in which European ships carried manufactured goods to Africa, then transported enslaved Africans to the Americas and the Caribbean, and finally conveyed American agricultural products back to Europe.

Militia Act (1862) Congressional measure that permitted formerly enslaved people to serve as laborers or soldiers in the U.S. Army.

militias Part-time "citizen-soldiers" called out to protect their towns from foreign invasion and ravages during the American Revolution.

Mississippi Plan (1890) Series of state constitutional amendments that sought to disenfranchise Black voters and was quickly adopted by nine other southern states.

Missouri Compromise (1820) Legislative decision to admit Missouri as a slave state while prohibiting slavery in the area west of the Mississippi River and north of the parallel 36°30′.

moderate Republicanism Promise to curb federal government and restore state and local government authority, spearheaded by President Eisenhower.

modernism An early twentieth-century cultural movement that rejected traditional notions of reality and adopted radical new forms of artistic expression.

money question Late nineteenth-century national debate over the nature of U.S. currency; supporters of a fixed gold standard were generally moneylenders and thus preferred to keep the value of money high, while supporters of silver (and gold) coinage were debtors who owed money, so they wanted to keep the value of money low by increasing the currency supply (inflation).

monopoly Corporation so large that it effectively controls the entire market for its products or services.

Monroe Doctrine (1823) U.S. foreign policy that barred further colonization in the Western Hemisphere by European powers and pledged that there would be no American interference with any existing European colonies.

Montgomery bus boycott Boycott of bus system in Montgomery, Alabama, organized by civil rights activists after the arrest of Rosa Parks in 1955.

Mormon Church The Church of Jesus Christ of Latter-day Saints, founded by Joseph Smith, emphasizing universal salvation and a modest lifestyle; often persecuted for separateness and practice of polygamy.

Morrill Land-Grant College Act (1862) Federal statute that granted federal lands to states to help fund the creation of land-grant colleges and universities, which were founded to provide technical education in agriculture, mining, and industry.

muckrakers Writers who exposed corruption and abuses in politics, business, consumer safety, working conditions, and more, spurring public interest in progressive reforms.

Mugwumps Reformers who bolted the Republican party in 1884 to support Democrat Grover Cleveland for president over Republican James G. Blaine, whose secret dealings on behalf of railroad companies had brought charges of corruption.

Mulattoes Mixed-race people who constituted most of the South's free Black population.

Nat Turner's Rebellion (1831) Insurrection in rural Virginia led by Black overseer Nat Turner, who murdered slave owners and their families; in turn, federal troops indiscriminately killed hundreds of enslaved people in the process of putting down Turner and his rebels.

National Association for the Advancement of Colored People (NAACP) Organization founded in 1910 by Black activists and White progressives that promoted education as a means of combating social problems and focused on legal action to secure the civil rights supposedly guaranteed by the Fourteenth and Fifteenth Amendments.

National Banking Act (1863) The U.S. Congress created a national banking system to finance the enormous expense of the Civil War. It enabled loans to the government and established a single national currency, including the issuance of paper money ("greenbacks").

National Recovery Administration (NRA) (1933) Controversial federal agency that brought together business and labor leaders to create "codes of fair competition" and "fair-labor" policies, including a national minimum wage.

National Security Act (1947) Congressional legislation that created the Department of Defense, the National Security Council, and the Central Intelligence Agency.

National Trades' Union Organization formed in 1834 to organize all local trade unions into a stronger national association; dissolved amid the economic depression in the late 1830s.

nativism Reactionary conservative movement characterized by heightened nationalism, anti-immigrant sentiment, and laws setting stricter regulations on immigration.

nativists Native-born Americans who viewed immigrants as a threat to their job opportunities and way of life.

natural rights An individual's basic rights (life, liberty, and property) that should not be violated by any government or community.

Navigation Acts (1651–1775) Restrictions passed by Parliament to control colonial trade and bolster the mercantile system.

neutrality laws Series of laws passed by Congress aimed at avoiding a Second World War; these included the Neutrality Act of 1935, which banned the selling of weapons to warring nations.

New Democrats Centrist ("moderate") Democrats led by President Bill Clinton that emerged in the late 1980s and early 1990s to challenge the "liberal" direction of the party.

new economy Period of sustained economic prosperity during the 1990s marked by federal budget surpluses, the explosion of dot-com industries, low inflation, and low unemployment.

New Freedom Program championed in 1912 by the Woodrow Wilson campaign that aimed to restore competition in the economy by eliminating all trusts rather than simply regulating them.

New Frontier Proposed domestic program championed by the incoming Kennedy administration in 1961 that aimed to jump-start the economy and trigger social progress.

new immigrants Wave of newcomers from southern and eastern Europe, including many Jews, who became a majority among immigrants to America after 1890.

New Left Term coined by the Students for a Democratic Society to distinguish their efforts at grassroots democracy from those of the 1930s Old Left, which had embraced orthodox Marxism and admired the Soviet Union under Stalin.

New Mexico A region in the American Southwest, originally established by the Spanish, who settled there in the sixteenth century, founded Catholic missions, and exploited the region's indigenous peoples.

New Netherland Dutch colony conquered by the English in 1667, out of which four new colonies were created—New York, New Jersey, Pennsylvania, and Delaware.

Nineteenth Amendment (1920) Constitutional amendment that granted women the right to vote in national elections.

nonviolent civil disobedience The principled tactic that Martin Luther King Jr. advocated: peaceful lawbreaking as a means of ending segregation.

North American Free Trade Agreement (NAFTA) (1994) Agreement eliminating trade barriers that was signed in 1994 by the United States, Canada, and Mexico, making North America the largest free-trade zone in the world.

North and South Carolina English proprietary colonies, originally formed as the Carolina colonies, officially separated into the colonies of North and South Carolina in 1712, whose semitropical climate made them profitable centers of rice, timber, and tar production.

North Atlantic Treaty Organization (NATO) Defensive political and military alliance formed in 1949 by the United States, Canada, and ten Western European nations to deter Soviet expansion in Europe.

Northwest Ordinance (1787) Land policy for new western territories in the Ohio Valley that established the terms and conditions for self-government and statehood while also banning slavery from the region.

***NSC-68* (1950)** Top-secret policy paper approved by President Truman that outlined a militaristic approach to combating the spread of global communism.

nullification Right claimed by some states to veto a federal law deemed unconstitutional.

Old Southwest Region covering western Georgia, Alabama, Mississippi, Louisiana, Arkansas, and Texas, where low land prices and fertile soil attracted droves of settlers after the American Revolution.

Open Door policy (1899) Official U.S. assertion that Chinese trade would be open to all nations; Secretary of State John Hay unilaterally announced the policy in 1899 in hopes of protecting the Chinese market for U.S. exports.

open shop Business policy of not requiring union membership as a condition of employment; such a policy, where legal, has the effect of weakening unions and diminishing workers' rights.

Operation Desert Storm (1991) Assault by American-led multinational forces that quickly defeated Iraqi forces under Saddam Hussein in the First Gulf War, ending the Iraqi occupation of Kuwait.

Operation Overlord The Allies' assault on Hitler's "Atlantic Wall," a seemingly impregnable series of fortifications and minefields along the French coastline that German forces had created using captive Europeans for laborers.

Oregon Fever The lure of fertile land and economic opportunities in the Oregon Country that drew hundreds of thousands of settlers westward, beginning in the late 1830s.

Overland Trails Trail routes followed by wagon trains bearing settlers and trade goods from Missouri to the Oregon Country, California, and New Mexico, beginning in the 1840s.

Pacific Railway Act (1862) Congress provided funding for a transcontinental railroad from Nebraska west to California.

Panic of 1819 A financial panic that began a three-year economic crisis triggered by reduced demand in Europe for American cotton, declining land values, and reckless practices by local and state banks.

Panic of 1837 A financial calamity in the United States brought on by a dramatic slowdown in the British economy and falling cotton prices, failed crops, high inflation, and reckless state banks.

Panic of 1873 Financial collapse triggered by President Grant's efforts to withdraw greenbacks from circulation and transition the economy back to hard currency.

Panic of 1893 A major collapse in the national economy after several major railroad companies declared bankruptcy, leading to a severe depression and several violent clashes between workers and management.

Parliament Legislature of Great Britain, composed of the House of Commons, whose members are elected, and the House of Lords, whose members are either hereditary or appointed.

party boss A powerful political leader who controlled a "machine" of associates and operatives to promote both individual and party interests, often using informal tactics such as intimidation or the patronage system.

Patriots Colonists who rebelled against British authority before and during the Revolutionary War.

patronage An informal system (sometimes called the "spoils system") used by politicians to reward their supporters with government appointments or contracts.

Pearl Harbor (1941) Surprise Japanese attack on the U.S. fleet at Pearl Harbor on December 7, which prompted the immediate American entry into the war.

peculiar institution Phrase used by Whites in the antebellum South to refer to slavery without using the word *slavery*.

People's party (Populists) Political party formed in 1892 following the success of Farmers' Alliance candidates; Populists advocated a variety of reforms, including free coinage of silver, a progressive income tax, postal savings banks, regulation of railroads, and direct election of U.S. senators.

perestroika Russian term for economic restructuring; applied to Mikhail Gorbachev's series of political and economic reforms that included shifting a centrally planned Communist economy to a mixed economy allowing for capitalism.

Personal Responsibility and Work Opportunity Act of 1996 (PRWOA) Comprehensive welfare-reform measure aiming to decrease the size of the "welfare state" by limiting the amount of government unemployment aid to encourage its recipients to find jobs.

plain white folk Yeoman farmers who lived and worked on their own small farms, growing food and cash crops to trade for necessities.

plantation mistress Matriarch of a planter's household, responsible for supervising the domestic aspects of the estate.

planters Owners of large farms in the South that were worked by twenty or more enslaved people and supervised by overseers.

Pontiac's Rebellion (1763) A series of Native American attacks on British forts and settlements after France ceded to the British its territory east of the Mississippi River as part of the Treaty of Paris without consulting France's Native American allies.

popular sovereignty Legal concept by which the White male settlers in a U.S. territory would vote to decide whether to permit slavery.

Powhatan Confederacy An alliance of several powerful Algonquian societies under the leadership of Chief Powhatan, organized into thirty chiefdoms along much of the Atlantic coast in the late sixteenth and early seventeenth centuries.

Proclamation Act of 1763 Proclamation drawing a boundary along the Appalachian Mountains from Canada to Georgia in order to minimize occurrences of settler–Native American violence; colonists were forbidden to go west of the line.

professions Occupations requiring specialized knowledge of a particular field; the Industrial Revolution and its new organization of labor created an array of professions in the nineteenth century.

Progressive party Political party founded by Theodore Roosevelt to support his bid to regain the presidency in 1912 after his split from the Taft Republicans.

Prohibition (1920–1933) National ban on the manufacture and sale of alcohol, though the law was widely violated and proved too difficult to enforce effectively.

Protestant Reformation Sixteenth-century religious movement initiated by Martin Luther, a German monk whose public criticism of corruption in the Roman Catholic Church and whose teaching that Christians can communicate directly with God gained a wide following.

public schools Elementary and secondary schools funded by the state and free of tuition.

Pullman Strike (1894) A national strike by the American Railway Union, whose members shut down major railways in sympathy with striking workers in Pullman, Illinois; ended with intervention of federal troops.

Puritans English religious dissenters who sought to "purify" the Church of England of its Catholic practices.

race-based slavery Institution that uses racial characteristics and myths to justify enslaving a people by force.

racial justice protests Largest collection of multiracial and intergenerational protests across the United States in opposition to racism toward Black people, prompted by the documented murder of George Floyd, a Black man, by a Minneapolis police officer.

Radical Republicans Congressmen who identified with the abolitionist cause and sought swift emancipation of the enslaved, punishment of the Rebels, and tight controls over former Confederate states.

railroads Steam-powered vehicles that improved passenger transportation, quickened western settlement, and enabled commercial agriculture in the nineteenth century.

Reaganomics President Reagan's "supply-side" economic philosophy combining tax cuts with the goals of decreased government spending, reduced regulation of business, and a balanced budget.

Reconstruction Finance Corporation (RFC) (1932) Federal program established under President Hoover to loan money to banks and other corporations to help them avoid bankruptcy.

redeemers Postwar White Democratic leaders in the South who supposedly saved the region from political, economic, and social domination by Northerners and Blacks.

Red Power Activism by militant Native American groups to protest living conditions on Indian reservations through demonstrations, legal action, and at times, violence.

republican ideology Political belief in representative democracy in which citizens govern themselves by electing representatives, or legislators, to make key decisions on the citizens' behalf.

republican simplicity Deliberate attitude of humility and frugality, as opposed to monarchical pomp and ceremony, adopted by Thomas Jefferson in his presidency.

return to normalcy Campaign promise of Republican presidential candidate Warren G. Harding in 1920, meant to contrast with Woodrow Wilson's progressivism and internationalism.

***Roe v. Wade* (1973)** Landmark Supreme Court decision striking down state laws that banned abortions during the first trimester of pregnancy.

Roman Catholicism The Christian faith and religious practices of the Roman Catholic Church, which exerted great political, economic, and social influence on much of western Europe and, through the Spanish and Portuguese Empires, on the Americas.

Roosevelt Corollary (1904) President Theodore Roosevelt's revision (1904) of the Monroe Doctrine (1823) in which he argued that the United States could use military force in Central and South America to prevent European nations from intervening in the Western Hemisphere.

Rough Riders The First Volunteer Cavalry, led in the Spanish-American War by Theodore Roosevelt; victorious in their only engagement, the Battle of San Juan Hill.

Sacco and Vanzetti case (1921) Trial of two Italian immigrants that occurred at the height of Italian immigration and against the backdrop of numerous terror attacks by anarchists; despite a lack of clear evidence, the two defendants, both self-professed anarchists, were convicted of murder and were executed.

salutary neglect Informal British policy during the first half of the eighteenth century that allowed the American colonies freedom to pursue their economic and political interests in exchange for colonial obedience.

Sand Creek Massacre (1864) Colonel Chivington's unprovoked slaughter of the Cheyenne and Arapaho in Colorado, initially reported as a justified battle but soon exposed for the despicable massacre it was.

Scopes Trial (1925) Highly publicized trial of a high-school teacher in Tennessee for violating a state law that prohibited the teaching of evolution; the trial was seen as the climax of the fundamentalist war on Darwinism.

Second Bank of the United States Established in 1816 after the first national bank's charter expired; it stabilized the economy by creating a sound national currency; by making loans to farmers, small manufacturers, and entrepreneurs; and by regulating the ability of state banks to issue their own paper currency.

Second Great Awakening Religious revival movement that arose in reaction to the growth of secularism and rationalist religion; spurred the growth of the Baptist and Methodist denominations.

Second Industrial Revolution Beginning in the late nineteenth century, a wave of technological innovations, especially in iron and steel production, steam and electrical power, and telegraphic communications, all of which spurred industrial development and urban growth.

Second New Deal (1935–1938) Expansive cluster of legislation proposed by President Roosevelt that established new regulatory agencies, strengthened the rights of workers to organize unions, and laid the foundation of a federal social welfare system through the creation of Social Security.

Securities and Exchange Commission (SEC) (1934) Federal agency established to regulate the issuance and trading of stocks and bonds in an effort to avoid financial panics and stock market crashes.

Seneca Falls Convention (1848) Convention organized by feminists Lucretia Mott and Elizabeth Cady Stanton to promote women's rights and issue the pathbreaking Declaration of Rights and Sentiments.

separate but equal Underlying principle behind segregation that was legitimized by the Supreme Court ruling in *Plessy v. Ferguson* (1896).

separation of powers Strict division of the powers of government among three separate branches (executive, legislative, and judicial), which in turn check and balance each other.

Seventeenth Amendment (1913) Constitutional amendment that provided for the public election of senators rather than the traditional practice allowing state legislatures to name them.

sharecropping A farming system developed after the Civil War by which landless workers farmed land in exchange with the landowner for farm supplies and a share of the crop.

Shays's Rebellion (1786–1787) Storming of the Massachusetts federal arsenal in 1787 by Daniel Shays and 1,200 armed farmers seeking debt relief from the state legislature through issuance of paper currency and lower taxes.

Sherman's "March to the Sea" (1864) The Union army's devastating march through Georgia from Atlanta to Savannah led by General William T. Sherman, intended to demoralize civilians and destroy the resources the Confederate army needed to fight.

silent majority Term popularized by President Richard Nixon to describe the great majority of American voters who did not express their political opinions publicly; "the non-demonstrators."

Sixteenth Amendment (1913) Constitutional amendment that authorized the federal income tax.

slave codes Laws passed by each colony and later states governing the treatment of enslaved people that were designed to deter freedom seekers and rebellions and often included severe punishments for infractions.

social Darwinism The application of Charles Darwin's theory of evolutionary natural selection to human society; social Darwinists used the concept of "survival of the fittest" to justify class distinctions, explain poverty, and oppose government intervention in the economy.

social gospel Mostly Protestant movement that stressed the Christian obligation to address the mounting social problems caused by urbanization and industrialization.

Social Security Act (1935) Legislation enacted to provide federal assistance to retired workers through tax-funded pension payments and benefit payments to the unemployed and disabled.

Sons of Liberty First organized by Samuel Adams in the 1770s, groups of colonists dedicated to militant resistance against British control of the colonies.

Southern Christian Leadership Conference (SCLC) Civil rights organization formed by Dr. Martin Luther King, Jr. that championed nonviolent direct action as a means of ending segregation.

Spanish Armada A massive Spanish fleet of 130 warships that was defeated at Plymouth in 1588 by the English navy during the reign of Queen Elizabeth I.

spirituals Songs with religious messages sung by enslaved people to help ease the strain of field labor and to voice their suffering at the hands of their masters and overseers.

Square Deal Theodore Roosevelt's progressive agenda of the "Three Cs": control of corporations, conservation of natural resources, and consumer protection.

stagflation Term coined by economists during the Nixon presidency to describe the unprecedented situation of stagnant economic growth and consumer price inflation occurring at the same time.

Stamp Act (1765) Act of Parliament requiring that all printed materials in the American colonies use paper with an official tax stamp in order to pay for British military protection of the colonies.

Standard Oil Company Corporation under the leadership of John D. Rockefeller that attempted to dominate the entire oil industry through horizontal and vertical integration.

staple crops Profitable market crops, such as cotton, tobacco, and rice, that predominate in a region.

state constitutions Charters that define the relationship between the state government and local governments and individuals, while also protecting individual rights and freedoms.

steamboats Ships and boats powered by wood-fired steam engines that made two-way traffic possible in eastern river systems, creating a transcontinental market and an agricultural empire.

Stonewall Uprising (1969) Violent clashes between police and gay patrons of New York City's Stonewall Inn, seen as the starting point of the modern gay rights movement.

Stono Rebellion A 1739 slave uprising in South Carolina that was brutally quashed, leading to executions as well as a severe tightening of the slave codes.

Strategic Arms Limitation Treaty (SALT I) Agreement signed by President Nixon and Premier Leonid Brezhnev prohibiting the development of missile defense systems in the United States and Soviet Union and limiting the quantity of nuclear warheads for both.

Strategic Defense Initiative (SDI) (1983) Ronald Reagan's proposed space-based anti-missile defense system, dubbed "Star Wars" by the media, which aroused great controversy and escalated the arms race between the United States and the Soviet Union.

Student Nonviolent Coordinating Committee (SNCC) Interracial organization formed in 1960 with the goal of intensifying the effort to end racial segregation.

suburbia Communities formed from mass migration of middle-class Whites from urban centers.

Suez crisis (1956) British, French, and Israeli attack on Egypt after Nasser's seizure of the Suez Canal; President Eisenhower interceded to demand the withdrawal of the British, French, and Israeli forces from the Sinai Peninsula and the strategic canal.

Taft-Hartley Labor Act (1947) Congressional legislation that banned "unfair labor practices" by unions, required union leaders to sign anti-Communist "loyalty oaths," and prohibited federal employees from going on strike.

Tariff of 1816 Taxes on various imported items, to protect America's emerging iron and textile industries from British competition.

Tariff of Abominations (1828) Tax on imported goods, including British cloth and clothing, that strengthened New England textile companies but hurt southern consumers, who experienced a decrease in British demand for raw cotton grown in the South.

tariff reform (1887) Effort led by the Democratic party to reduce taxes on imported goods, which Republicans argued were needed to protect American industries from foreign competition.

Taylorism Labor system based on detailed study of work tasks, championed by Frederick Winslow Taylor, intended to maximize efficiency and profits for employers.

Tea Party Right-wing populist movement, largely made up of middle-class, White male conservatives, that emerged as a response to the expansion of the federal government under the Obama administration.

Teapot Dome Scandal (1923) Harding administration scandal in which Secretary of the Interior Albert B. Fall profited from secret leasing of government oil reserves in Wyoming to private oil companies.

Tecumseh's Indian Confederacy A group of Native American nations under leadership of Shawnees Tecumseh and Tenskwatawa; its mission of fighting off American expansion was thwarted at the Battle of Tippecanoe (1811), when the Confederacy fell apart.

telegraph system System of electronic communication invented by Samuel F. B. Morse that could transmit messages instantaneously across great distances.

Teller Amendment (1898) Addition to the congressional war resolution of April 20, 1898, which marked the U.S. entry into the war with Spain; the amendment declared that the United States' goal in entering the war was to ensure Cuba's independence, not to annex Cuba as a territory.

temperance A widespread reform movement led by militant Christians that focused on reducing the use of alcoholic beverages.

tenements Shabby, low-cost inner-city apartment buildings that housed the urban poor in cramped, unventilated apartments.

Tet offensive (1968) Surprise attack by Viet Cong guerrillas and North Vietnamese army on U.S. and South Vietnamese forces that shocked the American public and led to widespread sentiment against the war.

Texas Revolution (1835–1836) Conflict between Texas colonists and the Mexican government that resulted in the creation of the separate Republic of Texas in 1836.

Thirteenth Amendment (1865) Amendment to the U.S. Constitution that ended slavery and freed all enslaved people in the United States.

tobacco A "cash crop" grown in the Caribbean as well as the Virginia and Maryland colonies, made increasingly profitable by the rapidly growing popularity of smoking in Europe after the voyages of Columbus.

Tonkin Gulf Resolution (1964) Congressional action that granted the president unlimited authority to defend U.S. forces abroad after an allegedly unprovoked attack on American warships off the coast of North Vietnam.

Townshend Acts (1767) Parliamentary measures to extract more revenue from the colonies; the Revenue Act of 1767, which taxed tea, paper, and other colonial imports, was one of the most notorious of these policies.

Trail of Tears (1838–1839) The Cherokees' 800-mile journey from the southern Appalachians to Indian Territory.

transcendentalism Philosophy of New England writers and thinkers who advocated personal spirituality, self-reliance, social reform, and harmony with nature.

Transcontinental Treaty (1819) Treaty between Spain and the United States that clarified the boundaries of the Louisiana Purchase and arranged for the transfer of Florida to the United States in exchange for cash.

Treaty of Ghent (1814) Agreement between Great Britain and the United States that ended the War of 1812.

Treaty of Guadalupe Hidalgo (1848) Treaty between United States and Mexico that ended the Mexican-American War.

Treaty of Paris (1763) Settlement between Great Britain and France that ended the French and Indian War.

Treaty of Paris (1783) The treaty that ended the Revolutionary War, recognized American independence from Britain, created the border between Canada and the United States, set the western border at the Mississippi, and ceded Florida to Spain.

Treaty of Versailles Peace treaty that ended the Great War, forcing Germany to dismantle its military, pay immense war reparations, and give up its colonies around the world.

trench warfare A form of prolonged combat between the entrenched positions of opposing armies, often with little tactical movement.

triangular trade A network of trade in which exports from one region were sold to a second region; the second sent its exports to a third region that exported its own goods back to the first country or colony.

Triple Alliance (Central Powers) One of the two sides during the Great War, including Germany, Austria-Hungary, Bulgaria, and Turkey (the Ottoman Empire).

Triple Entente (Allied Powers) Nations fighting the Central Powers during the Great War, including France, Great Britain, and Russia; later joined by Italy and, after Russia quit the war in 1917, the United States.

Truman Doctrine (1947) President Truman's program of "containing" communism in Eastern Europe and providing economic and military aid to any nations at risk of Communist takeover.

trust Business arrangement that gives a person or corporation (the "trustee") the legal power to manage another person's money or another company without owning those entities outright.

Tuskegee Airmen U.S. Army Air Corps unit of African American pilots whose combat success spurred military and civilian leaders to desegregate the armed forces after the war.

two-party system Domination of national politics by two major political parties, such as the Whigs and Democrats during the 1830s and 1840s.

U-boat German military submarine used during the Great War to attack warships as well as merchant ships of enemy and neutral nations.

Underground Railroad A secret system of routes, safe houses, and abolitionists that helped freedom seekers reach freedom in the North.

Unitarians Members of the liberal New England Congregationalist offshoot, who profess the oneness of God and the goodness of rational worshippers, often well-educated and wealthy.

United Farm Workers (UFW) Organization formed in 1962 to represent the interests of Mexican American migrant workers.

Universalists Generally working-class members of a New England religious movement, who believed in a merciful God and universal salvation.

USA Patriot Act (2001) Wide-reaching congressional legislation, triggered by the war on terror, which gave government agencies the right to eavesdrop on confidential conversations between prison inmates and their lawyers and permitted suspected terrorists to be tried in secret military courts.

U.S. battleship *Maine* American warship that exploded in the Cuban port of Havana on February 15, 1898; though later discovered to be the result of an accident, the destruction of the *Maine* was initially attributed by war-hungry Americans to Spain, contributing to the onset of the Spanish-American War.

utopian communities Ideal communities that offered innovative social and economic relationships to those who were interested in achieving salvation—now.

Valley Forge (1777–1778) American military encampment near Philadelphia, where more than 3,500 soldiers deserted or died from cold and hunger in the winter.

Viet Cong Communist guerrillas in South Vietnam who launched attacks on the Diem government.

Vietnamization Nixon-era policy of equipping and training South Vietnamese forces to take over the burden of combat from U.S. troops.

Virginia Statute of Religious Freedom (1786) A Virginia law, drafted by Thomas Jefferson in 1777 and enacted in 1786, that guarantees freedom of, and from, religion.

virtual representation The idea that the American colonies, although they had no actual representative in Parliament, were "virtually" represented by all members of Parliament.

Voting Rights Act of 1965 Legislation ensuring that all Americans were able to vote; ended literacy tests and other means of restricting voting rights.

Wagner Act (1935) Legislation that guaranteed workers the right to organize unions, granted them direct bargaining power, and barred employers from interfering with union activities.

War of 1812 (1812–1815) Conflict fought in North America and at sea between Great Britain and the United States over American shipping rights and British-inspired Indian attacks on American settlements. Canadians and Native Americans also fought in the war on each side.

war on terror Global crusade to root out anti-Western and anti-American Islamist terrorist cells launched by President George W. Bush as a response to the 9/11 attacks.

War Powers Act (1973) Legislation requiring the president to inform Congress within forty-eight hours of the deployment of U.S. troops abroad and to withdraw them after sixty days unless Congress approves their continued deployment.

War Production Board Federal agency created by Roosevelt in 1942 that converted America's industrial output to war production.

war relocation camps Detention camps housing thousands of Japanese Americans from the West Coast who were forcibly interned from 1942 until the end of the Second World War.

Watergate (1972–1974) Scandal that exposed the criminality and corruption of the Nixon administration and ultimately led to President Nixon's resignation in 1974.

weapons of mass destruction (WMD) Lethal nuclear, radiological, chemical, or biological devices aimed at harming people, institutions, and a nation's sense of security.

Western Front Contested frontier between the Central and Allied Powers that ran along northern France and across Belgium.

Whig party Political party founded in 1834 in opposition to the Jacksonian Democrats; supported federal funding for internal improvements, a national bank, and high tariffs on imports.

Whiskey Rebellion (1794) Violent protest by western Pennsylvania farmers against the federal excise tax on corn whiskey, put down by a federal army.

Wilmington Insurrection (1898) Led by Alfred Waddell in Wilmington, North Carolina, White supremacists rampaged through the Black community, overthrew the local government, and forced over 2,000 African Americans into exile.

Wilmot Proviso (1846) Proposal by Congressman David Wilmot, a Pennsylvania Democrat, to prohibit slavery in any lands acquired in the Mexican-American War.

Women's Army Corps Women's branch of the U.S. Army; by the end of the Second World War, nearly 150,000 women had served in the WAC.

women's movement Wave of activism sparked by Betty Friedan's *The Feminine Mystique* (1963); it argued for equal rights for women and fought against the cult of domesticity that limited women's roles to the home as wife, mother, and homemaker.

women's suffrage Movement to give women the right to vote through a constitutional amendment, spearheaded by Susan B. Anthony and Elizabeth Cady Stanton's National Woman Suffrage Association.

women's work Traditional term referring to routine tasks in the house, garden, and fields performed by women; eventually expanded in the colonies to include medicine, shopkeeping, upholstering, and the operation of inns and taverns.

Works Progress Administration (1935) Government agency established to manage several federal job programs created under the New Deal; it became the largest employer in the nation.

Yalta Conference (1945) Meeting of the "Big Three" Allied leaders—Franklin D. Roosevelt, Winston Churchill, and Josef Stalin—to discuss how to divide control of postwar Germany and eastern Europe.

yellow journalism A type of news reporting, epitomized in the 1890s by the newspaper empires of William Randolph Hearst and Joseph Pulitzer, that intentionally manipulates public opinion through sensational headlines, illustrations, and articles about both real and invented events.

Zimmermann telegram Message sent by a German official to the Mexican government urging an invasion of the United States; the telegram was intercepted by British intelligence agents and angered Americans, many of whom called for war against Germany.

Appendix

The Declaration of Independence (1776)

When in the Course of human events, it becomes necessary for one people to dissolve the political bands which have connected them with another, and to assume among the powers of the earth, the separate and equal station to which the Laws of Nature and of Nature's God entitle them, a decent respect to the opinions of mankind requires that they should declare the causes which impel them to the separation.

We hold these truths to be self-evident, that all men are created equal, that they are endowed by their Creator with certain unalienable Rights, that among these are Life, Liberty and the pursuit of Happiness. —That to secure these rights, Governments are instituted among Men, deriving their just powers from the consent of the governed, —That whenever any Form of Government becomes destructive of these ends, it is the Right of the People to alter or to abolish it, and to institute new Government, laying its foundation on such principles and organizing its powers in such form, as to them shall seem most likely to effect their Safety and Happiness. Prudence, indeed, will dictate that Governments long established should not be changed for light and transient causes; and accordingly all experience hath shewn, that mankind are more disposed to suffer, while evils are sufferable, than to right themselves by abolishing the forms to which they are accustomed. But when a long train of abuses and usurpations, pursuing invariably the same Object evinces a design to reduce them under absolute Despotism, it is their right, it is their duty, to throw off such Government, and to provide new Guards for their future security.—Such has been the patient sufferance of these Colonies; and such is now the necessity which constrains them to alter their former Systems of Government. The history of the present King of Great Britain is a history of repeated injuries and usurpations, all having in direct object the establishment of an absolute Tyranny over these States. To prove this, let Facts be submitted to a candid world.

He has refused his Assent to Laws, the most wholesome and necessary for the public good.

He has forbidden his Governors to pass Laws of immediate and pressing importance, unless suspended in their operation till his Assent should be obtained; and when so suspended, he has utterly neglected to attend to them.

He has refused to pass other Laws for the accommodation of large districts of people, unless those people would relinquish the right of Representation in the Legislature, a right inestimable to them and formidable to tyrants only.

He has called together legislative bodies at places unusual, uncomfortable, and distant from the depository of their public Records, for the sole purpose of fatiguing them into compliance with his measures.

He has dissolved Representative Houses repeatedly, for opposing with manly firmness his invasions on the rights of the people.

He has refused for a long time, after such dissolutions, to cause others to be elected; whereby the Legislative powers, incapable of Annihilation, have returned to the People at large for their exercise; the State remaining in the mean time exposed to all the dangers of invasion from without, and convulsions within.

He has endeavoured to prevent the population of these States; for that purpose obstructing the Laws for Naturalization of Foreigners; refusing to pass others to encourage their migrations hither, and raising the conditions of new Appropriations of Lands.

He has obstructed the Administration of Justice, by refusing his Assent to Laws for establishing Judiciary powers.

He has made Judges dependent on his Will alone, for the tenure of their offices, and the amount and payment of their salaries.

He has erected a multitude of New Offices, and sent hither swarms of Officers to harrass our people, and eat out their substance.

He has kept among us, in times of peace, Standing Armies without the Consent of our legislatures.

He has affected to render the Military independent of and superior to the Civil power.

He has combined with others to subject us to a jurisdiction foreign to our constitution, and unacknowledged by our laws; giving his Assent to their Acts of pretended Legislation:

For quartering large bodies of armed troops among us:

For protecting them, by a mock Trial, from punishment for any Murders which they should commit on the Inhabitants of these States:

For cutting off our Trade with all parts of the world:

For imposing Taxes on us without our Consent:

For depriving us in many cases, of the benefits of Trial by Jury:

For transporting us beyond Seas to be tried for pretended offences

For abolishing the free System of English Laws in a neighbouring Province, establishing therein an Arbitrary government, and enlarging its Boundaries so as to render it at once an example and fit instrument for introducing the same absolute rule into these Colonies:

For taking away our Charters, abolishing our most valuable Laws, and altering fundamentally the Forms of our Governments:

For suspending our own Legislatures, and declaring themselves invested with power to legislate for us in all cases whatsoever.

He has abdicated Government here, by declaring us out of his Protection and waging War against us.

He has plundered our seas, ravaged our Coasts, burnt our towns, and destroyed the lives of our people.

He is at this time transporting large Armies of foreign Mercenaries to compleat the works of death, desolation and tyranny, already begun with circumstances of Cruelty & perfidy scarcely paralleled in the most barbarous ages, and totally unworthy the Head of a civilized nation.

He has constrained our fellow Citizens taken Captive on the high Seas to bear Arms against their Country, to become the executioners of their friends and Brethren, or to fall themselves by their Hands.

He has excited domestic insurrections amongst us, and has endeavoured to bring on the inhabitants of our frontiers, the merciless Indian Savages, whose known rule of warfare, is an undistinguished destruction of all ages, sexes and conditions.

In every stage of these Oppressions We have Petitioned for Redress in the most humble terms: Our repeated Petitions have been answered only by repeated injury. A Prince whose character is thus marked by every act which may define a Tyrant, is unfit to be the ruler of a free people.

Nor have We been wanting in attentions to our Brittish brethren. We have warned them from time to time of attempts by their legislature to extend an unwarrantable jurisdiction over us. We have reminded them of the circumstances of our emigration and settlement here. We have appealed to their native justice and magnanimity, and we have conjured them by the ties of our common kindred to disavow these usurpations, which, would inevitably interrupt our connections and correspondence. They too have been deaf to the voice of justice and of consanguinity. We must, therefore, acquiesce in the necessity, which denounces our Separation, and hold them, as we hold the rest of mankind, Enemies in War, in Peace Friends.

We, therefore, the Representatives of the united States of America, in General Congress, Assembled, appealing to the Supreme Judge of the world for the rectitude of our intentions, do, in the Name, and by Authority of the good People of these Colonies, solemnly publish and declare, That these United Colonies are, and of Right ought to be Free and Independent States; that they are Absolved from all Allegiance to the British Crown, and that all political connection between them and the State of Great Britain, is and ought to be totally dissolved; and that as Free and Independent States, they have full Power to levy War, conclude Peace, contract Alliances, establish Commerce, and to do all other Acts and Things which Independent States may of right do. And for the support of this Declaration, with a firm reliance on the protection of divine Providence, we mutually pledge to each other our Lives, our Fortunes and our sacred Honor.

Georgia
Button Gwinnett
Lyman Hall
George Walton

North Carolina
William Hooper
Joseph Hewes
John Penn

South Carolina
Edward Rutledge
Thomas Heyward, Jr.
Thomas Lynch, Jr.
Arthur Middleton

Massachusetts
John Hancock

Maryland
Samuel Chase
William Paca
Thomas Stone
Charles Carroll of Carrollton

Virginia
George Wythe
Richard Henry Lee
Thomas Jefferson
Benjamin Harrison
Thomas Nelson, Jr.
Francis Lightfoot Lee
Carter Braxton

Pennsylvania
Robert Morris
Benjamin Rush
Benjamin Franklin
John Morton
George Clymer
James Smith
George Taylor
James Wilson
George Ross

Delaware
Caesar Rodney
George Read
Thomas McKean

New York
William Floyd
Philip Livingston
Francis Lewis
Lewis Morris

New Jersey
Richard Stockton
John Witherspoon
Francis Hopkinson
John Hart
Abraham Clark

New Hampshire
Josiah Bartlett
William Whipple

Massachusetts
Samuel Adams
John Adams
Robert Treat Paine
Elbridge Gerry

Rhode Island
Stephen Hopkins
William Ellery

Connecticut
Roger Sherman
Samuel Huntington
William Williams
Oliver Wolcott

New Hampshire
Matthew Thornton

Articles of Confederation (1787)

To all to whom these Presents shall come, we the undersigned Delegates of the States affixed to our Names send greeting.

Whereas the Delegates of the United States of America in Congress assembled did on the fifteenth day of November in the Year of our Lord One Thousand Seven Hundred and Seventy-seven, and in the Second Year of the Independence of America agree to certain articles of Confederation and perpetual Union between the States of Newhampshire, Massachusetts-bay, Rhodeisland and Providence Plantations, Connecticut, New York, New Jersey, Pennsylvania, Delaware, Maryland, Virginia, North-Carolina, South-Carolina and Georgia in the Words following, viz.

Articles of Confederation and perpetual Union between the States of Newhampshire, Massachusetts-bay, Rhodeisland and Providence Plantations, Connecticut, New-York, New-Jersey, Pennsylvania, Delaware, Maryland, Virginia, North-Carolina, South-Carolina and Georgia.

Article I. The stile of this confederacy shall be "The United States of America."

Article II. Each State retains its sovereignty, freedom and independence, and every power, jurisdiction and right, which is not by this confederation expressly delegated to the United States, in Congress assembled.

Article III. The said States hereby severally enter into a firm league of friendship with each other, for their common defence, the security of their liberties, and their mutual and general welfare, binding themselves to assist each other, against all force offered to, or attacks made upon them, or any of them, on account of religion, sovereignty, trade or any other pretence whatever.

Article IV. The better to secure and perpetuate mutual friendship and intercourse among the people of the different States in this Union, the free inhabitants of each of these States, paupers, vagabonds and fugitives from justice excepted, shall be entitled to all privileges and immunities of free citizens in the several States; and the people of each State shall have free ingress and regress to and from any other State, and shall enjoy therein all the privileges of trade and commerce, subject to the same duties, impositions and restrictions as the inhabitants thereof respectively, provided that such restrictions shall not extend so far as to prevent the removal of property imported into any State, to any other State of which the owner is an inhabitant; provided also that no imposition, duties or restriction shall be laid by any State, on the property of the United States, or either of them.

If any person guilty of, or charged with treason, felony, or other high misdemeanor in any State, shall flee from justice, and be found in any of the United States, he shall upon demand of the Governor or Executive power, of the State from which he fled, be delivered up and removed to the State having jurisdiction of his offence.

Full faith and credit shall be given in each of these States to the records, acts and judicial proceedings of the courts and magistrates of every other State.

Article V. For the more convenient management of the general interests of the United States, delegates shall be annually appointed in such manner as the legislature of each State shall direct, to meet in Congress on the first Monday in November, in every year, with a power reserved to each State, to recall its delegates, or any of them, at any time within the year, and to send others in their stead, for the remainder of the year.

No State shall be represented in Congress by less than two, nor by more than seven members; and no person shall be capable of being a delegate for more than three years in any term of six years; nor shall any person, being a delegate, be capable of holding any office under the United States, for which he, or another for his benefit receives any salary, fees or emolument of any kind.

Each State shall maintain its own delegates in a meeting of the States, and while they act as members of the committee of the States.

In determining questions in the United States, in Congress assembled, each State shall have one vote.

Freedom of speech and debate in Congress shall not be impeached or questioned in any court, or place out of Congress, and the members of Congress shall be protected in their persons from arrests and imprisonments, during the time of their going to and from, and attendance on Congress, except for treason, felony, or breach of the peace.

Article VI. No State without the consent of the United States in Congress assembled, shall send any embassy to, or receive any embassy from, or enter into any conference, agreement, alliance or treaty with any king, prince or state; nor shall any person holding any office of profit or trust under the United States, or any of them, accept of any present, emolument, office or title of any kind whatever from any king, prince or foreign state; nor shall the United States in Congress assembled, or any of them, grant any title of nobility.

No two or more States shall enter into any treaty, confederation or alliance whatever between them, without the consent of the United States in Congress assembled, specifying accurately the purposes for which the same is to be entered into, and how long it shall continue.

No State shall lay any imposts or duties, which may interfere with any stipulations in treaties, entered into by the United States in Congress assembled, with any king, prince or state, in pursuance of any treaties already proposed by Congress, to the courts of France and Spain.

No vessels of war shall be kept up in time of peace by any State, except such number only, as shall be deemed necessary by the United States in Congress assembled, for the defence of such State, or its trade; nor shall any body of forces be kept up by any State, in time of peace, except such number only, as in the judgment of the United States, in Congress assembled, shall be deemed requisite to garrison the forts necessary for the defence of such State; but every State shall always keep up a well regulated and disciplined militia, sufficiently armed and accoutred, and shall provide and constantly have ready for use, in public stores, a due number of field pieces and tents, and a proper quantity of arms, ammunition and camp equipage.

No State shall engage in any war without the consent of the United States in Congress assembled, unless such State be actually invaded by enemies, or shall have received certain advice of a resolution being formed by some nation of Indians to invade such State, and the danger is so imminent as not to admit of a delay, till the United States in Congress assembled can be consulted: nor shall any State grant commissions to any ships or vessels of war, nor letters of marque or reprisal, except it be after a declaration of war by the United States in Congress assembled, and then only against the kingdom or state and the subjects thereof, against which war has been so declared, and under such regulations as shall be established by the United States in Congress assembled, unless such State be infested by pirates, in which case vessels of war may be fitted out for that occasion, and kept so long as the danger shall continue, or until the United States in Congress assembled shall determine otherwise.

ARTICLE VII. When land-forces are raised by any State of the common defence, all officers of or under the rank of colonel, shall be appointed by the Legislature of each State respectively by whom such forces shall be raised, or in such manner as such State shall direct, and all vacancies shall be filled up by the State which first made the appointment.

ARTICLE VIII. All charges of war, and all other expenses that shall be incurred for the common defence or general welfare, and allowed by the United States in Congress assembled, shall be defrayed out of a common treasury, which shall be supplied by the several States, in proportion to the value of all land within each State, granted to or surveyed for any person, as such land and the buildings and improvements thereon shall be estimated according to such mode as the United States in Congress assembled, shall from time to time direct and appoint.

The taxes for paying that proportion shall be laid and levied by the authority and direction of the Legislatures of the several States within the time agreed upon by the United States in Congress assembled.

ARTICLE IX. The United States in Congress assembled, shall have the sole and exclusive right and power of determining on peace and war, except in the cases mentioned in the sixth article—of sending and receiving ambassadors—entering into treaties and alliances, provided that no treaty of commerce shall be made whereby the legislative power of the respective States shall be restrained from imposing such imposts and duties on foreigners, as their own people are subjected to, or from prohibiting the exportation or importation of and species of goods or commodities whatsoever—of establishing rules for deciding in all cases, what captures on land or water shall be legal, and in what manner prizes taken by land or naval forces in the service of the United States shall be divided or appropriated—of granting letters of marque and reprisal in times of peace—appointing courts for the trial of piracies and felonies committed on the high seas and establishing courts for receiving and determining finally appeals in all cases of captures, provided that no member of Congress shall be appointed a judge of any of the said courts.

The United States in Congress assembled shall also be the last resort on appeal in all disputes and differences now subsisting or that hereafter may arise between two or more States concerning boundary, jurisdiction or any other cause whatever; which authority shall always be exercised in the manner following. Whenever the legislative or executive authority or lawful agent of any State in controversy with another shall present a petition to Congress, stating the matter in question and praying for a hearing, notice thereof shall be given by order of Congress to the legislative or executive authority of the other State in controversy, and a day assigned for the appearance of the parties by their lawful agents, who shall then be directed to appoint by joint consent, commissioners or judges to constitute a court for hearing and determining the matter in question: but if they cannot agree, Congress shall name three persons out of each of the United States, and from the list of such persons each party shall alternately strike out one, the petitioners beginning, until the number shall be reduced to thirteen; and from that number not less than seven, nor more than nine names as Congress shall direct, shall in the presence of Congress be drawn out by lot, and the persons whose names shall be so drawn or any five of them, shall be commissioners or judges, to hear and finally determine the controversy, so always as a major part of the judges who shall hear the cause shall agree in the determination: and if either party shall neglect to attend at the day appointed, without reasons, which Congress shall judge sufficient, or being present shall refuse to strike, the Congress shall proceed to nominate three persons out of each State, and the Secretary of Congress shall strike in behalf of such party absent or refusing; and the judgment and sentence of the court to be appointed, in the manner before prescribed, shall be final and conclusive; and if any of the parties shall refuse to submit to the authority of such court, or to appear or defend their claim or cause, the court shall nevertheless proceed to pronounce sentence, or judgment, which shall in like manner be final and decisive, the judgment or sentence and other proceedings being in either case transmitted to Congress, and lodged among the acts of Congress for the security of the parties concerned: provided that every commissioner, before he sits in judgment, shall take an oath to be administered by one of the judges of the supreme or superior court of the State where the case shall be tried, "well and truly to hear and determine the matter in question, according to the best of his judgment, without favour, affection or hope of reward:" provided also that no State shall be deprived of territory for the benefit of the United States.

All controversies concerning the private right of soil claimed under different grants of two or more States, whose jurisdiction as they may respect such lands, and the states which passed such grants are adjusted, the said grants or either of them being at the same time claimed to have originated antecedent to such settlement of jurisdiction, shall on the petition of either party to the Congress of the United States, be finally determined as near as may be in the same manner as is before prescribed for deciding disputes respecting territorial jurisdiction between different States.

The United States in Congress assembled shall also have the sole and exclusive right and power of regulating the alloy and value of coin struck by their own authority, or by that of the respective States—fixing the standard of weights and measures throughout the United States—regulating the trade and managing all affairs with the Indians, not members of any of the States, provided that the legislative right of any State within its own limits be not infringed or violated—establishing and regulating post-offices from one State to another, throughout all of the United States, and exacting such postage on the papers passing thro' the same as may be requisite to defray the expenses of the said office—appointing all officers of the land forces, in the service of the United States, excepting regimental officers—appointing all the officers of the naval forces, and commissioning all officers whatever in the service of the United States—making rules for the government and regulation of the said land and naval forces, and directing their operations.

The United States in Congress assembled shall have authority to appoint a committee, to sit in the recess of Congress, to be denominated "a Committee of the States," and to consist of one delegate from each State; and to appoint such other committees and civil officers as may be necessary for managing the general affairs of the United States under their direction—to appoint one of their number to preside, provided that no person be allowed to serve in the office of president more than one year in any term of three years; to ascertain the necessary sums of money to be raised for the service of the United States, and to appropriate and apply the same for defraying the public expenses—to borrow money, or emit bills on the credit of the United States, transmitting every half year to the respective States an account of the sums of money so borrowed or emitted,—to build and equip a navy—to agree upon the number of land forces, and to make requisitions from each State for its quota, in proportion to the number of white inhabitants in such State; which requisition shall be binding, and thereupon the Legislature of each State shall appoint the regimental officers, raise the men and cloath, arm and equip them in a soldier like manner, at the expense of the United States; and the officers and men so cloathed, armed and equipped shall march to the place appointed, and within the time agreed on by the United States in Congress assembled: but if the United States in Congress assembled shall, on consideration of circumstances judge proper that any State should not raise men, or should raise a smaller number of men than the quota thereof, such extra number shall be raised, officered, cloathed, armed and equipped in the same manner as the quota of such State, unless the legislature of such State shall judge that such extra number cannot be safely spared out of the same, in which case they shall raise officer, cloath, arm and equip as many of such extra number as they judge can be safely spared. And the officers and men so cloathed, armed and equipped, shall march to the place appointed, and within the time agreed on by the United States in Congress assembled.

The United States in Congress assembled shall never engage in a war, nor grant letters of marque and reprisal in time of peace, nor enter into any treaties or alliances, nor coin money, nor regulate the value thereof, nor ascertain the sums and expenses necessary for the defence and welfare of the United States, or any of them, nor emit bills, nor borrow money on the credit of the United States, nor appropriate money, nor agree upon the number of vessels to be built or purchased, or the number of land or sea forces to be raised, nor appoint a commander in chief of the army or navy, unless nine States assent to the same: nor shall a question on any other point, except for adjourning from day to day be determined, unless by the votes of a majority of the United States in Congress assembled.

The Congress of the United States shall have power to adjourn to any time within the year, and to any place within the United States, so that no period of adjournment be for a longer duration than the space of six months, and shall publish the journal of their proceedings monthly, except such parts thereof relating to treaties, alliances or military operations, as in their judgment require secresy; and the yeas and nays of the delegates of each State on any question shall be entered on the Journal, when it is desired by any delegate; and the delegates of a State, or any of them, at his or their request shall be furnished with a transcript of the said journal, except such parts as are above excepted, to lay before the Legislatures of the several States.

ARTICLE X. The committee of the States, or any nine of them, shall be authorized to execute, in the recess of Congress, such of the powers of Congress as the United States in Congress assembled, by the consent of nine States, shall from time to time think expedient to vest them with; provided that no power be delegated to the said committee, for the exercise of which, by the articles of confederation, the voice of nine States in the Congress of the United States assembled is requisite.

ARTICLE XI. Canada acceding to this confederation, and joining in the measures of the United States, shall be admitted into, and entitled to all the advantages of this Union: but no other colony shall be admitted into the same, unless such admission be agreed to by nine States.

ARTICLE XII. All bills of credit emitted, monies borrowed and debts contracted by, or under the authority of Congress, before the assembling of the United States, in pursuance of the present confederation, shall be deemed and considered as a charge against the United States, for payment and satisfaction whereof the said United States, and the public faith are hereby solemnly pledged.

ARTICLE XIII. Every State shall abide by the determinations of the United States in Congress assembled, on all questions which by this confederation are submitted to them. And the articles of this confederation shall be inviolably observed by every State, and the Union shall be perpetual; nor shall any alteration at any time hereafter be made in any of them; unless such alteration be agreed to in a Congress of the United States, and be afterwards confirmed by the Legislatures of every State.

And whereas it has pleased the Great Governor of the world to incline the hearts of the Legislatures we respectively represent in Congress, to approve of, and to authorize us to ratify the said articles of confederation and perpetual union. Know ye that we the undersigned delegates, by virtue of the power and authority to us given for that purpose, do by these presents, in the name and in behalf of our respective constituents, fully and entirely ratify and confirm each and every of the said articles of confederation and perpetual union, and all and singular the matters and things therein contained: and we do further solemnly plight and engage the faith of our respective constituents, that they shall abide by the determinations of the United States in Congress assembled, on all questions, which by the said confederation are submitted to them. And that the articles thereof shall be inviolably observed by the States we respectively represent, and that the Union shall be perpetual.

In witness thereof we have hereunto set our hands in Congress. Done at Philadelphia in the State of Pennsylvania the ninth day of July in the year of our Lord one thousand seven hundred and seventy-eight, and in the third year of the independence of America.

The Constitution of the United States (1787)

We the People of the United States, in Order to form a more perfect Union, establish Justice, insure domestic Tranquility, provide for the common defence, promote the general Welfare, and secure the Blessings of Liberty to ourselves and our Posterity, do ordain and establish this Constitution for the United States of America.

Article. I.

Section. 1. All legislative Powers herein granted shall be vested in a Congress of the United States, which shall consist of a Senate and House of Representatives.

Section. 2. The House of Representatives shall be composed of Members chosen every second Year by the People of the several States, and the Electors in each State shall have the Qualifications requisite for Electors of the most numerous Branch of the State Legislature.

No Person shall be a Representative who shall not have attained to the Age of twenty five Years, and been seven Years a Citizen of the United States, and who shall not, when elected, be an Inhabitant of that State in which he shall be chosen.

Representatives and direct Taxes shall be apportioned among the several States which may be included within this Union, according to their respective Numbers, which shall be determined by adding to the whole Number of free Persons, including those bound to Service for a Term of Years, and excluding Indians not taxed, three fifths of all other Persons. The actual Enumeration shall be made within three Years after the first Meeting of the Congress of the United States, and within every subsequent Term of ten Years, in such Manner as they shall by Law direct. The Number of Representatives shall not exceed one for every thirty Thousand, but each State shall have at Least one Representative; and until such enumeration shall be made, the State of New Hampshire shall be entitled to chuse three, Massachusetts eight, Rhode-Island and Providence Plantations one, Connecticut five, New-York six, New Jersey four, Pennsylvania eight, Delaware one, Maryland six, Virginia ten, North Carolina five, South Carolina five, and Georgia three.

When vacancies happen in the Representation from any State, the Executive Authority thereof shall issue Writs of Election to fill such Vacancies.

The House of Representatives shall chuse their Speaker and other Officers; and shall have the sole Power of Impeachment.

Section. 3. The Senate of the United States shall be composed of two Senators from each State, chosen by the Legislature thereof for six Years; and each Senator shall have one Vote.

Immediately after they shall be assembled in Consequence of the first Election, they shall be divided as equally as may be into three Classes. The Seats of the Senators of the first Class shall be vacated at the Expiration of the second Year, of the second Class at the Expiration of the fourth Year, and of the third Class at the

Expiration of the sixth Year, so that one third may be chosen every second Year; and if Vacancies happen by Resignation, or otherwise, during the Recess of the Legislature of any State, the Executive thereof may make temporary Appointments until the next Meeting of the Legislature, which shall then fill such Vacancies.

No Person shall be a Senator who shall not have attained to the Age of thirty Years, and been nine Years a Citizen of the United States, and who shall not, when elected, be an Inhabitant of that State for which he shall be chosen.

The Vice President of the United States shall be President of the Senate, but shall have no Vote, unless they be equally divided.

The Senate shall chuse their other Officers, and also a President pro tempore, in the Absence of the Vice President, or when he shall exercise the Office of President of the United States.

The Senate shall have the sole Power to try all Impeachments. When sitting for that Purpose, they shall be on Oath or Affirmation. When the President of the United States is tried, the Chief Justice shall preside: And no Person shall be convicted without the Concurrence of two thirds of the Members present.

Judgment in Cases of Impeachment shall not extend further than to removal from Office, and disqualification to hold and enjoy any Office of honor, Trust or Profit under the United States: but the Party convicted shall nevertheless be liable and subject to Indictment, Trial, Judgment and Punishment, according to Law.

Section. 4. The Times, Places and Manner of holding Elections for Senators and Representatives, shall be prescribed in each State by the Legislature thereof; but the Congress may at any time by Law make or alter such Regulations, except as to the Places of chusing Senators.

The Congress shall assemble at least once in every Year, and such Meeting shall be on the first Monday in December, unless they shall by Law appoint a different Day.

Section. 5. Each House shall be the Judge of the Elections, Returns and Qualifications of its own Members, and a Majority of each shall constitute a Quorum to do Business; but a smaller Number may adjourn from day to day, and may be authorized to compel the Attendance of absent Members, in such Manner, and under such Penalties as each House may provide.

Each House may determine the Rules of its Proceedings, punish its Members for disorderly Behaviour, and, with the Concurrence of two thirds, expel a Member.

Each House shall keep a Journal of its Proceedings, and from time to time publish the same, excepting such Parts as may in their Judgment require Secrecy; and the Yeas and Nays of the Members of either House on any question shall, at the Desire of one fifth of those Present, be entered on the Journal.

Neither House, during the Session of Congress, shall, without the Consent of the other, adjourn for more than three days, nor to any other Place than that in which the two Houses shall be sitting.

Section. 6. The Senators and Representatives shall receive a Compensation for their Services, to be ascertained by Law, and paid out of the Treasury of the United States. They shall in all Cases, except Treason, Felony and Breach of the Peace, be privileged from Arrest during their Attendance at the Session of their respective Houses, and in going to and returning from the same; and for any Speech or Debate in either House, they shall not be questioned in any other Place.

No Senator or Representative shall, during the Time for which he was elected, be appointed to any civil Office under the Authority of the United States, which shall have been created, or the Emoluments whereof shall have been encreased during such time; and no Person holding any Office under the United States, shall be a Member of either House during his Continuance in Office.

Section. 7. All Bills for raising Revenue shall originate in the House of Representatives; but the Senate may propose or concur with Amendments as on other Bills.

Every Bill which shall have passed the House of Representatives and the Senate shall, before it become a Law, be presented to the President of the United States; If he approve he shall sign it, but if not he shall return it, with his Objections to that House in which it shall have originated, who shall enter the Objections at large on their Journal, and proceed to reconsider it. If after such Reconsideration two thirds of that House shall agree to pass the Bill, it shall be sent, together with the Objections, to the other House, by which it shall likewise be reconsidered, and if approved by two thirds of that House, it shall become a Law. But in all such Cases the Votes of both Houses shall be determined by yeas and Nays, and the Names of the Persons voting for and against the Bill shall be entered on the Journal of each House respectively. If any Bill shall not be returned by the President within ten Days (Sundays excepted) after it shall have been presented to him, the Same shall be a Law, in like Manner as if he had signed it, unless the Congress by their Adjournment prevent its Return, in which Case it shall not be a Law.

Every Order, Resolution, or Vote to which the Concurrence of the Senate and House of Representatives may be necessary (except on a question of Adjournment) shall be presented to the President of the United States; and before the Same shall take Effect, shall be approved by him, or being disapproved by him, shall be repassed by two thirds of the Senate and House of Representatives, according to the Rules and Limitations prescribed in the Case of a Bill.

Section. 8. The Congress shall have Power To lay and collect Taxes, Duties, Imposts and Excises, to pay the Debts and provide for the common Defence and general Welfare of the United States; but all Duties, Imposts and Excises shall be uniform throughout the United States;

To borrow Money on the credit of the United States;

To regulate Commerce with foreign Nations, and among the several States, and with the Indian Tribes;

To establish an uniform Rule of Naturalization, and uniform Laws on the subject of Bankruptcies throughout the United States;

To coin Money, regulate the Value thereof, and of foreign Coin, and fix the Standard of Weights and Measures;

To provide for the Punishment of counterfeiting the Securities and current Coin of the United States;

To establish Post Offices and post Roads;

To promote the Progress of Science and useful Arts, by securing for limited Times to Authors and Inventors the exclusive Right to their respective Writings and Discoveries;

To constitute Tribunals inferior to the supreme Court;

To define and punish Piracies and Felonies committed on the high Seas, and Offences against the Law of Nations;

To declare War, grant Letters of Marque and Reprisal, and make Rules concerning Captures on Land and Water;

To raise and support Armies, but no Appropriation of Money to that Use shall be for a longer Term than two Years;

To provide and maintain a Navy;

To make Rules for the Government and Regulation of the land and naval Forces;

To provide for calling forth the Militia to execute the Laws of the Union, suppress Insurrections and repel Invasions;

To provide for organizing, arming, and disciplining, the Militia, and for governing such Part of them as may be employed in the Service of the United States, reserving to the States respectively, the Appointment of the Officers, and the Authority of training the Militia according to the discipline prescribed by Congress;

To exercise exclusive Legislation in all Cases whatsoever, over such District (not exceeding ten Miles square) as may, by Cession of particular States, and the Acceptance of Congress, become the Seat of the Government of the United States, and to exercise like Authority over all Places purchased by the Consent of the Legislature of the State in which the Same shall be, for the Erection of Forts, Magazines, Arsenals, dock-Yards, and other needful Buildings;—And

To make all Laws which shall be necessary and proper for carrying into Execution the foregoing Powers, and all other Powers vested by this Constitution in the Government of the United States, or in any Department or Officer thereof.

Section. 9. The Migration or Importation of such Persons as any of the States now existing shall think proper to admit, shall not be prohibited by the Congress prior to the Year one thousand eight hundred and eight, but a Tax or duty may be imposed on such Importation, not exceeding ten dollars for each Person.

The Privilege of the Writ of Habeas Corpus shall not be suspended, unless when in Cases of Rebellion or Invasion the public Safety may require it.

No Bill of Attainder or ex post facto Law shall be passed.

No Capitation, or other direct, Tax shall be laid, unless in Proportion to the Census or enumeration herein before directed to be taken.

No Tax or Duty shall be laid on Articles exported from any State.

No Preference shall be given by any Regulation of Commerce or Revenue to the Ports of one State over those of another; nor shall Vessels bound to, or from, one State, be obliged to enter, clear, or pay Duties in another.

No Money shall be drawn from the Treasury, but in Consequence of Appropriations made by Law; and a regular Statement and Account of the Receipts and Expenditures of all public Money shall be published from time to time.

No Title of Nobility shall be granted by the United States: And no Person holding any Office of Profit or Trust under them, shall, without the Consent of the Congress, accept of any present, Emolument, Office, or Title, of any kind whatever, from any King, Prince, or foreign State.

Section. 10. No State shall enter into any Treaty, Alliance, or Confederation; grant Letters of Marque and Reprisal; coin Money; emit Bills of Credit; make any Thing but gold and silver Coin a Tender in Payment of Debts; pass any Bill of Attainder, ex post facto Law, or Law impairing the Obligation of Contracts, or grant any Title of Nobility.

No State shall, without the Consent of the Congress, lay any Imposts or Duties on Imports or Exports, except what may be absolutely necessary for executing it's inspection Laws: and the net Produce of all Duties and Imposts, laid by any State on Imports or Exports, shall be for the Use of the Treasury of the United States; and all such Laws shall be subject to the Revision and Controul of the Congress.

No State shall, without the Consent of Congress, lay any Duty of Tonnage, keep Troops, or Ships of War in time of Peace, enter into any Agreement or Compact with another State, or with a foreign Power, or engage in War, unless actually invaded, or in such imminent Danger as will not admit of delay.

Article. II.

Section. 1. The executive Power shall be vested in a President of the United States of America. He shall hold his Office during the Term of four Years, and, together with the Vice President, chosen for the same Term, be elected, as follows:

Each State shall appoint, in such Manner as the Legislature thereof may direct, a Number of Electors, equal to the whole Number of Senators and Representatives to which the State may be entitled in the Congress: but no Senator or Representative, or Person holding an Office of Trust or Profit under the United States, shall be appointed an Elector.

The Electors shall meet in their respective States, and vote by Ballot for two Persons, of whom one at least shall not be an Inhabitant of the same State with themselves. And they shall make a List of all the Persons voted for, and of the Number of Votes for each; which List they shall sign and certify, and transmit sealed to the Seat of the Government of the United States, directed to the President of the Senate. The President of the Senate shall, in the Presence of the Senate and House of Representatives, open all the Certificates, and the Votes shall then be counted. The Person having the greatest Number of Votes shall be the President, if such Number be a Majority of the whole Number of Electors appointed; and if there be more than one who have such Majority, and have an equal Number of Votes, then the House of Representatives shall immediately chuse by Ballot one of them for President; and if no Person have a Majority, then from the five highest on the List the said House shall in like Manner chuse the President. But in chusing the President, the Votes shall be taken by States, the Representation from each State having one Vote; A quorum for this purpose shall consist of a Member or Members from two thirds of the States, and a Majority of all the States shall be necessary to a Choice. In every Case, after the Choice of the President, the Person having the greatest Number of Votes of the Electors shall be the Vice President. But if there should remain two or more who have equal Votes, the Senate shall chuse from them by Ballot the Vice President.

The Congress may determine the Time of chusing the Electors, and the Day on which they shall give their Votes; which Day shall be the same throughout the United States.

No Person except a natural born Citizen, or a Citizen of the United States, at the time of the Adoption of this Constitution, shall be eligible to the Office of President; neither shall any Person be eligible to that Office who shall not have attained to the Age of thirty five Years, and been fourteen Years a Resident within the United States.

In Case of the Removal of the President from Office, or of his Death, Resignation, or Inability to discharge the Powers and Duties of the said Office, the Same shall devolve on the Vice President, and the Congress may by Law provide for the Case of Removal, Death, Resignation or Inability, both of the President and Vice President, declaring what Officer shall then act as President, and such Officer shall act accordingly, until the Disability be removed, or a President shall be elected.

The President shall, at stated Times, receive for his Services, a Compensation, which shall neither be increased nor diminished during the Period for which he shall have been elected, and he shall not receive within that Period any other Emolument from the United States, or any of them.

Before he enter on the Execution of his Office, he shall take the following Oath or Affirmation:—"I do solemnly swear (or affirm) that I will faithfully execute the Office of President of the United States, and will to the best of my Ability, preserve, protect and defend the Constitution of the United States."

Section. 2. The President shall be Commander in Chief of the Army and Navy of the United States, and of the Militia of the several States, when called into the actual Service of the United States; he may require the Opinion, in writing, of the principal Officer in each of the executive Departments, upon any Subject relating to the Duties of their respective Offices, and he shall have Power to grant Reprieves and Pardons for Offences against the United States, except in Cases of Impeachment.

He shall have Power, by and with the Advice and Consent of the Senate, to make Treaties, provided two thirds of the Senators present concur; and he shall nominate, and by and with the Advice and Consent of the Senate, shall appoint Ambassadors, other public Ministers and Consuls, Judges of the supreme Court, and all other Officers of the United States, whose Appointments are not herein otherwise provided for, and which shall be established by Law: but the Congress may by Law vest the Appointment of such inferior Officers, as they think proper, in the President alone, in the Courts of Law, or in the Heads of Departments.

The President shall have Power to fill up all Vacancies that may happen during the Recess of the Senate, by granting Commissions which shall expire at the End of their next Session.

Section. 3. He shall from time to time give to the Congress Information of the State of the Union, and recommend to their Consideration such Measures as he shall judge necessary and expedient; he may, on extraordinary Occasions, convene both Houses, or either of them, and in Case of Disagreement between them, with Respect to the Time of Adjournment, he may adjourn them to such Time as he shall think proper; he shall receive Ambassadors and other public Ministers; he shall take Care that the Laws be faithfully executed, and shall Commission all the Officers of the United States.

Section. 4. The President, Vice President and all civil Officers of the United States, shall be removed from Office on Impeachment for, and Conviction of, Treason, Bribery, or other high Crimes and Misdemeanors.

Article. III.

Section. 1. The judicial Power of the United States shall be vested in one supreme Court, and in such inferior Courts as the Congress may from time to time ordain and establish. The Judges, both of the supreme and inferior Courts, shall hold their Offices during good Behaviour, and shall, at stated Times, receive for their Services a Compensation, which shall not be diminished during their Continuance in Office.

Section. 2. The judicial Power shall extend to all Cases, in Law and Equity, arising under this Constitution, the Laws of the United States, and Treaties made, or which shall be made, under their Authority;—to all Cases affecting Ambassadors, other public Ministers and Consuls;—to all Cases of admiralty and maritime Jurisdiction;—to Controversies to which the United States shall be a Party;—to Controversies between two or more States;— between a State and Citizens of another State,—between Citizens of different States,—between Citizens of the same State claiming Lands under Grants of different States, and between a State, or the Citizens thereof, and foreign States, Citizens or Subjects.

In all Cases affecting Ambassadors, other public Ministers and Consuls, and those in which a State shall be Party, the supreme Court shall have original Jurisdiction. In all the other Cases before mentioned, the supreme Court shall have appellate Jurisdiction, both as to Law and Fact, with such Exceptions, and under such Regulations as the Congress shall make.

The Trial of all Crimes, except in Cases of Impeachment, shall be by Jury; and such Trial shall be held in the State where the said Crimes shall have been committed; but when not committed within any State, the Trial shall be at such Place or Places as the Congress may by Law have directed.

Section. 3. Treason against the United States, shall consist only in levying War against them, or in adhering to their Enemies, giving them Aid and Comfort. No Person shall be convicted of Treason unless on the Testimony of two Witnesses to the same overt Act, or on Confession in open Court.

The Congress shall have Power to declare the Punishment of Treason, but no Attainder of Treason shall work Corruption of Blood, or Forfeiture except during the Life of the Person attainted.

Article. IV.

Section. 1. Full Faith and Credit shall be given in each State to the public Acts, Records, and judicial Proceedings of every other State. And the Congress may by general Laws prescribe the Manner in which such Acts, Records and Proceedings shall be proved, and the Effect thereof.

Section. 2. The Citizens of each State shall be entitled to all Privileges and Immunities of Citizens in the several States.

A Person charged in any State with Treason, Felony, or other Crime, who shall flee from Justice, and be found in another State, shall on Demand of the executive Authority of the State from which he fled, be delivered up, to be removed to the State having Jurisdiction of the Crime.

No Person held to Service or Labour in one State, under the Laws thereof, escaping into another, shall, in Consequence of any Law or Regulation therein, be discharged from such Service or Labour, but shall be delivered up on Claim of the Party to whom such Service or Labour may be due.

Section. 3. New States may be admitted by the Congress into this Union; but no new State shall be formed or erected within the Jurisdiction of any other State; nor any State be formed by the Junction of two or more States, or Parts of States, without the Consent of the Legislatures of the States concerned as well as of the Congress.

The Congress shall have Power to dispose of and make all needful Rules and Regulations respecting the Territory or other Property belonging to the United States; and nothing in this Constitution shall be so construed as to Prejudice any Claims of the United States, or of any particular States.

Section. 4. The United States shall guarantee to every State in this Union a Republican Form of Government, and shall protect each of them against Invasion; and on Application of the Legislature, or of the Executive (when the Legislature cannot be convened), against domestic Violence.

Article. V.

The Congress, whenever two thirds of both Houses shall deem it necessary, shall propose Amendments to this Constitution, or, on the Application of the Legislatures of two thirds of the several States, shall call a Convention for proposing Amendments, which, in either Case, shall be valid to all Intents and Purposes, as Part of this Constitution, when ratified by the Legislatures of three fourths of the several States, or by Conventions in three fourths thereof, as the one or the other Mode of Ratification may be proposed by the Congress; Provided that no Amendment which may be made prior to the Year One thousand eight hundred and eight shall in any Manner affect the first and fourth Clauses in the Ninth Section of the first Article; and that no State, without its Consent, shall be deprived of its equal Suffrage in the Senate.

Article. VI.

All Debts contracted and Engagements entered into, before the Adoption of this Constitution, shall be as valid against the United States under this Constitution, as under the Confederation.

This Constitution, and the Laws of the United States which shall be made in Pursuance thereof; and all Treaties made, or which shall be made, under the Authority of the United States, shall be the supreme Law of the Land; and the Judges in every State shall be bound thereby, any Thing in the Constitution or Laws of any State to the Contrary notwithstanding.

The Senators and Representatives before mentioned, and the Members of the several State Legislatures, and all executive and judicial Officers, both of the United States and of the several States, shall be bound by Oath or Affirmation, to support this Constitution; but no religious Test shall ever be required as a Qualification to any Office or public Trust under the United States.

Article. VII.

The Ratification of the Conventions of nine States, shall be sufficient for the Establishment of this Constitution between the States so ratifying the Same.

The Word, "the," being interlined between the seventh and eighth Lines of the first Page, the Word "Thirty" being partly written on an Erazure in the fifteenth Line of the first Page, The Words "is tried" being interlined between the thirty second and thirty third Lines of the first Page and the Word "the" being interlined between the forty third and forty fourth Lines of the second Page.

Attest William Jackson Secretary

Done in Convention by the Unanimous Consent of the States present the Seventeenth Day of September in the Year of our Lord one thousand seven hundred and Eighty seven and of the Independance of the United States of America the Twelfth In witness whereof We have hereunto subscribed our Names,

G°. Washington
Presidt and deputy from Virginia

Delaware
- Geo: Read
- Gunning Bedford jun
- John Dickinson
- Richard Bassett
- Jaco: Broom

Maryland
- James McHenry
- Dan of St Thos. Jenifer
- Danl. Carrol

Virginia
- John Blair
- James Madison Jr.

North Carolina
- Wm. Blount
- Richd. Dobbs Spaight
- Hu Williamson

South Carolina
- J. Rutledge
- Charles Cotesworth Pinckney
- Charles Pinckney
- Pierce Butler

Georgia
- William Few
- Abr Baldwin

New Hampshire
- John Langdon
- Nicholas Gilman

Massachusetts
- Nathaniel Gorham
- Rufus King

Connecticut
- Wm. Saml. Johnson
- Roger Sherman

New York
- Alexander Hamilton

New Jersey
- Wil: Livingston
- David Brearley
- Wm. Paterson
- Jona: Dayton

Pennsylvania
- B Franklin
- Thomas Mifflin
- Robt. Morris
- Geo. Clymer
- Thos. FitzSimons
- Jared Ingersoll
- James Wilson
- Gouv Morris

Amendments to the Constitution

The Bill of Rights: A Transcription

The Preamble to The Bill of Rights

Congress of the United States
begun and held at the City of New-York, on
Wednesday the fourth of March, one thousand seven hundred and eighty nine.

THE Conventions of a number of the States, having at the time of their adopting the Constitution, expressed a desire, in order to prevent misconstruction or abuse of its powers, that further declaratory and restrictive clauses should be added: And as extending the ground of public confidence in the Government, will best ensure the beneficent ends of its institution.

RESOLVED by the Senate and House of Representatives of the United States of America, in Congress assembled, two thirds of both Houses concurring, that the following Articles be proposed to the Legislatures of the several States, as amendments to the Constitution of the United States, all, or any of which Articles, when ratified by three fourths of the said Legislatures, to be valid to all intents and purposes, as part of the said Constitution; viz.

ARTICLES in addition to, and Amendment of the Constitution of the United States of America, proposed by Congress, and ratified by the Legislatures of the several States, pursuant to the fifth Article of the original Constitution.

Note: The first ten amendments to the Constitution were ratified December 15, 1791, and form what is known as the "Bill of Rights."

Amendment I

Congress shall make no law respecting an establishment of religion, or prohibiting the free exercise thereof; or abridging the freedom of speech, or of the press; or the right of the people peaceably to assemble, and to petition the Government for a redress of grievances.

Amendment II

A well regulated Militia, being necessary to the security of a free State, the right of the people to keep and bear Arms, shall not be infringed.

Amendment III

No Soldier shall, in time of peace be quartered in any house, without the consent of the Owner, nor in time of war, but in a manner to be prescribed by law.

Amendment IV

The right of the people to be secure in their persons, houses, papers, and effects, against unreasonable searches and seizures, shall not be violated, and no Warrants shall issue, but upon probable cause, supported by Oath or affirmation, and particularly describing the place to be searched, and the persons or things to be seized.

Amendment V

No person shall be held to answer for a capital, or otherwise infamous crime, unless on a presentment or indictment of a Grand Jury, except in cases arising in the land or naval forces, or in the Militia, when in actual service in time of War or public danger; nor shall any person be subject for the same offence to be twice put in jeopardy of life or limb; nor shall be compelled in any criminal case to be a witness against himself, nor be deprived of life, liberty, or property, without due process of law; nor shall private property be taken for public use, without just compensation.

Amendment VI

In all criminal prosecutions, the accused shall enjoy the right to a speedy and public trial, by an impartial jury of the State and district wherein the crime shall have been committed, which district shall have been previously ascertained by law, and to be informed of the nature and cause of the accusation; to be confronted with the witnesses against him; to have compulsory process for obtaining witnesses in his favor, and to have the Assistance of Counsel for his defence.

Amendment VII

In Suits at common law, where the value in controversy shall exceed twenty dollars, the right of trial by jury shall be preserved, and no fact tried by a jury, shall be otherwise re-examined in any Court of the United States, than according to the rules of the common law.

Amendment VIII

Excessive bail shall not be required, nor excessive fines imposed, nor cruel and unusual punishments inflicted.

Amendment IX

The enumeration in the Constitution, of certain rights, shall not be construed to deny or disparage others retained by the people.

Amendment X

The powers not delegated to the United States by the Constitution, nor prohibited by it to the States, are reserved to the States respectively, or to the people.

Amendment XI

Passed by Congress March 4, 1794. Ratified February 7, 1795.

Note: Article III, section 2, of the Constitution was modified by amendment 11.

The Judicial power of the United States shall not be construed to extend to any suit in law or equity, commenced or prosecuted against one of the United States by Citizens of another State, or by Citizens or Subjects of any Foreign State.

Amendment XII

Passed by Congress December 9, 1803. Ratified June 15, 1804.

Note: A portion of Article II, section 1 of the Constitution was superseded by the 12th amendment.

The Electors shall meet in their respective states and vote by ballot for President and Vice-President, one of whom, at least, shall not be an inhabitant of the same state with themselves; they shall name in their ballots the person voted for as President, and in distinct ballots the person voted for as Vice-President, and they shall make distinct lists of all persons voted for as President, and of all persons voted for as Vice-President, and of the number of votes for each, which lists they shall sign and certify, and transmit sealed to the seat of the government of the United States, directed to the President of the Senate; — the President of the Senate shall, in the presence of the Senate and House of Representatives, open all the certificates and the votes shall then be counted; — The person having the greatest number of votes for President, shall be the President, if such number be a majority of the whole number of Electors appointed; and if no person have such majority, then from the persons having the highest numbers not exceeding three on the list of those voted for as President, the House of Representatives shall choose immediately, by ballot, the President. But in choosing the President, the votes shall be taken by states, the representation from each state having one vote; a quorum for this purpose shall consist of a member or members from two-thirds of the states, and a majority of all the states shall be necessary to a choice. [And if the House of Representatives shall not choose a President whenever the right of choice shall devolve upon them, before the fourth day of March next following, then the Vice-President shall act as President, as in case of the death or other constitutional disability of the President. —]* The person having the greatest number of votes as Vice-President, shall be the Vice-President, if such number be a majority of the whole number of Electors appointed, and if no person have a majority, then from the two highest numbers on the list, the Senate shall choose the Vice-President; a quorum for the purpose shall consist of two-thirds of the whole number of Senators, and a majority of the whole number shall be necessary to a choice. But no person constitutionally ineligible to the office of President shall be eligible to that of Vice-President of the United States.

**Superseded by section 3 of the 20th amendment.*

Amendment XIII

Passed by Congress January 31, 1865. Ratified December 6, 1865.

Note: A portion of Article IV, section 2, of the Constitution was superseded by the 13th amendment.

Section 1.

Neither slavery nor involuntary servitude, except as a punishment for crime whereof the party shall have been duly convicted, shall exist within the United States, or any place subject to their jurisdiction.

Section 2.

Congress shall have power to enforce this article by appropriate legislation.

Amendment XIV

Passed by Congress June 13, 1866. Ratified July 9, 1868.

Note: Article I, section 2, of the Constitution was modified by section 2 of the 14th amendment.

Section 1.

All persons born or naturalized in the United States, and subject to the jurisdiction thereof, are citizens of the United States and of the State wherein they reside. No State shall make or enforce any law which shall abridge the privileges or immunities of citizens of the United States; nor shall any State deprive any person of life, liberty, or property, without due process of law; nor deny to any person within its jurisdiction the equal protection of the laws.

Section 2.

Representatives shall be apportioned among the several States according to their respective numbers, counting the whole number of persons in each State, excluding Indians not taxed. But when the right to vote at any election for the choice of electors for President and Vice-President of the United States, Representatives in Congress, the Executive and Judicial officers of a State, or the members of the Legislature thereof, is denied to any of the male inhabitants of such State, being twenty-one years of age,* and citizens of the United States, or in any way abridged, except for participation in rebellion, or other crime, the basis of representation therein shall be reduced in the proportion which the number of such male citizens shall bear to the whole number of male citizens twenty-one years of age in such State.

Section 3.

No person shall be a Senator or Representative in Congress, or elector of President and Vice-President, or hold any office, civil or military, under the United States, or under any State, who, having previously taken an oath, as a member of Congress, or as an officer of the United States, or as a member of any State legislature, or as an executive or judicial officer of any State, to support the Constitution of the United States, shall have engaged in insurrection or rebellion against the same, or given aid or comfort to the enemies thereof. But Congress may by a vote of two-thirds of each House, remove such disability.

**Changed by section 1 of the 26th amendment.*

Section 4.
The validity of the public debt of the United States, authorized by law, including debts incurred for payment of pensions and bounties for services in suppressing insurrection or rebellion, shall not be questioned. But neither the United States nor any State shall assume or pay any debt or obligation incurred in aid of insurrection or rebellion against the United States, or any claim for the loss or emancipation of any slave; but all such debts, obligations and claims shall be held illegal and void.

Section 5.
The Congress shall have the power to enforce, by appropriate legislation, the provisions of this article.

Amendment XV

Passed by Congress February 26, 1869. Ratified February 3, 1870.

Section 1.
The right of citizens of the United States to vote shall not be denied or abridged by the United States or by any State on account of race, color, or previous condition of servitude—

Section 2.
The Congress shall have the power to enforce this article by appropriate legislation.

Amendment XVI

Passed by Congress July 2, 1909. Ratified February 3, 1913.

Note: Article I, section 9, of the Constitution was modified by amendment 16.

The Congress shall have power to lay and collect taxes on incomes, from whatever source derived, without apportionment among the several States, and without regard to any census or enumeration.

Amendment XVII

Passed by Congress May 13, 1912. Ratified April 8, 1913.

Note: Article I, section 3, of the Constitution was modified by the 17th amendment.

The Senate of the United States shall be composed of two Senators from each State, elected by the people thereof, for six years; and each Senator shall have one vote. The electors in each State shall have the qualifications requisite for electors of the most numerous branch of the State legislatures.

When vacancies happen in the representation of any State in the Senate, the executive authority of such State shall issue writs of election to fill such vacancies: *Provided,* That the legislature of any State may empower the executive thereof to make temporary appointments until the people fill the vacancies by election as the legislature may direct.

This amendment shall not be so construed as to affect the election or term of any Senator chosen before it becomes valid as part of the Constitution.

Amendment XVIII

Passed by Congress December 18, 1917. Ratified January 16, 1919. Repealed by amendment 21.

Section 1.
After one year from the ratification of this article the manufacture, sale, or transportation of intoxicating liquors within, the importation thereof into, or the exportation thereof from the United States and all territory subject to the jurisdiction thereof for beverage purposes is hereby prohibited.

Section 2.
The Congress and the several States shall have concurrent power to enforce this article by appropriate legislation.

Section 3.
This article shall be inoperative unless it shall have been ratified as an amendment to the Constitution by the legislatures of the several States, as provided in the Constitution, within seven years from the date of the submission hereof to the States by the Congress.

Amendment XIX

Passed by Congress June 4, 1919. Ratified August 18, 1920.

The right of citizens of the United States to vote shall not be denied or abridged by the United States or by any State on account of sex.

Congress shall have power to enforce this article by appropriate legislation.

Amendment XX

Passed by Congress March 2, 1932. Ratified January 23, 1933.

Note: Article I, section 4, of the Constitution was modified by section 2 of this amendment. In addition, a portion of the 12th amendment was superseded by section 3.

Section 1.
The terms of the President and the Vice President shall end at noon on the 20th day of January, and the terms of Senators and Representatives at noon on the 3rd day of January, of the years in which such terms would have ended if this article had not been ratified; and the terms of their successors shall then begin.

Section 2.
The Congress shall assemble at least once in every year, and such meeting shall begin at noon on the 3d day of January, unless they shall by law appoint a different day.

Section 3.
If, at the time fixed for the beginning of the term of the President, the President elect shall have died, the Vice President elect shall become President. If a President shall not have been chosen before the time fixed for the beginning of his term, or if the

President elect shall have failed to qualify, then the Vice President elect shall act as President until a President shall have qualified; and the Congress may by law provide for the case wherein neither a President elect nor a Vice President shall have qualified, declaring who shall then act as President, or the manner in which one who is to act shall be selected, and such person shall act accordingly until a President or Vice President shall have qualified.

Section 4.

The Congress may by law provide for the case of the death of any of the persons from whom the House of Representatives may choose a President whenever the right of choice shall have devolved upon them, and for the case of the death of any of the persons from whom the Senate may choose a Vice President whenever the right of choice shall have devolved upon them.

Section 5.

Sections 1 and 2 shall take effect on the 15th day of October following the ratification of this article.

Section 6.

This article shall be inoperative unless it shall have been ratified as an amendment to the Constitution by the legislatures of three-fourths of the several States within seven years from the date of its submission.

Amendment XXI

Passed by Congress February 20, 1933. Ratified December 5, 1933.

Section 1.

The eighteenth article of amendment to the Constitution of the United States is hereby repealed.

Section 2.

The transportation or importation into any State, Territory, or Possession of the United States for delivery or use therein of intoxicating liquors, in violation of the laws thereof, is hereby prohibited.

Section 3.

This article shall be inoperative unless it shall have been ratified as an amendment to the Constitution by conventions in the several States, as provided in the Constitution, within seven years from the date of the submission hereof to the States by the Congress.

Amendment XXII

Passed by Congress March 21, 1947. Ratified February 27, 1951.

Section 1.

No person shall be elected to the office of the President more than twice, and no person who has held the office of President, or acted as President, for more than two years of a term to which some other person was elected President shall be elected to the office of President more than once. But this Article shall not apply to any person holding the office of President when this Article was proposed by Congress, and shall not prevent any person who may be holding the office of President, or acting as President, during the term within which this Article becomes operative from holding the office of President or acting as President during the remainder of such term.

Section 2.
This article shall be inoperative unless it shall have been ratified as an amendment to the Constitution by the legislatures of three-fourths of the several States within seven years from the date of its submission to the States by the Congress.

Amendment XXIII

Passed by Congress June 16, 1960. Ratified March 29, 1961.

Section 1.
The District constituting the seat of Government of the United States shall appoint in such manner as Congress may direct:

A number of electors of President and Vice President equal to the whole number of Senators and Representatives in Congress to which the District would be entitled if it were a State, but in no event more than the least populous State; they shall be in addition to those appointed by the States, but they shall be considered, for the purposes of the election of President and Vice President, to be electors appointed by a State; and they shall meet in the District and perform such duties as provided by the twelfth article of amendment.

Section 2.
The Congress shall have power to enforce this article by appropriate legislation.

Amendment XXIV

Passed by Congress August 27, 1962. Ratified January 23, 1964.

Section 1.
The right of citizens of the United States to vote in any primary or other election for President or Vice President, for electors for President or Vice President, or for Senator or Representative in Congress, shall not be denied or abridged by the United States or any State by reason of failure to pay poll tax or other tax.

Section 2.
The Congress shall have power to enforce this article by appropriate legislation.

Amendment XXV

Passed by Congress July 6, 1965. Ratified February 10, 1967.

Note: Article II, section 1, of the Constitution was affected by the 25th amendment.

Section 1.
In case of the removal of the President from office or of his death or resignation, the Vice President shall become President.

Section 2.

Whenever there is a vacancy in the office of the Vice President, the President shall nominate a Vice President who shall take office upon confirmation by a majority vote of both Houses of Congress.

Section 3.

Whenever the President transmits to the President pro tempore of the Senate and the Speaker of the House of Representatives his written declaration that he is unable to discharge the powers and duties of his office, and until he transmits to them a written declaration to the contrary, such powers and duties shall be discharged by the Vice President as Acting President.

Section 4.

Whenever the Vice President and a majority of either the principal officers of the executive departments or of such other body as Congress may by law provide, transmit to the President pro tempore of the Senate and the Speaker of the House of Representatives their written declaration that the President is unable to discharge the powers and duties of his office, the Vice President shall immediately assume the powers and duties of the office as Acting President.

Thereafter, when the President transmits to the President pro tempore of the Senate and the Speaker of the House of Representatives his written declaration that no inability exists, he shall resume the powers and duties of his office unless the Vice President and a majority of either the principal officers of the executive department or of such other body as Congress may by law provide, transmit within four days to the President pro tempore of the Senate and the Speaker of the House of Representatives their written declaration that the President is unable to discharge the powers and duties of his office. Thereupon Congress shall decide the issue, assembling within forty-eight hours for that purpose if not in session. If the Congress, within twenty-one days after receipt of the latter written declaration, or, if Congress is not in session, within twenty-one days after Congress is required to assemble, determines by two-thirds vote of both Houses that the President is unable to discharge the powers and duties of his office, the Vice President shall continue to discharge the same as Acting President; otherwise, the President shall resume the powers and duties of his office.

Amendment XXVI

Passed by Congress March 23, 1971. Ratified July 1, 1971.

Note: Amendment 14, section 2, of the Constitution was modified by section 1 of the 26th amendment.

Section 1.

The right of citizens of the United States, who are eighteen years of age or older, to vote shall not be denied or abridged by the United States or by any State on account of age.

Section 2.

The Congress shall have power to enforce this article by appropriate legislation.

Amendment XXVI

Originally proposed Sept. 25, 1789. Ratified May 7, 1992.

No law, varying the compensation for the services of the Senators and Representatives, shall take effect, until an election of representatives shall have intervened.

PRESIDENTIAL ELECTIONS

Year	Number of States	Candidates	Parties	Popular Vote	% of Popular Vote	Electoral Vote	% Voter Participation
1789	11	**GEORGE WASHINGTON**	No party			69	
		John Adams	designations			34	
		Other candidates				35	
1792	15	**GEORGE WASHINGTON**	No party			132	
		John Adams	designations			77	
		George Clinton				50	
		Other candidates				5	
1796	16	**JOHN ADAMS**	Federalist			71	
		Thomas Jefferson	Democratic-Republican			68	
		Thomas Pinckney	Federalist			59	
		Aaron Burr	Democratic- Republican			30	
		Other candidates				48	
1800	16	**THOMAS JEFFERSON**	Democratic- Republican			73	
		Aaron Burr	Democratic- Republican			73	
		John Adams	Federalist			65	
		Charles C. Pinckney	Federalist			64	
		John Jay	Federalist			1	
1804	17	**THOMAS JEFFERSON**	Democratic-Republican			162	
		Charles C. Pinckney	Federalist			14	
1808	17	**JAMES MADISON**	Democratic-Republican			122	
		Charles C. Pinckney	Federalist			47	
		George Clinton	Democratic-Republican			6	
1812	18	**JAMES MADISON**	Democratic-Republican			128	
		DeWitt Clinton	Federalist			89	
1816	19	**JAMES MONROE**	Democratic-Republican			183	
		Rufus King	Federalist			34	
1820	24	**JAMES MONROE**	Democratic-Republican			231	
		John Quincy Adams	Independent			1	

1824	24	**JOHN QUINCY ADAMS**	Democratic-Republican	108,740	30.5	84	26.9
		Andrew Jackson	Democratic-Republican	153,544	43.1	99	
		Henry Clay	Democratic-Republican	47,136	13.2	37	
		William H. Crawford	Democratic-Republican	46,618	13.1	41	
1828	24	**ANDREW JACKSON**	Democratic	647,286	56.0	178	57.6
		John Quincy Adams	National-Republican	508,064	44.0	83	
1832	24	**ANDREW JACKSON**	Democratic	688,242	54.5	219	55.4
		Henry Clay	National-Republican	473,462	37.5	49	
		William Wirt	Anti-Masonic	101,051	8.0	7	
		John Floyd	Democratic			11	
1836	26	**MARTIN VAN BUREN**	Democratic	765,483	50.9	170	57.8
		William H. Harrison	Whig			73	
		Hugh L. White	Whig	739,795	49.1	26	
		Daniel Webster	Whig			14	
		W. P. Mangum	Whig			11	
1840	26	**WILLIAM H. HARRISON**	Whig	1,274,624	53.1	234	80.2
		Martin Van Buren	Democratic	1,127,781	46.9	60	
1844	26	**JAMES K. POLK**	Democratic	1,338,464	49.6	170	78.9
		Henry Clay	Whig	1,300,097	48.1	105	
		James G. Birney	Liberty	62,300	2.3		
1848	30	**ZACHARY TAYLOR**	Whig	1,360,967	47.4	163	72.7
		Lewis Cass	Democratic	1,222,342	42.5	127	
		Martin Van Buren	Free Soil	291,263	10.1		
1852	31	**FRANKLIN PIERCE**	Democratic	1,601,117	50.9	254	69.6
		Winfield Scott	Whig	1,385,453	44.1	42	
		John P. Hale	Free Soil	155,825	5.0		

Year	Number of States	Candidates	Parties	Popular Vote	% of Popular Vote	Electoral Vote	% Voter Participation
1856	31	**JAMES BUCHANAN**	Democratic	1,832,955	45.3	174	78.9
		John C. Frémont	Republican	1,339,932	33.1	114	
		Millard Fillmore	American	871,731	21.6	8	
1860	33	**ABRAHAM LINCOLN**	Republican	1,865,593	39.8	180	81.2
		Stephen A. Douglas	Democratic	1,382,713	29.5	12	
		John C. Breckinridge	Democratic	848,356	18.1	72	
		John Bell	Constitutional Union	592,906	12.6	39	
1864	36	**ABRAHAM LINCOLN**	Republican	2,206,938	55.0	212	73.8
		George B. McClellan	Democratic	1,803,787	45.0	21	
1868	37	**ULYSSES S. GRANT**	Republican	3,013,421	52.7	214	78.1
		Horatio Seymour	Democratic	2,706,829	47.3	80	
1872	37	**ULYSSES S. GRANT**	Republican	3,596,745	55.6	286	71.3
		Horace Greeley	Democratic	2,843,446	43.9	66	
1876	38	Rutherford B. Hayes	Republican	4,036,572	48.0	185	81.8
		Samuel J. Tilden	Democratic	4,284,020	51.0	184	
1880	38	**JAMES A. GARFIELD**	Republican	4,453,295	48.5	214	79.4
		Winfield S. Hancock	Democratic	4,414,082	48.1	155	
		James B. Weaver	Greenback-Labor	308,578	3.4		
1884	38	**GROVER CLEVELAND**	Democratic	4,879,507	48.5	219	77.5
		James G. Blaine	Republican	4,850,293	48.2	182	
		Benjamin F. Butler	Greenback-Labor	175,370	1.8		
		John P. St. John	Prohibition	150,369	1.5		
1888	38	**BENJAMIN HARRISON**	Republican	5,477,129	47.9	233	79.3
		Grover Cleveland	Democratic	5,537,857	48.6	168	
		Clinton B. Fisk	Prohibition	249,506	2.2		
		Anson J. Streeter	Union Labor	146,935	1.3		

1892	44	**GROVER CLEVELAND**	Democratic	5,555,426	46.1	277	74.7
		Benjamin Harrison	Republican	5,182,690	43.0	145	
		James B. Weaver	People's	1,029,846	8.5	22	
		John Bidwell	Prohibition	264,133	2.2		
1896	45	**WILLIAM MCKINLEY**	Republican	7,102,246	51.1	271	79.3
		William J. Bryan	Democratic	6,492,559	47.7	176	
1900	45	**WILLIAM MCKINLEY**	Republican	7,218,491	51.7	292	73.2
		William J. Bryan	Democratic; Populist	6,356,734	45.5	155	
		John C. Wooley	Prohibition	208,914	1.5		
1904	45	**THEODORE ROOSEVELT**	Republican	7,628,461	57.4	336	65.2
		Alton B. Parker	Democratic	5,084,223	37.6	140	
		Eugene V. Debs	Socialist	402,283	3.0		
		Silas C. Swallow	Prohibition	258,536	1.9		
1908	46	**WILLIAM H. TAFT**	Republican	7,675,320	51.6	321	65.4
		William J. Bryan	Democratic	6,412,294	43.1	162	
		Eugene V. Debs	Socialist	420,793	2.8		
		Eugene W. Chafin	Prohibition	253,840	1.7		
1912	48	**WOODROW WILSON**	Democratic	6,296,547	41.9	435	58.8
		Theodore Roosevelt	Progressive	4,118,571	27.4	88	
		William H. Taft	Republican	3,486,720	23.2	8	
		Eugene V. Debs	Socialist	900,672	6.0		
		Eugene W. Chafin	Prohibition	206,275	1.4		
1916	48	**WOODROW WILSON**	Democratic	9,127,695	49.4	277	61.6
		Charles E. Hughes	Republican	8,533,507	46.2	254	
		A. L. Benson	Socialist	585,113	3.2		
		J. Frank Hanly	Prohibition	220,506	1.2		
1920	48	**WARREN G. HARDING**	Republican	16,143,407	60.4	404	49.2
		James M. Cox	Democratic	9,130,328	34.2	127	
		Eugene V. Debs	Socialist	919,799	3.4		
		P. P. Christensen	Farmer-Labor	265,411	1.0		

Year	Number of States	Candidates	Parties	Popular Vote	% of Popular Vote	Electoral Vote	% Voter Participation
1924	48	**CALVIN COOLIDGE**	Republican	15,718,211	54.0	382	48.9
		John W. Davis	Democratic	8,385,283	28.8	136	
		Robert M. La Follette	Progressive	4,831,289	16.6	13	
1928	48	**HERBERT C. HOOVER**	Republican	21,391,993	58.2	444	56.9
		Alfred E. Smith	Democratic	15,016,169	40.9	87	
1932	48	**FRANKLIN D. ROOSEVELT**	Democratic	22,809,638	57.4	472	56.9
		Herbert C. Hoover	Republican	15,758,901	39.7	59	
		Norman Thomas	Socialist	881,951	2.2		
1936	48	**FRANKLIN D. ROOSEVELT**	Democratic	27,752,869	60.8	523	61.0
		Alfred M. Landon	Republican	16,674,665	36.5	8	
		William Lemke	Union	882,479	1.9		
1940	48	**FRANKLIN D. ROOSEVELT**	Democratic	27,307,819	54.8	449	62.5
		Wendell L. Willkie	Republican	22,321,018	44.8	82	
1944	48	**FRANKLIN D. ROOSEVELT**	Democratic	25,606,585	53.5	432	55.9
		Thomas E. Dewey	Republican	22,014,745	46.0	99	
1948	48	**HARRY S. TRUMAN**	Democratic	24,179,345	49.6	303	53.0
		Thomas E. Dewey	Republican	21,991,291	45.1	189	
		J. Strom Thurmond	States' Rights	1,176,125	2.4	39	
		Henry A. Wallace	Progressive	1,157,326	2.4		
1952	48	**DWIGHT D. EISENHOWER**	Republican	33,936,234	55.1	442	63.3
		Adlai E. Stevenson	Democratic	27,314,992	44.4	89	
1956	48	**DWIGHT D. EISENHOWER**	Republican	35,590,472	57.6	457	60.6
		Adlai E. Stevenson	Democratic	26,022,752	42.1	73	
1960	50	**JOHN F. KENNEDY**	Democratic	34,226,731	49.7	303	62.8
		Richard M. Nixon	Republican	34,108,157	49.5	219	
1964	50	**LYNDON B. JOHNSON**	Democratic	43,129,566	61.1	486	61.9
		Barry M. Goldwater	Republican	27,178,188	38.5	52	
1968	50	**RICHARD M. NIXON**	Republican	31,785,480	43.4	301	60.9
		Hubert H. Humphrey	Democratic	31,275,166	42.7	191	
		George C. Wallace	American Independent	9,906,473	13.5	46	

1972	50	**RICHARD M. NIXON**	Republican	47,169,911	60.7	520	55.2
		George S. McGovern	Democratic	29,170,383	37.5	17	
		John G. Schmitz	American	1,099,482	1.4		
1976	50	**James E. CARTER**	Democratic	40,830,763	50.1	297	53.5
		Gerald R. Ford	Republican	39,147,793	48.0	240	
1980	50	**RONALD REAGAN**	Republican	43,901,812	50.7	489	52.6
		James E. Carter	Democratic	35,483,820	41.0	49	
		John B. Anderson	Independent	5,719,437	6.6		
		Ed Clark	Libertarian	921,188	1.1		
1984	50	**RONALD REAGAN**	Republican	54,451,521	58.8	525	53.1
		Walter F. Mondale	Democratic	37,565,334	40.6	13	
1988	50	**GEORGE H. W. BUSH**	Republican	47,917,341	53.4	426	50.1
		Michael Dukakis	Democratic	41,013,030	45.6	111	
1992	50	**WILLIAM J. CLINTON**	Democratic	44,908,254	43.0	370	55.0
		George H. W. Bush	Republican	39,102,343	37.4	168	
		H. Ross Perot	Independent	19,741,065	18.9		
1996	50	**WILLIAM J. CLINTON**	Democratic	47,401,185	49.0	379	49.0
		Robert Dole	Republican	39,197,469	41.0	159	
		H. Ross Perot	Independent	8,085,295	8.0		
2000	50	**GEORGE W. BUSH**	Republican	50,455,156	47.9	271	50.4
		Al Gore	Democrat	50,997,335	48.4	266	
		Ralph Nader	Green	2,882,897	2.7		
2004	50	**GEORGE W. BUSH**	Republican	62,040,610	50.7	286	60.7
		John F. Kerry	Democrat	59,028,444	48.3	251	
2008	50	**BARACK OBAMA**	Democrat	69,456,897	52.9	365	63.0
		John McCain	Republican	59,934,814	45.7	173	
2012	50	**BARACK OBAMA**	Democrat	65,915,795	51.1	332	57.5
		Mitt Romney	Republican	60,933,504	47.2	206	
2016	50	**DONALD J. TRUMP**	Republican	62,979,636	46.1	304	60.2
		Hillary Rodham Clinton	Democrat	65,844,610	48.2	227	
2020	50	**JOSEPH R. BIDEN**	Democrat	81,268,924	51.31	302	66.8
		Donald J. Trump	Republican	74,216,154	46.86	232	

Candidates receiving less than 1 percent of the popular vote have been omitted. Thus the percentage of popular vote given for any election year may not total 100 percent. Before the passage of the Twelfth Amendment in 1804, the Electoral College voted for two presidential candidates; the runner-up became vice president.

ADMISSION OF STATES

Order of Admission	State	Date of Admission	Order of Admission	State	Date of Admission
1	Delaware	December 7,1787	26	Michigan	January 26,1837
2	Pennsylvania	December 12,1787	27	Florida	March 3,1845
3	New Jersey	December 18,1787	28	Texas	December 29,1845
4	Georgia	January 2,1788	29	Iowa	December 28,1846
5	Connecticut	January 9,1788	30	Wisconsin	May 29,1848
6	Massachusetts	February 7,1788	31	California	September 9,1850
7	Maryland	April 28,1788	32	Minnesota	May 11,1858
8	South Carolina	May 23,1788	33	Oregon	February 14,1859
9	New Hampshire	June 21,1788	34	Kansas	January 29,1861
10	Virginia	June 25,1788	35	West Virginia	June 30,1863
11	New York	July 26,1788	36	Nevada	October 31,1864
12	North Carolina	November 21,1789	37	Nebraska	March 1,1867
13	Rhode Island	May 29,1790	38	Colorado	August 1,1876
14	Vermont	March 4,1791	39	North Dakota	November 2,1889
15	Kentucky	June 1,1792	40	South Dakota	November 2,1889
16	Tennessee	June 1,1796	41	Montana	November 8,1889
17	Ohio	March 1,1803	42	Washington	November 11, 1889
18	Louisiana	April 30,1812	43	Idaho	July 3,1890
19	Indiana	December 11,1816	44	Wyoming	July 10,1890
20	Mississippi	December 10,1817	45	Utah	January 4,1896
21	Illinois	December 3,1818	46	Oklahoma	November 16,1907
22	Alabama	December 14,1819	47	New Mexico	January 6,1912
23	Maine	March 15,1820	48	Arizona	February 14, 1912
24	Missouri	August 10,1821	49	Alaska	January 3,1959
25	Arkansas	June 15,1836	50	Hawaii	August 21,1959

POPULATION OF THE UNITED STATES

Year	Number of States	Population	% Increase	Population per Square Mile
1790	13	3,929,214		4.5
1800	16	5,308,483	35.1	6.1
1810	17	7,239,881	36.4	4.3
1820	23	9,638,453	33.1	5.5
1830	24	12,866,020	33.5	7.4
1840	26	17,069,453	32.7	9.8
1850	31	23,191,876	35.9	7.9
1860	33	31,443,321	35.6	10.6
1870	37	39,818,449	26.6	13.4
1880	38	50,155,783	26.0	16.9
1890	44	62,947,714	25.5	21.1
1900	45	75,994,575	20.7	25.6
1910	46	91,972,266	21.0	31.0
1920	48	105,710,620	14.9	35.6
1930	48	122,775,046	16.1	41.2
1940	48	131,669,275	7.2	44.2
1950	48	150,697,361	14.5	50.7
1960	50	179,323,175	19.0	50.6
1970	50	203,235,298	13.3	57.5
1980	50	226,504,825	11.4	64.0
1985	50	237,839,000	5.0	67.2
1990	50	250,122,000	5.2	70.6
1995	50	263,411,707	5.3	74.4
2000	50	281,421,906	6.8	77.0
2005	50	296,410,404	5.3	77.9
2010	50	308,745,538	9.7	87.4
2015	50	321,931,311	4.3	91.1
2020	50	331,449,281	7.4	93.8

IMMIGRATION BY REGION AND SELECTED COUNTRY OF LAST RESIDENCE, FISCAL YEARS 1820–2020

Region and country of last residence	1820 to 1829	1830 to 1839	1840 to 1849	1850 to 1859	1860 to 1869	1870 to 1879	1880 to 1889	1890 to 1899
Total	128,502	538,381	1,427,337	2,814,554	2,081,261	2,742,137	5,248,568	3,694,294
Europe	99,272	422,771	1,369,259	2,619,680	1,877,726	2,251,878	4,638,677	3,576,411
Austria-Hungary	—	—	—	—	3,375	60,127	314,787	534,059
Austria	—	—	—	—	2,700	54,529	204,805	268,218
Hungary	—	—	—	—	483	5,598	109,982	203,350
Belgium	28	20	3,996	5,765	5,785	6,991	18,738	19,642
Bulgaria	—	—	—	—	—	—	—	52
*Former Czechoslovakia	—	—	—	—	—	—	—	—
Denmark	173	927	671	3,227	13,553	29,278	85,342	56,671
Finland	—	—	—	—	—	—	—	—
France	7,694	39,330	75,300	81,778	35,938	71,901	48,193	35,616
Germany	5,753	124,726	385,434	976,072	723,734	751,769	1,445,181	579,072
Greece	17	49	17	32	51	209	1,807	12,732
Ireland	51,617	170,672	656,145	1,029,486	427,419	422,264	674,061	405,710
Italy	430	2,225	1,476	8,643	9,853	46,296	267,660	603,761
Netherlands	1,105	1,377	7,624	11,122	8,387	14,267	52,715	29,349
Norway-Sweden	91	1,149	12,389	22,202	82,937	178,823	586,441	334,058
Norway	—	—	—	—	16,068	88,644	185,111	96,810
Sweden	—	—	—	—	24,224	90,179	401,330	237,248
Poland	19	366	105	1,087	1,886	11,016	42,910	107,793
Portugal	177	820	196	1,299	2,083	13,971	15,186	25,874
Romania	—	—	—	—	—	—	5,842	6,808
Russia	86	280	520	423	1,670	35,177	182,698	450,101
Spain	2,595	2,010	1,916	8,795	6,966	5,540	3,995	9,189
Switzerland	3,148	4,430	4,819	24,423	21,124	25,212	81,151	37,020
United Kingdom	26,336	74,350	218,572	445,322	532,956	578,447	810,900	328,759
*Former Yugoslavia	—	—	—	—	—	—	—	—
Other Europe	3	40	79	4	9	590	1,070	145

Asia	34	55	121	36,080	54,408	134,128	71,151	61,285
China	3	8	32	35,933	54,028	133,139	65,797	15,268
Hong Kong	—	—	—	—	—	—	—	102
India	9	38	33	42	50	166	247	102
Iran	—	—	—	—	—	—	—	—
*Israel	—	—	—	—	—	—	—	—
Japan	—	—	—	—	138	193	1,583	13,998
Jordan	—	—	—	—	—	—	—	—
*Korea	—	—	—	—	—	—	—	—
Philippines	—	—	—	—	—	—	—	—
Syria	—	—	—	—	—	—	—	—
Taiwan	—	—	—	—	—	—	—	—
Turkey	19	8	45	94	129	382	2,478	27,510
Vietnam	—	—	—	—	—	—	—	—
Other Asia	3	1	11	11	63	248	1,046	4,407
North America	9,655	31,905	50,516	84,145	130,292	345,010	524,826	37,350
Canada and Newfoundland	2,297	11,875	34,285	64,171	117,978	324,310	492,865	3,098
Mexico	3,835	7,187	3,069	3,446	1,957	5,133	2,405	734
Caribbean	3,061	11,792	11,803	12,447	8,751	14,285	27,323	31,480
Cuba	—	—	—	—	—	—	—	—
Dominican Republic	—	—	—	—	—	—	—	—
Haiti	—	—	—	—	—	—	—	—
Jamaica	—	—	—	—	—	—	—	—
Other Caribbean	3,061	11,792	11,803	12,447	8,751	14,285	27,323	31,480
Central America	57	94	297	512	70	173	279	649
Belize	—	—	—	—	—	—	—	—
Costa Rica	—	—	—	—	—	—	—	—
El Salvador	—	—	—	—	—	—	—	—
Guatemala	—	—	—	—	—	—	—	—
Honduras	—	—	—	—	—	—	—	—
Nicaragua	—	—	—	—	—	—	—	—
Panama	—	—	—	—	—	—	—	—
Other Central America	57	94	297	512	70	173	279	649

Region and country of last residence	1820 to 1829	1830 to 1839	1840 to 1849	1850 to 1859	1860 to 1869	1870 to 1879	1880 to 1889	1890 to 1899
South America	405	957	1,062	3,569	1,536	1,109	1,954	1,389
Argentina	—	—	—	—	—	—	—	—
Bolivia	—	—	—	—	—	—	—	—
Brazil	—	—	—	—	—	—	—	—
Chile	—	—	—	—	—	—	—	—
Colombia	—	—	—	—	—	—	—	—
Ecuador	—	—	—	—	—	—	—	—
Guyana	—	—	—	—	—	—	—	—
Paraguay	—	—	—	—	—	—	—	—
Peru	—	—	—	—	—	—	—	—
Suriname	—	—	—	—	—	—	—	—
Uruguay	—	—	—	—	—	—	—	—
Venezuela	—	—	—	—	—	—	—	—
Other South America	405	957	1,062	3,569	1,536	1,109	1,954	1,389
Other America	—	—	—	—	—	—	—	—
Africa	15	50	61	84	407	371	763	432
Egypt	—	—	—	—	4	29	145	51
Ethiopia	—	—	—	—	—	—	—	—
Liberia	1	8	5	7	43	52	21	9
Morocco	—	—	—	—	—	—	—	—
South Africa	—	—	—	—	35	48	23	9
Other Africa	14	42	56	77	325	242	574	363
Oceania	3	7	14	166	187	9,996	12,361	4,704
Australia	2	1	2	15	—	8,930	7,250	3,098
New Zealand	—	—	—	—	—	39	21	12
Other Oceania	1	6	12	151	187	1,027	5,090	1,594
Not Specified	19,523	83,593	7,366	74,399	18,241	754	790	14,112

Region and country of last residence	1900 to 1909	1910 to 1919	1920 to 1929	1930 to 1939	1940 to 1949	1950 to 1959	1960 to 1969	1980 to 1989
Total	8,202,388	6,347,380	4,295,510	699,375	856,608	2,499,268	3,213,749	6,244,379
Europe	7,572,569	4,985,411	2,560,340	444,399	472,524	1,404,973	1,133,443	668,866
Austria-Hungary	2,001,376	1,154,727	60,891	12,531	13,574	113,015	27,590	20,437
Austria	532,416	589,174	31,392	5,307	8,393	81,354	17,571	15,374
Hungary	685,567	565,553	29,499	7,224	5,181	31,661	10,019	5,063
Belgium	37,429	32,574	21,511	4,013	12,473	18,885	9,647	7,028
Bulgaria	34,651	27,180	2,824	1,062	449	97	598	1,124
*Former Czechoslovakia	—	—	101,182	17,757	8,475	1,624	2,758	5,678
Denmark	61,227	45,830	34,406	3,470	4,549	10,918	9,797	4,847
Finland	—	—	16,922	2,438	2,230	4,923	4,310	2,569
France	67,735	60,335	54,842	13,761	36,954	50,113	46,975	32,066
Germany	328,722	174,227	386,634	119,107	119,506	576,905	209,616	85,752
Greece	145,402	198,108	60,774	10,599	8,605	45,153	74,173	37,729
Ireland	344,940	166,445	202,854	28,195	15,701	47,189	37,788	22,210
Italy	1,930,475	1,229,916	528,133	85,053	50,509	184,576	200,111	55,562
Netherlands	42,463	46,065	29,397	7,791	13,877	46,703	37,918	11,234
Norway-Sweden	426,981	192,445	170,329	13,452	17,326	44,224	36,150	13,941
Norway	182,542	79,488	70,327	6,901	8,326	22,806	17,371	3,835
Sweden	244,439	112,957	100,002	6,551	9,000	21,418	18,779	10,106
Poland	—	—	223,316	25,555	7,577	6,465	55,742	63,483
Portugal	65,154	82,489	44,829	3,518	6,765	13,928	70,568	42,685
Romania	57,322	13,566	67,810	5,264	1,254	914	2,339	24,753
Russia	1,501,301	1,106,998	61,604	2,463	605	453	2,329	33,311
Spain	24,818	53,262	47,109	3,669	2,774	6,880	40,793	22,783
Switzerland	32,541	22,839	31,772	5,990	9,904	17,577	19,193	8,316
United Kingdom	469,518	371,878	341,552	61,813	131,794	195,709	220,213	53,644
*Former Yugoslavia	—	—	49,215	6,920	2,039	6,966	17,990	16,267
Other Europe	514	6,527	22,434	9,978	5,584	11,756	6,845	3,447

Region and country of last residence	1900 to 1909	1910 to 1919	1920 to 1929	1930 to 1939	1940 to 1949	1950 to 1959	1960 to 1969	1980 to 1989
Asia	299,836	269,736	126,740	19,231	34,532	135,844	358,605	2,391,356
China	19,884	20,916	30,648	5,874	16,072	8,836	14,060	170,897
Hong Kong	—	—	—	—	—	13,781	67,047	112,132
India	3,026	3,478	2,076	554	1,692	1,850	18,638	231,649
Iran	—	—	208	198	1,144	3,195	9,059	98,141
*Israel	—	—	—	—	98	21,376	30,911	43,669
Japan	139,712	77,125	42,057	2,683	1,557	40,651	40,956	44,150
Jordan	—	—	—	—	—	4,899	9,230	28,928
*Korea	—	—	—	—	83	4,845	27,048	322,708
Philippines	—	—	—	391	4,099	17,245	70,660	502,056
Syria	—	—	5,307	2,188	1,179	1,091	2,432	14,534
Taiwan	—	—	—	—	—	721	15,657	119,051
Turkey	127,999	160,717	40,450	1,327	754	2,980	9,464	19,208
Vietnam	—	—	—	—	—	290	2,949	200,632
Other Asia	9,215	7,500	5,994	6,016	7,854	14,084	40,494	483,601
North America	277,809	1,070,539	1,591,278	230,319	328,435	921,610	1,674,172	2,695,329
Canada and Newfoundland	123,067	708,715	949,286	162,703	160,911	353,169	433,128	156,313
Mexico	31,188	185,334	498,945	32,709	56,158	273,847	441,824	1,009,586
Caribbean	100,960	120,860	83,482	18,052	46,194	115,661	427,235	790,109
Cuba	—	—	12,769	10,641	25,976	73,221	202,030	132,552
Dominican Republic	—	—	—	1,026	4,802	10,219	83,552	221,552
Haiti	—	—	—	156	823	3,787	28,992	121,406
Jamaica	—	—	—	—	—	7,397	62,218	193,874
Other Caribbean	100,960	120,860	70,713	6,229	14,593	21,037	50,443	120,725
Central America	7,341	15,692	16,511	6,840	20,135	40,201	98,560	339,376
Belize	77	40	285	193	433	1,133	4,185	14,964
Costa Rica	—	—	—	431	1,965	4,044	17,975	25,017
El Salvador	—	—	—	597	4,885	5,094	14,405	137,418
Guatemala	—	—	—	423	1,303	4,197	14,357	58,847
Honduras	—	—	—	679	1,874	5,320	15,078	39,071
Nicaragua	—	—	—	405	4,393	7,812	10,383	31,102

Panama	—	—	—	1,452	5,282	12,601	22,177	32,957
Other Central America	7,264	15,652	16,226	2,660	—	—	—	—
South America	15,253	39,938	43,025	9,990	19,662	78,418	250,754	399,862
Argentina	—	—	—	1,067	3,108	16,346	49,384	23,442
Bolivia	—	—	—	50	893	2,759	6,205	9,798
Brazil	—	—	4,627	1,468	3,653	11,547	29,238	22,944
Chile	—	—	—	347	1,320	4,669	12,384	19,749
Colombia	—	—	—	1,027	3,454	15,567	68,371	105,494
Ecuador	—	—	—	244	2,207	8,574	34,107	48,015
Guyana	—	—	—	131	596	1,131	4,546	85,886
Paraguay	—	—	—	33	85	576	1,249	3,518
Peru	—	—	—	321	1,273	5,980	19,783	49,958
Suriname	—	—	—	25	130	299	612	1,357
Uruguay	—	—	—	112	754	1,026	4,089	7,235
Venezuela	—	—	—	1,155	2,182	9,927	20,758	22,405
Other South America	15,253	39,938	38,398	4,010	7	17	28	61
Other America	—	—	29	25	25,375	60,314	22,671	83
Africa	6,326	8,867	6,362	2,120	6,720	13,016	23,780	141,990
Egypt	—	—	1,063	781	1,613	1,996	5,581	26,744
Ethiopia	—	—	—	10	28	302	804	12,927
Liberia	—	—	—	35	37	289	841	6,420
Morocco	—	—	—	73	879	2,703	2,880	3,471
South Africa	—	—	—	312	1,022	2,278	4,360	15,505
Other Africa	6,326	8,867	5,299	909	3,141	5,448	9,314	76,923
Oceania	12,355	12,339	9,860	3,306	14,262	11,353	23,630	41,432
Australia	11,191	11,280	8,404	2,260	11,201	8,275	14,986	16,901
New Zealand	—	—	935	790	2,351	1,799	3,775	6,129
Other Oceania	1,164	1,059	521	256	710	1,279	4,869	18,402
Not Specified	33,493	488	930	—	135	12,472	119	305,406

Region and country of last residence	1990 to 1999	2000 to 2009	2010	2011	2012	2013	2014	2015
Total	9,775,398	10,299,430	1,042,625	1,062,040	1,031,631	779,929	653,416	730,259
Europe	1,348,612	1,349,609	95,429	90,712	86,956	80,,333	71,325	78,074
Austria-Hungary	27,529	33,929	4,325	4,703	3,208	1232	1,114	1148
Austria	18,234	21,151	3,319	3,654	2,199	248	223	207
Hungary	9,295	12,778	1,006	1,049	1,009	984	891	941
Belgium	7,077	8,157	732	700	698	513	408	505
Bulgaria	16,948	40,003	2,465	2,549	2,322	2,646	2,226	2,336
*Former Czechoslovakia	8,970	18,691	1,510	1,374	1,316	232	303	371
Denmark	6,189	6,049	545	473	492	127	129	243
Finland	3,970	3,970	414	398	373	300	274	301
France	35,945	45,637	4,339	3,967	4,201	2,534	2,589	2,784
Germany	92,207	122,373	7,929	7,072	6,732	4,066	4,375	4,380
Greece	25,403	16,841	966	1,196	1,264	938	780	867
Ireland	65,384	15,642	1,610	1,533	1,694	1,295	1,413	1,375
Italy	75,992	28,329	2,956	2,670	2,946	2,355	2,313	2,760
Netherlands	13,345	17,351	1,520	1,258	1,294	786	665	778
Norway-Sweden	17,825	19,382	1,662	1,530	1,441	863	816	965
Norway	5,211	4,599	363	405	314	80	92	80
Sweden	12,614	14,783	1,299	1,125	1,127	783	724	885
Poland	172,249	117,921	7,391	6,634	6,024	8,697	8,304	7,886
Portugal	25,497	11,479	759	878	837	1,585	1,587	1,690
Romania	48,136	52,154	3,735	3,679	3,477	4,050	3,267	3,478
Russia	433,427	167,152	7,502	8,548	10,114	8,222	6,824	6,552
Spain	18,443	17,695	2,040	2,319	2,316	1,367	1,326	1,414
Switzerland	11,768	12,173	868	861	916	452	388	411
United Kingdom	156,182	171,979	14,781	13,443	13,938	9, 459	8,906	10,095
*Former Yugoslavia	57,039	131,831	4,772	4,611	4,488	4,445	—	—
Other Europe	29,087	290,871	22,608	20,316	16,865	17,839	—	—

Asia	2,859,899	3,470,835	410,209	438,580	416,488	275,700	233,163	261,374
China	342,058	591,711	67,634	83,603	78,184	35,387	30,284	31,241
Hong Kong	116,894	57,583	3,263	3,149	2,642	2,093	1,801	1,716
India	352,528	590,464	66,185	66,331	63,320	49,897	37,854	42,213
Iran	76,899	76,755	9,078	9,015	8,955	11,623	9,620	10,344
*Israel	41,340	54,081	5,172	4,389	4,640	3,466	3,015	3,182
Japan	66,582	84,552	7,100	6,751	6,581	1,837	1,635	1,858
Jordan	42,755	53,550	9,327	8,211	7,014	2,816	2,427	2,461
*Korea	179,770	209,758	22,022	22,748	—	—	—	—
Philippines	534,338	545,463	56,399	55,251	55,441	43,489	34,591	40,815
Syria	22,906	30,807	7,424	7,983	6,674	2,196	1,832	2,004
Taiwan	132,647	92,657	6,785	6,206	5,295	5,255	4,326	4,420
Turkey	38,687	48,394	7,435	9,040	7,362	3,990	2,925	3.150
Vietnam	275,379	289,616	30,065	33,486	27,578	24,277	18,837	21,976
Other Asia	637,116	745,444	112,320	122,417	122,000	107,232	—	—
North America	5,137,743	4,441,529	426,981	423,277	409,664	271,807	222,547	247,492
Canada and Newfoundland	194,788	236,349	19,491	19,506	—	—	—	—
Mexico	2,757,418	1,704,166	138,717	142,823	145,326	99,385	94,889	105,958
Caribbean	1,004,687	1,053,357	139,389	133,012	126,615	121,349	—	—
Cuba	159,037	271,742	33,372	36,261	32,551	30,482	24,092	25,770
Dominican Republic	359,818	291,492	53,890	46,036	41,535	39,590	23,775	26,665
Haiti	177,446	203,827	22,336	21,802	22,446	23,480	13,676	14,053
Jamaica	177,143	172,523	19,439	19,298	20,300	16,442	13,547	16,566
Other Caribbean	181,243	113,773	10,352	9,615	9,783	9,384	—	—
Central America	610,189	591,130	43,597	43,249	39,837	44,056	—	—
Belize	12,600	9,682	997	933	875	966	773	851
Costa Rica	17,054	21,571	2,306	2,230	2,152	1,661	1,461	1,633
El Salvador	273,017	251,237	18,547	18,477	15,874	18,401	15,598	16,930
Guatemala	126,043	156,992	10,263	10,795	9,857	9,530	8,549	9,344
Honduras	72,880	63,513	6,381	6,053	6,773	5,462	4,433	5,039
Nicaragua	80,446	70,015	3,476	3,314	2,943	5,064	3,775	3,951
Panama	28,149	18,120	1,627	1,447	1,363	1,598	1,277	1,412
Other Central America	—			-	-	-		

Region and country of last residence	1990 to 1999	2000 to 2009	2010	2011	2012	2013	2014	2015
South America	570,624	856,508	85,783	84,687	77,748	76,167	60,665	67,927
Argentina	30,065	47,955	4,312	4,335	4,218	4,177	3,683	3,886
Bolivia	18,111	21,921	2,211	2,113	1,920	1,961	1,527	1,689
Brazil	50,744	115,404	12,057	11,643	11,248	9,565	8,625	10,516
Chile	18,200	19,792	1,940	1,854	1,628	1,649	1,435	1,486
Colombia	137,985	236,570	21,861	22,130	20,272	22,196	16,478	17,207
Ecuador	81,358	107,977	11,463	11,068	9,284	9,470	6,952	7,664
Guyana	74,407	70,373	6,441	6,288	5,282	6,295	4,327	5,162
Paraguay	6,082	4,623	449	501	454	331	256	338
Peru	110,117	137,614	14,063	13,836	12,414	11,782	9,572	10,701
Suriname	2,285	2,363	202	167	216	160	127	183
Uruguay	6,062	9,827	1,286	1,521	1,348	933	812	902
Venezuela	35,180	82,087	9,497	9,229	9,464	7,648	6,871	8,192
Other South America	28	2	1	2	—	1	—	—
Other America	37	19	4	—	—	1	—	—
Africa	346,416	759,734	98,246	97,429	103,685	71,872	62,175	71,492
Egypt	44,604	81,564	9,822	9,096	10,172	6,213	5,094	5,693
Ethiopia	40,097	87,207	13,853	13,985	15,400	8,323	7,002	8,312
Liberia	13,587	23,316	2,924	3,117	3,451	3,923	3,035	3,042
Morocco	15,768	40,844	4,847	4,249	3,534	3,768	3,538	3,805
South Africa	21,964	32,221	2,705	2,754	2,960	2,283	2,083	2,538
Other Africa	210,396	494,582	64,095	64,228	68,168	61,455	—	—
Oceania	56,800	65,793	5,946	5,825	5,573	3,849	3,399,	3,811
Australia	24,288	32,728	3,077	3,062	3,146	1,296	1,159	1,379
New Zealand	8,600	12,495	1,046	1,006	980	482	453	514
Other Oceania	23,912	20,570	1,823	1,757	1,447	1,505	—	—
Not Specified	25,928	211,930	5,814	6,217	9,265	10,127	—	—

— Represents zero or not available.

*Note that (a) Korea split into North Korea and South Korea in 1945; (b) Czechoslovakia separated into the Czech Republic and the Slovak Republic in 1993; (c) Former Yugoslavia, beginning in the 1990s, broke into the six nations of Serbia, Montenegro, Slovenia, Croatia, Macedonia, and Kosovo; (d) and due to the way United States immigration statistics are recognized and collected, immigrants from the Occupied Palestinian Territories are grouped together with immigrants from Israel.

Region and country of last residence[1]	2016	2017	2018	2019	2020
Total	1,183,505	1,127,167	1,096,611	1,031,765	
Europe	98,043	89,706	85,486	90,810	
Austria-Hungary[2,3]	2,620	2,886	3,154	2,247	
Austria[2,3]	1,621	1,962	2,289	1,201	
Hungary[2,3]	999	924	865	1,046	
Belgium	821	742	628	765	
Bulgaria[4]	2,560	2,070	1,717	1,697	
Czechoslovakia[5]	1,299	1,142	1,138	1,200	
Denmark	562	536	412	467	
Finland[6]	512	478	456	523	
France	5,473	4,973	4,537	5,009	
Germany[3]	5,895	5,369	5,022	5,276	
Greece	1,664	1,495	1,367	1,537	
Ireland[7]	1,895	1,685	1,477	1,912	
Italy	4,385	4,055	3,545	4,072	
Netherlands	1,550	1,285	1,154	1,348	
Norway-Sweden[8]	1,729	1,523	1,347	1,445	
Norway[8]	404	377	301	349	
Sweden[8]	1,325	1,146	1,046	1,096	
Poland[3]	5,287	4,592	4,161	4,561	
Portugal[9]	1,017	910	914	959	
Romania	3,322	2,722	2,397	2,532	
Russia[3,6,10]	9,280	8,841	8,883	10,006	
Spain	4,018	3,555	3,210	3,465	
Switzerland	1,090	837	732	730	
United Kingdom[11]	14,887	13,318	11,867	12,951	
Yugoslavia[12]	5,392	4,966	4,522	5,065	
Other Europe	22,785	21,726	22,846	23,043	
Asia	442,854	404,371	383,145	352,593	
China	77,658	66,479	61,848	60,029	
Hong Kong	2,982	2,893	2,480	2,377	
India	61,691	57,155	56,761	51,139	
Iran	9,596	9,311	5,334	4,463	
Israel	4,652	4,227	4,009	4,702	
Japan	5,709	5,176	4,760	4,897	
Jordan	7,345	8,219	15,417	7,442	
Korea[13]	21,329	18,559	17,253	18,120	
Philippines	50,609	46,542	44,776	43,478	
Syria[14]	3,800	3,010	1,877	1,708	

Region and country of last residence[1]	2016	2017	2018	2019	2020
Taiwan	5,062	4,787	5,093	5,770	
Turkey[14]	8,635	9,144	13,097	9,135	
Vietnam	40,412	37,541	33,236	38,944	
Other Asia	143,374	131,328	117,204	100,389	
America	502,639	489,676	489,291	452,941	
Canada and Newfoundland[15,16,17]	19,349	18,469	14,337	14,723	
Mexico[16,17]	172,726	168,980	160,132	153,502	
Caribbean	180,479	173,724	180,628	135,605	
Cuba	66,120	64,749	75,159	39,580	
Dominican Republic	60,613	58,384	57,286	49,815	
Haiti	23,185	21,501	21,091	16,991	
Jamaica[18]	22,833	21,517	19,986	21,337	
Other Caribbean[18]	7,728	7,573	7,106	7,882	
Central America	54,512	52,907	58,387	61,087	
Belize	878	754	637	817	
Costa Rica	2,295	2,259	2,241	2,466	
El Salvador	21,268	21,920	22,884	24,326	
Guatemala	12,548	12,792	15,172	13,111	
Honduras	12,996	11,147	13,492	15,543	
Nicaragua	3,397	3,014	2,967	3,689	
Panama[19]	1,130	1,021	994	1,135	
Other Central America	-	-	-	-	
South America	75,571	75,595	75,806	88,022	
Argentina	3,783	3,191	2,863	3,753	
Bolivia	1,481	1,399	1,398	1,425	
Brazil	13,528	14,832	15,286	19,607	
Chile	1,711	1,664	1,566	1,817	
Colombia	16,830	16,341	15,950	18,715	
Ecuador	10,779	10,826	11,775	11,189	
Guyana	4,909	4,683	4,573	4,837	
Paraguay	400	364	361	435	
Peru	10,519	9,767	9,488	9,873	
Suriname	130	111	161	149	
Uruguay	911	952	904	1,063	
Venezuela	10,590	11,465	11,481	15,159	
Other South America	-	-	-	-	
Other America	2	1	1	2	
Africa	110,754	116,667	112,745	110,048	

Region and country of last residence[1]	2016	2017	2018	2019	2020
Egypt	13,367	11,166	11,657	10,415	
Ethiopia	13,699	15,678	13,965	10,109	
Liberia	3,545	4,085	3,008	3,419	
Morocco	4,447	4,066	2,961	3,659	
South Africa	3,441	3,438	3,575	3,337	
Other Africa	72,255	78,234	77,579	79,109	
Oceania	6,489	5,986	5,422	6,209	
Australia[20]	4,173	3,818	3,394	3,823	
New Zealand[20]	939	900	831	979	
Other Oceania	1,377	1,268	1,197	1,407	
Not Specified[21]	22,726	20,761	20,522	19,164	

[1] Prior to 1906, refers to country of origin; from 1906 onward, refers to country of last residence. Because of changes in country boundaries, data for a particular country may not necessarily refer to the same geographic area over time.

[2] Austria and Hungary not reported separately for all years during 1860 to 1869, 1890 to 1899, and 1900 to 1909.

[3] Poland included in Austria, Germany, Hungary, and Russia from 1899 to 1919.

[4] Bulgaria included Serbia and Montenegro from 1899 to 1919.

[5] Includes Czechia, Czechoslovakia (former), and Slovakia.

[6] Finland included in Russia from 1899 to 1919.

[7] Northern Ireland included in Ireland prior to 1925.

[8] Norway and Sweden not reported separately until 1861.

[9] Cape Verde included in Portugal from 1892 to 1952.

[10] Refers to the Russian Empire from 1820 to 1920. Between 1920 and 1990, refers to the Soviet Union. From 1991 to 1999, refers to Russia, Armenia, Azerbaijan, Belarus, Georgia, Kazakhstan, Kyrgyzstan, Moldova, Tajikistan, Turkmenistan, Ukraine, and Uzbekistan. Beginning in 2000, refers to Russia only.

[11] United Kingdom refers to England, Scotland, Wales, and Northern Ireland since 1925.

[12] Includes Bosnia and Herzegovina, Croatia, Kosovo, Macedonia, Montenegro, Serbia, Serbia and Montenegro (former), and Slovenia.

[13] Includes North Korea and South Korea.

[14] Syria included in Turkey from 1886 to 1923.

[15] Includes British North America and Canadian provinces.

[16] Land arrivals not completely enumerated until 1908.

[17] No data available for Canada or Mexico from 1886 to 1893.

[18] Jamaica included in British West Indies from 1892 to 1952.

[19] Panama Canal Zone included in Panama from 1932 to 1972.

[20] New Zealand included in Australia from 1892 to 1924.

[21] Includes 32,897 persons returning in 1906 to their homes in the United States.

Note: Official recording of immigration to the United States began in 1820 after the passage of the Act of March 2, 1819. From 1820 to 1867, figures represent alien passenger arrivals at seaports; from 1868 to 1891 and 1895 to 1897, immigrant alien arrivals; from 1892 to 1894 and 1898 to 2014, immigrant aliens admitted for permanent residence; from 1892 to 1903, aliens entering by cabin class were not counted as immigrants. Land arrivals were not completely enumerated until 1908. For this table, Fiscal Year 1843 covers 9 months ending September 30, 1843; Fiscal Years 1832 and 1850 cover 15 months ending December 31 of the respective years; Fiscal Year 1868 covers 6 months ending June 30, 1868; and Fiscal Year 1976 covers 15 months ending September 30, 1976.

LEGAL IMMIGRATION TO THE UNITED STATES

	Number of Legal Immigrants
2016	1,183,505
2017	1,127,167
2018	1,096,611
2019	1,031,765
2020	TO BE RELEASED
Total	4,439,048

PRESIDENTS, VICE PRESIDENTS, AND SECRETARIES OF STATE

	President	Vice President	Secretary of State
1.	George Washington, Federalist 1789	John Adams, Federalist 1789	Thomas Jefferson 1789 Edmund Randolph 1794 Timothy Pickering 1795
2.	John Adams, Federalist 1797	Thomas Jefferson, Dem.-Rep. 1797	Timothy Pickering 1797 John Marshall 1800
3.	Thomas Jefferson, Dem.-Rep.1801	Aaron Burr, Dem.-Rep. 1801 George Clinton, Dem.-Rep. 1805	James Madison 1801
4.	James Madison, Dem.-Rep. 1809	George Clinton, Dem.-Rep. 1809 Elbridge Gerry, Dem.-Rep. 1813	Robert Smith 1809 James Monroe 1811
5.	James Monroe, Dem.-Rep. 1817	Daniel D. Tompkins, Dem.-Rep. 1817	John Q.Adams 1817
6.	John Quincy Adams, Dem.-Rep. 1825	John C. Calhoun, Dem.-Rep. 1825	Henry Clay 1825
7.	Andrew Jackson, Democratic 1829	John C. Calhoun, Democratic 1829 Martin Van Buren, Democratic 1833	Martin Van Buren 1829 Edward Livingston 1831 Louis McLane 1833 John Forsyth 1834
8.	Martin Van Buren, Democratic 1837	Richard M. Johnson, Democratic 1837	John Forsyth 1837
9.	William H. Harrison, Whig 1841	John Tyler, Whig 1841	Daniel Webster 1841

	President	Vice President	Secretary of State
10.	John Tyler, Whig and Democratic 1841	None	Daniel Webster 1841 Hugh S. Legaré 1843 Abel P. Upshur 1843 John C. Calhoun 1844
11.	James K. Polk, Democratic 1845	George M. Dallas, Democratic 1845	James Buchanan 1845
12.	Zachary Taylor, Whig 1849	Millard Fillmore, Whig 1848	John M. Clayton 1849
13.	Millard Fillmore, Whig 1850	None	Daniel Webster 1850 Edward Everett 1852
14.	Franklin Pierce, Democratic 1853	William R. King, Democratic 1853	William L. Marcy 1853
15.	James Buchanan, Democratic 1857	John C. Breckinridge, Democratic 1857	Lewis Cass 1857 Jeremiah S. Black 1860
16.	Abraham Lincoln, Republican 1861	Hannibal Hamlin, Republican 1861 Andrew Johnson, Unionist 1865	William H.Seward 1861
17.	Andrew Johnson, Unionist 1865	None	William H.Seward 1865
18.	Ulysses S. Grant, Republican 1869	Schuyler Colfax, Republican 1869 Henry Wilson, Republican 1873	Elihu B. Washburne 1869 Hamilton Fish 1869
19.	Rutherford B. Hayes, Republican 1877	William A. Wheeler, Republican 1877	William M. Evarts 1877

	President	Vice President	Secretary of State
20.	James A. Garfield, Republican 1881	Chester A. Arthur, Republican 1881	James G. Blaine 1881
21.	Chester A. Arthur, Republican 1881	None	Frederick T. Frelinghuysen 1881
22.	Grover Cleveland, Democratic 1885	Thomas A. Hendricks, Democratic 1885	Thomas F. Bayard 1885
23.	Benjamin Harrison, Republican 1889	Levi P. Morton, Republican 1889	James G. Blaine 1889 John W. Foster 1892
24.	Grover Cleveland, Democratic 1893	Adlai E. Stevenson, Democratic 1893	Walter Q. Gresham 1893 Richard Olney 1895
25.	William McKinley, Republican 1897	Garret A. Hobart, Republican 1897 Theodore Roosevelt, Republican 1901	John Sherman 1897 William R. Day 1898 John Hay 1898
26.	Theodore Roosevelt, Republican 1901	Charles Fairbanks, Republican 1905	John Hay 1901 Elihu Root 1905 Robert Bacon 1909
27.	William H. Taft, Republican 1909	James S. Sherman, Republican 1909	Philander C. Knox 1909
28.	Woodrow Wilson, Democratic 1913	Thomas R. Marshall, Democratic 1913	William J. Bryan 1913 Robert Lansing 1915 Bainbridge Colby 1920
29.	Warren G. Harding, Republican 1921	Calvin Coolidge, Republican 1921	Charles E. Hughes 1921
30.	Calvin Coolidge, Republican 1923	Charles G. Dawes, Republican 1925	Charles E. Hughes 1923 Frank B. Kellogg 1925

	President	Vice President	Secretary of State
31.	Herbert Hoover, Republican 1929	Charles Curtis, Republican 1929	Henry L. Stimson 1929
32.	Franklin D. Roosevelt, Democratic 1933	John Nance Garner, Democratic 1933 Henry A. Wallace, Democratic 1941 Harry S. Truman, Democratic 1945	Cordell Hull 1933 Edward R. Stettinius, Jr. 1944
33.	Harry S. Truman, Democratic 1945	Alben W. Barkley, Democratic 1949	Edward R. Stettinius, Jr. 1945 James F. Byrnes 1945 George C. Marshall 1947 Dean G. Acheson 1949
34.	Dwight D. Eisenhower, Republican 1953	Richard M. Nixon, Republican 1953	John F. Dulles 1953 Christian A. Herter 1959
35.	John F. Kennedy, Democratic 1961	Lyndon B. Johnson, Democratic 1961	Dean Rusk 1961
36.	Lyndon B. Johnson, Democratic 1963	Hubert H. Humphrey, Democratic 1965	Dean Rusk 1963
37.	Richard M. Nixon, Republican 1969	Spiro T. Agnew, Republican 1969 Gerald R. Ford, Republican 1973	William P. Rogers 1969 Henry Kissinger 1973
38.	Gerald R. Ford, Republican 1974	Nelson Rockefeller, Republican 1974	Henry Kissinger 1974
39.	James E. Carter, Democratic 1977	Walter Mondale, Democratic 1977	Cyrus Vance 1977 Edmund Muskie 1980

40.	Ronald Reagan, Republican 1981	George H. W. Bush, Republican 1981	Alexander Haig 1981 George Schultz 1982
41.	George H. W. Bush, Republican 1989	J. Danforth Quayle, Republican 1989	James A. Baker 1989 Lawrence Eagleburger 1992
42.	William J. Clinton, Democratic 1993	Albert Gore, Jr., Democratic 1993	Warren Christopher 1993 Madeleine Albright 1997
43.	George W. Bush, Republican 2001	Richard B. Cheney, Republican 2001	Colin L. Powell 2001 Condoleezza Rice 2005
44.	Barack Obama, Democratic 2009	Joseph R. Biden Jr., Democratic 2009	Hillary Rodham Clinton 2009 John Kerry 2013
45.	Donald J. Trump, Republican 2017	Michael R. Pence, Republican 2017	Rex W. Tillerson 2017 Michael R. Pompeo 2018
46.	Joseph R. Biden Jr., Democrat 2021	Kamala D. Harris, Democrat 2021	Antony J. Blinken, Democrat 2021

Further Readings

Chapter 1

A fascinating study of pre-Columbian migration is Gavin Menzies and Ian Hudson, *Who Discovered America? The Untold Story of the Peopling of the Americas* (2014). Clarissa Confer's *Daily Life in Pre-Columbian Native America* (2007) reveals what life was like before the arrival of Europeans. Erik Wahlgren describes the Norse settlements in the North Atlantic in *The Vikings and America* (2000). Alice B. Kehoe's *North American Indians: A Comprehensive Account*, 3rd ed. (2005), provides an encyclopedic treatment of Native Americans. Equally valuable is Anton Treuer's *Atlas of Indian Nations* (2014). See also Charles Mann's *1491: New Revelations of the Americas before Columbus* (2005) and *1493: Uncovering the New World that Columbus Created* (2011), Colin G. Calloway's *One Vast Winter Count: The Native American West* (2006), Daniel K. Richter, *Before the Revolution: America's Ancient Pasts* (2011), and Peter Silver's *Our Savage Neighbors: How Indian War Transformed Early America* (2008). On North America's largest Native American city, see Timothy R. Pauketat, *Cahokia: Ancient America's Great City on the Mississippi* (2010).

The conflict between Native Americans and Europeans is the focus of James Axtell's *The Invasion Within: The Contest of Cultures in Colonial North America* (1986) and *Beyond 1492: Encounters in Colonial North America* (1992). Colin G. Calloway's *New Worlds for All: Indians, Europeans, and the Remaking of Early America* (1997) explores the ecological effects of European settlement, while Peter Mitchell's *Horse Nations: The Worldwide Impact of the Horse on Indigenous Societies Post-1492* (2015) explains the transformational impact of horses on Native Americans.

On the religious turmoil of the era, see Matthew Carr's *Blood and Faith: The Purging of Muslim Spain* (2010), Carlos M. N. Eire's *Reformations: The Early Modern World, 1450–1650* (2016), Alec Ryrie's *Protestants: The Faith That Made the Modern World* (2017), Lyndal Roper's *Martin Luther: Renegade and Prophet* (2017), and Peter H. Wilson's *Europe's Tragedy: A History of the Thirty Years' War* (2009). Benjamin Friedman's *Religion and the Rise of Capitalism* (2021) examines the relationship of Protestantism and economics.

Laurence Bergreen examines the voyages of Columbus in *Columbus: The Four Voyages* (2011). To learn about the queen who sent Columbus to the New World, see Kristin Downey's *Isabella: The Warrior Queen* (2014). For sweeping overviews of Spain's creation of a global empire, see Hugh Thomas's *Rivers of Gold: The Rise of the Spanish Empire, from Columbus to Magellan* (2004) and *World without End: Spain, Philip II, and the First Global Empire* (2016) and Robert Goodwin, *Spain: The Center of the World, 1519–1682* (2015).

The Spanish conquest of the Mexica is the focus of David M. Carballo's *Collision of Worlds: A Deep History of the Fall of Aztec Mexico and the Forging of New Spain* (2021). For a more favorable view of the Spanish invaders, see Fernando Cervantes's *Conquistadores: A New History* (2021). David J. Weber examines Spanish colonization in *The Spanish Frontier in North America* (1992). For comprehensive overviews of the Hispanic influence in U.S. history, see Felipe Fernández-Armesto's *Our America: A Hispanic History of the United States* (2014), Carrie Gibson's *El Norte: The Epic and Forgotten Story of Hispanic North America* (2020), and Paul Ortiz's *An African American and Latinx History of the United States* (2018).

For the French experience in North America, see William J. Eccles's *France in America*, rev. ed. (1990). For an insightful comparison of Spanish and English modes of settlement, see J. H. Elliott, *Empires of the Atlantic World: Britain and Spain in America, 1492–1830* (2006). The Spanish settlement of what became the state of Texas is described in Donald E. Chipman's *Spanish Texas, 1519–1821* (1992).

Chapter 2

Two excellent surveys of early American history are Peter C. Hoffer's *The Brave New World: A History of Early America*, 2nd ed. (2006), and William R. Polk's *The Birth of America: From before Columbus to the Revolution* (2006).

Bernard Bailyn's *The Barbarous Years: The Peopling of British North America; The Conflict of Civilizations, 1600–1675* (2013) tells the often brutal story of British settlement in America during the seventeenth century. On the impact of the American environment on colonial settlement, see Malcolm Gaskill's *Between Two Worlds: How the English Became Americans* (2015) and Sam White's *A Cold Welcome: The Little Ice Age and Europe's Encounter with North America* (2019). The best overview of the colonization of North America is Alan Taylor's *American Colonies: The Settling of North America* (2001). On the interactions among Native American, European, and African cultures, see Andrew Lipman's *The Saltwater Frontier: Indians and the Contest for the American Coast* (2015), Gary B. Nash's *Red, White, and Black: The Peoples of Early North America*, 5th ed. (2005), and Margaret Ellen Newell's *Brethren by Nature: New England Indians, Colonists, and the Origins of American Slavery* (2016).

A good overview of the founding of Virginia and Maryland is Jean and Elliott Russo's *The Early Chesapeake in British North America* (2012). For information regarding the Puritan settlement of New England, see David D. Hall's two fine books, *A Reforming People: Puritanism and the Transformation of Public Life in New England* (2013) and *The Puritans: A Trans Altlantic History* (2019). On the Pilgrims and Plymouth, see Francis J. Bremer's *One Small Candle: The Plymouth Puritans* (2020) and Martyn Whittock's *Mayflower Lives: Pilgrims in a New World and the Early American Experience* (2019). The best biography of John Winthrop is Francis J. Bremer's *John Winthrop: America's Forgotten Founding Father* (2003). On Roger Williams, see John M. Barry's *Roger Williams and the Creation of the American Soul* (2012) and James A. Warren's *God, War, and Providence: The Epic Struggle of Roger Williams and the Narragansett Indians against the Puritans of New England* (2018).

The pattern of settlement in the middle colonies is the subject of Barry Levy's *Quakers and the American Family: British Settlement in the Delaware Valley* (1988). On the early history of New York, see Russell Shorto's *The Island at the Center of the World: The Epic Story of Dutch Manhattan and the Forgotten Colony That Shaped America* (2004). Settlement of the Chesapeake Bay region is the focus of James Horn's *Adapting to a New World: English Society in the Seventeenth-Century Chesapeake* (1994). On North Carolina, see Noeleen McIlvenna's *A Very Mutinous People: The Struggle for North Carolina, 1660–1713* (2009)

On the shifting political dynamics in England during the seventeenth century, see Peter Ackroyd, *The History of England from James I to the Glorious Revolution* (2015) and Steve Pincus, *1688: The First Modern Revolution* (2009). For a study of race and the settlement of South Carolina, see Peter H. Wood's *Black Majority: Negroes in Colonial South Carolina from 1670 through the Stono Rebellion* (1974). On the flourishing trade in captive Native Americans, see Alan Gallay's *The Indian Slave Trade: The Rise of the English Empire in the American South, 1670–1717* (2002) and Andres Resendez's *The Other Slavery: The Uncovered Story of Indian Enslavement in America* (2016). On the Yamasee War, see Steven J. Oatis's *A Colonial Complex: South Carolina's Frontiers in the Era of the Yamasee War, 1680–1730* (2004) and William L.

Ramsey's *The Yamasee War: A Study of Culture, Economy, and Conflict in the Colonial South* (2010).

Chapter 3

The diversity of colonial societies is featured in David Hackett Fischer's *Albion's Seed: Four British Folkways in America* (1989). John Frederick Martin's *Profits in the Wilderness: Entrepreneurship and the Founding of New England Towns in the Seventeenth Century* (1991) demonstrates how economic concerns rather than spiritual motives were driving forces in many New England towns.

Bernard Rosenthal challenges many myths concerning the Salem witch trials in *Salem Story: Reading the Witch Trials of 1692* (1993). Mary Beth Norton's *In the Devil's Snare: The Salem Witchcraft Crisis of 1692* (2002) emphasizes the role of Native American violence, while Stacy Schiff's *The Witches: Salem, 1692* (2016) provides a riveting analysis of the many factors influencing the outbreak of anti-witch hysteria. See also Benjamin C. Ray's *Satan and Salem: The Witch-Hunt Crisis of 1692* (2015).

Colorful discussions of women in the New England colonies can be found in Laurel Thatcher Ulrich's *Good Wives: Image and Reality in the Lives of Women in Northern New England, 1650–1750* (1980) and Mary Beth Norton, *Separated by Their Sex: Women in Public and Private in the Colonial Atlantic World* (2011). On women and religion, see Susan Juster's *Disorderly Women: Sexual Politics and Evangelicalism in Revolutionary New England* (1994). John Demos describes family life in *A Little Commonwealth: Family Life in Plymouth Colony*, new ed. (2000).

For analyses of Native American wars, see Alfred A. Cave's *The Pequot War* (1996), James D. Drake's *King Philip's War: Civil War in New England* (2000), and Jill Lepore's *The Name of War: King Philip's War and the Origins of American Identity* (1998). The story of the Iroquois is told well in Daniel K. Richter's *The Ordeal of the Longhouse: The Peoples of the Iroquois League in the Era of European Colonization* (1992). Native Americans in the southern colonies are the focus of James Axtell's *The Indians' New South: Cultural Change in the Colonial Southeast* (1997). On the fur trade, see Eric Jay Dolan, *Fur, Fortune, and Empire: The Epic Story of the Fur Trade in America* (2010). For insights into the Glorious Revolution in England, see Steve Pincus's *1688: The First Modern Revolution* (2009).

For the social history of the southern colonies, see Allan Kulikoff's *Tobacco and Slaves: The Development of Southern Cultures in the Chesapeake, 1680–1800* (1986). On the interaction of Blacks and Whites, see Mechal Sobel's *The World They Made Together: Black and White Values in Eighteenth-Century Virginia* (1987). On the selling of enslaved Africans, see William St. Clair's *The Door of No Return: The History of Cape Coast Castle and the Atlantic Slave Trade* (2007). African Americans during colonial settlement are the focus of Timothy H. Breen and Stephen Innes's *"Myne Owne Ground": Race and Freedom on Virginia's Eastern Shore, 1640–1676*, new ed. (2004). David W. Galenson's *White Servitude in Colonial America: An Economic Analysis* (1981) looks at the lives of indentured laborers.

Henry F. May's *The Enlightenment in America* (1976) and Donald H. Meyer's *The Democratic Enlightenment* (1976) examine intellectual trends in eighteenth-century America. See also Ritchie Robertson's *The Enlightenment: The Pursuit of Happiness, 1680–1790* (2020). On the Great Awakening, see Frank Lambert's *Inventing the "Great Awakening"* (1999) and Thomas S. Kidd's *The Great Awakening: The Roots of Evangelical Christianity in Colonial America* (2007). Excellent biographies of the key revivalists are Phillip F. Gura's *Jonathan Edwards: A Life* (2003) and Thomas S. Kidd's *George Whitefield: America's Spiritual Founding Father* (2015).

Chapter 4

A good introduction to the imperial phase of the colonial conflicts is Douglas Edward Leach's *Arms for Empire: A Military History of the British Colonies in North America, 1607–1763* (1973). Also useful is Brendan Simms's *Three Victories and a Defeat: The Rise and Fall of the First British Empire* (2008). Fred Anderson's *Crucible of War: The Seven Years' War and the Fate of Empire in British North America, 1754–1766* (2000) is the best history of the Seven Years' War. For the implications of the British victory in 1763, see Colin G. Calloway's *The Scratch of a Pen: 1763 and the Transformation of North America* (2006). On the French colonies in North America, see David W. J. Eccles, *The French in North America: 1500–1783* (2010), David Hackett Fischer's *Champlain's Dream* (2008), and Allan Greer's *The People of New France* (1997).

For a narrative survey of the events leading to the Revolution, see Nina Sankovitch's *American Rebels: How the Hancock, Adams, and Quincy Families Fanned the Flames of Revolution* (2020) and Eric Hinderaker's *Boston's Massacre* (2017). For Great Britain's perspective on the imperial conflict, see Ian R. Christie's *Crisis of Empire: Great Britain and the American Colonies, 1754–1783* (1966). Also see Jeremy Black's *George III: America's Last King* (2007), David Preston's *Braddock's Defeat: The Battle of the Monongahela and the Road to Revolution* (2015), and Nick Bunker's *An Empire on the Edge: How Britain Came to Fight America* (2015). For a social history of the Revolution, see Gary Nash's *The Unknown American Revolution: The Unruly Birth of Democracy and the Struggle to Create America* (2006).

The intellectual foundations of revolt are explored in Bernard Bailyn's *The Ideological Origins of the American Revolution* (1992). To understand how these views were connected to organized protest, see Jon Butler's *Becoming America: The Revolution before 1776* (2000) and Kevin Phillips's *1775: A Good Year for a Revolution* (2012). On the first major battle, see Nathaniel Philbrick's *Bunker Hill: A City, a Siege, a Revolution* (2013).

On the efforts of colonists to boycott the purchase of British goods, see T. H. Breen's *The Marketplace of Revolution: How Consumer Politics Shaped American Independence* (2004). For the critical events during the summer of 1776, see Joseph J. Ellis's *1776: The Summer the Revolution was Born* (2013). Pauline Maier's *American Scripture: Making the Declaration of Independence* (1997) remains the best analysis of the framing of that pathbreaking document. The best analysis of why Americans supported independence is Thomas Slaughter's *Independence: The Tangled Roots of the American Revolution* (2014).

Chapter 5

Military affairs in the early phases of the Revolutionary War are the focus of John Ferling's *Almost a Miracle: The American Victory in the War for Independence* (2009). The Revolutionary War is the subject of Holger Hoock's *Scars of Independence: America's Violent Birth* (2017) and Jeremy Black's *War for America: The Fight for Independence, 1775–1783* (1991). For a splendid account of Washington's generalship, see Robert Middlekauf's *Washington's Revolution: The Making of America's First Great Leader* (2015).

On the social history of the Revolutionary War, see John W. Shy's *A People Numerous and Armed: Reflections on the Military Struggle for American Independence*, rev. ed. (1990). Colin G. Calloway tells the neglected story of the Native American experiences in the Revolution in *The American Revolution in Indian Country: Crisis and Diversity in Native American Communities* (1995). For a continental assessment of the Revolution, see Alan Taylor's *American Revolutions: A Continental History* (2016).

Why many Americans remained loyal to the Crown is the subject of Thomas B. Allen's *Tories: Fighting for the King in America's First Civil War* (2010) and Maya Jasanoff's *Liberty's Exiles: American Loyalists in the Revolutionary War* (2011). A superb study of African Americans during the Revolutionary era is Douglas R. Egerton's *Death or Liberty: African Americans and Revolutionary America* (2009). For insights into the role of Native Americans in the war, see Colin G. Calloway's *The American Revolution in Indian Country* (1995). The strategic American victory at Saratoga is the focus of Richard M. Ketchum's *Saratoga: Turning Point of America's Revolutionary War* (1999).

Carol Berkin's *Revolutionary Mothers: Women in the Struggle for America's Independence* (2005) documents the role that women played in securing independence. A superb biography of Revolutionary America's most prominent woman is Woody Holton's *Abigail Adams* (2010). A fine new biography of America's commander in chief is Ron Chernow's *Washington: A Life* (2010). The best analysis of the British side of the war is Andrew Jackson O'Shaughnessy's *The Men Who Lost America: British Leadership, the American Revolution, and the Fate of Empire* (2013).

Chapter 6

A good overview of the Confederation period is Richard B. Morris's *The Forging of the Union, 1781–1789* (1987). For the role played by key leaders, see Joseph J. Ellis's *The Quartet: Orchestrating the Second American Revolution, 1783–1789* (2016). Daniel Bullen's *Daniel Shays's Honorable Rebellion: An American Story* (2021) covers that fateful incident.

An excellent overview of post-Revolutionary life is Joyce Appleby's *Inheriting the Revolution: The First Generation of Americans* (2000). For the dramatic story of the framers of the Constitution, see Richard Beeman's *Plain, Honest Men: The Making of the American Constitution* (2009). Woody Holton's *Unruly Americans and the Origins of the Constitution* (2007) emphasizes the role of taxes and monetary policies in the crafting of the Constitution. A more comprehensive study of the economic issues facing the new republic is Thomas K. McCraw's *The Founders and Finance: How Hamilton, Gallatin, and Other Immigrants Forged a New Economy* (2012). The complex story of ratification is well told in Pauline Maier's *Ratification: The People Debate the Constitution, 1787–1788* (2010). Excellent studies of James Madison's development as a political theorist are Michael Signer's *Becoming Madison: The Extraordinary Origins of the Least Likely Founding Father* (2015) and David O. Stewart's *Madison's Gift: Five Partnerships That Built America* (2015).

On attitudes toward religion in the new United States, see Jon Meacham's *American Gospel: God, the Founding Fathers, and the Making of a Nation* (2006).

The best introduction to the early Federalists remains John C. Miller's *The Federalist Era, 1789–1801* (2011). Other works analyze the ideological debates among the nation's first leaders. Richard Buel, Jr.'s *Securing the Revolution: Ideology in American Politics, 1789–1815* (1972) and Stanley Elkins and Eric McKitrick's *The Age of Federalism: The Early American Republic, 1788–1800* (1993) trace the persistence and transformation of ideas first fostered during the Revolutionary crisis. The best studies of George Washington's political career are John Ferling's *The Ascent of George Washington: The Hidden Political Genius of an American Icon* (2009) and Edward Larson's *The Return of George Washington: Uniting the States, 1783–1789* (2015).

The 1790s may also be understood through the views and behavior of national leaders. See the following biographies: Richard Brookhiser's *Founding Father: Rediscovering George Washington* (1996), *Alexander Hamilton, American* (1999), and *James Madison* (2013) and Joseph J. Ellis's *Passionate Sage: The Character and Legacy of John Adams* (1993). On social life, see Jack Larkin's *Everyday Life in America, 1790–1840* (1989). On the presidency of John Adams and his controversial crackdown on free speech, see Wendell Bird's *Criminal Dissent: Prosecutions under the Alien and Sedition Acts of 1798* (2020).

On the formation of the federal government and its economic policies, see Thomas K. McCraw's *The Founders and Finance: How Hamilton, Gallatin, and Other Immigrants Forged a New Economy* (2012). Federalist foreign policy is explored in Jerald A. Combs's *The Jay Treaty: Political Battleground of the Founding Fathers* (1970) and William Stinchcombe's *The XYZ Affair* (1980).

Chapter 7

The most comprehensive overviews of the first years of the new nation are Alan Taylor's *American Republics: A Continental History of the United States, 1783–1850* (2021) and Gordon S. Wood's *Empire of Liberty: A History of the Early Republic, 1789–1815* (2010). The best treatment of the election of 1800 is Edward J. Larson's *A Magnificent Catastrophe: The Tumultuous Election of 1800* (2007).

The standard biography of Jefferson is Joseph J. Ellis's *American Sphinx: The Character of Thomas Jefferson* (1996). More recent analyses include John Boles's *Jefferson: Architect of American Liberty* (2017) and Andrew Burstein's *Democracy's Muse: How Thomas Jefferson Became an FDR Liberal, a Reagan Republican, and a Tea Party Fanatic, All the While Being Dead* (2015). On the life of Jefferson's friend and successor, James Madison, see Drew R. McCoy's *The Last of the Fathers: James Madison and the Republican Legacy* (1989).

On the magisterial influence of John Marshall on American legal philosophy, see Richard Brookhiser's *John Marshall: The Man Who Made the Supreme Court* (2018) and Joel Richard Paul's *Without Precedent: John Marshall and His Times* (2018). The concept of judicial review and the courts can be studied in Cliff Sloan and David McKean's *The Great Decision: Jefferson, Adams, Marshall, and the Battle for the Supreme Court* (2009). A recent biography of Jefferson's political nemesis is Nancy Isenberg's *Fallen Founder: The Life of Aaron Burr* (2008). On the duel that saw Aaron Burr kill Alexander Hamilton, see John Sedgwick's *War of Two: Alexander Hamilton, Aaron Burr, and the Duel That Stunned the Nation* (2015).

For the Louisiana Purchase, consult Jon Kukla's *A Wilderness So Immense: The Louisiana Purchase and the Destiny of America* (2003). The development of the states bordering the Gulf of Mexico is told well in Jack E. Davis's *The Gulf: The Making of an American Sea* (2017). For a captivating account of the Lewis and Clark expedition, see Stephen Ambrose's *Undaunted Courage: Meriwether Lewis, Thomas Jefferson, and the Opening of the American West* (1996).

Burton Spivak's *Jefferson's English Crisis: Commerce, Embargo, and the Republican Revolution* (1979) discusses Anglo-American relations during Jefferson's administration; Clifford L. Egan's *Neither Peace nor War: Franco-American Relations, 1803–1812* (1983) covers America's relations with France. An excellent revisionist treatment of the events that brought on war in 1812 is J. C. A. Stagg's *Mr. Madison's War: Politics, Diplomacy, and Warfare in the Early American Republic, 1783–1830* (1983). See also Paul A. Gilje's *Free Trade and Sailors' Rights in the War of 1812* (2013) and Willard Sterne Randall's *Unshackling America: How the War of 1812 Truly Ended the American Revolution* (2017). The war itself is the focus of Donald R. Hickey's *The*

War of 1812: A Forgotten Conflict (1989). For the perspective of those who fought in the war, see A. J. Langguth's *Union 1812: The Americans Who Fought the Second War of Independence* (2007). See also Alan Taylor's award-winning *The Civil War of 1812: American Citizens, British Subjects, Irish Rebels, and Indian Allies* (2011).

Chapter 8

The best overview of the second quarter of the nineteenth century is Daniel Walker Howe, *What Hath God Wrought: The Transformation of America, 1815–1845* (2007). The classic study of transportation and economic growth during the early nineteenth century is George Rogers Taylor's *The Transportation Revolution, 1815–1860* (1951). A more recent treatment is Sarah H. Gordon's *Passage to Union: How the Railroads Transformed American Life, 1829–1929* (1996). On the Erie Canal, see Gerard Koeppel's *Bond of Union: Building the Erie Canal and the American Empire* (2009). On the development of clipper ships, see Stephen Ujifusa's *Barons of the Sea: The Race to Build Clipper Ships* (2018).

On the industrial revolution, see Charles R. Morris's *The Dawn of Innovation: The First American Industrial Revolution* (2013). The impact of technology is examined in David J. Jeremy Black's *Transatlantic Industrial Revolution: The Diffusion of Textile Technologies between Britain and America, 1790–1830s* (1981). On the invention of the telegraph, see Kenneth Silverman's *Lightning Man: The Accursed Life of Samuel F. B. Morse* (2003).

The outlook of the working class during this time of transition is surveyed in Edward E. Pessen's *Most Uncommon Jacksonians: The Radical Leaders of the Early Labor Movement* (1967). See also James R. Barrett's *History from the Bottom Up and Inside Out: Ethnicity, Race, and Identity in Working-Class History* (2017). Detailed case studies of working communities include Anthony F. C. Wallace's *Rockdale: The Growth of an American Village in the Early Industrial Revolution* (1978), Thomas Dublin's *Women at Work: The Transformation of Work and Community in Lowell, Massachusetts, 1826–1860* (1979), and Sean Wilentz's *Chants Democratic: New York and the Rise of the American Working Class, 1788–1850* (1984).

For a fine treatment of urbanization, see Charles N. Glaab and A. Theodore Brown's *A History of Urban America* (1967). On immigration, see John Bodnar's *The Transplanted: A History of Immigrants in Urban America* (1987), Roger Daniels's *Coming to America: A History of Immigration and Ethnicity in American Life* (2002), Leonard Dinnerstein's *Ethnic Americans: A History of Immigration* (2009), Jay P. Dolan's *The Irish Americans: A History* (2008), and John Kelly's *The Graves Are Walking: The Great Famine and the Saga of the Irish People* (2012). For a fascinating account of two sisters who became the first female physicians in America, see Janice Nimura's *The Doctors Blackwell: How Two Pioneering Sisters Brought Medicine to Women—and Women to Medicine* (2021).

Chapter 9

The standard overview of the Era of Good Feelings remains George Dangerfield's *The Awakening of American Nationalism, 1815–1828* (1965). A classic summary of the economic trends of the period is Douglass C. North's *The Economic Growth of the United States, 1790–1860* (1961). An excellent synthesis of the era is Charles Sellers's *The Market Revolution: Jacksonian America, 1815–1846* (1991).

On Monroe, see Harlow Giles Unger's *The Last Founding Father: James Monroe and a Nation's Call to Greatness* (2010) and Tim McGrath's *James Monroe: A Life*

(2020). On John Quincy Adams, see William J. Cooper's *The Lost Founding Father: John Quincy Adams and the Transformation of American Politics* (2017), Charles N. Edel's *John Quincy Adams and the Grand Strategy of the Republic* (2014), and Fred Kaplan's *John Quincy Adams: American Visionary* (2014). For diplomatic relations during James Monroe's presidency, see William Earl Weeks's *John Quincy Adams and American Global Empire* (1992).

Chapter 10

The best comprehensive surveys of politics and culture during the Jacksonian era are Daniel Walker Howe's *What Hath God Wrought: The Transformation of America, 1815–1848* (2007) and David S. Reynolds's *Waking Giant: America in the Age of Jackson* (2008). A more political focus can be found in Harry L. Watson's *Liberty and Power: The Politics of Jacksonian America* (1990). On the rise of urban political machines, see Terry Golway's *Machine Made: Tammany Hall and the Creation of Modern American Politics* (2014).

For an outstanding analysis of women in New York City during the Jacksonian period, see Christine Stansell's *City of Women: Sex and Class in New York, 1789–1860* (1986). In *Chants Democratic: New York City and the Rise of the American Working-Class, 1788–1850* (1984), Sean Wilentz analyzes the social basis of working-class politics. More recently, Wilentz has traced the democratization of politics in *The Rise of American Democracy: Jefferson to Lincoln* (2009).

The best biography of Jackson remains Robert Vincent Remini's three-volume work: *Andrew Jackson: The Course of American Empire, 1767–1821* (1977), *Andrew Jackson: The Course of American Freedom, 1822–1832* (1981), and *Andrew Jackson: The Course of American Democracy, 1833–1845* (1984). A more critical study of the seventh president is Andrew Burstein's *The Passions of Andrew Jackson* (2003). See also Jon Meacham's *American Lion: Andrew Jackson in the White House* (2009). On Jackson and the Native Americans, see Robert Remini's *Andrew Jackson and His Indian Wars* (2001). The story of the Trail of Tears is told in A. J. Langguth's *Driven West: Andrew Jackson and the Trail of Tears* (2011) and Claudio Saunt's *Unworthy Republic* (2020).

On Jackson's successor, consult Ted Widmer's *Martin Van Buren* (2005). Studies of other major figures of the period include Robert Elder's *Calhoun: American Heretic* (2021), Merrill D. Peterson's *The Great Triumvirate: Webster, Clay, and Calhoun* (1987), James C. Klotter's *Henry Clay: The Man Who Would Be President* (2018), and Robert Vincent Remini, *Daniel Webster: The Man and His Time* (1997).

The political philosophies of Jackson's opponents are treated in Michael F. Holt's *The Rise and Fall of the American Whig Party: Jacksonian Politics and the Onset of the Civil War* (1999) and Harry L. Watson's *Andrew Jackson vs. Henry Clay: Democracy and Development in Antebellum America* (1998). The outstanding book on the nullification issue remains William W. Freehling's *Prelude to Civil War: The Nullification Controversy in South Carolina, 1816–1836* (1965). John M. Belohlavek's *"Let the Eagle Soar!": The Foreign Policy of Andrew Jackson* (1985) is a thorough study of Jacksonian diplomacy.

Chapter 11

Three efforts to understand the mind of the Old South and its defense of slavery are Lacy K. Ford's *Deliver Us from Evil: The Slavery Question in the Old South* (2009), Eugene D. Genovese's *The Slaveholders' Dilemma: Freedom and Progress in*

Southern Conservative Thought, 1820–1860 (1992), William W. Freehling's *The Road to Disunion: Secessionists Triumphant, 1854–1861* (2007), and Walter Johnson's *River of Dark Dreams: Slavery and Empire in the Cotton Kingdom* (2013). Stephanie McCurry's *Masters of Small Worlds: Yeoman Households, Gender Relations, and the Political Culture of the Antebellum South Carolina Low Country* (1995) describes southern households, religion, and political culture. Erskine Clarke's *Dwelling Place: A Plantation Epic* (2005) focuses on a Georgia plantation owned by a Presbyterian minister and sustained by enslaved workers. The best recent book on the role of slavery in creating the cotton culture is Edward E. Baptist's *The Half Has Never Been Told: Slavery and the Making of American Capitalism* (2014).

Other essential works on southern culture and society include Bertram Wyatt-Brown's *Honor and Violence in the Old South* (1986), Elizabeth Fox-Genovese's *Within the Plantation Household: Black and White Women of the Old South* (1988), Joan E. Cashin's *A Family Venture: Men and Women on the Southern Frontier* (1991), and Theodore Rosengarten's *Tombee: Portrait of a Cotton Planter* (1986).

John W. Blassingame's *The Slave Community: Plantation Life in the Antebellum South*, rev. and enlarged ed. (1979), Eugene D. Genovese's *Roll, Jordan, Roll: The World the Slaves Made* (1974), and Herbert G. Gutman's *The Black Family in Slavery and Freedom, 1750–1925* (1976) all stress the theme of a persisting and identifiable culture emerging among the enslaved. The crucial role of religion and the church in African American culture is the focus of Henry Louis Gates, Jr.'s *The Black Church: This Is Our Story, This Is Our Song* (2021). The emergence of a political culture among African Americans in the northern states is the subject of Van Gosse's *The First Reconstruction: Black Politics in America from the Revolution to the Civil War* (2021) and Kate Masur's *Until Justice Be Done: America's First Civil Rights Movement* (2021).

On the question of slavery's profitability, see Sven Beckert's *Empire of Cotton: A Global History* (2014), Robert Johnson's *River of Dark Dreams: Slavery and Empire in the Cotton Kingdom* (2017), and Edward E. Baptist's *The Half Has Never Been Told: Slavery and the Making of American Capitalism* (2014). For the business aspects of selling enslaved people, see Joshua D. Rothman's *The Ledger and the Chain* (2021). A massive uprising of enslaved people in Louisiana is the subject of Daniel Rasmussen's *American Uprising: The Untold Story of America's Largest Slave Revolt* (2011).

Chapter 12

On the reform impulse, consult Ronald G. Walter's *American Reformers, 1815–1860*, rev. ed. (1997). Revivalist religion is treated in Nathan O. Hatch's *The Democratization of American Christianity* (1989), Christine Leigh Heyrman's *Southern Cross: The Beginnings of the Bible Belt* (1997), and Ellen Eslinger's *Citizens of Zion: The Social Origins of Camp Meeting Revivalism* (1999). On the Mormons, see Alex Beam's *American Crucifixion: The Murder of Joseph Smith and the Fate of the Mormon Church* (2014) and Benjamin E. Park's award-winning *Kingdom of Nauvoo: The Rise and Fall of a Religious Empire on the American Frontier* (2020).

The best treatment of transcendentalist thought is Robert Gross's The *Transcendentalists and Their World* (2021). On Henry D. Thoreau, see Michael Sims's *The Adventures of Henry Thoreau: A Young Man's Unlikely Path to Walden Pond* (2014). Edgar Allan Poe is the subject of Jerome McGann's *The Poet Edgar Allan Poe: Alien Angel* (2015). On Margaret Fuller, see Charles Capper's *Margaret Fuller: An American Romantic Life* (2009).

For the war against alcohol, see W. J. Rorabaugh's *The Alcoholic Republic: An American Tradition* (1979) and Barbara Leslie Epstein's *The Politics of Domesticity: Women, Evangelism, and Temperance in Nineteenth-Century America* (1981). On prison reform and other humanitarian projects, see David J. Rothman's *The Discovery of the Asylum: Social Order and Disorder in the New Republic*, rev. ed. (2002) and Thomas J. Brown's biography *Dorothea Dix: New England Reformer* (1998). On women's rights, see Louise Michele Newman's *White Women's Rights: The Racial Origins of Feminism* (1999).

Useful surveys of abolitionism include Manisha Sinha's *The Slave's Cause: A History of* Abolition (2017), James Brewer Stewart's *Holy Warriors: The Abolitionists and American Slavery*, rev. ed. (1997), and Julie Roy Jeffrey's *The Great Silent Army of Abolitionism: Ordinary Women in the Antislavery Movement* (1998). For the pro-slavery argument as it developed in the South, see Larry E. Tise's *Proslavery: A History of the Defense of Slavery in America, 1701–1840* (1987) and James Oakes's *The Ruling Race: A History of American Slaveholders* (1982). For the dramatic story of the role of the Underground Railroad in freeing slaves, see Eric Foner's *Gateway to Freedom: The Hidden History of the Underground Railroad* (2015).

Chapter 13

For background on Whig programs and ideas, see Michael F. Holt's *The Rise and Fall of the American Whig Party: Jacksonian Politics and the Onset of the Civil War* (1999). On John Tyler, see Edward P. Crapol's *John Tyler: The Accidental President* (2006), Richard J. Ellis's *Old Tip vs. The Sly Fox: The 1840 Election and the Making of a Partisan Nation* (2020), and Christopher Leahy's *President without a Party: The Life of John Tyler* (2020). On the expansionist impulse westward, see Walter Nugent's *Habits of Empire: A History of American Expansionism* (2008) and Richard White's *"It's Your Misfortune and None of My Own": A New History of the American West* (1991). On the creation of the California missions, see Steven W. Hackel's *Junípero Serra: California's Founding Father* (2013) and Gregory Orfalea's *Journey to the Sun: Junípero Serra's Dream and the Founding of California* (2014).

For the expansionism of the 1840s, see Steven E. Woodworth's *Manifest Destinies: Expansion and the Road to the Civil War* (2010). For the impact of post offices in facilitating western expansion, see Cameron Blevins's *Paper Trails: The US Post and the Making of the American West* (2021). The movement of settlers to the West is ably documented in John Mack Faragher's *Women and Men on the Overland Trail*, 2nd ed. (2001), David Dary's *The Santa Fe Trail: Its History, Legends, and Lore* (2000), and Rinker Buck's *The Oregon Trail: A New American Journey* (2015). On the Donner Party tragedy, see Michael Wallis's *The Best Land under Heaven: The Donner Party in the Age of Manifest Destiny* (2017).

Gene M. Brack's *Mexico Views Manifest Destiny, 1821–1846: An Essay on the Origins of the Mexican War* (1975) takes Mexico's viewpoint on U.S. designs on the West. Excellent overviews of the role of Mexico and Mexicans in American expansionism, see Neil Foley's *Mexicans in the Making of America* (2014) and Juan Gonzalez's *Harvest of Empire: A History of Latinos in America* (2011). For the American perspective on Texas, see Joel H. Silbey's *Storm over Texas: The Annexation Controversy and the Road to Civil War* (2005). On the siege of the Alamo, see Bryan Burrough and Chris Tomlinson's *Forget the Alamo: The Rise and Fall of an American Myth* (2021) and William C. Davis's *Three Roads to the Alamo: The Lives and Fortunes of David Crockett, James Bowie, and William Barret Travis* (1998). An excellent biography related to the emergence of Texas is Gregg Cantrell's *Stephen F. Austin: Empresario of Texas* (1999).

On James K. Polk, see Robert W. Merry's *A Country of Vast Designs: James K. Polk, the Mexican War, and the Conquest of the American Continent* (2009). The best survey of the military conflict is John S. D. Eisenhower's *So Far from God: The U.S. War with Mexico, 1846–1848* (1989). The Mexican War as viewed from the perspective of the soldiers is described in Richard Bruce Winders's *Mr. Polk's Army: American Military Experience in the Mexican War* (1997). On the diplomatic aspects of Mexican American relations, see David M. Pletcher's *The Diplomacy of Annexation: Texas, Oregon, and the Mexican War* (1973). Abraham Lincoln's early views of slavery are outlined in William W. Freehling's *Becoming Lincoln* (2019) and James Oakes's *The Crooked Path to Abolition: Abraham Lincoln and the Antislavery Constitution* (2021). The growing tensions in Congress during the 1850s are the focus of Joanne Freeman's *The Field of Blood: Violence in Congress and the Road to Civil War* (2019). The best surveys of the forces and events leading to the Civil War include James M. McPherson's *Battle Cry of Freedom: The Civil War Era* (1988) and *The War That Forged a Nation: Why the Civil War Still Matters* (2017), Stephen B. Oates's *The Approaching Fury: Voices of the Storm, 1820–1861* (1997), James Oakes's *The Scorpion's Sting: Antislavery and the Coming of the Civil War* (2015), and Bruce Levine's *Half Slave and Half Free: The Roots of Civil War* (1992). The most recent narrative of the political debate leading to secession is Michael A. Morrison's *Slavery and the American West: The Eclipse of Manifest Destiny and the Coming of the Civil War* (1997). The best brief history of the Civil War, at less than a hundred pages, is Louis Masur's *The Civil War: A Concise History* (2011).

Mark J. Stegmaier's *Texas, New Mexico, and the Compromise of 1850: Boundary Dispute and Sectional Crisis* (1996) probes that crucial dispute, while Michael F. Holt's *The Political Crisis of the 1850s* (1978) traces the demise of the Whigs. See also Fergus M. Bordewich's *America's Great Debate: Henry Clay, Stephen A. Douglas, and the Compromise That Preserved the Union* (2012). Eric Foner, in *Free Soil, Free Labor, Free Men: The Ideology of the Republican Party before the Civil War* (1970), shows how events and ideas combined in the formation of a new political party. The pivotal *Dred Scott* case is assessed in Earl M. Maltz's *Dred Scott and the Politics of Slavery* (2007).

On the role of John Brown in the sectional crisis, see Robert E. McGlone's *John Brown's War against Slavery* (2009). A detailed study of the South's journey to secession is William W. Freehling's *The Road to Disunion*, vol. 1, *Secessionists at Bay, 1776–1854* (1990) and *The Road to Disunion*, vol. 2, *Secessionists Triumphant, 1854–1861* (2007). Robert E. Bonner traces the emergence of Southern nationalism in *Mastering America: Southern Slaveholders and the Crisis of American Nationhood* (2009).

On the Buchanan presidency, see Jean H. Baker's *James Buchanan* (2004). Maury Klein's *Days of Defiance: Sumter, Secession, and the Coming of the Civil War* (1997) treats the Fort Sumter controversy. An excellent collection of interpretive essays is *Why the Civil War Came* (1996), edited by Gabor S. Boritt.

Chapter 14

On the start of the Civil War, see Adam Goodheart's *1861: The Civil War Awakening* (2011). The best one-volume overview of the Civil War period is James M. McPherson's *Battle Cry of Freedom: The Civil War Era* (1988). A more recent synthesis of the war and its effects is David Goldfield's *America Aflame: How the Civil War Created a Nation* (2011). The best brief history is Louis Masur's *The Civil War: A Concise History* (2011). A good introduction to the military events is Herman Hattaway's *Shades of Blue and Gray: An Introductory Military History of the Civil War* (1997). The outlook and experiences of the common soldier are explored in James M. McPherson's *For Cause and Comrades: Why Men Fought in the Civil War* (1997). For the global dimensions of the conflict, see Don H. Doyle's *The Cause of All Nations: An International History of the American Civil War* (2015).

The northern war effort is highlighted in Gary W. Gallagher's *The Union War* (2011). For emphasis on the South, see Gallagher's *The Confederate War* (1997). A sparkling account of the birth of the Rebel nation is William C. Davis's *"A Government of Our Own": The Making of the Confederacy* (1994). On the president of the Confederacy, see James M. McPherson's *Embattled Rebel: Jefferson Davis as Commander in Chief* (2014). On two of the leading Confederate commanders, see Michael Korda's *Clouds of Glory: The Life and Legend of Robert E. Lee* (2014) and S. C. Gwynne's *Rebel Yell: Stonewall Jackson* (2014). On the key Union generals, see Lee Kennett's *Sherman: A Soldier's Life* (2001) and Josiah Bunting III's *Ulysses S. Grant* (2004). The controversy over Sherman's March to the Sea is the focus of Matthew Carr's *Sherman's Ghosts: Soldiers, Civilians, and the American Way of War* (2015).

The history of the North during the war is surveyed in Philip Shaw Paludan's *A People's Contest: The Union and Civil War, 1861–1865*, 2nd ed. (1996) and J. Matthew Gallman's *The North Fights the Civil War: The Home Front* (1994). See also Jennifer L. Weber's *Copperheads: The Rise and Fall of Lincoln's Opponents in the North* (2006). The central northern political figure, Abraham Lincoln, is the subject of many books. See James McPherson's *Abraham Lincoln* (2009) and Ronald C. White, Jr., *A. Lincoln: A Biography* (2009).

The experience of the African American soldier is surveyed in Joseph T. Glatthaar's *Forged in Battle: The Civil War Alliance of Black Soldiers and White Officers* (1990) and Ira Berlin, Joseph P. Reidy, and Leslie S. Rowland's *Freedom's Soldiers: The Black Military Experience in the Civil War* (1998). On Lincoln's evolving racial views, see Eric Foner's *The Fiery Trial: Abraham Lincoln and American Slavery* (2010). The war's impact on slavery is the focus of James Oakes's *Freedom National: The Destruction of Slavery in the United States, 1861–1865* (2013) and Bruce Levine's *The Fall of the House of Dixie: The Civil War and the Social Revolution that Transformed the South* (2013). On the Emancipation Proclamation, see Louis P. Masur's *Lincoln's Hundred Days: The Emancipation Proclamation and the War for the Union* (2012). For a sensory perspective on the fighting, see Mark M. Smith's *The Smell of Battle, the Taste of Siege: A Sensory History of the Civil War* (2014).

An excellent analysis of Fredericksburg, one of the war's crucial battles, is John Matteson's *A Worse Place than Hell: How the Civil War Battle of Fredericksburg Changed a Nation* (2021). The Union siege of Petersburg is the focus of A. Wilson Greene's *A Campaign of Giants: The Battle for Petersburg* (2018). For the efforts of the Union navy to blockade southern ports, see Gil Hahn's *Campaign for the Confederate Coast* (2021).

Gender and ethnic studies include Nina Silber's *Gender and the Sectional Conflict* (2008), Drew Gilpin Faust's *Mothers of Invention: Women of the Slaveholding South in the American Civil War* (1996), Judith Giesberger and Randall Miller's *Women and the American Civil War: North-South Counterpoints* (2018), George C. Rable's *Civil Wars: Women and the Crisis of Southern Nationalism* (1989), and William L. Burton's *Melting Pot Soldiers: The Union's Ethnic Regiments*, 2nd ed. (1998). What Civil War veterans experienced after the conflict ended is the subject of Brian Matthew Jordan's *Marching Home: Union Veterans and Their Unending Civil War* (2015) and Gregory P. Downs's *After Appomattox: Military Occupation and the Ends of War* (2015).

Chapter 15

The most comprehensive treatment of Reconstruction is Eric Foner's *Reconstruction: America's Unfinished Revolution, 1863–1877* (1988). See also Foner's *The Second Founding: How the Civil War and Reconstruction Remade the Constitution* (2020).

Good brief histories include Michael W. Fitzgerald's *Splendid Failure: Postwar Reconstruction in the American South* (2007) and Alan Guelzo's *Reconstruction: A Concise History* (2018), and Kate Masur's *Until Justice Be Done: America's First Civil Rights Movement* (2021). On Andrew Johnson, see Hans L. Trefousse's *Andrew Johnson: A Biography* (1989) and David D. Stewart's *Impeached: The Trial of Andrew Johnson and the Fight for Lincoln's Legacy* (2009). Robert S. Levine's *The Failed Promise* (2021) analyzes Reconstruction through the relationship between President Andrew Johnson and Frederick Douglass, the most prominent African American leader.

Scholars have been sympathetic to the aims and motives of the Radical Republicans. See, for instance, Herman Belz's *Reconstructing the Union: Theory and Policy during the Civil War* (1969) and Richard Nelson Current's *Those Terrible Carpetbaggers: A Reinterpretation* (1988). A fine biography of one of the leading Radicals is Bruce Levine's *Thaddeus Stevens* (2021). The ideology of the Radicals is explored in Michael Les Benedict's *A Compromise of Principle: Congressional Republicans and Reconstruction, 1863–1869* (1974). On the Black political leaders, see Phillip Dray's *Capitol Men: The Epic Story of Reconstruction through the Lives of the First Black Congressmen* (2008).

The intransigence of southern White attitudes is examined in Michael Perman's *Reunion without Compromise: The South and Reconstruction, 1865– 1868* (1973) and Dan T. Carter's *When the War Was Over: The Failure of Self-Reconstruction in the South, 1865–1867* (1985). Allen W. Trelease's *White Terror: The Ku Klux Klan Conspiracy and Southern Reconstruction* (1971) covers the various organizations that practiced vigilante tactics. On the massacre of African Americans, see Charles Lane's *The Day Freedom Died: The Colfax Massacre, the Supreme Court, and the Betrayal of Reconstruction* (2008).

The difficulties former slaves had in adjusting to the new labor system are documented in James L. Roark's *Masters without Slaves: Southern Planters in the Civil War and Reconstruction* (1977). Books on southern politics during Reconstruction include Michael Perman's *The Road to Redemption: Southern Politics, 1869–1879* (1984), Terry L. Seip's *The South Returns to Congress: Men, Economic Measures, and Intersectional Relationships, 1868–1879* (1983), and Mark W. Summers's *Railroads, Reconstruction, and the Gospel of Prosperity: Aid under the Radical Republicans, 1865–1877* (1984).

Numerous works study the freed Blacks' experience in the South. Start with Leon F. Litwack's *Been in the Storm So Long: The Aftermath of Slavery* (1979). The Freedmen's Bureau is explored in William S. McFeely's *Yankee Stepfather: General O. O. Howard and the Freedmen* (1968). The situation of freed slave women is the focus of Jacqueline Jones's *Labor of Love, Labor of Sorrow: Black Women, Work and the Family, from Slavery to the Present* (1985). On the "scalawags," see James Alex Bagget's *The Scalawags: Southern Dissenters in the Civil War and Reconstruction* (2003). For a provocative interpretation of the lasting effects of the Civil War and Reconstruction, see Heather Cox Richardson's *How the South Won the Civil War: Oligarchy, Democracy, and the Continuing Fight for the Soul of America* (2020).

The politics of corruption outside the South is depicted in William S. McFeely's *Grant: A Biography* (1981). The best recent biography of the eighteenth president is Ron Chernow's *Grant* (2017). The political maneuvers of the election of 1876 and the resultant crisis and compromise are explained in Michael Holt's *By One Vote: The Disputed Presidential Election of 1876* (2008).

Credits

Text Credits

Chapter 4

P. 167: Excerpts reprinted by permission of the publisher from *The Ideological Origins of the American Revolution* by Bernard Bailyn, pp. xx-xxiii, Cambridge, Mass.: The Belknap Press of Harvard University Press, Copyright © 1967, 1992 by the President and Fellows of Harvard College.

PP. 167-168: Excerpts from "Social Change and the Growth of Prerevolutionary Urban Radicalism," by Gary B. Nash. From *The American Revolution: Explorations in History of American Radicalism,* by Alfred F. Young (ed.). Copyright © 1976 by Northern Illinois University Press. Used with permission of Northern Illinois University Press.

Chapter 7

p. 294-295: Excerpts from "Thomas Jefferson and the Character Issue," by Douglas L. Wilson. Originally published in *The Atlantic Monthly,* November 1992. Used by permission the author.

p. 295; Paul Finkelman, Excerpts from "Jefferson and Slavery," in *Jeffersonian Legacies,* edited by Peter S. Onuf. pp. 181–183, 210–211. © 1993 by the Rector and Visitors of the University of Virginia. Reprinted by permission of the University of Virginia Press.

Chapter 15

p. 627: Eric Foner, excerpt from *The Story of American Freedom.* Copyright © 1998 by Eric Foner. Reprinted by permission of W. W. Norton & Company, Inc., the author, and the Sandra Dijkstra Literary Agency.

Credits

Image Credits

Front Matter
Page v: Steamers Grey Eagle, Frank Steele, Jeannette Roberts and Time and Tide at the lower levee photographed by William Henry Illingworth, created in 1859/Minnesota Historical Society; p. viii and throughout: National Archives; p. xii: © New-York Historical Society/Bridgeman Images; p. xiii: dbimages/Alamy Stock Photo; p. xiv: Peter Newark American Pictures/Bridgeman Images; p. xv & p. xvi: Library of Congress; p. xvii: Everett Collection Historical/Alamy Stock Photo; p. xviii: World History Archive/Alamy Stock Photo; p. xix: Shawshots/Alamy Stock Photo; p. xx: Everett Collection Inc./Alamy Stock Photo; p. xxi: AP Photo/Jae C. Hong.

Chapter 1
Page 2: (Join or Die): Library of Congress; (Rapalje children): © New-York Historical Society/Bridgeman Images; (De Soto and Incas): bpk, Berlin/Kunstbibliothek, Staatliche Museen/Knud Petersen/Art Resource, NY; (Slaves singing): The Picture Art Collection/Alamy Stock Photo; (Columbus): Everett Collection/Shutterstock; p. 4: © The Trustees of the British Museum/Art Resource, NY; p. 5: Sarin Images/GRANGER; p. 6: Photo © Derek Bayes/Bridgeman Images; p. 10: DEA/G. Dagli Orti/De Agostini via Getty Images; p. 11: Science History Images/Alamy Stock Photo; 12: Library of Congress; p. 15: YinYang/Getty Images; p. 16: SuperStock/agefotostock; p.18: MPI/Archive Photos/Getty Images; p. 22: Sarin Images/GRANGER; p. 23 both: Bridgeman Images; p. 26: © Deutsches Historisches Museum/Bridgeman Images; p. 28: Bridgeman Images; p. 31: Benson Latin American Collection, LLILAS Benson Latin American Studies and Collections, The University of Texas at Austin; p. 34: Sarin Images/GRANGER; p. 38: Album/Oronoz/Newscom; p. 40: Werner Forman/Art Resource, NY; p 44: Sarin Images/GRANGER.

Chapter 2
Page 48: © British Library Board. All Rights Reserved/Bridgeman Images; p. 51: still light/Alamy Stock Photo; p. 52: GRANGER; p. 54: Sarin Images/GRANGER; p. 55 right: Bettmann/Getty Images; left: Sarin Images/GRANGER; p. 62: Sarin Images/GRANGER; p. 65 top: GRANGER; bottom: Library of Congress, Rare Book and Special Collections Division; p. 66: Everett Collection Inc./Alamy Stock Photo; p. 67: Sarin Images/GRANGER; p. 69: © British Library Board. All Rights Reserved/Bridgeman Images; p. 72: The New-York Historical Society/Getty Images; p. 73: Bettmann/Corbis/Getty Images; p. 78: Sarin Images/GRANGER; p. 80: GRANGER; p. 81: Plate on p. 80, from Latin translation of Thomas Harriot's *A brief and true report of the new found land of Virginia* (Frankfurt: Johann Wechel, 1590. 1608 edition). Copperplate engravings by Theodor de Bry after watercolors by John White/Duke University Libraries/Internet Archive; p. 82: Sarin Images/GRANGER: p. 83: GRANGER; p. 84: © The Trustees of the British Museum/Art Resource, NY; p. 85: Earl Gregg Swem Library, Special Collections Research Center, William & Mary Libraries; p. 87: GRANGER; p. 88: The Picture Art Collection/Alamy Stock Photo.

Chapter 3
Page 92: Sarin Images/GRANGER; p. 95: Sarin Images/GRANGER; p. 97: THE CONNECTICUT HISTORICAL SOCIETY; p. 98: Courtesy of The Charleston Museum, Charleston, South Carolina; p. 100: Sarin Images/GRANGER; p. 101: North Wind Picture Archive/Alamy; p. 102 left: Sarin Images/GRANGER; right: © Peabody Essex Museum/Bridgeman Images; p. 103: Sarin Images/GRANGER; p. 106: Germantown Historical Society/Historic Germantown; p. 109: Sarin Images/GRANGER; p. 111 & p.112: © New-York Historical Society/Bridgeman Images; p. 113: Library Company of Philadelphia; p. 116: Philadelphia Museum of Art, Gift of Mr. and Mrs. Wharton Sinkler/Bridgeman Images; p. 117: Sarin Images/GRANGER; p. 118: Bridgeman Images.

Chapter 4
Page 122: DeA Picture Library/GRANGER; p. 124: Snark/Art Resource, NY; p. 125: MPI/Getty Images; p. 129: The New York Public Library/Art Resource, NY; p. 131: Sarin Images/GRANGER; p. 134: Library of Congress; p. 135: New-York Historical Society/Bridgeman Images; p. 136: GRANGER; p. 140: North Wind Picture Archives/Alamy Stock Photo; p. 141: Library of Congress; p. 142 & 143: Library of Congress; p. 145: Peter Newark American Pictures/Bridgeman Images; p. 146: Library of Congress; p. 147: Sarin Images/GRANGER; p. 148 & 150: Library of Congress; p. 153: © Virginia Historical Society/Bridgeman Images; p. 154: Sarin Images/GRANGER; p. 158: © Philadelphia History Museum at the Atwater Kent/Courtesy of Historical Society of Pennsylvania Collection/Bridgeman Images; p.162: North Wind Picture Archives/Alamy Stock Photo.

Chapter 5
Page: 170 (pamphlet): Photo © Christie's Images/Bridgeman Images; (cartoon): Sarin Images/GRANGER; (frigate burning): © New-York Historical Society/Bridgeman Images; (Jefferson): GRANGER; (Allegiance to no crown): Photography by Erik Arnesen © Nicholas S. West; (pamphlet): Photo © Christie's Images/Bridgeman Images; p. 172: GRANGER; p. 174: Photo by Francis G. Mayer/Corbis/VCG via Getty Images; p. 176: Anne S.K. Brown Military Collection Brown University Library; p. 178: US Senate Collection; p. 181: Alonzo Chappel, Battle of Long Island, 1858; M1986.29.1; Brooklyn Public Library, Center for Brooklyn History; p. 183 left: Courtesy American Antiquarian Society; right: GRANGER; p. 187: GRANGER; p. 189: Sarin Images/GRANGER; p. 190: Bridgeman Images; p. 194: agefotostock/Alamy Stock Photo; p. 196: ART Collection/Alamy Stock Photo; p. 201: Library of Congress; p. 204 & 205: GRANGER; p. 206 Everett/Shutterstock; p. 207: GRANGER.

Chapter 6
Page 212: Ian Dagnall/Alamy Stock Photo; p. 216: GRANGER; p. 219: The Miriam and Ira D. Wallach Division of Art, Prints and Photographs: Print Collection, The New York Public Library; p. 221: North Wind Picture Archives/Alamy Stock Photo; p. 222: MPI/Getty Images; p. 223: Library of Congress; p. 226: The Picture Art Collection/Alamy Stock Photo; p. 229: Library of

Congress; p. 233: © New-York Historical Society/Bridgeman Images; p. 236: Albert Knapp/Alamy Stock Photo; p. 239: Everett Collection Historical/Alamy Stock Photo; p. 241: dbimages/Alamy Stock Photo; p. 242: Library of Congress; p. 244: Sarin Images/GRANGER; p. 245: Gift of Edgar William and Bernice Chrysler/The Metropolitan Museum of Art; p. 247: Art Collection 2/Alamy Stock Photo p. 249 top: National Portrait Gallery, Smithsonian Institution; bottom: Sarin Images/GRANGER; p. 251: Sarin Images/GRANGER.

Chapter 7
Page 256: Photography by Erik Arnesen © Nicholas S. West; p. 259: Library of Congress; p. 260: Art Collection 2/Alamy Stock Photo; p. 264: Historic Collection/Alamy Stock Photo; p. 266: © American Philosophical Society; p. 267: Greg Vaughn/Alamy Stock Photo; p. 269: The Picture Art Collection/Alamy Stock Photo; p. 270: Timothy H. O'Sullivan/Digital image courtesy of the Getty Museum's Open Content Program; p. 271: © New-York Historical Society/Bridgeman Images; p. 272: Library of Congress; p. 273: North Wind Picture Archives/Alamy Stock Photo; p. 274 & p. 276: Sarin Images/GRANGER; p. 277: Library of Congress; p. 279: © Courtesy, American Antiquarian Society/Bridgeman Images; p. 280: Niday Picture Library/Alamy Stock Photo; p. 284: Sarin Images/GRANGER; p. 286 & p.289: Library of Congress.

Chapter 8
Page 298 (Clay): National Currency Foundation/Wikimedia, public domain; (slaves): Peter Newark American Pictures/Bridgeman Images; (Blount & Dawson card): Courtesy of Swann Auction Galleries/Bridgeman Images; (school): GRANGER; (steamboats): Steamers Grey Eagle, Frank Steele, Jeannette Roberts and Time and Tide at the lower levee photographed by William Henry Illingworth, created in 1859/Minnesota Historical Society; (mill workers): Sarin Images/GRANGER; p. 300: Yale University Art Gallery; p. 301: Gift of Miss Sadie B. Feldman in memory of her brother, Samson Feldman, 1987, The Walters Art Museum, Baltimore; p. 302: Gift of Mrs. Huttleston Rogers, Courtesy National Gallery of Art, Washington; p. 307: Steamers Grey Eagle, Frank Steele, Jeannette Roberts and Time and Tide at the lower levee photographed by William Henry Illingworth, created in 1859/Minnesota Historical Society; p. 310: Messrs. Smith & Co. Ship Yard, 1833, by James Fulton Pringle, oil on canvas, H: 32 x W: 50.75 in., Fenimore Art Museum, Cooperstown, New York. Gift of Stephen C. Clark. N0394.1955. Photograph by Richard Walker; p. 312: North Wind Picture Archives/Alamy Stock Photo; p. 315: Sarin Images/GRANGER; p. 317: from the official catalog, Great Exhibition, Crystal Palace, London 1851; p. 319: Sarin Images/GRANGER; p. 323: Gift of Edgar William and Bernice Chrysler Garbisch, Courtesy National Gallery of Art, Washington; p. 325 & p. 327: Sarin Images/GRANGER; p. 328: The New York Public Library/Art Resource, NY; p. 330: Winslow Homer, American, 1836-1910; The Country School, 1871; oil on canvas; 21 1/4 x 38 1/4 inches; Saint Louis Art Museum, Museum Purchase 123:1946.

Chapter 9
Page: 334: Yale University Art Gallery; p. 338: Library of Congress; p. 340: Rogers Fund, 1942. Metropolitan Museum of Art; p. 341: National Currency Foundation/Wikimedia, public domain; p. 343: The History Collection/Alamy; p. 348: Sarin Images/GRANGER; p. 350: Yale University Art Gallery; p. 352: Library of Congress; p. 354: Gift of I. N. Phelps Stokes, Edward S. Hawes, Alice Mary Hawes, and Marion Augusta Hawes, 1937. The Metropolitan Museum of Art; p. 356: Library of Congress.

Chapter 10
Page 362: The Museum of the City of New York/Art Resource, NY; p. 365: Library of Congress; p. 367: History and Art Collection/Alamy Stock Photo; p. 368: Library of Congress; p. 369: Peter Newark American Pictures/Bridgeman Images; p. 371: Andrew Cribb/Alamy Stock Photo; p. 373: Sarin Images/GRANGER; p. 377: US Marine Corp and National Archives; p. 379 & p. 380: GRANGER; p. 384, p. 386, p. 387 & p. 389: Library of Congress.

Chapter 11
Page 394: Everett Collection/Shutterstock; p. 397: Contraband Collection/Alamy Stock Photo; p. 400: GRANGER; p. 405 left: Sarin Images/GRANGER; right: Fotosearch/Getty Images; p. 407: North Wind Picture Archives/Alamy Stock Photo; p. 410: GL Archive/Alamy Stock Photo; p. 411: Courtesy of Swann Auction Galleries/Bridgeman Images; p. 412: Sarin Images/GRANGER; p. 413: Photograph of Jack, Courtesy of the Peabody Museum of Archaeology and Ethnology, Harvard University, 35-5-10/53044; p. 415: The Colonial Williamsburg Foundation. Museum Purchase; p. 417: Peter Newark American Pictures/Bridgeman Images; p. 418: GL Archive/Alamy Stock Photo; p. 421: Everett Collection Historical/Alamy Stock Photo.

Chapter 12
Page 426: FineArt/Alamy Stock Photo; p. 429: Library of Congress; p, 430: GRANGER; p. 432 top: Classic Image/Alamy Stock Photo; bottom: Rogers Fund, 1942. The Metropolitan Museum of Art; p. 433: Schomburg Center for Research in Black Culture, Manuscripts, Archives and Rare Books Division. The New York Public Library Digital Collections; p. 435: Library of Congress; p. 437: Lordprice Collection/Alamy Stock Photo; p. 438: Gift of Mrs. Russell Sage, 1908. The Metropolitan Museum of Art; p 439: Library of Congress; p. 440: Science History Images/Alamy Stock Photo; p. 441: Everett Collection/Shutterstock; p. 442: IanDagnall Computing/Alamy Stock Photo; p. 444 Gift of Miss Sadie B. Feldman in memory of her brother, Samson Feldman, 1987, The Walters Art Museum, Baltimore; p. 446: World History Archive/Alamy Stock Photo; p. 448 left: Library of Congress; right: Everett Collection/Shutterstock; p. 450: Cultural Archive/Alamy Stock Photo; p. 452: The New York Public Library Digital Collections. p. 455: Everett/Shutterstock; p. 457 both: Library of Congress; p. 459 left: National Portrait Gallery, Smithsonian Institution; right: Library of Congress.

Chapter 13
Page: 470 (Clara Barton): Library of Congress; (handbill): Sarin Images/GRANGER; (Visit from the Old Mistress): Smithsonian American Art Museum, Gift of William T. Evans; (farm slaves): Library of Congress; (Ad for Uncle Tom's Cabin): Sarin Images/GRANGER; (John Brown): Library of Congress; (Greenback currency): Everett/Shutterstock; p. 472: © Civil War Archive/The Bridgeman Art Library; p. 474: Art Collection 3/Alamy Stock Photo; p. 478: Morris K. Jesup Fund, 1933. The Metropolitan Museum of Art; p. 479: North Wind Picture Archives/Alamy Stock Photo; p. 480 & 481: Peter Newark American Pictures/Bridgeman Images; p. 482: Sarin Images/GRANGER; p. 485: MPI/Getty Images; p. 486: © Museum of Fine Arts, Houston/The Bayou Bend

Collection, gift of Miss Ima Hogg/Bridgeman Images; p. 489: GRANGER; p. 494: The Art Archive/Shutterstock; p. 495: Herbert Orth/Contributor/The LIFE Image Collections/Getty Images; p. 498 © Courtesy, American Antiquarian Society/Bridgeman Images; p. 500: Library of Congress; p. 503: Art Resource, NY; p. 504: Sarin Images/GRANGER; p. 507: Library of Congress; p. 508: Library of Congress; p. 512: INTERFOTO/Alamy Stock Photo; p. 517: Art Resource, NY; p. 518 left: National Portrait Gallery, Smithsonian Institution; Frederick Hill Meserve Collection; right: Library of Congress; p. 520: Everett Collection/Shutterstock; p. 524: ZUMA Press, Inc./Alamy Stock Photo.

Chapter 14
Page: 530: Pictures Now/Alamy Stock Photo; p. 532: Library of Congress; p. 536 both: Library of Congress; p. 538: The Stapleton Collection/Bridgeman Images; p. 539: Courtesy Jackson K. Doane, Jr.; p. 540: Library of Congress; p. 542: Alpha Stock/Alamy Stock Photo; 543: Reading Room 2020/Alamy Stock Photo; p. 546, p. 549, p. 551, p. 552, & p. 553: Library of Congress; p. 556: Beinecke Rare Book and Manuscript Library, Yale University/Wikimedia Commons; p. 558 both: Library of Congress; p. 560: World History Archive/Alamy Stock Photo; p. 563, p. 565, & p. 566: Library of Congress; p. 570: Everett Collection Historical/Alamy Stock Photo; p. 575 & p. 578: Library of Congress.

Chapter 15
Page 584: Sarin Images/GRANGER; p. 587: Library of Congress; p. 590: Sarin Images/GRANGER; p. 591: Science History Images/Alamy Stock Photo; p. 592: Library of Congress; p. 594: Sarin Images/GRANGER; p. 595: Everett Collection/Shutterstock; p. 597: Library of Congress; p. 600: Science History Images/Alamy Stock Photo; p. 603: GRANGER; p. 605 & p. 606: Library of Congress; p. 608: Sarin Images/GRANGER; p. 611: John Kraljevich/John Kraljevich Americana p. 614: Library of Congress; p. 617: akg-images/Fototeca Gilardi; p. 622: Library of Congress.

Index

Page numbers in *italics* refer to illustrations.

K

L

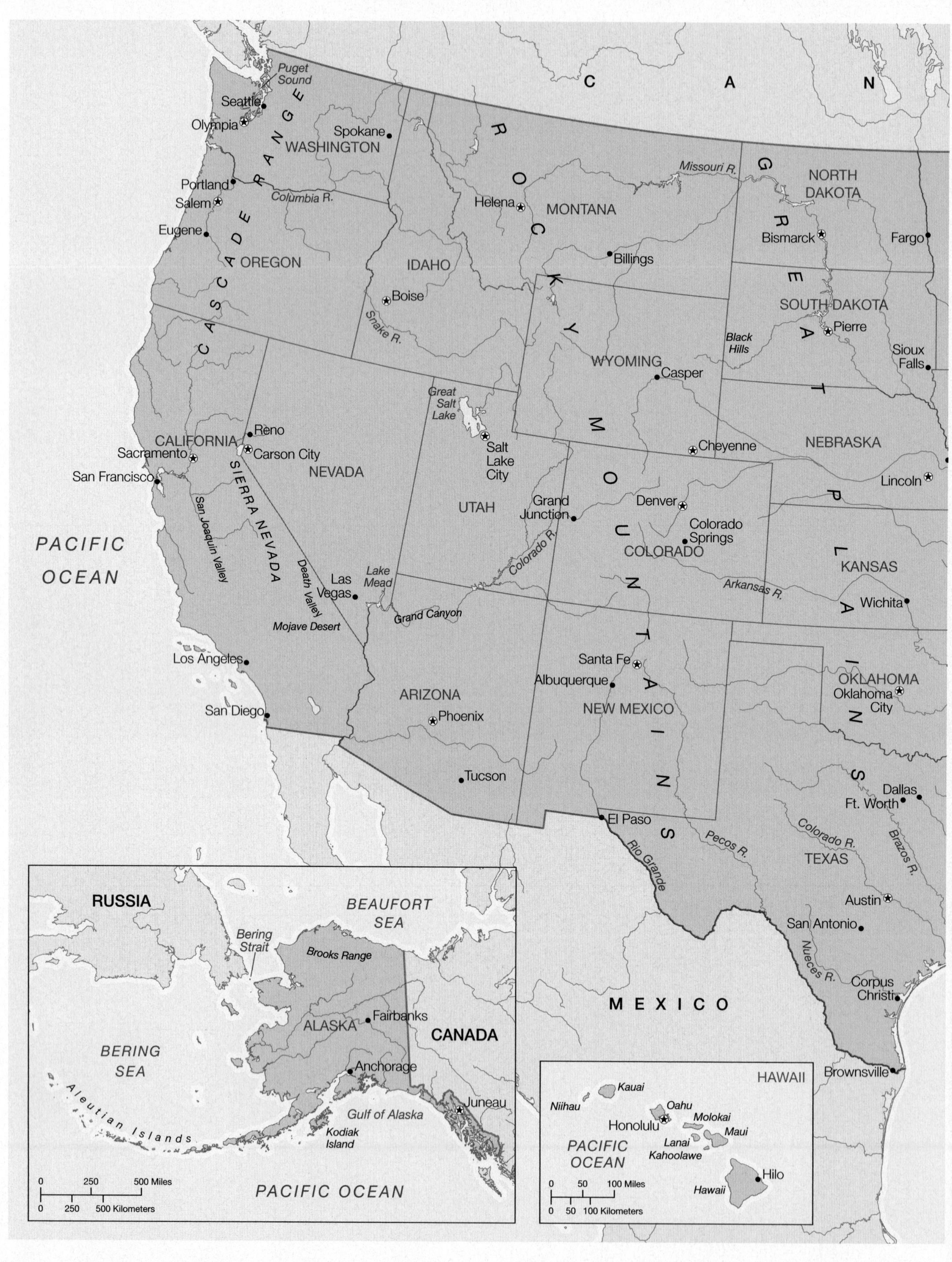

C A N
Puget Sound
Seattle
Olympia
Spokane
WASHINGTON
CASCADE RANGE
ROCKY MOUNTAINS
GREAT PLAINS
Missouri R.
NORTH DAKOTA
Portland
Salem
Columbia R.
Helena
MONTANA
Eugene
Bismarck
Fargo
OREGON
IDAHO
Billings
Boise
SOUTH DAKOTA
Pierre
Snake R.
Black Hills
Sioux Falls
WYOMING
Casper
Great Salt Lake
Reno
CALIFORNIA
Salt Lake City
Cheyenne
NEBRASKA
Sacramento
Carson City
NEVADA
San Francisco
SIERRA NEVADA
Lincoln
UTAH
Grand Junction
Denver
San Joaquin Valley
Colorado Springs
PACIFIC OCEAN
COLORADO
Colorado R.
KANSAS
Death Valley
Las Vegas
Lake Mead
Arkansas R.
Wichita
Grand Canyon
Mojave Desert
Los Angeles
Santa Fe
OKLAHOMA
Albuquerque
Oklahoma City
ARIZONA
San Diego
Phoenix
NEW MEXICO
Tucson
Dallas
Ft. Worth
El Paso
Colorado R.
Rio Grande
Pecos R.
Brazos R.
TEXAS
RUSSIA
BEAUFORT SEA
Austin
Bering Strait
Brooks Range
San Antonio
Nueces R.
Corpus Christi
MEXICO
ALASKA
Fairbanks
CANADA
BERING SEA
Anchorage
Brownsville
HAWAII
Aleutian Islands
Juneau
Kauai
Gulf of Alaska
Niihau
Oahu
Molokai
Honolulu
Maui
Kodiak Island
Lanai
PACIFIC OCEAN
Kahoolawe
0 250 500 Miles
0 250 500 Kilometers
PACIFIC OCEAN
Hilo
0 50 100 Miles
Hawaii
0 50 100 Kilometers

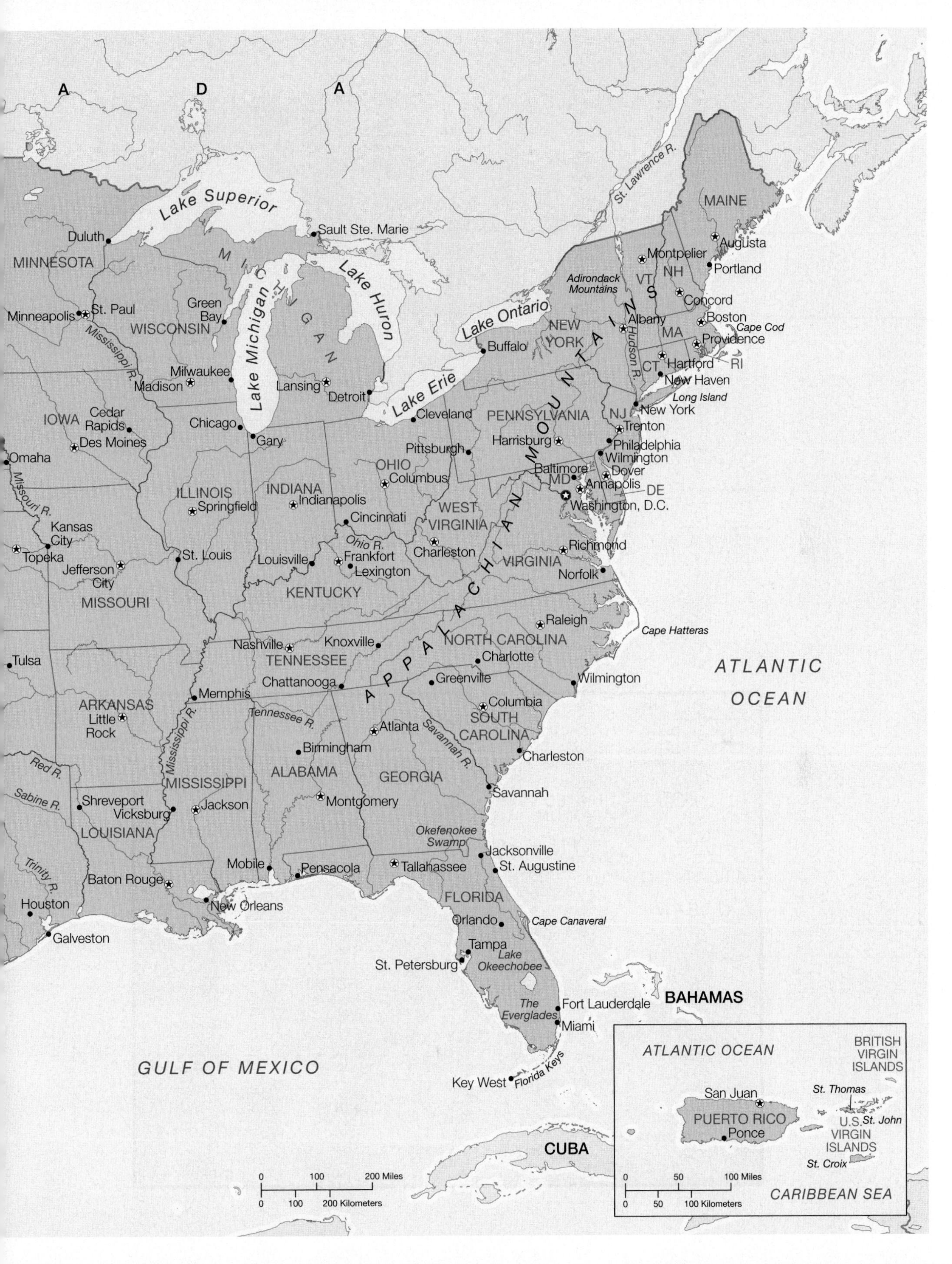

A
D
A
Lake Superior
Lake Michigan
Lake Huron
Lake Ontario
Lake Erie
St. Lawrence R.
MAINE
Augusta
Portland
Montpelier
VT
NH
Concord
Adirondack Mountains
Boston
Cape Cod
MA
Providence
RI
Hartford
CT
New Haven
Long Island
Albany
Hudson R.
NEW YORK
Buffalo
New York
NJ
Trenton
PENNSYLVANIA
Harrisburg
Philadelphia
Wilmington
Dover
DE
Baltimore
MD
Annapolis
Washington, D.C.
Pittsburgh
Cleveland
Sault Ste. Marie
MICHIGAN
Lansing
Detroit
Duluth
MINNESOTA
Minneapolis
St. Paul
WISCONSIN
Green Bay
Milwaukee
Madison
Mississippi R.
IOWA
Cedar Rapids
Des Moines
Omaha
Missouri R.
Chicago
Gary
ILLINOIS
Springfield
INDIANA
Indianapolis
OHIO
Columbus
Cincinnati
Ohio R.
WEST VIRGINIA
Charleston
Kansas City
Topeka
St. Louis
Jefferson City
MISSOURI
Louisville
Frankfort
Lexington
KENTUCKY
VIRGINIA
Richmond
Norfolk
APPALACHIAN MOUNTAINS
Raleigh
NORTH CAROLINA
Cape Hatteras
Charlotte
Wilmington
Nashville
Knoxville
TENNESSEE
Chattanooga
Greenville
Columbia
SOUTH CAROLINA
Charleston
ATLANTIC OCEAN
Tulsa
Memphis
ARKANSAS
Little Rock
Tennessee R.
Atlanta
Savannah R.
Birmingham
ALABAMA
GEORGIA
Savannah
Red R.
Sabine R.
Shreveport
Vicksburg
MISSISSIPPI
Jackson
Montgomery
LOUISIANA
Okefenokee Swamp
Jacksonville
St. Augustine
Trinity R.
Mobile
Pensacola
Tallahassee
Baton Rouge
New Orleans
Houston
Galveston
FLORIDA
Orlando
Cape Canaveral
Tampa
St. Petersburg
Lake Okeechobee
The Everglades
Fort Lauderdale
Miami
BAHAMAS
GULF OF MEXICO
Key West
Florida Keys
CUBA
0 100 200 Miles
0 100 200 Kilometers
ATLANTIC OCEAN
BRITISH VIRGIN ISLANDS
San Juan
St. Thomas
PUERTO RICO
Ponce
U.S. VIRGIN ISLANDS
St. John
St. Croix
0 50 100 Miles
0 50 100 Kilometers
CARIBBEAN SEA

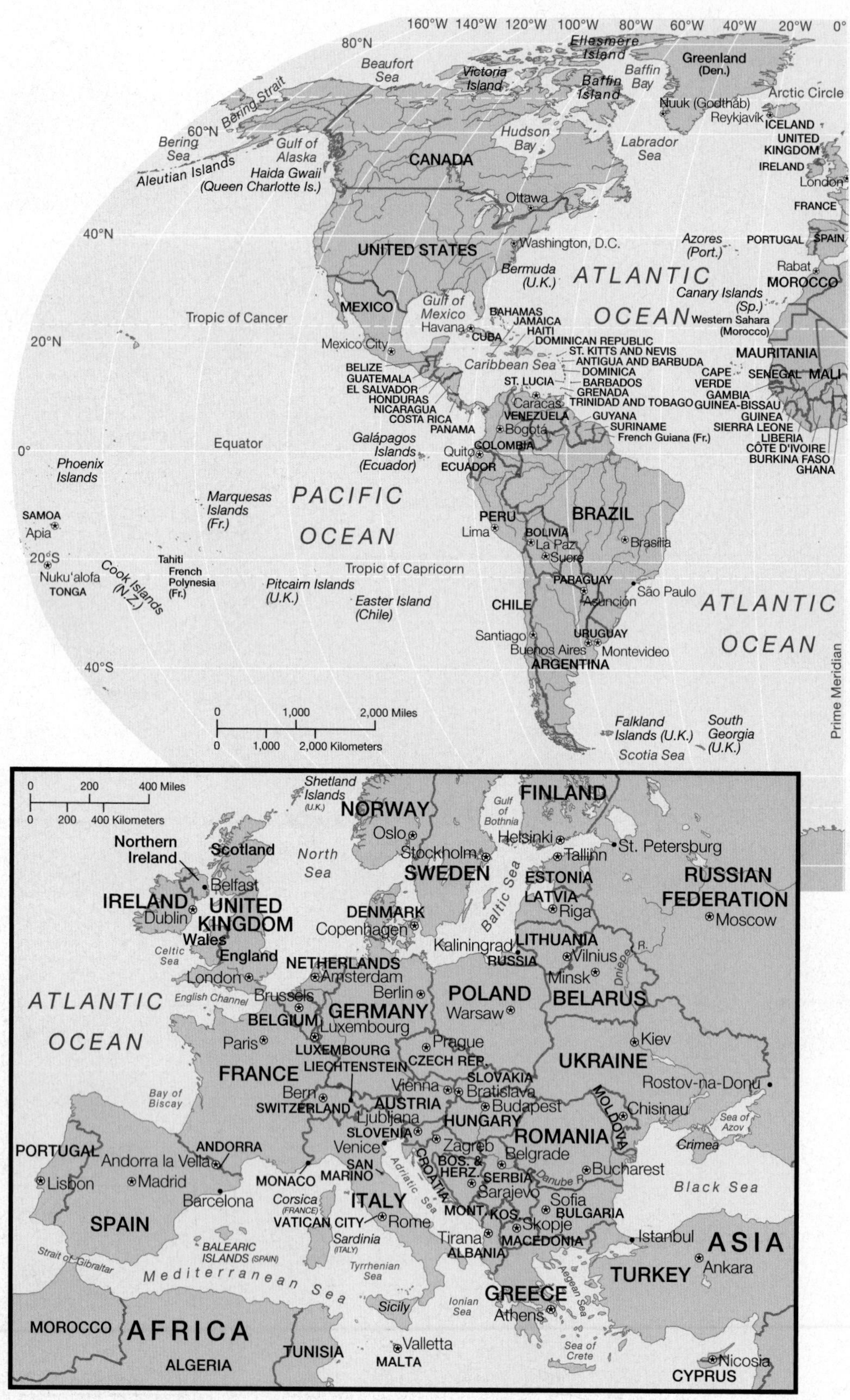

160°W 140°W 120°W 100°W 80°W 60°W 40°W 20°W 0°
80°N
60°N
40°N
20°N
0°
20°S
40°S
Ellesmere Island
Beaufort Sea
Victoria Island
Baffin Island
Baffin Bay
Greenland (Den.)
Arctic Circle
Nuuk (Godthåb)
Reykjavík
ICELAND
UNITED KINGDOM
IRELAND
London
FRANCE
Bering Strait
Bering Sea
Gulf of Alaska
Aleutian Islands
Haida Gwaii (Queen Charlotte Is.)
Hudson Bay
Labrador Sea
CANADA
Ottawa
UNITED STATES
Washington, D.C.
Azores (Port.)
PORTUGAL
SPAIN
Rabat
MOROCCO
Bermuda (U.K.)
ATLANTIC OCEAN
Canary Islands (Sp.)
Western Sahara (Morocco)
Tropic of Cancer
MEXICO
Gulf of Mexico
Havana
CUBA
BAHAMAS
JAMAICA
HAITI
DOMINICAN REPUBLIC
ST. KITTS AND NEVIS
ANTIGUA AND BARBUDA
DOMINICA
BARBADOS
ST. LUCIA
GRENADA
TRINIDAD AND TOBAGO
Mexico City
Caribbean Sea
MAURITANIA
CAPE VERDE
SENEGAL
MALI
GAMBIA
GUINEA-BISSAU
GUINEA
SIERRA LEONE
LIBERIA
CÔTE D'IVOIRE
BURKINA FASO
GHANA
BELIZE
GUATEMALA
EL SALVADOR
HONDURAS
NICARAGUA
COSTA RICA
PANAMA
Caracas
VENEZUELA
GUYANA
SURINAME
French Guiana (Fr.)
Bogotá
COLOMBIA
Quito
ECUADOR
Galápagos Islands (Ecuador)
Equator
Phoenix Islands
Marquesas Islands (Fr.)
PACIFIC OCEAN
SAMOA
Apia
Nuku'alofa
TONGA
Cook Islands (N.Z.)
Tahiti
French Polynesia (Fr.)
Pitcairn Islands (U.K.)
Easter Island (Chile)
Tropic of Capricorn
PERU
Lima
BRAZIL
BOLIVIA
La Paz
Sucre
Brasília
PARAGUAY
Asunción
São Paulo
CHILE
Santiago
URUGUAY
Buenos Aires
Montevideo
ARGENTINA
ATLANTIC OCEAN
Prime Meridian
0 1,000 2,000 Miles
0 1,000 2,000 Kilometers
Falkland Islands (U.K.)
South Georgia (U.K.)
Scotia Sea
0 200 400 Miles
0 200 400 Kilometers
Shetland Islands (U.K.)
NORWAY
Oslo
Gulf of Bothnia
FINLAND
Helsinki
St. Petersburg
Tallinn
Stockholm
SWEDEN
North Sea
Northern Ireland
Scotland
Belfast
IRELAND
Dublin
UNITED KINGDOM
Wales
England
Celtic Sea
London
ESTONIA
LATVIA
Riga
RUSSIAN FEDERATION
Moscow
Baltic Sea
DENMARK
Copenhagen
Kaliningrad
RUSSIA
LITHUANIA
Vilnius
Minsk
Dnieper R.
BELARUS
NETHERLANDS
Amsterdam
Berlin
POLAND
Warsaw
ATLANTIC OCEAN
English Channel
Brussels
BELGIUM
GERMANY
Luxembourg
LUXEMBOURG
Paris
Prague
CZECH REP.
Kiev
UKRAINE
FRANCE
LIECHTENSTEIN
SLOVAKIA
Vienna
Bratislava
Rostov-na-Donu
Bay of Biscay
Bern
SWITZERLAND
AUSTRIA
Budapest
HUNGARY
MOLDOVA
Chisinau
Sea of Azov
Crimea
Ljubljana
SLOVENIA
Zagreb
CROATIA
ROMANIA
Belgrade
PORTUGAL
ANDORRA
Andorra la Vella
Venice
SAN MARINO
BOS. & HERZ.
SERBIA
Danube R.
Bucharest
Lisbon
Madrid
MONACO
Sarajevo
Black Sea
Barcelona
Corsica (FRANCE)
ITALY
Adriatic Sea
MONT.
KOS.
Sofia
BULGARIA
SPAIN
VATICAN CITY
Rome
Skopje
Sardinia (ITALY)
Tirana
ALBANIA
MACEDONIA
Istanbul
ASIA
BALEARIC ISLANDS (SPAIN)
Ankara
TURKEY
Strait of Gibraltar
Mediterranean Sea
Tyrrhenian Sea
GREECE
Aegean Sea
Ionian Sea
Sicily
Athens
MOROCCO
AFRICA
Valletta
MALTA
TUNISIA
ALGERIA
Sea of Crete
Nicosia
CYPRUS

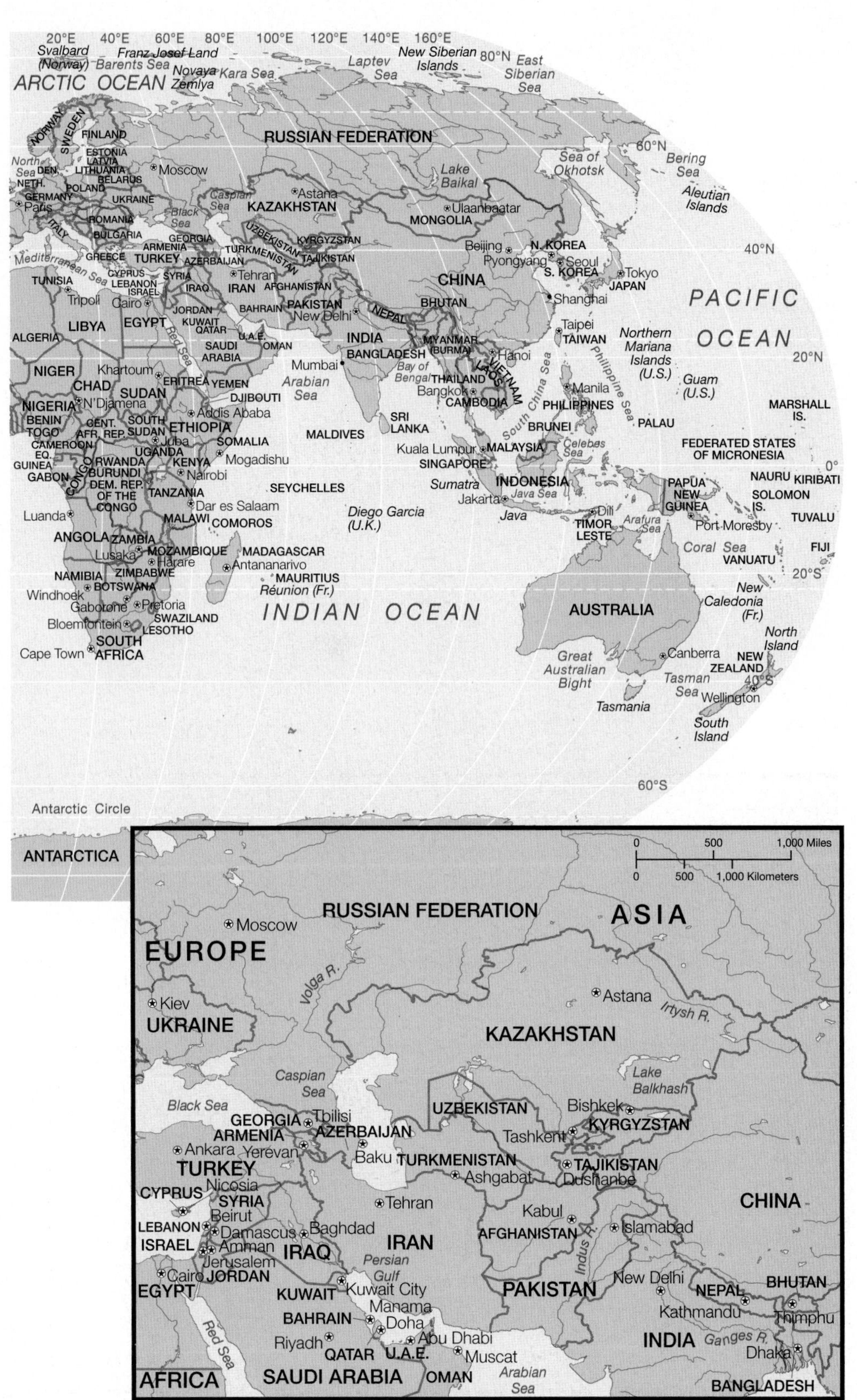

20°E
40°E
60°E
80°E
100°E
120°E
140°E
160°E
Svalbard (Norway)
Franz Josef Land
Barents Sea
Novaya Zemlya
Kara Sea
Laptev Sea
New Siberian Islands
80°N
East Siberian Sea
ARCTIC OCEAN
RUSSIAN FEDERATION
FINLAND
NORWAY
SWEDEN
ESTONIA
LATVIA
LITHUANIA
North Sea
DEN.
NETH.
BELARUS
POLAND
GERMANY
Moscow
Paris
UKRAINE
ROMANIA
ITALY
BULGARIA
Black Sea
Caspian Sea
Astana
KAZAKHSTAN
Lake Baikal
Ulaanbaatar
MONGOLIA
Sea of Okhotsk
60°N
Bering Sea
Aleutian Islands
GEORGIA
ARMENIA
AZERBAIJAN
GREECE
TURKEY
UZBEKISTAN
KYRGYZSTAN
TURKMENISTAN
TAJIKISTAN
Mediterranean Sea
CYPRUS
SYRIA
LEBANON
ISRAEL
IRAQ
Tehran
IRAN
AFGHANISTAN
Beijing
N. KOREA
Pyongyang
Seoul
S. KOREA
Tokyo
JAPAN
40°N
TUNISIA
Tripoli
Cairo
LIBYA
EGYPT
JORDAN
KUWAIT
QATAR
BAHRAIN
PAKISTAN
New Delhi
NEPAL
CHINA
BHUTAN
Shanghai
PACIFIC OCEAN
ALGERIA
Red Sea
U.A.E.
SAUDI ARABIA
OMAN
INDIA
BANGLADESH
MYANMAR (BURMA)
Hanoi
LAOS
Taipei
TAIWAN
Northern Mariana Islands (U.S.)
20°N
Guam (U.S.)
NIGER
CHAD
Khartoum
SUDAN
ERITREA
YEMEN
Mumbai
Arabian Sea
Bay of Bengal
THAILAND
Bangkok
VIETNAM
CAMBODIA
South China Sea
Philippine Sea
Manila
PHILIPPINES
MARSHALL IS.
NIGERIA
N'Djamena
DJIBOUTI
BENIN
TOGO
CENT. AFR. REP.
SOUTH SUDAN
ETHIOPIA
Addis Ababa
SRI LANKA
PALAU
CAMEROON
EQ. GUINEA
GABON
CONGO
Juba
UGANDA
RWANDA
BURUNDI
KENYA
SOMALIA
Mogadishu
MALDIVES
BRUNEI
Kuala Lumpur
MALAYSIA
Celebes Sea
FEDERATED STATES OF MICRONESIA
SINGAPORE
Nairobi
DEM. REP. OF THE CONGO
TANZANIA
SEYCHELLES
Sumatra
INDONESIA
Java Sea
Jakarta
PAPUA NEW GUINEA
NAURU
KIRIBATI
0°
Dar es Salaam
SOLOMON IS.
Luanda
MALAWI
COMOROS
Diego Garcia (U.K.)
Java
Dili
TIMOR LESTE
Arafura Sea
Port Moresby
TUVALU
ANGOLA
ZAMBIA
MOZAMBIQUE
Lusaka
Harare
MADAGASCAR
Antananarivo
Coral Sea
VANUATU
FIJI
NAMIBIA
ZIMBABWE
BOTSWANA
MAURITIUS
Réunion (Fr.)
20°S
Windhoek
Gaborone
Pretoria
New Caledonia (Fr.)
INDIAN OCEAN
AUSTRALIA
Bloemfontein
SWAZILAND
LESOTHO
SOUTH AFRICA
Cape Town
North Island
Great Australian Bight
Canberra
NEW ZEALAND
Tasman Sea
40°S
Wellington
Tasmania
South Island
60°S
Antarctic Circle
ANTARCTICA
0
500
1,000 Miles
0
500
1,000 Kilometers
RUSSIAN FEDERATION
ASIA
Moscow
EUROPE
Volga R.
Kiev
UKRAINE
Astana
Irtysh R.
KAZAKHSTAN
Caspian Sea
Lake Balkhash
Black Sea
GEORGIA
Tbilisi
ARMENIA
AZERBAIJAN
UZBEKISTAN
Bishkek
KYRGYZSTAN
Tashkent
Ankara
Yerevan
Baku
TURKMENISTAN
TAJIKISTAN
TURKEY
Ashgabat
Dushanbe
Nicosia
CYPRUS
SYRIA
Tehran
CHINA
Beirut
Kabul
LEBANON
Damascus
Baghdad
IRAN
AFGHANISTAN
Islamabad
ISRAEL
Amman
IRAQ
Jerusalem
Persian Gulf
Indus R.
Cairo
JORDAN
EGYPT
KUWAIT
Kuwait City
PAKISTAN
New Delhi
NEPAL
BHUTAN
Manama
BAHRAIN
Doha
Kathmandu
Thimphu
Red Sea
Riyadh
Abu Dhabi
INDIA
Ganges R.
QATAR
U.A.E.
Muscat
Dhaka
AFRICA
SAUDI ARABIA
OMAN
Arabian Sea
BANGLADESH